RICHARD OVERY

The Bombing War

Europe 1939–1945

PENGUIN BOOKS

PENGUIN BOOKS

Published by the Penguin Group
Penguin Books Ltd, 80 Strand, London WC2R ORL, England
Penguin Group (USA) Inc., 375 Hudson Street, New York, New York 10014, USA
Penguin Group (Canada), 90 Eglinton Avenue East, Suite 700, Toronto, Ontario, Canada M4P 2Y3
(a division of Pearson Penguin Canada Inc.)
Penguin Ireland, 25 St Stephen's Green, Dublin 2, Ireland (a division of Penguin Books Ltd)
Penguin Group (Australia), 707 Collins Street, Melbourne, Victoria 3008, Australia
(a division of Pearson Australia Group Pty Ltd)
Penguin Books India Pvt Ltd, 11 Community Centre, Panchsheel Park, New Delhi – 110 017, India
Penguin Group (NZ), 67 Apollo Drive, Rosedale, Auckland 0632, New Zealand
(a division of Pearson New Zealand Ltd)
Penguin Books (South Africa) (Pty) Ltd, Block D, Rosebank Office Park,
181 Jan Smuts Avenue, Parktown North, Gauteng 2193, South Africa

Penguin Books Ltd, Registered Offices: 80 Strand, London WC2R ORL, England

www.penguin.com

First published by Allen Lane 2013
Published in Penguin Books 2014
002

Copyright © Richard Overy, 2013

The moral right of the author has been asserted

The epigraph is from John Betjeman, *Collected Poems*, copyright © 2006 the Estate
of John Betjeman, reproduced by permission of John Murray (Publishers). The
quotations from Vera Brittain *England's Hour* are reproduced by permission of
Mark Bostridge and T. J. Brittain-Catlin, literary executors of the estate of Vera Brittain, 1970.

Typeset by Jouve (UK), Milton Keynes
Printed in Great Britain by Clays Ltd, St Ives plc

A CIP catalogue record for this book is available from the British Library

ISBN: 978-0-141-00321-4

www.greenpenguin.co.uk

MIX
Paper from
responsible sources
FSC
www.fsc.org   FSC™ C018179

Penguin Books is committed to a sustainable
future for our business, our readers and our planet.
This book is made from Forest Stewardship
Council™ certified paper.

'A provocative new take on the second world war . . . a much
needed breath of fresh air . . . he is master of his subject'
Keith Lowe, *Daily Telegraph*

'A richly detailed history which never shies away from questioning
conventional moral assumptions about the Second World War'
Independent, Books of the Year

'A tight, comprehensive narrative of the death that rained from
the sky across our continent for nearly sixty years'
Dan Jones, *Daily Telegraph*, Books of the Year

'The most important book on the Second World War in
decades . . . Magnificent . . . must now be regarded as the standard
work on the bombing war' Richard J. Evans, *Guardian*

'It is unlikely that a work of this scale, scope and merit will be
surpassed' Jill Stephenson, *Times Higher Education*

'The first full narrative of the bombing war in Europe . . . masterly'
Barney White-Spunner, *Country Life*, Books of the Year

'Magisterial . . . Overy's authoritative book, the product of
many years of archival research, is undoubtedly one of the most
important on the Second World War to appear in recent times'
Gary Sheffield, *New Statesman*

'Excellent . . . Overy is never less than an erudite and clear-eyed
guide whose research is impeccable and whose conclusions appear
sensible and convincing even when they run against the established
trends . . . he has set a new standard in the study of the air war'
Roger Moorhouse, *Financial Times*

'Remarkable . . . a powerful book' Hugh Macdonald, *Herald*

'Extraordinary and far-reaching history of Europe's bombing
war . . . incredibly broad and well-researched, also highly readable'
Tobias Grey, *Spectator*

PENGUIN BOOKS

THE BOMBING WAR

ABOUT THE AUTHOR

Richard Overy is the author of a series of remarkable books on the Second World War and the wider disasters of the twentieth century. *The Dictators: Hitler's Germany, Stalin's Russia* won both the Wolfson Prize for History and the Hessell-Tiltman Prize. *The Bombing War* was short-listed for the 2013 Guggenheim-Lehrman Prize in Military History. He is Professor of History at the University of Exeter. Penguin publishes *1939: Countdown to War, The Morbid Age, Russia's War, Interrogations, The Battle of Britain* and *The Dictators*. He lives in London.

Oh bountiful Gods of the air! Oh Science and Progress!
You great big wonderful world! Oh what have you done?

John Betjeman, '1940'

Contents

PART ONE
Germany's Bombing War

PART TWO
'The Greatest Battle': Allied Bombers
over Europe

PART THREE
'The Greatest Miscalculation'?

List of Illustrations

1. A crashed Junkers Ju88 bomber during the Battle of Britain
2. German aircrew take an athletic break from the bombing campaign
3. A British Midlands pub still doing business despite the bombing
4. A building in Manchester crashes onto the street during a Blitz raid
5. A civil defence rescue team in London hunts for survivors
6. A British businessman and civil defence personnel rescue office files
7. A funeral procession in East London in 1943 after a hit and run raid destroyed a school
8. Students of the Ivan Pavlov Medical School in Leningrad form a First Aid squad during the bombing of the city
9. Inhabitants rush for shelter during the heavy bombing of Stalingrad in August 1942
10. Leaflets from the political warfare campaign are loaded onto an RAF bomber
11. 500-lb bombs being stored during the early stages of the bombing of Germany, 1940
12. A dinner for the American and British commanders of the Combined Bomber Offensive, 1943
13. An American crew on an RAF bomber base scrawl messages on a bomb destined for Germany
14. Two RAF crewmen show the strain of the operation on their safe return to base
15. A B-24 Liberator bomber hit by anti-aircraft shells and on fire during an operation
16. A German fighter crashes in the German countryside during the 1944 'Battle of Germany'
17. The Fieseler aircraft works at Kassel, Germany, destroyed during the campaign against German aircraft production, 1944

Illustrations are reproduced courtesy of the Imperial War Museum, London (pictures 1–7, 10, 11, 13, 14, 18–22, 26, 30, 31), the Society for Cooperation in Russian and Soviet Studies, London (8, 9), the RAF Museum, Hendon (12), the Library of Congress, Washington DC (15–17), Hamburg Staatsarchiv (23), Stadtarchiv Kassel (24, 25), Archivio Storico della Città di Torino (28), and Santuario Basilica della Consolata, Torino (29).

Acknowledgements

This book owes much to the generosity of the Arts and Humanities Research Council and to the Leverhulme Trust, the first for funding a major research project on 'Bombing-States and Peoples in Western Europe' in the years 2007–10, which I helped to direct at the University of Exeter, the second for funding a year of research leave in 2010–11 to allow me to complete most of the archive research and begin writing. I would also like to thank the University of Exeter for allowing me a number of semesters of leave to work on the bombing project. I owe a particular debt to the support and help given by the team on the AHRC project – Claudia Baldoli, Vanessa Chambers, Lindsey Dodd, Stephan Glienke, Andy Knapp, Marc Wiggam – and I hope they find that the end product has been worth all our many brainstorming sessions. I would also like to thank Claire Keyte for all her unstinting assistance in helping us manage the AHRC project and its aftermath.

Over the course of the preparation and writing of this book I have relied on the help, advice and criticism of a great many people. I owe a particular debt to those who have helped me find archive material or have translated what I couldn't read. Dr Matthias Uhl devoted many hours to searching out and organizing material from the German and Soviet archives deposited in Moscow. To him and his anonymous assistants I owe a large debt of thanks. The Russian material has been rendered into English for me by Olesya Khromeychuk and Elena Minina, for which I am also deeply grateful. The Bulgarian account of the bombing of Bulgaria was made accessible to me thanks to the help of Professor Dobrinka Parusheva in Sofia and Vladislava Ibberson, who did the translation. Material on the Soviet bombing of Finland was very kindly supplied by Dr Anu Heiskanen from Helsinki and, for the bombing of Rotterdam, by Major Joris van Esch during his time at the US Military Academy. Pieter Serrien was generous in providing information on the bombing of Belgium. As ever I am indebted to the assistance given in the many archives I have visited, with the exception of the American National Archive at College Park, Maryland, which astonishingly still remains a researcher's nightmare.

Many other people have contributed in one way or another in helping to get this book finished and providing material, information or advice: in particular Martin Alexander, Monika Baar, Maria Bucur, Nicholas Chapman, Sebastian Cox, Jeremy Crang, Juliet Gardiner, Jim Goodchild, Hein Klemann, Sergei Kudryashov, James Mark, Phillips O'Brien, Anna Reid, Matthias Reiss, Laura Rowe, Nick Terry, Martin Thomas and Richard Toye. I would also like to offer a general thanks to all my students at Exeter who have taken my course on the history of bombing over the last five years and made the teaching so enjoyable. They have often made me think about issues differently, or reassess things I took for granted. I hope they will see some of that intellectual conversation reproduced here. For any remaining errors I have only myself to blame.

To my agent Gill Coleridge and her assistant Cara Jones my grateful thanks for their enthusiastic support. I am indebted as ever to the team at Penguin Press – Simon Winder, Richard Duguid, Penny Vogler – and to my copy-editor, Richard Mason, for all their help in turning the manuscript into its final polished form.

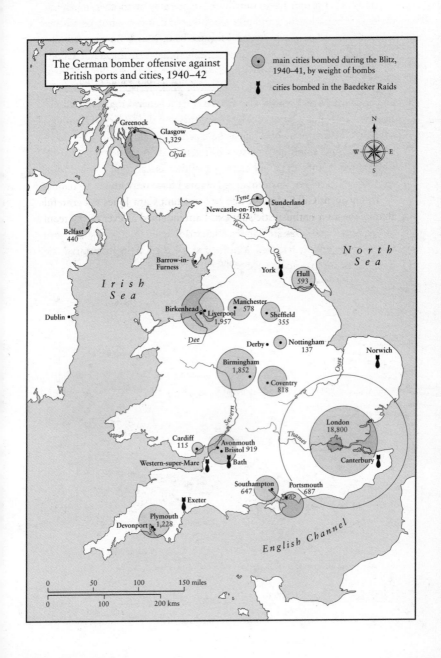

The German bomber offensive against British ports and cities, 1940–42

- main cities bombed during the Blitz, 1940–41, by weight of bombs
- cities bombed in the Baedeker Raids

Greenock
Glasgow
1,329
Clyde

N
W — *E*
S

Tyne
Newcastle-on-Tyne
152
Sunderland

Tees

Belfast
440

Barrow-in-Furness

*Irish
Sea*

*N o r t h
S e a*

York
Hull
593

Ouse

Dublin

Birkenhead
Liverpool
1,957

Manchester
578

Sheffield
355

Dee

Derby
Nottingham
137

Norwich

Birmingham
1,852

Coventry
818

Ouse

London
18,800

Thames

Cardiff
115

Avonmouth
Bristol 919
Bath

Canterbury

Western-super-Mare

Southampton
647

Portsmouth
687

Exeter

Plymouth
1,228
Devonport

English Channel

0   50   100   150 miles
0   100   200 kms

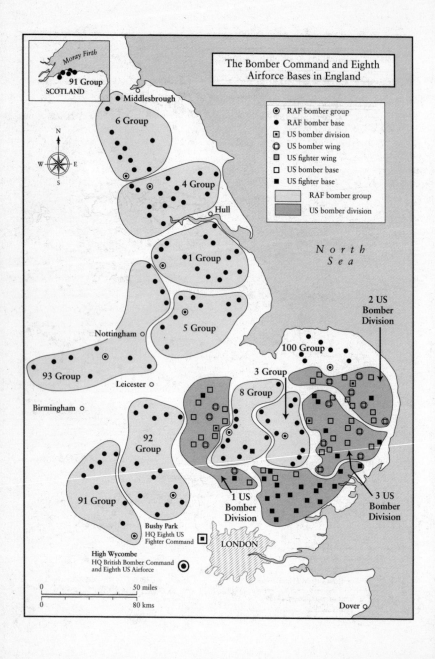

The Bomber Command and Eighth
Airforce Bases in England

Moray Firth
91 Group
SCOTLAND

Middlesbrough

6 Group

N
W   E
S

4 Group

Hull

North
Sea

1 Group

2 US
Bomber
Division

5 Group

100 Group

Nottingham

3 Group

8 Group

93 Group

Leicester

Birmingham

92
Group

1 US
Bomber
Division

3 US
Bomber
Division

91 Group

Bushy Park
HQ Eighth US
Fighter Command

High Wycombe
HQ British Bomber Command
and Eighth US Airforce

LONDON

0   50 miles
0   80 kms

Dover

Legend:
- ⊙ RAF bomber group
- ● RAF bomber base
- ▣ US bomber division
- ◉ US bomber wing
- ▦ US fighter wing
- ◻ US bomber base
- ■ US fighter base
- RAF bomber group
- US bomber division

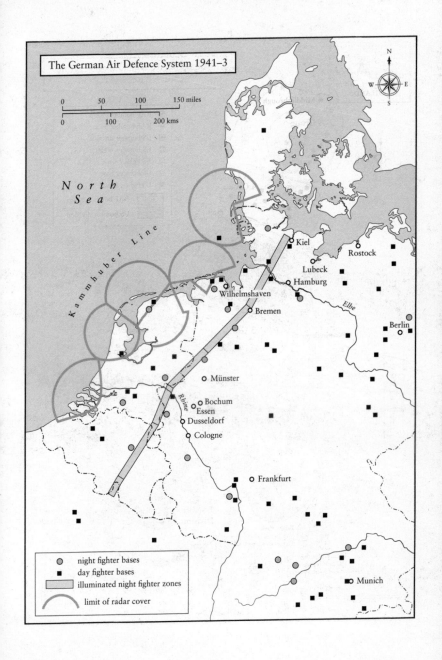

The German Air Defence System 1941–3

	miles
0	50	100	150 miles
0	100	200 kms

North Sea

Kammhuber Line

Kiel
Rostock
Lubeck
Hamburg
Wilhelmshaven
Bremen
Elbe
Berlin
Münster
Rhine
Bochum
Essen
Dusseldorf
Cologne
Frankfurt
Munich

- ● night fighter bases
- ■ day fighter bases
- ▬ illuminated night fighter zones
- ◠ limit of radar cover

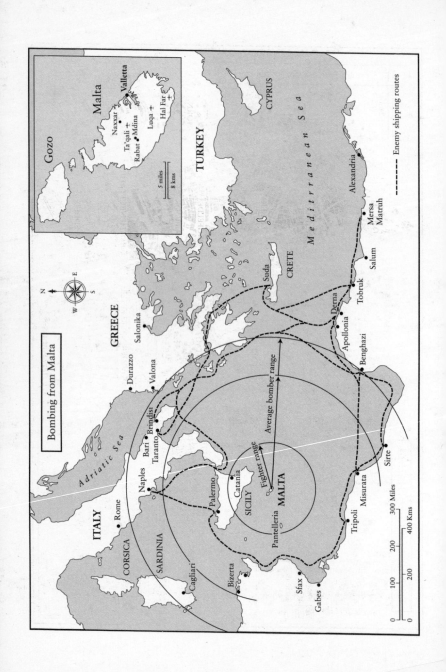

Bombing from Malta

Inset map (top):

Gozo

Malta

Naxxar •
Ta'qali ✝
Rabat • Mdina
Luqa ✝
Hal Far ✝

Valletta ●

5 miles
8 kms

Main map:

ITALY

Rome •

Naples •

CORSICA

SARDINIA

Cagliari •

Bizerta •

Gabes •

Sfax •

Tripoli •

Misurata •

Sirte •

GREECE

Salonika •

Durazzo •

Valona •

Brindisi •
Bari •
Taranto •

Adriatic Sea

Palermo •

Catania •

SICILY

Pantelleria •

MALTA

Average bomber range

Fighter range

300 Miles

400 Kms

TURKEY

CYPRUS

Mediterranean Sea

Alexandria •

Mersa Matruh •

Salum •

CRETE

Suda •

Tobruk •

Derna •

Apollonia •

Benghazi •

N
W   E
S

- - - - - Enemy shipping routes

0   100   200   300 Miles
0   200   400 Kms

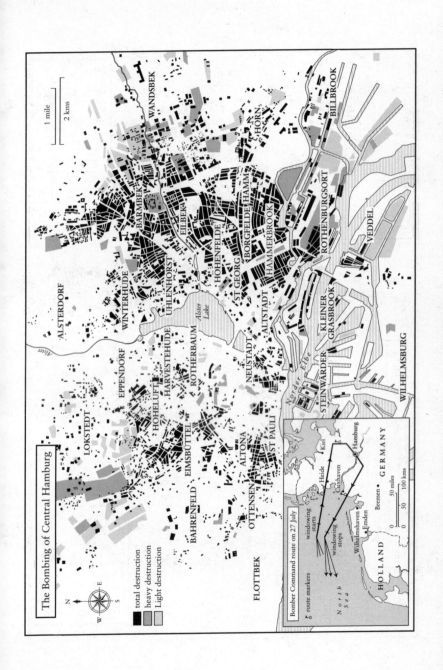

The Bombing of Central Hamburg

■ total destruction
▨ heavy destruction
░ Light destruction

N
W E
S

1 mile
2 kms

ALSTERDORF
LOKSTEDT
EPPENDORF
Alster
WINTERHUDE
HOHELUFT
HARVESTEHUDE
ROTHERBAUM
UHLENHORST
EILBEK
BARMBEK
WANDSBEK
HORN
HAMM
BORGFELDE
HAMMERBROOK
HOHENFELDE
ST GEORG
ALTSTADT
NEUSTADT
Alster Lake
ST PAULI
ALTONA
OTTENSEN
EIMSBÜTTEL
BAHRENFELD
FLOTTBEK
ROTHENBURGORT
BILLBROOK
VEDDEL
KLEINER GRASBROOK
STEINWARDER
WILHELMSBURG
Norder Elbe

Bomber Command route on 27 July

δ route markers

windowing starts
windowing stops

North
Sea

HOLLAND

GERMANY

Heide
Kiel
Cuxhaven
Hamburg
Wilhelmshaven
Emden
Bremen

0   50   100 kms
0   50 miles

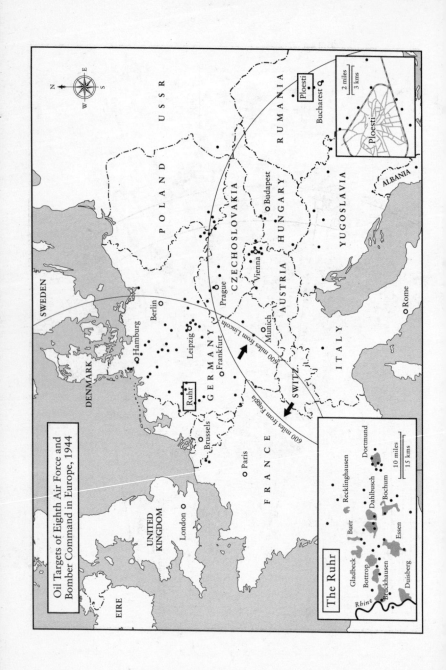

Oil Targets of Eighth Air Force and
Bomber Command in Europe, 1944

The Ruhr

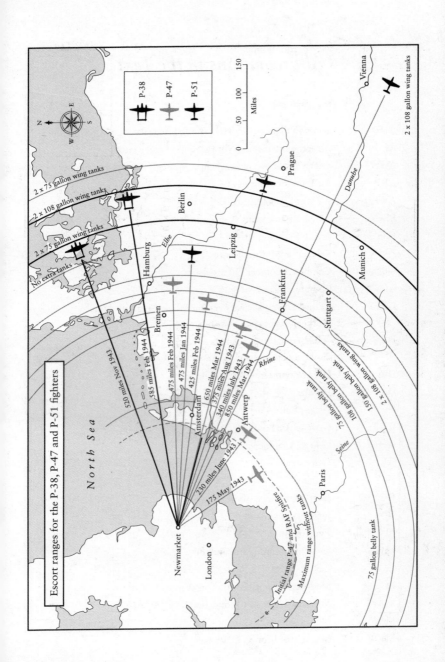

Escort ranges for the P-38, P-47 and P-51 fighters

P-38
P-47
P-51

Miles
0   50   100   150

North Sea

London
Newmarket
Paris
Amsterdam
Antwerp
Bremen
Hamburg
Berlin
Leipzig
Frankfurt
Stuttgart
Munich
Prague
Vienna

Rhine
Seine
Elbe
Danube

2 x 75 gallon wing tanks
2 x 108 gallon wing tanks
2 x 75 gallon wing tanks
No extra tanks

520 miles Nov 1943
585 miles Feb 1944
475 miles Feb 1944
475 miles Jan 1944
425 miles Feb 1944
650 miles Mar 1944
375 miles Aug 1943
340 miles July 1943
850 miles Mar 1944
230 miles June 1943
175 May 1943

Initial range P-47 and RAF Spitfire
Maximum range without tanks
75 gallon belly tank
108 gallon belly tank
150 gallon belly tank
2 x 108 gallon wing tanks
2 x 108 gallon wing tanks

Abbreviations in the Text

ADD	aviatsiya dalnego deystviya (Long-Range Aviation, USSR)
AI	Airborne Interception (British night-fighter radar)
AON	aviatsya osobovo naznachenya (Strategic Air Reserve, USSR)
ARP	Air Raid Precautions
AWPD	Air War Plans Division
BBC	British Broadcasting Corporation
BBSU	British Bombing Survey Unit
BMW	Bayerische Motorenwerke
CBO	Combined Bomber Offensive
CCS	Combined Chiefs of Staff
COSI	Comité Ouvrier de Secours Immédiat (Committee for Workers' Emergency Assistance)
DBA	dalnebombardirovochnaya aviatsiya (Soviet Long-Range Aviation)
DiCaT	Difesa Contraerea Territoriale
Do	Dornier
Fw	Focke-Wulf
GAF	German Air Force
GHQ	General Headquarters (USA)
GL-1	Gun-Laying radar
He	Heinkel
JIC	Joint Intelligence Committee (UK)
JPS	Joint Planning Staff
Ju	Junkers
LaGG	Lavochkin-Gorbunov-Gudkov
LMF	lack of moral fibre
MAAF	Mediterranean Allied Air Forces
MAP	Ministry of Aircraft Production
Me	Messerschmitt
MEW	Ministry of Economic Warfare

MiG	Mikoyan & Gurevich
MO	Mass Observation
MP	Member of Parliament (UK)
MPVO	mestnaia protivovozdushnaia oborona (Main Directorate of Local Air Defence, USSR)
NCO	Non-commissioned officer
NFPA	National Fire Protection Association
NFS	National Fire Service
NKVD	narodnyy komissariat vnutrennikh del (People's Commissariat of Internal Affairs, USSR)
NSV	Nationalsozialistische Volkswohlfahrt (National Socialist People's Welfare)
ORS	Operational Research Section
OSS	Office of Strategic Services (USA)
OTU	Operational Training Unit
PVO	protivovozdushnaia oborana strany (National Air Defence, USSR)
PWB	Psychological Warfare Branch (USA)
PWE	Political Warfare Executive
RAF	Royal Air Force
R&E	Research and Experiments Department (UK)
RFC	Royal Flying Corps
RLB	Reichsluftschutzbund (Reich Air Protection League)
RM	Reichsmark
SA	Sturmabteilung (literally 'storm section')
SAP	Securité Aérienne Publique (Public Air Protection)
SD	Sicherheitsdienst (Security Service – German secret home intelligence)
SHAEF	Supreme Headquarters Allied Expeditionary Force
SIPEG	Service Interministériel de Protection contre les Événements de Guerre (Interministerial Protection Service against the Events of War)
SNCF	Societé nationale des Chemins de Fer Français (French National Society for Railways)
SS	Schutzstaffel (literally 'protection squad')
T4	Tiergarten-4 (cover name for German euthanasia programme)
TFF	Target-Finding Force (UK)

UNPA	Unione Nazionale Protezione Antiaerea (National Union for Anti-Air Protection)
USAAF	United States Army Air Forces
USSBS	United States Strategic Bombing Survey
USSTAF	United States Strategic and Tactical Air Forces
VNOS	vozdusnogo nablyudeniya, opovescheniya i svyazi (Air Observation Warnings and Communication, USSR)
VVS	voyenno-vozdushnyye sily (Military Air Forces, USSR)
WAAF	Women's Auxiliary Air Force
WVS	Women's Voluntary Services for Air Raid Precautions (UK)
Yak	Yakovlev

Preface

Between 1939 and 1945 hundreds of European cities and hundreds more small townships and villages were subjected to aerial bombing. During the course of the conflict a staggering estimate of around 600,000 European civilians were killed by bomb attack and well over a million more were seriously injured, in some cases physically or mentally disabled for life. The landscape of much of Europe was temporarily transformed into a vision of ruin as complete as the dismal relics of the once triumphant Roman Empire. To anyone immediately after the end of the war wandering through the devastated urban wastelands the most obvious question was to ask how could this ever have been agreed to; then, a second thought, how would Europe ever recover?

These are not the questions usually asked about the bombing war. That bombing would be an integral part of future war had been taken for granted by most Europeans in the late 1930s; it would have seemed almost inconceivable that states should willingly forgo the most obvious instrument of total war. Technology shapes the nature of all wars but the Second World War more than most. Once the bombing weapon had been unleashed its potential was unpredictable. The ruins of Europe in 1945 were mute testament to the remorseless power of bombing and the inevitability of escalation. Yet the remarkable thing is that European cities did indeed recover in the decade that followed and became the flourishing centres of the consumer boom released by the post-war economic miracle. Walking along the boulevards and shopping precincts of modern cities in Germany, Italy or Britain, it now seems inconceivable that only 70 years ago they were the unwitting objects of violent aerial assault. In Europe only the fate of Belgrade at the hands of NATO air forces in 1999 is a reminder that bombing has continued to be viewed as a strategy of choice by the Western world.

Most of the history written about the bombing offensives in Europe focuses on two different questions: what were the strategic effects of bombing, and was it moral? The two have been linked more often in recent accounts, on the assumption that something that is strategically unjustifiable must also be ethically dubious, and vice versa. These arguments have generated as much heat as light, but the striking thing is that they have generally relied on a shallow base of evidence, culled still in the most part from the official histories and post-war surveys of the bombing war, and focused almost entirely on the bombing of Germany and Britain. There have been some excellent recent studies of the bombing war which have gone beyond the standard narrative (though still confined to Allied bombing of Germany), but in most general accounts of the air campaigns established myths and misrepresentations abound, while the philosophical effort to wrestle with the issue of its legality or morality has produced an outcome that is increasingly distanced from historical reality.

The purpose of the present study is to provide the first full narrative history of the bombing war in Europe. This is a resource still lacking after almost seven decades of post-war scrutiny. Three things distinguish this book from the conventional histories of bombing. First, it covers the whole of Europe. Between 1939 and 1945 almost all states were bombed, either deliberately or by accident (and including neutrals). The broad field of battle was dictated by the nature of the German New Order, carved out between 1938 and 1941, which turned most of Continental Europe into an involuntary war zone. The bombing of France and Italy (which in each case resulted in casualties the equal of the Blitz on Britain) is scarcely known in the existing historiography of the war, though an excellent recent study by Claudia Baldoli and Andrew Knapp has finally advertised it properly. The bombing of Scandinavia, Belgium, the Netherlands, Romania and Bulgaria by the Allies, and the German bombing of Soviet cities, is almost invisible in accounts of the conflict. These elements of the bombing war are all included in what follows.

Second, bombing has all too often been treated as if it could be abstracted in some way from what else was going on. Bombing, as the account here will show, was always only one part of a broad strategic picture, and a much smaller part than air force leaders liked to think. Even when bombing was chosen as an option it was often by default, always subject to the wider political and military priorities of the wartime leadership and influenced by the politics of inter-service rivalry which could limit what ambitious airmen wanted to achieve. Whatever claims might be made for air power in the Second World War, they need to be put into perspective. Bombing in Europe was never a war-winning strategy and the other services knew it.

Third, most accounts of bombing deal either with those doing the bombing or with the societies being bombed. Though links between these narratives are sometimes made, the operational history is all too often seen as distinct from the political, social and cultural consequences for the victim communities: a battle history rather than a history of societies at war. The following account looks at bombing from both perspectives – what bombing campaigns were designed to achieve, and what impact they had in reality on the populations that were bombed. Armed with this double narrative, the issues of effectiveness and ethical ambiguity can be assessed afresh.

No doubt this is an ambitious project, both in geographical scope and narrative range. Not everything can be given the coverage it deserves. This is not a book about the post-war memory of bombing, on which there is now a growing literature that is both original and conceptually mature. Nor does it deal with the reconstruction of Europe in the decade after the end of the war in more than an oblique way. Here once again there is a rich and expanding history, fuelled by other disciplines interested in issues of urban geography and community rebuilding. This is a history limited to the air war in Europe as it was fought between 1939 and 1945. The object has been to research areas where there is little available in the existing literature, or to revisit established narratives to see whether the archive record really supports them. I have been fortunate in gaining access to two new sources from the former Soviet archives. These include German Air Force documents covering the period of the Blitz, about which remarkably little has been written from the German side. There is also a rich supply of material on the Soviet air defence system and the civil defence organization, and the first statistics on Soviet casualties and material losses caused by German bombing. These can be found in the Russian State Military Archive (RGVA) in Moscow and the Central Archive of the Ministry of Defence of the Russian Federation (TsAMO), Podolsk. I am very grateful to Dr Matthias Uhl of the German Historical Institute in Moscow for obtaining access to these sources, which make it possible to reconstruct two important but neglected aspects of the bombing war. I have also been fortunate in finding a large collection of original Italian files from the Ministero dell'Aeronautica (Air Ministry) in the Imperial War Museum archive at Duxford, which cover both Italian anti-aircraft defences and the Italian bombing of Malta, the most heavily bombed site in Europe in 1941–2. I would like to record my thanks to Stephen Walton for making these records freely available to me.

My second purpose has been to re-examine the established narratives on the bombing war, chiefly British and American, by looking again at archive sources in both countries. For a long time the official histories have shaped the way the story has been told. Although the British history by Charles Webster and Noble Frankland published in 1961 is among the very best of the British official histories of the war (later dismissed by Air Marshal Harris as 'that schoolboy's essay'), the four volumes reflected the official record in The National Archive and focused narrowly on the bombing of Germany rather than Europe. The American seven-volume official history by Wesley Craven and James Cate also follows closely the operational history of the United States Army Air Forces, of which the bombing campaign was only a part. Written in the 1950s, the source base also reflected the official record, now deposited in National Archives II at College Park, Maryland, and the Air Force Historical Research Agency, Maxwell, Alabama. However, much of the history of the bombing campaign and the politics that surrounded it can only be fully understood by looking at private papers of individuals and institutions, or at areas of the official record not directly linked to bombing operations or which were originally closed to public scrutiny because they raised awkward questions. The extensive preparations for gas and biological warfare, for example, could not easily be talked about in the 1950s (and many of the records remained closed for far longer than the statutory minimum); nor could intelligence, whose secrets have gradually been unearthed over the past 30 years.

On the experience of being bombed there is less of an official voice. Only in Britain did the civil series of official histories cover civil defence, production and social policy. These are still a useful source but have been superseded in many cases by more detailed and critical historical writing. I have used less well-known local records to supplement the central archive. Particularly useful were the civil defence papers deposited at the Hull History Centre, which tell the story of a city subjected to bombing from summer 1940 to the last recorded raid on Britain, in March 1945, and the records covering the north-east deposited at the Discovery Museum in Newcastle-upon-Tyne. For other European societies there is no official history (though the volumes on the home front produced by the semi-official Military History Research Office [*Militärgeschichtliches Forschungsamt*] in Potsdam serve the same purpose very successfully), but there is a plethora of local studies on bombed cities in every state that was subjected to raids. These studies supply an invaluable source on local conditions, popular responses, civil defence performance and casualties; without them it would have been impossible to reconstruct the history of the bombed societies in France, Italy, the Low Countries and Germany. Where possible these studies have been supplemented by national records deposited in Berlin, Freiburg im Breisgau, Rome, Paris and on Malta (which has a useful civil defence archive positioned not many miles from Malta's beautiful beaches).

It is necessary to say something about the use of statistics throughout the book. Many wartime statistics are known to be deficient for one reason or another, not least those which have survived from the popular beliefs of the wartime period about levels of casualty. I have relied in the text on figures for the dead and injured from what is available in the archive record, though with the usual caveats about reliability and completeness. I have tried as scrupulously as possible to allow for reasonable margins of error, but there are nevertheless wide differences between the statistical picture presented here and many of the standard figures, particularly for Germany and the Soviet Union. In most cases figures of bomb casualties have had to be scaled down. This is not intended in any way to diminish the stark reality that hundreds of thousands of Europeans died or were seriously injured under the bombs. The search for more historically plausible statistics does not make the killing of civilians from the air any more or less legitimate; it simply registers a more reliable narrative account of what happened.

In a book of this scale it has been difficult to do full justice to the human element, either for those doing the bombing or for those being bombed. This is, nonetheless, a very human story, rooted in the wider narrative of twentieth-century violence. Throughout these pages there are individuals whose experiences have been chosen to illuminate an issue which touched thousands more, whether aircrew fighting the elements and the enemy at great physical and psychological costs, or the communities below them who became the victims of a technology that was never accurate enough to limit the wide destruction of civilian lives and the urban environment. It is one of the terrible paradoxes of total war that both the bomber crew and the bombed could be traumatized by their experience. Looking at the bombing war from the distance of 70 years, this paradox will, I hope, strengthen the resolve of the developed world never to repeat it.

Richard Overy
London, January 2013

Prologue

Bombing Bulgaria

The modern aerial bomb, with its distinctive elongated shape, stabilizing fins and nose-fitted detonator, is a Bulgarian invention. In the Balkan War of 1912, waged by Bulgaria, Greece, Serbia and Montenegro (the Balkan League) against Turkey, a Bulgarian army captain, Simeon Petrov, adapted and enlarged a number of grenades for use from an aeroplane. They were dropped on a Turkish railway station on 16 October 1912 from an Albatros F.2 biplane piloted by Radul Milkov. Petrov afterwards modified the design by adding a stabilized tail and a fuse designed to detonate on impact, and the 6-kg bomb became the standard Bulgarian issue until 1918. The plans of the so-called 'Chataldzha' bomb were later passed on to Germany, Bulgaria's ally during the First World War. The design, or something like it, soon became standard issue in all the world's first air forces.

Petrov's invention came back to haunt Bulgaria during the Second World War. On 14 November 1943 a force of 91 American B-25 Mitchell bombers escorted by 49 P-38 Lightning fighters attacked the marshalling yards in the Bulgarian capital, Sofia. The bombing was spread over a wide area, including three villages. The raid destroyed some of the rail system, the Vrajedna airfield and a further 187 buildings, resulting in around 150 casualties. A second attack 10 days later by B-24 Liberator bombers was less successful. There was poor weather across southern Bulgaria and only 17 of the force reached what they hoped was Sofia and bombed through cloud, hitting another seven villages around the capital.[1] The attacks were enough to spread panic through the city. In the absence of effective air defences or civil defence measures, thousands fled to the surrounding area. The Royal Bulgarian Air Force, though equipped with 16 Messerschmitt Me109G fighters supplied by Bulgaria's German ally, could do little against raids which, though not entirely unexpected, came as a complete surprise when they happened.[2]

The raid in November 1943 was not the first attack on a Bulgarian target during the war, though it was the heaviest and most destructive so far. Bulgaria became a target only because of the decision taken in March 1941 by the Bulgarian government, after much hesitation, to tie the country to Germany by signing the Tri-Partite Pact, which had been made between the principal Axis powers, Germany, Italy and Japan, the previous September.[3] When in spring 1941 German forces were based in Bulgaria to attack Greece and Yugoslavia, the RAF sent a force of six Wellington bombers to bomb the Sofia rail links in order to hamper the concentration of German troops. A British night raid on 13 April made a lucky hit on an ammunition train, causing major fires and widespread destruction. Further small raids occurred on 23 July and 11 August 1941, which the Bulgarian government blamed on the Soviet air force. Although Bulgaria did not actively participate in the Axis invasion of the Soviet Union on 22 June 1941, it gave supplies to Germany and allowed German ships to use the major ports of Varna and Burgas. On 13 September 1942 a further small Soviet raid hit Burgas where German ships, laden with oil-drilling equipment, were awaiting the signal to cross the Black Sea to supply German engineers with the materials they would need to restart production once the Caucasus oilfield had been captured. The Soviet Union was not at war with Bulgaria and denied the intrusions in 1941 and in 1942, for which it was almost certainly responsible, but the attacks were of such small scale that the Bulgarian government did not insist on reparations.[4]

The handful of pinprick attacks in 1941 and 1942 were enough to make Bulgaria anxious about what might happen if the Allies ever did decide to bomb its cities heavily. Bulgaria's position in the Second World War was an ambiguous one. The Tsar, Boris III, did not want his country to be actively engaged in fighting a war after the heavy territorial and financial losses Bulgaria had sustained in the peace settlement of 1919 as a punishment for joining with Germany and Austria-Hungary in the First World War. Only with great reluctance and under German pressure did the prime minister, Bogdan Filov, declare war on Britain and the United States on 13 December 1941. Aware of Bulgaria's vulnerability, the government and the Tsar wanted to avoid an actual state of belligerence with the Western powers, just as the country had refused to declare war on the Soviet Union. Bulgaria's small armed forces therefore undertook no operations against the Allies; instead they were used by the Germans as occupation troops in Macedonia and Thrace, territories given to Bulgaria after the German defeat of Yugoslavia and Greece in 1941. By 1943 it was evident to the Bulgarian government and people that they had once again backed the wrong side. Much of the population was anti-German and some of it pro-Soviet. In 1942 a left-wing Fatherland Front had been formed demanding an end to the war and the severing of links with Germany. Partisan movements in the occupied territories and in Bulgaria itself became more active during 1943 and in August that year they launched a major recruitment drive. The partisans were chiefly communist and campaigned not only for an end to the war but for a new social order and closer ties with the Soviet Union. In May 1943 and again in October, Filov authorized contacts with the Western Allies to see whether there was a possibility of reaching an agreement. He was told that only unconditional surrender and the evacuation of the occupied territories could be accepted.[5]

It is against this background that sense can be made of the Allied decision to launch a series of heavy air attacks on Bulgarian cities. Knowing that Bulgaria was facing a mounting crisis, caught between its German ally and the growing threat of a likely Soviet victory, Allied leaders were encouraged to use bombing as a political tool in the hope that it might produce a quick dividend by forcing Bulgaria out of the war. The idea that bombing was capable of a sudden decisive blow by demoralizing a population and causing a government crisis had been at the heart of much interwar thinking about the use of air power. It was the logic of the most famous statement of this principle made in 1921 by the Italian general, Giulio Douhet, in his classic study *The Command of the Air* (*Il dominio dell'aria*). The principle was also a central element in the view of air power held by the British prime minister, Winston Churchill, who had previously applied it to both Germany and Italy. It was not by chance that in a meeting with the British chiefs of staff on 19 October 1943, it was Churchill who should suggest that in his view the Bulgarians were a 'peccant people to whom a sharp lesson should be administered'. Their fault was to have sided once again with the Germans despite, Churchill claimed, his efforts to get them to see sense. Bombing was designed to undo the cord that bound Bulgaria to her German patron.

The sharp lesson was to be a heavy bombing attack on Sofia. Churchill justified the operation on political grounds: 'experience shows,' he told the meeting, 'that the effect of bombing a country where there were antagonistic elements was not to unite those elements, but rather to increase the anger of the anti-war party'.[6] Others present, including Air Chief Marshal Sir Charles Portal, chief of the air staff, and the chief of the general staff, General Alan Brooke, were less keen and insisted that leaflets should be dropped along with the bombs explaining that the Allies wanted Bulgaria to withdraw its occupation troops and surrender (in the end a leaflet was dropped with the curious headline 'This is not about Allied terror, but about Bulgarian insanity').[7] But the idea of a 'sharp lesson' quickly circulated. The American military chiefs thought that Sofia was so low a military priority that an attack was scarcely justified, but they were impressed by the possible 'great psychological effect'.[8] Both the British and American ambassadors in Ankara urged an attack so as to interrupt Turkish-German commercial rail traffic.[9] On 24 October the Anglo-American Combined Chiefs of Staff directed General Dwight D. Eisenhower, supreme commander in the Mediterranean, to give such a lesson as soon as this was operationally practical.[10] The Turkish government approved, hopeful perhaps despite neutrality to profit from Bulgaria's discomfiture in any post-war settlement. Churchill wanted Stalin's say-so as well because Bulgaria was clearly in the Soviet sphere of interest. On 29 October the British Foreign Minister, Anthony Eden, who was in Moscow for negotiations, was able to report back Stalin's comment that Sofia should certainly be bombed as it was nothing more than 'a province of Germany'.[11]

The Bulgarian government had expected bombing for some time. While the regime struggled to come to terms with internal dissent, the Soviet presence in the east and Allied demands for unconditional surrender, it also sought ways to appease the Germans in case they decided to occupy Bulgaria. In the course of 1943 the deportation of Jews from the occupied areas of Thrace was completed and, despite the hostility of the Tsar, the German authorities in Sofia persuaded the Bulgarian government to deport native Bulgarian Jews as well. It was agreed that they would first be transferred to 20 small towns in the hinterland around Sofia and in May 1943 some 16,000 Jews were taken at short notice from the capital and parcelled out among eight provinces. The Filov government linked the Jewish policy with bombing. When the Swiss ambassador asked Filov to stop sending Thracian Jews to Auschwitz on humanitarian grounds, Filov retorted that talk of humanity was misconceived when the Allies were busy obliterating the cities of Europe from the air. Moreover, when he failed to take up a British offer in February 1943 to transport 4,500 Jewish children from Bulgaria to Palestine, he feared that Sofia might be bombed in retaliation.[12] Once the Jews of Sofia had been deported to the provinces, anxiety revived again in Bulgaria that the Allies would now no longer hesitate to bomb from fear of killing Jews. In the end the Jews of Bulgaria not only escaped deportation to Auschwitz but also escaped the bombing, which left much of Sofia's Jewish quarter in ruins.

It was not the Jewish question that invited Allied bombing in November 1943, though many Bulgarians assumed that it was. The first raids seemed to presage an onslaught of aerial punishment and the population of the capital gave way to a temporary panic. Yet the first two attacks in November were followed by two desultory operations the following month and nothing more. Some 209 inhabitants in Sofia had been killed and 247 buildings damaged. The 'sharp lesson' was not sharp enough for the Allies because it did little to encourage Bulgaria to seek a political solution while the military value of the attacks was at best limited, hampered by poor bombing accuracy and gloomy Balkan weather. On Christmas Day 1943, Churchill wrote to Eden that the 'heaviest possible air attacks' were now planned for Sofia in the hope that this might produce more productive 'political reactions'.[13] On 4 January 1944 a large force of 108 B-17 Flying Fortresses was despatched to Sofia, but with poor visibility the attack was aborted after a few bombs were dropped on a bridge. Finally, on 10 January 1944 the first heavy attack was mounted by 141 B-17s, supported during the night of 10–11 January by a force of some 44 RAF Wellington bombers. This attack was devastating for the Bulgarian capital: there were 750 dead and 710 seriously injured, and there was widespread damage to residential housing and public buildings. The air-raid sirens failed to sound because of a power cut. This time the population panicked entirely, creating a mass exodus. By 16 January, 300,000 people had left the capital. The government abandoned the administrative district and moved out to nearby townships. It took more than two weeks to restore services in the capital, while much of the population abandoned it permanently from fear of a repeat attack. On 23 January the German ambassador telegraphed back to Berlin that the bombing changed completely the 'psychological-political situation', exposing the incompetence of the authorities and raising the danger of Bulgarian defection.[14] The government ordered church bells to be pealed as an air-raid warning, in case of further power cuts.[15]

The second major raid, of 10 January, did pay political dividends. While Filov tried unsuccessfully to persuade a visiting German general, Walter Warlimont, Deputy for Operations on Hitler's staff, to mount a revenge attack on neutral Istanbul – whose consequences might well have been even more disastrous for Bulgaria – most Bulgarian leaders had come to realize that the German connection had to be severed as

soon as possible and a deal struck with the Allies.[16] The Bishop of Sofia
used the occasion of the funeral for the victims of the bombing to launch
an attack on the government for tying Bulgaria to Germany and failing
to save the people from war. That month an effort was made to get the
Soviet Union to intercede with the Western Allies to stop the bombing,
but instead Moscow increased its pressure on Bulgaria to abandon its
support for the Axis.[17] In February the first informal contacts were
made with the Allies through a Bulgarian intermediary in Istanbul to see
whether terms could be agreed for an armistice. Although hope for
negotiation had been the principal reason for starting the bombing, the
Allied reaction to the first Bulgarian approach following the raids was
mixed. Roosevelt wrote to Churchill on 9 February suggesting that the
bombing should now be suspended if the Bulgarians wanted to talk, a
view shared by British diplomats in the Middle Eastern headquarters in
Cairo.[18] Churchill scrawled 'why?' in the margin of the letter. He was
opposed to ending the bombing despite a recent report from the British
Joint Intelligence Committee (JIC) which observed that the first bombing in November 1943 had achieved no 'decisive political result'. He
had already authorized the bombing of the Bulgarian ports of Burgas
and Varna, which were added to the list of priority targets, subject to
political considerations.[19] In January 1944 the British War Cabinet, in
the event of a German gas attack, considered the possibility of retaliatory gas bomb attacks against Germany and its allies, and included
Bulgaria on the list.[20] On 12 February Churchill replied to Roosevelt
that in his view the bombing had had 'exactly the effect we hoped for'
and urged him to accept the argument that bombing should continue
until the Bulgarians began full and formal negotiations: 'if the medicine
has done good, let them have more of it'.[21] Roosevelt immediately wired
back his full agreement: 'let the good work go on'.[22]

Some of the evidence coming out of Bulgaria seemed to support
Churchill's stance. Intelligence reports arrived detailing the rapid expansion of both the Communist partisan movement and the Fatherland
Front. The partisans contacted the Allies through a British liaison officer
stationed in Bulgaria, encouraging them to keep up the bombing in
order to provoke the collapse of the pro-German regime and help
expand support for the resistance. The partisans sent details about the
central administrative area in Sofia, bordered by the recently renamed
Adolfi Hitler Boulevard, which they said was ripe for attack; at the same
time partisan leaders asked the Allies not to bomb the working-class
districts of Sofia, from which most of their recruits were drawn. By

March the partisans were finally organized by the Bulgarian Communists into the National Liberation Revolutionary Army.[23] As a result of the evidence on the ground the Western Allies, with Stalin's continued though secret support (the Soviet Union did not want Bulgarians to think they had actively abetted the bombing), accepted Eden's argument that by 'turning on the heat' on Bulgarian cities it might shortly be possible either to provoke a *coup d'état* or to batter the government into suing for peace.[24] On 10 March Sir Charles Portal told Churchill that he had ordered heavy attacks on Sofia and other Bulgarian cities as soon as possible.[25]

On 16 March and then on 29–30 March the Allies launched the most destructive attacks of all on Sofia, as well as subsidiary attacks on Burgas, Varna, and Plovdiv in the interior, designed to disrupt rail communications and sea traffic for the Turkish trade with Germany. The attacks were aimed predominantly at the administrative city centre of Sofia and carried a proportion of incendiaries, 4,000 in all, in order to do to Sofia what had been done so effectively to German targets. The raid of 16 March burned down the royal palace; the heavy raid of 29–30 March by 367 B-17s and B-24s, this time carrying 30,000 incendiaries, created a widespread conflagration, destroying the Holy Synod of the Bulgarian Orthodox Church, the National Theatre, several ministries and a further 3,575 buildings, but killing only 139 of the population that had remained.[26] The last major raid, on 17 April by 350 American bombers, destroyed a further 750 buildings and heavily damaged the rail marshalling yard. During 1944 the death toll in Sofia was 1,165, a figure that would have been considerably higher had it not been for the voluntary evacuation of the capital. The incendiary attacks hastened the disintegration of Bulgarian politics and increased support for the Soviet Union, whose armies were now within striking distance. But only on 20 June 1944, several months after the bombing, did the new government of Ivan Bagryanov begin formal negotiations for an end to Bulgarian belligerency, still hoping to keep Bulgaria's territorial spoils and avoid Allied occupation.[27] By this time the Allies had lost interest in bombing Bulgaria, which slipped further down the list of priority targets as the bombers turned their attention to Budapest and Bucharest in the path of the oncoming Red Army.[28]

By the summer of 1944 the Allies had other preoccupations and it seemed evident that Bulgarian politics had been sufficiently destabilized by the bombing to make further attacks redundant. Nevertheless, the final assessment of the effects of the bombing was ambivalent. In July

the United States Joint Chiefs of Staff prepared an evaluation of the
Balkan bombings which suggested that the psychological effects desired
had largely been achieved; the report nevertheless suggested that the
enemy had sustained an effective propaganda campaign about the high
level of civilian casualties, which had undermined the prestige of both
the United States and Britain in the eyes of the Bulgarian people. The
chiefs directed that in the future any attacks in the region had to be confined to 'targets of definite military importance' and civilian casualties
minimized. The British chiefs of staff rejected the American claim and,
in defiance of what they well knew to be the case, insisted that only military targets had been subject to attack, even if this had involved damage
to housing and civilian deaths. Their report concluded that Allied bombers ought always to be able to act in this way and that operations 'should
not be prejudiced by undue regard for the probable scale of incidental
casualties'.[29] This was a view consistent with everything the RAF had
argued and practised since the switch to the deliberate bombing of
German civilians in 1941.

For the historian the judgement is more complex. Bombing almost
certainly contributed to the collapse of any pro-German consensus and
strengthened the hand both of the moderate centre-left in the Fatherland Front and of the radical partisan movement. But in the end this did
not result in a complete change of government until 9 September 1944,
when the Soviet presence produced a Fatherland Front administration
dominated by the Bulgarian Communist Party (a political outcome that
neither Churchill nor Eden had wanted from the bombing).[30] Moreover,
other factors played an important role in Bulgarian calculations: the
crisis provoked by Italian defeat and surrender in September 1943; the
German retreat in the Soviet Union; and fear of a possible Allied Balkan
invasion or of Turkish intervention.[31] Where Churchill saw bombing as
a primitive instrument for provoking political crisis and insisted
throughout the period from October 1943 to March 1944 that this was
the key to knocking Bulgaria out of the war, the American military
chiefs continued to give preference to the bombing of Italy and Germany and were less persuaded that a political dividend was certain. For
them the bombing fitted with the strategy of wearing down Germany's
capacity for waging war by interrupting the supply of vital war materials and forcing the diversion of German military units from the imminent
Normandy campaign. There was also a price to pay for the bombing. In
September 1944, following the Bulgarian surrender, some 332 American Air Force prisoners of war were sent by air shuttle to Istanbul and

then on to Cairo; some had crashed bombing Bulgaria, others on their
way to or from attacks on Romanian targets. An American report
suggested that the prisoners had been badly treated. Two air force prisoners were killed by the Bulgarian police, and an estimated 175 American
war dead were presumed to be on Bulgarian territory, although only
84 bodies could be located.[32]

The bombing of Bulgaria recreated in microcosm the many issues that
defined the wider bombing offensives during the Second World War. It
was a classic example of what has come to be called 'strategic bombing'.
The definition of strategic bombing is neither neat nor precise. The term
itself originated in the First World War when Allied officers sought
to describe the nature of long-range air operations carried out against
distant targets behind the enemy front line. These were operations
organized independently of the ground campaign, even though they
were intended to weaken the enemy and make success on the ground
more likely. The term 'strategic' (or sometimes 'strategical') was used by
British and American airmen to distinguish the strategy of attacking
and wearing down the enemy home front and economy from the strategy of directly assaulting the enemy's armed forces.

The term was also coined in order to separate independent bombing
operations from bombing in direct support of the army or navy. This
differentiation has its own problems, since direct support of surface
forces also involves the use of bombing planes and the elaboration of
target systems at or near the front whose destruction would weaken
enemy resistance. In Germany and France between the wars 'strategic'
air war meant using bombers to attack military and economic targets
several hundred kilometres from the fighting front, if they directly supported the enemy's land campaign. German and French military chiefs
regarded long-range attacks against distant urban targets, with no direct bearing on the fighting on the ground, as a poor use of strategic
resources. The German bombing of Warsaw, Belgrade, Rotterdam and
numerous Soviet cities fits this narrower definition of strategic bombing. Over the course of the Second World War the distinction between
the more limited conception of strategic air war and the conduct of
long-range, independent campaigns became increasingly blurred; distant operations against enemy military, economic or general urban
targets were carried out by bomber forces whose role was interchangeable with their direct support of ground operations. The aircraft of
the United States Army Air Forces in Italy, for example, bombed the

monastery of Monte Cassino in February 1944 in order to break the
German front line, but also bombed Rome, Florence and the distant
cities of northern Italy to provoke political crisis, weaken Axis economic potential and disrupt military communications. The German
bombing of British targets during the summer and autumn of 1940 was
designed to further the plan to invade southern Britain in September,
and was thus strategic in the narrower, German sense of the term. But
with the shift to the Blitz bombing from September 1940 to June 1941,
the campaign took on a more genuinely 'strategic' character, since its
purpose was to weaken British willingness and capacity to wage war
and to do so without the assistance of German ground forces. For the
unfortunate populations in the way of the bombing, in Italy or in Britain or elsewhere, there was never much point in trying to work out
whether they had been bombed strategically or not, for the destructive
effects on the ground were to all intents and purposes the same: high
levels of death and serious injury, the widespread destruction of the
urban landscape, the reduction of essential services and the arbitrary
loss of cultural treasure. Being bombed as part of a ground campaign
could, as in the case of the French port of Le Havre in September
1944 or the German city of Aachen in September and October the same
year, produce an outcome considerably worse than an attack regarded
as strategically independent.

In *The Bombing War* no sharp dividing line is drawn between these
different forms of strategic air warfare, but the principal focus of the
book is on bombing campaigns or operations that can be regarded as
independent of immediate surface operations either on land or at sea.
Such operations were distinct from the tactical assault by bombers and
fighter-bombers on fleeting battlefield targets, local troop concentrations, communications, oil stores, repair depots, or merchant shipping,
all of which belong more properly to the account of battlefield support
aviation. This definition makes it possible to include as 'strategic' those
operations that were designed to speed up the advance of ground forces
but were carried out independently, and often at a considerable distance
from the immediate battleground, such as those in Italy or the Soviet
Union, or the aerial assault on Malta. However, the heart of any history
of the bombing war is to be found in the major independent bombing
campaigns carried out to inflict heavy damage on the enemy home front
and if possible to provoke a political collapse. In all the cases where
large-scale strategic campaigns were conducted – Germany against Britain in 1940–41, Britain and the United States against Germany and

German-occupied Europe in 1940–45, Britain and the United States against Italian territory – there was an implicit understanding that bombing alone might unhinge the enemy war effort, demoralize the population and perhaps provoke the politicians to surrender before the need to undertake dangerous, large-scale and potentially costly amphibious operations. These political expectations from bombing are an essential element in the history of the bombing war.

The political imperatives are exemplified by the brief aerial assault on Bulgaria. The idea of what is now called a 'political dividend' is a dimension of the bombing war that has generally been relegated to second place behind the more strictly military analysis of what bombing did or did not do to the military capability and war economy of the enemy state. Yet it will be found that there are many examples between 1939 and 1945 of bombing campaigns or operations conducted not simply for their expected military outcome, but because they fulfilled one, or a number, of political objectives. The early bombing of Germany by the Royal Air Force in 1940 and 1941 was partly designed, for all its military ineffectiveness, to bring war back to the German people and to create a possible social and political crisis on the home front. It was also undertaken to impress the occupied states of Europe that Britain was serious about continuing the war, and to demonstrate to American opinion that democratic resistance was still alive and well. For the RAF, bombing was seen as the principal way in which the service could show its independence of the army and navy and carve out for itself a distinctive strategic niche. For the British public, during the difficult year that followed defeat in the Battle of France, bombing was one of the few visible things that could be done to the enemy. 'Our wonderful R.A.F. is giving the Ruhr a terrific bombing,' wrote one Midlands housewife in her diary. 'But one thinks also of the homes from where these men come and what it means to their families.'[33]

The political element of the bombing war was partly dictated by the direct involvement of politicians in decision-making about bombing. The bombing of Bulgaria was Churchill's idea and he remained the driving force behind the argument that air raids would provide a quick and relatively cheap way of forcing the country to change sides. In December 1943, when the Mediterranean commanders dragged their feet over the operations because of poor weather, an irritated Churchill scribbled at the foot of the telegram, 'I am sorry the weather is so adverse. The political moment may be fleeting.' Three months later, while the first Bulgarian peace feelers were being put out, Churchill wrote 'Bomb with high intensity *now*', underlining the final word three times.[34] The campaign in the Balkans also showed how casually politicians could decide on operations whose effectiveness they were scarcely in a position to judge from a strategic or operational point of view. The temptation to reach for air power when other means of exerting direct violent pressure were absent was hard to resist. Bombing had the virtues of being flexible, less expensive than other military options, and enjoying a high public visibility, rather like the gunboat in nineteenth-century diplomacy. Political intervention in bombing campaigns was a common feature during the war, culminating in the decision eventually taken to drop atomic weapons on Hiroshima and Nagasaki in August 1945. This (almost) final act in the bombing war has generated a continuing debate about the balance between political and military considerations, but it could equally be applied to other wartime contexts. Evaluating the effects of the bombing of Bulgaria and other Balkan states, it was observed that bombing possessed the common singular virtue of 'demonstrating to their peoples that the war is being brought home to them by the United Nations'.[35] In this sense the instrumental use of air power, recently and unambiguously expressed in the strategy of 'Shock and Awe', first articulated as a strategic aim at the United States National Defense University in the 1990s and applied spectacularly to Baghdad and other Iraqi cities in 2003, has its roots firmly in the pattern of 'political' bombing in the Second World War.

Bombing was, of course, much more than a set of convenient political tools and much of what follows describes the organizations, the forces and the technology that made bombing operations possible. Strategic bombing was a military activity which had to be organized very differently from operations of the army and navy and it was one fraught with difficulty under the technical conditions of the time. Air force commanders wanted to deliver what the politicians wanted, but as a consequence bomber forces were always trying to run before they could walk. All the major air services faced a long learning curve during the war as they struggled to overcome a whole range of inherent problems and limitations. Power was generally projected onto distant cities or industrial installations and in most cases involved long and hazardous flights, hampered by fickle weather, by enemy defences, and by complex issues of navigation and effective bomb-aiming. Fixed bases had to be secured near enough to enable the bombing to take place. The rate of loss of aircrew was high, though not exceptional if a comparison is made with other front-line forces. The most distinctive feature of

bomber operations was the capacity of aircraft to penetrate enemy airspace and to inflict damage on the domestic economy, military capability
and population according to the prevailing directives. No other service
could project power in this way, so by default the bomber became the
supreme instrument for waging what was defined at the time as total
war. The belief that modern, industrialized war was now to be fought
between whole societies, each mobilizing the material energies and willpower of their entire population for the task of fighting, arming and
supplying the mass armed forces of the modern age, took root in the
generation that grew up after the Great War. While it was generally
understood by the air forces themselves that bombing enemy populations for the sake of exerting terror was contrary to conventional rules
of engagement, attacking and killing armaments workers, destroying
port facilities or even burning down crops could all be construed, without too much sophistry, as legitimate objectives of total war.

Before the coming of the Second World War those air forces that had
considered the implications of war against the enemy home front had to
choose a set of targets which made strategic sense. These included all
military installations, heavy industry, energy supply, armaments production and communications. The German campaign against Britain
was based on a detailed gazetteer of industrial and military targets scrupulously compiled before 1939 from photo-reconnaissance evidence
and industrial intelligence.[36] In the summer of 1941 the United States
Army Air Forces drew up a plan for bombing Germany that identified
six key target systems and a total of 154 individual industrial targets,
whose destruction was supposed to lead to the collapse of the German
war economy and its supporting services.[37] Air force commanders were
reluctant to endorse operations that could not demonstrate some clear
military or war economic purpose, however broadly the net of total war
might be spread, or however forceful the political pressure. Even in Bulgaria, the brief political directive from Churchill was watered down
when it was passed on to the military chiefs to give it a spurious military
justification: 'Sofia is a centre of administration of belligerent government, an important railway centre, and has barracks, arsenals and
marshalling yards.'[38] The reluctance of the air commanders on the spot
to carry out the bombing of Bulgaria with the single-mindedness
demanded by Churchill, reflected their view that bombing was not likely
to achieve very much in practical terms, while the bombing of, for
example, Romanian oil supplies or the Viennese aircraft industry would
clearly have significant consequences. The short campaign against

Bulgaria illustrated the tension that existed between the exaggerated expectations of politicians and public about the likely political and psychological results from attacking an enemy from the air, and the demonstrable value of doing so in military and economic terms. This ambiguity underlay many of the wider wartime arguments between politicians, airmen and the military chiefs over what bombing could or could not deliver and it helps to explain a feature characteristic of all bombing campaigns: the escalation of the degree of indiscriminate damage.

The pattern of bombing in Bulgaria, from a limited raid on the railway facilities and the Vrajedna airfield in November 1943 to the final raids in March and April 1944 when the extensive use of incendiaries produced much higher levels of urban destruction, was not an accidental progression. In all the major campaigns in Europe (and in the campaigns mounted in eastern Asia) there occurred an evident escalation the longer the bombing went on and the more uncertain were its results. Air force commanders had an urgent need to demonstrate that their operations were militarily useful in the face of hostile criticism from the other services or the impatience of their political masters. This was true of the German bombing of British cities, the British bombing of Germany in 1940–42 and the Combined Bomber Offensive between 1943 and 1945. Perhaps the best example is the shift in British planning from the 1939 Western Air Plans for limited attacks on Ruhr industrial installations to the decision taken in 1941 to attack the central areas of German industrial cities with large quantities of incendiaries to destroy working-class housing and to kill workers. The reasons for escalation – the phenomenon that explains the exceptional or disproportionate level of civilian deaths in all bombed states – differ in historical detail from case to case. Nevertheless they suggest a common process dictated partly by technical frustration at poor accuracy and navigation or high losses; partly by political frustration at the absence of unambiguous results; partly by air force anxiety that failure might reflect badly on its claim on resources; and finally, and significantly, by the slow erosion of any relative moral constraints that might have acted to limit the damage to civilian targets. Among the many questions about the military conduct of the campaigns, the issue of escalation and its consequences remains the most important. It has significant implications for the current exercise of air power in the wars of the twenty-first century.

For the societies that suffered the bombing during the war there was only one reality that mattered: 'The bomber will always get through.'

The famous remark by the British deputy prime minister, Stanley Baldwin, on the eve of his departure for the Geneva Disarmament talks in November 1932, that the man in the street ought to understand there was no power on earth yet available to stop him from being bombed, has usually been taken for deliberate hyperbole, to scare delegates at Geneva into accepting a ban on bomber aircraft. Yet though it proved possible during the war to detect aircraft with radar and to intercept them by day and increasingly by night, and to inflict high-percentage rates of loss on an attacking force, in the context of the Second World War, Baldwin was right. Most bombers did reach the approximate target area and disgorge their bombs with limited accuracy on the ground below, turning wartime civilian society into an effective front line. That this would be so was widely expected by the 1930s among the populations of the world's major states, who saw bombing fatalistically, as something that would define future conflict. 'It is the height of folly,' wrote the British Air Minister, Lord Londonderry, to Baldwin in July 1934, 'to imagine that any war can be conducted without appreciable risk to the civil population.'[39] Brought up on a diet of scaremongering fiction and films, subject by the 1930s to regular drill or instruction or propaganda for air-raid precautions, civilian society came to take it for granted that it would become an object of attack, even that there might be some degree of democratic legitimacy in bombing if all of modern mass society had to be mobilized for war. The British pacifist Vera Brittain, writing in 1940 at the height of the Blitz, observed that in the First World War there had grown up a 'barrier of inconceivable experience' between the soldiers on the Western Front and the civilians at home in Britain. During the current conflict, she continued, 'both suffering and suspense are universal in England herself ... There is no emotional barrier between men and women, parents and children, the old and the young, since the battle is shared by all ages and both sexes.'[40]

The concept of civilian society, primarily urban society, as a new front line in war was in reality a novel, indeed unique, phenomenon in the context of the modern age. It gave to the strategic bombing war a second political dimension because it raised the problem of maintaining social cohesion and political allegiance in the face of extreme levels of direct military violence against the home front. The survival of positive 'morale' became central to the concerns of those governments whose populations were subject to attack. Morale as such was poorly defined at the time, was difficult to measure in any meaningful way and subject to a great many other pressures besides the effects of bombing. A British

Air Ministry report in autumn 1941 confessed that since 'morale is itself
a thing of opinion and not of fact, there is no likelihood even of experts
agreeing on the matter'.[41] Yet it was the bombing war in particular that
was popularly believed by rulers and ruled to have a fundamental
impact on the war-willingness and psychological state of the population
and it featured regularly in home intelligence reports on the public
mood in Britain, Germany, Italy and Japan. This was an equally difficult
assessment to make for those doing the bombing. They tried to estimate
with some precision what effect their attacks might have on the state of
mind of those they bombed, but the answers were more often than not
contradictory or confused. The JIC report on the bombing of Bulgaria,
produced in January 1944, highlighted social effects that were 'out of
proportion' to the modest scale of attack, but still concluded that the
political results had been negligible.

    There can be little room for doubt that the experience of bombing
was deeply demoralizing for many of those who survived it, though it
could also provoke sudden moments of exhilaration, or induce a profound apathy, but the difficulty in drawing any clear causal links
between bombing and popular response is simply that the response was
as varied, irregular, unpredictable and diverse as the society that made
it. The social reaction to bombing is often treated as if it must be uniform, but it differed widely between states and within communities.
This was a reality seldom appreciated by those doing the bombing for
whom 'Germans' or 'Italians' or even 'Bulgarians' became simply a
generic description of the human target. One of the key questions still
debated about the bombing war is why the bombed societies did not
collapse at once under the impact, as conventional wisdom before
1939 suggested they would. This is too simple an approach. Bombing
did place enormous strains on local communities, and some did experience a cumulative or temporary social breakdown as a result, but it was
always a long step from local social crisis to the complete collapse of a
war effort. To understand why 'morale' did not collapse in Britain or
Germany in the sense of a political upheaval is to engage with complex
issues of social cohesion defined by regional difference, the intensity of
the bombing experience, the nature of the prevailing state and local
administration, the peculiar structures of local society and the cultural
impact of propaganda. Any narrative of the bombing war has to address
the psychological, social and cultural response as well as the conventional military reality: the view from below as well as the view from
above. This dual approach has featured only rarely in the existing his-

tory of the bombing campaigns, yet it is the one sure way to assess just what effects bombing actually had on the target communities, and to suggest what those effects might be in any future war.

The story of the civilian front line in the air war is an aggregate story of loss of extraordinary proportions: an estimated 600,000 killed, a million seriously injured, millions more less severely hurt; millions dispossessed through bomb destruction; 50–60 per cent of the urban area of Germany obliterated; countless cultural monuments and works of art irreparably lost. It is only when these costs are summarized that the unique character of the bombing war can be properly understood. The dead were not accidental bystanders but the consequence of a technology generally incapable of distinguishing and hitting a small individual target, and which all sides knew was incapable of doing so with the prevailing science. This raises a number of questions about why the states involved never reined back campaigns with such a high civilian cost and in particular why Britain and the United States, liberal democracies which self-consciously occupied the moral high ground during the war, and had both deplored bombing before 1939, ended up organizing strategic bombing campaigns that killed around 1 million people in Europe and Asia. These seem obvious questions seventy years later but they can only be properly answered by understanding the terms in which the moral imperatives of war were perceived at the time. The assault on civilians signified an acceptance, even by the victim populations, of shifting norms about the conduct of war; what had seemed unacceptable legally or morally in 1939 was rapidly transformed by the relative ethics of survival or defeat.[42]

It is easy to deplore the losses and to condemn the strategy as immoral, even illegal – and a host of recent accounts of the bombing have done just that – but current ethical concerns get no nearer to an understanding of how these things were possible, even applauded, and why so few voices were raised during the war against the notion that the home front could legitimately be a target of attack.[43] The contemporary ethical view of bombing was far from straightforward, often paradoxical. It is striking, for example, that among those who were bombed there was seldom clear or persistent hatred for the enemy; there was a sense that 'war' itself was responsible and 'modern war' in particular, as if it enjoyed some kind of existence independent of the particular air fleets inflicting the damage. There could even be a sense that bombing was necessary to purge the world of the forces that had unleashed the barbarism in the first place, a blessing as much as a curse. A young

German soldier captured and interrogated in Italy early in 1945 told his captors: 'In the long run your bombings may be good for Germany. They have given her a taste, bitter though it may be, of what war is really like.'[44] The moral response to bombing and being bombed was historically complex and sometimes surprising. Issues that seemed black and white before the war and do so again today were coloured in many shades of grey during the conflict. Nonetheless, the figures on death, injury and destruction are shocking, just as the other forms of mass death of civilians in the Second World War. The grisly consequences of the bombing war would have outraged opinion in the 1930s just as they have attracted current opprobrium among historians and international lawyers.[45] Exploring how it was possible to legitimize this scale of damage in the brief span of total war between 1940 and 1945 forms the fourth and perhaps the most important element in *The Bombing War*, alongside the political context that shaped the development of the aerial conflict, the military operations that defined its precise character and extent, and the administrative, social and cultural responses that determined the limits of what bombing could actually achieve.

I

Bombing before 1940:
Imagined and Real

In 1938 the American critic Lewis Mumford, well known for his unflat-
tering views on the modern giant city, explored the rise and fall of what
he called 'Megalopolis' in his book *The Culture of Cities*. He described
'a vast pus-bag of vulgar pretense and power' in which civilization
became year by year more fragile and insecure until the day when the
air-raid sirens sound: 'Plainly, terrors more devastating and demoralizing than any known in the ancient jungle or cave have been re-introduced
into modern urban existence. Panting, choking, spluttering, cringing,
hating, the dweller in Megalopolis dies, by anticipation, a thousand
deaths.' A humane civic life, Mumford argued, was no longer possible
in modern cities during a bombing war. The end result of the destruction was a city of the dead, 'Nekropolis', 'a tomb for the dying . . . flesh
turned to ashes'.[1]

Mumford was one of hundreds of Europeans and Americans whose
powerful imaginative writing helped to define the popular idea of what
a bombing war would be like long before it became a possibility or a
reality. The most famous of them all was the English novelist H. G.
Wells whose *The War in the Air*, published as far back as 1908, set the
pattern for all subsequent literature, fiction and non-fiction, that
addressed the possible effects of a bombing war. In the novel, a fleet of
malevolent German airships destroys New York in a matter of hours, 'a
crimson furnace from which there was no escape'. The worldwide war
that develops engulfs civilization, whose misplaced sense of security and
progress is blotted out more rapidly than the fall of any earlier civilized
order: 'And this was no slow decadence that came to the Europeanized
world; those other civilizations rotted and crumbled down, the Europeanized civilization was, as it were, blown up.'[2] Wells used the book to
highlight a theme that he returned to regularly in the years leading up
to the outbreak of the Second World War: that the application of modern science to war was fraught with danger. The destruction of New

York in the novel was, he suggested, 'the logical outcome' of this unfortunate marriage. In a less well-known sequel, *The World Set Free*, written five years later in 1913, Wells anticipated the nuclear age, in which 200 of the world's great cities are destroyed in the 'unquenchable crimson conflagrations of the atomic bomb'.[3] Like Mumford, Wells saw urban life as both defining the modern age ('gigantic cities spreading gigantically') and uniquely susceptible to obliteration by the very science to which it had given birth.[4]

Neither the alleged fragility of the modern city nor the fears for the end of civilization were realized in the war that broke out in August 1914, yet they remained dominant tropes in the thirty years that separated Wells' early predictions from the reality of mass city bombing after 1940. Aircraft in the Great War were in their technical infancy. Although the war did witness the origins of what came to be called by its end 'strategic bombing', the scale of such bombing was tiny and its direct impact on the warring states subjected to it was negligible. The first major raids were mounted by dirigibles, as they were in Wells's novel. The German Navy approved long-range attacks by Zeppelin airships against British port cities and, eventually, against targets in London. The first of 52 raids was made on the night of 20–21 January 1915. Altogether during the war airships dropped 162 tons of bombs, mostly haphazardly, and killed 557 people.[5] Attacks by aeroplanes away from the front line began on 22 September 1914 when a handful of aircraft from the Royal Naval Air Service, on the orders of the First Lord of the Admiralty, Winston Churchill, attacked Zeppelin sheds in Cologne and Düsseldorf, followed on 23 November by a raid on the city of Friedrichshafen, where Zeppelins were built. The first German aircraft to bomb Britain did so in retaliation on 24 December. There were small raids by German, French and British units for the next two years but they achieved almost nothing until the German Air Force formed an 'England Squadron' in late 1916, commanded by Captain Ernst Brandenburg, to begin a series of day and night attacks against British ports, including 18 raids on London. The first raid was made on Folkestone on 25 May 1917, the last a year later, on the night of 19–20 May against London. The mixed force of Gotha-IV and R-Gigant multi-engine bombers dropped 110 tons in 52 raids, killing 836 and wounding 1,982. The original object had been to destroy 'the morale of the British people' to such an extent that the British government might consider withdrawing from the conflict. But the weight of attack failed entirely to support what was at best a speculative strategy. Small German raids were also made on

French industrial targets in Paris, killing 267 Parisians, but achieving little. The offensive petered out in spring 1918 following mounting losses.[6] Its principal achievement was to provoke the British into retaliation.

The German bombing, sporadic and limited though it was, helped give birth not only to an integrated air defence system, but also to what would have been the first strategic air offensive. The first anti-aircraft guns were in place across south-east England by spring 1915. The air defences were established formally as the Air Defence of Great Britain. At the heart of the system was the London Air Defence Area, set up in July 1917 under Maj. General Edward Ashmore. By the summer of 1918 the defence boasted 250 anti-aircraft guns (based on artillery developed on the Western Front), 323 searchlights, eight fighter squadrons for day-and-night interception and a personnel of 17,000. To track incoming aircraft, observer cordons were set up some 50 miles from vulnerable areas, manned by soldiers and policemen.[7] In the threatened cities a primitive civil defence structure was established in 1917, with improvised shelters, air-raid wardens and policemen armed with whistles for sounding the alarm. The system was seldom needed over the last two years of war, and not at all after the last raids in May 1918, but it created a precedent that was later revived in the 1930s when lessons from the Great War were needed for British air-raid precautions planning. The raids gave rise to moments of panic in the bombed towns; in the east coast port of Hull, an easy Zeppelin target, a portion of the population trekked out of the city to the surrounding countryside, as they were to do during the next war. In London, estimates of those who sought shelter in the Underground ranged from 100,000 to 300,000.[8]

The air raiding was widely condemned as a vicious and cowardly attack on the innocent. The final death toll of 1,239 from all Zeppelin and bomber raids included 366 women and 252 children. Bombing represented, according to *The Times*, 'relapses into barbarism', a language regularly applied to aerial bombing for the next twenty-five years.[9] There were widespread appeals for retaliation, using much the same language of moral justification that would later be used during the Blitz, and there followed a number of deliberate reprisal raids. The government, however, wanted a more systematic response. An Air Board, appointed in 1916, planned to create a separate, independent air force and, with the government's approval, to use it to undertake a systematic long-range bombing offensive against German military and economic targets within the limited range of the existing aircraft. In July 1917 the

South African soldier and politician, Field Marshal Jan Smuts, visiting London during an Imperial Conference, was invited by the prime minister, David Lloyd George, to produce recommendations for organizing Britain's air effort. Smuts suggested the establishment of a separate air ministry and air force and also endorsed the idea of long-range attacks against the enemy home front.[10] The idea was accepted and an initial bombing plan was drawn up by Lord Tiverton, a senior Royal Flying Corps staff officer, at the request of the first chief of the newly created air staff, Sir Frederick Sykes. The industrial plan picked out German iron and steel, chemicals, the aero-engine and magneto industries as the key objectives, and from October 1917 the RFC VIII Brigade, commanded by Lieutenant Colonel Cyril Newall (the future chief of the air staff in the late 1930s), began a limited assault on the cities that housed them.[11]

The force mainly composed of light De Havilland DH-9 bombers had little success. Crew had an average of 17 hours flying experience, were poorly trained for accurate navigation and target-finding, and carried 250-lb and 500-lb bombs that were later found to have inflicted little damage. The newly formed Air Policy Committee encouraged the crews to 'attack the important towns systematically' if they could not find a target, with the object of creating widespread disruption and demoralizing the workforce.[12] This offensive was also met by an effective German air defence system which, like the British, was first activated in 1915 in response to Allied incursions. The same year an Air Warning Service (*Flugmeldedienst*) was established using observation aircraft and ground-based observation posts. By 1917, when heavier Allied raids began, the defensive system combined interceptor aircraft and an extensive network of 400 searchlights and 1,200 anti-aircraft guns of different calibres. To hamper night-time raids, an extensive blackout was introduced in western Germany, together with illuminated fake targets. As in Britain, local civil defence measures were introduced to protect the civilian population. In total, 746 were killed and 1,843 injured; as in Britain, German propaganda deplored the 'frightfulness' (*Schrecklichkeit*) of attacks against the defenceless civilian population.[13]

The intention to mount a serious bombing offensive against Germany, as an indirect contribution to the ground war, finally resulted in April 1918 in the establishment of the Royal Air Force, a merger of the Royal Flying Corps and the Royal Naval Air Service. A Cabinet ruling on 13 May 1918 stressed that the force's independence was deliberately linked to the purpose 'of carrying out bombing raids on Germany on a large scale'. To underline this commitment, an integral element of the new RAF was activated on 5 June as the Independent Air Force (to distinguish it from the RAF aircraft still supporting the Army) and placed under the command of General (later Marshal of the Royal Air Force) Sir Hugh Trenchard.[14] Two weeks later an elaborate review of British air strategy was submitted to the War Cabinet by the RAF staff which laid out the principles on which all subsequent air offensives were to be based. Air power, it was suggested, was the most probable and efficient way of securing peace by attacking the 'root industries' of the enemy and 'the moral [sic] of his nation'. A detailed list of precise targets in the Ruhr-Rhineland industrial region was drawn up based on Tiverton's original plan; in cases when these could not be attacked, bombers were to raid 'densely populated industrial centres' in order 'to destroy the morale of the operatives'.[15]

The opportunity to test what a bomber force could do was never realized. In June the Independent Force dropped just 70 tons of bombs on Germany, in August only 100, in the last weeks of war a further 370 tons. Of this quantity most were dropped on tactical targets, either enemy airfields or communications serving the front line. For example, the thirteen attacks carried out during 1918 on the Baden town of Offenburg, within easy range of British bombers, were almost all aimed at the railway station or rail lines.[16] Overall the strategic force dropped just 8 per cent of the tonnage of bombs dropped by British aircraft throughout the war. Only 172 of its 650 mainly small-scale raids were on the German homeland and losses were high, 458 aircraft in total.[17] The French High Command was unenthusiastic about longer-range bombing, and the American and Italian bomber units that were supposed to join an expanded Inter-Allied Independent Force, formed in October 1918, had no time to see serious action.[18] Like Wells's science-fiction fantasies, the independent bombing offensive was more imagined than real.

The post-war assessments of the bombing of Germany carried out by a British Bombing Commission and a United States Bombing Survey in 1919 indicated very modest material achievements. But there were to be exaggerated expectations of the probable effect of bombing on home morale. Trenchard famously remarked that the moral, or psychological, effect of bombing was twenty times greater than the material effect, though there was little evidence to confirm this beyond occasional but temporary moments of panic during the war in British, French and

German cities, and the class prejudices of those who asserted it.[19] The
report on the 1923 annual RAF exercises, with Trenchard now chief of
the air staff, assumed that modern war was 'a contest of morale', in
which the febrile urban crowd would prove to be 'infinitely more susceptible to collapse'.[20] Much the same argument was formulated by the
Italian general, Giulio Douhet, whose *Command of the Air* (*Il dominio
dell'aria*) has become one of the classics of air-power theory. He argued
that the nature of warfare had been changed irrevocably by the advent
of the aeroplane, to the detriment of armies and navies. Future wars, he
argued, would be based on the rapid destruction of the enemy's air
force, in order to attack, as swiftly and ruthlessly as possible, the enemy
civilian economy and population. The temporary inhumanity (Douhet
also advocated using gas or bacteriological agents) was designed to
make wars short and sharp and, by implication, at lower human cost
than the long war of attrition that Europe had just experienced. 'A man
who is fighting a life-and-death struggle – as all wars are nowadays –
has the right,' Douhet claimed, 'to use any means to keep his life.'[21]
Douhet's vision of future war owed something to Wells – 'This is a dark
and bloody picture I am drawing for you' – but it was first and foremost
an expression of what soon came to be termed 'total war'.[22]

   Although Trenchard and Douhet are now hailed as pioneers in air
power theory, their conclusions were over-imaginative and unscientific
and, for the military establishments of the 1920s, an invitation to
indulge in what were still widely regarded as morally unacceptable violations of the laws of war. Despite the subsequent status enjoyed by
both men, they remained relative outsiders in the 1920s. Douhet was
briefly Air Minister in Mussolini's first Cabinet in 1922, but was then
retired from military service, sacked as minister, and left to argue his
case from the wings. Trenchard spent much of his term as chief of staff
fighting to retain air force independence and to forge a distinct strategic
identity for his force. Neither was a household name in the 1920s,
though Douhet's works became more widely known in the decade that
followed. No air force in the 1920s (or indeed in the 1930s) deliberately
created a strategic bombing capability to eliminate an enemy rapidly
and ruthlessly by assaulting civilian morale, a strategy crudely described
in the interwar years as 'the knockout blow'. What was significant
about both Douhet and Trenchard, and a great many other post-war
military thinkers, was the assumption that future war would be waged
between whole societies in which the citizen, whether in uniform or in
a factory, or driving a train or ploughing the fields, whether male or

female, would contribute to the national war effort. This assumption made industries, cities and workers objects of war as much as the armed forces and put into sharper focus the pre-war fiction about the menace to civilization.

The European public in the 1920s saw the limited bombing of the Great War in much starker terms than most of the military establishment. The critical change brought about by the war was the widespread realization among Europe's population that there was no possibility in any future war of civilian immunity. Small though the bombing effort had been during the Great War, it was taken to symbolize the crossing of an important threshold, in which science in the service of war could subvert conventional forms of military conflict in favour of a wilful assault on civilian society. Commenting in 1923 on a claim that hostile aircraft could poison the whole of London in three hours, the English historian, Goldsworthy Lowes Dickinson, wrote: 'war now means extermination, not of soldiers only, but of civilians and of civilisation'.[23] Lowes Dickinson was not a military expert, but much of the scaremongering literature in the interwar years was made more chilling because it was written by soldiers or ex-soldiers, or by scientists and engineers who paraded their expertise to the public to give their conclusions greater weight. The Earl of Halsbury, the author in 1926 of *1944*, a novel about a future gas attack to annihilate London, was the same Lord Tiverton (now elevated to higher noble rank) who had planned the strategic offensive against Germany in 1917. He claimed in his preface that there was nothing fantastic about his description of the gas attack, which he had based on current expertise on the possible effects of chemical weapons. In 1927 he elaborated for a popular newspaper audience the lessons of his novel: 'The central organisations essential to modern warfare are carried out in "open towns" and largely by civilians ... *The first conclusion that emerges is that an attack will be made upon the civilian population*.'[24] These sentiments had much in common with Douhet, and with a wave of alarmist literature on air warfare produced by military experts in France. In 1930 Lieutenant Colonel Arsène Vauthier in *The Aerial Threat and the Future of the Country* warned that in the next war French cities would be smothered with gas and bombs: 'the entire future of the country is at stake, the entire civil population will be placed abruptly on the warfront'.[25]

Two particular arguments can be identified in the scaremongering literature of the interwar years: first, that the destruction would be aimed at major cities; second, that the destruction would be swift and

the degree of damage annihilating. In most imagined accounts of bombing there were standard tropes about the surprise, speed and scope of
air attack. Douhet wrote in 'The War of 19—', published in Italy's leading aeronautical journal in March 1930, shortly after his death, about
an air war between France and Germany in which four French cities are
attacked by German aircraft with 500 tons of incendiary and poisonous
bombs, enough to destroy the cities completely. The raid takes just one
hour, and the four cities are burnt to the ground.[26] Frank Morison in
War on Great Cities, published in 1938, just months before the outbreak of the next war, talked of a million dead in London from a gas
attack, and millions more following swift British retaliation on Paris,
Rome or Berlin. One 5,000-lb bomb would be enough, he suggested, to
destroy completely the whole administrative and government centre
around Whitehall. Like many of the experts writing on bombing he
assured his readers that this was 'no fanciful picture' but a cold statement of fact.[27] Tom Wintringham, a former soldier and later a
commander of the British International Brigade during the Spanish
Civil War, painted an equally lurid picture in 1935 of the end of Europe's major cities: 5–6 million killed in London, Paris and Berlin by a
combination of gas, high explosive, exposure, disease and hunger.[28] In
all these accounts, and with special emphasis in Douhet, there is little
effective defence against bombing, and none against gas or germs.

Most of these pessimistic representations of air warfare were indeed
fanciful portraits, divorced from technical and scientific reality. What
they all shared was an understanding of the apparent vulnerability of
the modern city to the 'knockout blow'. This was so widely discussed
and endorsed that it requires some explanation. By the 1920s much of
urban Europe was of relatively recent construction, with cities filled
with migrants from the villages or immigrants from abroad. The large
new populations lived in congested, quickly constructed terraces and
tenements, and serviced the burgeoning ports and industries stimulated
by the rapid development of European trade and manufacturing. The
new cities were regarded by many social critics (and most of Europe's
conservative elite) as socially amorphous and alienating, with an under-
developed sense of community and unstable values. They were sites of
pre-war and post-war political radicalism and, in the case of Russia, of
revolution. The new cities were also popularly associated with a rising
tide of crime, vice and genetic defects. These views of urban life reflected
profound class and regional prejudices; they surfaced regularly in
accounts of future bombing precisely because the rootless urban crowd

was expected to be more prone to panic.[29] The account of the psychology of the crowd by Gustave Le Bon published in 1895, or William Trotter's study of the herd instinct which appeared in 1916, gave popular sanction to the view that the character of modern urban life predisposed individuals to merge at moments of crisis into an unmanageable mob. A British Air Ministry official reflecting in 1937 on what he regarded as the unstable behaviour of 'aliens' and 'the poorer sections of the community' during the German bombing of London in 1917, concluded that 'the capital cities constitute the popular nerve centres where the danger is greatest'.[30]

City vulnerability was also regarded as a product of the complexity and interconnectedness of the modern infrastructure that supported urban life. The sudden dislocation of any one part by bombing was expected to unravel the whole and provoke a social catastrophe. The working of this process was explained in an article by the British philosopher Cyril Joad, writing in 1937:

> Within a few days of the outbreak of the next war it seems reasonable to suppose that the gas and electric light systems will have broken down, that there will be no ventilation in the tube [metro] tunnels, that the drainage system will have been thrown out of gear and sewage will infect the streets, that large parts of London will be in flames, that the streets will be contaminated with gas, and that hordes of fugitives will spread outwards from the city, without petrol for their cars or food for their stomachs, pouring like locusts over the country in the hope of escaping the terror from the air.[31]

The military thinker J. F. C. Fuller suggested that within hours of a major bomb attack on London, the city would become 'one vast raving Bedlam': 'traffic will cease, the homeless will shriek for help, the city will be in pandemonium'. As city life collapses, Fuller continued, government would be swept away in an 'avalanche of terror'.[32]

Such anxieties reflected more profound fears about the ambiguous nature of modern 'civilization' and its capacity to survive after the descent into mass industrialized warfare between 1914 and 1918. The result was a profound paradox. There was throughout Europe and the United States in the interwar years a genuine and enthusiastic fascination with what the aeroplane represented. For the European dictatorships, right and left, aviation was commandeered as a way to express the vibrant modernity and technological sophistication of the new political movements.[33] In France, Britain and the United States aviation was a key product of the modern consumer age, capable of transforming lifestyles, easing modern communication and providing exhilarating opportunities for organized leisure. Here was science genuinely at the service of man. On the other hand, military aviation was regarded not only as a fascinating technical expression of the modern age, but also as the harbinger of its possible dissolution. Much of the apocalyptic language used to describe the threat of bombing was directed not so much at the threat from the air as such but at the self-destructive nature of a civilization capable of generating the technical means for obliterating modern cities in the first place. 'It is poor consolation,' Lord Halsbury told the British House of Lords in 1928, 'that the only answer we can find to the destruction of half of civilisation is that we should be able to destroy the other half.'[34]

The experts and novelists and film producers who sustained the idea of a bombing apocalypse had mixed motives for what they did. Some wanted the bombing scare to encourage pacifism and international agreement by making the image of future war unbearably bleak. Some wanted the opposite, using the fear of bombing to encourage higher levels of state spending on defence. Winston Churchill, for example, in 1934 spoke of an air threat that was 'ready to ... pulverise ... what is left of civilisation', but his aim was to encourage the government to speed up rearmament.[35] Military experts, scientists and architects hoped that civil defence preparation would be taken more seriously. Literature appropriated bombing because it presented easy metaphors or sold copies. Yet the fears that the future bombing war provoked were real enough and became embedded in popular public perception of what the terms of total war were likely to be. Psychiatrists expected air war to provoke widespread mental disorders. The existence of a specific psychological condition of 'air-raid phobia' was detected by psychologists in Britain once raiding began.[36] The public was easily stirred by the idea of destruction from the air, but the fear – or rather a nexus of 'fears' – was the product of uncertainty about the future and ignorance of the exact nature of the threat.[37] The popular view of science increased that fear, because science had evidently sprung numerous unpleasant surprises in the Great War. Scientists themselves could be confounded by what the military sciences might do. The Cambridge geneticist Joseph Needham, sketching notes for a lecture in 1936 on 'Can Science save Civilisation?', concluded that if science could be used 'for destroying civilisation by air warfare', saving it was unlikely.[38]

This catastrophic view of future air war did not take place in a vacuum. Politicians were easily persuaded of the fear themselves, often equally ignorant about the true state of possibilities, and sensitive to their responsibilities in trying to reduce any risk that bombing civilian populations might actually happen. The British prime minister, Stanley Baldwin, claimed in 1936 that after a gas and bomb attack 'the raging peoples of every country, torn with passion, suffering and horror, would wipe out every Government in Europe'.[39] A strong case can be made to show that the willingness of British statesmen to concede the dismemberment of Czechoslovakia during the 1938 Munich crisis was based on fear of air raids on British cities.[40] Since bombing was always imagined as a war directed at cities and civilians, the search in the interwar years for ways to avert or reduce the threat to the civilian population became a political question rather than a strictly military one, not least because 'total war' would mean reliance on civilian industry and workers if it were to be waged successfully. At first governments pursued ways of outlawing the bombing of non-military targets, or even outlawing military aircraft altogether. When that effort broke down in the 1930s, governments across Europe reacted by introducing national programmes of civil defence to try to mitigate the disastrous social and political effects bombing was expected to provoke.

The search for international agreement on the bombing threat raised numerous difficulties, as had all efforts to reach international agreement on the laws of war in the half-century since the 1874 Brussels Conference first tried to define them. The Hague Conventions of 1899 and 1907 explicitly prohibited the use of bombing from the air, and Convention IV in 1907 spelt out that this prohibition extended to attacks on civilians or the destruction of civilian property by aerial bombardment. Although the convention had the force of international law, not all of those states present at The Hague subsequently ratified its provisions, including Germany and France.[41] During the Great War these prohibitions were regularly violated in the bombing undertaken by both sides. At the Washington Disarmament Conference in 1922, which successfully limited naval armaments, agreement was reached to establish a committee of international jurists to draw up definite rules of engagement for air warfare. The Commission met at The Hague between December 1922 and February 1923 and drew up what became known as The Hague Rules for Air Warfare. No state ratified the rules, but they were widely understood to define what was regarded as acceptable practice in future air war and they were used as a reference point in subsequent discussions of the legal implications of civilian bombing. Bombing was governed by two principal articles: Article 22 outlawed any bombing deliberately intended to destroy civilian property or kill non-combatants; Article 24 restricted bombing only to known and identifiable military objectives and, most significantly, only permitted bombing of those objectives 'in the immediate vicinity of the operation of the land forces'. In this case bombing could be lawfully conducted, even when the military objective was close to habitation.[42]

The international effort to limit the air threat continued for at least the decade that followed the drafting of The Hague Rules. In June 1925 at Geneva the major powers agreed to a Protocol outlawing the use (though not the possession) of poisonous chemical or bacteriological weapons. The instrument came into force in 1928 but was ratified slowly by the states that might be affected by its provisions: Germany confirmed adherence in April 1929, Britain in April 1930, the United States only in 1975. The Protocol did not prevent continuing anxiety about the use of gas warfare, which many men had experienced at first hand in the trenches of the First World War. The persistent mistrust of the stated political intention not to use chemical or germ warfare highlighted a major problem in the attempt to create a legal framework to outlaw bombing, and indeed during the subsequent World War it was mutual deterrence rather than law that inhibited their use. The most important initiative to control the deployment of military aircraft came with the Geneva Disarmament Conference which convened in February 1932. All the major states that took part expressed a willingness to explore a number of distinct possibilities, including the international control of civil aviation, the abolition of bomber aircraft and the creation of an international air police force. The most comprehensive proposal, the French 'Tardieu Plan', presented to the conference in a revised version in November 1932 contained all three: a European Air Transport Union to oversee all civil air transport; the complete abolition of all bomber aircraft; and an 'organically international air force' run by the League of Nations to enforce its regulations with 'immediate intervention'.[43]

This and all other plans failed to produce any agreement on limiting the air threat. The French and British air forces remained opposed to any suggestion that offensive military aircraft should be abolished, while the loss of sovereignty implied by an international air police force could not be reconciled with fears for national security. The only delegation to support the abolition of all military aircraft was Spain; the only country to endorse the complete abolition of aerial bombing was the Netherlands.[44] In July 1932 a resolution from the Czech Foreign

Minister, Edouard Beneš, that 'air attack against the civilian population shall be absolutely prohibited', was approved, but its significance was much reduced by the failure to reach any agreement restricting the bombing aircraft that might carry it out. In March 1933 a fresh proposal was made by the British delegation, outlawing air bombardment and limiting the number of military aircraft on a sliding scale from 500 for the major powers (though none for Germany, which was still disarmed under the terms of the Versailles Settlement) down to just 25 each for Portugal and Finland.[45] The new proposal carried an important rider that bombing could still be carried out 'for police purposes in certain outlying regions'. Romania, Czechoslovakia and Yugoslavia at once tabled an amendment to add 'outside Europe', from fear perhaps that they might be regarded as outlying regions. But the rider was in effect an oblique reference to the British policy of using bombing as a cheap and efficient means to police the Empire and it suggested to other delegates that there would be one rule for Britain, another for the rest. The project finally collapsed, not to be revived during the brief surviving life of the conference.[46]

The idea of internationalizing aviation or creating an international air force or outlawing bombing did not disappear in 1933 for all its evident contradictions. For the following five years politicians and the wider public supported calls to restrict the air threat by agreement. In Britain, the Labour politician Philip Noel-Baker and the Liberal peer Lord David Davies campaigned vigorously for the idea of an air police force (H. G. Wells's 1933 fantasy, *The Shape of Things to Come*, ends optimistically with a benign world 'Air Dictatorship' based implausibly in the Iraqi city of Basra). Noel-Baker argued for a League of Nations air force to enforce peace, but ended up with the paradoxical argument that in the event of a state launching a bombing attack, the League should be able to use gas and high explosive 'to bombard *his* cities until he stopped'.[47] This paradox highlighted the central problems of trust and compliance in all attempts to internationalize aviation or control bombing in the absence of secure forms of verification. Restrictions on bombing never became a national political priority for any major state after the failure at Geneva, except in the curious case of Hitler's appeal to Britain and France to consider outlawing bombing, which he included in a more comprehensive 'Peace Plan' presented to them on 31 March 1936 in the wake of the remilitarization of the Rhineland two weeks before.

From among the thirty-two separate articles included in Hitler's plan,

Article 26 recommended convening a conference for the express purpose of bringing air warfare into 'the moral and humane atmosphere of the protection afforded to non-combatants or the wounded by the Geneva Convention'. Hitler proposed that priority should be given to outlawing by agreement the use of gas, poisonous or incendiary bombs, and to prohibiting air bombardment of any kind in localities further from the fighting front than the range of medium-heavy artillery.[48] It is hard to judge the extent to which Hitler's proposal should be regarded as a serious attempt to limit the damage to be done by bombing, though he returned to the theme several times. During the historic meeting with Neville Chamberlain in his apartment on 30 September shortly after signing the Munich Agreement, Hitler once again explained that he personally found the idea of bombing women and children repellent. But as he had presented his Peace Plan of March 1936 just a year after the declaration of German rearmament in April 1935 and a matter of weeks after German troops had re-entered the Rhineland, the Western powers were not inclined to regard his overture as anything more than a gesture, and no reply was given, though a distrustful British Foreign Office did inquire why germ warfare was not included on Hitler's list.[49] The last time an international effort was made to define the rules governing bombing came on 30 September 1938, the same day as Chamberlain's meeting with Hitler in Munich, when the League of Nations Assembly at Geneva passed unanimously a British resolution confirming the main provisions of The Hague Rules drawn up fifteen years before.[50] Although the resolution was not legally binding, it was regarded as if it represented collective legal opinion.

The international initiatives did little to allay the widespread popular anxiety about bombing and the next war. In 1934 the British League of Nations Union organized a national ballot on issues of peace and security, and the third question on the ballot – the abolition of military aircraft – won 9 million votes, a reflection of the extent to which the democratic nature of the bombing threat was well understood by the wider public.[51] The fear of bombing was nourished throughout the 1930s by news of bombing atrocities, first in China during the opening conflict with the Japanese army in 1931–2, then in 1935–6 with news that Italian aircraft in the war with Ethiopia had violated the 1925 Geneva agreement by dropping gas bombs on Ethiopian forces and civilians. The Italian case differed from the campaigns of colonial pacification carried out regularly by British and French aircraft against tribal enclaves and villages (which never got the same level of publicity), because it was an aggressive war waged against an independent sovereign state and a fellow member of the League of Nations. It was also the first time, as one journalist put it, that a 'White Power' had used gas from the air in defiance of international law.[52] Italy had ratified the Geneva Protocol in 1928, Ethiopia in October 1935. The dropping of mustard gas bombs began in December 1935 after Mussolini had personally approved it in a telegram to the Italian commander, Marshal Rodolfo Graziani, on 27 October. There were 103 attacks using mustard gas or phosgene bombs between 22 December 1935 and 29 March 1936, shortly before the Ethiopian surrender. Italy kept large stocks of gas bombs in East Africa and used them in regular pacification operations throughout 1936 and 1937.[53]

Among those who brought news of Italian gas bombing to Britain was the South African journalist, George Steer. By coincidence he was also the journalist who alerted the British public to what came to be regarded as the worst pre-war bombing atrocity, the German-Italian bombing of the ancient Basque town of Guernica (Gernika) on 26 April 1937. No single event played as large a part in confirming for the European public that the bombing of cities and civilians was now to be an established part of modern warfare. The raid took place as Spanish nationalist armies commanded by General Francisco Franco advanced into north-east Spain during the civil war campaign against the Spanish Second Republic, the consequence of a failed military coup in July 1936. Guernica was certainly not the first Spanish city to be bombed during the Civil War – much international attention was also paid to the bombing of Barcelona and Madrid – and the nationalists, supported by German and Italian air contingents sent to Spain, were not the only side to carry out bombing. Nor were the circumstances of the raid clear. Orders to the German air units, commanded by Wolfram von Richthofen, stated that the raid was supposed to target communications and enemy forces. Franco's propaganda asserted that Communists had burned down the town to discredit the enemy.[54] Nevertheless the destruction of Guernica, in Europe rather than the colonies or distant China, served as a lightning conductor for the accumulated anxieties of European populations.

The bombing was announced the following day in Paris and Manchester, thanks to a Reuters reporter who was with Steer in nearby Bilbao when the attack occurred; it was this initial report that prompted Pablo Picasso to paint his homage to Guernica as his contribution to the Spanish pavilion in the 1937 Paris World's Fair. But it was Steer's sombre and detailed dispatch, published with some hesitancy by *The Times* on 28 April (and with less hesitancy by *The New York Times*), that attracted most attention.[55] Steer emphasized the innocence of Guernica and of its victims, and much of the subsequent propaganda generated by the anti-Franco (and anti-fascist) lobbies in the democracies played on the ordinariness of the damaged town. A British cinema newsreel broadcast the voiceover, 'these were homes like yours'; a pamphlet on an earlier bombing by nationalist aircraft had carried the headlines 'Children Like Ours! Mothers Like Ours! Wives Like Ours!'[56] Steer had already witnessed the bombing of the Basque town of Durango some weeks before (and had regarded this as 'the most terrible bombardment of a population in the history of the world'), but he chose to highlight Guernica because it was the old Basque capital, with a famous oak tree in its main square around which the Basque people traditionally expressed their democratic consent to their governors. Some 1,400 of the population of 6,000 were reported to be dead, though the true figure is now thought to be around 240.[57] Widespread protests against the bombing led the League of Nations on 29 May 1937 to condemn the practice in the Spanish Civil War and to demand the withdrawal of non-Spanish forces from the conflict. Eventually, at the end of March 1938 Chamberlain was persuaded to make a House of Commons statement deploring 'the direct and deliberate bombing of non-combatants' in Spain as an illegal act.[58]

The failure to reach international agreement coupled with continued popular anxiety about bombing convinced European governments to look for other means to secure their civilian populations against the consequences of bomb attack. The state's interest in protecting urban populations was evidently affected by the pervasive imagery of social breakdown and political collapse that accompanied almost all descriptions of future war. In a speech to the House of Commons on 10 November 1932, the deputy prime minister, Stanley Baldwin, had warned that any town in reach of an aerodrome would be bombed within five minutes of the start of any war: 'the question is whose morale will be shattered quickest by preliminary bombing'. The speech is better remembered for his subsequent remark that 'The bomber will always get through', but Baldwin's chief concern was to find some way once again to exempt civilians 'from the worst perils of war'.[59] This meant finding an effective form of civilian air-raid protection. Most major states had begun to think about civil defence programmes in the 1920s. The British government established a Committee on Air Raid Precautions as early as May 1924 chaired by the permanent under-secretary at the Home Office (and the future head of wartime civil defence), Sir John Anderson. The committee concluded early on that the air menace was so great that protection would amount to essential 'palliatives'. Anderson himself accepted the reality that in a future total war 'the distinction between combatants and non-combatants would largely disappear'.[60] For years before the outbreak of war in 1939, the common assumption among those who planned civil defence, in Britain and elsewhere, was the unavoidability of war waged against civilians.

Most active civil defence preparations, however, dated from the breakdown of the disarmament conference and the growing international crisis spurred by the after-effects of the world economic crisis, Japanese aggression in China, German demands for treaty revision and American isolation. The failure to sustain any collective forms of security exposed all European states to the possibility of war. Because of the prevailing image of a war fought from the start by aircraft deployed swiftly and ruthlessly to knock an enemy out, civil defence became by the mid-1930s an urgent priority. The German Air Protection Law (*Luftschutzgesetz*) dated from 1935; an Italian inter-ministerial commission for civil defence was set up in 1930, the first civil defence legislation followed in 1932 and 1933; the British Home Office established an Air Raid Precautions department in 1935, followed by a comprehensive Air Raid Precautions law in December 1937; in France the major civil defence law dated from April 1935, in Poland from September 1934, in Switzerland (where a 'purple cross' association was established to oversee civil defence thinking and planning) from August 1934, in Hungary from July 1935; and so on.[61]

The details of civil defence organization and policies in the major states are covered in more detail in the chapters that follow. Here it is worth observing that they differed in scale and emphasis and in the extent to which the objective of even partial protection could be supplied in the few remaining years of peace. Most governments failed by the outbreak of war to do enough. One of the limiting factors was the substantial cost implied by effective civil defence measures. Many of these costs were defrayed by the central state through insisting that local authorities, who more closely represented the communities under threat, should bear much of the expense, but this resulted in uneven provision from city to city. In Britain it was calculated that the cost of providing deep (and therefore effective) shelter for the whole urban community, in a country more heavily urbanized than any other European state, was somewhere between £300 million and £400 million, more than the whole military budget for 1938, and beyond what any British government was prepared to pay.[62] In Germany, also heavily urbanized, the state agreed to subsidize the costs of civil defence only in major cities graded Air Defence I, chiefly in the industrial western provinces. In Italy the costs proved prohibitive after the expense of wars in Ethiopia and Spain; by 1939 there were public air-raid shelter places for only 72,000 out of a population of 44 million. In France the cost of deep shelters for Paris was calculated at 46 billion francs, half the military budget for 1939; French spending on civil defence in 1939 equalled just 0.9 per cent of the defence budget.[63]

Since not everything necessary to provide protection could be paid for, states opted for particular strategies to try to minimize the potential social damage. Evacuation was one way of ensuring the possible survival of large fractions of the urban community. In France, where there was profound concern throughout the interwar years about the problems for security posed by a sharply declining rate of population growth, the social body was to be preserved by moving women and children out of the city in an organized way as soon as war began, since they were the biological investment for the future. Extensive provision was made for evacuation in the late 1930s, and the delay in sending an ultimatum to Berlin following the German attack on Poland was excused by the need to transport the vulnerable population out of Paris in anticipation of a sudden, annihilating air attack.[64] In Germany, where pro-natalist priorities were equally evident, the Hitler government opted to avoid mass evacuations, first by encouraging local communities to establish 'self-protection' through rigorous civil defence training and the creation of private cellar and basement shelters, and second by reliance on an extensive military anti-air defence of guns, searchlights and radar. By making the population stay put, it was hoped that Germany's war economy would suffer less disruption; but it also met the ideological requirement to demonstrate family and community solidarity in the face of the aerial threat.[65] In Britain, limited evacuation was organized in the late 1930s, but greater emphasis was put on preparations for gas warfare, since fear of gas bombing remained at the forefront of British interwar anxieties about the bombing war. Gas masks were produced for the entire population, and decontamination squads organized earlier and trained more thoroughly than other civil defenders. In Germany masks were issued only to the population most likely to be under threat, in France they were issued late and in insufficient numbers, while in Italy masks had to be bought at considerable expense, and were poorly distributed. In the Soviet Union, where the gas mask was a symbol of a nationwide anti-air organization, Osoviakhim, supplies never exceeded more than 10 per cent of the population.[66]

Civil defence regimes everywhere in the 1930s depended on some level of popular participation. One of the implications of total war waged by bomber aircraft was the need for home populations to recognize that they would become, willy-nilly, a home army combating the effects of air raids. Levels of participation, not all of it voluntary, varied from state to state. In Germany and the Soviet Union, mass organizations were created – 13 million in the German Air Defence League (*Luftschutzbund*), founded in 1932, 15 million in the Soviet Osoviakhim, established in 1927. Neither organization was a formal civil defence service, but they provided propaganda and training for householders, students and workers. In both cases there was a strong ideological imperative to join, in the Soviet case to help preserve the new revolutionary state, in the German case to defend the National Socialist 'People's Community'. In other states there was greater reliance on volunteers for regular civil defence services, medical aid and welfare, but these numbered millions by the end of the 1930s. A conservative estimate of the number of Europeans involved in some form of civil defence activity by 1939 is somewhere between 30 and 32 million, the great majority German and Soviet. The motives for joining evidently varied widely. If some were motivated by apprehension at what the air war would be like, it seems more plausible that those who became full-time or part-time civil defence workers did so because they believed it was possible to ameliorate the physical and social effects of bombing, despite rather than because of the lurid images of its unbearable nature. A proportion was almost certainly animated by the ideology of community protection, though some, like the British novelist Henry Green, joined in order to avoid having to serve in the army.[67] A great many became civil defenders simply because of where they worked and lived.

The sense that here were urban communities about to become embattled reinforced the argument that in the next war whole societies would be on the front line. This did little to allay the anxieties about air warfare. Civil defence preparations could be seen as a rational response to threat, but they could also be seen as a sure indication that bombing and gassing were going to happen. In Germany by the late 1930s the civil defence authorities found evidence that side by side with community civil defence commitment there existed persistent anxiety and scepticism about the dangers to which the population was now exposed and the deficiencies of existing provision.[68] In Britain, popular reaction to increased civil defence activity provoked hostility from anti-war and pacifist lobbies which saw air-raid precautions as an invitation to militarize the nation and evidence that the government was preparing for war. The No More War Movement encouraged its members to acts of civil disobedience against civil defence requirements because they represented 'the psychological preparation for rearmament'. In December 1937 the National Peace Council, the umbrella organization for all pacifist and anti-war groups, agreed to investigate the establishment of ARP Vigilance Committees in every city to challenge the implicit militarism of civil defence measures and to argue that peace was a surer path to security. Some local boroughs with left-wing councils refused to introduce civil defence measures until compelled to do so during the early months of war.[69]

Much criticism was also levelled at what was seen as a deliberate failure on the part of government to provide even the minimum level of shelter and security.[70] Scientists and architects regularly recommended radical, if idealistic, responses to the air threat. In 1938 Frederick Towndrow, the editor of *Architectural Design and Construction*, argued in an article on 'The Great Fear – And After' for a systematic programme of urban decentralization, bomb-proof plans for building, and a network of bunkers and arterial roads underneath every city.[71] Another proposal published in 1937 for building 100 new small towns designed to limit the air threat recommended broad boulevards, wide recreational spaces (useful for segregating parts of the town 'which might happen to be on fire because of incendiary bombs'), and residential housing built around quadrangles to prevent the spread of gas and allow easy escape onto the street.[72] In Germany in the late 1930s all new residential housing was supposed to have an air-raid shelter built into its design, while plans were also elaborated for decentralizing the population into small towns of 20,000 people, or even in isolated homesteads, one for every four acres of territory.[73] In France, fantastic schemes were sketched out against the air threat, including an air defence skyscraper more than five times the height of the Eiffel Tower, with platforms for anti-aircraft guns, observer posts and fighter aircraft, and an underground city of the

future, its subterranean structure covered over with earth to allow farm-
ing to carry on above the sunken streets.[74] The integration of civil
defence into thinking about town planning and construction provides a
further illustration of the extent to which the expectation of future air
war had become embedded in popular European culture by the late
1930s.

There are several possible ways to interpret the popular and political
response to the bombing threat, either as prudent forethought or the
product of an over-anxious imagination or a fatalistic acceptance of the
unavoidable terms of modern conflict. Apprehension was not all fantasy, since modest bomb attack had already been experienced in the
Great War, but that experience came to be distorted through eager
extrapolation. All the popular and political responses to the air threat in
the Europe of the 1930s shared a collective understanding that bombing
would be a characteristic of future war, that it would involve assault on
civilians and civilian life, that it would be aimed principally at cities and
that it would involve destruction at a level likely to induce social chaos.
Unlike most military revolutions, where change is generated within the
military environment, the bombing war took shape first in the public
imagination, where it was incubated under the glare of public anxiety
long before most air forces had either the means or any doctrinal interest in creating a strategic capability aimed at the heart of an enemy
nation. Air forces were bound to be affected by the way in which future
war was framed in public discussion, because air power was at the
centre of all the predictions about how catastrophic the next war would
be. The attention given to air power flattered the infant air forces and
inflated the desire for organizational autonomy and a strategic profile
distinct from the other two services. There remained nevertheless a wide
gap between the air war as it was popularly imagined and the evolving
strategic outlook of the air forces themselves.

There were many factors inhibiting the development of a bombing
strategy. For most of the interwar period air forces had to struggle to
secure enough money to be able to construct the necessary infrastructure for the exercise of air power and to be able to keep abreast of a
rapidly changing technology. At the same time the persistent calls for air
disarmament, even for the abolition of all military aircraft, compelled
air force leaders to spend time and effort simply trying to retain any
military capability at all. Political effort also had to be devoted to contesting the aim of armies and navies to rein back air force ambitions for

independence and to compel air forces to think principally in terms of support for surface forces. 'The decision in war devolves to the forces on the ground,' wrote one German commentator on the air force experience in the Spanish Civil War, 'and on the forces that fight on the ground, not in the air or from the air.'[75] In the United States there remained persistent hostility from the army to the claims for air force independence and a strategic bombing force. Commenting on the Italian war effort in Ethiopia in late 1935, Deputy Chief of Staff General Stanley Embick concluded that air power was secondary: 'Italian progress from day to day is measured solely by the slow advance of the men in the mud . . . the role of military aviation must by its inherent nature be essentially of an auxiliary character.' In his view, the claims made for air power were exaggerated and unrealistic: 'They [aircraft] are fragile, vulnerable to the smallest missile, inoperable in bad weather, and exceedingly costly.'[76] In France the air force remained closely tied to the army, even after a measure of organizational independence was conceded in 1933. Some 86 per cent of all French aircraft remained attached to individual army units, at the disposal of army commanders.[77]

The most difficult problem confronting airmen after 1919 was the unstable and rapidly evolving nature of the air weapon. The gap between the biplanes and triplanes of 1918 – slow, cumbersome, easily damaged craft made of wood and wire – and the faster monoplane, metal-framed and heavily armed aircraft of 1939, was a quantum leap in technology. It was essential, given limited budgets and little practical experience, that right choices be made when modernizing an air force. Since the technology changed almost year by year, overcommitment to a particular aircraft model or strategic profile could prove costly; with such a potentially unstable technology, obsolescence was a high risk and security uncertain. This was no more evident than in the shifting balance between offensive and defensive air power. By the late 1920s light bombers were as fast, or faster, than the biplane fighters that might intercept them; by the late 1930s high-performance monoplane fighters were more than 100 miles per hour faster than the light and medium bombers they opposed, capable of much greater manoeuvrability and with powerfully destructive armament. In almost all major European states radar detection of incoming enemy aircraft was either operationally available or in the process of development. As the balance shifted towards defence, air forces had to choose carefully the kind of bomber aircraft they should now invest in. This perhaps explains the designation of 'Ideal Bomber' given by the RAF when it began to search in

1938 for a heavy aircraft (specification B19/38), capable of long range, a heavy bombload, and flying high enough and fast enough to be less troubled by enemy fighter aircraft.[78] In the end, the project remained idealistic: the bombers that the RAF relied on for its later offensive were twin-engine bombers hastily converted to a multi-engine heavy-bomber role in the first years of war.

Most air forces between the wars opted to develop battlefield light- and medium-bomber aircraft, supported by ground-attack fighter-bombers, rather than pursue the strategic aim of the 'knockout blow'. This was true even in Douhet's Italy, where the air force rejected mass fleets of bombers in favour of a variety of assault aircraft to support surface operations.[79] This choice depended to some extent on the prevailing role of the army in overall military planning and the army's belief that the most strategically efficient use of air power was in some form of combined arms operational structure. In France, Germany and the Soviet Union there existed a core of airmen who did favour an independent strategic air force, based around a bombing capability, but they lacked sufficient prestige or influence to overcome the preference of the ground army to exploit air power as an important adjunct to any ground campaign or the opposition of those airmen who thought air defence and air-to-air combat a better use of scarce resources.

In France, the armed forces were strongly influenced by the experience of the Great War, which seemed to demonstrate clearly that overwhelming air power on or near the fighting fronts was more strategically decisive than speculative long-range bombing of the enemy home front. The main statement of French bombing theory by Camille Rougeron, *L'Aviation de Bombardement*, argued that the ideal bomber aircraft should be derived from fighter design and be used both to attack military targets and to win air superiority over the battlefield.[80] The 1921 French *Instruction* for the armed forces laid down the principle that air power should be used in support of front-line operations. In 1936 the *Instruction* was modified by the Popular Front Air Minister, the radical left-wing politician Pierre Cot, to allow for the creation of an operationally independent strategic reserve. But even this reserve was designed to allow for mass attacks at critical points in the battle either to disrupt enemy supplies and reinforcements or to make possible a breakthrough on the ground. When Cot lost office in 1938, the strategic reserve was once again broken up and distributed among the defending armies along the French eastern frontier.[81] The French Army deeply distrusted Cot and his sympathy for the Soviet Union and came to identify his policy of independent, strategic air power as a Communist attempt to subvert the role of the army in determining French military doctrine. The 'strategic' use of air power was regarded as simply an extension of the main battle, not as an alternative.

In practice, aviation in the Soviet Union moved closer to the French model during the 1930s. In the late 1920s, when the Red Army began to think seriously about future strategy, the idea of creating a mobile strategic air reserve for use at critical points in the battle, or for effecting a breakthrough for the ground army, became accepted doctrine. Under the influence of two Soviet air theorists, A. N. Lapchinskii and Vasily Khripin, encouragement was given to the establishment of independent bomber units. In 1935 these were grouped together into a strategic reserve, *aviatsya osobovo naznachenya* (AON), but like Cot's plan, the object was to use them at critical stages of the ground battle. Some thought was given to the possibility of bombing distant targets in Germany or Japan in the event of war, but the thought was never enshrined in doctrine. In 1937 Stalin ordered an end to the heavy-bomber programme, partly because of the poor safety record of the aircraft, but largely as a result of the military purges in 1937 which decimated the group of army and air force leaders who favoured independent strategic operations. Priority was given thereafter to ground attack and medium-bomber aircraft designed to give direct support to ground armies. In 1940 AON was broken up and, like French bomber aircraft, redistributed to front-line army units.[82]

The German case proved to be similar, except that Germany's compulsory air disarmament after the Versailles Treaty of 1919 postponed the formal development of German air power until the advent of Hitler as chancellor in January 1933. In the absence of an air force, the War Ministry in the early 1920s established more than 40 study groups dedicated to evaluating the lessons of the earlier air war, but only four looked at bombing. Their conclusions shaped subsequent German air strategy. Aircraft were judged to be a primarily offensive weapon, and the principal object of an aerial offensive was the achievement of air superiority over the battlefront.[83] Long-range bombing of the enemy home front was not regarded as strategically worthwhile, partly because anti-air defences were expected to be able to blunt an air offensive, partly because it would disperse rather than concentrate a combined arms offensive. Among the former air force officers working in the War Ministry in the 1920s was a small group who favoured developing a more strategic role for a future air force, including Lieutenant Colonel Helmuth Felmy and the future chief of the air staff in 1935, Colonel Walter Wever. But even under their influence, the air force operational doctrine published in 1935 on 'The Conduct of the Air War' emphasized that the chief objective of the air force was to support the army's ground operations and to eliminate enemy air power, followed only if necessary by attacks on enemy war production to break a front-line stalemate: 'The will of the nation finds its greatest embodiment in its armed forces. Thus, the enemy armed forces are therefore the primary objectives in war.'[84]

This remained the central principle of German air force doctrine and it owed much to the fact that almost all the senior airmen responsible for shaping air strategy, including the commander-in-chief and former Prussian army cadet, Hermann Göring, originally came from a conventional army background, in which concentration of all available force on the battlefield mission was expected to be decisive. 'In the war of the future,' wrote Wever, echoing the doctrine laid down in 1935, 'the destruction of the armed forces will be of primary importance.'[85] The German Air Force Service Manual in 1936 excluded the use of aircraft in terror raids on cities in favour of bombing attacks on the depots, communications and troop concentrations deep in the enemy rear.[86] German airmen were confident that a network of high-quality anti-aircraft guns and searchlights, supported by defensive fighters and a system of effective communication, could prevent a bomber offensive from inflicting serious damage on Germany's war effort, either in the zone of battle or on the home front.[87] The experience of the German Condor Legion in the Spanish Civil War (which provided almost three years of practical combat, ideal for the refinement of the close-support strategy) confirmed the air force argument that front-line aviation made most strategic sense and that attacks on an amorphous target like morale were just as likely to be counter-productive by strengthening resistance.[88] Unlike the RAF, German airmen drew from the lessons of the Great War the conclusion that it made much more strategic sense to fight the enemy air force and to protect the ground army rather than squander men and machines on long-range bombing. The 'knockout blow' was to be inflicted at the battlefront, an intention dramatically fulfilled in all the German campaigns from Poland in 1939 to the Soviet Union in 1941.

The concept of the independent strategic air offensive as the decisive

means to undermine the enemy war effort took root between the wars
only in Britain and the United States. Even here the idea was hedged
about with restrictions, not only as a result of the dubious legality of a
campaign waged against the civilian home front, but because of pressure
from the two senior services, army and navy, to make air power conform to the general aim of the armed forces to defeat the enemy army
and navy in the field. In the United States the air forces remained a part
of the army, subject to army doctrine. In the 'Fundamental Principles for
the Employment of the Air Service', published by the War Department
in 1926, air force organization and training was based 'on the fundamental doctrine that their mission is to aid the ground forces to gain
decisive success'.[89] A board established in 1934 to reassess the role of
what was now called the Army Air Corps was told by the army deputy
chief of staff, Maj. General Hugh Drum, that in the army's opinion no
operations should be undertaken by air forces which did not contribute
directly to the success of the ground forces. 'Battle is the decisive element in warfare,' Drum continued, whereas independent air operations
'would be largely wasted'.[90] In 1935 the army agreed to the establishment of a GHQ Air Force, an independent component of the Air Corps,
but its object, like the Soviet AON, was to bring additional reserve air
power to bear at decisive points in repelling an unlikely enemy invasion,
not to conduct strategic operations distant from the battlefield.[91] In the
absence of any real danger and faced by an unhelpful Treasury, the Air
Corps mustered an exiguous force. In 1932 there were just 92 light-
bomber aircraft on hand.[92]

Under these circumstances American airmen found themselves compelled to elaborate an unofficial theory of strategic bombing in tandem
with the formal commitment to support the operations of the army. The
American airmen who had witnessed the bombing of London in 1917–18
were more impressed by its results than their German counterparts.
In the early 1920s the chief of the Air Service, Maj. General Mason
Patrick, publicly supported the idea that 'decisive blows from the air on
rear areas' might end future conflicts, even while he endorsed his service's formal commitment to direct army support.[93] His deputy, Brig.
General William ('Billy') Mitchell, was an even more outspoken advocate
of air power as a new way of war. His enthusiasm for an autonomous air
arm was based on his conviction that attacks on 'transportation
and industrial centres' with high explosive, incendiary and gas bombs
could prove to be a decisive contribution to victory. Mitchell elaborated

the concept of the 'vital centres' in the enemy's civilian war effort, whose destruction from the air might render surface operations by the army and navy redundant.[94] Although these views were not turned into doctrine – Mitchell was court-martialled in 1925 for his outspoken demands for an independent air force – they survived in air force circles as an unspoken commitment to the idea that in a future war between modern, highly urbanized and industrialized states, air power could uniquely destroy the key targets that kept that sophisticated network in being.

The idea of the vital centres lay at the root of the future elaboration of American bombing strategy in the Second World War. The commander appointed to the GHQ Air Force in 1935, Maj. General Frank Andrews, privately supported the idea that independent air operations against factories, refineries, power plants, utilities and centres of population were the most effective way to use bomber aircraft. The concept was elaborated and taught at the Air Corps Tactical School in the 1930s by a number of officers who were to become prominent organizers of the American bombing effort in the 1940s. Unlike European air forces, American airmen argued that attacking the more vulnerable home front made greater strategic sense. 'Civilization has rendered the economic and social life of a nation increasingly vulnerable to attack,' ran one lecture in 1935. 'Sound strategy requires that the main blow be struck where the enemy is weakest.' The will of the enemy population, it was argued, could be broken only by assaulting the 'social body', a metaphor for the elaborate web of services, supplies and amenities that held modern urban life together. In a list of factors that represented the capacity of a nation to sustain a war effort, the military system was placed fourth, behind the 'social, economic and political systems' that nourished the military effort in the first place.[95] Major Harold George, who later drafted the plan for the American air offensive against Germany, argued not only that modern industry had created an 'economic web' which could be interrupted by bombing, but that the moral effect on an enemy population 'by the breaking of this closely-knit web' might end the war on its own.[96] To confirm these speculations, the Air Corps Tactical School commandant, Major Muir Fairchild, conducted an elaborate exercise in April 1939 on the vulnerability of New York and its surrounding area as a model for all cities, 'the most important and the most vulnerable' element of the modern state. The conclusion was that two squadrons of bombers, attacking with 100 per cent precision, could

knock out the entire electricity-generating system in New York and par-
alyze the whole city at a stroke.[97]

The Air Corps operated in a vacuum in the 1930s in the absence of
permissive air doctrine and the necessary aircraft equipment to justify
the idea of a strategic offensive. In 1933 the Air Corps was allowed to
explore the development of a four-engine bomber in order to ensure
that military air technology kept abreast of the more rapid developments
in civil aviation. The development contract was won by the Boeing Airplane Company, which by 1935 had produced a prototype designated
the XB-17, forerunner of the B-17 'Flying Fortress', with a range of
1,800 miles, carrying 4,000 lbs of bombs.[98] The army had approved the
project only as a defensive aircraft for the long routes to Panama, Alaska
and Hawaii, but in 1936 army thinking changed and the production
order was cancelled. The army, impressed by the results of front-line
support operations in Spain, thought medium bombers promised
'greater efficiency, lessened complexity and decreased cost'.[99] The development of the B-17 was squeezed to the slenderest of margins. It was
saved only by a sudden revolution in political support for the Air Corps.
In late 1938 President Roosevelt authorized a large-scale expansion of
American military spending, including a major commitment to the
expansion of the air force (partly to ensure that France and Britain
could be supplied with aircraft for the growing crisis in Europe). An Air
Board appointed in March 1939 strongly supported the idea of a heavy
bomber and the B-17, from a single development model, became overnight the heart of American air strategy. Plans were developed to build
498 by 1941 and 1,520 by the end of 1942, the first commitment of any
air force to the employment of a heavy four-engine bomber.[100]

One of the companies asked to produce the B-17, the Consolidated
Airplane Company, instead designed its own bomber model in 1939 capable of carrying up to 8,000 lbs of bombs, with a higher speed and a
maximum range of over 2,000 miles. This was accepted by the Air
Corps after trials and modifications in 1940 and became the B-24 bomber,
nicknamed 'Liberator' by the RAF, when a number were sent to Britain
in 1941. It eventually became the standard American bomber, with
18,400 produced by 1945. The new bomber designs, together with the
revolutionary M-4 Norden stabilized bombsight, first developed by the
Dutch-American engineer Carl Norden for the United States Navy in
the late 1920s, meant that the United States was better placed to operate a strategic air campaign in the early 1940s than any of its potential
enemies. In 1939 permission was given to begin development of a

'superbomber' with a range sufficient to reach Europe. What the Air Corps still lacked was any plan or doctrine which would allow it to use its enhanced power for what most airmen assumed was the primary function of the air force: to assault the 'social body' of the enemy.

In Britain, commitment to some form of an independent bombing offensive was kept alive throughout the twenty years that separated the unfought air campaign against Germany in 1919 and the onset of a second war in 1939. In this case, too, the RAF did not enjoy unlimited opportunity to develop either the doctrine to support an air offensive or the technology necessary to sustain it. In the 1920s there was relatively little thinking about the nature of an air offensive beyond speculation on Trenchard's assertion about the probable vulnerability of civilian morale in any future conflict. When in the late 1920s the Air Ministry explored the possibility of a 'Locarno' war against France to help the Germans repel a possible French invasion in violation of the 1925 Locarno Pact, it was argued that even if the French bombed London, 'we can count on our superior morale and striking power to ensure that the Frenchman squeals first'.[101] In 1928 the British chiefs of staff insisted on securing a firm description from the RAF on 'The War Object of an Air Force'. In the meetings that followed, the navy and army chiefs of staff made it clear that in their view the vague commitment to attacking the enemy economy and population was not only contrary to international law but departed from the traditional principle of war that the main effort had to be devoted to defeating the enemy in the field. An uneasy truce was established between the services on the basis that the aim of the air force 'in concert with the Navy and Army' was to break enemy resistance, and to do so 'by attacks on objectives calculated to achieve this end'. This left Trenchard and the RAF with substantial leeway in defining just what those objectives were and how they might be attacked.[102]

Although the other services wanted the RAF to develop a balanced force, capable of offering them support and defending the country against air attack, the air force itself remained dominated by the idea that bombing defined its purpose as a modern force capable of revolutionizing warfare. In a survey of RAF development written after the end of the Second World War, Robert Saundby, deputy commander of Bomber Command during the war, claimed that the air staff in the 1920s 'saw clearly that the bomb was the offensive weapon of the Air Force'; and indeed in the first edition of the RAF *War Manual*, published in 1935, it was claimed that 'The bomb is the chief weapon of an air force and the principal means by which it may attain its aim in war'.[103] When it came to thinking about what the bomb or bombs might be used for, RAF leaders continued to rely on unverifiable assumptions about the social fragility of the enemy. In the 1928 discussion organized by the chiefs of staff, Trenchard, like American airmen, had suggested that air power would have to be exerted against the 'enemy's vital centres', where the enemy 'is at his weakest', but he made little effort to define what those might be.[104] For much of the decade that followed, those British airmen who followed the 'Trenchard doctrine' fell back on bland metaphors about the social body, using, like American airmen, an anatomical language that created a deliberate abstraction in place of the real bodies that bombing would damage.[105] The RAF *War Manual* claimed that all modern states 'have their nerve centres, main arteries, heart and brain'. By attacking them, air forces would delay, interrupt and disorganize the vital centres to such a degree that the enemy's 'national effort' would collapse, not only through injury to the social body, but by the effect this might have on the collective mind, as the *Manual* explained:

> Moral effect – Although the bombardment of suitable objectives should result in considerable material damage and loss, the most important and far-reaching effect of air bombardment is its moral effect ... The moral effect of bombing is always severe and usually cumulative, proportionately greater effect being obtained by continuous bombing especially of the enemy's vital centres.[106]

The conviction that bombing must cause the physical and mental collapse of an enemy state dominated British air theory, as it dominated public anxieties about total war.

One reason why the RAF stuck with the idea that a powerful striking force of bombers would be the most effective way to exploit the potential of air power can be found in the nature of the combat experience enjoyed by British airmen in the interwar years. Instead of drawing lessons from the Spanish Civil War about the advantages of close-support aviation and air superiority, which was the conclusion drawn by other air forces, RAF doctrine was mainly informed by the experience of what was called 'air policing' in the Empire and Afghanistan.[107] The use of aircraft to enforce local control against rebel tribes and tribesmen (described in the *Manual* as war against 'semi-civilised peoples') was taken as a paradigm to explain what might happen if a civilized state were subjected to a heavier level of bombing. Even tribal communities, it was argued, had vital centres which governed their existence; target intelligence on those centres would allow the small light bombers allocated to the operation to destroy them, and in doing so, to compel compliance from unruly subjects. John Slessor, Director of Plans in the Air Ministry in the late 1930s, gave a brutally frank description in his memoirs of why air policing worked: 'Whether the offender concerned was an Indian Frontier tribesman, a nomad Arab of the northern deserts, a Morelli slaver on the border of Kenya, or a web-footed savage of the swamps of the southern Sudan, there are almost always some essentials without which he cannot obtain his livelihood.'[108] A model example for the RAF was the bombing undertaken in Ovamboland in southern Africa in 1938, in which rebel chieftain Ipumbu of the Ukuambi tribe was brought to heel by three aircraft that destroyed his *kraal* (camp) and drove off his cattle. In this case, and others, emphasis was put on the 'moral effect' of coercive bombing, as well as its material impact.[109] The practice of air policing using bomber aircraft as a 'strategic' tool was shared by all those who later held high RAF office in the Second World War: Charles Portal, wartime chief of the air staff; Arthur Harris, commander-in-chief of Bomber Command; Richard Peirse, his predecessor as commander-in-chief; Norman Bottomley, Portal's wartime deputy. Later, in September 1941, Portal used the analogy to explain to Churchill the nature of the assault on the 'general activity of the community' in Germany: 'In short, it is an adaptation, though on a greatly magnified scale, of the policy of air control which has proved so outstandingly successful in recent years in the small wars in which the Air Force has been continuously engaged.'[110]

This perception of bombing serves to explain the wide gap between the strategic vision at the heart of the interwar RAF and the reality of Britain's bombing capability and defence strategy in the 1930s. Imperial air policing was undertaken in conditions of clear visibility, little or no opposition, and low-level attack, none of which would be true of an aerial offensive undertaken in Europe. As a result, colonial practice did not persuade Britain's military leaders to bank everything on the bomber. Indeed, fear of bombing, particularly once Hitler's Germany had been identified in the mid-1930s as the most likely potential enemy, acted as a powerful spur to change British priorities in the air to one that was more appropriately defensive. When the military Joint Planning Committee was asked in 1934 to estimate the probable effects of a German 'knockout blow' from the air, it was assumed that a week of bombing would produce 150,000 casualties and render millions homeless. Later estimates by the chiefs of staff continued to assume that these statistics were realistic – more than a match for the alarmist literature of the age.[111] In 1937 the newly appointed Minister for the Co-ordination of Defence, Sir Thomas Inskip, told the RAF that the role of the air force was not to inflict a knockout blow on the enemy (which it was incapable of doing) 'but to prevent the Germans from knocking us out'.[112] The Committee of Imperial Defence spelt out guidelines for air strategy in which the air force would have to support the navy and army, defend the mainland United Kingdom from air attack, and try to inflict aerial damage on the enemy's strike force. Instructions were given to prepare for a possible attack on German industry in the Ruhr, but only if political permission were given and only after the RAF had met its other commitments. Instead of a force dominated by a large component of bombers to assault the enemy's war effort, the British defence chiefs insisted on a balanced force, a view with which a number of senior airmen agreed, despite the prevailing culture that bombing is what the RAF should do. Between 1937 and the outbreak of war this meant devoting the lion's share of resources to Fighter Command, the air defence network and civil defence. As a result, RAF strategy seemed increasingly schizophrenic, one half emphasizing the strategic value of bombing, the other preparing to defend successfully against it.

For all the emphasis in air force circles on the value of a strike force, the technical preparations for an offensive were almost non-existent. Instead of the massed bomber fleets assumed to be necessary to inflict serious damage, the force was composed of a modest number of light and medium bombers, most of them incapable of reaching beyond the fringes of western Germany. More problematic was the absence of serious thinking about problems of navigation, bombing training, bombsights and bombing accuracy, reflecting an air force culture that played down the importance of technique and tactics.[113] The RAF made generalists of the senior staff, who moved regularly between command in the field and office duty in the Air Ministry, discouraging the development of a corps of technically qualified airmen to match the Technical Office of the German Air Force. The British scientist, Sir Henry Tizard, chaired a committee set up in 1938 to give scientific advice to the RAF on bombing, but found senior commanders unenthusiastic about collaborating with science.

When an Air Ministry Bombing Policy committee was finally set up in March 1938 to explore the problems of how to reach, find and hit a target, it was acknowledged that a great deal more needed to be done to be able to do any of them. The bombsight was little different from those used in the First World War and navigation was undertaken either visually by day or by the stars at night. At the committee's first meeting, the pessimistic conclusion was reached that new technical equipment was unlikely to produce any marked improvement in navigation or accuracy. Opportunities for accurate night-time bombing were expected to be 'rare'.[114] Bombing trials showed that with high-level bombing by day, the form most favoured, only 3 per cent of bombs were likely to hit their target, and in a shallow dive, 9 per cent.[115] By March 1939 the Air Ministry planning department bemoaned the failure to mobilize all the country's scientific resources to produce a better bombsight, and suggested that political pressure should be exerted on the United States to provide the Norden gyroscopic model, but it was largely a problem of their own making.[116] A month before the Munich crisis in late September 1938, the commander-in-chief of Bomber Command, Air Chief Marshal Edgar Ludlow-Hewitt, told the Air Ministry that under present circumstances it would be best to rely on the North Sea and air defences in the event of war with Germany. The attempt to bomb Germany 'might end in major disaster'.[117]

There was a profound irony in the fact that the one force in which commitment to a bombing offensive at some point was a matter of principle lacked the capability to conduct it, while the United States, with the necessary industrial and technical resources, had no intention of doing so. In the end, of course, both air forces did undertake large-scale and complex bomber offensives. It is therefore worth reflecting on why Britain and the United States, both liberal states committed in the 1930s to trying to keep the peace, both states in which there was widespread public condemnation of bombing civilians, whether in Ethiopia, China or Spain, should be the ones where the idea of destroying the 'vital centres' or 'the social body' were most fully elaborated. Part of the explanation lies in the geopolitical and military realities confronted by both states. Force projection for both had seldom involved a large army and the army remained, even after the Great War, a component of the defence establishment rather than its driving force, as it was in France, Germany or the Soviet Union. In conjunction with large navies, on which home security had been dependent, air power could be projected overseas with greater flexibility and potential striking power than overseas expeditionary forces. In Britain, defence of the Empire against threat meant that Germany was not the only potential enemy. In the discussions surrounding the development of the 'Ideal Bomber' in the mid-1930s, range was called for that could reach targets in Japan or the Soviet Union (in case of a Communist threat to India), as well as provide Empire reinforcement in areas as geographically distant as Canada or Sierra Leone. The threat from Soviet long-range bombers – anticipating the later Cold War – was expected to spread to British interests in the Middle East and eventually to menace British cities. The only response was expected to be a British strike force for use against Soviet cities.[118] In the United States, the arguments from the Air Corps for the survival of a heavy-bomber programme were all based on the idea that force would have to be projected across oceans to American Pacific possessions, and perhaps against targets in Europe from American airbases.

There was also in both Britain and the United States a real attraction to the idea that air warfare was a more modern and efficient form of fighting than the recent experience of a gruelling and costly land war. Since both were democracies, with political elites sensitive to popular anxieties and expectations, air power was intended to reduce the human costs of war on the ground. Arthur Harris famously argued that the army would fail next time to find 'sufficient morons willing to be sacrificed in a mud war in Flanders', but for Germany, France or the Soviet Union, a ground army and effective ground defences were essential elements in their security planning.[119] The idea that modern technology and science-based weaponry enhanced military efficiency was central to the American view of the potential of a bombing war. At the Air Corps Tactical School, airmen emphasized that air power was 'a new means of waging war', and one that would supply 'the most efficient action to bring us victory with the least expenditure of lives, time, money and material'.[120] Air power also appealed because it could make optimum use of the technical and industrial strengths of the two states, while minimizing casualties. In the United States, planning for possible industrial mobilization of resources to support large-scale air activity began in the 1920s and by the early 1930s produced detailed mobilization planning for 24,000 aircraft a year; in Britain plans for industrial mobilization dated from the mid-1930s with the development of so-called 'shadow factories', ready to be converted to military output if war broke out. In both cases, extensive manufacturing capacity and advanced technical skills were regarded as a critical dimension of future war-making, particularly in the air.[121] The modernity of air power was emphasized in other states as well, for propaganda reasons as well as military ones, but much less autonomy was allowed to those air forces to campaign for strategies that could be presented as more efficient and less costly than traditional ground war.

One important consequence of the equation of air power and modernity was the willingness of airmen in Britain and the United States to accept that modern 'total war' reflected a changed democratic reality, that war was between peoples as well as armed forces. In an age of modern industry, mass political mobilization and scientific advance, war, it was argued, could not be confined to the fighting front. Although the term 'total war' was first popularized by Erich Ludendorff, the German general who had masterminded much of Germany's war effort between 1916 and 1918, it was appropriated as a description of whole societies at war much more fully in Britain and America than it was in Continental Europe. 'There can be no doubt,' wrote the British aviation journalist, Oliver Stewart, in 1936, 'that a town in any industrial civilisation is a military objective; it provides the sinews of war; it houses those who direct the war; it is a nexus of communications; it is a centre of propaganda; and it is a seat of government.'[122] As a result, he continued, 'blind bombing of a town as a town might be logically defended'. In a lecture to the Naval Staff College, also in 1936, Air Vice Marshal Arthur Barrett asked his audience to recognize that it was no longer possible 'to draw a definite line between combatant and non-combatant'. This was, he claimed, a result of the 'power of democracy'; the more governments depended on the support of the governed, the more the morale and resources of the civil population became a legitimate object of attack.[123] The United States air force also based its argument in favour of offensive bombing on the nature of a modern democratic state:

> Where is that will to resist centered? How is it expressed? It is centered in the mass of the people. It is expressed through political government. The will to resist, the will to fight, the will to progress, are all ultimately centered in the mass of the people – the civil mass – the people in the street ... Hence, the ultimate aim of all military operations is to destroy the will of those people at home ... The Air Force can strike at once at its ultimate objective; the national will to resist.[124]

It may well be that in both Britain and the United States popular fears about a war from the air were more powerfully and publicly expressed, given the previous geographical immunity both states had enjoyed before the coming of the aeroplane, and that as a result popular phobias fuelled military speculation that bombing the home front would have immediate results. But whatever the source of this conviction, it governed most air force expectations about how the next war should be fought.

Did this make the bombing offensives of the Second World War inevitable? Certainly no force in 1939 was prepared to carry out an annihilating, war-winning 'knockout blow' of the kind Douhet had envisaged, with thousands of massed bombing aircraft, using every possible weapon to destroy the popular war-willingness of the enemy in a matter of days. The RAF was the only air force to consider the possibility, but it was restrained by everything – inadequate technical means, a shortage of aircraft, the prevailing political and legal restrictions on attacking civilians – from carrying out such a strike. In other air forces different cultures prevailed and produced contrasting strategic choices. Nevertheless, an independent, potentially war-winning air offensive was difficult to resist by air forces keen to assert their organizational independence – as were all three air forces that eventually mounted major offensives – and anxious to profit from the expansive commitment of scientific, industrial and research skills to air force procurement. Each air force was also very aware of the imperatives imposed by 'modern' war, not only the 'civilianization' of warfare implied by total war, but the need to keep abreast of technical developments (atomic weapons, jets, rockets, radar) that might transform the nature of air warfare itself and make escalation unavoidable.

In addition, there was the pervasive popular image of future war. Despite its apocalyptic language and fantastic imagery, there can be little doubt that the constant fictional representation of a bombing war created a widespread expectation that this is how the war was going to be waged, and would have to be waged to prevent one side or the other from gaining an overwhelming advantage. On 1 September 1939, the day that Germany invaded Poland, the air-raid sirens sounded in blacked-out Berlin in the early evening. Berliners panicked, grabbing gas masks and rushing for the shelters in case Polish bombers had somehow succeeded in breaking through to the capital. 'The ugly shrill of the sirens,' wrote the American journalist, William Shirer, 'the utter darkness of the night – how will human nerves stand that for long?'[125] During the night of 3 September, the date Britain declared war on Germany, the air-raid warning sounded all over southern England. The population braced itself for mass bombing and gas attack. The following morning, wrote one wartime diarist who had sat terrified all night, 'practically everyone is now carrying a gas mask. What a reflection on our civilisation!'[126] Both cases were false alarms, and they remained false for many more months. Yet it is a reasonable, if unverifiable, assumption that knowledge of such intense popular fear prompted air forces to go further than they would otherwise have gone when bombing offensives were finally launched. In this case imagination and reality became fatefully entwined.

PART ONE

Germany's Bombing War

2

The First Strategic Air Offensive, September 1940 to June 1941

In April 1939 Adolf Hitler sat in his private apartment at the Reich Chancellery in Berlin in conversation with the Romanian diplomat, Grigore Gafencu. He used the opportunity to complain vigorously about the obstructive policies of the British government and the pointlessness of a contest between the two states. In a rising temper he told Gafencu that if England wanted war, 'it will have it'. Not a war as in 1914, but one in which Germany would use new and terrible weapons, the fruit of her technical genius. 'Our Air Force leads the world,' he exclaimed, 'and no enemy town will be left standing!' Gafencu, silenced by the diatribe, listened as Hitler's voice grew calmer and graver. 'But after all,' he continued, 'why this unimaginable massacre? In the end victor or vanquished, we shall all be buried in the same ruins.' Only Stalin, he reflected, would benefit from a destructive air war.[1]

It would be a simple step to conclude from this that when German air fleets were unleashed against British cities from the autumn of 1940, Hitler was fulfilling his promise to annihilate the source of his strategic frustration with a campaign of terror bombing. In a speech to the assembled organizers of the Winter Help organization on 4 September 1940 Hitler apparently gave vent to that frustration following a number of small-scale air attacks on the German capital. He promised his listeners that German bombers would repay the British tenfold for what they were doing 'and raze their cities to the ground'. The American journalist William Shirer, who was present, observed the effect on a largely female audience, which by the end was on its feet baying approval.[2] The SS Security Service (SD), monitoring popular opinion, found that Hitler's speech made a deep impression on the public when it was reported, but most of all the threat to obliterate British cities.[3] Yet neither Hitler's prediction to Gafencu nor his promise to the German public can be taken at face value. Both were clearly designed for political effect and the threats rhetorical. In the confines of his headquarters Hitler took a more modest view of air power, whose development he had influenced to only a small degree. The air force that was turned against Britain in 1940 had not been designed to carry out a long-range 'strategic' campaign and when ordered to do so that autumn there was no directive to carry out obliteration bombing, though the effects on the ground were often construed as such by the victims. Though the popular view in the West has always been that German bombing was 'terror bombing', almost by definition, Hitler for once held back. In the first years of the war, until British area bombing called for retaliation in kind, Hitler refused to sanction 'terror bombing' and rejected requests from the German Air Staff to initiate it. Not until the onset of the V-Weapon attacks in June 1944 did he endorse the entirely indiscriminate assault of British targets.[4]

FROM WARSAW TO PARIS

For the first year of the war the German Air Force conducted what was called 'Operational Air War' as it had been laid down in the 'Guidelines for the Conduct of Air Warfare' drawn up by the infant force in 1935 and issued in a revised version in 1940. Although the air force sought to distinguish air strategy from that of the army and navy by virtue of its exceptional mobility, flexibility and striking power, in practice German air strategy was linked closely to the ground campaign. Air forces were expected to defeat the enemy air force and its sources of supply and operation; to provide direct battlefield support for the army or navy against the enemy surface forces; and to attack more distant targets, several hundred kilometres from the front line, which served the enemy air effort. These targets included energy supply, war production, food supply, imports, the transport network, military bases and centres of government and administration. The list did not include attacks on enemy morale or residential centres, which the air force regarded as a waste of strategic effort, but it *did* include provision for revenge attacks if an enemy bombed German civilians. All operations, except these last, were designed to undermine the enemy's capacity to sustain front-line resistance. Operational air warfare contributed to the central aim of forcing the enemy armed forces to give up the fight.[5]

In practice the limits of German air technology, with a heavy multi-engine bomber still at the development stage, meant that the air force was regarded principally as a powerful tool to unhinge the enemy front by using fighters to destroy the enemy air force while twin-engine medium bombers, heavy fighters and dive-bombers attacked the enemy field formations and more distant economic and military targets. The instructions for air support of the army, issued in July 1939, acknowledged that air power could be exercised indirectly in support of the army by undermining enemy supply and production and reducing the war-willingness of the enemy nation. But it was emphasized that the air force would be needed primarily to help speed up the movement of the army by attacking a wide number of targets, fixed or fleeting, on or just behind the battlefront, which stood in the army's way.[6] The decision to organize the air force in integrated air fleets, each with its own component of bombers, fighters, dive-bombers and reconnaissance aircraft, and each allocated to a particular army group, enhanced the flexible, multi-tasked character of air warfare, but also tied the air force to the land campaign. The critical element in air-army cooperation was rightly seen to be effective communication between ground and air, and air force directives in 1939 and 1940 made something of a fetish of precisely described links by radio or signal or liaison officer.[7]

This joint effort was the core of what later came to be called 'Blitzkrieg' and it was used to devastating effect in all the German land operations of the first two years of war (and would have been used in southern England, too, if German forces had got ashore in the autumn of 1940). Yet it is difficult to reconcile the idea of a German Air Force tied flexibly but surely to the land campaign with the popular recollection of the German bombing of Warsaw in September 1939 and of Rotterdam eight months later. Long before the onset of the 'Blitz', the Western world had come to assume that the German Air Force, for all its vaunted support of German armies, was an instrument for perpetrating aerial terror, as it was widely believed to have done at Guernica in April 1937, during the Spanish Civil War. A British wartime account claimed that Germany's earlier bombing would go down in history 'as an outstanding example of depraved conduct . . . murder on a scale that Christendom had never before experienced'.[8] So powerful is this conventional view of German bombing atrocity (which helped to legitimate the heavy bombing of German cities later in the war) that it is worth looking in greater detail at the story of German city-bombing before the onset of the campaign against Britain in September 1940.

The German aggression against Poland which began on 1 September 1939 was a model of the modern exercise of air power. On that day the 397 aircraft of the Polish Air Force, including 154 mainly obsolete bombers and 159 fighters, faced two German air fleets, Air Fleet 1 under

General Albert Kesselring and Air Fleet 4 under Lt General Alexander Löhr, with a total of 1,581 aircraft including 897 bombers and 439 fighters and fighter-bombers. Polish combat aircraft were outnumbered by more than four to one. During the first three days of the campaign waves of German bombers and dive-bombers attacked airfields, rail centres, military depots and radio stations. So rapidly was the Polish Air Force overwhelmed that resistance almost entirely disappeared; half their planes were lost in combat and those that remained flew on 17 September to bases in Romania rather than risk destruction or capture. From 4 September the German air fleets were able to concentrate attacks on communications to slow down the Polish army as it tried to re-form in the Polish interior. Between 6 and 13 September air attacks spread out further east towards the Vistula River and targets in Praga, the part of Warsaw on the far bank of the river. Resistance was light but the military targets which German aircraft were told to hit were obscured by smoke and haze and suffered little in the preliminary attacks. As the German armies closed the ring around Warsaw and the nearby fortress at Modlin, the air forces were ordered to bomb enemy troop concentrations in and around the city, but not to attack 'the streaming columns of refugees' on the roads leaving the Polish capital.[9] On 16 September the Polish commander in Warsaw was given six hours to surrender. He refused, declaring the capital to be a 'special military zone', and as a result German planes dropped leaflets warning the population to leave. As Warsaw was a defended city, it was legitimate for German air forces to join the German Army artillery in the siege. On 22 September Hitler ordered the final liquidation of Polish resistance in Warsaw, including air strikes on important military and economic targets, as well as buildings housing the military and political authorities.[10] The German Foreign Office requested that the air force make every effort to avoid damaging the Belvedere Palace; Hitler ordered special care to be taken not to hit the Soviet diplomats leaving the city after the Soviet invasion of eastern Poland on 17 September.[11] On 25 September there was extensive incendiary bombing and heavy damage to the centre of Warsaw in an attack which dropped some 632 tonnes of bombs, the largest air attack made by any air force until then. Troops of the German Third Army were killed when German aircraft strayed too far into areas already occupied by German forces, and on 26 September all bombing ceased. The following morning Warsaw surrendered.[12]

The air attacks on Warsaw were designed to speed up the capitulation of the armed forces defending the city, but no more than that. When

Colonel Wolfram von Richthofen, designated 'Air Leader for Special Tasks' (*Fliegerführer zur besonderen Verfügung*) and a veteran of the Guernica bombing, requested annihilating attacks on the whole urban area, the German Air Force chief of staff, Colonel-General Hans Jeschonnek, refused.[13] Nevertheless, the impression made on the Polish population and those foreigners unlucky enough to be caught in the path of the bombing was of deliberately random attack. A Polish doctor, Zygmunt Klukowski, drove through Lublin on 4 September, where he saw his first evidence of the bombing: 'three completely destroyed apartment buildings. Many buildings had broken windows and collapsed roofs.' Five days later he survived eight raids on Lublin in one day: 'Practically everyone prayed,' ran his diary. 'Some civilians were shaking with fright.' Klukowski observed that he had experienced nothing quite like this in the First World War.[14] Chaim Kaplan described in his diary the hell in Warsaw, worse than 'Dante's description of the Inferno'; everyone ran to shelter in 'dark holes', full of hysterical women.[15] An unlucky strike hit the American ambassador's residence outside Warsaw on 2 September.[16] The gap between the air force orders, which specified economic, military and administrative targets, and the reality on the ground, reflected the overwhelming air power German forces were able to bring to bear, but above all the problems faced in achieving a high degree of accuracy even when dive-bombing from low altitude, a problem that characterized almost all bombing operations throughout the war. German post-operational research showed that two aircraft factories at Mielec and Lublin, reported by the pilots who bombed them as destroyed, were untouched. Trains were seen steaming along tracks described by pilots as 'wrecked' shortly before.[17] A post-operational assessment made by General Hans Speidel in November highlighted the particular importance that had been attached to destroying sources of power (electricity, gas), but since many of these installations were located close to residential zones, the raids inevitably involved civilian casualties.[18] A final figure for the dead in Warsaw from bombing has never been calculated with any certainty. Many were the victims of artillery fire rather than bombing; Chaim Kaplan thought shelling to be the greater menace to the civilian population.[19] The claims that between 20,000 and 40,000 died is certainly an exaggeration, for fatalities on this scale would have required a firestorm on the scale of Hamburg in 1943 or Dresden in 1945, and of that there is no evidence, nor was the German Air Force at that stage capable of creating one. Current estimates suggest around 7,000 dead, on the assumption that casualty

rates per ton of bombs might have equalled the Dresden raid, but a casualty rate equivalent to the Blitz on London would mean around
2,500 deaths on the basis of the limited tonnage dropped.[20]

The German Air Force itself made the most of its contribution to victory in Poland and in doing so helped to nurture the myth of Warsaw's
destruction from the air. The propaganda arm produced the film *Baptism of Fire (Feuertaufe)*, a documentary deliberately designed to present
to the German public and to foreign audiences the image of awesome
aerial power exerted against the unfortunate Poles. In November
1939 the new Reich Commissar of the Polish 'General-Government',
Hans Frank, hosted neutral diplomats and military attachés formerly
accredited to Warsaw at a reception in the former capital. In his address
he asked them to examine closely the extensive bomb damage in Warsaw (it was claimed that out of 17,000 buildings only 300 had escaped
unscathed); as a result of their observations he suggested they should
'recommend to their respective Governments to intercede for peace'.[21]
By February 1940 Mussolini was openly talking of the 40,000 Poles
who he claimed had died in the ruins of Warsaw, though only 12 per
cent of the city had been destroyed or seriously damaged, and not all of
that was due to bombing.[22] The Hitler regime was happy to make political capital out of the bombing, just as the German Air Force clearly
exploited the Polish campaign to enhance its own political weight and
strategic status alongside the German Army. Yet the fact remains that
the air campaign in Poland was a model of the operational air warfare
elaborated before 1939, with air forces closely supporting the land campaign by destroying (with a wide margin of error) military, industrial
and infrastructure targets designed to weaken Polish military resistance – and not an example of ruthless Douhetism.

The second major city attack occurred in the early stages of the German aggression against the Low Countries and France, which began on
10 May 1940. Part of the plan was to move the right wing of the German Army Group B through the Netherlands using a combination of
surprise paratroop attack, air strikes on military targets and a ground
assault. The German priority was to seize Dutch airfields and key communication points, which was largely achieved, though at high cost. By
13 May German forces had reached and occupied southern Rotterdam,
but were facing stiff resistance around the bridges over the River Maas,
running through the centre of the city. The German Eighteenth Army
issued orders to General Schmidt's XXXIX Corps to break Dutch
resistance in the city using all means available, since speed was essential

for the rest of the campaign plan. Orders were given to carry out air attacks on 14 May against military targets in the area facing the German Army. That morning, following a German threat to destroy the city, the Dutch authorities began negotiating its surrender. A little after noon, Schmidt ordered the air force units to abandon plans for the raid: 'bombing attack Rotterdam postponed owing to surrender negotiations'.[23]

While talks continued, a large number of Heinkel He111s appeared in the sky, flying in two separate formations towards the centre of the city. Schmidt hastily ordered red flares to be fired; 'for God's sake,' he was heard to say, 'there'll be a catastrophe'. Half the 100 aircraft saw the flares and turned back, but 57 dropped their load as directed on Dutch army targets in an urban triangle to the north of the river, in the process burning down 2.8 square miles of the defended area and killing, according to the most recent estimate, 850 people.[24] Much of the damage was done by fire caused by leaking oil installations after the bombing. At 3.30 that afternoon the city formally surrendered and to avoid further damage and loss of civilian life, the Dutch Army capitulated a day later. In his memoirs the commander of Air Fleet 2, Albert Kesselring, claimed that radio contact with German forces in Rotterdam broke down at midday so that the cancellation order never got through, but the commander of the bombing squadrons involved later gave testimony that the surrender negotiations were known about and that red flares, fired by German forces from an island on the River Maas, were the signal to abandon the raid if negotiations were still being conducted. One group did see the flares; for the other group, heavy smoke from the battle below obscured them.[25] There has never been much doubt that the operation against Rotterdam was occasioned by the difficult situation faced by German soldiers in the south of the city as they tried to force the bridges. Like the bombing of Warsaw, the operations against Rotterdam imposed heavy civilian casualties because the Dutch Army chose to defend the area rather than declare it an 'open city' or surrender. In both cases substantial damage and death were also caused by artillery fire. Whether or not Göring was attracted to the idea of displaying German air power once again as irresistible and ruthless, which has sometimes been suggested but never proved, the bombing of Rotterdam excited the same kind of extravagant attention as Warsaw. An RAF air-training manual issued in March 1944 described the attack as an unexampled atrocity with 30,000 dead in 30 minutes.[26]

Paris might have suffered something of the same fate as Rotterdam if the French Army and government had insisted on defending the French capital to the last. A number of military targets were bombed around Paris on 3 June, in the later stages of the campaign in the West, but on 11 June it was declared an 'open city' by the French commander-in-chief, Maxime Weygand, and evacuated by the government and military high command.[27] The bombing that took place in France between 10 May and French surrender on 17 June was almost all of it tactical bombing, in support of the German offensive, or to prevent the evacuation of Allied (mainly British) troops in late May and the first half of June, or to destroy the French Air Force and its sources of supply. In the process, substantial damage was done to the towns and their civilian populations in the path of the oncoming German forces. Other places were declared 'open cities' to avoid the devastation of the First World War, including the cathedral town of Rheims. Once the Dunkirk pocket was eliminated, the German armies turned south towards Paris to complete the destruction of French military power. At this point German aircraft were free to roam over French territory; they were directed to attack rail communications, the aircraft and aero-engine industry and oil depots. Between 1 and 3 June long-range attacks destroyed the major rail links between Paris and most of the rest of France. During the first four days of June attacks were also mounted against the port areas at Marseilles (where there were oil storage tanks), Le Havre and the docks at the mouth of the River Rhône. On 3 June German bombers also hit nine French airfields and aircraft factories around Paris at Villacoublay, Les Mureaux and the Citroën works, killing 254 people, 195 of them civilians.[28] The bombing began a panic, accelerating the growing movement to abandon the capital; on 8 and 9 June ministry personnel were evacuated. But the bombing was not resumed and Paris's status as an 'open city' was respected for reasons that are still not entirely clear.[29] German forces concentrated on the direct support of their own operations against what remained of the French Army and its Air Force. The German Air Force ended the era of rapid conquests as it had begun in Poland, clearing the way for the army to roll forward and secure final victory.

THE 'ENGLAND-PROBLEM'

The exercise of German air power between September 1939 and June 1940 reflected a particular conception of 'strategic' air warfare in which victory was a combined achievement of the air forces and the army. The use of bombing was essentially tactical, even when targets distant from the actual front line were the object of attack. Although some German Air Force commanders thought that this form of force projection signified a new age of independent air warfare, and revelled in its novelty and power, there was a great difference between a campaign launched to support a major ground offensive and a campaign in which aircraft were working entirely on their own. The possibility in June 1940 that the German Air Force might be used to strike at Britain opened up for the first time the prospect of a genuinely independent bombing campaign, but it was by no means a certainty. In the summer of 1940 there were no plans for an air campaign against Britain that would last almost a year, though that is eventually what happened.

The priority for the German bombing force in June 1940 was to recuperate and reorganize after the effort made during the Western campaign. The bomber arm at the start of the invasion of France and the Low Countries had a strength of 1,711 aircraft with 1,084 available for service; by early July the regrouped bomber force had a strength of 1,437 with 993 serviceable aircraft. Between 10 May, when the campaign started, and 29 June, the air force had lost 1,241 combat aircraft, 51 per cent of them bombers. One-third of the bomber crew strength was lost during the same period, 446 out of 1,325 available.[30] During June and July new aircraft and replacement crew joined the two air fleets assigned to northern France and the Low Countries: Air Fleet 2 under the newly promoted Field Marshal Albert Kesselring occupied an area from northern Germany to Le Havre on the French Channel coast; Air Fleet 3 under Field Marshal Hugo Sperrle (another beneficiary of the crop of promotions announced by Hitler after the defeat of France) was spread out from south-west Germany across occupied France to the Atlantic coast and the Normandy peninsula. Most of their aircraft were stationed on bases close to the coastline facing Britain. *Fliegerkorps IV* (Air Corps IV), which specialized in anti-shipping operations, was moved from Kesselring's command to Sperrle's, so that it could attack shipping approaching the English coast from the Atlantic. A smaller Air Fleet 5, under General Hans Stumpff, was stationed in Norway for attacks against North Sea shipping and targets in Scotland and the north-east of England, though difficult flying conditions were to limit its contribution during the long aerial siege that unfolded from the autumn of 1940.

By late June it was not yet evident what direction German strategy would take now that German hegemony had been established over

Continental Europe. Hitler and much of the German leadership and public hoped that the war in the West was over and that Britain would now try to seek a way to extricate itself from an unwinnable contest. In late June Hitler withdrew to his headquarters near Kniebis in the Black Forest where, according to his air force adjutant, Nicolaus von Below, 'he sat in deep contemplation of his enemy'.[31] Hitler had already speculated about the prospect of offering Britain a way to end the war, but he was not confident that a Britain led by Churchill would be likely to embrace negotiation.[32] Another alternative was an invasion of southern England, the capture of London, and a dictated settlement. This possibility had already been suggested by the German Navy commander-in-chief, Grand-Admiral Erich Raeder, in meetings with Hitler on 21 May and 20 June, partly to ensure that the next campaign, if there were one, would give a higher profile to the navy. Raeder nevertheless repeatedly warned of the high risks involved with a cross-Channel assault; his personal preference was for another approach altogether, a concerted strategy of blockade directed at British trade using aircraft, submarines and surface raiders to reduce British imports and stocks to an insupportably low level.[33] This was a strategic choice with strong echoes from the First World War when the German Navy had promised that unrestricted submarine warfare, launched in 1917, would sink enough tonnage every month to force Britain out of the war. Blockade was also a strategy strongly supported by the air force. In November 1939 the air staff drew up detailed target plans for attacks on British shipping, ports and food stocks. The head of German Air Intelligence, Colonel Joseph 'Beppo' Schmid, in a paper entitled 'Proposal for the Conduct of Air Warfare against Britain', argued a powerful case that in this war it was Britain which was more vulnerable to blockade. 'Key is to paralyse British trade,' he wrote, to counter-blockade the blockader.[34]

In the end Hitler opted for all three possibilities, and achieved none of them. The air-sea blockade of Britain was already in being, based on a still-active directive first issued from Hitler's headquarters on 29 November 1939 in which he had ordered extensive aerial mining of British coastal waters and estuaries.[35] In early July Hitler finally decided to make an offer to Britain at the next session of the German Parliament, scheduled for 19 July, and asked his Foreign Secretary, Joachim von Ribbentrop, to draft a suitable speech. But at the same time, on 2 July, the armed forces were asked to begin exploratory planning for the possibility of invasion, and five days later were given a formal directive to prepare operational plans for the 'War against England'. The same day, 7 July, Hitler informed the Italian Foreign Minister, Count Galeazzo Ciano, who was visiting Berlin, that he was inclined to unleash 'a storm of wrath and of steel' on the recalcitrant British, but had not finally made up his mind. Ciano found Hitler 'calm and reserved, very reserved for a German who has won'.[36] On 16 July Hitler finally ordered the invasion as a priority. Given the codename 'Operation Sea Lion' (*Seelöwe*), the directive explained that a landing on the south-east coast of England between Ramsgate in Kent and the Isle of Wight would be possible only if the English Air Force could be so morally and physically disabled 'that it no longer showed any worthwhile capacity to attack the German crossing'.[37] No definite date was announced until it was certain that Britain would not agree to talks.

In the early evening of 19 July Hitler duly made his offer to Britain in a packed and uncharacteristically sombre session of the German Parliament, now invaded by the reality of war. Laurel wreaths had been laid in the seats of six deputies killed in action during the land campaign; the front rows of the chamber balconies were populated by senior military commanders, smothered in braid, their medals gleaming. Most of the speech was a triumphant review of German conquests. The war itself Hitler blamed on international Jewry; the 'offer' amounted to little more than an appeal to Britain to see sense.[38] It was brusquely rejected in London as Hitler had suspected it would be. Invasion became by default the next option. Discussions with senior commanders in the days following the offer to Britain showed Hitler just how difficult the operation was going to be. The navy commander-in-chief emphasized the essential role of the air force in providing a protective umbrella over the landing grounds and keeping the Royal Navy at bay, but his lack of confidence was shared by Hitler. A strong case was made by Hitler's chief of operations, Colonel Alfred Jodl, that Italy should play a full part in the defeat of Britain to make success more likely, by diverting Italian submarines to the Atlantic and Italian aircraft to northern France to take part in the bombing campaign. Although Hitler approved Jodl's idea in August, the German military chiefs were characteristically unenthusiastic. (Eventually, between October 1940 and January 1941, a handful of Italian fighter and bomber squadrons flew a number of desultory raids from Belgian bases, dropping 54 tonnes of bombs on East Anglian ports.)[39] The uncertainty about invasion is one of the explanations for Hitler's growing concern with the Soviet Union in the summer of 1940. At first Hitler hoped that Britain would abandon the war to free his hands for the more important clash with the Communist enemy and avoid a war on two fronts.[40] When it became clear that Britain would not consider a cessation of hostilities, he turned the argument round. At a conference with the service commanders-in-chief on 31 July 1940 he suggested that the Soviet Union was Britain's last hope in Europe and ordered that exploratory preparations begin for a massive blow to be struck against Soviet military power in the summer of 1941. On the same day in a conference with Raeder, Hitler nevertheless insisted on a final timetable for Sea Lion. The operation was to be ready by 15 September, to be launched at some point in the following ten days, but only if air superiority and adequate shipping could be guaranteed.[41]

Through all the arguments about German strategy during July 1940 the one consistent thread was the importance of the German Air Force as the key instrument for creating the possibility of British defeat. This reality pampered air force pretensions. A later wartime account of the summer of 1940 by the air force history office underlined the novelty of a situation in which the air force could now undertake the 'strategic offensive . . . on its own and independent of the other services'.[42] A paper prepared by the commander of Fliegerkorps I in July opened with the defiant assertion that Germany was by definition an 'air power' whereas Britain was a sea power: 'Its chief weapon against England is the Air Force, then the Navy, followed by the landing forces and the Army.'[43] Extensive intelligence on British targets had been gathered by the air force before the outbreak of war in case it should ever be needed. On 1 June 1939 the German Air Ministry had published a comprehensive volume on British air forces, anti-aircraft defences, war economic targets and flying conditions. Orientation Book Great Britain provided exceptionally detailed maps of British airbases, support depots and anti-aircraft defences. The maps of key economic targets included grain silos, oil storage tanks, the aircraft industry, the armaments industry, raw material production, iron ore fields, steelworks and aluminium plants. The graphs of cloud-cover frequency varied from an average of 40 to 50 per cent across the year over Croydon in the south to between 65 and 85 per cent over Tynemouth in the north.[44] A second gazetteer of the economic geography and meteorological pattern of the British Isles was available from 1938 and reissued in February 1940. Its 100 pages supplied a wealth of detailed information about every major city and port, including photographs of the dock areas and calculations of average wind speeds and direction over the course of a typical year. The climatic information painted a gloomy picture for a possible strategic air war. 'All in all,' concluded the document, 'it appears that the British Isles, particularly in the winter months of frequent storms, fog and dense cloud, present very difficult meteorological flying conditions, which without doubt belong among the most unpleasant to be found in any of those major countries regarded as civilised [*Kulturländer*].'[45]

Even before any decisions had been taken at Hitler's headquarters, the air force ordered training operations over targets in southern England using small numbers of aircraft, or sometimes only a single plane. Significantly these flights, known generally by the German term *Störangriffe* (nuisance raids), were undertaken both by day and by night to prepare German bomber pilots for raids of either kind. Some involved mining operations off the English coast. The so-called 'schooling flights' were intended to familiarize crews with the target areas, the pattern of enemy anti-aircraft defences, and the variety of routes available to attack a particular objective, so that when the real offensive was ordered there would be a greater prospect of operational success. Crews sent on the raids were told to alter the timings continually in order to confuse the defenders.[46] The British side found it difficult to understand what the object of the German intruders could be, since the bombs were scattered widely over often quite insubstantial targets. On one night bombs were distributed almost entirely on open country in Cornwall, Devon, Somerset, Gloucestershire, Shropshire and South Wales (where a lucky hit struck Monmouth railway station).[47] It was finally assumed by the RAF that the attacks were practice runs, testing the water before a larger campaign, as indeed they were.

The German Air Force drew some important lessons from the schooling, particularly about night-time attacks, which in contrast to the conventional image of German bombing during the Battle of Britain, were in the majority, even during July and August. In the London Borough of Balham, for example, there were eight small raids in the last week of August, two by day and six by night. In the first week of September, before the onset of the heavy bombing of the capital, there were ten more raids, seven of them at night, operations designed to help train crews with the more difficult task of navigating in the dark.[48] It was discovered that aircraft carried too few bombs of the right calibre to be sure of hitting anything successfully; rather than a small number of heavy high-explosive bombs, bomber units were told to carry larger numbers of smaller bombs to make it more likely that some of the bombs would hit their target. The same lesson was learned with incendiary bombs. It was realized that they had to smother an area in large numbers

to be sure of creating fires difficult to extinguish. These changes determined the tactics to be used throughout the campaign that followed.[49]

While the air force prepared with enthusiasm for its first independent
campaign, the planners at Hitler's headquarters moved to clip its wings.
The operational directives that eventually emerged during the course of
July were based on the experience gained in Poland and the Western
campaign. The aerial assault on England differed from the earlier operations only because, rather than operating simultaneously, the air force
would have to attack first, followed after a short time by the army.
Though the geography presented different challenges, the campaign
plan differed little from the successful pattern of combined operations
established in the first year of war. The air force was to provide an aerial
umbrella over the invasion force and powerful artillery support for the
army as it landed. Rather than undertake an independent campaign, the
whole air force was expected to facilitate the operation of surface
forces.[50] On 21 July Göring met the three air fleet commanders to discuss the operational planning, and three days later the following 'Tasks
and Goals' for the air force were distributed to air force units reflecting
these tactical priorities:

(1) Fighting for air supremacy, that is to say smashing the enemy air force
and its sources of power, in particular the engine-industry
(2) protection for the army crossing and the paratrooper operations
through:
    a) fight against the enemy fleet
    b) fight against attacking enemy air force
    c) direct support for the army
(3) reduction of England through paralysing its harbour installations.
Destruction of its stocks and obstruction of imports.[51]

The fighter arm was needed first, to destroy enemy fighters before they
could inflict damage on German bombers. Once air superiority was
achieved, bombers would be free to attack targets beyond the range of
fighter protection, which extended little further than London, and to attack
round the clock, by day and by night. The object was to move forward,
stage by stage across southern England to a line from King's Lynn to Leicester, destroying air force, military and economic targets systematically.[52]

For the crews impatiently waiting at airfields across northern Europe,
the critical factor was when the assault would start. The order to stand
by at full readiness had been sent out on 17 July 1940, but there was
still no D-Day. Uncertainty existed at every level about whether the

operation would really go ahead. Secret police reports on the mood of the population found a growing impatience with the postponement of 'the great attack on England', even more so as RAF bombers flew almost nightly to targets in north-west Germany, forcing millions of people into air-raid shelters and cellars.[53] Hitler's air force adjutant, von Below, observed that even Göring was unsure that an air campaign would be really necessary. 'We did not know what plan to evolve,' Göring complained to an interrogator at Nuremberg six years later. 'I did not know whether there would be an invasion or not, or what would be undertaken.'[54] Finally, in late July Göring was told to have his forces ready for action, so that when Hitler ordered the air assault it could start at 12 hours' notice, but no date was fixed.[55] Operational plans were finally put into the form of a directive from Hitler's headquarters only on 1 August, a reflection of Hitler's own hesitancy about the wisdom of the invasion and his growing preoccupation with Russia. The date for the start of the air assault, codenamed 'Eagle Day' (*Adlertag*), was fixed for 5 August, Britain's grim weather permitting. A separate note from Supreme Headquarters indicated that Hitler would decide whether Sea Lion would go ahead between 8 and 15 days after the start of the air campaign. The deciding factor was the success of the air force.[56] The concern with the weather had not been misplaced. Weather conditions were to play a critical part throughout the whole of the subsequent campaign, placing arbitrary limits on German action. During the first days of August large-scale air operations were impossible. On 6 August Göring summoned his air fleet commanders to his country estate at Carinhall, where they finalized the plan to destroy the RAF in four days, both its fighter arm and its bomber force, just as they had done in Poland and France. 'Eagle Day' was postponed until 10 August, then for a further three days. In Berlin, workmen could be seen building stands decorated with giant eagles and monumental replicas of an iron cross around the Brandenburg Gate, the backdrop, so it was rumoured, to the anticipated victory parade over Britain.[57]

THE 'ENGLAND-ATTACK'

The long aerial campaign that began in earnest in August 1940 has always been divided in British accounts into two distinct parts, the Battle of Britain, from July to October 1940, and the 'Blitz', from September 1940 to May 1941. The distinction owes something to the

fact that they were fought by two different forces, the Battle largely by
RAF Fighter Command, the Blitz by the civil defence forces, anti-aircraft
units and small numbers of RAF night-fighters. There were also differences of geography: the Battle was fought over southern England, the
Blitz across the whole of the British Isles. Looked at from the German
perspective the conflict has an entirely different shape. The German Air
Force fought a campaign almost a year long, from July 1940 to June
1941. It was almost always called the 'England-War' or the 'England-
Attack', and it was treated on the German side as a unity because it was
conducted by the same air forces, flying operations from the same bases
by day or by night, though increasingly the latter, with the aim of weakening British resistance, perhaps decisively. Accounts by the German Air
Force history office written in 1943 and 1944 describe the phases of a
ten- or eleven-month bombing campaign. German airmen were dismissive of the idea that there was a distinct 'Battle of Britain', though they
were familiar with the term; throughout the war they preferred to talk
about 'England' because of its distinct cultural resonance in Germany.[58]
When public announcements were made of British bombing attacks, it
was common to talk of the English 'Gentlemen' who had authorized
them – polite, hypocritical and ruthless.

The two forces that opposed each other in August 1940 were organized, equipped and led very differently. On 3 August the German Air
Force had a bomber strength of 1,438 aircraft of which 949 were serviceable, substantially fewer than in May; to conduct the war against
the RAF there were 878 serviceable Messerschmitt Me109E/F single-
engine fighters and 320 Messerschmitt Me110C twin-engine fighters
from an operational strength of 1,065 and 414 respectively.[59] The Ju87B
dive-bomber, which had proved so effective in the land campaign, was
withdrawn after the opening days of the 'England-Attack' when it was
discovered that its slow speed in the dive made it exceptionally vulnerable to fast fighter interception. The aircraft were divided between the
three air fleets: 44 combat squadrons (19 bomber) in Air Fleet 2; 33 combat squadrons (14 bomber) in Air Fleet 3; and six combat squadrons
(four bomber) in Air Fleet 5.[60] Unlike the British and American systems,
the German Air Force was not organized functionally but territorially.
Bombers, fighters, fighter-bombers and reconnaissance aircraft were
under a single air fleet commander responsible for a particular
geographical area. Air Fleet 2 was led by Albert Kesselring (former commander of Air Fleet 1), a jovial former cavalry officer, who had joined
the air force in 1934, served briefly as air force chief of staff in the

mid-1930s, and eventually rose to be commander-in-chief of Axis forces in the Mediterranean theatre, where his authorization of savage reprisals earned him the status of a war criminal in 1945, after the end of the war. His fellow commander of Air Fleet 3, Hugo Sperrle, like Kesselring a Bavarian and former army officer, boasted a commandingly large frame that dwarfed even the corpulent Göring. Air Fleet 5, stationed in Norway under General Stumpff, was the Cinderella of the air force. Short of aircraft, faced with dauntingly difficult and lengthy flights across the North Sea, Stumpff's force played a marginal part in the campaign.

Over them all presided Hermann Göring, both Air Minister and air force commander-in-chief, promoted to Reich Marshal in July 1940, the highest-ranking officer in the German armed forces. He was served by an Air Force General Staff which had liaison officers posted to Hitler's Supreme Headquarters to maintain regular contact. Most of the running of the air force was conducted by the general staff and the permanent officials in the Air Ministry, whose state secretary was the former Lufthansa director Erhard Milch, also recently created field marshal. The special political position enjoyed by their commander-in-chief, who was president of the German Parliament and Hitler's nominated successor as *Führer*, meant that Göring could argue the air force case from a position of considerable strength, though it also meant that his time and fluctuating energy had to be divided among a great many tasks.[61] He was a jealous and ambitious commander, almost childishly enthusiastic about the air force, yet almost all accounts of his leadership highlight the arbitrary, irregular and often ill-informed character of his interventions. One of the first American interrogators assigned to Göring in 1945 summed up the prevailing view among his subordinates, culled from the many interviews he had read: 'Lazy, superficial, arrogant, vain and above all a *bon viveur*.'[62] In practice he was a more assiduous and perceptive commander than this judgement suggests, but he did manipulate the air force to enhance his own standing. The role of the air force in the strategic bombing of Britain owed much to Göring's conviction that it could achieve things the other services could not. The political value of success for both the air force and its leader was a driving force of the strategic campaign.

The bomber arm, which would bear the brunt of the eleven-month campaign, was equipped with three aircraft types: two of them, the Dornier Do17Z and the Heinkel He111H/P, had first been developed in 1934–5 and were now nearing obsolescence. They were relatively slow,

poorly armed and could carry over most of the distances required
between 2,200 and 4,000 lbs of bombs; the third was the more recently
developed medium bomber, the Junkers Ju88A, which first saw service
on any scale in August 1940 and soon became the principal bomber
model as the Do17 and He111 were gradually phased out. The Ju88 had
been welcomed in the late 1930s as a versatile and effective aircraft,
also capable of a reconnaissance and night-fighter role, but it was
plagued with development problems and only in the autumn of 1940 did
it start to appear in quantity.[63] But instead of the promised speed and
enhanced striking power, the Junkers bomber, like the ones it was designed
to replace, carried a modest defensive armament, flew at around 280
miles per hour and could carry little more than the existing aircraft,
around 4,000 lbs of bombs, with even smaller weights for longer
flights.[64] Confidence that the Ju88 would fulfil all immediate requirements meant that there was no heavy bomber available in 1940, though
they were in the pipeline. The Heinkel He177 multi-engine long-range
bomber commissioned in 1938 was still in an early development stage,
which left nothing except for the slow Focke-Wulf Fw200 'Condor', a
converted airliner that was used to good effect in the early stages of the
war against shipping, but was far too vulnerable to risk in overland
attacks. The small German bombers also carried relatively small bombs,
principally the 50-kg or 250-kg fragmentation bomb, with a high
charge-to-weight ratio, the 1,000-kg landmine, and the 1-kg incendiary
bomb, packed in cases of 36 bombs each. Loaded with thermite (a mixture of ferrous oxide and powdered aluminium), and with a casing of
magnesium alloy, the incendiary core burned for around a minute, the
casing for twelve to fifteen minutes.[65]

The bombers enjoyed the benefit of sophisticated methods of electronic navigation developed in Germany in the 1930s. The *Knickebein*
(crooked leg) system, pioneered by the German Telefunken company,
used two beams of radio pulses sent from separate transmitters. One
sent Morse dashes, one dots. When the two merged, the aircraft was at
the point to release the bombs. The beams were based on the Lorenz
blind-landing equipment developed in the 1930s to guide aircraft back
to an airfield at night or in poor weather. The second system, known
as *X-Gerät* (Equipment X), was more complex. It utilized six Lorenz
beams, three pointing at the target, three designed to cross them at
intervals, the first 50 kilometres away from the objective, the second
5 kilometres away and the third just before the actual target zone.
A timer activated on the aircraft automatically released the bombs at

precisely the pre-calculated distance. In November 1940 *Y-Gerät* was added using just a single beam, which relied on signals sent back from the bomber to calculate its range. When the ground station was satisfied that the aircraft was precisely over the target, it transmitted an automatic bomb release.[66] The *Knickebein* method could be used in any bomber with blind-landing equipment, the *X-* and *Y-Gerät* only by specially converted aircraft. Experimental training began in 1938, and in late summer 1939, before the invasion of Poland, the new units were established as *Kampfgruppe 100*, Bomber Group for Special Operations, directly under Göring's control.[67] It was found that both systems could achieve a remarkable level of accuracy under the right conditions, in marked contrast to the poor navigational prospects for the RAF. Around 30 to 40 Heinkel 111s fitted with the new equipment were used to undertake pinpoint attacks or to act as a vanguard for a larger force by dropping flares and incendiaries in the target area. In the spring of 1941 a second unit was activated, *Kampfgruppe 26*, designed to use the *Y-Gerät*. Transmitter stations were set up from Stavangar in Norway to Cherbourg in western France, a total of seven by the summer of 1941.[68]

The British forces that opposed the German bomber offensive were organized in functional commands, under commanders-in-chief responsible to the air staff based at the Air Ministry in London. The one command that mattered during the German offensive was Fighter Command, which operated both day- and night-fighters. In early August 1940 there were 60 operational squadrons in Fighter Command, with 715 serviceable aircraft out of an establishment strength of 1,112, not far short of the German figure. There were 19 squadrons of the Supermarine Spitfire Mark IA and Mark II, which had begun to appear in numbers earlier in the year, and 29 of the Hawker Hurricane Mark I and Mark IIA.[69] Almost all Fighter Command's resources were devoted to defending southern and central England from air attack by day. There were only seven full night-fighter squadrons available by 7 September 1940, equipped with the Bristol Blenheim light bomber converted to a fighter role, and one squadron of Boulton-Paul Defiants. Both types had failed to prove their worth in daytime fighting, and were not much better as night-fighters. The fixed defences were organized by the Anti-Aircraft and Balloon Commands, both of which had been put under the control of Fighter Command headquarters at Stanmore in 1939. They presented a very porous front line against the bomber. By the start of the German campaign there were 52 balloon squadrons with a total of 1,865 balloons, giant gas-filled obstructions floating in rows above the cities, attached to long hawsers to damage low-flying aircraft. The Anti-Aircraft Command had been starved of resources in the late 1930s and was forced to expand rapidly during the course of 1940, but it failed to meet its plan. By the end of 1940 there were only 1,442 heavy anti-aircraft guns out of the 3,744 planned; as for the more effective Bofors light anti-aircraft gun, the deficit was even greater, 776 out of 4,410. The Inner Artillery Zone around London, first planned in 1923, had 92 heavy guns, only one-third of the number projected before the war.[70] The commander-in-chief of Fighter Command, Air Chief Marshal Hugh Dowding, admitted in his later despatch on the Battle of Britain that anti-aircraft artillery had been 'inadequate for the defence of all the vulnerable targets in the country', though without advanced gun-laying equipment and radar there was a limit to what anti-aircraft guns could do apart from induce prudence in the enemy and some sense of security among the threatened population.[71]

The one outstanding advantage enjoyed by Fighter Command was the system of integrated communication and intelligence-gathering on which the entire system rested. Its success was due in large part to Dowding, whose understanding of technical issues, organizational skills and fierce defence of his force made him a model commander. He was socially awkward, alternately garrulous and aloof (the quality that earned him the sobriquet 'Stuffy'); he was near the end of his career in 1940 and fought the contest against the German Air Force with compulsory retirement constantly threatened. Unlike in the German Air Force, Dowding enjoyed a good deal of independence from the air staff and from the Air Minister, Sir Archibald Sinclair, a career Liberal politician, appointed in June 1940, whose chief role was to act as the link between Parliament, Churchill and the RAF. Dowding operated a strongly centralized force. Only during the late 1930s did it become possible for the first time, thanks to the development of a chain of radar stations around the British coast, to gain effective advance intelligence of approaching aircraft. Many stations were still not complete early in 1940, but by the autumn the Chain Home network had 30 stations from Cornwall to the far north of Scotland, almost half of them on the south and east coasts, facing the German enemy. To avoid the danger that they might be destroyed by air attack, eleven of the most important had shadow stations set up a few miles distant. In addition there were 31 Chain Home Low stations, to detect aircraft flying under 1,000 feet.[72] The radar chain was far from perfect (estimating height proved difficult, particularly with crew trained too briefly), but it was supplemented by a

nationwide Observer Corps which took over observation once aircraft
had crossed the coast. The whole system was held together by telephone. Radar plots of incoming raids were fed into the central operations
room at Fighter Command headquarters and then relayed to Fighter
Command Groups and sector stations; Observer Corps sightings were
sent straight to Groups from Observer Corps Centres. The whole process could take as little as four minutes, which gave just enough time for
most intercepting fighter aircraft to be airborne. Once aloft, fighters
communicated with each other by radio.

The centrally controlled fighter defences and the special role played
by radar were among the many factors misunderstood by the German
Air Force when their air attacks were finally launched. It was assumed
on the German side that British radar was relatively unsophisticated,
and it got less bombing attention than had been expected. It was also
believed that RAF fighters were tied closely to the area around their
station and lacked precisely the flexibility and intelligence that the system in practice gave them. These misapprehensions were compounded
with a persistent underestimation of the size of Fighter Command and
the capacity to reinforce it continuously with men and aircraft. It was
assumed throughout the German campaign, well into 1941, that the
RAF could not replace losses fully and was a constantly declining
threat, even when the reality of high German losses in August and September 1940 suggested a quite different conclusion.[73]

The British had the opposite problem, persistently overestimating the
size and range of the German front-line air force, pilot numbers and
production levels. Air intelligence suggested a German aircraft output
of 24,400 in 1940 – the true figure was 10,247 – and a front-line force
in early August of 5,800 planes, including 2,550 bombers, when the
actual figure of serviceable bombers was 37 per cent of this figure.
Against Britain the three air fleets employed a total of only 2,445 serviceable aircraft of all types on the eve of Eagle Day. Early evaluations
wrongly assumed that German bombers and long-range fighters had
sufficient range to cover the whole of the British Isles from French bases,
while it was believed short-range fighters could reach as far as Hull
(when they could barely contest the airspace over London). The RAF
also assumed that the German enemy had generous numbers of pilots
and could make good losses of men and aircraft sufficiently to expand
the size of the air force even under combat conditions, which was
also never the case.[74] These contrasts in perception were important in
shaping the attitude both sides took to the conflict. German forces

assumed that what they did by day and by night seriously eroded the capability of an already meagre RAF; British air forces, on the other hand, were spurred to urgent expansion and heroic defiance against an enemy thought to be powerfully and dangerously endowed.

The German determination to start the full air assault with a flourish on Eagle Day was frustrated by grey skies and further rain. Substantial attacks had already been made since 8 August, and the first raids on radar installations and RAF fighter stations followed four days later, seriously damaging the Ventnor radar station on the Isle of Wight, and the airfields at Manston and Hawkinge in Kent. But this was not a real battle. German air units were finally told to prepare for Eagle Day on 13 August, but poor weather persisted and the attack was half-hearted. Units had been ordered not to fly, but the message had not been received by all of them and sorties began early in the morning and went on until evening. Some bombers arrived without their escorts, some escorts without their bombers. The German losses totalled 45 aircraft at the cost of 13 British fighters. Not a single Fighter Command airfield had been attacked. This is a well-known failure, but it nevertheless masks the fuller picture of German operational strategy during August, of which direct attacks on the RAF formed only a part. The fighter-to-fighter contest watched daily in the skies over southern England dramatically symbolized the struggle for the British public then and now, but it was only part of what the German Air Force actually did.

Throughout August and September, and on into the winter months, the German Air Force flew numerous, daily *Störangriffe*, small raids by day and night intended to lure the RAF into battle, to destroy individual military-economic targets, to trigger the air-raid alarm system, and to induce tiredness and despondency in the population. In August 1940 there were four major raids, employing hundreds of bomber aircraft, but 1,062 smaller raids spread out over the country, the largest number of the whole campaign.[75] The city of Hull, for example, was subjected to six small night raids between 20 June and 6 September, which between them destroyed only 17 houses and badly damaged a further 47, but kept the population in a state of perpetual alert.[76] Some of these raids were scarcely opposed by Fighter Command, at night almost none. In addition the German Air Force mounted *Zerstörerangriffe* (destroyer attacks) against key armaments and port installations, using larger numbers of heavy fighters or dive-bombers, as well as armed reconnaissance flights. For the war at sea, a number of specialized units dropped mines in coastal waters and estuaries. In August 1940 only

328 were dropped, but over the following three months 2,766.[77] There were also plans to attack RAF bomber bases north of London once air superiority was achieved – Operation 'Luftparade' – but the failure to dominate Fighter Command postponed the attempt. Only Driffield airfield in Yorkshire was severely hit by aircraft of Air Fleet 5 flying from Norway. The sheer range of targets and attack categories was an exhausting schedule for German air units and it was this, as much as the damage inflicted by Fighter Command, that by early September created a steady attrition of the force and growing strain on the pilots. Later in the war German appraisal of the campaign suggested that the air force had simply been asked to do too much, a view that is difficult to contest. Kesselring in his memoirs dismissed the strategy as 'muddle headed'.

The systematic assault on Fighter Command during the last two weeks of August 1940 was nevertheless the chief priority, and the great majority of German combat aircraft were assigned to the task. The counter-air campaign replicated the strategy adopted in Poland and the Western campaign. Waves of bombers and dive-bombers were to attack key airfields, installations and stores while fighter aircraft destroyed enemy fighter opposition. Between 12 August and 6 September a total of 53 major attacks were directed at RAF targets, the heaviest occurring between 24 August and 6 September. The German Air Force High Command presumed that the outcome of the campaign would also follow the pattern of previous successes, and early reports from the fighting suggested there was no reason to think otherwise. The German assumption that the RAF suffered declining figures of supply, falling pilot numbers and a crude dependence on local air control encouraged a pervasive optimism. The major raid on the Fighter Command station at Biggin Hill in Kent on 18 August was celebrated as a symbolic German triumph. Pilots were invited to give their accounts of the raid for use in air force propaganda. For many of them this attack was the first major raid they had undertaken against an English target; they returned with smug reports of feeble British defences:

> As the machines landed back again after exactly three hours, I saw all the ground personnel standing by the runway. The men worried about us, only wanted to know if all their 'birds' had returned unharmed. But we scrambled out of the machines, went over to them, shook them by the hand. 'Young men, that was nothing at all, we had imagined a quite different defence.' Is that all England can offer? Or is the English air force already so weakened?[78]

Another confirmed that anti-aircraft fire and enemy fighters had been invisible; the target airfields showed a sea of flames, shattered buildings, destroyed runways. 'The German pilots shook their heads,' the account concluded. 'Has it gone so quickly? Is England already finished?' Biggin Hill, ran a third account, 'completely destroyed ... wiped out of existence'.[79] In reality, Biggin Hill remained operational almost every day of the battle, its staff and pilots dispersed in nearby villages, an emergency operations room set up in a local shop, its aircraft carefully camouflaged.

It was the impression of overwhelming air superiority and accurate and destructive raids that fuelled the belief among the German Air Force leadership that the RAF was close to collapse in the last two weeks of August 1940. On 20 August Göring directed his forces to complete the elimination of Fighter Command in four days of 'ceaseless attacks' against targets that the RAF would be forced to defend, including aero-engine and aluminium production.[80] German Air Intelligence concluded by the end of August that 18 Fighter Command stations had been permanently destroyed and the rest disabled (when not one had been out of action for more than a few days); Fighter Command was estimated to be down to around 300 aircraft, including reserves and a monthly production of 280 (when Fighter Command strength was 738 serviceable aircraft on 6 September and fighter production for August totalled over 450). Between 12 and 19 August, based on the eyewitness reports of German pilots, 624 British aircraft were claimed for the loss of 174 German. At Hitler's headquarters it was recorded on 1 September, 'English fighter defence strongly affected ... the question is can England therefore continue the struggle?'[81]

It is this perception that explains the shift in the last week of August to a variety of other targets, many of them attacked by small groups of aircraft, but all of them designed to accelerate the decline of Britain's war effort and so create the conditions for a successful Channel crossing. On the night of 19–20 August there were more than 60 raids across the British Isles on aircraft industry targets and harbour installations. Heavy attacks were ordered on Portsmouth, Liverpool, Bristol and Birmingham, again almost all at night, although Göring excluded London from the list. Hitler's headquarters gave specific instructions on 24 August that only Hitler could authorize raids against the enemy capital, but the attacks edged ever closer.[82] On the night of 18–19 August the first bombs fell in the London suburbs, on Croydon, Wimbledon and the Maldens, and four nights later the first bombs fell by mistake on central London. There was nothing inadvertent about the next raids. On the night of 24–25 August there were bombs on Croydon, Banstead, Lewisham, Uxbridge, Harrow and Hayes. On the night of 28–29 August, London was under red alert for seven hours and bombing was reported in Finchley, St Pancras, Wembley, Wood Green, Southgate, Old Kent Road, Mill Hill, Ilford, Chigwell and Hendon.[83] Although the bombing of London, indeed the official start of the 'Blitz', is usually dated from the major daylight raids of 7 September 1940, industrial and military targets in the suburbs were under attack throughout the previous three weeks, paving the way for a final wave of attacks timed to take place shortly before the launch of Sea Lion. On 31 August Hitler gave the order to prepare for major attacks on London. A directive was issued by Göring on 2 September and approved by Hitler three days later.[84]

The decision to begin a systematic aerial campaign against London has always been seen from the British perspective as a merciful reprieve from the battering sustained by Fighter Command. It is argued that the switch to bombing London saved the RAF and exposed the German bomber forces to debilitating losses as they tried to bomb by day in large formations. It is usually explained as Hitler's indignant response to two small raids on Berlin on the nights of 25–26 and 29–30 August. These raids caused little damage but had a profound moral effect on the population of the German capital, which had been told repeatedly that German air defences would keep British bombers at bay. 'The Berliners are stunned,' wrote William Shirer, who witnessed the massive response of German anti-aircraft artillery and searchlights, 'a magnificent, a terrible sight'.[85] During the second raid on 29 August, 10 people were killed in Berlin and 21 seriously injured. So shocked was Hitler that he immediately returned from his headquarters to the capital. After the first raid the Propaganda Ministry ordered a modest six-line communiqué; after the second raid Goebbels ordered banner headlines condemning the raid. 'Berlin is now in the theatre of war,' he wrote in his diary. 'It is good that this is so.'[86] The raids gave Hitler the opportunity to present the planned attack on London to the German public as a reprisal and plans for the first major daylight raid were given the title 'revenge attack' (*Vergeltungsangriff*). His speech on 4 September condemning the British bombing of Berlin was given full publicity and the 'revenge attack' on 7 September was greeted in the German press with jubilation: 'one great cloud of smoke stretches tonight from the middle of London to the mouth of the Thames'.[87]

Revenge for the Berlin raids certainly played a part in explaining the timing of the campaign against London, but the issue is more complicated.

The decision to attack London was taken against a long background of British raids on urban targets in Germany. The first raid, on Mönchengladbach in the Ruhr, had been made on 11 May. Throughout the period from mid-May to the Berlin raids, British bombers attacked German targets on 103 days, mainly on the North Sea coast or the Ruhr-Rhineland area. The raids were seldom heavy and involved comparatively few casualties but they had the effect of forcing the German population into air-raid shelters for many hours over wide areas not directly affected. During most of August the number of night-time sorties flown by the RAF over Germany was approximately double the number flown by the German Air Force against Britain.[88] So inaccurate was the British bombing that the German authorities had great difficulty in working out the rationale behind it. After the first raids, the local civil defence units were warned to get everyone into air-raid shelters when the alarm went because enemy bombers 'drop their bombs planlessly just anywhere'.[89] By July the apparent aimlessness of attacks, even against small villages or farmsteads, forced civil defence alerts in remote rural areas. The civil defence authorities assumed from repeated attacks on residential districts that British pilots had been given the single task of 'dropping bombs only to do damage to the civilian population'.[90] The result of the regular raids on civilian targets in western Germany was to provoke a good deal of public anxiety and demands for retaliation, which grew louder as the British bombing expanded in scale. The Security Service report for 2 September summed up the growing impatience of the population: 'It is high time that something serious was done about measures of revenge threatened for months.'[91]

The possibility of mounting retaliatory attacks against enemy cities in response to enemy attacks was part of German Air Force doctrine and had been repeated in the instructions in July, subject only to Hitler's personal approval. London was kept in abeyance as a target perhaps to maximize the impact on the population when attacks finally began, but also to shield Berlin from the possibility of retaliation in turn. But given the pressure of popular opinion after four months of repeated British operations against German urban and rural targets, and the very public failure of the German air defence system to protect the capital, Hitler was compelled to make a gesture to meet public expectations. The attacks on Berlin seem to have affected him particularly: 'a calculated insult', according to his air force adjutant von Below, which required a response in kind.[92] There were no moral or legal qualms about the attack on cities, since the RAF raids were widely regarded as evidence that the enemy had already shown a deliberate disregard for civilian casualties in prosecuting the war. This was not mere special pleading. The view of British ruthlessness went back to memories of the wartime naval blockade, which were deeply embedded in the generation now in command of Germany's war effort. 'The British are realists,' Hitler told his dinner companions later in the war, 'devoid of any scruple, cold as ice.'[93] Once again Britain had declared an economic blockade on the day war broke out. Early air force wartime planning documents assumed that Britain might resort to 'terror measures' against German cities. Papers found after the defeat of France on Franco-British plans to bomb Soviet oilfields to cut off German oil supplies were used to show just how unscrupulous the British could be.[94] The operation carried out on 7 September was in this broader sense a 'revenge attack', designed to strike a powerful blow to satisfy German domestic opinion, to shock the population of London out of its enthusiasm for war, and perhaps bring RAF bombing to a halt.

The 'revenge attack' was nevertheless not intended to be random retaliation. The London raids fitted into the framework of the planned pattern of the campaign, which was still predicated on the idea of a cross-Channel invasion at some point in September. After the brief assault on the RAF, the air force schedule was to move to other urban targets further inland, employing predominantly night-time 'destroyer' raids, with a final heavy blow at London just before Operation Sea Lion to create a major refugee problem.[95] Operations against targets in the London area were already under way weeks before Hitler's speech and there were detailed target plans for the capital – known on the German side by the acronym *Loge*, from *Londongebiet* (London area) – showing dock areas, communication targets, power stations and armaments works, which had been distributed to the *Fliegerkorps* in July. The object of the attack was to do serious damage to London's capacity as Britain's major port, to undermine the infrastructure necessary for the war economy as well as to intimidate the population. German bombing was intended to affect morale indirectly, rather than undermine it by deliberately indiscriminate or terror attacks. It was recognized that operations against crowded port areas would necessarily involve damage to residential housing and civilian casualties, but this was not regarded as a sufficient reason to abandon port facilities as a target.[96] The combination of military-economic targeting and indirect pressure on morale was regarded, according to a later wartime account of the campaign, as 'the principal and most effective form of operation'.[97]

Air force units were under orders to identify and hit precise strategic targets. If they could not, an alternative target was to be found. In extreme cases they were under orders to bring back their bombload and, if conditions permitted, to jettison the bombs on approaching their home base at a height of 30 metres from the ground, low enough to prevent the fuse from being activated, so that the bombs could be used again.[98] The insistence on identifying and attacking strategic targets was no doubt done partly to emphasize the contrast between British and German practice, but it also made military sense because it maximized the impact on the enemy's war effort of a given weight of bombs. Tactical instructions to German pilots issued in the autumn of 1940 insisted on the importance of achieving a high concentration of strikes on a designated target. When the air force chief of staff asked Hitler in mid-September whether he approved of deliberate attacks on residential areas as well, Hitler said no. His rejection was recorded in his headquarters war diary: 'Terror attacks against purely residential areas will be held back as a very last resort, and for the moment will not be used.' War-essential targets in London, including airfields, were given priority; terror was only to be used if the RAF unleashed a similar programme against German towns.[99]

The German Air Force saw the opening assault on London on 7 September 1940 as the opportunity to achieve the operational success and wide publicity that had been denied on 'Eagle Day'. Bomber groups had been sent their instructions on 4 September. The London area was divided up into target zones for each group, each terminating in the London docks. The plan was to attack in three waves, the first attracting British fighters, but the second two free to bomb as enemy fighters were forced to land and refuel. The bombers were instructed to carry 20 per cent of their load as 'flame bombs' (*Flammenbombe C250*), large oil bombs designed to ignite the highly flammable material in London's docklands, and 30 per cent as delayed-action bombs, to hinder efforts to fight the fires. Close formation and concentration of effort were called for.[100] The raid itself was a considerable success because Fighter Command was positioned to expect further attacks on the fighter stations rather than a mass raid on London. A large formation of 348 bombers, escorted by 617 Me109s and Me110s, was able to penetrate through to the London docks and the Royal Arsenal at Woolwich and drop around 300 tonnes of bombs at 5 p.m. A second wave attacked at 8 p.m., dropping a further 330 tonnes, and bomber activity went on until the early hours of 8 September. Major fires started throughout the dock and port area and 436 Londoners were killed. The German Air Force lost 40 aircraft, the RAF 28. The sheer size of the fighter screen made it difficult for the enemy fighters to reach the bomber squadrons and a high concentration of effort was indeed achieved.

The day was chosen, like the 18 August attack on Biggin Hill, for the preparation of a special volume of reports from the pilots and crew about the first major 'vengeance-attack'. Though the reports were destined for the Propaganda Ministry, they reflected the view of German aircrew that the 7 September raids gave them a renewed sense of purpose after weeks of small-scale and costly conflicts. Air force medical personnel had already observed signs of nervous exhaustion and 'aversion to flying' among personnel who had had little respite for a month.[101] 'At last once again a splendid goal before us!' ran one account among the many. Talks to the crews had stressed the fact that bombing London was revenge for the destruction of German towns and the deaths of German civilians, and this view reappeared in a number of the accounts. 'Everyone knew about the last cowardly attacks on German cities,' wrote one reporter, 'and thought about wives, mothers and children. And then came that word "Vengeance!"' The reports once again contrasted German operational achievements with British failures:

> We steered towards London from the south. Still 50 or 60 kilometres away from Britain's capital, we saw already in the sky thick, black clouds of smoke, which grew up like giant mushrooms. This is a target one can no longer mistake! A blazing girdle of fire stretched round the city of millions! In a few minutes we reached the point where we had to drop our bombs. And where are Albion's proud fighters to be found? No Spitfire, no Hurricane in sight. Finished, quite finished is that British 'air supremacy'. Before us now lies the bend in the Thames to the east of the city. In this bend lies our target: an electricity works surrounded by giant gasworks and docks. Below us flames and smoke . . .[102]

Another pilot recalled the sight of a ruined airfield on the flight to London, with nothing visible save the charred foundations. The impression from the air, which was largely what German Air Intelligence had to go on, was of systematic devastation.

The conviction that the German Air Force was *winning* the battle helps to explain why over the week following the raids on 7 September, Göring insisted once again that the RAF was on the point of collapse and the invasion a possibility. London was attacked in force again by day on 9, 11 and 14 September, with the RAF taking heavy casualties and inflicting fewer than usual. Not even the events on 15 September, celebrated thereafter in Britain as 'Battle of Britain Day', seriously dented German air force confidence. That day German bomber forces were hit heavily by changed RAF tactics. The British side thought that 185 German aircraft had been brought down, but actual losses amounted to 30 bombers and 26 fighters destroyed and a further 20 bombers damaged. This was a high enough toll from the attacking force, and it accelerated the shift over to night-time raiding, which had been conducted intermittently up until then. But during the week between 7 and 15 September, Fighter Command lost 120 aircraft to 99 German fighters, a ratio that could not easily be sustained by the RAF for very long. The German view was that air superiority, which had eluded the air force in August, was now within its grasp. Göring told Goebbels on 4 September that the war in the west would be over in three weeks. Goebbels relished the initial reports from neutral observers in London, which conjured up 'really apocalyptic images'.[103]

None of this was in the end sufficient to convince Hitler that the risk of embarking on Sea Lion was worth taking. He had already expressed reservations in July about the possibility of defeating Britain. Against a background of wrangling between the army and the navy over how wide a beachhead could be supported, Hitler waited to see how the air war unfolded. On 3 September, D-Day was fixed for 20–21 September, but by mid-September it was evident from continued attacks by RAF Bomber Command against the assembled shipping and stores for the invasion that the enemy air force was far from defeated. Admiral Raeder and the army leadership began to explore indirect strategies – cutting Britain off in the Mediterranean by the occupation of Gibraltar, Malta and Suez, an intensified blockade – but Hitler still hesitated, perhaps in the hope that the new wave of bombing in London might still force the British leadership to negotiate. On 14 September in discussion with the three service chiefs he reasserted his view that the quickest way to end the war was to invade, but he concluded that the air force, though poised for victory, had not yet achieved air mastery.[104] Persistent poor weather and the threat of British naval power contributed to the declining prospects for Sea Lion. Hitler reviewed the situation again on 17 September but could see little change; two days later Sea Lion was postponed indefinitely. Hitler was in the end unimpressed by the performance of the air force. In September he was shown less optimistic estimates of RAF strength than the ones Göring used. These indicated, correctly, that there were still at least 600 fighters in RAF units; interviews with the fighter aces Adolf Galland and Werner Mölders in the week after the postponement confirmed that the situation in the air war was more even than Göring and air force propaganda had suggested. Galland later recalled that his candid account of an RAF far from defeat was greeted by Hitler with nods of agreement.[105]

It has never been entirely clear what Hitler expected the air force to do once Sea Lion failed to materialize. The air force failure was only relative, since a great deal of damage had been done by the German Air Force in August and September, but air force action had not been sufficient to establish air superiority over southern England for any length of time. The explanations for this failure are well known, but are worth reiterating. The intelligence assessment of the enemy played a part throughout in shaping the German approach to the battle. German estimates in mid-September were notoriously wide of the mark. Instead of 300, the RAF had 656 operational fighters on 19 September with 202 more in immediate reserve and 226 in preparation for transfer to units; there were over 1,500 pilots available in the second half of September. The German fighter arm, in contrast, was down to 74 per cent of its pilot strength (around 700–800) by the beginning of September, and suffered losses of 23.1 per cent of its personnel throughout the month; serviceable fighter strength hovered around 500. The loss of crew over England was permanent, 638 identified bodies, 967 prisoners. This was never the contest of the Few against the Many. High attrition – a total of 1,733 aircraft lost from 10 July to 31 October, against 915 RAF fighters – could not be made good from German production. Between June and October 1940 the German aircraft industry turned out 988 single-engine fighters, but British factories produced 2,091 Hurricanes and Spitfires. There were problems with the planning and organization of German aircraft production (to be explored later), but the central problem facing the German Air Force during the daylight fighting was the failure to anticipate serious, centrally directed fighter defences. The sustained strength of Fighter Command compelled the German fighter force to accompany the bombers more closely, exposing them as well to greater risk, increasing the level of combat attrition and making it in the end impossible to sustain the daylight campaign.[106]

THE FIRST STRATEGIC OFFENSIVE

The German Air Force as a whole was still a formidable weapon in the autumn of 1940. But after the cancellation of Sea Lion the rationale for its continued activity against Britain had to be reassessed. Hitler quickly lost interest in the air campaign and issued no fresh directives for it throughout the ten months that followed, except to reiterate the block-ade strategy. He was, claimed von Below, one of the first German leaders to recognize that the air war 'had neither achieved its objective nor was likely to'.[107] Historians too have shown much less interest in the Ger-man strategic bombing campaign, overshadowed as it is by the Battle of Britain at one end and the Barbarossa invasion at the other. In strategic terms the bombing campaign has generally been regarded as a failure. Yet it was here, between October 1940 and June 1941, that the first independent strategic bombing campaign took place. If the air force had been compelled to work within a broader inter-service strategy up until mid-September, it was now no longer obliged to do so and could fulfil its ambitions for independent action. On 16 September, unencumbered by Sea Lion, Göring ordered a new phase in the campaign of attacks across the breadth of the British Isles.[108]

It is possible that Hitler hoped the British could still be induced to give up the war because of the moral and material damage that would be wrought by the bombing and that the campaign was sustained in hope of a political dividend. There is no doubt that there was a popular expectation in Germany that the bombing might win Germany a reprieve from a second winter of war. 'When will Churchill capitulate?' asked Goebbels in his diary in late November 1940 after more news of devastating raids on Britain's cities.[109] Yet the surviving evidence sug-gests that Hitler remained sceptical about what air power might achieve and focused his attention on the campaign against the Soviet Union, whose successful outcome was intended to create the conditions that would make it possible to return to the problem of Britain a year hence. He was nonetheless trapped in a situation of his own making. He could not order the campaign to end because that would seem to admit defeat and privilege British resistance in the eyes of the German public and the wider world. Nor could he ignore what Stalin might think. The air cam-paign had to be kept going because it would persuade Stalin that Britain was still the principal object of German strategy and mask the eastward turn. Politics played its part in sustaining a campaign whose strategic purpose was no longer so clear-cut.

The bombing campaign can best be understood as a form of eco-nomic warfare. In his post-war interrogations at Nuremberg, Hitler's chief of staff at Supreme Headquarters, Field Marshal Wilhelm Keitel, explained that the bombing in 1940–41 was designed to have two important economic purposes: first, a contribution to the food blockade strategy, in collaboration with the navy's submarine arm, along the lines of the campaign in the Great War; second, a campaign of attrition against key military-economic targets.[110] These aims were to be met principally by large-scale night-bombing attacks, sea-mining and day-time raids by small numbers of high-flying fighters, some converted to carry a 250-kg bomb. These daytime raids were designed during late September and October to lure the RAF into combat, and to attack with as much precision as possible a suitable military or economic target. As the weather deteriorated, the raids became less frequent and eventually petered out. Although these daytime *Störangriffe* imposed heavy losses on RAF fighters, it was found that the single bomb was difficult to drop with any accuracy, and on occasion had to be jettisoned to allow the converted fighter to return to its fighter role in self-defence.[111] The pattern of German bombing operations over the course of the England campaign is set out in Table 2.1. The high point of German bombing was achieved in October and November 1940, while poor weather from December to February made continual raiding difficult and costly. The blockade campaign was carried out according to the instructions established in the directive from July 1940 on the conduct of the trade war. It potentially involved the air force in closer collaboration with the German

Table 2.1: Statistics on German Air Activity against Britain,
August 1940–June 1941

Date	Major attacks	*Störangriffe*	Mines laid
Aug 1940	4	1,062	328
Sept 1940	24 (22 London)	420	669
Oct 1940	27 (all London)	21	562
Nov 1940	21	840	1,215
Dec 1940	18	369	557
Jan 1941	15	103	144
Feb 1941	6	151	376
Mar 1941	19	234	410
Apr 1941	21	412	433
May 1941	10	440	363
June 1941	6	221	647
Total	171	5,173	5,704

Source: Calculated from BA-MA, RL2 IV/33, 'Angriffe auf England: Material-sammlung 1940–41', monthly reports from Luftflotten 2, 3, 5.

Navy, whose limited naval air arm and as yet small force of U-boats needed reinforcement by bombers and dive-bombers with experience of over-sea operations, but such cooperation threatened air force hopes that victory might be delivered by air power alone.

The naval High Command placed great hopes on the plan to destroy at least 750,000 tonnes of shipping a month on the calculation that sinking 40 per cent of Britain's 22 million shipping tonnage over a year would force Britain out of the war.[112] The air force High Command, however, preferred to run the bombing as a unitary campaign and in the end devoted only limited resources to the naval element of the trade war. In March 1941 Göring succeeded, in the face of naval hostility, in uniting control over aircraft operating over sea under an air force commander, the *Fliegerführer Atlantik*, based at the French Atlantic port of Lorient. The number of serviceable aircraft available totalled only 58, including 6 of the Focke-Wulf FW200 'Condor', whose initial successes were now compromised by improved British interception.[113] Between July and December 1940, aircraft sank 50 merchant ships with a gross tonnage of 149,414 tonnes. Over the following six months a further 68 ships were sunk, totalling 195,894 tonnes, an average over the year of just 28,775 tonnes per month, a mere 4 per cent of what was required.[114] The sea-mining campaign was similarly affected by the shortage of aircraft. In October 1940 a specialized unit, *IX Fliegerkorps*, was set up for mining operations, but it consisted of only 88 aircraft to cover all the waters around the British Isles. Moreover, out of the 11,167 mines dropped from the air between April 1940 and April 1941, more than one-third, 3,984, were dropped on land targets.[115] Sinkings were sparse, but German airmen claimed for themselves an unverifiably large tonnage sunk by their mines throughout the campaign from 1940 to 1943, even though many of them had been laid by naval vessels and submarines.

The German Air Force saw blockade as a strategy best carried out by destroying port facilities and existing stocks rather than ships at sea, and focused its efforts on urban targets. The blockade priorities are evident from the pattern of the major (and many minor) attacks carried out during the course of the ten-month campaign. Between August 1940 and June 1941 there were 171 major raids, of which 141 were directed at ports (including London). Major port attacks at night absorbed 2,667 tonnes (86 per cent) of incendiary bombs out of a total of 3,116, and 24,535 tonnes (85 per cent) of high explosive out of a total of 28,736.[116] Although some of the tonnage directed at Manchester and London was destined for non-port targets, the priority was for docks, warehouses, silos, oil storage and shipping. The economic war was seen above all as one means of closing off United States aid to Britain, which Hitler, among others, assumed to be an important source of sustenance for Britain's war effort even before the start of Lend-Lease in March 1941.[117] The flow of American goods was in reality a slender stream rather than a flood, but the German fear of American reinforcement of Britain's war effort plays some part in explaining the willingness to continue the campaign over the difficult winter months. An assessment of the RAF made by the German Air Force operations staff in January 1941 assumed that problems caused to the supply of American aircraft and equipment must be seriously undermining British air strength and operational performance.[118]

For the first months of the bombing campaign the principal target was London, which was attacked for 57 nights in a row and occasionally by nuisance raids during the day. Between 7 September and 31 October, 13,685 tonnes of high explosive and *Flammenbomben* and 13,000 incendiary canisters were dropped on the capital.[119] Unlike the early planning in the British and American bombing campaigns, the German Air Force did not draw up a list of vulnerable industrial target systems but relied more on the geographical pattern of British trade and distribution as a guide to blockade priorities, which explains the particular attention devoted to London. The one exception was the aircraft industry, and in particular the aero-engine industry, which was singled out as the priority industrial target, whose destruction would undermine RAF expansion and fighting capability. On 7 November 1940 Göring issued a new directive for the bombing campaign which left London as the principal target, but instructed the air fleets to undertake operations against the industrial region in the Midlands and Merseyside to destroy the British aircraft industry. The directive specified operations against Coventry ('Moonlight Sonata'), Birmingham ('Umbrella', after Chamberlain) and Wolverhampton ('All One Price', a confusion for the popular Woolworths stores).[120] Raids were carried out on the night of 14–15 November against Coventry and for three nights from 19–20 November against Birmingham. The raid against Wolverhampton was not attempted. For the Coventry raid 503 tonnes of bombs were dropped, including 139 1,000-kg mines, the heaviest available, and 881 canisters of incendiary bombs. The aiming point was a cluster of 30 aero-engine and component factories, including the Daimler and Alvis works. The German post-raid assessment was made difficult

by the presence of cloud and smoke, but at least 12 works were identified as severely damaged and a further 8 were presumed to have
suffered the same level of destruction. The close proximity of workers'
housing to the 30 aiming points resulted, according to the German raid
report, in 'considerable destruction to the residential areas', but this was
not the principal object of the attack. The raids against Birmingham
totalled 762 tonnes of bombs, including 166 of the 1,000-kg and
1,563 incendiary canisters. Here again post-raid images showed that
fire had destroyed much of the residential centre, and the few visible
industrial targets, particularly the Rover Motor Works, were also seen
to have sustained heavy damage. German estimates suggested that
60 per cent of Birmingham's armaments production had been hit in the
raids. The overall assessment of the damage sustained in the attack on
Midlands industry painted an optimistic image of German successes:
'The most important foundation of the British aircraft industry is for
the present to be regarded as severely shaken.'[121]

The raids undertaken in November represented an escalation of the
air war against inland targets. The destruction of residential districts
produced high levels of civilian casualties as it had already done in London. Between September and November 1940, 18,261 people were
killed in German raids.[122] German estimates of damage to London
reported the aerial evidence that around 50 per cent of the residential
area immediately north of the docks (described in the report with the
English word 'slums') had been rendered uninhabitable. British morale
was described as 'seriously damaged' now that bombing was no longer
confined to strictly military targets.[123] Although housing as such was
not a specific target and terror-bombing not its particular purpose, the
tactical changes initiated in bombing attack – the use of heavy high-
explosive bombs, the dropping of mines on land targets, the increased
proportion of incendiaries to around half the bombload, regular nuisance raids to maximize the air-raid alarm times and provoke anxiety
and fatigue – all contributed to raising the threshold of civilian disruption and casualty. But the chief reason was the declining accuracy of the
bomber force under difficult night-time conditions, often in poor weather. The British Meteorological Office produced a report on aimed
bombing which showed that on average there were favourable bombing
conditions over Britain for only one-quarter of the year; from 20,000 feet
there was reasonable visibility for only one-fifth of the year.[124]

The German Air Force leadership had a persistently exaggerated
view of just how accurate their bombing could be under such circum-

stances. Maps issued to bomber crew had very precise target zones marked in a series of cross-hatched blue rectangles or rhomboids; the precise targets (a gasometer, a power station) were indicated by a small solid circle, while open red circles indicated the presence of decoy sites.[125] They were expected to find these targets and not to waste their bombs. Instruction to crews in January 1941 identified inaccuracy as the principal problem confronting the force: 'too many bombs have fallen on open ground far away from the target area ordered'.[126] The RAF calculated that only between 10 per cent and 30 per cent of aircraft actually found their target (though on a fine moonlit night an estimated 47 per cent found Coventry).[127] For this there were many explanations. Crews arriving at the bomber bases in the winter of 1940–41 were less experienced than many of the crews lost in combat or accident. At the training schools bomber crew were taught to fly using electronic aids to within one degree of accuracy, but by September the British understood the German beam system, which had never worked perfectly, and were beginning a programme of countermeasures to jam the signals and confuse the pilots.[128] Although this did not usually prevent German bombers from finding a target city, it was sometimes the wrong one. A raid on the Rolls-Royce works in Derby in May 1941 ended up bombing the nearby city of Nottingham.[129]

   The ability of British scientific intelligence, then its infancy, to grasp the nature of the beam system and to effect countermeasures was entirely predictable. The RAF had itself been using the German blind-landing Lorenz system since the 1930s and was familiar with its basic principles. Prisoner interrogations in the spring of 1940 alerted the British to the existence of blind-bombing technology. In June, Churchill's scientific adviser, Frederick Lindemann, was convinced of the threat posed by the beams by a young Oxford scientist, R. V. Jones, who had been recruited by the Air Ministry as a scientific intelligence expert. Churchill himself insisted on action. An RAF unit, No. 80 Wing, was set up to research countermeasures and on 21 June 1940 the beam frequencies were finally detected. Under the codename 'Headache' a high-level research programme began to identify the source of the beams and to find ways of interfering with the signals. Transmitters were set up in southern and central England which could spoil the quality of the German Knickebein radio pulses, though they could not eliminate them altogether. Known as 'aspirins' (to cure the headache), there were 15 in place by October, 58 by summer 1941, 68 by the end of the year.[130] Additional jamming stations were used for the X- and Y-Gerät, which by spring 1941 proved capable of completely misleading the pathfinder forces. By May only one-quarter of German aircraft were getting the bomb-drop signal.[131]

Once it became evident that the beams could be distorted or interrupted, crews were advised to avoid complete reliance on the *Knickebein* system and to resort to using visible markers, including woods, railways, water landmarks (estuaries, rivers, coastline), but not roads, because the roadmaps were known to be out of date.[132] They were encouraged to imitate the British practice of *Koppelnavigation*, coupling electronic and visual methods to find the route and the target. All units were asked to choose the most experienced crews for each operation as 'illuminators' (*Beleuchter*) to guide less experienced crews, and to help them avoid British decoy fires which by the end of 1940 stretched across the English countryside.[133] Over the following months reliance on electronic navigation and the pathfinders of *Kampfgruppe 100* declined and crews had to resort to careful plotting and observation. This was a difficult task, as RAF crews were finding over Germany, and it made the German bomber force as a whole a much blunter instrument than it had been at the start of the campaign. At night, aircraft could achieve a relatively high concentration of bombs on a target area, but not on a precise target. German airmen shot down over Britain and held at the Trent Park interrogation centre in north London were overheard by hidden microphones to admit that the beams were no longer trusted.[134] They complained among themselves that bombing accuracy was a difficult thing to achieve, demanding high levels of competence. The tension between expectation and reality is well illustrated by the following recorded exchange between a German Air Force major and a lieutenant:

M: [*Knickebein*] is accurate enough for night work, so that I can simply drop the bombs at that moment.

L: But if you drop the bombs at that moment, then if you are at a height of 6,000 metres the bomb will drop 1½ km farther in front, won't it? It doesn't drop vertically.

M: It doesn't make any difference with such targets.

L: Well then, it can't be so accurate.

M: No, good heavens, as I have just said, it is so difficult even to get to the point of intersection ...

L: Yes, but why don't your bombs fall accurately?

M: ... you are just told to take the centre of the town and you must each find your own targets.[135]

German fliers knew that the levels of accuracy demanded were beyond them and that increasingly they hit the area in the target cities where the fires could be seen. It was even possible with a moment's inattention to miss a target as large as London. 'Göring should be told that we can't hit the target,' complained a German captain in another eavesdropping. 'We must tell him all we have to put up with here . . .'[136]

This was one among many problems faced by the German bombing campaign, though few of them were dictated by the enemy, whose capacity to inflict serious damage on enemy aircraft at night remained minimal for most of the period of German attack. The bomber crews sustained high losses from accidents caused by the difficulty of long night-time flights and poor weather conditions, which could alter suddenly in the course of an operation. The number of serviceable bombers stood at almost 1,000 at the start of August, but by the end of November was down to 706. That month Kesselring himself witnessed a crash between two Ju88s, one of them a new plane, and berated his crews for 'carelessness'. Figures for the period of poor weather from January to March 1941 show that out of 216 bombers lost and 190 damaged, 282 were as a result of flying accident.[137] The often poor state of airfields in France and the Low Countries, in some cases lacking solid concrete runways, made landing and take-off especially risky. Over the winter months the German aircraft industry went through a period of crisis, making it harder to replace lost or damaged aircraft or to maintain the supply of filled bombs and mines. The planned output of bombers during the whole period of the campaign was little higher than in 1939, an average of 240 a month. Actual output was even lower, reaching a figure of only 130 bombers in January.[138] The older He111 and Do17 bombers were being phased out, but a new generation of higher-performance aircraft were still in the development stage, facing accumulating technical difficulties, particularly the ill-fated Messerschmitt Me210, which was finally cancelled in April 1942. Plans for a 'Bomber B', a faster high-altitude bomber more suited to a strategic role, were still on the drawing board in 1940. Bombs were also a problem. In March 1941 the Air Ministry technical office warned the air force staff that there was not enough explosive to fill all the required bombs and mines, and empty bomb cases were piling up in warehouses. It was recommended filling fewer mines, which took a much larger explosive charge, in order to free explosive for regular bombs.[139]

The many pressures on German crews from the high accident rate, the stringent demands for accurate bombing, the injunction not to waste bombs, flying night after night in deteriorating meteorological conditions against a wide variety of scattered targets for a strategy whose end point was not entirely evident, all produced its own combat strain among the crews. Instructions to the bomber groups pointed out the necessity of giving flyers two days of proper rest after three days of combat. A long report on the medical condition of flying crews in late November 1940 noted increased signs of severe psychological and physical reaction to the pressure of constant combat and warned that the longer the campaign went on, the more likely it was that effective pilots would break down. The doctors recommended periods of leave in Paris or Brussels as a diversion, at least two weeks home leave every six months, and for all flying personnel, three weeks at a winter sports spa with plenty of good food and the best possible accommodation.[140] A rest home for psychiatric casualties was set up at the Hotel Boris in the Breton seaside town of Port Navalo. To give crews some sense of purpose, reports were prepared for distribution to every squadron on the estimated effects of their operations. An American report on impressions of London was circulated in early November: 'London is still working, but on a much reduced scale . . . the apparatus that keeps London going is under strong pressure . . . The damage sustained in the past six weeks can hardly be made good in two years.'[141] After the raids on Coventry and Birmingham, news was distributed about the crisis of the British steel and engineering industries, the collapsing morale of the British workforce and a widespread health crisis provoked, it was claimed, not altogether implausibly, by a combination of glassless windows and damp weather. On 23 November Göring sent out a communiqué to all the front-line squadrons assuring them that despite the difficult and tiring work in the face of enemy defences and the atrocious weather, and above all how seldom the success of operations could effectively be measured, the raid on Coventry showed that they were working for a historic victory.[142] He then took a period of leave himself until the middle of January.

If the German air forces faced problems in the autumn and winter of 1940, they were as nothing compared with the problems facing their enemy. The success against German daylight operations in September accelerated the German transition to night-bombing. Against night-time attack there was still in the autumn of 1940 almost no effective defence. As long as bombers flew well clear of the ceiling of anti-aircraft fire and searchlights, or chose routes with poor anti-aircraft defences, the only factor inhibiting the impact of a raid was the difficulty of getting bombs sufficiently concentrated on the chosen objectives. Otherwise the bomber always got through. The problems of defence against night attack had been fully appreciated in Britain after the outbreak of war, and a committee was established in March 1940 to consider its implications, but the pressure of daylight fighting throughout the first nine months of 1940 left night defence as a low priority. The switch to extensive night-bombing in September 1940 provoked an immediate crisis. There were very few dedicated night-fighter squadrons and the evidence from daylight attacks showed how few aircraft could be brought down by anti-aircraft fire. When Dowding was made to account for the poor state of night defences at a meeting in the Air Ministry on 18 October 1940, he confirmed that his force had been trying for a year to intercept enemy aircraft at night 'with negligible success'.[143]

One answer was to expand the fixed anti-aircraft defences. The balloon barrage was extended and balloons were painted black. Plans were made to arm balloon cables with an explosive device, but production was slow and success unpredictable.[144] In September the anti-aircraft artillery was reorganized into three regional commands (Southern, Midland and Northern) to give it greater flexibility, but the supply of guns was still far short of what was regarded as adequate to defend all vital targets in the three areas. Out of 100 designated priority zones only 60 were defended and some of those with only a handful of guns.[145] Although the importance of radar-controlled gun-laying was recognized, the GL MkI apparatus introduced in increasing numbers during the bombing campaign was not capable of accurate height prediction and proved difficult to use. There were still only 10 per cent of the required sets available by February 1941. Nor were the searchlight batteries served with effective radar equipment as they were later in the war; even by June 1941, when the bombing was almost over, Sir Frederick Pile, commander-in-chief of Anti-Aircraft Command, still had only 54 out of the promised 2,000 Search Light Control sets (known as 'Elsie') available.[146] A more sophisticated gun-laying equipment, GL MkII, arrived in small quantities from January but was difficult to operate except by highly skilled personnel. It came into its own only in 1942. Many of the anti-aircraft gun sites were not easily accessible and conditions for the crews amounted in many cases in 1940 to little more than a bunker dug out of the ground, prone to flooding and poor protection from the deafening sound of the guns. Anti-aircraft troops were low priority during the period of invasion scare, and many of those who manned guns against German raiders had come straight from training camp. So short of personnel was the Command that in 1941 Pile insisted on recruiting women to work at gun sites, but enrolment did not start until after the end of the bombing, in August 1941. The women, Churchill was assured, would have to be educated and 'preferably golf and tennis players'.[147]

Over the course of the bombing from July 1940 to June 1941, anti-aircraft artillery was relatively ineffective. It was claimed that 170 aircraft were shot down at night over the whole course of the campaign and perhaps 118 damaged, but precise verification was difficult and the temptation to claim success in a gruelling and noisy battle hard to resist. For this result it proved necessary to fire prodigious quantities of ammunition. Scientists brought in to advise the Air Ministry found that in autumn 1940 more than 6,000 shells were fired for every aircraft claimed, and even by April 1941 the number had only been reduced to 3,195. They regarded the idea of a 'barrage' as an illusion, since only 'aimed fire' had any chance of success, as with all artillery.[148] Yet in response to criticism that there was too little anti-aircraft fire during the first great raids on London, Pile ordered the 92 guns in the Inner Artillery Zone on 7 September 1940 increased to 203 in 48 hours and asked every unit to fire everything it could, regardless of results. In September 260,000 shells were fired. Although it was discovered that civilian morale was boosted by the noisy activity, civilians were exposed to a rain of shrapnel and the danger of unexploded shells, while gun barrels wore out faster than they could be replaced from new production. In November guns were shifted away from London towards the Midlands, to meet demands from industry for more effective protection, but the game of musical chairs simply exposed the fact that there was not enough artillery to go round. The Command was forced to cut back on firing and ordered searchlights to be extinguished, despite popular protest, because it was realized that with too few guns and lights, the target areas were easily distinguishable for enemy pilots as the ones defended. The blackout proved more effective than the lights in confusing the raiders but was in the end no substitute for an extensive belt across the country of radar-guided searchlights and guns. Fixed anti-aircraft defences, in the absence of effective radar equipment, were, as Pile later admitted in his memoirs, deficient.

Greater reliance came to be placed on decoy sites, known as Special Fire (SF) or 'Starfish', which were constructed during the last few months of 1940 in country areas around key targets. By November, 27 sites had been constructed and 5 more were in preparation. To reassure the rural population there were orders to ensure that no decoy was closer than 500 yards to any inhabited building, or closer than 800 yards to a village, though in reality these distances gave scant protection.[149] Raised tanks filled with a mixture of creosote, diesel oil or paraffin surrounded troughs filled with straw set out in the shape of a star. When the troughs were filled and set alight, the effect replicated the white and yellow blaze from incendiary bombs. Bristol, for example, was surrounded by 12 starfish sites, some almost 20 miles distant. The first became operational on Blackdown, in the Mendip Hills, in late November 1940 and a week later attracted its first bombs. In January over 1,000 incendiaries fell on the site. A decoy airfield laid out in fields near Uphill, on the outskirts of Weston-super-Mare, was attacked heavily the same month after it had been ignited by hand with matches and a bottle of petrol because the electric switch failed in heavy rain. Some 42 high-explosive bombs and 1,500 incendiaries fell during the raid. A nearby farmer found his herd of dairy cattle dead or mutilated, some still struggling to walk with their legs blown off.[150] During the rest of 1941 the Starfish were ignited 70 times, with mixed results; in some cases three-quarters of the bombs were dropped on the decoy site, in others none at all.[151]

Camouflage was another way of concealing the target, but the Camouflage Advisory Panel set up in 1939 and the Camouflage Policy Committee established in March 1940 both reached conclusions that camouflage was difficult to apply effectively and worked best only for daytime raids. Some effort went into providing steel-covered netting to mask the shadow of large buildings and painting trees and shrubs on hangars and storerooms, but it was concluded that heavy industrial haze, persistent fogs and an effective blackout served much the same purpose as camouflage. Plans to paint sections of railway line dark green to blend with the surrounding fields were rejected on the grounds that pilots would never be fooled by it, while the extensive use of paint on key buildings provoked a sudden scare that German agents would somehow find a way of adding their own patches of special chemically enhanced paint intended to make the targets visible to German infra-red equipment.[152] More attention was given to the idea that light-coloured concrete roads and runways could be covered with tarmac and coloured chippings to mask the glare, but the expense was considerable and the government refused to sanction road camouflage when local councils applied for funding.[153] In summer 1940 the Camouflage Committee stopped meeting.

Some of the solutions suggested by scientists brought in to advise the air force and the government were equally far-fetched. One idea was to lay a minefield in the sky in the path of oncoming bombers, on the same principle as a minefield at sea. The object was to attach a small one-pound explosive with a self-detonating mechanism to a long length of piano wire, with a parachute at one end. A line of mines would be laid from an aircraft at right angles to the approaching enemy and as the mines sank at a carefully calibrated speed they were supposed to land on the aircraft wings and explode. Dowding reluctantly agreed to tests in the summer of 1940 but unsurprisingly they proved disappointing.[154] At some point in October 1940 Churchill's personal scientific adviser, Frederick Lindemann, was converted to the idea of the long aerial mine and persuaded the prime minister to endorse it. Orders were placed for 1 million mines and 24 mine-laying aircraft, but the scheme was always overambitious, since it relied on very precise knowledge of where enemy aircraft would be flying and on perfect timing. It was discovered that the first 1,000 mines delivered all had defective self-detonating devices. When efforts were made in June 1941 to lay the first minefields, only three attempts were made, without any observable success. The scheme was quietly scrapped.[155] Lindemann was also the source of a second fanciful countermeasure. In November 1939 he suggested exploring the use of colloidal coal (a finely ground and treated coal dust) to cover rivers, canals and ports with a non-reflective film to frustrate their use as navigation markers on moonlit nights. Experiments continued throughout the bombing campaign but it was found that winds and tidal waters drove the dust to the edge of the water, making the estuaries or canals more rather than less visible. After two years of experiment a public exercise was conducted in February 1942 on the Thames between Westminster and Vauxhall bridges. Tons of dust was sprayed from converted barges; it gradually gathered at the river's edge and after two hours sank.[156]

It was generally recognized that the only effective way to be sure of destroying an enemy bomber was night-time interception by a dedicated night-fighter aircraft, but it proved beyond the capability of the RAF to achieve this for almost the whole of the German bombing campaign. The problem was regarded as so critical that on 14 September 1940 a committee was set up under the retired Air Chief Marshal Sir John Salmond to investigate the whole issue of night-fighter policy. Three days later the committee presented its findings, recommending a special night-fighter staff, a night-fighting training unit, the decentralization of control over night-fighters to increase speed of response and flexibility, and the introduction of effective radar aids. Great expectations were had of the transfer of a number of single-engine fighter squadrons to night work on clear moonlit nights.[157] Dowding opposed almost all of the recommendations and paid for his resistance with his command. On 1 October he attended a meeting of the Salmon committee where he explained that reorganizing his force would achieve nothing without effective airborne radar (AI = Airborne Interception), which was the only prospect for success. A week later he met Churchill and reiterated his view that the recommended changes would achieve little.[158] He was made to accept the proposed changes with reluctance and on 9 October ordered the activation of nine night-fighter squadrons, six of them in 11 Group in south-east England, including a number of converted Hurricane fighters. On 4 November he was told to introduce more Hurricanes to try to stem the new flow of bombing towards the Midlands, but he told the Air Ministry that without radar detection these efforts constituted nothing more than 'wishful flying'.[159]

It has been argued that the knives were already out for Dowding even before the crisis over night-fighting erupted in October 1940. A secret memorandum circulated in September claiming, among other things, that Dowding had 'a very slow brain', reached Churchill's close colleague Brendan Bracken.[160] Dowding was certainly not widely popular but did enjoy the backing of Churchill and the chief of the air staff, Sir Cyril Newall, with whom he had worked closely to mould the air defence system in the 1930s. Dowding's stubborn insistence that there was nothing very effective he could do about night-interception until the technology was ready was used against him, particularly by Churchill's friend Lord Beaverbrook, appointed Minister of Aircraft Production in May 1940, whose angry claims that aircraft production was facing a calamity as a result of bombing played an important part in the campaign to get Dowding finally retired. When Beaverbrook asked for aircraft squadrons to be stationed next to aircraft factories to afford them protection from night attack, Dowding refused. Dowding offered more anti-aircraft guns, but in October 1940 there were only 158 guns defending the entire aircraft industry, from Scotland to southern England.[161] By then opinion in the Air Ministry had hardened against him. On 2 October Air Chief Marshal Newall, his firmest ally, was forced to retire, to be replaced by Air Marshal Charles Portal, who remained chief-of-staff down to the end of the war.[162] A few days later Salmond wrote to Churchill insisting that Dowding should step down at once, and that all the senior commanders in the air force agreed.[163] Dowding's testy response to the effort to expand night defences in October must have convinced even Churchill that it was time for him to go. On 13 November Dowding was notified that he was to be succeeded by Air Vice Marshal Sholto Douglas, who was one of his many critics in the ministry. Dowding was the most senior casualty of the German bomber offensive.

Sholto Douglas tried immediately to demonstrate that he was more willing than his predecessor to find a way to challenge the German night offensive, but he soon found that Dowding's reservations had been justified. Douglas requested a minimum of 20 night-fighter squadrons, including 8 squadrons of Hurricanes, but by March 1941 he still had only 5 squadrons, while the introduction of the Beaufighter Mark II (now designated the principal night-fighter) and of Airborne Interception (AI-Mark IV) radar for night-time operations was much slower than required. In December 1940 Portal rejected Douglas's request for further expansion of the night force with the argument that there was not a single crew capable of regularly shooting down night-bombers. He allocated Beaufighter production to the war at sea.[164] The figures for night-fighter interception made it evident that Portal, and before him Dowding, were right. In the raids against Birmingham in mid-November 1940 there were 100 British aircraft airborne but only one German casualty, a victim of accident. Only a handful of bombers were shot down before the advent of the more effective AI-Mark IV radar sets in March 1941, almost at the end of the campaign. In January 1941 the RAF needed 198 sorties for every German aircraft shot down, but in March the figure fell dramatically to 47. During 1941 the night defences claimed a total of 435 German planes, but 357 of them from April onwards.[165] In January 1941 the first 6 inland Ground Control Interception (GCI) radars for tracking a single fighter on to an incoming bomber became operational, but they were faced with regular teething troubles and only began to work as planned by the summer, when 17 static and mobile stations were available out of a planned network of 150.[166] As with so much of the British response to the German campaign, improved operational and technical effectiveness came only after the bombing was almost over.

Only in the spring of 1941 did tactical instructions to German bomber units begin to take the threat of British night-fighters seriously The danger that British fighters might try to use the German radio beams to guide them to the bombers led to instructions to make irregular zigzag courses to confuse the enemy, to approach on a broad front, rather than grouped together, to fly at lower heights or, in some cases, to employ single aircraft to fly in very low at 200–300 metres.[167] In July 1941 it was finally admitted that German tactics would have to change to cope with the mounting evidence that RAF night-fighters could track incoming aircraft and find them over the target. Bomber units were instructed to mount decoy flights with weak forces on widely distant targets to shield the true destination of the main attacking force (a tactic soon adopted by the RAF over Germany). The main force was instructed to attack on a very broad front, flying from numerous different directions towards the chief objective, particularly on clear and moonlit nights, even though the effect of this and other tactical changes was to disperse German bomb attacks even more and to reduce the prospect of a heavy, concentrated blow.[168]

The exposure of Britain's cities and industries to heavy bomb attack with feeble defences provoked widespread anxiety in Whitehall. For much of the bombing campaign, the size of the German force continued to be greatly exaggerated. Air intelligence estimated that on 1 November 1940 the German Air Force had 1,800 bombers and 1,900 single-engine and twin-engine fighters, when the true figures for late October, unknown in London, were 833 serviceable bombers and 829 serviceable fighters.[169] When Churchill was told in December that the German Air Force was two and a half times larger than the RAF, he asked for the figures to be investigated. Understanding the size of the German force was, he thought, 'of capital importance to the whole future picture of the war'.[170] Lindemann discovered that air intelligence had been assuming a figure of 12 aircraft for each German squadron, plus reserves, when the available intercept intelligence suggested only 9 per squadron, with a reserve of 3. In January 1941 he was able to demonstrate that the German bomber force had 1,200 aircraft, which was closer to the reality than any previous estimates, and a better reflection of the actual impact German bombing was making.[171]

Churchill nevertheless remained apprehensive about German intentions. He expected the German Air Force to make a 'far more serious attempt' in the spring and early summer of 1941 to defeat Britain from the air. Intelligence from a Swiss source suggested that Germany had been conserving thousands of aircraft for a single supreme blow, an 'air banquet', to be mounted in the spring for a genuine knockout blow from the air and, improbable though this was, Churchill asked the air staff how many aircraft Britain could reply with if a banquet was

prepared with every available plane. He was told by a sceptical Portal
in the spring of 1941 that Germany could probably send 14,000 planes,
but the RAF could retaliate with only a feeble 6,500, including
2,000 trainers and 3,000 reserves.[172] Churchill was just as anxious
about the possibility of an overpowerful German Air Force resorting to
gas to finish the war quickly. In November 1940 he asked his de facto
deputy, the Labour Party leader, Clement Attlee, to make sure that British stocks of poison gas reached at least 2,000 tons of available
chemicals; the air staff informed Churchill that existing gas supplies
could be used for four or five days of concentrated gas attack on German cities, or for two weeks if gas and high explosive were dropped
together.[173] Concern over the supply of gas bombs had already arisen in
the summer of 1940 when it was evident that there were not enough
containers for the gas. Beaverbrook was instructed to accelerate production of gas bombs and spray canisters for mustard gas for the
moment, as Sinclair put it, 'when gas warfare commences', and by
October he could promise to meet the air staff requirement for a minimum of 200,000 gas bombs. By the spring of 1941, in anticipation of
a more extensive and deadly bombing campaign in the winter of 1941–2,
the RAF was primed to conduct a gas war against the German
homeland.[174]

The German Air Force was planning neither an aerial banquet nor a
programme of gas warfare. Instead, the operations staff took stock of
what had been achieved by the end of 1940 and produced a plan of
attack for the spring which was designed to be the 'culmination point'
of the campaign before the transfer to the war against the Soviet
Union.[175] In mid-January 1941 a list of priority targets was drawn up,
uniting the blockade strategy with the campaign against British aircraft
production (see Table 2.2). These formed the main objectives in the final
six months of the campaign between January and June 1941 and were
confirmed by a directive from Hitler's headquarters on 6 February,
which once again emphasized the military importance of attacking
war-essential targets rather than residential areas.[176] In January the air
fleets were sent new maps of ports, docks, principal naval installations
and aircraft industry targets. Attacks on the aircraft industry were divided between operations against areas of concentrated armaments
production (Coventry, Birmingham, Sheffield) and individual targets
suitable for attack by a small number of aircraft on clear nights.[177] Particular attention was to be paid to shipping and port facilities, which
were now thought to have suffered much less damage from the bomb-

Table 2.2: Principal Targets for German Bomb Attack, Spring 1941

Ports I Rank	Ports II Rank/ Naval Depots	Aircraft Industry I Rank	Aircraft Industry II Rank
Merseyside	Southampton	Manchester	Preston
London	Barrow-in-Furness	Birmingham	Gloucester
Clydeside	Port Talbot	Coventry	Cheltenham
Humber ports	Great Yarmouth	Glasgow	Oxford
Belfast	Portsmouth	Belfast	Chelmsford
Bristol	Plymouth	Bristol	Slough
Tyne ports	Chatham	Sheffield	Reading
Tees ports	Rosyth	Derby	Yeovil
Swansea		Luton	
Cardiff	Liverpool*		
Leith			

* Liverpool to be subjected to area attack as the principal port for American aircraft supplies.
Source: TsAMO, Fond 500/725168/110, Operations Staff, report on British targets and air strength, 14 Jan 1941.

ing in 1940 than at first believed. Air intelligence estimates for the port of London had at first assumed a decline of up to 80 per cent in the handling capacity of the main docks. By January the available intelligence suggested that London was still operating at almost three-quarters of its capacity despite months of heavy raiding, a figure that did indeed reflect the reality.[178] To ensure that the food blockade worked more effectively, bomber units were instructed to attack grain silos, sugar refineries and oilseed plants

German bombing followed the plan closely in 1941. Between January and May there were 61 major raids on ports and 9 major raids on armaments centres, as well as numerous smaller *Störangriffe* against industrial or naval targets. These included heavy raids on Glasgow-Clydeside on 13 and 14 March, 7 April and 5 May, and on the Merseyside area on 12 and 13 March and the first four nights in May, and on Hull on the 18 March and 7–8 May. Belfast, the Northern Ireland capital, was bombed heavily on 15 April (leaving 700 dead), and Dublin, the capital of neutral Ireland, was bombed by accident on 2–3 January and again on 31 May (causing 34 deaths).[179] Coventry was visited again on the night of 8 April with almost as large an attack as the one in November. The largest raids, however, were reserved for London. On 16 April,

681 bombers delivered 886 tonnes of bombs and three nights later 712 aircraft dropped 1,026 tonnes and 4,252 incendiary canisters, the largest raid of the whole campaign. These were again described as 'vengeance attacks' for the RAF bombing of central Berlin on 10 April, which destroyed the State Opera House, and damaged Humboldt University and the State Library. The opera house was to have hosted a leading Italian opera company the following week, which may well explain why Hitler chose to subject Göring to an angry tirade following the attack.[180] A final heavy 'vengeance' raid was inflicted on London on 10 May by 505 aircraft dropping 718 tonnes of high explosive and damaging the Houses of Parliament, but after that night-time bombing tailed away.

A high proportion of incendiaries were carried in the raids in 1941 and large-scale fires started. Photo-reconnaissance confirmed that incendiary bombs did more damage to port areas and storehouses than high explosives, with the result that the ratio between incendiary and high-explosive loads reached 1:1.[181] In the last weeks of the campaign German bombers undertook a wide variety of operations. In April the three air fleets flew 5,448 sorties; 3,681 on major raids, 1,292 on Störangriffe, 263 against shipping targets at sea and 212 for sea-mining. The constant activity produced continually high losses. Between January and June 1941, 572 bombers were destroyed and 496 damaged; the figures for fighters were 299 lost and 300 damaged.[182] By 17 May the bomber arm had 769 serviceable aircraft out of an established strength of 1,413, divided between the northern European and the Mediterranean theatres. This was 30 per cent smaller than the number of bombers available for the start of the campaign in France and it was to have serious repercussions on the impending operation against the Soviet Union. For the rest of the war the bomber arm never again achieved the size it had enjoyed on 10 May 1940.

For German aircrew the last months of the campaign were difficult to sustain. Thousands of casualties were taken for a campaign where there was no clear conclusion and results that could only be speculated over. Moreover, from March 1941 the air units in the west knew that the bulk of forces would be diverted to the war in the east; some forces were already detailed for combat in the Mediterranean and, from April, in the Balkan campaigns against Greece and Yugoslavia. Those that remained for the campaign against Britain were told to bomb with ever greater concentration and accuracy to compensate for the reduced numbers. On 16 March a directive was issued to the three air fleets explaining that part of Air Fleet 3 would stay behind in France during the Barbarossa campaign while the rest of the air force moved east. The remaining bomber force, including the small number posted in Norway (Air Fleet 5), was instructed to keep up the pressure on British supply by attacking ships in port and at sea and to raid aero-industry targets opportunistically. Attacks on London as 'vengeance' were to be carried out only when instructed by the air force High Command.[183] On 22 May the first stage in transferring Air Fleet 2 to the east began when command and organization units were sent to Posen in Poland. On 8 June air groups began a two-week transfer eastwards, leaving just 8 bomber groups out of 44. On 25 June Air Fleet 3 completed its reorganization across the whole of northern France. The reduced activity was immediately evident. In June only 6 major raids were mounted and 221 *Störangriffe*, in contrast to 31 major raids and 852 minor raids in April and May.[184] In France and the Low Countries the constant drone of German aircraft and the noisy presence of thousands of crewmen suddenly ceased. Londoners had their first month of almost uninterrupted sleep.

What did the eleven-month bombing campaign achieve? Although Hitler did not halt the bombing until the switch to the campaign against the Soviet Union, his few remarks show a sustained scepticism about the possibility of achieving anything decisive by air action alone. In December 1940 he dismissed the effects of bombing on British industry as minimal.[185] Göring later claimed that he had told Hitler repeatedly that raiding London would 'never force them to their knees'.[186] The prospect that bombing would bring about a political collapse faded the longer the campaign continued. When the navy commander-in-chief discussed the bombing campaign with Hitler in February 1941, he found the Führer in complete agreement with his view that morale in Britain had remained 'unshaken' by the bombs.[187] Hitler was generally more optimistic about the sea blockade and the submarine war, to which bombing contributed indirectly. In his directive of 6 February he emphasized the importance of attacks on shipping and ports, but concluded that the effects on the British willingness to fight had been the least successful aspect of the bombing.[188] In spring 1941 he assumed that Britain could be dealt with by bombing and invasion after the defeat of the Soviet Union, in the summer of 1942. 'We'll deal with them later,' he told a sceptical Göring, 'if the stubborn Churchill fails to see sense.'[189]

There were nevertheless strategic gains to be made from the bombing

campaign, which Hitler also recognized. The bombing kept up consistent pressure on the British war effort and always carried the possibility
that Britain's war willingness would decline to the point of abandoning
the struggle. It is also possible to read the bombing as a warning to the
United States not to support Britain or to intervene in the conflict. President Roosevelt received regular reports on the course of the air war and
it was some months before either he or the United States military leadership were confident enough of Britain's survival to send aid without
the risk that it would fall into German hands.[190] The bombing also supported German strategy in other parts of Europe. During the latter part
of 1940 Hitler became increasingly concerned with the Mediterranean
and Balkan theatres, not only because of Italian difficulties in the war
with British Commonwealth forces in North Africa and the Italian invasion of Greece, launched on 28 October 1940, but because he feared
that Britain might intervene militarily in the Balkans, opening up the
possibility of a third front, as had happened in the First World War.[191]
Bombing was one way to ensure that large resources would have to be
kept in mainland Britain rather than be diverted to other theatres,
weakening the British position in the Mediterranean, Middle East and
South-East Asia, where small numbers of obsolete aircraft would prove
no match for the German and, later, the Japanese air forces. In spring
1941 the British were expelled from Greece and Crete, unable to contest
German air superiority, and the way was open for Hitler's invasion to
the east.

Above all the bombing was intimately linked with the decision to
invade Russia in 1941. The two strands of Hitler's strategy are usually
described as if they were separate, but they were complementary: first
because bombing would persuade Moscow that the war in the west was
Hitler's priority; second because it would limit any help that Britain
might be able to give the Soviet Union once Barbarossa was under way.
The German air campaign certainly convinced Stalin that Hitler
intended to finish Britain off first and contributed to his conviction that
Germany would not attack the Soviet Union in 1941. The Soviet
ambassador to London, Ivan Maisky, confirmed in his memoirs the
Soviet view at the time that Hitler did not just want to use bombing as
pressure on Britain to negotiate, but as a prelude to the physical conquest of the British Isles.[192] It is not by chance that the German Air
Force indulged in a final heavy flourish against Britain in the weeks just
before the launch of Barbarossa. Moreover, the war against the Soviet
Union would have presented a greater element of risk if Britain

had been allowed the luxury to arm and prepare for military intervention or increased bombing of Germany once German forces were
occupied in the east, as a German wartime analysis of the bombing later
suggested:

> In general the 10 months of uninterrupted attacks on the British Isles were
> of considerable importance in the subsequent unfolding of events. Even if
> this purely strategic air offensive did not force any decisions, the damage
> to enemy supplies and economy was nevertheless great . . . It was two years
> before the RAF was able to deal any effective counter blows. Thus the
> time when the Reich would have come under heavy attack had been
> delayed. Our flyers had assured that the Russian offensive would not be
> undermined from the rear.[193]

When the invasion of the Soviet Union began in late June 1941, Goebbels observed in his diary that the RAF had 'by and large not exploited
the situation' beyond a handful of unsuccessful raids. German bombing
had pushed Britain onto the defensive at a critical juncture for German
strategy.[194]

The difficult task was to be able to gauge with any degree of certainty
exactly what effect bombing had had on Britain's supply of essential
food and materials or on British aircraft production. Unlike the British
and Americans at the end of the war, the German Air Force was never
able to carry out its own bombing survey. In general, its view was
over-optimistic about the degree of damage. The aggregate picture of
the campaign, the first of its kind, suggested to the Germans the possibility of really debilitating effects. (Details of the location and weight of
bombs dropped on major night raids are in Table 2.3.) Nevertheless, the
only material the air force had to go on to assess damage were pilots'
reports, photo-reconnaissance and occasional foreign news reports or
accounts by neutral observers. Such intelligence could be frustratingly
ambiguous, as British and American assessors were to discover later
in the war. The photo-reconnaissance of Coventry and Birmingham
after the major raids in November 1940 was inhibited by smoke and
cloud over the chief target areas, and conclusions had to be extrapo-
lated from the condition of the visible area.[195] The observations of
neutrals could be read a number of ways. The American report cited
earlier on the long-term damage to London's infrastructure also contained the author's opinion that the one important thing evident in the
capital among all classes was 'a mood of remarkable courage, phlegm,
an element of "aprés nous le deluge"'. As a result, he continued, 'the

Table 2.3: Major Night Raids on the British Isles and Weight of Bombs (Tonnes), 12 August 1940–26 June 1941

City	HE Bombs	Incendiaries	Number of Attacks
London	14,754	1,135	79
Liverpool	2,796	304	14
Birmingham	2,057	225	11
Bristol	1,237	248	10
Plymouth	1,125	207	8
Portsmouth	1,091	180	5
Southampton	971	88	7
Coventry	797	69	2
Glasgow	748	176	4
Manchester	703	106	4
Sheffield	587	70	3
Hull	474	57	3
Swansea	363	103	4
Cardiff	273	63	3
Belfast	180	25	2
Others	550	60	–
Total	**28,706**	**3,116**	**159**

Source: BA-MA, RL2 IV/27, Bechtle lecture, appendix, 'Grossangriffe bei Nacht gegen Lebenszentren Englands in der Zeit 12.8.1940–26.6.1941'.

majority of Londoners are firmly convinced that despite everything, England will win'.[196]

Air force conclusions were necessarily based on an extravagant and generous interpretation of what had been done. Exaggeration was built into air force estimates of achievement in this, as in most other bombing campaigns during the war. The sight of a blazing city below, the gutted ruins spied from the air a day or so later, suggested complete devastation. All bombing forces assumed that a bombed factory was a destroyed factory, when in reality it meant a factory that needed repairing or dispersing. Ships claimed as sunk by pilots, who could only briefly watch the plume of water or the fires on deck after the bombs fell, might just as easily limp to port hours later. Records show that German pilots regularly reported around four times the number of enemy aircraft actually shot down. In most of these cases there was no way of verifying the claims, though knowledge of the gap between published RAF claims and actual damage to German units ought to have raised serious doubts.

And indeed air intelligence used the evidence of physical damage to the British aero industry to try to assess RAF capability over the course of the Blitz rather than rely on pilot reports, though this too was largely conjectural. It was calculated that the output of British combat aircraft fell from a peak of 1,100 in July 1940 to a low of 550 by April 1941. A figure of 7,200 was suggested for total output in 1941. In fact, production in April alone was 1,529, and for the whole year, 20,094.[197]

On the other effects of bombing there was more reticence. No effort seems to have been made to calculate the number of deaths and the area of housing damaged. The eventual death toll of 43,384 from June 1940 to June 1941 was far in excess of the deaths inflicted on the German population by British bombing, which in 1940 numbered only 975. In the absence of any published statistics, it is unlikely that the German side could possibly have guessed how heavy the toll of civilians was. The population was not a specified target, though civilian deaths were to be expected. The high level of casualty was a result not only of the growing inaccuracy of German bombing already noted, but also of the congested nature of the working-class quarters around the major port areas that were bombed and the poor level of shelter provision generally available in inner-city precincts. What interested the German High Command more was damage to the British war effort, which shaped their view of what bombing was supposed to achieve. Throughout the campaign it was stressed how extensive must be the cost to British military output and the supply of military personnel. In a daily briefing to the air force in May 1941, Göring assured his crews that German attacks had achieved 'enormous damage to the point of complete destruction' of British armaments capacity. A later summary of the bombing campaign by the air force historical branch in July 1944 continued to assert that 'many armament factories and ports in England were destroyed and their reconstruction delayed due to the possibility of further attack'. All this was so much guesswork.

Fortunately for the historian, the British authorities undertook their own statistical surveys of German bombing. From October 1940 careful records were kept of all forms of casualty and damage to housing and industry. Estimates of the impact on production were derived from calculating fluctuations in the aggregate supply of electric power to bombed cities. By December there were calculations of the extensive average damage of one ton of German bombs on London: 6 people killed, 25 wounded, 35 rendered homeless, 80 made temporarily homeless,

10 houses destroyed, 25 temporarily uninhabitable, 80 slightly damaged.[198] These proved to be exceptional figures from the early heavy
raids. Over the whole course of the German offensive, according to the
government scientific adviser Patrick Blackett, German bombs killed
0.8 persons per ton (about four times the rate of RAF killing of Germans in 1941), a total of 44,652 people throughout 1940 and all of
1941. An additional 52,370 were seriously injured. Damaged housing
totalled over 2 million, though most were quickly repaired.[199]

The impact on the economy was much more modest. Official estimates suggested a loss of just 5 per cent of current production. Studies
of the effects of bombing on urban activity rates, measured by electric
power consumption, confirmed that except for the single exception of
Coventry, which took six weeks to recover from the attack in November
1940, most cities suffered only a temporary loss of 10, 15 or 25 per cent
of activity, and they made good that loss at an average of 3 percentage
points a day, or between three and eight days.[200] Railways, it was observed,
'continued to maintain nearly normal service' throughout the Blitz. In
most cases temporary repairs and re-routing resulted in no more than a
day's delay. The longest reported interruption to the water supply in
1941 was 24 hours. The grid system for electricity and gas supply meant
that industry was little affected by sporadic attacks on sources of energy.
Only 0.5 per cent of oil stocks were lost as a result of air raids.[201] The
blockade was similarly unimpressive. The Ministry of Home Security calculated that the bombing destroyed only 5 per cent of British flour-milling
capacity, 4 per cent of the production of margarine, 1.6 per cent of
oilseed output and 1.5 per cent of the capacity of cold-storage facilities.
At no time was the London docks outer basin unserviceable and bombing had 'no appreciable effect' on food supply to the capital.[202] The
measurement of morale was a more challenging task. In a comprehensive survey of the Blitz, produced in August 1941 by British Air
Intelligence, it was concluded that 'no town in England has suffered a
breakdown in morale', though it was admitted that it was not known at
what scale of attack, if any, morale actually would collapse.[203] The overall conclusion from the many assessments of German bombing was that
it achieved high levels of civilian death and damage to housing, but on
the critical issues of war economic performance, air force fighting power,
food supply and civilian morale its effects were limited and temporary.

None of these British assessments took sufficient account of the costs
to Britain's war effort of maintaining large active air defences and an
army of civil defence and emergency personnel, as later assessments of

the cost of bombing in Germany have always done. The most significant strategic effect of bombing was the diversion of very substantial military and civilian resources to anti-aircraft defences and civil air-raid precautions. The personnel cost was high, and had to be sustained throughout the war. British Anti-Aircraft Command had 330,000 men by the summer of 1941 and went on to recruit 74,000 women from the Auxiliary Territorial Service.[204] The civil defence services in June 1941 employed 216,000 full-time and 1,233,800 part-time personnel (ARP, casualty services, auxiliary police force).[205] The fire services at the end of 1940 employed 85,821 full-time and 139,300 part-time, but were supported by the wartime Auxiliary Fire Service, which supplied an additional 67,024 full-time and 125,973 part-time.[206] This totalled almost 700,000 full-time and 1.5 million part-time men and women, who would otherwise have been engaged in different wartime activities. The cost of sustaining this 'civil defence economy' – uniforms, equipment, provisions, welfare aid, coffins, shelters and so on – was a major item of national and local government expenditure.

The diversion of military resources was also very large. Fighter Command expanded its units in mainland Britain from 58 daytime squadrons in July 1940 to 75 day and night squadrons in January 1941 and 99 by September. As a result it proved impossible to send significant reinforcements of the most advanced fighters overseas. The Middle East and Far East were reinforced with growing numbers of technically inferior or obsolete British and American aircraft.[207] Anti-aircraft guns, shells and equipment, and the growing radar network, all diverted production away from any offensive military effort. Defence of Britain was the priority. These many demands on Britain's war effort as a result of the German bombing campaign represented a large net diversion of resources, regardless of whether the physical damage from German attacks was effective or not. In this sense German Air Force claims were right: Britain's offensive war effort was curtailed in 1940 and 1941 by the bombing campaign and the expectation of its renewal.

'HIGH SCHOOL FOR BOMBERS':
GERMAN BOMBING 1941–5

On 14 February 1944 a German Air Force Academy lecturer explored the many phases of the German bombing of Britain since 1941. For eighteen months, he told his audience, there had been no major inland attacks on England. Thanks to a solid and effective defence the only prospect for German bombers and fighter-bombers stationed in France was to undertake small hit-and-run raids on England's south coast. Even these operations had fallen from an average of 15 a month in 1942 to 5 or 6 a month by late 1943. The risks for the pilots, he continued, were considerable. The raids on England were a kind of 'high school for bombers': pilots either learned their trade or they died. The average crew survived no more than 16 to 18 missions. 'It's plain to see,' he concluded, 'that *in this way* England's war economy and morale cannot be hit in any war-decisive way.'[208]

In the summer of 1941 that is not how the future looked to either side. As noted, the German intention was to return to finish Britain off once the Soviet Union had been defeated in a six-month campaign. So confident was Hitler that the war would work out this way that in July 1941 he ordered the large-scale expansion of aircraft output and naval equipment to meet the expected renewal of the contest with Britain in 1942. Göring was able to extract a special priority order from Hitler (the so-called 'Göring Programme') to produce a fourfold increase in output, including a complement of around 400 heavier four-engine bombers (principally the Heinkel He177) in 1942 and around 1,000 in 1943.[209] The development of very long-range bombers – nicknamed the 'Amerikabomber' – was moving out of the realm of fantasy. The Messerschmitt company had begun work on the Me264, which with a maximum range of over 9,000 miles would be capable of reaching American cities and returning to Europe. The idea circulated at Hitler's headquarters from autumn 1940 of occupying the Azores as a potential base for long-range air attacks on the United States if, or when, they entered the war.[210] The object for Sperrle's Air Fleet 3 was to hold the line in 1941–2 until the full weight of German air strength could once again be brought to bear against the Western powers. It was this bleak scenario that British leaders also anticipated. Churchill harried the Air Ministry to expand night defences for the renewed 'night-bombing season' expected that autumn. Sholto Douglas, Dowding's replacement at Fighter Command, wanted to expand night-fighter squadrons to at least 30 (from the 16 he had) by the end of the year to deal with 'the heavy and prolonged attacks by night' against British cities once the German Air Force had deployed its bombers westward during the winter lull in the ground fighting in Russia.[211] It took some time before it was evident that German difficulties in the Soviet campaign would make it impossible ever again to mount a sustained bombing offensive against Britain.

In the second six months of 1941, Air Fleet 3 tried to find ways in which it could get at Britain with some strategic purpose despite its limited numbers. At first German bombers continued to carry out night raids on distant urban targets. Birmingham was hit three times in July 1941, Hull twice. In August the weather was so poor that there could be no raiding on 25 days of the month. In September the force switched to mining operations. In December small raids were made on Newcastle, Plymouth and Hull. German spirits were kept up by vastly exaggerating the losses inflicted on the enemy; for the cost of 236 German aircraft between July and December, the force claimed 1,223 RAF planes destroyed.[212] As the urgent demands of other theatres drew aircraft away, Sperrle was left by the winter of 1941–2 with just two bomber groups. The most obvious route for his shrunken force to take was to help the navy in the war against British shipping. On 7 April 1942 Air Fleet 3 also took over command of the air-sea forces of *Fliegerführer Atlantik* and played a more effective part in the blockade war against ships at sea and southern English ports.[213] Occasional raids were made by German night-fighters, flying low to attack RAF bomber stations, but these too petered out during 1942.

All this time British defences were being expanded and their level of technical performance transformed. By 1943 there was a network of 53 inland radar stations (GCI) spread across the country from the Scilly Isles to the Orkney Islands, and all night-fighters were fitted with AI Mark IV sets for radar interception of incoming German aircraft.[214] *Luftflotte 3* losses averaged 10 per cent, an unacceptably high rate for a small force, short of reinforcements. By the end of 1941, RAF night-fighters, now chiefly Bristol Beaufighters converted to a night-fighter role, were inflicting loss rates of up to 18 per cent on the small and infrequent German raids.[215] By spring 1942 Anti-Aircraft Command had supplies of new searchlights with radar detection and a new system for clustering them in 'Killer Zones' to achieve a more effective light trap, in conjunction with radar-directed guns and night-fighters. Improved gun-laying reduced the number of shells fired for each aircraft destroyed to 1,830, the lowest of the war.[216] A German bomber group commander told an investigation team sent to evaluate Air Fleet 3 in March 1943 that any attacks overland against British targets under existing air defence conditions would produce 'a catastrophe'.[217]

Nevertheless there were two final flurries of German bombing in the late spring of 1942 and the early spring of 1944, both of them inspired by a renewed desire to retaliate against the greatly expanded British

bombing of German cities. The first came in April and May 1942 with
the so-called Baedeker raids. The term 'Baedeker', after the well-known
German tourist guides, was invented by the deputy director of the Foreign Office press department, Baron von Stumm, and it stuck despite
Goebbels' hostility to the idea of publicly boasting about 'the destruction of things of cultural value'.[218] The raids have usually been explained
as a response to the RAF bombing of the ancient German ports of Rostock and Lübeck, which destroyed their medieval centres, but the main
RAF raids on Rostock occurred after the Baedeker raids had started. In
fact the origin of the renewed wave of bombing lay in an RAF attack
on Paris in early March 1942. Hitler was incensed by the threat to the
artistic and architectural heritage of the French capital, which had been
spared in 1940 by the German Air Force, and demanded that Air Fleet
3 prepare a revenge attack on London. Göring, who throughout the
long period of air force inactivity in the west chafed at the bit to start
bombing again, ordered Hans Jeschonnek, the German Air Force chief
of staff, to get Air Fleet 3 to start attacking British industry as well.[219]
Following the destruction of two-thirds of the historic port of Lübeck
on 28–29 March, Hitler changed the order to bomb London into
reprisal attacks against selected British cities with special historic or cultural value. This time bomber groups were permitted to carry out terror
raids against the population as revenge for RAF attacks, but Göring
told his crews that there was little to be gained from simply bombing
residential districts, and ordered them to find useful military or economic objectives instead.[220]

The raids were carried out by small forces of between 40 and 70 aircraft, starting with Exeter on 23–24 April, followed by attacks on Bath
on 25–26 April, Norwich on 27 and 29 April and, in between, York on
28 April. On 16 May Göring ordered raids against Canterbury too and
the city was attacked on 31 May and 2 June. Two raids against the seaside resort of Weston-super-Mare in late June were later recorded by the
German Air Force history office in the list of principal Baedeker targets,
though its cultural value was at best modest ('a popular watering-place',
according to the 1927 Baedeker *Great Britain*).[221] Over the summer
months some 30 raids were made, dropping a total of only 439 tonnes
on target, but by August the thick defence and declining numbers
brought the raids to a halt. The brief campaign had almost no strategic
effect except to provoke an even higher level of defensive alertness and
technical improvement on the part of the enemy. In the first three

months of 1943 only 67 tonnes of bombs were dropped on target, mostly along the English south coast. German aircraft were forced to fly low and to shift course constantly to avoid detection by enemy radar. Little reliance was made on radio navigation, and the results on poorly illuminated nights were regarded by the field commanders as 'worthless'.[222]

The second brief campaign occurred in the spring of 1944, following repeatedly heavy attacks against the German capital in the 'Battle of Berlin' in the autumn of 1943. The roots of what was codenamed Operation Steinbock lay in Hitler's angry insistence in the spring of 1943 that the German Air Force do something to intensify the air war against Britain in order to counter the remorseless impact of the Anglo-American Combined Bomber Offensive and satisfy growing popular demands for retaliation.[223] Secret missile development, which Hitler hoped would prove decisive, was still more than a year from operational readiness. In mid-March Göring's deputy, Field Marshal Erhard Milch, convened a meeting to discuss ways of rebuilding air striking power against Britain. One way, it was concluded, lay in improvements to the existing technology. Air Fleet 3 was promised increased supplies of the new fast medium bomber, the Messerschmitt Me410, the improved Junkers Ju188S and the Focke-Wulf Fw190 fighter-bomber version with additional drop fuel tanks; a more effective incendiary bomb and improved radar aids (Lichtenstein-R and Neptun-R) were also expected to raise the operational effectiveness of the force.[224] It was also promised larger numbers. Throughout 1943, despite growing pressure to give priority to fighters, plans were hatched to expand bomber output. By December 1943 Göring was calling for an increase in bomber output to 900 a month, from the modest 410 achieved in October. It was indicative of the declining political influence of the air force commander-in-chief that these ambitions remained in the realm of fantasy.[225]

On 1 April 1943 Colonel Dietrich Peltz was appointed *Angriffsführer England* (Attack Leader England) with instructions to find ways of reviving the enervated bombing campaign. He was a successful commander with experience of the 1940–41 bombing and was soon to be promoted general at the remarkably young age of 29. His reputation was his undoing. In May he was appointed Inspector of Bombers and in June a sudden emergency in the Mediterranean saw him transferred away from the revived England campaign before anything had been achieved. During his absence the airmen responsible for the anti-shipping campaign tried to get the promised new resources allocated instead to the blockade strategy on the grounds that land bombing had never proven its worth. In conjunction with the promised new submarines and the use of new long-range aircraft it was argued that the level of tonnage attrition might reach 1.5 million tonnes a month, enough to seriously damage Anglo-American invasion plans.[226] Some sense of the frustration felt by those in charge of the air-sea effort was expressed in a facetious letter to Hans Jeschonnek in early September 1943. 'If for example,' wrote the *Fliegerführer Atlantik*, Lt General Ulrich Kessler, 'bombs are dropped on an English country house where dances are taking place, there is little possibility of killing anyone of importance, since Churchill doesn't dance . . .'. But bombs on ships, he continued, 'is *the deciding factor in this war*'.[227] By the time the letter arrived, Jeschonnek had killed himself, unable to bear the continued pressure of coping with air force failures after the successful Allied raid on the air force research station at Peenemünde in August.

The attempt to shift strategy once again to a naval-air blockade failed to convince either Hitler or Göring. Peltz returned to his role as *Angriffsführer* and succeeded in scraping together 524 bombers and fighter-bombers for the renewed 'England-Attack', of which 462 were serviceable. The aircraft were mainly the older Ju88s and Dornier Do217s, and a handful of He177 heavy bombers. The promised new equipment failed to materialize. The standard of training and preparation for long-range attacks was known to be poor, and serviceability rates were low. Peltz relied on the target-marking *Kampfgruppe 66*, who had greater experience of city bombing, though they could still be misled by British countermeasures. To increase the damage, the aircraft were to carry 70 per cent incendiaries, as British bombers did.[228] On 1 December Hitler approved renewed operations for 'long-range warfare against England'. Göring saw the campaign as an opportunity to show once again what the air force could do. 'If we succeed in carrying out vengeance on the sharpest scale,' he announced, 'this will exercise the greatest effect on the war-weariness of the English people, stronger than anything else.'[229]

On 21 January 1944 the first raid of 'Operation Steinbock' was flown against London. One of the German casualties that night was an He177, the first time the Allies had ever seen a German heavy bomber over London. Out of the 500 tonnes destined for the city only 30 tonnes reached the target. Of the 14 raids on London between January and April, only 4 delivered even half the destined tonnage in the right place.

A typically abortive operation was undertaken by 13 He177s on 13 February: one burst a tyre on takeoff, eight turned back with engine trouble, one flew to Norwich by mistake and then jettisoned its bombload in the Zuyder Zee, and three reached London, where one was shot down. Attacks on Bristol and Hull failed to find the cities at all. On the nights when the pathfinders succeeded in reaching the target, there was a significant concentration of bombing. In London there were 890 deaths, the highest level of casualty since May 1941.[230] In the February raids the German crews used for the first time thousands of small strips of foiled paper known by the codename *Düppel* (first used by the RAF under the codename 'Window' for the devastating attack on Hamburg in July 1943). Though intended to blind British radar, it did not stop night-fighters and anti-aircraft fire from exacting a high toll on the attacking force.[231] Losses of between 5 and 8 per cent for a force that could not be replenished led to the collapse of the renewed campaign after a few weeks. The last attack, on Falmouth in Cornwall, took place on 29 May. By that stage Peltz had just 107 aircraft left, far too few to pose any threat to the Allied invasion of France, which took place a week later.

By this time Hitler was hoping to release the long-promised secret weapons for a real revenge attack. The first was the Fieseler FZG-76 cruise missile (generally known as the 'flying bomb'). Developed by air force engineers at the research facility at Peenemünde on the Baltic coast, the first missile was test flown in December 1942 and had a maximum range of around 150 miles. The second weapon was the A4 rocket designed for the German Army by a team led by Wernher von Braun. Successfully launched in June 1942, it was the world's first ballistic missile with a range of 220 miles. In June 1944 the first Fieseler flying bombs were launched at London, in September the first A4 rockets. Though the purpose of both weapons was to avenge the destruction of German cities – hence the name *Vergeltungswaffen* (weapons of vengeance) for what were known as the V-1 and the V-2 – and to try to buoy up German domestic morale, as many of the earlier bombing operations had been intended to do, neither weapon was strictly speaking a form of strategic air warfare.[232] They were fired randomly and exacted a high civilian death rate in the first few months, but had little effect on the wider strategic picture. The entire explosive weight of the A4 rockets fired at London, Paris and Antwerp was the equivalent of one large-scale RAF raid.[233] Only 517 rockets hit London, a further 598 falling short or into the sea. The flying bombs were more deadly, but their threat to the home front peaked in the first few months. Thereafter the number of bombs and casualties declined as launch sites were overrun or destroyed and effective defence against the flying bomb was developed. The RAF, using some of the new turbojet Gloster Meteor fighters, found ways to knock the flying bombs off course, while anti-aircraft guns, using shells with proximity fuses, shot down increasing numbers. Out of 10,492 aimed at London, only 2,419 reached their destination (although another 2,600 fell short in Kent, Sussex and Surrey thanks to double-cross information fed to German intelligence that the bombs were dropping too far north). More flying bombs fell on Belgium than on England.[234] Nevertheless, for the victim populations the effects of both weapons replicated a bombing raid and it is in that context that the V-weapons will be discussed more fully in the following chapters.

   The failure of Steinbock and the deteriorating situation in Germany under heavy bomb attack, where every fighter aircraft was needed to protect the surviving war economy, sealed the fate of Germany's bomber force. Bomber production had already fallen to a mere 16 per cent of overall monthly aircraft output as priority was given to fighters and fighter-bombers, including the Messerschmitt Me262 turbo-jet fighter, the first of its kind. In May 1944 Hitler insisted that the aircraft should be transformed from its intended fighter interception role, which posed a serious threat to Allied bombers, to the function of a fast fighter-bomber, for which it was less well suited. Although Hitler wanted the aircraft to be operated by the commander in charge of the bomber force, its object would be to mount harassing attacks on the advancing Allied armies and air forces, not to undertake long-distance operations.[235] The following month Hitler ordered absolute priority for aircraft defending the Reich and the final exclusion of all heavier bombers. The bomber groups were ordered to transfer their crews and training personnel to the fighter sector. In early July a new production programme for aircraft cut out the remaining bomber models He177, Ju288, Ju290, Ju390 and He111, and further development of a range of advanced prototypes. On 8 July Hitler formally approved the end of the German bomber and a week later Göring ordered all researchers, engineers and workers employed on the bomber programme to transfer their skills to the new priority sectors. This did not stop engineers at Daimler-Benz recommending an intercontinental 'superfast bomber' project in January 1945, coupling a six-engine carrier aircraft with a smaller bomber which would be released over the ocean as it neared an American target city.[236] German aeronautical technology entered the realm of science fiction as the war drew to a close. The German bomber force dwindled away in the last months of bitter combat under a weight of bombs greater each month than the quantity dropped throughout the entire first bombing offensive in 1940–41. In December 1944 just 37 bombers were produced.

In London anxiety remained that at some point Hitler might launch a macabre bombing finale as his empire crumbled around him. Churchill had worried in 1943 that the bombing of the dams in the Ruhr might provoke Germany to attack Britain's water supply.[237] The discovery of the V-weapons' threat fuelled the fears that Germany had not yet exhausted its arsenal of scientific surprises. Secret intelligence suggested that the enemy was developing an even larger rocket with a 20-ton warhead as well as a chemical fluid which would be dropped from aircraft and ignited in order to suck the oxygen out of the air and cause mass suffocation.[238] In March 1945 Portal had to reassure Churchill that a German spoiling attack on the Houses of Parliament was improbable. On 29 March the chiefs of staff considered the possibility of a once-and-for-all suicide attack by all the remaining German aircraft, but thought it unlikely since few German aircraft could now reach London from what remained of German-controlled territory. On 5 April 1945 Churchill still needed to be reassured by the military chiefs that a last throw by Hitler with bacteriological and chemical bombs was unlikely, though it could not be entirely ruled out.[239] Historians have speculated on the existence of so-called 'dirty bombs' in Germany in 1944–5, using the waste material from Germany's failed nuclear research programme. There is some evidence that small spherical bombs containing radioactive waste were stored in the Mittelbau-Dora works at Nordhausen, where the A4 rockets were being produced, but it is not conclusive. A case has recently been made that German scientists did finally achieve some form of atomic reaction at the very end of the war, but even if true, atomic weapons were still far away from operational realization.[240] By the end of 1944 the capacity of German aircraft to deliver anything significant in British airspace was negligible.

The failure of the German Air Force to return to strategic bombing after the summer of 1941 was not the product of an unwillingness to pursue an independent air strategy but a result of the heavy demands made of German forces on the many fighting fronts that opened up over the next three years. Combined operations became the principal focus of air force activity. If the Soviet Union had been defeated in 1941, as Hitler had hoped, then a renewed air offensive would almost certainly have been the outcome, despite Hitler's own reservations about the strategic effect of independent bombing, which he expressed to Goebbels in April 1942:

> the munitions industry . . . cannot be interfered with effectively by air raids. We learned that lesson during our raids on English armament centres in the autumn of 1940 . . . Usually the prescribed targets are not hit; often the fliers unload their bombs on fields camouflaged as plants . . .[241]

A fresh air offensive would nevertheless have required a substantial increase in bomber output and the development of more technically sophisticated aircraft, bombs and navigation aids. It is striking that despite the efforts to upgrade and modernize the German bomber force in the years 1941 to 1944, almost none of the vaunted new generation of aircraft proved of operational value. Aircraft production stagnated in 1941 and 1942, bomber output in particular; according to Field Marshal Wilhelm Keitel in one of his post-war interrogations, 'a sort of vacuum was created' where aeronautical innovation was concerned.[242] It cannot be certain that a renewed bomber offensive would have had the technological edge or scale that it enjoyed in 1940.

As it was, strategic bombing remained a relatively unimportant part of overall German strategy. Apart from the blockade campaign of 1940–41, whose material effects were at best disappointing, bombing in the west was confined largely to tactical support missions or small-scale spoiling attacks. Hitler did not share Churchill's or Roosevelt's enthusiasm for air power, nor did he fully grasp its political potential beyond the propaganda effects of 'vengeance' for the German public. Göring did appreciate that air power was transforming the nature of warfare. 'He looked at the army,' one of his adjutants told an American interrogator in 1945, 'and thought it a miserable, obsolete branch of the armed force. The fleet was in his eyes, superseded.'[243] Yet he failed to persuade Hitler to reshape German strategy to embrace air power more effectively, and failed to supervise the development of the usable, high-quality technology that Germany was capable of developing and producing during the war. Nor in the end did Göring think that air power could be decisive on its own. Air forces, he told one of his first interrogators, shortly after his capture, 'can only disrupt, interfere and destroy' as a vital adjunct to the decisive ground campaign.[244]

The German experience demonstrated the real limitations of bombing strategy under current conditions. The weapons used for the first strategic bombing offensive were insufficient to achieve its aims, despite the limited and poorly planned opposition the bomber force faced. The bomber aircraft had limited range, carried too small a bomb load, relied on a navigation system that was highly vulnerable to interruption and, most significantly, divided their operations among a wide number of targets, few of which were hit often enough, heavily enough or ruthlessly enough to undermine activity more than temporarily. The German air offensive was a classic example of a strategy pursued before its time.

3

Taking it? British Society
and the Blitz

In mid-September 1940 a London East End pacifist wrote a letter to the Quaker activist Ruth Fry refusing her offer of a bed outside the capital to escape the bombs, preferring to wait and be killed if fate so dictated. It was a frank and certainly prejudiced view of the crisis: 'People remain calm, yes, but happy? Certainly not.' The writer continued: 'No gas, tea shops closed, takes two hours to boil a kettle when a trickle of gas comes through. Thousands sleeping in the underground . . . but Churchill remains a great man, "the man of destiny" and the House of Commons just meets now and then to listen to a carefully studied speech. How low have we fallen?' The writer thought Churchill might even sell Britain short by reaching a backstairs agreement with Hitler. 'Some may well think that we deserve to be bombed,' the writer reflected, 'but the RIGHT people don't get hurt. A nice winter in prospect.'[1]

In almost every respect – except the perception of calmness – this letter defies the popular image of British society under the impact of the Blitz, and of the iconic status enjoyed by Britain's most famous prime minister. It suggests that in the face of the bombing, there were many historical realities, not one. Ordinary people responded to the sudden catastrophe in a myriad of ways, and if some fulfilled the popular image of placid fortitude, there were others like the letter-writer who saw injustice and bad faith in high places. Behind the rhetoric of 'we can take it' the social response to the German bombing was complex and fractured.

The British people were the first to experience a heavy and prolonged campaign of independent bombing. British society was the first to be tested to see whether the fantastic images of social disintegration suggested in the air culture of the pre-war years would really be the outcome. Moreover, British civilians had for centuries been spared the horrors of invasion, occupation and civil war that had regularly punctuated the history of Continental Europe. The violent death of over 43,000 people during the almost year-long German campaign was an unprecedented violation of British domestic life. The narrative of this violation differs remarkably from the narrative of the bombing itself, as it does for all bombing campaigns. Bombing raids took a matter of a few hours at most, but the act of ejecting the bombs took no more than a few seconds over the target. Bomber crews were not like soldiers, confined to the front lines, the battlefield strewn with corpses, the wreckage wrought by bombs and shells all too visible. Aircrews returned to base and an environment of relative calm. Yet for the bombed community the strike of the bombs was just the beginning. The material, social and psychological impact of bomb destruction persisted for weeks or months, sometimes for years. Bombing was a brief, if dangerous, operation for the bomber crew, but it was a profound social fact for the victims who lived more permanently with its consequences.

The British government was all too aware in the late 1930s of the extraordinary demands likely to be made on the fabric of the state and the resolution of the population if a major bombing campaign ever happened. Though preparations to cope with the air menace were launched nationwide from the mid-1930s, there remained intrinsic limitations as to what could be done. A report on evacuation plans in January 1939 put the problem bluntly: 'in a country of the size of England there is under the conditions of modern war no place of absolute safety'.[2] It was understood that safety was only relative and that high levels of casualty and destruction were almost certainly unavoidable. The one sure protection for the population was to provide bombproof shelter, but central government and local authorities alike appreciated that this was a counsel of perfection. An official leaflet on shelters produced in 1939 urged the public to realize that the idea of a 'bombproof' shelter was misleading. 'Literally it means a shelter conferring complete immunity from the direct hit of the heaviest piercing bomb,' ran the explanation. 'It is not considered practicable to design a structure … giving such immunity.'[3] The official British response to the coming bombing campaign was always to limit the damage, not to avoid it.

BUILDING THE NEW FRONT LINE: 1939–40

The view that civilian society was willy-nilly in the firing line in modern war turned the home front into a fighting front. This was a universal response in all societies threatened by bombing, reflected in the language used to describe civilian defence. When the editor of the *New States-man*, Kingsley Martin, visited the East End in September 1940 after the start of the heavy raids, he found 'in the most exact and non-metaphorical sense, the front line of an enormous battle'.[4] Local civil defence authorities divided their operational activities into two parts: the first they called 'the Battle', carried on when the bombs dropped; the second was 'the Aftermath', coping with the victims and the restoration of services.[5] As the war went on, those engaged in all the many branches of civilian defence came to view themselves as a fourth service, alongside the army, navy and air force.

The idea of a civilian front line raised innumerable questions about how to transform a predominantly urban population, organized by civilian authorities, into a community capable of withstanding and contesting the effects of heavy bombing. The local records make it clear that if the Blitz had begun on 3 September 1939, the consequences would have been much worse than they proved to be a year later. The long interval between the outbreak of war and the onset of the bombing gave both the government and the local administration the time to prepare their front line and to encourage the growing militarization of a large section of the population. The slow pace of recruitment of civil defence personnel before the start of the war ended with the onset of hostilities. Between 1939 and 1940 an army of regulars and volunteers was created capable of manning the front line; for the rest of the civil population habits of obedience to the blackout regulations, gas-mask drill, air-raid alerts and evacuation imposed on everyone an exceptional pattern of wartime behaviour that persisted until the very end of the war. Part of this regulation represented simple self-interest, but it survived even during the long periods after 1941 when the bombing was comparatively light and intermittent. The development of a civil defence mentality derived in part from the democratic nature of total war, which insisted that all citizens had a part to play and encouraged the view that wartime identity was linked to new ideals of the civil warrior.[6] When the government considered the idea that workers should carry on working even after the air-raid alarm had sounded, the risk was justified by the argument that all those engaged in vital war work 'are frontline troops'.[7] In 1945 Herbert Morrison, British Home Secretary through most of the Blitz, summed up the civil defence forces he had organized as a 'citizen army' filled with 'rank-and-file warriors', men and women alike.[8]

In reality civilians were not soldiers. The civil defence network had to be built up from the late 1930s using civilians who were neither armed nor uniformed nor used to the demands of regular, quasi-military discipline. Following the Air Raid Precautions Act in late 1937, local authorities were obliged to establish a local civil defence scheme to be approved by the Home Office Air Raid Precautions Department, set up in 1935 under Sir John Hodsoll. Central government undertook to fund 65–75 per cent of the cost, subject to Home Office approval. The local councils were expected to appoint an ARP Controller to coordinate all civil defence activity, and it was generally expected that in the threatened urban areas this would be the local town clerk, head of the municipal administration. He would be subject to a local Emergency Committee or War Executive Committee formed by elected councillors and municipal officials of whom the most important were expected to be the city's chief engineer, the local medical officer of health, the chief air-raid warden and the chief constable of police (who in some cases doubled as chief warden).[9] The decision was taken by the government that civil defence should be grafted onto the existing structure of local administration, which meant placing a heavy burden on officials who had no necessary understanding of the problems involved in organizing passive defences or in disciplining their populations to collaborate and conform. Some relief was to be found by establishing Group Units, which linked smaller local authorities together and allowed them to pool resources and share experiences.[10]

During the spring of 1939 a network of Regional Commissioners was established to compensate for the difficulties local authorities might experience, and although their executive responsibilities were defined rather inexactly, they represented an important link once war had broken out between the main ministries involved in civil defence or emergency work and the local ARP organizations. There were eventually twelve Civil Defence Regions covering the entire country, each with a major headquarters in a designated city and a large staff responsible for coordinating the welfare and emergency services. Because of its size and importance, London was awarded five commissioners.[11] The whole structure was to be controlled by the British Home Secretary, who on the outbreak of war would also hold the newly created post of Minister of Home Security. The man eventually chosen for this dual role was Sir John Anderson, a much-respected career civil servant, austere, sharp-minded and principled, but remote from the teeming city populations now under his care. The Ministry was activated on 4 September 1939.[12] The strength of the British wartime system rested on these clear ligaments linking local and central government and the fortunate absence of duplication of effort, but its success rested a great deal on the capacity of local civilian officials to respond to the strenuous demands of war, and this could by no means be taken for granted.

Local authorities built up their civil defence organization with no standard pattern and no common schedule. In those urban areas where there was strong political resistance from a wide spectrum of pacifist and anti-war groups to civil defence as an expression of militarism and war preparation, it proved possible to block the development of effective organization until close to the start of the war. Other authorities began preparation several years before it became a legal obligation. When the City Engineer in Hull wrote a circular letter to other urban authorities in early 1938 to find out what progress they had made with civil defence measures, he found schemes already in existence in Walsall, Doncaster, Coventry, Ealing, Stoke Newington, Manchester, Leeds, Newcastle and Birmingham, but no schemes at all in Sunderland, Bradford, York, Rotherham, Sheffield, Middlesborough and half a dozen other industrial cities. The most comprehensive schemes had been developed as early as 1935 in Coventry and Newcastle, covering every potential aspect of emergency work, training and public education; major schemes in Leeds and Manchester were ready by the autumn of 1936. Most cities had a scheme in place by the time of the Munich Agreement, in late September 1938.[13]

To cope with the new demands, local authorities appointed a full-time ARP controller, but much of the work was carried out by men, and occasionally women, who combined civil defence functions with their other duties. The key institution was the Control Room, which was usually set up in the local town hall in a bomb-safe basement, linked by telephone to other emergency centres or served by a troop of young messengers recruited from uniformed youth groups. By the outbreak of war, progress in constructing a functioning civil defence organization differed widely between areas, though the local records show that it was seldom ideal. In the London borough of Hampstead the ARP services were reported to be ready to function fully in an emergency by July 1939 and all gas masks had been issued to the population. The Control Room and first-Aid posts were fully manned round the clock from 31 August, but out of the planned 1,100 air-raid wardens only 220 were in place and from 45 cycle messengers, only three.[14] In York, less menaced than London, progress was even slower. By October the city's Emergency Committee had still not put up signs showing where warden posts and air-raid shelters could be found, a major domestic shelter programme had only just begun, gas masks had not yet been fully distributed for babies and children, and a full-time ARP officer had not yet been appointed. Out of 1,700 warden volunteers only 964 were effective and 500 had disappeared since the outbreak of war.[15]

The most difficult issue confronting local authorities was the recruitment of a sufficient number of local volunteers to man the civil defence and emergency services. A proportion of all jobs were full-time and in many cases well paid, attractive to a generation still experiencing relatively high unemployment. In Hampstead the post of principal assistant in the ARP department was advertised at £450 a year and drew 251 applications (a skilled worker earned perhaps £250). Less responsible posts still carried generous salaries of £250–£300 a year.[16] It was harder to secure full-time and part-time volunteers. Although large numbers did come forward, inspired by the threat of a real war, most local civil defence forces were always short of their full establishment. When the bombing began in earnest in the late summer of 1940, many local authorities found themselves forced to accept help from voluntary organizations which had not been included in civil defence planning. In this case the British tradition of voluntarism cut both ways, encouraging men and women to come forward as wardens, nurses, firemen and rescue workers but at the same time alienating those who resented the transformation of volunteers into a disciplined and state-directed force. Nevertheless by the summer of 1940 out of a required establishment of 803,963 civil defence personnel nationwide, there were 626,149 in place, one-fifth of them employed full-time, the rest volunteers. A further 353,740 were part-timers on call in an emergency but not part of the enrolled service, including many workers who were recruited by factories and businesses to undertake air-raid duties in an emergency.[17]

These figures did not include two organizations central to the effective working of the emergency services later in the year: the fire brigades and the Women's Voluntary Services. The regular fire services had always relied on extensive volunteer or part-time participation even in major urban areas. In 1937 there were approximately 5,000 full-time regular firemen who could not possibly cope with the requirements of heavy bombing raids on their own. The government ordered local authorities to set up an Auxiliary Fire Service (AFS) in 1938 to meet the possible threat of bombing, and by the outbreak of war the total fire service had swollen dramatically to 75,000 full-timers, around 85 per cent of them auxiliaries.[18] By the end of 1940 there were altogether 85,821 full-time and 139,300 part-time firemen, of which the AFS made up 67,024 and 125,973 respectively.[19] Relations between the two forces were notoriously poor, since many of the auxiliaries were from professional or clerical backgrounds while the regular firemen were overwhelmingly ex-servicemen or policemen. The author Henry Green, an early pre-war recruit, recalled the hostility in his wartime novel of life in the fire service, *Caught*: 'there's a prejudice against you lads,' the station officer tells him, 'you might as well know'.[20] The prejudice extended to women, who were introduced in significant numbers by the end of 1940, and to conscientious objectors who tried to join in 1940 when tribunals directed them to non-combatant jobs. In June 1940 the London Fire Brigade refused pacifist recruits on the grounds that they would be resented by the former soldiers among the regulars. The London Ambulance Service was also instructed to reject pacifist applicants and to weed out those with pacifist views among their ranks. The London County Council formally banned the employment of conscientious objectors on all civil defence duties the same month; a further 51 local authorities in England endorsed the same ban.[21]

Like the Auxiliary Fire Service, the Women's Voluntary Services for Air Raid Precautions (usually simply the Women's Voluntary Services, WVS) was established in response to the growing international crisis in 1938 and the imminent prospect of war. Launched on 8 June 1938 by the Dowager Marchioness of Reading at the suggestion of Neville Chamberlain, the organization had over 32,000 volunteers by the end of the year from all over the country, and eventually almost 1 million members.[22] Though the WVS was not strictly a public institution, the government provided funds and supported its activities. The initial object had been to recruit potential female air-raid personnel, but the organization quickly outgrew this purpose to provide a broad-based national welfare and relief service staffed and run entirely by volunteers. The distance from regular civil defence work was incorporated in a distinctive WVS uniform of green tweed suits and felt hats. There were WVS Centres set up in most cities where women were recruited and trained. Lecture courses were organized on air-raid precautions, yet the women were not expected to administer first aid or extinguish incendiaries but to supply advice, set up and run Rest Centres, and to feed the homeless and disorientated victims of bomb attack. Demonstrations were organized of 'street cooking' to show how primitive barbeques set up in the aftermath of a raid could provide hundreds of wholesome meals.[23] The WVS also ran local 'Housewives' Conferences' to try to spread the circle of volunteers by showing films or theatrical sketches of housewives in action. In many areas women who were unwilling or unable to become full-time WVS volunteers set up neighbourhood networks. In Hull a League of Good Neighbours was organized early in 1940 to help the local air-raid wardens by providing emergency shelters, buckets of water on the doorstep, blankets and plenty of hot drinks. A bright yellow poster printed with the words 'Good Neighbour' was displayed in the windows of more than a thousand Hull homes.[24]

The effort to recruit women focused on areas popularly perceived to be women's work – feeding, comforting, supplying household advice and goods. Yet from the outset it was clear that the civil defence services would not be able to recruit enough able-bodied men and would have to extend the service to women. This involved other judgements about the capability of women to fulfil civil defence roles. In York a recruitment drive to find women wardens specified that they should be 'of a reliable and worthwhile type' and should only be allowed to man posts on the outskirts of the town.[25] In Hull, where around one-fifth of all wardens were women, the duties of female wardens were defined in gender terms: keeping information on all the women resident in the air-raid sector, help with expectant mothers and the disabled, duty at Rest Centres, demonstration of child and infant gas masks, and relief for male wardens at posts during the day, when raiding was unlikely to happen.[26] In Newcastle the recruitment and appointment of air-raid shelter wardens was based on the ratio that three female wardens were equivalent to two males, seven women equivalent to five men; and so on. Women civil defence workers were paid 70 per cent of the men's rate, and received less compensation for injuries.[27] The recruitment of women was nevertheless essential. By June 1940 there were 151,000 employed full-time or part-time in ARP, and 158,000 in ambulance and first-aid work, over 72 per cent of the service.[28] Wartime accounts of the Blitz are full of stories of female heroism and stoical resolve. In *Post D*, John Strachey, the socialist politician and temporary air-raid warden in Chelsea, records a woman warden who extinguished 11 incendiary bombs on her own as they scattered around Chelsea Hospital.[29] The true heroes of Strachey's account are the imperturbable women who run his air-raid post. A long survey of the Blitz compiled by the Air Ministry in the autumn of 1941 observed that women wardens in general reacted more sensibly to the grim reality of death and mutilation than men. They also took casualties. In the civil defence services 618 women were killed or seriously injured over the course of the war; 102 women from the WVS were killed during the Blitz.[30]

All of these different services had to be forged into a home-front fighting force with high levels of discipline and paramilitary practices and equipment. The militarization of civil defence was evidently helped by the fact that many of those who ran it or were recruited to its ranks had experience of military service in the Great War or had been career servicemen. One of the first wardens killed in Hull, in July 1940, was an 'Old Contemptible' from the British Army expeditionary force of August 1914, who had lived through the entire first war.[31] Among the Regional Commissioners and their assistants there were eight generals, one admiral and nine other senior naval and army officers. In York the local ARP controller was a lieutenant general; an inspection of York civil defences in April 1940 was carried out by the national inspector of training and the regional training officer, the first an army captain, the second an admiral.[32] Some authorities unsuccessfully petitioned the Ministry of Home Security in September 1939 to create a genuinely paramilitary force with officers and NCOs.[33] At the least, the various civil defence services were keen to be in uniform as an indication of their status and a means of forging a distinct identity. 'Uniform,' ran a London Civil Defence Region circular, 'has a value of its own ... irrespective of the physique or personality of the wearer.'[34] The government was slow to respond to the local pressure to create uniformed services, partly because of the cost, but once the bombing started the metal helmets and armlets originally made available were supplemented by ever more elaborate uniforms. For men this included blue overalls, military-style blouses and trousers, greatcoats, leather boots and berets; for women, greatcoats, serge jackets and skirts, stout shoes, felt hats, raincoats, fleece linings and peaked caps.[35] The extravagant lists of equipment required by civil defence workers lacked only weapons. By the summer of 1940 civil defence personnel were permitted to join in local military parades to display their claim to be the fourth service.

The quasi-military character of the civil defence service extended to the training programmes first set up in the 1930s and the joint exercises civil defence personnel were required to take part in before the onset of the bombing. The training was undertaken both at a local level and in the main training centres set up by the Home Office before the war. During the war advanced courses were run from two Home Security schools, at Falfield in Gloucestershire and Easingwold in Yorkshire, supplemented by regional schools in each of the civil defence areas. Much of the early training concentrated on preparation for gas attack, which until 1940 was still regarded as the more serious threat. In most

of the syllabi set up for ARP personnel, anti-gas lessons greatly outnumbered instruction on dealing with high-explosive and incendiary
bombs. At Stoke Newington in north London eight out of nine ARP
lectures for recruits covered gas ('Nature and Property of Blister Gases',
'Protection of Eyes and Lungs', 'Gas Protection of Buildings'; and so
on), while most of the training equipment consisted of imitation gas
bombs, a smelling set of war gas specimens, and tins of mustard oil
and lewisite oil to substitute for the real thing.[36] In the summer of
1939 the Hull ARP organization ran regular training demonstrations of
bombs and their effects in local parks; after detonating a miniature but
very noisy high-explosive bomb, the training focused on gas bombs.
Persistent gases (mustard gas and lewisite) were identified by smell;
non-persistent gases were released in small quantities and the trainees
warned to stand upwind while they observed its passage.[37] The Home
Office undertook to supply 'Mobile Gas Chambers' – vans converted
for gas training – while some authorities set up intimidating 'gas chambers' where the public could test whether their gas masks were in
working order.[38]

    In the year or so before the onset of the Blitz civil defence personnel
moved from training to practice. Regular exercises were held on every
aspect from the blackout to evacuation. Since many of these exercises
also depended on the cooperation of the population, they were a test of
how disciplined the larger civilian body might be. This sometimes had
mixed results. The evacuation practice held on 26 August 1939 to prepare schoolchildren and parents for the real thing met with a low
turnout, for schools were still on vacation.[39] Blackout practices began
from the mid-1930s. Usually held in the middle of the night when most
people were fast asleep, they seem generally to have been judged a success. A large blackout test in Leicester in January 1938 also involved
mobilizing gas decontamination squads and firemen, although the effort
to judge it from the air was inhibited by steady drizzle. A large-scale
practice in the Manchester area in spring 1939 was given a higher
degree of verisimilitude by the decision of Salford ARP to use fireworks
and a controlled explosion to simulate a raid, followed by the demolition of an old property block to mimic bomb destruction.[40] With the
outbreak of war, combined exercises for all the emergency services (fire,
ARP, first-aid, rescue and demolition) took place on a regular basis.
In York there were eleven practices in November 1939 alone; in the
London Region major exercises were held throughout the Phoney
War, explained in detail in operational orders that replicated military

operations. Like military exercises, civil defence practice was run by umpires who awarded points to successful teams and observed deficiencies.[41] Whether the practices really prepared the domestic front line for what was to come is difficult to judge. 'We come here ready for at least death,' complains Henry Green's autobiographical hero, 'and then we get into trouble for not doing under our beds.' Green found the months of inactivity harder to bear than the real thing. 'Now it's on us,' he continued, 'not nearly as bad as we thought.'[42]

The period of almost a year between the outbreak of war and the onset of heavy city bombing exposed many problems in defending a large urban population against the anticipated horrors of air attack. Though the civil defence organization was largely in place by the end of the summer of 1940, and subject to regular rehearsals, the behaviour of the wider population, who were only compelled by law to comply with the blackout regulations but with no other aspect of ARP, was open to wide variation. The carrying of gas masks, almost universal at the onset of hostilities, declined rapidly. By March 1940 only 1 per cent of Londoners could be observed with them. Even after the onset of the Blitz, Factory Inspectors found many workers defying the instruction to carry their gas mask to work; the Ministry of Labour had to remind all firms to hold respirator practice at least once a week, preferably just before the dinner hour.[43]

Popular compliance with evacuation also declined sharply over the course of 1939–40 as homesick mothers and children returned to their families and homes. On 1 September 1939 a vast exodus of 1,473,500 people left the threatened cities to be rehoused in small town and rural areas – unaccompanied children, mothers with babies and pre-school infants, the disabled, the blind, and pregnant women.[44] This official transfer was accompanied by voluntary evacuation by those (generally wealthier) whose presence in the cities was not required by the war effort. The foster households were paid 10s 6d per week for each child (8s 6d if there were two children); those aged 16 or over yielded 15s each, but many were set to work on farms and in other small businesses to pay for their keep. The bulk of evacuees chose to return home, around 900,000 by January 1940. A large number had not even evacuated in September 1939. In London, for example, only 34 per cent of eligible schoolchildren actually left the city in 1939, in Birmingham only 14 per cent. By May 1940 there were only 254,000 schoolchildren still evacuated in the whole country. Poor organization, an absence of effective welfare facilities and a failure to make adequate health inspections all combined to undermine the initial plan. So hostile were many city-dwellers to repeating the experience that a new government plan to register all children for evacuation when the bombing really began met with wide indifference; over 1 million parents refused to register when asked or failed to respond at all. The effort to get the most vulnerable members of the urban community into relatively safer reception areas collapsed.[45]

The poor level of popular collaboration with ARP was also evident in the uneven spread of air-raid shelters across the country. The number of shelter spaces in public and domestic shelters by March 1940 was estimated at just under half of the 27.6 million people in the major cities and ports. Of this total, 39 per cent were domestic shelters of three main types: brick surface shelters, reinforced basements (with steel or wooden supports) and so-called 'Anderson shelters', curved metal sheets to be dug into back gardens and covered with up to a half-metre of soil, named after the engineer David Anderson who designed them.[46] None of these was remotely bombproof. Neither were most of the public shelters, which consisted of basements in public buildings, public trenches (some with proper covering and reinforced sides, some not), and a number of larger, purpose-built shelters. The government remained committed throughout 1940 to the argument that it was better to have the population dispersed in small, mainly domestic shelters than gathered together in large public bunkers, where there were greater health risks and problems of public order. Public shelters supplied spaces for around 10 per cent of the vulnerable population, domestic shelters almost 40 per cent.[47] This took no account of the large number of people who believed in 1940 that they had no secure access to an air-raid shelter or those who chose not to shelter at all. One opinion poll taken in July 1940 showed that 45 per cent of respondents had no domestic shelter and relied on the much smaller proportion of public shelters; a second showed that two-thirds of respondents blamed the government for not building more underground facilities.[48] Research undertaken later in the war by the government scientist Solly Zuckerman revealed that of those without a domestic shelter (45 per cent of households with children, 58 per cent of those without) only 9 and 17 per cent respectively claimed to have resorted to public shelters. Among families that did not evacuate, the survey found that just over half claimed to have no shelter during air raids.[49] Here lay the origins of the high level of Blitz casualties.

There were also wide differences dictated by topography and social geography in the nature and number of shelters built before the Blitz. In urban areas with unsuitable geological conditions or low-lying poorly drained ground, there were few cellars or basements and councils had to resort to large numbers of brick-built surface shelters, whose evident vulnerability made them unpopular with shelterers. In Hull the local council ordered almost 15,000 of them to be built because many working-class houses lacked gardens for Anderson shelters; even for those that did there was the constant menace of flooding. In Gateshead, across the River Tyne from Newcastle, surveys in 1939 showed that out of 31,000 households inspected, 24,000 were unsuitable for Anderson or basement shelters 'because of the restricted nature of the backyards', and surface shelters had to be built for 60,000 people.[50] In the London borough of West Ham the low-lying ground made it difficult to install any domestic shelters, either Anderson, surface or trench, while the absence of gardens in most working-class housing ruled out outside shelter. A wartime analysis of West Ham's Blitz observed that garden shelters were also disliked because they cut families off from the community around them; communal shelters came to be preferred for social as well as practical reasons.[51] There were also numerous cases of people rejecting the offer of shelters, or refusing to allow basements or cellars to be used. In Hull the same street-by-street survey of shelter options found a mixed response from those canvassed. In one street with 26 properties, 5 householders asked for a shelter, 9 refused, 3 had no available space, 2 were shops and 7 elicited no reply. Even when the canvass of the whole city was complete, 1,279 households cancelled their initial request.[52] When York civil defence services got the same response, the ARP committee insisted that people should be compelled to make a statement explaining why they had refused a shelter. Those who cancelled a request were to be denied any shelter in the future. Almost 10 per cent of Anderson shelters delivered were rejected on delivery.[53]

The problems of supplying shelters in the most vulnerable city-centre areas, with cramped streets, small backyards, narrow pavements and a working population immediately distrustful of the officials who canvassed them, highlighted the complex relationship between state and people occasioned by the menace of bombing. What should have been a straightforward consensus on providing effective shelter and emergency care became an area for political negotiation and public persuasion. Neither state nor community had any experience to go on, and although they shared an interest in protection from bombing, it was hard to enforce regulations or to participate willingly in the absence of any bombs. This partly explains why the shelters that were provided were so poorly resourced. Many were badly constructed because of shortages of material, particularly cement, and the reliance on local contractors, whose construction work varied widely in quality and cost. Little thought seems to have been given to what should be inside the shelters; almost all lacked bunks, and most had no toilet facilities, heating or effective light. The cost of even this degree of shelter was enormous. Local records show that civil defence expenditure increased dramatically between 1939 and 1940. In Hull expenditure was £18,200 in 1938–9 but £69,400 in 1939–40. In Newcastle the cost in 1938–9 was £18,600 but in 1939–40 was £244,000 and in 1940–41, £450,800.[54] The impact on the local economy was immediate and local councils found themselves competing for scarce resources and waiting months or more for the supply of civil defence equipment. What might be defined as a 'civil defence economy' was forced to compete with the pressing demands for military supplies. By the autumn of 1940 the Ministry of Home Security was asking for one-third of all cement production for shelters, but was allocated just 12 per cent. Churchill, who wanted priority for shelters to meet his promise that people might 'sleep as safe as possible', was told that priority had to be given to war production and the defence ministries, whose requirements were needed to protect the country from invasion.[55]

The relationship between state and people was also severely tested over the issues of air-raid alarms and the blackout. The alarm system was operated by the Royal Air Force, which reserved the right to use its advance intelligence of approaching aircraft, secured by radar and the Observer Corps, to decide when an alarm should be sounded. The system at the start of the war was a complex one. The country was divided into 111 warning districts and only those where the attacking aircraft seemed to be heading would be given first a restricted alert that aircraft were approaching (yellow), then a full alarm which triggered the sirens (red), followed by a 'raiders passed' message (green) and a final 'cancel caution' (white), when the state of alarm was ended.[56] This system raised many difficulties. German attacks were often small-scale and scattered, which made it difficult to decide when and where to sound the alarm. The policy was generally to avoid sounding an alarm for a small number of aircraft, but this meant that bombing might occur with no siren at all, which provoked public resentment. In July 1940 the manager of the National Oil Refinery at Llandarcy in South Wales complained that his plant had been bombed three times without receiving even a yellow warning. In Liverpool in August bombs dropped on

Merseyside after the all-clear, leaving workers reluctant to leave the shelters on 'green'. 'The general opinion,' wrote Liverpool's chief constable, 'is that the warning system is not to be relied on.'[57] The issuing of indiscriminate red alerts, on the other hand, stopped all work by day or by night and sharply reduced war production. Since the red alerts often produced no raid on most of the area where they were issued, people began to ignore them. In July 1940 the system was modified. The 'red' became an 'alert', when bombers were active but not yet a direct threat, while the alarm came only minutes before an attack. Workers were expected to continue working during an alert and to retreat to shelter only when roof-spotters reported approaching aircraft or could hear nearby gunfire. The reduction in alarms was welcome, though it still meant that bombs might fall without warning, while workers took to the role of roof-spotter with mixed enthusiasm.[58]

The blackout was in general a more successful measure, though it imposed on the whole of Britain an exceptional experience for almost six years of war. Detailed regulations for street lighting and vehicle lighting, instructions to paint white lines on kerbs and other obstacles, stringent scrutiny of blacked-out windows, all succeeded in creating an effectively darkened but navigable environment. In cities, air-raid wardens patrolled from day one of the war to report any chink of light, and because it was an offence, unlike other civil defence regulations, persistent offenders were fined.[59] This even extended to government departments where it was regularly reported that they failed to show a good example to the community. Officials tried to claim Crown immunity but the police insisted on charging someone for each offence. A senior officer was appointed in each government building, answerable in court for any negligence; it was agreed that any subsequent fine would be paid for by the government employer.[60] The blackout was in many ways the most obtrusive of civil defence measures for it had to be observed daily and completely. 'The lack of ventilation was stifling in hot weather,' wrote the Warwickshire housewife, Clara Milburn, in her wartime diary, 'but it is wonderful how one can conform to an order when it is absolutely necessary.'[61] Enforcement of the blackout nevertheless provoked tensions with the wardens. Civil defence personnel had no right of arrest, except for those who were also enrolled as special constables or auxiliary policemen. Arguments over the blackout or shelter provision seem to have been widespread. 'At present,' noted a Ministry of Health official in autumn 1940, 'anyone can assault an ARP warden.' His or her only remedy was to take out a private lawsuit.[62]

The tensions were at their highest through the long months of waiting for the bombing to start. On the one hand, some of the public
thought that civil defence personnel were shirkers, men who ought to be
in the armed forces (an irony given the hostility to employing conscientious objectors). The Ministry of Information was so concerned with
the popular attitude to civil defence workers that in June, Under-Secretary
of State Harold Nicolson recommended a concerted propaganda drive
to restore confidence in ARP and 'implicit obedience to the wardens'.[63]
On the other hand, civil defence personnel became restless and disillusioned by almost a year of inactivity. In Hampstead it was reported that
volunteer enthusiasm was on the wane by November 1939, exacerbated
by long hours of unpaid work and poorly furnished ARP posts. Wardens
were resigning at the rate of eight a day.[64] The Regional Commissioner
for the Northern Region later admitted to an audience that the monot-
ony of standing-by for months had been 'the first enemy to be fought'.[65]
When the first bombs dropped in late June and some civil defence
services found themselves in action, the Ministry of Home Security
announced to the nation that the fourth arm of the services alongside
the army, navy and air force had finally gone into action. 'You've had a
long period of waiting,' ran the broadcast. 'Sometimes your purpose has
been misunderstood.'[66] The preparation to meet the bombing war was
nevertheless mixed: limited evacuation, disliked by many; a poor level
of shelter provision with almost no amenities in place; an alarm system
which invited distrust; emergency services untested in the crucible of
home-front war.

RESCUE AND SHELTER

When the bombing began in earnest from August 1940 its effects were
not uniform. Across the country the experience of bombing varied
according to the strategy pursued by the enemy. Most of the population
experienced alarms and disturbed sleep, but more than half were never
bombed, and many of those towns and cities on which bombs fell were
the victims just once or twice of stray or jettisoned bombloads. In rural
areas bombing was a very occasional interruption. In North Devon, for
example, a handful of bombs fell on villages which were on the flightpath to South Wales, and a bomb on Barnstaple, the largest town, left a
crater in a road. Villagers watched the burning port of Plymouth in the
far distance or went as bomb tourists to inspect the damage in local

towns. The only three wartime fatalities in the region were the result of crashed RAF aircraft.[67]

It was the ports and cities on the German Air Force priority lists which suffered repeated and heavy bombing. Even small coastal towns were not immune if they were on the German routes. Ramsgate on the Kent coast, 'that defenceless watering place' Churchill called it, had 62 raids between 1940 and 1944; many of the attacks were made by only one or two aircraft and on some occasions the handful of bombs fell into the sea or on the local golf course. The one major and deliberate raid was on 24 August 1940. Over the course of the war 76 towns-people were killed.[68] The port of Hull by contrast was deliberately targeted 84 times, 20 modest raids in 1940, 10 heavy raids in 1941, and then hit-and-run raids until March 1945, all at the cost of 1,104 dead.[69] Plymouth, hit 59 times between July 1940 and April 1944 and subject to 602 air-raid alerts, claimed to be proportionately the 'worst blitzed city', with 1,172 dead. The total number of damaged housing units exceeded the city's entire pre-war total because repaired houses were hit again, sometimes two or three times.[70] The impact on major conurba-tions also differed widely. In the northern region there were 118 raids in 1940, 131 in 1941, but thereafter only 49 small raids. In Newcastle these resulted in 141 deaths and in Sunderland 273, yet in Gateshead, across the river from Newcastle, there were only five fatalities and in Durham and in Darlington, both at the heart of the nearby coalfield region, there was not one.[71] The overall pattern of bombing in Britain presented a patchy and uneven picture both geographically and chronologically.

The priority throughout the period popularly known as the Blitz (a term mistakenly derived from the German *Blitzkrieg*, or lightning war) was to limit casualties either by temporary or permanent evacuation of the bombed area or through shelter and rescue. The effort to ensure that vulnerable women and children were evacuated was renewed as bomb-ing began, but there remained extensive resistance to the transfer. A study of ten London boroughs found that among the most heavily bombed quarters of central London the percentage of households affected by evacuation ranged from 20 per cent in West Ham to 11 per cent in Islington. The proportion in suburban Barnes was only 8 per cent.[72] From the whole London area, now the object of sustained daily bombing, only 20,500 children were moved in September, and in December only 760. By September 1941 there were just 60,000 un-accompanied evacuee children from a population of over 7 million. In

December 1940 the Minister of Health, Malcolm MacDonald, concluded in a report for the government civil defence executive committee
that there was no need to compel children to leave the capital: 'the general picture is that London children are healthy and are even less affected
by bombing than adults'.[73] By the spring of 1941, from the whole country, there were 1.368 million evacuated children, babies and mothers,
teachers, disabled and blind, a lower figure than in 1939; some had
remained in the reception areas since 1939, others joined in what was
called a 'trickle evacuation' over the winter months, many from cities
outside London. The number of unofficial or unassisted evacuees has
been difficult to estimate but may well have been greater than the number who left under official aegis. By 1941 the population of Greater
London had fallen by one-fifth. Many private evacuees could be found
among better-off households which could bear the cost of moving to the
country or a long sojourn in a hotel. In September Home Intelligence
reported that it was impossible to get a hotel room anywhere within
70 miles of London.[74]

Temporary evacuation after a raid was a common and rational
response to the impact of heavy bomb attack, but it was frowned on by
the authorities. 'Trekking', as it came to be called, was regarded as a
social menace and a threat to wartime productivity. Those who either
would not or could not evacuate formally were encouraged to stay put.
'It is undesirable,' ran a Ministry of Home Security report from March
1941, 'that considerable numbers of people ... should become a night
vagrant population.'[75] Yet from the start of the Blitz urban populations
voted with their feet. Workers from the dock areas of London after the
first major attacks tried to reach safer areas at night. Home Intelligence
warned of 'nerves cracking from constant ordeals'. A large part of the
population of Plymouth and Southampton slept in the country or in
tents after the first raids; even by the spring some 10,000 people, led by
the local mayor, trekked out of Southampton every night, in Plymouth
around 6,000–7,000. After the heavy raiding of Liverpool, 50,000 dockworkers were bussed in and out of the city. In Clydebank after the raids
in spring 1941, thousands trekked to the railway tunnel at Greenock
while 2,000 slept in the open on local hillsides. A total of nearly
40,000 people eventually left the stricken city.[76] These evacuations were
in many cases brief and improvised, affected by the pattern of raiding,
but they did raise difficult issues of temporary accommodation and
feeding, and the government reluctantly had to concede the establishment of 'cushion areas' around the worst-affected cities, where

temporary billets could be found and Rest Centres and canteens provided.

The most notorious case was the east coast port of Hull where severe damage to the residential areas around the docks created a large population of trekkers who moved into schools and improvised dormitories in the rural areas north of the city. Sustained bombing through the summer of 1941, against a target that was easy to find across the North Sea, turned the trekking into a permanent evacuation every night of around 7,000–9,000 people. Some slept in barns or pigsties, some in schools, chapels and cinemas. The government tried to control the movement, but eventually conceded that dockworkers were disciplined enough to return each day to work and the problem of homelessness was a real one. A cushion belt with facilities for up to 35,000 people was organized and properly resourced. Even by 1943 there were still over 1,600 trekking regularly out of the city every night.[77] The government was most worried about the loss of workers, but research showed that workers who fled the worst effects of a raid returned to work remarkably quickly. A survey of Liverpool after the major raids in 1941 showed that labour shortage accounted for only 5 per cent of the delay to the port's activity. In Clydebank, only a few days after the Blitz, five major firms reported that out of a workforce of 12,300 around two-thirds were back at work. Only 6 per cent of workers were lost through death, injury or flight.[78] Local surveys found that many of those who fled the raids soon returned to their damaged houses, preferring home to an alien billet.

The sudden evacuations following a raid highlighted the generally poor state of shelter provision, particularly among the most vulnerable working-class populations in the congested city centres, many of whom lacked a domestic shelter or easy access to nearby safety. The government priority of dispersing the population worked only where there was confidence in the level of shelter provision. The public distrusted most the numerous trench and brick surface shelters. A nearby hit would often be enough to kill or maim those inside, a direct hit a certainty; the heavy concrete roofs of brick shelters collapsed on those inside when the weak brick walls gave way. Trenches were prone to flooding and in some cases were not braced laterally, so that a blast could sweep down a trench killing all its occupants. It took only a few bombs to persuade people to boycott a shelter they regarded as a potential tomb. When a survey was made in London, 1,400 surface shelters were condemned as unsafe.[79] In Newcastle news that Londoners had rejected surface shelters led to a city-wide investigation and 560 shelters were closed down. Heavy rain had in some cases been sufficient to make the shelters collapse without the help of bombs. The poor level of provision meant that in central London only 3 per cent of the population used public shelters, in the suburban areas only 1 per cent. A shelter census showed that a mere 7 per cent of the available capacity of trench shelters and 8 per cent of brick surface shelters were actually occupied by the spring of 1941. Propaganda designed to show that brick and trench shelters were safe enough was disregarded.[80] Even the domestic Anderson shelters were not fully utilized since they too were easily destroyed by nearby bombs. Basements were safe only as long as they could withstand the collapse of the building above them. In Tynemouth a single bomb killed 102 people when the basement ceiling of a large communal shelter gave way, burying the occupants in debris. In Stoke Newington, north London, in October 1940, 154 people were drowned or mutilated when a basement collapsed, fracturing the water mains.[81]

The shelter crisis may well help to explain why casualties were so high during the early major bombing raids. In September the 6,968 deaths and 9,488 serious injuries was the highest monthly total of the Blitz. But it was also evident from the start of the bombing that many people deliberately chose not to shelter or found the most rudimentary and imperfect solutions. Mass Observation (MO) reporters in the late summer and autumn of 1940 were struck by the lackadaisical response to taking shelter.[82] Later in 1941 the government scientist Solly Zuckerman tried to find an answer to the question of why so many people had run the risk of not sheltering. He drafted a set of possible explanations based on interviews with civil defence personnel who had worked through the Blitz: 'Whether people have fatalistic attitude i.e. "name on bomb"', 'Whether truly apathetic or careless of life'.[83] There was almost certainly no single or even obvious explanation, but the evidence is overwhelming that many of those killed in London and in the bombed provincial cities died in the open, or in bed, or in unprotected spaces. Like the pacifist whose letter opens this chapter, there was an element of fatalism in popular attitudes to the bombing, or an exhilarating willingness to run risks, or simply a stubborn desire to defy an enemy who expected his victims to cower underground. After the first raids the author F. Tennyson Jesse wrote from London to an American friend, 'the English get bored so much more quickly than they get anything else, and nobody is taking cover much any longer'.[84]

These were hardly rational responses but it is unlikely that any general psychological account would explain them. Circumstance clearly played a part. One of Clara Milburn's neighbours had no garden shelter and sat during raids in an opening under the stairs decorated with Union Jacks. Many civil defence workers were compelled to sit in their posts during raids with minimal protection. John Strachey at Post D complained to the local council, but it was months before the wardens' room in which he served was given strengthened joists and pillars to protect it.[85] In many cases the refusal to shelter was deliberate if often temporary. The journalist Virginia Cowles found many examples in London of an active choice not to shelter: the caretaker and his wife in her block of flats eating supper with a raid overhead; a soldier and his wife arguing about whether to drive home during a raid; Cowles herself choosing to sleep in her bed because a shelter 'was no safer against a direct hit than staying at home'.[86] There was an element of bravado as well. Vera Brittain reported the popular society game 'Playing No Man's Land', which involved bright young things dodging bombs on their way from one party to the next. Even Brittain, sober by comparison, slept in her bed some nights from sheer exhaustion rather than go to the shelter. The attitude she found among Londoners of 'grim, resigned patience' could be mobilized for running risks. 'It's them that are careless what get it,' she was told by an ARP worker.[87]

The high level of casualties and poor level of shelter provision forced the population of London to take events into their own hands. People gravitated to structures they regarded as sufficiently sturdy, such as railway arches, where informal shelter communities were set up despite the evidence that they were as vulnerable to a direct hit as anything else. The Chislehurst Caves in Kent were occupied by migrants from London's East End. In West Ham three large underground stores were forced open and occupied by local people, though one area had no ventilation, sanitation, or a floor fit to sleep on. On 14 September 1940 the Stepney communist, Phil Piratin, led a group of 70 protestors from the borough to occupy the plush basement shelter of the Savoy Hotel on the Strand in the heart of London's prosperous West End. They found a shelter divided into sections painted pink, blue and green, with matching bedding and towels, and an array of armchairs and deckchairs assembled for the long wait underground. The group settled down in the chairs and refused to leave when police were called; sympathetic waiters served bread and butter and tea on silver trays. Piratin led them out again when the bombing that day was over.[88]

This incident was part of an uncoordinated but widespread demand for deep shelters, which were not unreasonably regarded as the only real guarantee of safety. Roy Harrod, one of the economists brought into the government Statistical Branch, wrote to Churchill's senior scientific adviser, Frederick Lindemann, that the time had come for a deep-shelter policy, despite the official hostility to them:

> a very formidable discontent is now arising. On all sides one hears the same opinion. People do not mind risk by day but ask for a safe and quiet night. It is not only noise but also risk that keeps people awake and impairs their efficiency. It also impairs their morale and loyalty. It is generally thought that deep shelters were provided in Spain. It is thought that the Government is inert or pig-headed in not doing so here.[89]

Churchill and his Cabinet colleagues were not persuaded and dispersal remained the priority. When local authorities applied for permission to build deep shelters, the Ministry of Home Security refused or made them a secondary priority. Newcastle's ARP Controller wanted local tunnels to be converted for the poorer dockside population, who it was felt would be difficult to control if serious bombing began. The Ministry allowed surveying to continue but did not regard it as a priority. In the London borough of Islington demands were made for deep shelters at least 100 feet (30 metres) underground because of popular pressure to abandon the poorly constructed trench shelters, but the government refused; in West Ham local protesters constructed models of deep shelters to demonstrate their viability and relative value for money (less per head of population, it was claimed, than the cost of their funerals), but failed in their bid.[90]

The question of deep shelters had been a political issue even before the war when the communist scientist J. B. S. Haldane launched a campaign in 1937 to get adequate protection for the urban working class.[91] After the outbreak of war the British far left, and particularly the Communist Party, faced the problem that they opposed what Moscow had declared to be an imperialist war. Leading Marxists were expelled from the Labour Party, including the radical lawyer Denis Pritt, and the Home Office and Ministry of Information closely monitored left-wing activity. For the radical left the shelter issue became a way of avoiding the accusation of unpatriotic behaviour and turning the tables on the government. In the late summer of 1940 the People's Vigilance movement was set up by Pritt and other Communists with a manifesto that called, among other things, for 'Adequate protection from air raids'.[92] In January 1941, the same month that the Communist *Daily Worker* was banned, the movement launched the People's Convention to try to mobilize popular demands for accountable government and a programme of what were now called Haldane shelters, as well as financial compensation for the threatened urban communities. But by the summer of 1941 the movement began to peter out; political activity of all kinds was difficult to sustain under persistent air attack and official pressure not to undermine the political truce established between the main parties in 1940, while the German invasion of the Soviet Union turned Communists overnight into enthusiasts for the war effort.[93]

In the end the onset of heavy and persistent bombing in London in September forced the government's hand. On 7 September, the first day and night of heavy bombing in London, several thousand Londoners bought tickets for the Underground and stayed put in the stations and tunnels. Over the following weeks the numbers increased to a level that neither the police nor local London Transport officials could control. At first they blamed 'husky men, foreigners and Jews', but it soon became clear that there were plenty of what police reporters later chose to call 'Aryans'.[94] The official position, already decided before the war, was not to open the Underground rail system for use as shelter because the priority was for traffic through the capital. On 21 September Churchill asked Anderson why the ban could not be lifted and received the reply that in the absence of any means of preventing access except military force, he had agreed to allow shelterers onto platforms at night. Not every station could easily be used, but the decision soon led to a regular influx of Londoners every night, sleeping on station floors, escalators and platforms, with the minimum of comfort. In September over 120,000 used these new deep shelters; as the bombing declined over the winter the number hovered around 65,000.[95] This was a small fraction of the population that needed shelter, but the occupation of the Underground highlighted the widespread public disquiet over the lack of safety, and at the same time highlighted the poor conditions and limited welfare available to the mainly working-class communities seeking shelter. Investigations were carried out in Underground stations to monitor their levels of comfort and hygiene. The lower platforms at South Kensington were found to house around 1,500 people, mostly women packed closely together; there were no beds but a mass of dirty bedding and litter, ventilation was poor, there was no hot or cold water supply, no canteen and no effective first aid.[96] Other stations revealed the same improvised and insanitary conditions.

The poor level of amenity and hygiene in all public shelters was imme-

diately evident once the bombing began. One of the most notorious
shelters was the 'Tilbury' shelter in Stepney in east London, a warehouse
and cellar area near Liverpool Street Station. Part of it was an official
public shelter, the rest not, and an estimated 14,000–16,000 clustered
into the area during raids. When the Minister of Health, Malcolm Mac-
Donald, visited the site in early October he told Churchill that the
sanitary facilities were appalling. Churchill wrote back a despairing
note: 'If we cannot cope with a problem like this, we are certainly not
going to be able to beat the Hun.'[97] Other public figures visited the shelters and reported back to the government. Kingsley Martin, the editor of
the *New Statesman*, sent his account of the shelters to MacDonald in
September, who passed it on to Churchill. Martin found the stench indescribable. At the Aldgate shelter there was one tap serving the whole
shelter, situated by the men's toilet; the floor was soiled and dotted with
contraceptives; the racial mix, he thought, promoted conflict. The most
severe critic was Clementine Churchill, the prime minister's wife, who
complained after trips to view East End shelters that people continued to
live in conditions of 'cold, wet, dirt, darkness and stench'. She observed
few first-aid posts, overcrowding, latrines side by side with the beds, no
hot drinks, few washing facilities, poor lighting and ventilation. Hers
was by no means the only account presented to the government but her
avenue to her famous husband was direct and, from the evidence of the
correspondence, forcefully exploited.[98]

The lack of amenities did not reflect an absence of planning and
preparation. There had been no intention of turning either public or
domestic shelters into dormitories, since it was expected that most of
the bombing would be done by day. The preoccupation with the prospect of gas attack had also distorted pre-raid training. There were
thousands of decontamination squads, decontamination chambers and
civil defence and nursing personnel thoroughly trained to cope with the
consequences of every type of poison gas. This remained an idle resource
while the shock of heavy explosive and incendiary raids had to be met
without sufficient forethought or experience. Even the nature of the
casualties had not been properly calculated. Solly Zuckerman with Lindemann's support persuaded the Ministry of Health in October to
establish a Casualty Survey under his direction, which would examine
the physiological effects of bombing to better understand how to protect the body against its effects and reduce death and injury. Bomb blast
was a particular concern since it was capable of killing a victim without
any external signs of injury. On the other hand, blast could also inflict

mutilating damage; wounds to the eyes were typical, including numerous cases where glasses had been driven into the wearer's eyeballs by
shock waves.[99] The effect of blast on air-raid shelters was also poorly
understood. The Building Research Laboratory was recruited in 1939 to
study the physical blast effects, but many of the inquiries were not
undertaken until after the raiding had started and there were ruined
shelters to examine.[100] In both cases the completed surveys and reports
were available only after the main bombing was over.

    The sudden shock of heavy raiding did not prevent the civil defence
structure from operating as an organization, but the immediate assistance needed for the bombed population was in some cases poorly
understood. The system of Rest Centres set up by each authority had
few beds, no centre for giving information to the homeless and disorientated population, and a standard and inadequate diet of tea, biscuits
and bully beef. The lack of bunks and beds was a severe difficulty. In
Streatham and Wandsworth, in south London, the local authorities
distributed hammocks, which Churchill also favoured, but they were
unpopular with the public ('Stout women do not like hammocks, nor
do pear-shaped men,' ran one report) and were eventually rejected by
the Ministry of Home Security.[101] There was a lack of canteen facilities
for aid workers and for the bombed-out which was most marked in the
East End, where the heaviest bombing took place. In September 1940 in
West Ham there were no shelter canteens, mobile canteens or communal feeding centres. A local pie-maker, working among the ruins of his
neighbourhood and his shop, improvised the sale of 2,700 dinners to
the homeless after a major raid. The ARP Controller was eventually
replaced at the insistence of the Regional Commissioners.[102] It was in
the East End that the absence of sufficient first-aid posts with adequate
stocks was also most marked. By late September 1940 there were fears
that the front line in parts of London might well give way.

    The reaction to raiding varied widely from area to area, but in the
opening weeks it was clear that the civil defence system could not deliver
everything the bombed population needed. The problem was in some
respects worse in the smaller cities outside London where a heavy raid
could destroy much of the civil defence structure and dislocate a higher
proportion of the population. The major raids on Southampton on
30 November and 1 December 1940 exposed the problems of dealing
with a sudden disaster even when it had been anticipated. The attacks
destroyed the telephone system and made communication difficult; the
Control Room in the city's civic centre building was knocked out but,

contrary to instructions, no auxiliary control centre had been prepared; the water mains were severely disrupted, producing an acute water shortage; food was available but not distributed effectively; the thousands of evacuees who fled into the countryside could not be properly provisioned or disciplined; a number of full-time first-aid staff abandoned their posts at the risk of prosecution; the almost 3,000 soldiers and workers who were sent to help could not be properly fed or housed. In his report for the government, the Regional Commissioner admitted that 'The Civic Authorities were overwhelmed by the magnitude of the disaster.'[103] An official of the Ministry of Food, sent to Southampton after the raids, found the remaining population 'dazed, bewildered, unemployed and uninstructed'. In the bombed areas people stayed in their houses without food or safe water; information on the location of Rest Centres and canteens could not be passed on because of a complete breakdown of communication. The five mobile canteens visited had no more than a handful of customers, and only tea and sandwiches to dispense; one arrived from London driven by two women with only supplies of tea, sugar and soap. The official could find no communal feeding facilities. 'Over and above everything,' he wrote in his report, 'local authorities must once and for all be condemned. They have everywhere, I think, proved inefficient ... they are parochial, slow and indecisive.' Among 'islands of good work' he found half-measures and ad hoc arrangements which threatened 'the progressive deterioration of morale in every English city'.[104]

The relative failure of the efforts to shelter and rescue the bombed communities provoked a crisis at the centre of the war effort by the end of September 1940 not unlike the crisis facing the RAF with the switch to night-bombing. Churchill pressured Anderson to do something urgently about the shelter crisis and to restore confidence in the ARP structure, but for all his widely acknowledged competence, Anderson was not an inspiring home-front commander. Beaverbrook suggested to Churchill in early October that a change was needed at the top. Anderson became Lord President of the Council, responsible for home-front mobilization of resources, and on 3 October his place was taken by the former Labour Party chair of the London County Council, Herbert Morrison. Morrison was a popular political figure, a barrow boy from Lambeth and a conscientious objector in the First World War, who dedicated himself in the interwar years to promoting the welfare of poorer Londoners. He was a blunt, intelligent and politically astute politician, capable much more readily than Anderson of engaging with public

concerns and demonstrating the government's desire to act. He recruited
the radical Labour MP for Jarrow, Ellen Wilkinson, as his under-secretary
responsible for shelter. Nicknamed 'Miss Perky' by her parliamentary
colleagues, her energy and forthrightness were deemed to be the right
qualities for one of the hardest jobs to be faced in the winter of 1940.[105]

The first priority was to reform and expand the provision of shelter
and welfare. Anderson had already set in motion programmes for
improvement, though much still depended on the initiative and resource-
fulness of local authorities. In mid-September Lord Horder, chairman
of the British Medical Association, had been asked to report on shelters
in London in view of the potential threat of epidemics and public disorder. He had recommended installing bunks and proper sanitary
facilities, spraying the walls with antiseptic, delousing bedding (and
sleepers), appointing shelter marshals, and regular inspections by the
local medical officers of health.[106] Morrison, together with the Minister
of Health, Malcolm MacDonald, set about implementing many of the
recommendations. In late September a set of standard by-laws for conduct in shelters was drawn up and finally published as an Order in
Council on 4 December. The orders prohibited smoking, animals, cooking, noisy conduct and musical instruments, and denied access to anyone
drunk or whose 'person or clothing is offensively unclean or verminous'
or who spat or defecated in the shelter.[107] Social discrimination was
encouraged by the new regulations. Vagrants and alcoholics were barred
from shelters and in London were accommodated during raids by a volunteer pacifist group in Westminster. Wardens were also told to police
prostitution by 'firmly and discreetly' telling a woman to desist from
soliciting, as long as they were reasonably certain that that was what
she was doing. Popular hostility to East End Jews, who became the butt
of some of the protest during the early raids for allegedly sitting all day
in the shelters, was mitigated by the establishment of separate Jewish
rest and feeding centres where kosher food was provided and Yiddish
spoken.[108]

The shelter programme nevertheless required more than rules for
exclusion and shelter discipline. A programme was begun to install
thousands of bunk beds in two or three tiers in all public and many
domestic shelters. Morrison introduced a ticketing system to control
entry to London shelters. Heating and lighting, mainly absent from surface shelters, were slowly introduced, while programmes to drain and
cover over the floors of flooded Anderson and brick shelters were begun.
The shortage of labour and materials meant dividing the country into A,

B and C zones, with priority for shelter improvement in the A zone of major urban areas. Each of the twelve civil defence regions was asked to appoint a Regional Shelter Officer to coordinate the activity.[109] Morrison also introduced a new portable shelter which bore his name to supply the many thousands who chose to stay in their homes rather than use garden or public shelters. It was designed by an engineer in the ministry's Research and Experiments Division late in 1940 and approved after a demonstration on New Year's Day 1941 in front of Churchill. Shaped like a large table, it had a flat surface top, steel frame and wire mesh sides and could withstand a fall of debris. Production depended on the availability of steel and the first models were ready only in March 1941 when the Blitz was nearing its end. By August 298,000 had been delivered.[110] By this stage 1,330,000 bunks had been installed in Underground stations, communal shelters, basements and Andersons with orders on hand for a further 3 million; half a million Anderson shelters (60 per cent of the whole) had been given concrete flooring. In May 1941 London could sleep 461,000 in bunks and had public and domestic shelter accommodation for 86 per cent of the population, though much of it still remained unused.[111]

The medical and welfare conditions for the homeless and for shelterers were also subjected to a thorough overhaul. It was decided in December 1940 that responsibility for this aspect of shelter and rescue should be given over fully to the Ministry of Health. One of the problems in organizing effective welfare since September was the absence of a clear demarcation of function. On 31 December the Ministry of Home Security took over responsibility for the number, siting and construction of shelters, while the Ministry of Health assumed control over everything that went on inside – health, welfare, public order, food and entertainment. This still produced some overlap, since Morrison remained responsible for the welfare provided by local civil defence authorities outside the shelters, but it eased the confusion that had existed when the bombing began.[112]

The first fruit of the new order was to institute shelter committees and a system of shelter wardens, distinct from the ARP organization, whose responsibility was to keep public order, note infractions and organize shelter activities. The Ministry of Health recommended people who could be firm and polite without bullying or domineering and encouraged the choice of one of the 'House Mothers', women who had already established a reputation in the larger shelters for sorting out the frictions and anxieties generated in their small, claustrophobic communities.[113]

In January 1941 the Ministry appointed a welfare director to organize programmes of welfare for the shelter population and in May each local authority was encouraged to appoint a welfare officer to supervise the new activities. These included educational programmes, entertainments, games and excursions. The shelter population was regarded as 'almost terrifyingly receptive' after weeks of boredom and darkness. Nevertheless, dull talks were arranged on practical subjects such as furniture covering and how to keep fit, and included a suggested lecture on 'National Savings – the danger of carrying about or hiding large sums of money.' For children aged 5–14 there were separate talks for girls and boys which reflected the prevailing gender values: for boys there were 'careers', 'life in the armed forces', 'a farmer's work', 'aeroplane construction'; for girls, 'dressmaking', 'cookery and housekeeping', 'nursing as a career', 'elementary first aid'. A central film library was set up for shelter committees to choose a programme of information films; the list included *The Manufacture of Gas* (the first and most unfortunate title), *The Life Cycle of the Tadpole* and *Kill that Rat*, for which a better case could be made. Shelters established choirs, which competed with other shelters, while some shelter committees organized excursions during the day to concerts, theatres and to London Zoo.[114] The class bias of much of the effort to improve shelter life was unavoidable, given the social background of senior officials dealing with a predominantly working-class constituency. Among the evening classes recommended in February 1941 for the cockney borough of Hackney was 'elocution'; for the more cosmopolitan Soho, 'English for Foreigners'.[115]

One of the principal concerns since September 1940 had been the threat of epidemic disease created by insanitary conditions and the close proximity of large numbers of people. Under the Ministry of Health the programme of establishing first-aid centres was accelerated. By January 1941 there were posts in most Underground stations and major shelters with more than 500 people. Face masks were distributed from February, though seem not to have been used. Education was seen as an important element of the programme and an information film titled *Atishoo!* was distributed to cinemas the same month to encourage the use of handkerchiefs. The close links between the medical personnel and shelter wardens created what one local authority called 'a miniature social service'. The spread of satisfactory conditions was slow (there were complaints in Norwich in March that people still fouled the streets because there were no shelter toilets), but by the early summer issues of hygiene and health were under control. The equipment detailed for medical posts was extensive, turning them into small well-equipped clinics just at the point when large-scale bombing tailed off.[116] At the same time the problem of Rest Centres and feeding was tackled. Most local authorities expanded the capacity of Rest Centres and provided improved meals. In Newcastle the number of places expanded from 2,400 in August 1940 to 12,200 a year later, with 3,300 volunteer workers to man the centres. There were 22 emergency feeding centres which provided a narrow but wholesome menu of traditional English food. The government undertook to supply extensive stocks of food-stuffs for emergency purposes and by autumn 1941 had allocated '"blitz" food stocks' capable of feeding 10 million people for three days and an Emergency Meals Service for feeding at least 10 per cent of the population of the most vulnerable 147 cities.[117] The Rest Centres also became places where the WVS and other volunteers supplied informa-tion to the homeless or bomb victims on where to go to find official assistance. By the end of the Blitz there were 78 information centres functioning, while the Citizens Advice Bureaux, set up before the war, expanded the number of offices from around 200 to more than 1,000 by 1942.[118]

From late 1940 a concerted effort was made by the government to learn lessons from the early experience of the bombing and to make sure that those lessons were communicated widely to the authorities responsible for civil defence. After the Coventry raid in November 1940 a number of 'Coventry Conferences' were held for local ARP Controllers where problems were discussed and recommendations made. The key issues isolated were the need for mobile canteens pre-pared for an emergency, the establishment of temporary information centres and posters or loudspeaker vans to announce exactly where they could be found, and the effective use of outside aid for emergency fire-fighting and repair work.[119] The success of the learning curve can be judged by the reaction to raids later in the Blitz. The major raids on Hull on 7–8 and 8–9 May 1941, which followed smaller raids during March and April, showed that lessons had been learned from the problems experienced in Coventry and Southampton, highlighted at the Coventry Conference. Although the city guildhall was hit and the surrounding area was set on fire, the Control Room in its basement continued to function, using messengers when phone lines were ruptured. Although 24 reception centres were damaged and the WVS worked even during the raids without the promised steel helmets, 41 centres remained open on the first night and 46 on the second, coping with a total of 13,000 people.

Clothing, tea and biscuits were supplied and over 13,000 garments distributed. The centres had representatives from the key welfare departments who could answer queries immediately. Volunteers were under instructions not to send anyone away even in crowded halls. On the following day the local authority opened district offices in the damaged areas to deal with the homeless and claims for assistance. The officials dealt with the long queues as quickly as they could and diverted people to slacker offices when that was possible. Over 36,000 people were seen during the week after the raids. During the first few days mobile canteens and emergency feeding centres provided 367,000 meals, most of them a midday dinner. Out of the 39 mobile canteens, 30 were supplied from outside the city. Meals were free for the first four days. The government authorized the release of 4,000 cases of oranges for the bomb victims. The result was an outcome very different from the experience of Southampton.[120]

The state had learned much since the start of the Blitz, but there had been much to learn. Casualties still remained high in the spring of 1941 as the bombing spread out into areas less prepared to cope with it and starved of the resources now being provided for London. In late March 1941 Churchill wrote to Morrison and MacDonald urging them to speed up the programme of improvements to cope with the expected intensification of the Blitz later in the year. The moment of crisis evident in September 1940 had temporarily subsided. At least one of the explanations was the effective response of the government to the deficiencies in shelter and welfare provision exposed by the reality of heavy bombing. Another lay in efforts to limit the amount of material damage that bombing could do.

DAMAGE LIMITATION

No amount of effective blackout, camouflage or firepower could prevent damage on the ground to industry, commercial buildings and housing. People could be moved or sheltered, or choose to stay and be bombed, but physical assets were generally static, except for foodstuffs and machine tools. The government and the armed forces needed to guarantee the continued operation of the war economy by keeping factories working as many hours as possible. They needed to ensure a continuous supply of foodstuffs for the population by protecting stocks and maintaining the activity of the ports. Finally, the population needed to be housed in the bombed cities where they worked to keep production going. These were the elements of Britain's war effort that German airmen were ordered to erode; damage limitation was critical to Britain's survival.

British industry and commerce was an easy target. Concentrated in major industrial regions in the centre, north-west and north-east, and in the large port cities from London in the south to Glasgow in the north, industry and commerce lay open to attack once German air forces had secured bases in France and Belgium. Britain was also exceptionally urbanized, with the majority of the population crowded into cities and towns, most of which had swollen in the nineteenth and early twentieth centuries with low-rise, poorly built terraced housing or tenement blocks to house a large industrial and commercial workforce. No planning had ever anticipated heavy bombing attack; cities grew haphazardly, the working classes concentrated in the centres around the docks or industries they worked in, the better off moving to larger, sturdier and more spacious suburban houses. This pattern of growth made individual industrial or port targets difficult to find and hit, but it also maximized the prospect of widespread physical damage to the urban infrastructure and residential housing. The exception was the expansion of new technology manufacture – aircraft, radios, electrical goods, scientific instruments – which developed in southern Britain and London during the interwar years. These new factories were often sited on the outskirts of smaller towns and cities; they were easier to locate from the air than factories in crowded urban areas, but also more dispersed.

Protection for industry and the industrial workforce followed standard civil defence procedure. Shelters were constructed in many key industrial and commercial undertakings (though less effectively in dock areas); the blackout was closely observed, with exceptions for undertakings that could not black out all their operations entirely; many firms ran their own ARP branch, while key equipment and machinery were protected by sandbags and blast walls.[121] These provisions gave limited protection during a raid but in the early attacks did little to protect workers from falling glass from roofs and windows, which accounted for up to 80 per cent of the casualties in the aircraft industry. Instead glass was replaced with solid material, which eliminated all daylight and left workers labouring in artificial light by day and by night.[122] The necessity for keeping production going for as long as possible, even during red alerts, led to the introduction in the autumn of 1940 of roof-spotters whose role was to watch for local gunfire and approaching

aircraft before alerting the rest of the workforce to take shelter. The initial loss of production time was substantial. The steel industry calculated
that up to the end of August bomb damage to plant had caused a loss of
only 1,000 tons of steel products, but alerts had cost 147,000 tons. This
was more than was lost when heavy attacks were eventually made on
the steel industry in December.[123] The spotter scheme was approved by
the War Cabinet in September. It was provoked initially during the
months of the Battle of Britain by the need to keep aircraft production
going at all costs, which was the responsibility of Lord Beaverbrook, the
first Minister of Aircraft Production. Beaverbrook favoured conscript-
ing all workers to stand to their duties 'as soldiers and sailors are
required to conform to the orders of the Commanding Officer', but
discussions between employers and unions led to the adoption of the
look-out scheme.[124]

The necessity for the system was demonstrated on the day agreement
was reached. At the Vickers aircraft plant in Weybridge, south of London, a surprise attack by a handful of dive-bombers on 3 September
1940 killed 89 workers and resulted in the disappearance of a further
3,000 and a cut in production by two-thirds.[125] Roof-spotting had the
advantage that it gave more precise warning of impending attack than
reliance on official alerts, and it cut to a fraction the amount of time lost
by needlessly sending the workforce to shelter. In early November
1940 the Minister of Labour, Ernest Bevin, forwarded to Churchill statistics from one firm which had instituted 'Air Watching' to show what
it could achieve. Between 24 August and 19 October there had been
124 air-raid alerts, lasting a little over 233 hours; instead of losing the
equivalent of ten working days, the roof-spotting had resulted in a loss
of just one hour twenty minutes.[126] Calculations made over the war in
industrial localities suggest gains of 60–70 per cent in work-time by
carrying on after the siren. In total, an estimated 11 million man-hours
were saved.

Roof-spotting nevertheless placed a severe strain on those workers
who were sent on rotas to sit for hours on the roof in all weathers when
for most of the time there was no direct threat, and from 1941 onwards
almost none. The first cohorts were trained by the RAF and then sent
back to their localities to train a wider circle of recruits, approximately
4,000 each week. The scheme was not legally binding, and most industries began negotiating with the unions on how to cope with raiding in
order to avoid industrial unrest. Schemes of compensation were worked
out for the time when air raids really did compel workers to shelter: full

pay for up to eight hours a week and half-pay thereafter.[127] Workers who found themselves temporarily unemployed as a result of raids, or who suffered injury, could apply to local Assistance Boards and 100,000 payments were made over the course of the Blitz to the injured, in addition to temporary cash payments and clothing coupons for post-raid homeless. Many firms working on war contracts collaborated in Local Production Defence Committees to pool spotter information and provide adequate shelter for the labour force. One set up in Birmingham in March 1941 eventually covered 800,000 workers. To try to limit the time lost in reconstructing damaged premises the government insisted that Reconstruction Panels and Emergency Repair Committees be set up by local firms working with the civil defence authorities and local trade unions. By summer 1941, 120 Panels were in operation and had organized the repair of around 4,000 damaged plants.[128]

The easiest way to limit damage was to disperse production into a larger number of smaller premises or to duplicate vital production in two or more places. Much armaments production lent itself to dispersed production of components, particularly the aircraft industry, so that some degree of decentralization was already in place by the time war broke out. There were also thousands of small engineering and manufacturing firms which could be mobilized to meet the expected production crisis. The dispersal of the aircraft industry became policy at the Ministry of Aircraft Production several months before the bombing began and it continued on a wide scale throughout the Blitz.[129] The object was to split up major production units so that there would be at least two and sometimes three production lines for individual components and for finished aircraft; small components or sub-assemblies were to have emergency sites on stand-by in case of air-raid damage; small hangers ('Hangerettes') were to be constructed some distance from aircraft plants so that finished planes would not be destroyed before they had been delivered.[130] This pattern was followed successfully by most firms. The Castle Bromwich Spitfire plant in Birmingham was split into 23 premises spread over eight towns, each component manufactured in at least three places. The Vickers Weybridge plant bombed in September dispersed to 42 sites within a radius of 20 miles, employing 10,000 workers but no more than 500 on each site. In some cases the firm shared premises: a film studio was used to assemble Wellington bomber wings while films were still being made; a coffin-maker, keen no doubt to profit from the coming business boom, refused to evacuate his premises until compelled to do so and left his tools and equipment for Vickers to use. The Bristol Aeroplane Company dispersed its aero-engine production into the local Corporation Electricity Department, the bus garage and a cigarette factory.[131] A more serious problem was dispersing labour to follow the machines. The government set up a scheme to build hostels for 200,000 workers engaged on war orders, but this did little for labour that dispersed itself after a raid. The search for nearby sites for dispersal had the advantage that a firm might miss the bombs but still hold its workforce together. The Bristol Company observed the sensible rule of finding 'premises not near, and yet not too far'.[132]

The results of the efforts to restrict damage to military production were mixed. Intense raids on the arsenal at Woolwich in the attack on 7 September resulted in heavy temporary losses of munitions output (except for bombs, ironically enough, which lost only 2 per cent); raids on Southampton damaged 30 per cent of Spitfire production based there.[133] But these figures were often only temporary disruptions. Work was either further dispersed or the plant repaired, covered with tarpaulins and running at almost full capacity within days. For all the anxiety about Britain's war industries, it was found that among the smoke and debris much less damage was done than at first appeared. Reporting to Churchill on the bombing of the Midlands aero-industry in November and December 1940, Beaverbrook found that only 700 machine tools had been destroyed and 5,000 damaged out of a total regional stock of 120,000. A study of 200 Birmingham city-centre factories after five heavy raids found that only 15 per cent had called in repair services and only 22 per cent had suffered serious damage but with most tools intact. The heavy raids on Merseyside in December left 'negligible' damage to factories in Bootle and all machines intact in the aircraft plants in Manchester. The Regional Commissioner in his report concluded that 'permanent damage is very small indeed'.[134] The pattern in 1941 was similar. The Ministry of Home Security calculated that out of 6,699 economic 'key points' – industry, utilities, food stocks, oil – only 884 had been hit; a mere eight out of 558 factories attacked had been destroyed beyond repair. Figures for weekly output of iron and steel show a higher output figure for every month of the Blitz compared with September 1940. By the end of the bombing, the monthly output of aircraft was almost a quarter higher than it had been before it started. The report concluded that the War Material Production Index was affected more in April 1941 by the Easter holidays than by bombing. More effective damage, as the Manchester report suggested, required far greater numbers of aircraft, more effective bombs, repeated raiding and the occasional lucky hit.[135]

The protection of food stocks and food supplies was a greater challenge, since food could only be imported through a handful of major ports and perishable food was stored in large quantities on or near the quayside. So anxious was the government to protect food stocks that air-raid precautions were introduced in 1940 at embarkation points for food supplies from West Africa and southern Asia.[136] The supply of food from overseas depended on keeping open Britain's major ports, which is why the German Air Force attacked them with such regularity. Ports could not be dispersed like factories, though the shipping could be diverted to smaller and less vulnerable coastal towns. But the attacks seldom succeeded in closing an entire port, damaging though they were. In Liverpool, subject to a detailed study after the Blitz, only the raids in May 1941 seriously affected the operation of the dock area, resulting in the loss of the equivalent of three working days. In the five weeks before the raid an average of 91,000 tons had been unloaded each week; in the week of the raids the figure fell to 35,000 tons, but a week later was back up to 86,000. During the same period the average weekly number of stevedores was 510,000; during the week of bombing this number fell to 299,000, but by the third week of May had risen to 518,000. The damage had been extensive, including 69 out of 144 berths, but arriving ships were instead unloaded in midstream while the docks were repaired.[137] In most cases there seems to have been only a temporary decline in dock work following the raids, though workers depended on the local authorities providing them with food, temporary accommodation and transport.

The greatest amount of damage was done by fire, when it destroyed existing stocks of food. Much of the food and animal feedstuff was stored close to the quayside in wooden warehouses. In Liverpool 100 sheds were destroyed in the bombing, with the loss of 31,500 tons of food. Records of food losses were compiled every week and presented to the Cabinet in close detail. By the end of December 1940 141,000 tons of foodstuffs had been lost, including 27,000 tons of wheat and 25,000 tons of sugar.[138] The following week a granary with 30,000 tons of cereals was destroyed next to the Manchester Ship Canal, but in this case most of the grain that spilled out was salvaged. Between January and May 1941 a further 271,000 tons of food was affected by raiding, but only 70,500 tons was reckoned a complete loss. The Ministry of Food set up a salvage branch in January 1941 and managed to rescue

162,900 tons for consumption and 39,000 tons for agricultural uses. The Ministry gradually moved food stocks away from vulnerable areas, so that by the end of 1941 only 45 per cent was still close to the docks.[139] This proved to be a slow process: in Hull the food crisis that hit in May 1941 finally prompted the authorities to abandon storage near the port area; in Newcastle a bomb on a quayside warehouse in September 1941 resulted in a congealed syrup of flour, fat and sugar that nourished swarms of fat flies so dense that local people had to drink their tea through a straw from covered cups to prevent it being contaminated.[140] Nonetheless by the autumn of 1941 the food situation had improved from the worst days of the Blitz. Most stocks had been decentralized into 104 food-storage zones across the country, providing enough stock to feed the entire population for two weeks, three times the level before the war.[141]

Alongside food the most important factor for the millions of ordinary people caught up in the campaign was to have somewhere secure to live. As German bombing shifted to night operations and became less accurate, damage to residential housing in the inner-city areas escalated. The most poignant images of the Blitz are the rows of demolished terraces and the huddle of the homeless and dispossessed in the brick-strewn streets. 'Never before have I seen houses completely reduced to this thick and gritty powder,' wrote Tennyson Jesse to an American friend in October 1940. John Strachey, reflecting on the ordinariness of the small houses blown open to view by the bombs, described 'a domestic sort of war' in which its catastrophes were 'made terrible not by strangeness but by familiarity'.[142]

It is nonetheless possible to exaggerate the degree of damage to housing and the extent of homelessness as a result of the Blitz. Homelessness was for most bomb victims a temporary state. Every effort was made by local authorities to return people to hastily repaired housing, or to allocate those whose homes had been obliterated to temporary billets or new accommodation. In Birmingham, where 67,000 were registered as homeless after the bombing, people returned to damaged housing even in bombed areas, or moved into housing standing vacant in the neighbourhood. Out of every 300 families rendered homeless, 280 in fact returned to their homes. Observers found that among the remainder whose houses had been destroyed, a 'strong tendency exists towards moving into a house in the immediate neighbourhood'. To ease the congestion, the Ministry of Health waived the slum-clearance orders on condemned housing to allow the homeless a temporary new home, so long as it was

cleaned and repaired in advance.[143] Nor was the percentage of uninhabitable housing as high as the initial scenes of devastation suggested. Once
the smoke had cleared and the debris had been shunted aside, most
houses were quickly reparable and the remainder capable of returning to
use within a matter of weeks. By January 1941, 80 per cent of the half
million houses damaged in London had been repaired, and 70 per cent
of the 70,000 in Birmingham. By the end of the Blitz 1.6 million houses
had been returned to use, leaving just 271,000 still undergoing repairs.[144]

The task of rehabilitation and rescue began as soon as a raid was over.
Local authorities set up schemes for Mutual Aid so that immediately
after an incident there would be lorry-loads of labourers, craftsmen and
equipment arriving from neighbouring towns. In the Northern Civil
Defence Region seven cities could supply at once a total of 44 vehicles
and 1,150 men for mutual aid. Each man arrived with a pick, shovel and
a meal, while every five men had a crowbar and a wheelbarrow between
them. The first help would be followed by heavy equipment – hydraulic
jacks, steamrollers, bulldozers, excavators, concrete mixers and cranes.[145]
The work could be interrupted by unexploded or delayed-action bombs
or the fall of badly damaged masonry, but temporary repairs could be
undertaken very quickly. In Liverpool there were 7,000 workers
employed on clearing and repairing the damage the day after the heavy
raids in May 1941. Sometimes cities that sent mutual aid found themselves the victim of bombing before their crews had returned. Manchester
in late December had 24 rescue squads away in Liverpool and had to call
for assistance from Bury, Oldham, Bolton, Huddersfield and Nottingham to compensate. A month before, Manchester had sent 12 squads to
help in Coventry alongside 52 from neighbouring Midlands towns.[146]
The rescue services worked in difficult conditions, sometimes short of
food and comfortable accommodation, but they were able to restore
housing, road traffic and utility services in a remarkably short period of
time. In Coventry electricity was restored two days after the raid,
two-thirds of the water supply a week later, half the private telephone
lines after a week, all but one train line and all bus routes after just four
days. After six weeks 22,000 houses had been made habitable. Clara
Milburn and her village neighbours took in a number of temporary refugees from Coventry but found after four or five days that many preferred
to go back to bomb-damaged homes, including a woman with just one
intact room for her, her daughter and the piano accordion she refused to
abandon.[147]

The urge to return home in cases other than complete destruction is not difficult to explain. Householders were anxious to salvage what they could from badly damaged housing or to find where salvaged furnishings had been sent in their absence. The Ministry of Home Security issued detailed regulations on salvage in August 1940 but made it clear that primary responsibility lay with the owner for recovery and protection of 'removable goods'. As the bombing intensified, this responsibility had to be shared increasingly with the civil defence authority, particularly in cases where the owners could not be traced.[148] Goods were transported and stored free of charge; storage facilities could be requisitioned and piles of fire-damaged, damp and dusty possessions made their way to a motley number of church halls, warehouses, theatres and equipment stores where they ran the risk of pilfering. Demolition workers stole anything they regarded as both useful and portable, though a Mass Observation report pointed out that many refused to steal from poorer houses if there was a street of middle-class villas available.[149] During the Blitz there were almost 8,000 reported cases of looting, of which only a quarter resulted in arrests. The opportunity to steal was widespread, but over the course of the war, crime and punishment remained little different from pre-war levels, though looting was punished with increasing severity because it challenged the community values of a country at war.[150]

As many people as could returned to live in familiar surroundings and with familiar things, however damaged. The immediate repair of housing was undertaken by the Ministry of Health, which may well explain why it was called 'first aid'. A great many houses had windows blown in and slates removed from the roof. Stocks of likely materials had been established in advance and could be utilized at once; lists of contractors willing to be part of the programme were drawn up beforehand and mobilized when repairs were needed. Instructions were issued to replace windows with linoleum, cardboard or plasterboard, leaving some ventilation and, in habitable rooms, between one-third and one-half covered with translucent fabric to let in a pale daylight. Ceilings were repaired with stiff cardboard screwed to the joists above. Roofs were covered with tarpaulins and retiled as soon as labour was available.[151] The results were neither attractive nor comfortable but, in the absence of a further explosion, habitable.

Churchill was among those whose view of the ruined cities focused on the visible destruction as a loss difficult to recover. In December 1940 he pressed the Minister of Works to set up repair squads for the rows of windowless housing he saw 'deserted and neglected'. The Ministry had already begun a programme of urgent repairs to factories and severely damaged housing. Because there was little for the army to do, thousands of building workers were temporarily released from their units to cope with more extensive house reconstruction. Housing in the intermediate category of badly damaged was always a much smaller proportion of the whole. Following the heavy raid on Hull on 8 May 1941, 561 houses were destroyed or beyond repair, 1,345 were damaged but needed extensive work, but 8,352 were still usable subject to minor repair.[152] The First Aid programme was designed for this larger category. The statistics show that the programme of repairs kept reasonable pace with the renewed bombing in the spring of 1941. By March 1941 there were only 5,100 damaged houses in London awaiting repair out of 719,000; in the provincial cities 50,800 out of 335,000. By November, with the bombing almost at an end, over 2 million houses had been dealt with. Of the severely damaged houses, over one-third had been restored to use by 1942.[153] The bare statistics render dumb the acres of burnt out and ruptured urban landscape and the improvised nature of life in damaged houses and apartments, but they do show that nationwide programmes of repair and rehabilitation worked to limit the damage that bombing might have inflicted on a less prepared and economically poorer community.

The one factor responsible for a large part of the damage was fire, and the extent of incendiary bombing was one of the aspects of the bombing campaign that had not been anticipated or adequately prepared for. Fire chiefs were asked to estimate after the Blitz how much of the damage in their regions could be attributed to fire and their replies ranged between 80 and 98 per cent; 90 per cent of the damage in London, Plymouth, Southampton and Portsmouth was the result of conflagrations caused by large clusters of incendiaries.[154] Firefighting in wartime differed from peacetime not only because of the danger of high-explosive bombs or delayed-action incendiaries, each with a high-explosive capsule inside designed to maim, but because buildings became fully ventilated at once as windows were blown out, creating a rapid blaze and spreading quickly to become what fire chiefs called a 'fire zone'. Water supplies were fractured, forcing brigades to pump water from rivers and canals, often at considerable distance from the blaze. British cities were fortunate that the scale of attack never made possible a firestorm like Hamburg or Dresden.

The existing fire services were, despite the expansion of their numbers, ill-prepared to cope with this degree of fire damage. The country remained divided into more than 1,600 firefighting authorities, all nominally independent. Some had modern equipment and a core of experienced firemen alongside the new volunteers, but some major urban areas had kept their 'police brigades', composed of local policemen with limited professional training. The poor performance of the firefighting in Plymouth, Liverpool, Southampton and Manchester resulted from this dependence on local police who doubled as firemen.[155] Many brigades could not help neighbouring services fully because hose and hydrant equipment was incompatible. There was a shortage of modern fire tenders and automatic equipment. The AFS had been trained as thoroughly as possible during each year since 1939, but in some cases it was abandoned to operate on its own without the help of the professional force. Henry Green, anxious for action in wartime London, found the reality on 7 September 1940, when he and his AFS crews were sent in a taxi drawing a pump to stem the large timber fires in the docks, a scene of complete confusion: 'When at last we drove through the Dock ... there was not one officer to report to, no one to give orders, we simply drove on up a road towards what seemed to be our blaze.' After finding the burning timber, Green found himself 'pitchforked into chaos ... doing practically no good at all ... no orders whatever'. He was struck by the sorry sight of burning pigeons in flight.[156] Even allowing for literary licence, Green's experience reflected the existing inadequacies of the force. By the autumn of 1940, wrote the Home Office Chief of Fire Staff – the improbably named Sir Aylmer Firebrace – the service had reached 'the limit of its possibilities'.[157]

Some effort was made to cope with the effects of bombing and there is no question that the fire services responded readily and bravely to the challenge. Some 700 firemen and 20 firewomen lost their lives and over 6,000 were seriously injured. The work was exhausting and in the case of London, continuous for almost two months, during which 13,000 fires were tackled by men who were allowed only 24 hours off between 48-hour shifts. The local services were grouped into mutual aid schemes like the civil defence services, with instructions to pool operational experience, and share equipment and men. At Coventry 150 pumps were supplied by other forces, a level of aid that brought all but 5 of 200 fires under control after two days.[158] In major cities contingency plans were made against the prospect of fire. Large water tanks, holding from 5,000 to 1 million gallons of water, were placed in vulnerable areas. Householders were encouraged to keep their own supply of water ready in bathtubs and buckets to use against incendiary fires.

The number of fireboats, to deal with dock and ship fires, increased from 5 to 250. The fire services laid 1,200 miles of black 6-inch water pipe along main urban city-centre streets to which hoses could be attached in an emergency.[159] In September 1940 the first steps were taken to spread responsibility among the wider population by introducing the Fire Watchers Order to compel businesses to appoint fire guards to watch for incendiaries which they could either fight themselves or call others for help. In October the Access to Property Order at last gave civil defence staff the legal right to enter private property to extinguish fire-bombs.[160]

None of these reforms worked well enough to cope with the escalating impact of incendiary bombing from November 1940 onwards. Firms which had instituted fire-watching schemes sometimes left the premises untended in the evening or at weekends, when bombing was just as likely. In other cases fire-watchers turned up late or drunk for a duty they regarded as an imposition.[161] The front line against incendiaries was supplied by ordinary householders, equipped if they were lucky with a stirrup pump and buckets of sand, supported by air-raid wardens and trained firefighters. Firemen often arrived only once a building was already well alight. A report to the Ministry of Home Security in December highlighted the disastrous experience of recent raids and recommended that a concerted firefighting organization be established which involved volunteers from the public, civil defences and the fire services.[162] The turning point was probably the heavy raids on Manchester in late December. A few weeks before, the Ministry of Aircraft Production (MAP) area officer in Manchester had complained to Beaverbrook that Manchester lacked a fire-prevention scheme and encouraged him to set one up. The fires that destroyed much of Merseyside between 20 and 24 December were blamed on the inadequate fire-watching provision sponsored by local business. The managing director of *The Manchester Guardian* reported that when the firemen arrived they failed entirely to cope, refusing to enter dangerous buildings or to tackle early conflagrations.[163]

In late December Herbert Morrison introduced to Cabinet a scheme for compulsory fire-watching. This was part of a broader drive to recruit more civil defence personnel, since the first months of bombing had exposed the gaps in its organization. The decision to introduce compulsion was presented as a form of civil conscription, with appeals to duty: 'some of you lately, in more cities than one,' Morrison announced in a New Year's Eve broadcast, 'have failed your country. This must never happen again.'[164] He wanted fire-watching parties to be set up in every street and business and empowered the local authorities to compel compliance if there were not enough volunteers. A further instrument for compulsion was introduced on 10 April 1941 with a new National Service Bill, which allowed compulsory recruitment of additional civil defence workers, classified key civil defence personnel as reserved occupation (free of the possibility of military conscription), and compelled local authorities to employ pacifists and conscientious objectors in civil defence and firefighting.[165] The move brought additional volunteers and fire-watchers; street fire parties were trained, equipped where possible with helmets, pumps, ladders and shovels, and linked more closely with the local firefighting authorities. Eventually as many as 6 million people registered for fire duty. Nevertheless, the increased level of compulsory mobilization reached those parts of the population generally less committed to the civic militarization that had gone on during the Phoney War, before the fighting started in April 1940. Some pacifists, content to undertake voluntary fire-watching, refused to be conscripted to do the same job; by April there were 24 cases going through the courts, followed in all but two by a brief prison sentence.[166] In Newcastle out of 57,444 registered for compulsory duty, 44,785 claimed exemption on grounds of ill-health, family commitments or vital war work. By 1943 the city had 57,000 people organized in fire-guard units but they were all volunteers.[167]

The new programme of fire prevention almost certainly came too late to make a great difference to the effects of the Blitz. Morrison faced hostility from the trade unions over issues of compensation and conditions for the new fire-watching groups. The relation between the fire services and the new organization was also not clearly defined and the fires that engulfed London, Plymouth, Hull and Merseyside in the spring of 1941 showed the limits of reform. On 8 May the War Cabinet approved the creation of a National Fire Service and Morrison railroaded the agreement into law two weeks later. The NFS became operational in August 1941, organized in 11 regional divisions and a separate service for Scotland. Across the country there were a total of 143 local fire forces. The fire-watchers became the Fire Guard, with white metal helmets and better equipment, under the direction of Ellen Wilkinson. The police brigades and all the smaller forces were scrapped. The reform made possible a standard chain of command so that a single officer would be in charge of the fire services after a raid; it also allowed standardization of equipment and operational technique. A National

Fire College was set up in a former hotel outside Brighton, and six volumes of a Manual of Firemanship were published.[168] By 1943 a comprehensive, well-equipped fire-prevention and firefighting system had been created, although difficulties were still experienced in coping with major conflagrations, as the later Baedeker raids demonstrated. How the new system would have stood up to bombing renewed on the scale of 1940–41 was never tested. The new service had to cope with only 10,000 fires, whereas the firemen in the Blitz had had to tackle 50,000.[169] The improvement in firefighting, like the efforts to cope with shelter, rescue and welfare, was one of the many stable doors locked long after the horses had bolted.

'THE MENTAL STABILITY OF HULL': MORALE IN THE BLITZ

In November 1941 the section of the Ministry of Home Security devoted to research on the effects of bombing began a survey under the direction of Solly Zuckerman on the psychological effects of air raids. A team of psychiatrists was sent to Hull to investigate the mental stability of its population in the aftermath of a series of shattering raids in the spring and summer of 1941. The object was to try to isolate factors that might explain how a city could be brought to the point of collapse. Hull was chosen because of the large numbers of trekkers who still left the city every night even though the major raids had stopped. The popular view in Whitehall was that the people of Hull exhibited less moral fibre than other city populations. Zuckerman's team set out to test as scientifically as possible the extent to which bombing produced psychological collapse.[170]

There was more to the research than simple academic curiosity. Long before 1939 there had been a widespread popular assumption that bombing would be unendurable for an urban population and that the panic induced by air attack might provoke some form of social breakdown. 'Morale' was the term popularly used, a military concept more easily defined in the context of the battlefield than it was in the wider world of civilian society. It was not easy to measure or to identify, and Zuckerman's team spent the first weeks trying to decide what questions to ask in order to determine the degree of abnormality or normality in the large sample of 900 men and women they initially selected. The selection was not entirely random, since many were trekkers, but they were chosen from a variety of occupations, from different areas of the city and from both sexes. The doctors prepared to look for hysteria, anxiety or depression as more or less extreme symptoms of neurosis; they also had a mixed category of anxiety and depression which they thought reflected a common psychological mix among those faced with death, dispossession and homelessness. They found almost no evidence of hysteria, the most serious medical condition, and therefore discounted it. Among the raid victims the psychiatrists found that 4.2 per cent of the men remained seriously neurotic six months after the attacks, while among women in heavily bombed areas the figure was 13.7 per cent. Moderate or slight neurosis persisted in 20 per cent of men and 53 per cent of women, but from the 706 subjects eventually assessed, 374 appeared on examination to have suffered no symptoms at all.[171]

The psychiatrists took this evidence to mean that the fears about the mental state of Hull's population had been exaggerated and that psychiatric help for bomb victims was superfluous, capable of doing 'more harm than good'. They recommended reliance on common sense and plenty of food: 'the stability in mental health of the population depends much more on their nutritional state'.[172] Zuckerman and his colleague, the physicist J. D. Bernal, completed their report for the government based on these findings. They concluded that there was no evidence of bad morale in Hull, neither panic nor excessive neurosis. 'Hull to-day looks like a badly blitzed town,' concluded their report, 'but a visitor is not impressed by any peculiarities of the population.'[173] Zuckerman was interested in statistical observation, which is why the figures on neurosis in Hull seemed so compelling. Elsewhere judgements about morale had been made impressionistically, although they generally confirmed the Hull findings, even in places such as Coventry where the initial fear had been of mass hysteria.[174] The wider psychological press had also produced regular articles in 1940 and 1941 confirming that admissions for psychiatric treatment had in many cases gone down during the Blitz, while those with marked psychosis induced by bombing were already psychiatric cases before the war.[175] In the London region hospitals an average of only two psychiatric cases a week were recorded in the first three months of raiding.[176]

The Hull figures nevertheless masked a much grimmer social and psychological reality for the victims of bombing. Each interviewee had the record of their Blitz experience, their previous mental and physical state and their current condition recorded on case sheets by the

psychiatrists. A high proportion displayed symptoms that were anything but normal. Many women revealed that they had become prone
to fainting, cried incessantly or vomited at the sound of the siren. Men
admitted to depression, insomnia, extreme tension and severe dyspep-
sia. Case 17, a housewife judged to have 'fair stability but marked
timidity', confessed that she shook uncontrollably 'like an electric clock'
throughout the raids and for hours afterwards. Case 20, a housewife of
'dull, solitary disposition', wet herself in the shelter, refused to undress
at night and dreamt of Germans dropping out of planes. Case 7, a
docker, had changed from being cheerful and adaptable, after seeing his
brother and sister-in-law killed in his house; he now drank eight pints a
night and smoked 30–40 cigarettes a day to calm his nerves. Another
docker lost his mother and three nieces in a shelter, dug out his brother
and sister-in-law trapped for four days, and witnessed a shelter with
20 people in it blown apart. He told the interviewer that he thought life
'not worth living'.[177]

In the worst cases, the psychological survival of the victim was in
itself remarkable. Two examples out of many illustrate the dimensions
of the crises to which survivors were exposed, often two or three times:

Case 1: Male Worker. Married, 4 children
'He heard the mine come down and rushed to the floor of his cloakroom
with his wife. He felt the explosion hit his stomach, and for 2 to 3 minutes
he had considerable difficulty in getting his breath . . . On recovery he saw
the whole house in ruins except for the walls of the room where he was.
He heard moaning, and set about digging for his children – this was the
worst experience of all; he felt "in a mental frenzy" . . . His wife sat about
dazed. Then he called for the ambulances, and fainted – to wake up later
in hospital. Two of the family were found dead . . .'

Case 37: Mrs C, housewife 'with a good personality'. Married, 4
children
'In the May blitz her house was demolished and after being imprisoned
for ¾ of an hour she was released by the wardens. She had been in this
house only a couple of hours, having moved from a house which was
demolished the night before. She had already been bombed out of a third
house in March. Her sister, with her 5 children, were killed in a raid . . . She
dreamt of raids and used to lie awake imagining horrors. She could not
forget the death of her sister's children and used to cry all day. She had
headaches and fits of dizziness and was terrified of the siren.'[178]

These experiences almost certainly produced profound trauma in many of the victims, though the language now used to describe it and the therapies to assist it have all been post-war developments. Few claimed to have gone to a doctor, and the men returned to work within days or weeks. The psychiatrists observed that all their interviewees were willing, even eager to talk. Their somatic experiences were evidently not unique to Hull and could be traced in every bombing raid across Europe. But they constituted a private crisis, veiled by the official bland assertions that Hull was, after all, 'mentally stable'.

This kind of hidden damage was not what interested the authorities. The ministries and armed forces worried about defeatism, fifth-columns, political radicalism, pacifism and rumours. The population was monitored by numerous agencies to seek out evidence of collective disaffection or social breakdown – the Ministry of Information Home Intelligence department, the Ministry of Home Security, the intelligence services of the three armed forces, the Ministry of Food Research Department and MI5, the internal security police. In this process the reaction to the bombing formed only one element among many potential sources of discontent and disillusionment. Even at the height of the bombing in March 1941, opinion polls found that only 8 per cent of respondents thought air raids the most important war problem; an April poll found that 62 per cent claimed to feel no more anxious about air raids than they had before the bombing started.[179] The Home Intelligence reports of the Ministry of Information also reveal a patchwork of reactions during the months of the Blitz in which the strength of concern over bombing fluctuated sharply. There was nevertheless an assumption that bombing must affect 'morale' more than other problems because of its violent interruption of daily life and the deliberate targeting of working-class areas, which the largely professional and educated classes who monitored them thought likely to display less robust willpower under attack.

The Ministry of Information began to think seriously about how to influence popular outlook on air raids as early as May 1940 after a Home Morale Emergency Committee gave its first report. The committee recommended using actors to keep people cheerful in the shelters and the distribution of song sheets, the start of a long catalogue of misplaced schemes. In June it identified 'the lonely woman' as the weakest link in the chain of public courage and suggested concerted efforts to encourage a sense of community and neighbourliness to help them. The committee also worried that class antagonism might be exacerbated by air raids, and suggested replacing the cultured voice of the BBC with more local dialects and giving radio air-time to left-wing speakers.[180] In July the Treasury granted £100,000 for schemes to sustain morale. The Ministry used some of the money to sponsor public meetings and lectures all over the country to give the public a stronger sense of what they were fighting for and what role they could now play in total war. Lectures on 'The Civilian's Part in Defence' or 'The Home Front' were interspersed with 'What German Occupation Means' and 'The Nazi Record'. By the end of July 1940 well over 5,000 meetings had been held, attended by more than half a million people. The same month Kenneth Clark, the art historian seconded to the Ministry, launched an 'anti-rumour' and 'anti-gossip' campaign under the slogan 'The Silent Column', which proved an immediate disaster among a public hostile to what one of them called 'the Gestapo over here'.[181]

Nevertheless a rumour department continued to operate during the Blitz, trying to counteract the more bizarre stories and exaggerated death tolls circulated by word of mouth. The official position on air-raid damage was to give away as little as possible and to release no figures on deaths or material losses. Among all the issues bombing raised with the wider public, this was one that provoked strong feelings. The Ministry of Information finally agreed to release limited raid details to their Regional Information Officers for wider publication, but Morrison stopped it. After the Coventry raid in November 1940 – which fuelled exaggerated reports of thousands dead, and shelters sealed up with the bodies still inside – the Ministry pressed again for a more flexible policy. A compromise was finally reached by the end of December which allowed discretionary release of casualty figures in a bombed locality if it was felt this would reduce damage to morale. Monthly figures of the dead were to be posted in town halls when required, but it was agreed that the figures for Coventry could be released as a special case.[182] But when Duff Cooper pressed for real post-raid information to counter the popular view that the government was 'hiding the truth from them', Churchill sent a firm rebuttal: 'I am not aware of any "depressing effect" produced upon the public morale, and as a matter of fact I thought they were settling down very well to the job.'[183]

Churchill epitomized the slogan chosen to buoy up popular sentiment during the Blitz that 'We [sometimes London, sometimes Britain] can take it.' This seemed a clever choice of slogan because it combined defiance with a sense of collective effort and left little space for those who thought differently (though it also provoked resentment from

those who did). Much of the popular writing by journalists and essay-
ists viewing British urban society under bombing reinforced the
propaganda. 'There was no break in the dam here as there was in
France,' wrote Virginia Cowles in a book published in June 1941. 'Even
the weakest link in the chain was reliable. From the highest to the hum-
blest, each person played his part.'[184] Vera Brittain, while deploring the
war that made such sacrifices necessary, nevertheless portrayed in *England's Hour*, written in London in 1940 in between air raids, a heroic
British morale: 'Never, I suppose, has the sum total of civilian courage
in this country proved so great as it is to-day . . . Day after day, men and
women working in offices, in factories, or in their homes, fight their
human fears with a brave show of cheerful indifference.'[185]

The Ministry of Information found that, contrary to its early predictions, 'gloomy apprehension' was more marked among the middle
classes and least evident among workers. Police fears that the 'poorer
classes' would stand up less well to raids was quickly exposed as an illusion. Early reports from local Metropolitan Police stations in London
confirmed that the poorer areas displayed no signs of panic or alarm.
'Public morale in these areas, which are poor class,' ran a report from
Tooting, in south London, 'was splendid.' Middle-class shelterers, on
the other hand, were easily distinguished by their sombre aloofness
from the shelter community.[186] It was also found once bombing had
started that communities which had not been bombed were much more
prone to 'self-pity and exaggeration' than those on the receiving end. At
the height of the London bombing, morale was judged to be generally
good; an opinion poll conducted in November 1940 found 80 per cent
confident that Britain would win.[187] Local reports after raids also suggested that after the initial shock and disorientation, panic subsided.
'The spirit of the people,' according to guidance notes issued to local
army commands in November 1940, 'though temporarily shocked, is
never lost, perhaps it slacks a little.' A Ministry of Home Security report
in January on lessons learned from 'intensive air attacks' concluded that
civil defence had 'stood up well to a severe test'.[188]

The construction of the image of stoical endurance was designed to
augment the public pressure to participate in civil defence work, good
neighbour associations, women's voluntary organizations, and fire-
watching. The government commissioned a documentary on the Blitz
with the title *London Can Take It!* Produced by Humphrey Jennings
and Harry Watt, with an American journalist as scriptwriter and
voice-over, the film was aimed at the American market, where it was

distributed by Warner Brothers to 15,000 American cinemas.[189] The
10-minute documentary was built around the contrast between the
smoke and noise of a night-time raid on the capital and the population's
calm return to work the following morning; the script described the
bombed communities as 'the greatest civilian army in the world'. When
it was released in Britain in October 1940, the film was prudently
retitled *Britain Can Take It!* and the commentary altered to show that
in each British city resistance was 'every bit as heroic' as in London.
It proved popular with cinema audiences (though by the height of
the Blitz in 1940, cinema audiences in London had fallen to 46 per cent
of the pre-raid level).[190] In late 1942 the image of a courageous civilian
army defying the German Air Force was solidified in the publication of
Front Line, the official account of the population under fire in 1940–41.
Like the film, *Front Line* emphasized the contribution of ordinary
people, 'the achievement of the many' in the face of brute force. By
January 1943, 1.3 million copies had been sold.[191] The image of British
defiance and endurance was easily borrowed by the public trying to find
a cognitive shape and a shared language for expressing their ordeal. The
American journalist Virginia Cowles asked two young girls carrying
bedding for the night to an East End shelter whether they were still in
danger: 'Every bloody night! Cor, don't you know we're the front
line?'[192]

The Ministry of Information nevertheless understood that there were
limits to the campaign. 'Taking it' was a rallying-cry as much as a
description of reality and it invited hostility from those who experienced bombing first hand. In February 1941, following heavy raids on
the Welsh port of Swansea, a BBC reporter broadcast a cheerful eyewitness account of what he saw:

> But there are the usual smiles; even those who have lost friends or relatives
> are not really depressed . . . I saw some elderly men and women running
> through the streets clutching small cases and parcels in their hands . . . Many
> of them raised their hand and gave us a cheery greeting . . . The attitude
> of everyone here is just grand.

The broadcast was deplored by the Swansea authorities and the population, and the Ministry reminded the BBC to clear broadcasts with
their officials beforehand to avoid local protests. But a month later, in
March, another broadcast insisted that an air raid on Cardiff had had
only moderate effects. A local woman wrote to Churchill to complain
that the city had been 'a positive inferno' and asked him to broadcast on

the evening news to explain how he was going to stop the city from being bombed again.[193] When Churchill did broadcast to the nation in April that morale was firmest in the most heavily bombed cities, Edward Stebbing, a young conscript convalescing in a Scottish hospital, heard another patient call out 'You ------ liar!' A few weeks before, Stebbing had listened to the grumbles of his unit forced to do fire-watching duty. 'If only people knew,' he wrote in his diary, 'of the discontent that seethes behind the façade of unity!'[194] The Ministry was also assailed by critics of a different sort who wanted the slogan to be 'We can give it', to show that Britain's war effort was not simply about absorbing punishment. In early October 1940 local informers noted that reprisals against German cities were being widely discussed. By December reports suggested abandoning the slogan 'Britain can take it!' because the public 'is more concerned about "giving it"'. Propaganda on being 'front-line minded' was abandoned and in April 1941 the Home Morale Policy Committee recommended dropping 'We can take it!' and substituting something more constructive.[195]

What has been called 'the myth of the Blitz', shaped by the public discourse on civilian endurance and pluck, was not entirely myth, though historians have been sensibly critical of some of its central claims.[196] There is no dispute that hundreds of thousands of ordinary citizens did behave with a remarkable degree of courage, good sense and self-sacrifice in situations they could never have imagined having to endure. James Doherty, a warden in Belfast during the Blitz, remarked in his memoir that 'War has an impact on human character. It makes heroes out of quiet fellows.'[197] There was no gender division in the qualities required. Sir Aylmer Firebrace observed incidents of exceptional bravery across the fire service. 'Neither sex,' he wrote in 1946, 'had a monopoly of courage and staying power.'[198] The experiences of the Blitz tested civil defence workers to extremes, whatever their social background or the nature of their personality. Barbara Nixon, a young woman volunteer warden in east London, kept a diary in which she confessed her uncertainty about whether she could cope when the bombing started. The first bomb she experienced blew her off her bicycle. She picked herself up and ran to help survivors. The first thing she saw was a baby in the road, burst open from the force of the blast. She wrapped it in a curtain and went on to cover up half a dozen more mutilated bodies in the street. The hope that she could 'control her nerves' had been a personal obstacle to overcome, as it was for a great many people. She reflected that civil defence workers were like soldiers waiting apprehensively for their first taste of enemy fire. After the first few times 'one forgot oneself entirely in the job on hand'; people worked with a 'dogged equanimity'.[199] The mundane context in which local disasters occurred, in familiar neighbourhoods, among friends or acquaintances, nevertheless differed from the serviceman's experience. Nixon met RAF crew on leave in her area more frightened of bombing than she was.

The myth nevertheless tells only part of the story of how people reacted to the bombing campaign and how they coped with its consequences. There was no simple linear pattern of social and psychological response – remarkable quiet courage, class solidarity, stolid resilience – but instead a vast patchwork of responses determined by a rich array of situational and dispositional factors. Unsurprisingly, there were profound distinctions in the capacity of individuals to cope with the mental pressures of disaster, as the research in Hull later demonstrated. There were also clear differences of geography, not only between small towns bombed only once or major cities bombed more than fifty times, but between a small self-contained urban area with one city centre, where the shock of destruction was often very great, and a large conurbation more able to absorb the disaster, shelter the homeless and provide alternative amenities. There were evident social differences dictated by contrasts in wealth and opportunity. Better-off or more educated households were able to buy more assistance, drive out of bombed cities, stay with friends in houses large enough to absorb the influx, replace lost or damaged possessions and navigate the complex system of post-raid administration. Workers in most cases lacked those choices, social skills, material advantages and time, and as a result suffered disproportionately from the consequences of bombing. Finally there were differences over time. The reaction of populations bombed repeatedly was observably different from a community hit for the first time. Home Intelligence reports by October 1940 noted a more cheerful outlook in London because raids were less frightening 'once you have got used to them'. A post-Blitz analysis of morale produced by the Air Ministry put 'conditioning' high on the list of factors that helped people cope. A survey showed that between the first London raids on 7 September and the end of the month the number of Londoners claiming to get no sleep fell from 31 to 3 per cent, while two-thirds said they could sleep at least four hours despite the bombing outside.[200]

These many contrasts make it difficult to construct an aggregate account of popular behaviour and moral outlook during the Blitz that does not distort this diversity. Nevertheless, a number of broader conclusions suggest themselves. Almost all contemporary accounts of bombing show that the immediate reaction among the bombed population (including a number of civil defence and medical personnel) was one of shock, disorientation, fear and anxiety. The experience of being bombed was a physical and psychological challenge of an extreme kind. One woman who lived through the first raids on London (and refused to take shelter) tried to describe the experience in a letter a week later:

> we were very frightened … Sunday night was the limit. No sleep was possible, crashes came from all sides and then suddenly the most brutal shattering roar … I cannot describe to you what a curious note of brutality a bomb has … The screaming bomb I can cope with … its noise doesn't sound to me as appalling as the noise of high explosive.[201]

There were evidently extremes of fear and panic at the moment of the raid itself, and it would be remarkable if the reaction had been very different among an untrained and poorly protected population, though it was also far from universal. The letter-writer's three maids were said to turn up each morning from the shelter 'amazingly courageous and unruffled'. In the Hull survey 349 bombed housewives were asked what they considered the worst aspects of a raid, and despite the long-term traumatic effects from which they suffered, 286 identified the actual moment of bombing as the worst – the whistling noise of the bombs, the roar of aircraft engines overhead and the explosion of landmines. Only 20 picked out fear for the family, and 17 the burning ruins and scenes of devastation.[202] Almost all official accounts acknowledged that the initial reaction to a raid was one of 'despondency' or 'depression' or 'confusion', but experience showed that the demoralization and loss of nerve was always temporary, even if the psychological scarring lasted longer. The initial shock was also local, even if the shock-waves rippled out to the surrounding area. The government scientist Patrick Blackett concluded in his analysis of morale in August 1941 that 'people who are not being bombed do not worry too much about those who are'.[203]

There were many other reactions, some of which could coexist with fear and despondency, some of which transcended them. There are accounts of bravado, exhilaration, curiosity, anger, detachment that defy any attempt to impose generic categories on the victims of bombing. Harold Nicolson, Duff Cooper's deputy at the Ministry of Information, wrote the following in his diary after the bombing of his offices in the University of London Senate House building in November

1940: 'It was all great fun and I enjoyed it. This is not a pose. I was exhilarated. I am odd about that. I have no nerves for this sort of thing.'[204] One London warden, whose letters were published while the Blitz was still happening, recalled a mixture of emotions but no fear: 'For my part, I am beginning to bear all perils with a certain philosophical detachment, a kind of intellectual courage ... I climbed to the top of one of the city's highest buildings and there excitedly awaited the battle.'[205] The aftermath of bombing, particularly in smaller cities where bombing was uncommon, brought trails of sightseers, curious to view the damage. Police had to set up roadblocks outside Coventry following the raid on 14–15 November to keep visitors out of the city; at the tiny port of Whitley Bay in Northumberland, bombed sporadically in 1941 and 1942, the incidents attracted visitors in such numbers that rescue work was hampered and police and civil defence workers had to be employed to keep the crowds under control.[206]

Bombing also generated an instant cultural response. Artists, photographers, writers, poets, and critics embraced bombing and its aftermath despite the horrors. This could be done with official approval. The paintings of John Piper (who arrived in Coventry almost immediately after the bombing to record the damage) or Edward Ardizzone were part of the War Artists programme. Henry Moore's drawings of the shelterers in the Underground are the best-remembered images of the Blitz (though at the time Londoners were reported to be 'baffled and insulted' by his modernist idiom).[207] Writers and poets found in the bombed cities a rich source of inspiration, 'half masonry, half pain' in the words of the poet Mervyn Peake. A number became civil defence workers – Henry Green, Stephen Spender, Graham Greene, Rose Macaulay – and gave literary expression to their experience of what one literary warden called 'a splendid violence'.[208] The poet Louis MacNeice, looking at the aftermath of a raid, could not help himself 'regarding it as a spectacle', the colours and textures of smoke, fire and water like 'the subtlest of Impressionist paintings'.[209] The cultural voyeurism was a tribute to the democratic character of the new home-front war because the images were of ordinary people and the descriptions were of the mundane and everyday, even if most of those who experienced the bombing were unlikely to see the pictures or read the novels that so vividly captured their suffering.

Among the many ambivalent reactions to bombing was the popular attitude towards the Germans. Where it might seem self-evident that a bombed population would want to be revenged on a hateful enemy, the effect of the raiding produced a complex response. There was certainly no shortage of anger.[210] The general secretary of the National Union of Railwaymen, writing in the *Railway Review* in November 1940, urged a bombing policy that spared the German people 'none of the terrors that we have endured . . . bomb for bomb, blow for blow, by night and day'.[211] Lady Hilda Wittenham gave a forthright response to a letter in the press from Lord Queensborough, which had deplored the deaths of German women and babies:

> The lesson we wish to teach is this. Let the German women get out of their homes and rush into their shelters and let their homes be razed to the ground . . . Let this lesson be taught to German women all over Germany so that not a single home stands. Then they will understand what their brutal work has done here.[212]

Diaries and memoirs also illustrate moments of intense hatred. 'The wickedness of this enemy is beyond words,' wrote Clara Milburn after the bombing of neighbouring Coventry; Edward Stebbing was told by an old soldier who had spent his leave in London in October 1940 that even after the war if he met a German, 'he would want to murder him'. The Ministry of Information received a letter after the bombing of Southampton from an eyewitness claiming that morale would be raised only by the knowledge that Britain was going to hit back 'to give the Boche some of his own medicine and to hell with the Boche women and children'. The Ministry declined to reply on the ground that the author seemed too panic-stricken for reasonable argument.[213]

More surprising is the widespread evidence that simple vengeance against the Germans was disapproved of by much of the British public. Policy at the Ministry of Information, on Churchill's instructions, was to play down the idea of reprisals. Home Intelligence reports showed that popular interest in reprisal was declining by the late autumn. Two RAF training stations organized debates on the motion 'Should we bomb Berlin?', but both registered strong majorities against.[214] Opinion polls taken over the course of the Blitz showed that in the bombed areas in particular there was no overwhelming desire for retaliation. In October 1940 the British Institute of Public Opinion (Gallup Polls) asked whether respondents would approve or disapprove of the RAF bombing of civilians and found the population exactly divided, 46 per cent for and 46 per cent against. The same question was asked again in April 1941, after six further months of bombing, and this time found 55 per cent in favour and 38 per cent against. But when the responses were divided by geographical area they revealed that in London more people were opposed to bombing enemy civilians than favoured it (47 per cent to 45 per cent), while the areas where there had been no bombing registered the highest proportion in favour and the lowest against (55 per cent to 36 per cent).[215] During the last months of 1940 a campaign began to take shape in London against the RAF night-bombing of Germany which finally resulted in the formation, in August 1941, of the Committee for the Abolition of Night-Bombing whose most prominent members were the economist Stanley Jevons, the writer Vera Brittain and the Quaker Corder Catchpool. It was supported not only by pacifist organizations, some of which ran a public campaign of propaganda against reprisal raids, but by non-pacifist public figures who risked popular hostility to maintain their objection to the idea that British interests could be served by bombing Germans indiscriminately.[216] In April 1941 the Bishop of Chichester, George Bell, followed shortly afterwards by the playwright George Bernard Shaw and the classical scholar Gilbert Murray, published letters in *The Times* deploring night-bombing. The protests made no difference to RAF policy, but they did provoke debate about the legitimacy and purpose of bombing Germany back and showed that bombing did not necessarily encourage a thirst for vengeance.

None of these reactions brought British society remotely to the edge of crisis during the year of heavy bombing. Although much has been written about the dark side of the Blitz, the narrative suggests that moments of social breakdown or acute protest were rare, confined to particular areas and brief in extent. The authorities could not be certain of this in advance, so that there evolved a continuous process of monitoring, adjustment, negotiation and reform to cope with bombing disasters and their immediate consequences. 'Morale' in this sense was not something static, 'susceptible of quantitative measurement', as the Air Ministry put it, but reflected a variety of public opinions and emotional states, some of them positive, some negative.[217] How much of this reflected the impact of the air war is open to question. It is evident that many other issues on the home front and the fighting front preoccupied the wider public as well. A Mass Observation survey in August 1940 found that three-quarters of respondents could not name a British air marshal; included on the list of responses was Hermann Göring. A second MO report on the attitude of demolition labourers showed that they discussed the bombing hardly at all, but spent most of the time bantering

about sex, race and loot, with an occasional comment on the war overseas.[218] Diaries and letters from the Blitz contain very full entries on the
bombing at the start of the offensive, but both the regularity and the
level of detail decline markedly after the first month. The war in Africa
against Italy features widely; the debacle at Dakar, when a combined
British/Free French force was repulsed by the Vichy garrison, was a
humiliation that lingered on in the public mind; the Battle of the Atlantic and food supplies took top place in polls about war problems taken
in November 1940 and March 1941, 20 per cent in the first case, 44 per
cent in the second. Night-bombing was chosen by 12 per cent in November, but only 8 per cent four months later.[219]

The maintenance of social and psychological stability in the bombed
areas was not, of course, automatic. Two factors were of critical importance in explaining how British society coped with the Blitz. The role of
the state and local authorities in managing the consequences of bomb
attack was a major test of Britain's capacity to survive its effects. The civil
defence and emergency services played as full a part as the resources and
planning would allow, and the performance of all services improved
steadily over the period of the Blitz. The formal structures for coping with
bombing came to be reinforced by a substantial fraction of the population that endorsed the public discourse on 'front-line civilians' and wanted
to play a part, however limited, in a democratic war effort. In doing so
they acted both as agents of authority but also as informal community
monitors, reinforcing consensus and broadening the field of participation.
One example may illustrate this process. In the Northumberland town of
North Shields the residents of just two streets established a formal committee to run their fire-fighting party, with regular meetings and a minute
book. The committee was elected by 85 per cent of the householders, who
had to pay 5 shillings (25 pence) each to defray the expenses of ladders,
stirrup pumps and water drums. Four fire parties, composed of a designated leader and five men, were allocated in shifts to watch for six hours
every night. Women were allocated to day duty in parties led by two men.
The few households that refused to participate received house visits to
encourage them to join in. The rotas were observed until 1944 without a
single incendiary threat.[220] This represented an exceptional level of commitment on the part of this and hundreds of other small communities,
which can perhaps best be explained in terms of a strong impulse towards
democratic identification with the war effort. The bombing threat was
uniquely able to mobilize these forms of popular engagement and to limit
the space for non-compliance.

The authorities had to combine popular mobilization with a capacity to deliver what the population needed after bomb attack. The bombed populations became dependent on public authorities as the only potential source of aid in ways quite different from peacetime. Official analyses of the Blitz conducted later in 1941 suggested that the critical thing was to provide concrete, material assistance and to be able to do so rapidly after a raid. This meant the ability to provide solid information at once about where to go to find assistance, food and shelter. The initial problems in Southampton and Coventry were caused by a failure of communication. In Coventry loudspeaker vans were eventually brought in inviting the public to come and ask questions, which officials noted down: 'where they could get a meal'; 'where they could get coal'; 'how they could be evacuated'; 'how soon would the "pictures" be resumed?'; and many more questions on housing repair and food.[221] Instructions to Regional Commissioners after the crisis in Southampton emphasized how important it was that the situation 'should be taken in hand <u>at once</u>. Speed in re-establishing effective machinery of town management is the essence.'[222] In all cases it was observed that the morale of the population depended more 'upon material factors acutely involving their lives, than upon the ebb and flow of the events of the war'.[223] The Regional Commissioners instructed local authorities to focus everything on 'energetic action' immediately after a raid to cope with welfare, food supply, communications, repair and salvage. Of all these factors food (particularly hot meals) and a secure place to sleep were the most important. The Air Ministry report on the Blitz concluded that civilians could stand up to continuous night raids if they could be sure 'that there is a safe refuge <u>somewhere</u> for themselves and their families'.[224] The record in the bombed areas was uneven, and took time to develop, but the capacity to feed, shelter and rehouse the bombed communities was sufficient to prevent social breakdown and to encourage reliance on the state even in the worst-affected inner-city areas.

The second factor was the capacity of ordinary people to find ways of 'normalizing' daily life under bombing by restoring some sense of order or devising psychological mechanisms for coping. The authorities also placed a premium on restoring 'the wheels of Civic Government and normal life' as quickly as possible.[225] Life after bombing was for a fraction of the population far from normal, but there are numerous eyewitness accounts which suggest that establishing new routines or restoring some or all of pre-bombing habits was an essential aid to coping with disaster. 'The better we wrest order out of potential chaos,' wrote Vera Brittain in 1940, 'the more effectively we counter not merely the attacking Nazis but war itself.'[226] Observers were sometimes surprised to find life continuing much as usual despite the bombs. Even Clara Milburn, so shocked by the major raid on Coventry, drove into the city a few weeks later to buy a new car battery and found the car dealer open and working with broken doors and cracked walls.[227] In the shelters and Rest Centres displaced families, where they could, turned a temporary billet into a space they could regard as home. A survey in south-east London in 1941 found that shelterers would pass four or five available shelters in a raid in order to get to the one they had first started to shelter in. Poorly constructed shelters were sometimes boarded up for repair, but users would tear the boarding down and re-enter a familiar space rather than change to a more comfortable shelter. Shelters could be decorated with paint provided by the council, while curtains, lampshades and pictures were common. 'These small points,' ran the report, 'add up to definite aid against fear and help to keep the atmosphere normal.'[228] This also explains the strong desire expressed by the temporarily homeless to return to a damaged house rather than have to live somewhere unfamiliar.

Coping mechanisms took many forms: increased interest in horoscopes and prediction; a return to religious belief (fostered by the exceptional practical assistance supplied by many priests in bombed areas); a show of fatalistic bravado. Accounts confirm that Londoners really did say that they were safe from everything except the bomb with their name on it. In areas with prolonged bombing, individuals could become insensitive to the sufferings of others as a way of protecting their own psychological stability. One London woman working for ARP wrote that 'We have adjusted our minds to the fact that tragedies do happen ... Thank God for the adaptability of the human mind.'[229] This view of death was encouraged by the authorities, who wanted to limit the emotional space available to express grief by carefully controlling the mass burials made necessary by the number and condition of the corpses. Popular hostility to the idea of burial in a common grave, with its stigma of pauperism, was allayed to some extent by militarizing the burial ceremonies.[230] Public expressions of grief or strain were common enough during a raid itself, but shelter marshals had instructions to try to isolate or remove hysterical or emotionally disturbed shelterers, not all of whom, as had been assumed, were women. The habits of British emotional reserve and *sangfroid* were adopted as cultural archetypes which ordinary people should, as far as they were able, try to approximate. Virginia Cowles found her caretaker and his wife eating supper calmly in their kitchen with the noise of bombs falling in the distance and the windows rattling. 'I asked them if they weren't afraid and Mrs K. said: "Oh, no. If we were, what good would it do us?"' Cowles decided that if they could take it, she could too, and went to bed 'hoping that if death came it would be instantaneous'.[231] Though reality might often be very different, the repetition of images of imperturbability helped to reinforce and validate imperturbable behaviour.

After the Blitz declined in intensity in June 1941, a number of surveys were conducted to try to understand why British society had not broken down under the bombs. This was a matter of judgement, and for the historian too any attempt to suggest what might have led to social breakdown even in one city is an exercise in speculation. In the end, despite a level of casualty higher than it might have been with better shelters and better shelter discipline, the Blitz resulted in the deaths of only 0.1 per cent of the population and serious injury to a further 0.15 per cent. Most of the damaged houses were fit enough for habitation after a few weeks or months. Food supplies were effectively maintained and food stocks increased. Air Intelligence calculated that if the German Air Force had more than doubled its effort it might have pushed the population 'to breaking point', but there was no supporting evidence to underpin the claim. The surveys carried out by government scientists concluded that a city like Birmingham might require four times the weight of bombs to overwhelm the civil defences; their final judgement in April 1942 suggested that to achieve real results the offensive should have been at least five times greater in scale. Even here no attempt was made to define properly what it meant to 'knock out' a city or to demoralize a population to the point of social collapse.[232]

TAKING IT AGAIN: BOMBING 1941-5

In December 1940 Sir George Gater, Permanent Secretary at the Ministry of Home Security, chaired a committee meeting on 'intensive air attacks' which concluded unanimously that the type of attack experienced in the Blitz 'was very much what had been originally anticipated'.[233] This was far from the truth. The authorities had anticipated daytime raids and had made almost no provision for dormitory shelters; raids were expected to be of brief duration rather than lasting for six to eight hours; the high proportion of incendiaries had not been prepared for;

a great deal of redundant effort had gone into anticipating gas attack with a variety of toxic elements. Over the course of the four wartime years following the Blitz most of these deficiencies were rectified. Civil defence was much better placed to cope with a heavy bombing offensive in 1944 than it had been in 1940.

There was no certainty in the summer of 1941 that the temporary pause brought about by the German invasion of the Soviet Union would not end in a matter of months, after which the German Air Force could renew the offensive on Britain with even greater intensity. 'We must prepare for worse attacks than we have yet known,' announced a report from the Ministry of Home Security in August 1941, and the same month a poll found that three-quarters of respondents expected renewed heavy raiding, though the sudden period of relief was welcome enough. Mass Observation found that within weeks Londoners seemed to forget the daily routine of siren and shelter and luxuriate in 'momentary peace'.[234] The sudden cessation of heavy raiding was reflected in a dramatic fall in monthly casualty rates, which was sustained into 1942 and 1943 (Table 3.1). The main weight of the limited German attacks was borne by the coastal towns of the south and east. Sunderland on the east coast had been little bombed during the Blitz, but suffered 8 small raids in 1942 and 1943 which killed 191 people and demolished over 500 houses.[235]

Yet in the absence of any firm evidence that the bombing offensive would not be renewed at some point in the future, civil defence and emergency services were continually upgraded and professionalized and shelter and welfare amenities expanded. By the autumn of 1941 there were approximately a quarter of a million hospital beds immediately available for bomb casualties and 1,000 decontamination centres for gas cleansing either built or under construction.[236] Civil defence personnel and the emergency services were all finally issued with helmets, uniforms and standard equipment to make them into an identifiable service. The peak strength of the civil defence forces was reached in December 1943 at 1.86 million. Shortages of male personnel as a result of military conscription forced civil defence to rationalize its use of manpower and to recruit more women, whose service was made compulsory in April 1942. By 1943 there were fewer full-time civil defence workers, but 33,000 more part-timers, most of them female.[237] In London there was an impressive expansion of facilities: in 1941 there had been 540 ambulances, in late 1942 there were 1,344; instead of 180 medical centres, there were 451; the number of rescue squads almost trebled, from 350 to 1,367.[238] Only in 1944 did numbers begin to decline.

Table 3.1: Monthly Casualties from Bombing, August 1940–December 1941

Month	Killed					Seriously Injured			
	M	F	C	U	Total	M	F	C	Total
Aug 1940	649	368	126	6	1,149	871	531	128	1,530
Sept 1940	3,023	3,013	920	12	6,968	4,543	4,164	781	9,488
Oct 1940	2,767	2,910	629	7	6,313	3,853	3,433	663	7,949
Nov 1940	2,329	2,066	604	5	5,004	3,244	2,465	538	6,247
Dec 1940	1,813	1,561	580	34	3,988	2,686	1,816	362	4,864
Jan 1941	801	630	216	1	1,648	1,195	663	179	2,037
Feb 1941	448	310	98	3	859	598	354	102	1,054
Mar 1941	2,222	1,683	602	106	4,613	2,743	1,876	404	5,023
Apr 1941	3,048	2,487	744	196	6,475	3,572	2,603	494	6,669
May 1941	2,617	2,095	791	109	5,612	2,904	1,819	416	5,139
June 1941	185	163	62	–	410	232	176	44	452
July 1941	201	194	81	3	479	225	193	73	491
Aug 1941	52	79	31	–	162	77	58	19	154
Sept 1941	109	82	48	–	239	125	97	31	253
Oct 1941	134	93	35	–	262	181	127	45	353
Nov 1941	39	37	13	–	89	78	68	17	163
Dec 1941	17	14	6	–	37	19	27	7	53

M = men; F = women; C = children; U = unidentified
Source: TNA, HO 191/11, MHS, 'Statement of Civilian Casualties in the United Kingdom from the Outbreak of War to 31 May 1945', 31 July 1945.

Despite the low level of enemy activity, Britain retained almost 2 million active civil defence workers for most of the war.

A great effort was made to improve shelter and welfare provision to avoid the mistakes of 1940–41, but the demands of the war economy meant that shelter repair and improvement remained a low priority. Fortunately the decline in raiding turned out to make the programme less urgent. In London, shelter was available for 5.5 million people by the end of 1941. Public shelters accounted for 1 million places, but in December 1941 they housed just 47,000 people, 0.8 per cent of London's population.[239] Surface and trench shelters were overhauled but became no more popular than before; bunks were slowly distributed to local authorities as steel supplies became available. Reconstruction and rehabilitation work was carried out alongside shelter improvement. In the spring of 1942 in Hull there were over 2,000 building workers engaged in completing the repair of houses damaged in the major raids of 1941; at the same time 2,000 shelters were given either steel reinforcement or an extra 'skin' of bricks and reinforced concrete.[240]

Welfare and food supply were also overhauled. By autumn 1941 there were 14,000 Rest Centres countrywide capable of holding 5 per cent of the population, and plans to expand capacity to 8 per cent together with permanent hostels for around 200,000 people. The Ministry of Food took responsibility for the provision of food in all shelters accommodating more than 200 people. Detailed regulations were issued for shelter canteens: they could be open during the evening until 10.30 p.m., serving only hot food that could be held in the hand, to prevent the demand for mass feeding. In a 'poor borough' cheap tea, pies and buns were recommended; in a 'better-off borough' higher-priced coffee might also be served as well as tea, but no buns. Each city had to develop an Emergency Feeding Scheme with cooks and helpers standing by and generous supplies of emergency foodstuffs in special food centres. The city of Leicester, for example, appointed a City Feeding Officer and a Dining Officer supported by the WVS in an emergency. On receipt of the message 'Prepare to feed!' six mobile canteens and emergency feeding centres were to go into operation. A typical feeding centre had a warehouse full of stock – 224 lbs of sugar, 2,900 lbs of biscuits, 200 lbs of tea, 50 cases of pork and beans, 23 cases of beef hash; and so on.[241] Substantial supplies of food were held in reserve across the country until the autumn of 1944, when the Ministry finally asked local authorities to surrender what they had in store so that it could be used to feed refugees in Europe.

For this extensive and expensive structure, there was relatively little to do between the summer of 1941 and the spring of 1944. The most significant raiding occurred in the spring and early summer of 1942 with the Baedeker raids. The raids on Exeter and Bath resulted in serious fires which took time to overcome. Two attacks on the centre of the West Country seaside resort of Weston-super-Mare at the end of June resulted in 93 deaths and damage to 5,000 houses, but the fires were contained more effectively by the rapid response of neighbouring emergency services, following the lessons of earlier raids in the region. Though packed with holiday-makers, morale in the town was regarded as high; the day after the raids, children could be observed playing in bomb craters on the beach.[242] Norwich suffered more heavily than other towns targeted by Baedeker raiding, with four raids in late April 1942. The first one hit with complete surprise and although there was an alert, many people did not shelter and 158 were killed. In the second raid there were 67 deaths, none in the third, and on the final night only one bomb actually hit the city. The city ARP Controller concluded that the Report Centre worked efficiently, largely thanks to a major civil defence exercise – Exercise 'Scorch' – carried out some time before. Mutual Aid delivered 81 rescue parties from the eastern region, together with 24 ambulances and 45 first-aid parties, and within days 2,000 building workers were giving first aid to residential housing. The volunteer Fire Guard was judged to have performed poorly under combat conditions, while large numbers trekked from the city each night.[243] But when one of the psychiatrists monitoring Hull visited Norwich shortly after the raids, he once again found little evidence of serious psychiatric disorder beyond the category of 'mildly upset'. A survey of four of the Baedeker-targeted cities (Norwich, Exeter, Canterbury and York) showed that in all but York, where bombing was less concentrated, there were initially high levels of anxiety, substantial absenteeism and evacuation. Exeter lost the equivalent of 3.1 citywide working days, Canterbury and Norwich 2.2 and York 0.6. Nevertheless workers soon returned to work as the raids died away. Two weeks after the raids only 4 per cent of Norwich workers were still absent, 1 per cent in York (a level considerably lower than the usual level of absenteeism), 10 per cent in Canterbury and 10 per cent in Exeter.[244] Trekking and evacuation levels declined steeply after the first two weeks as the threat evaporated. Popular behaviour did not differ greatly from the experience of the Blitz.

For the rest of the country and for most of 1942 and 1943 the few raids had only a nuisance value. Yet the system was never able to relax from fear that the Germans might choose to repeat a heavy attack. The RAF was asked by London County Council in autumn 1942 whether it was possible or likely that the German Air Force would retaliate with the kind of heavy area attack (known at the time as 'Crash Raids') inflicted by Bomber Command. The Air Ministry replied that it was both possible and likely, if there were enough German aircraft. The Crash Raid differed from previous attacks because of the sheer weight of bombs dropped, the high proportion of incendiaries, and the short duration and concentration of the raid. Fear of German retaliation forced the civil defence authorities to plan on the basis of what the RAF was doing nightly to German cities. The conclusion they drew was that bombing on this scale broke down centralized control of a city area and fractured communications; British cities now organized the decentralization of incident control to smaller sectors and created mobile emergency columns to move from area to area, almost the exact tactic adopted by German civil defence.[245] In summer 1943, following the 'Dambuster' raid on the German dams, there were warnings about a possible German campaign against the British water supply. After the Hamburg firestorm in July 1943, authorities were put on high alert to expect a possible 'overwhelming' raid.[246] All these fears proved entirely at odds with reality. When German raiding began again in 1944, it was a shadow of the threat it had once posed.

The talk of Crash Raids and overwhelming bombing had the one advantage that it kept the entire civil defence structure in a state of permanent alert through long periods of inactivity and dull routine. The civil defence forces found themselves in a country still at war but with most of their battles behind them. This placed a growing strain on the permanent personnel and on the millions of volunteers. One local authority asked to reorganize the Fire Guard scheme in 1943 complained that after four years of war 'the general public has grown apathetic to further re-organisations'.[247] The Ministry of Home Security recommended refresher courses at Home Office schools for senior ARP workers and courses were still being run late in 1944. In early 1944 it was decided to distribute live mustard gas to local authorities to try to make decontamination training more challenging. (Gas Identification Officers were instructed to keep the small grey cylinders of gas in a cool, dry place until they needed it for a class; they were to demonstrate it cautiously, standing upwind, holding the cylinder close to the ground and taking care not to shake it.)[248] Civil defence workers tried to overcome the inactivity by promoting a sense of corporate identity beyond the shared responsibilities and duties. They organized newspapers and journals, produced artworks for civil defence exhibitions, established choirs and drama societies and ran sports clubs. Tynemouth civil defence performed Handel's *Messiah* at Christmas 1943 and arranged concerts for the Stalingrad fund.[249] In Belfast, wardens' posts competed for the Hayes Cup, an annual competition on all aspects of a warden's duties. James Doherty, whose post won the trophy, recalled that quizzes and sports matches helped to fill the time 'during the long, dreary war years'.[250] This shared sense of identity was stimulated by the establishment of a fully uniformed service and regular parades or paramilitary training. Even some pacifist groups engaged on civil defence work compromised their hostility to militarism by adopting a distinctive uniform, with combat jackets, berets and shoulder flashes.

The most serious threat faced in the last years of the war came from the bombs and missiles directed chiefly at south-east England between January 1944 and March 1945. The first attacks of Operation Steinbock (the 'Baby Blitz' in spring 1944) caught the population and the authorities by surprise. There were 1,300 deaths from raids on London and a number of port cities, most of them in the first few weeks before a fresh wave of evacuation and greater care with sheltering once again reduced the level of human damage. By this stage of the war there was shelter provision for over 28 million people nationwide and 6.8 million bunks in public dormitories, but with the first heavy raids Londoners again clamoured to be able to use the Underground system. At the Oval police lost control of the crowd and 200 people broke into the station. The Regional Commissioner and London Transport agreed to reopen the system on 23 February and by early March 150,000 were sheltering each evening, 63,000 sleeping all night. Work had begun on a number of deep shelters in 1941, but although many had been completed they were kept in reserve for military purposes and were not yet open to the public. Despite public demands, the Cabinet decided on 29 February to keep them closed.[251] Health officials found the remaining shelters for the most part well lit, clean and catering drinks and food.[252] The civil defence organization had its first serious test for two years and coped effectively enough against a modest bombing effort. German aircraft scattered their loads widely and started a large number of small fires, but volunteer Fire Guards succeeded in extinguishing an estimated 75 per cent of them. 'Bombs dropped haphazard,' ran London civil defence instructions, 'though unpleasant, can be dealt with.'[253]

The impact of the Second Blitz on the public was limited after a first initial shock. Published diaries from the period show little interest or anxiety over the raids, but a constant concern about when and where the second front in northern Europe would open.[254] The same could not be said of the missile attacks which began in June 1944 and continued until almost the end of the war. The first warnings about a possible German secret weapon had been confirmed in April 1943 and a committee established under Churchill's son-in-law, Duncan Sandys, to estimate the nature and seriousness of the threat. Intelligence sources confirmed that there were two possible weapons, a flying bomb and a long-range rocket. Coordination for all forms of defence against the new weapons was made the responsibility of the Home Defence Executive, the military equivalent of the civil defence apparatus. Scientific opinion was divided over the possibility of effective rocket technology. Some forecasts suggested a rocket of 10 tons, capable of killing 100,000 in the first month and turning London into a wasteland in six.[255] By early 1944 intelligence estimates began to scale down the threat and a sceptical Churchill admonished his Cabinet colleagues for becoming 'slaves to our fears'. It was judged that civil defence could deal with any fresh emergency, whatever the scale of the new aerial assault, and the judgement proved sound.[256] Four flying bombs (or 'doodle-bugs' as the RAF christened them) first fell on the night of 12–13 June, one of them in London at Bethnal Green, killing six people. On 15–16 June a further 40 fell in the London area and the attack continued at a high rate for a further few weeks until anti-aircraft fire, fighter interception and the Allied advance on the firing sites reduced the threat to a fraction.[257]

Unlike the Second Blitz, the flying bombs provoked a flurry of activity in the capital. Popular discussion of the new weapons sounded, according to the writer George Stonier, like 'a high-pitched buzz'. Edward Stebbing found the talk endless and the fear greater: 'I must admit that these things have put my nerves on edge more than ordinary raids. I suppose the novelty of them, the devilish ingenuity, has something to do with it.'[258] The arrival of the new menace coincided with the successful Allied landings in France, dampening morale during what should have been a period of growing public confidence. One of the first official reports suggested that popular opinion in London had moved from bewilderment to consternation as the random nature of the threat became clear. 'The incongruous effect,' continued the report, 'was a greater disturbance of morale by a form of attack that caused fewer casualties.'[259] Local firms in London reported rising absenteeism and evidence of fatigue, which it was claimed 'undermined the tonic effect of D Day'. In one company in Battersea, an area in the path of the new weapon, morale was thought to be 'at the lowest in the history of this war', with 50 per cent decline in production.[260] Opinion polls found that exactly half of respondents thought the new bombs harder to bear than the Blitz. 'It's not like the old Blitz,' complained one Londoner. 'People are just getting down and disheartened.'[261]

Evacuation, which had fallen to a countrywide total of 343,000 by March 1944, was resumed again in July with the transfer of 307,600 under formal schemes, and more limited assistance for a further 552,000 women and children voluntary evacuees.[262] The civil defences called on resources from other parts of the country. An extra 7,000 wardens were sent along with thousands of spare Anderson and Morrison shelters. Special 'flying squads' were recruited to be sent rapidly from one incident to the next.[263] Yet in the end the emergency services found the flying-bomb attacks easier to cope with than a conventional raid because they were isolated, easy to spot at once and did little damage below ground level. 'An almost clock-work precision has been reached,' ran a Home Security report on the response to the flying-bomb campaign.[264] Many incidents were cleared up in an hour; fires were infrequent except with a lucky hit. Casualties were nevertheless high because attacks came by day and by night, with only the briefest warning. Estimates showed an average of around 20 dead and injured for each flying bomb that landed in an urban area, higher than the average of 16 for a landmine or 14 for a ton of regular bombs.[265] The worst injuries were caused by flying glass as windows repaired after the Blitz were shattered once more. Research showed that sheltering levels were again low among people who only had access to public shelters, overwhelmingly among the poorer neighbourhoods. Tube shelters were hastily refilled, reaching a peak of 81,240 at the end of July, and three of the reserved deep shelters were finally handed over. During June, July and August 5,482 were killed and 15,900 injured, the highest figures since May 1941.[266] The blast effect of the bombs resulted in extensive housing damage once again, but out of more than 1 million homes hit but habitable, only 27,000 still needed 'first-aid' repairs by September.

The rocket was an altogether more formidable weapon but its uneven range, poor technical performance and random targeting meant that like the flying bomb, civil defence services could cope with its consequences more effectively than had been expected. The precise nature of the weapon remained uncertain until fresh intelligence arrived shortly before the first two rockets hit the outskirts of London at Chiswick and Epping on 8 September 1944. Because of that uncertainty, Morrison had persuaded the Cabinet in late July to set up a Rocket Consequences Committee to organize emergency measures to cope with the imagined scale of the threat. Fresh evacuation was planned, and the transfer of 120,000 men, including soldiers, to help to restore battered services and utilities. But by the middle of August a report from Air Intelligence finally indicated correctly a small rocket with a 1-ton warhead. The emergency was scaled down and finally abandoned on 1 September.

The rockets proved to be far less devastating than the science-fiction fears had supposed. Only 15 struck in September and 25 the following month. Rockets caused an exceptional amount of physical damage because of the velocity of impact, but with no more than two to six incidents a day during the autumn months, civil defence found it could cope as efficiently with rockets as it had with flying bombs. The public reacted to the rocket threat with less anxiety, partly because simply going to the shelter was no safeguard, partly because the number of incidents was generally small. Mass Observation found a widespread fatalism: 'If it's going to hit you, you'll probably be dead, and there's nothing you can do about it.'[267] Incidents brought large numbers of sightseers each day, curious rather than fearful. An opinion poll showed that as many as 61 per cent claimed not to be much affected by the rockets, while the numbers using the public shelters as a result of rocket attack were recorded as zero.[268] Numbers crowded into the Underground shelters up to August, but during the first two months of rocket attacks the shelter population fell to around 18,000 a night. Evacuation was sharply reversed once again as families judged the rocket a lesser threat and the risks manageable. Between October and December 734,000 evacuees returned to the capital. By March 1945 there were just 454,200 still billeted away from home.[269] Missile attacks continued at a higher level in January and February 1945, a bizarre toll extracted from a civilian population whose front-line role had been in abeyance for years and which waited with mounting impatience for an end to the war in Europe. Altogether 2,618 died from rocket attacks and 5,661 were injured, a rate of 5 fatalities for each missile. The last rocket fell on 27 March, the last flying bomb two days later. The last bombing raid hit Hull on 17 March, damaging 64 houses. Total wartime casualties from all forms of bombing were 60,595 killed and 86,182 seriously injured.[270]

The threat of the new weapons slowed down the rate at which the whole civil defence system was to be wound down. Local authorities were told after the first flying-bomb attacks that nowhere could be considered immune and were instructed to keep shelters in good condition, well lit and locked, to avoid widespread vandalism. The reduction in personnel was finally ordered in August and September once it was realized that the threat from secret weapons could be contained. At the same time blackout restrictions were relaxed to a state known as 'dim out', with reduced lighting but not total darkness. People reacted to the sudden return of illumination very cautiously after five years of habitual observation. 'My first impression,' wrote one Mass Observer, after leaving the window lit, 'was that the room seemed naked, uncomfortable, incomplete.' Londoners were found in general to err on the side of continued caution and few lit windows were visible until the end of the war.[271] In practice many authorities outside the threatened districts had already begun to slim down the civil defence organization and to prepare for the massive task of dismantling the physical apparatus of protection and welfare. Some of the dismantling was done illegally by the community. It was reported in Newcastle in July 1944 that gangs of youths were stealing doors and bunks from shelters and selling them for firewood. In London so-called 'marauders' stole doors, pipes, taps and fencing, while prostitutes openly used shelters as business premises. Householders were breaking up metal Anderson shelters and bunks for other uses or turning the garden shelters into workshops and coalhouses. Authorities were still trying to demolish surface shelters, collect Andersons and Morrison tables and sell off civil defence vehicles well into 1946 and 1947.[272] In one case a candidate in the July 1945 General Election was given permission to use a number of surface shelters as Committee Rooms for electioneering as long as all parties were given the same opportunity and he paid rent for the privilege.[273] In London sheltering in the Underground declined steadily during the rocket campaign. By January 1945 it was down to 16,000, by April around 10,000. A notice to quit was served on 4 May. On 6 May there were still 334 intrepid sleepers. On 7 May, when Germany surrendered unconditionally, there were none.[274]

The Ministry of Home Security, created for the emergency in 1939, was peremptorily closed down on 30 May 1945 and its powers transferred back to the Home Office. The five years in which it had taken the lead in preparing British society for total war on the home front and conducting its civilian offensive had represented an exceptional intervention by the state in the daily lives of Britain's urban inhabitants. This had been achieved with evident areas of friction, social tension and occasional delinquency. The state provided a relatively sound organization but, in the beginning, poor facilities and limited material resources contributed to a high level of civilian casualties and community disruption. Fortunately for Britain's war economy there was only a limited and temporary disruption of output. Over the course of the war the civil defence system became a large, expensively equipped and uniformed service with a higher operational capacity and potential effectiveness than it had enjoyed during the major bombing offensive.

Unlike the German home front, British society was not faced with an escalating and devastating offensive over five years of war, though the persistent threat of attack, including the final flourish with missiles instead of bombs, forced Britain to divert very substantial resources to keeping the home-front forces in being – resources that might well have been diverted to other more productive wartime purposes. Probably only in two months of the war, in September 1940 and May 1941, did the scale of attack and level of casualty suggest the possibility of a serious social or political crisis, but it would be wrong to argue that in either case the government was likely to compromise on the war effort. What is clear from the experience of bombing is the difficulty, later found in trying to evaluate 'morale' in defeated Germany and Japan, in separating out the effects of bombing from the many other sources of public concern. Bombing itself affects only very particular areas in clearly defined time. The scientist Patrick Blackett pointed out in his account of morale written in August 1941 the simple fact that no air force 'will ever be large enough to bomb all the people all the time'.[275]

4

The Untold Chapter: The Bombing
of Soviet Cities

In late September 1941 the British Under-Secretary of State for Air, Harold Balfour, found himself in Moscow attached to a mission headed by Lord Beaverbrook and the American diplomat Averell Harriman to discuss aid for the Soviet Union. Having experienced nine months of the Blitz on London, Balfour suddenly found himself again in the firing line from German bombers. He thought the blackout a model of its kind, 'not a glimmer anywhere', with cars dangerously invisible on the Moscow streets. The city was encircled by a thick apron of barrage balloons. On 2 October, as agreement was finally being signed on schedules of supplies for the Soviet war effort, the air-raid alarm went. Beaverbrook and Harriman were ushered down into the Moscow metro, where they dined and played cards to pass the time. Balfour instead disobeyed Soviet requests to shelter and went to the roof of the British Embassy, from which he was afforded a remarkable view of the heaviest anti-aircraft barrage he had ever witnessed. He reflected that for a country desperate for material aid from the West, their use of anti-aircraft ammunition was prodigal, but nonetheless apparently effective. Despite almost daily raids he saw comparatively little air-raid damage.[1]

The journalist Alexander Werth, who was in Moscow during the heaviest raids in July and early August 1941, had wondered whether Muscovites could stand a Blitz as steadfastly as Londoners had done. He found Muscovites grim and tired after the experience of long hours of compulsory fire-watching in a city where failure to extinguish incendiaries could end with execution. He witnessed one of the largest raids from a trench shelter near the British Embassy, though no bombs hit the city centre that night. Surrounded by the loud clatter of shrapnel, Werth gazed at a sky 'filled with the lights of exploding shells, and tracer bullets, and all kinds of rockets'.[2] Other visitors to Moscow that autumn found conditions there very different from war-damaged London. Sir Walter Citrine, head of the British Trade Union Congress, arrived shortly

before the major evacuation of the city in October 1941 and was told
by other non-Russians that German aircraft seldom got through to the
centre of the city. Citrine found the blackout 'impenetrable', the shelters
comfortable (but reserved for women and children), and the population
unruffled; 'most British cities,' he concluded, 'have suffered far more
from the depredations by raiding aircraft than has Moscow.'[3] The German campaign against Moscow was, in truth, a shadow of the bombing
of England in 1940. The first and heaviest raid, on the night of 21 July
1941, involved only 195 aircraft, of which 127 reached the target, a
fraction of the number that had pounded London in the autumn of
1940. Over the following month there were 19 raids, most with only a
few aircraft; this resulted in the destruction of a handful of factories and
residential buildings and the death of 569 Muscovites.[4] By December
the German Air Force made only small nuisance raids, killing that
month 67 people and damaging a small number of buildings. After
April 1942 the raids on the capital petered out.[5]

    After a year of continuous long-range bombing of British cities, the
German Air Force returned to a predominantly tactical role. The Soviet
Union had prepared extensively for a repeat of the Blitz on Soviet
soil, which explains the thunderous roar of the guns heard by Harold
Balfour and the pyrotechnic performance watched by Alexander Werth.
There was nevertheless persistent, if small-scale, German bombing against
more distant targets beyond the front line over the course of the four
years of the German-Soviet war. This resulted not in the 500,000 dead
from bombing later claimed in Soviet publications, but in a little over
51,000 deaths and serious injury to 136,000 others. Buildings, industry
and communications were attacked, but unsystematically and with
limited effect. The story of this confrontation between Soviet air and
civil defences and the German Air Force remains one of the least-explored
areas of Europe's bombing war.

'A PROPER WAR': AIR POWER
ON THE EASTERN FRONT

Before the onset of the German invasion of the Soviet Union, the air
force chief of staff, Hans Jeschonnek, was heard to say 'At last a proper
war'.[6] After months of indecisive strategic operations against Britain, the
German Air Force returned to the role for which it had been principally
prepared, supporting a combined arms offensive against the enemy's

armed forces. The directive for Operation Barbarossa, published on 18 December 1940, required the German Air Force to focus all its efforts 'against the enemy air force and direct support for the army'. Attacks on the enemy arms industry were reserved for the unlikely point when mobile warfare ended and the industries of the Ural region came within range.[7]

The deliberate rejection of long-range bombing against industrial targets reflected Hitler's own scepticism about the effect of strategic attacks and overweening confidence in the ability of the German armed forces to knock out the Soviet Union in a brief summer campaign, in which case Soviet industry would fall into German hands in a few weeks. There were also questions of geography. The air campaign against the Soviet Union was entirely different from the one being waged against British ports and cities. Britain was a small, compact island with many key targets no more than a short flight away. The Soviet Union was the world's largest nation, with much of its modern industry hundreds or thousands of miles away from the closest German airbases. Göring told his first post-war interrogators that even for the Russian campaign he had 'always believed in strategic use of air power' but the problem was the lack of 'concentrated targets'.[8] The vast campaign, along a front of more than 1,000 miles, also spread German air resources thinly. The invasion of the Soviet Union was undertaken with 200 fewer bomber aircraft than the invasion of France in 1940, thanks largely to the long attrition war against Britain in the first half of 1941. High losses in the first three months of the campaign – a total of 1,499 aircraft – spread German air forces more thinly still and ruled out any large-scale independent bombing campaign.[9]

The Soviet Air Force, like the German, concentrated on close support for the front-line armies with short-range bombing attacks aimed at tactical targets in the rear of the enemy army. This was an outcome with both military and political causes. In the early 1930s the Soviet air forces had developed major bombing capability and encouraged designers to develop multi-engine bombers. By 1935 almost two-thirds of the combat air force was composed of bombers. During the Spanish Civil War, Soviet close-support aviation demonstrated its utility and encouraged the air force to focus increasingly on battlefront aircraft and medium/light bombers for attacks on rear areas close to the front. The change in emphasis was underscored by the effects of the Soviet purges in 1937 when senior airmen close to the ill-fated Marshal Tukhachevsky were arrested and executed. Air force commanders had broadly favoured

large bombers and independent operations, but practical experience
and political intervention pushed them towards the German ideal of
operational air warfare against enemy armed forces. Independent
bombing came to be regarded as a bourgeois deviation that 'overrates
equipment and underrates man'.[10] One of the victims of the Terror was
the celebrated aircraft designer Andrei Tupolev, who was arrested in
October 1937 implausibly accused of handing over blueprints to the
Germans to help them design the Me110 heavy fighter. One of the pioneers of heavy-bomber design, he was confined to a prison complex on
Radio Street, Moscow, where he continued to design aircraft with a
team of imprisoned engineers.[11] The key contributions of his group of
150 prisoners were the medium bombers Pe-2 and Tu-2, which performed a significant battlefront role during the war.

The Red Air Force (VVS) in 1940 created a separate Long-Range
Aviation section (DBA), but the bombers were, like the German and
British, relatively short-range twin-engine aircraft, the DB-3 and TB-3,
intended principally for battlefield support. In May 1941, shortly before
the German invasion, the bomber and transport aircraft were reorganized in a Long-Range Aviation (ADD) force, but this, too, was designed
chiefly for attacks on the enemy armed forces and supply chain and
was long-range only by comparison with the short-range fighter and
fighter-bomber units. The long-range force had 1,332 bombers in June
1941 out of a total of 8,465 VVS aircraft. A separate air organization
was activated in 1932 for the defence of Soviet cities, composed of
fighter aircraft, anti-aircraft guns, searchlights and the air-warning system. Known as *protivovozdushnaia oborona strany* (PVO), the units
were organized in thirteen PVO zones corresponding to local military
districts. Although PVO units cooperated with the combat air force,
they retained a separate organization and status throughout the war.[12]

On the eve of the war PVO fighter forces totalled an estimated 1,500;
most were obsolete models, but by the summer of 1941 a new generation of fast monoplane fighters, the MiG-3, Yak-1 and LaGG-3, were
beginning to reach the fighter defence squadrons.[13] The PVO personnel
numbered 182,000, many of them assigned to the 58 anti-aircraft artillery regiments and 120 anti-aircraft units. Around the major cities an
outer circle of anti-aircraft artillery and searchlights was set up, and an
inner zone of machine guns and lighter anti-aircraft fire. Throughout
the Soviet Union there were 3,659 heavy guns (including the powerful
85mm), 330 light guns and 650 anti-aircraft machine guns, supported
by 1,597 searchlights. PVO defence was concentrated on the urban

areas closest to the German threat; more distant urban targets were less well protected. By summer 1941 the zones facing the Axis attack had between 86 and 100 per cent of the protection assigned to them; Moscow had 89 per cent, but more distant Kharkov only 15 per cent.[14] The whole organization was supported by the Air Observation Warnings and Communication (VNOS), which gave advance notice of approaching enemy aircraft. Located some 10–12 kilometres apart, the observer posts stretched along the whole western frontier from the White Sea to the Black Sea. The first line of observers was supported by a second line further east that was to be manned on mobilization. Although radar was in the process of introduction in 1941, the observer system relied extensively on visual observation, sound detectors and telephone reporting.[15]

In the first weeks of Operation Barbarossa, which was launched on 22 June 1941 by German, Hungarian, Finnish, Romanian and Slovakian forces across an entire front from the far Arctic north to the Black Sea in the south, both sides used their aircraft almost entirely for tactical support of the attacking and defending armies. Heavy raids were mounted against cities in the path of the approaching Axis armies, particularly the Belorussian capital of Minsk, but the main targets were airbases, railway hubs and military installations. The Soviet authorities counted 627 daylight and 212 night-time attacks. As in Poland in 1939, the damage to residential and non-military targets was extensive but not in this case deliberate. The 21 raids on Minsk left much of the wooden area of the city burnt out; the 15 raids on Smolensk inflicted heavy damage on the town and the rail network; 15 raids on Kiev wrecked areas of the city. Provisional estimates suggested 1,715 dead, 4,864 injured.[16]

There were many opportunities to inflict serious damage on the Soviet war effort during the opening weeks when the Soviet government authorized a frantic dispersal of threatened industrial production to areas remote from the German attack. A Committee of Evacuation was set up on 24 June, two days after the Axis assault began. Within weeks the first factories had been dismantled and were being transported by lorry or rail further east, including important elements of the aircraft industry. In the six months from July to December, 2,593 enterprises were moved, along with 25 million workers and their families. The industrial workforce in the Ural region increased by 36 per cent, that in western Siberia by one-quarter.[17] The moves were made under the most difficult of circumstances, and sustained bombing by German aircraft might well have disrupted them further. Although Soviet aircraft production was dented by the evacuation, nonetheless 5,173 modern fighter aircraft were produced between July and December against a German output of just 1,619. The following year 9,918 Soviet fighters were produced, all of them the latest high-performance models, against 4,542 German.[18]

The first long-range bombing attacks were carried out not by German aircraft, but by the hard-pressed Soviet Air Force against the German capital, Berlin. The motive seems to have been largely political, since the small scale of the raids and modest bombloads were unlikely to achieve more than a pinprick effect. The first bombers carried German translations of Stalin's speech of 3 July 1941 in which he summoned his countrymen to fight a war to the death against the invader. The first attack came on the night of 7 August when 15 DB-3 bombers belonging to the Soviet Baltic Fleet flew from the Baltic Sea base at Kagul on the island of Ösel. Only five reached the centre of Berlin where they dropped leaflet packs and 30 bombs. There were seven more raids by early September, but two failed to reach Berlin at all and the damage was insignificant.[19] Two heavier RAF raids were made during the same period, the only time the two allies cooperated on bombing missions. The small number of Soviet aircraft and the tactic of flying high to avoid detection meant that on the night of the first raid the sirens sounded only 23 minutes after the bombs had dropped. The following day, the German papers referred only to 'enemy planes', rather than advertise the Soviet Air Force's modest achievement.[20]

Small attacks were also made on targets in German-occupied Poland and East Prussia, but the demands of the fighting front limited further raids on rear areas. Only 549 sorties were made against more distant targets during the war, including raids on the oil-producing region at Ploeşti in Romania (attacked between 22 and 26 June and again by six bombers on 14 July) and the small raids on Bulgarian ports.[21] German long-range bombing attacks were confined chiefly to Moscow, partly, according to Hitler's directive, in revenge for the attacks on Helsinki and Bucharest – a repeat of the decision a year before to attack London in retaliation for the first RAF raids on Berlin.[22] No doubt Hitler, like Stalin, wanted to make a political gesture in bombing the enemy capital, but he was also bent on its complete destruction once that became possible. Moscow together with the second Soviet city, Leningrad, was to be erased as an urban centre, and although the German Air Force certainly lacked the means to achieve that in the late summer of 1941, the bombing could be interpreted as an opening salvo. Although most of the objectives had a military-economic importance, the Kremlin was also targeted as the centre of Soviet government and hit on occasion by showers of incendiaries. The bombing was limited chiefly by the diversion of bomber forces to help the ground campaign. It also seemed less urgent as confidence grew at Hitler's headquarters that the Soviet capital would be captured easily in the next operational wave of the ground war, 'to deprive the enemy before the coming of winter', as a new directive in mid-August 1941 stated, 'of his governmental, armament and traffic centre around Moscow'.[23] Once that was achieved, he told his head of household, Otto Günsche, in September 1941, he had a powerful air force to deal with any possible Russian revival beyond the Urals. Günsche recalled how confident Hitler appeared: 'Moscow will be attacked and then fall, then we will have won the war.'[24]

The air raids carried out against Moscow contributed very little to the coming ground assault. Between 21 July and 22 August there were 19 raids, among them the few heavy attacks of the campaign. According to Soviet records these resulted in 569 deaths and serious injury to 1,030; 18 enterprises were heavily damaged, 220 suffered some damage, and 153 residential buildings were destroyed.[25] The German aircraft were supposed to be intercepted by the 6th Air Defence Corps of the PVO and a ring of anti-aircraft fire. Around Moscow, in an arc some 75 kilometres from the centre, were 800 guns and 600 searchlights; the commander of the fighter force, Colonel I. D. Klimov, had 420 aircraft under his command, but only eight of the 494 pilots available had been trained for night-flying. Although the anti-aircraft defences of Moscow recorded the use of 29,000 shells on 21–22 July, German records show that only one aircraft was lost in the first attacks.[26] Soviet air units were for the most part less well trained than their German counterparts; the use of radio control for aircraft was still not developed effectively and Soviet air forces lacked a purpose-built radar chain like those in use in Britain and Germany. Some pilots resorted to simply ramming an enemy bomber when they met one. To help detect the approach of enemy bombers, the Soviet PVO used listening apparatus, the SP-2, and later the ST-4. Four large cones, like so many giant ear trumpets, were carried on the back of a lorry, three on one side of a fixed frame, one on the other, with two listeners for each apparatus. The SP-2 was supposed to detect aircraft at 5–6 kilometres distance, the larger ST-4 (with square rather than conical trumpets) at distances up to 12 kilometres. Various means were devised to cut out the noise of the wind, but it is difficult to imagine that much warning could have been given using such equipment. German aircraft were advised to throttle back their engines to reduce even further the prospect of being heard.[27]

The raids on Moscow soon faded away. Out of 75 raids on the capital between July 1941 and April 1942, 59 were carried out with fewer than 10 aircraft, only 9 with more than 50. A total of little more than 1,000 tons was dropped, where London had received 16,000.[28] The last raid on Moscow itself occurred on 5–6 April 1942, killing just 5 people and wounding 10 others.[29] From September 1941 the focus shifted to the bombing of Leningrad by the aircraft attached to Army Group North as it completed the encirclement of the city. In August the VIII Air Corps under General Wolfram von Richthofen had transferred 262 aircraft north to join General Alfred Keller's First Air Fleet in support of the campaign towards Leningrad. Regular attrition caused by poor airfield conditions, high accident rates and the slow progress of repairs meant that seldom more than 50–60 per cent of German aircraft were now serviceable. At first German air forces concentrated on breaking the Soviet line and cutting Leningrad off from essential supplies rather than bombing the city. The air raids when they finally began were an extension of the military siege, rather than an independent operation, and they were combined throughout the winter of 1941–2 with heavy shelling of the surrounded city, which exacted a considerably higher toll of human and material losses than the bombs. Hitler planned to wear Leningrad down by starvation and the constant threat of death, but the small number of aircraft available and the hostile climate meant that the army had the more important role to play. Systematic bombing of the main urban area only began once the city was finally cut off and surrounded on 8 September, but the effect of the raids was blunted by the demands for air support for the ground fighting around Leningrad as Soviet armies struggled to break the German stranglehold. Help for the army left fewer bombers free to fulfil Hitler's new directive on 22 September that Leningrad should be 'erased from the earth' by continuous artillery and air bombardment.[30]

Leningrad itself was divided into four PVO regions. The city was protected by PVO 2nd Air Corps and the regular VII Fighter Aviation Corps. Since the air defence and front-line zones were now the same, the air defence system was subordinated to the Leningrad front to allow more efficient use of resources. The air defence of the city was led by a young air force colonel, Alexander Novikov, whose success earned him rapid promotion to become air force commander-in-chief in April 1942.

Alongside around 800 aircraft on the Leningrad Front, there were 160 anti-aircraft batteries with 600 guns, and 300 large balloons that floated gauntly above the city.[31] German Air Fleet I, assigned to the northern front, began the campaign with an estimated 1,200 aircraft. The bombing was directed as far as possible at vital targets, and for the besieged population the most important object was food. On 8 September a group of German bombers attacked the large wooden Badeyev warehouses, burning them to the ground and creating a three-mile high column of pungent smoke from the burning meat and sugar. It was, recalled one Soviet eyewitness, an 'immense spectacle of stunning beauty'.[32] During September there were a further 23 raids, among them, as in Moscow, some of the heaviest of the war. In November there were 35, in December, as the weather worsened, only eight. In January, February and March 1942 there were no air raids. In April bombing started again with larger numbers of aircraft, but in May there were no attacks and in June only two. The casualties from bombing and shelling were counted together until April 1942, a total of 10,218 killed and injured. Deaths from artillery fire, which was less predictable and more lethal in its effects, were higher than deaths from bombing. In June 1942, 43 were killed as a result of two raids, but 258 were killed by routine shelling.[33]

There was little strategic gain from the bombing, which was too irregular and small-scale to do much serious damage. German bombers nevertheless tried to hit industrial centres, railway lines and hubs, and the port area in order to reduce the capacity of Leningrad, despite the famine, to continue to produce weapons and equipment for the front line. Throughout the period from 22 June 1941, when the invasion began, to the halt before Moscow in December 1941, German bombers also attacked a variety of military-economic targets across the western Soviet Union, principally railways and marshalling yards, often at considerable distance from the front lines. The majority of these raids were *Störangriffe* carried out predominantly in daylight, like the small raids made before the Blitz on Britain, designed to interrupt briefly the flow of traffic or the military support network, and to gather intelligence. Out of 839 raids recorded by the Soviet authorities in the first month of the war, 640 were made with fewer than 12 aircraft.[34] There were later attacks as far away as Stalingrad, hit on 1 November by three Heinkel He111 bombers which destroyed three buildings and part of a timber mill, killing 36 people. More small raids followed on the rail network in and around the city, resulting in the loss of 15 locomotives,

359 carriages and 5 metres of track. Unprepared for attack and with no established civil defence system, 330 were killed and 522 injured. There were other raids on distant targets: Kuibyshev, far to the south-east of Moscow, where much of the government apparatus had been evacuated to apparent safety in October 1941 as German forces converged on Moscow; Kursk (to become famous later in the war as the site of a major German defeat), where three bombers attacked the main railway station with just five bombs; and Novorossiisk on the Black Sea coast, where large numbers of incendiaries were used to try to burn down the supply station of the Black Sea Fleet.[35]

The long-distance raids exposed numerous problems for the anti-air defences in areas which had been regarded as less likely to be under threat. In a raid by one aircraft on Rostov-on-Don on 28 August 1941, no air-raid alarm sounded because of poorly coordinated communications. The local PVO commander, whose failure it was, nevertheless threatened the head of civil defence in Rostov that if a single bomb hit a residential building, 'you will be the one to pay with your life'. In other cities there were no bomb-disposal units, and local soldiers, ordered to try to defuse unexploded bombs with no proper equipment, sensibly refused.[36] In the Yaroslav region, German aircraft attacked the rail network at low altitude either singly or in small groups, almost immune from the local PVO organization which had only six fighters, 20 anti-aircraft guns and half the required manpower to cover the entire area.[37] Although the PVO organization was expanded before the coming of war, 40 per cent of its guns and aircraft defended just three cities, Moscow, Leningrad and the southern oil city of Baku. The whole organization lacked 40 per cent of the required fighters, one-third of the necessary anti-aircraft guns and half the barrage balloons. Its decentralized character also made effective cooperation difficult between regions and on 9 November 1941 the State Defence Committee (set up in July 1941 with Stalin as its head) placed the PVO under a central commander in Moscow, Maj. General M. S. Gromadin. Under the new PVO regime defence facilities slowly expanded; by May 1942 there were 4,576 anti-aircraft guns, by September 1943, 9,134, including a threefold increase in guns to defend the rail network.[38] Even then the anti-aircraft fire was of limited utility without radar-aided gun-laying equipment or proximity fuses. The large number of guns depended on a crude barrage effect that destroyed enemy bombers largely by chance.

Most German attacks were made against rail targets and bridges. Not only did this make military sense in order to hamper the movements of the Red Army, but many of these smaller targets were poorly defended. In many cases Soviet records show that a heavier tonnage was dropped on smaller rail targets than in the urban attacks. Between July and December 1941 there were 8,752 raids on communications; between January and June 1942, 1,304; in the first period 533 locomotives and 7,819 wagons were destroyed, in the second period 428 and 6,693. Since the attacks were generally carried out against stations or marshalling yards, casualties were considerable. In the period from January to June 1942, 3,080 people were killed in railway attacks, 5,675 injured.[39] The German Air Force soon identified the most suitable targets. Air units were encouraged to attack locomotives, either stationary or moving, and to focus on the principal rail hubs, with repair facilities and supply centres. It was discovered that attacking stretches of rail line had little effect, particularly once the ground had become frozen, since bombs failed to penetrate effectively, 'mostly bouncing away, to detonate harmlessly beside the rails'. Snowy conditions in general made air operations difficult, not only because of low serviceability and the difficulty of flying from and landing on snow-covered bases, but because of the poor visibility of targets once they were protected by the natural camouflage of winter.[40]

The futility of attacking railway lines was made evident by the rapid recovery carried out by emergency repair teams, using stocks stored near the critical stretches of track. The normal time required to repair short lengths of track was from two to four hours, though it could take some hours before the emergency team arrived. More serious craters could be bypassed by laying new track around them. The cases where the rail link was severed for longer were sufficiently unusual for them to feature in the reports of the War Communications Office. At the Shuvaevo-Zhukopa station, near the Kalinin front north of Moscow, the network was interrupted for 43 hours; on another stretch in the same area between Goritsa and Zhukopa, the track was only fully restored after 79 hours. The cumulative effect could be more substantial. The lines leading to the Kalinin front were the most heavily attacked between March and June 1942, resulting in a loss of 1,988 hours of traffic over a four-month period. Bridges took on average longer to repair, but were in general functioning again 8 to 36 hours later. The Soviet assessment of the railway campaign concluded that it was more strategically useful to mount more frequent attacks against fewer objectives, rather than less frequent attacks against many, as the German Air Force was doing. The overall conclusion by the summer of 1942 was that despite regular interruptions to stations and marshalling yards, rail traffic 'has never been discontinued entirely'.[41]

The changing strategic focus of Axis forces in the summer of 1942 for the southern assault towards the Volga and the Caucasus ('Operation Blue') was signalled by the sudden increase in air attacks on railway communications across the southern zone as a prelude to the new campaign. In May and June a majority of attacks were directed at the southern Ukraine, the area around Voronezh and the Krasnodar region on the Black Sea coast leading to the Caucasus, 59 per cent of all German sorties. By the time Operation Blue started on 28 June the German Air Force had already inflicted substantial damage on rail centres and killed an estimated 1,400 people, including the two deadliest raids so far, when 415 mostly evacuees were burned to death at Kavkazskaia station and 466 killed at the rail centre at Kochetkova.[42] In July attacks on railways targets more than 100 kilometres from the front line intensified, taking up almost two-thirds of all raids. These included the preliminary raids on Stalingrad and the region around the city as it became clear with German operational successes that the city would soon be an object within the grasp of Army Group South. There were 59 raids on the Stalingrad region, four on the city itself, doing little damage but killing 99 people. By August the German Air Force devoted one-third of all raids on the Eastern Front to the Stalingrad area, 17 per cent to the Caucasus.[43]

The commander of the German Fourth Air Fleet for the campaign against Stalingrad was Wolfram von Richthofen, the officer who had commanded the bombing of Guernica in 1937 and the bombing of Warsaw in 1939 and who had led the ferocious aerial assault on the Crimean city of Sebastopol in June 1942. This month-long campaign saw the progressive destruction of the fortress city by a combination of repeated air strikes and the effects of 2,000 artillery pieces around its perimeter. The 390 bombers and dive-bombers available to von Richthofen pounded the city into ruins, leaving at the end only 11 undamaged buildings. When they did not drop bombs, the aircraft carried scrap metal – old engines, ploughs, rail track – which they dropped on the defenders. Sometimes they dropped leaflets asking *Wie geht es?* ('How's it going?'). Thousands of civilians were evacuated across the Black Sea, attacked by aircraft as they went. Those who chose to stay or were ordered to do so lived a subterranean existence in the hundreds of caves, tunnels and storerooms on the rocky peninsula which gave a natural protection. The local authorities counted only 173 dead after the first days of bombing, though many more died from the powerful artillery barrage. The shelters were filled with stale air, making it difficult to breathe, and were piled high with a jumble of goods and luggage. The Russian journalist Boris Voyetekhov found himself in one of the largest underground caverns, where machinery turned out a stream of grenades, newspapers were typeset and printed, the party officials worked on their reports and artists worked on posters encouraging greater effort.[44] In the underground post office, the postmen wrote 'to be looked for after the war' on letters that could not be delivered to the streets of rubble on the surface. Sebastopol finally fell on 1 July.

Much against his will, von Richthofen was moved from the Sebastopol campaign shortly before its conclusion to set up headquarters for the new operation in which he was to play a leading part.[45] The German Air Force allocated more than half of all aircraft to the Eastern Front, 1,155 in total, for Operation Blue. But the number of serviceable aircraft available to von Richthofen for the drive on the Volga and the Caucasus that developed from mid-July was only around 750, divided between the VIIIth and IVth air corps, the first for the drive across the Don steppe to Stalingrad, the second to support operations further south in the Caucasus.[46] Most of the air force action was in direct support of ground forces and in combat against the Soviet Air Force which proved unable to contest air superiority successfully, although night-bombing attacks against German bases inflicted some effective damage. As Army Group B, under the command of General Friedrich Paulus, pushed its way rapidly across the steppe towards Stalingrad, the way was paved for a bombing assault on the city. This has always been treated in the literature as the most deadly bombing operation not only of the entire Eastern war, but of any day of raiding before Hiroshima.

The situation at Stalingrad, both at the time and since, has encouraged a popular sense of historical extremes, and there is no disguising the mounting drama as German armies, the Sixth Army under Paulus, the Fourth Panzer Army under General Hoth, pushed back the embattled Stalingrad defenders of the Soviet 62nd and 64th Armies into a narrowing zone in front of the city and, by September, back into the city itself. The Soviet Eighth Air Army commanded by General T. Khriukin had only 454 aircraft when the assault started, of which just 172 were fighters. There were too few heavy anti-aircraft guns, since Stalingrad had not been expected to be a major target. The balance of air power lay for the moment with the German Air Force. On 21 August the German army crossed the Don River and pushed on towards the city;

the bank of the Volga was reached on 23 August. On that day von Richthofen was apparently ordered by Hitler's headquarters to bring together as many of his scattered air units as possible to support a major bombing attack on the city. Around 400 Ju88 and He111 bombers were available. There is no record in the War Diary at Supreme Headquarters, where Hitler watched closely the course of the campaign, to indicate that a heavy bombing of the city was ordered that day, but air force records show that the bomber force flew 1,600 sorties against targets in Stalingrad, dropping around 1,000 tons of bombs, though it seems likely that this took place over a six-day period and not all on 23 August. Because of poor anti-aircraft defence, bombers could fly at around 2,000–3,000 metres to drop their bombs. Soviet records show that they came in waves of 70–90 aircraft, sometimes in much smaller formations.[47]

The attacks were not simply directed at destroying the city, which would be of little help in trying to capture it a few days later, but were concentrated on key military, administrative and economic targets, including the large oil-storage depots on the bank of the Volga. German air intelligence had produced detailed maps of Stalingrad, along with other cities, showing the key industrial sites and military installations. These included the vast 'Dzerzhinskii' tractor factory and the Red October metalworks, as well as an oil refinery.[48] From early August the Soviet reports indicate attacks on warehouses, quays and industrial installations. The attacks on 23 August produced extensive damage to the main industrial installations and the communications system. The burning oil produced a vast fog of black smoke that contributed more than anything else to the sense that the raids on that day had substantially destroyed the city, but it was the bombing of the city centre the following day, 24 August, that did the most damage. Destruction of the central water supply system that day robbed the fire service of water at a critical juncture and allowed the fires to take hold, destroying or damaging around 95 per cent of the buildings in the central district.[49] The standard figure cited for the losses of the Soviet population who remained in the city has been put at 40,000, which would indeed make 23 August 1942 the most deadly day of bombing before the atomic attacks.[50]

There can be little doubt that this figure, like the exaggerated death toll at Rotterdam, will not stand up to scrutiny. No one doubts that by mid-September, pounded by a circle of heavy guns and tanks, bombed and dive-bombed regularly to destroy military resistance, the city was heavily destroyed. When Churchill's interpreter, Arthur Birse, was invited to tour Stalingrad later in 1943, he found it an incredible sight: 'A collection of scattered and broken remains . . . The streets, as far as I could distinguish any, were mounds of rubble. The inhabitants lived in dugouts and cellars.'[51] Yet the Soviet records of the damage to Stalingrad from the air (rather than the massive damage inflicted by artillery and tanks) present quite a different picture. The bombing of 23 August was not given particular prominence in the reports produced at the time, which focused instead on the regular raiding that took place over the whole period from 23 to 29 August, resulting in a cumulatively severe level of damage. The death from bombing of 40,000 people would almost certainly have been treated, as it was in Hamburg in July 1943, as a disaster without precedent and could have been produced only by a major firestorm. The report from the local air defence authorities for August simply records 'Starting from mid-August the city experienced non-stop air bombing by large groups of enemy planes.' The assessment of casualties for the six-day period of heavier raiding arrived at a figure of over 1,815 dead and 2,698 severely injured, many of the fatalities inflicted at the Volga River crossings.[52] In September the number of raids fell from 100 to 69, mostly on the city, burning down many of the buildings still standing. Data was recorded as incomplete, which under the circumstances is unsurprising, but the recorded death toll was 1,500 for the whole month, not including those killed by the continuous artillery fire. Death statistics for October were again incomplete, but those recorded numbered 380. Between July and October 1942 the local civil defence authorities counted 3,931 deaths, a figure much more consistent with the scale of the raiding and the tonnage of bombs dropped.[53]

There is little doubt that these figures understated the actual deaths from bombing, given poor communications and the emergency conditions, but no margin of error could turn this figure into 40,000. There are other factors to bring into account in reducing this statistic: Stalingrad was a city of 440,000, many of whom were in fact evacuated (or fled) across the Volga as the German army approached; no pre-atomic bombing succeeded anywhere in killing at least 10 per cent of the population in a single day. The German bomber force was anyway much smaller than the later Allied forces which could indeed obliterate half a city under the right circumstances. There were only 400 aircraft, all of them medium bombers, and the final tally of 1,000 tons represented what the same force had dropped on London in one night without exacting more than 1,000–2,000 deaths. Stalingrad was a modern city, with wide roads, parks, and a great many more stone and concrete buildings than less modern Russian cities. As in other more modern cities it would have been difficult to generate a firestorm sufficient to consume 40,000 people. As it was, the figures of over 1,800 in August and 1,500 in September were the highest death tolls recorded in the Soviet Union from bombing throughout the war. In the end the figure of 40,000, like the '20,000 dead' in Rotterdam, has fitted a popular view of German atrociousness, but not the facts.

After the bombing in August 1942 the capability of von Richthofen's Fourth Air Fleet declined steadily, the victim of persistent attrition from a reviving Red Air Force, and of the deteriorating weather and supply lines. By 20 September there were only 129 fully operational bombers left, some of which were used to attack Soviet oil production at Grozny in a raid on 10 October. At the same time the PVO defence of the region was greatly expanded. By November there were 1,400 Soviet aircraft on the Stalingrad front, with more in reserve, and thanks to reforms introduced by Novikov, following his promotion to air force commander-in-chief in April, the air units were centrally controlled, fitted with radio communication and more tactically adept. When Paulus and his Army Group were finally cut off and encircled at Stalingrad, Göring promised to supply the pocket using all the transport and bomber aircraft that could be spared. The result was the loss not only of 495 transport and bomber aircraft, but also of some of the experienced training officers brought out of Germany to boost the declining pool of regular pilots. One of the aircraft lost was a Heinkel He177, one of a first group of 20 sent to southern Russia for trials. Only seven were fit for service and the group commander was shot down on his first mission.[54] The failure of the supply programme to keep the Sixth Army fighting contributed to the cooling of relations between Hitler and Göring, and marked a turning point in the offensive capabilities of the German Air Force. In his first post-war interrogation, Göring complained, without much justification, about the crisis of the German bomber arm prompted by the events in Russia: 'I built the Luftwaffe as the finest bomber fleet, only to see it wasted at Stalingrad. My beautiful bomber fleet was used up in transporting munitions and supplies . . . I always was against the Russian campaign.'[55]

THE SOVIET 'BLITZ'

The German bombing of the Soviet Union differed in intensity and scale from the bombing of Britain or of Germany. Most bombing was undertaken in support of ground operations. The deliberate bombing of more distant targets was intermittent and, usually, small-scale. It included not only cities and the rail transport system, but could at times hit rural areas as well. German aircrews were encouraged to destroy local villages when they hit an airbase in the belief that they housed many of the local Soviet workers and airmen.[56] The construction of a 'front-line' mentality was unnecessary in areas far in the rear as little or no bombing occurred there; for the population of the western and southern Soviet Union, the front line was real and dangerous and swept over and past them with inexorable momentum and violence. In Leningrad or Sebastopol or Stalingrad bombing was part of the war on the ground going on all around the city. The same was true for Soviet industry. Programmes of dispersal were not the fruit of the bombing threat but a dire necessity in the face of the rapid Axis advance. From this perspective, bombing was one of the least of the wartime concerns confronting the embattled Soviet people.

Nevertheless, the Soviet government had for many years encouraged popular identification with civil defence measures and, from 1932, made civil defence a formal part of the military system. Aviation was one of the key elements of Bolshevik modernity after 1917, both a military necessity but also a tool to advertise the success of the young revolutionary state through pioneering aviation technology, record-making and breaking, and high-profile air exploration. In the 1920s popular organizations designed to promote air-mindedness were created, first Aviakhim (Society of Friends of the Aviation and Chemical Industries) and then in 1927, following a merger between Aviakhim and the Society for Assistance to Defence, a unitary association known as Osoviakhim. The new organization became the vehicle for encouraging not only military-style training of the population, but preparing for civil defence tasks against the prospect of bomb or chemical attack. By 1933 the organization had 13 million members, including 3 million women, and was treated by the regime as an instrument for collective mobilization against any threat to the revolutionary heritage.[57] In 1932 the regime formally founded the Main Directorate of Local Air

Defence (*mestnaia protivovozdushnaia oborona*, or MPVO), which
was organized on paramilitary lines but was under the control of the
People's Commissariat of Internal Affairs (NKVD). The responsibilities
of the new organization covered all aspects of civil defence – training
personnel, distributing gas masks, helping to convert cellars into shelters, and eventually creating a mass movement of 'self-defence groups'
whose purpose was to mobilize a large part of Soviet urban society to
defend its new cities and factories through their own collective efforts.

The MPVO was, despite its extensive organization and size by the
early 1940s, unevenly prepared for the possibility of a bombing war.
Like the active anti-air defences of the PVO, its efforts were concentrated on those zones closest to the possible threat of bombing. Here it
was organized much as the rest of the Soviet system on a decentralization of responsibility first to the level of republic, then region (*oblast*),
district (*raion*) and city. The local MPVO offices were linked to the
national NKVD structure, and local officials were ultimately responsible to the Commissar of the Interior, who for the period from 1938 to
1945 was Stalin's Georgian ally, Lavrentii Beria. The exception was the
MPVO organization for industry and for transport, which was run by
the commissariats responsible until 7 October 1940, when all MPVO
work was centralized under the NKVD.[58] In 1941 before the outbreak
of war there were 2,780 designated civil defence sites, mostly in the
central and western Soviet Union, monitored by 121 cities designated
as MPVO stations. They were run by a local network of full-time staff,
which numbered just 3,838 in 1941, and were supported by around
half a million workers, who combined regular work with their civil
defence role. The main divisions were in Moscow, Leningrad and Baku,
with battalions stationed in Minsk, Zaporozhie, L'vov and Kiev. The
organizers were poorly trained; two-thirds had had no experience or
formal training, just 9 per cent had attended courses of one or two
months' duration. Training exercises were held regularly but attendance
was poor. Most officials relied on two or three hours of practical training a week. Industrial and transport sites also had dedicated firefighting
brigades, 680 in number, but in May 1941 they possessed not a single
fire engine.[59]

Despite the popular emphasis on collective efforts for civil defence,
Osoviakhim was not integrated into the MPVO system. It is unclear
how many of the population had had basic anti-gas, first-aid or air-raid
training by the time war broke out. Self-defence groups existed, but
their mobilization depended on the state of the local MPVO organiza-

tion. Most of the records of MPVO units before the war show a poor level of preparation. In the city of Kursk, for example, it was found at the start of the war that although camouflage of local targets was satisfactory, staff were poorly trained, little effort had gone into planning protection of the population, what basement shelters existed were poorly resourced and insanitary, fire brigades lacked hoses and tenders, emergency units had no equipment for clearing debris, or jacks or cables, and not one MPVO brigade had motor-transport.[60] Across the country, little effort had gone into preparing for the possibility of gas attack. There were just 10,000 old-fashioned army gas masks available for the civilian population and few gas-proof shelters. Decontamination teams lacked essential equipment and chemical laboratories capable of dealing with gas attack existed only in the larger cities, Moscow, Leningrad and Kiev. The few men trained in decontamination work were mobilized into the army on the outbreak of war along with an estimated 35 per cent of the rest of the MPVO workforce.[61] In cities where the sheer distance from the front was thought to confer immunity from raiding, little was done to train and prepare the population for the possibility. In the 'tank' city of Cheliabinsk shelters were only checked for the first time in May 1942 when it was discovered that the authorities had so far issued no instructions on what to do in an air attack even though German aircraft were now very much closer.[62]

The poor level of practical preparation can be explained by the lack of urgency occasioned by the German-Soviet Pact of 23 August 1939, which made the two dictatorships into temporary allies and postponed the prospect of war as long as Britain remained undefeated. The German bombing offensive against Britain was still being conducted just a matter of weeks before the onset of Barbarossa and it must have seemed unlikely that it could suddenly be diverted eastwards at such short notice. The failure can also be explained by the wide number of other urgent defensive tasks on which the regime focused, including military production and frontier fortifications, and by the belief that most of the Soviet Union would be relatively safe from bombing, given the long distances from German bases and the Soviet operational plan in the event of war to mobilize rapidly, push forward and compel the enemy to fight on his own territory. Soviet cities by the early 1940s were still in the throes of adjusting to a massive influx of population and rapid programmes of building, which made the regular organization of civil defence less straightforward because there were fewer established local communities and less sense of civic identity. The effect of the Axis assault on 22 June 1941 was to overturn all these assumptions and to accelerate the preparation of the population for its own defence against bombing. If the German Air Force had undertaken a strategic bombing campaign from the start, Soviet cities and industry would have been at their most vulnerable in the first year of fighting.

On 2 July the government issued a resolution on the 'universal and compulsory anti-air-raid and anti-chemical defence preparation of the population'. The MPVO organization was quickly expanded with new personnel to replace those conscripted, but the Axis campaign soon overran 94 cities designated as MPVO stations, and forced the whole organization to move its activities eastwards, where another 102 cities, including Stalingrad, were added to the list of MPVO stations as the risk of air attack suddenly became real.[63] In the remaining area of the Soviet Union, MPVO numbers expanded rapidly. By 1944 there were 85,000 MPVO troops (including 9,621 army officers) supported by a civilian apparatus of 135,000 people. Additional civil defence groups which numbered 527,000 were formed for specialized work – decontamination, rescue, reconstruction. Urban 'self-defence' units were also established to help fight the consequences of bombing, a total of 2,990,000 women and men. In addition more than half the remaining population, 71 million people, were given rudimentary anti-gas and civil defence training, 40 million in the first year of the war, 15 million in the territories liberated in late 1943 and 1944 when bombing had all but disappeared as a threat. In the liberated areas 75 cities regained their status as MPVO stations.[64]

The Soviet Union introduced a comprehensive programme of civil defence protection only once war was under way. The statistics show a remarkable programme of achievement even allowing for a measure of exaggeration about the number and quality of shelters or the level of training really acquired or the speed of reconstruction. Since the system was never severely tested, except in Leningrad and Stalingrad, its capacity to withstand a sustained aerial campaign cannot easily be judged. The regime nevertheless placed substantial emphasis on the necessity for protecting the population and encouraging popular participation in their own preservation. Expenditure on MPVO work was 182 million roubles in the second half of 1941, 468 million in 1942, 474 million in 1943. Including all civil defence and reconstruction expenditure, the total wartime expenditure for MPVO was 3.22 billion roubles.[65] The money was spent on a variety of essential civil defence resources. During the war 6,699 first-aid centres were set up in which 135,000 people

were treated for air-raid injuries and an estimated 108,000 returned to
work. The fire service expanded rapidly, as it did in other bombed states,
from 680 brigades in summer 1941 to 12,149 in 1945, and from
18,269 firefighters to 170,786. From having no fire engines, the
expanded service eventually fielded 469. Anti-gas preparations, rudimentary in 1941, were extended to all the areas where gassing was
possible. Because of the disruption caused by the loss of the western
territories, gas-mask production could not begin until late 1942. Two
new civilian types, GP-1 and GP-2, were eventually produced in
modest quantities, 10.1 million for a population of over 120 million in
the unoccupied areas, and another 3.6 million for the armed forces. The
number of laboratories for anti-gas work increased threefold during the
war to a peak of 1,194 in 1945; by the end of 1942 there were 295 decontamination squads. As in Britain, fear that German forces would be
tempted to use chemical weapons encouraged the construction of a
large but, as it proved, mainly redundant sector of the civil defence
apparatus.[66]

The main requirement was to provide adequate shelter for the threatened urban areas. This was a problem with many practical difficulties.
Much housing in the Soviet Union was constructed of wood without
cellars or basements that could easily double-up as shelters. Some 70 per
cent of housing in Moscow was wooden. New buildings were supposed
to be constructed with basement protection, but the rule was not uni-
versally applied. In the capital an estimated 400,000 out of a population
of 4 million could be sheltered by the outbreak of war, but most of the
shelter places were in the newly built Moscow metro system where Stalin himself set up his underground headquarters close to the Kremlin.
The metro had been intended for use as a shelter when it was constructed and MPVO personnel set up first-aid posts, water taps and
loudspeakers in the stations when raiding started. People slept on
boards placed over the rails in the tunnels. In the evenings there were
lectures and film shows and concerts.[67] For the population further from
the centre, in low-rise wooden buildings, trench shelters and fox-holes
were built. The national programme for sheltering the population posed
prodigious problems of cost and materials and most provision was
made in cellars and basements, where they existed, or in trenches and
dugouts. Purpose-built shelters (category I) were deep under the ground
and, where necessary, reinforced with concrete; out of an estimated
15 million in need of shelter by 1942, category I supplied just
349,500 places (2.3 per cent). Category II comprised the converted

spaces underneath buildings and accommodated by 1942 some 2.388 million people. Each basement was protected by a wooden door 15 centimetres thick, faced with metal on both sides; they contained emergency lighting, tubs of sand and water, and crude benches or bunks. Additional gas-proof shelters were gradually constructed to provide space for 745,000 by the summer of 1942, and 1.9 million by 1945. For the rest of the population there were either temporary shelters excavated in the ground, or, for 60 per cent of those under threat, no shelter at all.[68]

The lengthiest bombing took place against Moscow and Leningrad, where there had been more pre-war civil defence preparation than elsewhere. When the war broke out the blackout in Moscow was enforced at once; street lighting was operated from a wide number of sources and had to be converted to central control so that it could be doused simultaneously across the city. The blackout was regulated by local self-defence units, the MPVO officials and the police. Cars drove slowly and without headlights; matches could not be struck outdoors or torches used. So anxious were Soviet citizens about not violating the blackout that when an American journalist found himself one night in a dark and windowless basement shelter, the women around him asked him to cover the luminous dial of his watch.[69] Each Moscow district had its own MPVO brigades recruited from municipal workers and local volunteers. At neighbourhood level the self-defence units, wearing red armbands with 'MPVO' stitched on them, were responsible for ensuring that shelters were sanitary and orderly and also played a role in post-raid rescue and welfare.[70] Every multi-storey building had fire-watchers responsible not only for giving the alert when incendiaries were dropped but for tackling any bomb that landed on their roof-space. They were issued with asbestos gloves, long tongs, and boxes of sand, and told to douse the bombs in buckets of water or to throw them into the street. They were not supposed to shelter during a raid. Harold Balfour was told in September 1941 that the efficiency of the system depended on the simple equation that if a fire started the fire-watcher responsible was shot, an outcome less implausible in the context of the Soviet dictatorship than elsewhere.[71] Alexander Werth was introduced to a number of girls from the Communist Youth organization (Komsomol) who did volunteer fire-watching duty. One gave the Party line, 'we couldn't allow even a little house to be destroyed by the Fascists', but the other blushed and stammered about the fear she felt as she had stood her ground on a roof, surrounded by incendiaries and the boom of high-explosive bombs.[72]

Moscow's bombing was disruptive for the first weeks after it began, but considerable effort was made to repair the damage quickly or to board up and conceal what could not be rebuilt at once. From September 1941 onwards the attacks were what the British Air Ministry later smugly described as mere 'harassing raids'.[73] In December there were 20 raids, but eight were merely reconnaissance patrols. The raid on 1 December involved only eight bombs, one on 4 December dropped 23 bombs, while the next raid on 6 December amounted to three. In January 1942 just three incendiary bombs reached the city. The last raid, in April, killed five people and injured ten, destroyed one wooden house and two buildings, and damaged a water pipe.[74] Compared with the other problems faced by Muscovites as a result of the invasion, bombing was secondary. The MPVO troops in Moscow found themselves in a war zone by the late autumn. They laid 25,000 anti-tank and anti-personnel mines in the approaches to the city and were responsible for laying explosives on 27 bridges in case they had to be demolished when the Germans arrived.[75] In October a rushed evacuation took place in conditions of mounting chaos as a German breakthrough to surround and capture the capital seemed likely, but it was not an evacuation prompted by bombing. Walter Citrine observed in mid-October lorries loaded with women and children heading out of the city, and long lines leaving on foot, mostly women, clutching what possessions they could: 'As they went out on one side of the road, on the other came in the troops, tanks, anti-tank guns, howitzers and mechanized infantry in one continuous stream.'[76]

In Leningrad, too, bombing was just one of many issues confronting the population as the ring of enemy forces tightened, Germans from the south and south-west and Finns from the north. The Finns were embarking on what was called the 'Continuation War' to win back territory conceded in March 1940 after the four-month war with the Soviet Union. The MPVO station in Leningrad had 1,335 officers and men, supported by 124,000 civil defence workers organized in 3,500 units. As in Moscow, they found themselves drafted into the land battle as the enemy drew closer; they laid 2,600 landmines and prepared four bridges for demolition, as well as helping to build defensive structures on the approaches to the city, some among 900 eventually constructed by MPVO during the war.[77] They helped to clear debris and to demolish dangerous structures; under the ruins of the State Bank they found and returned some 13.5 million roubles in cash. In September 1942 there were 23 German raids, many directed at military targets in Leningrad, which killed or injured some 4,409 people. This was the heaviest of the bombing. After that, and for the next two years, the city was subject to intermittent nuisance raids. By contrast there were 272 shellings by heavy artillery between September and December 1941, which resulted in smashed buildings, fires and a large number of dead and mutilated victims, both civilian and military, largely indistinguishable from the damage inflicted by bombs. The MPVO in the end ordered the alarms for both shelling and bombing.[78]

Many of the recollections and diaries of the Leningrad siege reveal a casual attitude to the bombing by much of the population. Svetlana Magaieva, a young girl during the siege, lived in an apartment block with no shelter. Her mother and their neighbours stayed in the apartment during raids, playing games to pass the time. When bombs detonated nearby, crockery would fall on the floor and smash and the wooden furniture move across the room as it might in an earthquake. Most people around her did not go to the basement or trench shelters, which were regarded as little safer than home.[79] Shelter discipline was not strictly enforced in Leningrad and was lax elsewhere. Policemen were supposed to alert householders with whistles, since sheltering was nominally compulsory, but people braved the raids regardless. An MPVO report in April 1942 noted the persistent 'undisciplined behaviour' of the population during warnings, when they chose to stay in their homes rather than seek shelter. The lapses were blamed on an insufficient level of political education. Discipline was particularly bad among soldiers, who took a more insouciant view of the threat. A report in May 1942 noted that three-quarters of all bomb casualties in Kalinin province, north of Moscow, were military personnel who displayed a 'careless attitude' towards air-raid rules.[80]

For the people of Leningrad the chief problem was first hunger, then famine. The destruction of the Badeyev warehouses on 8 September 1941 was the start of a long winter of terrible starvation as the slender stocks remaining evaporated, leaving rations that could not, for almost a million Leningraders, sustain life. By December, Svetlana Magaieva lay in bed all day too weak to move, listening to the shells and bombs 'which did not frighten me any more'.[81] The young fire-watcher, Evgenii Moniushko, found it progressively more difficult to climb the stairs to his lookout post or heave his emaciated body through the skylight onto the roof.[82] Workers continued to produce goods, chiefly weapons and munitions for the Leningrad front, until the raw materials ran out; they stayed in the factories after their shifts and those resting also took their turn fire-watching or extinguishing incendiaries. The MPVO found itself performing rescue and first-aid for the victims of shelling as well as the bombs, and it was also called on to help find and supply food rations for the citizens it was supposed to protect. In April 1942 the raids worsened with six attacks by an estimated 350 aircraft. The raids left 192 dead, but that same month the MPVO helped to move 104,880 decomposing corpses out of hospitals and makeshift morgues for mass burial.[83] In this case, as in Moscow, the crisis caused by the consequences of the wider war posed a more substantial challenge to the morale of the population. During 1942 the number of air raids on Leningrad itself declined until September (there were only three raids between May and August), when a renewed German attack on the Leningrad front brought more than 60 minor raids on the encircled city and its surroundings. During 1942 and 1943 most casualties were caused by shelling, which did not cease until the successful Soviet counter-offensive in January 1944.

The only other major Soviet city to experience sustained and heavy bombing was Stalingrad, whose raids have already been described. Unlike Moscow or Leningrad, Stalingrad was deemed to be too far away from the threat of bombing for the same level of protection to be offered. The MPVO station was only activated in early 1942 and by the time of the attacks on the city training had still not reached a level necessary to cope with the scale of raids. The first light attacks in the summer were nevertheless coped with satisfactorily by the existing structure of 'self-defence' groups, and the blackout functioned well. In July the bombing increased in intensity, but still only involved a small number of aircraft and damage that could easily be contained.[84] Only in the last 10 days of August did the level of raiding temporarily overwhelm the civil defenders. After the destruction of workers' housing blocks on 20 August, the population began to pour across the Volga to safety on the other side. The MPVO units managed to bring the first wave of fires under control, but the heavy bombing on the 24 August, which damaged the water supply, infected the civil defenders with panic too. 'The centre of the city is in ruins and ashes,' wrote the local MPVO commander. 'The scope of the destruction is phenomenal. The debris on the streets are impassable.'[85] He calculated that half his personnel fled over the river, but 500 workers volunteered to act as emergency units and came under MPVO control. Nevertheless, if the reports are to be believed, the emergency services succeeded in restoring damaged infrastructure as the bombing eased off. By 30 August water supply and high-voltage electric power were back in operation, linked to surviving industry. Telecommunications were restored in three districts by 29 August and in five more by the following day. Reconstruction of key roads and clearing of debris was completed at the same time.[86] It proved a meagre triumph (though it demonstrated once again the limits of aerial bombing); Stalingrad ceased its function as a city during September and became simply a battlefield.

Once the early raiding was finished there was less need for the expanding MPVO organization. Like the civil defence organization in Britain, the MPVO reached its highest level of preparation and efficiency after the main bombing was over. By July 1944 there were shelter spaces for almost half the 18 million city dwellers who were deemed to qualify for protection. Some 6.5 million civilian gas masks were produced in 1943 and 1944 when the need was slight. By January 1943 there were 3,742 MPVO protection sites, for a far smaller territory than in summer 1941.[87] The organization was nevertheless far from redundant. Small-scale raiding went on through 1943 and 1944, the large part of it on railway targets – approximately 60–70 per cent – with many raids by lone aircraft. Three-quarters of the raids were undertaken at night and a proportion were reconnaissance rather than bombing operations. Between March 1943 and March 1944 Soviet sources counted 4,930 incursions, which produced a cumulative death toll of 9,416 people. In 1944 German aircraft concentrated on railway targets at some distance from the fighting front, and out of 16,632 casualties recorded in 1944, 87 per cent were inflicted at or around railway targets. In 1945, with the Red Army on the brink of invading the German homeland, there were just two brief German raids recorded, one on Estonia on 16 January and the last incursion on 16 February over Lithuania by one German bomber.[88]

The changing pattern of German air activity and the large pool of manpower and equipment led to a reorganization of the MPVO structure. On 10 June 1943 resolution N3592 of the State Defence Committee created a separate MPVO organization for industry and transport to help cope with the persistent threat to the rail network. Experience had shown that the emergency and repair units fielded by the MPVO were generally far too small to cope with the practical consequences of a raid; after the June decree larger emergency columns of 100–500 people were established in 44 cities to try to cope with the restoration of damage to rail transport and, more occasionally, to industry. The number of MPVO personnel assigned to the rail network doubled from 76,000 to

149,000. The industrial units were also responsible for camouflaging factories and transport targets, a task that was undertaken with help from the national Academy of Architecture and the Academy of Science.[89] As the fighting front moved westwards again with the Axis retreat, MPVO stations were restored in the liberated areas, allowing MPVO personnel to extend the work of reconstruction and repair as a direct contribution to the operations of the Red Army.

The new role adopted by the MPVO was reflected in the range of activities between 1941 and 1945 claimed as part of its contribution to the Soviet war effort. These included rebuilding 273 bridges (among them the vital bridge over the Dnieper through which the Red Army's reconquest of Ukraine could be supplied); repairing 1,014 kilometres of rail and tram track, 412 kilometres of roads; and repairing and reconstructing 11,309 apartment blocks, industrial facilities and civic buildings.[90] In Leningrad, despite the persistent shelling, 860,000 square metres of roofing had been repaired by 1944, and 3 million square metres of window, each aperture covered with plywood and a small inset of glass, to let in the light.[91] The MPVO became the equivalent of the technical troops of the armed forces, restoring water supply in Kiev, Kharkov, Krivoi Rog and Smolensk, and electric power in Kharkov, L'vov, Smolensk and half a dozen other cities where the German army had practised a scorched-earth policy. A total of 8 million man-days were spent by MPVO personnel on reconstruction and repair work, almost 5 million of them in 1944.[92] Civil defence in a more conventional sense declined. By 1944 trench and dugout shelters were being demolished or filled in. In Stalingrad the rebuilding had already begun.

The effects of the bombing on the Soviet population subjected to it are difficult to assess. Since air attack was conducted in most cases in conjunction with a destructive land campaign, its effects merged with the damage and dislocation caused by conquest or forced evacuation. In Leningrad the shelling was regarded as more menacing than the bombing, while the famine eclipsed everything. Most eyewitness accounts, however, remark on the calmness of the population. The head of the Leningrad Health Department told Alexander Werth that in his view the most remarkable thing was the absence of 'cases of insanity or other nervous diseases due to bombing or shelling'.[93] A worker at the Putilov armaments works recalled that the bombing made him and his comrades frightened but also angry. He described one night when 300 incendiaries landed on the plant: 'Our people were putting the fires out with a sort of concentrated rage and fury; like a thousand squirrels they rushed around, putting out the flames. They had realized by then that they were in the front line – and that was all. No more shelters.'[94] Children in Leningrad played games with the shrapnel picked up after the anti-aircraft barrage. Svetlana Magaieva and her companions even stayed outside while the shrapnel fell, on the promise that whoever stood nearest to a fallen fragment would have the right to claim it.[95] There was occasional evidence that bombing was used as an opportunity to express political views impossible under normal conditions. Leaflets appeared calling for Leningrad to be declared, like Paris in 1940, an open city; as occupation of the city seemed imminent, swastikas were daubed on walls and pro-Hitler comments overheard. Later, during the famine, resentment spilled over at times from the knowledge that the Party elite were still able to enjoy food rations long denied to the rest of the population.[96] Yet anti-Soviet sentiment, where it existed, did not need bombing to stimulate it. In most areas outside Leningrad, the bombing was a brief interruption, small raids that exacted a rising level of casualties, chiefly among those living too close to transport targets, but never severe enough to distort the way the population felt about the war effort, whether positive or negative. The conditions in Sebastopol and Stalingrad were different, dictated by the fact that both cities were defended battlefields upon which a fraction of the civilian population was trapped in a storm of shells and bombs and bullets.

The strategic and economic impact of bombing was, like the effects of the offensive against Britain, mixed. The Soviet Union was compelled to maintain a large active air defence and to expend large amounts of ammunition without much effect on the attacking aircraft, though once the threat to the cities had subsided the fighter aircraft and anti-aircraft guns could be used to supplement the fighting front. The MPVO involved at its peak 747,000 full-time workers and 2.9 million in the civil defence units, though in this case too many of the workers and full-time troops contributed directly to the Soviet advance towards Germany rather than providing redundant civil defence on the home front. In economic terms the limited amount of bombing had little effect. Soviet productive effort was affected critically by the loss of territory in the western Soviet Union, but was sustained thereafter by the success of the evacuation programme and the flow of Lend Lease from Britain and the United States. German efforts to interrupt the flow of supplies through the port of Murmansk by bombing proved futile in the face of severe weather conditions and concentrated ground defences. The damage to Soviet industry was slight. The MPVO calculated that industrial sites made up just 5.7 per cent of the destruction inflicted by bombing, communications some 38 per cent, and residential and public buildings, 48 per cent.[97] Although attacks on railways had a cumulative effect in the number of hours of transport time lost, railway lines could not be permanently disrupted any more than had proved to be the case in Britain in 1940–41.

The bombing did of course exact continuous human casualties. The figures for those killed and injured from bombing attacks on population centres were collected by the local MPVO offices and submitted to the headquarters in Moscow. The figures for the whole war period are set out in Table 4.1. Given the difficulty of trying to distinguish between death from bombing and death from shelling, the figures will be less exact than the chart suggests. The detailed casualty statistics presented every month from each MPVO region were on occasion corrected when additional casualties came to light, which suggests that a considerable effort went in to ensuring that the casualty lists were as accurate as war conditions would allow. The large death rate in 1942 reflects the damage done in Leningrad, Kharkov, the Crimea and at Stalingrad. The half-million deaths from bombing claimed in later Soviet publications must be regarded as a rhetorical statistic, to demonstrate the level of sacrifice of the Soviet people and the wickedness of the German enemy; it bears no relation to the detailed wartime documentary evidence. An inflated figure was perhaps a useful tool for demonstrating that the sacrifice of Soviet citizens in the Soviet Blitz greatly exceeded the losses

Table 4.1: Soviet Civilian Casualties from Bombing, 1941–5

Time Period	Killed	Injured	Total
22 June 1941–1 Jan 1942	5,979	11,957	17,936
1 Jan 1942–1 Jul 1942	22,745	87,103	109,848
1 Jul 1942–1 Jan 1943	7,846	11,976	19,822
1 Jan 1943–1 Jul 1943	5,272	10,556	15,828
1 Jul 1943–1 Jan 1944	2,527	3,757	6,284
1 Jan 1944–1 Jul 1944	5,470	8,017	13,487
1 Jul 1944–1 Jan 1945	1,687	3,059	4,746
1 Jan 1945–9 May 1945	0	0	0
Total	51,526	136,425	187,951

Source: RGVA, Fond 500, 37878-1/722, Medical Dept, HQ MPVO, 'Losses as a result of bombing by the enemy aviation of the population centres of the USSR', 20 June 1945.

sustained in the Blitz on Britain, the Soviet Union's erstwhile ally. The figure of 51,526 is much more consistent with the nature of the German bombing effort and the declining capability of the German bomber force as it struggled to sustain support for the ground war with dwindling resources.

THE FATE OF THE 'URALBOMBER': 1943-4

In May 1943 Hitler called German aviation industrialists together for a meeting. Ernst Heinkel, one of those present, recalled the Führer's impatient demand for a high-performance bomber: 'For three years I've been waiting for a long-distance bomber. I can't bomb the convoys in the North Sea, nor can I bomb the Urals.'[98] A few months before, Hitler had told the air force chief of staff that the most urgent priority was a long-range heavy bomber for the Eastern Front to undertake raids by night 'against long-distance targets which lie so far from our front that they [cannot] be reached by other aircraft types'.[99] Hitler's view – almost certainly correct – was that the air force made too many technical demands in the development of new aircraft and as a result produced persistent delays in providing the front line with what was strategically necessary.[100] The Barbarossa Directive in December 1941 had anticipated a campaign against the Soviet armaments industry once the mobile war was over, but no campaign materialized, and no heavy bomber. The history of the air war against the Soviet Union would certainly have been different had an effective aircraft been available sooner and in sufficient quantities.

The story of the so-called 'Uralbomber' was a long one. In 1934 the then chief of the air staff, Colonel Walter Wever, was an enthusiastic supporter of the idea that in any future war a large multi-engine bomber would be needed. According to Andreas Nielsen, one of the German Air Force officers later recruited by the American Air Force to write historical studies on the war, Wever was convinced that the important target areas 'would be Soviet industries and the outermost corners of European Russia' and even beyond, in the Siberian regions to the east of the Urals.[101] Two companies, Junkers and Dornier, were commissioned to produce an aircraft that soon attracted the nickname 'Uralbomber'; the result was the Do19 and the Ju89, both of which first flew in 1936. Wever's untimely death reduced the lobby in the Air Ministry in favour

of a long-range bomber. His successor, Albert Kesselring, an army officer seconded to the air force, promoted greater army-air cooperation,
and on 29 April 1937 the bomber programme was wound up. Research
on bombing carried out by a special unit under the command of the
future chief of staff, Hans Jeschonnek, confirmed an air force prejudice
that precision bombing with highly trained crews carried out in bombers that could dive, to increase accuracy, was preferable to mass bombing
with level-flying heavy aircraft.[102] Air force technical development was
led by a former fighter pilot, Ernst Udet, who understood the virtues of
dive-bombing but had little sympathy for the large bomber. The Junkers
Ju88, the bomber developed under Udet's stewardship, carried a modest
weight of bombs, but could dive to increase the impact of the bombs
against a visible target on the ground. All bombers were supposed to be
at the same time dive-bombers, whatever their size.

This was not the end of the German heavy bomber, as is usually
argued, but only a pause. It was understood that a new generation of
high-performance aircraft would be needed in the 1940s and that this
should at least include a modern large bomber to supersede the obsolescent Do17 and He111 on which the force currently relied. On 2 June
1937, only weeks after the cancellation of the 'Uralbomber', the Ernst
Heinkel works was given the contract to develop Project 1041 for a
multi-engine long-range bomber. The aircraft was given the designation
He177 and the prototype flew for the first time on 20 November 1939.
By then it was already included in long-range planning for output from
1942 onwards, as successor to the ageing generation of medium bombers. It was intended to produce 350–450 bombers in 1942, rising to
900 in 1943 and over 1,500 in 1944.[103] The new bomber had a limited
performance compared with the new generation of British and American aircraft, the Avro Lancaster and the B-29 'Superfortress' then under
development. With a full load of 6,000 lbs of bombs the He177 had an
operational range of only 745 miles, which would not take it to the
Urals and back. The greatest handicap for the new long-range bomber
was the requirement that despite its great bulk and weight, it should
have the capacity to perform a shallow dive as well, a requirement
entirely at odds with the size of the aircraft and its strategic purpose.
Heinkel solved the problem by coupling two pairs of Daimler Benz
DB-606 engines together, giving the aircraft four engines but only two
nacelles, to reduce the drag during a dive. The engine configuration was
not the only difficulty experienced with the aircraft – there were 56 files
on modifications and technical problems on the He177 in Heinkel's

office – but it was the principal one.[104] The aircraft as a result was prone to engine failure and engine fires, so much so that crews nicknamed it the *Luftwaffenfeuerzeug*, the 'air force lighter', and disliked having to fly it.

The slow pace of development of the He177 dictated by problems of design mattered less in the early part of the war when quick victories could be achieved with the prevailing technology. The German Air Force nevertheless expected that it would be their replacement bomber and by 1942, with the Soviet war prolonged beyond the first phase of fast-moving mobile warfare, the necessity for a bomber with greater bomblift and longer range became obvious. The strategic gap that this opened up for the air force was exacerbated by the insistent demands of the army for close support and the low level of serviceability and supply for the eastern theatre. An air force study written in late 1943 claimed that air force commanders had wanted to bomb Soviet industry from at least the autumn of 1941, but found that army requirements left the air force 'completely harnessed to close support' throughout the campaign.[105] Although Hitler deplored the absence of a heavy bomber, his role as commander-in-chief of the army, assumed in December 1941, inclined him to place priority on air support for ground operations when these faced crisis. The main handicap, however, was the failure of the He177 to fulfil its early promise.

The sorry story of the He177 reflected more profound problems in the technical evolution of the air force. Uncertainty about the course of the war or the reliability of the aircraft had led to two cancellations, only for the model to be reinstated months later. Decision-making at a technical level was hampered by the interference of both Udet and Göring, neither of whom understood the nature of technical planning or grasped the extent to which industrial rivalry encouraged Heinkel to shield the seriousness of the design problems from fear that the heavy bomber would be placed with another company.[106] Only in August 1942 did the chief of the air force development and testing office supply Göring with a comprehensive survey of all the faults of the He177, with the conclusion that the model could only be introduced successfully into combat by March 1944 at the earliest. Erhard Milch, Göring's deputy, reflected that 'one could weep' over the failure of the air force's one available strategic bomber.[107] When Hitler was finally informed in May 1943 that the coupled engine was the explanation for the failure to get the He177 into combat he is supposed to have retorted: 'But that's mad-ness . . . is it possible that there could be so many idiots?'[108] The air force

technical branch had already arrived at the same conclusion and other
bomber models were now in the pipeline, though years away from
large-scale operation. Heinkel was ordered to convert the bomber to
four regular but different engines (the DB-610) and the model was
renamed the He277. It was ready for testing only by July 1944, by
which time the bomber programme had been wound up in favour of
fighters. Until then plans continued to produce the ill-starred He177 at
the rate of 100 a month.

The crisis of the German field army in the Soviet Union from Stalingrad onwards prompted the air force to argue the case for greater
operational independence so that it could find ways to interrupt the
flood of Soviet weapons and aircraft before they reached the front. In
the summer of 1943 serious research began on what the chief bottleneck targets in the Soviet industrial system might be. The driving force
behind the plan was the commander of the Sixth Air Fleet stationed in
central Russia, Col. General Robert Ritter von Greim (who briefly
replaced Göring as air force commander-in-chief in late April 1945).
His staff drew up detailed contingency plans in June 1943 for a 'Campaign against Soviet Russian War Economy', but particularly the
aero-engine industry, aviation fuel, locomotive production, tanks and
vehicles.[109] Two civilian experts, Professor Heinrich Steinmann and
Dr Rudolf Carl, undertook their own analysis after being prompted by
Armaments Minister Albert Speer, whose experience of Allied bombing
of German industry inclined him to think that systematic destruction of
the electricity-generating industry in the Moscow/Volga area might
have decisive effects. The Carl Committee for 'Economic Objectives for
Air Attacks' recommended destroying 56 generating stations in the
region as the fastest way to impede Soviet war production. Models were
made of the power stations and shown to Hitler. On Speer's insistence,
Hitler finally approved in December 1943 'Aktion Russland' (Russian
Action) for a single surprise attack against the Soviet energy system.[110]

Most of this planning was delusional. Although the air force staff
now led by General Günther Korten (following Jeschonnek's suicide in
August 1943), with Karl Koller as operations chief, strongly favoured a
strategic campaign against selected Soviet targets, there were a great
many obstacles to overcome. On 9 November 1943 Koller circulated a
memorandum on 'The Campaign against the Russian Arms Industry',
which at last won the army's approval as a possibly surer way to destroy Soviet armaments at source rather than having to wait to destroy
them at the fighting front.[111] But the army preferred attacks against

armament factories rather than energy supply, and was anyway soon demanding every bomber to stem the Soviet advance around Kiev. Specialist training units were set up for crews assigned to long-range night-bombing – something that had not been kept up after the end of the Blitz against Britain – but the shortage of He177 aircraft left them training on He111 and Ju88 medium bombers, with limited range. The crews needed time to learn how to use the new and more accurate Lotfe 7D bombsight, and the Fritz X gliding bomb, to maximize the impact of each raid. Navigation lagged behind Allied achievements. Air units were recommended to use a 'command aircraft' to circle over the chosen target, directing incoming bombers by radio to achieve the optimum impact, an arrangement that had already achieved some success in attacking tactical targets.[112] It was difficult to find bases that could handle the new campaign and at the same time keep their purpose concealed. As Soviet forces advanced, so some of the targets chosen fell out of range. In January 1944 the experts concluded that attacks on the limited number of objectives still near enough to bomb 'can lead to no decisive results'.[113] By this stage of the war German bomber losses were exceeding production every month; from October 1943 to March 1944 the air force lost 2,623 bombers on all fronts against production of 2,109.[114] In February 'Aktion Russland' was abandoned.

Instead, the 350 bombers that had been gathered on the Eastern Front for long-range operations were diverted back to a three-month railway campaign which proved unable to affect Soviet mobility materially and exposed the extent to which the speculations about doing serious damage to Soviet industry had been so much wishful thinking. Between January and May 1944 German aircraft destroyed no more than 34 kilometres of track, 15 railway bridges and 41 locomotives in more than 1,000 small raids. During the whole of 1944, 166 locomotives were destroyed and 441 damaged; during the same period only 11 factories were destroyed, together with 85 warehouses and shops.[115] Nevertheless, in May 1944 Koller once again pressed unsuccessfully for a pre-emptive bombing campaign in the east, as the German strategic situation continued to deteriorate. The idea of bombing Soviet industry lingered on well past any point of operational reality. Late in 1944 Speer, von Greim and Koller persisted in arguing the case for long-range operations against economic targets. In April 1945 Koller, now chief of staff following Korten's death from injuries sustained when the bomb exploded in Hitler's headquarters in July 1944, recommended for the last time the idea of bombing more distant Soviet objectives. Hitler agreed, only to cancel his approval a few days later when every bomber was needed to defend the approaches to Berlin. Right to the end there remained a wide gap between ends and means in air force ambitions, a pattern that could be traced back to the illusions harboured about the degree of damage done to the British war effort during the Blitz. Despite the hope of many German Air Force leaders that they would be permitted to project a more strategic form of air power, the air force ended the war as it had begun it, conducting operational air warfare alongside the army.[116]

There are many reasons why the transition to strategic bombing failed in the war on the Eastern Front: a shortage of aircraft given the demands of the fighting front; difficulties in maintaining adequate serviceability rates and the effects of the harsh climate; the muddled development of the one heavy bomber that might have fulfilled the task in time; the absence of a clear strategic view of what bombing might or might not achieve after the relative failure over Britain; and by 1943 the demand for long-range aircraft to support the Atlantic war and to renew the bombing of Britain. Whether or not a campaign to inhibit Soviet industrial production would have succeeded is open to speculation, given the capacity of the Soviet system to absorb massive shock and to improvise creatively, and the strongly coercive nature of Soviet labour policy. Soviet industrial building was certainly vulnerable to concentrated incendiary attack, as the fate of Stalingrad's industry demonstrated, but the industrial economy was vast and much of it far distant from German bases. The Soviet Air Force, on the other hand, recognized the nature of the campaign being waged and focused attention on close support for the fighting fronts, leaving long-range bombing to the Western Allies. Soviet bomber production was a fraction of the output of all combat aircraft, just 15 per cent between 1943 and 1945.[117] A number of small raids continued to be made on European targets, but again largely for political effect. Soviet bombers raided Berlin three times in the autumn of 1942, on 26–27 and 28–29 August and 9–10 September, partly in the expectation that the RAF would be bombing at the same time, a promise Churchill had made to Stalin when he visited him in Moscow in August, but failed to redeem. Small raids were made at the same time on Budapest, Bucharest, Warsaw and Helsinki, but after that long-range attacks were suspended until the spring of 1944 when the Finnish capital was bombed once again to try to coerce Finland into making a separate peace.[118]

The brief offensive against Finland was the only time that the Soviet

Union used air power on its own as a way to achieve a strategic end. Helsinki had been bombed once in the Winter War of 1939–40, but by units of the Baltic Fleet air force, which had contravened orders not to attack the city area.[119] The three raids on Helsinki in 1944 coincided with the short campaign conducted by the Mediterranean Allied Air Forces against Bulgarian targets, which Stalin refused to support. There were three main raids, on the nights of 6–7, 16–17 and 26–27 February 1944, carried out by large bombing forces, 785 on the first night, 406 on the second and 929 on the third. The aircraft carried around 2,600 tons of bombs, but the raids were a complete failure. Although Soviet histories subsequently asserted that the bombing successfully hit industry, administrative centres and military targets, Finnish sources indicate that around 95 per cent of the bombs failed to hit the target area of the city, 48 square kilometres, and most fell in the sea. Thirty Soviet aircraft were lost to the defence forces and to accident.[120] The raids did little to persuade the Finns to seek an armistice. This they did later in the year, in September, when it was evident that the war was lost.

The closest the Soviet side came to collaboration with the strategic offensive conducted by the British and American air forces against Germany was in the summer of 1944. This followed an agreement made with the American Air Force to allow American bombers to undertake shuttle-bombing of targets in eastern Germany and German-occupied Europe using Soviet airfields as the shuttle base. It was a surprising decision given the suspicious hostility displayed to Western offers of air assistance in the Caucasus in late 1942.[121] Roosevelt raised the question of shuttle-bombing with Stalin at the Teheran Conference in late November 1943, at a time when the United States Army Air Force stationed in England was searching for a way to hit German industry without suffering heavy losses from unescorted missions. The American Air Force hoped that this might open the way for negotiating bases in the far east of the Soviet Union for attacks on Japan; there was some hope that military collaboration might contribute to warmer political ties between the two allies. Stalin finally agreed at the end of December, for reasons which are not entirely clear given the subsequent months of often fractious negotiation between the two sides. The Soviet priority remained front-line support for the advancing army, for which shuttle-bombing would provide little assistance.[122]

An American delegation headed by Colonel John Griffith, who had fought with the American anti-Bolshevik intervention force in Russia in 1918, finally secured use of three sites in the liberated area of Ukraine at Poltava, Piryatin and Mirgorod. An American 'Eastern Command' was established under Colonel Alfred Kessler, an early replacement for Griffith, who found his anti-Soviet feeling difficult to disguise. After months of planning, 'Operation Frantic' finally began on 2 June 1944, by which time the rationale for shuttle-bombing had largely disappeared, thanks to the introduction of the American P-38 and P-51 fighters. The first operation was mounted against targets in southern Germany from bases in Italy occupied by the US Fifteenth Air Force. The commander in the Mediterranean, General Ira Eaker, flew on the first mission to ensure that it enjoyed a high political profile, and he was duly feted on his arrival in the Ukraine. The second operation, flown on 21 June from Eighth Air Force bases in England, was a disaster. A few hours after landing, the 73 B-17 'Flying Fortresses' on the field at Poltava were subjected to a devastating attack by German bombers which flew in low against negligible defences. Colonel Archie Old, commander of the task force, described the attack in a report for the Eighth Air Force commander:

> About ten minutes after the first flares were dropped the first bombs started falling and then for almost two hours, the bastards bombed hell out of the flying field, especially that part where the task force B-17s were dispersed. It was one of the most accurate bombing raids that the task force commander has seen or heard of, many thousands of bombs were dropped and approximately 95% of them fell on the flying field . . . of seventy-three B-17s on the field 100% were either destroyed or damaged.[123]

Soviet personnel were forced by their commanders to try to combat the effects of the bombing while it was still going on; when it was over, Soviet soldiers picked up the unstable anti-personnel 'butterfly' bombs with their bare hands, or shot at them to make them explode. Between 30 and 40 of the soldiers were killed, as well as two Americans. The German commander was Lt. General Rudolf Meister, the man chosen to organize the pinpoint bombing of Soviet power stations the previous year.[124] Only a handful of further operations were conducted by Eastern Command, including supply for the Polish Home Army in its uprising against the German occupiers, launched on 1 August 1944. This proved too much for the Soviet regime to stomach and in late August the Soviet Foreign Minister, Vyacheslav Molotov, told the Americans that the bases were now needed for the Soviet Air Force. On 4 October Operation Frantic was wound up, though the last American personnel did not leave until June 1945.

The air war on the Eastern Front remained for almost all its course a tactical one. Only 5 per cent of Soviet sorties were made against distant targets; the German Air Force flew a higher proportion of long-range sorties for reconnaissance and occasional bombing missions, and bombed cities in the path of the ground campaign, but did not develop a campaign of independent bombing of military-economic targets despite the growing pressure from Hitler and the air force High Command to do so. The Soviet Air Force was nevertheless not entirely opposed to the development of strategic air power in the future. Andrei Tupolev was allowed to renew work on a heavy four-engine bomber and the result was the Pe-8/TB7, the first modern heavy bomber of the Soviet Air Force; in the end only 91 were ever produced because of the urgent need for front-line aviation, but a few of them took part in the bombing of Helsinki in 1944.[125]

Tupolev was also given the opportunity to exploit three Boeing B-29 'Superfortresses', interned by the Russians after they landed on Soviet soil following missions over Japan in the summer of 1945. These became the basis for the development of a new Soviet super-bomber, the Tu-4, which ushered the Soviet Union into the strategic air age.[126] The head of the MPVO, reflecting on what lessons might be learned from the civil defence effort during the war, favoured retaining all deep shelters against the possibility that bigger and better bombs would be developed in the future from which the Soviet people would need sounder and more extensive shelter.[127] While Tupolev worked on the new Soviet super-bomber, Lavrentii Beria, the Minister of the Interior, headed a project to develop the Soviet atomic bomb. When the bomb was successfully detonated on a remote site in central Asia on 29 August 1949, the Soviet Union entered the nuclear age. The heavy bombers, missiles and nuclear weapons of the 1950s overturned the Soviet preference for close-support aviation as the principal way to project air power and presented the new German Federal Republic, in the front line of the Cold War, with a strategic threat unrecognizable from the bombing war on the Eastern Front just a decade before.

PART TWO

'The Greatest Battle': Allied
Bombers over Europe

5

The Sorceror's Apprentice: Bomber Command 1939–42

On 1 September 1939 President Roosevelt sent an appeal to all the major European powers involved in the crisis over Poland to give a public undertaking that they would abstain from any air attacks against civilians or unfortified cities. The same day Hitler told the American chargé d'affaires in Berlin that this had always been his preference and assured Roosevelt that German aircraft would only attack military objectives. The British prime minister, Neville Chamberlain, gave his guarantee the same day; a joint Anglo-French declaration followed on 3 September, only reserving the right to act as they saw fit if the enemy failed to observe the same restrictions.[1] The Polish ambassador in Washington, whose country was already at war, agreed that Polish pilots would be told not to bomb open cities as long as the enemy did the same.[2] None of these expressions of goodwill was legally binding in international law.

The idea that bombing warfare could somehow be 'humanized' had been explored by a British committee set up in July 1938 with the cumbersome title 'Limitation of Armaments Committee, Sub-Committee on the Humanisation of Aerial Warfare'. The discussions of the committee, chaired by Sir William Malkin, went round in circles. The terms for a possible international agreement on limiting bombing to military objectives suffered not only from the realistic objection that such terms would be unenforceable in a real war, but from the difficulty of defining what was meant by a military objective. In the end the committee proved more useful in giving the Air Ministry the opportunity to defend the idea that bombing arms factories and armaments workers was as legitimate as a naval blockade, than it was in finding grounds for a diplomatic solution.[3] In the absence of international agreement, the RAF was told to abide by The Hague Rules for air warfare, first drafted in 1923 but never ratified, but to do so only as long as the enemy did the same. The rules were spelt out in a Cabinet decision and repeated regularly up to and beyond the outbreak of war: intentional bombing of civilians was illegal; only identifiable military objectives could be attacked from the air; and any such attack must be undertaken without negligent harm to civilians. In August 1939 the Air Ministry concluded that attacks on targets difficult to identify through cloud or at night would also be illegal, as would any operation in which the civil population, hospitals, cultural monuments or historic sites were targeted. An inter-departmental committee, set up the same month to draft detailed instructions on rules of engagement for the British armed forces, stipulated 'that it is clearly illegal to bombard a populated area in the hope of hitting a legitimate target'.[4]

These legal limitations reflected decisions taken in military staff talks between the British and French High Commands in the spring of 1939 as they planned for a possible war. In April the two military staffs had agreed only to attack military targets in the narrowest sense of the term, at sea or at the fighting front. British bombers were to be used to help the battle on land, not to attack distant targets in Germany. The French were insistent that the RAF should not attack German cities while the balance of air resources so obviously favoured Germany, and French industry was not yet adequately protected.[5] A few days before the outbreak of war the British Chief of the Air Staff, Sir Cyril Newall, warned Air Chief Marshal Edgar Ludlow-Hewitt, commander-in-chief of Bomber Command, that his activities were bound to be restricted 'for political reasons', though Ludlow-Hewitt knew that Bomber Command's small size and operational difficulties were enough on their own to inhibit offensive action.[6] Newall worried that even if the RAF bombed legitimate objectives, the Germans would claim that they had killed civilians. There was strong political pressure to ensure that the democracies were not seen to violate the bombing proscription first. It was decided in October 1939 that only if German aircraft started to kill large numbers of civilians from the air – 'promiscuous bombardment' as it was called – would the RAF 'take the gloves off'.[7]

Both sides at first stuck to their pledge not to attack targets in each other's cities where civilians were at risk (though this did not prevent the German Air Force from killing non-combatants during its operations in Poland). Chamberlain had no interest in provoking German bombing of British towns despite appeals from the Polish government in early September to begin bombing Germany as a gesture of assistance.[8] It was nonetheless the case that for the first months of the war Bomber Command strained at the leash to be able to do what years of planning had prepared it for. A half-hearted agreement was reached with the French High Command to initiate bombing of the German Ruhr-Rhineland industrial region – usually capitalized in British documents simply as the RUHR– if a sudden German attack threatened Belgium or menaced Franco-British forces decisively, but the French remained cautious about risking German retaliation, even during the invasion in May 1940.[9] In the end it was the British who ended the international embargo agreed in September. On the night of 11–12 May, two days after the German invasion in western Europe, 37 medium and light bombers attacked industrial and transport targets in the Rhineland city of München Gladbach (now Mönchengladbach), killing four people, including an Englishwoman who happened to live there. British raids were to continue throughout the war. The last was made on 2–3 May 1945 on the north German port of Kiel, just 36 hours before Allied troops occupied the city.[10]

'TAKING THE GLOVES OFF', 1939–40

The political and legal restrictions imposed on Bomber Command were consistent with the widely held view in Britain that indiscriminate bombing was the hallmark of barbarism, whereas self-restraint was a feature of being civilized. Yet there were also powerful prudential arguments for not undertaking bombing from the start of the war, as the French realized. In the autumn of 1939 Bomber Command was not yet ready to launch any major offensive campaign. For all the talk in the 1930s of developing a 'striking force' capable of taking the fight to the enemy heartland, progress in developing the technology of aircraft, bombs, bombsights and navigation aids had been painfully slow. One of Chamberlain's more desperate acts before the war was to ask Roosevelt on 25 August 1939, a week before his appeal, to supply the American Norden bombsight for British use. Roosevelt declined, not because it would compromise his subsequent appeal to abstain from bombing, but because agreeing to this request would make it seem that the United States had taken sides in the conflict.[11] At the outbreak of war Ludlow-Hewitt was well aware of the deficiencies of his force, which had already been exposed when the Air Ministry at last began in 1938 to consider the practicalities of long-range bombing. The gap between ambition and reality was remarkably wide for a force committed to a bombing strategy, a reflection of the poor technical experience of much of the RAF leadership and the failure to define doctrine clearly. There were too few airfields capable of handling heavier aircraft, little experience in bombing training, a shortage of maps of north-west Germany and a total of only 488 bombers of all kinds, including light bombers destined to form part of the Advanced Air Striking Force when it was sent to France in late 1939. 'Unrestricted air warfare,' ran an Air Ministry instruction, 'is not in the interests of Great Britain.'[12]

RAF Bomber Command dated from the reorganization of the air arm in 1936. Unlike the German Air Force, all bomber units were grouped together under a single commander-in-chief, based at Bomber Command headquarters near High Wycombe, north-west of London. This had important implications for the identity of the Command, because its sole function was to bomb. As a force it was only offensive, and its main duty was to define what targets to bomb, to produce the technology to enable those targets to be destroyed and to train the manpower to do it. This functional identity encouraged Bomber Command to construct a doctrine and a force independent of the army and navy, capable of striking a potential enemy at what was perceived to be their most vulnerable point. The Command was disinclined to accept the role of auxiliary to the requirements of surface forces, and there was almost no planning for army cooperation to match German Air Force doctrine. Right up to the outbreak of war and beyond, the RAF argued that its contribution to the battlefield would be of little significance: attacks on railway communications were regarded as difficult and ineffective, while raids against marching columns of men were deemed to be a waste of bombing resources.[13] Instead the Air Ministry drew up what were known as the Western Air Plans, a series of 16 individual plans, some of which committed the bomber force to assist the Admiralty in the war at sea, but none of which committed the bombers to help the army in the field. Only two of the plans were seriously prepared for: W. A.4 involved long-range attacks against communications targets in Germany to slow up a German advance; W. A.5 was for attacks on the German industrial economy, particularly the Ruhr area and the German oil industry.[14] An Industrial Intelligence Centre, first established in 1931 under Desmond Morton (later Churchill's intelligence adviser), drew up lists of vulnerable targets in German industry. Most of them could not be hit from British bases with existing aircraft, but they formed the basis for the RAF insistence that the most efficient use of bomber aircraft was against the enemy home front, not its armed forces.[15] Yet vulnerable targets on the home front could not be hit as long as the government insisted on the letter of the law.

The bomber force was organized in September 1939 in five Groups, spread out across east-central England and East Anglia, each Group made up of between six and eight squadrons, a total of 33 in all. Although some of the aircraft were called heavy bombers at the time, the Groups were actually equipped like the German Air Force with twin-engine light or medium bombers. The light bombers made up 16 squadrons, 10 consisting of the Fairey Battle, six of the Bristol Blenheim IV. The Battle emerged from a 1933 requirement for a monoplane light bomber but was obsolescent by 1939 and unsuited to daylight raiding; its operational function was unclear and its striking power negligible. They were sent to France as part of the air expeditionary force but were sitting ducks for German fighters. On 14 May 1940 as many as 40 out of a force of 71 Battles were shot down in a single disastrous operation against the crossings at Sedan in the Ardennes, close to the Belgian border. The Blenheim was developed from 1935 as a fast medium bomber. It was weakly armed but could reach a maximum speed of 266 mph. It could carry only 1,000 lbs of bombs around 700 miles. Its limited range and small bombload made it unsuitable for a strategic role and it played a larger part in the anti-shipping war along the German-occupied northern shores of Europe. Light bombers were sensibly phased out as the war progressed.[16]

Bomber Command had three principal long-range bombers in 1939, the Vickers Wellington, the Armstrong Whitworth Whitley and the Handley Page Hampden. The Hampden came from a 1932 specification, the Whitley from 1934, making them both considerably older than their German counterparts. The Hampden had a top speed of 255 mph and could carry up to 4,000 lbs of bombs around 600 miles; the Whitley Mark V with Rolls-Royce Merlin engines was the mainstay of Bomber Command in the first year, with a range of 800 miles with 3,000 lbs of bombs and a top speed of 222 mph. They were lightly armed and easy prey on unescorted sorties by day. The most successful of the medium bombers was the Vickers Wellington Mk IC (succeeded in 1941 by the Mk II and III), which made up more than half of Bomber Command's strategic force by 1942. It was powered by Bristol Pegasus engines, had a top speed of 235 mph and could carry 4,500 lbs of bombs some 600 miles. Its geodetic construction – a lattice-like fuselage shell – made it exceptionally robust compared with the Hampden and Whitley, and later marks of the Wellington remained in service throughout the war.[17] What the medium bombers lacked were effective navigational aids to match the German electronic systems (navigators and pilots were still taught astral navigation), powerful armament to be able to defend themselves against fighter assault, and bombs of sufficient destructive power. The standard British 250- and 500-lb bombs had a low charge-to-weight ratio (around one-quarter was explosive, against one-half in German bombs), but they also contained less destructive explosive content without the addition of aluminium powder (standard in German bombs), and were prone not to detonate. The standard incendiary bomb was the 4-lb Mk I magnesium bomb, which remained in production, with small modifications, throughout the war. Larger 'firepot' bombs were developed in 1939 and 1940, designed to distribute a high number of incendiary devices, but they were plagued with technical difficulties. Only later in the war did Bomber Command acquire heavier oil-based incendiaries.[18] The technical level of the force that went to war in 1939 – aircraft, bombs and equipment – can be described charitably as unsophisticated.

The early experience of the bomber force during the Phoney War confirmed the wisdom of not pressing for an immediate bombing offensive. The political restrictions confined the RAF to attacks on German naval vessels at sea and naval targets on the North Sea islands of Sylt and Heligoland, and on the German coast at Wilhelmshaven. Even these limited operations brought insupportable casualty rates: a small raid on the German coast on 4 September cost 23 per cent of the bomber force; a raid by Hampdens against Heligoland on 29 September cost half the force. In October 1939 the 'heavy bombers' were ordered to operate chiefly at night, as the Air Ministry had always expected.[19] The only operations permitted in German air space were propaganda runs, dropping millions of leaflets. Some aircrews, struggling to cope with the excessive cold, chucked out the heavy bundles without cutting them first, making them a potentially more lethal weapon than had been intended. By March 1940 it was reported that the morale of Bomber Command crews was close to cracking after long and dangerous propaganda operations which seemed to contribute nothing to winning the war and exposed crew to excessive risk of accident.[20] The night-time flights posed all kinds of difficulties. Interviews with operational crews confirmed that intense cold and long, risky flights over sea were compounded with the difficulty experienced over Germany itself, which they found to be 'very black'. It proved almost impossible to find and hit a specific target in the midst of the blackout, even with leaflets, a fact that RAF planners had already realized some months before when drawing up a 'Night Plan' to accommodate the shift from daylight to night-time operations, in which it was admitted that hitting anything at night 'will be largely a matter of chance'.[21] In late March, shortly before the campaign in Norway, the chiefs of staff concluded that Bomber Command was too weak and unprepared to be able to do anything effective in the foreseeable future.[22] In April, just prior to the German invasion of the Low Countries and France, the new head of Bomber Command, Air Marshal Charles Portal, who replaced Ludlow-Hewitt that month, told the air staff that he had only 260 serviceable bombers and 384 crews; he estimated that they would be capable of dropping 100 tons of bombs in the first week of bombing operations but only 30 tons by week three. Because of the high rate of loss anticipated, the force would be capable of only 36 sorties a day after two weeks of conflict.[23] This was a negligible effort on the eve of the German offensive.

It is all the more surprising under these circumstances that the RAF should have decided to take the gloves off in May 1940 when the German invasion began. The decision to permit British bombers to attack military-economic targets on German soil close to civilian populations was not an invitation to undertake the heavy city-bombings of the later war years, if only because Bomber Command was manifestly incapable of inflicting them. But it was a threshold that had to be crossed consciously, given the heavy weight of political and ethical restrictions laid on the force from the start of the war. What was judged to be illegal in August 1939 had to be presented as legitimate when it was undertaken in the summer of 1940. Most explanations for the start of the British campaign have assumed that it was a response to the German bombing of Rotterdam on 14 May, but the first raid, on München Gladbach, had already taken place three days before, while Rotterdam was not mentioned in any of the Cabinet discussions about initiating the bombing of German targets. The decision was taken because of the crisis in the Battle of France, not because of German air raids.[24] The actual circumstances surrounding the onset of bombing were more complex. By chance the German attack in the west on 10 May 1940 began on the same day that the Chamberlain government was replaced by a new one headed by Winston Churchill. Chamberlain had always opposed the use of bombers against urban targets, but Churchill had no conscientious or legal objections. As Minister of Munitions in 1917, he had been a prominent supporter of an independent air force and a campaign of long-range bombing against German industrial objectives. Later, as Minister for Air after the war, he had played a key role in securing the independent future of the RAF. He accepted the argument that bombing could be expected to produce important strategic results. A government headed by Churchill rather than Chamberlain was always more likely to endorse a bombing campaign.[25]

One of the first issues discussed by Churchill's new War Cabinet on 12 May was the virtue of initiating what was described as 'unrestricted air warfare'. It was agreed that the RAF should no longer be bound by any moral or legal scruples to abstain from bombing; Germany's wartime actions, Churchill claimed, had already given the Allies 'ample justification' for retaliation. The chiefs of staff had since the outbreak of war approved the idea that if urgent military necessity made bombing imperative, it should not be limited by humanitarian considerations. On 13 May the Cabinet considered again whether the crisis in the Battle of France was severe enough to justify bombing. Though there were arguments against running the risk of German retaliation, approval was given for a bombing attack against oil and rail targets in Germany on the night of 14–15 May. On 15 May the Cabinet finally took the decision to approve a full bombing strategy against German targets where civilians might be casualties, as long as they were 'suitable *military* objectives'.[26] The driving force behind the decision was the deputy prime minister, Clement Attlee, who had been absent from the earlier Cabinet discussions but who strongly favoured raids on Germany, and continued to do so throughout the war. Churchill was anxious about the effect on American opinion if Britain began the bombing war, but the dire state of the ground campaign turned the tide. It was hoped that German bombers would be forced to strike back at Britain, while German fighters would be withdrawn from the land battle to defend Germany, though neither eventuality materialized. On the night of 15–16 May Bomber Command launched its first large-scale raid with 99 medium bombers on targets scattered across the Ruhr. To prevent further heavy losses of bombers in the land campaign in France the air staff decided on 19 May to use the medium bombers only for attacks on Germany; on 30 May as the front in France collapsed, Bomber Command was ordered to stop using any bombers for direct support of the land battle and to concentrate on German industry, an admission of just how disastrously the British light bombers had performed in battlefront conditions against an air force which had advanced air technology and a sound doctrine for aircraft use.[27]

The change in priorities necessitated a revision of the rules on the conduct of air warfare laid down in August 1939, which had made it illegal to attack targets in which civilians might be 'negligently' killed.

On 4 June 1940 the Air Ministry issued new guidelines for Bomber Command, cancelling the earlier instructions. The intentional killing of civilians was still regarded as a violation of international law, but attacks could be made on military targets 'in the widest sense' (factories, shipyards, communications, power supply, oil installations) in which civilian casualties would be unavoidable but should be proportional.[28] 'Undue loss of civil life' was still to be avoided, which meant returning to base or jettisoning bombs safely if the target could not be properly identified.[29] Nevertheless, the ethical restraints imposed at the start of the war were eroded step by step as a result of the decision to initiate 'unrestricted' bombing of targets in urban areas. In July, Bomber Command War Orders were modified to allow pilots discretion in choosing any military or military-economic target (defined increasingly broadly) if the primary target was obscured or difficult to find, a policy almost certain at night to involve extensive damage to civilian life since, as Portal reminded the Air Ministry, a high percentage of bombs 'inevitably miss the actual target'.[30] The final restraints were lifted in September and October 1940 after the first German attacks on London, though there had already been growing pressure from Bomber Command to be allowed to bomb less discriminately.[31] In September the policy of bringing back unused bombs was suspended in favour of bombing anything that could be found worth bombing, though not merely at random. On 30 October Bomber Command was directed to focus on enemy morale by causing 'heavy material destruction in large towns' to teach the German population what bombing could do.[32] This decision brought to an end the first stage in setting aside the political and legal limitations that had operated during the Phoney War, and it paved the way for the escalation of the RAF campaign during 1941 and 1942 into full-scale city-bombing.

The onset of the RAF bombing campaign in summer 1940 can certainly be explained by the change in government and the military necessity imposed by the German breakthrough and triumph in the west, but neither argument is entirely convincing. Unrestricted (though not yet unlimited) air warfare against Germany owed its genesis partly to the intense pressure applied by the RAF from the start of the war to be allowed to commence bombing operations over Germany regardless of the possible human cost. Military expediency also played a part, for RAF leaders had a force whose chief purpose was long-distance bombing; used in any other way, the strike force would no longer give the RAF the chance to demonstrate what strategic bombing could achieve.

246

Bombing policy was predicated on offensive action and nourished by the idea, widespread among RAF leaders, that total war, if it came, would see the erosion of any distinction between the fighting man and the civilian war worker.[33] In the first few months of the war senior airmen argued repeatedly for attacks on the Ruhr as Germany's Achilles' heel. It was always recognized, by politicians as well as airmen, that such attacks would involve heavy civilian losses, as a War Cabinet paper in October 1939 made clear:

> Germany's weakest spot is the Rhur [sic], the heart of which is about the size of Greater London, and in which is concentrated approximately 60% of Germany's vital industry. It contains, moreover, a population which might be expected to crack under intensive air attack. Such attacks would involve a heavy casualty roll among civilians, including women and children.[34]

A planning document in October 1939 claimed that Bomber Command could, if allowed, bring industry in the Ruhr 'practically to a standstill'; a few weeks later the Air Ministry produced a precise schedule of sorties needed to 'K.O. the Ruhr' in a matter of weeks.[35] By the spring of 1940 there was a chorus of demands to allow the Ruhr plan to be put into action. Early in May Viscount Trenchard, the doyen of the bombing lobby, expressed his regret to Portal that bombing had not yet been attempted 'when I and others think it would probably have ended the war by now'. Portal himself, two days before the start of the German invasion, pressured Newall, the chief of the air staff, to reserve Bomber Command for attacks on German industry, rather than fritter it away in direct support for the army.[36] All such views were represented by Newall to the chiefs of staff and the War Cabinet. The decision in May was clearly influenced by the widespread but unverifiable assertion that bombing would achieve something worthwhile.

The bombing lobby rested its case on a number of evident exaggerations. Both the accuracy and power of British bombing and its capacity to inflict decisive material and psychological damage on Germany were presented in terms quite incompatible with the reality of Bomber Command's strength, range and capability. The detailed study on the Ruhr bombing suggested that somewhere between 1,000 and 4,000 sorties were all that was required to knock it out. Calculations suggested that 8 bomb hits would eradicate a power plant, 64 hits destroy a coking plant and 12 hits destroy an aqueduct; average bombing error was given as 75 yards (69 m) from low level, 300 yards (276 m) from high altitude, figures that had never been verified under combat conditions (and proved entirely unattainable in practice).[37] It would take Germany months, so it was claimed, to recover from such an assault. There was no sense in this, as in other planning documents, of the exceptional operational and technical difficulties that would be encountered in carrying out such a programme.

The effects these operations would have on the German war economy and German morale, even if they could be executed, were subject to similar distortions. In the late 1930s intelligence assessments of German economic capacity for war almost all emphasized the fragility of an industrial economy regarded as taut and overburdened. Planners in the Air Ministry assumed that they faced an enemy whose strength was a facade, 'politically rotten, weak in financial and economic resources', and that the results of bombing were likely to be 'decisive' for the outcome of the war.[38] This remained the prevailing view for much of the war despite all the evidence to the contrary. It also coloured the first over-optimistic reports of the impact of RAF raids in summer 1940 once the gloves were off. A Foreign Office intelligence report compiled from neutral eyewitnesses on 30 May suggested 'terrible effects' in the Ruhr and a serious crisis of morale spreading through the German home front; a second report sent on to Churchill in early June by the Foreign Secretary, Lord Halifax, talked of the profound depression in Germany caused by the 'violence and efficacy' of British bombing.[39] An Air Intelligence evaluation suggested 'general dislocation of rail traffic' throughout Germany. The RAF planning staff considered that the first three weeks of bombing had produced 'valuable results', apparently justifying the decision to start it in the first place.[40]

There was also the moral dimension. To abandon the principle that killing civilians from the air was wrong owed a good deal to the British perception of the German enemy. The legal issue involved was sidestepped by two arguments: first, that the Germans had begun unrestricted bombing and would do it again, given the chance; second, that Hitler's Reich represented such a profound menace to Western civilization that the greater moral imperative was to use every means available to destroy it. The view that the Germans were responsible for bombing civilians first had a long pedigree, stretching back to the Zeppelin and Gotha raids of the First World War, which many RAF commanders had experienced as young officers just over 20 years before. During the 1930s, popular prejudices revived about German science and the German military conniving to produce lethal weapons of mass destruction to be unleashed from the air on an unsuspecting opponent.[41] The bomb-ing of the Basque town of Guernica in April 1937 by the German Condor Legion was popularly regarded in the West as evidence that the Germans had once again abandoned any pretence of civilized behav-iour. The campaign in Poland was scrutinized for evidence that German bombers were deployed for terrorizing and murdering civilians. Although the evidence was ambiguous – since it was understood that the German raids were directed at military targets as part of a combined-arms ground campaign – the RAF preferred to assume that the Germans had bombed indiscriminately. A report published by the RAF Tactical Committee in October 1939 of a speech made by a Ger-man air staff officer on the Polish campaign claimed that on the Germans' own admission their operations went beyond the terms of The Hague Rules.[42] That same month Newall told the commander of the Advanced Air Striking Force in France that because of German action in Poland, 'we are no longer bound by restrictions under the instructions governing naval and air bombardment ... Our action is now governed entirely by expediency.'[43] Churchill himself later came to cite the German bombing of Warsaw and Rotterdam as moral justifica-tion for what was to be done to the German civilian population.

The assumption in all the discussions about restricting bombing was that it had force only so long as the enemy observed the same limitation, and in this sense Poland played an important part in paving the way for British action. Of course, German bombers had not yet bombed British cities, so the argument for attacking Germany came to be based on pre-emptive retaliation. Even before the war the RAF had taken for granted that the German Air Force would be bound by no scruples and would be 'ruthless and indiscriminate' when the time came for a knockout blow.[44] When a German raid on the Royal Navy base at Scapa Flow in March 1940 killed a nearby cottager (the first civilian casualty of the war), Churchill angrily berated the Air Ministry for not giving it maximum publicity as the likely start of 'deliberate horror raids on civilians', for which the Germans would carry the blame.[45] In April the propaganda department of the new Ministry of Economic Warfare recommended describing German reconnaissance missions as frustrated bombing raids – 'driven off before they were able to drop their bombs' – so as to justify any British retaliation.[46] In May 1940 one of the arguments for bombing Germany was that sooner or later Ger-man leaders would do the same when it suited their strategic interests. 'Do [the government] think,' wrote one bombing lobbyist, Marshal of the RAF Sir John Salmond, 'that Hitler, who does not consider for a moment the slaughter of thousands on the ground and of devastating countries with which he has no quarrel, will shrink from killing civilians in this country?'[47] In the Cabinet discussion on 15 May, Sir Hugh Dowding, commander-in-chief of Fighter Command, argued in favour of anticipatory attacks because he felt convinced that sooner or later the German Air Force would start indiscriminate bombing.[48] Yet very soon the argument that Germany started the bombing became the standard version, both among the wider public and in the RAF, and it has remained firmly rooted in the British public mind ever since.

The view that German crimes, or potential crimes, made British bombing legitimate was legally dubious, since it amounted to claiming that two wrongs make a right, but it was morally rooted in the belief that German bombing was just one manifestation of the profound threat that Hitler and the National Socialist movement represented to the survival of the West. The terms of the contest in 1940 were easily presented as a struggle of light against dark, civilization against barbarism, to a public anxious not to see the war as a repeat of the pointless slaughter of 1914-18. The claim to the moral high ground gave an ethical purpose to British strategy that could be used to justify an air policy that in the 1930s would have been widely regarded as a moral lapse, like the Italian bombing of Ethiopians or the Japanese bombing in China. Churchill was among the foremost champions of the idea that every effort should be made to root out the source of Europe's political poison. 'The whole world is against Hitler and Hitlerism,' he announced in a radio broadcast in November 1939. 'Men of every race and clime feel that this monstrous apparition stands between them and the forward movement that is their due, and for which the age is ripe.'[49] And although Churchill sometimes made the distinction between 'Nazis' and 'Germans', he commonly used the pejorative 'Huns' to describe the enemy, a term deliberately chosen in the First World War to contrast German barbarity with Western civility.

There was also widespread popular support for the argument that Hitler's Germany was so wicked that any methods, even if they were morally questionable, should be used to destroy it. This was true across the political spectrum, even among those who had campaigned for peace in the 1930s. In an article on 'Nazism and Civilisation', Sir Charles Trevelyan, who had once advocated mass resistance to war, defined the war as a necessary crusade against a barbarous system that had discarded 'all moral, international and public law' and had bombed women and children.[50] Philip Noel-Baker, director of the International Peace campaign in the late 1930s, observed that the bombing of Germany, of which he approved, was almost civilized 'compared to the concentration camp and to the Himmler terror'. In a newspaper article just after the onset of the Blitz he pointed out that Hitler had smashed 'every last remnant of the Laws of War' and that British hands were now free to take any measures to 'bring his monstrous aggression to an end'.[51] A leading member of the Women's League for Peace and Freedom, which had publicly condemned bombing in the 1930s, abandoned her pacifism in 1940 on the grounds that 'Nazism is a menace of evil corruption and lying and of all the forces of evil', which could only be eradicated by the use of force. When pacifist clergy lobbied the archbishops of Canterbury and York in 1940 to condemn the British use of bombing, they received the following reply: '. . . the moral issue involved in the victory of the allies is of greater importance than the harsh fact of fighting by methods that one deplores'.[52] Many prominent churchmen, politicians and intellectuals, who might have condemned bombing under different circumstances, supported it as a necessary evil. Already predisposed to see the German threat in crude moral terms, it was a relatively simple step to the argument that the greater moral obligation was to secure the continued freedom of the West than to abstain from killing German civilians.

The British government and the RAF leadership were nevertheless aware that it was necessary to present the bombing as distinct from German practice to avoid the accusation that the British were no less barbarous than the Germans. In late April 1940 the Minister for Air, Sir Samuel Hoare, stated in a radio broadcast that the British would never imitate the enemy's 'dastardly conduct': 'We will not bomb open towns. We will not attempt to defeat the Germans by terrorizing their women and children.'[53] When the decision was finally taken on 15 May to start bombing, Churchill advised the Ministry of Information to publish a discreet press release on German killing of civilians from the air in France and the Low Countries, but to say nothing about British retaliation.[54] Pilots were at first instructed to ensure they could identify and hit specific targets before bombing them. Emphasis was put in every subsequent discussion on RAF bombing that it was directed only at military targets, even though the term was stretched almost to meaninglessness by the long list of economic and social objectives eventually classified as military, and the decision in October 1940 to permit the targeting of morale through attacks on city areas.[55] Throughout the war the public presentation of the bombing offensive in Parliament and in the press never deviated from the claim that the RAF only bombed military targets, unlike the enemy. When attacks against 'industrial populations' was included in a draft directive in August 1942, the Air Ministry insisted that the term be altered to 'industrial centres' to avoid the impression that civilians were deliberate targets, 'which is contrary to the principles of international law – such as they are'.[56] When Air Marshal Harris tried to persuade the Air Ministry in the autumn of 1943 to be more honest in their publicity about bombing by showing that killing civilian workers was a stated aim of the bombing campaign, the Ministry refused to change. 'It is desirable,' ran the reply, 'to present the bomber offensive in such a light as to provoke the minimum of public controversy.'[57] Discretion was always observed in describing British bombing as directed at military targets, even to the crews who could see the real results of later raids that obliterated whole cities.

Much of the argument about whether to bomb or what to bomb was rendered void by the reality of Bomber Command's offensive across the summer months of 1940. The optimistic intelligence reports were belied by the evidence of just how little Bomber Command could do with limited numbers and a small bomblift. Taking the gloves off revealed not a clenched fist but a limp hand. In late May priority was given to oil (Western Air Plan W.A.6) and communications targets, since their destruction was expected to affect the campaign in France directly. After the French defeat the priority given to oil remained in place, but a new directive on 20 June added the German aircraft industry to the list and suggested the firebombing of forests to induce a food crisis in Germany (it was argued that game driven from the forests by fire would be forced to eat the crops on the surrounding farmland). On 30 July Bomber Command was also directed to hit electric power stations where they could be located easily by night, while over the whole summer raids had to be carried out on targets in the ports from which an invasion might be launched.[58] Between June and August the modest bombload of 2,806 tons was divided between these eight different objectives, spread across northern France, the Low Countries and northern Germany, a little under one-quarter of the tonnage directed at enemy airfields.[59] The constant shifts in priority prevented the Command from focusing on any one target system. Most operations had to be conducted in unfavourable conditions when the primary target was obscured by haze or cloud or shrouded by the blackout. Irregular, small-scale, dispersed and difficult to assess, the early raids had the sole merit of forcing large numbers of Germans in north-west Germany to seek shelter during the summer nights until ways were devised by German civil defence to minimize the time lost because of the alarms.

The large number of German targets and sudden shifts in allocation required a tactical approach that reduced even further any prospect of serious damage. In most cases only 20–30 aircraft were dispatched to each location, and only a fraction allocated to each specific target on the assumption that a handful of bombs dropped by five or six aircraft would be enough to do effective damage. Out of 89 attacks made on Hamburg in 1940, 58 were made with fewer than 10 aircraft.[60] Most bombs carried were high explosive; incendiaries were spread in small quantities throughout the attacking force, which eliminated any prospect of a concentrated fire-raising operation. The number of bombers available for sorties declined over the summer months after the losses sustained in the Battle of France and because of the need to divert bomber aircraft to training units. The total number of sorties carried out between June and August was 8,681, but over 1,000 were against targets in France and the Low Countries, and around two-fifths were light-bomber sorties. The tonnage of bombs dropped was just 0.9 per cent of the tonnage dropped by Bomber Command in the same months in 1944.[61]

It soon became clear that the bombs were dropped with no particular accuracy. In the absence of electronic navigation or an effective bomb-sight, Portal's claim that bombing would be inherently inaccurate proved entirely justified. A photographic survey of bombing raids on the German aircraft industry in July 1940 found that out of 10 attacks only a couple of hangars had been destroyed; out of 31 oil installations bombed, only one appeared damaged.[62] An American eyewitness account of an RAF attempt to bomb a Daimler-Benz factory in Stuttgart highlighted the exceptional efforts bomber pilots made to identify their target, circling the city for half an hour, but reported that not a single one of the bombs they subsequently dropped hit the plant.[63] One Bomber Command pilot later wrote that precise objectives in summer 1940 'were pointless' when crews could not even find the city they were supposed to target.[64] Most RAF bombs dropped in the German countryside, but even those deliberately dropped on forests between June and August 1940, following repeated pressure from Churchill to try to burn down German woodland, failed to ignite a fire. Experiments with setting fire to woods or crops continued for more than a year, when it was finally conceded that even under ideal climatic conditions most incendiaries burnt only the few inches around where they landed.[65]

Little of this problem was due to German defences. As the British were themselves to find during the Blitz, little preparation had been made for the defence against night-bombing. German anti-aircraft fire could force enemy aircraft to fly higher at night but could hit them mainly by chance, and this despite a formidable array of anti-aircraft weapons. By June 1940 there were 3,095 heavy guns, 9,815 light guns and 4,035 searchlights organized into defensive zones around the vulnerable industrial areas. Guns were moved back from the frontier areas following the defeat of France, strengthening the home defence even more. Yet between January and June 1940 only two aircraft were claimed from anti-aircraft fire, and in August and September not a single one. The principal effect was to force the attacking bombers to break formation, exacerbating the existing dispersion of the British effort.[66] Most of Bomber Command's problems were self-inflicted. A post-war presentation of the early bombing effort by an official of the British Bombing Survey Unit in 1946 concluded that the forces were too small, the weapons incapable of a high degree of damage, targets could not be found, and too much effort was devoted to subsidiary operations: 'great call on Air Force,' ran the lecture notes, 'to attack and destroy targets beyond its power'.[67]

Under these circumstances it is perhaps surprising that the offensive was continued at all. Its survival owed much to the confidence of Bomber Command's new commander-in-chief, Charles Portal, that bombing would eventually deliver strategic dividends. Portal was a successful career airman who began flying in the First World War and was among the first airmen to drop bombs on German soil. He played a key part in building up RAF strength in the late 1930s as director of organization. He was in charge of training when he was called to command the bombing war in April 1940. He was widely respected – 'honest and unprejudiced' according to one former colleague, 'not much small talk' according to another – and liked by Americans for his straightforward character and shrewd intelligence. A shy man who lunched alone day after day at the same London club, the private man was sealed off from his staff. He was convinced that bombing was a more effective way to wage modern war and remained a staunch defender of the bombing force when he was appointed chief of the air staff in October 1940.[68] He argued steadily through the summer months that Bomber Command should be allowed to do what it had been prepared for, despite all the operational difficulties, and he shielded the force from criticism through the years that followed.

The second factor was the unstinting support of Churchill whose interest in bombing waxed through the months after the fall of France. He asked to be informed about the operational performance of Bomber Command and intervened in every aspect of its activities, from the supply of bombers and bombs to the plan to burn down forests. His enthusiasm for bombing was a creature of the emergency facing Britain during the summer and autumn of 1940 when British forces had to demonstrate to the United States and to the peoples of occupied Europe that they still had some capacity for offensive action, however limited. It was also necessary to impress the British public that military action against Germany had not been abandoned after the evacuation from Dunkirk in late May and early June.[69] On 8 July Churchill wrote to the Minister of Aircraft Production, Lord Beaverbrook, summing up his view of how bombing could help decisively in the overthrow of Hitler: 'But there is one thing that will bring him back and bring him down, and that is an absolutely devastating, exterminating attack by very heavy bombers from this country upon the Nazi homeland.'[70] The choice of words was unfortunate and Churchill's comment has contributed to the recent debate about whether the bombing campaign from the outset had a genocidal purpose.[71] This is almost certainly not what Churchill had in mind, since he wrote the letter months before the onset of the Blitz (this *did* prompt in him a rhetorical language of violent retribution). He also reproduced it later on in his history of the war, when he had had time to reflect on what to leave out, and indeed deliberately omitted much of the story of British bombing and his part in it.[72] But it did express Churchill's desperate hope that bombing Germany was perhaps, as RAF leaders had repeatedly asserted, one possible means to compel Hitler to abandon invasion plans or even to dislocate the German war effort decisively. Harris kept a copy of the Beaverbrook letter with him after the war; 'That was the RAF mandate,' he told the biographer Andrew Boyle in 1979, shortly before his death.[73]

From the point of view of British strategy, approval of bombing was a decision that came at a high price. Bomber Command achieved negligible results against German targets and invited German retaliation. In early September Hitler finally responded to British attacks by permitting a campaign against London and other cities which dwarfed anything that could be done in return. It is possible that the Blitz would have been launched anyway, as British air leaders had expected, but it is also possible that without a British bombing campaign, British cities might have been spared the full horrors of the winter of 1940–41.

GERMAN LESSONS: 1940-41

The onset of heavy German night-bombing in September 1940 showed Bomber Command at last what a serious bombing offensive looked like. Attacks were made with hundreds of bomber aircraft concentrated against a single target, while diversionary or nuisance raids were made to confuse the defences and create widespread disruption. Heavy use of incendiaries contrasted with the British preference for high-explosive bombs, and produced widespread area damage. At first the RAF thought the German campaign was flawed because they assumed the attacks were designed to terrorize the population. A survey of 'Lessons to be Learned from German Mistakes', produced two weeks after the first heavy raid on London, concluded that 'the indiscriminate attack of cities is invariably uneconomical', a view with which German air commanders would have concurred.[74] But it soon became clear that the pattern was to attack ports, food supplies and the aircraft industry, and the evident ability of German bombers to attack at will and achieve a relatively high concentration of hits turned the RAF towards the idea of learning lessons from what the Germans got right. After nine months the Air Ministry arrived at the view that regular 'Blitz' attacks on German city areas demonstrated the most profitable use to which Bomber Command could be put.[75] The shift in 1941 and 1942 to a policy of 'area' bombing came about not as a result of the poor accuracy achieved in attacks on specific objectives, as is usually suggested, but as a result of copying the Germans.

The German offensive was from this point of view a valuable learning tool, since it was difficult to evaluate clearly what Bomber Command was itself achieving over Germany. From June 1940 onwards, Britain was cut off from Europe by German military successes. Until the autumn the RAF relied on hearsay and occasional news reports to form a picture of the effects of British bombing. The sustained German attacks could now be used to assess with greater scientific, technical and statistical precision exactly what an air raid might achieve. The programme of evaluation began almost immediately. In late September 1940 the Research and Experiments Department of the Ministry of Home Security supplied a detailed study of the effects of German bombs on different types of target – oil storage, gas works, power stations, aircraft factories, and so on – and reached a conclusion that was to have far-reaching consequences for the development of Bomber Command's offensive.

'It is axiomatic,' ran the report, 'that fire will always be the optimum agent for the complete destruction of buildings, factories etc.' The department recommended using high-explosive bombs to create the 'essential draught conditions' in damaged buildings, followed by heavy incendiary loads, and completed with more high explosive to hamper the enemy emergency services.[76] The evidence that concentrated use of incendiaries was the most effective form of air assault against large industrial centres gradually emerged as the key lesson to be learned from the experience of the Blitz. It was the seed from which area bombing slowly germinated during the year that followed.

The work of the Research and Experiments Department made an essential contribution to understanding what bombing could achieve. The department was set up in spring 1939 to help the Home Office evaluate the effects of bombing and was run by the former director of the Building Research Station, Dr Reginald Stradling. He co-opted scientists and statisticians onto the staff, including the zoologist Solly Zuckerman and the physicist (and former pacifist) J. D. Bernal. In November 1941 Bernal established division RE8 to supply the Air Ministry directly with calculations on the effects of German bombs on British cities, the productive loss caused by bombing and the likely impact of British bombing on German cities.[77] This work was supplemented by the Air Warfare Analysis Section, which looked at the weight and type of bombs to be dropped, and by the work of the Road Research Laboratory and Building Research Laboratory, both of which helped to estimate the nature of bomb damage and the vulnerability of German building structures.[78] Bombing research was in its infancy during the Blitz, but it benefited from the long experience in the 1930s of recruiting senior scientists to work on particular aspects of air warfare.[79] Although the relationship between scientists and airmen was never formalized, the Air Ministry knew that it needed scientific input not only to provide effective technology (particularly radar and navigation aids) but to be able to make better sense of operations. Research questions were usually framed by the air staff and the subsequent expert reports circulated to those who needed them; sometimes it was the experts who took the initiative. This was particularly the case with the German-born Oxford physicist Frederick Lindemann (later Lord Cherwell), who was recruited by Churchill in 1939 to form a small statistical section in the Admiralty, and then followed Churchill to Downing Street in 1940. Lindemann took a special interest in bombing and was perhaps more responsible than anyone in keeping Churchill abreast of the many problems faced by Bomber Command in its early years.[80] His Statistical Section began at once in September 1940 to produce accurate figures on the damage inflicted by German bombs, and to relate those figures to the density of urban population in different city zones. These figures were then applied to German cities, to try to determine the areas where the highest damage could be done in terms of lives lost and houses destroyed.[81] Why Lindemann was so committed to the idea of destroying the country of his birth has never been clear, but he played an important part in deriving conclusions about German bombing and projecting them onto potential German targets.

Of all the lessons drawn from what was thought to be German practice, the possibility of urban destruction was the most important. It was gradually assumed that the German intention was to undermine British morale by inflicting concentrated attacks on ports and industrial cities, reducing the will to work by the destruction of services, amenities and housing, and reducing food supplies. Planners at the Air Ministry described German bombing as the direct opposite of British practice: instead of attempting to hit precise targets, the German Air Force carried out attacks on particular industrial or commercial areas where multiple targets were clustered; German raids were concentrated but too inaccurate for any purpose, it was argued, other than 'the "blitzkrieg" of fairly extensive regions'.[82] Studies of British cities also confirmed that the critical level of damage was inflicted by incendiary bombs dropped in large numbers. Particular attention was paid to the German bombing of London, Coventry and Liverpool, but special studies were commissioned of the bombing of Hull and Birmingham with a view to understanding how fire combined with high explosive affected areas of different housing and population density. Damage was heaviest in the congested working-class districts, which suggested that these were optimum targets. A draft directive from the bombing operations office in the Air Ministry in June 1941 drew heavily from this research on the Blitz: 'The output of the German heavy industry depends almost exclusively on the workers. Continuous and relentless bombing of these workers and their utility services, over a period of time, will inevitably lower their morale, kill a number of them, and thus appreciably reduce their industrial output.'[83]

These arguments signalled an important change in the way 'morale' was interpreted. The politicians, Churchill included, generally understood morale in political terms: heavy pressure from bombing would induce a social and political collapse, perhaps even a revolution. The

German attacks on morale were more clearly economic in intent. In May 1941 the Ministry of Economic Warfare, which had been monitoring the ineffective impact of Bomber Command on precise economic objectives in Germany, sent a memorandum recommending that the RAF abandon military targets and focus instead on economic warfare against major industrial concentrations or 'whole cities'. The idea stemmed from the effects of German bombing on the British workforce: 'British experience leads us to believe that loss of output ... through absenteeism and other dislocation consequent upon the destruction of workers' dwellings and shopping centres is likely to be as great as, if not greater than the production loss which we can expect to inflict by heavy damage.'[84] Although the hope for a political dividend from bombing was not abandoned entirely, particularly by Churchill, the Air Ministry came to view morale as a barometer of productive performance rather than political outlook. The same term was used to cover both, but by the time morale became a specified objective in July 1941, it was used as a description of economic attrition – a form of 'industrial blockade' – in which the working-class population was attacked as an abstract factor of production whose deaths, disablement or absence would have economic consequences.[85]

By the spring of 1941, the arguments in favour of imitating what was thought to be German practice had come to be widely broadcast and from a variety of different sources. The debt owed to German bombing was evident in the choice of the term 'Blitz' to describe the nature of the new strategy. In April 1941 a review of bombing policy recommended 'carefully planned, concentrated and continuous "BLITZ" attacks delivered on the centre of the working-class area of the German cities and towns'. Notes produced in the Bombing Operations department of the Air Ministry a month later on the use of the bomber force also stressed 'continuous blitz attacks on the densely populated workers [sic] and industrial areas'.[86] Later in 1941, when calculations were made of the ratio between weight of bombs and expected deaths among German workers, the measurements were given as '1 Coventry', '2 Coventries', etc.; an attack on the scale of '4 Coventries' was expected to yield 22,515 German deaths.[87] It is important to recognize that the emphasis on killing German workers and destroying their milieu was deliberate, not an unintended consequence of bombing factories. In November 1940 a memorandum on bombing policy, almost certainly penned by Harris, asked whether the time had not come to strike in full force 'against the people themselves'. In May 1941 the director of Air Intelligence welcomed an attack on 'the livelihood, the homes, the cooking, heating, lighting and family life of that section of the population which, in any country, is least mobile and most vulnerable to a general air attack – the working class'. The chiefs of staff in June finally endorsed morale attacks that induced 'fear of death and mutilation'.[88] The idea of collateral damage had been turned on its head: instead of the death of workers and the destruction of their housing being a side-effect of hitting factories, damage to factories was a collateral effect of destroying working-class neighbourhoods.

However, deliberate attacks on densely populated areas, aimed at killing workers and disrupting civilian life, once again raised awkward moral questions. A further memorandum drafted in May 1941 by the Director of Bombing Operations pointed out that since October 1940 Churchill had freed Bomber Command from having to bomb with discrimination, so that 'attacking the workers' was now permissible. 'We do not mean by this,' he continued, 'that we shall ever profess the German doctrine that terrorism constitutes an effective weapon of war.' Nevertheless, he recommended that no announcement of the policy should be made, and the details of plans for attacking the population should have very limited circulation; in the wrong hands, 'all sort of false and misleading deductions might be made'.[89] In late November 1941 Sir Richard Peirse, the then commander-in-chief of Bomber Command, addressing a sympathetic audience of the Thirty Club, explained that for almost a year his force had been attacking 'the people themselves' intentionally. 'I mention this,' he continued, 'because, for a long time, the Government for excellent reasons has preferred the world to think that we still held some scruples and attacked only what the humanitarians are pleased to call Military Targets . . . I can assure you, Gentlemen, that we tolerate no scruples.'[90]

There were also lessons to learn about how a Blitz attack should be carried out. An Air Staff memorandum on area attack pointed out how unwise it would be 'if we fail to pick the brains of an enemy who has had so much experience in developing the required technique'.[91] The method consisted of a high concentration of incendiary bombs dropped in a short period of time with the use of a target-marking force to indicate the urban area to be devastated. The proportion of incendiaries carried by German bombers was known to vary between 30 and 60 per cent, concentrated in the first attack groups, while RAF bombers carried between 15 and 30 per cent, diluted throughout the force. The critical problem was to drop enough incendiaries to create fires that ran out of control, which meant smothering an area with firebombs. The attack on the City of London on 29 December 1940 was used as the model. The raid started 28 conflagrations, 51 serious fires, 101 medium fires and 1,286 small ones, and it was this level of assault that could be expected to overwhelm the emergency services.[92] Detailed evidence from Britain's other blitzed cities suggested that incendiary bombs had five times the destructive potential of heavy explosive per ton. They were best used, it was suggested by Air Intelligence, against cities with narrow streets and wooden structures. Germany's old town centres were 'ideal targets for large-scale incendiary attack' because German urban areas were denser and taller than their British equivalents. A salvo of 30,000 British 4-lb incendiaries dropped in 20 minutes was regarded as a necessary minimum, though much larger quantities were found to be necessary later on. High explosive was needed to reduce the water supply and ventilate the buildings.[93] It was realized in the Air Ministry by the summer of 1941 that to maximize the effect of firebomb attack the equivalent of the German *Kampfgruppe 100* was required, skilled in navigation so that it could carry out a fire-raising attack which the following bombers could use for their own navigation.[94] Portal used *Kampfgruppe 100* as his example when he suggested in August 1941 to the government scientific adviser, Sir Henry Tizard, the need to move to a target-marking system as soon as possible.[95]

These lessons were learned in the end both slowly and piecemeal. The structure for decision-making in the RAF and the Air Ministry made it difficult to change quickly, while there remained honest differences of opinion about the most effective use for bombers. Major changes in policy over bombing required the approval of the chiefs of staff and Churchill's Defence Committee. They had to be properly formulated and presented to the Air Council and the Air Staff in the ministry before they could be presented to higher authority. Much of the work on trying to understand German strategy and tactics was dispersed among different departments and usually written up in the first instance by junior staff. This situation improved when a Directorate of Bombing Operations was finally set up under Air Commodore John Baker in September 1940, at the prompting of the then deputy chief of the air staff, Air Marshal Harris. While strategy was decided at the highest level, the operational conduct of Bomber Command was left largely to the discretion of the commander-in-chief, who could modify or ignore instructions from the air staff with which he disagreed. Bombing policy was also subject to external civilian influence. The Ministry of Economic Warfare

1. A crashed Junkers Ju88 medium bomber on an airfield in northern France, autumn 1940. Accidents took a high toll on German aircraft during the Blitz in the difficult winter weather.

2. During the campaign against Britain, German airmen take a break with organized sports. Air force psychiatrists also recommended three weeks at a winter sports spa to overcome combat fatigue.

3. 'Britain Can Take It'. A British pub somewhere in the Midlands after a bombing raid, still serving beer to the rescue squad. Pictures like this helped to sustain the popular image of British stoicism in the face of peril.

4. Here the photographer has managed to capture the moment during a Blitz raid when a large building collapses on the corner of Deansgate and St Mary's gate in Manchester, which was raided heavily in December 1940.

5. Civil defence workers scramble to rescue Londoners trapped under rubble during a daylight raid on London in the autumn of 1940. More than 43,000 people died in the bombing in 1940–41.

6. Class war. A cheerful civil defence team helps a banker rescue files from a bombed business in the heart of the City of London, which was hit dramatically on 29 December 1940.

7. A funeral procession in London for thirty-one schoolchildren killed in a hit-and-run raid on London in January 1943. Such raids were small and few, but still deadly, long after the Blitz.

8. Soviet medical students from the Ivan Pavlov Medical School in Leningrad form an emergency civil defence first-aid team during the bombing and shelling of the city in the siege that began in September 1941.

9. People in Stalingrad running for their lives during the bombing of the city by the German Air Force Fourth Air Fleet in August 1942. An estimated 4,000 were killed in a month of heavy bombing.

10. Political warfare leaflets are loaded onto an RAF bomber for delivery over occupied Europe and Germany. During the war more than 1.4 billion leaflets were dropped by aircraft in the propaganda war, and a further 95 million by balloon.

11. An RAF bomb store in October 1940. Rows of 500-lb bombs are waiting to be loaded onto Bomber Command aircraft for another night raid against Germany after five months of almost uninterrupted operations against German targets.

12. The Combined Bomber Offensive at work. The picture shows British and American air leaders at dinner in 1943. Seated facing the camera from left to right are Carl Spaatz, Charles Portal, Frederick Anderson, Ira Eaker (standing), Arthur Harris and James Doolittle. In the centre foreground is Trafford Leigh-Mallory.

13. Though relations between the RAF and the US Eighth Air Force could be strained, publicity stunts, like this one at an RAF base, were designed to ease the tension. Here US aircrew write messages on a British bomb destined for Germany.

14. Two RAF crewmen after their return from a combat mission. The strain is evident from operations that resulted overall in the death of almost half the men who flew. Fear was the emotion most commonly remembered by those who survived, and courage their chief characteristic.

15. The dangers faced by bomber crew came from enemy fighters, anti-aircraft fire and the weather. Here a stricken B-24 'Liberator' bomber from the US Eighth Air Force, on fire and damaged by anti-aircraft shells, struggles to keep flying.

under the Labour minister Hugh Dalton and the ad hoc Lloyd Committee, set up in 1939 under Geoffrey Lloyd to deal specifically with the German oil situation, could make recommendations to the politicians that simply bypassed the RAF.[96] Air policy was not entirely haphazard, but it moved in the first years of war in fits and starts, trapped between exaggerated expectations and a beleaguered reality.

Portal's successor as commander-in-chief of Bomber Command in October 1940 was Sir Richard Peirse, a senior career airman, who had been vice-chief of staff before his appointment. He was a supporter of precision bombing, though more of a realist about what could be achieved, and not in principle opposed to area bombing. He stuck to the directives that called for attacks on oil, communications and the aircraft industry, but his force remained small and divided between numerous targets. The number of sorties per month fell steadily, exacerbated by the slow supply of bombers and crew and the deteriorating weather, which grounded bombers on both sides through much of December and January. In September 1940 there were 3,597 sorties, by November only 2,039 and in January 1941 only 1,131. Even by the summer of 1941 the figures were little better than they had been a year before, reaching a peak of 3,989 in July.[97] The RAF also experienced, like the German Air Force, a high rate of wastage due chiefly to accidents. The Bomber Command Groups had 290 serviceable bombers at the beginning of October 1940, but only 212 at the end of November. Peirse told Portal that for every aircraft shot down by the enemy, he was losing six to accidents.[98] Part of the problem he attributed to the declining skill of bomber crews, too many of whom were rushed from the Operational Training Units (OTUs) to the front-line squadrons. The decision to accelerate promotion to allow sergeants to pilot aircraft produced evidence, so it was claimed, of 'slackness and inefficiency'. A report from 7 Group in January 1941 highlighted poor discipline among recruits from the OTUs: 'unpunctuality and absence without leave ... some of them seem to think they can turn up when they like'.[99] For many crewmen in the winter of 1940–41 the reality was to fly long, dangerous operations over German territory in poor weather, with inadequate equipment, returning to bomber stations which were still improvised and poorly lit, and in the knowledge that most of the target photographs they took were of somewhere other than the place to which they had been directed.

The poor performance of Bomber Command owed a good deal to the priorities that had been given to home defence during the summer and autumn of 1940. But since this was one of Britain's few offensive options, its deficiencies were very public. In early November Churchill complained to Portal that bomb tonnage on Germany was 'lamentably small', given the amount of money and material devoted to it: 'I wish I could persuade you to realize that there is a great failure of *quantitative delivery*.' In December 1940 he returned again to attack the 'stagnant condition' of the command and its 'deplorable' operational perform-ance.[100] Peirse was sensitive to the accusations and continued to insist that his force would be a cardinal factor in reducing Germany's war economy and will to wage war by the spring of 1941, while para-doxically explaining that weather and poor training were likely to inhibit anything his force could do.[101] Churchill's frustration contrib-uted to pushing Bomber Command slowly towards a strategy that favoured city bombing. He tried unsuccessfully to insist that Bomber Command attack Berlin in October. He told Peirse that he hoped his Command would soon be bombing 'every "Hun corner" every night'.[102]

In late November 1940 the War Cabinet endorsed a decision to retaliate for the attack on Coventry by bombing a German city indis-criminately. Portal supplied a list of four cities – Hanover, Mannheim, Cologne and Düsseldorf – and told Peirse to mobilize every aircraft he could, even from the training units. Bombing was to continue all night, replicating the German practice of heavy incendiary attack, followed by high explosive, and then further incendiaries. Codenamed ABIGAIL RACHEL, Peirse chose Mannheim as his target and attacked it on 16–17 December 'based on the experience we have gained from Coventry, Bris-tol etc.' But because of poor weather only 101 out of a planned 235 aircraft could be sent. Most claimed to have bombed the target, but in fact the advance group of Wellingtons failed to mark the centre of the city, while other bombers scattered their loads widely over residential areas. There were 34 deaths and 476 houses were destroyed. When Peirse asked whether he could conduct a similar raid against Hanover, Churchill was non-committal.[103]

The city attacks were not repeated, though not from any moral qualms. The Blitz had finally eroded any serious concern about the mor-ality of bombing the civilians of a state whose air force had killed almost 30,000 British civilians in four months. They were held in abeyance by the striking news given to the Cabinet in mid-December that the small effort against German oil targets had probably reduced German sup-plies by 15 per cent. The figure was a gross distortion of reality, as photo-reconnaissance intelligence of plants bombed in December made

clear, but Portal snatched at the news as a chance to redeem Bomber
Command at one of the many critical moments in its survival over the
early war years. The air staff worked out that there were enough aircraft to knock out 17 oil plants and that the attack could be repeated
every four months to ensure that they remained inoperable.[104] The chiefs
of staff approved the policy on 7 January 1941 and the War Cabinet a
week later, with the rider that in adverse conditions area attacks might
be made instead. The decision to focus on a single target made little
sense in the light of what had already been learned about the pattern of
German bombing, and the failure of the plan was evident within weeks.
At the end of February 1941 Peirse had to confess to Portal that he had
only been able to attack oil targets on three nights in the whole of January and February; towns had been attacked six times, but most of
Bomber Command's effort had in fact been devoted to German naval
and port targets, which were easier to find and hit.[105] The oil plan was
a peculiar fantasy given the current technical capability and evident
inaccuracy of the bomber force. Its failure was masked by the sudden
decision taken by Churchill in early March to focus the effort of Bomber
Command entirely on the Battle of the Atlantic to try to break the
blockade imposed by German sea and air attack. Portal lacked Göring's
political muscle and was unable to resist the diversion. Naval priorities
prevailed and for four months Bomber Command began a largely fruitless campaign against German submarine pens and warships.

By the time Bomber Command was permitted to return to priorities
in Germany the weight of opinion inside and outside the RAF had consolidated in favour of morale attacks on working-class urban areas.
Early in June 1941 the Air Ministry produced a new discussion document rejecting oil as a primary target. What was proposed was a
compromise between what remained of the principle of precision and
the desire to replicate German area attacks. Using material supplied by
the Ministry of Economic Warfare, a concerted attack on railway transport in the Ruhr-Rhineland area was proposed. Precise targets were to
be located in city areas so that '"shorts and overs" [which constituted
most British bombs] will kill'. For most nights, however, it was proposed that the bomber force be used to attack the industrial workforce
in the same Ruhr area.[106] Following German practice, it was also suggested that city targets on or near water would be more suitable to
make sure that a sufficient proportion of the attacking force could find
them. On 9 July the new proposals were issued as a directive to Bomber
Command, after the phrase 'the morals of the German people' had been

altered to read 'morale'. A list of suitable railway targets was appended
with the caveat that for 75 per cent of any month bombers would not
be able to see their targets clearly enough for precision; for three-quarters
of each month Bomber Command was expected to undertake 'heavy,
concentrated and continuous attacks of working class and industrial
areas'.[107] There was no certainty how long this directive would remain
in force. Peirse complained to Portal about the constant changes in priority: 'I do not feel I am fully in touch with your ideas. I may be working
with you or against you, I am not sure. But it is certainly difficult to
work to any plan with this ever-changing background.'[108] Peirse came to
accept that winning the bombing war required 'attack of the German
people themselves', and this part of the directive remained in place, in
one form or another, for the rest of the war.[109]

   The one lesson that the RAF and the government failed to learn from
the German experience was, paradoxically, the reality of relative failure.
German bombing did not dislocate the economy seriously nor did it
undermine civilian commitment to the war effort, as the Air Ministry
could clearly see. It was difficult to argue that German 'morale' would
somehow crack if British morale had remained intact after nine months
of remorseless assault. When the new directive was shown to the American chiefs of staff at the Argentia meeting between Churchill and
Roosevelt in August 1941, they found it hard to reconcile the morale
bombing of Germany with the 'valorous experience' of the British
people under German bombardment.[110] The RAF could not ignore this
paradox. It was resolved by suggesting that the Germans lacked the
qualities of endurance and pluck displayed by the British under fire. The
general prejudice among senior airmen was that the German people, as
one intelligence report put it, 'will not stand a quarter of the bombing'
dished out to Britain, though there were few sensible grounds for believing it.[111] A report in July 1941 following a meeting in Lisbon with
American diplomatic personnel from Germany, suggested that the average German worker displayed a 'lack of moral fibre'.[112] An Air Staff
memorandum produced in September 1941 accepted that in the British
case bombing tended to stiffen rather than weaken morale, but went on
to argue that the Germans had based their campaign on judging the
poor morale of their own people. Made of sterner stuff, British morale
had not given way, but, the report concluded, 'the wheel has gone full
cycle, and it has become increasingly clear that one of the most (if not
the most) serious chinks in the German armour is the morale of the civil

population'.[113] The paper concluded with an unambiguous statement of the purpose that now lay behind the British bombing offensive:

> The ultimate aim of the attack of a town area is to break the morale of the population which occupies it. To achieve this we must achieve two things: first, we must make the town physically uninhabitable and, secondly, we must make the people conscious of constant personal danger. The immediate aim is, therefore, twofold, namely, to produce:
>
> (i) Destruction, and (ii) The fear of death.

Here was a German lesson to be taught to the Germans.

BOMBER COMMAND IN CRISIS: 1941–2

By the time the July 1941 directive was issued, the war had suddenly changed its character. Heavy German bombing of British cities stopped in early June, and on 22 June as many as 4 million Axis forces poured across the Soviet border in the largest invasion in history. That same evening Churchill broadcast to the nation, pledging British support for the Soviet Union against 'the bloodthirsty guttersnipe' who had now unleashed war against another suffering people. He announced that he had offered Stalin all technical and economic assistance, but the one military pledge he made was to promise 'to bomb Germany by day as well as by night with ever-increasing measure' to give the German people a taste of their own medicine.[114] On 7 July Churchill sent a telegram to Stalin explaining that the best Britain could offer as direct military assistance was bombing; this, Churchill continued, would force Germany to divert fighters to the west, and ease the pressure on the Soviet front.[115] Churchill hoped privately that the new campaign would prompt Soviet bombers to attack Germany from the east: 'A lot of German war industry should be vulnerable especially if we are bombing from the other side.' Stalin replied that he would prefer Britain to open a second front in northern France or Scandinavia.[116]

Churchill exaggerated what Bomber Command was capable of achieving and misunderstood the nature of Soviet air strategy, which favoured ground support over long-range bombing. But Bomber Command used the German-Soviet war as a way to improve its low political stock. On 21 July 1941 Churchill and Attlee were invited to view a demonstration by the heavy bombers that were scheduled to come into large-scale service over the coming year. The party watched as five heavy four-engine bombers flew past at low altitude: a Short Stirling, an Avro Lancaster, a Handley Page Halifax and two American bombers promised to Britain under the Lend-Lease scheme authorized in March 1941, the Boeing B-17 'Flying Fortress' and the Consolidated B-24 'Liberator'. The party was impressed in particular by the Lancaster, but there were reservations in the RAF about the American bombers with their more limited bombloads.[117] The political imperative of supporting the Soviet war effort suited Bomber Command in summer 1941 because it gave the Command a prominence that its poor operational record scarcely warranted. Churchill needed bombing as something to trade with Stalin. Later in the war Air Vice-Marshal Richard Peck, in a speech surveying the course of British bombing, reminded his audience that in summer 1941 the air forces were given the task of supporting Russia by bombing Germany: 'Not everyone has appreciated,' he continued, 'the extent to which the bomber offensive was applied to aid the Russian armies.'[118]

The political imperative masked the operational reality. On 22 June, the night of the German invasion, 70 medium bombers raided the north German port of Bremen; it was covered in haze and the bombing was scattered. The following night 62 bombers raided Cologne where a few bombs fell on the city but there were no reported casualties; 41 bombers raided Düsseldorf with no clear result; 26 aircraft attacked Kiel with little effect and one death.[119] These were no larger than the attacks still being mounted by the exiguous German force left in northern France – raids on Birmingham with 94 and 88 aircraft, on Hull with 78, 64 and 114, on London with 60 – and considerably less destructive.[120] Most RAF attacks were still being made on targets on the French coast. On 7 July Churchill complained to Portal that he should stop bombing these Battle of the Atlantic targets and concentrate on 'the devastation of the German cities' to take the weight off Russia. The war diary written up at Hitler's supreme headquarters failed even to mention any of the British raids.[121]

Summer 1941 was not the first time that bombing had been promoted for political reasons, but the fear that Germany might defeat the Soviet Union and turn back to Britain with all the resources of Eurasia at its disposal gave bombing an added urgency. It also made the operational inadequacy of Bomber Command more obtrusive. In early July Churchill complained to Lindemann, Portal and the Air Minister, Sir Archibald Sinclair, that the bomber force was little larger than it had been the year before, though it was supposed to be 'indispensable for victory'.[122] High losses and the slow build-up of bomber production had indeed reduced the plans for expansion. There was worse to come. In July 1941 Lindemann asked Bomber Command whether he might investigate bombing accuracy by analysing photographs taken during operations. This was a project that had only become possible since the early summer. When the war broke out the RAF had day cameras but none suitable for night photography. Trials were carried out with the standard F.24 camera using a shutter mechanism and a large flash unit released manually through the bomber's flare shute. When the flare was at maximum intensity, one of the bomber crew had to close the shutter. The result was a complex operation designed to be undertaken at the most dangerous point over the target. Research began on an automatic night camera but it was not ready until 1942. The force had to make do in 1941 with a simplified camera with no shutter, which produced a poorer image but one regarded as adequate. In December 1940 there were still only 13 cameras available; Peirse asked for 500 so that most bombers could carry them. By March 1941 there were 75, by September there were 200.[123] Taking an effective photograph was always difficult, with the ground obscured by smoke and the camera confused by flares, gunbursts and searchlights. Pilots disliked the order to keep a level flightpath while the picture was taken. Nevertheless, from June 1941 a growing stream of images became available for the first time, interpreted by a special unit set up at RAF Mednenham. Now that a fuller photographic record was possible, Portal willingly agreed to Lindemann's request, perhaps not fully aware of what the results might show.[124]

Lindemann instructed a young economist on his staff in the Statistical Section, David Bensusan-Butt, to examine 650 photographs taken from 100 raids between 2 June and 25 July 1941. The report was ready by 18 August. The analysis showed that in general only one in five of all bomber aircraft sent on a mission reached within five miles of the assigned target; of those recorded as actually bombing, the proportion was one in four over Germany, one in 10 over the Ruhr industrial area, and on moonless or hazy nights one in 15.[125] Churchill was alarmed by the revelations: 'It is an awful thought,' he wrote to Portal, 'that perhaps three-quarters of our bombs go astray.'[126] The RAF response was, not surprisingly, defensive. Portal pointed out that weather over Germany had been very poor in June and July; that the Butt Report covered only one-tenth of Bomber Command sorties; that inexperienced navigators probably took images too long after the release of the bombs (almost certainly the case, given the difficulty of operating the camera and seeing the bomb burst below); and, above all, that German raids tracked over Britain showed only 24 per cent of German bombers reaching the target area. Even Lindemann admitted that conditions had not been ideal for photographic analysis in the summer months.[127] Portal was no doubt correct to argue that the Butt Report was subject to substantial methodological flaws, but the RAF's own operational evidence gathered since 1940 had consistently shown a very wide margin of error between what the crews reported and what had actually been bombed. Given Bomber Command's continued practice of sending raids to two or three cities on the same night, and in relatively small numbers, the aircraft likely to be hitting a particular aiming point in Germany on any one raid would be in single figures.

The Butt Report has generally been regarded as a turning point in the British bomber offensive, but its significance can easily be exaggerated. Peirse had asked the Air Ministry in December 1940 to speed up camera supply so that a proper survey of accuracy and bombing effort could be made.[128] Detailed examination of photographic evidence had already been carried out by Bomber Command in April, and again in June 1941, each time showing how over-optimistic were the reports of the crews and how wide the margin of error. Exaggerated reports were common to both sides in the bomber war, but the sober reality was often understood by those who flew. Robert Kee, a bomber pilot and future historian, later reflected on what his diary entries from late 1941 showed him:

> . . . it read pretty depressingly in terms of successful operations . . . Here is an attempt to bomb Brunswick, hopelessly dark, bombed some incendiaries at what we hoped was Hanover. Düsseldorf also hopeless, bombed searchlight concentration. Kiel, this is three in succession. Kiel, hopeless again, very bad weather . . . Mannheim, too much cloud, bombed searchlights.[129]

In October the Operational Research Section of Bomber Command, established at Peirse's request in September under the direction of Dr Basil Dickens, reviewed accuracy for the three months following the Butt Report. It was found that the average performance was even worse than feared: only 15 per cent of aircraft bombed within five miles of the target point.[130]

In truth, the Butt Report highlighted just one of the many problems facing the force in the late summer of 1941, important though it was. Losses began to increase substantially as the result of stronger German defences, placing a heavier burden on a training programme which turned out a growing number of crewmen with limited understanding of what was required of them. 'The one failing of the whole training system,' recalled a rear gunner, 'was that we weren't told more of what to expect. We just learned it strictly from experience.' Peirse told the Air Ministry that up to 40 per cent of the operational squadrons' work consisted of essential additional training, which resulted in regular accidents. Most of the non-operational flying was done during the day, which also prepared crew poorly for what to expect of night-time conditions.[131] In August Bomber Command lost 525 aircraft destroyed or severely damaged (a wastage rate of 13 per cent, many lost to accidents) but received only 106 replacements. In the following three months a further 578 aircraft were written off, many again on non-operational flights. Raids carried out on Berlin for political effect had losses of 30 per cent.[132] Between July and December 1941 the force showed a steady decline in its capability (see Table 5.1).

There are many explanations for the crisis now confronted by Bomber Command. The new strategy of attacks on city areas was only possible with better equipment, and the directives failed to take sufficient account of what technology was currently available. The most

Table 5.1: Bomber Command Statistics, July 1941–February 1942[133]

Month	Bomb Tonnage	Bomber Sorties	Aircraft/Crews (average)	Aircraft Missing
July 1941	4,384	3,989	449	152
August	4,242	3,988	486	156
September	2,889	3,021	485	95
October	2,984	2,715	517	86
November	1,907	1,765	507	83
December	1,794	1,582	530	47
January 1942	2,292	2,226	410	56
February	1,011	1,506	374	41

(Aircraft missing are missing on operations. The number damaged or lost to accidents was higher; figures include all heavy, medium and light-bomber operations)
Sources: TNA, AIR 9/150, DBOps to DCAS, 11 Sept 1941; AIR 22/203, War Room Manual of Bomber Command Operations, 1939–1945, 20–21; AIR 41/41, RAF Narrative, 'The RAF in the Bombing Offensive Against Germany: Vol III', App C, E1.

pressing need was for larger aircraft capable of carrying a much greater tonnage, dropped with greater accuracy. This was an obvious solution and the pressure to accelerate output and improve navigation came from all sides. Yet the heavy bombers that Churchill had been shown in July were still only available in very small numbers because of persistent problems with technical development, while improved navigation was still at the experimental stage despite more than 18 months of war. The Stirling and the Halifax made their first sorties in February and March 1941. The Short Stirling Mk I was the only one of Britain's wartime bombers designed from the start to have four engines. First commissioned in 1936, the prototype made its first successful flight in December 1939 and the first aircraft came into service late in 1940. Powered by four Bristol Hercules engines, the Stirling had a top speed of 270 mph and a range of 590 miles with a full bombload of 14,000 lbs. It had a limited flying ceiling but good defensive capabilities with three powered turrets, yet it was plagued with technical problems which had to be ironed out in 1941 and early 1942. The same was true for the Handley Page Halifax, which also stemmed from a 1936 specification and was originally designed as a twin-engine medium/heavy bomber. In 1937 it was converted to four Rolls-Royce Merlin engines and the prototype flew in October 1939. The Halifax Mk I was developed rapidly and was in service by November 1940. Its first operation, against the French port of Le Havre, was made in March 1941. It had a low operational ceiling of 18,000 feet, a top speed of 265 mph and a range of 1,260 miles with a maximum bombload of 13,000 lbs. The aircraft exhibited persistent development problems, had slow handling characteristics and took high losses. Output continued because it was difficult to disrupt production schedules already laid down, but it was an unpopular aircraft with bomber crews.[134]

The third heavy bomber, the Avro Lancaster, grew out of another twin-engine development, the Manchester, also first specified in 1936. The Manchester was designed around twin Rolls-Royce Vulture engines, but these proved to be a constant source of technical delays. The prototype flew in July 1939, the first service aircraft were delivered in November 1940. The first raid was against the French port of Brest in February 1941, but repeated engine failure led to the cancellation of further production and only 209 were built. In late 1940 a Manchester Mk III was produced with four Rolls-Royce Merlin engines. It was renamed the 'Lancaster' and for Bomber Command it was an unexpected godsend. The Lancaster had a much better performance, a top speed of 287 mph, a ceiling of almost 25,000 feet and a range of over 1,000 miles even with its heaviest load of 22,000 lbs. The usual load was somewhere between 14,000 and 18,000 lbs and the range correspondingly farther. Its carrying capacity was larger than any other bomber used in the European theatre, and four or five times that of the standard German medium bombers. Some 6,750 Lancasters were produced during the war, the mainstay of the later force. Unlike the Halifax, the Lancaster had a more modest loss rate (3.92 per cent compared with 5.75 per cent), absorbed less production effort, carried an average of almost twice as much bomb weight and was easier to service.[135] But it only began operations in modest numbers in 1942. In 1941 the small total of heavy bombers dropped only 4,000 tons against the 31,500 tons dropped by the Wellington medium bombers.[136]

The advent of heavier aircraft would mean that the RAF could take advantage of both a new generation of heavier bombs under development and the rapid expansion of bomb production. The prospect of increasing the aggregate payload was regarded as the critical factor in the offensive, but it had to be postponed until the heavy-bomber force became available. The 250-lb and 500-lb General Purpose bombs were still extensively in use in 1941; larger 1,000, 2,000 and 4,000-lb bombs, more suitable for the larger bomber models, were developed during the Blitz and brought into use in small numbers. These Medium Capacity (MC) and High Capacity (HC) bombs had a higher charge-to-weight ratio, a thinner metal shell and a much greater blast effect. However, they still lacked aluminized explosive, which would have increased that effect more than threefold; only later in the war was Lindemann finally able to persuade the RAF to adopt it. The 4-lb incendiary bomb remained standard equipment but was supplemented by the larger 30-lb firebomb with a blend of phosphorous, rubber and benzol gel, 400,000 of which were ordered in June 1941 and 3 million used by the end of the war.[137] All these bombs became available in quantities too large for the existing bomber force to use. In April 1941, 12 million incendiaries were ordered for the rest of the year and 36 million for 1942; because of magnesium shortages, however, output was only 2.2 million in the nine months of 1941 and 11.8 million in 1942, but these figures were more than enough for a force not yet converted fully to mass incendiary bombing. By the end of 1941 there was a surplus of more than 2 million bombs and monthly production was double monthly expenditure.[138] By summer 1941 around 11,000 tons of high-explosive bombs were being produced and filled every month, though Bomber Command had dropped a monthly average on Germany of just 948 tons between January and April and averaged only 1,884 tons between July and December. In October 1941 there were unused stocks of 121,000 tons of bombs.[139] This was the reverse of the German problem during the Blitz, when there had been the aeroplanes but insufficient filled bombs; the RAF had the bombs but not enough heavy and medium bombers to use them.

Both the new aircraft and the new bombs were slow to join Bomber Command in any significant numbers. Only 41 heavy bombers were produced in 1940 and 498 in 1941, compared with an output of 4,703 medium bombers.[140] These were modest figures against the plans drawn up in spring 1941 to create a force of 4,000 heavy bombers by the spring of 1943. Bomber production had taken a back seat during the summer and autumn of 1940 when priority went to fighter aircraft for defence against German raids. The Minister of Aircraft Production, Lord Beaverbrook, was later blamed by the Air Ministry for trying to kill off 'the Big Bomber programme', but this ignored the serious technical problems encountered in trying to develop and get into service large and complex aircraft in a matter of months.[141] In May 1941 Portal informed Beaverbrook's successor, John Moore-Brabazon, that he did not want any further heavy bombers developed during the war because of the long lead time between designing a bomber and seeing it into service.[142] The '4,000 Plan' was always unrealistic. It called for production of at least 1,000 bombers a month over a two-year period, more than twice the number produced during 1941 and 1942. It was already evident by the summer of 1941 that bomber production had hit a serious bottleneck. The RAF pinned its hopes on being able to persuade the United States to make up the shortfall.

The efforts to get America to solve Britain's bomber crisis went back to the early spring of 1941, when Lend-Lease was finally approved. The RAF delegation in Washington had the challenging task of persuading the American service chiefs to accept the transfer of substantial quantities of modern aircraft, and in particular heavy bombers, from their own rearmament programme. Air Vice Marshal Slessor negotiated the aircraft requirements with the Army Air Corps, commanded by General Henry 'Hap' Arnold ('Hap' for 'Happy'). The American offers were enshrined in what became known as the 'Slessor-Arnold Agreement', a generous commitment, subject to circumstances, to supply Britain on a 50–50 basis from all American aircraft production.[143] The agreement failed, however, to address the problem of the heavy bomber, where Britain's deficiency was most marked and American output still in its infancy. Arnold visited Britain in April 1941 and was told that the British aircraft industry could not produce more than 500 of the 1,000 heavy bombers needed each month. The United States was asked to fill the gap. Arnold agreed that up to four-fifths of American heavy-bomber output could go to Bomber Command by summer 1942, but this would consist of fewer than 800 aircraft. By then it was evident that the American Air Force would renege on the original agreement as relations with Japan deteriorated. At the staff discussions at the Churchill-Roosevelt Argentia summit at Placentia Bay in August 1941, Arnold refused to confirm the American offer. In his diary he noted: 'What the British want – my God what a list and what things – no promises.'[144] During September the full extent of American withdrawal from the initial Slessor agreement became clear. The bombers destined for Britain had been fitted with the Norden bombsight, which was still embargoed for British use, and ensured that the bombers could not be released to the RAF. Instead of the 800 bombers expected, the British were granted 238 with no promise of any further deliveries beyond July 1942. It marked the end of the Slessor agreement and the end of any prospect of developing a force of 4,000 bombers.

The most urgent problem facing Bomber Command was the search for some form of electronic aid for navigation without which even larger numbers of bombers would still have restricted striking power. In the summer of 1941 the problem was not simply the failure to hit a precise industrial or railway target, but the inability, under conditions of night, poor weather and German defences, to find an entire city. Given that these failures almost nullified what Bomber Command was trying to do, the long period that elapsed in trying to find appropriate tactics or technology is difficult to explain. The technology itself was not exotic, and the capacity to interfere with German electronic navigation in the winter of 1940–41 made evident that British science was capable of replicating German practice. The Telecommunications Research Establishment had begun work on a system using radio pulse transmitters in 1938, known as 'G' (for Grid), but usually described as 'Gee'. The system worked by sending pulses from three ground stations which could be measured on a cathode-ray tube carried in the receiving aircraft; where the coordinates intersected it was possible to estimate between a mile and six miles the aircraft's position. Like the German system, it had limited range and was less accurate the further away from the ground stations the aircraft was. It worked generally no further than western Germany. The system was shown to Bomber Command in

October 1940 and service trials began in May 1941. The first experimental operation using 'Gee' was conducted by two Wellington bombers on 11 August 1941, but one crashed on German soil. The delay in introducing 'Gee' was partly a result of delays in the production of one of its valves, but the main problem was the argument between those who favoured putting 'Gee' in a small number of target-finding aircraft, which would lead in the rest of the force, and those who argued that it was something which should be made widely available for the benefit of all. This was to become a central conflict in deciding the best tactics for attacking German cities and it undermined efforts to develop a more appropriate operational system more rapidly. The use of 'Gee' was postponed until enough sets were available to supply much of the Command; its first operational use was not until 8 March 1942.[145]

The arguments over the introduction of 'Gee' also involved the best tactics to adopt to achieve Bomber Command's new objectives and to counter the threat posed by German anti-aircraft defences. Since the summer of 1940, when the German Air Force had relied principally on anti-aircraft fire, a more sophisticated defensive system had been constructed combining anti-aircraft fire, night-fighters, searchlights and radar. The original air defence system, like that of the British, had been based on the assumption that attacks would come by day. The German defenders soon realized that the pattern of British bombing was difficult to predict. A few daylight raids were made, but most raids were small night attacks defined because of their modest scale as nuisance raids (*Störangriffe*), whose object, it was assumed, was to intimidate the population and disturb the rhythm of industrial labour. Then came heavier raids in spring 1941, again scattered and unpredictable but deliberately directed, so the German authorities believed, against 'open cities and residential areas' as simple terror attacks.[146] Night attacks meant that anti-aircraft fire, without radar assistance, was effectively blind. The decentralized pattern of British raiding made it difficult to know what to protect. German air observation posts were set up around 15–20 kilometres from predicted target areas, but night-time conditions reduced the prospect of accurate information. The numerous sound detectors used in conjunction with searchlights were found to be vulnerable to the British tactic of throttling back the engines to dampen the noise as aircraft approached a potential danger zone. (British crews also believed that throwing empty milk bottles or beer bottles out of their aircraft confused enemy equipment. The 'whistling bottle' was said to interfere with sound location and triggered the searchlights to switch off.)[147] For the German side a concerted defence was difficult to mount because RAF bombers failed to damage essential war-economic targets, which were guarded by 'air defence strongpoints', and instead scattered and their loads over an extended area with few evident objectives. The Butt Report could essentially have been written by the Germans months before.[148]

On 3 March 1941 the German Air Force established a new command system to cope with the British offensive. General Hubert Weise was appointed *Luftwaffenbefehlshaber Mitte* (Air Force Commander, Centre) with the task of constructing an effective air defence wall around northern Germany. He centralized air defence by taking over the defensive functions of the *Luftgaue* (Air Regions) in northern, western and central Germany. On 1 May 1941 he set up the first dedicated night-fighter organization under General Josef Kammhuber as *Jagdführer Mitte* (Fighter Leader, Centre) and integrated it with the searchlight and anti-aircraft artillery batteries deployed in northern Germany and the Low Countries. A 'Kammhuber Line' – generally known in German as *Himmelbett* (heavenly bed) – was constructed from the Swiss border, through the Belgian city of Liège to the German-Danish border, consisting of a series of map 'boxes' in each of which a small number of fighters were controlled by a new and improved radar, codenamed *Würzburg*.[149] Only one fighter could be controlled at a time, but once a bomber had been identified it became with practice easier to direct a fighter to combat position. The night-fighters were not yet fitted with AI radar, like British night-fighters. But the German version, codenamed *Lichtenstein*, was in the process of development and was finally installed in 1942, though it was not popular with pilots, who assumed the large external aerials would reduce performance. The searchlights were numerous and powerful, but it was found they were wrongly positioned. From mid-1941 they were spaced out at least three kilometres apart to ensure a better prospect of trapping a bomber overhead. The anti-aircraft batteries were gradually supplied with the new *Würzburg* radar, which, like the British experience with anti-aircraft radar, proved difficult to operate with poorly trained personnel and was prone to technical problems. As radar-guided fire improved, the batteries found the supply of radar too slow. By spring 1942 only one-third of anti-aircraft guns had the new apparatus.[150]

The fighters worked in two distinct ways. The first echelon engaged in what was called 'dark' night-fighting, using radar-equipped ground controllers to guide them to their target; behind the night-fighter boxes was a line of searchlights, soon to have their own radar guidance system, which was used by a second echelon of night-fighters for 'light' fighting against bombers trapped in a searchlight cone. No dedicated night-fighter had been developed before the start of British bombing, but the Junkers Ju88, the Messerschmitt Me110 and the Dornier Do17 (later Do217) were converted to the role in 1940 and formed the mainstay of the force thereafter. The night-fighter force had expanded by the start of 1942 to four night-fighter groups totalling 265 aircraft, a modest fraction of the total German Air Force establishment. The British tactic of allowing bomber crews to work out their own route to the target meant that the raiding group became spread out in area and time, making it easier for each German night-fighter to locate and destroy them in their individual boxes. By September 1941, night-fighters assisted by searchlights had claimed 325 enemy aircraft, while 'dark' night-fighting added a further 50.[151] Anti-aircraft fire claimed 439 aircraft shot down between January and September 1941, though many of these, if true, were from daylight operations mounted by other RAF commands.

The steady increase in losses might well have pushed Bomber Command to adopt new tactics. The decision to focus on incendiary bombing of urban areas ought to have encouraged a tactical shift to larger and more concentrated raids. The advantages were obvious: the concentration of the bomber stream would mean that the individual fighter boxes in the *Himmelbett* line and the searchlight wall behind them would be swamped; most bombers would be through the line and to relative safety until they reached one of the inland gun belts. Above all, tight formation and a bomber stream would allow a raiding group to drop all its bombs in a short period of time, maximizing their impact and reducing bomber casualties.[152] Opinion in the Air Ministry and the Air Staff nevertheless remained divided. Peirse favoured retaining the loose, decentralized formations and encouraging the crews to find the best way to their target and back. A tighter formation, it was claimed, would place a heavier burden on pilots, while it would become easy prey for the 'dark' night-fighters waiting in the Kammhuber Line. Bomber Command had reached an impasse, exaggerating the threat from the German defences, yet incapable of responding creatively to the new strategic imperatives.

Peirse's lacklustre command finally produced a growing chorus of criticism. The Directorate of Bombing Operations insisted that Bomber Command begin serious operational preparations for large-scale incendiary attacks on enemy cities. Assessments were produced by Air Intelligence of the degree of necessary concentration based on German practice. The Air Warfare Analysis Section tested the possible effects of heavy salvos of incendiaries on a large-scale map of the City of Westminster to see what damage might be done. Around 100,000 incendiary bombs were now considered a suitable load to begin a major conflagration. Zone maps of German cities were drawn up showing the most densely populated residential areas (Zones 1 and 2a), the suburban areas (Zones 2b and 3) and the outer industrial area (Zone 4), with recommendations to deliver the maximum bombload on the two central zones where large numbers of workers were packed together and to leave the industrial areas alone. In October Peirse was sent detailed instructions on carrying out an experimental incendiary raid on a German city. The subsequent raid on Nuremberg on the night of 14–15 October proved an inauspicious start: most aircraft bombed a small town outside Nuremberg and only one Stirling hit targets in the city, injuring six people. No major fires were started.[153]

The most dangerous criticism came from the top. In response to a paper from Portal in late September 1941 spelling out the long-term plan for 4,000 bombers, Churchill replied: 'It is very disputable whether bombing by itself will be a decisive factor in the present war. On the contrary, all that we have learnt since the war began shows that its effects, both physical and moral, are greatly exaggerated.'[154] Portal objected that he saw no reason to regard the bomber 'as a weapon of declining importance', but went on to ask Churchill whether the RAF should now be looking for a new strategic concept. Churchill's reply in early October was equivocal. On the one hand he assured Portal that bombing was still a strategic priority, but on the other he played down the likelihood of a satisfactory strategic outcome:

> I deprecate, however, placing unbounded confidence in this means of attack, and still more expressing that confidence in terms of arithmetic ... Even if all the towns of Germany were rendered uninhabitable, it does not follow that the military control would be weakened or even that war industry could not be carried on. The Air Staff would make a mistake to put their claim too high.[155]

This was the start of Churchill's growing disillusionment with what bombing could deliver. His initial enthusiasm had been based on a very limited understanding of what bombers were currently capable of achieving. As a politician he was interested in the prospect that air attack might provoke a political reaction in Germany, but the erratic intelligence available suggested that bombing had done very little to undermine German war-willingness, while the clearer evidence nearer home showed that the British political system and social structure had survived intact. Morale was now viewed by the RAF less as a means of political pressure, more as a war of economic and social attrition or, as Portal put it, 'interference with all that goes to make up the general activity of a community'. But to Churchill, who had imagined a more immediate and politically significant effect from bombing, the idea of long-term and unpredictable attrition was an unexciting prospect.

Peirse made one final effort to redeem his reputation and that of his force. On the night of 7–8 November 1941 he marshalled the largest force yet sent out on operations over Germany, some 392 aircraft, including 43 heavy bombers. The weather forecast was poor but he persisted with the operation. The chief target was Berlin but of the 169 bombers sent there, only 73 reached the capital where they distributed their bombloads, with limited effect. Only 14 houses were destroyed, 9 people killed and 32 injured. Other bombers attacked Cologne, which suffered five deaths and two houses destroyed, and Mannheim, where no bombs fell at all. During the night 37 bombers were lost, more than 9 per cent of the force; for the task force sent to Berlin the loss rate was 12.4 per cent. One squadron recorded in its diary that the mission was 'practically abortive'.[156] Berlin was not bombed again until January 1943. Peirse was summoned to see Churchill on the following day and told to suspend the offensive over the winter to conserve his shrinking force. Small raids were carried out when possible, but the assault on morale ordered in the summer of 1941 effectively came to an end with little achieved. The Air Staff investigated the Berlin raid and concluded that Peirse had been negligent in sending out his force in the knowledge that high winds, storms and iceing would be met by the crews. The decision was taken in December to replace him and he was finally removed in early January 1942 after Churchill had been shown the documents on the disastrous Berlin raid. On 8 January Peirse was appointed to command Allied air forces in Asia, facing the Japanese. Air Vice Marshal John Baldwin, commander of 3 Group, became his temporary replacement until a new commander-in-chief was in post.[157]

Bomber Command found itself in a state of limbo in the last months of 1941 and the first two months of 1942. The crews were only too aware of the crisis surrounding their commander-in-chief and the failures of the force. Over 3,000 had been casualties during 1941. In December the Directorate of Bombing Operations investigated the views of the Group commanders about the state of the force and found evidence of a feeling of 'hopelessness and ineffectiveness' among the operational units, largely on account of the difficulties in navigating and target-marking. When they found a target, the report continued, 'they stumbled on it more by luck than judgement'.[158] The overwhelming evidence that British raids were still widespread and ineffective exposed Bomber Command to close scrutiny by the chiefs of staff. The talk in the interregnum imposed by Peirse's redeployment was about the possibility of winding up the offensive. In a note on the 'Use of the Bomber Force' drafted early in 1942, the government scientist Patrick Blackett speculated that with a few more reverses the navy and army might insist on the 'dismemberment of the Air Force as a unit'.[159] Sir Stafford Cripps, Lord Privy Seal, told the House of Commons late in February 1942, winding up a debate on the current strategic situation, that bombing strategy was among the things under consideration: 'the Government are fully aware of the other uses to which our resources could be put'.[160] The day before this speech the new deputy director of bombing operations, Group Captain Sydney Bufton, fresh from command of a bomber squadron and a champion of concentration and target-marking, warned his superior of the situation now faced by the Command:

> At the present time there is a great deal of criticism of our strategic bombing offensive. This is being voiced not only in Army and Navy circles and in Parliament, but also more generally by members of the public. The criticism cannot be countered by promises of results which we expect to obtain in the future, and rightly cannot be met by evidence of any decisive results which our bomber force has achieved in the past. These results so far have been nebulous, inconsistent and indecisive.[161]

One week before this a new commander-in-chief had been appointed to Bomber Command – Air Marshal Sir Arthur Harris.

HARRIS AND THE AMERICANS

Harris was in Washington on the morning the Japanese Navy bombed Pearl Harbor, 7 December 1941. He had been sent in July as a member of the delegation negotiating for American aircraft deliveries to the RAF. His telegrams back to London said much about his personality.

In September he dismissed the prospect of American belligerency – 'these people are not going to fight ... they have nothing to fight with' – and thought they engaged in 'plain double cross' in reducing aircraft allocations to Britain.[162] Harris complained to Air Chief Marshal Freeman, vice chief of the air staff, about how hard it was to carry out missionary work 'with a people so arrogant as to their own ability and infallibility as to be comparable only to the Jews and the Roman Catholics'. The problem, Harris continued, was the American conviction 'of their own superiority and super efficiency – and of our mental, physical and moral decrepitude'.[163] During the morning of 8 December he was summoned to see Henry Stimson, Roosevelt's Secretary for War, and Robert Lovett, Assistant Secretary for the Army Air Forces, to discuss supplies for Britain in the wake of the Japanese attack. 'They were dazed,' Harris wrote to Portal, 'and Stimson himself hardly able to speak.' The American politicians asked Harris to give back at once 250 aircraft already supplied to the RAF so that they could defend Hawaii. Harris telegrammed Portal for urgent instructions about what to 'save from the wreck if wreck is unavoidable'.[164] Two weeks later Portal arrived in Washington to attend the first major wartime conference between Roosevelt, Churchill and the Allied military chiefs. During the first week of January 1942, Portal told Harris that he wanted him to replace Peirse; Harris agreed and Churchill approved the appointment, which was made official from 22 February 1942, after Harris had sailed back to England.[165]

The Japanese attack promised to transform the bombing war more certainly than the German invasion of the Soviet Union because it brought into the conflict a power capable of colossal military output, and an air force already committed to the concept of long-range strategic bombing. Yet the outcome of the Arcadia Conference in Washington between 22 December 1941 and 14 January 1942 left the bomber offensive as one small part of the wider strategic objectives agreed between the two leaders. On the way to the conference Churchill cabled to Roosevelt a long memorandum on Allied strategy, which included a short passage on bombing asking the United States to send at least 20 bomber squadrons to help boost Britain's offensive. 'Our own bomber programme,' he added, 'has fallen short of our hopes.'[166] During the 12 meetings between the British and American teams, however, bombing was discussed only once, when the US side insisted that their bombers would be manned only by American crews, confirming that

Britain would get no further heavy bombers from American production.[167] In the list of strategic priorities bombing was included as a contribution to item '(d)': 'wearing down and undermining German resistance by air bombardment, blockade, subversive activities and propaganda'.[168] On 7 January Churchill, briefly in Florida for his health, summed up what the two men had agreed. Bombing hardly featured except for Churchill's fears that the Blitz might be renewed. He assumed that most American air power, including the bombers, would have to focus on the Pacific War for the coming year.[169] The role of bombing in Allied strategy for the foreseeable future was regarded as modest and peripheral.

The Americans were not unprepared for involvement in the European bombing war. Indeed as early as 1935 American airmen had begun thinking about building bomber aircraft that could fly across the Atlantic to project long-distance air power against a hostile state. Writing in 1939, General Arnold, Chief of the Army Air Corps, addressed the question 'Can We Be Bombed?' and concluded that the answer was yes: 'We are vulnerable to bombing. Such bombing is feasible.'[170] On the day the German army invaded in the west, 10 May 1940, Arnold proposed the development of a new bomber with a 4,000-mile radius of action capable of attacking European ports to disrupt 'the launching of expeditionary forces against the Western hemisphere'.[171] During 1940 and 1941 the US Army Air Forces had been instructed by Arnold to collect detailed intelligence information on German industrial and economic targets, much of it supplied by the British Air Ministry. Consistent with air force thinking, this material was designed to support the idea that attacks against the vulnerable industrial web would unravel the enemy's capacity to make war. When Roosevelt instructed the American armed forces to draw up a 'Victory Program' in the summer of 1941, the air force was asked to prepare a plan of the resources needed to fulfil a strategic air campaign against Germany. In six stifling days in Washington in August 1941, a team assembled by Lt. Colonel Harold George worked day and night to produce a detailed plan for a putative offensive. The result was AWPD-1, a detailed survey of 154 German targets in three key target areas: electric power, fuel oils and communications. Production of 11,800 heavy bombers, to be employed on precision bombing in daylight, was considered sufficient for the task, though the air force currently had only a few hundred. Unlike the RAF, which had never embraced a serious counter-force strategy, the American planners – like the German Air Force in 1940 – assumed that enemy air power would be an essential intermediate target, whose destruction would make the obliteration of the primary objectives possible.[172] Morale was not considered a useful target and was not included on the list. Unlike the RAF, the American planners did not argue about the legality of bombing urban targets or hitting civilians.[173] The German economic web, with its vital centres, was treated as an abstraction; the metaphor of the 'social body' created a language that distanced those planning the bombing from the reality of civilian deaths.

Roosevelt was pleased with the plan. He had supported American air rearmament steadily since 1938 and in spring 1941 authorized a schedule of production which included 500 heavy four-engine bombers a month.[174] Despite his appeal in September 1939 to avoid bombing civilians, he shared Churchill's uncritical view that bombing was a possible war winner in the face of German aggression. He had a long personal hostility to Germany and the Germans, and an abhorrence of Hitlerism. American reports sent back to Washington at the start of the war in Poland highlighted the ruthless destruction of Polish towns from the air and underlined how shallow had been Hitler's positive response to Roosevelt's plea.[175] Roosevelt, like Churchill, proved susceptible to the extravagant fears of German air power and scientific ingenuity painted by unreliable intelligence. Since the Munich crisis, when the president had advocated to his Cabinet the idea that European states should bomb Germany in concert to halt Hitler's aggression, Roosevelt had retained extravagant notions of what air power might achieve. His special adviser Harry Hopkins noted in August 1941 Roosevelt's conviction that bombing was 'the only means of gaining a victory'.[176] In the United States as in Britain the air forces became the unexpected beneficiaries of political support at the highest level, without which the complaints and blandishments of the other services would have been more difficult to resist.

The sudden coming of war with Japan, Germany and Italy in December 1941 nevertheless exposed how flimsy were the American preparations made so far. The United States possessed no strategic bomber force and had to build one from scratch. Most of the small number of B-17 'Flying Fortress' bombers were stationed in Hawaii and the Philippines to protect against possible Japanese aggression. A real fear was the possibility of air attack either on the Eastern seaboard from German bases or by Japanese carrier aircraft from the Pacific. Civil defence preparations were already in place, organized by the Office of Civilian Defense set up in May 1941, and were activated at once in vulnerable areas on the outbreak of war. War-essential factories in coastal areas were ordered to begin a programme of camouflage and to black out windows with black paper and layers of opaque paint. All aircraft plant, even in areas not obviously exposed to risk, had to prepare concealment and obscurement plans while the American Chemical Warfare Service developed units to distribute a five-mile smokescreen around vulnerable targets.[177] Air-raid wardens patrolled Washington streets to enforce the blackout drills, and in June 1942 it was decided that coastal cities should operate a permanent 'dim-out' against the threat of air raids, with veiled vehicle lighting and low-visibility street lamps.[178]

Strict civil defence instructions were issued for the control of traffic during air-raid alerts and in August 1942 the Federal Works Agency produced a 173-page air-raid protection code, covering every subject from behaviour in air-raid shelters to compulsory fire-watching. As in Britain, dispersed sheltering was favoured, with no more than 50 people in any one shelter, but unlike the European experience, basements and cellars were regarded as hazardous. In tall buildings with a reinforced skeleton it was recommended that shelters should be constructed on the upper floors, though not on the top floor; the exact position could be calculated by working out the load-bearing properties of the ceiling once debris had collapsed onto it. The structure of the air-raid precautions system resembled the British, with volunteer auxiliary firemen, fire-watching units, first-aid volunteers, decontamination and rescue battalions.[179]

The Office of Civilian Defense, run in 1942 by James Landis, a Harvard law professor, was responsible for organizing the volunteer and full-time personnel. Thousands of Americans spent much of the war period engaged in drills and practices that made increasingly less sense as the war went on, though continued speculation about the possibility of German bombing kept the civil defence force in being. In May 1943 there were fears after German defeat in Tunisia that Hitler would seek a propaganda coup by launching bombing aircraft from German submarines against East Coast cities. The gas threat was also an ever-present anxiety. In June 1943 Roosevelt announced that any use of gas by the Axis powers would provoke immediate retaliation 'throughout the whole extent of the territory' of the enemy state.[180] As in Europe, civil defence was also designed to get the American public to identify

with the war effort as democratic participants; since American bombing
was predicated on attacking the social and economic web of the enemy,
the American people could now be viewed as an active part of the war.
The Civilian Defense journal was deliberately titled *Civilian Front* to
reflect war in the modern age. This rationale was explained by Landis in
an editorial in 1943:

> Civilian Defense is more than insurance for ourselves. It is a military duty.
> Modern war is not confined to battle lines. It is all the arms, resources and
> production of one people against all the arms, resources and production
> of another. A food warehouse or a machine tool plant 3,000 miles from
> the spot where the land forces are locked in combat is as legitimate a mili-
> tary objective as a pillbox on the battle line . . . That is our assignment and
> it is a military assignment as definite as that given an armed task force
> ordered to take and hold an enemy position.[181]

Imagination rather than reality shaped these views as they had in pre-
war Europe, but in the eyes of the American public they helped to
legitimate American bombing of German urban targets when this began
early in 1943.

The American bombing campaign took a long time to evolve. The
Eighth Air Force was activated on 28 January 1942 in Savannah, Geor-
gia, under the initial command of Colonel Asa Duncan. Because of the
commitment made at the Arcadia Conference to mount an invasion of
Europe, or possibly North Africa, during the coming year, the Eighth
Air Force was expected to play an air support role as well as prepare for
strategic operations from airfields in England. Arnold sent Colonel Ira
Eaker to Britain to establish contact with Bomber Command and to
learn about its operations. Eaker met Harris in Washington before they
both left in late February and an immediate rapport was established
between the two men, despite the differences in their personality: Eaker
was diffident and earnest, Harris opinionated and brusque. Eaker
arrived in London on 21 February, a day before Harris assumed command at High Wycombe. After a period staying with Harris, Eaker in
April set up an American headquarters in the nearby Wycombe Abbey
School for Girls, after the pupils had been forced to leave. Codenamed
PINETREE, the site became the command centre for the Eighth Bomber
Command, with Eaker (now Brig. General) as its commander, but as yet
with no aircraft or personnel.[182] It was made clear from the start that
the American force was not under RAF command, though it was
expected to learn a great deal from British experience. Eaker wrote to

Harris later in the summer that he regarded him as 'the senior member in our firm – the older brother in our bomber team'.[183] Arnold appointed Maj. General Carl Spaatz, one of the most senior American airmen, as overall commander of the Eighth Air Force, including its fighter, reconnaissance and service branches, but Spaatz remained in the United States for five months while the air force organization was established, the training programmes initiated, and the service and procurement system organized. He finally took over from Duncan on 10 May 1942.[184] Both Eaker and Spaatz were selected by Arnold because they had shared with him the struggle to establish American air forces during the years of isolation and both supported his view of the strategic importance of independent air power. Spaatz had visited Britain in July and August 1940 and had been unimpressed by what appeared to be indiscriminate German night-bombing, but impressed by the possibility that daylight bombing in close formation could afford sufficient protection against fighter penetration and achieve greater bombing precision.[185] These were lessons that governed the operational and tactical development of the American bomber force in 1942 and 1943.

The first echelon of American Air Force personnel arrived on 11 May, a second one a week later, but the first 180 aircraft only arrived in mid-July, and just 40 were heavy bombers. American planning, unlike British, had to be based from the start on the assumption that an invasion might take place somewhere in 1942, so that most of the initial aircraft deliveries were of light or medium bombers for army support roles at the expense of a strategic bombing capability.[186] Until the decision taken by Churchill and Roosevelt in July 1942, against strong American objection, to undertake a limited invasion in North Africa (codenamed 'Torch'), American air planning had to be based on the assumption that a landing in France would be undertaken before October. The result would have been to divert American aircraft almost entirely to a role in support of surface forces, and this possibility compromised the early efforts to turn the Eighth Air Force into a principally strategic force. The prospect of an invasion of Europe (codenamed 'Sledgehammer') also prompted the head of the American military mission (Special Observer Group) appointed in spring 1941, Maj. General James Chaney, to insist that Eaker and Spaatz integrate with his organization rather than set up a new independent command. The jurisdictional battle was resolved only because Eaker refused to be based in London under Chaney's close supervision. The arguments over invasion also affected relations with the British, who tried to insist for the sake of operational efficiency that American fighter aircraft be absorbed into RAF Fighter Command and that at least 400 American heavy bombers should be given in the first instance to Bomber Command, which could utilize them immediately. Arnold visited London in late May 1942 and succeeded in reducing this demand to a tentative 54 but could not promise that American-flown bombers would be in action much before the autumn.[187] He found London very different from his last visit during the Blitz: 'men, women and children have lost that expression of dreaded expectancy,' he wrote in his diary, 'they have a cheerful look on their faces ... Pianos are playing, men are whistling. London is changed.'[188] He returned to Washington with enough achieved to prevent the further emasculation of the Eighth Air Force's still non-existent capability.

Harris had arrived in England shortly before Eaker and moved at once to High Wycombe to take up the command left in abeyance by the sacking of Peirse. He remained the longest-serving bomber commander of the war. He began his air career in the First World War when he left Rhodesia, where he had emigrated as an adventurous teenager in 1910, to join the Royal Flying Corps. He became a major and ended a dramatic operational career in 1918 as a training officer. He remained in the fledgling RAF and saw active service in the Middle East, where he helped to define 'air policing' methods by using light bombers to intimidate recalcitrant populations in Iraq and Palestine. He held high office in the Air Ministry in the 1930s, and played a key part in planning what was known as the 'Ideal Bomber' (the Lancaster was a distant descendant). In 1939 he became commander of 5 Group, Bomber Command, before becoming Portal's deputy when he was appointed chief of staff in October 1940. From June 1941 Harris was in Washington, absent from the ongoing arguments about air tactics and the diminishing impact of the command, though not unaware of the problems.[189]

On most accounts Harris was judged an effective officer and he impressed many of those who met him with a shrewd intelligence and a mordant wit. He established a working relationship – though not always frictionless – with Churchill and the American air leaders. He gave the impression of a straightforward, no-nonsense personality, who spoke his mind and changed it little. He had scant sympathy with those of his colleagues or his men who displayed any weakness. The crews who followed behind the target markers he termed 'rabbits'; the crewmen who expressed doubts about bombing civilians were 'weaker sisters'. The civilian critics of bombing were 'Fifth Columnists', his junior critics at the ministry simply 'impertinent'.[190] His blunt talking became a hall-mark of his relations with anyone who crossed him, however senior. In April 1942 Wilfrid Freeman, then vice chief of staff, told Harris after a typically robust exchange that he had spent years getting used to his 'truculent style, loose expression and flamboyant hyperbole', but could still be surprised by the level of verbal injury Harris was willing to inflict. So fearsome was Harris's reputation that when in early 1947 the Air Ministry proposed a conference on the wartime bombing campaign based on the critical report of the British Bombing Survey Unit, Claude Pelly wrote to his co-author Solly Zuckerman that they needed adequate warning if Harris decided to come from retirement in South Africa so that they could 'make the best of a couple of Continents' start. Iceland or Southern Pacific?'[191]

Harris had two important prejudices which coloured his entire period as commander-in-chief. He held an exceptional hostility to the Germans, which made it possible for him not only to run a campaign of city-bombing with high civilian casualties in mind, but to relish in his own choice of words 'this lethal campaign'. Harris was known to see the First World War as unfinished business, and he had an instinctive hostility to totalitarian systems, right or left. But neither perhaps explains sufficiently why he regarded the death of ordinary Germans as something to be sought in its own right. 'We have got to kill a lot of Boche,' he famously wrote in April 1942, 'before we win this war.'[192] During 1943 and 1944 he wanted the Air Ministry to state unequivo-cally that killing the German people was what his Command was for. In later life he never wavered from his conviction that there was nothing ethically objectionable to killing the enemy civilian in total war, which was a view widely shared at the time, but his complete indifference to the fate of the Germans he bombed, even in Dresden, is more difficult to understand. When the biographer Andrew Boyle asked Harris in 1979 about his 'aggressive philosophy where Germans were concerned', Harris did not respond.[193] His second conviction was his unyielding belief that the heavy bombing of urban areas was the best use to which the current bombing technology could be put. He contested, often bitterly, any attempt to divert the forces under his command to other purposes and when compelled to do so, fought to have his bombers returned to what he saw as their only rational function as soon as pos-sible. The destruction of cities, Harris insisted to the end of the conflict, would 'shorten the war and so preserve the lives of Allied soldiers', though it cost the lives of half his operational crews.[194] This stubborn refusal to accept that any other strategy might yield more strategically useful and less damaging results made him into the Haig of the Second World War. Harris's reputation, like Haig's before him, has been a historical bone of contention ever since.

Though Harris's appointment no doubt marked a turning point in the bombing war, he was not, as is so often suggested, the originator of the area-bombing campaign. He arrived at his command after a brief interregnum in which the officers in the Air Ministry in favour of large-scale incendiary attacks on residential areas had been able to exploit the absence of a field commander to put in place an unambiguous commitment to the strategy they preferred. A new directive was sent to Baldwin as acting commander-in-chief on 14 February 1942, modifying the directive of July 1941 by removing communications as a primary target and focusing the force entirely on 'the morale of the enemy civil population and in particular of the industrial workers'. A list of cities was appended to the directive, with the vulnerable central zones highlighted and the bomb tonnage necessary to destroy them recommended.[195] In February 1942 the Directorate of Bombing Operations, which had prepared the directive, explored the vulnerability of particular cities to large-scale conflagration and chose Hamburg (rated 'outstanding'), followed by Hanover, Cologne, Düsseldorf, Bremen, Dortmund and Essen.[196] The zoning system developed in 1941 was now applied to these cities to show the value of hitting the 'closely built-up city centre' (Zone 1) and the 'completely built-up residential area' (Zone 2a). Attacks on these central zones were estimated to be up to 20 times more effective than attacks on the outer industrial and suburban zones. The damage done to a large working-class area was expected to affect the output of numerous factories through absenteeism or death, where an attack on a single factory target would affect only that one.[197] This was the background to the famous minute sent to Churchill by Lord Cherwell on 30 March 1942 in which he calculated that 10,000 RAF bombers would by mid-1943 be able to drop enough bombs to de-house one-third of Germany's urban population. 'Investigation,' ran the minute, 'seems to show that having one's house demolished is most damaging to morale.' Churchill was so impressed that he insisted on circulating the minute to the War Cabinet. It generated at the time a great deal of argument from other scientists who criticized the arithmetic (Patrick Blackett thought it exaggerated by a factor of 600 per cent), and it has attracted much discussion from historians, but in effect it simply advertised a shift in bombing priorities that had already been agreed and was now in place.[198]

Harris did make a difference when he took over Bomber Command because he was an aggressive and single-minded defender of his force against all efforts to divert it to other purposes or to compromise the directive he had been given. He also argued forcefully against the widespread criticism of the Command – 'ignorant and uninstructed chatter,' he called it – because of the damaging effect on bomber crew morale to be regularly reminded that their efforts were 'futile'.[199] But Harris did realize how limited bombing still was without a substantial increase in the size of the bomber force and an end to the dispersion of bomber aircraft to other theatres. When he arrived at the Command he had at his disposal only a few hundred bombers, of which a large part were still medium Wellingtons. He understood that this force was incapable of achieving what the new city-bombing directive suggested. He complained to Norman Bottomley, deputy chief of staff, that what he needed was a force of at least 2,000 bombers; such a force, he claimed, would not only destroy his list of 20 cities, but 'knock Germany out of the war'.[200]

Harris nevertheless set out to demonstrate what his limited numbers could achieve. On 8–9 March 1942, 211 aircraft (including 37 heavy bombers) armed with 'Gee' navigation attacked Essen and the Krupps complex. Dense industrial smoke obscured the city; no bombs hit Krupps, a handful of houses were destroyed and 10 people killed. A second raid on Essen two days later killed only five people; the bombs were scattered over 61 different villages and towns.[201] A raid on Cologne on 13–14 March proved more effective thanks to better target-marking despite a gloomy night. The most successful attack was made against the Baltic Sea port of Lübeck on the night of 28–29 March. Although beyond the range of 'Gee', there was a full moon and good visibility. The 234 bombers attacked in three waves, carrying two-thirds incendiaries against the lightly defended and densely constructed 'old town' area. Around 60 per cent of buildings in the city were damaged and 312 people killed, the heaviest casualties in Germany so far. A series of four raids were then made against the northern port of Rostock between 23–24 and 26–27 April, again aiming for the main city area, 60 per cent of which was damaged or destroyed, though thanks to effective civil defence only 216 inhabitants died. These were the first raids where incendiary damage could be inflicted on the central areas of a combustible target along the lines planned in 1941 and they inflicted high levels of urban destruction. They were also the first raids that the German authorities took seriously; following the Rostock raid a special category of 'great catastrophe' was introduced to define larger and more destructive attacks.[202]

The reaction to the first 'Gee' raids at the Air Ministry was nevertheless unenthusiastic. The Director of Bombing Operations, John Baker, accused Harris of misunderstanding the nature of the incendiary attacks he had recommended, by carrying too much high explosive. Harris was sent a memorandum summing up the opinion of British fire chiefs about the relative value of high explosive and incendiary, which showed that in almost all cases more than 90 per cent of the damage had been caused by fire. Baker suggested carrying at least 200,000 4-lb incendiary bombs to maximize the damage.[203] On 8 May, following the Rostock raids, Baker's deputy, Sydney Bufton, also wrote to Harris with the evidence from plotted photographs that his attacks on Essen in March and again in April showed 90 per cent of bombs had fallen from between 5 to 100 miles from the Essen aiming point. Plots of 12 raids on Essen between March and June 1942 showed that in seven of them fewer than 5 per cent of aircraft got within three miles. The raids on Rostock, which was easier to locate being near the coast, showed that 78 per cent of the photographs taken were not of the town.[204] A few weeks before this, on 14 April, the chiefs of staff had asked Churchill to authorize a second study of bombing results by Justice Sir John Singleton, to see what might be expected from bombing over the following 18 months. The decision was prompted by Cherwell's minute on 'de-housing', which suggested very significant consequences by the end of that period with more bombers and greater accuracy.[205] Singleton's report was produced by 20 May using material supplied by Baker and Bufton, though without the statistical foundation used in the Butt Report from the previous August. Singleton concluded that the use of 'Gee' had had mixed results, but that in general efforts to improve the level of accuracy and concentration had been a failure. He did not believe that over the following six months 'great results can be hoped for'.[206] Cherwell wrote to Churchill a week later that Singleton had been disappointed 'as any layman would be, by the inaccuracy of our bombing'.[207]

On the question of greater accuracy Harris was generally unhelpful. The arguments over developing a target-finding force equivalent to the German *Kampfgruppe 100* had begun in 1941 but were still unresolved when Harris took over. He was opposed to the idea of using the introduction of 'Gee' as an opportunity to develop specialized units to find, identify and illuminate a target city. Together with other senior commanders, he thought the creation of an elite corps would leave poorer-quality crews to follow behind and would sap the morale of the rest of the force. He favoured keeping 'lead crews' in each bomber Group to find and mark the target, and was impervious to the evidence that this practice failed to produce a concentration of bombing effort. At a meeting with Group commanders and the Directorate of Bombing Operations in mid-March, Harris made it clear that he entirely rejected the idea of a target force and was supported by all five Group commanders.[208] The argument highlighted the extent to which the individual commanders-in-chief and their commanders enjoyed independence from the Air Staff at the ministry in the way they chose to run their campaigns. It was nevertheless difficult for Harris to ignore all the evidence of continued inaccuracy and the political and service pressure to improve it. Failure to do so might, as an Air Staff memorandum pointed out in May, make it increasingly difficult 'truthfully and logically' to resist pressure to divert bombers to other uses.[209] In March, Bufton sent out a questionnaire to squadron and station commanders in Bomber Command asking them whether they approved the creation of a Target-Finding Force. The replies were unanimously in favour. A squadron commander based at Oakington, near Cambridge, told Bufton that the senior officers' First World War experience was valueless in the new conflict: 'The crocks ... must be swept from the board.'[210]

Bufton sent the results of the survey to Harris but it made little difference. Harris found five squadron commanders who were prepared to argue the opposite case. The most he would concede was the idea of raid leaders for each Group, which built on existing practice. The crisis point came in June when Wilfrid Freeman, acting on Portal's behalf as vice chief of staff, finally seized the initiative after weeks of fruitless argument with Harris over tactical issues. He told Harris that he would have to accept the logic of a specialized force. Harris met Portal and despite a trenchant rearguard action finally agreed to the establishment of what he insisted on calling the Pathfinder Force to distinguish it from the Air Staff title of target-finding. Even then Harris found ways to obstruct the proper functioning of the new force, which remained short of the most effective aircraft and highly trained crews. An Australian pilot, Group Captain Donald Bennett, was appointed on 5 July 1942 to command the new units; the Pathfinder Force was activated on 15 August and undertook its first operation three days later against the north German coast port of Flensburg. It proved an awkward baptism. Strong winds drove both the Pathfinders and the main force off course and instead of bombing the German city, the bombs fell on two Danish towns and injured four Danes.[211] An Air Ministry minute in early August noted that despite the agreement to form a target-finding force, 'a lack of enthusiasm and sense of urgency in high quarters permeates the whole command, and will inevitably result in a complete failure of the T.F.F. [Target-Finding Force] at its inception'.[212]

Harris found himself, like Peirse before him, fighting against a chorus of criticism both inside and outside the RAF. During May he began to plan a sensational air raid to try to still public criticism and stamp his mark on his new Command. He won approval from Portal and Churchill for the plan to send 1,000 bombers against a single German city. It was a risky promise because it depended on the cooperation of Coastal Command in releasing their bomber aircraft for the raid and the use of aircraft from the training units. Bomber Command itself had just over 400 front-line aircraft. The city chosen was Hamburg, which like Lübeck and Rostock was easily identifiable as near the coast. The object, Harris wrote, was to wipe it out in one night, or at most two. The target was large, near and 'suitably combustible'. The aim was to carry every single incendiary possible and to create an 'unextinguishable conflagration' by bombing in a continuous stream and in a short period of time, a gesture towards the tactical recommendations made by the Air Ministry.[213] The codename 'Operation Millennium', like later codenames, betrayed its apocalyptic purpose. By 23 May plans were prepared with details of German defences and three routes to the target. Coastal Command agreed to release 250 aircraft, only to find that the Admiralty countermanded the offer. Harris had at the last moment to recruit training personnel and trainee pilots to raise his force to a total of just over 1,000. The weather worsened over the week that followed and by 26 May Cologne was chosen as a possible alternative. Hamburg was finally abandoned as the primary target and waited another year for its firestorm.

After first approving, then cancelling, then reinstating the operation on 30 May, the raid against Cologne was authorized by Harris for that night. A total of 1,047 bombers were sent off, but only 868 claimed to have attacked the main target, dropping 1,455 tons of bombs, two-thirds of them incendiaries, though only 800 tons fell on the city itself. The concentrated stream allowed the bombers to complete the raid in just an hour and a half, which may explain why the first reports from the city suggested that only between 50 and 100 bombers had been overhead. A later report from the local National Socialist regional leader confirmed the actual scale: it was, he wrote, 'the most successful concentrated enemy air attack to date'.[214] Some 3,330 buildings were destroyed and 7,908 damaged; 486 people were killed and over 5,000 injured; 59,100 were rendered temporarily homeless. This represented a loss of 5.2 per cent of Cologne's buildings. Heavy though the raid was, it was impossible to wipe a city out, as Harris had hoped.[215] He planned to continue the large raids as long as he had the force of bombers acting together. On 1–2 June another '1,000' raid was made on Essen, with far less success: only 11 houses were destroyed and 15 people killed. The last large '1,000' raid, Millennium II, was against the port of Bremen on the night of 25–26 June. Out of a force of 960 aircraft, 696 claimed to have hit the city, but destroyed only 572 buildings and killed 85 people, suggesting that many of the bombs missed the target area altogether.[216] This was the end of the '1,000' plan. Despite the effort to overwhelm the Kammhuber Line by using a concentrated bomber stream, losses were the highest of the war, 123 bombers from the three raids. This threatened to eat into Bomber Command's training system and the large raids were discontinued. Some of the OTUs were close to mutiny at the loss of training staff and the demands placed on novice crews sometimes forced to fly obsolescent aircraft to make up the numbers on each raid.[217]

The gesture did something to reinstate Bomber Command's reputation, particularly with the British public impatient for more rapid progress, but the situation faced by both Bomber Command and the Eighth Air Force in the summer and early autumn of 1942 was more dangerous to the future of the bombing campaign than the crisis in 1941. The summer of 1942 represented a low point in Allied fortunes. The Pacific and southern Asia were dominated by a rampant Japan, held at bay by the victory at Midway in early June, but a formidable obstacle for sustained counter-attack. In North Africa the British Commonwealth forces abandoned most of Libya, lost Tobruk and retreated into Egypt. Field Marshal Erwin Rommel seemed poised to seize the Suez Canal. The Battle of the Atlantic had reached a critical point and on the Eastern Front German forces poured towards the oilfields of the Caucasus and the Volga city of Stalingrad. The many areas of crisis left Allied strategy in confusion and the bombing offensive was the unwitting victim of efforts to plug the many strategic gaps that were opening up with Axis success. Field Marshal Smuts, recruited to Churchill's War Cabinet, urged the prime minister to send Bomber Command to North Africa where he thought it would do more good.[218] To try to allay these pressures Harris wrote direct to Churchill to persuade him that Bomber Command was still the potentially war-winning instrument it had hoped to be two years before:

> We ourselves are now at the crossroads. We are free, if we will, to employ our rapidly increasing air strength in the proper manner. In such a manner as would avail to knock Germany out of the War in a matter of months, if we decide upon the right course. If we decide upon the wrong course, then our Air power will now, and increasingly in the future, become inextricably implicated as a subsidiary weapon in the prosecution of vastly protracted and avoidable land and sea campaigns.[219]

Harris appended a document to show that his force had at present just 36 squadrons with 584 aircraft, or exactly 11 per cent of the entire RAF and Fleet Air Arm, and added that of this percentage half the operational effort went to help the Royal Navy. A few weeks later Harris calculated that his force had dwindled to 22 effective squadrons available for bombing Germany.[220]

In the last months of 1942 Bomber Command waited to see what the strategic outcome would be. Harris knew that the Command would benefit from a number of technical and tactical innovations that were in the pipeline. As predicted, 'Gee' had had a very short life. It was first jammed by German countermeasures on 4 August and a wide network of stations were set up to interfere regularly with the Gee transmissions. Two new systems had been in development at the Telecommunications Research Establishment. The first was known as 'Oboe' (the transmission noise resembled the sound of the instrument). Two ground radar transmitters, one at Dover and one at Cromer in Norfolk, emitted pulses which were received by an aircraft transmitter and relayed back to the master station, allowing an exact fix of the plane's position. When the aircraft was over the aiming point, the second station sent out a bomb-release signal. The system was accurate but could only reach 270 miles into Germany, covering the Ruhr but little else, and could only be used by one aircraft at a time. The second system was a more radical innovation. Taking advantage of the British discovery of the cavity magnetron, which permitted much narrower radar wavelengths, an airborne radar device, H2S, was devised which gave a map of the ground area by recording stronger echoes from built-up areas. This could be used over longer distances and could not be jammed as beams could be. Both instruments were available for operational use in early 1943. Their potential effectiveness was magnified by the fortuitous development of a new fast twin-engine bomber, the de Havilland Mosquito. Begun initially as a private venture in October 1938, the aircraft was uniquely made of wood, and powered by two Rolls-Royce Merlin engines. It was designed as a light bomber and relied on its high speed to avoid enemy fighter interception. The Air Ministry showed little interest until Air Marshal Freeman, in charge of research and development, saw the aircraft late in 1939 and ordered work on a prototype. It first flew on 25 November 1940 and saw operational service a year later, where it was used extensively for daylight bombing. It could fly at almost 400 mph (faster than Battle of Britain fighters) and had a service ceiling of at least 28,000 feet. It was so difficult to intercept that it had lower losses than any other Bomber Command aircraft. Its special operational character-istics made it a natural choice for the new Pathfinder units, but in January 1943 there were still only 16 Mosquitos available as target markers.

Bomber Command was nevertheless unable to demonstrate after the Cologne raid of late May 1942 that it merited the kind of strategic pro-file that Harris had argued for in June. The hope that American entry into the war might soon lead to a strengthened bombing effort was undermined by the slow establishment of the Eighth Air Force, which until July did not know whether there would be time to mount any raids against German targets at all before starting direct preparations to aid a cross-Channel invasion. Even more than Bomber Command, the American bomber force lived in the future. The slow build-up of aircraft and personnel postponed any serious possibility of action against Ger-many into 1943. Table 5.2 shows the build-up of the Eighth Air Force

Table 5.2: Eighth Bomber Command Operational Statistics,
August–December 1942

Month	Sorties	Bomb Tonnage	Operational Bombers	Crews Available	Losses
August	90	135	24	21	2
September	106	215	56	55	7
October	157	334	90	110	11
November	382	612	99	113	14
December	243	417	115	114	34

Sources: AFHRA, Maxwell, AL, Eighth Air Force collection, 520.056-188, Statistical Summary of Eighth Air Force Operations, 17 August 1942–8 May 1945; Richard G. Davis, *Carl A. Spaatz* (Washington, DC: 1993), App 17.

during 1942, but none of the operations it describes took place over Germany.

Like the German Air Force and Bomber Command, an operational learning curve had to be followed before crews with no operational experience could be released against improving German defences. Pressure from Washington insisted that Spaatz and Eaker organize a demonstration to satisfy American and British opinion, and Arnold named Independence Day, 4 July, as the day to carry it out. Spaatz had no aircraft of his own, so he recruited six Douglas A-20 light bombers serving with the RAF to make a suicidal attack against four German airfields on the Dutch coast. The RAF colours were painted over and the six aircraft sent off on the morning of the 4 July. By the end, one third of the force was lost, seven aircrew were dead and one a prisoner. Three weeks later a surviving crewman committed suicide. The press on both sides of the Atlantic made the most of the raid, but it was a futile gesture.[221] Arnold pressed his commanders to speed up the organization of real operations. The United States bomber offensive was launched on 17 August with an attack by 12 Boeing B-17 'Flying Fortress' bombers on the railway sheds at Rouen in northern France. Eaker flew with the mission, which was protected by RAF fighters. All aircraft returned safely after striking the target. Ten days later, after three more missions over occupied Europe, Eaker reported to Spaatz the current assessments of accuracy. The bomb plots seemed to show that 90 per cent of the bombs dropped fell within a one-mile radius of the aiming point, almost half within 500 yards. He concluded from this that daytime bombing with the Norden bombsight was 10 times more accurate than RAF night-bombing. Limited though this experience was, Eaker, like Harris, thought that Allied bombing by day and night would be adequate 'completely to dislocate German industry and communications'.[222] But unlike the British and German learning curve, the early raids convinced the American side that daylight raids were possible.

While Harris waited for a response from Churchill on the future of the offensive, the prime minister flew to Moscow on 12 August for urgent talks with Stalin. The object was to explain to Stalin why the Western powers had decided in July to abandon the idea of a cross-Channel invasion in 1942. The meeting was famously combative: Stalin argued against every explanation provided by Churchill in insulting terms until the point when Churchill explained the plans for an Anglo-American bomber offensive. Roosevelt's representative, Averell Harriman, wired back the result to his leader: 'Stalin took over the argument himself and said that homes as well as factories should be destroyed . . . Between the two of them they soon destroyed most of the important industrial cities in Germany.'[223] Harris and Spaatz were both fortunate that bombing was still required in summer 1942 as a means to placate the Soviet Union over the failure to open a second front. Although Churchill knew about the poor progress of the offensive, it could not easily be abandoned now that there was to be no cross-Channel operation. On 17 August Churchill asked Portal and Sinclair to lay on an operation against Berlin to show Stalin that he had been in earnest, but he was told that Harris regarded the operation as too costly with only 300 serviceable bombers and a great many inexperienced crews. Though Churchill argued angrily in favour of an attack, Harris told Portal that it would seriously damage the expansion of the Command. 'As I have frequently pointed out to you,' he wrote in late August, 'Bomber Command is now quite definitely too small for the tasks it is expected to carry out.'[224]

As a result, when Harris asked Churchill for a 'firm and final decision' on 4 September about the future of the bomber offensive, he received a guarded response. Churchill remained committed to bombing Germany, since he could not easily terminate such a conspicuous element of Britain's war effort, but he thought it would have no decisive results in 1943 nor bring the war to an end; 'better than doing nothing,' he concluded.[225] This was a view widely shared in military and political circles by the autumn of 1942, for whom the chief priority was breaking the submarine blockade, using bombers if necessary, and supporting American participation in the ground offensives planned for North Africa and Europe. Leo Amery, one of Churchill's Cabinet colleagues, found the Harris memorandum 'entirely unconvincing' and thought bombers should be used for 'tactical co-operation with the army and navy'.[226] One of the scientists at the Air Warfare Analysis Section warned the Air Ministry that Bomber Command could not hit enough of Germany industry to do any decisive damage. 'I am aware that this view of night bombing,' he continued, 'is shared by a very large number of thoughtful people.'[227] When the chiefs of staff considered the future of the bombing campaign in November 1942, Portal was subjected to a hostile cross-examination by his colleagues. General Alan Brooke, chief of the imperial general staff, thought the air force lacked a clear plan of campaign, underestimated the German defences, exaggerated the possible bomblift and overstated the damage likely with blind bombing. The one slim advantage, he concluded, was its political value, bringing 'the horrors of war home to the German people'.[228]

Harris took out his own frustration on others. He deplored the decision by the Canadian bomber squadrons, which composed a growing fraction of the Command, 'to huddle into a corner by themselves', even more the prospect of supplying them with Lancaster bombers at the expense of British crews.[229] He was scathing about the American Eighth Air Force, despite the public image of friendly collaboration, for taking airfields in East Anglia away from British squadrons, forcing them to fly dangerous return routes to bases further west and north, and without contributing 'the smallest assistance' to the bombing campaign against Germany. He asked the Air Ministry to challenge American leaders to state categorically 'whether it is their intention to proceed with the air bombardment of Germany', and, if so, when it would start. If no adequate answer was forthcoming, Harris recommended taking some of the airfields back, to which the Ministry gave qualified agreement.[230] To Portal he sent a bitterly sarcastic denunciation of the efforts to divert his force to what he called panacea targets: 'In sum,' he concluded, 'they spell the end of our effective Bomber offensive against Germany.' He spent the rest of the war grimly contesting every attempt by what he called 'Panacea Target mongers' and 'Diversionists' to prevent him bombing city areas.[231]

There was little that Bomber Command could do over the autumn months to still the chorus of complaints. Evidence from attacks on Germany showed that despite the advent of the Pathfinders, levels of accuracy were still strikingly low. In December 1942 the government scientist Henry Tizard asked the Command for details of its performance in recent weeks against Ruhr targets and was told that in good weather around one-third of bombs were landing within three miles of the aiming point, but in most raids the figure was still 15 per cent, and sometimes zero.[232] Surveys of raids on Mainz and Munich showed a wide spread of bombs, with most incendiaries destined for Munich falling in open country. 'There is at the present time,' wrote Bufton in response to these findings, 'a lack of grasp throughout the Command of a common tactical doctrine.'[233] There was also no effective way of measuring what impact the bombing was having on the German economy, military machine and popular morale. During 1942 the Command dropped 37,192 tons of bombs on German soil compared with 22,996 in 1941, but not only did most of these bombs fail to hit the target area, the raids cost some 2,716 bombers lost on operations or through accident.[234] The first scientific analysis of a major raid was supplied in November 1942 by division RE8 of the Research and Experiments Department, which used British models to calculate the likely degree of homelessness, lost man-months and financial cost of the 1,000-bomber raid on Cologne seven months before. The first statistical assessments of acreage destroyed and of the ratio between high-explosive and incendiary damage were only ready in January 1943.[235] Until then, claims that cities had been wiped out or obliterated were mere guesswork. In fact, during 1942 the damage to German economy and society remained limited. A small number of spectacular raids in the late spring had not been sustained and the German civil defence and repair organization coped with the consequences with little pressure. The German economy cushioned the bombing and expanded weapons output by more than 50 per cent during the year. Post-war calculations in the US Bombing Survey suggested a loss of potential overall production of 2.5 per cent due to British bombing, or roughly half the impact of the German Blitz on Britain. During the course of 1942 4,900 Germans had been killed, two for every bomber lost.[236] The one solid achievement was to compel the German enemy to divert aircraft, guns and ammunition to defence against bombing, when they could have been used for the fighting fronts in Italy and Russia.

At the chiefs of staff meeting on 18 November 1942, Churchill opened the discussion on bombing with the remark that at the moment it had 'petered out'. He continued that the answer was not megalomania – a none-too-oblique reference to Harris – but a more modest and achievable programme.[237] There are a number of familiar explanations given for the failure to produce an operationally effective and sustained bomber offensive in the first three years of war – economic restraints on aircraft production, the demands of other theatres, the long programme of training and preparation – but none of them is sufficient to understand why evident tactical, operational and technical changes were not made sooner and consistently or a clear and convincing plan devised (or indeed why the whole strategy was not abandoned in favour of using the resources more productively). By the autumn of 1942 neither the British nor American air forces had a bombing plan beyond destroying working-class districts and attacking a limited number of industrial objectives in western Germany, and no effective effort had been made to evaluate what even this modest programme might achieve strategically. The British War Cabinet finally asked the Joint

Planning Staff to draw up a bombing plan in late August 1942, but nothing was approved before the end of the year.[238] Roosevelt the same month ordered Arnold to produce a comprehensive plan for the future air war, and the result, AWPD-42, was the clearest outline yet produced of how a bombing offensive should be organized and with what object, though it was still not a definite operational directive. Arnold complained to Harry Hopkins a few weeks later that what was still missing was 'a simple, direct plan, tied to a definite date'.[239] American frustration at the lack of strategic direction and the slow build-up of the Eighth Air Force made Arnold decide to send Spaatz to join Eisenhower in North Africa with a view to eventually making him overall commander of all American air forces in Europe. Spaatz was reluctant to lose operational control of the Eighth Air Force, which was now taken over by Eaker, while the start of operations in Africa, as had been feared, diverted the bombing effort to the Battle of the Atlantic and postponed even longer the start of American bombing over Germany.[240]

The most remarkable failure in the British offensive was the slow development of target-finding and marking, the dilatory development of effective electronic aids, marker bombs and bombsights, and the inability to relate means and ends more rationally to maximize effectiveness and cope with enemy defences. The lengthy learning curve cost Bomber Command 14,000 dead from September 1939 to September 1942. A central explanation is the poorly defined relationship between the Air Ministry, the Air Staff and the commanding officers. A great deal of responsibility was delegated to the commander-in-chief, which in turn was delegated to the Group commanders in the field. This created a wide gap between the essential scientific and tactical evaluation available from the staff in the Ministry and the officers whose task it was to organize operations. The Ministry of Economic Warfare in a letter to the Air Minister observed that this gap reduced the prospect of learning from experience and of collectively evaluating the best use to be made of the bomber force. The Ministry wanted a greater say in bombing operations, and was thus a scarcely neutral observer, but the predicament was a real one, made worse by Harris's strident defence of his independence.[241] At the same time, directives were worked out by Ministry officials for the Air Staff with too little reference to the commanders in the field on questions of technical requirements and operational feasibility, and with no clearly articulated strategy behind them, since this was not the officials' job. The result, as a memorandum produced in May 1942 suggested, was 'considerable criticism and loss of faith on both sides'.[242] The crews were caught between these two poles, asked to perform impossible tasks, taking high casualties and receiving little explanation for the wider purpose of their missions. Bufton, himself a former squadron commander, summed up this sense of frustration: 'They feel that they can do more than they are doing; they grope somewhat blindly in an effort to find where the failure lies.'[243]

6

The Combined Bomber Offensive:
Germany 1943–5

At lunchtime on 18 January 1943, Air Vice Marshal John Slessor, RAF assistant chief of staff, sat on top of the roof of the Anfa Hotel in Casablanca watching 'the long Atlantic rollers breaking on the beaches' while he sketched out a compromise agreement between the American and British chiefs of staff over the future of Allied strategy. Chief of Staff Charles Portal then read it through and changed a few words. In the list of strategic commitments jotted in his notebook, Slessor had included: 'The heaviest possible bomber offensive from the UK against GERMANY direct.'[1] His hastily concocted notes were typed up and agreed when the Combined Chiefs of Staff reassembled for the afternoon session and became the basis for the document on Allied strategy endorsed by Roosevelt and Churchill three days later. Slessor elaborated the idea of a heavy-bomber offensive into a full draft directive, and this was presented to the Combined Chiefs on 21 January with only minor changes in the wording. It was approved and the Casablanca Directive for a joint bomber offensive against Germany was released as policy document CCS 166 two days later.[2]

The Casablanca Conference (14–24 January) came at a critical point for the Allies. Stalin declined to come, being too occupied with the battle of Stalingrad, so the discussions focused on the future of Western Allied strategy. At stake was the balance between expanding the Mediterranean theatre of war, which the United States had joined with the landings of Operation Torch in November 1942, and the plan to open a Second Front in France in 1943 or 1944. For the bomber forces there was more at stake. The conference opened at the end of a period of growing criticism of Bomber Command and the Eighth Air Force; it presented both forces with the opportunity to argue their case for sticking with an independent bombing strategy. This entailed a public-relations exercise to sell bombing to a potentially sceptical audience.

General Arnold instructed his staff to prepare detailed statistics, maps, reports and coloured charts for him to take to Casablanca, a list of props that ran to over three pages.[3] Harris took pains to ensure that a regular flow of publicity material, including good aerial photographs of damaged cities, reached the American press. The Air Ministry organized an exhibition in Washington in early January 1943, which was visited by Vice President Henry Wallace and later taken to the White House to show to Roosevelt. Wallace, it was reported, was 'completely sold on the necessity of bombing Germany' as a result of what he had seen, and keen to pass on his impressions to the president. The RAF delegation in America thought of producing a film to assist Arnold's efforts to present the bombing offensive to the American public.[4] At Casablanca, Arnold fielded a full team with both Eaker and Spaatz in attendance to argue the air force case; Portal had chosen to take Slessor, who was a sociable air force diplomat with planning experience, rather than Harris, whose bluntness would have been out of place in the delicate discussions to follow.

It is difficult to assess whether these propaganda efforts really affected the final decision to approve a combined offensive. The outcome for the two bomber forces was in the end mixed. The Casablanca Directive was a loosely worded document, a set of hopeful intentions rather than a clear plan 'that could have been made by any schoolboy', as one senior RAF officer later put it.[5] Months went by before a real planning document was produced. It was also designed to fit in with the priorities of the other services and the political leadership. Bombing was accepted at Casablanca as one way of weakening Germany before invasion rather than as an independent offensive in its own right, the same role that the German Air Force had had before the aborted Operation Sea Lion. Bombing survived as an option not because it was central to the strategic outlook of the Western allies, but because it was secondary.

THE CASABLANCA DIRECTIVE

Straightforward as the final decision for CCS 166 has seemed to later historians, the conference highlighted many of the conflicts and arguments that surrounded the bombing campaign in the last months of 1942. The commitment of the two war leaders and their military staffs to a sustained bombing campaign was not a foregone conclusion.

Churchill had shown increasing impatience with Bomber Command since August 1942, when he had assured Stalin on his visit to Moscow that a heavy raid on Berlin was imminent. Harris refused to attack the German capital until he had an adequate force at his disposal and the eventual raid, codenamed 'Tannenberg', only took place on 17 January, in the middle of the conference, long after Stalin too had lost patience with the constant delays.[6] In the end Churchill had to be content with sending Stalin a list of the 16 German cities that had been attacked between July and September 1942. Not until March 1943 did Stalin finally acknowledge the news that Berlin had been raided, more than six months after Churchill's first promise.[7] There was impatience, too, in both London and Washington, with the slow progress of the Eighth Air Force. Churchill thought that American bombers should be allocated to the war at sea and support for the landings of Operation Torch, and the plans for a daylight offensive against Germany be abandoned. In December Spaatz warned Eaker that the Eighth had to start operations 'projected into Germany' or face the prospect of diversion to the Mediterranean theatre, but the first American raid on a German target was launched only on 27 January 1943, when 59 bombers attacked the port at Wilhelmshaven three days after the end of the conference.[8] Arnold later reported to his chief of staff that at Casablanca he had been put permanently on the defensive by the British and American delegations 'for not having our heavy bombers bombard Germany'.[9]

The air forces' case at Casablanca had to be made to a disillusioned audience and it had to be made as far as possible together. Yet from the autumn of 1942 there were evident strains in the relationship between the RAF and the US Army Air Forces, despite the public commitment to combined operations. Both air forces realized that bombing had to be presented as a more coherent strategic option than it had offered for much of 1942. In September 1942 Portal and Slessor drew up a paper on 'Future Strategy', which argued for a combined offensive that would create the conditions for an easier invasion of Continental Europe by weakening German resistance and might knock Italy out of the war entirely, but no effort was made to articulate what kind of bombing was needed and against which targets.[10] Arnold bemoaned the absence of any definite plan from a British air force 'without strength in any one place to win decisively'.[11] On 19 September 1942 his planning staff in Washington produced a detailed operational plan, AWPD-42, which resembled the British commitment to wearing Germany down prior to a land invasion, but spelt out in fine detail how this was to be achieved. The American plan committed their bomber force to bomb by day a list of 177 targets vital to the German war effort, dropping 132,090 tons of bombs on 66,045 operational sorties; the seven chosen target systems were the German Air Force, submarine building, communications, electric power, oil, alumina and synthetic rubber. A counter-force strategy against the German fighter fleet was described as a key intermediate aim, whose achievement would make it possible to complete the rest of the programme in time for invasion, but counter-force strategy never appealed to the RAF.[12] Portal told Arnold politely that he had read AWPD-42 'with great interest', but it does not seem to have brought the two sides to a common view except that bombing mattered to ultimate victory. Arnold complained to the American Joint Chiefs at Casablanca that the British in his view seemed incapable of thinking in global strategic terms but simply chased 'the next operation'; he did not think the British 'had ever had a definite bombing program', and at his insistence the Combined Chiefs of Staff were asked to draft a priority bombing programme, which provided the trigger for the Casablanca Directive a few days later. Even this amounted to a compromise between the British statement of general aims about undermining German morale and American articulation of a list of priority targets.[13]

The most awkward issue at Casablanca was the argument over daylight bombing. This had been a running sore through 1942 as the Eighth Air Force built up its capability. Churchill was strongly sceptical of the claim that daylight bombing would work. Neither the RAF nor the German Air Force had been able to sustain daylight operations against effective fighter and anti-aircraft defences, and until January 1943 the Eighth Air Force had only flown against light resistance in France. Churchill began a sustained campaign in autumn 1942 to persuade the American side that day-bombing was too risky over Germany: 'They will probably experience a heavy disaster,' he minuted to Portal, 'as soon as they do.'[14] Churchill thought it more sensible for American bombers and crew to be converted for night work and integrated with Bomber Command. In October he asked Dwight D. Eisenhower, recently appointed Supreme Commander for Operation Torch, if American bombers could not be changed over to night-fighting.[15] On the advice of both Portal and Sir Archibald Sinclair, the Air Minister, Churchill restrained himself from pressing the point too far in case the American leadership decided to switch their bombing effort to another theatre.

RAF leaders waited to see what would happen with daylight attacks before deciding whether to insist that the American Air Force accept the alternative of night-bombing.[16] The American Air Force delegates at Casablanca knew that this was an argument they had to win. After clearing the request with Eisenhower on 13 January, Arnold invited Eaker to fly to Morocco to help him present the case for the American offensive. Arnold warned him at once that Churchill had already suggested to Roosevelt that the Eighth Air Force switch to night-bombing under RAF control. Eaker was asked to draft notes for 'The Case for Day Bombing'; he prepared a one-page synopsis with seven principal arguments to show to Churchill and a fuller version to help Arnold influence the Combined Chiefs of Staff.[17]

Although it was unlikely that Churchill would get his way, given the weight of British and American opinion in favour of trying out the day-bombing experiment, the risk existed that Roosevelt would be too preoccupied with other issues to notice. At a high-level discussion with the president on 18 January, Eisenhower and Spaatz secured agreement that neither bomber force should have the right to 'alter the technique or method of operating' of the other. American fears that Harris might be placed in overall command of a joint bomber offensive were set aside by the decision to make Portal, who was a popular choice with the Americans, the nominal director of the whole bombing campaign.[18] On 20 January Eaker was given a brief appointment to see Churchill so that he could present his paper. Churchill greeted him dressed up in the uniform of an RAF air commodore and the two men sat down on a couch to talk. The prime minister read aloud the page-long list of reasons for day-bombing. Eaker later recalled that when he came to the sentence about round-the-clock bombing, Churchill 'rolled the words off his tongue as if they were tasty morsels'.[19] Later that day Churchill was heard to remark, 'Eaker almost convinced me', but he had nonetheless agreed to give day-bombing over Germany a preliminary trial. At a meeting that evening Roosevelt and the army chief of staff, General Marshall, also gave daylight bombing their blessing and the following day Slessor was able to draft his directive for bombing by day and by night, one of the few features of the subsequent combined campaign on which both sides were agreed.[20]

The records of the many discussions held at Casablanca give little hint of the arguments over bombing taking place in the wings. In the minutes of the American Joint Chiefs of Staff the bombing campaign was mentioned briefly only three times; during the plenary sessions bombing was discussed on only two occasions, again at no length. In the list of priorities finally agreed by the Combined Chiefs the critical issues were the commitment to an invasion of Italian territory in the Mediterranean and an eventual campaign in north-west Europe, for which bombing would be a necessary prelude to maximize the chances of success for a major combined-arms operation. Churchill telegraphed the War Cabinet from Morocco the results of the conference, but included no mention of bombing.[21] The army and navy commanders at Casablanca devoted almost nothing in their memoirs to the arguments over bomber strategy. The projection of air power against Germany was essentially subsidiary to the wider strategic intention of re-occupying Europe during 1943 and 1944. The Casablanca Directive itself was a brief set of instructions to destroy and dislocate the German 'military, industrial and economic system' and to undermine the morale of the German people to the point where the German power of resistance was 'fatally weakened'. This was worded in terms that were permissive rather than prescriptive, and its force was immediately compromised by the list of other tasks bombing could be called upon to perform: bombing the submarine bases in France; attacking Berlin to keep the Russians happy; a campaign against Italy when required; objectives of fleeting importance (including German naval vessels); and full support 'whenever Allied Armies re-enter the Continent'.[22] This was a wish-list that encouraged the continued dispersion of Allied bomber forces.

When Eaker arrived back in England on 26 January he ordered the first American raid on Germany for the following day, and then dined that night with Harris to discuss what had happened. Two days later Norman Bottomley, the deputy chief of staff, was asked to send the new directive to Bomber Command. His original letter included the decision to make Portal responsible for the strategic direction of the bomber offensive, but Portal thought it more prudent not to advertise the change to his prickly subordinate, and on 4 February Harris was sent only the Casablanca Directive.[23] Although it was suggested that the new directive replaced the one issued to Bomber Command in February 1942, it is clear that Harris did not regard it as anything more than a statement of intent. In his memoirs Slessor described the Casablanca Directive, which he had drafted, as a policy statement rather than a proper directive.[24] Both air forces could read into it what they wanted.

A COMBINED OFFENSIVE?
JANUARY–JULY 1943

In the last months of 1942 the term 'combined offensive' began to be used more commonly. In August 1942 the Joint Planning Staff had drawn up recommendations for a concerted Anglo-American programme of bombing which provided the background for the eventual directive at Casablanca.[25] The preamble to AWPD-42 stipulated that the offensive was 'a combined effort' of the two air forces, the one concentrating on destroying precision objectives by day, the RAF on night-bombing of areas to break down morale. The passage was underlined to give it added force.[26] The combination was little more than a marriage of convenience. American air forces based their planning and preparation on isolating and destroying Germany's key industrial and economic targets and eliminating German air power – much as the German Air Force had done against Britain – while Bomber Command continued, when able, its unremitting destruction of the central areas of German industrial cities.

Like any marriage of convenience, the partners had separate beds. There had been suggestions before Casablanca that there should be a single commander for the bomber offensive. Arnold wanted a supreme air commander for the whole European theatre, but the British preferred separate commands in Britain and the Mediterranean, and Arnold waited for almost a year before appointing Spaatz as supreme commander of all American strategic and tactical air forces in Europe in the face of British objections.[27] The decision to accept bombing by day and by night underlined the need for two separate organizations, and although Portal had been given overall responsibility for coordinating the bomber offensive, he was not in command of either the Eighth Air Force or Bomber Command. This produced an awkward structure in which it remained unclear exactly the limits of Portal's power or the degree of collaboration between the two Allied bomber forces. Eaker had made it evident well before the Casablanca Conference that he did not regard the Eighth Air Force as in any sense under British command, though he did submit plans to Portal for approval and looked to him for protection from the demands of other theatres and services. 'We always feel,' Eaker wrote to Portal in late August 1943, 'that our guardian and greatest friend is away when you are absent.'[28] The American air forces in Britain found the formal command lines all the way back to Washington difficult to operate smoothly; in turn air force officials in the US capital were often poorly informed about conditions in Europe, and frustrated by the long distances. Eaker relied on Portal to supply bases and equipment and benefited from the chief of staff's familiarity with the offensive and with the political arguments that surrounded it. Harris had none of these difficulties. He communicated regularly with Portal and Churchill in defence of his command prerogatives and tolerated as little interference as possible. The two air forces maintained liaison staff at each other's headquarters, and on occasion collaborated on a common target, but there was no mechanism for shared command. The American mission statement for the offensive described the bombing as 'a *joint* assignment, completely complementary', which it was, but it remained combined in name rather than fact.[29]

The divide between the two air forces was explicit on the question of their strategic priorities. The Casablanca Directive required little adjustment for Bomber Command, which had been attacking German morale and destroying industrial cities for several years with the aim of fatally weakening the enemy. Harris remained doggedly resistant to the idea that specific target systems were strategically valuable in themselves and hostile to the diversion of his force for other purposes. Bomber Command was committed to accruing a growing register of destruction in German cities in the hope that the attrition might at some unspecified point and in an indefinable way weaken German capacity to wage war to the point of collapse. Harris, unlike the American Air Force commanders, remained convinced that bombing, combined with Soviet pressure, would bring victory in 1944 without the need for an expensive ground invasion.[30]

In the discussions following Casablanca, Harris summed up for the American side his strategic achievements so far and his plans for 1943. Essen, he claimed, was 'smashed out of recognition' and out of action for two months; Berlin, Nuremberg, Munich, Cologne and Wilhelmshaven were 'badly knocked about' but not devastated; Hamburg, Duisburg and Stuttgart had had 'lucky escapes'. His plan was to devastate one city and to damage three others badly each month up to September:[31]

This will mean 6 cities "Essenised" and another 18 badly knocked about. Taking cities more or less at random from last year's chief targets, this might work out as follows:–

<u>Devastated</u> Hamburg (counted as two by virtue of its size), Bremen, Duisburg, Wilhelmshaven, Kiel.

<u>Badly Hit</u> Berlin, Bochum, Cassell [sic], Munich, Nuremberg, Dusseldorf, Cologne, Leipsig [sic], Hanover, Stuttgart, Gelsenkirchen, Brunswick, Emden, Frankfurt, Mannheim, Magdeburg, Dortmund, Essen.

This was a crude strategy, crudely expressed, and it greatly exaggerated what Bomber Command could actually do to a city, including Essen. The ambition was not random only in the sense that most German cities housed some industry and could therefore be subject to attack; it could also be given a scientific gloss in the calculations supplied by the RE8 division and the Ministry of Economic Warfare (MEW) on the estimated economic damage already done and the potential economic gains from further destruction. This had allowed Portal in November 1942 to present the chiefs of staff with the grisly prediction that Bomber Command in 18 months could kill 900,000 Germans, seriously injure another 1 million, destroy 6 million homes and de-house 25 million people.[32] The MEW drew up a detailed list of all the important industrial and commercial targets in the so-called 'Bombers' Baedeker' (once again after the famous German tourist guides). Each installation was awarded a point score: 1+ for factories of leading importance to the war effort; 1 for major plants in major industries; 2 for minor plants in major industries or major plants in minor industries; and 3 for factories of small importance.[33] These scores were then calculated with population size to produce a league table of German cities which Harris kept with him at his headquarters. The list eventually reached over 100 cities, with 'key-point ratings' attached to each one – ranging from Berlin at number 1 with 545 to Wittenberg at number 104 with a rating of just 9. Harris crossed through each city on the list as it was attacked.[34]

American commanders rejected the idea of city-bombing and were sceptical of the claim that morale attacks would diminish the German war effort or create a widespread crisis. Portal tried to persuade Eaker in February 1943 that round-the-clock attacks on cities would be strategically valuable – 'heavy blows delivered on German cities have far greater effect than they did' – but Eaker would not be drawn in.[35] The gulf between the two strategic conceptions, as has often been emphasized, reflected two very different military cultures. American strategic practice was much closer to the German model than it was to the British. Eighth Air Force officers could be genuinely puzzled by exactly what the British strategic aim was. At a meeting called in the Air Ministry in March 1943 by Sydney Bufton, now promoted to Director of Bombing Operations, the American representative asked for an explanation of what Bomber Command was trying to do: 'Was it to kill Germans; to cause them to expend man hours; or was it to do specific damage to some certain installation?'[36] There was an awkward pause until Bufton announced that it was to neutralize German man-hours, a strategic commitment not expressed in any directive. When Eaker sent a draft of the American plans for fulfilling Casablanca to Spaatz in April, Bomber Command's effort was described no fewer than four times as little more than 'concentrated attacks against related areas and cities'.[37] The assumption in American planning was that Bomber Command would now help the Eighth Air Force, not the other way round.

Unlike Harris, Arnold and Eaker wanted to build on the Casablanca Directive to produce a strategic directive that made greater sense. The driving force behind American planning was the belief that whatever the air forces did over the coming year, they should contribute to making the invasion of Europe possible. The air force mission statement defined 'fatally weakened' as 'so weakened as to permit initiation of final combined operations on the Continent', which gave bombing a defined strategic purpose.[38] Arnold asked the Committee of Operations Analysts in Washington, set up in December 1942 under the prominent lawyer Elihu Root Jr., to draft a list of targets whose destruction would contribute to Axis defeat; staffed by men from business and the professions, the Committee supplied the data on 19 industrial target systems by March 1943.[39] Arnold instructed Eaker to work out with Portal the precise number of targets and the degree of operational effort required to destroy them, and by early April the draft plan for a Combined Bomber Offensive (CBO) was ready. The final version identified 76 key targets, with the aircraft industry at the top, submarines second and ball-bearings third.[40] It was sent on to Bufton by an Air Ministry colleague with a covering note that it was 'dull as hell' and needed to be shorter and brighter. It had been drafted chiefly by Eaker and his staff and was based on their fundamental realization that the German air forces had to be defeated first before the subsequent precision bombing of key industrial targets could be carried out without insupportable losses, and it was this argument that separated American from British bombing strategy most clearly. The adoption of a counter-force priority proved to be strategically well founded, as it had been for the German Air Force in 1940.[41] The 'intermediate target' became in effect the primary target.

The Air Ministry planning department had already tried to alert

Portal to the growing threat of the German single-engine fighter force before Eaker's report was available, so that there was support from both air forces for the shift in priority. Harris sent Eaker a fulsome response, since the new plan was clearly designed for the American market and impinged little on what he hoped to do.[42] The report was sent to Washington for Arnold's approval and in late April Eaker travelled back to the United States to defend his plan before the Joint Chiefs, who approved it on 29 April. This was in some ways a more important moment than the argument at Casablanca since the whole offensive critically relied on political approval in Washington for speeding up bomber allocation for the Eighth Air Force. Late in May Eaker was informed from Air Force headquarters in Washington that the plan had been approved by the president and by Churchill; the Combined Chiefs of Staff endorsed it with Portal's strong support on 18 May.[43] The new Directive for what was codenamed 'Operation Pointblank' was issued to Harris and Eaker on 10 June 1943. The close link with the planning for Operation Overlord was explicit. The Combined Chiefs asked for regular reports on the progress of the CBO to help them judge when conditions for invasion were ripe. Portal set up a regular flow of monthly reports from the Joint Intelligence Committee, while Eaker promised Washington that Arnold would get an analysis every two weeks together with a monthly summary. In September the Combined Chiefs confirmed that the CBO was now the 'prerequisite to "Overlord"', with the highest strategic priority.[44] Air supremacy was the key to successful invasion, and bombing was its instrument. In America there was at last a sense that a proper air strategy was in place. Assistant Secretary for War Robert Lovett wrote to Eaker in July that the combined offensive 'ought to have the effect of the famous old "one-two" in prize fighting'.[45]

These differences in command and strategy were compounded with the gulf separating the two forces in terms of current striking power. Bomber Command had been slowly expanded and modernized for three years before Casablanca and was closer to being able to redeem some of its tarnished promise in the spring of 1943 than the Eighth Air Force, which was still in the difficult throes of constructing a viable organization. Building up an effective bomber force differed markedly from the development of a major land army. Bomber commands consisted of volunteers with a high degree of long-term, expensive and specialized training. The initial equipment was complex and industrially demanding. On both counts loss rates had to be kept as far as possible to a supportable minimum. The nature of air battle required numerous well-equipped permanent bases, an extensive maintenance organization, a large stock of spares and, in the case of the Eighth Air Force, a long trans-oceanic logistics tail. The sharp end of air combat was supported by a ground organization many times larger than the aircrew on which the campaign rested. There was no supporting infantry in air combat.

Bomber Command became a substantial force only in the spring of 1943 as the changeover from medium to heavy-bomber production was finally completed. By March 1943 it was planned to have 49 heavy-bomber squadrons, by June as many as 60 out of a worldwide total of 431 RAF units of all types. Heavy-bomber squadrons made up 7 per cent of RAF squadron strength in September 1942, 14 per cent by the summer of 1943.[46] This was still far short of what Harris had wanted. In January 1943 there were still only an average of 514 heavy bombers and crews operationally ready. Harris's Command reached its peak strength in heavy bombers only in 1944 and 1945; the same was true for pilot strength, which was not much greater in 1943 than it had been in late 1941, though each of the heavier aircraft they flew dropped up to four times the weight of bombs (see Table 6.1 for the growth of Bomber Command). The overall size of the Command was dictated by the need for specialized ground personnel, which meant by the start of 1943 a combat strength of 23,000 aircrew (including training and OTU personnel) and a supporting force of 138,000 men and women, a ratio of 1:6. As the force of heavy bombers and pilots expanded, the ratio changed. By the end of the war there were 49,000 aircrew supported by 174,000 ground staff, a ratio of 1:3.5.[47] Women made up 17 per cent of the force by 1944.

The aggregate figures disguised manpower problems. By the summer of 1943 there were substantial shortages of skilled labour, much of it required by industry or by overseas air squadrons. This included a deficiency of 65 per cent of aircraft fitters (I Class), the most important category, and an overall shortage of two-fifths of skilled technicians and more than a third of all other trades.[48] There was also a persistent shortage of construction labour for airfields, both for Bomber Command and the Eighth Air Force. Heavy bombers required larger airfields, solid runways and extensive depots. In January 1943 there were 32,000 working on building airbases for the American force, 42,000 working for Bomber Command. As demands for training facilities also expanded, so more new bases had to be built. In addition to the 81 Bomber Command operational fields ready by January 1944, there were also 47 for training

Table 6.1: Bomber Command Strength in the United Kingdom, 1939–45

Year	Squadrons (including training units)			Pilots	All Aircrew	Ground Staff	WAAF	Airfields
	LB	MB	HB					
1939 (Sept)	6	17	–	–	–	–	–	20
1940	6	17	–	1,110	6,702	49,685	2,408	–
1941	9	32	3	2,133	20,633	99,515	10,169	–
1942	9	33	15	1,468	23,003	115,570	22,092	45
1943	10	16	36	2,403	45,330	127,914	34,080	60
1944	5	0.5	60.5	3,747	52,476	134,834	38,157	81
1945	10	0	73	3,501	49,418	136,629	37,292	71

Figures for columns 1–3: 1 Jan each year. Figures for columns 4–7: July 1940, December 1941–December 1944, May 1945. Column 8: February 1942, January 1943–5.

Sources: Compiled from TNA, AIR 22/203, War Room Manual of Bomber Command Operations 1939–1945, chart 1; AIR 20/2025, RAF personnel, establishment and casualties; UEA, Zuckerman Archive, SZ/BBSU/3, Exercise Thunderbolt, Précis no. 10, 'Administrative Aspects of the Bomber Offensive'.

purposes.[49] The Eighth Air Force initially calculated that it would need 61 completed airfields by the end of 1943, but eventually built 120, utilizing 1 million man-months of labour and laying 46 million square yards of concrete. The Royal Canadian Air Force No. 6 Group was promised 15 airfields, but ended up with only 10.[50]

The pressure on airfield space was reduced by the decision very early in the war to disperse most of the basic training overseas. It is seldom sufficiently acknowledged that the British bombing effort during the war was in reality a British Commonwealth undertaking. Britain was never 'alone' during the Second World War. On 17 December 1939 an agreement had been signed with the Canadian government to set up the British Commonwealth Air Training Scheme on bases in Canada. During the course of the war a peak of 73 schools were set up under the scheme, with a further 24 under RAF control. The Scheme turned out 131,000 trained aircrew, including 49,808 pilots and 29,963 navigators. By 1944 over 3,000 completed training each month. The majority (55 per cent) went into the Royal Canadian Air Force (a high proportion for Canadian units in Bomber Command), while the RAF took one-third; the remainder went to the Australian and New Zealand air forces.[51] Other British aircrew were also posted to training schools in the United States under the so-called Arnold Scheme. In April 1941 the American Army agreed to allow British participation in the Southeast Air Corps Training Program in the southern United States and 7,885 pilots were sent for basic training, together with 1,200 navigators. The programme was linked with Canadian training, but the failure rate in the United States was high because of the poor level of scientific education among British recruits and the scheme petered out in 1942.[52] Although crew were trained for a variety of different combat roles, the most pressing need was for bomber crew and it was here that overseas training had its greatest impact.

The training programme was the prelude to a great expansion of Commonwealth and European participation in the bombing war. There were Free French, Dutch, Norwegian, Czech and Polish crew in Bomber Command, but by far the largest contingents came from the main Dominion states, Canada, Australia and New Zealand. Only the Canadian units were large enough to be organized into a separate national organization because Canada, unlike Australia and New Zealand, was not directly menaced by Axis aggression and could confidently send its forces overseas. The RAF had not initially warmed to the idea of separate national units, partly because the complex training pattern made it difficult to keep crew from the same nationalities together as they went through the system. This was the problem with the limited number of Australians who contributed to the bombing war from British bases. Three Australian squadrons were activated, but even these could not be replenished regularly with only Australian airmen, while two-thirds of the ground personnel were British. In the spring of 1943 an effort was made by the Australian War Cabinet to stimulate creation of a distinctly Australian bomber group; there was resistance from the crews, already integrated with RAF units, and eventually an acknowledgement that the personnel needed to operate a full Group could not be freed from the limited labour supply in Australia needed for the Pacific War and wartime industry.[53] The pressure from the Canadian government for the 'Canadianization' of the units organized in Bomber Command had more success. On 1 January 1943 an entirely Canadian Group, no. 6, was activated under the command of Air Vice Marshal G. E. Brookes. It was spread out across the Yorkshire countryside with headquarters at Allerton Hall, nicknamed 'Dismal Castle' on account of its gloomy aspect. In total, 15 Canadian squadrons were formed, though like the Australian units they were not composed entirely of Canadians. The exception was the French Canadian squadron, formed in autumn 1942, where a great effort was made to ensure that it received only French-speaking aircrew.[54]

The Eighth Air Force was, by contrast, an almost entirely American effort. The structure of the force set up by Spaatz and then Eaker differed from Bomber Command because it also included its own fighter, training and air service commands, which were regarded as integral to the bombing campaign. When Eaker replaced Spaatz as commander of the Eighth Air Force late in 1942, he appointed Colonel Newton Longfellow, commander of the 2nd Bombardment Wing, to take over the Eighth Bomber Command. The force was divided into three Air Divisions, and then into Combat Wings each with their own tactical headquarters, each wing made up of three heavy bombardment Groups, or squadrons, and modelled, despite the differences in vocabulary, on Bomber Command practice. The force was still very small at the start of 1943, partly because of the decision to take a large component of aircraft and crew to establish the Twelfth Air Force in the Mediterranean theatre. Some 27,000 men and 1,072 aircraft were transferred at a critical point in the build-up of the offensive, leaving Eaker temporarily with just 27,000 men and 248 heavy bombers.[55] The diversion left the Eighth Air Force as little more than a skeleton. By April there were still only 250 heavy bombers, of which around half were serviceable at any one time, a reflection of the difficulty in establishing an effective supply organization and the need for extensive modification of the B-17s for actual combat conditions. Even by June 1943 the serviceability rates for heavy-bomber units was little more than half.[56] In the second half of 1943, however, the Eighth Air Force began to expand rapidly, reaching its peak strengths, like Bomber Command, in late 1944 and early 1945 (see Table 6.2 for the build-up of the Eighth Air Force).

Even more than the RAF, the American organization relied on very extensive base facilities and a large non-combat cohort to service and maintain the force. Among the many problems facing the Eighth Air Force in the first half of 1943, the issue of supply – everything from air-crew to spare parts – was the most pressing. For Bomber Command the logistics were straightforward. For the Eighth Air Force all the combat material, except for heavy aircraft, which could be flown across the northern Atlantic, had to come by ship and be stored in large service depots set up at each bomber base to handle the incoming resources. A Truck Transport system was established which by the end of 1943 could move 1.5 million ton-miles each month. The seven principal storage depots covered an area of more than 9 million square feet.[57] The most urgent need was for service personnel. In the late spring Arnold sent Maj. General Follett Bradley, Inspector General of the Army Air Forces, to England to help organize an effective programme to supply the trained manpower necessary to keep the Eighth Air Force flying. The 'Bradley Plan' called for 190,000 personnel in the Service Command to

Table 6.2: The Build-Up of the Eighth Air Force, 1943-5

Date	Heavy Bombers		Crews Available	Officers	Enlisted Men	Service Command
	Assigned	Operational				
1943 Jan	225	80	85	4,525	31,716	10,181
1943 Jul	800	378	315	11,966	89,685	20,236
1944 Jan	1,630	842	1,113	19,087	137,580	58,557*
1944 Jul	2,688	2,036	2,007	31,586	168,055	–
1945 Jan	2,799	1,750	2,295	27,187	148,498	–

* figure for December 1943.
Sources: AFHRA, 520.056-188, Statistical Summary Eighth Air Force Operations 1942–1945; CD A5835, Eighth Air Force, Growth, Development and Operations, December 1942–December 1943, Personnel Status, Exhibit 1.

match the planned size of the force, but the figures were always behind
target in 1943, partly because around 88 per cent of the air force had to
be shipped across the Atlantic in competition with vital supplies for the
Mediterranean and the build-up of forces for the eventual invasion of
France.[58] By June 1943 five bomber Groups had arrived in England
without their ground crews or operational equipment and had to double
up on bases which had them.[59] The Service Command rejected the offer
of help from the RAF and insisted that American aircraft should only
be maintained by American workmen, but many aircraft arrived in
England in need of extensive modification. To Arnold's complaints
about the low level of combat readiness of the Eighth Air Force by
the summer of 1943, Eaker retorted that aircraft should have been
prepared for combat in the United States rather than rely on modification depots in England, which lacked the means to convert aircraft
quickly.[60] It took most of the year before serviceability and replacement
rates for American heavy bombers could keep more than half the air
force flying.

The Eighth Air Force also suffered from the absence of a large corps
of trained officers and men from the pre-war air force. Some senior airmen had combat experience from the First World War, but most younger
officers had not had to fire a gun or drop a bomb in anger. Arnold
acknowledged that with only 1,500 regular officers in 1941, spread
worldwide a year later, 'the experience level is very thin'.[61] Tactical
thinking about the conduct of long-range bomber operations was in its
infancy and relied on learning from both the British and German experience. The large number of volunteers in the United States for service in
the air force had not, like those in the RAF, witnessed the battles over
northern France and southern England or seen what bombing might
achieve. Eaker called them 'sturdy amateurs', not lacking in enthusiasm
or courage, but not the equivalent of a highly trained peacetime force.[62]
Brig. General Haywood Hansell, temporarily in command of the Eighth
Bomber Command before Longfellow's appointment (hitherto commander of the First Bombardment Wing), produced a report for Eaker
in February 1943 suggesting that the force was simply not ready yet for
a major offensive against Germany. Hansell added that for the following months crews should be asked to undertake shallow attacks against
German targets to keep losses to a minimum and to practise with the
new target-finding apparatus, Oboe and H2S, taken over from the
RAF.[63] Nevertheless, the pressure on the Command to show that it
could produce results made it difficult for Eaker to limit what was done,

even when the early raids sustained high losses and resulted in extensive combat fatigue. Between January and April the monthly loss rate averaged almost 7 per cent, too high a figure for such a small force.[64] The slow expansion of the bomber units meant that crews arriving together from the United States might be broken up to fill the losses in existing Groups. This process, Eaker told Arnold, created 'an understandable and definite loss of morale'.[65]

The problems faced by the Eighth Air Force in adjusting to new conditions of combat, thousands of miles from the United States with thousands of freshmen aircrew, were exacerbated by the often poor relations between American airmen and the British communities that had to accommodate and service them. The relationship with the air force suffered from the instinctive sense of competition between the Eighth and Bomber Command, since they were the only servicemen actively in battle against the German homeland. The numbers involved were also very large – by December 1943 there were 283,000 servicemen and civilians in the Eighth Air Force – while the irregular nature of air combat gave aircrew long periods when they lived among predominantly civilian communities. One woman, keeping a diary for Mass Observation, condemned Americans as 'loud, bombastic, bragging, self-righteous'. Opinion polls showed that the British public most disliked American 'boastfulness', 'immaturity' and 'materialism'.[66] Though established prejudices might explain some of this reaction, the behaviour of mostly very young men a long way from home, learning 'British English', contributed to the confrontation. Eighth Air Force commanders were warned in December 1942 that 'unbridled speech' was causing embarrassment to Anglo-American relations and that all supplies of alcohol to the Command would be suspended if it continued.[67] General Marshall wrote to all senior commanders that American officers had encouraged a 'marked hostility and contempt for the British', and great efforts were made to introduce activities that would educate the American servicemen into treating their British hosts with greater respect and dignity. The Provost Marshal of the Eighth Air Force, in a lengthy report on the conduct of airmen towards the British, complained of the persistent 'Limey complex' which made them largely indifferent to their hosts unless there was the prospect of sex. A Special Service Study found that only 2 per cent of the air force had actually visited a British home.[68] The Eighth Air Force set up a speakers' pool with officers assigned to give talks to British audiences about American customs and manners; between April and September 1943 the speakers averaged 15 lectures a month, a grand total of 241. Eaker joked that out of the three possible crimes his men might indulge in – murder, rape and 'interference with Anglo-American relations' – the first two might under certain circumstances be pardoned, 'but the third one, never'.[69]

British criticism was not confined to popular areas of social friction. Over the first half of 1943 there was evidence of mounting frustration from the Air Ministry and Bomber Command over the long apprenticeship and unredeemed promises from the American Air Force. Harris and Portal both pressed Eaker to collaborate more fully in the renewed offensive in the spring of 1943, though both well knew that Bomber Command had taken three years to reach its current size and capability. There were British complaints about the quality of the B-17 'Flying Fortress' as a daylight bomber and arguments over the effectiveness of the new American oil-based incendiary bomb, the 6-lb M69. British tests suggested that the new bomb lacked penetration, had an unreliable fuse and relatively low incendiary efficiency, and despite American objections to the test results, the RAF continued to use the standard 4-lb incendiary.[70] There were strong objections to the British view of the B-17, but the American judgement on the bombers currently employed also accepted that the two main bombers, the 'Flying Fortress' and the B-24 'Liberator' were rapidly reaching the end of their useful life.[71] Indeed the harshest criticism of Eighth Air Force performance came from the American side, not from the RAF. Arnold, whose health deteriorated badly during 1943, finally lost patience with Eaker's force in June 1943. Citing the number of aircraft already sent to Britain, Arnold telegraphed Eaker that the number of bombers sent out on each mission 'is not rpt not satisfactory', and told him bluntly to change his commanders and staff to find officers who could organize attacks in 'a highly efficient manner'.[72]

In the short correspondence that followed, Eaker was defensive about his force and resentful of Arnold's intervention. Arnold ought certainly to have known better, since the ratio between aircraft supplied and aircraft on missions always had to take account of those awaiting repair, modification, or used for training purposes. 'Neither of us,' Eaker replied, 'has been able to accomplish ideal for reasons both should appreciate. We get nowhere with recrimination.'[73] Nevertheless Eaker agreed to make major changes in his command structure, anxious perhaps about the security of his own position. Longfellow, who Arnold regarded as insufficiently aggressive, was redeployed to Washington; Hansell was passed over (too 'nervous and highly strung', according to

Eaker); responsibility for the Eighth Bomber Command was given on 1 July 1943 to Brig. General Frederick Anderson, commander of the Third Bombardment Wing, while Hansell was replaced as commander of the First Bombardment Wing in June. The Third Wing was taken over by a young commander admired by both Arnold and Eaker, Colonel Curtis LeMay, future chief of the Strategic Air Command after the war. Anderson had arrived in England in February, flew his first mission to Rouen on 15 March ('enjoyed it thoroughly'), and in his diary looked forward to the day when a stream of B-17s would be taking off every day 'as they carry out their joy, dropping bombs on Germany'. He flew regularly with his crews and took the same risks.[74] Though Anderson had only been a few months in active service, Eaker judged that he had the right character for high command, though he regretted losing Longfellow, who was a close friend. 'This Bomber Command job of ours is a killer,' he told Arnold. 'It will break anybody down in six months unless he is a very unusual fellow.'[75] What had most concerned Arnold during the Command crisis was not the virtue of the bomber offensive itself and its achievements, but the extent to which it represented the claims to a distinct air force identity and a distinct strategy. For Arnold this meant a clear demonstration to the American public that the offensive was producing results which would inspire their 'faith in *our way of making war*'.[76]

The different force profiles and levels of preparation were no more sharply evident than in the contrast between the operational performance of the two bomber forces over the course of 1943, when Harris launched what have come to be seen as the three major battles of the bomber offensive, against the Ruhr-Rhineland in late spring and early summer 1943, against Hamburg in July, and against Berlin in the autumn. The campaign against the Ruhr-Rhineland was not in any sense a new one, since it had been a first priority for bombing ever since the onset of the campaign in May 1940. The difference in the spring of 1943 was the advent of substantial numbers of heavy bombers, particularly the Lancaster. During the months from March to June when the Ruhr 'battle' took place, the operational strength of Bomber Command averaged 794 heavy bombers, of which 578 (or 73 per cent) were serviceable. Each bomber dropped an average of just over 7,000 lbs of bombs, against an average load of 4,970 for the Eighth Air Force throughout 1943.[77] The Pathfinder Force was now fully equipped with the Mosquito Mk IX, which utilized the new electronic aids, Oboe Mark IA and H2S, which were both now available in sufficient quantity, though H2S proved a disappointment over heavily urbanized areas. Raids on the Ruhr had always been subject to the hazards of cloud and industrial smog, and the effective use of decoy sites. Navigation equipment no longer dependent on visual sighting was expected to allow a much greater degree of concentration at or near the principal aiming point. Over the target, new systems of marking had been developed using bright white markers when the ground was visible, or red, green and yellow sky-markers when it was not. The colourful flares were known by the codename 'Wanganui'; the German public called them Christmas trees. Once at the target the new Mk XIV bombsight could be used even when the aircraft took evasive action.[78] Radio counter-measures were available to block the German *Freya* radar, codenamed 'Mandrel', and to interfere with German ground-control transmissions, known as 'Tinsel', while new airborne devices to warn of German night-fighters and radar ('Monica' and 'Boozer') were finally being used, though again with only mixed effect.[79] All of these many technical and tactical innovations made Bomber Command a much more formidable threat. In a speech later in the war Harris admitted to an army audience that the bomber offensive only started seriously in March 1943.[80]

The first major raid on the Ruhr was made on the night of 5–6 March against Essen. A force of 442 aircraft attacked with 1,014 tons of bombs, two-thirds of them incendiaries. The Pathfinders worked well and an estimated 75 per cent bombed within three miles of the city centre, which was the principal aiming point. The apparent success of the raid gave Harris his verb 'to essenize' the target, but the next raid on Essen was less successful and a major raid on Duisburg on 26–27 March was scattered, largely because five out of nine of the Pathfinder Mosquito aircraft had to turn back with technical problems. A major raid on Berlin, conducted at Churchill's suggestion, lost direction and hit the capital with only 10 high-explosive bombs; the next raid missed the city altogether. Although the Ruhr plan was the first time Bomber Command had concentrated on a single coherent target, major raids were also made on more distant cities, reducing the impact on the Ruhr-Rhineland to no great effect. Attacks on Munich and Stuttgart recorded between one-fifth and one-third of bombs within three miles of the aiming point, levels of accuracy not significantly better than the year before.[81] Between March and June, when the battle against the Ruhr came to an end, Bomber Command had launched 28 raids against cities in the Ruhr-Rhineland area, but another 18 raids against targets in central Germany, Italy and France. Though the pattern of destruction varied widely between the different operations, the attacks on the Ruhr-Rhineland were the first raids to inflict serious levels of destruction on the urban area.[82]

The reaction from the German side was to search for new ways to cope with the sudden escalation of RAF capability. Hitler was preoccupied with stabilizing the war in Russia and North Africa but angered by what he saw as the continued failures in air defence. His air adjutant von Below recalled long evening conversations with Hitler about the inadequacy of anti-aircraft fire, the incompetence of Göring and the shortage of modern aircraft designs, but Hitler remained, according to von Below, 'at a loss' on questions of air power.[83] To stifle widespread popular anxiety Goebbels ordered the press and propaganda agencies to stop using the word 'mood' to describe public attitudes, which could evidently be widely variable, and to write only about 'high morale'.[84] Security Service intelligence reports showed the population in the bombed regions dismayed and restless at the apparent absence of effective defence, while exaggerated rumours of the extent of the destruction and casualties in the Ruhr were in circulation throughout the unbombed areas and could not be stopped. 'Even sensible people,' ran one report, 'have given these rumours credence.'[85]

The German defences against night-bombing were nevertheless stronger than they had been a year before. General Josef Kammhuber had around 400 night-fighters, double the level of the previous year, organized in five wings. There were around 500 day-fighters in the Western theatre protecting the Reich against daylight incursions. Each box in the *Himmelbett* system now had enough radars to control three fighters at a time, and had developed the means to pass on information to neighbouring boxes, but the rigid nature of the fixed line of air defence made less sense against large concentrations of heavy bombers that could routinely swamp the line as they crossed into Germany. Kammhuber proposed a single central authority to control the whole night-defence system and a fivefold increase in the night-fighter force, but the proposal was rejected by Hitler in favour of strengthening anti-aircraft and searchlight defences around the vulnerable inland areas.[86] As a result the night-fighter force stagnated, taking losses of 282 aircraft during the period of the Ruhr battle, against an overall loss of 600 RAF bombers from all causes. Pressure to change to a more flexible system of defence was rejected. The idea of using ground-control stations to direct night-fighters into the bomber stream so that they could fly with it, shooting down any bomber that came within range, a tactic known as *Zahme Sau* ('Tame Boar'), was turned down because it would drain resources away from the Kammhuber Line; a second proposal from Major Hans-Joachim Hermann to use single-engine day-fighters at night against bombers illuminated by searchlights, flares and target markers, known as *Wilde Sau* ('Wild Boar'), arrived too late for the spring attacks and was again difficult to integrate with the existing system.[87] Kammhuber's insistence that his aerial fortification was the only way to combat the bombers brought him into conflict with Göring and his deputy, Erhard Milch, and in November he was finally relieved of his command and sent to run the rump Air Fleet 5 in Norway.

In the midst of the campaign against the Ruhr, Harris was compelled to organize an operation of which he fundamentally disapproved. The engineer Barnes Wallis had begun work in 1940 on the kind of explosive device needed to breach a major dam wall. In March 1941 an Air Attack on Dams Committee was set up to study the possibility, using the Road Research Laboratory as a base. In April 1942 Wallis developed the idea of a cylindrical bomb, dropped from a low height, to bounce across the water and drop to the foot of the dam wall; codenamed 'Upkeep', the bomb tests represented a real technical challenge but were convincing enough by February for the air staff to approve a possible operation against the German Möhne, Sorpe and Eder dams.[88] When the report was passed to Harris he scrawled at the bottom: 'This is tripe of the wildest description ... not the smallest chance of it working.'[89] Nevertheless, more trials were conducted to determine whether the 'bouncing bomb' was a viable operational proposition. A squadron of Lancasters under Wing Commander Guy Gibson, no. 617 squadron, was activated on 21 March 1943 and trained rigorously for an operation against the reservoir dams that supplied water for the Ruhr. Harris remained adamantly unconvinced: 'As I always thought,' he minuted in April, 'the weapon is balmy [sic] ... get some of these lunatics controlled or if possible locked up.'[90] His scepticism was ignored. On the night of 16–17 May, under the codename 'Operation Chastise', 19 Lancasters were despatched of which 12 attacked the three dams, breaching the Möhne and the Eder, but doing only superficial damage to the Sorpe dam. Two-thirds of the water escaped from the reservoirs and 1,294 were drowned in the inundation, including 493 foreign workers. The destroyed dams lost an estimated 25,000–30,000 tons of masonry but both were repaired by October, while the long-term damage to the industrial water supply was less than had been hoped.[91] Further attacks were ruled out, partly because of the high loss rate. Only 8 Lancasters returned from the raid and 56 out of the 113 aircrew were lost.

The early raids against the Ruhr were regarded by Harris as less than satisfactory. The proportion of aircraft dropping bombs within three miles of the aiming point varied greatly. The experiment with sky-marking showed that out of 11 raids that used it, one resulted in severe damage, one in considerable damage, eight in 'scattered damage', and one in no damage at all. The photo-reconnaissance evidence on major raids showed that the percentage of hits within three miles varied from 80 per cent to 25 per cent, with most less than 50 per cent.[92] Harris assumed that 'weaker brethren', as he called them, were failing to press home attacks, while he singled out the tactic of violent evasive action (an instinctive response to intense searchlight and anti-aircraft activity) as a key culprit. In early May 1943 he circulated a tactical memoran-dum to groups on 'Evasive Action by Bombers' to replace existing instructions, which had given pilots advice on what forms of evasion to take under different circumstances. The new memorandum insisted that most forms of evasion were 'useless', since an anti-aircraft barrage was indiscriminate and inaccurate (a claim scarcely justified by the 1,496 bombers damaged by anti-aircraft fire during the campaign). Evasion, the report continued, increased the chance of collision, kept bombers for longer in the danger zone, and placed serious strain on the aircraft structure. Crews were told to fly 'straight and level' through the target area to increase the concentration of bomb hits.[93] Whether crews really did respond to the instruction, or whether the growing experience of the Pathfinders and the surviving pilots reduced losses and increased concentration, the major raids carried out between May and July against Cologne, Duisburg and Wuppertal-Barmen resulted in the most destruc-tive and lethal attacks so far.

These last raids produced very heavy damage to the centre of the city, and in the case of Barmen, attacked on the night of 29–30 May by 719 bombers, created a major conflagration that consumed four-fifths of the built-up area and killed 3,400 people, the largest number in any one raid until then. Wuppertal, the other half of the town of Wuppertal-Barmen, was raided on 24–25 June by 630 aircraft and 94 per cent of its urban area was destroyed or damaged, with 1,800 deaths. In the four months of the heavy 'crash raids', as they were called, an estimated 22,200 were killed, almost twice the number killed in the whole period since May 1940. Some 55,700 buildings were rendered for the moment uninhabitable. 'They had ruined the Ruhr,' complained Hitler in June, though only 5 per cent of buildings were actually destroyed.[94] The exact nature of the damage could not be known to Bomber Command, but intelligence estimates of the damage to the Ruhr were constructed in the summer to give Harris the necessary material to defend his city-bombing campaign. This was difficult to do and had to be based on extrapolation from the detailed statistical surveys of housing damage and man-hour losses in British cities bombed in 1941 and 1942. The Joint Intelligence Committee estimated that 9 per cent of the population of the most heavily raided cities were homeless (422,500) and 38.5 per cent (1,816,000) had housing damage. The committee estimated that 68,750 houses had been destroyed, a figure closer to the reality than might be expected from simple photo-reconnaissance. Estimating the impact on the economy was more difficult. The Krupp works in Essen were thought to have lost between one-quarter and one-half of planned output over the summer. The MEW estimated a total loss to German production of 10–12 per cent from attacks on the Ruhr-Rhineland (including 2–2.5 million tons of steel) and a bad state of morale.[95] A study by the RE8 department two months later of the impact of the raids on Essen, based on studies of British workers during the Baedeker raids, concluded that if German workers reacted in the same way as British workers to the loss of housing and amenities, then Essen lost the equivalent of 50 city-days of work output. None of these efforts at calculating what Bomber Command was achieving were coordinated or consistent. Nor could they confirm whether bombing was a strategically sensible use of British resources.[96]

Alongside the night-bombing, the Eighth Air Force, as one senior American commander put it, 'can only nibble at the fringes of German strength'.[97] There were three small raids on German territory in March; one in April (a mission to Bremen which cost the loss of 15 per cent of the force); six attacks on the north German coast in May; and three in June, including the only attack on the Ruhr, against the synthetic rubber plant at Hüls on 22 June, where the loss rate was almost 9 per cent.[98] The two forces were at quite different stages. In the first six months of 1943 Bomber Command dropped 63,000 tons of bombs, the Eighth Air Force only 8,400 tons more. For the American command, Operation Pointblank had not yet started; in contrast, the RAF, as the Director of Plans explained in March 1943, hoped that bombing 'may well produce decisive results this year'. There was nevertheless no prospect that the two bomber forces would constitute what the Joint Intelligence Committee called after the Ruhr offensive 'an organic whole', because of continued American resistance to the idea that bombing cities was strategically useful. The Ruhr battle was one of a long line of Bomber Command campaigns in which the Eighth Air Force was largely absent.[99]

OPERATION GOMORRAH: THE DESTRUCTION OF HAMBURG

Back in November 1941 the Bombing Operations Directorate in the Air Ministry had concluded from a study of urban targets in northern Germany that Hamburg was the city which presented the best general conditions for a large-scale incendiary attack. Since the area was large, 'saturation point' would be harder to achieve. The report continued that if Hamburg was selected for special incendiary attack, 'the whole of the effort should be confined to the congested city and housing areas North of the Elbe'. To get a clear picture of what saturation point might look like, the Directorate used a map of central London as a model, placing transparencies with a typical incendiary bomb salvo printed on them over the London streets to work out how widely the bombs would spread and how vulnerable the buildings might be.[100] Over the winter of 1941-2 a great deal of effort went in to working out how to create a major conflagration with the existing technology. In February 1942 a further memorandum on choosing a German city to burn down had Hamburg at the top of the list, its vulnerability rated 'outstanding'.[101]

Harris might well have tried to exploit that vulnerability in May 1942 when he planned the first 1,000-bomber raid, but poor weather prevented it. Had he done so, Hamburg would certainly have sustained far less damage and loss of life than proved to be the case when Harris finally decided, on 27 May 1943, that Hamburg would suffer next what he was inflicting on the cities of the Ruhr-Rhineland. What resulted in a series of raids appositely titled 'Operation Gomorrah' was the single largest loss of civilian life in one city throughout the whole European war, exceeded only by the 250,000 Japanese killed in the firebombing of Tokyo and the atomic attacks on Hiroshima and Nagasaki. The destruction of Hamburg in an uncontrollable firestorm on the night of 27-28 July 1943 is often presented as if it were an accident, the result of exceptional meteorological conditions and the failure of German defences, and not a product of deliberate intention. This is to misunderstand entirely the purpose of the city-bombing campaign, which was predicated from the start on causing as much general damage and loss of life as possible by means of large-scale fires. The firebombing of Hamburg was not exceptional. Not for nothing was its vulnerability rated 'outstanding'; it was expected to burn well.

To understand the capacity of Bomber Command to inflict a conflagration of such intensity on Hamburg, it is useful to place it in the context of the long operational and scientific effort devoted by the Air Ministry to understanding how incendiarism worked. When the RE8 department was established in the summer of 1942, one of the first tasks given to it by the Air Ministry was research into the spread of fire and the role of wind speeds in turning a strong blaze into a conflagration. It was assumed that city fires could be acted upon much as a pair of bellows on a domestic hearth if the wind speed and direction were favourable. 'Once a large conflagration has become established,' wrote one of the department's scientific advisers, 'the "fire-storm" which it induces is sufficient to ensure its further spread.'[102] On the advice of J. D. Bernal, wind trials were conducted by the Porton Down Experimental Station in Wiltshire using models of urban areas, while the RAF Photo-Interpretation section provided night photographs to help in identifying the factors which accelerated the spread of fire.[103] It was also necessary to determine scientifically the vulnerability to firebombs of German urban structures, in particular town houses and apartment blocks, and the quantity and mix of bombs necessary to overwhelm the fire services in a single raid. Work on German structures began in 1942 and was more or less complete by the time of the final RE8 report on 'German Domestic Architecture' issued early in 1943. Tests on models of different kinds of German roofs were carried out at the Road Research Laboratory at Harmondsworth, outside London, while material on German staircases and stairwells was supplied from a German publication on 'Residences and Houses of the Middle Classes'.[104] The study of German architecture had involved a good deal of argument over the average thickness of wood beams and the penetrative power of the standard 4-lb incendiary bomb, which had only been resolved by recruiting émigré German architects, including the Bauhaus founder, Walter Gropius, to confirm the details of construction. The conclusion from studies of roof coverings, joists and floor density typical of construction in north-western Germany and Berlin was that 'a German house will burn well'.[105]

The most important issue was to decide what mix and weight of bombs would best achieve a conflagration that was beyond the control of the ground defences. The quantity of incendiary and high-explosive bombs judged to be necessary to destroy each square mile of the target city was cranked up regularly during the two years before Operation Gomorrah. Initial research suggested that between 100,000 and 200,000 4-lb bombs would swamp any fire-watching and firefighting force, but they had to be dropped in large salvos, not in small packets.[106] By late 1942 incendiary technique was better understood. Its purpose, as one Air Ministry report put it, was 'the complete destruction by fire of the built-up area of a city'. This required a fire-raising group to isolate the target and start fires pronounced enough for the follow-up force to drop 25,000 incendiaries for each square mile attacked as well as high-explosive bombs to destroy windows, crater the streets, and intimidate civil defence and fire-workers. In order to start a conflagration the target area had to be the most densely packed residential areas of the city centre, Zones 1 and 2A on the zone maps supplied to Bomber Command. Igniting the 'terraces of box-like buildings dating from the Middle Ages' was, according to the Bombing Directorate, expected to 'yield good dividend'.[107]

To prevent effective firefighting the incendiary load had to contain not only regular incendiaries but also the delayed-action explosive incendiary, capable of maiming or killing enemy civil defence workers and deterring them from action. These devices were deliberately timed to detonate at irregular intervals, some after three minutes, a small proportion only after ten.[108] In late 1942 a small anti-personnel high-explosive bomb with a trigger fuse was developed, which could be activated by any object, even a jet of water, and would kill those immediately around it without warning.[109] It was suggested that a high proportion of delayed-action bombs should be used in 'incendiary attacks on virgin towns' to create a powerful deterrent effect on the enemy emergency services.[110] There was also considerable argument about the merits of complementing the conventional magnesium bomb with larger oil-based incendiaries, which were also subjected to rigorous scientific testing. The result was the selection of the 30-lb Mark II containing a mix of white phosphorous and benzol gel, capable of greater penetration than the 4-lb incendiary, and effective in spreading fire quickly over a wider area.[111] All of these bombs were eventually produced and used in substantial quantities over the last three years of war, peaking in 1943 (see Table 6.3).

Table 6.3: Incendiary Bombs Dropped by the RAF, 1940–45

Year	4-lb bomb	4-lb explosive bomb	30-lb bomb	No. 14 IB Cluster (106 × 4-lb)
1940	508,993	–	–	–
1941	2,082,669	–	758	–
1942	8,010,920	–	309,200	–
1943	25,898,290	1,469,853	1,728,949	–
1944	18,392,077	1,498,723	979,182	6,288,460
1945	6,761,544	690,523	–	3,764,670

Source: TNA, AIR 22/203, Bomber Command, War Room Manual of Operations 1939–1945, 54.

There was strong American interest in the development of incendiary bombing. The conventional view that the Eighth Air Force used predominantly high-explosive bombs for precision air attacks in contrast to the fire-raising tactics of Bomber Command is not borne out by the evidence. The Bombing Directorate in the Air Ministry collaborated closely with the American Office of Scientific Research and Development, which produced studies on the 'Theory and Practice of Incendiary Bombing', and supplied the British with illustrated volumes on major conflagrations in American cities, which were more common and more destructive than in Europe. The photographs resemble closely the aftermath of the major city-bombing in Germany.[112] In October 1942 America's foremost expert on fire in foreign countries, Boris Laiming, filed a report which was passed on to the Air Ministry in December. He argued that the only way to start a major conflagration under conditions normally prevailing in Germany was to start a great many smaller fires simultaneously on long strips of urban territory on a day when there was a reasonable wind and low humidity.[113] In the United States, experiments were made at the Chemical Warfare Service depot in Utah in burning down different kinds of structure and at a facility in New Jersey on penetrating simulated German roofing with incendiaries.[114] American expertise was also invited to Britain. Horatio Bond, chief engineer of the National Fire Protection Association, visited London for four months in late 1942 to give advice on large-scale fire destruction, followed a few months later by James McElroy, another senior NFPA engineer, who worked for the rest of the war at the RE8 headquarters at Princes Risborough in Buckinghamshire, first producing so-called 'fire division maps' of German cities, showing each urban 'cell' that needed to be set alight, then going on to produce vulnerability maps of major industrial targets for the Eighth Air Force Operational Research Section, to show what proportion and what type of incendiary bomb should be carried by aircraft.[115]

The American Air Force was impressed by British incendiary practice. In April 1943 Arnold spelt out for his assistant chief of staff for materiel the ways in which the Eighth Air Force would be expected to use incendiary bombs: first, for burning down precise industrial targets when a greater degree of destruction was possible using fire; second, by starting fires 'in the densely built-up portions of cities and towns' to create a beacon for RAF attacks at night on the same city or town; third, for burning down densely built-up areas 'when the occasion warrants'.[116] American forces used principally the 4-lb incendiary (renamed the M-50), the M-17 110-bomb cluster, the M-47 70-lb oil and rubber bomb, and the M-76 473-lb oil bomb. Extensive plans were laid in 1942 for incendiary bomb production, 39 million bomb cases in that year, 107 million in 1943, divided between the different services and Lend-Lease supplies for Britain.[117] Extensive research on the effects of incendiary bombing resulted in a set of recommendations for the Eighth Air Force in September 1942, which differed from RAF practice principally by preferring the 473-lb oil bomb over the 4-lb incendiary and identifying weather as a vital condition: 'a high wind is still the best weapon'. Bomb patterns were to be dense enough 'to *guarantee* real conflagrations'.[118] Extensive experiments were carried out in Britain on the use of oil bombs of different weights, and in April large quantities were finally shipped to American bases for operational use. They were first employed extensively in July 1943, the month of Operation Gomorrah. By the end of the war the Eighth Air Force had dropped a total of 90,357 tons of incendiaries and incendiary clusters, totalling 27 million 4-lb bombs and 795,000 heavy incendiaries.[119]

The two-thirds load of incendiary bombs aimed at the residential areas in Hamburg north of the River Elbe to try to stimulate an uncontrollable conflagration was thus no accident. The choice of Hamburg is not difficult to explain. The Air Ministry Target Committee in April 1943 defined Hamburg as 'No 1 priority' because of its shipbuilding industry.[120] It had been attacked repeatedly since 1940, usually in small raids which inflicted light damage on Germany's second-largest city. There were 127 small raids between 1940 and the end of 1942; the 10 raids in 1943 before Gomorrah resulted in just 142 deaths and the destruction of 220 buildings.[121] Hamburg was fourth on the MEW list, behind Berlin, Duisburg and Bochum, all three of which had been attacked in the late spring. The MEW rankings in the 'Bomber's Baedeker' had 21 industrial targets ranked 1+ or 1 and 25 ranked 2, substantially more than most other cities.[122] The vulnerability of Hamburg was magnified by its proximity to British bases, the conspicuous coastline and its sheer size. In a survey of German cities already subject to incendiary attack, the ratio of incendiary to high-explosive damage in Hamburg was judged to have been 13:1, higher than any other except the port of Wilhelmshaven.[123] It is not clear whether Harris was ever shown these figures, but his desire to launch a spectacular operation fitted with the geographical pattern of the new attacks and Air Ministry ambitions. Not to have attacked Hamburg in force would have been more difficult to explain.

The decision was nevertheless not easily endorsed and rested in the end on Churchill's approval. The chief argument was over the decision whether to use a simple tactical device to temporarily blind all German radar, known by the codename 'Window'. The tactic consisted of dropping very large quantities of small aluminized strips which would create a confused blur of echoes on enemy radar screens and make accurate detection of the bomber stream impossible. It was first developed in late 1941 by Robert Cockburn at the Telecommunications Research Establishment in Malvern, and early trials led to the manufacture of the material with a view to using it against German radar in May 1942. Frederick Lindemann persuaded Portal to cancel the instruction and a fresh set of tests showed that the latest British ground and airborne radar was highly susceptible to 'Window' if the Germans retaliated with it. Lindemann insisted that it should not be used operationally until an antidote could be found. The Germans did develop the same technique, known as *Düppel*, but like the RAF, hesitated to develop and use it. However, by late 1942 new British AI radar for night-fighters and GCI radar for ground control, together with a new American airborne radar, SCR-270, all had the capacity to survive a 'Window' assault. American experiments also showed that maximum effect would come from a large number of narrow strips, about half as long as the wavelengths of the German *Würzburg* radar, which controlled the German air defences. 'Window' was manufactured in 30-cm strips, 1.5-cm wide, with paper on one side and aluminium foil on the other, in bundles of 2,000 for release from each aircraft in the bomber stream.[124]

The combination of improved British defences and the weakness of the German bomber arm in the west finally persuaded Portal to approve the employment of 'Window', but now the chiefs of staff objected to its operational use before the invasion of Sicily in early July, in case the German Air Force used it to confuse Allied air support during the landing. As a result its use was postponed until Operation Gomorrah, following approval by Churchill on 15 July.[125] A few days later Churchill was faced with another objection, this time to the choice of Hamburg as a target at all. Henry Tizard, the government's chief scientific adviser, wrote to Churchill and Portal deploring the planned destruction of Hamburg on the grounds that it would be a useful capital for the Allies to occupy when they ran post-war Germany, and that its population was 'anti-Russian, anti-Prussian and anti-Nazi', and might soon be 'anti-war'. Churchill sent the letter to the chiefs of staff, but Portal had already answered Tizard, explaining that Hamburg was too important a target to ignore. 'It is a moot point,' he continued, 'whether bombing produces a more desirable effect when directed upon anti-Nazis than upon the faithful', but he was content for Harris to find out whether Hamburg's anti-Nazi sentiment would be stung into action by bombing. Churchill took this for approval.[126] By then the first of the Gomorrah raids had already taken place.

The operation against Hamburg, like the heavy bombing of Cologne in late June and early July 1943, was spread over 10 days from the first RAF raid on 24-25 July to the final raid on 2-3 August.[127] The opening night-bombing raid by 728 aircraft was the first to use 'Window'. Around 80 miles from the target the Pathfinder force and the main force that followed emptied bundles of foil strips at the rate of one bundle a minute. The strips worked perfectly, creating numerous echoes on the cathode-ray radar screens and presenting German night-fighters with a confusion of false information. Searchlights and anti-aircraft artillery had to improvise a barrage of light and fire in the hope that bombers might be deterred anyway. In just under one hour 2,284 tons of bombs were dropped, including an average of 17,000 incendiaries for every square kilometre.[128] Although fewer than 50 per cent of the bombers hit the three-mile aiming zone, the rest hit the large central and north-western residential districts, killing, according to the Reich Statistical Office, 10,289 people, three times more than the worst raid so far.[129] Over the following two days the Eighth Air Force attacked targets by day in north-west Germany. On 25 July, 218 bombers bombed shipbuilding targets in Hamburg and Kiel, losing 19 aircraft in the process; on 26 July, 96 aircraft attacked Hanover and 54 raided Hamburg, with the loss of a further 18 aircraft, a rate over the two days of more than 10 per cent, an indication that the warnings about the dangers of day-time bombing voiced at Casablanca had not been misplaced. The two American raids killed 468 people in Hamburg.[130]

The RAF raid that followed on the night of 27–28 July was a text-book example of the incendiary planning of the previous two years. It was helped by the prevailing meteorological conditions. There had been rainfall on 22 July, but the remainder of the week was dry. Humidity levels, which had been high earlier in the month, fell abnormally, reaching 46 per cent on 25 July and only 30 per cent on 27 July. Temperatures soared in the last week, reaching 32C (90F) on the evening of 27 July; low humidity and high temperatures remained over the following two days. These summertime conditions favoured the chances of a major conflagration.[131] The Pathfinder force dropped markers several miles east of the centre of Hamburg, but the 729 aircraft concentrated their 2,326 tons well on the packed working-class districts of Hammerbrook, Borgfelde, Hamm, Billwärder, Hohenfelde and Rothenburgsort. The raid lasted just over an hour. The concentration of approximately 1,200 tons of incendiaries on an area of two square miles created numerous major fires that soon merged together into a roaring inferno. Water shortages caused by the earlier heavy raid hampered firefighting. Many emergency workers and vehicles were further west in the city still coping with the aftermath of the first fires where the civil defence control room had been destroyed. Efforts to stem the fires proved useless. What followed, in the words of Hamburg's police president, was a 'hurricane of fire ... against which all human resistance seemed vain'.[132] The illusion of a hurricane was caused by the scale and intense heat of the conflagration which caused fire winds that drove the flames across natural firebreaks. The inferno created a pillar of hot air and debris that rose quickly to a height of more than two miles above the city. Greedy for more oxygen, the fire drew in cold air from the surrounding area with such force that the new winds reached hurricane-force strength in the area of the fire, collapsing buildings, uprooting trees and sucking human bodies into the flames where they were swiftly incinerated or mummified. Acting like giant bellows, the winds created temperatures in excess of 800C that destroyed everything combustible barring brick and stone. Oxygen was sucked out of the thousands of basement and cellar shelters, leaving their inhabitants to die slowly of carbon monoxide poisoning.[133] An estimated 18,474 people died during the night. An area of more than 12 square miles was burnt out.

This was not the end for Hamburg. Harris's intention of destroying the city brought two more major raids on 29–30 July and 2–3 August. The first, carried out by 707 bombers, dropped a higher tonnage than the firestorm night, but did not create a second thermal hurricane. Large residential areas were again burnt out and an estimated 9,666 killed. The final raid in August was abortive. Large thunderstorms protected Hamburg. The Pathfinder force failed to mark the city and most aircraft dropped their bombs over northern Germany or in the North Sea. The final raid killed 78 people. The cumulative total for Operation Gomorrah calculated by the local police authorities by December 1943 was 31,647; the figure was revised in May 1944 to 38,975, which is close to the figure currently favoured of 37,000.[134] Around 900,000 people evacuated the city and 61 per cent of Hamburg's houses and apartments were destroyed or damaged together with 580 industrial premises and 2,632 shops. The RAF bomber force lost only 87 aircraft, or 2.5 per cent of all sorties, thanks partly to the use of 'Window', partly to the shock effect on Hamburg's defences. The post-raid report noted that smoke obscured much of the evidence of destruction but confirmed that the 'amount of residential damage is very great'.[135]

The consequences for the German air defence system were profound. The catastrophe at Hamburg even more than the raids on the Ruhr catapulted the German Air Force into abandoning the principle of the fixed front, embodied in the Kammhuber Line and heavy reliance on anti-aircraft fire, and substituting instead a much larger fighter force based on new forms of combat. Even before the conflagration at Hamburg, Göring, despite his anxiety to begin offensive air operations against Britain, admitted to his staff that 'Air defence is now in my opinion decisive.' The terrible events in Hamburg accelerated the shift to priority for fighter production and intense efforts to combat the scientific lead in radar and radio countermeasures which the Allied air force had established over the summer months.[136] By October 1943, Göring's deputy, Erhard Milch, had drawn up firm plans for the output of more than 3,000 fighter aircraft a month, and more speculative plans for 5,000 fighters every month during 1945, at the expense of further bomber production.[137] By simplifying production methods, reducing the large number of aircraft types and abandoning the habit of regular modification, Milch calculated that the output could be achieved without a large increase in labour.[138] He had already taken over central responsibility for radar and radio development in May and had begun an immediate acceleration of research and production. In July a new office for high-frequency research was set up under Dr Hans Plendl, which drew in 3,000 scientific personnel to combat the variety of devices that had fallen into German hands during the Ruhr battle, thanks to the recovery of equipment from crashed bombers.[139]

After the success of 'Window', priority was given by the Germans to developing radar that would be more immune to its effects in order to increase as rapidly as possible the hitting-power of the German fighter force. Permission was now given to build up units trained for Hermann's *Wilde Sau* technique while on the day following the final heavy raid on Hamburg, 30 July, the *Zahme Sau* tactic of controlled infiltration of the bomber stream was approved by Milch and Hubert Weise, overall commander of the German home-front air defence. The result was a substantial diversion of guns and aircraft away from the fighting fronts where they were needed more than ever by the summer of 1943. By late August there were over 1,000 fighter aircraft stationed in Germany, 45.5 per cent of all German fighter strength, and a further 224 in northern France. Over the same period the number of heavy anti-aircraft guns on the home front increased from 4,800 before Gomorrah to over 6,000 by the end of August, including more of the heavier 10.5-cm and 12.8-cm models. Shortages of skilled personnel hampered the anti-aircraft effort throughout the year, and for the first time substantial numbers of women and young people were recruited as *Flakhelfer*; on Hitler's orders training began in August 1943 for 250 units of Reich Labour Service boys to undertake air defence duty in the year before they joined the armed forces.[140]

In Britain the Hamburg raids were treated as a great success. The Director of Intelligence in the Air Ministry thought that the operation confirmed the superiority of incendiary over high-explosive bombs: 'the complete wipe-out of a residential area by fire is quite another and better conception. May it long continue!'[141] Robert Lovett wrote to Eaker from Washington that the War Department was keen to see the photo-reconnaissance images of Hamburg's destruction as soon as possible: 'The pasting Hamburg got must have been terrific.' Eaker replied that the raids had 'a tremendous effect'.[142] For Harris, Operation Gomorrah was more than he could have hoped for. The post-raid assessments, now based on RE8 research on man-months lost and acreage destroyed, transformed the statistical image of Bomber Command's achievements and gave Harris the weapons he needed to argue the case that bombing was capable of knocking Germany out of the war. If there had been a defensiveness about Bomber Command strategy before Hamburg, the new evidence could be used to strengthen Harris's hand. On 12 August he wrote to Portal, who was with the Combined Chiefs at the Quadrant conference in Quebec, that in his view the bombing war was 'on the verge of a final show-down'. Harris was certain that with the same concentration of effort 'we can push Germany over by bombing this year'.[143]

The results of Operation Gomorrah could only be assessed by the crudest measurements, since the detailed effects were not yet known even to the German authorities. This meant chiefly an assessment of the acreage of Zones 1 and 2A, the inner-city residential areas, 'devastated' predominantly by incendiary attack. The Hamburg raid had the effect of doubling the amount of damage inflicted on German cities so far. Up to the end of June it was estimated that 12.27 per cent of the inner-city areas had been destroyed; by the end of September this figure had increased to 23.31 per cent, 18,738 acres against 9,583.[144] The intelligence staff at Bomber Command headquarters used this material to present a statistical way of measuring success based on the following three criteria:

Tons of bombs claimed dropped per built-up acre attacked = 'Effort'
Acres of devastation per ton of bombs claimed dropped = 'Efficiency'
Acres of devastation per acre of built-up area attacked = 'Success'

On this basis it could be demonstrated that 'success' (acres destroyed per acres attacked) had increased from 0.001 at the end of 1941, 0.032 at the end of 1942, to 0.249 at the end of October 1943. The acres of Germany's central urban area devastated had increased by a factor of 24 in the course of 1943.[145] These figures gave no indication of what effect this was likely to have either on Germany's war effort or on the state of mind of those bombed. The MEW warned the Air Ministry that it was hard to judge German conditions. They estimated that Operation Gomorrah had cost Hamburg the equivalent of 1.25 million man-months, or 12 per cent of the city's annual production. The cumulative effect of all Bomber Command's attacks during the late spring and summer was estimated at a more modest 3 per cent of Germany's potential production effort.[146]

Evidence soon became available to show that the damage was not as crippling as had at first been hoped. The port of Hamburg, which had been less severely damaged than the city, was estimated by the MEW to be operating at 70 per cent of its capacity again by the end of August; intelligence on the Blohm and Voss shipyards, one of the principal targets for the Eighth Air Force, suggested that they had not been destroyed and

were still functioning.[147] By November the city was back to 80 per cent
of its pre-raid output. When Göring was captured at the end of the war
with a train full of possessions, the American army found among them
a presentation folio of more than a hundred charts and graphs on the
remarkable recovery of Hamburg.[148] The one statistic that could only be
guessed at was the number of dead. This was not a measurement used
by Bomber Command, whose calculations of 'effort', 'efficiency' and
'success' became increasingly more abstract as the war went on. The
acreage destroyed was released to the British press as early as the
6 August, though the RAF communiqué emphasized that the damage
'particularly covers the principal manufacturing districts and the docks
and wharves'.[149] Sources in Sweden suggested the figure of 58,000 dead,
which was reprinted in British newspapers later in August. News of the
firestorm only became available from a correspondent of the Swiss
paper *Baseler Nachrichten* in November 1943 when it was circulated
among the anti-bombing lobby in Britain and published in the *New
Statesman*. The claims that 20,000 bodies had been found, incinerated
to a degree not even found in a crematorium, were contested by British
scientists who were shown the material. They dismissed the description
of the firestorm as scientific nonsense, an 'intrinsic absurdity'.[150]

STALEMATE OVER GERMANY

In the aftermath of Operation Gomorrah both Allied bomber forces
expected a growing success rate and both were impatient to achieve it.
There was a growing confidence that the aims laid down at Casablanca
might now be operationally in their grasp. Lovett wrote to Eaker in
early July about the wave of optimism surging through the United States
'that the Air Forces will knock Germany over by Christmas'.[151] A report
on the Combined Offensive produced by Eaker in early August
1943 talked of knocking out the industrial props of Germany one by
one until 'the German military machine comes closer and closer to collapse'.[152] Harris telegraphed Portal at the Combined Chiefs of Staff
conference in Quebec in mid-August that the combined efforts of the
two forces should be enough, once again, to 'knock Germany stiff'.[153]
Portal was keen for Harris to attack Berlin with the same force as Hamburg: 'In present war situation,' he telegraphed from Quebec, 'attacks
on Berlin on anything like Hamburg scale must have enormous effect
on Germany as a whole.' Harris explained that this would need

40,000 tons of bombs and good weather, but the battle of Berlin was to be next on his list.[154]

For both bomber forces there was a race against time. The Eighth Air Force needed to be able to show that it was meeting the Pointblank requirement to undermine the German Air Force in time for the projected invasion of France in May 1944. Whatever the American public expected of the bombing campaign, Eaker's directive was to use air power to prepare the way for the ground armies, and the progress of the combined offensive was regularly measured against this requirement. The Quadrant conference in Quebec in August 1943 reiterated that destruction of German air power was to have 'the highest strategic priority'.[155] By October it was evident that the German fighter force was growing in strength and that the efforts to reduce it had been ineffective. The Eighth Air Force was directed to speed up its assault on its list of essential German targets; out of 128 attacks on Europe, only 50 had so far been against Germany.[156] Throughout the last weeks of 1943 and the first months of 1944, Eaker, and his successor in January, Brig. General James Doolittle, were told insistently by Arnold and Spaatz that Pointblank 'must be pressed to the limit'. In January 1944 the chiefs of staff wanted the offensive to focus only on German fighter strength during the preparatory period for Operation Overlord, as the German Air Force had been asked to do before Sea Lion in 1940.[157]

Harris and Bomber Command ran a different race. He wanted city-bombing to bring the war to a conclusion without an extensive and costly ground invasion, and this meant doing such severe damage to Germany's urban population and environment in the months after Gomorrah that the German war effort would crumble. A joint report on the progress of the combined offensive drawn up in November 1943, but clearly influenced by Harris, played down the impact of American raids and highlighted the significance of area attacks on industrial cities, which had already reduced German war potential, it was claimed, by 10 per cent and 'may well be fatal' if the figure could be doubled in the next few months.[158] Harris drew up a list the same month of the different urban target areas (with Berlin the priority) for 'the continuation and intensification' of the offensive, each city defined as 'largely destroyed', 'seriously damaged', 'damaged' or 'undamaged', and with the added hope that the Eighth Air Force would soon join in the bombing of the German capital.[159] In December Harris used the urban damage figures in a report to Portal and Sinclair in which he claimed that the physical destruction of 40–50 per cent of the urban area of the principal towns of Germany would produce, by April 1944, the month before Overlord, 'a state of devastation in which surrender is inevitable'.[160]

The two ambitions were not easily compatible, and in the event difficult to achieve. Over the course of the late summer and autumn both forces carried out major raids that became large-scale air battles of increasing severity and intensity as German defences were strengthened and the German Air Force was freed at last to pursue more effective operational tactics. On 12 August 133 B-17 'Flying Fortresses' attacked Bochum in the Ruhr-Rhineland and lost 23 of their 133 aircraft (17 per cent of the force). The next major battle came on 17 August, deliberately chosen as the anniversary of the Eighth Air Force's first mission in 1942. The object was to inflict a spectacular blow. The targets selected were the ball-bearing works at Schweinfurt and Messerschmitt Me109 fighter production at Regensburg. For this raid American bombers were divided up; those destined for Regensburg under the command of Curtis LeMay would continue on to North African bases, those for Schweinfurt, commanded by Brig. General Robert Williams, had to fight their way there and back. Both cities were the furthest the Eighth Air Force had yet flown into German airspace and involved the largest number of bombers so far dispatched, a total of 376 B-17s – a reflection of a sudden escalation in the supply of both crews and aircraft. The Messerschmitt works produced 18 per cent of all Messerschmitt Me109 production; the ball-bearing works at Schweinfurt produced 45 per cent of the supplies of German ball-bearings. The aircraft set off in the late morning of 17 August and were attacked by German fighters from the moment Allied fighter cover ended, at Antwerp on the Channel coast. The group destined for Regensburg reached the target near midday and dropped 298 tons, killing 400 people and causing the temporary loss of 20 per cent of fighter output. On the way there 12 B-17s were shot down, 12 more were lost in the aftermath as they flew on across the Alps to Tunisia. Poor repair facilities in North Africa left more bombers grounded, and after a long return flight with further losses, only 55 out of the original 146 returned to English bases.[161]

The First Bomber Division faced an even greater battle. For more than three hours in the afternoon flight the bomber stream was subjected to persistent fighter attack, losing a total of 36 aircraft. Around 3 o'clock, 424 tons of bombs were dropped on the Schweinfurt works, killing 141 people, destroying two works completely and seriously damaging a number of others. The German Armaments Ministry recorded a temporary loss of 34 per cent of ball-bearing production, though large reserve stocks were available to cushion the blow.[162] For the Eighth Air Force the cost for just two targets on their list was exceptional. Together with the 60 aircraft shot down, 176 were damaged and 30 remained in North Africa. Including those lightly damaged, the casualty rate was 71 per cent; counting those destroyed, severely damaged or out of theatre, the loss rate was 31 per cent, levels that could scarcely be sustained for more than a few more raids. The German Air Force lost 28 fighters to the concentrated fire of the B-17s, though in common with almost all air-to-air engagements, American aircrew claimed to have shot down a remarkable 288 enemy aircraft.[163] In September a raid on Stuttgart, undertaken while Arnold was visiting Britain, saw the loss of 65 bombers (19 per cent) out of a force of 338, with little damage to the city itself.

The Eighth Bomber Command nursed its wounds for more than a month before beginning a new series of deep-penetration attacks in October. A raid on the coastal city of Anklam on 9 October cost 18 bombers out of a force of 106, but the most famous battle of the bomber war took place during a second raid on Schweinfurt on 14 October when 65 bombers were lost out of an attacking force of 229, a total loss rate of over 28 per cent of the force. Fighters accompanied the aircraft as far as Aachen, thanks to the addition of extra fuel tanks, which pushed their range to 350 miles, but after that the bomber stream was subjected to hundreds of attacks with rocket and cannon fire from enemy fighters. Eaker wrote to Arnold after the raid: 'This does not represent disaster; it does indicate that the air battle has reached its climax.'[164] But so severe was the risk on any raid past fighter cover that for the next four months operations were only carried out with increasing numbers of bombers on cities within easy range. As a result Kiel, Bremen, Wilhelmshaven and Emden – already the victims of the first year of Bomber Command raids thanks to their proximity – became the recipients of occasional heavy bombing, while the majority of American attacks now took place once again over France. The Eighth Air Force, like the German Air Force and Bomber Command years before, began to think about the possibility of night attacks, and in September 90 B-17s were converted for practice and training in night-flying.[165] In three months of raiding the Eighth Bomber Command lost 358 B-17s in combat, achieving the highest loss rate of the war in October. The campaign did not come to a complete halt, but the next raid deep into Germany was made only on 20 February 1944 in very different circumstances.[166]

Bomber Command also began to experience higher losses and, despite the advent of the target-finding apparatus Oboe and H2S, continued to hit urban targets with intermittent success. The rate of expansion in the first half of the year was not sustained: operationally ready aircraft within the Command increased by more than two-thirds between February and June, but only by another quarter between July and December. Pilot strength was 2,415 in June, 2,403 in December.[167] On 17–18 August Harris was ordered to mount a more precise attack on the German Air Force research station on the Baltic coast at Peenemünde. The raid by 560 aircraft dropped 1,800 tons of mainly high explosive on the research stations and accommodation (also killing 500 Polish forced labourers in a nearby labour camp). Extensive damage was done to the rocket-research programme in one of the few 'precision' raids attempted by the Command in 1943, but 40 aircraft were shot down, a loss rate of 6.7 per cent. Harris then shifted his focus to Berlin. The first raid on 23–24 August missed the centre of the capital and hit the southern suburbs, killing 854 people, and destroying or damaging 2,600 buildings. The loss rate of 7.9 per cent was the highest on any raid since the start of the offensive. A second raid on 31 August–1 September cost 7.6 per cent of the attacking force while H2S marking was erratic, causing the bomber stream to drop bombs up to 30 miles from the aiming point. Only 85 houses were destroyed in Berlin and 68 people killed. So heavy were the losses to Stirling and Halifax squadrons that the third attack, on 3–4 September, was made only with Lancasters, but not only did the H2S marking once again miss the main aiming point, 7 per cent of the Lancaster force was lost. The first 'Battle of Berlin' petered out until November in favour of less dangerous targets.[168] On the night of 22–23 October a second firestorm was created in the small city of Kassel, where H2S marking was for once accurate. The raid report noted that the whole city area 'was virtually devastated'.[169] The death of an estimated 6,000 people was a higher percentage of the city population than in Hamburg. Some 59 per cent of Kassel was burnt out and 6,636 residential buildings destroyed. Armaments production was hit heavily by the destruction of the workers' quarters, but like Hamburg revived after two or three months to around 90 per cent of the pre-raid level.[170] The raid put Kassel for the moment at the top of Bomber Command's list of the proportion of city buildings destroyed or damaged, ahead of Hamburg, 58 per cent to 51 per cent.[171] But Bomber Command lost 43 aircraft, 7.6 per cent of the force, a steady attrition of its strength.

Over the course of 1943 the Command lost 4,026 aircraft, 2,823 in combat.[172]

The high losses of the autumn months created a growing sense of urgency and uncertainty in both bomber forces, despite the brave face turned to the outside world. The claims that had been made from Casablanca onwards served the cause of service politics as well as Allied strategy; the stalemate developing in late 1943 as the balance shifted away from offensive towards defensive air power exposed the bomber force to the risk of relative failure. Although both forces advertised their success in diverting ever-increasing numbers of German fighters to the defence of the Reich, this was in some sense a Pyrrhic victory, since the bomber forces were now subject to escalating and possibly insupportable levels of loss and damage. Lovett reminded Eaker in September that if Germany did not collapse over the winter, the public would think 'our "full-out" offensive doesn't work'.[173] A paper prepared for Portal in October argued that a failure to demonstrate what strategic bombing could do would have 'dangerous repercussions upon post-war policy'.[174] Both forces wanted the other to help more in pursuit of what was seldom a common ambition. In October Portal told Eaker and Harris that the Pointblank aim to eliminate the German Air Force as a preliminary to a more sustained offensive had so far failed. 'Unless the present build-up of the G.A.F. fighter force is checked,' he continued, 'there is a real danger that the average overall efficiency and effectiveness of our bombing attacks will fall to a level at which the enemy can sustain them.' The operational evidence showed that Bomber Command had so far devoted only 2 per cent of its effort to fighter aircraft assembly plants (as by-products of area attacks) and Harris was now instructed to launch operations against six principal cities associated with fighter production.[175]

Harris treated the request as he had treated other 'panacea' targets. In July he had been briefed to attack Schweinfurt as the most vulnerable link in the chain of German war production. Alongside claims for its importance he scribbled 'sez you!' in the margin, and no night raid was made. In December he was told again that his Command should bomb Schweinfurt at night. He rejected the idea on the grounds that his force even now could not hit a small city with any certainty, and would not waste time on a single target when there were bigger cities to destroy and 'only four months left!'[176] To the Air Ministry's complaints that Bomber Command should have done more to support the Eighth Air Force campaign against German air power, Harris retorted that he would not do their job for them. The two forces could not be regarded as complementary, Harris continued, since his Command had dropped 134,000 tons in 1943 and the Eighth Air Force only 16,000, much of it on less important targets.[177] When RE8 researchers suggested that Bomber Command attacks had by their estimate actually done little more than reduce German economic potential by 9 per cent in 1943 (even this figure turned out after the war to have been over-optimistic), Harris responded angrily that in the cities his force had devastated the proportion must self-evidently be higher. Even this devastation, as the Air Ministry reminded him, had affected only 11 per cent of the whole German population, but Harris was a figure difficult to gainsay even over an issue of real strategic significance.[178] He stuck to area bombing in preference to selected targets and as a result made Pointblank harder to achieve, while paradoxically contributing to the stalemate he was trying to break.

While the two forces argued over priorities, the greatest battles of the bomber war were being played out in the skies over Germany. In all cases the majority of bombers succeeded in carrying out their bombing mission; there was never a point when the bomber did not get through. Although the bombloads were often spread over areas widely distant from the actual target, wherever they landed they did serious damage to the home population, in town or countryside, on which they fell. These aerial battles were nevertheless distinct from the bombing itself. They were fought between the enemy defensive forces – guns, night- and day-fighter aircraft, searchlights, decoys and barrage balloons – and the intruding enemy. At this stage of the war the problems facing both sides, though supported by increasingly sophisticated scientific and technical equipment and weaponry, remained the same as they had been since the onset of the bombing war in 1940: weather conditions, bombing accuracy, the balance between defensive and offensive tactics, operational organization and force morale. These factors profoundly affected what the two bomber commands were capable of achieving.

In an age where radar aids to navigation and electronic guidance systems were in their infancy, weather continued to play an arbitrary and intrusive role in the conduct of air warfare. The final United States Bombing Survey report on weather effects regarded them as 'a major controlling factor' in the operation of Allied bomber forces. For the Eighth Air Force, which relied more on visual bombing, weather prevented any operations for a quarter of the time, while 10 per cent of all aircraft that did take off aborted because of weather conditions. It was calculated from unit records that the operational rate of the Eighth Air Force was only 55 per cent of the potential effort because of the effects of northern Europe's rainy climate. Low cloud and fog were the main culprits.[179] Calculations by the Army Air Forces' Director of Weather in late 1942 found that the average number of days per month when the sky over the target was absolutely clear was one or two in the winter months, rising to a peak of seven in June, a total of 31 days in the year. Days when the major limiting factors of high wind, ice or more than 3/10ths cloud cover were absent were more numerous, but still numbered only 113 out of the year, again with a low of 6 in the winter months and a peak of 12 in June.[180] The air force weather service developed a sophisticated pattern of weather prediction, based on the experience of the burgeoning civilian airline business in the 1930s, providing regular climate data, forecasts of current weather trends, and a precise operational forecast for particular missions.[181] Even with reasonably accurate forecasting, weather conditions could alter rapidly and unexpectedly. The combat diary of the 305th Bombardment Group in 1942-3 can be taken as an example: 23 November, Lorient 'covered by cloud'; 12 December, Lille 'cloud cover at the target'; 23 January, Brest 'obscured by the cloud cover'; 4 February, Emden 'no bombs were dropped due to the clouds'; and so on.[182]

Bomber Command was less affected by the weather because area bombing could be carried out in weather conditions that were less than ideal, but British experience also showed that 'average good visibility' was only available between five and nine nights in the summer months and three to five during the winter.[183] To the end of the war, Harris continued to cite the weather as a principal explanation for why Bomber Command could not switch to attacks on precise target systems.[184] With the arrival of electronic aids to navigation, bombing could be carried out through cloud and smoke, though the return to a base suddenly shrouded in fog caused regular accidents. Weather did make severe demands on pilots as they struggled at night to cope with the elements, as the following recollection of the last night of Operation Gomorrah illustrates:

> we set course north to the targets and flew into thunderstorms resulting in heavy icing. We could hear the ice breaking off the sides of the aeroplane and the propellers, and then we were losing power virtually on four engines with heavy icing and I then lost control of the aeroplane . . . It started to descend with the weight of ice and at that stage we were hit by anti-aircraft

fire ... The aeroplane by this stage was completely out of control with
icing ... a very frightening experience.

On this occasion pilot and crew survived.[185]

Of all the problems posed by the generally poor weather conditions
over Germany, maintaining adequate levels of bombing accuracy was
the most significant. For the Eighth Air Force clear weather was essential if precise targeting was to survive. In ideal conditions the early raids
on France showed an average error range of 1,000 yards, but conditions
were seldom ideal. An investigation carried out in February 1943 highlighted problems of poor accuracy and, alongside weather and enemy
defences, blamed poor onboard teamwork and inexperienced pilots. It
was found that the method of bombing in squadron (or Group) formation reduced accuracy substantially for the last formations to bomb; up
to July 1943 an average of only 13.6 per cent of bombs fell within
1,000 feet of the aiming point, but for the last formation to bomb the
figure fell to only 5 per cent.[186] Anderson pressed his commanders to
focus all their efforts on putting more bombs 'on the critical points of
the targets'. 'It is evident,' he continued, 'that our bombing is still not up
to the standards that it can be.'[187] Cloud, industrial haze and smoke-
screens made this inevitable. The American offensive began without a
Pathfinder force and no electronic aids to navigation. In March 1943 Eaker
had asked Portal to supply both the Oboe and H2S equipment for use
by the American formation leaders. Portal offered equipment for only
eight aircraft and training facilities for the crews. By the early autumn
there were three Pathfinder units forming, one with H2S, two with the
American version of the technology, known as H2X.[188] Eaker found the
temptation irresistible to use the new guidance system to allow bombing when the target was obscured. In September 1943 the Eighth Air
Force undertook its first deliberate blind-bombing attack on the German port of Emden. The bombing was scattered around Emden and the
surrounding region, but the fact that it was now possible to arrive over
the area of the target in poor weather introduced the American air
forces to area bombing.

Escalation in this case *was* dictated by the technical impossibility of
bombing accurately for more than a few days a month. From September
1943 onwards American bombers were directed to attack city areas
through cloud in the hope that this would hit the precise targets obscured
by the elements. Sensitive to opinion, the raids on city areas were
defined, like Bomber Command, as attacks on industrial centres or,

increasingly, as 'marshalling yards'.[189] The distinction for most, though not all, American raiding from British area bombing was intention. The civilian and the civilian milieu were never defined as targets in their own right, even if the eventual outcome might make the distinction seem merely academic. Around three-quarters of the effort against German targets between 1943 and 1945 was carried out by 'blind bombing' using H2X equipment; from October to December 1943 only 20 per cent of bombs dropped using radar aids came within five miles of the aiming point, an outcome little different from Bomber Command in 1941-2.[190] High levels of accuracy were reserved for primary industrial targets in good weather, where accuracy levels increased from 36 per cent within 2,000 feet in July 1943 to 62 per cent in December. American practice became one of selective precision when visibility was good, and less discriminate attacks when visual conditions were poor.[191] The result, as with Bomber Command, was to increase the number of German civilians killed and houses destroyed by American bombers, which now carried much higher incendiary loads for blind-bombing raids. Even precision bombing resulted in widespread damage to the surrounding civilian area. The USAAF in-house history of radar bombing was more candid than the public image: 'Neither visual nor radar bombing ever achieved pin-point bombing; both methods were, in effect, methods of area bombing in the sense that a certain percentage of bombs fell within an area of a certain size, the rest falling without.'[192]

The problem for Bomber Command was different. Here unacceptably inaccurate bombing had to be improved to achieve higher concentrations on the chosen urban areas. The introduction of Oboe and H2S contributed to raising the average accuracy of the attacking force, but concentration could be lost if the weather deteriorated or the Pathfinder force missed the aiming point, or German decoys were successful in diverting a proportion of the attacking force. In raids using Oboe in 1943, the number of aircraft which bombed within three miles of the target ranged from 77 per cent against Cologne in July to 32 per cent against Bochum in September, but poor weather prevented evaluation of at least half the raids. Oboe proved to be the more successful of the two methods but could only reach as far as the Ruhr-Rhineland. For H2S operations the scale of accuracy was even longer: 86 per cent against Kassel in October to 2.1 per cent against Berlin on the 31 August. The average for the 23 H2S raids that could be plotted was 32 per cent, a substantial improvement on the Butt Report evidence, but still a low level of concentration.[193] Research on the first large-scale blind-bombing raid using H2S in poor weather, against Mannheim-Ludwigshafen on 17–18 November, estimated that perhaps 60 per cent of the attacking aircraft had hit the conurbation itself. These figures indicated that the force had at last adopted a technology and tactics that might reduce the amount of wasted effort. This was partly due to the additional training for Pathfinder navigators organized by the Bombing Development Unit, set up in late 1942, consisting of flights over British cities. These simulated raids showed wide deviation from the putative aiming point, but an average of 50 per cent of 'hits' within a three-mile radius (four miles for London). The trials showed that H2S worked well over certain urban targets, but poorly over sprawling urban areas or cities surrounded by hills, as had already been found over Germany. The Operational Research Section of Bomber Command calculated that this was probably the best to be hoped for when bombing cities. Improved though Bomber Command accuracy was from the poor state of 1941, every second bomb was still miles from the aiming point.[194]

The problems of weather and bombing accuracy highlight a factor about the bombing war that is seldom given the weight it deserves in assessing what was and was not possible for the forces at the Allies' disposal. The operations mounted week after week during the last two years of war were of unprecedented scale and complexity, employing some of the war's most sophisticated equipment. For both air forces the pre-raid preparation required all the conventional demands of battle – tactical, logistical and technical; the intelligence and operational research reports had to be factored into each calculation and the weather closely monitored. Organizing a raid with hundreds of aircraft coordinated over long distances promised all kinds of hazard; pilots had to create formation while avoiding accidents and synchronize their flight with the escorting fighters as far as their range would allow. Along the target run and over the target itself there were precise instructions about combat, evasion, target recognition, heights and speeds. On return there was the process of debriefing crews, coping with casualties and estimating the outcome of the raid. Each battle was self-contained, but for commanders and their crews the campaign was continuous, more so than for almost any other form of combat over the four or five years of war.

The typical instructions for a Bomber Command raid illustrate the close attention to planning detail and the range of demands made of the crews. Aircraft from four or five bomber Groups were given instructions about force size, composition of the bombload, routes to the destination target (or for the decoy attacks), and the timing of each of five waves of attacking aircraft, which had to drop their bombs within a 20-minute period to maximize impact. There were instructions on 'Window', on the Mandrel jammer, radar and wireless use, and the chosen target-marking pattern, which could either be ground-marking with illuminating flares followed by red and/or green target indicators or sky-marking with red and green star flares. The Master Bomber and the supporting Pathfinders had to drop their markers and repeat markers over an 11-minute period, while the main force had to watch for the markers, bomb the centre of them if they could and then turn for home. The whole combat force typically extended for 20 miles, was six miles wide and flew in staggered formation, the highest aircraft some 4,000 feet above the lowest. Crews had to fly low over England, then climb to 14,000-15,000 feet, then increase speed and fly at 18,000-20,000 feet for bombing, finally falling away from the target zone to 12,000 feet, back to 18,000 feet for the return flight across Germany, 12,000 feet again at the European coast, and not below 7,000 feet on crossing back over English territory. Then came the de-briefing interviews, and the PR assessments.[195]

The Eighth Air Force derived a lot from British experience, but typical raid preparations and combat showed an even greater awareness of the complexity of the task. The principles guiding target selection dwarfed the simple list of cities and their industrial importance given to Harris. Target selection involved assessing the strategic importance of a target, working out the degree of 'cushion' in the economy for substituting or dispersing output, calculating the depth of a target system (how far away a product might be from front-line use), judging the recuperative possibilities of a target, and weighing up its vulnerability and the capacity of the air forces to destroy it by researching its potential structural weaknesses and susceptibility to damage.[196] The material was collected and evaluated by the Enemy Objectives Unit based in the American Embassy in London under the leadership of Colonel Richard D'Oyly Hughes, a former British officer who had taken American citizenship in the early 1930s. His team of economists visited British industrial plants to work out the most vulnerable part of each type of target and then applied the knowledge to detailed photographic material on the German equivalent. In the evenings they relaxed from their efforts by working out fruitless statistical teasers – 'How many sheep are there in Bavaria?', 'What is the most economical land route from Gdansk to Gibraltar?'[197] Their labours proved most effective with assessments of damage to capital-intensive targets such as oil refineries or synthetic oil and rubber producers. This material was taken and put into operationally useful form for air force units.

The typical Eighth Air Force operational procedure reflected a managerial ethos that was quite distinct from British practice. American officers had in many cases been drafted in to the air force from business and professional backgrounds, which prepared them for the vocabulary and categories typical of modern managerial practice. The formal procedure laid down in July 1943 reflected that culture: a conference of key personnel at 4.00 on the afternoon before the operation at which the prospective weather determined the target to be attacked; target folders checked, fighter escort informed; calculation of type and weight of bombs and number of aircraft; notification of assigned combat groups; finally, determination of axis of attack, rendezvous point, route out, initial point (near the target run-in), altitudes, aiming point, rally point (just outside target area), and route back. The resulting field order was then sent by teletype to the combat units involved.[198] A second procedure then took place at the airbases of the different bombardment wings with an operational briefing for all commanders and crew for approximately two and a half hours covering the following: plan for formation (general), approximate time for turns, sun position, power settings, intelligence information and weather prospects. Detailed planning was essential because in daytime bombing the force had to fly in tight formation. The Eighth Air Force flew at 25,000 feet, each wing flying in three staggered combat boxes, covering a height of 3,000 feet to maximize the firepower of the group, before breaking into bombing formation in approach to the target. Separate briefings were then held for pilots and co-pilots (16 items), navigators and bombardiers (six items), gunners and radio operators (three items). Watches were then synchronized. At 8 a.m. on the morning of the operation a decision to go ahead or postpone had to be taken based on the current state of the weather. Commanders had an obligation, according to a manual on tactics, 'to work out each mission in *minute* detail. The struggle here is of the life and death variety.'[199]

Somehow or other all the detailed calculations, operating plans and contingencies had to be mastered and put into effect by the expensively trained crews. There was always to be a gap between the ideal operation laid down by the military bureaucracy that ran the offensives and the reality of combat. Unanticipated factors of all kinds, not least the extent and combativeness of the enemy forces, undermined the best-laid operational procedures. Given the technical sophistication of much of the equipment, the large number of freshmen crews to be initiated on each operation, the vagaries of weather and navigation, it is perhaps surprising that bombing operations achieved as much as they did. Almost all the flight crew were between the ages of 18 and 25, a large number of them between 18 and 21; a few who lied about their age flew heavy bombers aged just 17. Almost nothing of what they experienced in training could prepare them for what happened by day or by night over Germany. For Bomber Command crew there was extreme cold for much of the time unless they wore layer upon layer of protective clothing; there was a numbing tiredness on operations that could last eight or nine hours, using up the body's natural adrenalin supplies and requiring chemical stimulants (commonly amphetamines); with the decision taken in spring 1942 to have just one pilot, the crew had to hope that one of their number had enough basic flying skills to get them to their target and back if the pilot was killed or incapacitated. There was the constant fear of night-fighters and anti-aircraft fire or of being coned by searchlights, to which large night-time formations added the danger of collision or bombs from the invisible aircraft above in the bomber stream.

The Eighth Air Force crew had some advantages: the B-17 'Flying Fortress' was less cold to fly in and they were provided with good thermal clothing; each aircraft had a pilot and co-pilot; attacking aircraft were more easily visible, though the limited range of the B-17 machine guns meant that rocket- and cannon-firing fighters could damage the bombers before facing risk themselves. Other factors were shared. The experience was frightening and the accounts of a great many airmen understandably recall fear as a very primary emotion. 'I was scared all the time,' recalled one veteran, 'but I was more scared of letting the rest of the crew see.' Aircrew were commonly sick as a result of the long, bumpy flights. Their priority was to complete the mission and return to base. 'You bombed a target and got the hell out and got home, there wasn't much glamour about it,' remembered another. Their primary loyalty was to the other crews about them. 'I never worried about the people down below,' said one pilot. 'I was more concerned with the ones in the air.' This was perhaps an understandable moral concern. The permanent dangers to which an aircrew were exposed and the sheer mental and physical demands of combat, surrounded at times by dead or dying companions, with jammed guns, or engines knocked out, created a temporary nightmare world in which the one hope was that their aircraft and crew would not be next. After the Regensburg raid one American commander who reached Tunisia reported that he and his crew 'felt the reaction of men who had not expected to see another sunset'. He recommended reducing the standard tour of 30 operations to 25 if crew were not to collapse from the psychological pressure. 'Survival was our thing,' concluded one veteran.[200]

The success of bombing operations depended almost entirely on the quality and training of the crews, but the pressures to which they were subject placed often insupportable demands on their psychological equilibrium. This situation arose not only because of the natural stresses of combat, but because of the curious social situation in which bomber crew found themselves. Although regularly recruited for operations which provided hours of tension and endeavour, once back at base it might be days, sometimes longer, before the next operation. In that interval crews were free to go to the local town, meet girls, reunite with wives or partners, enjoy a variety of forms of recreation. Cinema attendance at Eighth Air Force bases reached a million a month by November 1943, stage-show attendance 150,000.[201] This meant that bomber crew had a cycle of relief and anxiety distinct from the emotional pattern of ground combat troops. In the first years of the offensive survival rates were low, so that life at base was also about reconciling the loss of companions, relishing survival and anticipating the next operation. Casualties were high not only from combat but because of routine fly-ing accidents. In Bomber Command some 6,000 crew were killed in accidents in 1943–4; the Eighth Air Force suffered in 1943 as many as 8,800 losses in combat and a further 2,000 from non-combat acci-dents.[202] Death or German imprisonment was more common than serious injury, which numbered only 1,315 in the Eighth Air Force up to the end of 1943, mostly to the hands, neck and head. The American statistical record described those who had finished their tour of 30 oper-ations and returned to the United States as 'Happy Warriors'; they were certainly lucky warriors, constituting less than one-fifth of the crews sent to Europe.

The one form of often hidden casualty which bombing encouraged was psychiatric. The stress of combat, or combat fatigue, was not in doubt. Questionnaires from the USAAF Psychological Branch to squadron commanders found that they valued 'judgment' and 'emo-tional control' far higher than practical skills among cohorts of incoming pilots.[203] The psychological reaction to flying stress depended partly on the personality of the individual crew member, partly on the nature of the experiences or dangers to which he had been exposed. Most crew on a tour of 25 or 30 operations died before they reached their total. Of those who survived, a small proportion became medical casualties as a result of stress, but almost all suffered from some degree of fear-induced anxiety, which was observed to get worse the longer the operational tour lasted. American psychiatrists reported heavy drinking, psycho-somatic disorders and long periods of depression among crew who carried on flying.[204] In Bomber Command the tendency was to blame any exaggerated state of anxiety on 'lack of moral fibre' (LMF), a stigma designed as an emasculating deterrent to any sign of weakness. Harris thought that among his crews only a quarter were effective bombers, the rest merely there to give German anti-aircraft guns something to shoot at.[205] Air force medical staff, on the other hand, found that there were very few records of cowardice, despite the popular fear among air-crew that they might be regarded that way if they broke down. In both the RAF and the Eighth Air Force it came to be recognized that regular air operations induced particular forms of neurosis which had little to do with a lack of spirit and everything to do with the harsh experiences of daily flying. Eighth Air Force was instructed to rest and rotate tired crews but to isolate those whose behaviour might contaminate the effi-ciency of their unit. These cases were divided between the categories of 'flying fatigue' and 'lack of moral fibre'. To the former there was no stigma attached, but the latter were to be removed from flying status, stripped of their commission and sent home in disgrace.[206] Those who developed serious psychoneurotic symptoms were sent to special hospi-tals to undergo narcosis therapy, and many were subsequently returned to duty including combat flying. By early 1944 it was found that around 3 per cent of flying officers (of those who survived) were removed from flying status before completing a tour of 25 operations.[207]

In Bomber Command the treatment of flying fatigue could be much harsher if unit commanders were prejudiced against the idea of psychi-atric casualty.[208] But like the Eighth Air Force, a system of classification came into use which allowed the neuropsychiatrists in the RAF medical service to distinguish between those with neurotic conditions capable of diagnosis and possible treatment and those classified as 'waverers', defined as fully fit but fearful. Flying stress was accepted as an under-standable reaction to 'severe combats, crash landings, "bale-outs" and "shaky-dos" in general'. Those who ended up in front of the psych-iatrist were classified in four categories based on a predisposition to neurotic behaviour (usually defined by character assessments or family history) and degree of flying stress. Those with a high predisposition or a high level of stress were deemed to be medical casualties and withdrawn from flying without penalty. Those with low predisposition but marked flying stress or those with neither predisposition nor serious evidence of stress were defined as lacking in confidence, and a judgement had to be made about whether they were also guilty of 'lack of moral fibre'. It was never easy, as one RAF psychiatrist put it, to tell 'whether a man's inability to continue flying is his fault or his misfortune, whether in fact it is due to simple lack of confidence or of courage, or whether it results from nervous predisposition or illness outside his control'.[209]

These were fateful decisions for the men involved, since those deemed not to be medical cases (approximately 25 per cent of those referred for assessment) were dealt with by an executive board which tended to assume cowardice on the part of the men in front of them. Yet the medical casebooks show that individuals were often subjected to a series of traumatic combat experiences sufficient to challenge the mental stability of even the toughest character:

> Flight engineer, 20 raids, 150 operational flying hours: 'He had been badly shot up on four occasions. On the last of these, after being attacked by a night-fighter, the port engine of his machine caught fire, the mid-upper gunner was badly injured and the rear gunner was killed ... The rear-gunner's body was burning and motionless ... He had to use an axe to hack off bits of the blazing turret and also parts of the rear-gunner's clothing and body, finally letting the slip-stream blow them all away ... The wireless, the hydraulics and the tyres had all gone and a crash-landing was made ... 10 days later he was in a nervous state with tremulous hands and sweaty palms. He had some headaches, felt unable to relax, was depressed, preoccupied and unable to concentrate. His appetite was bad ... When I asked him how he would sum up his feelings in one word, he said "fear".'[210]

On this occasion the decision was made to allow the officer a spell of non-combat duty, rather than assume cowardice. But there were other cases where fear was imputed by the psychiatrists, often unjustifiably, with the result that an airman could be stripped of his commission and the right to fly. In the RAF 8,402 aircrew were examined for neurosis from 1942 to 1945, of whom 1,029 were declared LMF, 34 per cent of them pilots. The best post-war estimate has suggested that Bomber Command crews provided one-third of those figures, which works out at perhaps 20 per month, a remarkably small proportion of all those regularly exposed to the stress of combat flying.[211] Most medical reports on the air forces indicated high morale despite the high casualty rate. Eaker claimed that morale was not affected so much by losses as by the knowledge that a raid had been ineffective.[212] Psychiatrists nevertheless found that one of the most important motivations was the desire to make it through to the end of the tour still alive. Since only 1 in 4 survived one tour, and 1 in 10 a second one, survival remained a primary drive despite the stresses. Research in the Eighth Air Force found that a large proportion of men returning to the United States after a completed tour of duty displayed 'subjective anxiety' symptoms: 'weight loss, insomnia, severe operational fatigue, and loss of efficiency'.[213]

These were the men sent by night and by day against German targets in the context of steadily increasing losses on the major raids. During 1943 Bomber Command lost 15,678 killed or prisoners of war, while the Eighth Air Force lost 9,497, almost all of them in missions against German targets.[214] The escalating costs of the offensive presented the bomber commanders once again with questions about the strategic value of what they were doing. The reality of tactical stalemate coincided by chance with a revival of the hope, largely abandoned since 1941, that bombing might induce a social or political crisis so severe that it would critically undermine the German war effort. Though Harris saw area bombing chiefly as a form of economic attrition, he never entirely excluded the possibility that his bombing might provoke a political bonus, even to the point of German surrender, and he was happy to fuel such speculation if it strengthened his hand. Air Intelligence, for example, were impressed by his claim that the destruction of half the German urban area would provoke collapse, even if the Gestapo and the SS were determined to 'prevent insurrection'.[215] For some months political intelligence in Britain, encouraged by German difficulties on the Soviet front and in the Mediterranean, had been suggesting that there might be a positive answer to the question 'Will Germany crack?', and that bombing could supply it. In September 1943 the Joint Intelligence Committee prepared a long paper on the 'Probabilities of a German Collapse' in which Germany's situation in autumn 1943 was compared with the historical reality of the collapse of the German home front in the autumn of 1918. The JIC thought the conditions of life in the bombed cities much worse than in 1918 and the signs of revolutionary discontent increasingly evident despite the brutal nature of the dictatorship.[216] In November 1943 an even more optimistic evaluation was produced by the British Political Warfare Executive on the creation in bombed cities of a 'new proletariat' with a communist mentality, which might yet create a revolutionary crisis in Germany before the winter was over. In January further intelligence was sent to Churchill on social unrest in Germany which suggested that 'the more we bomb, the more satisfactory the effect'. Churchill underlined the sentence with his trademark red pencil.[217]

For Churchill the promise of a German collapse revived the confident assumptions about the political impact of bombing which he had harboured ever since the offensive began in 1940. The evidence in the autumn and winter of 1943 was nevertheless slender, based to some extent on imagining what bombing on such a scale might have meant if it had been British rather than German cities under the hail of bombs. American political intelligence was in general dismissive of the idea that bombing alone could generate a German collapse. Spaatz rejected entirely the value of popular war-willingness as a target: 'Morale in a totalitarian society is irrelevant so long as the control patterns function effectively.'[218] American assessments of the revolutionary potential of the German working class focused on the 'negative character of its assumption of power' in 1918, following the Kaiser's abdication, and the failure of the German left to stop Hitler. Arnold asked a 'Committee of Historians' for their analysis of the prospects for German collapse. The nine historians included distinguished names – Bernadotte Schmitt, Edward Earle, Louis Gottschalk –with experience of writing the history of war and revolution. They concluded that although German morale had deteriorated during 1943, the existence of Nazi control 'gives no encouragement to the supposition that any political upheaval can be anticipated in Germany in the near future'. They acknowledged that there was a superficial resemblance to the final days of 1918, but their report concluded that insistence on unconditional surrender, the lack of any effective avenue for popular discontent and the contrast in the military situation 'make the seeming analogy invalid'.[219] The key problem identified by all the critics of the idea that Germany would imminently crack was the exceptional capacity of a totalitarian state to exact obedience. If the German people were 'discouraged, disillusioned and bewildered', as intelligence reports suggested, they still appeared to have a fear of state terror more powerful than the fear of further bombing.[220] 'Even when public morale is desperately low,' remarked Portal's deputy, Norman Bottomley, in a speech in the spring of 1944, 'general collapse can for a long while be staved off by a ruthless and desperate party system and a corps of brutal Gestapo hangmen and gangsters.'[221]

These projections were, as it turned out, broadly correct. The bombing made the German population more rather than less dependent on the state and the party. Like the Blitz, Allied bombing created largely passive responses to the problem of survival. In its monthly news digest in March 1944, American air intelligence published a translated article on the air offensive from the German *Berliner Börsen-Zeitung*, which seemed to sum up the frustrating reality of an attrition war in the air:

> A war with its focal point centred in the air is not the shortest, as was once believed, but on the contrary the longest and most meaningless in its accumulation of destruction ... particularly as even the greatest terror gradually wears off or corresponding counter-measures are found. Thus the time when it was thought that air offensives alone could force Europe to capitulate and that the Anglo-Americans could then march in with music had disappeared into the dim distance.[222]

The Committee of Historians concluded from their assessment of Allied strategy and German staying-power that the defeat of Germany was only possible with continued Soviet pressure from the east, continuous bombing from Britain and Italy, and one or more large-scale invasions of German-occupied Western Europe. 'It seems clear,' continued the report, 'that bombing alone cannot bring about that defeat in the spring of 1944.'[223] The stalemate in the bombing war could only be reversed by military means. 'Our first objective,' wrote General Doolittle to his commanders on assuming control of the Eighth Air Force in January 1944, 'is to neutralize the German fighter opposition at the earliest possible moment.'[224]

THE 'BATTLE OF GERMANY': 1944

In June 1943 Robert Lovett, Assistant Secretary for War responsible for the air force, wrote a long memorandum for Arnold in which he analysed the problems facing the American air offensive and suggested solutions. The most important issue he identified and emphasized was 'supply *long range fighter* protection to help the B-17s'. He suggested designing built-in additional fuel tanks for American fighter aircraft but in the interim adding two wing tanks to the new P-51 'Mustang' fighter. He concluded, 'This is a "must".'[225] The P-51 did not see long-range service over Germany until the spring of 1944, by which time other fighter aircraft converted to longer range were already in service to protect the American bombers part of the way to their targets. The need for long-range fighters matched the needs the German Air Force had faced in the Battle of Britain. Success in defeating the German Air Force in their own airspace – the 'Battle of Germany' – depended on establishing air supremacy and this in turn relied on the extent to which the Eighth Air Force could use large fighter forces to destroy enemy air power. Fighter-to-fighter combat and counter-force bombing was the solution not only to the expansion of the bomber offensive but also to the eventual success of Allied invasion in the west. What the Eighth (supported by the Fifteenth Air Force flying from Italy) was now engaged in was less a strategic air offensive, more the conduct of a 'grand tactical' air battle.

There has been since the war much discussion of why it took so long for the United States air forces to develop fighter aircraft with long-range capability. Spaatz had been a witness to the German raids on England in 1940 when the need for fighter cover to protect German daylight bombing had been self-evident. The planners in 1941 who drew up AWPD-1 emphasized that the development of escort fighters that could fly as far as the bombers was 'mandatory'.[226] Arnold as early as February 1942 had asked for all new fighters to be developed with auxiliary tanks. In June 1943 he ordered a crash programme to ensure that full bomber escort could be provided by early 1944.[227] There was no shortage of high-quality fighter aircraft designed with longer range than the British Spitfire (which had supplied limited fighter escort in 1943). The P-38 Lockheed 'Lightning', a radical twin-engine, twin-boom fighter was a pre-war development which had long-range extra fuel tanks built into the design. Its development was delayed and it entered service in summer 1942, used in North Africa as a low-altitude battlefield aircraft, in a role that suited it poorly. Late in 1943 two Groups were allocated to Eighth Air Force and at once extended potential escort range as far as Leipzig, though in numbers too small to transform the offensive, and with persistent technical problems with the engine. The mainstay of the Eighth Fighter Command in 1943 was the Republic P-47 Thunderbolt, a high-performance fighter/fighter-bomber designed in 1940 around the Pratt and Whitney R-2800 radial engine. It could carry two external fuel tanks to boost range as far as the German frontier when drop tanks were first installed in July 1943, but little effort went into modifying the P-47 so that it could reach far into Germany. Eaker gave auxiliary tanks a low priority among his many other problems. Yet with larger tanks the P-47 could by the spring of 1944 fly as far as Hamburg, where before it had been confined to an arc that reached little further than the Low Countries.[228]

The one aircraft that did promise to transform the air war over Germany was the North American P-51 'Mustang' recommended by Lovett. Originally designed to meet a British requirement in 1940, it began service with the RAF (under the name 'Apache') in November 1941. British engineers fitted it with a Rolls-Royce Merlin engine and revolutionized its performance, increasing speed, rate of climb and manoeuvrability. News reached Washington via the American Embassy in London and Arnold immediately saw the aircraft's potential. By November 1942 he had placed initial orders for 2,200, fitted with Merlin engines made under licence in the United States.[229] Since the P-51 was supposed to fulfil British orders, Arnold had once again to renege on the agreement. After a stormy exchange with Portal in the late autumn of 1943, Arnold got his way.[230] The P-51 entered service in early December 1943 with drop tanks that could take it 475 miles into Germany; when it finally came on stream in significant numbers in spring 1944 its range, with new tanks, could take it further than Berlin and even as far as Vienna. Most accounts of the battle for air supremacy credit the P-51 with the destruction of German fighter defences, but rather like accounts of the Battle of Britain, in which the Spitfire has always been privileged over the Hurricane, the sturdy and less glamorous P-47 Thunderbolt bore the brunt of the first months of the Battle of Germany. On the day the P-51 was introduced to combat against targets in France, 5 December 1943, there were 266 P-47s but only 36 P-51s. Three months later, on the first deep daylight raid into Germany against Leipzig, there were 688 P-47s and just 73 P-51s. By the end of March 1944, the point that some historians have seen as the moment when air superiority passed to the Eighth Air Force, there were still more than twice as many Thunderbolts as Mustangs.[231]

The explanation for the slow evolution of a long-range fighter capability lies not with the technology but with the Eighth Air Force commanders. Eaker had always believed in the self-defending capability of the large daylight bomber formation. The prevailing tactical assumption in operations was 'the security of the force'; the larger the bomber stream, the more secure it would be.[232] The Eighth Fighter Command under Brig. General Frank Hunter shared Eaker's view that unescorted bomber operations were possible, and for much of the summer and autumn, when Eighth Bomber Command losses were rising, he ordered fighter-sweeps across northern France and the Low Countries which on some occasions encountered no German aircraft at all. When it was insisted that the P-47s escort the bombers more effectively, the range was still too short to provide more than limited assistance, and made shorter still by the order to fly a weaving route next to the bomber formation to match its speed. In August 1943, after the first Schweinfurt raid, Arnold insisted on sacking Hunter and replacing him with Maj. General William Kepner, a dedicated fighter general, popular with his crews, who saw the role of his command to fly deep into Germany in order to destroy the German fighter force. Eaker opposed the change of commander and remained lukewarm about the effort to use fighters, rather than his bombers, to achieve the air superiority required from the Pointblank offensive. Destroying enemy fighters he saw as 'the secondary job'; the primary task was dropping bombloads as accurately as possible on strategic air force targets.[233]

Arnold's persistent dissatisfaction with the performance of the Eighth Air Force speeded up the decision to activate the Fifteenth Air Force in the Mediterranean to attack Pointblank targets from the south, where the weather was better. Without notifying Eaker, Arnold asked the Combined Chiefs at their meeting on 18 November to approve the reorganization of American air forces by appointing an American strategic air commander for both European theatres, responsible for the Eighth, Fifteenth and Ninth Air Forces and, if possible, Bomber Command. The Combined Chiefs agreed to the rearrangement on 4 December (with the exception of Bomber Command, which Portal refused to hand over) and Arnold got support from Roosevelt and Churchill.[234] Arnold asked Spaatz to return to Britain to take up the post of Commanding General, Strategic Air Forces, on 1 January 1944. He brought with him Maj. General James Doolittle, commander of the Northwest African Strategic Air Force, and a firm advocate of bomber escorts. Spaatz took over Eaker's headquarters, while Doolittle commanded the Eighth from 'Widewing', up until then headquarters for Anderson's Bomber Command. Anderson became chief of operations to Spaatz. Arnold had been insensitive enough to notify Eaker of the change in command by telegraph back on 19 December, rather than in person, consistent with his testy treatment of Eaker earlier in the summer. Eaker objected vehemently to the change but his objections were overruled; on 6 January Doolittle took over the Eighth and Eaker left to command strategic forces in the Mediterranean at just the point when large numbers of bombers and escort fighters were at last coming through the pipeline to transform the capability of the air force Eaker was compelled to abandon.[235]

In any assessment of the success in establishing air superiority over Germany, the change in American leadership is clearly central. Spaatz, Doolittle and Kepner shared a common strategic outlook on the import- ance of combining the indirect assault on air force production and supplies through bombing with the calculated attrition of the German fighter force through air-to-air combat and fighter sweeps over German soil. Spaatz spent some weeks reviewing the offensive in January 1944 and then told Doolittle that destroying German fighter strength and increasing the tempo of attacks on German aircraft production was 'a critical deciding factor in Germany's defeat'.[236] Doolittle was from the start anxious to use his large force, now with more than 1,000 bomb- ers and 1,200 fighters, to destroy the German air arm. Commenting to Spaatz on the plans for completing the Combined Bomber Offensive, he was critical of the idea of pursuing 'economic' bombing, and argued for making attacks on the enemy fighter force in the air and on the ground the 'primary consideration', as it had been when he was a commander in the Mediterranean.[237]

Kepner had already begun to transform the tactics of fighter support before Doolittle's appointment. The key was to allow the fighter escorts to engage the enemy fighter force and not simply protect the bombers; this had been the dilemma facing German fighters in the Battle of Brit- ain, when they were eventually compelled to fly as close support for the bomber stream, and lost their combat flexibility. From January 1944 onwards American fighter units were ordered to 'pursue the Hun until he was destroyed'.[238] The new tactic of 'Free Lance' allocated some fighter planes to abandon the bombers entirely and seek the German force wherever it was to be found. The escort aircraft, flying in loose groups of four, ranged up to seven or eight miles away from the bomber stream in search of combat. On the return flight they were encouraged to fly at low level to strafe German airfields or attack German fighters taking off or returning to base. To maximize combat time a system of escort relays was set up in which each stage of a bomber's flight would be protected by fighter units assigned to a particular stretch, so that they could fly direct to the rendezvous point rather than lose precious fuel flying slowly with the bombers. P-47s guarded the first and last legs of the route, P-38s the intermediate stretch, and the very long-range P-51s the area close to the target zone. The success of the change in tactics depended first on a much-enlarged supply of fighter aircraft and pilots, with improved levels of maintenance, and on the exploitation of the RAF 'Y' radio-intercept service, which made it possible for American fighters to be directed to the point where German aircraft were themselves assembling in formation.[239] The object was to leave the German enemy no respite from the threat of combat and to impose an insupportable level of attrition.

The German Air Force did not remain passive in the face of the growing American threat. The driving force behind the reorganization of air defence and the expansion of fighter output was Göring's deputy, Erhard Milch, who understood more clearly than his master that 'the homeland is more important than the front'.[240] The allocation of priority to the defence of the Reich and to fighter production brought about not only a regular process of tactical and technical readjustment, but a major change in command and organization as well. In August 1943 the chief of staff, Hans Jeschonnek, who effectively carried the weight of high command in Göring's increasing absence, found the constant criticism and abuse from his commander-in-chief over the bombing offensive impossible to withstand. On 19 August he shot himself, leaving behind two letters for Hitler's air adjutant condemning Göring's incompetent leadership. Jeschonnek was not entirely blameless since he had continually emphasized the importance of air power at the fighting front rather than defence of the home territory.[241] He was replaced by Col. General Günther Korten, whose relationship with Göring was better, but unlike Jeschonnek he was committed to the idea of strengthening home air defences and had Hitler's support for doing so. In November, Kammhuber was removed from his post, one of the remaining obstacles to reorganizing the defensive system. In northern Germany, Fighter Corps I (*Jagdkorps I*), responsible for the fighter defence of most of western and central Germany, was expanded and placed under the command of Lt. General Josef 'Beppo' Schmid, best known for supplying over-optimistic intelligence during the Battle of Britain. From a single fighter wing in January 1943, Schmid's new command had 11 wings and 20 fighter Groups by the end of the year. In December 1943, Hubert Weise, *Luftwaffenbefehlshaber Mitte*, was replaced by Col. General Hans-Jürgen Stumpff, the former commander of Air Fleet 5; on 27 January the command was renamed the Reich Air Fleet (*Luftflotte Reich*), now responsible for the coordinated control of the entire defensive air war against the Allied bombers.[242] The process of creating a single centralized air defence of Germany was completed in February 1944 with the transfer of anti-aircraft artillery and the German air-warning system to direct control by the Reich Air Fleet and the local fighter divisions. The system now more closely resembled the centralized control structure set up by Fighter Command in Britain in 1940. From Stumpff's headquarters in Berlin it was possible, using the radar information from Fighter Korps I, to communicate a running account of the air battle to the fighter units to ensure a concentrated response; for his part, Schmid had no fewer than 148 direct telephone lines to fighter stations and control centres.[243]

The German Air Force knew a remarkable amount about the British and American air forces. Most of the information came from downed Allied aircraft and interrogated prisoners. The bombers' predictable tactics and long flying time over German territory in the last months of 1943 had contributed to the escalating loss rates imposed on each bombing mission.[244] The electronic war, which had swung briefly in the Allies' favour with the use of 'Window' over Hamburg, was more evenly balanced by the end of the year. German researchers quickly discovered ways to neutralize the effects of 'Window' with two devices, *Würzlaus* and *Nürnberg*, which allowed the more skilful radar operators to distinguish between 'Window' echoes and an aeroplane; by the end of the year 1,500 *Würzburg* radar had been modified. The German Telefunken researchers came up with a new air radar device, codenamed SN-2, which could operate impervious to 'Window' interference, and a crash production programme was begun. The new Allied H2S radar navigation could also be tracked by the end of 1943 using a new homing device, *Naxos-Z*, which enabled German night-fighters to track the RAF Pathfinder force; it also proved possible to get a bearing on the Allied bombers that were not carrying H2S by using their Identification Friend-or-Foe mechanism. Both breakthroughs contributed to Bomber Command's escalating losses. The Eighth Air Force began to use 'Window' (codenamed 'Chaff' in the United States) on 20 December 1943 at the same time as introducing a *Würzburg* jammer known as 'Carpet' to reduce losses by radar-guided anti-aircraft fire. Here again German radio engineers later found a partial solution by introducing a modification known as *Wismar*, which allowed the radar to switch frequencies and avoid the effects of 'Carpet', though by this time the tactical battle between the two air forces had rendered electronic protection less important.[245]

The keys to German air defence were assumed to be production and manpower. To meet the threat of daylight bombing the anti-aircraft artillery was substantially increased in early 1944, with 1,508 heavy batteries (5,325 guns), 623 light batteries (9,359 guns) and 375 search-light batteries (5,000 lights of 200 or 150 cm diameter). Output of anti-aircraft guns reached a peak in 1944 of 8,402 heavy and 50,917 light guns, but the wastage rate of barrels doubled over 1943 because of the increased bomber activity.[246] An additional 250,000 personnel had to be found in 1944, mainly recruited from Soviet prisoners of war, Italian volunteers from Mussolini's Italian Social Republic, air force wounded and young German volunteers. This represented a damaging dilution of the quality of anti-aircraft personnel. By spring 1944 some 111,000 women also served in the German anti-aircraft defence system. To navigate the regime's confused stance on employing women, posters reminded the female volunteers: 'The woman in a soldier's post but still a woman!'[247] The anti-aircraft batteries by 1944 were organized increasingly in large groups of heavy guns – Grossbatterien made up of three regular batter-ies – to produce more concentrated fire, but this made heavy demands on a less skilled and less robust workforce. Yet over the course of the year anti-aircraft artillery came to replace the fighters as the main means for destroying or damaging enemy aircraft; the major industrial targets were protected by defensive strongpoints of no fewer than three Gross-batterien.[248] Throughout the campaigns of 1943 and 1944 anti-aircraft damage to Allied aircraft was extensive. An American raid on Berlin on 6 March 1944 resulted in damage to 48 per cent of the 672 bombers who reached the target. Only faltering supplies of ammunition pre-vented anti-aircraft fire from being more effective.[249]

The accelerated production of fighter aircraft also faced problems in late 1943, partly because aircraft production was still controlled by the Air Ministry while the rest of the armaments economy had been central-ized under Albert Speer's Ministry of Armaments and War Production, and partly because of Göring's renewed efforts to revive German offen-sive air power by switching resources to bombers again in the winter of 1943. The current plans for producing more than 30,000 fighters in 1944 and 48,000 in 1945, drawn up by Milch's planning staff in the German Air Ministry, also lacked realism, not least because of the prob-lem of fuel supply. Yet the figures matched what the crisis in the skies over Germany seemed to require.[250] Milch collaborated closely with Speer and the head of his technical office, Karl-Otto Saur, to reduce the different models of each aircraft type – eventually reducing the models from 42 to 5 – and to speed up dispersal programmes. But the problems posed by Göring's revival of bomber plans pushed Milch, for political as well as practical reasons, to offer control over aircraft production to Speer to achieve a long-overdue rationalization of the whole production structure.[251] In February the two men reached an agreement to run together an emergency 'Fighter Staff' (*Jägerstab*) with Saur as its director, and it was established with Hitler's agreement on 1 March 1944. As a result in 1944 three times as many fighters were produced than in 1943, in the hope that this would be sufficient to hold back the Allied bombers long enough to allow the whole German aircraft programme to revive and expand.[252]

It was nevertheless evident by the end of 1943 that sheer numbers of German fighter aircraft were not the entire solution. The production of aircraft had to be balanced against losses and despite the success rate of German day-fighters and night-fighters against the major raids of the autumn and winter, the cumulative attrition of the fighter force made it difficult to expand overall force strength despite the very substantial increases in output. Although 3,700 day-fighters and night-fighters were produced between September and December 1943, the force at Stumpff's disposal when he assumed command in December numbered just 774 day-fighters and 381 night-fighters, with serviceability levels of 60-70 per cent because of shortages of spares and skilled ground personnel.[253] This paradox can be explained in a number of ways. Fighter aircraft were compelled to fight in poor weather conditions against bombers now using blind-flying techniques. Commanders sent aircraft out in dangerous conditions (though not usually in fog or heavy cloud) with the result that the accident rate rose sharply again. Icing and misting of the fighter cockpit windows was a particular hazard. Between September and December 1943 the German fighter force lost 967 aircraft in combat, principally with the American P-47 Thunderbolt, but a further 1,052 to accidents.[254] The second factor was pilot strength and quality. The high loss rates could not easily be made good by the flying schools which were under intense pressure to supply crew to every combat theatre. The result was a sharp reduction in the length of time devoted to training, which was exacerbated by the careful use of fuel. The hours devoted to training for a new German fighter pilot fell from 210 in 1942 to 112 by 1944; operational training was reduced from 50 hours to 20, and crews could be sent to squadrons with only a few hours' training on the front-line aircraft they were to fly in combat. Pilots who returned from combat on the Eastern Front found it difficult to adjust to dogfighting with skilled opponents, while pilots drafted in from other branches of the air force, or from air-ferrying, were not the equal of enemy crew who enjoyed dedicated fighter training in an entirely bomb-free environment.[255] The result was that by early 1944 the German fighter force was obtaining an average net gain every month of only 26 new pilots. The stalemate inflicted on the bomber forces in the autumn created the illusion of German success. In reality the German Air Force was a brittle shield.

The declining skills and rising losses of the German day-fighter force were magnified by the insistence that the object for the force as a whole was to destroy the enemy bomber. This, too, had been a problem for RAF Fighter Command in 1940 when the choice had to be made between stopping the German bombers or fighting their intruding fighter force. German Air Force tactics worked effectively as long as their fighters could seek combat in areas where the bomber force was unescorted. The introduction of longer escort runs in late 1943 transformed the battlefield, though the German Air Force was slow to adapt to the changed reality. Göring famously insisted that the first long-range American fighters to crash near Aachen must have drifted there with the prevailing wind.[256] The existing German fighter force was divided between the Me110/Me410 'destroyer' aircraft, armed with rockets and cannon against the Allied bombers, and the more versatile Me109 and Fw190 fighters which were responsible when necessary for air-to-air combat with enemy fighters. Once American escorts appeared, the slower twin-engine German 'destroyers' were sitting ducks. The first reaction was to move defence units further into Germany in the hope that Allied escort fighters would still have a limit to their range. But the heavier destroyers now had to be escorted by the single-engine fighters, which meant that they too would be tied to a role in which they would be at a persistent disadvantage. In March the destroyers were finally withdrawn altogether after one wing of 43 aircraft lost 26 in one raid, but the prevailing German view was still that their single-engine fighters had to try to get close to the enemy bombers to inflict damage, leaving those fighters easier prey to the increasingly aggressive Americans.[257] The more flexible the tactics of the Eighth Fighter Command became, the more inflexible the tactical demands on the German Air Force.

These weaknesses were cruelly exposed when Spaatz unleashed his campaign for air superiority over Germany. The eventual success of this campaign could not be taken for granted, not because of the German enemy but because of arguments over strategy among the Allies. There was no question that undermining the German Air Force was now a top priority. But Spaatz had to achieve Pointblank in competition with the demands for the 'Crossbow' operation authorized by Allied leaders in late 1943 against the V-weapon silos and installations, and the early onset of bombing tactical targets in support of Operation Overlord, which was expected in February 1944 to absorb at least three months' bombing effort by the strategic air forces.[258] The tension between pursuing Pointblank targets in Germany, and the diversion to targets in occupied Europe more directly related to invasion, was evident to Spaatz and his commanders. It resulted in prolonged arguments over target priorities, which were finally resolved at a meeting between Eisenhower and the senior Allied commanders in Europe on 25 March 1944 in favour of the 'Transportation Plan' for interrupting German rail traffic in north-west Europe. Spaatz was able to start his assault on the German Air Force before these arguments had been properly formulated and resolved – and in the event between January and May 1944 the Eighth and Ninth air forces based in Britain dropped 111,546 (75%) tons of bombs on strategic targets against 38,119 (25%) on tactical ones.[259] The real problem for Spaatz was the difficulty in persuading Harris to share in the task of defeating the German Air Force.

Harris was determined in early 1944 not to abandon the city attacks for a more concentrated assault on German Air Force targets. In January his Command was asked directly to abandon indiscriminate area attack (Harris scrawled 'never has been' in the margin of the memorandum) in favour of raids on ball-bearings factories and fighter output as a contribution to the Eighth Air Force effort to establish 'free deployment' for the day campaign over Germany.[260] Figures were produced by Bomber Command intelligence to show that over one-third of German man-hours had been lost in the bombed cities. Harris told the Air Ministry in early March 1944 that if his force stopped city-bombing, German industry would quickly recover and nullify all the efforts his force had made over the previous year.[261] When the Air Minister, Sir Archibald Sinclair, asked Portal for the opinion of the air staff on Harris's strategy, Portal replied candidly enough that the effort to calculate when Germany might collapse under a certain weight of bombs was 'little more than a waste of time'; the air staff, he continued, preferred a strategy of isolating and attacking the vulnerable points in the German structure whereas Harris just believed in 'piling the maximum on the whole structure'.[262] Portal nevertheless made little effort to get Harris to comply with the American plan to hit air force targets, until pressured to do so by Sydney Bufton, Director of Bombing Operations. Harris was finally ordered to bomb Schweinfurt by a special directive, and Bomber Command obliged on 24–25 February. Target-marking was generally poor and the damage to the city and its ball-bearing industry 'nominal'; only 22 bombs fell within the city boundaries, the rest in open country. In this sense Harris's fear that his force could not hit a small urban target effectively was right.[263]

Further raids were made to support the American campaign against Leipzig, Augsburg and Stuttgart, where there were aircraft and component firms, but the raid on Leipzig missed the Erla aircraft works entirely at a cost of 11 per cent of the attacking force, while the raid on Augsburg did little industrial damage but burnt out the whole medieval centre of the city. The raids on Stuttgart mainly through cloud were scattered, though a lucky hit was made on the Bosch magneto plant. Throughout the period when Spaatz was attacking the German Air Force, Harris persisted in continuing the Battle of Berlin where losses remained high and the impact limited. An assessment of the attacks on the capital between November 1943 and February 1944 by RE8 showed that only 5 per cent of residential buildings and 5 per cent of industrial plant had been damaged in heavy raiding.[264] The attacks made in March on Berlin still brought loss rates of between 5 and 9 per cent on each raid. The last major British raid of the war on Berlin, on 24–25 March, experienced high winds and resulted in scattered bombing across 126 villages and townships. Some 72 aircraft were shot down, 8.9 per cent of the force. In April the final city raid against Nuremberg before the switch to the Overlord campaign showed the persistent limitations of area bombing. A total of 95 aircraft were lost out of the 795 despatched, the highest loss rate of the war, 11.9 per cent. At least 120 aircraft bombed Schweinfurt by mistake, but missed the main area of the city; the remainder bombed a wide area of the German countryside north of Nuremberg, killing 69 villagers. Harris at last recognized that the effectiveness of the German night defences, as he told the Air Ministry, might soon create a situation in which loss rates 'could not in the end be sustained'.[265] Between November 1943 and March 1944, Bomber Command lost 1,128 aircraft for little evident strategic gain. Losses among the expanding German night-fighter force were also high, but by the spring they could see that they were gaining as close to a victory as air war would allow.[266]

In the end the defeat of the German Air Force was an American achievement. Spaatz divided the campaign into three elements: Operation Argument to undermine German aircraft production; a follow-up campaign against the German oil industry to starve the air force of its most precious resource; and finally continuous counter-force attacks against German fighters and their organization. The attack on the aircraft industry, which came to be known as 'Big Week', was postponed regularly through late January and early February 1944 by poor weather. Attacks were carried out against targets in France and a few deeper raids into Germany, but the cloud and snow kept German fighters grounded and increased the risk of accident to American aircrews. On 19 February the weather finally cleared and for the week until 26 February the Eighth Air Force flew 6,200 sorties against 18 aircraft assembly plants and two ball-bearing factories. The raids on the first day, 20 February, divided the bombers between 12 major targets in Rostock, Brunswick, Leipzig and half a dozen other, smaller towns. The losses totalled only 15 bombers from the 880 which attacked – a rate of only 1.7 per cent – and four fighters. Losses climbed as the German Air Force grasped the pattern of attacks, and the cost during the week was eventually 158 for the Eighth Air Force (imposed when, for some reason, escorting lapsed) and 89 for the Fifteenth, which attacked from Italy entirely without escort. Only 28 American fighters were lost from the large numbers despatched on each raid, but the German Air Force lost one-third of its single-engine fighters during February and almost one-fifth of its fighter crew. By contrast, the number of P-51 'Mustang' fighters available was 90 per cent higher at the end of 'Big Week' than it had been at the beginning.[267]

The damage sustained by the German aircraft industry was difficult for the Allies to gauge, not least because air intelligence estimates of German production by this stage of the war greatly understated the reality. The MEW estimates of German fighter production for the first half of 1944 was 655 a month, whereas the reality was 1,581 and rising steadily.[268] The aero-engine industry, more difficult to disperse and more vulnerable, was not attacked, a failure that Göring later pointed out to his post-war interrogators.[269] The attacks accelerated the further dispersal of the industry and prompted a programme for underground construction in which aircraft had a priority, a planned 48 million square metres of floorspace out of a provisional total of 93 million.[270] Output nevertheless continued to increase rapidly despite the bombing, which has encouraged the view that Operation Argument effectively failed. The figures show, however, that the Allied attacks, which continued intermittently thereafter, did reduce *planned* fighter output substantially below expectations. Between January and June 1944, 9,255 German single-engine fighters were produced instead of the planned 12,667, a shortfall of 27 per cent. The heaviest loss was experienced in February 1944 with a shortfall of 38.5 per cent of planned output.[271] Not all of this loss was due to bombing, since many other factors affected industrial performance by 1944, but the impact in February almost certainly was. The problem for Allied calculations was the failure to apprehend the rapid conversion in Germany to fighter priority and the successful rationalization and reorganization of aircraft production.

Spaatz also planned to attack oil facilities, particularly those producing aviation fuel, which were more vulnerable than aircraft assembly halls because of the large capital plant involved and the difficulty of dispersing or concealing them. Intelligence on German oil supplies was the reverse of aircraft production, consistently overestimating German synthetic production and imports. Reluctance to renew an oil offensive after the RAF failures of 1940 and 1941 was based partly on the belief that Germany had large concealed stocks available. By spring 1944, however, Allied intelligence indicated a growing oil vulnerability in Germany. Spaatz set up a planning committee in February 1944 composed of members of the Enemy Objectives Unit to report on other target systems that would accelerate German Air Force decline, and the committee report, presented to him on 5 March, highlighted oil as the principal factor, followed by rubber and bomber production. The economists calculated that enough damage could be done to current oil production to force the German armed forces to consume remaining stocks and that this was the quickest way to undermine fighting power.[272] Spaatz willingly accepted the argument and used the new oil plan to make his case, unsuccessfully, against the diversion of his resources to the tactical 'Transportation Plan'. The aim to destroy or immobilize 27 key oil targets was presented to Portal and Eisenhower as a surer way to undermine German military mobility at the front line, but the estimate that it might take three months to do so made oil plants, in Portal's view, a long-term objective. Instead, the 'Transportation Plan' won the day.

In the end Spaatz succeeded in undertaking attacks on German oil targets by sleight of hand. In April 1944 the Fifteenth Air Force began a number of raids against the Romanian oil-producing city of Ploeşti, nominally against 'marshalling yards'. In fact the raids hit the oilfield, as intended, and in early May, Eaker gave approval for further attacks on Romanian oil production. Spaatz managed to persuade Eisenhower that German Air Force dependence on oil made it effectively a Point-blank target too and got a verbal assurance that on days when he was not attacking French targets, he could attack synthetic oil production.[273] On 12 May Spaatz finally sent 886 bombers escorted by 735 fighters to attack six major oil plants across Germany. The force lost 46 bombers (32 of them from a bomber division whose escort failed to rendezvous correctly), but the swarms of American fighters destroyed 65 enemy air-craft for the loss of just seven planes. Ultra intelligence revealed the following day an urgent German order to move all available anti-aircraft artillery to protect the synthetic oil plants, including guns that until then had been guarding the aircraft industry. The next raid on 28 May was even more devastating, temporarily destroying output at the oil plants at Leuna and Pölitz in eastern Germany. Spaatz was proved right: the oil targets not only encouraged fierce defence by the German fighter force, but quickly proved debilitating to German forces reliant on a shrinking supply of fuel. Production of aviation fuel was 180,000 tons in March, but had fallen to 54,000 tons in June. So successful were the first attacks that on 4 June, two days before the invasion of France, Eisenhower gave formal approval for the oil offensive.[274]

All the while Spaatz was driving the Eighth Air Force to impose insupportable levels of attrition on the enemy fighter force. When there were no bomber raids, Kepner was encouraged to send his long-range fighters in wide sweeps over German territory, attacking German air-bases and seeking opportunities for combat. For bombing operations Spaatz chose long-distance targets which would compel German fight-ers to attack the bombers. In March he launched a number of major raids at aircraft production in Berlin, briefly overlapping with the battle Harris had been waging since November. The raids were among the costliest of the Pointblank campaign. On 6 March 730 bombers and 801 fighters left for the first raid on the capital. Fierce battles erupted over the city so that not only was the bombing inaccurate but the raid cost the Allies 75 bombers, though only 11 escorts were lost for the destruction of 43 German fighters. Raids continued throughout March and April, culminating in a final assault on Berlin on 29 April in which the bombing was ineffective and 63 bombers were lost. The German Air Force had reacted to the advent of the long-range escort fighter by creat-ing large concentrations of up to 150 fighters – the 'Big Wing' used in the last stages of the Battle of Britain – which were designed to batter their way through to the bomber stream, or, when opportunity pre-sented, to focus entirely on bombers whose escort had failed to materialize. The results for both sides were the highest losses of the war. In April the Eighth Air Force lost 422 heavy bombers, 25 per cent of the total; the German fighter force lost 43 per cent of its strength in the same month.[275]

The arena of daylight air combat over Germany was among the harshest of the air war. American commanders expected a great deal of their crews. They were able to accept high losses only because a generous spring tide of aircraft and crew was now flowing across the Atlantic. For the German fighter force, high losses made it difficult to keep more than 500 serviceable fighters in the Reich Air Fleet at any one time. The result was that in air-to-air combat, fighter to fighter, the German force was completely outnumbered and the concentrations easily broken up. 'An enormous number of us arrived, a crowd of 30, 50, sometimes 60 aircraft,' a captured German fighter wing commander explained, 'but each pilot simply attacked wildly at random. Result: each of them was shot down wildly at random.'[276] The same officer described the decline in German pilot morale over the spring of 1944 as the order persisted to attack only the bombers, when their instinct was to protect themselves by engaging the enemy fighters first. One of Germany's surviving pilots, Heinz Knocke, later published a vivid diary account of what air combat was like for German pilots in the spring of 1944:

> During the ensuing dogfight with the Thunderbolts my tail-plane was shot full of holes, and my engine and left wing were badly hit also. It is all I can do to limp home to our field . . . Immediately I order a reserve aircraft to be prepared for me to take off on a third mission. It is destroyed during a low-level strafing attack. Two of the mechanics are seriously wounded. No. 4 flight places one of its aircraft at my disposal . . . When we attempt to attack a formation of Liberators over Lüneberg Heath, we are taken by surprise by approximately forty Thunderbolts. In the ensuing dogfight our two wingmen are both shot down. After a wild chase right down to ground level the Commanding Officer and I finally escape with great difficulty.

Knocke sat in the crew-room that evening with the one remaining pilot from his squadron.[277] Declining morale was not difficult to explain with a one in two chance of surviving, repeated sorties each day, regular and unpredictable low-level attacks, irregular supplies and little chance of leave. Missions for German pilots became all but suicidal by the time of the Normandy invasion, when hundreds of fighter aircraft were sent west from Germany against odds even greater than the ones they had met in the spring.

For American aircrews the situation was less rosy than German accounts might suggest. Morale dropped for them too during the spring offensive, partly because of high losses, partly because of the demands made on the crew from bad-weather flying. In March and April 1944, 89 bomber crews chose to fly to Swiss or Swedish bases for internment. Conditions were made worse by the decision to abandon automatic repatriation of crews to the United States after 25 missions in order to keep up the number of experienced aircrew available.[278] German interrogation reports of crashed American aircrew found a deep fear of anti-aircraft fire, and a strong dislike of the order to conduct low-level attacks against German airfields because of light *Flak* and the tactic of stringing thick steel hawsers (*Drahtsperre*) across narrow valley approaches to slice into an attacking fighter.[279] A major hazard was the return flight with battle damage and the difficulty of landing away from base. The crew of one B-24 'Liberator' bomber, hit by anti-aircraft fire over Brussels, bailed out over Kent at the last moment before the damaged aircraft exploded: 'I broke an ankle and incurred internal injuries,' recalled the pilot. 'The navigator hit a tree and broke his back ... The flight engineer had a scalp injury from hitting his head on a rock. In all, we were pretty lucky.'[280] The high casualty rate made it difficult for American aircrew to form any sense of whether they were winning the battle or not. In the period from January to the end of May 1944 the Eighth and Fifteenth air forces lost 2,605 bombers. Between March and May the American fighter forces lost 1,045 aircraft over Germany and France.

Success only gradually became evident in May and June when Allied bomber losses suddenly fell sharply from the peak in April. By the summer the percentage of attacking bombers actually hit by enemy fighters fell from 3.7 per cent in March and April to only 0.4 per cent in July and August.[281] The reason can be found in the corresponding German statistics. Between January and June, German aircraft losses on all fronts equalled 137 per cent of established strength, 6,259 lost in combat, 3,608 due to accidents, predominantly due to poor weather or pilot error. Despite fighting much of the time over German territory, the German Air Force also lost 2,262 pilots. Most of the losses occurred in Germany or on the Western Front in France and the Low Countries. In June 1944 losses totalled 3,534, only slightly less than the 3,626 aircraft of all types produced that month.[282] This was an insupportable attrition cycle of both German material and manpower: even with the increases in fighter output that peaked later in the year, new production was sucked into a whirlpool of rapid destruction. Fighter pilots waited for the Me262 jet fighter, which first flew in March, in the hope that, produced in volume, it might turn the tide.

The point at which Allied air supremacy was established in German air space is difficult to estimate because of the continuous, fluid and incoherent nature of air combat. Some historians date it from the first attrition battles in March 1944, others from the early attacks on oil installations. The German head of the Historical Section of the German Air Force, Maj. General Hans-Detlef von Rohden, argued in a post-war assessment that Allied air supremacy over Germany had been achieved by the time of the Normandy invasion: 'Germany had lost the struggle for Air Control.'[283] A Joint Intelligence Committee evaluation in August 1944 concluded that the German Air Force 'can no longer affect the military situation on any front', which was not entirely true, but did reflect the exceptional degree of operational flexibility now available to American and, increasingly, British aircraft over Germany.[284] No date is entirely satisfactory, but by June, when German reserves were sucked into the aerial maelstrom in France, the attrition cycle was, for the moment, complete. This was a situation the German Air Force wanted to reverse. In September 1944 a staff paper reflected on the lessons of the Battle of Britain: 'We must try to achieve what England achieved in 1940.'[285] The larger question posed by the 'Battle of Germany' is why the German Air Force failed where in 1940 the RAF – by a narrow margin – succeeded.

There are certainly grounds for comparison. The German Air Force had a substantial fighter force with technology at the cutting edge, particularly after the Me109 fighter was refitted with the more powerful Daimler-Benz 605A engine; aircraft production was concentrated on an emergency fighter programme; a large pool of more than 2,000 fighter pilots were regularly available; there was a complex advance-warning system based on sophisticated radar equipment; and the organizational reforms during the winter of 1943–4 created a central control and communication system not unlike the centralized structure available to Hugh Dowding in 1940. The German Air Force had good intelligence warning of incoming attacks and a thorough understanding of enemy tactical weaknesses. Like Fighter Command, the men who fought in the German fighter force were defending their homeland and prepared to take high losses in doing so. Like their opponents in the Battle of Britain, the German Air Force leaders believed that success in the air was in 1944 'the most decisive precondition for victory'.[286]

The comparison is nevertheless a superficial one. Germany's strategic position in 1944 was very different from Britain's in 1940, fighting on two major fronts in the Soviet Union and Italy and facing growing resistance in other areas of German-occupied Europe. The German priority was not simply to frustrate the Allied search for air superiority but to try to defend a fortress area in central Europe against overwhelming material superiority on all fronts. The strategic crisis explains the emergency programme of fighter production, like the British crisis of summer 1940. German fighter output reached its wartime peak between the last months of 1943 and the autumn of 1944, though this was achieved in an environment of heavy and continuous bombing. As a result, the gap between German fighter production and Anglo-American fighter output (produced in an almost entirely bomb-free environment) was not as significant as the gap in economic resources might suggest. British and American fighter output between January and June 1944 was 11,817; German production over the same six months was 9,489.[287] In both cases this production was spread among a number of fighting fronts. Yet the Eighth Fighter Command had more than twice the number of fighters available when compared with the Reich Air Fleet, as well as additional support from RAF Fighter Command and the Ninth Tactical Air Force. In May 1944 the Reich Air Fleet had 437 serviceable fighters, the Eighth Air Force 1,174. The explanation lies partly in the difference between the two training regimes already noted, which put novice German pilots at a permanent disadvantage. There was also a major contrast in serviceability rates, which were higher for Allied aircraft once the American logistical system was working effectively. Under constant air attack and short of manpower, the production and distribution of spares and the supply of adequate ground engineering staff all declined in Germany. More than 9,000 German aircraft in 1944 were lost in transit from Allied air attack before they reached the combat squadrons.

These contrasts were reflected in rates of operational readiness and rates of loss. During the Battle of Britain the peak loss rate for Fighter Command reached 25 per cent in September 1940. German Air Force monthly fighter losses were already 30 per cent of the force in January 1944 and more than 50 per cent by May (see Table 6.4). Numerical inferiority was then compounded with the demand that German fighters seek out the Allied bombers rather than fighters, which made them more vulnerable at the moment of attack, and by the decision to assemble large numbers of fighters together (like Douglas Bader's 'Big Wings'

Table 6.4: Comparative Fighter Statistics, German Air Force and
Eighth/Ninth US Air Forces, January–June 1944

Month	German Air Force		Eighth/Ninth Air Force	
	Strength	% Loss Rate	Strength	% Loss Rate
Jan 1944	1,590	30.3	2,528	2.7
Feb 1944	1,767	33.8	2,998	3.4
March 1944	1,714	56.4	3,419	5.6
April 1944	1,700	43.0	3,685	7.6
May 1944	1,720	50.4	3,382	10.0
June 1944	1,560	48.3	3,046	17.7

Sources: Calculated from Richard Davis, *Carl A. Spaatz and the Air War in Europe*
(Washington, DC: 1993), App 9, 22–4; Horst Boog et al., *Das Deutsche Reich und der
Zweite Weltkrieg: Band 7: Das Deutsche Reich in der Defensive* (Stuttgart: 2001), 105.

in the Battle of Britain); this meant time lost in flight to assembly points
and, for pilots who had flown on the Eastern Front in pairs or loose
groups of four, a difficult adjustment to flying in larger formations.[288]
The RAF in 1940 avoided both these operational handicaps by using
Spitfires against enemy fighters, Hurricanes against the bombers, while
Dowding judiciously resisted the switch to 'Big Wings'. The difference
between the two sides was not simply a product of economic resources,
as is usually argued, but stemmed from operational and tactical choices
which rested in the end with those in command.

German Air Force commanders were also quick to point out to their
interrogators after the war that the principal problem they faced was
leadership. This is more difficult to assess, and air force commanders
were scarcely without prejudice. Most accounts blamed the air force
commander-in-chief, Hermann Göring. Minutes of the regular meetings
in late 1943 and early 1944 show a commander full of irate bluster and
frustration, prone to impulsive gestures and trite solutions. Though he
was capable of sudden bursts of activity, his subordinates found him a
bizarre, sadly comical figure. A paratroop general, secretly tape-recorded
in captivity in October 1944, entertained his fellow officers to a description of a recent interview with Göring at Karinhall: 'there stood the
figure and I thought: is it Nero II or a Chinese mandarin? [*laughter*] ... A
cloud of all the perfumes of the orient and occident met you half-way
exuding over the fat cheeks ... [All: *laughing helplessly*].'[289] Göring,
however, blamed Hitler: 'You had a great ally in your aerial warfare –
the Führer,' he told interrogators in June 1945.[290] From 1942 onwards,

and particularly after the failure of the air force to supply the encircled forces at Stalingrad, few major decisions in the air war could be taken without Hitler's approval or intervention. Yet Hitler did many things right in relation to the air war: he did not in the end obstruct the shift to fighter priority, favoured a heavy anti-aircraft defence, authorized the dispersal of industry underground, and bullied the air force into prioritizing improvements in electronic warfare.

Göring aside, the other leadership problems stemmed from lower down the air force tree. The coordinated aerial defence of German territory in 1944 fell to an organization that for years had been accustomed to conducting operational air warfare at the fighting fronts. The shift of three-quarters of the fighter force to Germany and the sharp decline in the bomber arm forced a rapid adjustment to an unfamiliar air environment. Stumpff, Schmid and Korten were relatively inexperienced for the kind of contest they fought in the 'Battle of Germany'. Spaatz, Kepner and Doolittle had solid experience with just the kind of battle they faced in 1944 and suffered little direct interference from Arnold or Roosevelt in Washington. Although Arnold was also capable at times of irate bluster, he grasped quickly key technical and organizational issues – the importance of the P-51 fighter, the absolute priority for extra fuel tanks, the critical role of logistics – which made his style of management more effective than Göring's was in 1944, or had been in 1940.[291] One factor did link the Battle of Britain and the 'Battle of Germany': the German Air Force did not admit that they had lost either battle. In the same document that reflected on how the German Air Force should emulate Fighter Command in 1940, optimistic plans were sketched out for a possible revival of effective fighter defence and a renewed bombing effort, despite the profound crisis now facing German air power: 'the war can only be brought to a satisfactory conclusion if we take the offensive'.[292]

RELEASING THE HURRICANE:
SEPTEMBER 1944–MAY 1945

The Combined Offensive was formally reactivated in September 1944 after three months in which the priority for Allied air forces had been supporting the invasion of France and the defeat of German armies in the west. Eisenhower eventually relinquished control of the strategic air forces on 14 September 1944, though he retained the right to request help

with the land war when needed. Both bomber commanders were anxious to return to what they saw as their primary mission. Spaatz reported
to Arnold on the revival of the pre-invasion command structure with
the comment that 'the Hun has still got a lot of fight left in him . . . we
must concentrate to kill him off'.[293] By July, Harris was impatient
to restart full-scale bombing, because he expected Germany to have
recovered fully in five bomb-free months. In August, Portal warned
Churchill that there were evident signs of German revival which would
have to be snuffed out by a bombing policy of 'continuous attrition'.[294]

What followed from September 1944 to May 1945 was an Allied
campaign with the heaviest weight of bombs and the highest level of
German casualties of the war. Over the eight months until German
surrender the Eighth and Fifteenth Air Forces together with Bomber
Command dropped three-quarters of the wartime bomb total against a
deteriorating German defence; approximately half of all German deaths
from bombing occurred over the same period. It is the extravagant
power of this final bombing campaign, and its massive damage to Germany's civilian population, urban infrastructure and cultural heritage
that has occasioned most post-war criticism of bombing strategy.
To understand why the offensive was continued on such a devastating
scale it is necessary to reconstruct the strategic situation as it seemed to
the Western Allies in autumn 1944.

The most obvious answer is that there was no compelling reason
after the rapid victory in France to ease the pressure on an enemy who,
it was hoped, might be defeated before Christmas. There was wide
popular endorsement of the bombing campaign among the home populations. The percentages in favour of bombing German civilians
expressed in British opinion polls rose from less than half in 1940 to
almost two-thirds by 1944, a reflection of popular anxiety to end the
war quickly and a growing familiarity with bombing as a central pillar
of Allied strategy.[295] The BBC air commentaries in 1944 by 'Squadron
Leader Strachey' (the left-wing politician John Strachey, now a temporary member of Bufton's Bombing Directorate) had record radio
audiences.[296] There was little reason for Churchill or Roosevelt to shut
down the bombing offensive given the exceptional commitment to its
organization and supply, and both leaders were by now anxious to
accelerate an end to the conflict and frustrated by an enemy whose willingness to continue fighting showed little sign of wilting. When Churchill
was shown yet another political intelligence report confirming that the
German people lacked the 'energy, the courage or the organization'

necessary to overthrow Hitler's dictatorship, he asked to be spared any further reports on German morale.[297] From the military point of view, bombing was now part of the combined arms offensive to defeat Germany on the ground, and although the targets were distant from the front line in eastern France, the Combined Chiefs of Staff expected that bombing would be used in general against targets that promised to expedite the army's advance. The achievement of air superiority in the summer of 1944 required constant and vigilant defence against any prospect of German recovery, since superiority was always relative. It was feared that if the German war effort were not suppressed, the conflict might run on well into 1945, or might even reach stalemate. There was always the persistent fear, going back many years, that the German leadership might be able to turn the tide of war by jumping a stage ahead in the race for new science-based weapons.

Of all the factors that encouraged the final months of heavy bombing, the fear that the German military situation might be reversed by new weapons, secret or otherwise, kept bombers at their task. Though some of these fears might appear with hindsight mere fantasy, the launch of the V-weapons and the first employment of the Me262 jet fighter/fighter-bomber provoked the Allied view that Germany's military situation might abruptly improve. The Me262 was a crude fighter, easily adapted to mass production, but with its high speeds it was capable of posing a serious challenge to the bomber fleets had it been available in sufficient numbers. The few units equipped with the Me262 by the end of the war claimed to have shot down 300 heavy bombers. The new aircraft was certainly welcomed by German air leaders as a possible war-winner. Evaluations of the war situation produced in September 1944 and January 1945 by German Air Force intelligence presented the possibility of a 'final victory' given the apparent decline in Anglo-American military capability and enthusiasm since the summer and the clutch of dangerous new technical developments available to Germany; these included the *Wasserfall* ground-to-air missile (V-4), proximity fuses, jet fighters (Me262 and Me163), jet bombers (Arado Ar243), rocket fighters (Heinkel He162), and equipment for non-visual detection and destruction of enemy aircraft.[298] Some of these developments were well known to the Allies, others merely speculation. The correspondence between Spaatz and Arnold on the threat of the German jet fighters reveals the extent to which the Allies feared for the future of the bombing offensive. Spaatz wanted top priority for the development of the American jet fighter, the Lockheed P-80, and suggested the possibility that American bombers would have to change to night-bombing or shallow penetration raids to keep losses to jet fighters within acceptable limits.[299] Doolittle told Arnold in August 1944 that he was not 'awed' by German potential, and proposed to challenge jet and rocket-propelled fighters by head-on attack and superior turning. But by October he warned that jet aircraft and enhanced weaponry, includ-ing the powerful 30-mm cannon, might well 'overwhelm our defenses' in attacks on Germany.[300] Anglo-American air intelligence confirmed, as Harris had warned, that by the autumn the German single-engine fighter force would be larger than at any point in 1944. Hence the arguments in favour of continued heavy bombing of German industrial and mili-tary targets.

The greatest fear was that the German leadership, like some wounded stag at bay, would unleash what are now called weapons of mass destruction. The United States Chemical Warfare Committee in January 1945 warned that although German leaders had not yet authorized the use of gas, the strategic situation they faced had changed for the worse: 'The Germans are now fighting with their backs to the wall, on their homeland, and may out of zealousness, in defense of their own soil, or the fanatical desperation of the Nazi leadership, resort to the gas weapon.'[301] These fears had a long pedigree. Extensive preparations had been made by the RAF during the Blitz to prepare for a gas campaign against Germany. When the United States entered the war, gas warfare plans were coordinated between the two allies.[302] In late 1943 these anxieties revived. Intelligence from a captured Italian diplomat sug-gested that Germany had large stocks of gas but would only use them 'in a last resort'. Churchill, who had been the motor behind expanding Britain's gas capability in 1941, underlined on the report the words 'Gas', 'no new gas has been produced', 'Germans would not use' as evi-dence of his continued concern.[303] A report from the Analysis of Foreign Weapons Division in October 1943 to the War Department concluded that 'Germany is well prepared with the necessary weapons and agents to start gas warfare at any moment', using a variety of new toxins and means of delivery. This was indeed the case: by the beginning of 1944 the German armed forces had thousands of tons of chemical weapons on hand, including the deadly agents Sarin and Tabun.[304] In December the Joint Chiefs of Staff were supplied with full details of the toxic gases available for American forces for the conduct of gas warfare from the air in both the European and Pacific theatres, and in 1944 an acceler-ated programme for the production of gas bombs was set in motion. In

January 1945 Arnold's headquarters could confirm that the air force 'can be effectively employed for waging gas warfare'.[305]

British preparations for gas warfare were much further advanced and more likely to be used. In January 1944 Portal told Churchill that he was toying with the idea of using gas to attack V-weapon installations, but hesitated to do so because the repercussions of starting gas warfare 'would be far-reaching'. The RAF was nevertheless alert for the first whiff of German gas in order to activate the extensive plans for airborne gas attacks. The War Cabinet was notified by the Air Staff the same month that if Germany should ever use it, the air force would immediately unleash six area attacks with mustard gas and two with Phosgene every month. The attacks were to be divided between lighter, harassing raids and heavy concentrated raids using a mix of gas bombs, incendiaries and high explosive, which would have to be repeated regularly 'on the most densely populated centres'.[306] The Air Staff understood that even if the German forces used gas against the invading troops in June 1944, Churchill favoured gas attacks not only on enemy troops but also on 'the cities of Germany'. A list of suitable cities was drawn up in case such attacks were needed, 15 for Bomber Command, 30 for the Eighth Air Force and 15 for American bombers from Italy. For the Normandy landings Bomber Command planned 11,000 sorties using gas and other bombs against a variety of military and civilian targets.[307] The stalemate in Normandy and the onset of the V-weapons campaign brought further pressure from Churchill to use gas to speed up German defeat: 'I want a cold-blooded calculation made,' he wrote on 6 July, 'as to how it would pay us to use poison gas ... we could drench the cities of the Ruhr.'[308] But the chiefs of staff remained opposed to the risk, while all the available intelligence suggested that there were no German plans to use it (though it was certainly discussed by Hitler and other German leaders during 1944).[309] Nevertheless, by early 1945 the American Chemical Warfare Service had sufficient stocks of gas in theatre to maintain a campaign equivalent to 25 per cent of the total available bomblift. Almost all gas attacks would be made from the air.[310]

Less well known are the plans for biological warfare against Germany developed in 1944-5. These, too, were the result of growing fears that a desperate enemy might utilize bacteriological warfare, possibly projected by some form of rocket propulsion. In 1942 Roosevelt authorized a War Research Board directed by George Merck, with an advisory board of prominent scientists, disguised simply as the 'ABC Committee', whose first task was to work out ways to protect the American population from a possible German or Japanese bacteriological attack. In late 1942 the work was taken over by the Chemical Warfare Service, which set up a research facility at Camp Detrick in Frederick, Maryland. As with gas warfare, intelligence began to appear in 1943 that suggested Germany was planning the use of biological warfare agents, and in particular 'bacillus botulinus' (now known as *Clostridium botulinum*, the cause of botulism), which was impossible to detect in an airborne attack, caused symptoms in four to five hours and death by embolism in most cases. The assumption was that Germany would only hesitate to use biological weapons because of the threat of 'instant reprisal' and as a result a programme to produce lethal pathogens was accelerated. A further report in January 1944 warned that rocket or air attacks using bacteria might be imminent, and their effects 'devastating'. This included the probability of using anthrax spores directed at human populations.[311] Three plants were set up for experiment and production in Mississippi, Indiana and Utah; 60 workers were infected, but none died.[312] Before biological agents became available in sufficient quantities, which would not be before April 1945, it was recommended that retaliation should be with gas.[313]

Would the Allies have used either gas or germ warfare? The question was never tested, since Hitler was opposed to their use and more concerned about defence against a possible Allied biological attack.[314] But the development of both Allied programmes shows the extent to which perception of the German enemy coloured the decision to continue heavy bombing in case worse weapons were to hand. The most significant factor is that fear of chemical and biological weapons prompted the Allies to think in terms of retaliation against civilian populations on a large scale, turning interwar fantasies about gas and germs into potential reality. The RAF staff thought that incendiary and high-explosive raids were more strategically efficient, in that they destroyed property and equipment and not just people, but in any of these cases – blown apart, burnt alive or asphyxiated – deliberate damage to civilian populations was now taken for granted. This paved the way for the possibility of using atomic weapons on German targets in 1945 if the war had dragged on late into the year, a fact that is easily forgotten. Echoes can be found in the later extravagant planning for second-strike nuclear destruction during the first decades of the Cold War, when up to 80 million Soviet citizens were expected to be casualties.[315]

It is against this strategic background that sense can be made of the decision to intensify the bombing offensive to be certain of securing

German defeat. The summer diversion to the ground war, however, had done nothing to settle the inter-Allied arguments over bombing strategy that surfaced in the early months of 1944. Indeed, a renewed eagerness to demonstrate what air forces were now capable of gave them fresh impetus. The first step following the decision to return the bomber forces to air force control was to change the overall command structure to more properly reflect the balance of power between the two Allied bomber forces. This was now heavily tilted towards the Eighth and Fifteenth Air Forces, which had on hand between them more than 5,000 heavy bombers in the European theatre and could call on over 5,000 fighters, including by November around 2,000 P-51s. One major Eighth Air Force raid late in 1944 employed 2,074 bombers and 923 fighters. Against this Harris could field around 1,400 heavy bombers, mainly Lancasters, a fraction of what had been hoped for.[316] Spaatz refused to return to Portal's direct control and preferred to retain his close relationship with Eisenhower. Under pressure from the British chiefs of staff Arnold agreed to relinquish the link with SHAEF, but only on condition that he would now be the representative of the Combined Chiefs of Staff for directing the American Strategic and Tactical Air Forces in Europe rather than Portal. To mollify the British, Spaatz was also formally appointed as Portal's deputy chief of staff, together with Norman Bottomley. In practice Spaatz was left free to organize an independent campaign; he left Anderson in London and based himself in a forward headquarters next to Eisenhower, first in Paris, then Rheims. He told Arnold in late September that he preferred to keep the two forces separate.[317] Harris also understood that the change would give him once again more control over his force; since he was now the junior partner after years in which Bomber Command had been the senior manager, the guardianship of his campaign loomed larger than ever in his mind.[318]

The changed command structure made a common plan for the strategic air war less likely. The Bombing Directorate in the Air Ministry in August 1944 argued for a major operation against German morale, codenamed 'Thunderclap', for 'laying on a "Rotterdam"' on the centre of Berlin. The aim was to shatter any German hope of sustaining the war effort by 'the *obliteration* of the visible signs of an organized Government', using 2,000 tons of bombs dropped in accurate concentration on a 2.5-square-mile area of central Berlin. The likely shock effect on German morale was compared with the shock effect on the Dutch government in 1940, which surrendered the day after the Rotterdam raid.[319]

The proposal came, for the moment, to nothing. The Combined Chiefs of Staff preferred to wait until German morale was evidently at its most fragile. The two bomber forces continued for the moment to attack what they had targeted before Normandy, Harris against city areas, Spaatz against oil and air force targets. During September Spaatz searched for a combination of targets that would put maximum pressure on the German military war effort. Since it was now evident that the Allies, sitting on the German frontier, would not find it as easy to invade as had been hoped, Spaatz preferred a strategy that would maximize the help the air forces could give to Eisenhower. His staff worked on a programme to attack major military industries and communications in the Ruhr-Rhineland, Saarland and south-west Germany to create the maximum dislocation and demoralization of the military and administrative structures. The plan was divided in two parts: 'Hurricane I' was to be directed in general at areas which contained valuable targets in western Germany during periods when visual bombing was difficult; 'Hurricane II' was for precise attacks in good weather on oil installations, motor transport depots and communications. The directive was issued on 13 October to both Harris and Spaatz, but persistent poor weather rendered 'Hurricane II' unworkable while 'Hurricane I' was too amorphous in ambition and was largely ignored.[320]

The search for an agreed plan did not stop the Allied bomber forces from heavy and regular attacks on German targets, almost all of them non-visual on account of the deteriorating weather. On 18 October the two forces agreed to set up a Combined Strategic Targets Committee, chaired jointly by Bufton and Colonel Maxwell from Spaatz's staff, to work out a better set of priorities. Air Marshal Arthur Tedder, Eisenhower's deputy, was invited by Portal to contribute to the evaluation process. Tedder deplored what he described as a 'patchwork quilt' of targets with no comprehensive pattern and recommended concentration on oil and communications as the two targets most likely to undermine German capacity to wage war. Tedder had been a firm supporter of the transport plan in Italy in 1943–4, then of the invasion of France. He was strongly supported by Solly Zuckerman, who had been responsible for working out the Italian plan, and was now advising SHAEF.[321] Tedder's intervention proved decisive. Ultra intelligence in late October confirmed that attacks on transportation had already had a substantial effect on coal movements. A meeting at SHAEF headquarters on 28 October agreed on priority being given to oil targets and communications, and a new instruction, Strategic Directive No. 2, was issued on 1 November to Spaatz and Harris. The new directive, however, was a compromise, as most directives had been since the Casablanca Conference. Alongside oil and transport, the directive allowed attacks on 'important industrial areas' when visual bombing was impaired, as well as policing attacks on the German Air Force organization and, when required, direct support of land operations.[322] Bombing preferences in fact remained divided: Spaatz, Doolittle and Bufton preferred the oil campaign; Tedder and Zuckerman sponsored communications; Harris, who had a strong personal antipathy to Zuckerman ('the "expert" Mr Solly Zuckerman') and to Bufton ('one of my ex-Station commanders'), remained wedded to the idea that oil and transport were expensive, dangerous and futile objectives when the destruction of cities could be more easily accomplished.[323] In a famous exchange of letters with Portal (his were drafted by Bufton) in December 1944, Harris rejected the oil plan on the grounds that it would need a quarter of a million tons of bombs and months of effort to achieve it.[324]

The effect of differences of opinion can be exaggerated. Allied air power was now so overwhelming and technically sophisticated that attacks anywhere contributed to the cumulative collapse of the German war effort, and could be carried out with small losses. Harris diverted some of his area raids to the Ruhr-Rhineland synthetic oil installations in November and December, and ordered a heavy attack on Leuna-Merseburg on 6–7 December which, though deep in German territory, cost only 5 bombers from a force of 475. From 6 per cent of its bombing total on oil in October, Bomber Command increased the total to 24 per cent the following month. That same month the Eighth Air Force devoted 39 per cent of its total on oil targets, the Fifteenth Air Force 32 per cent. Despite justified fears that German efforts would be focused entirely on reconstituting oil production, the long-term trend of the oil attacks since the beginning of the year was to create a critical level of loss, whose effects on German military mobility and air power were indeed fundamentally debilitating (see Table 6.5). Most of Harris's attacks were nevertheless devoted to night raids on urban targets, particularly on smaller cities that had not so far been the object of attack. Between October and April, when area attacks were ordered to cease, Bomber Command launched heavy attacks against cities across Germany. Some contained important rail junctions or marshalling yards, some chemical and oil plant, but most of the time the heavy bombloads destroyed wide urban areas or continued to fall on open ground. Although a number of daylight raids were made, Harris refused

Table 6.5: German Oil Production and Imports, 1944–5 (000 tonnes)

Month	Synthetic Production	Oil Refined in Germany	Imports	Total
Jan 1944	498	175	179	852
Feb 1944	478	160	200	838
Mar 1944	542	191	186	919
Apr 1944	501	157	104	762
May 1944	436	170	81	687
June 1944	298	129	40	467
July 1944	229	115	56	400
Aug 1944	184	134	11	329
Sept 1944	152	113	11	276
Oct 1944	155	124	34	313
Nov 1944	185	105	37	327
Dec 1944	164	108	22	294

Source: Calculated from Webster, Frankland, *Strategic Air Offensive*, vol 4, 516.

to convert his force to day-bombing, perhaps to ensure that the contribution of his Command remained distinctive to the last.

By contrast, American bombing, though intended to be directed at oil and transport targets, was often little distinguishable from area raiding. Much of the air policing of the German Air Force and attacks on targets of opportunity on the German transport network were carried out by fighters and fighter-bombers, which swarmed over Germany. The heavy bombers focused on major industrial and rail targets, but poor visibility for much of the winter meant that most bombs again fell widely scattered. From every 100 bombs dropped on an oil plant, 87 missed the target entirely and only 2 hit the buildings and equipment.[325] A conference on bombing accuracy called in March 1945 confirmed that most bombing since September 1944 had been blind-bombing, much through 10/10 cloud cover. From September to December 1944 only 14 per cent of bombing was done with good to fair visibility, a further 10 per cent visually aimed with poor visibility; 76 per cent was carried out non-visually, using a variety of electronic aids. In good visibility, at least four-fifths of bombs were found to fall within one mile of the aiming point, but through 10/10 cloud cover only 5.6 per cent.[326] The instructions given to the Eighth Air Force in October 1944 on bombing procedure encouraged attacks in poor weather on any towns visible with the aid of H2X, for the reason that they were certain to contain some vital military targets. The effect, like the directives to Bomber Command three years before, was to encourage escalating damage to the civilian milieu and higher civilian casualties.[327]

Whatever the operational drawbacks to flying in poor weather against heavily defended targets, enough bombs struck the oil plants and transport network to cause sufficient disruption. The transport plan was put into effect by the Eighth Air Force in early September, but serious assaults on the main rail junctions and marshalling yards began in October against Cologne, Hamm and Duisburg. The Rhine was blocked at Cologne by a lucky strike on the Cologne-Mulheimer Bridge, which collapsed into the water, blocking one of Germany's main traffic waterways. By November the German Railway was down to 11 days' supply of coal, by 12 December down to five days. Southern and eastern parts of Germany were starved of coal; locomotives and wagons were routinely strafed by fighters and fighter-bombers. Out of 250,000 goods wagons available, almost half were inoperable by late November. Total rail freight traffic fell by 46 per cent from September 1944 to January 1945. In the Ruhr, rolling stock available for daily use was by late October half the level of September. Rolling stock was withdrawn further away from the attacks in western Germany, but the result was to block supplies of coal and coke from the Ruhr, and force a reduction of one-third in electricity generation.[328] Serious damage to the Mittelland Canal, the main link between the Ruhr and central Germany, left it unusable for much of October and November. Coal traffic on inland waterways was 2.2 million tons in September, but 422,000 in December.[329] Hitler ordered the transfer of 1,000 heavy and 2,000 light anti-aircraft guns to defend key transport junctions, but as a result denuded the defence available to other vital war industries. Ultra intelligence decrypts kept the Allies regularly aware of the impact the transport plan was having and encouraged its expansion.[330]

Somehow or other, amidst the accumulating chaos of smashed rail lines, burnt-out cities and crumpled factories, the German Air Force continued to sustain a threat to the ubiquitous enemy. Despite the long battle of attrition, there were 2,500 serviceable fighters and night-fighters still available by December. Moreover, Allied losses on a number of daylight raids began to mount again: 40 bombers were lost in raids on oil targets on 7 October, 40 again on 2 November. But most of the raids recorded in the Eighth Air Force war diary show negligible losses and in many cases no losses to combat at all. Overall loss rates fluctuated between 1 and 2 per cent throughout the period from September 1944 to

the end of the war, an increasing number due to anti-aircraft fire. Allied
fighter losses were never high (the peak in September 1944 was only
1.9 per cent of sorties); losses amounted to just 1.37 per cent of all sorties in the last eight months of the war.[331] Meanwhile the German Air
Force remained trapped in the attrition cycle set in motion earlier in the
year. Combat in large formations proved dangerous even to experienced
pilots. The Allied raid on 2 November that lost 40 bombers cost the
German fighter force 120 planes. The collapse of aviation fuel supply
played an important part; training was cut back even further and strict
instructions were given on flight times and procedures to reduce fuel
consumption. Both day-fighter and night-fighter squadrons found they
had a surplus of pilots with available aircraft, but they could not
fly because of the restrictions. The enthusiastic expectations of the
Me262 jet fighter were disappointed by the slow pace of development
and continued technical problems with the jet turbines. Although 564 jets
were produced in 1944, the first fighter squadron armed with the new
model began operations only in November.[332]

The situation for the night-fighters was also seriously affected by fuel
shortages. Bomber Command losses fell dramatically from the high
point of the summer when attacks were still suffering average losses of
6–7 per cent. Over the last months of the war loss rates dropped to an
average of 1.5 per cent. In 1943 a Lancaster bomber had lasted on average for 22 combat sorties, whereas by 1945 the figure was 60.[333] The
more experience the crews got, the better their chances of survival. The
German night-fighter force, on the other hand, was hit by the collapse
in fuel supply in a number of ways. It was essential to be able to run full
training programmes for crews in the use of the complex scanning
equipment, the SN3 and FuG218, now available to locate the bomber
aircraft. The dynamos needed to charge the radar equipment could not
be operated because of fuel shortages; electricity supply to the radar
stations was intermittent by the winter months of 1944, which also
reduced training time on the new detection instruments.[334] Most night-
fighters were now the high-quality Junkers Ju88G, fitted with SN2 and
Naxos equipment, and the *Flensburg* detector used to home onto an
Allied bomber's 'Monica' signals. By chance this equipment fell undamaged into British hands when a disorientated German night-fighter
pilot landed in error on a Bomber Command station at Woodbridge
in Suffolk in July 1944. Extensive testing soon showed that the
simple expedient of turning off both the 'Monica' tail radar and the
H2S set would blind the enemy night-fighters. New devices – 'Perfectos',

'Piperack' and 'Serrate IV' – were developed to give warning of enemy fighters and to confuse German radar.[335] Although a new round of research began in Germany, there was too little time or opportunity to profit from it as the infrastructure collapsed. The see-saw electronic war ended in the Allies' favour. By 1945 the night-fighter force was a wasted asset.

In November 1944 the crisis in the German Air Force reached a peak. Göring found himself caught between two poles, Hitler's harsh accusations over the failure of the air force and the stark reality of Allied air supremacy. He took out his own frustration by blaming his aircrew for lack of courage and loyalty. On 11 November Göring convened a tribunal ('Aeropag') in Berlin with his senior air force commanders at which he announced that German air power had failed and asked for solutions. It became, recorded one of those present, 'a dreary forum which harped on about National Socialist influences within the Luftwaffe' but resolved nothing.[336] The anxieties in the West about the revival of German air power now scarcely reflected the reality. The air force relied increasingly on gestures. New *Sturmjäger* (storm fighter) units were created from skilled pilots who flew their aircraft, armed with heavy new 30-mm cannon, straight at the bomber stream, regardless of the powerful fighter escort. The suicidal tactics were occasionally accompanied by ramming, despite Hitler's disapproval of the idea of German *kamikaze*. To cope with the impossibility of day-to-day combat in small formations – usually groups of 10 or 20 aircraft, now directed mainly at fighter-bombers and fighter-intruders rather than the bomber stream – Adolf Galland, the General of Fighters, organized a plan for a 'Great Blow' by building up a reserve of fighters and fuel to release a sudden devastating attack on a large bomber stream. By 12 November there were 3,700 fighters of all kinds available, around 2,500 assigned for the blow. The object was to shoot down at least 400 bombers in one raid to try to deter the Allied offensive and buy time for the build-up of modern air equipment, 'the shock the enemy needed', one of the pilots later told his American captors, 'to make them cease their inroads into the heart of Germany'.[337]

At just the point that Galland and his commanders were waiting for the weather to clear, the units were ordered westward to the Ardennes to take part in Operation Autumn Mist (*Herbstnebel*), better known as the Battle of the Bulge. The reserves were lost and later decimated in operation *Bodenplatte* directed against Allied airfields in early January, when almost 300 German fighters were shot down. Galland was sacked by Göring a week later on suspicion of instigating a pilots' rebellion against his leadership. A mutiny finally surfaced in a grim confrontation at the Air Ministry after Karl Koller, the successor to Korten as chief of staff, sent a delegation to meet Göring to request changes in command, the re-equipment of fighter units with the Me262 jet, and greater respect for what the fighter arm was trying to do. Göring threatened them with court martial, but in the end the ringleaders were simply posted away from Berlin. Hitler, however, finally conceded that the jet ought to be used as a fighter rather than an ineffective fighter-bomber. Galland was sent to lead one of the first converted Me262 squadrons. On his last mission, flown on 26 April, 11 days before the end of the war in Europe, he was attacked by an undetected Mustang and limped back to his base with a smashed instrument panel, and both turbines damaged. As he arrived, the airfield was being bombed and strafed by Thunderbolts. He landed among them and dived into a bomb crater from his battered aircraft. Two weeks later he was explaining to his American captors the most effective way to put airfields out of commission.[338]

By January 1945 there was accumulating Ultra evidence that the choice of oil and the transport network as targets had been sensible. The stabilization of the front after the Battle of the Bulge made it evident that German forces were near the end of their fighting power, yet the assault on Germany itself promised a costly finale. The possibility of using Operation Thunderclap as a way to bring about sudden collapse was raised again. The Bombing Directorate wrote to SHAEF suggesting a bombing operation of exceptional density designed to provoke 'a state of terror by air attack' in which any individual in the vicinity of the raid would realize that the chances of escaping death or serious injury 'are extremely remote'.[339] This was one of a number of voices raised over the winter in favour of punitive raids designed to spread the bombing over wider sections of the population. The Joint Intelligence Committee at SHAEF suggested in October 1944 that surplus bombing capacity before German surrender might be usefully employed in attacks against parts of Germany which had not yet been affected 'in order to bring home to the whole population the consequences of military defeat and the realities of air bombing'.[340] Post-war interpretations of the last three months of bombing on a collapsing German war effort and a disorientated population have also come to regard the final flourish of bombing against a weakened enemy, with overwhelming force, as merely punitive, neither necessary nor, as a result, morally justified. The American air forces alone between January and April 1945 dropped more than four times the bomb tonnage used by Germany during the 10-month Blitz on Britain. For both Allied air forces the fact that it was now possible to demonstrate the full potential of air power at a critical point of the European war played some part in their willingness to push the offensive to the maximum, in case air power really could deliver the *coup de grâce*. But the calls for punitive attacks were not reflected in the prevailing directives, which still presented German resistance, particularly after the crisis in the Ardennes, as substantial enough to merit unrelenting attack. Robert Lovett wrote to Arnold early in January 1945 that despite everything, Germany showed no signs of cracking, while the German forces were fighting with such 'skill and fanaticism' that it might produce 'a type of dug-in, trench warfare which will be slow, costly in lives and difficult to synchronize with the increased demands of accelerated Pacific operations'. Only air power, Lovett concluded, could break the stalemate.[341]

The story of the last months of desperate German resistance is now well known, but at the time the intelligence picture for the Allies was less coherent and full of potential menace. Persistent rumours of German plans to build a 'redoubt' in southern Germany or the Alps were taken more seriously than they deserved. The capacity of the Red Army to complete its victory on the Eastern Front was regarded as more imponderable than it should have been. These uncertainties help to explain the decision that led on the night of 13-14 February in the Saxon city of Dresden to the third major firestorm of the war, which killed approximately 25,000 people in a few hours. No other raid of the war, not even Operation Gomorrah, has generated so much critical attention. Harris has regularly been blamed for conducting a needlessly destructive and strategically unnecessary raid against Dresden, but the irony is that the purpose on this occasion was dictated by the conditions of the ground war rather than the area campaign. It was Dresden's misfortune to be not only in the path of the oncoming Soviet armies, but a possible transfer route for the phantom last stand of German armies in the south. Although the city was ranked number 22 on the MEW list of target cities, with a key-point rating of 70, Harris had not yet attacked it in force, partly because of the long distance, but almost certainly because it contained no major industries linked to the current directive.[342] By the autumn of 1944 Dresden was also routinely included on target lists issued to the Fifteenth Air Force stationed in Italy, along with other targets in southern and eastern Germany, but had not yet been attacked.[343] When the Combined Strategic Targets Committee met in late November 1944, it listed cities for possible area attack when blind-bombing was necessary, with an 'x' to indicate oil targets present and '+' to indicate a key communications centre. All 13 cities in western Germany had one or both targets indicated; of the 11 selected in eastern Germany, seven were marked '+' but four – Dresden, Leipzig, Dessau and Danzig – had no key target marked.[344]

The origin of the decision to bomb Dresden has been obfuscated by the long post-war debate over who should accept responsibility or blame for what happened. The historical narrative seems, however, clear enough. The possibility of an area attack on Dresden first surfaced in October 1944 when Portal responded to a request from Churchill for a list of 'area targets' that the advancing Soviet Air Force might be able to bomb, which included Dresden among the seven suggested.[345] Discussion about bombing cities in eastern Germany was always related to the progress of Soviet forces and the possibility of helping their advance by a display of Allied air power. In mid-January 1945 Tedder met with Stalin to discuss the progress of the campaign against oil targets. Stalin showed great interest in the effects of bombing on German military fuel supplies and then showed Tedder the Soviet plans for the main Oder operation, launched five days later, on 20 January.[346] This discussion seems to have prompted two separate responses. The JIC on 25 January concluded that the Soviet offensive would be greatly helped by heavy attacks on Berlin, though priority was still to be assigned to oil targets. Portal and the Air Staff assessed the evidence but were unconvinced, and on 26 January their preference was still for attacks on oil and jet-fighter targets.[347] However, the same day Churchill, who must have read the report, asked Sinclair whether there were any plans to help the Soviet offensive. Dissatisfied with Sinclair's equivocal response, he dashed off a note on 26 January demanding to know whether Berlin 'and no doubt other large cities in East Germany' were now to be considered valuable targets. Sinclair replied on 27 January that Berlin, Dresden, Leipzig and Chemnitz were all now on the list for possible attack when the weather had improved.[348] The next day Portal wrote to Churchill that oil targets remained a key priority of the bombing war, but added the following: 'We also intend, as you know, to apply as much bomber effort as we can to the cities of Eastern Germany, including Berlin: but oil must come first.'[349] Two days later Portal and Churchill both travelled to Malta for discussions with the Americans before going on to the conference at Yalta.

The second response was to set in motion actual operations. On 27 January Bottomley sent Harris the JIC report and asked him to prepare attacks on Berlin, as well as the three principal Saxon cities, Dresden, Leipzig and Chemnitz.[350] He then drafted a paper for the chiefs of staff meeting, due to convene in Malta on 31 January, which effectively summarized the grounds for the bombing:

Evacuation Areas: Evacuees from German and German-Occupied Provinces to the East of Berlin are streaming westward through Berlin itself and through Leipzig, Dresden and other cities in the East of Germany. The administrative problems involved in receiving the refugees and re-distributing them are likely to be immense. The strain on the administration and upon the communications must be considerably increased by the need for handling military reinforcements on their way to the Eastern Front. A series of heavy attacks by day and night upon these administrative and control centres is likely to create considerable delays in the deployment of troops at the Front and may well result in establishing a state of chaos . . . It is for these reasons that instructions have been issued for heavy scale attacks to be delivered on these centres at the earliest possible moment.[351]

The initiative now passed to Tedder at Eisenhower's headquarters in Paris. After discussions with Spaatz and Bottomley, he drew up a planning document on 31 January incorporating the city attacks, which would involve both British and American bombers. Spaatz, who thought that Operation Thunderclap was now the plan, preferred a heavy attack on Berlin, with high casualties, but he did not demur at a broader programme.[352]

The only barrier to carrying out the raids was raised by the Soviet delegation at the Yalta conference. The Soviet side demanded agreement on a formal 'bombline' in eastern Germany, running through Berlin, Leipzig and Vienna, beyond which Western air forces would not bomb for fear of hitting Soviet forces and equipment. The discussions at Yalta were resolved on 7 February by agreeing on the term 'zone of limitation' to describe areas which either side could currently bomb, freeing Dresden and other cities from the Soviet proscription. It has often been argued that the Soviet side at Yalta asked for raids on Berlin, Leipzig and Dresden, but the discussion with the Soviet chief of staff, Marshal Aleksei Antonov, recorded in the minutes, only mentions the bombing of Berlin and Leipzig; Portal seems to have insisted on including

Dresden, since this was already on the list of cities suggested by the Air Ministry.[353] Though Harris later argued at the height of the Cold War that the request to bomb Dresden had come 'from the other side of the Iron Curtain', there can be no doubt that the plan was always a Western one.[354] On 7 February the American military representative in Moscow, General John Deane, was notified by Spaatz that the bombing had been planned, and Soviet leaders were finally told five days later that the raid on Dresden was imminent. On 8 February SHAEF issued a formal operational instruction to Bomber Command and the Eighth Air Force to attack cities in eastern Germany when the weather was favourable.

The question for Dresden and the other cities of eastern Germany was not why they were attacked, which conformed with Allied policy on raids in support of the ground war, from Monte Cassino to Le Havre, but the way in which the raids were conducted and the weight of attack. Consistent with the new directive, Spaatz ordered a major daylight raid on Berlin on 3 February 1945 with 1,000 B-17 'Flying Fortresses' and almost 1,000 fighters. For once he ordered the aircraft to attack the centre of the city along the lines first suggested in Operation Thunderclap, despite Doolittle's unhappiness about the deliberate targeting of civilian areas. On the operational directive Spaatz scrawled 'Beat 'em up!' (though much later he chose to remember the raid as just another military target). The toll was high for an American raid, indeed the highest German death toll from any of the raids on the capital. An estimated 2,890 were killed and 120,000 rendered temporarily homeless. A second heavy raid on Berlin with 1,135 bombers was made on 26 February.[355] On 6 February Chemnitz was also hit, by 474 American bombers; on 14–15 February a second attack was made by Bomber Command with 499 Lancasters, though cloud obscured the city and most bombs fell wide of it; a further raid was made by the Eighth Air Force on 2 March. Seen from this perspective, it is evident that the raid on Dresden was made as part of a series of agreed attacks on the cities of eastern Germany. All of these raids, and not just the attack on Dresden, were undertaken in the full knowledge that these were cities filled with civilian refugees from further east, whose destruction was likely to cause not just dislocation but high casualties as well.

The Dresden raid on 13–14 February 1945 was carried out by Bomber Command in two successive waves with 796 Lancasters, carrying 2,646 tons of bombs (including 1,181 tons of incendiaries). Light defences resulted first from the transfer of anti-aircraft artillery to the

Eastern Front, and second from a successful diversionary raid which attracted the nearby night-fighters. The first wave was not very effective, but the follow-up raid with the bulk of the Lancaster force in clear conditions achieved an exceptional level of concentration. Low humidity and dry, cold weather, combined with a very large number of small fires quickly started, proved ideal conditions for the generation of another firestorm. The flames consumed 15 square miles of the city, an area that exceeded the damage at Hamburg. Recent estimates from a historical commission in Dresden have confirmed that the original figure suggested by the police president of Dresden in March 1945 of approximately 25,000 dead is the best available estimate. Out of 220,000 homes, 75,000 were destroyed.[356] The firestorm, like the Hamburg conflagration, left bodies mummified or reduced to ash, making the final count difficult. A further 1,858 skeletons were unearthed when the city was slowly rebuilt after 1945. The aiming point in this, as in all area attacks, was the historic city centre, which was entirely burnt out. The next day the Eighth Air Force carried out its first raid on the marshalling yards of the city, but the smoke from the previous night's bombing obscured the target and the 700 tons of bombs destroyed more of Dresden's hapless streets. In the afternoon 210 B-17s, unable to bomb their primary oil target, blind-bombed the city with another 461 tons. In all, almost 4,000 tons of bombs were dropped on a single target in less than 24 hours.

Unlike any of the other major raids in the last months of war, the Dresden attack had immediate repercussions on Allied opinion. Two days after the raid an RAF officer at SHAEF headquarters gave a news conference in which he talked about bombing cities deliberately to cause panic and destroy morale. An Associated Press correspondent, Howard Cowan, filed a report successfully past the SHAEF censor, and by 18 February the American press was full of the news that the Allies had at last decided 'to adopt deliberate terror bombing'. Arnold was compelled to run a campaign to reassure the American public that Dresden had been attacked, like Chemnitz, as a major communications centre, entirely consistent with American bombing policy.[357] It was hard to stifle the debate. Goebbels released to the neutral press news that 250,000 people had been killed in Dresden (by the judicious addition of an additional zero to the provisional casualty estimate). In Britain and America news of the death toll was soon public knowledge. The Bombing Restrictions Committee in London publicized the figure of 250,000 at once and provoked a furious correspondence accusing the committee of acting as the mouthpiece for German propaganda. Air Ministry statements in the Commons dismissed the accusations of terror-bombing by claiming that no one, air marshals or pilots, was trying to work out 'how many women and children they can kill'.[358] But for the first time the real nature of area and blind-bombing attacks came under public scrutiny.

This may explain Churchill's now well-known decision to send a minute to Portal on 28 March 1945 protesting that the policy of bombing 'for the sake of increasing the terror, though under other pretexts, should be reviewed'. He asked Portal to focus on oil and transport, as the strategic directives had intended, instead of 'mere acts of terror and wanton destruction'. Harris was told of the document by Bottomley, who suggested that Churchill might have been worried about the shortage of German building materials, but Harris was outraged. He replied that city-bombing had always been strategically justified because it would shorten the war and save the lives of Allied soldiers, an assertion difficult to reconcile with the five long years of British bombing. Portal persuaded Churchill to moderate his original minute for the chiefs of staff, which he did, but area bombing's days were now numbered. Churchill did not indicate his motives, and the entire episode of Dresden is missing from his history of the Second World War. It is possible that the publicity surrounding bombing as a result of Dresden worried Churchill as he contemplated a general election at some point in the next few months; it probably reflected his persistent ambivalence about bombing ever since its first disappointments in 1940 and 1941; or it may be that he finally realized, as Allied forces now poured into the broken cities of the Ruhr, just what bombing had done (on 26 March he lunched on the banks of the Rhine with General Montgomery) and was affected by its enormity, as he had been when he wandered through British cities during the Blitz. Harris much later in life dismissed the episode as unimportant; he told his biographer that Churchill's attitude to him did not alter 'in any perceivable way' between 1942 and 1945. But the rift was important enough to be suppressed until its publication in the official history in 1961.[359]

Whatever Churchill's misgivings, British city-bombing continued in ways that were evidently punitive in nature and excessive in scale. Just 10 days after Dresden, Bomber Command attacked the small town of Pforzheim. The marking worked well and the bombers dropped their loads from just 8,000 feet (instead of 18,000–20,000 feet on raids against defended targets); the subsequent conflagration consumed 83 per cent of the city area, until then the worst in any raid of the war, and killed an estimated 17,600 people, though the death toll, the third highest in the European bombing war, has never had the publicity accorded to Dresden. The ruins of Cologne, hit by more than 250 wartime raids, were raked over again by a massive Bomber Command attack on 2 March by over 700 Lancasters, just four days before it was occupied by American forces. Essen suffered the same fate on 11 March, with a macabre finale by over 1,000 bombers dropping 4,661 tons on a desolate landscape only hours before it fell to the advancing army. On 24 March Bomber Command headquarters portentously announced that, thanks to bombing, the 'Battle of the Ruhr', then in its last furious days of ground combat, 'is already over – and Germany has lost it'.[360] On 16-17 March, 1,127 tons of bombs were dropped on the small medieval city of Würzburg, killing between 4,000 and 5,000 people and destroying 89 per cent of the city, a wartime record. Hildesheim was half destroyed on 22 March (the town centre 'should make a good fire', the crews were told).[361] The small city of Paderborn was destroyed on 27 March, and half of Plauen on 10-11 April. The final catalogue of area attacks could not be restrained even by Churchill. On 4 April Portal, spurred perhaps by Churchill's minute, had notified the chiefs of staff that area attacks on industrial districts for the sake of destruction would now cease. When Harris destroyed Potsdam in a devastating raid on 14-15 April, Churchill wrote angrily to Sinclair 'What was the point of going and blowing down Potsdam?' Portal replied a day later assuring the prime minister that Harris had already been told to discontinue industrial area attacks.[362] The directive sent to Harris on 16 April for the first time since February 1942 no longer contained industrial areas or morale as dedicated objectives.[363]

The American air forces wound down operations in April 1945. Much of the bombing since the February attacks was tactical in nature, directed at almost any target that could be deemed to be an element of German resistance. Operation Clarion was carried out with mixed success against a range of smaller communications targets. On 5 April all objectives were defined henceforth as tactical, but American bombing of the shrinking German area reached a climax, dropping 46,628 tons in 19 days of raiding, almost the same weight dropped during the German Blitz, but in just three weeks. The last raid by the Eighth Air Force was made on 25 April against the Skoda works at Pilsen; the last by the Fifteenth was on 26 April against the Austrian city of Klagenfurt.[364] Spaatz attended the surrender ceremony in Berlin on 8 May as the senior air commander in Europe. The Soviet delegation, however, refused to allow him to sign as the equal of Marshal Zhukov, the conqueror of Berlin, and he had to add his name underneath as a witness.[365]

Spaatz already knew that the Eighth Air Force was destined to go to the Pacific under his command to help complete the defeat of Japan. British bombers were also expected to contribute, and preparations were already in hand to undertake operations against Japanese cities that had already been reduced to ash in a series of extensive incendiary attacks carried out by the former Eighth Air Force divisional commander, Curtis LeMay. RE8 produced a report on 25 May 1945, two weeks after the German surrender, on 'Area Attack Against Japan', recommending that since everything easily combustible had already been burned down, Bomber Command should use 4,000-lb blast bombs to destroy any urban areas or industrial targets still standing. From previous analysis carried out on the vulnerability of Japanese housing, it was calculated that each bomb would destroy more than 10 built-up acres, whereas in Germany the figure had been only 1.5.[366] The air war in Europe was over, but Japan was soon to profit from its grim lessons.

SURVEYING THE WRECKAGE: 1945

In August 1944 Spaatz had asked his air force commanders to speed up the defeat and surrender of Germany so that a special committee could review what bombing had achieved in Europe in order to apply their conclusions to the war against Japan.[367] The idea of undertaking a serious scientific survey of the bombing campaign had first been aired in the spring of 1944 and was enthusiastically supported by Spaatz, who approached Arnold and Lovett on the subject in April. Arnold wanted an independent assessment of the question, 'Was strategic bombing as good as we thought it was?', and with Lovett's strong support the air force put together a plan which they presented to the president in September. Roosevelt approved the project and asked the Secretary of War, Henry Stimson, to establish the new office. Arnold chose a businessman, Franklin D'Olier, President of the Prudential Life Assurance Company, to head a board of professional economists, academics and analysts, and on 3 November Stimson formally set up the United States Strategic Bombing Survey (USSBS), based in London; a forward base was set up after the end of the war in the resort town of Bad Nauheim, with branches in other German cities. Approval was given to enlist 300 civilians and 850 officers and men from the armed forces.[368] Their task was to produce comprehensive reports not only on the results of American bombing but also on the RAF offensive. The survey began its operations before the end of the war, as territory was gradually liberated from German occupation.

The RAF also began to plan for a possible survey in the spring of 1944. The British side assumed that they would collaborate with the Americans, and on 10 August 1944 the chiefs of staff authorized the Air Ministry to prepare an inter-Allied survey organization. Arnold was solidly opposed to any joint venture, though it did not stop the USSBS commenting at length on British bombing. By the time Sinclair finally proposed a survey to Churchill in December 1944, it was to be a British project. Churchill brusquely dismissed the idea of what was now called the British Bombing Research Mission, partly because of the assumption that it would take at least 18 months to report – and hence be of no use in the war against Japan – but also because he deprecated tying up 'the use of manpower and brainpower on this scale'.[369] Instead of the large staff envisaged by the Ministry, Churchill recommended a limited group of 20–30 people. His intervention invited months of bureaucratic wrangling over who should take part and at what cost, until Portal finally lost patience, abandoned the idea of the Mission, and recruited a small unit already established at SHAEF, the Bombing Analysis Unit, as the core of a British Bombing Survey Unit (BBSU). The new organization was formally launched on 13 June 1945, months after the American survey had begun its work.[370] The Unit was to be run by an air force officer, Air Commodore Claude Pelly, and the SHAEF target adviser, Solly Zuckerman, assisted by staff from the RE8 division of the Ministry of Home Security, which was to be closed down when the war ended.[371] Both men were committed enthusiasts of the attack on communications, and their work and the subsequent reports reflected their bias. Their terms of reference were to examine the effects of bombing on German fighting capacity, the effectiveness of German defences and the accuracy of assessments of damage.[372] Already hostage to the small size and limited resources of the new Unit, the BBSU became a vehicle for Zuckerman to argue his transport case at in contrast to the disinterested analysis sought by the American Air Force. Much of the work of the BBSU was reliant on American research and expertise, a reflection of the rapid shift in the balance of power between the two air forces.

The process of collecting files and statistics and interrogating senior German personnel began at once. By the end of May a great many of the key figures had already been interrogated, including Göring, whose transcripts reveal an almost boyish desire to share his knowledge of the German Air Force with the victors. The provisional conclusions among the cohort of German airmen, engineers and ministerial staff subject to interrogation were almost unanimous. A British intelligence assessment, 'Factors in Germany's Defeat', produced by 17 May, included an interrogation with Adolf Galland, who ranked the offensive against transport, then oil, then the air force as the most decisive.[373] In mid-June a full report of interrogation extracts was produced by the director of American Air Force Intelligence at SHAEF, George McDonald. They also showed that the three critical targets were considered to be oil facilities ('The general opinion of the German leaders is that the attack on synthetic oil was the decisive factor'), communications ('brought about the final disruption of the German war effort'), and the German Air Force – achieved through attacks on aircraft production, airfields and combat attrition.[374] Göring thought the collapse of oil supply to be the single most critical factor – 'without fuel, nobody can conduct a war' – while Albert Speer, Hitler's Minister for Armaments and War Production, ranked communications at the top of the list of critical targets. Erhard Milch, Göring's deputy at the Air Ministry, ranked 'synthetic oil plants and railway communications' together.[375] On area bombing the German judgement was largely negative. It did not 'cause the collapse of the German people' and was regarded, according to McDonald, as 'the least important of the major target complexes'. When Göring was asked in one of his first interrogations on 10 May whether precision or area bombing was more effective in Germany's defeat, he replied: 'The precision bombing, because it was decisive. Destroyed cities could be evacuated but destroyed industry was difficult to replace.'[376] In a USSBS interview on 24 May with Karl Koller, the last German Air Force chief of staff, Koller claimed, not altogether plausibly, that without precision attacks 'Germany would have won the war'. He confirmed that oil and transport facilities were fatal targets for Germany.[377]

In general, Allied assessments reached the same conclusion. The USSBS produced over 200 detailed reports on every aspect of the bombing war, but the Over-all Report reflected the views of those interrogated. The Survey board had an interest in arguing that in the Western theatre air power was decisive, thanks chiefly to the air victory achieved over Germany in the spring and summer of 1944, 'which made devastating

THE COMBINED BOMBER OFFENSIVE: GERMANY 1943-5

attack on [the German] economy possible'. The report highlighted the relative failure of area attacks, which 'had little effect on production', while singling out oil and communications as critical. The attack on Ruhr steel in late 1944 was also added as a key factor, but the choice of this period rather than Harris's 'Battle of the Ruhr' in 1943 added weight to the implication that it was American bombing that had been decisive. The treatment of city attacks (four pages out of 109) minimized their impact on economic output. Statistics were presented which showed that city attacks, overwhelmingly by the RAF, cost only around 2.7 per cent of German economic potential in the target areas. It was calculated that the combined offensive cost 2.5 per cent of potential German output in 1942, 9 per cent in 1943 and 17 per cent in 1944 (figures that were roughly consistent with the claim that 5 per cent of British output was lost during the lighter Blitz). Since area bombing in 1944 experienced diminishing returns, ton for ton, by dropping on previously destroyed areas, the implication again was that most of the production loss was due to American bombing of selected target systems.[378]

Perhaps more surprisingly, this was the conclusion also arrived at by the BBSU when its main report was finally completed in draft in June 1946, almost a year after the USSBS. There were months of delay in arguments with the senior commanders who had been responsible for the offensive, except Harris, whose views were not canvassed. Unlike the USSBS reports, which were easily available, the BBSU final survey and subsidiary reports were given only a limited circulation. The final report was critical of almost all phases of Bomber Command's activities except the final phase against oil and communications targets. A good deal of the report was devoted to demonstrating that the final industrial and military crisis in Germany was a result of the disintegration of rail and water traffic: 'Enough has been said to show that the collapse of the German transport system . . . was the fundamental and main reason for the contemporaneous collapse of German war industry.'[379] This fitted with Zuckerman's own prejudices. Even the assessment of oil supply, which the report regarded as critically disabling, concluded that the offensive against transport was responsible for preventing the recovery of Germany's oil position.[380] The judgement of the report on area bombing of German cities was even more damning than the USSBS. Using methods pioneered earlier by the RE8 department, Zuckerman's team calculated on the basis of 21 heavily bombed industrial cities that area bombing reduced potential war production by 0.5 per cent in 1942,

3.2 per cent in the first six months of 1943, 6.9 per cent in the second six months of 1943, and then approximately 1 per cent throughout 1944, when bombing again brought diminishing returns and area bombing was only one of the factors affecting output. The figures were lower than the USSBS estimates (which had been speculative extrapolations) because they were based on careful research across a range of cities and because they measured potential loss against a rising trend of output. In all 21 cities studied, war production expanded faster than it had done in a control cohort of 14 cities not subject to attack.[381]

Damning though this indictment was, and partial though Zuckerman's position appeared to be, it fitted not only with the interrogation evidence but with the views among Air Ministry officials and RAF commanders in the two years after the war when hard thinking had to be done about what had been achieved by Bomber Command, rather than the Combined Offensive as a whole. Sydney Bufton, once an advocate of incendiary attacks on cities, produced a long critical assessment of area bombing in January 1945, in which he admitted the failure at Hamburg in 1943 as an example of misplaced confidence in the economic or morale effects of heavy urban destruction.[382] Norman Bottomley, Portal's deputy for the last three years of the war, and Harris's successor as commander-in-chief at Bomber Command, contributed an assessment of British bombing at a workshop organized by Tedder, now chief of staff, in August 1947 under the codename 'Exercise Thunderbolt'. The effect of area attack, he concluded, was 'great but never critical', nor was enemy morale ever 'critically undermined', a fact he blamed on poor intelligence. 'Offensive against oil and transportation proved most effective,' he wrote, but only after the achievement of the vital precondition of air superiority.[383] A lecture given in 1946 by one of the RAF officers on the British survey highlighted air force attrition, oil and transport again, but argued that 'little worthwhile' was achieved by area attacks before 1943, and thereafter the resistance of the German population and the reserve capacity of German industry made them 'resilient to area attack'.[384] Given the uniformity of opinion on both the German and Allied side, the one based on experience, the other on extensive research, it is surprising that the effects of bombing have occasioned so much debate ever since. The proximate causes – defeating the German Air Force and emasculating oil supply and transport – are unlikely to be undermined by further research.

The statistics nevertheless require some explanation about why the overall impact of bombing for much of the war period should have been so much lower than expectations. At its simplest level, as Henry Tizard put it after the war, 'You can't destroy an economy.'[385] American economists drafted in to advise the United States war effort in Europe were critical of the idea that bombing either areas or specific industries would of itself produce cumulative damage. The Hungarian émigré economist, Nicholas Kaldor, a member of the USSBS team, argued that the critical factors in choosing economic targets were the degree of 'cushion', the degree of 'depth' and the degree of 'vulnerability'. The first was governed by the existing elasticity of the economy in terms of finding additional or substitute resources for those lost to bombing; the second measured the extent to which a particular product or resource was close to actual military use, since the further back in the production chain, the longer the time before bombing would affect military performance; the third was governed by the extent to which concentrated, and relatively inflexible, capital industries could be effectively destroyed from the air.[386] Kaldor and his economist colleagues argued that for most of the war period Germany had a large cushion of resources of capital stock, labour and raw materials that could be allocated to sustaining war production. His conclusion was based partly on the assumption, now generally regarded by historians as invalid, that Hitler did not order full-scale mobilization until 1944. The degree of allocation of productive resources to war purposes was in fact high from the start of the war, but many of the economies of scale characteristic of large-scale industrial production became effective only by 1942-3, while the unanticipated length of the campaign against the Soviet Union distorted war production plans at a critical juncture in 1941-2.[387]

Yet Kaldor was not wrong to argue that a cushion existed. The index of armaments output showed that German production increased threefold between 1941 and 1944, despite all the bombing; some individual categories of weapon expanded more than this, fighter aircraft by a factor of 13, tanks by a factor of five, heavy guns by a factor of four.[388] As a result of the conquest of much of Continental Europe, Germany had access to large resources beyond her borders. Although this also involved economic costs to Germany, occupation meant that over 119 billion marks were contributed to Germany's war budget, one-quarter of all the costs of the armed forces; 7.9 million forced workers and prisoners of war were compelled to work in Germany, while an estimated 20 million more worked on orders for the German war effort in the occupied zones.[389] Moreover, German technical and organizational ingenuity made it possible to find substitute products or productive capacity even for 'bottleneck' industries like ball-bearings, where, as Kaldor argued, the target had 'run away' by the time the Allies attacked it again in 1944.[390] The German economy, wrote the USSBS economist J. K. Galbraith in an early evaluation, was 'expanding and resilient, not static and brittle'.[391]

For most of the Allied bombing offensive these factors were either insufficiently known or not understood and bombing, as a result, was relatively ineffective. Only in 1944, with the American decision to focus on enemy air power, oil and transport were three targets chosen which fortuitously matched Kaldor's calculation. The attack on the German aircraft assembly industry, as part of the assault against enemy air power, was the least successful because of the substantial cushion that existed in dispersing the final stages of production; all German leaders claimed, however, that repeated attacks on aero-engine production would have been critical. Oil and transport facilities, on the other hand, had poor cushioning possibilities once heavy attacks began, were highly vulnerable to sustained attack, and had a positive 'depth' factor because both were needed almost immediately by the armed forces and by industry to sustain fighting capability and output. The campaign against the German Air Force was indeed a precondition for the success of the campaigns against oil and transport , and was a direct result of the changing tactics of day-bombing and the high priority given by Spaatz to suppressing German air power as fully as possible. When German oil installations and air force operations both threatened a limited revival in late 1944, Spaatz shifted once again to priority oil and counter-force attacks. It is difficult not to argue that the United States air forces had a surer strategic grasp and a clearer set of strategic objectives than did Bomber Command. Counter-force operations and the search for target systems that would unhinge the enemy's military efforts were central elements in American wartime air doctrine. The RAF, by contrast, thought of air power more as a form of blockade, and was never enthusiastic about counter-force operations or attacks on transport, though both had been adopted in the Mediterranean campaign. The defeat of the German Air Force over Germany and the massive dislocation of German transport were primarily American achievements.

Area bombing was nevertheless, despite its critics, not entirely without impact on the German war effort. The random and scattered nature of much of the city-bombing campaign had evident opportunity costs for the German war effort, in addition to the effects of substantial civilian casualties and damage to housing. Consumer goods production had to be increased in 1943, against the trend of total war mobilization, to meet the needs of bombed-out families. The night-bombing interrupted utility services, hit shops and occasionally factories, necessitating the allocation of additional resources of manpower to cope. There is no way in which these kind of costs can be computed, any more than there was in Britain as a result of the Blitz. The real question concerns assessment of the damage done to the German industrial working class, since this was the whole rationale behind the campaign. It has never proved possible to calculate the number of workers killed, rather than non-workers (elderly, women with families, children, etc.), but some sense of the limitations of any such assessment can be found in the death statistics in Hamburg, where on the night of the firestorm in 1943 which killed over 18,000 people, only 280 were killed in the factory district, away from the main area of bombing.[392] Workers were not always the most likely victims, but even if the estimated total of 350,000 German dead from bombing were all workers, that would still have represented only 1.6 per cent of the German industrial and rural workforce, some of whom would have been killed by American daytime bombs rather than by the RAF.

The other argument for area bombing was the high level of absenteeism it would induce, though the British evidence, on which the strategy was based, was scarcely convincing. German records show that absenteeism as a direct result of bombing made up 4.5 per cent of hours lost at the height of the bombing in 1944; an additional 10.8 per cent of hours were lost due to illness or leave, though these may well have been a response to circumstances caused by bombing. Figures of hours lost due to bombing were higher in targeted industries (7.9 per cent in shipbuilding, 10.6 per cent in vehicle production), but much of this loss was the result of precise attacks by day rather than by Bomber Command at night.[393] The state of 'morale' among the German population, which was also a stated objective, will be examined in greater detail in Chapter 7.

The emphasis that has usually been put on the economic impact of bombing, in part a result of the very full economic data supplied by the bombing surveys, has had the effect of avoiding the more important question about the effect of bombing on the German military effort. Here the impact is more evident, though it would be prudent not to take at face value the USSBS claim that bombing was decisive. The air war over Germany was, in Albert Speer's phrase, 'the greatest lost battle'.[394] But it was a battle that was won alongside the Allied armies and navies; no particular service was decisive on its own. At the end of the war,

Bufton observed that the whole purpose of the bombing offensive in 1944 'has been designed to weaken the German war machine as a whole so that it could not resist successfully when the Allied Armies made their final attack'.[395] One of the principal criticisms of the BBSU report made by Portal (now Lord Portal of Hungerford) was the failure of its authors to grasp that 'from 1941 onwards, if not before, the object of the bomber offensive from the U.K. was to weaken Germany to such an extent that an invasion of the Continent would succeed'.[396] The problem with such claims is to be able to find a way to calculate the extent to which bombing really did inhibit German fighting power. As in the British case, the critical factor was the distorting effect that bombing had on German strategy once it became necessary to divert large resources to the military combat against the air offensive. Bombing, as Speer recognized, really did come to constitute a 'Second Front' by 1943, preventing German military leaders from using air power effectively at the fighting front as they had done in all the campaigns from 1939 to 1941. Failure in Russia, in the Mediterranean theatre and against the Allied invasion of France owed a great deal to the fact that German fighter aircraft, guns, ammunition and radar equipment were tied up in the Reich. This had not necessarily been the Allied intention, which focused on unhinging the domestic war effort, but it undoubtedly contributed to the military outcome at the fighting fronts throughout the last three years of war and compensated for whatever weaknesses might have existed in Allied combat experience or skills.

There are two ways in which the effects of bombing on Germany's military effort can be directly measured. The Combined Offensive distorted German military strategy by imposing a heavy cost in active and passive anti-aircraft defence. One of the keys to Germany's early battlefield successes was the employment of fighters, fighter-bombers and medium bombers in support of ground forces. The Allied bombing forced the German leadership to switch aircraft back to the defence of the Reich and to reduce sharply the proportion of output devoted to front-line bombers and fighter-bombers, as the following table demonstrates (see Table 6.6). This had the immediate effect of limiting severely the offensive air power available on the battlefield.

In early 1943, 59 per cent of German fighters were in the western theatre facing the bombing; in January 1944, 68 per cent; by October 1944, 81 per cent. At the beginning of 1944 German aircraft available on the Soviet front were little more than a year before, in the Mediterranean theatre they were 40 per cent fewer, but in defence of Germany

Table 6.6: German Fighter and Bomber Strength and
Production, 1943-4

Date	Fighter Output	Bomber Output	Fighter Strength	Bomber Strength
Mar 1943	962	757	2,028	1,522
June 1943	1,134	710	2,403	1,663
Sept 1943	1,072	678	2,220	1,080
Dec 1943	1,555*	522*	2,172	1,604
Mar 1944	1,638	605	2,261	1,331
June 1944	2,449	703	2,301	1,089
Sept 1944	3,375	428	3,002	929
Dec 1944	2,630	262	3,516	528

* Figures for January 1944.
Source: Calculated from Webster, Frankland, *Strategic Air Offensive*, vol 4, 494-5, 501-2.

the number increased by 82 per cent. The same was true for the distribution of anti-aircraft guns: in summer 1944 there were 2,172 batteries of light and heavy anti-aircraft artillery on the home front, but only 443 batteries in the Mediterranean theatre, and 301 on the whole of the Eastern Front.[397] This situation left German armies denuded of air protection at a critical juncture of the ground war on the eastern and Mediterranean fronts, while the diversion to the defence of Germany created just the conditions the American air forces needed to be able to overcome the German Air Force in the 'Battle of Germany', perhaps the single most significant military achievement of the offensive.

For the German war effort the costs of all forms of air defence by 1943-4 were substantial in terms of both manpower and equipment. The anti-aircraft service absorbed 255,000 personnel in 1940, but 889,000 at its peak in 1944; the 14,400 heavy and 42,000 light guns by 1944 required production of 4,000 new guns a month; anti-aircraft units consumed one-fifth of all ammunition, half the production of the electronics industry and one-third of all optical equipment.[398] The passive civil defence personnel numbered around 900,000 (supported by 15 million members of the Air Protection League); the numbers involved in post-raid clearance fluctuated over time, but they totalled by 1944 in the hundreds of thousands. Civil defence and medical equipment had to be maintained in the face of wide losses, hospitals had to be built and repaired, and fire services expanded. Few of those involved would have been potential soldiers, but many would have been potential war-workers, if they were not already combining civil defence activities with paid work. This does not mean that civilians were *ipso facto* legitimate targets, but as in the British case, it shows that bombing compelled German resources to be allocated in ways that directly affected German military potential at the fighting front and the pattern of strategic choices. Without bombing, the German war effort would have been as free to optimize the use of resources and conduct the military war effort as was the United States. The military consequences of the bombing campaign were clearly more important than the economic, psychological or political ones.

This still begs the question of what it meant for the Allies. J. K. Galbraith, one of the USSBS team, later wrote in his memoirs that the man-hours, aircraft and bombs 'had cost the American economy far more in output than they had cost Germany'.[399] Both air forces were sensitive to this charge and calculated themselves what proportion of the national effort could be attributed to the bombing. In the British case the proportion was calculated to be 7 per cent of all man-hour equivalents, in the American case an estimated 12 per cent of wartime expenditure, both figures that did not distort exceptionally the structure of either war effort, unless account is taken of just how wasteful much of the bombing was.[400] Moreover, these were positive choices made about the allocation of resources, where in the German case the choice was involuntary, an addition to the other choices made about the distribution of strategic resources. Nevertheless the cost in manpower and aircraft lost in combat was substantial. In RAF Bomber Command, 47,268 were killed in action (or died as prisoners of war) and 8,195 in accidents. According to Harris, an estimated 135,000 flew in combat with Bomber Command, a loss rate of 41 per cent. Total RAF dead during the war from all causes totalled 101,223, so that Bomber Command deaths amounted to 54.7 per cent of all RAF losses.[401] Of these, the largest non-British contingent was composed of Canadians, 9,919 of whom died in Bomber Command.[402] Total wastage of Bomber Command aircraft from all causes was 16,454.[403] American heavy-bomber losses against Germany totalled 10,152 between 1942 and 1945, and the total killed in all theatres against Germany was 30,099.[404]

Balancing the Allied losses against the German figures for aircraft and personnel says little about the final outcome. The costs were modest compared with the 9 million Soviet military dead and 5 million German dead, reflecting the priority of both Western Allies to avoid repeating the losses of the Great War for publics likely to be less tolerant of the escalating human cost to themselves than were populations under dictatorship. For Britain and the United States, the political advantages of preferring bombing to other forms of combat were to be found in the desire to limit the cost to the home population while maximizing the use of advanced technology and large manufacturing capacity to impose insupportable costs on the population, economy and military structure of the enemy. Bombing could be used to maintain domestic morale and to exert leverage on the enemy in ways which were rendered easily visible in the democratic media. That the campaign could have been conducted differently, at lower cost (to both sides) and with greater efficacy, is not in doubt, but it is evident from the historical record why these opportunities, strategic and technical, were missed or ignored or misunderstood, or incompetently attempted. War is always easier to fight looking backwards.

7

The Logic of Total War: German Society under the Bombs

After the war in Europe ended in May 1945, many of those who had helped direct the bombing of Germany were curious to see the destruction for themselves. General Spaatz flew to Augsburg in Bavaria on 10 May to meet Hermann Göring, who had just been captured by American troops. The American official historian, Bruce Hopper, was with Spaatz and recorded the two-hour interrogation in a small office in the Augsburg Riding School in which Göring reflected on why his air force had failed to halt the bombing. It was, Hopper wrote, a historic meeting of the 'Homeric Chiefs of the Air War'. All around was evidence of the destruction of the national economic and civil life of a great nation, doomed, so he thought, to be set back by a century as a result. 'That,' he added, 'has never happened before in history.'[1]

Other senior American airmen followed suit. General Anderson flew around the captured areas of western Germany, landing where he could and unloading a jeep to get a better look at the ruins. The diary record of his trip – 'Jeeping the Targets in a Country that Was' – recorded a shocking catalogue of destruction: 'Mainz, a shimmering shell . . . Darmstadt, a shambles . . . Frankfurt. Largely roofless. Looks like Pompeii magnified . . . Ludwigshafen. Frightful, fantastic spectacle.' Anderson flew across the Ruhr-Rhineland industrial basin where the language he used to describe the spectacle was stretched to extremes: 'Dusseldorf, not even a ghost . . . all ruins begin to look alike . . . Cologne, indescribable. One gets a feeling of horror: nothing, nothing is left.' His plane took him back to France five days later. His diarist breathed a sigh of relief, 'escape from Götterdamerung [sic] back to civilization'.[2] Sydney Bufton went to look at Hamburg and was 'greatly impressed', but shocked at the sight of people living in wrecked buildings 'into which I would not care to venture'.[3] Around the same time Solly Zuckerman, the British government scientist and champion of the Transportation Plan, visited the same Ruhr cities where he witnessed a similar desolate landscape: 'so much destruction one longed for open fields and to get away from the trail of our bombs'. Here and there he saw women sweeping the pavement in front of houses that were no more than neat piles of rubble; in the eradicated city of Essen he observed people who looked neat and tidy and in no obvious sense dejected. He was puzzled by this behaviour, so at odds with what he had expected. 'How the German civilians stuck the bombardments,' he wrote a few days later, 'is a mystery.'[4]

The survival of German society under the bombs has generally attracted less attention than explanations of British survival during the Blitz. Yet the German population of the major cities had to endure more than four years of increasingly heavy bombardment, fighting a war that was evidently lost long before its end. Despite Germany's growing debilitation, industrial production, food supply and welfare were all maintained until the very last weeks when Allied armies were on German soil and Allied bombers were pounding ruins into ruins. The capacity of the state and the National Socialist Party to absorb this level of punishment and manage its consequences demonstrated some remarkable strengths in the system, as well as its harsher characteristics. The question asked by the Allies before 1945 was typically 'When will Germany crack?' For the historian the issue needs to be approached the other way round. As for Zuckerman, the real issue is how German civilian life, trapped between remorseless bombardment and a suicidal dictatorship, adapted to the material and psychological pressures of progressive urban obliteration.

COMMUNITY SELF-PROTECTION

In 1935 the German *Reichsluftschutzbund* (Reich Air Protection League) published a poster featuring a stern-faced Hermann Göring above the slogan 'Air defence fighters have as much responsibility and as much honour as every soldier at the front!' The civil defence structure built up in Germany in the 1930s was from the outset more military in character than its British counterpart. The purpose of preparations for a possible bombing war was not simply to provide adequate protection from gas and bombs but to use air-raid precautions as a form of collective social mobilization. Civil defence was a community obligation which matched the wider claims of the German dictatorship to have created a rearmed and psychologically reinvigorated people after years in the democratic wilderness. By 1939, 15 million Germans had joined the *Luftschutzbund*; by 1942 there were 22 million, almost one-quarter of the population.[5]

The formal civil defence structure in Germany was intentionally military in nature because it was set up and commanded by the German Air Force when the armed forces were reconstituted in March 1935 in defiance of the Versailles Treaty. From 1933 to 1935 air-raid defence was an office in the German Air Ministry, first set up in September 1933 with Göring as minister. In March 1935 it became part of the new air force structure and on 4 July the Air Protection Law was published, defining the responsibilities of the new organization. The Air Protection Department was run by Dr Kurt Knipfer, an air-protection expert previously with the Prussian Ministry of Commerce, who held the office down to 1945, despite numerous changes in the organization of the ministry and the nature of civil defence activity. In 1939 the department was placed under Air Force Inspectorate 13 (Air Protection), but Knipfer was able to avoid too much interference from the military side of the air force, which regarded civil defence as a passive subsidiary to the combat role enjoyed by the rest of the service. With the creation of 12 Regional Air Commands (*Luftgaukommandos*) in 1938, a territorial structure was established for running air-raid protection at local level. The regional commands were responsible for all active and passive air defence in their area, including the air-raid warning service (*Luftschutzwarndienst*), emergency repairs, medical aid, decontamination squads, blackout, camouflage policy and fire protection.[6]

The question of organization was in practice far from straightforward. The Reich Interior Ministry, which had hitherto been responsible for air-raid protection, objected to the changed ownership of civil defence, and retained some responsibilities in areas of public health, civil administration and post-raid organization which survived until well into the war, though without very clear definition.[7] More significant was the claim made by the leader of the SS, Heinrich Himmler, when he was appointed Chief of German Police in June 1936. At local level the responsible leader of air-raid protection was usually the city police president, together with a committee composed of the local heads of the various emergency services. In smaller towns or the countryside the control post could be assumed by the local mayor, or rural officials, but in the threatened urban areas, the regular Order Police assumed responsibility. Himmler claimed that the police, rather than the air force, should run the fire service, provide medical help (in collaboration with the German Red Cross), organize gas decontamination and co-ordinate the emergency rescue services (*Sicherheits- und Hilfsdienst*). Confusion was temporarily set aside by an agreement between Göring's deputy, Erhard Milch, and Himmler in 1938, which confirmed that the Regional Air Commands had overall responsibility for active and passive air defence, but the Order Police would operate the rescue and welfare services once an air raid had taken place. The arguments over responsibility continued into the war as Himmler sought to exploit civil defence as an instrument for internal security as much as civil protec-tion.[8] The emergency services were in July 1942 turned into the Air Protection Police (*Luftschutzpolizei*) to make clear that they served the police authorities, not the air force. Such dualism was characteristic of the institutional competition provoked in the Third Reich by the efforts of the Party and the SS to penetrate or subvert or substitute conven-tional forms of authority.[9]

The creation of a national fire service was a typical example. The fire service was decentralized before 1933, the responsibility of local cities or provinces, with no technical compatibility between the different forces in equipment, hydrants or hose couplings, and dependent on a large number of volunteer auxiliaries. In 1933 the Air Ministry began a programme to encourage manufacturers to standardize fire-service equipment. In Prussia, the largest German province, fire and police ser-vices were tied more closely together and instructions on standardized practices and technical standards introduced; these were confirmed in the 1935 Air Protection Law. In 1936 the Interior Ministry planned to extend the Air Ministry guidelines to other provinces in order to pro-mote national standards. Himmler, however, wanted the fire service under his control as Chief of Police and prepared legislation to create a National Fire Service, run on standard lines defined by the police authorities and including both professional firemen and volunteers. A National Fire Service Law came into force on 23 December 1938, dis-solving all existing fire services and placing the new national organization under the control of the Order Police. Firemen were now to be known as Fire Defence Police (*Feuerschutzpolizei*), the volunteers as police auxiliaries.[10] By 1940 standard and interchangeable equipment was available, including a single model light-alloy hose coupling which could be used for all types of hose, and three standard pump appli-ances.[11] In the end, the contest for jurisdictional control did not inhibit the development of a more effective service to meet the needs of a future air war. German practice was the example used when a national fire service was created in England in 1941.

The German public was largely free from these jurisdictional conflicts. Unlike other European states, the most important aspects of air-raid protection were to be undertaken by the German population on its own behalf. The *Luftschutzbund* very quickly established itself as the national agent for educating, training and supervising the community in every aspect of air-raid protection. By 1937 there were 2,300 local branches with over 400,000 officials and 11 million members. By 1942–3 there were 1.5 million office-holders, 22 million members. They paid just one mark a year in subscription. In return, members attended one of 3,400 air-raid schools, or local courses in first aid, self-protection and firefighting.[12] For potential leaders there were Air Protection Academies to attend. In May 1937 the public's civil defence role was defined in a law on 'Self-Protection'. Three distinct forms of self-help were identified: 'Self-Protection' (*Selbstschutz*); 'Extended Self-Protection' (*Erweiterter Selbstschutz*); and 'Work Protection' (*Werkluftschutz*). Individual householders were expected to create their own 'air-protection community' in each house or apartment block, responsible for creating an air defence room (a cellar, or basement if possible), providing effective escape routes through adjoining walls, and maintaining in good working order a complete set of tools and equipment for post-raid assistance. These generally had to be paid for by the householders but were a statutory requirement; they included rope, a fire hose, ladders, a home first-aid kit, sand buckets, water storage, an axe, a shovel, and armbands for those who were 'lay helpers' or wardens.[13] The intention was to ensure that every citizen assumed responsibility for their own protection, in their own home; if required they would have to help protect the immediate neighbourhood as well. This was an extreme form of decentralization, but at the same time a commitment by every member of the 'people's community' (*Volksgemeinschaft*) to a common defence of the nation. Self-protection was voluntary in only a limited sense, since *Luftschutzbund* officials were supposed to check every household to make sure that blackout material, anti-incendiary equipment and a secure air-protection room were available. Failure to comply with civil defence regulations could involve a fine or imprisonment.

The other forms of self-protection involved sites outside the home. 'Extended Self-Protection' was designed for all those buildings which were unoccupied in the evening or at weekends, including commercial offices, warehouses, museums, theatres, or administrative buildings. The system was not needed until war broke out and took time to establish, but it ensured that empty buildings did not become easy targets when incendiary bombing began. Work air-raid protection was placed in 1937 under the supervision of Reich Group Industry (*Reichsgruppe Industrie*). Each factory or plant had its own air defence unit, usually headed by a manager in charge of an emergency organization. Factories had to provide their own shelters and organize lookout schemes, and each one was linked by telephone with the main police control centre in the city.[14] Again the object was to ensure that a high degree of community commitment would minimize damage and casualties and remove much of the air-protection burden from the public authorities. In the event that a building or workshop was bombed or set on fire, the local self-protection community had to tackle it first, then notify the local officials if it was too difficult to master, only finally receiving intervention from the police and emergency authorities when the incident was too serious. The onus in defending a locality from the effects of a bombing raid lay in the first instance, despite all the claims of the police and the air force, on those who lived and worked there.

The key figure in self-protection was the air-raid warden (*Luftschutzwart*). These were generally volunteers, men or women, most commonly members or officials from the *Luftschutzbund*, responsible for a group of apartment houses or a street. Their function was to ensure that air-raid rooms had been prepared, equipment was up-to-date and available, the blackout was observed, attics and cellars were cleared of waste and rubbish, air supply and escape routes both adequate and behaviour in the shelters orderly. They lacked the power of arrest, but did enjoy the right to compel local people to help with bombing incidents, even while the bombing was still going on.[15] Before the war many of the wardens combined their role with that of local Party 'block leader', responsible for checking on each block of houses or apartments to make sure that Party instructions and propaganda were disseminated and no visible signs of dissent expressed. But by the time war broke out the role was generally divided to make sure that both functions could be performed effectively, adequate civil defence and adequate Party surveillance. With military mobilization in 1939, male wardens had to be replaced by women. Regular appeals were made in the early years of the war for female volunteers; at least 200,000 *Luftschutzbund* officials were women. The air-raid warden was to be chosen for evident qualities of leadership, an obsessive requirement in a system dominated by the

'leadership principle'. The definition of typical leadership qualities produced early in 1942 presented a formidable range of requirements:
'Personal example, involvement of the leader at the site of greatest
danger, superlative capability, firm will, calmness, steadfastness and
confidence in the most difficult situation, trustworthiness, pleasure in
responsibility . . .'.[16] Regular circulars were sent round in the war with
stories of heroic individuals displaying, it is to be supposed, some or all
of these characteristics.[17] This was the front line on the German home
front: ordinary people called upon to perform, if they could, extraordinary acts of heroism.

Nonetheless, the introduction of civil defence measures before the
outbreak of war was far less extensive than the large organization and
popular propaganda of civic mobilization might have suggested. This
was partly a result of geography. Though the object was to involve
the whole population, the Reich was divided into three zones to reflect
the degree of imminent danger from air warfare. Zone I included all the
major industrial cities in Germany, 94 in total, with augmented civil
defences; Zone II covered 201 Air Defence Sites (*Luftschutzorten*) of
lesser importance; and Zone III included small towns and rural areas,
or regions too far distant for existing enemy aircraft to reach.[18] Only
those communities in Zone I were promised state finance to fund civil
defence preparations. In late 1938 the association of municipalities
complained to Göring that a lack of money for Zones II and III made
it difficult either to build public shelters or to provide firefighting equipment, but the Air Ministry remained adamant and local Regional Air
Commands were told to reject applications for less urgent air-raid facilities.[19] Not until November 1941 was the order reversed and funds were
made available for exceptional expenditure in areas still designated
Zone II or III.[20] Air-protection facilities and expenditure were targeted
at the key areas only; the countryside had almost no organization,
though its inhabitants were required to observe the blackout regulations. Only 12 million gas masks were distributed, again on the
assumption that most people would not need them. A further explanation for the slow and uneven spread of air-raid protection lay in the air
force conviction that anti-aircraft fire would be sufficiently concentrated to deter enemy aircraft even if they succeeded in penetrating
Reich territory, a judgement largely shared at first by the wider German
public. For all the fear earlier in the decade that Germany was exposed
to a circle of hostile states capable of bombing the German heartland,

preparation on the home front came later and on a more limited scale than in either Britain or France.

The most obvious deficiency came in the provision of public air-raid shelters and the supply of material to make the air defence room (*Luftschutzraum*) a safe and reliable refuge. The quality of the 'room' varied a great deal, sometimes an extensive cellar under an apartment block, sometimes little more than a small storeroom or a corridor. Most German industrial regions were of recent construction and the communal housing was large in scale and concentrated, though there was usually a basement or cellar. Older housing varied, though the evidence suggests that there were few people in the threatened cities who did not have access to local domestic shelter of some kind. Guidelines were regularly published about the ideal 'room', which had to be gasproof, blastproof, clearly indicated, clear of obstruction, and provided with lighting and seating: 'Everything prepared for the emergency!'[21] In the summer of 1939 the Air Ministry calculated that it would cost 50 *Reichsmark* (RM) per person to provide adequate shelter for the 60 million people who needed it, a total of 3 billion marks for which the money was simply not available.[22] The gap between ideal and reality was difficult to breach and cellars and basements had to be slowly improved over the war years. The same problems existed with public shelters. In late 1939, for example, it was discovered that the shelter programme for schools was well behind schedule, particularly in the areas outside Zone I. Many schools in more remote areas had neither cellar nor basement and had to be provided with trench shelters covered with concrete, or a strengthened ground-floor room, when the materials were available.[23]

The provision of shelter varied from area to area, since there was no common policy, but in 1939–40 the number of places available was far below what would eventually be required. In Hamburg in September 1939 there were just 88 public shelters for 7,000 people; by April 1940, 549 shelters for 51,000 out of a population of 1.7 million. Building work was directed at the 80,000 cellars in the city, of which three-quarters were provided with shoring and blast protection.[24] In the west German town of Münster, likely to be in the path of incoming bombers, there were by April 1940 public shelter places for just 4,550 people, 3.3 per cent of the population. Only by the end of the year was this increased to 20,000, with room for an estimated 40,000 in private air defence rooms.[25] Most public shelters were designed for those who were caught in the street during a raid; the preference was to ensure that people returned if they could to their house shelter in order to carry out their 'self-protection' duties. The one major difference between German practice and other European states was the legal compulsion to seek shelter during a raid, which almost certainly contributed to reducing casualties in the first war years. The wartime version of the Air Protection Law of 1935 carried the legal requirement to seek an air defence room or trench as soon as the alarm sounded, or to ask the nearest warden for help in finding a shelter place. In July 1940, after the first few RAF raids, the *Luftschutzbund* included in its regular bulletin for members a reminder that failing to take shelter was an offence: 'The police have been instructed to take steps against offenders and report them for punishment.'[26] Although it is unlikely that this happened in more than a few of the many cases, and merited little more than a nominal fine, shelter discipline was regarded as a serious question. Shelterers had to observe the simple rules of community, not smoke in the shelter, nor drink alcohol nor bring in animals except dogs for the blind. To ensure that the local wardens or 'self-protection' leaders could monitor the households for which they were responsible, formal notice had to be given of any overnight absence from home and copies of keys for all locked doors deposited with the officials. Once the bombing started in the summer, the rules became a ready instrument, with legal force, to control who would or would not have access in particular shelters.[27]

Rules for the blackout and evacuation also showed less immediate concern with the threat of bombing than had been apparent in Britain before the declaration of war. Blackout preparations in Germany had been insisted upon from the mid-1930s when extensive blackout exercises were held in major cities, though with mixed success. The main law covering the blackout was issued on 23 May 1939, with a subsidiary order on domestic lighting issued on 1 September, the day Germany attacked Poland.[28] All householders had a responsibility to ensure that the blackout was effective; in offices or commercial buildings one designated person was held to be responsible, in multi-storey apartment blocks one person was required to extinguish the lights in the halls and stairwells. In the first months of the war blackout discipline was variable. Building sites and factories showed more light than permitted; street lighting was 60 per cent gas-fired and more difficult to turn off and on than electric lighting, so that in many cities dim lighting remained. Helpful propaganda and advice was liberally supplied to help the population cope with the sudden plunge into darkness. In March 1940 Himmler, as Chief of Police, issued detailed guidelines on blackout behaviour which included walking on pavements no more than two abreast, and avoiding excessive alcohol: 'Drunk pedestrians bring not only themselves, but others into danger.' Blackout infringements brought regular fines of up to 150 RM, but later on householders could also have their electricity supply cut off as a reminder not to leave a light showing.[29]

State-sponsored evacuation against bombing was, by contrast, almost non-existent. In October 1939 Göring announced that there would be no assisted evacuation from the threatened urban areas, though plans could be made to transfer schoolchildren if necessary. Voluntary evacuation was neither prevented nor encouraged. Decisions on evacuation were reserved for Göring himself.[30] The initial wartime movements of population were away from the frontier (Red Zone) opposite France, only loosely connected with the bombing threat. Not until October 1940, more than a year after the start of the war, and six months after the start of British bombing, did the first trainloads of children leave Berlin at Hitler's instigation. They went as part of a scheme authorized in late September 1940, under the direction of the head of the Hitler Youth, Baldur von Schirach, as an extension to the existing programme to send city children for invigorating breaks in the countryside (*Kinderlandverschickung*), first begun in the late nineteenth century. In 1938 alone 875,000 had benefited from the peacetime scheme. Now, to reduce public alarm, the pretence was kept up that what children subjected to regular air-raid alerts needed was an extended rest in rural areas, rather than permanent life in a bomb-free region. The first cities where the programme was introduced were Berlin and Hamburg, followed some months later by cities in the Ruhr. The children, all aged between 10 and 14, flowed out to youth hostels, summer camps and small guest houses, a total of 2,500 destinations with 100,000 places where they stayed for up to six months, unless cold, homesickness or the severe routine of the Hitler Youth sent them home sooner.[31]

The 'phoney war' period in the air war in Germany lasted a shorter time than in Britain. On 10 May 1940 the first bombs fell on the south German city of Freiburg im Breisgau, killing 57 people, including 13 children. The German press deplored the evidence of Allied butchery, but the town had been bombed in error by three German aircraft that had lost their way on a flight to attack the French town of Dijon on the first day of the German offensive. Freiburg was later bombed 25 times by Allied aircraft.[32] It was the following night, on 11 May, that the first British bombs fell on the Rhineland; from then on across the summer months bombs fell on a German urban target almost every night. Since the raids were small and the bombing was scattered, the principal effect was to trigger the alarm system over wide parts of western Germany, compelling the population to seek shelter. In Münster in Westphalia there were 157 alarms in 1940, lasting a total of 295 hours, all but seven of them at night.[33] The onset of bombing did not, however, signal the onset of a front-line mentality. Bombing was geographically restricted and distributed in small packets over villages as well as major cities. German propaganda immediately began to condemn the attacks as simple terror bombing, but this was also the view of the German Air Force which assumed on the basis of the random pattern of the bombs that the British object must be to terrorize the population rather than attack the war economy. This thinking dominated German perception of the Allied offensive for much of the rest of the war. The propaganda apparatus played down the actual effects of RAF raids, but suspicious foreign journalists soon discovered for themselves almost no evidence of damage in Berlin or the Ruhr cities, and what small damage there was quickly repaired or covered by wooden hoarding.[34]

The absence of a clear urban front line fitted oddly with the large organization dedicated to civil defence and the prevailing image of the Third Reich as an embattled 'people's community'. The secret intelligence (SD) reports of the first few raids indicated that the population kept calm, except in places where the air-raid sirens failed to sound.[35] Air-raid discipline proved at first to be shallower than anticipated from the endless training courses and the 4 to 5 million-strong army of trained civilian 'self-protection' helpers. In May 1940 it was observed that out of simple curiosity people stayed out on the street to watch the bombing, or stood at open windows or on balconies. The *Luftschutzbund* circulated warnings in May and July that as soon as searchlights and anti-aircraft gunfire began it was an obligation to seek shelter, even more to ensure that no light was left visible given the planless character of British aircrew who 'threw their bombs wherever they saw a light'.[36] But when the bombing spread to Berlin in late August, the same pattern became evident and sterner warnings had to be issued. In September the president of the *Luftschutzbund*, Lt. General Ludwig von Schröder, announced that anyone who sustained injury while deliberately failing to shelter would not be given any state medical assistance. A propaganda campaign was launched to advertise the air-raid room as the safest place to be in a raid and to highlight the numbers still being killed in the open, but the complaints disappeared in 1941 as the bombing became heavier and more deadly.[37] During the summer and autumn of 1940 the population viewed the war differently from the embattled British; buoyed up by the sense of a historic victory and expecting Britain soon to abandon the war, the bombing did not seem to demand the same sense of battle.

The regular bombing nevertheless forced the German government to accelerate the programme for better protection and to ensure regular welfare. Since the attacks were small and irregular, the costs could be absorbed with relative ease. From the start the government agreed that compensation would be paid for injuries or losses sustained as a result of enemy air action, perhaps unaware of what such a commitment might mean in the long term. After the first raid in mid-May 1940 the Interior Ministry reminded all local authorities that compensation for bomb damage, or loss of livelihood or removal of personal possessions, was a direct charge on the Reich.[38] The question of loss of earnings was more difficult, since it would mean paying workers for doing nothing while they sat in the air-raid shelter, or took time off while their work premises were repaired. Random though British bombing was, the social geography of the raids showed that the key targets were industrial and port cities, and the majority of victims likely to be workers. The air-raid legislation of 1 September 1939 promised payment of 90 per cent of wages lost, but this had not anticipated the long periods of alarm when there were no attacks. One solution was to change the alarm system to ensure that as little time as possible was lost from productive work, and eventually the two-tier system of general alarm, followed by all-clear, was changed in favour of a series of step alarms in which the local civil defence would be notified first, followed by a 'raid possible' siren, then a general alarm. Industries were expected to work through the general alarm until a final six-minute warning was sounded to give workers time to get to the shelters.[39]

In summer 1940 it was decided that the 90 per cent wage compensation should be changed into an obligation to work extra time to make up for lost production or to help in repair and debris clearance after a raid, to make sure that workers were being paid for actual work. But this decision produced many anomalies and provoked working-class resentment, as had other restrictions on pay introduced with the onset of war.[40] Salary-earners, for example, were paid 100 per cent loss of earnings, while in February 1941 the Ministry of Labour agreed that porters and ancillary staff were also entitled to pay during alarms, but could not be expected to make up lost time for non-productive work.

By contrast, it was decided that home-workers were entitled to nothing since they could work extra hours when they chose.[41] The consequence was that some workers were paid compensation for doing nothing whereas others were paid nothing and made to work extra hours. It was evident that the escalating air attacks in 1941 made working-class morale a critical issue. A meeting in October between the Labour Ministry, the giant Labour Front union (representing 26 million workers), the Propaganda Ministry and the Party Chancellery concluded that morale was more important and insisted that the Labour Ministry find ways of improving compensation and assistance for workers faced as a result of bombing with increased travel costs or short-term unemployment; though not before the Labour Ministry representative had argued that workers saved money sitting in the shelters because there was nothing for them to buy there.[42] The issue remained unresolved, since firms were free to interpret themselves whether workers ought to be paid at all for interruption to their work or should earn only by working more. Pressure was applied increasingly by the Party through the local Gau Economic Offices to ensure that the law was not applied at the workers' expense. By late 1943 there had been 19 different pieces of legislation to try to cope with the consequences of work interrupted by bombing.[43]

Anxieties about compensation for German workers and German households were not extended to Germany's Jews. A decree in December 1940 instructed all local labour offices to ensure that no compensation for loss of earnings would be paid to Jewish workers on the grounds that the war 'to a not inconsiderable extent can be traced back to the influence of World Jewry'.[44] A second order on 23 July 1941 excluded German Jews or Jewish-owned businesses from making any claim for damage compensation under the 'War Damage Order'.[45] Efforts were made from early in the RAF campaign to help the bombed out (*Obdachlose*) by housing them in apartments owned by German Jews. In the Rhineland city of Soest the decision was taken in the late autumn of 1940, and although the Interior Ministry highlighted the possible legal problems with doing so, the policy of replacing Jewish householders with 'Aryans' became established by the time of the heavy raids in spring 1942.[46] In Cologne the Jewish occupiers were removed to crude barracks while Jewish houses and apartments were redistributed. The Party Chancellery confirmed in April 1942 that if British raids continued, 'we will pursue this measure completely and clear out all the Jewish homes'.[47] By this stage the preparations were well under way for transporting Germany's Jews to camps in the east and seizing the remaining Jewish housing and assets. Rules published in November 1941 made it possible to sell expropriated Jewish furnishings and possessions to survivors in bomb-damaged cities. Between October 1941 and March 1942, 60,000 German Jews were sent east, most to their deaths, and in the next three months a further 55,000.[48]

The bombing also forced the pace in providing more effective shelter and protection. Because of the poor accuracy of British bombing, many bombs fell in the open countryside or on villages, a result that had not been anticipated when planning air-raid protection. By the summer of 1940 it was evident that the emergency services would have to supply units to help with rescue, bomb disposal and repairs 'even in small, or the smallest localities, and outside them'.[49] Villages were helped by the local police, but the rural population was expected to form 'rural air-protection communities' as well, even in outlying areas with scattered homesteads. The blackout was strictly enforced in rural areas, though villagers could sometimes be the victims of bomb attacks on the many decoy sites set up across western Germany in country districts.[50] For farmers, the Reich Air Protection Law provided a statutory veterinary first-aid chest, one for the first 10 animals, two for more than 20, and three for farms with over 40 horses, cattle or pigs.[51] The destruction of housing, in town and countryside, was relatively small-scale in 1940 and 1941 because the RAF were not yet using incendiaries systematically on a large scale, but the regime was sensitive to the need to show that rehabilitation was an urgent priority. On 14 September 1940 the General Plenipotentiary for Construction, Fritz Todt, published a decree on repair to bomb-damaged housing, which gave it top ranking ahead of the list of urgent war-essential construction projects, as long as the repairs could be carried out quickly and the labour and materials found easily from local contractors. Todt's deputy for construction in Berlin, Albert Speer, promised in December 1940 that all lightly damaged houses (windows, roofs, etc.) would be repaired in 36 hours, and all plasterwork repaired in four days. These were promises not difficult to fulfil as long as the damage remained modest.[52]

The onset of bombing highlighted particularly the inadequate protection offered by the converted air-raid room and the modest amount of public shelter. In Hamburg an emergency programme was started which saw the number of places in public shelters expand from 51,000 in April 1940 to 233,207 a year later; by the time of Operation Gomorrah, the bombing of the city in July 1943, around three-quarters of the cellars had been converted to air-raid rooms.[53] In other cities, schemes were set up to strengthen the air-raid rooms by providing a reinforced ceiling, props and escape routes, but shortages of material and labour made it difficult to complete the work. In Münster around 5,000 cellars were improved between autumn 1940 and spring 1941, but a survey in early 1942 showed that still only 4.7 per cent of the population had rooms that were considered entirely safe in a raid.[54] In Berlin in the autumn of 1940 only one-tenth of the capital's population had air-raid rooms, partly on the assumption that it was relatively safe from long-range bomb attack, which it was not. Following the first raids on the capital in August 1940, Hitler ordered a programme to build between 1,000 and 2,000 bunkers in the capital, each capable of holding 100 people. He told the air-protection authorities that 'damage to property was bearable, but in no case were human losses'. Every house had to have its own air-protection room, if possible with light, heating and somewhere to sleep, and the cost would now be borne by the state.[55] On 10 October Hitler finally published an 'Immediate Programme' empowering the Air Ministry to undertake an extensive programme to ensure that the urban population had access to a proper air-raid room, as well as bunkers and shelters for businesses, schools, museums, galleries and ministries.[56] The cost in labour, cement and iron in an economy already facing rigorous restrictions and priorities proved impossible to meet and in mid-1941 and again in December that year, work on larger bunkers was curtailed where possible in favour of blast-proof trenches and reinforced cellars.[57]

Nevertheless, concrete bunkers were built both above and below ground in the major threatened cities, particularly in the Ruhr-Rhineland. In Cologne a total of at least 58 were built between 1940 and 1942, 15 of them concentrated in the inner city centre.[58] In all, some 76 cities undertook to construct a total of 2,055 bunker shelters between November 1941 and 1943, of which 1,215 were finished by early 1942, though not yet fully equipped. Shortages of material and the competing claims of armaments production, the Atlantic Wall defences (which consumed twice as much concrete as the bunker programme), and the giant concrete pens for submarines, meant that much of the programme remained incomplete by the time the heaviest raids began in 1943.[59] Even this number of new shelters could provide only a fraction of the population with protection. The first wave of building up until summer 1941 provided places for 500,000; a second, smaller wave resulted in places for 740,000 by summer 1943, or only 3.87 per cent of the population in the 76 cities involved. There were in addition converted cellars and 'air-raid rooms' for 11.6 million, though many were scarcely bombproof. For millions of Germans there was no immediate prospect of secure shelter, particularly in the cities ranked in Zone II and III, which became the object of heavy attacks in the last year of the war.[60]

A few weeks before the 'Immediate Programme', Hitler had also ordered the construction of six vast 'Flak-towers' in Berlin. The extraordinary scale of the buildings appealed to his sense of the architecturally gigantic, like the plans for the rebuilding of the capital. Their solid design, modelled on a towered Gothic castle, was deliberately intended to express both grim defiance and grotesque physical power, a blend of function and ideology, 'like a fantastic monstrosity,' one eyewitness wrote, 'from a lost world, or another planet'.[61] They were planned to provide not only enhanced anti-aircraft fire but protection for up to 20,000 people, artworks, museum collections, essential defence services, hospitals and a Gestapo office. Towering above the surrounding Berlin townscape, coated in green paint to make them less visible from the sky, the colossal towers were prestige buildings. Their cost in labour and resources was prodigious, the 'Berlin-Zoo' tower consisting of almost 200,000 tons of concrete, stone and gravel. The first was completed by April 1941, the second by October and the third by spring 1942. Hitler approved two more tower sets to guard the port in Hamburg; one was finished by October 1942, a second just before 'Gomorrah', in July 1943. Between them they could hold 30,000 people. Two more tower pairs were built in Vienna in 1943 and 1944, capable of holding not only the cultural treasures of the city, but at least 40,000 of its inhabitants. The Vienna towers were to be literally monumental; the ornamental marble to cover the exterior walls was quarried in France but in the end could not be shipped because of the Allied invasion of Normandy in June 1944.[62]

The development of effective protection and compensation was a reaction to the onset of British bombing, rather than a result of advanced planning for the possibility. Until well into 1941, while there was still a prospect that Britain would abandon the war, the plans for civil defence might still be regarded as temporary; the war against the Soviet Union made it clear that Hitler had abandoned the prospect of defeating Britain quickly and that the bombing offensive was likely to increase in intensity before German forces were free once again to concentrate on the British enemy. This strategic reorientation made it more important for the German state and the Party to be able to provide sufficient support to prevent bombing from damaging domestic support for the war effort. In 1940 only 950 people had been killed in all the bomb attacks (which suggests that the air-raid cellar offered better protection than the authorities feared). In 1941 the level of civilian casualties and damage to property began steadily to increase. In Münster there were 24 raids between July and December 1940, which killed 8 and wounded 59; just three raids in July 1941 killed 43 and injured 196. In Hamburg 69 attacks in 1940 had resulted in 125 deaths and 567 injured; a further 143 raids up to the time of 'Gomorrah' in July 1943 killed 1,431, injured 4,657, and left 24,000 temporarily homeless.[63] In 1941 an estimated 5,029 were killed and perhaps 12,000 injured in a total of 295 raids across Germany. Small though these statistics are by comparison with the casualties of the Blitz, it represented the first serious loss of civilian life for a population more accustomed to the roll-call of the military dead.[64]

During 1941 the pattern of RAF bombing also changed. From spring onwards bombers carried a higher proportion of incendiaries and began to concentrate them more effectively. Training in fighting incendiaries had been part of routine civil defence education, but now detailed pamphlets were issued on every type of British incendiary device with instructions on how to tackle them, including the recommendation to wear a gas mask. The schedule for 'self-protection' classes was changed so that almost all the practical elements were devoted to fighting fire and extinguishing incendiaries. Training centres had an 'air-protection exercise house' where trainees learned to overcome any anxieties about tackling a real fire by exposure to a controlled blaze.[65] Göring put his name to a list of ten principles to observe when combating incendiaries, under the slogans 'Incendiary bombs must be tackled immediately!' and 'Everyone fights for his own property and goods!'[66] A greater effort was made to get householders to remove clutter and stores from all attic spaces to prevent the rapid spread of fires. Hitler Youth groups and other Party organizations were detailed to carry out house-to-house clearance of all unnecessary stocks and furnishings, while local civil defence authorities were instructed to remove stored grain and foodstuffs from endangered storerooms. Air-raid wardens were authorized to set up small gangs of two or more residents to go out, even before the all-clear, to check on fires and try to get them under control. Anyone who refused to help was liable in the worst cases, according to the Air Ministry, to a spell in a concentration camp. No house was to be left empty and unwatched.[67] In March 1941 Hitler's Supreme Headquarters issued an order to local military commanders to establish an Armed Forces Emergency Service to provide military assistance in cases of major raids where the local civil defence and police units were not sufficient to cope with the scale of the damage or where fires threatened to destroy militarily important stocks or buildings. Armed forces stationed at home were to become an important source of emergency assistance over the following three years.[68]

The impact on popular opinion of the increased bombing is difficult to gauge in a state where the media was centrally controlled and public expressions of anxiety were likely to bring severe reprimand. In the spring of 1941 the authorities began to think about more formal programmes of evacuation from the most bomb-threatened regions, though the preference was for movement to safer suburban areas of the same city, or to the immediate rural hinterland. It was only available for women, children and the elderly, but not for any German Jews, for whom no official provision was allowed.[69] Evacuation remained voluntary and was presented to the population as a welfare measure, run exclusively by the Party through the National Socialist People's Welfare (NSV), another vast Party organization, with 15 million members, mostly volunteers and predominantly female. The first wave of evacuation from Berlin, Hamburg and the Ruhr cities involved only a small fraction, perhaps 10 per cent, of the children and mothers who qualified. Most parents preferred to wait and see what the risks were or were unenthusiastic about handing their children over to Party organizations.[70] The SD Reports for 1941 show a declining concern among the wider public over the air raids, but regular interest in the wider news of the war, particularly the successful campaigns against Yugoslavia and Greece and then against the Soviet Union from June 1941, all of which once again raised the possibility of a rapid end to the conflict, which would make all the effort at air-raid protection suddenly redundant. Bombing nevertheless persisted whatever was happening elsewhere in Europe. In July 1941 von Schröder sent a report to all *Luftschutzbund* officials praising the 'decisive bravery' and 'will to resist' of the German population subjected to bombing. The aim, he continued, was to overturn the 'legend' that the English held the record for steadfastness by demonstrating to the world the inner resolve of the German people.[71]

'GREAT CATASTROPHES': 1942–3

The German home front was suddenly rocked in March 1942 by the first concentrated and heavy incendiary raid on the coastal town of Lübeck. Two-thirds of the 400 tons were firebombs, dropped from only

2,000 feet on the old city centre, consisting of half-timbered houses. Rumours immediately circulated in the surrounding area that 3,000 had been killed and 30,000 rendered homeless (just over 300 died in the raid, the worst casualties so far); reports to Berlin observed an immediate improvement in air defence discipline in other cities.[72] The raid was swiftly followed by a series of devastating incendiary attacks on the port of Rostock, which produced for the first time an outcome classified under the term 'great catastrophe'.

The first attack on Rostock, on 23–24 April, was relatively limited. The *Gauleiter* reported to the Party chancellery that the population was calm and the raid well under the control of Party and state authorities. But three more raids in quick succession imposed more serious dislocation, damaging three-quarters of Rostock's 12,000 buildings. A state of emergency was declared and troops and SA men were brought in from the surrounding area. By the third day 100,000 of the population had been evacuated or had fled into the surrounding countryside. Rumours began to spread that Sweden had suddenly declared war on Germany and bombed Rostock as the first act.[73] When on the fourth day an alarm went off in error in the afternoon, the population began to panic and armed SS men were called in to make sure order could be maintained. Two looters were caught and one condemned to death within a day. Loudspeaker vans toured the area to call for calm while supplies of chocolate and butter (both commodities that had almost disappeared) were handed out from stocks found hoarded in the city. Fifteen military field kitchens were brought in to hand out hot meals, while an emergency supply column with 100 tons of food was sent to the stricken city from the 'catastrophe stores' kept for just such an occasion.[74] By 2 May the population was starting to return to collect goods stacked in the street while groups of artisans were brought in to begin work on reroofing and reglazing damaged buildings to make them habitable again. It was observed that among the 165 dead so far recorded were six Hitler Youth, eight local National Socialist political leaders and three SA men. The regional authorities found little evidence of 'hostile opinion against Party or state'. Their aim was rapidly to recreate 'the normal conditions of daily life in every area'.[75]

Although the authorities in Rostock judged that the civil defence services had coped well with the consequences of the raid, the onset of 'catastrophic air attacks' prompted a fundamental overhaul of the way civil defence and post-raid welfare was organized. The driving force behind the change was the Party hierarchy, which understood that the social and psychological consequences of heavy bombing were likely to have wider ramifications for social cohesion and war-willingness. During 1942 the balance in the air-protection structure swung heavily towards the Party and away from the Air Ministry and the police. The key figure was the Minister for Popular Enlightenment and Propaganda, Joseph Goebbels. In late April Hitler agreed to give him special responsibility as commissar for organizing immediate help measures for those areas where the local authorities could not cope. All local Party *Gaue* (and not the Regional Air Commands or the Order Police) were to notify Goebbels' ministry at once if help were needed. Goebbels told the *Gauleiter* that the watchwords were 'unity and planning'.[76] The choice of the new commissar was not an obvious one and his actual powers, as so often in the Third Reich, were poorly defined, though he evidently benefited from direct and regular access to Hitler. Goebbels' principal claim was his concern with monitoring and moulding popular opinion, which his local propaganda offices watched closely. Reports on raids were routinely sent to Goebbels' office as Party Reich Leader of Propaganda, which left him better informed about the national picture than most other political or military leaders. Moreover, Goebbels was a *Gauleiter* himself, representing Berlin; his new office was designed to ensure that the local Party leadership should play a fuller part in managing bombed communities. His appointment confirmed the increasing 'partification' of the whole civil defence project.

The roots of this new configuration could be found much earlier in the war. The Party Chancellery, directed by Rudolf Hess, had a 'Mobilization Department' (*Abteilung-M*), which drew up guidelines for the role of Party organizations in the event of war. The NSV was detailed to take on responsibility for providing post-raid welfare, including evacuation, and to wear green armbands with 'Luftschutz-NSDAP' sewn on them, to show that they were independent of the air force or police. In autumn 1940 Martin Bormann, Hess's deputy, drew up a list of nine civil defence activities formally under Göring's authority, in which the Party claimed a role. They included controlling behaviour in shelters, checking on the blackout, supplying candidates for air-raid warden who possessed impeccable racial and Party credentials, and providing morale support when it was needed.[77] These claims had at first a nominal value, given the limited raiding activity and the extensive civil defence organization already in place. But Party insinuation was insidious and remorseless. By the time Goebbels was granted his new powers, the Party had already made itself conspicuous in supplying SA and SS assistance when needed, Hitler Youth as messenger boys, the NSV as the organizers of evacuation, and the necessary pomp and ceremony at the burial of bomb victims. The post of Reich Defence Commissar (*Reichsverteidigungs-Kommissar*), established on 1 September 1939 and generally given to the local *Gauleiter* as a largely nominal title, was elevated by the war into an instrument for Party leaders to play a fuller part in home front mobilization. On 16 November 1942 the posts of commissar and regional Party leader were formally merged and the *Gau* became the administrative unit for the home front. The *Gauleiter* of Munich later recalled that from 1942 onwards his work came to consist almost entirely of 'defence from the enemy air war, activation of civilian air protection'.[78]

The claims of the Party had the paradoxical effect of demilitarizing the home front, as the air force role was confined progressively to the more evidently military aspects of air defence. Goebbels was to be the direct beneficiary of this process, though Bormann, now director of the Party Chancellery following Rudolf Hess's flight to Scotland in May 1941, resented Hitler's choice and took every opportunity to increase his influence over post-raid policy. The other competitor was Göring, whose role as general overseer of air defence was challenged by Goebbels' new powers. In May 1942 Goebbels, Göring and Wilhelm Frick, the Interior Minister representing the interest of the police and local authorities, drew up a formal document confirming the new pattern of responsibility between them. 'Pure air defence' was left in the hands of the Air Force and the police; all civil administrative tasks were the province of the Reich Defence Commissars (usually the local *Gauleiter*); the job of managing the care and morale of the population in the face of bombardment was the sole responsibility of the Party. Goebbels was confirmed in his new capacity as emergency commissar, for when the existing system could no longer cope.[79] The arrangement made explicit the shift of responsibility towards the Party and the collapse of the Air Force monopoly, but the demarcation left a great many grey areas. In December 1942 Göring issued a further directive to try to make the set-up clearer: in the event of a catastrophic raid, beyond the scope of the Reich Defence Commissar or the Air Protection Leader, help should be requested from the Party Chancellery, the Propaganda Ministry and the Interior Ministry. But this arrangement merely confirmed a state of improvised confusion.[80] At the beginning of 1943 Hitler finally agreed to set up an Inter-Ministerial Air Protection Committee (ILA), based in the Propaganda Ministry, with Goebbels as nominal head. The object was at last to create a single, national clearing-house for all emergencies, with no new powers and limited organization, but with a sufficient overview to be able to send resources in a crisis where and when they were needed.[81]

The struggle over competency between the power-brokers of the dictatorship proved less damaging than it might have been because intervention from the centre was confined principally to the most conspicuous and damaging raids, where the role of the Party or the political leadership could be effectively advertised. At local level the onset of heavy raiding provoked a greater effort to ensure that the local administration and Party organs were better prepared to meet the demand to provide effective welfare and emergency rations, re-house the homeless, and compensate those who had lost everything in the raids. The watchword was *Einsatz*, a difficult word to render in English, suggesting action that is decisive and purposeful. After the bombings of Lübeck and Rostock, cities were encouraged to develop an 'action-mentality' by creating an *Einsatzstab* (Action Staff) under a designated *Einsatzführer* (Action Leader), who was to be chosen from among the local air protection leaders as an individual of outstanding merit. The staff was to consist of representatives of all the local state and Party offices for welfare, food, building, repair, transport and local economy, but the Leader was the key figure, given temporary emergency powers to get help from within and outside the raided area and to apply it swiftly and ruthlessly to the catastrophe.[82] 'Self-protection' was to be strengthened by creating local 'self-protection squads' (*Selbstschutztruppen*) run by yet another, lower-level *Einsatzführer* whose job was to tackle raids on streets and small communities in a more coordinated and vigorous way. An 'action plan' was made a legal requirement for all *Einsatzführer* in October 1942. In August 1943 service in a self-protection squad was made a legal obligation for every German citizen, man and woman.[83] In practice, not everyone was required to serve, but the proportion could be very substantial. In the small Rhineland town of Bingen with a population of 16,600 people, 4,783, more than one quarter, were enrolled as active civil defenders.[84]

According to yet another Hitler decree, published in August 1943 after Operation Gomorrah, the aim of all the new emergency arrangements for coping with air raids was 'the restoration of normal life as quickly as possible'.[85] Though this was not easy in the few major cities where repeated heavy bombing began in 1943, the object of the new 'action culture' was to make sure that one way or another the problems of welfare, compensation, re-housing, damage repair and evacuation allowed an adequate community life to continue. A good example of how this worked was the post-raid activity in the Berlin suburb of Schöneberg, bombed heavily on 1–2 March 1943, leaving 11,000 temporarily homeless. They were gathered first in the 71 emergency rest centres, with room for between 25,000 and 40,000 people in converted cafés, schools, restaurants and boarding houses.[86] Here they were given food, spirits, cigarettes, substitute ration cards and a provisional sum, in cash or vouchers, for the most urgent replacement clothing and household goods. Those who could not be placed with friends or relatives at once could be found substitute housing, particularly former Jewish homes, with priority for families with children whose houses had been completely destroyed. Evacuation was recommended only in exceptional circumstances, and then to areas if possible within the same urban region, or the same *Gau*. Over 7,000 were re-housed within two days. The salvaged goods had to be left in the street, clearly marked (to prevent looting), where they were collected in municipal street-cleaning lorries or military vehicles and stored in requisitioned warehouses or shops. Glass from the shattered windows was quickly cleaned up and returned to glass-makers for recycling.[87]

The guidelines for re-housing, house repair and compensation were laid down in a number of decrees issued by the Interior Ministry and the Organisation Todt in the course of 1941.[88] In Schöneberg housing was tackled at once by a special unit (*Baugruppe Pfeil*) organized by the city mayor. The unit turned up the morning after a raid to classify all housing into four categories of totally destroyed, badly damaged, partially damaged and lightly damaged. The first had to be made secure, the second repaired if possible, the last two restored to a habitable state. The Interior Ministry instruction was to do no more than ensure that the buildings could be lived in – roofs covered over with boards or broken slates and tiles replaced.[89] In the aftermath of the Berlin raid there were 300 roofers, 460 glaziers and 485 bricklayers at work at once, covering over roofs first to protect the rooms exposed to the elements, then covering windows and doors temporarily with card or wood, and covering damaged walls with a coat of paint instead of wallpaper. Though there were complaints about the standard, most of those rehabilitated, according to the official report on reconstruction, showed the necessary resoluteness in returning to homes that were now far less comfortable places to live.[90] Most of the light damage from Allied bombing consisted of broken windows and damaged roofs. Three raids on Nuremberg in 1942 and 1943 destroyed 1.75 million square metres of glass and 2 million square metres of roofing; but out of 19,184 bomb-damaged buildings, only 662 were totally destroyed and 973 severely damaged, making it possible for those rendered homeless, as in Britain, to return to where they had lived after first-aid repairs were completed.[91] It was calculated that 324,000 homes had been destroyed or badly damaged throughout Germany by November 1943, but by then 3,184,000 people had been successfully rehabilitated or re-housed.[92]

The most complex procedure was to provide compensating goods for those who had lost some or all of their possessions and to calculate the extent of war-damage compensation to which people were entitled. The evidence from Schöneberg shows that the population took this issue more seriously than any other and that it gave rise to a greater degree of friction.[93] The procedures were time-consuming and the regulations irksome to those who saw themselves as victims. At the emergency centres, the bombed-out were given preliminary vouchers for clothes, shoes, soap and washing powder, without having to make a formal written application. Clothes included a suit or a dress, underwear, stockings, handkerchiefs and nightwear, and one pair of sturdy shoes. In March 1943 the welfare offices handed out 10,432 textile vouchers and 10,810 for shoes and 750 furniture certificates. So complex was the rationing system in Germany set up in September 1939 that bomb damage could destroy cards for household articles, furniture, coal, petrol, soap and tobacco, all of which had to be queued for, often for hours, in order to argue for a replacement. The new card or voucher was an entitlement only, whose redemption depended on the local supply of goods. Schöneberg was fortunate since there were stocks of second-hand goods and Jewish possessions, as well as goods from occupied or Axis Europe, France and Hungary in particular. In spring 1943 Hitler had ordered that labour and materials needed to overcome bomb damage and losses should be secured first from the occupied territories.[94] Berlin still had a large number of small traders and manufacturers who could supply what else was needed, and the stocks used up in March 1943 were soon replenished.[95]

The claims for financial compensation were altogether more fraught. A report from the Schöneberg regional office explained that the officials and the claimants worked in different directions, the first seeking to limit what had to be paid out only to genuinely verifiable losses, the victims with an interest in setting their claim as high as they could.

Forms had been distributed to householders so that they could list in detail all their possessions in anticipation of a raid.[96] Some filled out the claim form in only the most general terms, others supplied a detailed description of what was lost including, at times, photographs of the missing objects. Where the owner had been killed, legatees gave their own description of what they had expected to inherit. The officials based their assessments on the credibility of the claimant, including esti- mates of social class and likely earnings, as a guide to what a claimant might possibly own. One Berlin toolmaker claimed 12,000 RM of fur- nishings from a one-room apartment, including 143 separate items; the claims office dismissed the claim and paid out 1,500 RM. A building engineer living in a four-room household with his wife and four chil- dren claimed a loss of 50,000 RM, including a table valued at 4,800 RM (around three times the annual wage of a semi-skilled worker); he was granted just 6,000 RM pending further investigation. The harassed office staff treated few claims as deliberately false, but the bombed-out all over Germany inflated the value of their losses once their possessions could no longer be checked.[97] The total number of cases involved and the sums claimed represented a major administrative and financial effort for the state to cope with in the middle of a major war. In Nurem- berg alone, there were 27,977 claims for compensation by spring 1943 amounting to 44.8 million marks; of this sum 8.8 million were paid out in cash, 14 million in kind.[98] By late 1943 payments at national level were running at over 700 million RM a month; claims totalling 31.7 billion RM had been filed, of which 11.6 billion had already been paid out.[99] These were sums that could never have been imagined when the initial commitment was made to pay for the direct costs of the bombing war.

The greatest test of the evolving civil defence and emergency struc- ture came with the bombing of Hamburg in July and August 1943. The 137 small raids (and 782 air-raid alarms) up to July 1943 had given Hamburg more experience than most cities in coping with the conse- quences of bombing.[100] The idea of an Action Staff for catastrophic raids had been pioneered in Hamburg. By July 1943 there was public shelter available for 378,000 people; attics had been cleared, fire-risk stocks had been stored safely, and a programme of fire-retarding wood treatment – the 'Fire Protection Chemical Scheme' – had been ordered in spring 1943 for completion by the summer. There was a large cohort of 9,300 *Luftschutzpolizei*, and a citywide fire-watching scheme, which involved 15,000 people in the dock area alone. There had been

11,000 demonstrations organized in the city on how to extinguish incendiary bombs. Some 70,000 men and women had been trained for first aid by the German Red Cross. Hamburg's police president later in the year described the city as 'one large Air Protection community'.[101] The heavy British raids on other cities earlier in the year gave little indication of what Hamburg could expect in Operation Gomorrah. An attack on Stuttgart on 14–15 April had killed 118; a heavy raid on Dortmund on 23–24 May left 345 dead; another on Krefeld in June resulted in 149 deaths.[102] Hamburg itself had suffered 626 deaths in 42 raids in 1941, 494 deaths in 15 raids in 1942, and 142 deaths in 10 small raids in 1943. The first reports to reach Berlin of the Hamburg bombing gave little indication of how much more serious the raids in Operation Gomorrah proved to be.[103]

Hamburg was not unprepared for its ordeal, but the scale of the three nights of attack on 24–25, 27–28 and 29–30 July overwhelmed the thousands of trained personnel. After declaring a state of emergency, the Reich Defence Commissar, *Gauleiter* Karl Kaufmann, called in mutual assistance from outside the city from as far away as Dresden. At the height of the crisis there were 14,000 firefighters, 12,000 soldiers and 8,000 emergency workers, but although they were able to achieve limited containment of the fire area, the conflagrations soon grew out of control, consuming everything in their path.[104] The firestorm caused by the second raid fed on the oxygen in the thousands of cellars used as 'air-protection rooms', where people sat slowly asphyxiating from carbon monoxide poisoning or were burnt so completely that doctors afterwards had to estimate the number of dead by measuring the ash left on the floor. Others died with apparently no external injuries because their body temperature rose above 42 degrees centigrade, causing the body's natural regulator to collapse from 'over-warming'.[105] By the end of the year it was estimated that 85 per cent of deaths in German cities were caused by fire rather than high-explosive bombs.[106] The Hamburg police president later wrote that 'speech is impotent' to describe the scene that he confronted after the fire had ebbed away, but the description in his official report is vivid enough:

> The streets were covered with hundreds of corpses. Mothers with their children, youths, old men, burnt, charred, untouched and unclothed, naked with a waxen pallor like dummies in a shop window, they lay in every posture, quiet and peaceful or cramped, the death-struggle shown in the expression on their faces.[107]

By the end of November 1943, records had been compiled to confirm 31,647 dead, of which only 15,802 could be identified; a further 2,322 were known to have died outside the city. The final death toll will never be known with certainty, but it is generally assumed to be between 34,000 (shown by police records) and 40,000 (the figure widely used in Germany before the end of the war). The Hamburg Fire Department calculated that all the wartime bombing in Hamburg, from 1940 to 1945, resulted in the deaths of 48,572 people.[108]

The aftermath of the raids saw an awful calm descend on the damaged city. One million people fled unorganized over the course of the week and had to be absorbed into the surrounding countryside and small towns; 315,000 houses and apartments were destroyed or badly damaged, 61 per cent of the city. Over the course of the war 902,000 people in Hamburg lost all their possessions, including the novelist Hans Nossack, who by chance had gone to a summer cottage outside the city just before the raids began. He watched the columns and truckloads of refugees, some still in their nightwear: 'They brought with them an uncanny silence . . . crouched and remote . . . No lamenting anywhere, no tears.' Nossack returned to the city a few days later, losing his way through the ruined landscape, and the swarms of rats and flies, 'insolent and fat'.[109] The heat that had allowed the firestorm to take hold persisted after the bombing. Another eyewitness, Gretl Büttner, found the contrast uncanny between a deep blue sky dotted with pretty white clouds and the 'image of unending misery and terrible devastation', made starker by the fickle weather. She joined hundreds of others searching through the corpses, laid out in neat rows in squares free of debris, to try to find her companions.[110] The police set up a record-card index divided into four categories: identified and registered dead, unknown bodies and their place of discovery and burial, property salvaged and assigned to bodies, and articles found but unclaimed. Any goods that were not claimed were sold second-hand to the homeless. There were hundreds of orphaned children, or children separated from their parents, who had to be identified and housed. In the aftermath of the Hamburg bombings the Inter-Ministerial Committee made it compulsory for all children up to age four to wear a wooden or cardboard tag with their name, date of birth and address.[111]

The most urgent need in Hamburg in the first days after the firestorm was to supply clean drinking water and to avert a health disaster as refugees began to return to the devastated areas and in some cases to reoccupy the ruined remains of their homes. The drinking-water system was destroyed in the raids and regular water sources contaminated. The emergency services brought in disinfected street-cleaning lorries filled with fresh spring water immediately the bombing had finished. Water lorries were sent from as far afield as Stettin, Breslau, Berlin and Leipzig, mostly cleaned and converted petrol-tankers. The level of hygiene was poor and the population was warned to boil water even from the lorries. Two days after the last raid the local Hygiene Institute laboratory was working again, monitoring the quality of water from the main springs and the wells which were opened up for use. Epidemic illness was avoided.[112] The medical conditions in the city were nevertheless far from ideal. Instead of the usual 20,000 hospital beds there were now only 8,000 following the destruction of 24 hospitals. Emergency medical stations were set up to give immediate treatment. The many corpses were covered in quicklime and buried in mass graves, or doused with petrol and burnt.[113] The most damaged areas of the city were walled up to prevent people returning to areas where there was a risk to health; buildings which had been checked for bodies and cleared were marked with a blob of green paint.[114] Much of the gruesome work was carried out by camp prisoners whose survival worried the authorities less. Looters were few since the penalties were severe. By 5 August the first seven had been sentenced to death; in total, 31 cases were tried in the four months following the raids and 15 looters executed.[115]

Operation Gomorrah represented a profound challenge to German society and the German war effort but not one that could not in the end be met. Hermann Göring visited Hamburg on 6 August to an apparently enthusiastic welcome, though informers also heard widespread criticism of his leadership of the air force. The SD Report following the raids spoke of the 'exceptional shock effect' across the whole country, but also recorded the still widespread belief that Germany had the means to 'end the war victoriously'.[116] Albert Speer famously recalled in his memoirs his claim at the time that after six more Hamburgs, Germany would be finished. But he also remembered Hitler's reply: 'You'll straighten it out again.'[117] Following the raids, Speer was authorized by Hitler to set up yet another emergency organization based on three Air Raid Damage Staffs stationed in Hamburg, Berlin and Stuttgart. In the event of a new catastrophe, he would move in mobile columns of workers, relief supplies and equipment to get workers provided for as soon as possible and damaged industry and utilities working again.[118] Over the course of the year following Gomorrah, 50,000 emergency homes were built for Hamburg's workforce. Though small (between 30 and

40 square metres) and crudely built, the new housing clustered near the factories, which supplied the workforce with subsidized electricity at one fifth of the regular price.[119] The number of households in Hamburg fell from 500,000 to 300,000, reducing pressure on local amenities and housing so that within months around 90 per cent of the remaining population could be accommodated in regular housing.[120] The social consequences of the raids, which had killed around 2.4 per cent of the city's population, were gradually absorbed as services were restored, the rationing system reinstituted, and urgent house repair completed.

There were important lessons to be learned from the worst of Germany's air raids. Although he concluded that the city's civil defence system was basically sound, the police president added 20 pages of helpful advice to his report on practical and technical improvements to aspects of air-raid protection. His most urgent recommendation was to ensure that there were adequate escape routes, known to all shelter users, to prevent the mass deaths that had occurred in apparently safe air-raid rooms. The problems this presented were advertised in a *Luftschutzbund* report in July 1943 about a woman who succeeded in the nick of time in saving her fellow-shelterers:

> There was darkness in the cellar. We were all thrown on top of each other. The light failed. If we had only put ready an axe for opening up the break-through at a fixed point on the wall, we would have saved ourselves fearful minutes of alarm. We found the axe only after a good quarter of an hour. As the air in the cellar quickly became worse, I bashed at the break-through like someone possessed. Now it got its revenge, because we had never bothered particularly about the added bit of wall. Only after 20 minutes had I cut a hole just large enough to slip through.[121]

In the months after the bombing of Hamburg, air-protection instructions sent out monthly by the Air Ministry to local police authorities emphasized repeatedly the need to keep cellar shelters clear of obstacles, with a clearly marked break-through point, made of shallow mortar. More difficult was the realization that the constant repetition of the slogan earlier in the war that 'the air-protection room is the safest place' was no longer always the case. Air-raid wardens and Action Leaders were now encouraged to teach their communities the right moment to leave a shelter if a fire threatened to run out of control. When leaving a cellar in a firestorm, people were advised to wear a coat soaked with water and a damp hood. A coat, it was claimed, was more difficult for the fiery wind to tear off the body.[122]

After the experience of Hamburg, priority was given to finding more effective ways to prevent or to fight a firestorm, challenging though this was. Civil defence and firefighting units were instructed to start attacking fires as soon as they appeared, even during the raid, since casualties were certain to be lower than they would be once a firestorm took hold. 'The first half hour is of decisive importance in the development of fires,' ran the Air Ministry instructions. 'It is possible to prevent the genesis of a major conflagration, under circumstances where the fires started by the bombs are extinguished along whole streets.'[123] If a firestorm took hold, firefighters were told to concentrate on the area around the edges, where buildings were not yet completely on fire, in order to contain it; at the same time they were encouraged to search for pathways through the waves of fire which could be opened up to allow some of the trapped inhabitants to make their escape. In Hamburg, few of the population engulfed by the hurricane of fire survived relatively unscathed in blastproof surface shelters.[124] All self-protection leaders were charged with making sure that householders in every building or apartment kept adequate quantities of water available to tackle a small fire before it spread. The more water stored, the better; use was to be made of '*all* available containers whatever, not only buckets, pails, bathtubs and rain barrels, but even washbasins, washtubs etc.' Water could even be removed from central-heating systems.[125] Each air-protection room now had to contain its own supplies of water and sand. Self-protection units also had to appoint groups to go out during a raid to spot fires and to tackle them at once; empty buildings were no longer obliged to observe the blackout, so that fires could more easily be identified through the uncovered windows. 'Fires,' ran one piece of *Luftschutzbund* advice, 'always look much worse than they are, and are much easier to extinguish than appears in the first moment.'[126]

How effective civilians were in tackling a fire clearly varied from case to case, and it placed a heavy responsibility on householders, whose first thought was often for their own family and possessions. A Cologne journalist recorded in his diary how well his neighbours coped with the 1,000-bomber raid in May 1942: 'The incendiaries which clattered down around our house: one on the balcony of our neighbour Feuser, immediately extinguished by our neighbour Brassart, one in front of the garage of our neighbour Uhlenbruck, which the coal merchant snatched up, one by the garage of neighbour Gessert, which the householder put out.'[127] For the regular fire service, the onset of heavy firebombing raids placed a strain on units that were already depleted by regular culls of manpower for the armed forces. In September 1943 a second national inspector was appointed for the fire service, Hans Rumpf, who made it his job to visit more than 150 fire-service units over the following year, checking their equipment and practices. The system depended increasingly on volunteer firefighters, around 1.7 million by 1944. After the heavy fire raids in 1943, the local volunteers were organized in 'firefighting emergency units' so that they could be summoned at once from the surrounding area to help with fires in the major cities, an estimated 700 units made up of 100,000 firefighters. They were all brought under police jurisdiction, and those who were also members of the SS were permitted to wear the familiar silver runes on their uniform. The numbers of German men in the service fell steadily, so that during 1943 it became necessary to recruit foreign workers – Poles, Czechs and Ukrainians – into the fire service. In Hamburg by the end of the war around one-quarter of the regular fire service was made up of Ukrainians. A more radical departure was the call in April 1943 for women to volunteer for the fire service, not only in auxiliary roles but as regular firefighters. From October 1943 they could be subject to compulsory mobilization and by autumn 1944 an estimated 275,000 female firefighters, aged between 18 and 40, took their part in combating Allied incendiarism.[128] The popular myth that German women did nothing more than guard hearth and home during the war is demonstrably untrue for this most dangerous of activities.

Hamburg also signalled the onset of widespread urban evacuation following the first two years of war in which it had been discouraged or temporarily indulged. The veiled evacuation permitted under the *Kinderlandverschickung* organization tailed off during 1942 and 1943; from a peak of over 160,000 children in organized camps in July 1941, there were only 40,000 by May 1942, and a similar number in spring 1944. The peak figure accounted for only 2 per cent of all eligible 10 to 14-year-olds. Most stayed for no more than a few months in the Hitler Youth camps before returning home because the accommodation was not suitable for winter; mothers and younger children sent away to the country also stayed for short periods or tried to find friends or relatives to stay with as an alternative to close supervision by the National Socialist People's Welfare. Altogether the Party organizations accounted for around 2 million temporary refugees from the cities, but not for a system of permanent evacuation.[129] In July 1942 local authorities were reminded that 're-housing' (rather than evacuation) would be approved and covered by public funds only if it was necessary to remove the population from areas of severe bomb damage or unexploded ordnance, or in cases where population transfers were socially useful, and only with Göring's approval.[130] In February 1943 Hitler finally agreed that whole school classes could be evacuated from danger areas, but insisted that parents should have the choice whether or not to split the family. Numbers of schoolchildren formally evacuated remained small. In August 1943 in Berlin out of 260,000 eligible schoolchildren, only 32,000 were in organized evacuation, 132,000 placed with relatives or acquaintances.[131]

Only in the spring of 1943, with the onset of the heavy bombing of the Ruhr-Rhineland, did evacuation begin on any scale. On 19 April the Interior Ministry published a decree on organized evacuation (*Umquartierung*), either to accommodation in the same city, or in the rural hinterland, or, for the population not essential for the war effort, transfer to a more distant and safer region.[132] There were no firm plans in place to cope with the growing stream of refugees from the heavily bombed areas who were evacuating themselves. To avoid a growing chaos, the Interior Ministry finally published in July 1943 a list of city populations scheduled for evacuation and quotas for the regions (based on the Party *Gaue*) where the evacuees – mainly the old and the very young – would be sent. It was the crisis in Hamburg that shocked the German population into greater acceptance of evacuation as a clear necessity. Up until June 1943 the German railway authorities estimated that no more than 140,000–150,000 people had been moved under formal schemes to more distant areas; by the end of 1943 more than 2 million people had been transferred under official programmes.[133] The immediate evacuation of 900,000 from Hamburg was a result of the panic that occurred as Operation Gomorrah intensified. By the end of September 1943, 545,000 had been settled in regions across Germany, more than one-quarter in the neighbouring rural areas of Schleswig-Holstein, almost one-third in and around the south German town of Bayreuth.[134] The firestorm in Hamburg provoked widespread fear that Berlin would be next. From a marked reluctance to accept transfer away from the city, Berliners now flooded out, 691,000 by mid-September. Around 1.1 million altogether left the German capital, one-quarter of the pre-war population.

The urban exodus provoked widespread problems, not least because it had not been systematically planned for, as it had been in Britain, and finding and allocating spare accommodation – often just a room in a village house – had to be improvised at short notice. There were obvious sources of friction between a small-town and rural population, not yet much exposed to the physical effects of the bombing war, and an urban population used to different standards or from a very different social milieu. A report sent to the Party Chancellery from Upper Silesia in May 1943 highlighted some of these issues:

> The attitude of these racial comrades towards the guest region appears incomprehensible, for it must be observed that at the moment the women, scarcely having set foot on the soil of Upper Silesia, exclaim: 'If I have to come to a nest like this, then I'd rather go back to a heap of ruins'; another woman declared, 'I am surprised that the sluttish wives that crawl around here can still attract men' . . . The Germans from the west have often criticized the 'Heil Hitler' greeting with the remark that people don't greet each other like that in the old Reich.[135]

In August 1943 Goebbels' Inter-Ministerial Committee sent recommendations out to all *Gauleiter* to combat the 'spiritual depression' evident among the evacuee populations in their new surroundings, including the provision of a well-heated community room, with a radio, games, magazines and newspapers from the evacuated cities, as well as film shows, using equipment salvaged from bombed cinemas.[136] But the temptation to return home was strong. By the end of November 1943, 217,000 Berliners had returned despite efforts of the authorities to use compulsory ration-card registration in the evacuation areas as a means of ensuring that the rail network would not be overburdened with those who chose to return. In some areas the quota for evacuees from the major cities had to compete with local evacuation from small towns and cities not yet threatened. In Württemberg in southern Germany, out of 169,000 evacuees in February 1944, at least 52,000 (and perhaps as many as half) had abandoned the region's own towns for safety in the countryside. In other areas, the number of evacuees threatened to overwhelm small communities, which were expected to accommodate evacuee populations that were not far short of the number of permanent residents. In some cases, an apparently safe rural retreat was bombed anyway by aircrew who could not see where they were aiming, making both inhabitants and evacuees into refugees together.[137]

The evacuation crisis following Operation Gomorrah also exposed the serious state of the German medical service as it wrestled to cope with a much-reduced medical profession, the destruction of hospitals and clinics, and a sudden increase in the number of casualties, many of them serious, brought about by the intensified bombing. After the

Hamburg firestorm, many doctors and nurses left with the evacuees; clinics and medical practices were destroyed, leaving doctors with few alternatives but to find occupation away from the stricken city. When evacuation set in elsewhere, doctors were among those who accompanied the transferred communities. By late August an estimated 35–40 doctors a day were leaving Berlin, some with the evacuees, some with the 11,500 bedridden patients who were transferred to hospitals in safer areas.[138] The evacuation from the Ruhr-Rhineland had been carried out too quickly to match medical needs to the evacuee community, and since the majority were children, old people and women, many of them pregnant, the need for doctors, child nurses, and midwives was more rather than less urgent. In the reception areas the problem was made worse by the fact that the armed forces had taken many of the doctors from the zones classified II or III, not having realized the extent of the later bombing threat.[139] The aim of the Reich Health Chief, Leonardo Conti (one of those responsible for the T4 'euthanasia' programme), was to try to keep an acceptable proportion between the population and the number of doctors, but by October 1943 the profession was down to 35,000 for the whole population, from a pre-war level of 80,000. Around 5,500 were too old to practise effectively and 3,883 died between 1939 and 1942, some in military service. The ideal of one doctor for every 2,000 or 2,500 people could not be met, and of those available, many were themselves the victims of overwork, tiredness and illness. For evacuees Conti's aim was only one doctor for every 10,000.[140]

The onset of heavy bombing made it necessary to find a solution or risk a breakdown of effective medical services. Military casualty rates rose sharply during 1943 and 1944, making it more necessary to find ways to rationalize the civilian system. Lorries and vans were requisitioned as less than adequate ambulances, while efforts were made to find hotel or guest-house accommodation to use as hospitals. Doctors were ordered to place their instruments and medicines in bomb-safe basements every evening to avoid damage, while equipment from ruined clinics was given or sold to doctors still practising.[141] The German Red Cross, which controlled most of the ambulance service, instructed local branches to set up an emergency controller in major cities, with responsibility to call in emergency medical columns, prepared in advance with lorries, temporary barracks, beds, stretchers, sanitary materials and water filters, and a staff of one or two doctors and up to six nurses. Most bomb victims who survived were only lightly injured, a great many with eye injuries from glass, smoke, soot and dust from debris.

It was decided that these walking wounded would have to be treated in first-aid centres rather than hospitals, which would be used for the serious cases. Operations were suspended for hopeless cases so that resources could be devoted to those who might survive.[142] The main shortage was hospital space, since both military and civilian victims competed for this. In August 1941 Hitler authorized construction of emergency hospitals in bomb-threatened areas at the expense of the state.[143] The scheme made slow progress and in May 1943 Hitler approved the appointment of óne of the doctors on his staff, Karl Brandt, as General Commissar for Sanitary and Health Issues, with responsibility for creating additional emergency hospital space and planning its distribution. Conti immediately objected, since Brandt's appointment trespassed directly on his own role, but the purpose of the new appointment was to focus on hospital beds rather than areas of general medical policy. Brandt immediately bustled about planning 19 new hospital sites and 54,000 more hospital beds, but the 'Brandt Action' cut across existing planning, creating, in Conti's words, 'a permanent state of chaos'. Allocation of hospital space continued on an improvised basis.[144] The one area where extra provision proved unnecessary was psychiatric casualty. As in Britain, the assumption at first was that bombing was bound to increase the degree of serious mental disorder, particularly as many of those subjected to bombing were female. Yet it soon became clear that although fear and nervous anxiety were widespread, this did not lead to evident psychotic states. Psychiatric casualty was generally nursed in private. Only after the war were the traumatic consequences of exposure to the bombing threat eventually observable.[145]

Along with the evacuees came not only problems of welfare and medical provision but a treasure-trove of rumours spread by an urban population that suddenly found itself the centre of attention in the reception areas. Rumours performed a number of functions: they gave the evacuees a sense of temporary importance as they regaled their hosts with overblown accounts of the horrors of being bombed; they were a safety valve for people whose opportunity for criticizing the authorities was severely circumscribed; and they acted as an instant form of information and communication for communities who were starved of anything other than the official line peddled by German propaganda. Responsibility for controlling and combating rumours lay with Goebbels' Propaganda Ministry. As in Britain during the Blitz, the decision about how much information to release was a difficult one, not only because the effect on the public had to be monitored, but because hard information could be used by the enemy. The heavy raids on the Ruhr-Rhineland in spring 1943 immediately opened up, according to the Party propaganda office, 'the worst outcome, a flood of rumours'.[146] In areas that had not been bombed, rumours often reinforced a self-interested sense of immunity. Common rumours centred on the invulnerability of a region thanks to unspecified British interests in leaving it intact, or the depth of industrial and urban smog covering the area, or the excessive distance from British bases. Others focused on the most likely time to be bombed – on Fridays, on national festivals, on Hitler's birthday, on days specified in Allied leaflets.[147] One rumour involved lurid tales, which spread across Germany, of people stuck in melted asphalt and burned alive, or ignited by some form of phosphorous rain, half-truths from the sight of those struggling against the firestorm.[148]

In other cases rumours took on a more solid shape. In Munich following a heavy raid in September 1942, strong rumours were overheard, first that it was Germany's fault that civilian bombing had begun in the first place; second, and more significant, the view that bombing was God's punishment for having 'pushed the Jews over the frontier and thrown them into poverty'.[149] In July 1943 the rumour took root that volcanoes were to be bombed to bring about the end of the world. Rumours about the apocalypse were, Goebbels thought, quite understandable when faced with the sight of dead children laid out after a raid, but had to be contested nonetheless.[150] One child, hearing adults talking about 'the end' in a shelter, was unsure whether they meant the end of the war or in fact 'the end of the world'.[151] The summer of 1943 encouraged a sense of extremes. The news from Hamburg, which reached Bavaria in August, was, wrote one diarist, 'beyond the grasp of the imagination ... streets of boiling asphalt into which the victims sank ... 200,000 dead'. He witnessed a group of Hamburg refugees trying to force their way into a railway car, until one battered suitcase carried along by 'a half-crazed woman' dropped open to reveal clothes, a toy and the shrivelled, carbonized body of a child. He reflected that the terrible news from Hamburg meant the end of the old world for good: 'this time those riders now saddling their black steeds are none other than the Four Horsemen of the Apocalypse'.[152]

The issue of rumours was bound up with the more profound question of how to sustain popular commitment to the war effort and avoid more serious social or political crisis. These issues came to the forefront only in 1943 when casualty lists grew longer and the means to obstruct

Allied bombing became clearly ineffectual. In the Ruhr-Rhineland in spring 1943 the first evidence of possible social crisis emerged as the authorities struggled to cope with homelessness and temporary unemployment. Information fed into the Propaganda Ministry highlighted a growing sense of desperation. The raid on Duisburg on 19–20 March 1943 left thousands homeless, destroyed the city's major department stores, and left just two restaurants still functioning for 200,000 people. The local population complained that the promise of revenge against British cities had not been met while the Ruhr was reaching breaking point: 'We see no end. We cannot keep this up for long. How will it go?'[153] Even Goebbels was affected by the evidence of the first really sustained bombing campaign. On 13 March he wrote in his diary that 'Air warfare is at present our greatest worry. Things simply cannot go on like this.'[154] The difficulty for those charged with the psychological welfare of the population – the Party called it *Menschenführung* – was to separate out the different factors affecting the public mood, of which bombing was just one. In February 1943 Goebbels had delivered his famous speech about total war in Berlin to a selected Party audience, an oration designed to reinvigorate the war-willingness of the population after the defeat at Stalingrad. But its impact was limited and failed to address the question of how to cope with the consequences of air attack upon morale, though the speech was popular with the armed forces, who wanted the civilian population to grasp the true dimensions of the conflict.[155] The SD Reports showed that some of the population blamed the intensified bombing on Goebbels' speech, which seemed to be an invitation to the enemy to wage unrestricted war against the German people. Resentment against Berlin as the source of the 'total war' idea provoked a verse that soon had wide currency in western Germany: 'Lieber Tommy fliege weiter/wir sind alle Bergarbeiter./Fliege weiter nach Berlin/die haben alle "ja" geschrien' ['Dear Tommy fly on further/ we are all miners here./Fly further to Berlin/they have all screamed "yes"'].[156]

From spring 1943 onwards the regime for moulding opinion in Germany struggled to find a way to influence the response to bombing in ways that were more positive for the German war effort. Rumours were tackled by insinuating SA or Party officials into crowds and queues with instructions to challenge the substance of rumours; some rumours were deliberately started by propaganda officials to counter a local mood of depression or hopelessness; home intelligence regularly recommended tackling rumours at source by publicly announcing their false nature and providing some nuggets of more plausible information.[157] The difficult thing was to gauge how much hard information should be given out. The formal policy, approved by the High Command, was to announce no details about the number of casualties and the damage to buildings. In March 1943 a brief but clear communiqué was given about a raid on Berlin, immediately winning wide public approval.[158] But only in the case of the raid on the Rhineland dams were precise casualty figures given, to stop the rumours that 10,000–30,000 people had died.[159] Rather than give in to public pressure to give precise information, public anxiety was to be mediated by propaganda that highlighted the achievements of the German Air Force against the bomber offensive. Propaganda-Companies from the military propaganda arm began to work in the bombed cities from June 1943 to provide local stories on successful air defence or air-to-air combat. Goebbels had already orchestrated a campaign to convince the public that the German Air Force was taking revenge on the enemy population and would do so with new, powerful but secret weapons in the near future.[160]

The idea of vengeance (*Vergeltung*) was itself problematic, since it depended for its propaganda success on more than just promises. In 1943 the German Air Force activity against British targets reached its lowest point. Goebbels hoped that the successful test launch of the V1 and the V2 by early 1943 indicated a rapid move to large-scale revenge attacks; the substantial time lag meant that the public became first sceptical, then widely critical of the regime's promises. In late April 1943 the SD Reports noted widespread longing for the 'revenge announced "already so often"', and popular calls for revenge punctuated all the weekly reports throughout the year. By September the following joke was in circulation in the Ruhr and Berlin: 'The English and the Americans were given an ultimatum: if they do not cease the air war at once, another vengeance speech will follow.'[161] By then rumours about a new missile were in circulation and popular hopes that a definite deadline would be announced for its use. Goebbels had by then realized that vengeance propaganda was counter-productive and on 6 July 1943 he ordered the German press to stop using the term, though it retained its public currency. The armed forces' propaganda branch set up a commission to study the potential of the new weapons and concluded that they were not capable of turning the tide of war and should no longer be used for propaganda purposes.[162] Instead Goebbels used the Jewish question both as a way to explain the bombing war and as an instrument to encourage German resistance. In a speech on 5 June

1943 he denounced British bombing and the 'Jewish instigators' behind it. After Operation Gomorrah, Party propaganda played on 'the Jews' will to extermination' expressed through the 'bombing murder of the Jewish-plutocratic enemy', and called for a fanatical defence of German race and culture.[163]

On some issues the German public felt strongly, though it is not widely evident that the struggle against 'world Jewry' meant very much to the population in the front line against bombing. There were strong demands that the dead in bombing raids should be marked in the newspapers with an iron cross, like the military dead. The Propaganda Ministry approved of the idea in December 1941, but it was overturned by Hitler in January 1942 (who did not want women to be honoured that way) and rejected by the armed forces, who thought that it would diminish the value of the symbol for the military dead.[164] Attempts to describe the bomb victims with the military terms 'fallen' or 'wounded' (*Gefallene* or *Verwundete*) were also rejected by the armed forces, since many of those who died did so from wilful failure to seek shelter, including a notorious case in Bremen when 14 partygoers were killed because they wanted to finish their food and drink before going down to the cellar. In the end a compromise was reached, allowing civil defence workers of either sex who died while carrying out dangerous duties to have their death notices marked with an iron cross. They could also be described as 'fallen' for the Fatherland, but the rest of the bomb victims could not, a distinction confirmed by Goebbels in May 1943.[165]

Opportunity for more serious political or social dissent was limited, given the willingness of the regime to impose severe punishment on any open or dangerous forms of protest; where it existed, political resistance was fuelled by ideological difference rather than by bombing. Nevertheless, a growing pessimistic realism about the future jostled in public opinion with evidence of a firmer resolve and persistent confidence in Hitler's capacity to stabilize the situation. The SD Reports speculated, as did British intelligence, that the mass of homeless and disgruntled evacuees might be a possible source of an 'inner collapse' if the bombing got worse, but an estimated one-third of the evacuees returned home. Those who remained, mainly women and children, were unlikely instigators of revolt, though there were isolated acts of protest against the treatment of evacuees or the withholding of ration cards. The most famous case was in October 1943 at Witten in the Ruhr, where the police refused to intervene.[166] In some ways bombing actually created a safety valve for popular disaffection. Rumours could represent a surreptitious challenge to prescribed public discourse without amounting to serious dissent. In the shelters it was sometimes possible for the small communities that inhabited them to complain about their hardships or to satirize the regime without fear of punishment. In one Berlin bunker, Hitler was always referred to as 'The Hitler', an intentionally less flattering epithet than 'our Führer'. The local warden turned a blind eye both to this and to harsher complaints directed at the dictatorship.[167] For the bombed-out, the opportunity to let off steam could also be tolerated. One generic story, cited by a number of observers, told of a hysterical woman evacuee challenging the police to arrest her for some trivial offence because at least she would have a roof over her head. In each version of the story, the police do nothing.[168] The SD Reports noted a widely circulating rumour in August 1943 that the Allies had promised to stop the bombing if the government was changed; this was a brave rumour to pass on, but it was overheard in towns as far apart as Innsbruck and Königsberg.[169] It was also evident that the anxieties and fears generated by bombing in particular affected not only the home front but the fighting front as well. Censors intercepted letters giving painful details of the effects of heavy raids; soldiers on leave could see these effects for themselves. An SD Report in early September 1943 described a typical front-line response: 'What is the point in defending the homeland at the front if everything at home is smashed to pieces and there is nothing left afterwards when we come back.'[170] Efforts were made to ensure that news reached soldiers quickly to allay their fears. Special 'bomb postcards' could be written from raided towns with express delivery to military units.[171]

The heavy bombing of 1943, and the shock effect of the destruction of Hamburg in particular, did not in reality provoke serious political or social crisis, though it prompted growing public criticism and anxiety, and occasional, local acts of grumbling protest, which could be tolerated by the authorities. There is no single explanation for this, since the response varied a great deal between different regions and cities, or between different social groups and public organizations, but a number of factors played a part. The bombing was geographically concentrated still in 1942 and 1943, principally on the coastal towns and the industrial regions of western Germany, though an estimated half of British bombs fell in open country. Although regular warnings, compulsory sheltering and waves of morbid rumours affected much of the rest of the population, bombing was not directly experienced. For those who were principally affected, the chief concern was to survive the catastrophe, to find adequate welfare, food and shelter, and to protect and re-establish the private sphere. Hans Nossack found among his fellow Hamburgers a preoccupation with the mundane: 'if by chance a newspaper came into our hands, we didn't bother to read the war bulletins ... We would immediately turn to the page with the announcements that concerned us directly. Whatever happened outside of us simply did not exist.'[172]

Since the regime was exaggeratedly anxious about the state of public opinion, the duplication of effort by the air force, local authorities, the Party and the police meant that whatever jurisdictional friction might be generated, problems were identified and tackled. The plethora of mobile emergency columns, bringing food or medical care or construction teams, meant that none of the afflicted cities was likely to be short of some form of effective assistance. The range of civil defence activities was extensive and the mobilization of more women and young people in 1943 spread the mantle of responsibility over a large fraction of the urban population. The combination of state, party and community initiatives helped German society to cope with the rigours of a long-term bombing campaign and dampened any prospect of social disquiet. 'Everything went on very quietly,' wrote Nossack, reflecting on the absence of latent rebellion, 'and with a definite concern for order, and the State took its bearings from this order.'[173] Only in 1944–5, when bombing overwhelmed German society, was the search for order challenged.

ECONOMIC MIRACLES

It has become fashionable in recent accounts of the German economy during the Second World War to dismiss the idea that there was anything very miraculous about its ability to expand war production continuously between 1939 and 1944.[174] All war economies did this, the German more slowly at first than the others, then more rapidly towards the end of the war. The difference is that German industrial cities were subjected to heavy bomb attack from at least the spring of 1943 onwards, and in 1944 to a weight of bombs many times greater than the Blitz on Britain. In September 1944 Hitler addressed the leaders of German war production on what had been achieved 'despite the growing damage from air attacks'. The new peak in war production achieved in August, he continued, showed that German industry could be trusted, even in the shrunken and battered area still remaining to

Germany, to concentrate everything on war production 'in order to be able to increase yet further the output of the most important weapons and equipment'.[175]

If the 'miracle' of expanded German production has very material explanations in the effective exploitation of both capital and labour, and efforts to rationalize the distribution of resources, the ability to sustain exceptional levels of war production in the face of the bombing offensive cannot be taken for granted. If bombing eventually placed a ceiling on what could be produced, the performance of the key sectors of German industry over the last two years of war did have something of an 'economic miracle' about it. Above all it was the exact reverse of what the Allies thought would be possible once the offensive got going, as the statistics in Table 7.1 make evident. Whatever the other resource and organizational issues confronting the German war economy, which is not the subject here, the extent to which German war-economic potential could be safeguarded against the impact of bombing became a central concern of the German war machine and allowed the German armed forces to continue fighting forlorn campaigns well into 1945.

The geography of German industry at the outbreak of war had something in common with the British pattern. Older industrial sectors – coal, steel, machinery – were concentrated in the Ruhr-Rhineland and Saar basins, but had been supplemented in the 1930s by expanding domestic production in new greenfield sites, particularly on the Salzgitter orefield in Brunswick, and the seizure of additional iron-ore, steel, coal and machinery production in Austria, the Sudetenland and Bohemia/Moravia. Modern industrial sectors, however, including chemicals, electronics, radio, the aeronautical industry and motor vehicles, were sited away

Table 7.1: Selected Statistics on German Military Production, 1940–44

Weapon type	Unit	1940	1941	1942	1943	1944
Munitions	tonnes	865,000	540,000	1,270,000	2,558,000	3,350,000
Armour	tonnes	37,235	83,188	140,454	369,416	622,322
Artillery	over 7.5 cm	5,964	8,124	14,316	35,796	55,936
Aircraft	number	10,250	11,030	14,700	25,220	37,950
Submarines	tonnes	–	162,000	193,000	221,000	234,000

Source: IWM, S363, Saur papers, 'Auszug aus dem Leistungsbericht von Minister Speer, 27.1.1945'.

from the old industrial regions, in Bavaria, Württemberg, Berlin, Saxony, and a fringe of smaller industrial cities. After 1933, with the new regime's emphasis on military and economic rearmament, conscious efforts were made to disperse industry away from the more exposed industrial regions behind the western frontier and to place it in relatively bomb-safe areas in central, southern and eastern Germany, a process known as *Verballung*, literally, breaking up the industrial 'ball'. German territorial expansion in 1938–40 ensured that the balance of industrial output in the enlarged 'Greater Germany' tilted further east, creating a cushion to absorb any potential damage done to the Ruhr-Rhineland. The Ruhr supplied three-quarters of German iron and steel output in 1939 but less than two-thirds by 1943.[176] The vast Reichswerke 'Hermann Göring', a state holding company for iron, steel, coal and armaments set up in 1937, controlled 71 firms in Germany but 241 in occupied Austria, Czechoslovakia and Poland. Until 1944 a proportion of German war production was protected by its geographical dispersal and the long aerial ranges needed to reach it.

The vulnerability of German industrial and service sectors to bombing was well understood and 'Work Self-Protection' (*Werkluftschutz*) featured in the 1937 'Self-Protection' law. But like air-raid protection in general, the factory system was introduced piecemeal; those plants furthest from the bombing threat were less inclined to introduce rigorous air-protection procedures for their workforce, provide them with effective shelters or install blast protection for machinery and equipment. When the Heinkel aircraft plant in Rostock suffered damage in the raids in 1942, it was found that the firm had not followed the Air Ministry's advice in building protective bomb walls.[177] In the cities in Zone I effective work protection was mandatory. From 1939 onwards vulnerable firms were asked to transfer some of their production to less endangered areas, and an effort was made, as in Britain, to ensure that vital components or even whole products (aircraft, aero-engines, tanks, etc.) were produced in at least three geographically distinct sites. Some of this early dispersal was effective – the Weser aircraft works at Bremen moved one-third of its production of the Ju87 'Stuka' to Berlin; the Focke-Wulf plant, also in Bremen, was decentralized to three separate sites further east in 1940 and 1941; the Blohm & Voss flying-boat production was transferred from Hamburg to Bodensee, in south Germany – while new capacity was built in areas far removed from the current bombing threat. In 1938–9 Messerschmitt Me109 production was set up at Wiener Neustadt outside Vienna (five other assembly plants in Austria and Bohemia were added later); another production centre was established at the Erla works in Leipzig. None could easily be bombed until 1944.[178]

As in Britain, a programme of camouflage and decoy sites was set up to confuse bombers trying to identify industrial targets in difficult night-time conditions. The largest and most effective site was at Essen, where the vast Krupp works was reproduced in effigy in the countryside outside the city and sustained, according to German Air Force estimates, around three-quarters of the bombing attacks aimed at the real plant. Decoy sites outside Stuttgart and Karlsruhe attracted well over half of all bombs in 1941.[179] In Berlin elaborate efforts were made to disguise the government quarter to avoid the danger of bombing. The Brandenburg Gate was reconstructed along with mock ministries further from the centre while prominent landmarks were concealed. The east-west axis road in the centre of Berlin was covered with a canopy of wire netting and green gauze, while lamp posts were covered with green material to look like trees. A lake in west Berlin was covered with green netting with a length of grey material laid across it to resemble a road.[180] Outside the city 16 major dummy industrial sites were set up, which attracted British bombs throughout the war. When firebombing became the principal RAF method, the German Air Force set up fire sites in small walled enclosures to mimic the appearance of blazing buildings. These, too, proved highly effective for much of the war. To accentuate the disruptive effect of industrially generated smog, the air force also introduced artificial smoke to screen vulnerable targets. Once daylight raids began in earnest in 1943, the programme was expanded so that by the end of the war there were 100 smoke companies composed of 50,000 men and women.[181]

Of the many problems faced by the German economy between 1940 and 1942, bombing was not one of them. Small-scale, incidental damage could be compensated while dispersal and decoys reduced what limited prospect there was of accurate raiding against economic targets. The German economy from 1939 onwards experienced a rapid and extensive transfer to war production priorities, cutting private consumer spending by one-quarter by 1942 (against a 14 per cent reduction in Britain) and increasing the percentage of workers in manufacturing who produced goods for the armed forces, from 28 per cent in May 1939 to 70 per cent in May 1942.[182] Arms production expanded steadily in the first years of war, though not without considerable difficulties. These were not caused, as has often been argued, by an unwillingness

on the part of the regime to commit to large-scale economic mobilization for war – indeed it is possible to describe as early as 1941 a problem
of *over*-mobilization – but by poor facilities for national planning of
resource use, competition between the three services, and a fraught relationship between the military and industry; the one was concerned with
rapid innovation and constant tactical alterations in design, the other
with finding profitable ways to convert the large resources of allocated
manpower and machinery to efficient and uninterrupted flow production. Productive performance was held back as much by poor planning
as it was by potential resource bottlenecks, which only really inhibited
war production in Germany at the end of 1944 when bombing, the collapse of the economic New Order, and the disruption of trade finally
reduced German access to key materials. The effect of production politics in the first years of war was to hold back the full rationalization of
war production. The gradual introduction of a system of production
rings and committees in 1941–2 to oversee each branch of production,
together with the establishment in March 1942 of an organization for
coordinated resource allocation known as Central Planning, saw the
creation of a framework within which the substantial earlier investment
in war output capacity could be used to expand the supply of armaments exponentially over the last three years of war.[183]

Bombing only became one of the factors that German industry had
to take more fully into account during 1943 and early 1944, as a result
of the RAF campaigns against the Ruhr, Hamburg and Berlin, and the
American attacks on aircraft production and ball-bearing factories.
Although the Ruhr campaign led to a temporary reduction in iron and
steel supply, it failed to halt the upward direction of German war production, which reached new peaks during 1943. The main Krupp works
in Essen lost only 7.6 per cent of its planned output in 1943; the giant
August-Thyssen concern produced more iron in 1943 than in either of
the previous two years.[184] At the same time sales of iron and steel from
the new plants in central Germany and occupied eastern Europe controlled by the Reichswerke 'Hermann Göring' expanded by 87 per cent
between 1941 and 1943 to compensate for declining Ruhr production.
The Reichswerke supplied one-fifth of all iron and steel, one-quarter of
German coal.[185] Bombing, as already noted in Chapter 6, only reduced
potential German industrial output by around 9 per cent in 1943. That
loss has to be set against a threefold expansion of war production
between 1941 and 1944 evident for all major classes of weapons. Total
munitions output for large-calibre artillery was 100 per cent greater in

1943 than 1942, production of tank guns 60 per cent higher, aircraft output up by 61 per cent; in 1944 these statistics were once again exceeded by a wide margin. Bombing caused local and temporary dislocation, but could not prevent German industry from adapting to the pressures and expanding output.[186] The central problem facing the German war economy in the last years of war was not the bombing but the escalating loss rates at the fighting front. In the first years of the war, losses both of manpower and equipment had been relatively low; from the Stalingrad battles on the Eastern Front to the collapse of Axis forces in North Africa and the rising attrition in the Battle of the Atlantic, the toll on Germany's armed forces escalated sharply. The demand for higher production reflected higher losses and the subsequent demands from the armed forces for more rapid and extensive replacement of stocks. Army stocks of tanks and self-propelled guns on hand were by 1944 almost four times greater than in 1941; stocks of anti-tank guns five times greater than in 1942; supply of aircraft, both new and repaired, expanded from a monthly average of 1,381 in 1940 to an average of 3,609 in 1944.[187] The continuous campaigning in 1943 and 1944 for greater rationalization and concentration of production was driven by the military necessity of supplying the fighting fronts, including the anti-aircraft defences, with larger quantities of weapons in a context of high wastage. Hitler's response to losses was always to call on the industrial economy to produce more; the priority for German industrialists and planners was to meet those demands, irrespective of the impact of the bombs.

Clearly production would have been easier to organize and have imposed a lesser toll on managers and workers alike in an entirely bomb-free environment. Bombing inhibited the wartime development of new technologies, though it did not prevent it. Indeed in some well-known cases – the Heinkel He177 heavy bomber, for example – the problems were self-inflicted. Improvisation proved successful, but it also came at a cost in organizational effort and problem-solving that did not affect managers in the United States or the far Soviet Union. As the bombing grew heavier in 1943 and 1944, the initial attempts to offer protection or immunity to German industry were extended and consolidated. The first possibility was to provide better protection on site. Anti-aircraft guns were concentrated in special defensive zones around the most threatened areas of war production. Special 'action units' were established for industry which, like their urban counterparts, were sent to bombed industrial sites to try to restart production as rapidly as possible. In August 1943, following the Hamburg raids, Speer was authorized to declare emergency 'Damage Regions' (*Schadensbereiche*), which would receive priority in the restoration of productive activity.[188] Individual plants were encouraged to develop comprehensive protective installations for their machinery and to increase the level of training for their workforces in simple air-raid protection procedures. Factories that had been bombed but were still able to function were told not to put on a new roof but to construct a black cover below roof level to simulate an empty building; fire-damaged external walls were kept in place to make it look as though the plant had been abandoned. Other undamaged buildings had camouflage damage painted on the sides.[189] All combustible stores of materials had to be moved to safer storage sites, and by autumn 1943 the Economics Ministry was able to report that the policy was working well. Stocks were moved to the edge of the endangered cities and stored by small firms more remote from the threat of attack.[190] The result was that even in cities badly hit, it was still possible to maintain a large proportion of pre-raid production. In Augsburg, for example, where industry was among the most heavily damaged, the average value of monthly production was 964,000 RM in the last five months of 1943; in the five months of heavy raiding in 1944 the average was 814,000 RM. In Hagen, hit by four heavy attacks in 1943, the pre-raid average value was 5.2 million RM, the post-raid value 5.17 million. Much of any loss was absorbed by cutting consumer production and concentrating on war-essential products.[191]

The second necessity was to ensure that the working population in the bombed cities could be assisted enough to ensure that labour productivity was maintained and absenteeism kept to a minimum. This was a more complex problem by 1943 because of the introduction of an increasing number of foreign compulsory workers and the rising proportion of women in the workforce, though in both cases work discipline could be imposed more ruthlessly by male German supervisors. Foreign workers were treated as effective captives; they had restricted access to air-raid shelters or had to make do with slit trenches, so as to emphasize the difference in status between them and skilled German workers. In a controlled economy, with no right to strike and heavy penalties for dissent, worker unrest could still be displayed through slow working or sabotage. It remained in the interest of employers and the state to ensure that the German labour force was given both stick and carrot to keep it productive. Priority was given to repairing workers' housing or replacing it with temporary barracks. Workers engaged in repair work following a raid were given a bonus of between 52 and 65 per cent an hour depending on their particular skills.[192] Workers who were rendered homeless had to report to their employer within two days to qualify for compensation and to be allowed a brief period of compassionate leave.[193]

Other rewards or bonuses were introduced to sustain worker loyalty despite the long hours and greater danger. Hourly wage rates for all German workers were increased to 25 per cent extra for overtime, 50 per cent extra for Sunday work and 100 per cent extra on holidays. Firms were encouraged to set up nurseries for working women, hostels for workers and midday hot meals. The Daimler-Benz company increased its 'social spending' on workforce facilities and bonuses from 1.6 million RM in 1939 to 2.1 million in 1944; in the last year of war, 4.6 million RM were spent on air-raid protection.[194] In October 1942 arrangements were made to provide additional food rations for the population in raided cities, predominantly in the western industrial areas: 50 grammes of extra meat a week for a minimum of four weeks, and extra fats and bread at the discretion of the local Reich Defence Commissar. Later in the war, when overtime incentives were declining, special 'Speer recognition' awards were made for exceptional efforts, usually paid in kind – alcohol and tobacco for men, health tonics, tinned vegetables and condensed milk for women and youths. But at the same time German workers were subject to closer discipline. In the Ruhr cities 'labour control' units were organized by the German Labour Front, checking on attendance and hours worked, granting leave to bombed-out workers, and searching out workers absent without leave to return them to work. Thought was given to militarizing the labour force as 'soldiers on the home front', but although the term was regularly used in propaganda, it was not carried through from fear that it would make labour less rather than more efficient.[195] In summer 1944 instructions were given to compel workers aged over 18 to serve 10 times a month (eight for women) in the works' 'self-protection' squads to make sure there were enough people to fight the fires, though for much of the war the factory was almost certainly a safer place to be than at home.[196] Yet in the end the greatest incentive for workers to remain at work was the need for regular wages to support them and their families, and the fear that defeat would usher in a return to the Depression days of high unemployment and short-time working and the possible dismemberment of Germany. Bombing gave them no incentive to give up.[197]

The most common response to the increased bombing was some form of dispersal. For several years production had been dispersed to different units in order to expand capacity. From the summer of 1943 dispersal policy was designed to provide substitute sites rather than extra ones. On 28 June 1943 Hitler issued a decree for securing factory space and accommodation for workers in those areas where production was to be dispersed.[198] Two weeks later Speer's ministry sent orders implementing the decree, which included a prohibition on any 'wild dispersal' undertaken without approval and an injunction not to move everything to the eastern regions just because they were still beyond range of regular air attacks. Instead firms were encouraged to disperse into local rural areas, which would allow them to keep their workforce intact and maintain links with local service and component contractors.[199] The Air Ministry had already begun a programme of dispersal in October 1942, when orders were issued to move all production out of the most endangered areas and to ensure that each product was manufactured in at last two or three different places. Sometimes by chance the same component was bombed simultaneously in two separate places – a Ju87 component, for example, in two raids on Bremen and Osnabrück in 1942 – but in general multiple production gave an added cushion of flexibility. By November 1942 most of the 290 businesses producing 100 per cent for the air force west of the line Stettin-Berlin-Munich had dispersal plans prepared.[200] Over the following months much aircraft production was moved to the Protectorate, Slovakia, Poland, Silesia and Saxony, but there still remained much to be done by the time Hitler published his decree in June 1943. The next month, Göring as Plenipotentiary for the Four Year Plan, ordered complete 'evacuation of war-essential industry from the core of major cities'.[201]

The success of the dispersal policy, which allowed German production to expand significantly despite the escalating bombardment, can best be illustrated by looking at the two industries chosen by the US Eighth Air Force as potential bottlenecks: ball-bearings and aircraft assembly. Both cases demonstrate the substantial cushion available in a heavily industrialized state when manufacture needed to be decentralized. The potentially disruptive effects of this process were mitigated by the simultaneous insistence, laid down in regular orders from Hitler himself, on simplifying and standardizing production and design, concentrating on a narrow range of model types, searching for substitute materials or parts for those in short supply, and eliminating any production, whether civilian or military, that was classified as less essential. Bombing forced the German productive system to become more flexible and improvisatory in ways that the Allied air forces had not anticipated. The attack on the production of ball-bearings at Schweinfurt failed in its purpose for just this reason. Four days after the attack Speer flew to Nuremberg on Hitler's orders to inspect the damage; the following day, 19 October 1943, Philipp Kessler, a member of Speer's Armaments Advisory Council, was appointed General Commissar for Restarting Ball-Bearing Production. Disliking the rather ponderous title, he established a 'Ball-Bearing Rapid Action' (*Kugellager-Schnellaktion*) organization under his direction. Schweinfurt represented only 45 per cent of available ball-bearing production; stocks were immediately taken over from the other producers and from contractors who held substantial reserves, a total equivalent to two months' production. The careful husbanding of stocks meant that by January 1944 reserves of ball-bearings were three times greater than in January 1943. Machine tools for production at Schweinfurt were by January 1944 back to 94 per cent of requirements. Production was decentralized so that under half was left in Schweinfurt itself, the rest spread out among 20 other producers. The whole ball-bearing industry in Germany was served in the end by 49 dispersal plants; only 20 per cent of national production remained in Schweinfurt a year after the main attack. The output of aircraft and tanks, which relied extensively on ball-bearings, was affected hardly at all thanks to design changes. By the time ball-bearing supply was back to its pre-raid level, aircraft production was 58 per cent greater, tank production 54 per cent.[202]

The dispersal of the aircraft industry indicated another cushion of productive capacity, even if in some cases in 1944 assembly or repair had to be improvised in farm barns, wooded shelters or road tunnels. The second wave of dispersal following the planned decentralization in 1942–3 came following the Allied air attacks in 'Big Week' in February 1944. Although the production loss was small and soon made good, the decision was taken by the German Fighter Staff to decentralize all aircraft and aero-engine production even further in case the campaign intensified. The 27 main assembly plants were divided out among 729 smaller units, though in the end only around 300 were used; aero-engine output was divided from 51 plants (in many cases already dispersed once) to 249 new sites. Up to the end of 1943 some 3.3 million square metres had been made available as dispersed capacity, but the new programmes involved a further 2.4 million.[203] The result was a complex mosaic of productive sites for each of the main producers. The Erla Works in Leipzig, producing one-third of Me109 production, was split up among 18 dispersal plants, 13 component plants and 5 main assembly points, and although output was temporarily safeguarded, the six-month transfer of production lines cost 2,800 lost aircraft. The Me109 production at Wiener-Neustadt also had to be decentralized in spring 1944, and was also achieved with mixed success because sites were chosen where too much new installation and reconstruction was needed. Efficiency was hit by the requirement to have no unit capable of producing more than 150 aircraft a month. Nevertheless the company managed to build 50 per cent more fighter aircraft in 1944 than in 1943. By contrast, Me110 production at the Gothaer Waggonfabrik in Gotha was more successfully dispersed after the raids in February, so that full production was restored after only a few weeks.[204] The whole dispersal policy ensured that aircraft output would reach a peak of almost 40,000 aircraft in a year when 1 million tons of bombs were dropped on German and German-occupied targets. Bombing might have prevented higher output, but the aircraft industry would anyway have faced limitations from raw material and labour supplies in trying to produce more, with or without bombing.

The decentralization of production did come at a cost, and no doubt overall output would have been higher in 1943 and 1944 without it. The success of the transfer to above-ground sites ensured that overall output could continue its upward trajectory. For those who had to undertake the reorganization, or for the workers forced to transfer to different sites, almost 850,000 by late 1944, the social and psychological costs were considerable. For one thing managerial and technical personnel had to be divided out among a larger number of small plants, increasing individual responsibility and diluting a firm's leadership corps; more workers were engaged indirectly on military orders for which they had not been trained, or other workers (usually foreign or camp labourers) had to be transferred from one camp barrack to another; shorter production runs undermined the time and cost savings of large-scale assembly; tools and jigs had to be supplied in multiples, though in this case the large number of general-purpose machine tools available in Germany made the transfer to fragmented production easier to carry out. Above all, dispersal placed strains on the communication system and in particular the carefully controlled distribution of equipment and parts run by the Armaments Ministry, designed to ensure that components and tools only arrived at the time and in the quantities needed. With an exceptional amount of organizational and labouring effort, German industry succeeded in maximizing production despite the obstacles presented by dispersal. The object, as one manager put it, was for 'the impossible to be made possible'.[205]

Doing the impossible might well have described the coincidence of peak bombing and peak production. The factors that kept war production expanding during 1942 and 1943 played a critical part in sustaining the expansion of output during 1944. The concentration of production on the most essential equipment reached its high point in the spring of 1944 as older models of weapons and equipment were eliminated and standard models introduced. Types of light-infantry weapons were to be reduced from 14 to 5, anti-tank weapons from 12 to just 1, anti-aircraft guns from 10 to 2; the number of vehicle models was reduced from 55 to 14; and so on.[206] All inessential or non-military manufacture was combed through one more time to weed out unneeded production: the 117 firms still making carpets were reduced to 5; the 23 firms making 300 types of prismatic glass were reduced to 7, making just 14 types; the 900 machine-tool firms were reduced to 369. Where possible, the floorspace and labour were allocated to direct military output. In the machinery industry 415,700 workers were freed by early 1944 to work directly on war material.[207] Rationalization, defined by the regime as extracting as much military equipment as possible from existing machinery, materials and labour, was pushed to its limits during 1944. The major constraint on the German war effort, labour supply, was ameliorated by drawing in resources from occupied Europe, exploiting camp labour more extensively, and finding ways to get women with children to undertake part-time work or work at home. To cope with the large-scale movement of the population as a result of bombing, the Plenipotentiary for Labour, the Gauleiter of Thuringia, Fritz Sauckel, issued an order on 17 January 1944 obliging those who had been evacuated and were not yet working to report to local labour offices for work. The first order produced only 65,000 volunteers, but as the number of evacuees increased, the second and third 'Report Orders', which applied to women with children under seven and women aged 45–50, reaped a larger harvest. By October 1944, 1.6 million had registered, out of whom 303,000 were given work, three-quarters of them half-day shifts in dispersed factories. Almost all of these were women, joining the 3.5 million female workers already on half-shifts. Women constituted more than 50 per cent of the total German workforce by the end of the war.[208]

The changing composition of the industrial workforce brought advantages and disadvantages for German war production. The foreign workforce made up 1.6 million (15 per cent) of industrial labour in July 1942, 2.7 million (22 per cent) in July 1943, and by summer 1944, 3.2 million (29 per cent). Their presence could present problems of language, discipline and training, and there was anxiety that they would not cope as well as German workers under the pressure of bombing. At Daimler-Benz, 31 different nationalities were recorded in the workforce, including one lone Afghan and one Peruvian.[209] Women came to make up a growing proportion of the labour force, many of them forced labourers from the east. Female employment raised problems about family care, physical exhaustion and the struggle to secure rationed goods, but the economy would not have functioned without them. Efforts were made to sustain their productivity too with bonuses or extra rations and appropriate training. Of the total of 6.2 million employed in the arms industry, more than half of all industrial employment by October 1944, 35 per cent were women, 37 per cent foreign workers or prisoners of war.[210] This heterogeneous labour force was subject to persistent and heavy bombing throughout 1944 and the first months of 1945.

The assumption for Allied planners was that urban destruction would create a growing problem of absenteeism, which would contribute to undermining armaments production. Yet the statistics show that bombing contributed only a small proportion of lost hours in 1944. According to records compiled by the Economics Ministry, in October 1944 only 2.5 per cent of hours lost nationally was attributed to air raids. Absenteeism was a result of illness, leave, truancy or workplace policy – a total of 16 per cent lost work hours – but was not directly caused by bomb attack.[211] The aggregate figure nevertheless disguised wide variations from one branch of industry to another, and between different areas of the Reich. The absenteeism rates for the main industrial groups between March and October 1944 are set out in Table 7.2: Absenteeism rates were higher in the western areas of Germany, in Hamburg and in Munich. Yet over the course of 1944, despite the losses, the total number of hours worked in the 12,000 war production firms surveyed by the Ministry actually increased from 976 million in March to 1,063 million in October.[212] One explanation is that the large proportion of foreign, prisoner of war and concentration camp workers made it possible to use coercion to keep them working. At the Ford Works in Cologne, absenteeism was a problem only among German workers. In

Table 7.2: Hours Worked and Hours Lost in German Industry, March–October 1944 (%)

Industrial Branch	Hours Worked	Hours Lost	Air Raids	Illness/ Leave
Iron and Steel	84.7	15.3	5.1	10.2
Machinery	83.3	16.7	6.2	10.5
Vehicles	77.0	23.0	10.6	12.4
Aircraft industry	85.6	14.4	4.6	9.8
Shipbuilding	82.2	17.8	7.9	9.9

Source: BA-B, R3102/10031, Statistical Office, 'Vermerk über die Auswirkung der Feindlichen Luftangriffe auf die Arbeiterstundenleistung der Industrie', 27 Jan 1945.

1944 it was estimated that 25 per cent of the German workforce was absent on average over the year, whereas the figure for the Eastern workers (Russians, Poles, Ukrainians) was only 3 per cent. German workers either absented themselves permanently – a total of 1,000 at Ford in 1944, two-thirds of them women – or returned slowly after a raid, one-tenth after one to two days, two-thirds after two weeks.[213] For the German war economy one of the major advantages of exploiting captive labour on a large scale in 1944 and 1945 was the possibility of controlling their work effort even in the adverse conditions imposed by heavy bombing.

The large captive workforce also made it possible to contemplate from summer 1943 onwards a more radical solution to the policy of dispersal by placing the most important war production under the ground, either in converted mines, caves and tunnels, or in new purpose-built underground facilities, covered with up to seven metres of concrete. Interest in the programme was generated from a number of quarters. In July 1943 Hitler asked that production of the new A4 rocket (the later V2) should be made as safe as possible from bombing, preferably underground; Himmler undertook to carry it out because he had access to a rapidly expanding concentration camp population for the supply of labour. The Air Ministry had already asked the mining section of the Economics Ministry to compile a list of all potential sites in Germany and the nearest occupied territories with underground floorspace for the aeronautical industry to escape the raids.[214] The list of possible sites ran to 22 pages, 15 with German locations, 7 more for those identified

Table 7.3: Programmes of Underground Construction,
November 1944 (sq m)

Industry	Planned	Abandoned	Under Construction	Completed
Airframes	20,766,800	645,000	16,570,400	3,550,800
Air Components	6,391,400	–	5,347,700	1,043,720
Aero-engines	20,992,700	1,345,000	15,871,000	3,776,800
Tanks	2,109,000	–	1,818,400	290,500
Motor Vehicles	2,808,360	–	2,711,500	96,800
V-Weapons	1,538,700	–	387,400	1,151,300
Shipbuilding	1,775,400	–	1,248,200	527,200
Weapons	2,173,500	–	2,119,720	53,800
Machine Tools	7,101,600	–	6,079,400	1,022,200
Total	65,657,460	1,990,000	52,153,720	11,513,120

Source: TNA, AIR 10/3873, BBSU, 'German Experience in the Underground Transfer of War Industries', 12.

in Hungary, Slovakia, Bohemia/Moravia and Poland. Limited progress was made in 1943, but in the spring of 1944, with the onset of more targeted bombing of key industries, comprehensive plans were drawn up for a colossal construction programme to embrace eventually 93 million square metres of underground room, to include separate programmes for oil and SS projects, among them the A4 rocket. The distribution of underground plant, planned, completed and in hand, is set out in Table 7.3.

The plans were by 1944 difficult to implement, though the SS control of slave labour in the camps provided a ready-made supply of workers for the rocket programme, set up in the notorious Mittelbau-Dora works at Nordhausen. Only 17 per cent of the programme was completed by the end of 1944, and not all of that was occupied or functioning by the end of the war. The initial programme was designed to get aircraft production into shelters so that increased output of planes could be used to turn back the bombers and perhaps render the rest of the programme redundant. By May 1944 some 10 per cent of aircraft construction was underground, more by the end of the year. Saur developed a plan to create large underground sites in Hungary, first for fighter aircraft, then one for fuel oil, finally an integrated plant for weapons, munitions and vehicles, even though the Red Army was now within striking distance. The underground programme has always been viewed as a waste of resources: 'burrowing away from reality', was the judgement of the British Bombing Survey Unit.[215] It is true that most of the dispersal underground was wasted effort. The transfer of BMW aero-engine output into salt mines began in May 1944, was scheduled for occupation by December, but was not in the end utilized. The access shafts were narrow, the subterranean corridors only 10–30 metres wide, the salt a threat to the workforce and the machinery. Many of the underground installations suffered from poor ventilation, condensation, and the danger of rockfalls; conditions for workers were so poor that preference was given to using the captive workforce, which in the case of BMW made up 13,000 out of 17,000 at the main plant. By the time the vast Volkswagen works at Wolfsburg was ordered to disperse underground in August 1944, only 15 per cent of its 17,000 workers were German.[216] It is nonetheless difficult to see what other long-term solution remained to a regime that refused to surrender and over-optimistically assessed the prospects of survival into 1945 and 1946. When Allied bombing was finally directed at oil production in May 1944, the threat to the vulnerable capital-intensive sectors of German industry could only be solved by finding effective ways of sheltering it from the bombs, or giving up the conflict.

Allied bombing was at its most dangerous in 1944 when it targeted large capital projects in oil and chemicals which could not easily be moved or substituted, unlike ball-bearings or aircraft. Following the first bombing, Hitler on 31 May 1944 approved the appointment of Edmund Geilenberg as yet another emergency manager, this time as General Plenipotentiary for Emergency Measures, with the task of putting fuel production underground or moving it into less exposed above-ground installations. The plan was to create 98 dispersed sites, 22 of them under the earth, capable of producing up to four-fifths of all aviation fuel and 88 per cent of diesel fuel for tanks. By the end of the war around three-fifths of the preparatory work had been done, but only a small amount of equipment had been installed. German fuel supply relied in the end on being able to repair quickly enough the damage to the existing plants.[217] The problems posed by trying to repair damage and supply replacement components were critical in explaining the final collapse of the German war economy under the remorseless punishment inflicted in the last months of the war. Even before the onset of the transportation plan in September 1944, random interruption to an overstretched communications system led to regular hold-ups in getting damaged plant repaired, machines replaced or vital components and equipment supplied. The weekly reports on economic conditions produced by the Economics Ministry throughout 1944 reiterate the problems presented by interrupted rail lines and damaged rolling stock.[218] The department heads from Speer's renamed War Production Ministry all highlighted in their post-war interrogations the damage to production imposed because repairs could not be effected or components and parts supplied.[219] This situation was exacerbated by the decision to disperse production often long distances from the main plant. At the Henschel aircraft works 200 couriers were on hand to collect and distribute vital materials and parts to and from subcontractors in order to keep production going at all.[220]

Given the artificial concentration on war production at all costs, the chronic stress on the workforce labouring 60–70 hours a week, and the rapid contraction of the European supply base, there were limits to how far the German war economy could be pushed, even without the effects of bombing. The economist J. K. Galbraith, drafted in to assess the German economy at the end of the war, judged that in 1944 German production, bombing or not, was approaching 'what might be called a *general* bottleneck'.[221] The weight of attack from September 1944 on a taut economic structure confirmed that the German war economy had reached its limit. There was a sudden increase in the number of firms reporting air-raid damage. In July there were 421, of which 150 were totally or severely damaged; in September there were 674, with 253 in the worst categories; in November 1944, 311 out of 664 firms had suffered total or severe loss.[222] The economy kept going during the last eight months of war using accumulated stocks to compensate for the slow decline in the supply of basic materials – steel, iron, aluminium, machine tools – and the cumulative effect of the loss of rail and water transport for the supply of coal. As a result, peak wartime production for artillery, armoured fighting vehicles and fighter aircraft was actually reached in the last three months of 1944.[223] After that, production collapsed rapidly as the encircling armies and the enveloping air fleets tightened their noose around the German neck.

The German leadership continued, nevertheless, to throw emergency solutions at a collapsing structure. On 1 August 1944 an Armaments Staff responsible for eight priority production programmes was established, bringing together under the direction of Speer and Saur 25 department heads with supreme authority to squeeze what weapons they could out of the shrinking economic base. In December 1944 Germany was divided up into seven Armaments Zones (*Rüstungsbezirke*), in each of which an autonomous military economy was supposed to flourish. Production declined by more than half. During the last weeks of the war the system continued to hover between fantasy and reality. The army planned a slimmed-down 'Storm-Programme' for army weapons, deciding what the forces could do without while still able to keep on fighting successfully.[224] In early March Speer set up an emergency 'Transport Staff' to coordinate all communications; on 8 March he finally established three Armaments Plenipotentiaries in areas he thought were suitable for an 'autarkic economy'. One was based in Heidelberg, one in Prague and one in the Rhine-Ruhr, just days before its surrender.[225]

Bombing critically affected the German productive economy only during the last months of the war, but even though a ceiling was placed on further expansion, war production continued to increase until the crisis provoked by the loss of territory, the failure of the dispersal schemes and the collapse of the repair cycle. A combination of effective work protection, control of the workforce, concealment and deception, dispersal of key production, and insistent policies on concentration and rationalization, had succeeded in limiting the damage air attack could inflict on industry, though not on the cityscapes and urban populations that surrounded it. On 19 March 1945 Hitler published his 'scorched earth' decree in which he ordered the destruction of all that remained of Germany's industry, transport network and food supplies. It was never implemented, thanks partly to the intervention of Albert Speer, but it would certainly have imposed a higher level of damage on the industrial economy and infrastructure than the bombing. Hans Rumpf, chief inspector of the German fire service, later observed that the dismantling and reparation regime established by the Allies in the occupied zones of Germany after the war's end took a much higher proportion of German industrial capacity than the fraction destroyed by bombing. Of German engineering capacity, 20 per cent was destroyed from the air, 70 per cent by Allied requisitioning.[226]

'WILL GERMANY CRACK?': 1944-5

In February 1944 Heinrich Himmler, appointed Minister of the Interior in August 1943, in addition to his other offices, announced that 'no German city will be abandoned' as a result of bombing.[227] The situation facing Germany's urban area in 1944 was nevertheless a daunting one.

In the last 17 months of the war three-quarters of all bombs were dropped and approximately two-thirds of all bombing deaths were caused. In Munich, 89 per cent of bombs on the city fell in 1944 and 1945; in Mainz, 93 per cent of the deaths from bombing occurred in the same two years.[228] By spring 1945, no part of the contracting German Empire remained untouched. Bombing by day and by night did not affect every area simultaneously and many towns were bombed just once, but bombing and its social and cultural consequences came to dominate the daily lives of millions of Germans, a majority of them female. One young schoolgirl in Berlin, Waltraud Süssmilch, subject to compulsory civil defence training and playground demonstrations, surrounded by bombed areas of the city, straining to distinguish the different rush and explosion of each type of bomb, later recalled the bizarre wartime world in her memoir: 'Bombs belonged to my life. I was confronted with them daily. I could not do otherwise . . . I was no longer a child.'[229]

The presence of Himmler as Minister of the Interior as well as Chief of German Police continued a process begun in the 1930s to extend the responsibility of the SS and police system over all areas of air-raid protection and civil defence policy. During 1944 Himmler continued to undermine the position of the Air Ministry and in August the Air Force Inspectorate 13, responsible for air-raid protection, was abruptly abolished at Hitler's insistence. Responsibility for air-raid protection and the air-raid warning service transferred unconditionally to the SS and police. On 5 February 1945, just weeks before the end of the war, Himmler also succeeded in removing the Regional Air Commands from any responsibility for civil defence, leaving only a handful of mobile 'Air Protection Regiments' under air force control.[230] His new role introduced a fresh element of menace into the regular work of civil defence. On 14 April he published a decree threatening tough punishment for any civil defender who failed in their duty. While most citizens were said to display an 'exemplary self-sacrifice', the slackers and feckless were to be dealt with sharply under the terms of the Air Protection Law. Persistent negligence, malice or deliberate defiance was to result in a court appearance, which by 1944 meant facing a justice system dominated by a narrow ideological outlook and a search for vengeance.[231] For many of those engaged in civil defence, whether Ukrainians in the fire service or camp prisoners detailed to clear up urban debris, the SS was effectively their lawless master.

Goebbels found it difficult to maintain his position in the face of

Himmler's ambitions. In December 1943, frustrated that the Inter-Ministerial Committee had too little power, Goebbels convinced Hitler to make him Reich Inspector for Civil Air Protection. With the *Gauleiter* of Westphalia-South, Albert Hoffmann, as his deputy, and a collaborator from the committee, Alfred Berndt, as his office director, Goebbels used his new position to review civil defence all over Germany and to insist on improvements in self-protection organization and communal services.[232] By this stage the local responsibility for coping with the aftermath of raids had passed entirely to the Reich Defence Commissars, with whom Goebbels kept in close contact. In September 1944 the Commissars were formally acknowledged as the key coordinating figures in the defence of the Reich, at which point the Party also assumed the public political role of preparing the German people for their final ordeal. By this time Goebbels had abandoned the Inspectorate, which had done little more than report the state of affairs rather than initiate action; on 25 July 1944 he was named Reich Plenipotentiary for Total War, another emergency appointment which bore little relation to the conditions on the ground for which he was now ostensibly responsible.[233] It is questionable whether Goebbels' initiatives did anything more than simply confuse the existing structure. In February 1944 the Gauleiter of the Sudetenland complained that there was 'an alarming confusion' of orders issuing from a system that had become 'more and more bureaucratic'. The Reich Defence Commissar in Hanover-East pointed out in August that he was the subject of five separate streams of instructions on air-raid questions, producing simply a 'flood of paper' rather than a single, clear administrative path.[234]

The evidence on the ground suggests that the real responsibility for coping with air raids and their consequences still lay principally with local authorities and the millions of civilian volunteers who fought as best they could against the rising tide of destruction and demoralization. In August 1943 the police authorities issued an order compelling every resident or visitor in an air-protection zone to take part in self-protection action during a raid. Every street and apartment block had its wardens, self-protection troop, house-fire defenders, lay helpers and messengers, led by the local Leader of the Self-Protection Area.[235] In January 1944 Hitler approved further measures to increase the active participation of the population in their own defence, despite the growing risks they faced. He compared their experience with the front-line soldier who had to get over his fear of attacking tanks at close quarters: 'the one who has actually seen and practised extinguishing incendiary

bombs, loses a large part of his fear of this kind of weapon'.[236] The
schoolgirl in Berlin whose life was dominated by bombs was expected
to tackle and extinguish one of a number of types of Allied incendiary
('Would you trust yourself to extinguish such a bomb?' asked the fire-
man demonstrator. 'Yes,' she replied.)[237] In May the *Luftschutzbund*
issued instructions to air-protection officials to undertake home visits to
every house and apartment in their sector to provide up-to-date information for each householder, to ensure that every resident was materially
prepared to assist, and to try and strengthen the 'spiritual resolve' of the
community for the difficult task ahead.[238]

The priority by 1944, with heavy raids on Berlin and other cities
deeper in German territory, was to try to save as much as possible of
German urban life and the populations still living there. Even while
Allied aircraft remorselessly reduced the habitable areas of major cities,
the effort to repair or recondition damaged housing continued so that
workers who remained could have some kind of shelter. The repair of
bomb-damaged housing was governed by two decrees issued by Speer
as General-Plenipotentiary for Construction on 15 and 16 September
1943, which gave priority to getting working-class housing habitable
again to reduce lost work-time. Only those houses that could be repaired
easily and immediately were to be tackled; nothing was permitted that
took more than three months.[239] Local repair was allocated to a construction team organized by the Reich Defence Commissar, with help
from mobile columns of skilled workers organized by the Reich Group
Handwork. These motorized emergency units – for doors/windows,
roof repair, shop windows and room interiors – were functioning by
October 1943 and fully funded by July the following year. They arrived
in a bombed town, parked their vehicles in undamaged streets or
squares, and began work on reconstruction at once.[240] The quantity of
residential housing destroyed in 1943 was estimated at 5 per cent of the
housing stock, but during 1944 the figures mounted sharply, making it
difficult to keep pace with the programme of repair. In the most heavily
bombed cities, houses that were lightly damaged in one raid might be
hit again in the next more seriously. In the Ruhr city of Bochum residential damage by spring 1944 was 147 per cent of all homes, in Düsseldorf
130 per cent, in Essen 126 per cent, a result of counting some repaired
houses two, three or more times.[241] Between January and October
1944 the number of destroyed or heavily damaged residential buildings
was 311,807 against 119,668 in the first nine months of 1943, leaving
3.5 million temporarily, or in some cases permanently, homeless.[242]

From autumn 1944 it became difficult any longer to construct an accurate statistical picture of housing losses. The last recorded figures, in
November, showed the loss of 57,000 buildings in one month.[243]

The urban population also depended on the survival of services – gas,
electricity and clean drinking water. The problem of water supply
became acute by the summer of 1944 and emergency measures were
prepared for a population that had to share water with the fire service.
In all cities under attack the authorities were told to put up notices
indicating where people could find a stand-tap with clean water, and
warnings where water was not drinkable and would have to be boiled.[244]
The Interior Ministry drew up a list of all tanker lorries available nationally to help distribute clean water; the Reich Inspector for Water and
Energy sent out detailed instructions in August 1944 on how to keep
the water supply going by protecting or establishing plants that could
filter and purify contaminated water.[245] In Berlin the local association of
brewers was asked in autumn 1943 to supply a complete list of the
water sources (springs, streams) used in brewing and mineral water production; by June 1944, 286 usable sources had been identified. The
same month the Interior Ministry drew up an inventory of unused
bottles that could be requisitioned to supply water, which included
357,000 beer bottles and 312,000 used for Coca-Cola.[246]

Gas supply, on which a large number of German households
depended, faced the same problems of random but cumulative damage
to the gas network. It was found in 1943, even in heavy raids, that the
loss of supply could be kept within manageable boundaries. Surplus
capacity in the network actually exceeded by a significant margin the
damage done by bombing. A heavy raid on Berlin on 3–4 September
1943 resulted in the loss of gas in some districts for only a few hours, in
others for only a day. It was possible to find supplies from other parts
of the network when local gasworks were damaged; after the raid
on Leipzig on 3–4 December 1944, the main gasworks, supplying
250,000 cubic metres of gas, was temporarily put out of action, but
long-distance supply managed to restore 90 per cent of what was
needed.[247] But the expanded raiding in 1944 resulted in widespread and
unpredictable damage to both the gas and water networks. By June
1944 there were 94 badly damaged gasworks and waterworks countrywide; by the autumn gasworks were forced to cease operation in many
places because of the loss of vital pieces of equipment that could no
longer be supplied.[248] Millions of householders found that by 1945 gas
supply was non-existent or confined to a slender stream. 'The gas is

running on a tiny, dying flicker,' wrote one Berlin woman in her diary in April 1945. 'The potatoes have been cooking for hours . . . I swallowed one half-raw.'[249]

The damage done to German cities in 1944 and 1945 was extensive and indiscriminate. Goebbels ordered lists to be compiled of the destruction of all cultural monuments and cultural treasures. Church authorities sent in regular reports of damage to ecclesiastical property.[250] Table 7.4 shows the tonnage of bombs dropped by both Allied air forces on major German cities (by comparison total tonnage on London in the Blitz was 18,800 tons, and on the second most heavily bombed urban area, Liverpool/Birkenhead, only 1,957 tons). The detailed histories of individual cities show the extent of the cumulative losses inflicted in the final raids. Munich, unscathed for the first three years of war, suffered 30 major raids from September 1942. This involved the loss of 10,600 residential buildings; only 2.5 per cent of all buildings in the city remained completely unscathed by the bombing. Some 45 per cent of the physical substance of the city was destroyed, an average figure that disguises wide differences: areas of the central old city were three-quarters destroyed, but in the industrial zone of Munich-Allach only 0.4 per cent. Of cultural

Table 7.4: Bomb Tonnage Dropped on Major Urban Targets in Germany, 1940–45

City	Bomber Command	USAAF	Total
Berlin	45,517	22,768	68,285
Cologne	34,712	13,302	48,014
Hamburg	22,583	15,736	38,319
Essen	36,420	432	36,852
Duisburg	30,025	510	30,535
Kiel	16,748	13,198	29,946
Frankfurt am Main	15,696	12,513	28,209
Bremen	12,844	12,669	25,513
Mannheim	18,114	7,067	25,181
Stuttgart	21,014	3,905	24,919
Dortmund	22,242	2,541	24,783
Nuremberg	13,020	7,381	20,401
Munich	7,858	10,993	18,851

Source: Olaf Groehler, *Bombenkrieg gegen Deutschland* (Berlin: 1990), 432.

and religious buildings, 92 were totally destroyed, 182 damaged, including the cathedral, the old town hall, the council room, the state library (losses of half a million books), the Residence, the Maxburg, the National Theatre: and so on. In total, Munich had 7.2 million cubic metres of rubble that needed clearing away at the end of the war.[251] These statistics could be repeated for almost all German cities or towns by the war's end, large or small. The small community of Bingerbrück, on the Rhine, had 470 buildings; 327 were destroyed or heavily damaged, and only 2 avoided any damage at all.[252]

The heavy destruction of the infrastructure and residential districts of German cities and towns made it increasingly difficult to protect the population from death, injury and enforced displacement. The evacuation programme was expanded rapidly to try to reduce the risk to sections of the population who were not regarded as essential to the war effort. It was now evident that nowhere was safe, so that the proportion of the population who might need to move was unmanageably large. In January 1944 Hitler told Goebbels that not everyone eligible to move could go, since this involved an estimated 8 million children, mothers and the old from the 32 million inhabitants of every city over 50,000 people.[253] The following month Himmler sent out guidelines on evacuation with the object of limiting it as far as possible in order to avoid too much pressure on reception areas that in some cases were already full, and to ensure that work and air defence could be maintained. City dwellers were encouraged to move away from city centres, where the majority of deaths from fire were caused. In an ironic reversal of the RAF zoning system, Himmler ordered local authorities to move people away from the inner zone, with its narrow, tightly packed streets, to the less densely populated outer zones, the commuter suburbs and the farthest 'weekend commuter' belt; the priority was to ensure that most evacuees stayed close to the cities they had left.[254]

In practice restrictions were difficult to enforce and the rising tide of urban casualties accelerated the pace of both official and unofficial evacuation. Arrangements had to be made between the Party regions to see how many people could be accommodated and what transport was available for them, but by September 1944 there were 5.6 million evacuees, by November 7.8 million and by the beginning of 1945, 8.9 million. Not all of these were evacuees from bombing. Of the final figure for 1945 an estimated 1.76 million had left, while 2.41 million had been compulsorily evacuated or had fled from the frontier areas imminently threatened with invasion and 841,000 had been moved with dispersed factories.[255] No figures are available for those who remained in the suburbs or commuter belts of damaged cities, but in Hamburg the numbers displaced from the destroyed central areas to other parts of the city numbered half a million, leading to a sudden increase in the level of population density in the unbombed zones.[256] During the last half of 1944 and the first months of 1945, Germany was an exceptionally mobile society; Germans moved westwards from the threat of Soviet invasion, eastwards from the approaching Anglo-American armies, away from the bombed cities and, in an unknown number of cases, back again. Accommodation became rudimentary, food and welfare supplies exiguous, and pilfering and petty crime more widespread. Those who returned to living in familiar cellars and ruins could tell themselves that life was preferable there, for all the risks and violence of the air war. 'My cellar home in Hamburg,' wrote a woman evacuated to Linz, 'was a thousand times better.'[257]

For those who remained in the cities, fighting the raids and their consequences was only one of the problems confronted in the last year of the war. The problems of poor health, the difficulty of obtaining rationed goods, long hours of work, and declining transport all owed something to the effects of bombing, but were also derived from the exceptional demands made in the last year of war to sustain war production and military campaigning from an exhausted people. For almost 8 million forced foreign workers and prisoners of war, and the 700,000 concentration camp prisoners, there was no choice about running the risks of being bombed or the dangers of its aftermath. German cities changed their social geography markedly over the last year of war. The population of major cities in the Ruhr-Rhineland shrank to a fraction of their total before the bomber offensive: Essen, Düsseldorf and Frankfurt had less than half their pre-war population by May 1945, but Cologne had just 20,000 left out of 770,000. The population of Munich declined by 337,000 (41 per cent) between 1939 and 1945, the population of Berlin by 1.7 million (40 per cent), that of Hamburg by half a million (35 per cent).[258] Among those who remained were a rising proportion of non-Germans, or of German workers transferred from other industrial sites, but a shrinking number of young and middle-aged men. This was the population that suffered the high casualty rates of the last 18 months of the war.

The exact figure of deaths from bombing up to the end of the war has never been established with certainty, partly because of the sudden influx of refugees from the eastern regions in the last weeks of the conflict, partly because figures for casualties were collected by a number of different agencies – the Air Ministry, the Interior Ministry, the Economics Ministry and the Party Chancellery – and partly because in the final weeks of the war accurate record-keeping was no longer possible. The statistical series collected during the war differed from each other because some distinguished between civilian casualties, uniformed casualties, POWs and foreign workers, whereas others listed only civilian casualties. In August 1944, for example, Air Ministry records show 11,070 dead, but Economics Ministry records show 8,562; the first includes all categories of bomb victims, the second only civilians.[259] Table 7.5 shows the full record for November 1944 provided by the Air Ministry Air Protection Staff.

This source was used by the United States Bombing Survey after the war to estimate German casualties. The total number of dead for 1943 and 1944 from Air Protection Staff records was 100,107 in 1943, 146,300 for 1944, and 13,553 for the month of January 1945. The overall figure for those injured is 305,455. No further aggregate statistics are available for the last three months of the war. Using the same proportions as November 1944, it can be estimated that of this 259,960 dead, approximately 80 per cent were German civilians.[260] There are also archive records to show deaths from bombing in the years 1940 to 1942, a total of 11,228, of whom 6,824 died in 1942 and approximately 4,000 in 1941.[261] Based on these archive sources, the figure for those who died from May 1940 to January 1945 comes to 271,188. No doubt this does not include all those who were killed or died of wounds, but it does include uniformed personnel, POWs and foreign workers, and it applies to the whole of the Greater German area, including those territories incorporated from March 1938 onwards.

Table 7.5: The Dead and Seriously Injured from Bombing, November 1944 (Greater German Area)

Category	Dead	Injured
Armed forces	1,118	1,680
Police/Air Protection	129	161
Civilians	14,590	22,145
POWs	371	372
Foreign workers	1,232	1,677

Source: BA-B, R3102/10031, Air Ministry, LS-Arbeitsstab, 'Übersicht über Luftangriffe und Bombenabwürfe', Nov 1944.

It is difficult to reconcile these figures with the much larger totals arrived at in post-war calculations. The difference can largely be explained by the speculative nature of the estimates made for the number who died in the last four months of heavy bombing. In 1956 Hans Sperling published in the German official statistical journal *Wirtschaft und Statistik* (*Economy and Statistics*) a detailed account of his reconstruction of the dead from bombing. His total of civilians killed came to 570,000 for the wartime German area. Together with 23,000 uniformed dead and an estimated 32,000 POWs and foreign workers, his sum reached 625,000, the figure commonly quoted today for the total killed in Germany by Allied bombing.[262] Sperling's figures rested on speculations about the number of German civilians and foreign workers who died in the last four months of war, and in particular on the number of refugees fleeing westwards into the path of the raids. He guessed that 111,000 of them died between January 1945 and the end of the war, including the greatly inflated figure of 60,000 dead in Dresden. This would mean that around 300,000 people in total were killed in Germany in the final flourish of bombing, a statistic that has no supporting evidence. In 1990 the East German historian Olaf Groehler published revised figures. Although acknowledging the speculative nature of some of his own calculations, particularly for those who died in 1945, Groehler suggested a much lower figure of 420,000 for all categories of victim and for the enlarged German wartime area.[263]

There are ways to arrive at a more plausible total. If it is assumed that the figure of 271,000 dead by January 1945 is a realistic, if not precise, total (and there are archive figures which suggest a lower sum), it is possible to extrapolate from the last five months of heavy raiding for which records exist (September 1944 to January 1945) in order to find a possible order of magnitude for deaths in the last three months of the war. The average death toll for these five months was 18,777, which would give an aggregate figure for the whole war period of 328,000, though it would not allow for the exceptional casualty level at Dresden, confirmed by the latest research at approximately 25,000. Adding this would produce a total figure of approximately 353,000, representing 82,000 deaths in the last months. Detailed reconstruction of deaths caused by Royal Air Force bombing from February to May 1945, though incomplete, suggests a total of at least 57,000.[264] If casualties inflicted by the American air forces are assumed to be lower, since their bombing was less clearly aimed at cities, an overall death toll of 82,000 is again statistically realistic. In the absence of unambiguous statistical evidence, the figure of 353,000 gives an approximate scale consistent with the evidence. It is a little over half the figure of 625,000 arrived at in the 1950s.

The lower figure of 353,000 still represents an exceptional level of unnatural deaths compared with the impact of bombing elsewhere, and with the much lower level of casualties in Germany up until the summer of 1943. The obvious explanation is that repeated raids with 600 or 700 heavy bombers will eventually overwhelm the capacity of civil defence to limit casualties. This was certainly true for smaller cities hit just once, such as Pforzheim or Hildesheim, but also large cities such as Hamburg, whose defences could not cope with the firestorm, though they could cope effectively with raids of lesser intensity. But there are other reasons for an escalating level of casualties. Shelter provision had never been ideal, but in 1943 and 1944 resources were no longer available for a comprehensive shelter programme. Towns in Zones II and III became victims of bombing with inadequate public shelters. The air-protection room yielded mixed results, but in areas already heavily bombed, the cellar or basement under a heavily damaged building offered much less protection than a shelter under an intact building. Medical aid, despite the exceptional efforts of the profession, was a declining resource in 1944 and 1945, increasing the risk of death from infection or loss of blood. Finally, the mobile population was more exposed to risk, particularly once Allied aircraft began routine strafing of vehicles and trains, and evacuees found themselves in areas thought to be safe from bombs, but now subject to random attack. With at least 9 million people accommodated away from their homes, where they had had air-protection rooms and established self-protection routines, the risks of higher casualty levels increased. People who stayed in Berlin, despite the bombing, had established shelters to which they could go. 'Finally we're in our shelter,' wrote the Berlin diarist, 'behind an iron door that weighs a hundred pounds, with rubber seals around the edges and two levers to lock it shut ... the people here are convinced that their cave is one of the safest. There's nothing more alien than an unknown shelter.'[265]

The reaction of the population to this wave of destruction was never uniform. Over the last year of war ordinary people had many different pressures with which to cope, so that distinguishing what was particular about the bombing war from wider fears about defeat, dread of the arrival of the Soviet armies, fear of the security apparatus, and anxiety about the mounting military losses, is historically complex. Popular opinion was diverse and fluctuating. On bombing, the SD Reports in late 1943 and early 1944 show a pendulum swinging between hopes that the air terror would be ended by German retaliation and pessimistic realization that it was likely to get worse. In April 1944, for example, home intelligence found alongside anxious fears for survival and doubts that the war would end well, the hope expressed that Fate would still take a hand in Germany's favour because 'one simply cannot believe that everything had been in vain'.[266] For much of the year the principal source of anxiety was the state of the war on the Eastern Front; from June 1944 onwards the invasion from the west temporarily eclipsed it. Popular concern with bombing briefly revived with the onset of the V-weapons campaign in the summer, but the unrealistic expectation that it would reverse the tide of the air war at once was disappointed and by late June the intelligence reports found a widespread scepticism that anything could stop the bombing. By July, when every German front line had collapsed, in Belorussia, Italy and France, 'pessimistic opinion' prevailed everywhere. It was judged that this did not mean that the 'will to resist' had evaporated, simply that there was widespread doubt that it would be of any use.[267]

The German population lived through this period with a sustained sense of drama in which the experience of bombing played only a part. The Party played increasingly with the idea that the German people were bound in a 'community of fate' (Schicksalsgemeinschaft), in which the final struggles would test their racial qualities to extremes. Some of this propaganda may explain the evidence of a popular mentality of 'Victory or Death' detected by the SD, but most of the home intelligence reports over the last year of the war show that ordinary Germans felt themselves to be trapped between a rock and a hard place – unable to give up because of the consequences expected from a coercive and vindictive dictatorship, but fearful of the consequences of defeat, particularly at the hands of the Red Army. There is little evidence from the intelligence reports that bombing as such strengthened the resolve of the urban population to hold out longer or fight harder. Bombing was a demoralizing and exhausting experience: 'nervous anxiety', 'fear', 'worry', 'searching for survival' punctuate the reports of popular reaction to the air raids.[268] Regular air-raid alarms forced civilians to shelter for hundreds of hours in what were often uncomfortable and airless rooms. The American post-war morale survey found among the cohort of interviewees that 38 per cent experienced 'intense fear, nervous collapse', 31 per cent 'temporary or less severe fright'. One woman gave a vivid account of her ordeal: 'I saw people killed by falling bricks and heard the screams of others dying in the fire. I dragged my best friend from a burning building and she died in my arms. I saw others who went stark mad.'[269] These experiences were no doubt what the survey was looking for. In answer, however, to the question about why people thought the war was lost, only 15 per cent identified air raids as the reason, 48 per cent military defeats.[270]

What bombing did do was to increase the dependence of the population on both the state apparatus and the Party organizations responsible for welfare, reducing even further the space for more serious dissent. Survival depended on not challenging the system. Throughout the heaviest period of bombing both state and Party, assisted increasingly by the armed forces stationed in the Reich, were able to sustain the supply of replacement goods, the distribution of food and water, planned evacuation and rehabilitation, though transport difficulties and the declining access to European food supplies meant that living standards continued to fall throughout 1944.[271] Indeed, for most of the urban population official sources were the only ones available. The risks from black-marketeering and looting grew greater as the war drew to a close and the terror more arbitrary for the German people; military policemen shot or hanged those they caught on the spot. Even in Berlin in the last days before the Russians arrived, hungry survivors were able to find supplies of food dispensed by whatever authority was still functioning. It proved impossible at this stage to re-establish 'normal life' as had been attempted earlier in the war (and had been the aim in Britain, too, during the Blitz), but routines did not break down completely. Rather than greater communal resolve, accounts of the bombed populations show a growing apathy and demoralization: 'a weight like lead hangs on all our actions,' wrote one diarist in January 1945.[272]

The more surprising result of the bombing was the absence of sustained popular hatred directed towards those who were carrying it out. A long report on popular attitudes to the enemy produced in February 1944 indicated occasional evidence of anger directed at British aircrew, but concluded 'hatred against the English people in general cannot be spoken of'. The Soviet people were feared rather than hated, driven by 'an alien and incomprehensible mentality'. Paradoxically, wide popular hostility was reserved almost exclusively for the Italians for betraying Germany in 1943 by surrendering to the Allies.[273] There were, nevertheless, acts of spontaneous violence directed by the bombed population against aircrew who were caught after they had to bale out and land on

German soil. The number who became victims of 'lynch murder' has been estimated at between 225 and 350, a small fraction of the total of air force prisoners of war. The first recorded incident was during Operation Gomorrah on 25 July 1943, when two American airmen were killed. The pressure from above for people to take the law into their own hands increased during 1944 after Hitler endorsed popular vengeance against pilots guilty of strafing civilians, trains or hospitals. The peak of popular lynching occurred in March 1945, with 37 killings.[274]

The violence is not difficult to explain. Official propaganda had always described Allied bombing as 'terror-bombing' and the aircrew as gangsters or air pirates. The word 'vengeance' had become part of the public vocabulary of the air war. On 27 May 1944 Goebbels published a widely read article in the Party newspaper calling for 'an eye for an eye, a tooth for a tooth' in subjecting Allied flyers to German 'self-justice', echoing views expressed by Hitler as early as autumn 1942.[275] Many of the cases of lynching were associated with Party members or SA men, or policemen, who expected not to be punished. Spontaneous popular violence was rarer, though again explicable by the level of destruction and casualties imposed in the last years of war. What is surprising is that the violence was not more widespread given the increasingly lawless character of German justice. Reports after Goebbels' article indicated public concern that killing captured Allied aircrew would result in the killing of captured German airmen too in retaliation. The uniformed services would not endorse the killing and Allied survivors attested to the intervention of soldiers or policemen in saving them from angry crowds. In the aftermath of heavy bombing violent reaction against its perpetrators seems often to have taken second place to the relief at having survived and concern for others. Hans Nossack observed in Hamburg in the days after Operation Gomorrah that 'no-one comforted himself with thoughts of revenge'; the enemy was at most, Nossack continued, 'an instrument of unknowable forces that sought to annihilate us'.[276]

Somehow the German civilian population survived under the sharply deteriorating conditions of daily life, in a milieu that became progressively abnormal. The civil defence structure built up and renewed over the course of the war proved in the end sufficiently flexible to continue the task of combating the raids and coping with their consequences. 'Self-protection' is evident in the hundreds of photographs that survive of civilians forming human chains to supply water or to remove rubble, of volunteer firemen and salvage workers struggling to contain the

flames. After the heavy raid on Stuttgart in July 1944, one girl recalled
how her father had saved their home: 'our row of houses only remained
standing because my father had dread of being installed just anywhere
after the loss of his house. His view was: "If I cannot save my home, I
have nothing left in life." So during the raid he stayed up on top so that
he could throw the incendiary bombs straight onto the street.'[277] Waltraud Süssmilch found herself with other classmates after each all-clear
joining a long human chain passing buckets filled with water or sand by
hand to the next person, or in school hours packing parcels for the
bombed-out, or visiting the wounded.[278] Throughout 1944 advice on
firefighting and training for self-protection continued to be published
and distributed; blackout regulations were insisted upon and air-raid
instructions issued for areas where until late 1944 there had been very
little air action and little familiarity with the pattern of air-raid crises.

Right to the very last days of the war, air-raid protection continued
to function. The record of two of the air force Air Protection Regiments,
mobile units designed to bring immediate assistance to bombed cities,
even at considerable distance, illustrates the extent to which positive
efforts continued to be made to combat or ameliorate the effects of
remorseless daily bombing. Regiment 3, based in Berlin, in action almost
every day, travelled 190 kilometres in response to the bombing of
Magdeburg on 5–6 August 1944. One company tackled the damaged
Krupp-Gruson plant. It succeeded in extinguishing the blazing coal
bunkers, rescuing the machinery, putting out the large fires threatening
the material stores, and saving cellars full of military supplies. A second
company worked in the burning city, extinguishing five small fires where
the bombs fell, six roof fires, 11 storey fires, 14 'total fires' (preventing
them from spreading), six burning provision stores and five larger conflagrations. It handled 63 civil defence first-aid cases, 402 civilian
injuries, sent 138 off in ambulances, recovered 38 buried bodies and
33 people still alive.[279] Two weeks later Regiment 3 sent three companies to Stettin, where the raid had devastating effects. They rescued
501 people alive, and dug out 53 dead, extinguished 127 smaller house
fires, 29 'total fires', fought 12 industrial and commercial blazes, and
prevented 18 fires from spreading any further. The narrow streets in
Stettin made it difficult to get equipment into the heart of the blaze, and
only after three hours was it possible to create a corridor covered with
water jets to get through to the shelters. There they found 50 dead near
the shelter entrance who had tried to escape through the fire by their
own efforts, their corpses 'completely carbonated'. In the last weeks of

bombing in 1945, Regiment 7 reported a gruelling schedule of operations starting with a major fire-raid on Nuremberg on 20–21 February, where the unit extinguished 119 small and 60 major fires, and extracted 36 bodies from the rubble, followed by summons to a further 17 raids between 27 February and 21 March.[280] As the military fronts contracted, so it proved possible for technical troops from the armed forces to be deployed more extensively in trying to protect the surviving urban areas, working side by side with the remaining civil defenders.

One of the cities in need of urgent aid in 1945 was the Saxon capital at Dresden, destroyed in a firestorm on the night of 13–14 February. Dresden had already experienced two American daylight raids, on 7 October 1944 and 16 January 1945, which had killed 591 people. Little effort had gone into constructing adequate public shelters and one witness recalled that the sirens failed to sound that night. The day before the February raid was, according to Victor Klemperer, a German-Jewish philologist who had survived in Dresden married to a non-Jew, one of 'perfect spring weather'.[281] By a strange historical quirk, Klemperer was among the small population of surviving Jews in Dresden who that same day had been ordered to turn up 72 hours later to be transported away for 'outside labour duty'. When the main raid began in the middle of the night he ran at once to the Jewish shelter but scrambled on through the fires and bombs when the shelter became too hot. He managed to get down to the Elbe River, battered by the wind of the firestorm, slipping on the black rain that fell from the condensation caused by the rising column of hot air. He joined the flow of refugees the following morning with his wife, who had been saved only because someone had pulled her from the Jewish into the 'Aryan' shelter below their apartments:

> Fires were still burning in many of the buildings on the road above. At times, small and no more than a bundle of clothes, the dead were scattered across our path. The skull of one had been torn away, the top of the head was a dark red bowl. Once an arm lay there with a pale, quite fine hand, like a model made of wax such as one sees in barbers' shop windows ... Crowds streamed unceasingly between these islands, past these corpses and the smashed vehicles, up and down the Elbe, a silent, agitated procession.[282]

Klemperer was fortunate to survive. He was treated by first-aid workers that morning as American aircraft returned to bomb what was left of the city. By the evening food arrived and then water. The following morning the refugees were moved to the nearby towns of Klotsche and Meissen, where there were plentiful bowls of soup. Klemperer tore off the yellow star all Jews were required to wear and survived the war.

Klemperer's story is a reminder that the system being bombed still practised its lethal racism to the very last weeks of the war, though it also demonstrates that even as a German Jew he could get medical attention and food and emergency accommodation. Dresden became for the authorities a major emergency. The General of Technical Troops, Erich Hampe, was sent from Berlin on the morning of 14 February to supervise the re-establishment of rail communications over the surviving railway bridge. He found the burnt-out area of Dresden utterly deserted, except for a llama escaped from Dresden zoo. Within only two days an emergency rail service had been set up and the wounded could be moved to hospitals in nearby cities.[283] Altogether 2,212 were severely wounded and 13,718 lightly, but the death toll was much higher. By mid-March the police president reported that 18,375 dead had been accounted for, but estimated the final figure as likely to be 25,000, the number recently agreed as the upper limit by a historical commission set up by the mayor of Dresden in 2004. The bodies were collected in large pyres and those not already incinerated were burned quickly to avoid a health crisis.[284] Out of 220,000 homes in Dresden, 75,000 were totally destroyed and 18,500 severely damaged; there were 18 million cubic metres of rubble. By the end of February Dresden, a city formerly of 600,000, housing an unknown number of refugees from the east, had only 369,000 inhabitants left. It was submitted to two further heavy attacks by 406 B-17s on 2 March and 580 B-17s on 17 April, leaving a further 453 dead.[285]

By this stage of the war the bombing had to compete with fear of the oncoming Soviet forces, whose offensive the bombing of Dresden had been supposed to serve. Victor Klemperer noted in his diary, once he was safe in emergency housing, that he shared with those around him fear of bombing but also their profound fear of the Russians, confirmed by the long trails of refugees in carts and buggies making their way westward against the tide of German forces moving the other way. Another survivor wrote two weeks after the firestorm: 'Why are we still living? Only to wait until the Russians come.'[286] Other diaries show that growing horror at the thought of Soviet occupation, fuelled by grim rumours of the primitive behaviour of Soviet soldiers, put into perspective the bombing, whose dimensions and effects were more familiar. 'Masses and masses of fugitives are crossing the Oder,' wrote one

eyewitness in February 1945. 'Dead people have been temporarily buried in the snow. The Russians are coming! Napoleon's retreat from
Moscow must have been child's play by comparison.'[287] The Berlin
schoolgirl, Waltraud Süssmilch, was fascinated and horrified by the stories brought by the tide of refugees from the east that flowed into Berlin
in the last weeks of war. One story of the sadistic murder of a pregnant
woman by Red Army soldiers filled her with complete dread, even
though almost every day bombs were exacting a brutal physical toll all
around her.[288] In the last week before the end of the war Berliners stayed
in their shelters which doubled as protection from Soviet shelling, since
here, as over most of Germany, the bombing had ceased, in order to prevent the bombers from hitting Allied forces by mistake. The Berlin
diarist found the population of her shelter still agitated and nervous, as
though they were waiting for a bombing raid. Some of them speculated
that the Russians might not be as bad as German propaganda had
painted them. A refugee from the east, camped out in the shelter, began
to shout: 'Broken sentences – she can't find the right words. She flails
her arms and screams. "They'll find out all right," and then goes silent
once again.'[289]

One of the final raids of the war touched a small town that had been
spared the bombing, despite its notoriety. Berchtesgaden, where Hitler
had his Bavarian headquarters and retreat, was bombed by British aircraft on 25 April 1945 with considerable accuracy, leaving behind 'a
chaotic brown-and-black mess' in place of the pretty Alpine woods and
the smart modern villas of the Party elite. The town itself was not hit, an
outcome that local people treated as a miracle, apparently evidenced, as
one young eyewitness later wrote, by the sign of the Cross visible in the
sky. She was puzzled by this: 'Why of all places should He protect Berchtesgaden, when all of Europe was in ashes?' Her neighbours expected
Hitler to arrive at any moment to make his operatic last stand.[290] But
Hitler was cut off in Berlin, amidst the ruins of his new Chancellery
building. Thousands of Berliners crowded into the vast Flak-towers for
safety from the battle going on around them, though the bombing of the
capital was over. Waltraud Süssmilch and her family had taken shelter
in one tower but had to leave when it began to fill with water. The sight
of the ruined city, even after years of bombing, struck her as extraordinary. Like General Anderson, former commander of Eighth Bomber
Command, who toured the bombed cities later that summer, she thought
the bombed-out houses, burning roofs and broken windows looked like
the picture of Pompeii in her school history book.[291]

The bombing imposed on Germany exceptional demands for organizing the home front, quite different from the experience of the First World War. The dictatorship relied on sustaining a high degree of participation, willing or otherwise, in the organizations and institutions that were supposed to bind together the new 'People's Community'. Any explanation for the capacity of German society to absorb bombing destruction and levels of casualty on this scale must include the willingness of millions of ordinary Germans, in addition to all the other pressures of wartime work and survival, to participate in schemes of self-protection, civil defence work, first-aid organization and welfare provision, without which the consequences of bombing could not have been sustained, however coercive the regime or however narrow the space within which social protest could operate. The effect of bombing was not, in the end, as the Allies hoped, to drive a wedge between people and regime, but the opposite, to increase dependence on the state and the Party and to prompt willing participation by civilians in structures designed for their own defence with a remarkable degree of social discipline. The experience of being bombed did indeed create widespread anxiety, demoralization, social conflict and limited political criticism, but it was balanced in the end by the capacity of the dictatorship to exploit racial policy unscrupulously to its advantage (redistributing Jewish apartments and furnishings, using camp and foreign labour to clear up debris, etc.), while ensuring that minimum levels of social provision, flexible propaganda, administrative competence and targeted coercion would prevent anything like collapse.

8

Italy: The War of Bombs and Words

Italy was bombed for only a month less than Germany during the Second World War. Yet the story of the bombing of most of Italy's cities failed to attract the attention of the wider world in 1945 and has remained on the margins in most narratives of the conflict ever since. As many Italians were killed by bombing as died in the Blitz on Britain; more tons were dropped on Rome than on all British cities put together. Moreover, the damage to Italy's ancient heritage filled two volumes when it was investigated by a British committee in 1945, set up to preserve for future generations the 'artistic wealth' that Allied aircraft had been busy bombarding only months before.[1]

Italy's part in the bombing war was more complex than that of any other European state. For at least three years, from 10 June 1940, when Benito Mussolini declared war on Britain and France, the Italian Air Force (*Regia Aeronautica*) had carried out an active bombing campaign: briefly against targets in France (before the French sued for an armistice in June 1940), against England in the late autumn of 1940, and throughout the Mediterranean and North Africa until final defeat there in May 1943. Some of this air activity had been carried out in loose collaboration with German air forces. Throughout this period, though not continuously, Italian territory was itself bombed by the RAF, from bases in England as well as bases in Malta and North Africa. On 8 September 1943, following an Italian request for an armistice, the Italian state ceased to be an Axis enemy and became, after a short interval, a co-belligerent with the United Nations and an enemy of Germany, whose forces now occupied two-thirds of the Italian Peninsula. For the next two years, the few Italian pilots and aircraft remaining in the area not occupied by the Germans were used to attack German forces in the Balkans and the Ionian Islands, the first raids taking place against targets on Corfu and Kefallonia as early as September 1943.[2] Meanwhile in the occupied zones of central and northern Italy a new government under Mussolini was set up under German protection in what was now called the Italian Social Republic, and here a small Italian contingent, the National Republican Air Force (*Aeronautica Nazionale Repubblicana*) fought in German aircraft against the Allies.[3] Since German forces were in occupation, northern and central Italy remained a target for Allied bombing up until the very last days of the war, while the southern liberated zone was subject to occasional German air raids. The bulk of the Italian population was the object of air attack first as an enemy people, then as a population waiting to be liberated. The only constant in the Italian experience of war was the threat from the air.

FAREWELL TO DOUHET: ITALY'S BOMBING WAR

The Italian Fascist regime was from the start strongly committed to the belief that promoting air power would be a triumphant manifestation of Fascist strength, technical capability and military elan. The daring pilot became a symbol of the Fascist 'new man', pushing human endeavour to the limits. Fascism shared with the Italian Futurists, and particularly the founder, Filippo Marinetti, a fascination with modern technique and violent speed. Italian aircraft regularly won the Schneider speed trophy in the late 1920s and early 1930s; the Air Minister, Italo Balbo, famously led a flight of seaplanes in 1933 across the Atlantic to New York and Chicago. Mussolini, first prime minister in 1922, then from 1926 effective dictator, helped to shape the identification of Italian aviation with the values of the new Fascist state. In 1921 he was enthusiastic enough to take flying lessons, though he failed to qualify. Later, in power, Mussolini was often photographed in the open cockpit of an aircraft, though always in the co-pilot's seat. In the mid-1930s he began flying again and in January 1937 it was announced that he had been awarded his military pilot's licence.[4] The myth of Mussolini, the Italian superman, was served by the image of Mussolini the courageous and intrepid flyer, and he did nothing to deflate it. He evidently enjoyed flying. In 1942 the Air Ministry was asked to provide a complete list of all Mussolini's flights since December 1938, both inside Italy and abroad, and the final tally was 117, some to Libya and Russia, most of them short-haul journeys to Italian cities.[5] There was a cruel irony in his enthusiasm. In August 1941 his son Bruno, who had joined the air force and flown in Ethiopia and Spain, was killed test-flying the new four-engine Italian bomber, the Piaggio P.108, one of a number of modern Italian aircraft designs plagued with development defects.

The mobilization of Italian aviation to serve the political and cultural ambitions of the regime distorted the evolution of the Italian Air Force, which found itself trapped between Mussolini's pompous air-power rhetoric and the reality of Italy's limited economic and military potential. A good example of the dilemma was the place assigned to Giulio Douhet, Mussolini's first Air Minister. Although Douhet did not last long in office, his theoretical writing on the power of the massed bomber, used to strike a sudden, violent and annihilating blow against enemy cities to end wars quickly and decisively, suited Fascism's self-image as a movement dedicated to impulsive action and flamboyant gestures. Mussolini famously committed his armed forces to the idea of 'the war of rapid course' (*la guerra di rapido corso*), the Italian equivalent of *Blitzkrieg*.[6] He liked the idea of the surprise air strike to impose terror on an enemy population and had few scruples about ordering it during the Spanish Civil War. The bombing of Barcelona from 16 to 18 March 1938 followed Mussolini's direct order from Rome to bomb 'the demographic centre' of the city. The future chief of staff of the Italian Air Force, General Francesco Pricolo, wrote in 1938 that 'the effective arm of the air fleet is terror'.[7] Like Douhet, Pricolo was attracted to the 'decisive power' of an air force to secure victory.[8] When Italian airmen assessed the swift German defeat of Poland in the autumn of 1939, they described it as a classic example of 'the fundamental concept of Douhet', first achieving command of the air, then using overwhelming air power to finish off Polish resistance through the collapse of morale. The German bombing of Britain in the winter of 1940–41 was again used to underline the argument that only bombing could overcome the risk of a stalemate like Italy's gruelling trench war against Austria in 1915–18. 'Bombing aviation,' wrote Lt. Colonel Bruno Montanari in February 1941, 'is always the fundamental speciality of the air arm.'[9]

However, the actual development of air force doctrine and capability reflected the influence of Douhet hardly at all. The development of a large bomber fleet, whose purpose was to smash enemy war-willingness in days, fitted poorly with the actual requirements of the army and navy for support in probable surface operations in the Mediterranean basin or the Italian empire in North and East Africa. The most influential critic of Douhet was the young air force officer Amedeo Mecozzi, who thought that command of the air was always a local and temporary phenomenon. He argued for close cooperation with the army or navy using high-quality assault aircraft, capable of a fighter and fighter-bomber role, and for the overriding importance of counter-force operations. He drew different lessons from the role of Italian aircraft in Spain and the German success in Poland, both of which confirmed for Mecozzi the vital role to be played by aircraft on the field of battle rather than against enemy cities.[10] Though there remained a culture of 'Douhetism' in the Italian Air Force, much of the actual experience of air warfare in the wars in Ethiopia and Spain confirmed Mecozzi's arguments; Italian ground units preferred to be given close air support and expected Italian fighters and bombers to share that responsibility. One airman reflecting on Spain concluded that opportunities for the strategic use of aircraft were rare, whereas ground support had shown itself to be the 'principal task' and was likely to remain so into the future. Even General Pricolo was forced to conclude from German success the necessity of 'a closer and closer collaboration between the three armed forces'. Unlike Douhet, Pricolo admitted that no one thought any longer of 'a hypothetical independence' for the air force.[11]

The factor that affected Italian air development fundamentally was Mussolini's impatient pursuit of a new Italian Empire and a major role in European affairs. Unlike the other major powers, Italian forces were fighting almost continuously for four years before the outbreak of war in September 1939, first in Ethiopia from October 1935 to May 1936, then in Spain from July 1936 to March 1939 after Mussolini had decided to send an expeditionary force to help Franco in the civil war. This commitment was costly for a relatively poor economy with limited natural resources. Moreover, it locked Italy into a production cycle in which proven but obsolescent designs had to be produced in large numbers, while the evolution of a new generation of high-powered, monoplane fighters and bombers was delayed, at exactly the time when other air forces were moving on to a new range of advanced designs. Because Italian forces were deployed against weaker opponents, with little capacity to oppose Italian air operations, Italian air leaders could comfort themselves with the illusion of continuous triumph. Pricolo in 1940 could point to four years of war waged 'victoriously' and assume that having 'personally experienced wartime reality', the Italian Air Force had a substantial advantage over any potential enemy.[12] The truth was rather different. Italy began and ended the four years of war-before-the-war still in the biplane age. The culture of air aces and stunt flying,

inherited from the Balbo years, and sustained by Mussolini when he
became Air Minister in Balbo's place in 1933, gave a privileged place to
the pilot's view of war. The biplane Fiat Cr.32 (replaced in 1939 by the
biplane Cr.42) was liked by Italian airmen because it was exceptionally
manoeuvrable and easy to fly and, in the absence of radios, the open
cockpit allowed pilots to signal and gesture to each other. Biplane light
bombers eventually gave way to monoplane bombers with limited power
and carrying capacity, the Savoia-Marchetti Sm.79 and Sm.81, both of
which saw service in Spain alongside a small number of other models.[13]

The experience of fighting in Ethiopia and Spain nonetheless persuaded the Italian Air Force that it was technically advanced enough for
current air warfare. In Ethiopia around 450 aircraft were committed, of
which 80 were shot down or written off in accidents, and 100 aircrew
killed. Although the Italian Air Force was told that it could bomb to
terrorize the population, most bombing, with high explosive or gas, was
tactical, directed at lines of communication and assembled Ethiopian
forces. Attacks on towns were suspended from December 1935 following the international outcry at the destruction of Red Cross facilities,
but the army demands for close support to overcome stiffening Ethiopian resistance in 1936 would anyway have focused bombing on the
battlefront. An estimated 1,890 tons of bombs were dropped and a
further 1,813 in the year-long pacification operations conducted after
Ethiopian surrender. Ethiopia had no effective counter-air capability.[14]
Two months after the end of the war, Mussolini committed Italian
forces to intervention in Spain at the side of the Nationalist rebels
against the Spanish Second Republic. The air force sent an expeditionary force (l'aviazione legionaria) composed of fighters and light bombers.
Over the three years of intervention 197 bombers were deployed, flying
782 bombing missions. As in Ethiopia, most bombing was undertaken
in support of ground operations (a handful of Sm.79s took part in the
raid on Guernica).[15] But Mussolini was keen for the air force to demonstrate its debt to 'Douhetism' and in 1938 bombers stationed in the
Balearic Islands – the so-called 'falcons of the Balearics' – began systematic attacks on Barcelona and southern coastal towns still in the hands
of the Republic, aimed not only at oil and shipping but also at the morale of the population. The force seldom numbered more than 30 aircraft,
and is remembered chiefly for the three-day bombardment of Barcelona
from 16 to 18 March 1938 in which a modest 44 tons of bombs
destroyed 80 buildings and killed, according to different estimates,
between 550 and 1,043 civilians. Barcelona suffered 57 attacks during

the civil war but a number of other cities were also regularly raided by both Italian and German bombers: Valencia 69 times, Sagunto 47, Castellón de la Plana 39, and Tarragona a total of 29. Over the three years of civil war, bombing killed an estimated 2,600 and injured 5,798.[16]

Losses in combat were relatively modest in Spain, but all the aviation equipment, including the aircraft, was left behind when the air legion returned to Italy in May 1939. The biplane fighters had proved their worth even against the few poor-performance monoplanes supplied by the Soviet Union (although 41 per cent of the fighter force was lost, mostly to non-combat causes). The bombers had faced little opposition; Barcelona in early 1938 was defended by just two anti-aircraft batteries of eight guns and a few anti-air machine guns. The eventual nationalist victory in Spain was used to justify the propaganda claims that in aerial warfare Italy was a vanguard state, possessing, as one commentator put it, 'all the necessary elements to construct a superb air power' and blessed with a government willing to achieve it.[17] Success, in this case, was the enemy of progress. The gap between illusion and reality was wider by 1940, when Mussolini began seriously to contemplate joining his German Axis ally in the war against Britain and France, than it had been three years before. The list of factors limiting the Italian Air Force in a war with the rapidly modernizing Western states was prodigious, not least the absence of a uniform doctrine for the employment of the air force. The navy and army assumed that aircraft would chiefly be used to assist them in an imminent war. An independent air defence system was almost entirely lacking. Bomber units were numerous, but the air force remained divided between the commitment to assault aviation in support of a ground campaign and the shadow of Douhet. In the end, the air force undertook a mix of tactical and long-range operations to support the general campaign of the armed forces rather than pursue a more ambitious independent air strategy.

The state of readiness left a great deal to be desired. Although the air force claimed on the eve of the Italian declaration of war on 10 June 1940 to have a grand total of 1,569 bombers, only 783 were serviceable.[18] Of these the majority were the Sm.79, Sm.81 and the Fiat Br.20 light/medium bombers. Their performance was mixed: an average of 250–280 miles per hour, a range of 1,100 miles with around 2,250 lbs of bombs compared reasonably with the performance of some of the current British and German medium bombers, but the bombload was one-quarter of the load of a Wellington and half that of the Junkers

Ju88.[19] The aircraft generally lacked radios, had no modern navigational equipment for night-time bombing, lacked a sophisticated bombsight, and were weakly armed with three or four small machine guns against the fast, heavily armed fighters they were likely to encounter. Radar had been developed in Italy from the mid-1930s, and was in some respects in advance of other countries, but its introduction stalled through the hostility and indifference of the air force High Command until it became essential in 1942–3. Airbases were poorly resourced and in some cases still laid to grass rather than concrete.[20] The Italian aircraft industry was certainly capable of producing more advanced designs, but the choice of a new generation of aircraft to replace those that had fought in Spain was the victim of the organizational structure responsible for technical innovation. Italo Balbo, during his period as Air Minister, had separated the development and experimental branch from the air force organization in charge of procurement and production. Although large numbers of experimental prototypes were produced in the 1930s and early 1940s, the final decision on which to produce rested with the air staff and, in his role as Air Minister, with Mussolini. Development of a heavier four-engine bomber began in 1937, but the final choice of the Piaggio P.108, in preference to other more effective development models, was the result of judgements by individuals who lacked the technical competence to make them. Both this model and the successor to the Sm.79, the three-engine Sm.84, proved to be dangerous to fly and little better than the older models. The Cant Z.1007, developed in the late 1930s, became the most up-to-date Italian medium bomber, but it was prone to engine problems and deterioration of its wooden structure, was insufficiently powered, lightly armed, and could carry only 2,500 lbs of bombs over a range of 625 miles.[21] The confusion over modernizing the air force was compounded with Italy's shortages of fuel, steel, coal and machinery, which severely inhibited the scale of the Italian war economy. In 1940 Italy produced 3,257 aircraft of all types, in 1942 only 2,821, one-tenth of the quantity produced for Britain's air force.[22]

There has never been any doubt that Mussolini's decision to launch Italy into the world war was taken in defiance of the real economic and military situation faced by the armed forces and Italian industry. Almost as soon as war was declared on 10 June, Italian aircraft bombed targets in southern France; the first raid on the British air and naval base on Malta took place on 11 June. France soon sued for an armistice, leaving Mussolini as the junior partner in German victory. On 26 June he offered to help the German armed forces to defeat Britain by sending

10 divisions and 30 squadrons of aircraft to assist in any subsequent invasion. Hitler and Göring rejected the proposal on the ground that Italian forces would be better concentrated in the Mediterranean rather than dispersed around Europe. Air force commanders warned against sending Italian units to an area where climatic conditions were entirely different from the Mediterranean, and with aircraft whose performance was dangerously lower than those of the RAF.[23] Mussolini persisted because of the propaganda value he attached to Italian participation in a direct attack on the British homeland, and by mid-August German leaders finally accepted the offer in order to demonstrate to the wider world a common Axis bond in a struggle now described by the German Foreign Minister, Joachim von Ribbentrop, as 'a question of life and death'. But instead of the promised aerial armada, the Italian Air Force sent an Italian Air Corps (*Corpo Aereo Italiano*) composed of two bomber groups, a group of fighters and a reconnaissance squadron, a total of 180 aircraft, 66 of them bombers.[24] Finally sent north in late September 1940, several weeks after the abandonment of Operation Sea Lion, the force lost seven aircraft on route to its Belgian base at Ursel as a result of bad weather. The first attack was made on 24 October 1940 against coastal towns in East Anglia, the last on 2 January 1941. The force found the weather a continuous problem, while the technical means to keep the aircraft flying were damagingly deficient. It was a tribute to the skill of Italian pilots that the targets were found at all. A total of 64 tons of bombs were dropped in 24 operations against Harwich, Ipswich, Great Yarmouth and the Kent port of Ramsgate. Out of 104 sorties, 22 bombers and 14 fighters were lost, a rate of one-third. In February the force was withdrawn to meet urgent needs in the war in North Africa and the Mediterranean.[25]

The Italian contribution to the Blitz was negligible, but Italian propaganda managed to make the most of the experience. A poster was produced showing London in flames below an Italian hand with the traditional Roman gesture of thumbs down, though not a single Italian aircraft attacked the British capital.[26] A photograph showed one of the crew at Ursel painting slogans on the bombs before they were loaded on the aircraft – 'for dear Eden', 'for Churchill', 'Buckingham Palace'.[27] The Italian contribution was presented to the home population as equivalent to the German and relations between the two forces one of ideal 'comradeship'. Mecozzi, writing in autumn 1940, chose the headline 'Fascist wings dominate the war'.[28] The image presented to the Italian public was a military fantasy. German forces regarded the Italian Air

Corps as an oddity; detailed reports of German operations were sent regularly to the Italian Air Ministry, perhaps to rub salt in the wounds of Italian incompetence by showing what a modern air force could really do.[29] The Italian Air Force drew some obvious lessons from a difficult experience. It was evident that even the German Air Force had sustained high losses during the air operations in 1940, requiring a shift to night-time bombing, for which Italian airmen were poorly prepared. By day, it was reported, a heavy fighter escort three to four times larger than the number of bombers was required, a practice adopted by Italian units in raids carried out in the Mediterranean. German claims that ports or cities had been destroyed were regarded sceptically by Italian observers, who understood that for much of the time cloud and smoke obscured effective post-raid reconnaissance.[30] Above all, Italian commanders could see that the Italian Air Corps was out of its depth in a modern bomber offensive. Reflecting in May 1941 on the Italian experience, Colonel Andrea Zotti ruefully concluded that bombing would only be effective against a much weaker enemy.[31]

The British enemy in the Mediterranean was certainly much weaker than the RAF and the Anti-Aircraft Command in metropolitan Britain. The Italian Air Force was under strong pressure from Mussolini to demonstrate that bombing would contribute to the establishment of Italian hegemony in the Mediterranean basin, and as a result a number of long-range operations were undertaken against Palestine, Cyprus, Gibraltar, British bases on the Egyptian coast, and the island of Malta. Some 30 per cent of operations in the first year of the Italian war were conducted by bombers.[32] The raids were usually small in scale and the damage insignificant, though in the attack on Tel Aviv on 9 September 1940 from bases in the Italian Dodecanese Islands, 137 people were killed and 350 injured. There was no anti-aircraft defence of Palestinian ports, and the death toll was the highest from any Italian raid. A further raid on Tel Aviv in June 1941, from bases in Syria, left 13 dead.[33] Most attacks were made against the port of Haifa, raided 30 times with 61 tons of bombs. Most of the operations were tiny in scale. A lone raid on the Persian Gulf port of Bahrain was made by four bombers; the average number of aircraft for the long-distance raids, including the operations against Britain, was just 3.4.[34] The official objectives were ports, naval bases, railway communications and oil refineries (which alone accounted for one-third of all operations), though bombs also destroyed residential housing and public buildings. The pattern of long-range Italian air attacks is set out in Table 8.1:

Table 8.1: Italian Air Force Long-Range Operations,
June 1940–September 1942

Operational Zone	Number of Operations	Aircraft Sorties	Bomb Tonnage
Great Britain	24	104	55.1
Gibraltar	11	17	23.4
Egypt (Alexandria)	63	162	113.7
Palestine	32	110	66.9
Bahrain	1	4	2.1
Cyprus	34	125	75.8

Source: IWM, Italian Series (Air Force), Box 25, 'Relazione Statistica sull'attività Operativa dell'Aeronautica', 13–16.

In addition a great many operations were undertaken against shipping convoys, against merchant and naval ships in port and against enemy targets in North Africa, but these can more properly be regarded as tactical raids in support of Italian operations in Greece, from October 1940, and in Libya throughout the period of Italian hostility against Britain.

Even the limited Mediterranean air offensive strained Italian resources to the limit. The number of pilots planned for training each year was 900, and a total of only 1,920 were trained throughout the period 1940–43. By the autumn of 1942, 2,293 pilots had become casualties (killed, wounded or prisoner of war), and a further 4,422 aircrew and navigators. Some 3,511 aircraft were lost, 37 per cent through accidents; this figure included 997 bombers, lost either on long-range missions or in the fighting in Greece and North Africa.[35] By autumn 1942 the bomber arm had just 427 serviceable bombers, only half the number at the start of the war, and a fraction of the resources available to the Allies. The bomber units remained short of high-quality aircraft, sufficient fuel for training, effective onboard armament and radio communication between the attacking units. Tactical recommendations from the Germans were not welcomed and were introduced only slowly. Operational training units (*Gruppi Complementari*) were established only towards the end of 1941.[36] The strain on Italian pilots from long periods in action with high losses was considerable. The commander of the 30th Stormo (Group) stationed in Sicily complained in August 1941 that his crew had had no relief for 14 months, during which they were sometimes asked to fly 8–10 hours daily. Pilots were invalided out from physical exhaustion or nervous breakdown; the rest, he continued, resisted collapse through sheer willpower.[37] The effects of their efforts were also clearly limited, for Italy's war in Africa and the Mediterranean reached crisis point in 1941. An article in August 1941 in the major air force journal admitted that bombing was much more problematic than had been realized before the war: 'experience teaches that the destructive effect sought is powerfully limited by the wide dispersion of the bombs'. The system of relying on the bomber pilots to fly in behind the squadron leader to drop bombs 'in imitation' magnified the statistical likelihood of hitting the target with only 'the tiniest fraction of the bombs dropped'.[38] The legacy of Douhet melted away under the harsh glare of operational reality.

MALTA: 'THE MOST BOMBED PLACE ON EARTH'

The limitations of Italy's aerial war effort, and indeed the limitations of a bombing offensive, were no more clearly demonstrated than in the strategic campaign waged for more than two years against the tiny island of Malta. Only 58 miles from the southern shore of Sicily, its strategic position as a British seabase and airbase was perilous once Italy had declared war. The island measures only 13 miles by 7, with the islet of Gozo at its northern tip; defending the area successfully against a determined invasion seemed in 1940 unlikely, even more so once German attention was turned to the Mediterranean in early 1941. Malta instead became 'the most bombed place on earth', attacked 3,302 times between 1940 and August 1944, when the last small German raid occurred.[39] Under this continuous aerial assault, neither the British garrison nor the 260,000 inhabitants of the islands could be forced to abandon their resistance, an outcome that defied all the pre-war assumptions about the psychological fragility of heavily bombed populations.

Malta had been a British crown colony since the Treaty of Paris in 1814. Its population was predominantly Maltese, but there were a sizeable number of Italian descent. Italian was spoken among the Maltese elite and in the law courts and administration. It was this connection that attracted Mussolini to the idea that Malta was an outpost of an oppressed and 'Italianized' people, who should be liberated from British rule and given the dubious benefits of Italian Fascism. A Maltese Nationalist Party, led by Enrico Mizzi, agitated in the 1930s for Maltese autonomy and looked towards Mussolini's Rome for support. Between 1932 and 1934 the British colonial administration banned Italian in Maltese primary schools, the administration and the courts, and declared English and Malti the official languages of the islands.[40] The potential threat from Italy was well understood in Malta; Italian irredentism challenged the British authorities and raised the problem of a possible 'fifth column' if war broke out. From 1934 onwards the local authorities suppressed Italian and Fascist activity on the island, while preparing a civil defence programme against the possibility of Italian air attack.

The first meetings of the island's Air Raid Precautions Committee took place in December 1934 under the chairmanship of the lieutenant governor, General David Campbell.[41] The decision to establish what was called the Passive Defence system was implemented slowly, inhibited by the absence of an immediate menace and the shortage of funds from London to set it up. Most effort was devoted to the anti-air defence of the Grand Harbour in the capital, Valletta, where some 70,000 Maltese lived and worked. Training in gas decontamination and first aid was set up and recruitment of a mixed British-Maltese Passive Defence Reserve was begun. But when war broke out in September 1939, the chief air protection officer on Malta complained that the Passive Defenders had never been more than a 'force in embryo': only 3 out of 14 Passive Defence centres had been fitted out with equipment, about one-fifth of the volunteers had had any training, and the male recruits were rapidly leaving to join the armed forces.[42] By 1940 most air-raid wardens were women. The active defence of the island was poorly prepared. When Italy declared war on 10 June 1940 the air defence famously consisted of three naval Gloster Gladiator biplane fighters – christened *Faith*, *Hope* and *Charity* – supported by 32 heavy and 8 light anti-aircraft guns and 24 searchlights, clustered around the ports and the three RAF airbases then under construction at Luqa, Hal Far and Ta'Qali.[43] Warning of air raids was poorly coordinated and the sirens (or 'syrens' as they were always known on Malta) were a recent innovation not fully understood by the local population. Malta's fragile defence was masked in the summer of 1940 only by the looming presence of the British fleet in the Mediterranean, which acted as a major deterrent to Italian action until the advent of German forces.

The Italian campaign against Malta began at seven o'clock in the morning of 11 June, one day after the declaration of war. The blackout had begun the night before, but most Italian attacks were undertaken during daylight hours. Mussolini boasted that Malta would be Italian in a matter of hours, at the most three weeks. Although the capture of the island fitted with the propaganda of Malta as a stolen 'Italian' territory, there were important strategic considerations. Malta lay across the principal Italian supply routes to the Italian armies in North Africa, which were being prepared for an invasion of Egypt and the capture of the Suez Canal. The island became a base for British bombers in transit to the campaign in Africa, and for British submarines sent to interrupt Italian merchant traffic. It was also what the Italian Air Ministry called an 'aerial springboard' for the defence of Britain's long communications route across the Mediterranean to the Middle East.[44] The Italian High Command believed that the island could not easily be bombed into surrender or captured, so the principal but more limited objective became the neutralization of Malta's capacity to damage the long Italian logistics chain. The bombing offensive in 1940 was continuous but so limited in scale that the islanders and the garrison soon began to abandon the rush to the shelters. The Italian Air Force account of the campaign produced in October 1942 identified three major air offensives against Malta, but did not include the bombing in 1940 among them. During the opening months of the campaign the air force sent small numbers of bomber aircraft, escorted by more numerous fighters, on attacks against military targets in and around the main harbour and the three airbases. Italian records show that in the first 10 months of the war the air force mounted 103 operations against Malta, but the average size of the attacking force was just five planes.[45] The British authorities in Malta counted many more attacks, but it is likely that Italian aircraft sent from different bases arrived at different times over the island, and were classified as separate raids. The damage to military targets was slight and it was soon observed that with anti-aircraft and fighter defence – the Gladiators were soon joined by squadrons of Hurricanes – Italian bombers often failed to press home their attacks. In numerous raid reports, there was no damage and no casualties. The raids seldom lasted more than 20–30 minutes. The small numbers and operational caution meant that Italian losses remained low. In the first 10 months only 25 fighters and bombers were lost; the effects of the campaign were correspondingly meagre.[46]

The British chiefs of staff had at first assumed that the costs of trying to hold Malta would outweigh the advantages, but Churchill was an enthusiast for holding onto the island in case a base in the central Mediterranean became essential, as it did once France was defeated in June

1940.[47] Over the course of 1940 and 1941 the air force and anti-aircraft resources on the island were strengthened, though the limited effort expended by the Italian Air Force meant that reinforcement was treated with less urgency than was necessary. The Italian invasion of Greece, on 28 October 1940, encouraged the RAF to think of using Malta as a staging post for bomber aircraft destined for Egypt, in order to begin a counter-offensive against Italian ports. A force of eight Wellington bombers was sent out to Malta en route to Egypt. It was ordered to bomb Naples and Rome, but the Italian capital was taken off the list and replaced with orders to attack southern Italian ports at Brindisi and Taranto, and if possible Albanian ports where Italian resources and troops were being disembarked.[48] The raids were carried out by a handful of bombers and were little more effective than Italian attacks. Heavily loaded Wellingtons could not take off easily from the short runway at the Luqa base (two crashed with their bombloads) and urgent orders were sent to begin lengthening the runway as soon as possible. In November and December the RAF commander in Malta was ordered to undertake leaflet drops on Italian towns as long as the contents of the propaganda made them 'more effective than bombs'.[49] The drops began in late November with leaflets titled 'Goodbye Mare Nostrum' and 'Mussolini Is Always Right?' In January a new leaflet appeared under the slogan 'THIS IS WAR! Bombs, Death, Destruction', threatening more bombs until Mussolini was overthrown.[50] It was to be a long time before this threat could be redeemed, but a few weeks before, Portal had directed that even though Italian aircraft continued to aim for military targets, British bombers should bomb 'in centres of Italian population' if a primary target could not be located.[51]

The population on Malta soon adjusted to the strain of repeated small raids. When the bombing began, immediate steps were taken to evacuate women and children from the main towns. Since Malta was so small, evacuation meant moving a few miles to a village or small town in the north or west of the island, where there were fewer inviting targets. Houses were subject to inspection and under-utilized households were subject to compulsory billeting (though the governor's residence, the palace of the Archbishop of Malta and convents were formally exempted).[52] The policy was to keep families together as far as possible to avoid affecting morale and although evacuation was not legally compulsory, thousands made the short journey by bus or on foot away from the main ports and airbases, taking with them as many possessions as they could, despite the regulation to take only items that were portable and indispensable. The British families were taken to the village of Naxxar, where they slept in large dormitories in three-tier bunks set up in a prominent Maltese palace.[53] One of the few natural advantages Malta enjoyed was the large number of caves, tunnels and cellars carved into the island's rocky core. These were used at once as shelters. The British Home Office had already conducted experiments in 1937 to test what depth of rock on the island would withstand a bomb and recommended at least 60 feet, but in most cases the depth was less than this, and occasional bomb hits above ground sent shock waves capable of bringing down tunnel sides or ceilings.[54] Some of the population spent the first nights after the outbreak of war in uncomfortable and unsanitary quarters. A large disused railway tunnel outside Valletta housed hundreds from the town, sleeping on mattresses or in deck-chairs. Images of the Virgin Mary or the Sacred Heart of Jesus were hastily put up on the tunnel walls alongside small placards printed with words in Malti, *Ikun Imbierek Alla* ('Blessed be God').[55] As the bombing continued, the government took more responsibility for converting the rock shelters into permanent dormitories with the necessary equipment and facilities, but with the Italian preference for daylight bombing (in all bombing operations from 1940 to 1942 daylight attacks outnumbered night attacks by 3 to 1), many on the island took to ignoring the threat and sleeping in their own beds.[56]

The growing confidence of the population after the first anxious days was in contrast to the fears of the authorities that the Maltese population would not cope with air attack. The regulations applied to civilians reflected the British view of the Maltese as a colonial people. Italian nationalists were interned, and a strict curfew and censorship regime was imposed on the rest of the island. District Commissioners and Regional Protection Officers were appointed to cover the whole area so that close watch could be kept on the popular mood.[57] The idea was suggested of barricading bombed villages to prevent the panicked population from leaving and infecting others with their demoralization, and although the suggestion went no further, roadblocks and checkpoints were set up around the island to monitor closely the movement of civilians. Regulations in July allowed for air-raid wardens to be arrested if found outside after curfew hours, except when an alarm had sounded. One 18-year-old Passive Defender, caught riding his bicycle between villages after curfew, was arrested, fined and dismissed from the volunteer force.[58] A campaign against spreading rumours was begun at once, prompted partly by an unhelpful story begun two days after the start of the war that the Italian government had surrendered. Instructions sent out by the government Information Office on 14 June warned of the insidious effects of rumour and asked leading citizens to 'discourage the babbler'. To give force to the recommendation Sir William Dobbie, the new lieutenant governor, used a radio broadcast to announce the introduction of strengthened legislation and the punishment of the first culprits.[59]

In reality, the population reacted to the first months of bombing with an evident *sangfroid*. People were killed watching the aerial battles, or standing at shelter entrances despite the warnings, but casualties and damage were both too limited to disrupt the continuation of a more normal life. A familiar bedroom was preferred to a hard wooden shelter bunk. Tamara Marks, wife of a British serviceman, abandoned the evacuation station at Naxxar after a few weeks to return to a room in the bombed capital some fifty yards from the sea, where she swam and read. 'One bathed off the rocks,' she later wrote. 'Undressing was easy; one just slipped one's frock off and appeared in a bathing costume.' After just a matter of weeks she and her companions treated the raids as an irritating diversion rather than a menace.[60] It was commonly understood that Italian airmen flew high, seldom accepted combat, and dropped small quantities of bombs. Italian operational reports reflected this reality: poor weather, the failure to rendezvous with fighter escort, the heights compelled by anti-aircraft fire, the tiny number of bombs dropped, are characteristic features.[61] All of this changed on 16 January 1941, when the first major raid was made by the German Air Force against the British aircraft carrier *Illustrious*, which had limped into the Grand Harbour after enduring regular dive-bombing attacks through the western Mediterranean.[62] Repeated attacks by Ju87 and Ju88 aircraft failed to sink the ship, but for the first time showed how much damage a heavy raid could do to the surrounding port and housing. Tamara Marks visited the wrecked area the following day, stumbling over mountains of rubble full of the 'pitiful remnants of frocks, shoes and hats' and remains of goats brought earlier into the city for the sale of milk. The war, she thought, 'had started in earnest'. All that could be found of her best friend after a raid a few weeks later was her handbag.[63]

The presence of the German Air Force marked a profound change in the nature of the Italian war effort. From offers of military assistance to Hitler in July 1940 in what was called a 'parallel war' (*la guerra parallela*) fought by the two Axis states, the Italian leadership had to accept

German reinforcement to avoid complete defeat in Greece and Libya. Although the Italian armed forces wanted their reliance on Germany to be an expression of mutual assistance, it was difficult to disguise the onset of what has come to be called the 'subaltern war' (*la guerra subalterna*).[64] The German Air Force was large enough and well-organized enough to fight a parallel 'Blitz' against Malta while most German aircraft were engaged in the offensive against the British Isles. While a handful of Italian aircraft in Belgium gave token help to the Germans, a large force of high-quality German aircraft were sent south to bases in Sicily and southern Italy following Hitler's decision in late November 1940 to make the Mediterranean 'the grave of the English fleet'.[65] Air Corps X (*Fliegerkorps X*), commanded by the anti-shipping expert, General Hans Geisler, arrived at eight bases in Sicily in January 1941 with around 350 Ju88 and He111 bombers, Me110 heavy fighters, Ju87 dive-bombers and Me109 fighters.[66] In the absence of effective Italian defences, the German force brought its own anti-aircraft equipment, consisting of 20 batteries spread between Catania, Palermo, Trapani and Reggio Calabria. The Italians christened the force the German Air Corps (*Corpo Aereo Tedesco*) in an endeavour to match the title of the Italian corps sent to Belgium, but its performance far outdistanced the Italian contribution further north.[67] Malta was not yet a principal German objective, though it was bombed heavily in order to secure the sea route to North Africa, where in February 1941 a German army corps was sent under the command of Field Marshal Erwin Rommel to help prevent an Italian collapse in Libya. Air Corps X was directed to attack British naval vessels and merchant ships, and in the three months of intensive attack, German aircraft sank three times the volume of shipping sunk by the Italian Air Force. Against Malta, the Air Corps directed 53 raids between January and April, flying almost 50 per cent more sorties than Italian aircraft, at an average strength per operation almost three times the Italian one.[68]

Despite the intensity of the German attacks, Malta survived the first serious offensive. German aircraft were soon required to support the campaigns in Libya, and in April and May operations against Yugoslavia, then Greece and Crete, absorbed more of the German air effort. The German Navy commander-in-chief, Grand Admiral Erich Raeder, asked Hitler in March 1941 to approve an airborne operation to seize Malta, but Hitler was hesitant.[69] The Italian Air Force could see that neutralizing Malta was a larger task than it had seemed: 'the end of the offensive,' ran the official Italian Air Ministry account, 'found enemy forces on Malta almost intact'.[70] After May 1941, Air Corps X abandoned Sicily in favour of bases in the eastern Mediterranean, leaving Italian air and naval forces to cope with the problem of preventing Malta from interrupting Italian supply lines to North Africa. The same pattern of continuous but small-scale raids carried on over the summer and autumn against a growing fighter and anti-aircraft strength on the island. By September 1941 there were 120 serviceable aircraft on Malta, together with submarines and torpedo boats. The seriousness of the failure to take Malta now became apparent: by the autumn the transport of supplies to the Axis armies in North Africa had reached a crisis point; 204,000 tons of shipping had been sunk or damaged by forces from Malta in five months.[71] Raeder told Hitler that the problem was Italian 'operational and tactical impotence'.[72] On 2 October 1941 Göring told Pricolo that the German Air Force was going to send aircraft once again to Sicily and at the end of the month Hitler promised Mussolini that this time the German Air Force would make sure that Malta was permanently neutralized. The German Second Air Fleet commanded by Field Marshal Kesselring was sent south from the front in Russia to cover the Mediterranean; the fleet's Air Corps II was posted to Sicily and southern Italy under the command of General Bruno Loerzer, with approximately 400 aircraft, including 190 bombers.[73] The German force arrived in waves in late 1941 and early 1942, when flying on the Russian front was restricted by the poor weather conditions. The operational orders were to defend Italian convoys, to attack the ports and airfields on Malta, and to destroy any merchant ships attempting to break the siege of the island.[74] German operations opened against Malta on 18 December 1941 and grew in strength and intensity into what became, by March, the Malta Blitz.

The air defences on Malta were inadequate to meet the renewed offensive, which reached a climax of uninterrupted day and night attacks by the early spring of 1942, chiefly carried out by German aircraft in an offensive that matched in intensity and operational shape, though not in scale, the Battle of Britain. The statistics of the German assault are set out in Table 8.2. Italian aircraft by contrast carried out only 22 small raids against Malta involving 135 sorties.[75] Most of the tonnage was directed at the three airfields and the small number of aircraft which were difficult to conceal or disperse.[76] The worst month for the island was April 1942 when attacks were made at times by over 200 bomber and fighter aircraft against an island force of around 80 fighters commanded by Air Vice Marshal Hugh Lloyd, and a remarkable 230

Table 8.2: Statistics on the German Air Effort against
Malta, January–April 1942

Date	Sorties	Bomb Tonnage	German Losses	Estimated Enemy Losses
Jan 42	1,659	609	11	40
Feb 42	2,132	623	19	43
Mar 42	4,882	1,750	37	59
Apr 42	7,557	4,623	8	97
Total	16,230	7,605	75	239

Source: IWM, Italian Series, Box 14, E2545, Ministero dell'Aeronautica,
Servizio informazioni, Bollettino Periodico, 20 May 1942.

anti-aircraft guns crammed around the island's key points. On 14 April
the airbases at Hal Far and Ta'Qali were no longer serviceable; the main
base at Luqa was rendered unusable by 21 April. Much of the dock area
sustained damage that could not be repaired.[77] By early April, Kesselring was confident enough to report that air superiority had been
established over the island, something his air fleet had been unable to
achieve over southern England (though German estimates of RAF
losses of 239 aircraft were a gross distortion of the true figure of 36 lost,
44 damaged).[78] The next step was to use that advantage to mount an
invasion of the island to eliminate permanently any possibility that
Malta might revive over the summer. Air superiority was valuable only
as long as it could be maintained, but by the late spring German plans
for renewed offensives on the Soviet front meant that many of the aircraft used for bombing Malta would have to return east. This gave the
occupation of Malta an added urgency.

Mussolini favoured a dramatic operation – 'a surprise with formidable results' – to seize Malta in a sudden paratroop attack, backed up
by seaborne forces.[79] The idea was presented to Hitler in March, and
although he was reluctant to release forces from other operational theatres, he finally agreed to allow preparations to go ahead, including
the training and preparation of three German paratroop regiments to
support the small Italian airborne force. The German operation was
codenamed 'Operation Herkules'; the Italian plan, an updated version
of an operation first examined in the 1930s, carried the title 'Requirement C.3'.[80] The object was to launch an unexpected night-time attack
with airborne forces on the south-west of the island, followed by an
amphibious landing with army units and armour. The air force was to

maintain a continuous heavy bombardment, using delayed-action bombs and fake gas bombs to force the enemy into the awkward use of gas masks and to encourage 'declining morale' among the defenders.[81] The initial plan had been based on an invasion in late May, but the poor level of Italian preparation and the successful advance of Rommel's army towards Egypt led to a further postponement. On 30 April Hitler and Mussolini met at Berchtesgaden to discuss the future of the war in the south. Hitler, noted the Italian Foreign Minister, Galeazzo Ciano, 'talks and talks and talks' while Mussolini, used to doing the talking himself, visibly suffered from his unaccustomed and almost complete silence. At the end of his monologues Hitler agreed to support the Malta invasion fully as long as it took place after Rommel had succeeded in defeating the British in Egypt. Since this was expected to happen by the summer, a tentative date of mid-July was set.[82] But by June Hitler was once again uncertain that it should be undertaken while fighting on the German-Soviet front continued, and 'especially not with Italian troops', whose value was regarded by German leaders with profound scepticism.[83]

There is a strong case for arguing that Hitler was never as enthusiastic about the capture of Malta as his subaltern ally, Mussolini. The neutralization of the island as an air and submarine base through bombing had apparently been achieved by the early summer, and the German High Command was now much more concerned with the campaign in southern Russia and the prospect that Rommel might soon occupy the Suez Canal. The growing confidence that in the summer of 1942 decisive defeats might be inflicted on the Allies in both these theatres consigned Malta for the present to a subsidiary status. There were also considerable risks with even so modest an amphibious operation. The Italian Navy staff, which had been inclined to exaggerate Malta's defensive strength from the start of the war, thought the invasion 'without doubt, one of the most difficult operations that could be undertaken', against an area believed to possess 'one of the greatest concentrations of defensive power in the world'. The navy assumed that anti-shipping artillery, beach obstacles and a countryside riddled with machine-gun nests would be a formidable challenge for a force that had not yet undertaken an opposed landing.[84] The operation had to be carried out by August at the latest to gain favourable tides. Despite the intensive and destructive bombing, it was evident by May, once the first squadrons of Spitfires arrived on Malta and German aircraft began to move back to Russia, that Maltese resistance had not been broken, either materially or morally by the bombing. After two months of continuous operations, Kesselring by the end of May had only 83 serviceable aircraft left. By August 1942 there were 165 Spitfires available, a remarkable concentration of high-quality air power on one small territory, and a force which allowed the RAF, now commanded by Air Vice Marshal Keith Park, one of the victors of the Battle of Britain against Kesselring, to adopt a far more aggressive posture against enemy incursions.[85] Neither the German commander of Air Corps II nor the new commander-in-chief of the Italian Air Force, General Rino Fougier, favoured taking risks with invasion. By default the continued neutralization of the island by bombing became the only option and every effort was devoted to trying to deny Malta the convoyed supplies needed to sustain island resistance.[86] In October, in anticipation of a decisive battle around the small Egyptian settlement of El Alamein, the decision was taken to undertake once again a determined air offensive against the island to reduce its threat to the Axis supply chain, but the resources now available, particularly to the shrunken Italian Air Force, resulted in an indecisive and limited offensive. In the first week of October 114 Axis aircraft were shot down, for the loss of 27 Spitfires. By November the Axis effort against Malta declined to a long series of nuisance raids. Over the course of the war the RAF lost 707 aircraft in all operations from Malta, and 2,301 crew.[87]

The most remarkable aspect of the 'Blitzes' on Malta was the capacity of the population, the military garrison and the British colonial authorities to cope with almost daily bombing over a period of more than two years of aerial siege, and particularly through the two months of intense and destructive bombing in spring 1942, without a serious social crisis or a movement to surrender. 'The Maltese have nothing to laugh about,' observed Goebbels in his diary in April 1942. 'At the moment, they are the population tormented the most in the entire globe by air attacks.'[88] The anxiety felt by the authorities in 1940 that the population might panic entirely under bombing was soon replaced by positive efforts to find ways to turn Malta into a veritable fortress capable of withstanding a long aerial siege. Despite evacuation, there were such small distances between the main targets and the inland villages that almost all areas of the island were bombed at some time. By 1942 it was observed that a high proportion of bombs hit buildings already destroyed in earlier raids. Fields and roads became pitted with bomb craters and unexploded bombs (including unstable anti-personnel bombs) and live ammunition could be found all over the island. Warnings were issued in September 1940 and again in May 1941 to stop people removing or playing with the ordnance, but there were regular civilian injuries, some caused by the occasional juvenile practice of hitting live bullets with a hammer to make them explode.[89]

For the Maltese people the two most important factors were shelter and food. The provision of public or private shelter was eventually extended by early 1942 to a shelter space for almost the entire population of Malta and Gozo. These included spaces for 149,000 in shelters built or renovated by the Maltese government, employing 2,000 miners and stonemasons.[90] Each shelter had to be provided with bunks and sanitary equipment and, where it was possible, separate cubicles were excavated into which whole families could move possessions and furniture and the ubiquitous small shrines to the Madonna. The authorities also set up a scheme for the '1,000 head store' to make sure that for every 1,000 shelterers there would be a dedicated stock of food, kerosene and water in case of emergency.[91] Nevertheless there were numerous problems in trying to maintain standards in a situation where raiding sometimes occurred as often as eight times in 24 hours. In January 1942 the government established a Select Committee to investigate public concerns over shelter provision. The public was invited to submit their complaints and 95 people did so, highlighting chiefly the problems of overcrowding, poor lighting and water seepage. The committee also identified a shortage of bunks and poor sanitary arrangements and recommended regular inspection, a ticketing system for entry to the shelters, and better links between the underground shelters and the emergency stores. In some cases shelters lacked a shelter warden to supervise the shelter community and an effort was subsequently made to recruit more volunteers to help organize and control what for most Maltese had become an uncomfortable way of life.[92]

The most critical factor was the supply of food and fresh water. Malta was intensively farmed but lacked a great many essential foodstuffs. The traditional Maltese diet consisted mainly of macaroni, spaghetti, and bread covered with olive oil and tomato paste. Fish and goat meat supplemented a cuisine high in carbohydrates. Sugar was highly prized. In the first years of war rationing was limited, partly to avoid any possible friction with the population, partly because it did not seem necessary. Hoarding occurred in the first weeks, and the islanders conducted their own black market, concealed from the authorities by traditional networks of family or kin (and by the linguistic veil of Malti). The government was slow to implement a scheme for building up food stocks or for rationing, though a Director of Rabbit Production was appointed since rabbits were easy to raise on scraps and waste and were plentiful on the island. In February 1941 a Maltese nobleman, Marquis Barbaro, was made Food Distribution Officer and limited rationing was imposed from April 1941, but bread and flour paste remained unrationed until the height of the spring Blitz in 1942, while tea, butter and cheese remained outside the ration.[93] For islanders rendered unemployed by the war, or for the young and old with restricted access to food, the government brought in a welfare scheme of cash coupons or relief in kind. In 1941 a chain of Victory Kitchens was established, where a standard and monotonous menu of soup and spaghetti and goat stew was served at low prices to ensure that everyone who needed it could get a midday meal, however limited its nourishment.[94]

Once the heaviest bombing began in spring 1942, food needs became more urgent; the convoy crisis of the summer faced Malta with the prospect of widespread hunger. In June a delegation of food experts arrived from Britain to investigate what could be done to ensure Malta's survival. They reported that the urgency had been exaggerated: 'neither the troops nor the people in the streets showed any obvious signs of underfeeding'. They found the black market rife on the island and encouraged tighter controls. Their final report recommended suspending brewing, slaughtering livestock, cutting onion growing, expanding tomato cultivation, and possibly killing domestic pets. 'Rabbits,' the report concluded, 'should be maintained as long as possible.'[95] Rationing was tightened up on a range of supplies, including a standard 10.5 oz of bread a day, and 14 oz of sugar, 15 oz of fats and oils, and 12 oz of canned meat every two weeks, while at the same time an effort was made to improve the standard of Victory Kitchen meals, about which there were wide complaints. Stocks of food on the island in June 1942 amounted to 7,319 tons of flour, 783 tons of oils and fats, 1,287 tons of tinned meat, 1,021 tons of sugar and 129 tons of tea, but the island's Food and Distribution Board found that only flour and wheat supplies posed any real danger. Black-market hoards were investigated more vigorously and new punishments (one month in prison and confiscation of all goods) instituted.[96] Fresh-water stocks were increased to 17 million gallons from the 9.8 million gallons available in autumn 1941, while the government aimed to maintain a food reserve equivalent to at least ten months' consumption.[97] Just enough food got through to the island during the convoy battles of the summer of 1942 to allow the island to survive the siege.

The 'morale' of the island throughout the long months of bombing was sustained, as it was in Britain and Germany, by adequate enough provision of shelter, welfare and food supplies for the whole Maltese population. There was also a marked hostility of the Maltese directed towards the Italians, whose efforts to claim Malta as an Italian outpost did not prevent them from bombing it repeatedly. After the first raid on 11 June 1940, according to one account, 'the air grew blue with blasphemy' as angry Maltese cursed Mussolini and shook their fists at the air. The town council changed the traditional Italian street names to English.[98] There was no shortage of Maltese volunteers to man the anti-aircraft guns and 1,700 joined the Maltese 'Home Guard' volunteers.[99] The Catholic population also relied on their deep religiosity, a sentiment shared with the devoutly Christian lieutenant governor, Sir William Dobbie, who arrived in Malta in April 1940. From early in the war, priests held open-air masses (to avoid the danger of a sudden bomb on a church) and officiated at shelter services. One Spitfire pilot, on arriving at his base in the medieval walled city of Mdina (the old capital), was told by his Maltese driver that it was a sacred site: 'The Holy Father will not let the Germans bomb it.'[100] The British in Malta were impressed by the way the local population ignored the raids, staying on in cinemas when the air-raid warning sounded or refusing the formal requirement to take cover when bombing started. As in most bombing in Europe during the war, the raids evoked a range of attitudes, but in this case the bombing was relentless and there was nowhere to escape its effects. Almost 30,000 buildings were destroyed or damaged, though only 5,200 were rendered permanently uninhabitable.[101] The same Spitfire pilot later wrote that the Maltese people endured the bombing with an enviable stoicism and a level of bravery that had to be witnessed rather than imagined, since he found the situation 'unsettling and claustrophobic'.[102] Formal reports on the outlook of the Maltese population also highlighted the capacity to absorb the shock of bombing ('have stood up to their ordeal magnificently') and although this assertion suited the colonial authorities, there is no reason to doubt that it described a certain reality.[103] Malta was, nevertheless, a colony. Censorship, internment, compulsory conscription of male labour, regular checks and controls were built into the ruling system, while the British forces, officials and residents formed an elite that dominated the Maltese and restricted opportunities for protest or abdication. Among that elite, there seems to have been no moment when surrender was seriously contemplated.

Alongside the bombing, the persistent threat of invasion hung over the island for three years. Even as late as October 1942, the Italian Air Force concluded that despite every effort to neutralize the island by bombing, including the 'concrete results' of the heavy Blitz in spring 1942, the only solution to maintaining traffic with the Italian forces in North Africa was 'the territorial occupation of the island'.[104] The British authorities remained alive to this threat well into 1943 and regarded it as more damaging to morale than the air attacks. In early 1942 the War Office in London tried to persuade the British commanders in Malta to adopt a ruthless scorched-earth policy in the event of invasion, with plans to destroy all materials, equipment, oil, coal and port facilities. The Maltese troop commander refused, since it was tantamount to admitting defeat. The Maltese Defence Committee concluded in June 1942, '100% "Scorched Earth" <u>NOT</u> possible' because the civilian population still had to be fed and supplied; their morale was likely to plummet if they witnessed 'wanton destruction'.[105] Anti-invasion preparations were extensive. Under the codewords 'Volcano' (attack imminent) and 'Cyclone' (general attack started), the British authorities planned to repel as rapidly as possible any Italian or German attempt to occupy the island. The air-raid shelters doubled up as shelters for the invasion, when the entire population not needed for defence purposes would be placed underground. The signal for invasion was a continuous blast on the air-raid siren.[106] No invasion came and the siege was lifted with the arrival of a convoy from Alexandria on 20 November 1942. In February 1943 censorship was eased (though mention of air raids was only allowed four months after they had occurred). In November 1943 the blackout restrictions were relaxed.[107] The failed Axis offensive cost the islanders 1,486 dead and around 4,000 injured, as well as the massive destruction of the urban and port areas of the island, but it confirmed again that sustained and heavy bombing, in the face of even modest military defences and an organized civil defence programme, had clear strategic limits.

'GREAT DELAY TO THE TRAINS': ALLIED BOMBING 1940–43

The possibility that Italy might take advantage of the Allies' war with Germany to open up a new theatre in the Mediterranean was evident long before Mussolini finally seized the opportunity of imminent French collapse to join his Axis partner. The prospect presented the RAF with additional bombing opportunities to consider if, or when, bombing targets in enemy cities was permitted. In the last week of April the commander of British air forces in France, Air Marshal Arthur Barrett, wrote to the Air Ministry suggesting that bomber forces could operate from bases in southern France against industrial cities in northern Italy.[108] After the War Cabinet on 1 June 1940 had considered ways to cope with Italian belligerency, Barrett was instructed to begin planning the supply and maintenance of British bombers on southern French bases. In case of war, Italy was to be attacked 'without warning'.[109] By the time Italy declared war on 10 June, 'Haddock Force', as it was known, had operational bases, fuel and supplies on two southern French airfields. On 11 June a dozen Wellington bombers arrived, but the French military authorities were now opposed to any bombing of Italy that might provoke retaliation against French cities, and parked lorries on the runway to prevent takeoff. Only after days of inter-Allied argument did a force of eight aircraft set off on the night of 15–16 June to bomb the port of Genoa, but only one found it; the following night six out of nine managed to locate and bomb Milan. Then the order came to evacuate following the French surrender and the 950 men of Haddock Force left on ships from Marseille on 18 June, leaving all their stores and equipment behind.[110] Only on the eve of the armistice between France and Italy did French aircraft attack Italian targets in Sicily on 23 and 24 June, killing 45 people in a gesture of pointless defiance.[111]

The decision to begin bombing Italy – a campaign that continued uninterrupted in one form or another for five years – brought none of the anxieties over legality or retaliation that had governed the decision to begin bombing Germany four weeks earlier, in mid-May. From the outset it was assumed that Italian morale under Fascism was likely to be a more brittle target than German society under Hitler. Bombing could hence be justified by the expectation of rapid and significant political consequences rather than slow economic attrition. The first raids on northern Italy carried out by Bomber Command from British bases in June and August 1940 – three in all involving only 17 aircraft – were reported to have had 'a "stunning" effect on Italian morale'.[112] Intelligence fed to the RAF leadership suggested that Italy was 'the heel of Achilles' in the Axis war effort, short of resources and with a population unhappy about having to fight Mussolini's war.[113] Since Italy was difficult to reach from British bases or from bases in Egypt with existing aircraft, heavy bombing was not yet an option. But since Italy was regarded as politically fragile, a leaflet war was mounted to try to persuade the population to give up the fight. Leaflets could be dropped by small numbers of aircraft operating out of Maltese bases or occasionally in long-distance drops from Britain. One of the first leaflets drafted on Malta in November 1940 called for an Italian uprising: 'On hearing the great signal all of you on to the Square – armed with whatever you can lay your hands on, hoes, pickaxes, shotguns, even sticks.' The text called on Italians to create a civilized and democratic Italy and to be ready for the call (in block capitals) to 'COUNTER-REVOLUTION'.[114] Much of the campaign linked the call for Italian political resistance with the threat of bombing. A leaflet printed in January 1941 asked Italians to choose, 'Mussolini or bombs?', and 100,000 copies were flown from Luqa airfield to cities in southern Italy. In April 1941 a new leaflet under the headline 'ROME IS IN DANGER' threatened to bomb the Italian capital if Mussolini ordered the bombing of Athens or Cairo.[115]

Nothing came of the political initiative and the bombing was in reality small-scale and intermittent, a 'small switch', as Portal put it, rather than 'a big stick'.[116] Throughout 1940 and 1941 there were 24 small raids by Bomber Command (only four of them in 1941) and 95 raids from Malta, most of them by handfuls of Wellington bombers, seldom more than 10 at a time, on their way to bases in the Middle East.[117] In November 1940, for example, six Wellingtons attacked Naples, where they reported a poor blackout, no searchlights or enemy aircraft and inaccurate anti-aircraft fire. A raid on Taranto by 10 Wellingtons on 13–14 November could be carried out from 5,000 feet because there were once again no searchlights, aircraft or barrage balloons, and inaccurate gunfire. The blackout was poor in all areas and trains could be seen running between towns fully lit.[118] There were points in 1941 at which intensified bombing of Italy was considered, but the priority in the Mediterranean was to prevent Axis victory in North Africa and to keep the sea lanes open, and this absorbed all the RAF effort in the theatre. In October 1941 the Foreign Office suggested that at the right moment, when Italian morale was judged to be cracking, a heavy bomb attack might prove to be 'a knock-out blow', but Portal insisted that the war in Libya took priority.[119] The Foreign Office suggested again in January 1942 a surprise raid on Kesselring's headquarters at Frascati, near Rome, but the Air Ministry again demurred in favour of military targets in North Africa.[120] In the first nine months of 1942 there was only one Bomber Command raid on Italy, in April against Savona on the Ligurian coast, and 34 small raids from Malta against airbases and ports, despite the heavy Axis bombing of the island. For most of the period from late 1940 to the late autumn of 1942 much of Italy was spared anything more than damaging nuisance raids.[121]

This situation changed suddenly and dramatically for the Italian population in late October 1942 when the war in North Africa turned in the Allies' favour at El Alamein, followed by the invasion of north-west Africa in November. Imminent Italian defeat encouraged the view, as Churchill put it in early December, that 'the heat should be turned on Italy'.[122] Portal assured him that Italy would become 'Bombing Target No. 1', absorbing the same tonnage of bombs against the main ports and industrial cities as Germany.[123] Bomber Command was ordered to begin area bombing of northern Italian cities as the weather deteriorated over Germany. In the last two months of 1942 six area raids were made on Genoa, seven raids on Turin and one daylight raid against Milan. There was negligible resistance to the daytime raid by 88 Lancasters and bombs could be released over Milan from as low as 2,500 feet, though the post-raid report indicated that there had been too few incendiaries dropped to cause the kind of fire damage common in area attacks on Germany. Indeed detailed research by the RE8 department for the Air Ministry showed that Italian architecture was less prone to either lateral or vertical fire damage than German because of the extensive use of stone and marble, the solid stone flooring, the thickness and mass of the walls, and the wide courtyards and streets. RE8 recommended dropping high explosive on modern multi-storey apartment blocks, which were more vulnerable than traditional pre-nineteenth century construction, and where a lucky strike in the enclosed courtyard would maximize the blast effect of a bomb.[124] The Air Ministry nevertheless remained confident that incendiary damage in Italian cities would still be greater than damage from high explosive, as long as firebombs were dropped accurately enough on the most congested city-centre areas, Zones 1 and 2A, and included a proportion of explosive incendiaries to discourage the firefighters.[125]

The onset of the air offensive in October 1942 revealed the extent to which the Italian armed forces, the Fascist Party and the civil defence organization were unprepared for the effective protection, either active or passive, of the civilian population, and of the economic and industrial resources sustaining Italy's war effort. The Italian Air Force had devoted little effort to constructing a network of air defences to match the system in Britain or Germany. After three years of war the chief of the air staff, Rino Fougier, was forced to admit that Italy was 'in practice without effective defence'.[126] Most fighter aircraft had been used in support of the ground armies, while a night-fighter capability scarcely existed despite the fact that most raids until 1943 were by night. By September 1942 Italian night-fighters had flown only 380 hours on operations compared with 158,100 hours for day-fighters.[127] Search-lights, anti-aircraft batteries and radar were available in limited quantities, but were not integrated into a national system of communi-cation to cope with identifying and challenging incoming aircraft (even the daylight raid on Milan had prompted the air-raid alarm only after the bombs were already falling). Italian air defences relied heavily on light 20-mm guns, which could not reach high-flying bombers; the plans for 300 batteries of 90-mm guns were never met.[128] Fighters were supposed to provide protection during the day, when there were few, if any, raids, while anti-aircraft fire was supposed to defend at night, but neither operated at local level under a coordinated command, since anti-aircraft artillery was a branch of the army.[129] There were severe shortages of aviation fuel and of modern aircraft while air-to-ground radio communication had still not been introduced by the end of 1942. Reports from fighter units in the south, now facing daylight raids by American air forces, showed that in many cases scrambled fighters arrived too late to intercept bombers, or in other cases lacked the speed to catch them. One squadron in January 1943 was compelled to send aircraft out just one or two at a time; another group was forced to oper-ate six different types of fighter, some biplanes, some monoplanes, one of them German and eight of them French, with all the problems of coordination and maintenance likely to arise from a hybrid unit.[130]

Following the first major raids in late 1942, an effort was made to find a way of disposing the limited defensive resources to maximize their effectiveness. It was decided that the German system should be carefully investigated to see whether lessons could be drawn for the Ital-ian air defence system; in June 1943 Josef Kammhuber, commander of the German air defences, came to Italy to discuss how to set up a collab-orative air defence structure using Italian and German units and radar. By the summer only one Italian radar station had been completed, while the rest required between six weeks and two months before they would be available.[131] Some Italian pilots were sent for night-fighter training in Germany, but on their return found it difficult to cope with the very different conditions on an Italian airbase.[132] The organization of an integrated and unified air defence system had still not been agreed when the Mussolini regime collapsed in July. As Italy's military capability evidently declined from late 1942, so German forces stationed in the peninsula came to rely more on their own anti-air defences. By 1943, 300 German anti-aircraft batteries had been transferred to Italy but German forces refused to allow Italian troops to man them, as had been agreed. By June 1943 the German Air Force had night-fighter bases and radar installed along Italy's coastline in 33 'boxes', imitating the Kammhuber Line in Germany; two months later there were also 10 German night-fighter units protecting Turin, Milan, Genoa and other north Italian cities as far as Brescia and Venice.[133] This situation could produce its own friction. In Milan in February 1943, German anti-aircraft guns opened up on four Italian fighters, forcing them to abandon their operation. When the local Italian commander complained, the German anti-aircraft unit told him that as far as they were concerned Italian fighter pilots flew at their own risk.[134]

Italian air force leaders had counted from at least 1941 onwards on German assistance in supplying aircraft, aero-engines and advanced machine tools for the Italian aviation industry, but supply never matched requirements. A total of 706 German aircraft were delivered to Italian units over the whole course of the war, some 448 in the period when Italy was an Axis ally. The figure was a fraction of German output, and was divided between 15 different types, of varying quality. Some 300 were Me109s, but most of these were supplied in 1943 and 1944 to the new National Republican Air Force; there were 155 Ju87 'Stuka' dive-bombers, but the rest were small packets of aircraft for airborne operations or bombing. The Italian Air Force was supplied with only 14 night-fighters for the campaign against night-bombing.[135] Italy also relied on German supplies of radar equipment. In the course of 1942, 5 *Freya* and 10 *Würzburg* sets were made available, a fraction of what was needed. When a new air observation system was organized in the summer of 1943, the Italian *Difesa Contraerea Territoriale* (DiCaT), which had hitherto employed an observer corps based on acoustic devices, was supposed to operate a system of radar 'boxes' alongside German radar, but it had to wait for the slow supply of equipment from the German Telefunken manufacturer in order to be able to protect even the major target areas of Milan, Naples, Rome, Turin and Genoa.[136] German reluctance to supply more was based on a number of considerations. When the Italian Air Force asked for machinery to help them modernize the aircraft industry in the summer of 1941, the German Air Ministry replied that supplies were placed in three categories: essential equipment for German industry; essential machinery for industry in occupied Europe working directly to German orders or for neutrals supplying vital raw materials; and inessential orders, including Italian. The German side took the view that if they helped Italy, they would be assisting a potential competitor when regular commercial activity restarted after the war.[137]

The failure of Italian air defence was matched by the poor state of preparation of civil defence and the welfare and rescue services on which it relied. By a law of 5 March 1934 the provincial prefects, representing the state rather than the Fascist Party, were to assume responsibility for all local civil defence measures. Comprehensive instructions on all aspects of civil defence, including evacuation, shelters, anti-gas preparations and firefighting, were first issued in 1938 by the War Ministry.[138] In 1939, to avoid confusion between military and civil responsibilities, the War Ministry confirmed that the prefects rather than the local commanders of Italy's military zones had to organize the protection of the population under the Ministry of the Interior, but instructions continued to be sent from the War Ministry department, *Protezione Antiaerea*, on into the war, creating regular arguments over jurisdiction between the two ministries. Each local prefecture had a Provincial Inspectorate for Anti-Air Protection to oversee civil defence measures, but action in the 1930s was slow and piecemeal. For one thing, the funds available were severely limited, around one-tenth of the sums allocated to active air defence.[139] Given these limitations, the state had to decide on an order of priority. It was assumed that major industrial and military targets should be protected, but in case of total war it might be necessary to protect 'all the centres of population, based on a scale of the number of inhabitants'.[140] Since there was neither the money nor the materials and equipment to provide universal civil defence, resources were concentrated in the most likely target areas. Gas masks, for example, were produced in 1939 for only 2 million out of a population of 45 million, the majority allocated to Rome, Milan, Turin, Genoa and Naples, the rest to just 11 other cities. The shelter programme had scarcely begun in 1939, with places in public shelters for just 72,000 people and in domestic shelters for a further 190,000.[141] Not until the day war was declared, 10 June 1940, did the War Ministry send out to prefects a list of cities ranked in order of priority for civil defence activity, including the blackout. Category 'P' included 28 major ports and industrial centres, where civil defence measures were to be introduced 'with maximum intensity and speed'; category 'M' covered 23 smaller cities where civil defence provisions could be introduced 'with a slower rhythm and lesser intensity'; category 'S' left 41 cities (some of which, like Grosseto, were to be almost completely destroyed by bombing) where the authorities were free to carry out measures if they wanted to, 'within the limits of possibility'.[142]

Unlike the German and Soviet dictatorships, Fascist Italy failed to mobilize a large mass movement for voluntary civil defence. Instead a more modest *Unione Nazionale Protezione Antiaerea* (UNPA) was set up in August 1934 under the direction of the War Ministry to help educate the civilian population on how to observe civil defence requirements, to prepare for the blackout, to convert cellars and basements into improvised air-raid shelters, and to train volunteers for post-raid welfare and rescue work. By 1937 UNPA had recruited only 150,000 volunteers, in contrast to 11 million in Germany, and was constantly short of adequate funds.[143] UNPA organizers had to be members of the Fascist Party, and local block or house wardens (*capi fabbricato*), responsible for organizing civil defence in their neighbourhood buildings, were also appointed directly by the Party from among UNPA members. Most of them were men over 45 (all younger men were reserved for the armed services), women or youths; they had in many cases only limited training, and numerous civil defence exercises before 1940 demonstrated a persistent confusion between the responsibilities of the police, civil defence workers and the military air defence authorities.[144] There can be little doubt that Italy entered the Second World War with inadequate resources to protect the civilian population and a civil defence organization uncertain of its functions and short of trained personnel. The inadequacies were fatally exposed when nine RAF bombers arrived over Turin and two over Genoa on the night of 10–11 June 1940 to find both cities entirely illuminated despite a plethora of instructions on operating the blackout in priority areas and regular blackout practices for years. Although detailed orders for observing the blackout had been distributed in May, there were regular complaints throughout the early period of raiding about its inadequacy, conspicuously so on air force bases and in ministry buildings in Rome. When Ciampino airbase, near the capital, was asked in October 1940 to explain the bright lights visible through a large window, the commandant replied that they had been unable to find a curtain large enough to cover it.[145]

The first raids were militarily insignificant but they prompted an immediate sense of crisis among a population unprepared for the realities of war. On 18 June the prefect of Genoa complained to the Interior Ministry in Rome that the raids and alerts (three raids and 17 aircraft) 'have caused great delay to the trains'.[146] It was immediately realized that alerts had the effect of halting production for long periods as workers scrambled to use the factory shelters or disappeared for hours in panic, leaving machines unattended and electricity and gas switched off. Factories working on war orders were circulated with stern instructions to treat workers 'like a soldier, who has an obligation to stay at his post in front of enemy fire'.[147] Although factory workers were not in the end militarized, the UNPA personnel found themselves transformed into the status of 'mobilized civilian' in August 1940 to maintain standards of discipline and to prevent members from trying to abandon civil defence responsibilities in the face of the real menace of bombing. The *capo fabbricato* by a law of 1 November 1940 became a public official to emphasize their role in serving the community.[148] For most of Italy beyond the major ports in the south and Sicily serving the Axis armies in North Africa, the bombing ceased to be a serious threat almost at once. Throughout 1941 and the first nine months of 1942 there were almost no raids, and as a result much less pressure to speed up effective civil defence preparations. Shelter provision remained poor (the War Ministry told prefects to let civilians use shelters in factories and public buildings because of the evident deficiency in domestic shelter) while basic protection for industry, including blast walls or sandbagging, depended on the funds available or the good sense of the owner. The same problem confronted the effort to organize the protection of Italy's vast artistic and architectural heritage. Decrees and instructions on protection were regularly published from 1934 onwards, but a general law on the Protection of Objects of Artistic or Historic Value was only published by the Ministry of Education in June 1939.[149] Its provisions had scarcely begun to be introduced when on 6 June 1940, just days before the declaration of war, the local superintendents, responsible for the artistic heritage, were instructed to begin packing up and moving any portable artworks and putting sandbags and cladding over major churches and buildings. Around 100 depositories were established in Italy and hundreds of monuments given minimum protection, enough to cope with shrapnel or a distant blast, but not enough for a direct hit.[150]

All of this changed with the start of the Allied offensive in the autumn of 1942. The poor level of preparation for attacks on this scale helps to explain their substantial material and psychological impact compared with raiding on Germany. The bombing of Turin, particularly the heavy raids of 20–21 and 28–29 November by aircraft of Bomber Command, which hit both the industrial zone and the city centre, resulted in extensive and random destruction. Over 100 firms indicated some damage, but in important cases the loss was almost total. A radar workshop was 'entirely destroyed' along with 90 per cent of its machinery; a firm producing magnetos for aero-engines was almost completely eliminated by just one bomb; a major aircraft repair factory, Aeronautica d'Italia, was burnt out, leaving only one production line still operating. A report on the raids on Genoa on 13–14 and 15–16 November listed damage to rails, electric power lines and tunnels, much of which could be repaired, but at the Marconi radio works production was 'completely paralysed' and had to be transferred to a nearby town.[151] The threat to Italian production, already suffering from severe shortages of materials and equipment, was immediate. The War Ministry on 15 November circulated to all ministries a warning that war industry would now have to be decentralized and dispersed to areas where it could continue to function without the threat of paralysing air attack.

A few days later the Supreme Command agreed to a comprehensive dispersal programme from the main industrial regions. Firms were to try to find tunnels or underground facilities nearby to prevent too much disruption to work patterns or the loss of workers; where these were not available, decentralization into smaller firms in the locality was recommended; in extreme cases a radical transfer to a different zone was required where inessential plants could be closed down and their labour and factory space used by the evacuated firm.[152] For businesses that could not easily be moved – steel production, for example – efforts were at last to be made to supply more anti-aircraft batteries, smoke generators to obscure the zone, and a programme of camouflage. A Special Committee was set up in December 1942 composed of representatives from the defence ministries and the Ministry of Corporations to draw up lists week by week of firms that were ordered to disperse their production. Most went to towns or villages nearby, some into caves or man-made caverns. The dispersal provoked its own problems: shortages of lorries for transport, inadequate rail links, a shortage of skilled workers to assist the transfer, arguments with the Finance Ministry over subsidies and compensation for bombed-out businesses.[153] Italian war production continued to decline during 1943 as firms tried to cope with the sudden demand to improvise the transfer of their production or to cope with the continued heavy bombing of the industrial regions. Firms that had chosen to stay put, like Alfa Romeo, were forced by the summer of 1943 to move, in this case to the Grotte di San Rocco, a system of caves where, despite the stale air and high humidity, it was hoped that the workforce would be more productive than had been possible with regular alerts.[154]

The psychological and physical shock to the Italian population was much greater, as the British had hoped. Secure from the bombing war since the small raids in late 1940, the home front had not developed the infrastructure for civil defence nor the mindset to cope with sudden heavy raiding. Much of the damage was done to residential areas, since these were intended to be area raids. In Turin some 3,230 residential buildings and 46 schools were destroyed or heavily damaged in the November raids. The local prefect of Turin, whence some 400,000 had fled by December 1942, reported that the demoralized population were 'depressed, nervous, irritable and alarmed' not only by the bombing but by a general 'sense of exhaustion at the length of the war'.[155] Evacuees made their way out to the surrounding countryside or more distant provinces. Iris Origo, an Anglo-American married to an Italian marquis, recorded in her diary the sight of families arriving in Tuscany from Genoa after living for weeks in tunnels under the city 'without light, without sufficient water, and in bitter cold', displaying a 'healthy, elementary resentment' against those dropping the bombs but a profound anger at the incompetence and mismanagement of the Fascist system which had exposed them to bombing in the first place.[156] The failure to prepare for or to oppose the raids was regarded as a standing indictment of the Mussolini regime. The workers who stayed behind in Turin, according to one report, had calmed down after displaying an 'understandable agitation' at being bombed; but they remained in a continued state of anxiety largely because Allied aircraft could regularly be seen circling low over the city by day quite undisturbed. According to another report from Varese, north of Milan, the absence of any effective Italian defence against two Allied aircraft casually photographing the area below left the population 'perplexed and alarmed'.[157] Leaflets dropped during the raids in November and December listed major cities slated for future bombing (including the ones already bombed) and an appeal to 'evacuate the cities' as soon as possible while casualties were still by comparison 'very few'. Perhaps to rub the message home, small stickers were dropped printed in red letters with the single word 'Merda!' ('Oh shit!').[158]

Evacuation was not by 1942 an easy option. In the 1930s evacuating the population from the major cities had been seen as a way of reducing the threat of casualties in the absence of shelters or gas masks. A plan had been distributed to prefects in 1939 designed to halve the city population by encouraging voluntary evacuation where possible and insisting on the compulsory evacuation of children, the elderly and the sick (as well as convicts, a category more difficult to understand). Those who remained were generally obliged to do so because of the nature of their work or responsibilities. In June 1940 the scheme was virtually abandoned. Voluntary evacuation was uncontrolled, and soon led to prefects insisting that people return home. In the absence of persistent or heavy bombing, urban populations generally remained where they were.[159] The first raids in October 1942 transformed the situation overnight. In November new regulations governing evacuation were drawn up and circulated to all prefects; once again there were compulsory categories, help for voluntary evacuees, and provision for a new category of 'evening evacuees' who worked in the city during the day and returned in the evening to families in nearby suburban or rural areas. On 2 December Mussolini publicly endorsed the new wave of evacuations as a 'duty' to the community.[160] The mass exodus in November and December was largely unorganized, though Fascist Party workers, mainly youths and women, helped provide food and find accommodation. Since many Italian city-dwellers had family or friends in nearby rural areas (an estimated 40 per cent in Turin), the social problems were less severe than they might have been, but the problem of overcrowding, the difficulty of organizing regular transport for the 'evening' evacuees, and shortages of food soon made themselves felt. Protests from the prefects in March 1943 led to a reversal of policy and evacuees were encouraged instead to return home and run the risk of being bombed. The appeal had little effect. Half of the population of Turin remained away from the city at night, 55 per cent in the hinterland, 45 per cent in other provinces. A second wave of evacuation occurred in the summer of 1943, reaching two-thirds of the city population, many of the newcomers sleeping in woods and fields in conditions of deteriorating hygiene and widespread hunger.[161]

The crisis induced by bombing was more severe than anything experienced in Britain or Germany. As intelligence information filtered through to the Allies, the idea of bombing Italy out of the war suddenly became less fanciful. Sinclair told Churchill in late 1942 that Fascist morale would be badly rocked by bombing war industry and transport but that a final flamboyant attack on Rome 'might bring the Fascist state toppling down'.[162] An intelligence report to the American Office of Strategic Services (OSS) in April 1943 from Lisbon claimed that the Italian ambassador 'expects revolt within a month'. A second report a few weeks later passed on news that Pope Pius XII was unhappy about the bombings and now hoped that the generals might seize power and take Italy over to the side of the Allies.[163] As a result the political war on Italy was stepped up in the first months of 1943. American aircraft of the Ninth Air Force, which joined the campaign in December 1942, interspersed the bombing of Italian cities from North African bases with massive leaflet drops, 64 million items in the first eight months of the year. Their purpose, according to the Psychological Warfare Branch, was to 'harden Italian opposition to Mussolini, to Germany and the war'. Bombing strengthened the message. There was, the PWB claimed, a special connection between air power and propaganda.[164] The leaflets explained that bombing was necessary as long as Italy fought at Germany's side. 'Why We Bomb You', dropped in late 1942, challenged the Italian people 'to refuse to fight the war of Hitler and Mussolini', but warned them that the innocent would suffer if they did not.[165] This propaganda effort did not go unopposed. Side by side with the leaflets, the Allies were accused by the Italian authorities of dropping explosive pencils to kill Italian children: 'in one hand a hypocritical lying message,' wrote the Gazzetta del Popolo, 'in the other a vile death trap'.[166] The Fascist press issued its own leaflet accusing the Americans of using black airmen, 'the worst men ... the new tribes of savages'.[167] A number of Allied leaflets were sent to Mussolini in July 1943 by his Interior Ministry with the assurance that Italians who read them remained calm and unaffected. Allied propaganda, so it was claimed, 'has not produced any effect on public order'.[168]

The most difficult thing for the Allies to judge was the right moment to bomb Rome. The idea of bombing the Italian capital went back to the start of the war but was postponed again and again on political, cultural and religious grounds. When bombers were based in Malta in the autumn of 1940 the practical possibility of hitting the capital was hard to resist. On 28 October 1940, following the Italian invasion of Greece, the British Air Ministry immediately ordered the bombing of Rome in retaliation, but the following day the instruction was cancelled. Churchill was happy to order the bombing of Rome ('let them have a good dose') but only when the time seemed appropriate.[169] In the spring of 1941 the Air Ministry told the RAF headquarters in the Middle East that Rome could be bombed at once, without further authorization, if Italian aircraft bombed the centre of Athens or Cairo. When an Italian aircraft eventually dropped bombs on an army depot at Abbassia on the outskirts of Cairo in September 1941, the RAF Command in the

Middle East wanted to bomb Rome without delay, hitting Mussolini's official residence in the Palazzo Venezia and the central railway station, but again the War Cabinet demurred from fear of heavy reprisals against the Egyptian capital.[170] 'The selection of the right moment to bomb Rome,' wrote Portal to the Foreign Office, 'is clearly a matter of some delicacy.'[171]

The arguments about bombing Rome rested in the end on its exceptional symbolic status. Rome was the heart of the Catholic world, home to the neutral Vatican City, whose neutrality had to be respected or risk worldwide condemnation from Catholic communities. It was the heart of the classical Roman Empire, taught to generations of British public schoolboys, including those who now commanded the wartime RAF, as a model for the greater British Empire. It was also a primary centre of European culture, packed with treasures from the classical world to the age of the High Baroque. 'Liberal opinion,' complained Sinclair to Churchill in December 1942, 'regards Rome as one of the shrines of European civilization. This liberal opinion is a bit sticky about bombing ...'[172] Portal told Sinclair that reluctance could even be found among Bomber Command crews to bombing not only Rome but also Florence or Venice. Sinclair, though a Liberal politician himself, had no cultural scruples – 'we must not hedge our airmen round with meticulous restrictions', he scribbled at the side of a memorandum on bombing Rome – but he could see that there were political risks in damaging 'churches, works of art, Cardinals and priests' until the moment when a sudden blow might produce political dividends that outweighed the disadvantages.[173] Anthony Eden, the Foreign Secretary, was strongly opposed to bombing Rome except as a last resort; he resisted several offers from Arthur Harris to use 617 Squadron (the 'Dambusters') for bombing Mussolini's official residence, the Palazzo Venezia, or his private Villa Torlonia, on the grounds that the attacks were unlikely to kill him and more likely to reverse the decline in popular support for the dictator.[174]

The long hesitation over whether or when to bomb Rome was finally ended in June 1943 as the Allies prepared to invade Sicily after final victory in North Africa on 13 May. To prevent German reinforcement, Eisenhower's headquarters in Algiers favoured bombing two important rail marshalling yards at Littorio and San Lorenzo, the second close to the ancient basilica of the same name. Churchill wrote to Roosevelt on 10 June asking whether he approved the raid, and a week later Roosevelt replied that he was *wholly* in agreement' as long as the crews were given the strictest instructions to avoid dropping bombs on the Vatican or on Papal property in Rome.[175] This did not end the political arguments. At the Combined Chiefs of Staff meeting a few days later the prospect of damaging Rome's monuments and churches was discussed again. General Marshall, the US Army chief of staff, endorsed the raid on the ground that after the bombing of St Paul's, Westminster Abbey and the churches on Malta, the United States would 'have no qualms about Rome', and the chiefs sent Eisenhower their approval.[176] In early July the Archbishop of Canterbury, William Temple, wrote to Sinclair asking for assurance that the ancient and medieval centres of Rome, Florence and Venice would be excluded from the risk of attack. The Air Ministry told Sinclair that the lives of Allied soldiers should not be placed in jeopardy for the sake of a sacred edifice – 'are we to place the monuments of the past before the hopes for the future?' – and two days before the operation to attack the marshalling yards Sinclair told Archbishop Temple that the Allies could not refrain from bombing a military objective even if it was near old or beautiful buildings.[177]

Warnings were dropped by air on Rome on 3 and 18 July, and on 19 July, 150 B-17s and B-24s from the Northwest African Strategic Air Force, accompanied by 240 B-26s of the US Ninth Air Force, dropped around 1,000 tons on the railway at San Lorenzo and Littorio, and the two airbases at Ciampino. Since the bombing of the marshalling yards was from altitudes of between 19,000 and 24,000 feet, there was extensive damage to the surrounding area. Only 80 bombs were observed to hit the target area around Littorio, and a post-raid interpretation showed that there was heavy damage to the Basilica of San Lorenzo and across 27 residential streets.[178] The following day the Pope drove in his black Mercedes through Rome, the first time during the war that he had left Vatican City. The population greeted him with hysterical enthusiasm while aides distributed money among the crowd. There were over 700 dead reported by the emergency services, many in the working-class areas around San Lorenzo, the least Fascist quarter of Rome, but later estimates put the number killed between 1,700 and 2,000.[179] When the king, Victor Emanuel III, visited the ruins he was met by a sullen crowd which blamed him for the war. 'The population is mute, hostile,' wrote an aide, 'we pass through tears and an icy silence.'[180]

Rome's symbolic status ensured that the raid would attract wide publicity. The Combined Chiefs sent Eisenhower instructions that he was to publish a communiqué promptly after the bombing, attesting to the fact that only military objectives had been hit, in order to avoid accusations that the 'Shrine of Christendom' had been violated.[181] According to an OSS report, cities in northern Italy welcomed the fact that Fascists in Rome 'were getting their medicine at last', and there was evident dour satisfaction among populations already bombed that the cause of their ordeal was suffering too.[182] The Papacy, which had appealed several times to turn Rome into an 'open city', used the bombing as the opportunity to launch a major diplomatic offensive over the months that followed to try to secure immunity from further attacks. The most significant consequence was the fate of the Mussolini dictatorship, for Rome also symbolized the heart of the Fascist regime. Mussolini had been meeting Hitler at Feltre in north-east Italy on the day Rome was bombed. A 'pale and agitated official' had interrupted the two men with the news and Mussolini had hurried back to the capital. The days immediately following the bombing witnessed an atmosphere of mounting political tension. In the evening of 24 July a meeting was summoned of the Fascist Grand Council to which Mussolini was to report on the state of the Italian war effort. That afternoon, Mussolini later wrote, the tension was so acute that 'Rome turned pale'.[183] At the meeting he admitted that he was for the moment the most loathed man in Italy, but defended his record. By the morning of 25 July there had been a palace revolt; senior Fascists, army commanders and the king withdrew their support, and Mussolini's rule abruptly ended. The American Psychological Warfare Branch drew an obvious though speculative inference: the bombing of Rome on 19 July meant that by 25 July 'the Government was out'.[184]

Did bombing bring about the collapse of Mussolini's regime? A good case can be made that the sudden intensification of bombing in 1943 provoked a people already tired of war and fearful of its consequences to reject twenty years of Fascism and to hope for peace. The bombing from the winter of 1942–3 was on an unprecedented scale, 1,592 tons in 1942 but 110,474 tons in 1943, twice the tonnage dropped in the Blitz on Britain.[185] From modest losses in the early raids, the destruction of housing escalated dramatically, 122,000 buildings by March 1943.[186] Most of the operations were now carried out by American air forces which flew high and bombed with poor accuracy. The small town of Grosseto, for example, was largely destroyed when 24 B-17s were sent to attack an air force base but hit the residential districts, leaving 134 dead. Attacks on the airbase at Foggia, near the east coast, provoked an extraordinary crisis when bombs destroyed the town. After the raid on 31 May, some 40 per cent of the population fled, leaving shops and factories without manpower and services in disarray. The prefect reported that his city was a spectacle of desolation, 'infested by the fumes from putrifying bodies not yet recovered'.[187] The ports of the south were heavily bombed in anticipation of the Allied invasion of Sicily: 43 raids on Palermo; 32 on Messina; 45 on Catania. Naples was struck repeatedly throughout the war, small raids at first from Malta, but from the first heavy raid on 4 December 1942 there were repeated strikes that left 72,000 buildings damaged or destroyed by the spring of 1943. Neapolitans reacted to the bombing as a new war against the home front. 'My war started,' wrote one, 'on the 4 December.' The raid, recalled another, 'grew infinitely in the memory ... a monstrous roar of engines seemed to enter the room, in the brain, in every fibre of the body ... everyone was resigned to die'.[188] In Naples and elsewhere in Italy the raids exposed the failure of the regime to provide enough shelter space, to organize effective post-raid welfare, to train sufficient civil defenders or to mount a serious defence against Allied incursions. Protests dated from the first raids in 1941 against poor food supply, long queues and the inequality of sacrifice; the decline of support for a failing state long pre-dated the raid on Rome on 19 July 1943.[189]

The evolution of popular disillusionment with the regime can certainly be linked to the more general failure of the state to cope with the consequences of the new offensive. In the spring of 1943 at the Fiat works in Turin spontaneous strikes erupted between 5 and 8 March in protest at the failure to provide an indemnity for all bombed workers, and not just for those 'evening' evacuees who went back and forth to their families in the countryside. Mingled with protest at rising prices and poor food distribution, the strike movement spread to other factories and eventually as far as Genoa and Milan, until they petered out in April. In Genoa protests against the lack of shelters had already followed the first raids, when crowds of angry women tried to storm the bunkers belonging to the rich.[190] During 1943 a stream of reports reached Rome from provincial prefects indicating the growing demoralization and hostility of the population, though only some of this was due to bombing and much to do with Italy's ineffective war effort. A report from Genoa in May 1943 indicated that 'public morale is very depressed' due to food shortages and the complete incapacity of the Italian military, as well as the material and morale damage caused by the bombs. From Turin it was reported that workers could no longer see any point in working for a failed system but displayed instead 'apathy and indifference'. Palermo, hit repeatedly by bombing in 1943, reported in May that almost all civilian activities were paralysed, the population terrorized and the streets deserted. Even the reports from Rome, not yet bombed, indicated a population that was now 'mistrustful and desperate', awaiting a political upheaval of some kind: 'Faith in victory seems to be almost completely lost . . . the conviction of the uselessness of past and present efforts is almost general.'[191] Iris Origo, listening to discussions going on around her in Tuscany, complained that it was all 'talk, talk, talk, and no action', reflecting a 'dumb, fatalistic apathy' among a people no longer willing to go on with the war, but unable to find a means to end it.[192] Ordinary Italians turned to religion or superstition to help cope with the dilemma of being trapped between a remorseless bombing and a failed state. In Livorno (Leghorn) the absence of bombing until late May 1943 was attributed to the protection of the Madonna of Montenero (though it was also rumoured that Churchill had a lover in the city, which explained its immunity). In Sardinia a prayer was composed against the bombing: 'Ave Maria, full of grace, make it so the sirens do not sound, the aeroplanes do not come . . . Jesus, Joseph, Mary, make it that the English lose their way.'[193]

The bombing of Rome was neither the occasion nor the cause of the overthrow of Mussolini, but a symptom of a state in the final throes of disintegration. In a body wracked with ailments, it is not always easy to identify the precise cause of death. Moreover, the fall of the dictator brought neither peace to the Italian people nor an end to the bombing. Indeed, a better case can be made for the argument that bombing accelerated the decision of Mussolini's successor, Marshal Pietro Badoglio, together with the king, to seek an armistice in early September to take Italy out of the war after the initial decision to continue it. At first the Allies were uncertain how to react to the news of Mussolini's fall and bombing was briefly suspended. But on 31 July, after a four-day respite, Portal told Air Marshal Arthur Tedder, commander of the Mediterranean Air Force, to start bombing Naples and Rome again in order to pressure the Badoglio government to seek 'peace terms'.[194] BBC Radio Algiers broadcast the news to Italian listeners that bombing would start again on 1 August. Three million leaflets were distributed which suggested that abandoning the Germans was better than more 'iron and fire'; another 6 million dropped in mid-August explained that as long as the government in Rome continued the war, so the bombing would continue.[195]

The situation was confused by the request from the Badoglio regime in late July to make Rome an open city. American bombing was halted while the implications were examined. On 2 August Marshall drew up the American War Department's view of what constituted an open city – removal of all Italian and German forces, evacuation of all government agencies, cessation of all war production, and no roads or rail links to be used for military purposes – but a day later the War Cabinet in London rejected any idea of allowing Rome this status, even if the rigorous American demands could be met, as long as the war in Italy continued. On 13 August Eisenhower was notified that bombing could start again and Rome was bombed once more, the first of 51 further raids. The Pope again visited the damaged area accompanied by shouts from the crowd of 'Long live peace!'[196] Bombing spread out from Rome to other cities in central Italy. Pisa was struck on 31 August by 144 aircraft, leaving 953 dead and wide destruction in the residential areas of the city. Foggia was struck again, leading to its almost complete evacuation. On 27 August Pescara was bombed, with 1,600 dead. American intelligence reports suggested widespread rioting and anti-Fascist demonstrations once the bombing restarted.[197] On 3 September Badoglio bowed to reality, despite the looming menace of German occupation, and signed an armistice. On 8 September news of Italy's surrender was announced but for most Italians the war at the side of Germany was simply exchanged overnight for a war under German control.

'CERTAINLY BOMB': THE LIBERATION OF ITALY

The bombing campaign in Italy from September 1943 until the end of the war had not been planned for. The sudden collapse of Italian belligerency provoked an immediate and violent reaction from the large German armed forces now stationed throughout the peninsula. The Italian armed forces were disarmed, interned, and in most cases sent north to Greater Germany as forced labour. Italy became an occupied country, like France, with the difference that in this case a new Mussolini regime, the Italian Social Republic (usually known as the Salò Republic after the town on Lake Garda), was set up following Mussolini's dramatic rescue by German special forces from imprisonment. It was in effect a puppet government, entirely subservient to the military requirements of the German Commander-in-Chief South, Field Marshal Kesselring, but a number of Italian airmen and soldiers remained loyal to Fascism and served alongside German forces. German leaders were not much concerned with the idea of recreating the Fascist state since their priority was to prevent the Allies from reaching central Europe, but for the Italian people Fascist government remained in place, widely unpopular and despised, until Mussolini's death at the hands of Italian partisans in late April 1945.

For the Allies Italy presented both problems and opportunities. The priority from September 1943, after the conquest of Sicily and the first tentative landings on the toe of the peninsula, was to defeat the German armed forces and, if that could be done quickly, to liberate Italy and prepare to assault the German Empire from the south. If it could not be done easily, as soon appeared the case, Allied air forces would be used to support the land war and to bomb when necessary more distant targets. Even a limited presence on mainland Italy, however, presented the opportunity of raiding German targets from the Mediterranean which were difficult to reach from British bases. These differing aims required a reorganization of the confused mix of air force commands that had grown up with the expansion of the Mediterranean and North African air forces, both British and American. In early 1943 targets in Italy were hit by the Northwest African Strategic Air Force and the combined Tactical Bomber Force, made up of some RAF units and the American Twelfth and Ninth air forces. Other RAF units under Air Marshal Tedder formed the Mediterranean Air Force, which had operated chiefly in the desert war, but had begun to raid Italy after the defeat of the Axis in Tunisia in May 1943. In the autumn of 1943 these forces were amalgamated into the Mediterranean Allied Air Forces (MAAF), including both British and American air units. The British component was limited in size; the American element was enlarged to create a Fifteenth Air Force for long-range bombing missions, first under General Doolittle (until he replaced Ira Eaker in Britain as commander of the Eighth) and then under Maj. General Nathan Twining. The Twelfth Air Force under the command of Maj. General John Cannon was assigned to tactical missions, including bombing, to replace the Ninth which was sent to support the Normandy invasion of June 1944. The overall command of MAAF, which was activated on 10 December 1943, was given to Eaker, who took up his post in January; his deputy was the British Air Marshal John Slessor. On 4 January 1944 the American component of MAAF came formally under the control of General Spaatz when he was appointed overall commander of all American strategic and tactical air forces in Europe, but in practice only the strategic Fifteenth Air Force was responsible to Spaatz, while the tactical air forces answered to the

Mediterranean Supreme Commander, first Eisenhower then, from January 1944, General Maitland Wilson. The Fifteenth Air Force was activated on 1 November 1943 with its headquarters near the ruined town of Foggia. Its squadrons were spread over a dozen bomber bases from where they flew missions to Austria, southern Germany and the Balkans, as well as Italian targets. The RAF strategic force was composed mainly of Wellington medium-bombers and then Liberators in RAF markings, sharing bases with the Americans.[198]

A clear distinction between strategic and tactical bombing was difficult to make, since there were occasions when strategic forces were needed to support the ground war or to destroy communication in the rear of German armies. For the rest of the time they were expected to raid German targets. In December 1943, for example, out of a list of 48 strategic targets for Operation Pointblank supplied by the American Economic Warfare Division, only seven were in Italy, and only two (both ball-bearing factories) were included on the list of priorities.[199] In November 1943 the operations director at MAAF, Brig. General Lauris Norstad, ordered the tactical air forces to concentrate on supporting the ground war and bombing communications targets up to a line from Civita Vecchia (near Rome) to Ancona on the east coast; the strategic air forces, by this time principally the Fifteenth Air Force, were to bomb all communications targets north of this line, using either B-26 Martin Marauder medium bombers or their B-17s and B-24s when necessary.[200] The line shifted with the fortunes of the ground battle, but not until 1 March 1945 did the tactical air forces assume responsibility for the whole area of northern Italy still under German occupation.[201] The difference between a tactical and a strategic raid often made little difference to the population around the target, but the distinction was maintained in air force records. Out of 124,000 tons dropped on Italian targets in the first five months of 1944, 78,700 were deemed to be strategic, the rest tactical.[202] .

Most of the raiding in the last 20 months of the war was carried out by American air forces. The statistical breakdown of air raids by the different Allied air forces is set out in Table 8.3 The American raids were generally larger than those of the RAF. By the end of the campaign in the spring of 1945 there were over 1,900 American heavy bombers based in the Mediterranean out of an overall total of almost 4,300 American combat aircraft. Heavy bombers flew a total of 18,518 sorties in 1943, 90,383 in 1944, though some of their bombload was directed at German or Balkan targets. From 1943 to the end of the war, American heavy

Table 8.3: Major raids by British and American Air Forces, 1940–45

Year	Bomber Com.	RAF Med.	US 9th	US 12th	US 15th
1940	20	15	–	–	–
1941	4	92	–	–	–
1942	15	40	5	–	–
1943	13	136	92	145	27
1944	–	76	–	73	164
1945	–	22	–	12	42
Total	52	381	97	230	233

(Of the 381 raids by the RAF Med., 135 were small raids mounted from Maltese bases.)
Source: Calculated from Marco Gioannini, Giulio Massobrio, *Bombardate l'Italia* (Milan: 2007), website appendix.

bombers stationed in the Mediterranean dropped 112,000 tons on Italian targets and 143,000 tons on Greater Germany and German-occupied central Europe; tactical bombers dropped another 163,000 tons on Italian targets, a grand total of 276,312 tons on Italy.[203]

For the bomber crews flying in Italy the dangers were considerably less than in Germany, though the weather remained a persistent hazard despite the claim made by Harris that bombing could be conducted on all but 8 per cent of days in the Mediterranean in January and 5 per cent in July (compared with 51 per cent and 21 per cent lost days flying from English bases).[204] In late 1942 the Italian Air Force had only 44 serviceable night-fighters, most of them biplanes incapable of effective intervention.[205] The opposition from Italian anti-aircraft guns and fighters disappeared in autumn 1943, to be replaced with a large concentration of German anti-aircraft artillery around key targets. But the overwhelming air superiority enjoyed by Allied forces following the Axis defeat in Africa and the conquest of Sicily meant that there was little effective fighter opposition from the German Air Force, with the result that higher levels of accuracy were possible than could be achieved over Germany. Bomber Command raids in summer 1943 using H2S radar dropped between 70 and 87 per cent of bombs within three miles of their target, while most raids on Berlin at the same time could only achieve 30 per cent; not precise by any standard, but more concentrated and hence more destructive.[206] By late 1943 there were only 470 German aircraft dispersed between Sardinia, mainland Italy and the Aegean.

Maintenance problems meant a low level of serviceability, while numerical inferiority, a result of the diversion of aircraft to defend the Reich, provoked a constant attrition cycle that could not be reversed. By summer 1944 there were only 370 serviceable aircraft in the theatre, most of them single-engine fighters flown both by German and Italian pilots.[207] American bomber losses in 1944 and 1945 were largely due to anti-aircraft fire or accident, 1,829 against 626 credited to fighter interception.[208] Not for nothing was Joseph Heller's anti-hero in *Catch 22*, a novel about the American air experience in Italy, afraid of the 'goddam foul black tiers of flak ... bursting, and booming and billowing all around'.[209]

Though the defensive threat was less, the question of what to bomb was not easily answered, partly because detailed intelligence on Italian industry and communications after the German occupation in September 1943 was difficult to acquire and partly because of the persistent uncertainty surrounding the fate of Italy's historic heritage. There were disagreements not only over what to bomb, but what not to bomb. Unlike the British attitude, Washington recognized that it was politically expedient to preserve Italian culture from unnecessary damage in order to limit accusations of Allied barbarism. Therefore, on 20 August 1943 Roosevelt gave his approval for the establishment of the American Commission for the Protection and Salvage of Artistic and Historic Monuments in Europe. The Commission was advised by an academic working group set up by the American Council of Learned Societies, which produced 160 detailed maps of Italian cities using the Italian Baedeker guide, with most cultural monuments clearly marked. These were sent to MAAF and added to the dossiers for briefing officers when organizing an operation.[210] In April 1944 a list was distributed to all Allied air forces in Italy, listing cities in three categories for bombing purposes. The first category comprised Rome, Florence, Venice and Torcello, which could only be bombed with specific instructions from the High Command; the second category of 19 historic cities, including Ravenna, Assisi, Pavia, Parma and Montepulciano, were not regarded *prima facie* as militarily important, but could be bombed under circumstances of military necessity; the third category was made up of 24 cities, most with architecturally outstanding city centres, such as Brescia, Siena, Pisa, Bologna and Viterbo, which were deemed to contain or be near military objectives. These could be bombed freely 'and any consequential damage accepted'.[211] If any city in categories two and three was occupied by the enemy in a zone of operations, no restrictions were to be observed. Otherwise crews were instructed only to bomb objectives by day if not obscured by cloud, and by night if illumination made the precise military objective sufficiently clear. The rules gave a great deal of discretion to the individual pilot, and in practice, given the wide inaccuracy of high-level bombing, in Italy as elsewhere, protection for cultural monuments was observed only within wide operational limits.

Even the cities in category one came to be bombed when military circumstances dictated. 'Nothing,' wrote Eisenhower for the Allied forces in Italy, 'can stand against the argument of military necessity.'[212] In February 1944 MAAF headquarters decided that the rail centre at Florence would have to be bombed as part of the effort to cut German communications. British Air Marshal John Slessor told the Air Ministry that only the most experienced crews would be used. He pointed out that the famous Duomo was at least a mile distant from the target: 'it would be very bad luck if any of the really famous buildings were hit'. On 1 March Churchill was asked for his view; he scribbled on the letter 'certainly bomb', and the following day the chiefs of staff approved the raid.[213] Luck stayed with the bomber crews this time and the Duomo remained intact. They were told that some damage to the city was inevitable, but should not be construed as 'limiting your operations', which explains the damage to two hospitals and the death of 215 Florentines.[214] On 20 April 1944, bombs fell on Venice for the first time, contrary to instructions. An investigation showed that 54 American bombers, finding their targets in Trieste covered by cloud, defied orders and bombed the port of Venice as a target of opportunity from 24,000 feet. Once again, luck was in their favour; the historic heart of Venice suffered no damage.[215]

This was not the case with the efforts to avoid bombing Vatican City. The bombing of Rome was continued despite the persistent efforts by the Papacy, the Badoglio government (now based in southern Italy in the Allied zone) and even Mussolini's new Salò regime to get the Allies to accept the status of open city for the capital. Roosevelt, with a large Catholic minority in the United States, was more inclined to discuss the possibility, but Churchill worried that if Rome were made an open city, it would hamper Allied military efforts to pursue the Germans up the western side of the peninsula. The Combined Chiefs discussed the issue in late September but it remained deadlocked.[216] Then on 5 November four bombs were dropped on the Vatican, causing serious damage to the Governatorato Palace, the seat of Vatican government. The first reaction from the British ambassador to the Vatican, Sir Francis D'Arcy

Osborne, was to blame the Germans for the raid as a propaganda stunt, but a few days later investigations showed that one American aircraft, bombing at night, had lost contact with the rest of the force and dropped bombs in error.[217] Roosevelt once again tried to revive British interest in the demilitarization of Rome, but the British remained adamant that it would place too many restrictions on the Allied ground campaign, and on 7 December Roosevelt finally conceded that it was 'inadvisable' to pursue the matter any further.[218] Rome continued to be bombed and over 7,000 Romans died in the course of the year from the first bombing in July 1943 to the Allied capture of the city in June 1944. The accidental raid on the Vatican showed how difficult it was under conditions of night, poor weather, or human error to avoid widespread damage to Italy's cultural heritage even with the best of intentions.

There was nevertheless nothing accidental about the most controversial raid of all, against the fourteenth-century Benedictine abbey on the mountain top overlooking the small town of Cassino on 15 February 1944. The building dominated the Liri Valley position where the Allied armies were attempting to unhinge the German defences along the so-called Gustav Line, which stretched from the coast north of Naples to Ortona on the Italian Adriatic coast. On 4 November 1943 Eisenhower wrote to the Allied Fifteenth Army Group that the Monte Cassino abbey was a protected building; the Pope asked both the Germans and the Allies to respect its sacred status. When Eisenhower was replaced by Wilson as Supreme Commander in January 1944, the principle that historic buildings would only be hit under conditions of 'absolute necessity' still prevailed, though it did not prevent the bombing of the Papal estate at Castel Gandolfo on 11 February, which destroyed the convent and killed 27 nuns.[219] At Cassino all attempts to dislodge the German forces from the small town or the hilltop had failed and it is not difficult to understand why frustration with the slow progress of the campaign and the likelihood of high casualties encouraged the local army units to ask for air assistance. There were strong rumours (but no hard evidence) that the abbey was already occupied by German forces. On 11 February the 4th Indian Division, planning its assault, made a request for 'intense bombing' of the hilltop and its surroundings, including the monastery; on 12 February the commander of the Indian Division, Maj. General Francis Tuker, insisted that the monastery should be destroyed whether it was occupied by the Germans or not, since it would easily become a strongpoint if the Germans chose to use it.[220] The decision should have been made at the highest level by the Combined Chiefs of Staff and agreed by Spaatz, but in the end it was made by General Harold Alexander, overall army commander, and endorsed by Wilson. Eaker was instructed to launch an attack on 15 February using both strategic and tactical forces. He flew in a light plane over the abbey the day before and later wrote, to justify the attack, that he could see it was full of soldiers, radio masts and machine-gun nests, though his initial judgement was quite different.[221] The following day wave after wave of heavy and medium bombers pounded the monastery with 351 tons of bombs, killing 230 of the Italian civilians who had taken refuge in the abbey precincts.

The destruction was welcomed by the troops on the ground, who were seen to cheer as the bombers flew in, but the results of these raids (and attacks by Kittyhawk and Mustang fighter-bombers during the two days that followed) were mixed. The vast abbey walls remained intact, in places to a height of 30 feet, making the gutted building ideal for the German forces who now obligingly occupied it as a hilltop fortress from where they repelled the Indian and New Zealand efforts to dislodge them. The operation suffered from the usual bomb pattern, some bombs destroying the headquarters of the local Eighth Army Commander, General Oliver Leese, three miles from the abbey, and the French Corps headquarters 12 miles away.[222] The publicity surrounding the destruction, much of it hostile, forced the chiefs of staff to investigate who had ordered the bombing and why. On 9 March Wilson replied that the abbey building was undoubtedly 'part of the German main defensive position' and had to be eliminated to ensure success.[223] Slessor, Eaker's deputy, recalled in his memoirs that no one among the troops would have believed for a moment that the Germans were not using the building as a fortress, 'so the Abbey had to go', but he was critical of what the bombing actually achieved given that it took three more months to capture the hilltop, now fully occupied by the enemy.[224] A War Office investigation in 1949 into the circumstances of the bombing finally confirmed that there had been no evidence of German occupation to justify the raids, except for an unsubstantiated claim that a telescope had been glimpsed from a window. Eyewitness accounts were collected from Italian women who had sheltered in the abbey during the bombing. 'Even allowing for the excitable tendencies of women of Latin race,' ran the report, their testimony gave a credible if 'prosaic' account of what happened. Some 2,000 from the population of Cassino had sought shelter on German advice in the church of San Giuseppe behind the abbey; on 3 February, after angry protests from the crowd of evacuees, some of whom had been wounded by shellfire, the monks let them into the abbey. There were no German soldiers or equipment to be seen, except for two German medical officers tending to the wounded Italians. After the bombing, the civilians made their way where they could. The four women who gave accounts of the abbey reached Allied lines and were interviewed less than two weeks after the raid had taken place.[225]

The Monte Cassino raid was one of the few times that the strategic bombers were asked to support a ground operation directly. A few days later they also obliterated what was left of the town of Cassino itself. In both cases the result was to hamper army efforts to profit from the bombing. On 16 April 1944 Slessor wrote to Portal to complain about how counterproductive heavy bombing was on the battlefield itself: 'we hamper our own movement by throwing the debris of houses across roads and making craters that become tank obstacles ... we are inevitably bound – as we did at Cassino – to cause casualties to our own people ...'.[226] Most of the bombing that took place in 1944 and 1945 was directed further away from the battlefront, designed to hamper German communications throughout Italy and to destroy Italian industries working directly to German orders. The communications campaign was the more important. Italian geography worked both for and against the Allies. The narrow peninsula with its mountainous spine meant that communication by road and rail was mainly confined to narrow channels running down the eastern and western coasts of Italy. These channels represented tempting targets for interruption. On the other hand, the Allied armies were also confined to the hilly coastal zones where there were innumerable natural barriers to favour a defending army. In the winter, mud, heavy rain and snow slowed up any ground advance, while poor weather restricted air attacks on transport and allowed the enemy time to restock and reinforce.

The origins of the planning for a systematic campaign against communications lay in the hurried survey of the bombing of Sicily carried out by Solly Zuckerman, who among his many duties had been allocated in 1942 to the British Combined Operations headquarters as a scientific adviser. In January 1943 he was sent out to the Mediterranean theatre to investigate how Rommel had managed to escape across Libya despite massive Allied superiority on the ground and in the air. Zuckerman stayed on in an advisory role and was asked to supply evaluations for the invasion of Sicily in July 1943, for which he recommended attacking the 'nodal points' of the Sicilian and south Italian railway network, and particularly railway repair shops, depots and shunting yards. His advice was followed and his eventual report, based on a survey of the results in Sicily and southern Italy, suggested the campaign had been 'an outstanding success'.[227] Early in 1944 MAAF discussed the possibility of applying the Zuckerman model to the railway system in central and northern Italy to cut Kesselring's forces off from the supply chain. The preference was for attacks on rail centres rather than bridges and viaducts, which Zuckerman thought were too difficult to destroy, but there was considerable support among American planners for bridge-bombing using fighter-bombers and medium bombers for a task which called for effective precision. In the end, the communications campaign targeted both.

On 18 February Eaker issued a directive for the communications campaign, detailing the northern marshalling yards for the strategic air forces and the rail links further south for the tactical forces.[228] The Fifteenth Air Force targets were the main railway yards at Padua, Verona, Bolzano, Turin, Genoa and Milan, with secondary targets at Treviso, Venice Mestre, Vicenza and Alessandria. The tactical air forces were detailed to attack rail facilities in central Italy, at least 100 miles from the German front line to maximize the strain on enemy road traffic.[229] The campaign was given the codename Operation 'Strangle', to indicate its purpose, and lasted from 15 March until 11 May using every kind of aircraft available. The heavy bombers dropped 10,649 tons, the tactical air forces a total of 22,454, for a total loss of 365 aircraft, chiefly fighter-bombers and mainly to anti-aircraft fire.[230] Of this total, two-thirds were dropped on communication lines. In April a second campaign was ordered to coincide with an Allied ground assault designed to push the German army back past Rome. This operation was codenamed 'Diadem' and lasted to 22 June, by which time Rome was in Allied hands and German forces were retreating rapidly towards a new defensive 'Gothic Line' north of Florence. This time 51,500 tons of bombs were dropped, 19,000 by the Fifteenth Air Force, for the loss of only 108 bombers, a rate of only 0.4 per cent of all sorties. Of this total tonnage, three-quarters fell on transport targets.[231] The outcome was again mixed. The destruction of bridges and viaducts proved more effective than the assault on marshalling yards, which could be used for through traffic even when there was extensive damage. A disappointed evaluation by the MAAF Analysis Section showed that repairs were quickly carried out on rail centres in northern Italy and through tracks reopened. 'Military traffic was not hindered to a significant degree by these attacks,' the report concluded. Nor did they cause 'complete internal economic collapse'.[232] Kesselring, when interviewed in August 1945 after the end of the war, confirmed that the transport plan had not been a great success. Bridges were quickly replaced by pontoon bridges, camouflaged in some way; urgent countermeasures had been taken to restore road and rail links. An air strategy exclusively centred on cutting off supplies, Kesselring concluded, was not likely to be effective.[233]

The second set of targets for strategic attack lay in the surviving industry of the area occupied by German forces in northern and central Italy. As soon as the Italian surrender was certain, Albert Speer, the German Minister for Armaments and War Production, was appointed on 13 September 1943 plenipotentiary for Italian war production; General Hans Leyers acted as his permanent deputy in Italy.[234] The decision to exploit Italian production was taken for a number of reasons: first, to be able to supply German forces in the field with finished or repaired weapons; second, to supply Germany with additional equipment, resources and raw materials; and third, to act as a large subcontracting base for components, engines or subassemblies where there was a shortage of capacity in Germany. A number of committees were established to oversee the transition of Italian industry to German orders, but the priority was the exploitation of the Italian aircraft industry. Four companies made parts for Focke-Wulf, Heinkel, Messerschmitt and Junkers, while Alfa Romeo, Fiat and Isotta Fraschini produced the Daimler Benz DB605 and the Junkers Jumo 213 aero-engines. Once it was evident that production could be continued rather than have machines and labour transferred to Germany, Italian producers cooperated with the German occupiers; workers, though in general hostile to both the Germans and the new Mussolini republic, had little choice but to work or face unemployment or deportation.[235] In some cases German intervention encouraged industrial modernization and increased productivity in an industry that had failed to adapt to the needs of war, but the revival of production faced numerous obstacles in the supply of materials, transport facilities and machinery. Yet once it had begun, the major industrial regions again became targets for the Allied strategic air forces. Heavy raids were made in the spring and summer of 1944, hitting a total of 420 plants, particularly in the armaments, engineering and steel sectors, and Italian oil depots at Trieste, Fiume and Marghera.[236] Extensive damage was done to industrial buildings, but a regular toll of Italian civilian lives was exacted with each raid, which included low-level strafing of workers. One of the worst was the raid on Milan on 20 October

1944, which resulted in some of the aircraft dropping their bombs in error on residential districts, killing 614 people, including 184 pupils and 19 teachers at the Francesco Crispi school, more than three times the number killed in all the other 17 raids on the city in the course of the year.[237]

The renewal of bombing prompted the German authorities to continue the programme of dispersal that had begun in haste in the winter of 1942–3 and been suspended with the armistice. Advantage was taken of the extensive road tunnels and caves available in northern Italy. Work on parts for the Me262 turbo-jet fighter continued in the first months of 1945 in tunnels around Bolzano; the Fiat works moved production to a stretch of tunnel between Riva and Gargnano on the coast of Lake Garda, where 1,300 labourers continued to work until April of that year; Caproni produced parts for the V-weapons and the Me262 in a hydraulic tunnel between the River Adige and Garda. Of the 28 sites chosen for underground dispersal, only 10 actually reached the stage of production.[238] From early 1945 onwards, before the final offensive to drive the Germans across the Po Valley towards the Alps, a renewed communications campaign against rail centres and bridges across northern Italy undermined the frantic efforts of the German authorities to extract what they could from the shrunken Italian industrial economy. By February the MAAF targets committee had difficulty finding any targets left in northern Italy that had not already been hit or were regarded as worth the effort of bombing. Nevertheless raids continued to be made until the last days of the conflict. As in Germany, Allied air forces by the end of the war possessed a good deal of excess capacity for which there were no longer suitable objectives.[239]

The cost of the bombing campaign to the Italian economy is difficult to compute, not least because of the extensive damage done by artillery and battlefront aviation which resembled the consequences of bombing. The effect on German efforts to extract additional war production in northern Italy has been estimated at a loss of 30 per cent in productive performance due to absenteeism and regular alarms. The overall loss of capacity for Italian industry has been estimated at 10 per cent, since most industry was not an object of bombing; the loss for war-related industries was much higher, one-half for naval production, 21 per cent for the metallurgical industries, 12 per cent for machine engineering.[240] By contrast, the textile sector lost 0.5 per cent, the electrical industry 4 per cent and the chemical industry 6 per cent of capacity. Damage to housing, though heavy in particular cities, has been estimated at only

6 per cent of total housing stock. The chief target was the Italian transport system where two-fifths of the rail network was destroyed along with half the rolling stock and an estimated 90 per cent of all Italian lorries. The five years of war reduced Italian national income by 1945 to one-half the level of 1938.[241] This mainly affected not the German occupiers but a large part of the Italian civil population, which endured widespread losses of housing and possessions, unemployment and food shortages until well after the end of the conflict.

The Italian population was faced in the last two years of war with the bleak prospect of living on a wide and dangerous battlefield, caught between the German occupiers, the new Fascist regime and the slowly advancing Allies. Most of the casualties from bombing occurred in the period after the armistice, since air power was the one thing the Allies could project easily into the occupied zones. The Allied powers recognized the nature of the dilemma facing most Italians who had not yet been liberated, but they also wanted them to undermine the German occupation from within by acts of resistance or sabotage. An OSS report on the situation in Italy in September 1943 suggested a propaganda campaign to make Italians realize 'that the real people's war of liberation has started for them', and to encourage them to make life miserable for the Germans.[242] It was also recognized that bombing was likely to be politically counterproductive if it seemed to bring liberation no nearer. The ambassador D'Arcy Osborne warned the Foreign Office in March 1944 that bombing was 'slowly but surely turning Italian opinion against us' because of the evident disproportion between civilian damage and military results. The Italians, D'Arcy Osborne continued, were beginning to think that German occupation was a lesser evil 'than Anglo-Saxon liberation'.[243] Eden was sufficiently concerned to ask Sinclair in May to ensure that bombing was carried out with strict precautions against a 'friendly population', whose will to resist the Germans was weakened, rather than strengthened, by bombing and who were likely to harbour 'bitter memories of our method of liberation'.[244] The first priority for both Allies was, nevertheless, to defeat Germany rather than inhibit military action from fear of alienating Italian sentiments. When in May 1944 news reached London of the bombing of the village of Sonnino, where 45 people were killed, including 30 children, Churchill complained that the air force should not treat a co-belligerent population the same way as an enemy. Sinclair replied that it was not up to him to tell the air forces in the Mediterranean how to conduct their campaign; the vice chief of air staff, Air Marshal Evill, told Churchill that it was the fault of the Italian population for continuing to live near bombing targets.[245] Throughout the campaign the political necessity of defeating Germany overrode any political considerations towards the population held hostage on the battlefield.

There is no doubt that the long experience of bombing did strain Italian support for their imminent liberation. Iris Origo noted in her diary in the summer of 1944 how much British propaganda was resented with its 'bland assumption that peace at any price will be welcomed by the Italians'.[246] Corrado di Pompeo, a ministry official in Rome, recorded in his diary in February 1944 that at first his heart rejoiced 'when American aircraft passed overhead', but after regular raiding and the routine sight of blood-smeared corpses, he changed his mind: 'Americans are zero; they only know how to destroy and how to kill the defenceless.'[247] Nevertheless, the prospects for widespread rebellion against the authority of the Salò Republic or the German armed forces were unrealistic and throughout the period acts of violent resistance were met by the Germans with atrocious reprisals.[248] Under these circumstances rumour and superstition increased in importance as a mechanism for coping with the real dilemmas of occupation. The most remarkable was the claim, widely repeated, that Padre Pio, the Apulian monk (and now a saint), had safeguarded the region where he lived by rising in the air to the level of the bombers and staring the pilots in the eye until they turned back to base, their bombloads still on board.[249] In numerous cases, appeals were made to city saints or Madonnas to safeguard buildings and family from bomb damage. The Catholic Church also encouraged a mood of consolation and resignation. When he visited the damaged area of San Giovanni in Rome on 15 August 1943, the Pope told the crowd 'Follow the path of virtue and faith in God.'[250] Priests in Tuscany, writing of the bombing in 1944, talked of a 'Calvary', or 'our hour has come', or 'for us the hour of trial', as they prepared themselves and their congregations to endure the cruelties of air war.[251] By 1945, with the authority of the Salò republic collapsing in northern Italy, the Church came to play an increasingly important part in the daily lives of many ordinary Italians confronted with the continuous hardships imposed by bombing.

More important in terms of survival was the expansion of civil defence facilities and the widespread flight from the cities. For those who remained in urban areas, air-raid alerts became an almost daily occurrence. In Bologna province, for example, there were 94 air raids from July 1943 to April 1945, which killed an estimated 2,481 people, injured another 2,000 and destroyed 13 per cent of Bologna's buildings. In 1942 there was one alert lasting 1 hour 29 minutes; in 1943 the alerts lasted for 115 hours, in 1944 for 285 hours, and in 1945, 77 hours.[252] In Bologna, as in many other cities, the provision of shelter spaces had expanded rapidly with the onset of regular bombing. In October 1943 there had been spaces for 26,000 people out of a population of more than 600,000; by spring 1945 it was estimated that the 84 bomb-proof shelters, 15 trenches and 25 tunnels could accommodate 100,000.[253] In Milan, where trenches, school shelters and public shelters could hold 177,000 by October 1942, plans were begun to build a further 179 shelters to house another 38,000 people, while 8,000 domestic shelters were in the process of being overhauled to meet shelter standards.[254] Since most raids occurred during the day from 1943 onwards, it was important that there was adequate temporary shelter in inner-city areas for daytime workers. In many cases the shelters provided little protection from bomb blast and suffered from poor ventilation and overcrowding. In two cases overcrowding caused heavy casualties, one in Genoa's Le Grazie tunnel, where 354 people died, and one at Porta San Gennaro in Naples, where 286 perished. There was wide distrust of shelter provision and with the onset of bombing, millions of Italians either left for the nearby countryside or found refuge in a local cellar or basement.[255] The Prefect of Palermo reported in May 1943 that all the public shelters hit had collapsed, leaving the population with 'no faith in the remaining ones'. The Inspector of Air Raid Protection in Rome, reporting on the raids in July and August 1943, found that no signs had been put up indicating where the shelters were, and that there was no list of domestic shelters, making it impossible to know where their entombed occupants might be.[256]

The response to rising danger in the cities was a widespread wave of largely uncoordinated evacuation from all the threatened cities and towns, accompanied by compulsory evacuation insisted on by the German authorities from major combat zones and the Italian littoral.[257] As in Germany, the Fascist Party used evacuation as a way to try to tie the refugees more closely to the systems for party welfare and assistance, but the often spontaneous and large-scale evacuations were difficult to control, and were often followed by reverse evacuations as people returned to the risks of the city from poorly resourced rural retreats or realized that bombing could happen anywhere there was a railway. Most evacuees found temporary accommodation in nearby villages and small towns. In Turin province the population of nearby towns grew by up to 150 per cent as 165,000 people abandoned the city.[258] By May 1944 the number of evacuees in the main northern provinces had reached 646,000, of which 426,000 came from the main industrial cities of Milan, Turin and Genoa.[259] The total number of evacuees and refugees was estimated at 2.28 million by the spring of 1944, spread out among 51 separate Italian provinces.[260] The crowds of evacuees were distrusted by the authorities as a potential source of social protest and closely monitored, but for most the chief issue was to find enough food to survive on. Italy by 1944 was a very mobile society as people sought to find areas of greater safety, or were forced to move from military zones, or tried to return to the liberated south.[261]

Even in southern Italy safety was not guaranteed, for German aircraft bombed southern towns on occasion, including six raids on the already heavily bombed port of Naples. On the evening of 2 December 1943 a small raid by 35 German aircraft on the crowded dock at Bari led to widespread devastation and, unknown to the local population, the release of a toxic mix of oil and liquid mustard gas. The presence of this deadly mixture was suppressed by British authorities in the post-raid communiqué but was evident on the wounded men taken from the water and tended in the local hospital, where the staff were only notified that gas burns were to be expected when the symptoms were already well-established and patients dying.[262] Unknown to the Italian population, the Allies held large stocks of chemical weapons in Italy, ready to be used at a moment's notice. Since Mussolini had been responsible for using gas in Italy's war in Ethiopia, the prospect of a desperate act by the enemy in Italy was not entirely out of the question, but Allied chemical resources in Italy dwarfed the quantities used by Italians in Africa. By 1945, American forces had over 10 million lbs of mustard gas and 3 million lbs of other gases in the theatre, to be used principally by the air forces, which had 110,000 gas bombs in store.[263] The air force was ordered to keep on hand sufficient weapons to be able to carry out at least 45 days of continuous gas warfare from the air, aimed at enemy ports and military installations. In the event of a chemical attack by German or Italian forces in Italy, the Mediterranean Tactical Air Forces were ordered to use gas weapons in the immediate battle area without restriction, and to drop gas bombs on other military targets away from 'heavily populated areas' but, by implication, on areas which were nevertheless populated. Stocks of gas weapons were held in store in the area around Foggia, which explains the ship at Bari whose contents were destined to boost existing supplies in southern Italy.[264]

Throughout the peninsula, air-raid protection for the cultural sites threatened by widespread bombing assumed a fresh urgency. In November 1942 the education minister, Giuseppe Bottai, issued directives to intensify the work of protecting cultural buildings and churches, but it proved impossible to provide adequate physical covering that would withstand a direct hit or the effects of large-scale conflagrations. In Naples the destruction of the church of Santa Chiara by fire was only intensified by the protective covering outside, which increased the internal temperature.[265] After Rome tried to claim status as an 'open city', so other cities followed suit to avoid damage to their historic centres and collections of books and pictures. Padua, attacked 40 times, finally submitted its request on 1 February 1945, by which time the damage had been done. With the advancing battlefront it was also decided that much of the movable art and book collections stored in depositories in the countryside were in danger from air warfare and the retreating German armed forces, and the order was issued in October 1943 to bring the collections back to the cities where local art superintendents could safeguard them as best they could in underground storage facilities.[266] In the end the survival or otherwise of cultural treasures was arbitrary, dependent on where the bombs were strewn, or the intelligence of the curators who guarded them, or the attitude of the local German officials of the *Kunstschutz* (Art Protection) organization. In Turin some 13 churches had protected status, but only six survived relatively unscathed. In the convent of Santa Maria della Grazie in Milan, Leonardo's fresco of *The Last Supper* survived a direct hit by a miracle, as the rest of the refectory which housed it was demolished.[267] Among the other providential survivals was Botticelli's *Primavera*, spotted by two journalists sent to interview Indian soldiers in a villa outside Florence in sight of German tanks, the painting unboxed on the floor among the men brewing tea.[268] The strenuous efforts made meant that in the end much was saved, but a good deal of an invaluable patrimony was also destroyed or stolen.

The Allied hope that the bombing offensive might encourage Italian resistance to German exploitation, theft and savagery was as ambiguous as the early ambition to unseat Mussolini by bombing Rome. Opposition to the German occupiers certainly did not need bombing as a spur. Indeed, some case can be made to show that bombing actually harmed the prospects for the resistance and alienated potential supporters of the Allied cause. This was not the case with strike movement in northern Italy, which was linked to the onset of repeated and heavy raids from the autumn of 1943 onwards. Strikers at the Fiat works in November 1943 cited bombing as one of the reasons for running the risk of German intervention and Fascist brutality. The risks were substantial. In Turin a German deputy, sent to calm down the social protests, executed the protest leaders and deported 1,000 workers to Germany.[269] In the summer of 1944 further large-scale protests against dispersal plans brought so many workers out on strike that the German authorities were unable to cope. In December 1944 a strike crippled Milan's factories. Among these workers were those who risked acts of sabotage to accompany the bombing, while many workers who refused to be deported to work in Germany disappeared into the mountains to join the partisans. The partisan movement had close contacts with the Allies from 1944, and used these channels to explain that the poor accuracy, high-flying and inadvertent damage caused by Allied bombing alienated potential resisters, particularly as many of the areas hit were working class and anti-Fascist.[270] Partisan protests in late 1944 highlighted many examples where tactical bombing hit neither the Germans nor an evident military target, making a 'tragic situation' for the population all the harder. For the Allies this ran the risk, as intelligence information made clear, that the population might turn to supporting Soviet communism rather than continue to identify with the forces responsible for killing them. D'Arcy Osborne, in one of his despatches from Vatican City, pointed out that many Italians contrasted the Western Allies unkindly with the Red Army, which was 'the only one that gets results by fair military means', unlike Anglo-American forces who 'compensate their military inferiority by murder and destructive bombing'.[271] In this sense bombing had a much greater social and political impact in Italy than it did in the bombing of Britain or Germany, and one that fitted imperfectly with the 'liberating' image that Allied propaganda sought to convey. Communism continued to thrive in post-war Italy in cities where the housing losses, food shortages and unemployment compromised the achievements of peace.

The human costs of the bombing war in Italy are difficult to compute, because Sicily and the Italian Peninsula were the sites of two years of harsh warfare that raked its way slowly across the whole territory. Deaths, damage to buildings and the loss of artworks were caused by artillery fire, rockets, fighter aircraft, and some of it by naval fire along Italy's coastline, and from both sides, Allied and Axis. The 8,549 deaths in Sicily, for example, before the armistice were the result of all forms of military action whereas the 7,000 in Rome were due almost entirely to bombing.[272] The post-war statistical record drawn up to show the cause of deaths as a result of the war indicated a very precise total of 59,796, though other categories of 'poorly specified' or 'poorly defined' or 'various acts of war' count a further 27,762, some of whom were almost certainly bombing victims.[273] The total number of seriously injured has not been recorded. In cases where urban records provide a list of injured – for example in Bologna – the number is around the same as those killed, in this case 2,000. The number of those injured, whether severely or lightly, is not likely to be less than the figure of around 60,000 killed. Of the number of dead, about 32,000 were men, 27,000 women, a reflection of the extent of female evacuation and the compulsory requirement for men to carry on working in the cities on German orders or to help with post-raid rescue and clearance. The fact that the level of casualty was not much higher, given that the weight of bombs was almost six times the weight dropped on Britain, may owe something to the fact that many of the objectives for the tactical bombing attacks in 1943–5 were against rural or small-town targets rather than major cities. The Allied view was that Mussolini had brought this destruction on Italy's head by daring to attack Britain side by side with Germany in 1940: 'He insisted in participating in the bombing of England,' claimed one British propaganda leaflet, 'and so doing sowed the wind and condemned [Italians] to harvest the tempest.' In another leaflet, produced in July 1943, the British Political Warfare Executive (PWE) reminded Italian readers that 'the bombardment of the civil population is an official Fascist theory'.[274] In the war of words and bombs, Douhet, in the end, came home to roost.

9

Bombing Friends, Bombing Enemies: Germany's New Order

In early 1944 the US Eighth Air Force published a widely circulated publicity booklet, *Target Germany*. It purported to tell the story of the first year of the American bombing of the German enemy, 'raining havoc and destruction on the Nazi war machine'. The inside covers show a map of Europe where the force's bombs had fallen: there are 19 German targets but 45 in France, Belgium and the Netherlands. For much of the first year the apprentice American force took the short route across the Channel to bombard military-economic installations working for the German war effort. Most of the photographs in the richly illustrated text are of raids made on France and the Low Countries. The first raid on German territory finally took place late in January 1943, but more accessible European objectives were still seen as a useful way to get the crews to cut their teeth on combat.[1]

The bombing of European targets outside Germany and Italy was in reality more complex than this and was large in scale. The occupied territories of western and northern Europe – France, Belgium, The Netherlands, Norway and Denmark – absorbed almost 30 per cent of the bomb tonnage dropped by the American and British bomber forces. The occupied or satellite countries in eastern Europe and the Balkans absorbed another 6.7 per cent.[2] Well over one-third of all Allied bombs dropped on Europe fell on the German territorial New Order, making the experience of bombing in the Second World War a European-wide experience. The purpose behind these bombings, and their consequences for the populations caught in the coils of German expansion, are seldom treated as systematically as accounts of the bombing of Germany, yet they cost at least 70,000–75,000 lives, most of them among peoples sympathetic to the Allied cause. The majority of those losses, and most of the bomb tonnage that caused them, occurred in western Europe, principally France. These areas were near enough to reach and, in 1944, provided the territorial springboard for the Allied invasion of the western half of the German empire. Much of the bombing in the later period was in a loose sense tactical, intended to achieve a direct military end for the ground forces; but much of it was long-distance and heavy, designed to nibble away at war production for Germany in occupied territory, but also to promote wider political aims. According to the British Political Warfare Executive, set up in 1941, bombing of occupied areas promoted both 'morale breaking' and 'morale making'. Collaborators and Germans would be demoralized by the experience; those who did not collaborate would be encouraged at the prospect of liberation.[3] To be bombed in order to be free now seems paradoxical, but the policy governed much of the bombing that spread out across the entire European Continent between 1940 and 1945.

DISORDERING THE 'NEW ORDER'

The rapid German victories between 1939 and spring 1941 brought most of Continental Europe under German control. Neutral states were compelled to work with the changed balance of power while those states that were allied with Germany – Slovakia, Hungary, Romania, Croatia, Bulgaria – were satellites of the powerful German core. In Berlin the sudden transformation in German fortunes brought a flood of plans and projects for a European New Order which would secure Germany's permanent political and economic hegemony. The conquered states became involuntary participants in this larger project, compelled to provide economic resources, finance and labour for the German war effort, and doomed to be the battlefields on which the enlarged German empire would defend its borders. Right to the end of the war there were still German forces fighting in The Netherlands, Italy, Hungary and Czechoslovakia, alongside the defence of the German homeland.

It was inevitable under these circumstances that Britain, and later the United States, would have to engage the enemy on the territory of occupied or satellite states where German forces were dispersed. Until the Western states were in a position to mount a major land invasion, air power was regarded as the principal means available to attack Axis military resources across Europe and to undermine the extended war economy established throughout the German New Order. Because of the problem of aircraft range and the danger of flying for long periods over heavily defended territory, it was only possible in the first years of war to attack targets in western and northern Europe. Eastern and south-eastern Europe were only struck regularly from late 1943 onwards, chiefly by the American Fifteenth Air Force based in southern Italy. An alternative was to rely on local resistance and sabotage, and throughout the period in which air forces bombed targets in New Order Europe, the Allies tried to encourage the occupied peoples to take a hand in their own liberation even while subject to regular bomb attacks. Throughout the war period this resulted in awkward decisions for the Allies about the level of damage that should be inflicted on targets situated among potentially friendly civilian communities forced to work for the German war machine or, in some cases, voluntarily collaborating with it. The erosion of ethical restraints on bombing German industrial cities was a simpler issue than the moral dilemma of causing civilian casualties among those held hostage by German military success.

The debate about bombing friends as well as enemies began as soon as Britain was expelled from the Continent and France defeated. In July 1940 the War Cabinet agreed that any military target could be bombed in the northern and western parts of France occupied by German forces (though not in the unoccupied zone ruled from the new government seat at Vichy).[4] The problem was to decide what counted as a military target since it was already assumed that in the German case this meant industry, utilities and worker morale alongside more evidently military objectives. On 17 August Air Intelligence provided a list of what were defined as 'Fringe Targets' around the edge of occupied Europe which could be subjected to air attack. The fringe included targets up to 30 miles inland in Norway, Denmark, The Netherlands, Belgium and France. In Scandinavia there were 25 targets, consisting chiefly of oil installations and airbases (but including the Norwegian port of Kristiansund, already heavily bombed by German aircraft); in the Low Countries 61 targets were identified, ranging from electricity-generating stations to iron and steelworks; in France 31 targets were listed around the coast from Dunkirk to Bordeaux, including an aero-engine works at Le Havre, a power station at Nantes and a marshalling yard at Lille, a little over 30 miles from the coast.[5] Over the course of the autumn additional target information was processed and detailed target maps supplied. The list for France expanded to 58 objectives located in the 30-mile zone: 9 oil installations, 8 chemical plants, 11 aircraft works, 7 blast furnaces/steel mills, 11 shipbuilding firms and another dozen smaller targets. The targets were given star ratings to indicate their importance, three stars for the highest priority, of which there were 77 by spring 1941.[6] In May 1941 it was agreed that the RAF could undertake attacks on 'deep penetration targets' where these could be reached easily by day without excessive risk.[7] Conscientious anxieties played little part in these early raids. Escalation was soon built into the process of deciding what could be hit and under what conditions.

Many of the early raids around the fringe were tactical bombing operations carried out to forestall the possibility of German invasion and to hit at targets that supported the German air-sea blockade. They were carried out not only by Bomber Command but also by Coastal Command aircraft; in 1941, once the invasion threat had receded, Fighter Command also attacked coastal targets in large-scale fighter sweeps – the so-called 'Circus' operations – planned to lure the German Air Force into combat and undermine air force organization. The strategic assault of economic and military targets nevertheless remained limited at first, partly from concern over the political implications, partly from the military risks of attacks in daylight (night-bombing had not yet been approved for non-German targets) against the large German air forces stationed across north-west Europe. The reaction of the communities subjected to fringe bombing was mixed. There was evidence that the occupied peoples positively wanted the RAF to bomb the military and industrial targets in their midst. A Dutch request arrived in August 1940 to bomb the Fokker aircraft works in Amsterdam and a munitions plant at Hemburg ('working full capacity. Please bomb it').[8] A long letter from a French sympathizer forwarded to the Foreign Office in July 1941 claimed that many people in occupied France wanted the RAF to bomb factories working for the Germans: 'The bombardments not only have a considerable material effect, but are of primary importance for the future morale of the anglophile population.'[9] More letters arrived via Lisbon from Belgian sources explaining that the failure to bomb collaborating factories was attributed in Belgium to British 'decadence'. A Belgian Resistance newspaper, Le Peuple, published a report of an informal referendum on bombing taken among workers in factories exploited by the Germans. 'Not a single discordant voice,' ran the report. 'They all wish for the destruction of plants which work for the enemy.'[10]

Alongside this more positive evidence, there were regular protests from the localities which were the object of the early fringe bombing and concern expressed by the governments in exile in London (Dutch, Belgian, Norwegian) as well as the Fighting French led by General Charles de Gaulle. The Dutch government-in-exile wanted assurances in 1940 that bombing would not harm Dutch civilians or civilian property.[11] The objections from French sources were a response to the regular small raiding that occurred throughout 1940 and 1941, a total according to French records of 210 raids in 1940 and 439 in 1941 in which 1,650 people were killed and 2,311 injured.[12] In May 1941 the mayors of the coastal towns of Dieppe, Brest, Lorient and Bordeaux protested through the United States Legation at Vichy about heavy bombing of residential areas. The British Foreign Secretary, Anthony Eden, asked the Air Ministry to take every care to minimize damage to civilian property and civilian casualties, but the raids continued nonetheless. Intelligence information suggested that the French population still believed that the RAF bombed only the military targets, while it was the Germans who bombed residential districts to try to stoke up popular hatred of the British.[13] In August the Vichy regime made a formal diplomatic protest to the British government via the British Embassy in Madrid about the inaccuracy of British bombing, followed by further representations in September about the continual bombing of the Channel port of Le Havre, where it was claimed that British aircraft had attacked the town 55 times in a year (it was, indeed, a regular RAF target), scattering bombs all over the residential quarters, and killing 205 people. The Municipal Council of Le Havre recognized that the port was 'on "the front" in the war between Germany and England' but also pointed out that 'no state of war between France and England exists'.[14] The Air Ministry declined to reply to the French protest, but instead told the Foreign Office that accuracy was impossible when operations had to be carried out under indifferent weather conditions and the German habit of generating a smokescreen as soon as the bombers were sighted. The Bombing Directorate suspected that the protests were part of an orchestrated German plot to compel the RAF to reduce their offensive against French targets.[15]

A number of factors explain the escalating scale and lethality of bomber attacks on non-German targets from late 1941 onwards. The military situation brought increasing pressure to bomb targets in occupied Europe which served the German submarine and air blockade. The prime targets were to be found in the ports of western France and the airfields and bases across the Channel in northern France and the Low Countries. It was also soon evident that armaments, aviation and shipbuilding firms in the occupied zones were being utilized by the Germans, either directly taken over or the result of a collaborative agreement.[16] The Ministry of Economic Warfare considered these to be necessary targets for air attack, not only because they were more accessible than most targets in Germany, but because their destruction might reduce the willingness of occupied populations to work for the extended German war effort. On 23 June 1941 the War Cabinet approved the bombing of factories throughout occupied France, but only by daylight, to ensure a better level of accuracy, though the RAF still held back on political grounds from bombing targets far inland, including Paris. Small raids on German shipping at Brest had begun in January 1941, but the first heavy raids against Brest and Lorient, including in this case night attacks, started later in the spring, though these too remained intermittent and ineffective until the War Cabinet recommended a sustained campaign in October 1941 to reduce the dangerous threat to the Atlantic sea lanes, which it failed to do.[17] At the same Cabinet meeting Churchill agreed to attacks on goods trains in northern France, which were assumed to be carrying supplies or ammunition for German forces. Step by step the military imperatives for bombing targets in occupied Europe pushed the RAF across the thresholds established in 1940.

The second factor was political. During the course of 1941, as it became clear that the war was to be a long drawn-out conflict, the conduct of political warfare assumed a larger place. The Ministry of Economic Warfare, under the Labour politician Hugh Dalton, was at the heart of the indirect strategy laid down in 1940 to use bombing, blockade, propaganda and subversion as the means to undermine German control of occupied Europe. In the summer of 1941 the Minister of Information, Brendan Bracken, proposed setting up a separate organization, the Political Warfare Executive (PWE), jointly run by the Foreign Office and the Ministries of Information and Economic Warfare, to coordinate the political initiatives directed at occupied Europe. It was formally constituted in the late summer under Robert Bruce Lockhart, with the journalist Ritchie Calder as Director of Plans and Propaganda.[18] The PWE directors immediately saw the connection between British bombing strategy and political propaganda. The Joint Planning Staff in June 1941 had already indicated that active armed resistance in Europe would never work 'until bombing has created suitable conditions'.[19] Calder began to lobby for a bombing policy governed not only by military and economic considerations, but by political calculation. He was impressed by the apparent enthusiasm for being bombed expressed in contacts with the occupied populations. The Norwegians wanted to feel that they were still part of the war. Bombing, he thought, would 'prove British interest in Norway'; Air Intelligence confirmed that Norwegians were 'puzzled and bewildered' by the absence of raiding.[20] In a memorandum for the Foreign Office on 'The RAF and Morale-Making', Calder recommended bombing as a way to show the occupied populations that even if Britain could not invade, the German occupiers would not be immune from attack. On the other hand, he continued, 'lack of British activity creates the impression that we have "abandoned" the Occupied Territories'. Calder thought that 'demonstration raids', as he called them, would counter a mood of 'listlessness and despair', and invigorate militant forces among the occupied peoples.[21]

The weapon of political warfare was the leaflet rather than the bomb. Throughout the conflict the political warfare and intelligence establishment remained convinced that propaganda from the air was worthwhile, and millions of small sheets, or pamphlets or newsletters, were jettisoned over the target populations, both enemy and ally. Aircrews seem to have been less persuaded of the value and the PWE directed some of its propaganda effort to instilling confidence among them that leaflets – or 'nickels' as they were known – were just another, and equally effective, tool in the Allies' armoury. 'They are a weapon aimed not at men's bodies,' ran one training manual, 'but at their minds.'[22] The task of drafting, translating, printing and distributing the material was enormous. The statistics of RAF leaflet drops are set out in Table 9.1; the wartime total was 1.4 billion.

Each piece of aerial propaganda had to be discussed in terms of the current political and military situation, and the language adjusted accordingly. It also had to be considered that for many of those who risked picking up and reading the material, this was the only way they could get news of what was happening in the wider war. Allied confidence in the effects of leafleting was sustained by regular intelligence about the popular demand for more. In Belgium it was reported that children sold the leaflets they picked up for pocket money; French peasants concluded that if the RAF could waste time dropping leaflets, it 'must be very strong'.[23] On the actual effect of leaflet drops the evidence remains speculative. In Germany and Italy it was a crime to pick them up at all.

There is little doubt that the PWE greatly exaggerated the political effects likely to be derived from a combination of propaganda and judicious bombing. Like the optimistic assessments of imminent social crisis in Germany in 1940 or 1941, every straw of information was eagerly clutched. Violations of air-raid precautions were particularly highlighted. It was reported that 17 Dutchmen had been heavily fined in the

Table 9.1 British Leaflet Distribution from Aircraft over Europe by Year and Territory, 1939–45 ('000s)

Year	1939	1940	1941	1942	1943	1944	1945
Germany	31,095	43,179	29,243	125,536	240,259	176,272	63,762
France	–	21,045	25,870	151,999	282,173	163,330	–
Belgium	–	232	210	5,175	1,888	3,294	–
Netherlands	–	51	463	2,250	6,260	294	960
Denmark	–	–	797	546	856	2,419	1,175
Norway	–	32	700	1,497	1,320	222	6,782
Poland	–	1,421	–	–	–	–	–
Italy	–	891	164	3,726	13,828	–	–
Czechoslovakia	–	2,250	59	–	1,344	–	–
Misc.	–	702	–	665	295	–	–
Total	31,095	69,803	57,506	291,394	548,243	345,831	72,679

Source: Calculated from TNA, FO 898/457, 'Annual Dissemination of Leaflets by Aircraft and Balloon 1939–1945'.

summer of 1941 for staying out on the street during a raid singing 'Who's Afraid of the Big Bad Wolf?' News from Denmark suggested that 20,672 prosecutions for blackout irregularities had been pursued in 1941.[24] British political warfare assumed that the working class would be the most likely to challenge the occupiers because they were by definition supposed to be anti-fascist. Directives to the BBC European Service in early 1942 asked broadcasters to 'take *absolutely for granted* the workmen in enslaved countries are unhesitatingly behind our bombing policy, and will do all they can to help it'.[25] Bombing was supposed to suggest that liberation was close behind it and to encourage hatred of the German enemy. The leaflet campaign was deliberately designed to reflect this two-pronged argument. In spring 1941 messages to Belgium were to be divided into 'Hope – 45%', 'Hatred – 40%', 'Self-interest – 10%' and 'Self-respect – 5%'. Propaganda aimed at The Netherlands had 'Certainty of Allied Victory' top of the list with 35 per cent. In between the leaflet drops, the idea was to bomb intermittently to keep such hopes alive. In 1941 this appeal was possible. A Belgian woman who had escaped to Britain in October 1941 claimed the raids 'were the best propaganda the British had done'.[26] The years of apparent inactivity that followed undermined confidence in occupied Europe and dampened the hopes of Britain's political warriors.

By the end of 1941 these military and political considerations combined to push the RAF towards a more vigorous and less discriminate bombing strategy for the occupied regions. At a War Cabinet discussion in November 1941, the Air Minister pressed for permission to begin night-time raids against industrial targets across occupied Europe, including the major Renault works at Boulogne-Billancourt in Paris. Churchill insisted on postponing any decision until the political outcome was properly evaluated, but following RAF representations early in 1942, which claimed that the morale of the occupied population was better in areas that had been bombed than in those so far neglected, Churchill finally agreed to allow general bombing of European targets and the Cabinet confirmed the change at its meeting on 5 February 1942.[27] The RAF scarcely needed to be prompted. The Air Ministry in November 1941 had already discussed the use of incendiary bombs in attacks on industrial targets in occupied Europe to achieve maximum damage and 'to gladden the hearts of all men and women loyal ... to the Allied cause'.[28] In April 1942 Bomber Command was instructed to bomb targets in France, the Low Countries and Denmark ('knock them about'), so that local people would demand proper protection and hence disperse the German anti-air defences.[29] The PWE reached an agreement with the RAF to ensure that political considerations would play a part in target planning. The link between political propaganda and bombing policy became institutionalized and remained throughout the war a central element in bombing all the areas under German control.[30]

FRANCE: BOMBED INTO FREEDOM

The long arguments over whether or not to bomb targets in Paris were finally resolved by the decision in February 1942 to allow raids against important industrial targets throughout Europe. The raid on the Renault works became a test case of the dual strategy of economic attrition and morale-making. On the night of 3–4 March Bomber Command sent off 235 bombers, the largest number yet for a single raid. Flying in to bomb from between 2,000 and 4,000 feet with no anti-aircraft fire to distract them, 222 aircraft dropped 419 tons on the factory and the surrounding workers' housing. Much of the factory area was destroyed, though not the machinery in the buildings, at the cost of only one aircraft lost. No alarm had sounded and casualties among the local population were high: French civil defence first reported 513 killed and more than 1,500 injured, but the Paris prefecture eventually confirmed 391 dead and 558 seriously injured, more than twice the number inflicted so far by the RAF on any one night over Germany. An estimated 300 buildings were destroyed and another 160 severely damaged.[31]

The works were bombed not only for the potential damage to German vehicle output in the plant, but also to test how French opinion might react to an escalation of the bombing war. Leaflets were dropped beforehand 'To the populations of Occupied France', explaining that any factory working for the Germans would now be bombed and encouraging workers to get a job in the countryside or to go on strike for better protection; a BBC broadcast warned French people to stay away from collaborating businesses.[32] The PWE wanted to find out as soon as possible after the raid how French workers had reacted 'because it is the workers who have been killed, the workers who "go slow" and sabotage'.[33] Although the French authorities orchestrated elaborate public funerary events, the British soon received indications that the reaction had not been as adverse as the public outcry might have suggested. A report from Roosevelt's special emissary in the new French capital at Vichy, William Leahy, explained that the propaganda campaign fostered by the regime with German support had been ineffective and that there was little evidence of anti-British feeling either in Paris or in the rest of unoccupied France. Eden, who had been anxious about the political effect, was pleased with the results of a 'well-executed blow', which he believed evoked 'admiration and respect' among the people who suffered it. He was now willing to support further raids.[34] In Paris itself the operation was welcomed by many as a sign that liberation might be one step nearer. 'Nobody was indignant,' wrote one witness. 'Most hid their jubilation badly.' Blame was directed much more at the French and German authorities for failing to sound the alert, or to enforce the blackout effectively, or to provide adequate shelters.[35] Rumours quickly circulated outside Paris that the Germans had deliberately locked the workers inside the factory or had barred entry to the shelters. It was said that Parisians called out 'Long Live Great Britain!' as they lay dying.[36] The raid itself had limited results. Reports reached London in June that only 10 per cent of the machine tools had been lost as a result of the bombing and that the Renault works was operating at between 75 and 100 per cent of its pre-raid capacity.[37]

The heavy bombing of French targets between 1942 and 1944 by Bomber Command and the Eighth Air Force was undertaken in the hope that casualties could be kept to a minimum to avoid alienating the French population, while serious damage was done to Germany's western war effort. It was unfortunate for the French people that heavy bombers were seen as the necessary weapon for a number of very different strategic purposes for which they were far from ideal.[38] From 1942 onwards bombers were used to try to destroy the German submarine presence on the French west coast by bombing the almost indestructible submarine pens and the surrounding port areas; in 1943–4 bombers were directed at small V-weapons sites which were difficult to find and to damage; in the months running up to the invasion of Normandy, the 'Transportation Plan' similarly directed all Allied bomber forces (including the Fifteenth Air Force in Italy) against small rail targets, many of them embedded in urban areas; finally the months of campaigning across France in the summer of 1944 led to regular calls from the ground forces for heavy-bomber support, producing some of the most devastating raids of the war against French towns defended by German troops. The result was to strain popular French support for the bombing of the enemy in their midst.[39] Although anti-German sentiment was not reversed by the air campaign, there was a widespread belief that a less damaging strategy could have been found to achieve the same end.

The anti-submarine campaign exemplified the many contradictions that plagued the decisions to bomb France more heavily. When Bomber Command was directed to attack German naval targets on the French west coast, the orders were to attack only the dock areas and in conditions of good visibility. In April 1942 Harris wrote to Portal suggesting that the best way to slow down the German submarine war and to drive fear into the French workforce was to carry out 'real blitzes' on Brest, Lorient, St Nazaire, La Rochelle and Bordeaux.[40] Portal demurred since this was still contrary to government policy; in October 1942 guidelines were issued to Bomber Command to ensure that the air force would understand that only identifiable objectives in clear weather could be bombed and only if it was certain that heavy loss of civilian life would not result.[41] But when the Atlantic battle reached its climax in late 1942, the Anti-U-Boat Committee, under pressure from the Admiralty, finally recommended abandoning all caution by destroying through area attacks the towns that involuntarily hosted the German submarines. The War Cabinet approved the decision on 11 January 1943 and although by now Harris no longer wanted operational distractions from his attacks on Germany, his desire for 'real blitzes' on the French ports could now be fulfilled.[42] Harris described the French interlude in his memoirs as 'one of the most infuriating episodes' in the whole bomber offensive and an evident 'misuse of air power'.[43] He blamed the Admiralty for the change in priority, and there is no doubt that the driving force behind the change was the chief of the naval staff, Admiral Sir Dudley Pound, who in this case was able to persuade Churchill and Eden to swallow their scruples over bombing civilians for the sake of the survival of British sea traffic.

There had already been more than 20 attacks on the ports since 1940, which had served to encourage the Germans to take every precaution to protect submarine operations.[44] In the summer of 1942 a British propaganda campaign had been launched from the air against coastal towns from Dunkirk to St Nazaire warning the populations to evacuate: 'we must carry on a war to the death [*guerre à l'outrance*] against the submarines'.[45] Most evacuation did not occur until the bombing started in earnest. The heaviest raiding was reserved for Lorient where nine major attacks by Bomber Command in January and February dropped 4,286 tons of bombs (including 2,500 tons of incendiaries) with the specific purpose of burning down the town. On one raid the bombers carried 1,000 tons of bombs, the same quantity dropped a few months before by the German Air Force in the major raid on the city of Stalingrad.[46] The French report following the bombing described the raids as an example of a new RAF strategy of 'scorched earth'; not a building in the town remained standing or unscathed, a 'dead city', except for the submarine pens undamaged by the rain of bombs. In a 30-kilometre radius from the town thousands of village buildings had been destroyed and farms incinerated.[47] The PWE published an uncompromising statement following the bombing that the innocent must inevitably suffer with the guilty: 'The violence and frequency of attacks involving hardship to civilians must increase.'[48] Naval Intelligence assessments were nevertheless unimpressed by Bomber Command's strategy 'of the bludgeon', which failed to halt the rate of submarine operation significantly in any of the major targets, despite Pound's earlier insistence that it would. In April Harris was instructed to stop and to turn once again to Germany.[49] The submarine threat was defeated in spring 1943 by using aircraft to attack submarines at sea rather than in their concrete pens. The pens themselves became vulnerable only after the development of two giant bombs – 'Tallboy' and 'Grand Slam' – both the brainchild of Barnes Wallis, the engineer who designed the bomb used to breach the Ruhr dams. But the first 5-ton Tallboy was used against Brest only on 5 August 1944, and Lorient a day later, while the 10-ton Grand Slam was available only for the last weeks of the war.[50]

Bomber Command was joined by the Eighth Air Force for the submarine campaign and the round-the-clock bombing gave the local population, most of whom had been evacuated or had sensibly evacuated themselves, no respite from the raiding. Daylight bombing was carried out from a considerable height by crews who were still learning their way. The wide spread of bombs dropped from high altitude and the rising casualty rates that resulted provoked a sudden change in French attitudes during the course of 1943. A French Resistance worker who arrived in Britain in April 1943 warned his new hosts that the population was deeply hostile to high-level American raids, which threatened to undermine irretrievably 'the friendly feelings of the entire French population towards the Allies'.[51] This shift in opinion coincided with the decision to spread the bombing over all French territory following the German occupation of the southern, unoccupied zone in November 1942. On 21 December the Air Ministry was informed by the Foreign Office that raids on southern French cities were now legally permitted, and on 29 December the BBC broadcast the same warning to the population living there to stay away from military and industrial targets that had been given to the occupied north earlier in the year.[52] The guidelines issued in October 1942 on the conduct of raids now applied to the whole of France but they were not binding on the Eighth Air Force, and when the Renault works in Boulogne-Billancourt were bombed again on 4 April 1943 by 85 B-17 'Flying Fortresses', the results were very different from a year before. Just under half the bombs hit the industrial complex, but the rest were scattered over a wide residential area. One bomb penetrated the *métro* station at Pont-de-Sèvres; 80 corpses were identified and the unidentified human remains put into 26 coffins.[53] There was little anti-aircraft fire or fighter pursuit and only four aircraft were lost. The alarm had sounded only one minute before the bombs began to fall, giving the population out on the streets in the hour after lunch little chance to find shelter. The civil defence counted 403 dead and 600 injured; 118 buildings were destroyed and 480 heavily damaged.[54] A few days later, René Massigli, the French ambassador (representing the provisional government in London), met Eden to complain about the 'feeling of exasperation' in France caused by civilian losses from careless American bombing. In Brittany, he claimed, the reaction of the population was to cry out 'Vive la R.A.F.!', but also 'À bas l'Américain Air Force'.[55]

Raids over the summer by both air forces were reined back. The Eighth Air Force was asked to confine raids just to the submarine bases and to try to find an operational pattern that would reduce French civilian deaths. Arnold objected to British requests to restrict what American air forces could do and an agreed list was drawn up of objectives in France that could be attacked after a warning to the population. Massigli was told by Eden that the American air forces would only bomb certain selected targets and would try to do so with greater care, but by the autumn Eaker was keen to extend the Pointblank attacks to aircraft industry targets in France.[56] The French aircraft industry, much of it sheltered in the unoccupied zone until November 1942, produced 668 aircraft for Germany in 1942 and 1,285 in 1943, many of them trainer aircraft to free German factories for the production of combat models. German manufacturers used French capacity for their own experimental work, away from the threat of bombs on Germany.[57] As a result, French industry became a military priority for the American Air Force even at the risk of inflicting heavy casualties on the population. On 3 and 15 September 1943 Eighth Air Force raids on factories in

Paris spread damage once again across residential streets packed with workers and shoppers and killed 377 civilians.[58] The raids on the western port city of Nantes on 16 and 23 September exacted the highest casualties so far from bombing in France. The targets included a German naval vessel, a French locomotive works and an aircraft factory, which was hit heavily. On 16 September 131 B-17s hit the town with 385 tons of bombs; on 23 September 46 out of 117 B-17s despatched to Nantes in the morning dropped a further 134 tons in poor weather, followed by a less accurate raid by 30 aircraft in the evening.[59] In the first raid the bomb pattern once again spread out over a wide area of the city, destroying 400 buildings and severely damaging another 600. The civil defence authorities counted 1,110 dead and 800 severely injured. While the local emergency services struggled to cope with the damage, they were hit by the two attacks on 23 September, which not only struck the ruins but spread out over an area of more than 500 hectares. Because much of the centre of the city was already abandoned, deaths from the second two raids were 172, but a further 300 buildings were completely destroyed. This time the population panicked entirely and 100,000 abandoned the city. The raids on Nantes resembled completely the pattern of raids on a German city, with the exception that Eighth Air Force losses were modest, a total of seven aircraft on 16 September and no losses a week later.[60]

The raids of autumn 1943 provoked a mixture of outrage and incomprehension in France. Total deaths from bombing in 1943 reached 7,458, almost three times the level of 1942. A French report on public opinion, which reached the Allies early in 1944, highlighted the damaging effect of persistently inaccurate high-level bombing on a people 'tired, worn out by all its miseries, all its privations, all its separations, unnerved by too prolonged a wait for its liberation'.[61] The French Air Force, reduced under the armistice terms with Germany to a skeleton organization, tried to assess what object the Allied raids could have. Raids on Paris and against the Dunlop works at Montluçon (this time by Bomber Command) puzzled French airmen, who assumed there must be some secondary purpose behind the pattern of scattered bombing that they had not yet worked out.[62] Since the French Air Force could not do its own bombing, much time was spent in 1943 and 1944 observing Allied practice in order to understand the techniques and tactics involved as well as the effects of bombs on urban society, industrial architecture and popular morale.[63] Many of the reports on individual raids highlighted the sheer squandering of resources involved in a bombing operation when three-quarters of the bombs typically missed the target: 'The results obtained,' ran a report on the bombing of St Étienne, 'have no relation to the means employed, and this bombardment represents, like all the others, a waste of material – without counting the unnecessary losses in human life that they provoke.'[64] The air force worked out the pattern of bombing accuracy to show just how wide the dispersion of effort was. In raids against Lille the area in which bombs fell was a rectangle 8 by 4 kilometres; against Rouen 8 by 3 kilometres; a raid on the railway station at Cambrai in 1944 covered an area 3 kilometres in length and 1.5 kilometres wide. The impact varied from raid to raid, but studies showed that many raids covered an area of between 200 and 400 hectares, which explained the escalating losses of life and property. The French Air Force was impressed most by low-level dive-bombing and rocket attacks using the American P-47 'Thunderbolt' and the Hawker 1-B Typhoon, which achieved their object with much greater operational economy, and matched French strategic preferences before 1939.[65]

The French government and population were not unprepared for a bombing war. As in Britain, the French state had begun to plan for passive defence against air attack as early as 1923; a law for compulsory passive defence organization was passed in April 1935, compelling local authorities to begin the organization of civil defence measures. In July 1938 a Director of Passive Defence was appointed in the Defence Ministry to coordinate the protection of civilian lives and property with the committees of passive defence set up in each French administrative *département*.[66] The problem for French civil defence was the sudden defeat and occupation in the summer of 1940. In the area occupied by the Germans, civil defence was likely to be a necessary safeguard against British air activity; in the unoccupied zone, the urgency for continued civil defence seemed less evident. The Vichy government set up the Directorate of Passive Defence in the southern city of Lyon in 1941 under General Louis Sérant, but it was starved of funds and personnel. Spending on passive defence had totalled more than 1 billion francs in 1939 but by 1941 was down to just 250 million.[67] In both zones of France the difficult task was to reach a satisfactory working relationship with the German occupiers. The active air defence of the occupied zone was in the hands of Field Marshal Sperrle's Air Fleet 3. Following the switch to the war against the Soviet Union, the number of fighter aircraft and anti-aircraft guns left in France was seldom adequate for the weight of Allied attack. German priority was given to the protection of the most important military sites, including the submarine pens and German airbases. Air-raid alarms could only be activated on German orders, though French observers were expected to supply information to allow German officers to calculate whether it was worth sounding an alert. In the occupied zone the blackout was enforced on German orders. Mobile emergency units for air protection were sent from Germany to help with firefighting and rescue work alongside the residual French passive defence organization. They found the French attitude at times lackadaisical. German firemen fighting a blaze in Dunkirk in April 1942 were astonished at the lack of discipline among French colleagues who 'stood around on the corners smoking'.[68]

The relationship with the unoccupied zone was a constant source of friction for the German air command in Paris and the Italian occupation zone set up in 1940 in south-eastern France. The Italian Armistice Commission insisted that Vichy impose a blackout throughout the area abutting the Italian occupied regions to avoid giving British bombers an easy aid to navigation against Italian targets, but even when the French Air Force agreed, it proved difficult to enforce.[69] In November 1941 the German Armistice Commission in Wiesbaden complained that British aircraft regularly flew over the unoccupied zone without any blackout below: 'The contrast between the occupied zone, plunged into darkness, and the unoccupied zone, where the blackout is up to now only intermittent, nicely indicates to enemy planes the frontier of the two zones.'[70] The German Air Force demanded complete blackout every night along a cordon 100 kilometres from the occupation zone, and effective blackout over the whole of unoccupied France when aircraft were sighted. French officials regarded the request as 'inopportune' and prevaricated for months until August 1942, when the French government finally accepted a blackout of the frontier zones.[71] A German aerial inspection a few weeks later showed that many houses had not bothered to take blackout measures; vehicles could be seen driving with full headlights; in Lyon the blackout occurred only after the anti-aircraft artillery had begun to fire.[72] The long delay reflected a more general reluctance on the part of the French military leadership to comply with German demands. Failure to observe the blackout was also a simple way to express noncompliance. Free French radio broadcasts encouraged householders to keep lights on throughout the night to help the RAF find German targets. Only when the whole of France was occupied could the German occupiers insist on the blackout, but even then complaints continued about its inadequacy.

The occupation of the southern zone on 10 November 1942 coincided with the intensification of Allied bombing. As this became heavier, so the French authorities recognized that failure to collaborate fully with the German occupiers would expose the population to unnecessary risks. The ambivalence remained, however. When German Air Fleet 3 asked for French anti-aircraft gunners in 1943 to man batteries in the north of the country, French officials preferred to site them in central France where they could be used for training purposes rather than to fire at Allied aircraft.[73] In February 1943 the German military command in Paris insisted that a unitary French anti-air defence system should be set up covering the newly occupied French territory and working in close collaboration with the thinly spread German anti-air resources. The Vichy regime was asked to establish a Secretariat for Air Defence, including a national director for 'Passive Defence', and it was the German intention that the French organization would eventually operate over the whole of France.[74] The new French defences included anti-aircraft batteries which were, unlike their German counterparts, controlled by the army. The German Air Force command in France insisted that the new French units come under air force control, and the army was forced to comply.[75] A new air-raid warning system, the *Securité Aérienne Publique* (SAP), was activated in February 1943, manned by French personnel under French Air Force control, using a mixture of radar and visual observation. In the southern zone the force numbered 3,800 officers and men; in the northern occupation zone the German Air Force still kept its own system of alerts, but Vichy officials and officers were posted to the main air-defence centres to help coordinate air defence measures across the whole country.[76] The system suffered from the same problems found in the northern zone, since alerts could only be authorized by the Germans on information passed to them by French observers, except in more remote areas where there were no German officials.[77] The result once again was that alerts were sometimes sounded only when aircraft were already overhead, minutes before the bombs dropped.

The Passive Defence system insisted on by the German Air Force already existed in a skeleton form throughout Vichy France, organized by local prefects and mayors. In the southern zone the system had not been properly tested and required a rapid expansion. The Vichy regime, now led by Pierre Laval as premier, established an Interministerial Protection Service against the Events of War (SIPEG), not unlike the committee established in February 1943 by Joseph Goebbels in Germany,

16. The 'Battle of Germany'. The US strategic air forces aimed to destroy German aircraft production and defeat the German fighter force in the air. Here two German officials survey the smoking ruins of the Fieseler aircraft plant at Kassel.

17. A rare image of a fighter 'kill' in the air battle over Germany. A German fighter crashes into fields, photographed by the pursuing aircraft. By May 1944, German fighter-pilot losses were running at more than 50 per cent a month.

18. Two German women wander through the haze and devastation of a raid on Ebenfurth in September 1943, surrounded by civil defence personnel and fire engines. Nine million Germans eventually joined the stream of evacuees from the stricken cities.

19. Women and girls played a large part in the German civil defence effort. Here a young member of the German Girls' League (BDM) works alongside civil defenders during a raid on Düsseldorf in July 1943.

20. An artist's impression of RAF Lancaster bombers flying low over the Ruhr city of Essen to destroy industrial targets. The caption claimed that this would 'ensure accuracy'. In reality raids were made from safer heights against whole cities rather than just factories.

21. The reality of inaccurate bombing can be seen in the ruins of this farm, bombed during a raid on the Ruhr city of Dortmund on 23–24 May 1943. German farmers were also under instructions to douse lights at night and to keep civil defence equipment at hand.

22. Two circus elephants recruited in the aftermath of Operation Gomorrah against Hamburg help to move a car destroyed in the bombing, which killed an estimated 37,000 people over a week of heavy bombing in July 1943.

23. Concentration camp workers, wearing the familiar striped suits, work to clear the piles of rubble left in the aftermath of the bombing of Hamburg. Prisoners came to play an important part in the emergency repair services and the clearing of debris. By summer 1944 there were over half a million camp prisoners in Germany.

24. In his role as coordinator for air-raid emergencies Joseph Goebbels, the Minister for Propaganda and Public Enlightenment, visits the ruined city of Kassel after the firestorm of 22–23 October 1943.

25. The grisly aftermath of the Kassel firestorm. Incinerated bodies and body parts are laid out among the ruins. An estimated 6,000 died in the raid, a higher proportion of the city population than in the heavy raids on Hamburg in July 1943.

26. Among the bomb rubble in the Maltese capital of Valetta, children wait to collect fresh water from a roadside well. Malta became 'the most bombed place on earth' in 1941–2, but survived the siege.

27. The ruins of a railway marshalling yard in Rome after the American raid of 19 July 1943. Though the damage was extensive, rail communications were soon re-established and Rome did not fall to the Allies for almost a year. The Fascist Party symbol can clearly be seen on the front wall of the ruined station.

ation of bombing and imminent invasion forced the French government to produce coordinated plans to move their wartime refugees more successfully than in 1940.[86]

Evacuation had already begun in 1942 on an improvised basis and by early 1944 over 200,000 children had been moved from the most vulnerable cities. In December 1941 a scheme was established between the bombed city of Brest and the southern city of Lyon in which the bombed-out (*sinistrés*) were to be housed in Lyon and given welfare and funds by the council and population which adopted them. The scheme failed to attract even 100 children since parents were reluctant to accept separation and the children were reluctant to go.[87] In 1942 other bombed towns either sought or were offered adoption by cities regarded as safe, including Le Havre, which was eventually adopted by Algiers, but much of the aid came in the form of money or clothes or books for the homeless rather than a new home. Most French evacuees moved to family or friends in nearby villages, and French planners insisted, against German objections, that on practical and political grounds it made more sense to house evacuees locally rather than in remote areas in central France. With the heavy bombing of Lorient, St Nazaire and Brest in early 1943, the population flowed out into the surrounding countryside in tens of thousands.[88] On 4 February 1944 Laval issued comprehensive guidelines on evacuation policy following the severe bombing of the winter and the expectation that the military threat would escalate. The guiding principles of the programme were the need for an ordered transfer of population and the consent of those to be transferred, 'voluntary but organised'. The government favoured persuasion, using a programme of posters, radio broadcasts and public meetings. Priority was to be given to 'the human capital of the Nation', above all to children, who carried the demographic future of a post-war France.[89] Mothers and children and pregnant women were the chief categories, though the elderly and disabled were also included; those who remained were classified as 'indispensable' (administrators and officials), 'necessary' (labourers and white-collar workers, doctors, welfare workers) and 'useful' (those who helped to maintain the activity of the indispensable and necessary). Families nevertheless remained unenthusiastic about evacuation; they feared looting if they left their homes, and disliked the loss of independence and reliance on welfare in the destination zones. Eventually around 1.2 million moved as refugees, evacuees or bombed-out, most in reaction to the urgent imperative of survival.[90]

It has sometimes been remarked that the French failed to exhibit the

'Blitz spirit' evident in Britain, and later in Germany, in the face of bombing. In a great many ways the opposite is true. The French population faced an inescapable dilemma that made it difficult to know how to respond to the raids: they wanted the Allies who were bombing them to win, and they wanted the Germans who protected them to lose. Since they were not themselves at war, the sense that they represented a national 'front line' against a barbarous enemy could not easily be used to mobilize the population as it could in Britain and Germany. The bombing was not part of an orchestrated offensive against French morale, and civilians were not supposed to be a target; nor was bombing experienced either regularly or over a wide area, except for the bombing of northern France during the Allied invasion. French towns and cities were nevertheless caught between two dangerous forces, the German occupiers and Vichy collaborators on the one hand and the Allied air forces (including the B-24 'Liberator') on the other. Resisting the Germans by helping Allied aircrew or sabotaging what had not been bombed meant running risks of discovery, torture and execution that no one in Britain's Blitz was expected to run. Lesser infractions – deliberate refusal to observe the blackout, or absenteeism from a civil defence unit – could be interpreted by the occupiers not simply as an act of negligence but as an act of resistance. When evacuees returned without authorization, the local German commanders withdrew ration cards or threatened the returnees with a labour camp. French people exposed to the bombs experienced double jeopardy, both the damage and deaths from raids and the harsh authority of the occupiers.

This dilemma was exploited politically by both sides during the war. The German propaganda apparatus presented the Allied air forces as terror flyers, as in Germany, and the French press was encouraged to focus on the barbarous and indiscriminate nature of the attacks. The Vichy authorities shared this perspective, and may indeed have believed it. Cinema newsreels on the bombing of French targets broadcast by *France-Actualités* carried titles such as 'War on civilians', 'Wounded France', 'The Calvary continues', while after every major raid there were elaborate official funerals with full pageantry and speeches condemning the massacre of the innocents.[91] Since the Vichy regime was widely unpopular among important sections of the urban population, the bombing was used as a way to show that the authorities cared about the welfare of the damaged communities and to forge links between state and people. The bombed-out were entitled to state welfare at fixed rates; the state paid the funeral expenses of bomb victims; evacuation

costs could be met in full for transfers of less than 15 kilometres distance; pensions were introduced for those disabled by the bombs, and
for those widowed or orphaned in the raids.[92] In addition, bomb victims
were entitled to welfare assistance from two voluntary welfare organizations, the *Secours National* (National Assistance), re-established in
1940 with Marshal Pétain as its president, and the *Comité Ouvrier de
Secours Immédiat* (COSI, the Committee for Workers' Emergency
Assistance) set up following the Billancourt raid in 1942 under the
collaborationist René Mesnard. Both relied on state funds as well as
voluntary contributions, and both echoed the propaganda of the Vichy
regime in condemning the bombing and highlighting the efforts to aid
the victims as a means of binding together the national community. The
COSI took funds directly from the German authorities and in reality
distributed little of it to the bombed-out and much of it to the officials
who ran it.[93] The committee did play a part in redistributing to the
victims of bombing some of the Jewish apartments and furnishings con-
fiscated under German supervision, while the money given to the
committee by the Germans came from expropriated Jewish assets. The
first consignment of Jewish-owned furniture was handed over to COSI
in April 1942 and large quantities continued to be diverted to help the
bombed-out until 1944, though an even greater volume was shipped
directly to the Reich from France and the Low Countries to supply
German civilian victims of bombing, a total of 735 train-loads during
the course of the occupation.[94]

The Allies, on the other hand, needed to present to the French population a clear justification for the bombing as the key to eventual
liberation. This message worked well early in the war when there was
hope that RAF raids signalled the possibility of an early invasion, but
less well after years of waiting and in the face of rising casualties. The
Allies tried to combine the bombing with direct support for the French
Resistance movement, but at the same time to avoid operations that
would undermine the credibility of resistance and push the French
population towards grudging support for Vichy. Broadcasts from the
BBC, which were widely listened to in France, encouraged the French
population to see resistance and bombing as two sides of the same
coin.[95] The leaflet war was designed to offer clear warnings to the areas
scheduled for raiding as well as justification for attacks on German
targets or collaborating businesses. Millions of propaganda notices and
news reviews were dropped throughout the period, reaching a climax in
1943–4. The RAF dropped 155 million leaflets in 1942, 294 million in

1943, the great majority from aircraft, some from balloons sent with the prevailing winds.[96] The Eighth Air Force began leafleting operations in late 1942 only after the initial effects of American raids had been assessed to see what kind of political message should be delivered. A special force of 12 B-17 and B-24 bombers was set up in 1943 tasked with distributing leaflets over the occupied territories as well as across Germany.[97] By February 1944 the Americans had dropped 41 million items, including the French-language paper *America at War* which was used to explain the course of the conflict and the necessity for bombing French targets. In spring 1944 the quantity increased substantially to 130 million in March on the eve of the transportation campaign against French railways, and more than 100 million each month until D-Day. So heavy was the bombardment of paper that the German authorities in France organized leaflet-squads with sharpened sticks to collect them before they were picked up by the local population.[98]

The impact of the leaflet and broadcasting campaign was difficult for the Allies to assess since almost all the public media in Vichy France treated the bombing as an unmitigated crime. Allied intelligence was faced with a barrage of information showing that the bombing was defined by its 'terror character'. One newspaper, the *Petit Parisien*, following the bombing of Paris in September 1943, claimed that 'the barbarians of the West are worthy allies of the barbarians in the East'.[99] The *Mémorial de St Étienne* asked 'Will this destructive Sadism have no end? One is appalled before this mounting barbarity, this barbarity behind the mask of civilization.' The Allies recognized that the French reaction was not as simple as that, but there was increasing evidence that even among pro-Allied circles the mixed results of bombing raids provoked anxiety and hostility without at the same time undermining the acknowledgement that German targets were both legitimate and necessary.[100] This ambiguity was evident from the reaction to two raids on Toulon on 7 March 1944. The first killed or injured an estimated 900 German soldiers and won wide approval; the second four days later missed the target and killed 110 French civilians to widespread complaints. One of the American crews shot down on the second raid was black, prompting racist comments about the quality and competence of American airmen.[101] American bombing was identified in information from the French Resistance as the major source of resentment because of its apparently 'careless and casual' attitude to the communities being bombed: 'The Americans make it a sport,' ran one report, 'and amuse themselves by bombing from such altitudes.'[102] In May 1944 the French

Catholic cardinals sent an appeal to the Catholic episcopate in Britain and the United States asking them to lobby the air forces to bomb military objectives with greater care and avoid the 'humble dwellings of women and children'. The Archbishop of Westminster replied that his government had given every assurance that casualties would be kept to a minimum.[103]

There was nevertheless widespread resistance or non-compliance prompted by the bombing campaign as well. The Resistance took the view that those killed in Allied bombings were in some sense not victims, but combatants in a war for the liberation and salvation of the nation.[104] Those who chose to operate networks for the escape of Allied airmen certainly ran the risks of any combatant if they were caught. The death penalty was introduced in a decree on 14 July 1941 for helping Allied airmen, but an estimated 2,000–3,000 British and American servicemen were smuggled out of France and back to combat. In cases following heavy bombing, as at Lorient in 1943, some airmen were surrendered to the Germans, but Allied intelligence found that in many cases the Resistance distinguished between the regrettable effects of a heavy bombardment and their view of Allied aircrew as liberators.[105] The Resistance also regarded bombing as complementary to forms of active opposition to the occupiers, though it was seldom integrated as closely as it could have been despite their insistence that sabotage could often be a more effective tool than bombing.[106] There also existed many lesser levels of protest or non-compliance derived from the bombing war. The funerals of Allied aircrew killed in action attracted large crowds despite German efforts to obstruct them; wreaths were laid by the graveside dedicated 'To Our Heroes' or 'To Our Allies' or 'To Our Liberators' until seized or destroyed by the occupiers. There were numerous public demonstrations under the occupation, 753 in total, some orchestrated by Vichy to protest against bombing, but hundreds directed at shortages of food or adequate shelter.[107] The police reports from the provinces in 1943 found that despite, or because of, the bombings, the population talked openly of their hope for Allied invasion and the horrors of occupation: 'No-one,' ran a report from Charente in north-west France, 'believes any longer in a German victory.'[108]

The German occupiers found regular evidence of dissent among the French officials and servicemen organizing the air defence system. The slow introduction of French anti-aircraft units in the summer of 1943 was blamed by the German Air Force on the existence of a network of Freemasons among the French officials involved. French anti-aircraft personnel were made to sign a 'declaration of duty' not to reveal military secrets, and both anti-aircraft units and the French emergency services were monitored by the German Security Service (SD) for their alleged sympathies with de Gaulle and the Free French.[109] In August 1943, 15 anti-aircraft servicemen abandoned their posts and could not be found; the following month another 15 men from the Air Force Security School took two cars and a lorry and absconded to the Massif Central to join the partisan Resistance. In November 1943 a group of SAP soldiers were caught listening to French broadcasts from Britain; on the wall of their common room a poster was found proclaiming 'Vive les Gaullistes! Vive l'U.R.S.S! Vive de Gaulle!'[110] German Air Intelligence found that by the autumn of 1943 Allied success in the Mediterranean had changed the attitude of the French population to one of anxious longing for the moment of Allied invasion and celebration of every German defeat. 'The expected Anglo-American landing in France,' concluded a report in August, 'is now the daily topic of conversation.'[111]

Allied planning for the liberation of France was indeed far advanced by the autumn of 1943, but from the Allied point of view it was bound to cause high casualties and perhaps compromise at the last moment the sympathies of the French people for the Allied cause. Churchill remained continually anxious, as he told the War Cabinet in April 1944, that pre-invasion bombing might create an 'unhealable breach' between France and the Western Allies.[112] The principal issue was the decision to use the heavy-bomber forces, including the Fifteenth Air Force in Italy, to attack the French transport system before invasion and to support the army as it consolidated its position on the bridgeheads in Normandy in June and July 1944 and, a month later, in southern France. To this was added the decision to use Allied bomber forces in the 'Crossbow' operations against German V-weapon sites across northern France. Neither Harris nor Spaatz was enthusiastic about using the bomber force this way, since it was not what the bombing was supposed to be for, while the aircraft had not been designed for use against small tactical targets. In January 1944, following an order to intensify raids on V-weapon sites, Harris rejected the use of Bomber Command to attack 'Crossbow' targets as 'not reasonable operations of war'.[113] His reaction to the idea that bombers should support the ground offensive was just as negative. Bombers used for ground support would, he argued, 'be entirely ineffective', leading 'directly to disaster' for the invasion force.[114] Spaatz objected to Eisenhower that support for invasion was 'an uneconomical use' of the heavy-bomber force and preferred to leave the operations to the large tactical air forces assigned to the Allied Expeditionary Air Force under Air Marshal Trafford Leigh-Mallory, whose fighter-bomber and light-bomber aircraft were intended to attack small targets and could react quickly and flexibly to battlefield requirements.[115] Both bomber forces wished to be able to concentrate on Pointblank operations against Germany as a more strategically valuable way to limit the German response to invasion. Arnold told Spaatz in late April 1944, after the decision had already been taken to focus on the French railway system, that Pointblank should 'still be pressed to the limit'.[116] The arguments put forward in favour of the 'Transportation Plan' by Tedder and his scientific adviser, Solly Zuckerman, have already been discussed. Zuckerman's paper produced in January 1944 on 'Delay and Disorganisation of Enemy Movement by Rail' formed the basis of the eventual pre-invasion plan. On 25 March in a long and hotly debated meeting, Eisenhower finally came down in favour of using the bomber forces, under his own direct command, to attack the French railway system and other strategic targets both before and during the invasion period.[117]

This decision still left unresolved the political anxieties about possible levels of casualty. Portal informed Churchill after the meeting of 25 March that there were bound to be very heavy casualties as a result of the decision to hit 76 key points in the French railway network. Bomber Command suggested a figure of between 80,000 and 160,000 casualties, partly to confirm Harris's argument that heavy bombers were the wrong weapon.[118] Zuckerman calculated on the basis of damage done to British targets earlier in the war a more modest casualty figure of 12,000 dead and 6,000 seriously injured. In a discussion with the Defence Committee on 5 April, Churchill deplored a strategy that might result in 'the butchery of large numbers of helpless French people', but despite his reservations and the opposition of Eden and General Brooke, chief of the general staff, the campaign was allowed to start on the understanding that casualty levels would be carefully monitored over the weeks that followed and warnings sent to French communities to evacuate the threatened areas.[119] By mid-April casualties from the first nine raids were estimated at 1,103, well within the limits set by Zuckerman's estimate. The Defence Committee was supplied with the outraged French reports ('In Anglo-American eyes, to be European is enough to be wiped off the list of the living') and Churchill hesitated to give the campaign full approval.[120] Zuckerman and the

RE8 department of the Ministry of Home Security continued to monitor reports on a daily basis and by late April the available evidence
suggested that casualties had been approximately 50 per cent lower
than anticipated.[121] Only after Roosevelt had insisted that there should
be no restriction on military action if Operation Overlord were to
succeed, did Churchill finally on 11 May give his full approval to the
campaign.[122] For the four weeks before D-Day a furious crescendo of
bombing descended on the French railway system and the unfortunate
housing that surrounded its nodal points.

Zuckerman's calculations in fact underestimated French casualties
by a wide margin because transport targets were only part of what
Allied air forces were expected to bomb in the weeks leading to invasion. French civil defence officials counted 712 dead in March, 5,144 in
April, 9,893 in May and an estimated 9,517 in June. The total of
25,266 over the four months was almost certainly not complete, given
the difficulty of constructing exact records in a dangerous war zone; nor
did all the casualties come from attacks on rail targets, but also against
bridges and military installations, and German forces.[123] They nevertheless represented the overall human cost of the decision to use bombing
as the means to reduce the capacity of the German Army and Air Force
to oppose the landings in Normandy. The high casualties resulted chiefly
from the wide dispersion of bombs against relatively small targets and
the large tonnage employed. The 63,636 tons dropped on transport targets exceeded the entire tonnage dropped by the German Air Force
during the Blitz on Britain. The French air defence counted 71,000 high-
explosive bombs between January and March 1944, but 291,000 from
April to June.[124] Some attacks achieved a high level of precision, but in
many cases bombs were scattered over a wide area. The attack on the
rail centre at St Pierre des Corps on 11 April struck the whole area of
the town; the raid on Lille on 10 April hit an area of 32 square kilometres; that on Noisy-le-Sec on 18 April covered 30 square kilometres; on
Rouen a day later, the area was 24 square kilometres.[125] In May the
French authorities counted a total of 1,284 raids in which bombs fell on
793 different localities, 630 of them along the northern coast and the
area north-east of Paris. Only 8 per cent of the attacks were undertaken
at night, which ought to have increased the possibility of more accurate
raiding, but many of the daylight raids were carried out at heights of
3,000–4,000 metres (10,000–13,000 feet). In some cases, high casualties resulted from what the Passive Defence called 'imprudence' – people
standing at their windows to watch the bombing, others out in the

street, or in their gardens. In a raid on Nice on 26 May, 438 people were killed, two-thirds of them on the street, one-third in their houses. The shelters, for the most part either trenches or converted cellars, had uneven fortunes during the raiding; some stood up well even to direct hits, others, like one at Rouen on 30 May, were blown apart and most of the occupants killed.[126]

Some of the heaviest losses of life occurred in targets in the former unoccupied zone, which were hit by American aircraft of the Fifteenth Air Force operating from bases in Italy. For the crews involved, the bombing of precise railway targets with a view to reducing damage to civilian lives and property was very different from the long-range raids against Pointblank targets in southern Germany, which had been the main activity of the force since its formation in November 1943. Two raids, one on St Étienne on 26 May 1944 and one on Marseille the following day, resulted in heavy loss of civilian life. At St Étienne the alert sounded in good time; the 150 B-17s attacked in waves from around 13,000 feet, and half the bombs fell in the zone around the rail links. But there were too few proper shelters for a population unused to the air threat and more than 1,084 were killed. The effect on rail traffic was limited. Rail lines remained open and the damage, such as it was, could be overcome in four days. The attack on Marseille on 27 May flown at an estimated 20,000 feet, against stations at St-Charles and Blancarde, both situated in the heart of the city's residential area, scattered bombs over 10 of the city's quarters, destroyed 500 buildings and killed 1,752 people. Again Passive Defence observed the 'insouciance' of a population hit by an air raid for the first time and the absence of effective civil defence training. The stations were unimportant (one was a railway cul-de-sac), but the effect of the raid was to create a crisis of public morale and strong hostility to the air forces that carried out the attack.[127] The scale of the raiding and the damage inflicted brought protests from the French Resistance and the French authorities in London. The French Commissariat for Foreign Affairs warned the Foreign Office in early May that the raids were having a damaging effect on French opinion; in early June a resolution from the Resistance Group Assembly was passed on by Massigli, calling on the bomber forces to change their tactics and for an active propaganda campaign 'to dissipate the growing ill-feeling' among the victim populations.[128] An OSS report from Madrid relayed the Resistance view that the French population now believed their situation to be no better than 'the Nazis in Germany'.[129] This knowledge made little difference to Allied operations. In June, however, the bombing reached its high point as Allied forces poured ashore on D-Day and spread out into the Normandy countryside.

The results of the 'Transportation Plan' were the subject of keen argument both at the time and since. French investigations showed that by the beginning of June rail traffic was down to around half the level in January 1944, and in the key regions of the north and west, down to 15 and 10 per cent. There were 2,234 cases of damage to rail lines between January and June 1944, but as in Britain or Germany or the Soviet Union, these were relatively easy to repair.[130] Much damage was also done by sabotage, which the Resistance thought was a more effective way of achieving the same end, and with fewer losses to the French population, particularly the railwaymen, who were regarded as key Resistance workers.[131] Between January and July bombing and strafing destroyed or severely damaged 2,536 French locomotives, sabotage a further 1,605. But according to the SNCF (the French national railway), sabotage accounted for 70,000 goods wagons compared with 55,000 from air attack.[132] In the three months from April to June there were 1,020 bomb attacks on the rail network, but 1,713 acts of sabotage.[133] Of these the two most significant causes of delay to traffic were the attacks on repair depots, which created a cumulative backlog of repair to the rolling stock hit by raids or sabotage, and the attacks on rail bridges. Many of these were carried out by the tactical air forces using fighter-bombers and light bombers, and they proved decisive in cutting the key regions off from rapid German reinforcement. Most rail centres could be made operable again in an average of seven days, but bridges took from 10 to 16 days.[134] The German authorities made strenuous efforts to keep the rail system going and succeeded for much of the period of the transport campaign. By suspending almost all civilian traffic and helped by persistent poor weather for bombing, it proved possible to maintain military through-traffic up to June (when 535 loaded troop trains could still be deployed), but a slow decline set in from July. Total German ton-kilometres were 300 million for the month to mid-March, 400 million for each of the next three months, but 150 million in July, by which time the loss of raid traffic had compromised the possibility of effective German defence.[135] The argument from the French viewpoint, however, was not whether German fighting power was affected, but whether the high cost in civilian lives and buildings could not have been avoided by wielding an aerial weapon that was less blunt. French authorities found that major raids by heavy bombers placed between half and four-fifths of the bombs outside the target area;

in this sense Harris and Spaatz had been right to insist that large formations of heavy bombers were not the most suitable means to achieve the aim of precise destruction and limited French losses.

This conclusion was even more evident in the efforts of the two bomber forces to destroy the sites from which V-weapons were to be fired rather than raid the factories where they were being made. The first raids against the construction sites and depots in France were made in November 1943 after the Central Interpretation Unit at Medmenham had identified the first V-1 bunkers. The campaign against the V-weapons was codenamed 'Crossbow', but the bombing operations were known as 'Noball'. The quantities of bomb tonnage over the course of the campaign, from early December 1943 to mid-September 1944, exceeded by a wide margin the total devoted to the transportation plan, a final tally of 118,000 tons of bombs, 86,000 of which were dropped between 12 June and 12 September 1944 on targets considerably smaller than the marshalling yards and viaducts targeted for D-Day. The first bombings in the winter of 1943–4 were thought to have set back the onset of the V-weapons campaign by six months, but after the first attacks the Germans abandoned the system of 'ski-jump' launch sites (so called after their shape) because of their visibility and vulnerability, but let the impression remain that work was still being done on them in order to attract the bombers.[136] Eventually most of the original sites were identified and destroyed, but the newly modified launch sites were hard to find or hit. The German campaign was held up chiefly because of technical problems in producing sufficient operational V-1s to be able to start the offensive any sooner.[137] After the first V-1s fell on London from the middle of June 1944 onwards, a renewed order went out to both bomber forces to try to stamp out the threat. From December 1943 to May 1944, 'Crossbow' targets had taken 12 per cent of the bombing effort, but between June and August 1944 the proportion was 33 per cent.[138] This represented a very large diversion of resources from any assistance that could be given to the Allied armies in France against targets that were almost immune to bomb attack. In April 1944 RE8 had explained to the Air Ministry that small sites protected by 20 feet of concrete had a low level of vulnerability.[139] In July Sinclair instructed Portal to give the 'Crossbow' sites a lower priority because 'they are hard to destroy and easy to repair'. When Eighth Air Force B-17s attacked 10 sites in July, they missed eight and dropped only four bombs on the remaining two.[140] Although Churchill had been keen for Bomber Command to try to blunt the V-weapon assault, the

Air Ministry recognized by July that any effects were likely to be ephemeral. An Air Intelligence report in July on the V-1 sites captured by the American army in Cherbourg showed that although they had been heavily bombed, the design of the sites made them almost impervious to bomb damage and easily repaired if a chance hit achieved anything.[141] The bombing continued until September, when most of the sites were captured by the advancing army, but both air forces recognized the limitation of using heavy bombers for what were in effect tactical targets.

The same limitations operated with the decision to use heavy bombers in support of Eisenhower's ground campaign in France. For almost three months, northern France was a battlefield. Like the German attack on France in 1940, or the Soviet Union in 1941, it proved just as difficult for the advancing Allied armies and air forces to avoid heavy damage to the towns, cities and civilians in their path. In northern Normandy, where the battle lasted longest and was at its most intense, 14,000 French civilians died, 57 per cent as a result of bombing. Heavy air raids began from the first morning, 6 June, after warning leaflets had been dropped at dawn encouraging the Normandy population to 'Leave for the Fields! You Haven't a Minute to Lose!' In Caen on 6 June around 600 were killed by an American air raid, another 200 the following day amidst the ruins of much of the city; on 7 June a raid by more than 1,000 Bomber Command aircraft against six small towns, including Vire, St Lô, Lisieux and Coutances, eradicated the urban areas almost entirely. In the first two days of the campaign, 3,000 French civilians were killed.[142] The village of Aunay-sur-Odon, bombed to stop the movement of German tanks a few days later, was literally erased from the map. Pictures taken after the raid showed a single church spire in an otherwise entirely level landscape. The French authorities counted 2,307 bombardments in June, 1,016 of them on the north coast provinces, most against railway targets. In July there were fewer raids, 1,195 in total, in August 1,121.[143] The great majority of the raids were tactical, carried out by the Allied Expeditionary Air Force, but on occasion the heavy bombers were asked to bring overwhelming firepower to bear. Two attacks on Caen, one on 7 July and a second on 18 July, were among the heaviest of the Overlord campaign. The raid on 7 July involved 467 bombers, dropping 2,276 tons on the northern outskirts of the town. There were few German defenders and the main effect of the raid, which left a moonscape on the approaches to Caen, was to force the British and Canadian troops to clear the roads before any further advance could be made.[144] The raid on 18 July by 942 bombers dropped an extraordinary 6,800 tons on the city and its eastern environs; the result did little to the German defenders, who had largely withdrawn to a defensive line south of Caen, nor to the population, 12,000 of whom eked out a precarious existence in caves outside the town at Fleury, but the raid once again left a ruined landscape which slowed down the advance of ground forces. By the end of the invasion a combination of bombing and shelling had left habitable housing for only 8,000 out of the 60,000 people who had lived there.[145]

The weight of attack that could now be employed by the bomber commands was out of all proportion to the nature of the ground threat and on balance did little to speed up the course of the campaign. The establishment of air superiority over the battlefield was assured by the thousands of fighters and fighter-bombers available to Leigh-Mallory to establish a protective air umbrella over the Allied armies. Occasionally the bluntness of the bombing weapon spilled over to impose friendly fire on Allied troops. On 24 July, on the eve of the American breakout into Brittany, codenamed Operation 'Cobra', hundreds of Eighth Air Force bombers were ordered to shatter the German defences in front of General Omar Bradley's armies. 'Ground grunted and heaved as the first cascade of bombs came down,' wrote Captain Chester Hanson in Bradley's war diary, 'horrible noise and the shuddering thunder that makes the sound of the bomb so different from the artillery.' It was followed by the sight of ambulances streaming to the front line to pick up the dead and injured from among the American troops hit by the bombardment, a total of 25 killed and 131 wounded. Among the victims was Lt. General Lesley McNair whose mangled body was thrown 60 feet by a bomb and could only be identified by the three stars on his collar.[146] More bombs dropped on American troops the following day, bringing the total dead to 101. Eisenhower decided not to use heavy bombers again to support the ground battle but to use them against targets he properly regarded as strategic, but Bradley once again called in heavy bombers to help unblock German opposition in Aachen in November 1944.[147] This time elaborate precautions were taken to ensure that the 2,400 American and British bombers used did not impose friendly fire on American forces. Large panels visible from the air were used as checkpoints in Allied lines to indicate clearly where the army was; a line of vertical radar beams was then set up by mobile units which could be distinguished by onboard radar in the approaching bombers; barrage balloons with special cerise markings flew at 1,500 feet in front of the American line, and anti-aircraft guns were set up to fire coloured flares at 2,000 feet below the bombers. Despite the most elaborate of precautions, two bomb batches still fell on American troops, but with only one casualty.[148] Aachen was turned into a wasteland.

The gulf separating means and ends in the application of heavy bombers to the campaign in France was no more evident than in the fate of two coastal towns which were obliterated by the Allied bomber commands. Both towns held stubborn German garrisons which refused to surrender even when all France had been liberated. The·Channel port of Le Havre, subject to 153 small attacks since 1940, was no stranger to bombardment. It was strategically important as a potential port for Allied supply as Eisenhower's armies moved rapidly eastwards towards Germany, but it was defended by a garrison of over 11,000 German troops commanded by Colonel Eberhard Wildermuth. Since Le Havre was heavily fortified and he was under orders to prevent the port falling to the enemy for as long as possible, he rejected a request to surrender on 3 September. Bomber Command was then ordered to bombard the city for a week before a ground assault could finally seize the port. A remarkable 9,631 tons of bombs were dropped and 82 per cent of the town was destroyed at a cost of at least 1,536 French civilians. The German commander refused to give up and a brief ground assault soon captured the port and the entire garrison. The post-raid analysis carried out by SHAEF concluded that the bombing had not done much to assist the eventual ground assault, a view that Harris shared.[149] Wildermuth cited artillery as the real source of the Allies' rapid success on the ground; bombing killed only a tiny handful of German soldiers.

The second port was Royan at the mouth of the River Gironde, where the garrison had also refused to surrender when the whole surrounding area had been liberated. The presence of German forces made it difficult for the Allies to use the neighbouring port of Bordeaux and in December 1944 SHAEF was requested by the local American army commander to lay on a heavy bombing to push the garrison to abandon the fight. On the night of 4–5 January 1945, 347 Lancasters dropped 1,576 tons, including 285 4,000-lb 'blockbusters'; around 85 per cent of the town was destroyed and 490 French civilians (and 47 German soldiers) were killed. Poor communication had failed to alert Harris to the fact that targets outside the town had in fact been requested, not the town itself, while the French authorities had insisted that the civilian population had already been evacuated, which was not true.[150] The raid achieved nothing. The German commander refused to surrender until two further attacks by the Eighth Air Force on 14 and 15 April, which dropped another 5,555 tons, destroying everything still standing. The two raids, one of 1,133 bombers, the second with 1,278, were the largest operations mounted against any target in France. The Germans surrendered three days later. A French journalist 'defied anyone to find even a single blade of grass'.[151]

The overall cost from bombing in French lives and property during the war was exceptionally high and it resulted in the main from using the overwhelming power of the bomber forces against modest targets that might more easily have been attacked by tactical air forces with greater accuracy. It was this lack of proportionality that attracted most criticism from French sources sympathetic to the Allies and anxious that German targets should be bombed. 'That which revolts the vast majority,' ran an intelligence report from December 1943, '*of whom a great number are members of the Resistance* is the *inaccuracy* of aim.'[152] The result of using large heavy-bomber forces in level flying from high altitude was to exact forms of damage not very different from the impact on German targets. The following table (Table 9.2) shows the overall cost of the bombing on France. The official figures presented here are lower than the figure of 67,000 for overall deaths regularly cited in the post-war literature, and the Passive Defence authorities regarded the initial statistics as a minimum. But although there are minor discrepancies in the figures published by different agencies in 1945, and a more general problem in classifying deaths caused by

Table 9.2 French Losses from Bombing, 1940–45

Year	Deaths	Injured	Buildings Destroyed	Buildings Damaged
1940	3,543	2,649	25,471	53,465
1941	1,357	1,670	3,265	9,740
1942	2,579	5,822	2,000	9,300
1943	7,446	13,779	12,050	23,300
1944	37,128	49,007	42,230	86,498
1945	1,548	692	300	800
Total	53,601	73,619	85,316	183,103

Source: BN, Bulletin d'Information de la Défense Passive, May 1945, 4.

bombing, tactical air raids or artillery fire in a battle zone, a figure between 53,000 and 54,000 dead is unlikely to be superseded by anything more precise.[153] The figure for 1940 includes deaths and destruction from the air inflicted by all air forces during the German invasion in May and June.

Why did the Allies use the bomber force in France, in the face of the political anxieties regularly expressed in London, with such apparent disregard for civilian losses? The bomber commanders were themselves unhappy with what was being asked of them. Spaatz considered the tactical air forces adequate for giving effective ground support. In notes for Eisenhower he argued that strategic bombers would not yield a sufficient strategic return if used for the invasion: 'The advantages gained by such use would be very small compared to the effort put forth.'[154] The Eighth Air Force commander, Jimmy Doolittle, told Eisenhower and Spaatz in August that the use of strategic bombers with insufficient training and planning time in support of ground operations was bound to produce errors in execution and admitted that 'the fighters have done a better job of supporting the Army than the bombers'.[155] The persistent use of the strategic forces has a number of explanations. For the Allied Supreme Command in Europe and the Combined Chiefs of Staff, bombing had evident advantages: it would speed up the invasion after years in which demands for the Second Front had failed to be met; it would help to bring the end of the war closer for democratic populations anxious that hostilities should end sooner rather than later; it would make victory in France more certain and less hazardous; and it would finally allow the Allies to cash in the very large investment already made in strategic bombing which had not yet delivered what had been promised from the Combined Bomber Offensive. The bomber commanders also bear some of the responsibility. By making repeated and often strident claims about the capacity of strategic bombing to make a decisive contribution to shortening the war, they invited the ground forces to exploit those claims in a campaign that was regarded as decisive for the war effort. In the end, the balance between operational and political calculation was bound to fall in favour of the anticipated military outcome. When Eaker asked Portal in 1943, before starting the heavy bombing of French targets, how to overcome political objections to French losses, Portal replied that the government 'have never shrunk from loss of civilian life where this can be shown to be an inevitable consequence of a considered and agreed plan'.[156]

EASTERN EUROPE: EVERYWHERE
BUT AUSCHWITZ

The first time the RAF was invited to bomb the camp at Auschwitz (Oświęcim) in Poland was in January 1941. At that time it was not the extermination and labour complex of Auschwitz-Birkenau, where more than 1 million European Jews were murdered between the spring of 1942 and the end of the war, but a camp for 20,000 Polish prisoners of war. The request came, according to General Sikorski's Polish Army headquarters in Britain, from the prisoners themselves, who would welcome a bombing raid that would allow them to escape en masse. Air Marshal Peirse, commander-in-chief of Bomber Command, replied that it was impossible. On clear nights every bomber had to be deployed against German industry. The German war economy, Peirse explained, was likely to experience a crisis in 1941. 'Sporadic attacks' against a target such as Auschwitz were unlikely to be accurate enough to do more than kill many of the prisoners.[157]

The next time the RAF was asked to bomb Auschwitz was in July 1944 when it was no longer a prisoner-of-war camp, but the centre for the mass murder of European Jews. The complex consisted of three main areas: an extermination camp at Auschwitz-Birkenau; a camp for forced labour selected from those deemed fit enough from among the arrivals; and an industrial complex at nearby Monowitz where the chemical giant I. G. Farben was constructing a plant to produce synthetic rubber and other war-related chemicals. On 7 July, following an interview with Chaim Weizmann, president of the Jewish Agency, Eden wrote to Sinclair asking whether it was possible to bomb the camp or the railtracks leading to it. Churchill was keen to pursue this, but Sinclair, like Peirse, was unsympathetic. He told Eden that interrupting rail traffic in France had proved difficult even with the full weight of Bomber Command behind it; to find and cut a single line far away in Poland was beyond the power of the bomber force. Sinclair doubted that bombing the camp or dropping arms to the prisoners 'would really help the victims'. He thought the American air forces might be in a better position to do it, and promised to discuss the issue with Spaatz, overall commander of American air forces in Europe.[158] Spaatz was sympathetic, but claimed that nothing could be done without better photographic intelligence of the camp itself. There was extensive reconnaissance material on the nearby Monowitz plant and other war-economic targets around Auschwitz, but although some photographs showed areas of the camp, the extermination centre had not been the object of a specific reconnaissance operation.[159] Unknown to Spaatz, the War Department in Washington had already been lobbied several times in the summer of 1944 to undertake bombing of the rail lines or the gas chambers but had deemed the operation to be 'impracticable'. On 14 August the Assistant Secretary of War, John McCloy, rejected the request (and did so again when lobbied in November).[160] Two weeks later the Foreign Office informed Sinclair that since the deportation of Hungarian Jews to Auschwitz-Birkenau appeared to have been halted, there was no longer any need to consider an operation to bomb it. On 1 September 1944 Spaatz was instructed to pursue the idea no further.[161]

There has been much academic argument over the question of whether an operation against the Birkenau extermination facility or the railway lines was feasible or not.[162] There is no doubt that had it been a priority target for the Allies, it certainly could have been bombed. At just the time that the Allies were considering the requests from the Jewish Agency to undertake the bombing, the United States Fifteenth Air Force began a series of raids on the I. G. Farben complex at Monowitz where the prisoners in the Auschwitz labour camp were marched to work every day. Auschwitz had been on the Mediterranean Allied Air Forces target list since at least December 1943 when plans were drawn up for attacks on German oil and chemical plants in eastern Europe.[163] The first raid on 20 August 1944 hit Monowitz accurately, a second on 13 September was hampered by enhanced German anti-air defences, the third and fourth attacks on 18 and 26 December did more damage to the plant, and it was finally abandoned in January 1945 as the Red Army drew near. The damage was not extensive and output of methanol (from one of the completed parts of the site) was reduced by only 12 per cent. The raids showed, however, that operations over Auschwitz were indeed feasible; only six aircraft were lost despite the strengthening of German defensive measures.[164]

The raids against Monowitz took place against the background of a second request for 'political' bombing. On 1 August 1944 the Polish Home Army began an armed rising against the German garrison in Warsaw. The Polish army in London requested help from the RAF in the form of military supplies dropped from low altitude over the city. Churchill was once again keen that something should be done.[165] The Operation 'Frantic' shuttle-bombing to bases in the Ukraine had been temporarily suspended at Soviet insistence, which ruled out supply missions by the Eighth Air Force. Although Portal and Slessor, Eaker's second-in-command in the Mediterranean, regarded the operations as 'not practicable' because of the distance and the prospect of high losses, it was decided that the pressure from the Poles and the expectation that the Red Army would soon capture Warsaw were sufficient grounds for undertaking limited operations.[166] The RAF 205 Group, based at Brindisi in southern Italy (considerably closer to Warsaw than bases in England), was ordered to begin night-time operations. An unofficial mission had already been flown on the night of 4–5 August to drop weapons to Polish partisans, but only six aircraft arrived at the target and four were shot down. On 8 August Moscow was informed that an airlift to the Poles was about to begin, which almost certainly confirmed the Soviet side in the decision not to allow further shuttle-bombing until mid-September, when Polish resistance was almost over.[167] On the night of 8–9 August three Polish aircrews successfully reached Warsaw without loss; a total of 19 missions were flown, the largest on 14–15 August when 12 out of the 27 aircraft despatched found Warsaw, for the loss of eight aircraft. Total losses were 35 bombers (19 per cent) out of 195 sorties, but substantial quantities of ammunition and weapons reached the Home Army in the areas of the city where they still held out.[168] In this case the operational conditions were similar to a putative attack on Auschwitz-Birkenau. The difference in the Allied response in the late summer of 1944 can perhaps best be explained in military terms, for the Poles were fighting against the common German enemy. Appeals to help with civilian victims, whether refugees or those slated for genocide, were regarded as outside the remit of Allied military forces, whatever the moral force of the argument. The PWE rejected a Jewish appeal in December 1943 to take action against the Romanians over the killing of Romanian Jews ('considering the constant spate of requests for warning or appeal from Jewish organisations'), but were happy to suggest bombs on Bucharest in March 1944 to speed up the surrender of Romania's armed forces and to help the approaching Russians.[169] In the end, whether bombing Auschwitz-Birkenau would have had any impact on the conduct of a genocide that had almost run its macabre course by August 1944 remains open to speculation.

The arguments about what was possible in the bombing of eastern Europe, and under what operational conditions, highlight the very different circumstances faced by Allied air forces when confronted with the challenges of distance and geography. For at least the first half of the war, targets in eastern and south-eastern Europe were difficult to reach from any bases the RAF might have in the Middle East or North Africa. Navigation problems were magnified for flights from desert airfields across inhospitable terrain with poor mapping and reconnaissance, while maintaining heavy bombers in the heat and dust of the Middle East, thousands of miles from the sophisticated maintenance and logistical system in Britain, was a Sisyphean task. From bases in England, however, most aircraft could not reach distant targets; with the advent of the Lancaster and the Mosquito it took time before serious raids could be mounted even against Berlin, and most of the flight was across the heavily defended areas of the Low Countries and Germany. A large-scale offensive against the Balkan states, Austria, Hungary and Poland became possible only once bases were available in Italy, from the autumn of 1943.

Some sense of how difficult raiding was to be against targets quite remote from the aerial battlefield in western Europe had already become evident when in 1940, and again in 1941, the RAF undertook preparations to bomb the Soviet oilfields in the Caucasus region in order to deny Germany and Italy vital supplies of fuel. The plans in 1940 were prompted first by the French High Command, which wanted to strike at Soviet oil not only to undermine the trade with the Axis states but also to create a possible political crisis for the Soviet Union among the Moslem peoples of southern Russia. French military leaders were much happier about bombing the Soviet Union than bombing Germany.[170] The British side agreed with the plan and drew up a detailed study in April 1940 for deploying 48 Blenheim light bombers from bases in Syria and Iraq, supported by 65 Glenn Martin bombers bought by the French from American production. RAF planners thought little of Soviet air and anti-aircraft defences, and like the French, hoped that a three-month attack on Batum, Baku and Grozny might lead sooner or later 'to the complete collapse of the war potential of the USSR', as well as disastrous repercussions for Germany.[171] Chamberlain's Cabinet thought the campaign too risky, and following the German attack on France on 10 May, the French abandoned the idea. But the RAF remained in a state of readiness to eliminate the entire Soviet oil industry in three months, assuming an average margin of error of 75 yards, a conclusion entirely at odds with all the bombing trials conducted in 1939 and 1940.[172] The plan was revived again in June 1941 in the knowledge that Germany was about to attack the Soviet Union. There were strong recommendations from the British Embassy in Cairo and the chiefs of staff to use two squadrons of Wellington bombers and two of Blenheims for a month of intensive attacks, not only to deny the oil to the Germans but 'to remind the Soviet of consequences of acceding to German demands'.[173] Planning was completed by August 1941, but once again operational and strategic reality prevented a campaign in which the means were manifestly inadequate for the military and political ends desired. When an impromptu attack was finally made on German oil supplies in Romania on 11 June 1942 by 13 B-24 Liberator bombers from the airbase at Fayid in Egypt, the result was described by the Middle East RAF headquarters as a fiasco. The aircraft flew singly and independently; not one reached the oilfield at Ploeşti but instead dropped their bombs wherever they could; three returning aircraft landed at Ankara airport, two at Aleppo in Syria, one at Mosul, two more at other desert airfields, and only four reached the planned return base at Habbaniya in Iraq. The unlucky thirteenth aircraft was reported missing.[174]

By the summer of 1943 these conditions had altered a great deal. Victory in North Africa in May 1943 opened the way for the invasion and occupation first of Sicily, then of the southern provinces of mainland Italy. Based in Algiers, the Mediterranean High Command, first under Eisenhower, then under the British general, Henry Maitland Wilson, began to consider at last a full air offensive, combining both political propaganda and bombs, against the Balkan region and more distant targets in central Europe. The North African Air Forces were transformed into the Mediterranean Allied Air Forces; the American Ninth Air Force (replaced in November by the Fifteenth) was based in southern Italy at Foggia, and the smaller RAF 205 Group at Brindisi. The political offensive mirrored the activity of the PWE and the RAF in western Europe and Germany. It was based on calculations about how populations in the occupied or satellite areas of eastern Europe might react to leaflet propaganda as well as occasional bombing to enhance political pressure. In the Mediterranean, the American Psychological Warfare Branch (PWB) oversaw the production and distribution of most of the Allied political effort in cooperation with officials from the PWE; how that worked in the Italian campaign has already been described. Out of the more than 1.5 billion leaflets produced at the PWB centre at Bari and dropped by air or fired in propaganda 'shells' whose paper contents burst over enemy lines, hundreds of millions were targeted at Albania, Greece, Hungary, Bulgaria, Romania, Czechoslovakia, and the Yugoslav territories, Serbia, Croatia and Slovenia.[175]

The United States demonstrated the same confident enthusiasm for political warfare as the British. 'History may well show,' wrote the Eighth Air Force assistant chief of staff, 'that no single factor has contributed more to the raising and sustaining of morale in the occupied countries.' The combined effect of the British and American leaflet campaigns, he continued, 'will shorten the war as a certainty'.[176] A pamphlet produced under Spaatz's signature to explain the value of airborne propaganda to American crews (who like RAF flyers preferred dropping bombs to paper) claimed that the millions of RAF leaflets had brought 'truth, hope and comfort' to the oppressed and sustained the will for sabotage and resistance. 'In occupied territory the spirit of rebellion is being fanned,' Spaatz continued. 'The output of the factories suffers as surely as if they had been struck by bombs.'[177] A sophisticated technology was developed to ensure that the leaflets fluttered down over a wide area. A single bomber could carry up to 2 million leaflets at a time. Two large canisters were installed in the bomb bay, each holding 60 bundles of approximately 16,000 leaflets bound by a cord fixed to a barometric device. On release from the aircraft each bundle tumbled down until the change in air pressure acted on the release mechanism, scattering the individual leaflets over a wide area. The system was not foolproof: sometimes the bundles opened prematurely, scattering the loads in the wrong place; sometimes they failed to open and whole bundles, each weighing around 55 lbs, fell dangerously on the target population.[178]

Both the American PWB and the British PWE understood that for eastern Europe the propaganda had to be carefully calibrated to match the circumstances of individual countries, some of which were satellite states of Germany, others the victims of invasion and occupation. For the satellites the propaganda had to suggest the option of abandoning the German alliance and helping the Allies. The leaflet 'Take a Decision' dropped in May 1944 on Hungary, Bulgaria, Romania and Finland had this object in mind. Occupied Czechoslovakia, on the other hand, had to be appealed to differently. Intelligence sources suggested that the Czechs felt abandoned by the Allies as they had been at Munich in September 1938, and the figures show that Czechoslovakia indeed received only a fraction of the leaflet drops made on other areas.[179] Above all, the political initiative had to be related to the possibility or probability of bombing, either as a threat or a promise. The Czech sources confirmed that workers were waiting for the bombing to start and would add sabotage to anything the bombs failed to destroy. For the satellite states, bombing was seen, like the case of Bulgaria, as a means to bring the war home to these distant and formerly immune peoples. In the summer of 1944 the Western Allies also had to take account of the onrush of the Red Army, which was by now poised to invade central and south-eastern Europe. The PWE assessment of bombing Bucharest, for example, pointed out that bombs might increase Romanian 'depression', but were unlikely to induce defection from the war as the Romanian Army struggled desperately to keep the Soviet invaders at bay. Bombs dropped on Hungary were regarded as more useful since they would remind the Hungarian government and population that they had to do more to sever their connection with Germany.[180] Even against satellite states, the political warfare officers recommended attacks only on evidently military targets so as to avoid alienating the populations that were to be liberated from German domination. Czech informers made it clear that as allies, the Czech people should not be subjected to area bombing, which would provoke 'serious resentment'.[181] The Yugoslav partisan armies welcomed precise raids on German targets, but not raids on the major cities. The propaganda made much of Allied claims for bombing accuracy against military targets but was occasionally let down by the translation. A leaflet destined for Axis Bulgaria in late 1943 had the English 'blockbuster bomb' (designed to destroy factories or military facilities) translated into Bulgarian as 'homewrecker'.[182]

These political imperatives were integrated as far as possible with the military planning directed at eastern Europe, although the promise of accuracy was as difficult to fulfil in this case as it had been in the west. For the Western Allies there was only one principal target in eastern Europe once the area came within effective bombing range. The oil-producing region around Ploești in Romania supplied around 3 million tons of oil annually to Germany and Italy out of a total production of 5–6 million tons. For Germany, Romanian exports in 1943 amounted to one-third of all German oil products.[183] Since oil was a major target for the Combined Bomber Offensive, the interruption of Romanian supplies assumed a high priority. The RAF had begun to explore the possibility of raiding Ploești in the spring of 1942 to aid the Soviet Union but the operation, at the limit of aircraft range, was regarded as impossible with current strengths. The Combined Chiefs of Staff at the Casablanca Conference in January 1943 called for the immediate bombing of the oilfield, but when Churchill asked Portal to consider the operation he was told that it was still too risky, not only because it would require flying over Turkish airspace to be feasible, but because it would have to be a single, heavy and demobilizing strike which current air strengths in the North African theatre could not promise.[184] Although Churchill was willing, as he told Eden, 'to put the screw very hard on Turkey' to modify its neutrality for the RAF, the attack on Ploeşti when it came was made by American air forces acting under pressure from the American Joint Chiefs to act quickly to block Axis oil supplies.[185] The British contribution to the opening raid was to supply good maps of the region and large-scale models of the refineries. Portal was keen to allocate three skilled Lancaster crews because he was not confident that American pilots would be able to navigate the 1,850-mile trip successfully, but in the end the raid launched on 1 August 1943 was made only by the B-24 aircraft of the recently constituted Ninth Air Force.[186]

The American operation was first codenamed 'Statesman' then changed in May to 'Soapsuds'. Churchill disliked the new choice – 'unworthy of those who would face the hazards' – and it was eventually christened, with Roosevelt's approval, 'Operation Tidalwave'.[187] The operation required a great deal of preparation. It was originally scheduled for 23 June 1943, but postponed not only because priority was given to air support for the invasion of Sicily in July 1943, but because the period of intelligence research and crew training took much longer than anticipated. For the American airmen involved the raid was a daunting prospect. When a British adviser appeared at the airbase at Benghazi from which the raid was to be mounted, he found the morale of the crew 'about as bad as it could possibly be': they told him that they lacked experience of the low-level bombing chosen to maximize the impact of the attack; that they had no previous experience of operations over such long distances; that the countries over which they had to fly were completely exotic, 'populated by cannibals' for all they knew. Rigorous training and better information on the value of the raid contributed to overcoming the worst fears, but there could be no disguising the fact that Ploeşti was one of the most heavily defended targets in Europe.[188] American intelligence on German defences was in general poor, because the target was remote from the main operational theatres. Instead of the 100 anti-aircraft guns identified, there proved to be well over 200; instead of a token force of fighter aircraft, there were more than 200 Me109, Me110 and Ju88 aircraft, as well as the Romanian and Bulgarian air forces along the line of attack. The defence of Ploeşti was under the command of Lt. General Alfred Gerstenberg, who was also the unofficial German 'protector' of Romania. He long expected an Allied attack and introduced regular exercises for the defences as well as establishing a line of radar stations and a corps of visual observers in the

Balkan region. Chemical-smoke battalions were ready to obscure the target, while two dummy sites were constructed north-west and east of the complex to distract any attacker.[189] This was as formidable a defence as any available in Germany itself. For the American crews it meant an operation that was likely to be more suicidal than any they would encounter in western Europe.

The raid on 1 August 1943 began early in the morning. Under the command of Brig. General Uzal Ent, 175 aircraft flew off on a course designed to take them to the north-west of Ploești, in order to avoid the guns and the barrage of 100 balloons. Over Romania the lead commander turned east at the wrong point, bringing most of the force close to Bucharest where the German defenders were put on full alert. The force turned north into the teeth of the anti-aircraft and fighter defences. Some small groups flew low into the oil complex and bombed designated targets from 500 feet, but most, on Ent's orders, bombed what they could and escaped. The planned return route was abandoned as aircraft damaged by anti-aircraft fire and harried by German fighters flew south in disarray. Only 88 returned to Benghazi; 11 landed in Cyprus, eight in Sicily, four on Malta, eight were interned at Turkish bases and two crashed into the sea. A total of 54 aircraft were lost, many in acts of extraordinary courage in low-level attacks against massed defences. Almost all those that returned had suffered damage. Two weeks later the survivors were sent on a further long-range mission against the Wiener-Neustadt aircraft plant in Austria, but on this occasion suffered only two losses against the lightest of resistance.[190]

The results of the Ploești raid fell short of the ambition to knock the complex out for months, but enough serious damage was done to reduce output substantially at three major refineries and to destroy two completely. Spare capacity and rapid repair nevertheless reduced the effects on German supplies of crude oil. The effect on the local population was to produce a sudden exodus into the surrounding countryside, but casualties were relatively low save for 84 women killed when one aircraft crashed onto their prison.[191] The oilfield was allowed an eight-month respite during which time the pre-raid levels of output were once again restored. Losses of 40 per cent of the force could not be sustained and the Allied air forces had other urgent priorities in Italy and southern Germany. At a conference on bombing strategy in Gibraltar in November 1943 between Spaatz, Eaker, Tedder and Doolittle, the main concern was coordinating attacks on German targets from England and Italy. It was agreed that Balkan capitals might make a good morale target, and

Sofia was bombed shortly afterwards, but oil in south-eastern Europe had for the moment disappeared as a priority.[192] Not until 17 March 1944 was Spaatz informed by Arnold that the Combined Chiefs of Staff favoured a renewed attack on Ploeşti when good weather permitted, but the changing strategic situation, with Soviet forces driving on south-eastern Europe, gave priority to bombing communications around Bucharest rather than oil and the target was again postponed.[193] The change back to oil came later after Spaatz lost his argument with Portal over the best strategy for the pre-Normandy bombing and had to accept the Transportation Plan. In order to get at oil surreptitiously he allowed Eaker to send aircraft not only against the communications targets around Bucharest, but to attack once again the Romanian oilfield.

The result was a devastating series of 24 raids against Ploeşti between 5 April and 19 August 1944 under the command of Maj. General Nathan Twining. Twenty of the raids were undertaken by the Fifteenth Air Force, four at night by RAF 205 Group. Between them they dropped 13,863 tons of bombs, all but 577 from American aircraft. German and Romanian defences had been strengthened since the first raid. Alongside 34 heavy and 16 light anti-aircraft batteries and 7 searchlight batteries, there were between 200 and 250 aircraft.[194] By the close of the offensive there were 278 heavy and 280 light guns, including the new heavy-calibre 10.5 and 12.8 cm, supported by 1,900 smoke generators. The oilfield was designated a German 'stronghold' and Gerstenberg was appointed by the German High Command as 'German Commandant of the Romanian Oil Region'.[195] But this time the American bombers flew at high altitude, protected by large numbers of long-range P-38 and P-51 fighters. As a result the contest proved more one-sided than the raid in August 1943. Axis air forces managed to mount 182 sorties against the first raid, on 5 April, when 13 out of 200 bombers were lost. But by July the sortie rate had fallen to an average of 53 against the five raids that month. On the final raid, on 19 August, there was no fighter opposition.[196] Total losses were 230 American bombers, many to anti-aircraft fire. Destruction of the refineries was as complete as it could be, with half a million tons of oil destroyed, and more sunk through the successful mining operations on the Danube carried out mainly at night by RAF 205 Group. Some 1,400 mines were dropped and traffic on the Danube was reduced by two-thirds, though 15 per cent of the RAF force was lost in raids carried out dangerously at between 100 and 200 feet above the river.[197]

In a final gesture, on the eve of the Soviet entry into Romania, Gerstenberg gathered together any German troops he could find together with the oilfield anti-aircraft division in a bid to seize Bucharest (where the young King Michael had overthrown the Antonescu government) and bring the capital under German control. To support the coup, the German Air Force mounted a heavy raid on the centre of Bucharest on 24 August, destroying some of the administrative centre around the royal palace. The population, according to the German ambassador, was taken completely by surprise, perplexed by the sudden change from German ally to German enemy. But the German coup was stifled by the Romanian Army and the German presence replaced by a Soviet one.[198] In September 1944 Eaker was given permission by the authorities in Moscow to visit Romania, which had been occupied by Soviet forces on 30 August. He found the devastation at Ploeşti worse than any photo-reconnaissance image he had seen. The information Eaker was given showed that refining capacity had been reduced by 90 per cent. By the last attack on 19 August, remaining German personnel were only able to transport an estimated 2–4 per cent of Romanian capacity. He found his reception cordial and the Red Army commanders astonished at what high-level bombing could achieve. The Romanian people, Eaker reported to Washington, 'look upon us as liberators'.[199]

In truth the bombing of Romania did not liberate the population but contributed to the collapse of German resistance and the onset of half a century of Soviet domination. Whatever the political ambitions to intimidate the Balkan satellites into surrender or to boost the morale of Czechs and Yugoslavs, the pattern of bombing across eastern Europe was to a great extent governed by the military interest of the Allies in weakening German military resistance to the advancing Red Army. The priority given to communications and oil during the course of the summer of 1944 matched the priorities agreed for the bombing of Germany from English bases, and brought a great many more locations in Czechoslovakia, Poland and the Balkans onto the list of key targets assigned to the MAAF. The strategic commitment to attacking German communications in the region was made in April 1944 when it was realized how successful the Soviet advance had been during the winter months.[200] The MAAF drew up a survey at the end of April 1944 to see what could be done in 'giving direct aid to the Russian army', first by cutting German supplies then by interrupting any German withdrawal in the event of a Russian breakthrough.[201] In May, Portal instructed Spaatz to give top priority to bombing communications in Romania and Hungary and to treat the whole European transport system 'as one' when undermining German mobility.[202] Eighteen marshalling yards were singled out for attack, with high priority given to the yards at Bucharest where the Romanian authorities told Eaker later that a Fifteenth Air Force raid had killed 12,000 people, 6,000 of them refugees sitting in trains on the track in the belief that the air-raid siren was only a test. The raid was indeed a heavy one, hitting part of the residential area of the city, but official figures showed only 231 killed but 1,567 buildings destroyed or damaged.[203] From June 1944 oil was finally given a top priority and oil sites in Czechoslovakia and Poland were added to the list of potential targets throughout the region.[204] Right to the end politics played a part in bombing calculations. Strategic attacks against targets in Germany, Austria and Hungary could be undertaken either by visual or by blind-bombing technique against any military target defined in the broadest sense, including 'targets of opportunity'. Over Czech and Polish territory crews were only permitted to bomb the designated military target visually or in exceptional cases by blind-bombing, but no opportunity targets were permitted, to minimize the risk of casualties amongst allied populations.[205]

The most urgent need was to devise a way of ensuring that American and British aircraft did not accidentally bomb or strafe the advancing Soviet lines. In April 1944 a bomb line was agreed with the Soviet side in south-eastern Europe from Constanza, on the Romanian coast, through Bucharest, Ploeşti and Budapest. Only the last three could be the object of bomb attack, and American airmen were warned to learn the silhouettes and markings of Soviet aircraft.[206] The Soviet forces continued to inform their allies of the changing front line through the Allied missions in Moscow, though the MAAF had also posted representatives informally at the headquarters of the Soviet army group in the Balkans to try to minimize any hazard. A zone of 40 miles in front of the advancing Red Army was agreed as the limit for British and American bomber operations, but information about where the line was had to come through a cumbersome process of consultation in the Soviet capital. As the Allied air forces converged from east and west, the danger of inadvertent bombing increased. On 7 November 1944 a force of 27 P-38 'Lightnings' strafed and bombed a Soviet column in Yugoslavia 50 miles behind the Soviet front line, killing the commander and five others. Three of the nine Soviet fighters sent to protect the column were shot down.[207] Stalin's military headquarters made a strong protest and suggested a bomb line running from Stettin on the Baltic Coast down through Vienna to Zagreb and Sarajevo in Yugoslavia, leaving many designated oil and transport targets out of bounds to Western air forces. The Combined Chiefs of Staff refused to accept a bomb line further north than the Danube, but offered to set up a proper liaison organization with advancing Soviet armies to avoid further mishaps. When Moscow rejected the idea of any collaboration on the ground, Spaatz and Eaker worked out their own bomb line and communicated it to Moscow, sealing Dresden's fate a few weeks later.[208] The Soviet desire to reduce the bombing in eastern Europe was not disinterested, since by that stage of the war Moscow was more concerned to capture resources, equipment and plant intact rather than watch the strategic air forces obliterate them shortly before they fell into the Soviet sphere. After the war, the formal Communist line was to argue that bombing in the teeth of the Red Army advance had been carried out by the agents of capitalist imperialism to weaken the future socialist economy.

Unlike the situation in the western zones of Germany and Austria, it proved impossible for American or British intelligence teams to survey systematically the damage bombing had done to the industrial and infrastructure targets in eastern Europe, or to establish how effective the political offensive against the satellite and occupied populations had been. An American Military Mission arrived in Sofia in November 1944, but the Red Army command proved uncooperative. Eaker's visit to Ploeşti in September 1944 was the closest that Allied air commanders got to assessment of the damage, and his judgement that the offensive was 'a perfect example of what bombing can do to industry' is supported by the German figures on oil supply.[209] By the end of the war relations between the Allies were already cooling and Stalin was unwilling to allow Western intelligence officers access to the bomb sites in the Soviet-controlled regions of Europe. In July 1945 some of the USSBS team arrived in Berlin where amidst the chaos they tracked down Speer's chief economist, Rolf Wagenführ, who was already working for the Russian occupiers. An American team broke into his house in Soviet East Berlin, dragged him out of bed and bundled him onto an aeroplane to the American zone where he gave advice on German statistics for two weeks before being sent back. A key was also found to the German Air Ministry document safe where additional information was discovered; a discreet foray into the Soviet zone secured more German papers.[210] But all this was little substitute for ground-level reconnaissance of the targets bombed in Czechoslovakia, Poland and the Balkan states. Assessment of whether bombing had delivered the political dividend in

encouraging Axis populations to abandon the link with Germany was
open to speculation. In Bulgaria, Romania and Slovakia the political
scene was dominated by the imminent arrival of the Red Army. The
resentment and anxiety provoked by sporadic bombing of civilian areas,
evident from intelligence sources, paled into insignificance at the prospect of a Soviet Empire.[211] This was not the political outcome the West
had wished for when the air forces were at last in the position to rain
down bombs and leaflets on the distant East.

ROTTERDAM ONCE AGAIN

The situation for the smaller states in the German New Order on the
northern fringes of Europe – Belgium, The Netherlands, Denmark and
Norway – differed from the fate of France and of eastern Europe. In
both these latter cases invasion displaced the German occupier well
before the final end of the war in Europe. Belgium was finally fully liberated by November 1944, but not before heavy bombing by the Allies
and V-weapon attack by the German side had inflicted wide destruction
and casualties. The Netherlands, Denmark and Norway remained under
German occupation until the end of the war. A raid by British bombers
which hit residential districts of The Hague on 3 March 1945, killing
more than 500 people, occurred just weeks before liberation.[212] Over
the course of the war the enthusiasm relayed to the Allies by Dutch,
Belgian or Norwegian resisters about bombing German targets became
tempered by growing resentment at the cost in lives and livelihoods
imposed on those caught in the crossfire of war.

There was also an important political difference in the case of Norway, The Netherlands and Belgium. Each had a government-in-exile in
London, with a miniature apparatus of state. Unlike any other bombed
state, the exile governments could represent directly to the British
government their views on bombing policy and their objection to or
approval of its conduct. This in turn placed considerable pressure on the
RAF, and later the United States air forces, to ensure that the guidelines
governing the bombing of targets in the region clearly expressed its limits. Damage to civilian targets and civilian deaths had to be explained or
apologized for unlike raiding against most other targets in Europe. This
was even more the case when bombs intended for a German destination
instead fell inadvertently on Dutch or Belgian cities. Both states lay on
the flight paths to German targets for the whole war period. The Dutch

town of Groningen was bombed by mistake on 26 July 1940 and two people were killed; it was bombed again in error when the German port of Emden was shrouded in fog on the night of 26–27 September 1941 and this time six people died.[213] Maastricht was bombed by mistake for Aachen in February 1942, prompting Dutch protests that the RAF used trainee crews for nearer and easier targets, as they did, making mischance more likely. Raids deliberately targeted against Dutch cities provoked even higher casualties. Operations against targets in Rotterdam in October 1941 and January 1942 cost 177 Dutch lives; a raid in October 1942 on Geelen and one two months later on the Philips electrical works at Eindhoven killed a further 221.[214] Although the British Foreign Office believed that the Dutch took the robust view that 'war is war', Eden remained keen to ensure that proper guidelines were drawn up and crews instructed in their observance.[215] Belgian and Dutch targets were governed by the same rules drawn up in October 1942 for bombing occupied France, with the difference that attacks on trains by night could only take place between the hours of 11 o'clock in the evening and 4 o'clock in the morning rather than throughout the hours of darkness. Military targets had to be identified and if the prospect of a 'large error' occurred that was likely to lead to civilian casualties, the operation was supposed to be aborted.[216]

The systematic bombing of military and industrial targets in the Low Countries only began in 1943 when the Eighth Air Force used its heavy and medium bombers for attacks on targets near enough for fighter protection so that novice crews could be initiated into operational practice with fewer immediate risks, the very policy condemned by the Dutch when bombing started in 1941. The result was an immediate disaster. A daylight raid on Rotterdam on 31 March 1943 cost an estimated 400 lives; an attack that was supposed to hit the German ERLA aircraft plant near Antwerp instead devastated the town of Mortsel, killing 926 Belgians, including 209 children in four schools hit by the bombs. The bombing of Mortsel resulted in the worst casualties of the war from a single raid on the Low Countries. No warning leaflets had been dropped and the town was crowded with people. In addition to the dead, a further 1,342 were injured, 587 seriously, while 3,424 houses were damaged or destroyed. In the ERLA works 222 workers were killed.[217] Although heavy damage was done to the aircraft plant, the bombs were strewn over a wide residential area. The Eighth Air Force post-raid assessment showed that only 78 out of 383 bombs dropped came within 2,000 feet (600 metres) of the target.[218] For the residents of the town the raid was a shocking realization of the horrors of aerial war. 'I heard the screams of dying schoolchildren,' recalled one witness. 'I heard the grief-stricken cries of desperate mothers and fathers, searching in the ruins for their beloved children . . . I saw fires, heaps of ruins and people wringing their hands.'[219] A Foreign Office official wrote to the PWE a few days later describing the raid as 'catastrophic'; the 'bad shooting' of the Eighth Air Force, he complained, had done serious damage to the reputation of Allied air forces in a country which had hitherto welcomed the idea of bombs on German targets.[220]

The poor record of American bombing soon provoked a wider crisis. Eaker was first asked by the Air Ministry to take special care in bombing centres where civilians were likely to be hurt, then told to suspend bombing in occupied areas altogether pending a decision about which specific targets should be allowed. Despite protests from Washington, a list was agreed between the two air forces and Eaker and Harris were asked to avoid using freshmen crews against targets in major cities. The 20 agreed targets included only one in The Netherlands and five in Belgium. Bomber Command agreed to use only reliable and experienced crews, but Eaker insisted on the continued right of the American bomber force to use novices.[221] No sooner was the list agreed when the new Pointblank directive, drawn up for the Combined Bomber Offensive, apparently reversed the decision by listing targets in densely populated areas of occupied Europe as part of the overall plan. Eaker at once asked whether he was now free to bomb what he liked, but the issue could only be resolved at the highest level. Eden worried that civilian casualties in Belgium and The Netherlands would deeply affect 'the morale and spirit' of the local population and asked that radio broadcasts and leaflets should notify the people of impending bombing, but only after agreement had been reached with the Dutch and Belgian governments in London.[222] Leaflets were drafted warning the population that it would be dangerous to work in any factories assembling aircraft, locomotives, submarines and vehicles, or any one of their component parts. On 25 June 1943 the Belgian government-in-exile agreed to allow the new targets to be bombed once warning had been given; the Dutch government followed suit on 15 July but only after making it clear that they would only tolerate operations conducted in such a way 'as to minimize the danger to the civilian population'.[223]

Once again the raiding habit of flying at high altitude against targets which even when visible could not be hit with sufficient accuracy broke the pledge to bomb with greater discretion. The Eighth Air Force began

operations with B-17 'Flying Fortresses' against Dutch targets just two
days after receiving approval from the Dutch government. The target
chosen was the Fokker aircraft plant in Amsterdam, first bombed by the
RAF in 1940 with little effect.[224] The American operation on 17 July
killed 185 people and missed the factory. One bomb hit the church of
St Rita, filled with 500 schoolchildren who were singing an 'Ave Maria'
to ward off danger after the siren sounded. Eleven were killed in the
church; another 29 died when a bomb hit a doctor's waiting room.
Around 130 buildings were destroyed.[225] The Dutch government-in-exile
immediately protested and Eaker was asked to explain how he was
going to avoid a repetition. The Eighth Air Force switched temporarily
from using B-17s to using the medium twin-engine Glen Martin
'Marauder' B-26 bombers for attacks on Dutch and Belgian targets
from lower altitude. On their second raid, against a Dutch power station at Ijmuiden, all 11 B-26s were shot down.[226] Over the months that
followed the B-26s were instructed to fly higher and casualties on the
ground mounted again. The bombing of Ghent on 4 September
1943 resulted in 111 dead, that of Brussels on 7 September using B-17s
caused a further 327 deaths.[227] An American raid on Enschede on
10 October, again using B-17s, killed 150. The damage to the German
war effort was limited. The Fokker works completed a programme
of dispersal and decentralization into 43 smaller locations scattered
around the Amsterdam region.[228] For Dutch workers and producers, as
in Belgium and France, the choice of refusing to work for the German
military was to run the risk that both the machinery and the workers
would be transferred to Germany. By 1944 over 40,000 workers had
been sent from Rotterdam to work in the Reich; repeated raids, which
killed a total of 748 people in the city during the war, encouraged the
German occupiers to move workers to industry in Germany, where
there was effective protection and the means to compel compliance.[229]

   The inclusion of Dutch and Belgian firms in the Pointblank plan
came about as a result of the contribution made by their industries to
German aircraft and submarine production, as well as the supply of
machinery and steel. There were no complete aircraft produced in Belgium, although hundreds of small firms supplied components; in The
Netherlands, however, 414 aircraft were built in 1943 and 442 in 1944,
while Dutch shipbuilders supplied an important source of additional
capacity for the submarine industry and for the production of smaller
naval vessels.[230] By the end of 1943 around 75,000 Belgian and
109,000 Dutch workers were employed on German arms contracts.[231]

The transfer of German production to the occupied territories gave the occupiers sufficient reason to provide limited protection from air attack. Anti-aircraft guns and fighters stationed in the Low Countries formed, as in France, part of the air-defence rampart around the European fortress, which in The Netherlands included 10 squadrons of night-fighters by 1944 and 74 sites for radar and electronic warfare.[232] Regiments of German fire-protection police were also stationed in the Low Countries to supplement the efforts of the local population organized, in the Dutch case, in an Air Protection Service (*Luchtbeschermingsdienst*) first set up in April 1936 and organized by urban district, street and housing block. The attitude of the population to the raiding was complex since many Allied aircraft crashed in the Low Countries, and in many cases surviving crew were helped by the local population or benefited from escape networks. The local press generally condemned the raids with high civilian casualties, although in no occupied territory was the press free from German controls or from the numerous German communiqués on terror bombing they were given. An article in the *Haagische Courant* on a bombing attack with 22 dead carried the headline 'That's It: Murder' and ended with the question 'Is that not terroristic?' Another article following the bombing of Rotterdam on 29 January 1942 carried the headline 'Bloody Work of the English Air Pirates!'[233] British intelligence from Belgium and The Netherlands, however, only suggested that the barometer of popular support for bombing fluctuated as it did in France with the perceived accuracy or inaccuracy of a raid. There was, however, little sign of open resistance as there had been in the early years of war. A report sent to the PWE in November 1943 observed that the people 'are just weak and passive'.[234]

The most intensive period of bombing came in 1944 with the preparations for the Normandy invasion and the 'Crossbow' raids against sites intended for the V-1 and V-2 missiles. Most of the raids were small tactical raids against rail and air targets carried out by medium bombers and fighter-bombers. But as Belgium and The Netherlands became involuntary parts of the vast aerial battlefield in north-western Europe, so the pace of destruction and loss of life quickened. There descended on both populations a rain of bombs and leaflets, the second designed to explain the liberating effects of the first. In April and May 1944 the Eighth Air Force undertook 1,111 sorties against German airbases in the two countries, and in May 759 sorties against marshalling yards, losing only 20 aircraft in the process.[235] The preparatory raids by heavy bombers involved some of the highest casualties of the war. In Belgium

252 were killed in Kortrijk on 26 March and 428 in Ghent on 10 April. The peak in Belgium came between 10 and 12 May, when more than 1,500 died, culminating in a raid on Leuven in which 246 were killed. The 'Overlord' preparations cost Belgium a total of 2,180 civilian dead.[236] The Netherlands was bombed less heavily during the late spring, but on 22 February 1944 it had suffered the severest raid of the war when the city centre of Nijmegen was hit by a group of B-24 bombers returning from an aborted mission over Germany. The aircrew aimed for a marshalling yard on the edge of the town, still believing that they were over German territory. Instead the lead bombardier misjudged the speed, dropping bombs in the crowded city centre, followed by the rest of the combat box. The estimated 800 dead were caught in the open after the all-clear had been given a few minutes before the bombs began to fall. Some 1,270 buildings were destroyed or badly damaged. On this occasion the Dutch government, not fully aware of the results of the raid, lodged no protest.[237] Over the following three months more than 50 million leaflets were dropped on Belgium, 55 million on the Netherlands, preparing both populations for their liberation but including a leaflet apologizing for the bombing of Nijmegen and regretting that under the circumstances of modern air war 'sometimes harm and grief was caused to our friends'.[238]

During the period when the noose was tightened around the German New Order, little attention was given to conditions in Scandinavia. Denmark, like the Low Countries, was astride the bombing runs to targets in Germany and became the inadvertent target from occasional errors of navigation as well as the site of numerous Allied aircraft that either crashed or were forced to land. Most of the raiding against German naval targets and airfields was carried out by aircraft of Coastal Command until the end of 1941, when Bomber Command Blenheims and Mosquitos were detailed to attack land targets, while Coastal Command concentrated on targets at sea. The German occupiers collaborated with the Danish civil defence organization, *Statens Civile Luftvaern*, in observing incoming aircraft. A large number of light anti-aircraft guns protected military installations and when the Kammhuber Line was extended into Denmark to give better protection against RAF raids in 1941, squadrons of German night-fighters were also based at Danish airfields.[239] There were almost no strategic Allied air attacks on Denmark. Most bombs were jettisoned or dropped in error, a total of 3,269 high explosive and 22,298 incendiaries counted by Danish civil defence. The only planned attack on an industrial target took place on

27 January 1943 when eight Mosquitos attacked the Burmeister &
Wain Diesel Engine factory in Copenhagen. Some damage was done,
and a sugar plant was set on fire. The raid resulted from PWE pressure
to undertake an attack on at least one industrial target in each occupied
state to discourage collaboration and to reinforce local morale. In the
Danish case the raid proved a success: there were few casualties, and in
the aftermath Danes took to wearing RAF colours as a mark of sympathy with a distant ally. The only raid by the Eighth Air Force was
against Esbjerg airfield on the west coast of Jutland on 27 August 1944,
bombed as a target of opportunity following an aborted raid on Berlin.
Over the whole course of the war 307 Danes were killed as a result of
all Allied air activity and 788 injured.[240]

Operations against Norway were also linked closely to the air-sea
war, but Norway differed from Denmark because there were important
industrial and raw-material resources which the Germans exploited
throughout the occupation, particularly aluminium production and the
development of 'heavy water' for the German nuclear research programme. Both were attacked by the Eighth Air Force, the aluminium
plant at Herøya on 24 July 1943, the Norsk Hydro plant on 16 November. Spaatz was pleased with the result and thought 'it was heartening to
the Norwegians'.[241] Far from being heartened, the Norwegian government complained that the destruction of the Norsk Hydro plant, which
produced a large quantity of Scandinavia's much-needed fertilizer, had
provoked 'bewilderment and dismay' among the Norwegian population
as they contemplated declining food output. The small 'heavy water'
plant had been successfully sabotaged by the Norwegian Resistance
some months before. The Norwegian Foreign Minister, Trygve Lie,
asked the Allies to agree a means of collaborating on the choice of targets to avoid further mishaps. It took almost a year of argument before
an agreed list was drawn up. British air marshals, Lie complained, were
a law unto themselves.[242] When the Air Ministry presented a list of
seven targets they would like to bomb, the Norwegian High Command
responded that some were wrong, some had ceased operating, and
others were essential to Norway's economy when the war was over.[243] A
second list was worked out with Norwegian advice and finally agreed
on 2 November 1944. But only four days before that, Bomber Command had tried to hit the submarine pens at Bergen in poor weather.
The bombs struck the town centre, killing 52 civilians and burning
down Europe's oldest theatre. The Norwegian government again

warned the Foreign Office that raids without an evident military purpose merely alienated a potentially friendly population. Though on the agreed list, Bergen had been attacked by 47 Lancasters, against instructions, through almost complete cloud cover.[244]

For Norway and Denmark the price of remaining occupied was substantially lower than the price paid by Belgium and The Netherlands as they became the focus of the ground campaign from the autumn of 1944. As was the case in France, operational requirements soon came to replace political calculations when deciding on targets to attack. Belgium was caught in between the fighting powers as Allied armies occupied Belgian territory in September 1944. From sites in western Germany, the V-weapons were turned against Allied forces in Antwerp and the surrounding territory, while a few were launched against Paris. The first V-2 rocket fell on 7 October in Brasschaat on the outskirts of Antwerp, the first V-1 flying bomb on 21 October. The last V-1 struck on 28 March 1945. Around 12,000 V-1s were launched at Belgian targets, and 1,600 V-2s.[245] The port of Antwerp suffered most. The worst incident occurred on 16 December when a V-2 fell on the Rex Cinema, killing 271 Belgians and an estimated 300 soldiers.[246] Late in 1944 a British civil defence Mobile Column was sent to Belgium at the request of Montgomery's 21st Army Group, complete with canteens, ambulances and fire units; three British rescue instructors were sent to Brussels, Antwerp and Eindhoven to train soldiers for emergency work after a rocket strike.[247] In November 1944 the American Brig. General C. H. Armstrong was appointed commander of Flying Bomb Command Antwerp X, and three belts of anti-aircraft guns were set up in a ring around the city to shoot down the flying bombs. RAF Fighter Command set up a Continental Crossbow Forward Unit in December 1944 to add fighter interception of the flying bombs to the effects of anti-aircraft fire. By February almost three-quarters of the V-1s were destroyed before they hit the city, a total of 7,412 over the course of the campaign. Only 73 fell in the dock area of Antwerp and only 101 on the built-up area. The effect on the flow of Allied supplies through the port was described in the official account of the campaign as 'negligible'.[248] Against the V-2 rocket, however, there was no defence; the Belgian population became once again hostage to their geographical location and suffered a heavy toll. In total 6,500 were killed and 22,500 injured in the last flurry of bombardment from the air, almost exactly the same number of casualties exacted by the V-weapon attacks on England. This final German aerial assault greatly increased the overall Belgian casualties from air bombardment during the war. An estimated total of 18,000 Belgians were killed, one-third from German operations.[249]

Since The Netherlands was used as a *base* for firing V-weapons, the threat of Allied bombing hung over the Dutch population until almost the end of the war. The battle for Arnhem in September 1944 brought further heavy raids against German military targets by both the Eighth Air Force and Bomber Command. The continuous bombardment of London by V-2 rockets from sites in the Netherlands finally prompted a decision to try to neutralize the threat by bombing, despite their proximity to residential areas. On 3 March 1945 RAF bombers of the Second Tactical Air Force flew from bases in Belgium to bomb a V-2 site in a large park in the north of The Hague. The weather was poor – cloudy and with a strong wind – and the briefing officer had confused the map coordinates, instructing the force to bomb more than a kilometre away from the intended target. The 60 B-25 Mitchell and A-20 Boston/ Havoc aircraft dropped 67 tons of bombs on a residential area of the Dutch capital, killing an estimated 520 and rendering 12,000 homeless. A stream of up to 50,000 refugees fled from the area, some of them, one eyewitness wrote, still in their pyjamas: 'a long procession of people and children crying ... some were all white from lying under the ruins. Others bled from a variety of injuries, which were half-bandaged or not covered at all ... More and yet more.'[250] Over the course of the war an estimated total of between 8,000 and 10,000 Dutch deaths came from bombing, around one-tenth of them caused by German raids.[251]

The bombing, so close to the end of the war, provoked a furious response from the Dutch government in London and strong criticism from Churchill. A broadcast apology was made later in the month, promising a full inquiry, but nothing was relayed to the Dutch authorities, who repeated the request in June 1945 for an explanation.[252] The Air Ministry told the Foreign Office at the end of June that the internal investigation had discovered the error in plotting the coordinates for the raid and had court-martialled the officer responsible. There was, however, little sense of contrition. The operation, claimed the Ministry, was a difficult one: 'the extent of the disaster must to some extent be set down to the mischances of war'.[253] Six months later a Dutch woman wrote to King George VI asking him to pay compensation for the total loss of her house and possessions in the 3 March raid. The letter summed up the ambivalence felt by the liberated peoples about being bombed into freedom:

I humbly come to you, first to express my great gratitude for all you, the English Government and the English people have done to deliver us from those awful huns. Second to ask you for help. On March 3 my house (home) with all that was therein, was bombed and nothing could be saved ... And now after nearly ten months, I sit here as poor and forlorn as on March 3 ... It may seem rather impudent from me, to ask you for help, but I know you are righteous and honest, above all, and that in no way you will have a widow been left in solicitude [sic] and affliction, where there is still a debt for the RAF to be redeemed.[254]

The Foreign Office contacted the Air Ministry for confirmation that nothing could be done for what was clearly 'a hazard of war'. The Ministry replied that nothing should be done: 'If we started paying for this kind of loss there would be no end to our liability.'[255]

In all the bombing of New Order Europe a balance was supposed to be struck between political calculation and military imperatives, since the peoples to be bombed were allies or potential allies. The cautious bombing of the first two years of war reflected a balance in favour of political restraint. In some cases bombing was used as a 'calling card', to remind populations under German domination not to collaborate or to encourage confidence in eventual liberation. In some cases the resistance movements called for bombing because they accepted the airmen's claims about its accuracy and power. However, by the spring of 1942 and on to the end of the war, the pendulum swung slowly in favour of military necessity, while European resisters became disillusioned about what bombing might achieve. In June 1943 Sinclair asked Eden to reconsider the principle that causing casualties to non-German civilians was a sufficient ground for restraint. Eden had a politician's instinct that killing Allied civilians was the wrong course but his reply to Sinclair symbolized the shift in priorities: 'if the new bombing plan is strategically necessary, I shall not of course stand in its way'.[256] American airmen were in general less affected by political calculation, partly because the State Department was geographically remote, partly because Americans were outsiders in the European theatre, less aware of the political realities they faced. As the Western war entered Europe, bombing became more widespread and its effects usually indiscriminate. By 1944 Allied commanders were increasingly 'bomb happy', summoning bombing whenever there was a problem to solve. This produced dangerous paradoxes for the peoples of the New Order: the closer to victory and liberation, the more deadly became the bombing; as the bombing intensified, so German anti-aircraft resources were spread ever more thinly around the perimeter of the German empire, exposing the subject peoples more fully to the rigours of bombardment. The occupied states had their own civil defence organizations, but they were in general less well resourced than in Britain or Germany. This would have mattered less if the bombing of military objectives had been as accurate as the Allies claimed (and on occasion achieved). The bombing of Brest, Le Havre, Caen, Mortsel, The Hague, Bucharest and a dozen or more other cities exposed the hollowness of any claim to operational precision. Bombing was a blunt instrument as the Allies knew full well, but its bluntness was more evident and more awkward when the bombs fell outside Germany.

PART THREE

'The Greatest Miscalculation'?

10

The Balance Sheet of Bombing

Reflecting on his time as an economist mobilized to help prepare the United States Strategic Bombing Survey in 1945, J. K. Galbraith explained how shocked he and his colleagues were to discover that the German economy had not suffered the severe damage the whole world had been led to expect. Instead, the raw German statistics showed that war output grew dramatically under the pressure of Germany's many military commitments, even while the bombing became heavier and more damaging. The economists were forced to conclude, as Galbraith later wrote, that 'strategic bombing had not won the war'. On the most favourable account it had simply eased the path of the ground troops who did. 'We were beginning to see that we were encountering,' he wrote in his memoirs, 'one of the greatest, perhaps the greatest miscalculation of the war.'[1]

Whatever the merits of Galbraith's judgement, the bombing offensives in the Second World War were all relative failures in their own terms. Before 1939, bombing wars were popularly expected to be short and sharp and probably decisive. The major offensives conducted by Germany, Britain and the United States were instead long drawn-out affairs, wars of attrition with high losses of men and machines, with no clear-cut end and a wide gap between ambition and outcome, a Western Front of the air. The more minor operations conducted by the German Air Force in the Soviet Union or the Italian Air Force in the Mediterranean were poorly resourced and ineffective. Little of this had been predicted. The bomber offensives were regarded as unique expressions of the changing form of war, thought to be more appropriate for an age of mass politics and scientific modernity, in which whole societies were mobilized to fight each other using cutting-edge technology to do so. 'The advent of air power,' wrote one American airman after the war, 'created total war. Prior to air power, opportunities for destruction of another nation's total strength were limited almost entirely to the

destruction of the armed forces.'[2] That is why the history of the bombing war is not only about the strategic planning and operational reality
of the campaigns, but also about the response of the societies subjected
to attack, whose resilience helped to prolong and intensify the campaigns and fostered the cruel materialization of the 'total war' metaphors
of the interwar years.

All of the bombing offensives share some generic characteristics. In
the first place, despite all the thinking that had gone into the air war of
the future, they were all 'accidental' campaigns. None of the three major
offensives had been fully anticipated or prepared for. The German
bombing of Britain came about by chance after the German victory over
the Western Allies in summer 1940 and the failure to stifle RAF defensive power in the Battle of Britain. The British bombing of Germany had
been thought about more carefully before 1939, but little hard preparation had gone with the thinking either in terms of the necessary
technical and scientific support needed or the strategic aims worth
pursuing when an offensive was unexpectedly permitted in May
1940 during the Battle of France. At the end of the war, in an atmosphere of greater critical awareness of the drawbacks of the bombing
campaign, John Slessor defended the record of Bomber Command with
the argument that no one before the war knew what a bomber offensive
really entailed:

> We certainly grossly underestimated the time it would take to build up our
> air power. But ... *in 1939 we embarked on the first Air War*. The only
> previous war of any size in which aircraft played any part provided us
> with no previous experience worth having at all and we had no opportunity
> even of full-scale trials in peace time. Looking back now on our abysmal
> ignorance in 1939 of the potentialities of air warfare, what amazes me is,
> not that we made a lot of mistakes, but that we didn't make far more.[3]

The United States air campaign in Europe was also quite unanticipated,
even if air force leaders had spent time in the 1930s thinking about
what a future air war might entail. No American in 1939 had expected
to be dropping bombs on Germany and Italy in four years' time. When
war suddenly became a probability, plans were hastily drawn up in late
summer 1941, but the reality of forging an air weapon from the ground
up meant that the American bombing campaign took frustrating years
to realize its potential. This was very different from preparation for war
in the Cold War era, with defined enemies and a technology that could
be mobilized and lethally deployed in a matter of minutes.

The accidental nature of the campaigns explains much about their limited achievements. Each of the major offensives had muddled strategies precisely because so little was known about what effect large-scale bombing was really having on an enemy economy or on enemy war-willingness. Bombing results, wrote the British scientist Patrick Blackett in 1942, were largely 'a matter of speculation'.[4] Hard information for either side was generally lacking. This made it difficult in all cases properly to relate means and ends. The German offensive hovered between trying to gain air superiority against the RAF, preparation for invasion, contributing to the blockade by sea of British trade, degrading Britain's industrial war potential and vague expectations of a crisis afflicting the enemy's morale. In an interrogation at Nuremberg in 1946, while his post-war trial was in progress, Göring told his interviewer that thanks to Hitler's style of decision-making he never knew 'what would be undertaken, or what would be left alone'. As a result, he continued, 'I could never concentrate my energy on any one particular plan, and that was a decided disadvantage.'[5] The last German Air Force chief of staff, Karl Koller, who had been Sperrle's operations chief throughout the Blitz, blamed the failure of the campaign on the fact that 'the actual pattern of attacks on British targets was never consistent and fluctuated from one system to another'.[6] The British offensive also suffered from a failure to define its purpose clearly and from the multitude of different tasks expected of it. The many directives issued during the war show the extent to which Bomber Command was treated as a kind of fire service, summoned for every emergency. In the same post-war evaluation, Slessor confessed that thanks to 'every sort and kind of inroad' on bombing resources, 'we never had a consistent policy of how we [the air force] proposed to win the war'.[7] The American bombing effort was similarly divided between different theatres and different strategic objectives. Only in 1944, with the focus on establishing and retaining air superiority, was a strategy found that finally promised decisive results.

The air force view during the conflict was, of course, more positive, prompted as it was by service self-interest. All the air commanders in Europe wanted to be able to demonstrate that air power from its inception possessed unique qualities that needed to be exploited for their own sake, not at the behest of armies or navies. Since air forces consumed around 40 per cent of the direct budget for the armed forces, and recruited highly trained and expensive personnel, they were under considerable pressure to demonstrate that they were value for money. Portal was delighted to learn in 1944 that a single Lancaster allegedly

eliminated more German man-hours on its first sortie than the number
of British man-hours needed to build it ('the results of all subsequent
sorties,' ran the report, 'will be clear profit').[8] Bomber offensives were
certainly sustained, despite the absence of clear evidence of their effect,
because air force leaders wanted air power to rival or even to supersede
the achievements of armies and navies. Hence the claim made by Harris
in March 1945 that it was Bomber Command that had won the 'Battle
of the Ruhr' long before the arrival of Montgomery's 21st Army Group.
Karl Koller, asked to reflect in captivity on the achievements of air
power, gave an airman's answer: 'If someone denies today that even in
spite of the heroic efforts of the Armies and Navies the wars in Europe
and the Pacific were decided only by the Air Force, then he is either
malevolent or stupid.'[9] Most airmen who favoured independent bombing as a strategy assumed that much more would be achieved if only the
army or the navy would let them get on with the job. Air Vice Marshal
Saundby, Harris's deputy at Bomber Command, called D-Day 'an
unnecessary "boating expedition"', and thought the war would be won
more quickly by the strategic bombing of towns than by supporting
invasion.[10] The strategic confusion surrounding bombing campaigns
owed a great deal to the fact that armies and navies (and a substantial
number of air force commanders) looked at air force support for surface operations as a key element in the conduct of the war, whereas
other air force leaders believed their identity and future military-political
influence depended on the pursuit of a clearly defined independent air
strategy. The extent of enthusiasm for bombing strategy reflected these
different service cultures as well as the political balance between the
three services.

Air forces hoped to dress up their wartime credentials by exploiting
vanguard technologies that made air power distinct from land power
and made heavy demands of industrial and scientific resources which it
would be difficult to reverse. Bombing aircraft were large and complex
pieces of engineering, requiring an extensive technical commitment and
a large servicing apparatus once in combat. The development of the
American B-29 'Superfortress' cost more than the Manhattan Project
for the development of the atomic bomb. The navigation and aiming
technologies demanded sophisticated scientific support and a burgeoning scientific intelligence establishment. Operational research became
increasingly complex and science-based in the effort to find optimum
ways of getting the bomber's payload onto a precise target or a defined
area. A report produced in February 1945 by the British Air Warfare

Analysis Section, 'On a Problem in Maximising the Expectation of Damage to a Target', showed that with 'N' bombs dropped with modulus 'h' the outcome would be '$H = 2\pi \int_0^r (1-q^n) \rho\alpha\rho$'.[11] Harris suggested that the reports distributed to him and others by the operational research agencies ought if possible to be expressed in a language they could all understand, though even he came to appreciate the extent to which the bomber offensive relied on scientific input.[12]

Yet for all the scientific sophistication, long-range bombing in the Second World War was a crude strategy. It was designed to carry large quantities of explosive and incendiary chemical weapons from point A to point B and to drop them, usually from a considerable height and without much accuracy, on the ground below. Artillery remained far more accurate and more destructive, as was short-range dive-bombing. (The exception here was anti-aircraft artillery, which expended millions of shells over the course of the war, most of which, even with improved radar guidance, failed to disable an aircraft.) Without so-called 'smart' weapons, strategic bombing was a wasteful use of resources, since most bombs did not hit the intended target, even when that target was the size of a city centre. The sheer weight of bombs or acres burnt out became by default the only practical ways to measure what was being achieved. The obsession with the quantity of 'bomb-lift' displayed by Allied air forces was a reflection of the extent to which weight or scale was the driving force of the campaign, when the key variable was evidently accurate and effective destruction of a particular target. The German development of guided bombs and ground-to-air missiles, incomplete though it was, would prove to be the way forward.[13] By contrast the American Air Force boasted by autumn 1944, after the one-millionth ton had been dropped, that three tons of bombs were falling every minute on Axis targets.[14] As late as April 1945, when it was possible to bomb by day as well, the British Air Ministry argued that because accuracy was still compromised by the weather and uncertain navigation, area attacks had to be maintained with 'maximum continuity and weight of attack' on the implausible claim that even heavier raids might still shorten the war.[15] Instead of smarter weapons, the Western Allies focused vanguard research on nuclear development, which promised nothing but infinitely larger areas of destruction and levels of casualty. This paradox of a strategy that required advanced technology to achieve a blunt end was epitomized by the firebombing of Japanese cities begun in March 1945 and the dropping of the two atomic bombs, on Hiroshima and Nagasaki, in August.

The strategic bombing offensives were expected to yield three kinds of dividend: dislocation and destruction of the enemy war economy; progressive demoralization of the enemy population subjected to bombing; and specific political ends related to the current war situation. The first of these strategic objectives was shared by all three major bombing offensives, and it lay behind the plans of the German Air Force in Russia in 1943 to bomb Soviet industry in order to try to reduce the pressure on the embattled ground forces. Nothing of the previous experience of bombing suggested that an economy was a potentially fruitful target. Modern industrial economies were indeed large and inert objectives, with substantial flexibility and a large cushion of industrial capacity and labour to absorb temporary damage, even of a severe nature, as was evident in both the British and German case, and would almost certainly have been the result in the Soviet Union if the German Air Force had been able to carry out a serious campaign against Soviet industry. The answer, it was generally recognized, was to try to isolate some particular element vulnerable to destruction and likely to have a multiplier effect in undermining the rest of the structure. In October 1939 the British economist John Jewkes wrote a paper for the Ministry of Economic Warfare exploring the possibility of doing just that. 'Every economic system,' he wrote, 'has a series of "weak links" or "bottle necks". If they can be identified and destroyed,' he wrote, 'the whole system may be thrown out of proportion and a partial collapse induced.' He identified power supply, transport, chemicals and synthetic materials as the principal targets, because in this case bomb destruction would cause 'the greatest *disproportionality* in the enemy's industrial system'.[16]

All three air forces tried to work out just what would cause this level of disruption, yet evaluation depended not only on what was operationally possible (which limited the choice substantially for much of the war), but on selecting target systems that were likely to have a severe impact on an integrated economic structure, and to try to hit them repeatedly. The German Air Force chose trade and food blockade and the British aero-engine industry. The latter represented a classic example of an industry with substantial 'cushion', while trade was an amorphous target. The German view, which Koller explained after the war, had been to attack London heavily because it was thought to handle a high proportion of British seaborne traffic: 'the destruction of its dock areas would place an insuperable burden on other ports'.[17] The bombing of British ports certainly had the effect of causing high levels of casualty, but it had a very limited effect on trade and stocks, which could be

shifted to other coastal towns, or unloaded and stored in more improvised ways in the bombed docks. The submarine campaign and long-range
air attacks at sea promised more. The British offensive focused first on
the 'Ruhr', another amorphous target, then oil and communications,
but it finally abandoned the limited effort given the problems of range
and accuracy and opted for destroying working-class homes, services
and lives on the assumption that at a certain but unspecified level of
death and destruction an industrial economy would cease to function
effectively. In November 1942 Lord Cherwell informed Churchill that
by the end of 1944 he thought one-third of Germany's urban population would be homeless and every house in the main cities damaged or
destroyed, but little effort was made to relate these grim statistics to the
capacity of the German war economy to continue to function or to
assess the actual effect on the German armed forces, and indeed no
attempt was made during the war to estimate either.[18] Both the German
and the British offensives were persisted with because over-optimistic
intelligence suggested that much more damage was being done to the
enemy economy than was in fact the case. Accurate assessments of
economic loss were almost impossible to construct.

The American approach to bombing as economic warfare was the
only one to take seriously the idea of describing and quantifying the
likely bottleneck sectors of the German war economy, and to bring in
qualified economists and businessmen to contribute to the planning.
But even here it took time before it was realized that industries with
substantial 'cushion' were much less vulnerable than they seemed. The
aircraft industry, which was the primary economic target, adjusted in
weeks to the threat and increased output by 50 per cent in the months
that followed.[19] The danger here, as one economist pointed out in 1945,
was that the concentration on vulnerable points 'renders the success of
the air offensive as a whole more hazardous – in much the same way as
the gambler assumes a great risk of failure by playing for high stakes'.
If the calculation on vulnerability proves to be inadequate, 'the results
of the attacks may turn out not to be disproportionally high, but disproportionally low'.[20] This was true for much of the American air effort
against Germany and Italy, until two target systems were selected that
met the economic criteria. Oil was a concentrated product, for which it
was difficult to find compensatory production or 'cushion', while transport was a general target system that promised immediate and direct
effects on a wide variety of military and economic operations. For the
last nine months of the war, targets for daylight bombing were chosen

which had an immediate and obvious impact on the German war effort. Even then they had to be attacked heavily and often, since the natural response to any crisis induced by bombing was to find ways to reduce its critical impact. When Field Marshal Kesselring was interviewed after the war by Solly Zuckerman about the Transportation Plan for Italy that Zuckerman had helped to draft, Kesselring claimed that the effectiveness of the attack on communications, thanks to countermeasures, 'had not been the success the Allies had thought it to be'.[21] Zuckerman was so keen to prove the value of transport as a target that in 1974 he went to visit Albert Speer after he had been released from prison to get further corroboration, but Speer too proved unhelpful, critical instead of the Allied failure to attack chemicals or the aero-engine industry.[22]

The three air offensives against the war economy achieved much less than had been expected and much less than the limited intelligence had suggested. The British war economy was reduced by an estimated 5 per cent against a rapidly rising production trend. The German economy lost an estimated 3–5 per cent of its potential armaments output in 1943, 11 per cent in 1944, but again against a graph of steeply rising output. The German bombing of Soviet targets hardly dented the remarkable expansion of Soviet war production and there is good reason to think that even a far more coordinated campaign would have been absorbed by an economy used to improvisation and managing chaos with little effect on the upward trajectory of production. By the time the bombing of Germany did have observable effects on economic performance, there were many other factors inhibiting further expansion, not least the fact that the Allied armies, east and west, were now at the borders of Greater Germany and in occupation of much of southern and south-eastern Europe. Only in Italy did bombing have some effect in reducing economic performance, but the Italian war economy suffered from a whole range of problems endemic to its mobilization and not only or even principally from bombing.

The second dividend widely expected from bombing was the impact on the bombed population. Pre-war expectations about the potentially insupportable impact of bombing on civilian communities conjured up lurid images of social breakdown. Cities in particular were expected to become sites of anarchic chaos. Yet this, too, was a potential strategic gain for which there was not much practical evidence and a great deal of speculation. One British scientist in the mid-1930s thought it might be enough just to drop leaflets on German workers threatening to bomb them for there to be mass strikes and sabotage, or acts of political desperation among the relatives of 'murdered and tortured workers'.[23] In reality, the wartime bombing offensives began as campaigns of economic warfare, in which any moral consequences might be regarded as a bonus. The German bombing of Britain evidently had profound effects on the (chiefly) working-class city areas where the bombs fell, while the issue of how to monitor 'morale' and cope with its possible deterioration exercised the British authorities a good deal. But for all the anxieties, and the exceptional level of casualty, British society absorbed the bombing, continued to work, adjusted to temporary moments of social crisis, mourned losses, but did not in any meaningful sense break down. In 1941 Churchill surveyed the gap between illusion and reality in a letter to Portal:

> Before the war we were greatly misled by the pictures they [the Air Staff] painted of the destruction that would be wrought by Air raids. This picture of Air destruction was so exaggerated it depressed the Statesmen responsible for pre-war policy ... Again the Air Staff, after the war had begun, taught us sedulously to believe that if the enemy acquired the Low Countries, to say nothing of France, our position would be impossible owing to Air attacks. However, by not paying too much attention to such ideas, we have found quite a good means of keeping going.[24]

Portal replied that the air staff had simply been prudent.

The RAF, by contrast, soon abandoned conventional economic warfare in favour of deliberately attacking the German civilian workforce and their urban environment. This was done not simply because night-time bombing was so inaccurate – and continued to be throughout the war – but because the bombing of a city or urban quarter was deemed to be an effective economic target. Killing workers, destroying their houses and amenities, and reducing their willingness to work were designed in the long run to reduce German war production in many rather than a few factories. In a people's war, 'the people themselves', as Sir Richard Peirse put it, became a legitimate objective. This meant particular people, those living and working in industrial cities, where the population was attacked indiscriminately. The campaign against people also carried with it the possibility that 'morale' in a broader sense might disintegrate and the German dictatorship be challenged by its own population. Nothing like this occurred despite an escalating level of urban destruction and losses that greatly exceeded those in the Blitz. 'I think their endurance,' wrote Slessor in 1947, 'was the greatest marvel of the war.'[25] At the time it was assumed that the British population would not have withstood a similar level of damage and this judgement justified persisting with the strategy regardless of the absence of firm evidence of its effects. Lord Cherwell defended his argument in favour of 'dehousing' and killing Germans by suggesting that studies of the bombing of Hull and Birmingham showed that even this level of raiding, spread over a whole country, 'would be catastrophic'.[26] Slessor recalled that the bombing of Liverpool was believed at the time to have had a 'devastating effect on morale'.[27] These speculations about fragile social endurance were projected onto the German urban population even though the real fruit of the research conducted by the Ministry of Home Security in 1941 and 1942, including studies of Birmingham and Hull, showed that 'morale' withstood the effects of the Blitz well. After the war, cities quickly rebuilt their physical environment and social function.[28]

The United States Air Force did not consider morale, in either its political or economic sense, as a worthwhile target in its own right, even though by 1944 bomber crews were instructed to attack urban targets through cloud and haze in which civilian casualties and house destruction were likely to be extensive. Reports from Germany on the mood of the population, supplied by the Office of Strategic Services, gave mixed messages about the social and political effects of the offensive. A report from the Stockholm station in August 1943 from a source regarded as reliable claimed that German labour was 'discontented and disinclined to work' and the home front as a result 'endangered'. But a report a month later from the same station cited a source that indicated little prospect of an upheaval in Germany: 'The people see little difference between Churchill and Stalin and their present rulers.'[29] A report from the Bern station in November 1943 suggested that there were 10 million bomb refugees in Germany, many of whom 'have grown strongly sympathetic to Bolshevik ideology', while a second report in December argued the opposite, that bombing may even have given rise to a momentary improvement in morale 'through sheer gratitude at being saved'.[30] The American Air Force generally took the view that this information was too unreliable to base a strategic commitment on it, but the British intelligence agencies continued throughout this period to suggest that bombing must in the end produce serious social, economic or even political consequences. After the war Norman Bottomley, deputy chief of the air staff for most of the period of the bomber offensive, picked out intelligence as the key failure of the campaign: 'the machinery which existed before and throughout the war for the acquisition and the proper assessment of economic, industrial and social information concerning our enemy was certainly inadequate'. Slessor put it more bluntly: 'It was rotten.'[31]

'Morale' as a target failed to fulfil the expectations of those who sought to undermine it and was little understood at the time. Despite unprecedented levels of civilian casualty – over 600,000 civilian dead – no European society collapsed under the impact of bombing. War-willingness depended on a wide variety of variables; it fluctuated a great deal over time and in response to changing circumstances; it was carefully monitored by every warring regime and adjustments were made, where possible, to ensure that a temporary crisis of morale would not become more socially or politically corrosive. The experience of being bombed was demoralizing and terrifying, not only for civilians but for soldiers in the field. Fear was a primitive but rational response, although the evidence suggests that with repeated bombing the psychological reaction became less marked, in much the same way as infantrymen became adjusted to the rigours of an artillery bombardment. Bombing also induced moments of widespread panic. In Clydebank, Hull, Rostock, Turin, Stalingrad, Sofia and many other cities, bombing could induce a sudden and chaotic flight, rather like the image of panicked refugees popular in the pre-war literature on the vulnerability of the urban crowd. But in almost all cases the population returned to work, found accommodation outside the city when necessary, and tried to re-establish elements of pre-raid normality. Even in Stalingrad, inhabitants returned in spring 1943 to live in cellars and dugouts in familiar ruins despite the decision of the regime not to begin rebuilding the residential areas until after the war.[32]

A number of factors played a part in preventing these moments of panic from having more profound consequences. Bombing raids had the effect of increasing the dependence of the population on authority, whether national or local. Where the state, or the party, was sufficiently competent and responsive (and occasionally ruthless), it was possible to create a compact between authority and people in which welfare, rehabilitation and evacuation were organized on their behalf in return for continued labour, civil defence participation, voluntary welfare work and social peace. In cases where that competence was lacking, as in Italy for most of the war period, bombing could have more serious consequences. Coping mechanisms, both public and private, broke down in Italy, undermining allegiance to the regime and prompting widespread reliance on traditional family networks and religious faith in place of a failed state and a corrupt and inept party machine. Italy proved the exception in a number of ways, not least the failure to mobilize a substantial proportion of the urban population for its own defence. In Britain, Germany, the Soviet Union and to a lesser extent France, local volunteers from the threatened and bombed cities played a vital part in combating the effects of raids and protecting their own property and neighbourhoods. In Germany and the Soviet Union there was pressure from the National Socialist movement or the Communist Party to join the mass organizations for civil defence, but the core of the civil defence network lay in the civilian 'self-protection' units in Germany and the 'self-defence' groups in the Soviet Union, which were trained to a higher level and were supposed to play a lead in raids, even to the extent of staying out of the shelters while raiding was going on. In Britain the civil defence system relied more on a genuine voluntarism, but did not want for volunteers. Millions of householders and workers across Europe found themselves in uniform, often little more than an armband and a helmet, performing the entire range of civil defence activities from first-aid to heavy rescue work. Without the participation of urban populations in their own defence, the consequences of bombing would have been far more serious.

With hindsight, the mass participation of European civilians in dangerous and exposed activity, constantly subject to the threat of death or injury, coping with unprecedented scenes of material destruction and mutilated human remains, requires explanation beyond the obvious pressures of collective social responsibility and state inducement. The way in which future war was represented and defined in the 1930s played an important part in shaping the response of civilians to mobilization on the home front. The prevailing discourse of total war, or totalitarian war, as it was sometimes called in Britain, presented European populations with an entirely novel way of viewing future warfare, in which all the social, material and psychological resources of a nation at war would have to be mobilized in its defence and, by extension, become objects of potential attack and disablement. The home front in the First World War was understood to have been perhaps decisive in its eventual outcome, following the collapse of the Russian, Austrian and eventually the German war effort. By the 1930s the assumption was widespread that thanks to bombs, gas and even germ warfare, the means existed to turn even a distant home front into a battlefield; all through the rearmament of the 1930s it was expected that future war would once again be a war of mass armies, like 1914–18, which would need to be resourced by domestic industry and agriculture, making the home front at once a critical element in determining survival and, hence, a critical element to assault. By the time the war broke out, civil defence was already prepared, turning the home front into a potential front line manned by ordinary people in their own defence. Rather than see this as fundamentally illegitimate, many civilians came to accept that it was the inevitable consequence of the way war had developed in an age of modern science and mass democracy. The British Red Cross Society changed its statutory role in 1940 from helping sick and wounded soldiers in the field so that it could also meet the demands of 'wounded, injured and even mentally-distressed civilian victims' which had arisen 'as a consequence of modern warfare'.[33]

The changing perception of war as something waged collectively, by the people, for the people, was not confined only to the collectivist German and Soviet dictatorships. The nature of the apparent threat posed by fascism to the future of Western civilization turned Britain's war effort into a collective 'people's war' (a term first widely used in 1940). Many of the diaries and letters from the time show that civilians saw the sacrifices imposed by the bombing war as something that gave them the opportunity to participate in a practical way in fighting a war no longer confined to soldiers, in which work for the community provided a shared wartime identity and the opportunity to display the courage, comradeship and discipline usually associated with the military. It is striking how much of this home-front effort was owed to women, who played a major part in coping with bombing as the young and middle-aged men left the cities for the armed forces. Women donned civil defence uniforms in every European country. They were disproportionately targeted by the bombing war and disproportionately active in the vast welfare, feeding, evacuation and first-aid campaigns dictated by bomb destruction. Women were also disproportionately responsible for trying to salvage the household and keep families together. When Hans Nossack walked past the ruined apartments in Hamburg days after the firestorm of July 1943, he was struck by the scenes of ruined domesticity around him. 'Everything that men have to say about this is a lie,' wrote Nossack. 'It is not permissible to talk about it except in the language of women.'[34]

The very nature of civil defence for both men and women defined the wide boundaries of the collective social endeavour: the blackout had to be observed by every household, throughout the war, even in remote rural areas; every street and block of houses was monitored and reported on by local air-raid officials, in Germany the 'block warden', in the Soviet Union the 'house committee', in Britain the corps of air-raid wardens; fire-watching became a compulsory obligation in all bombed cities. Individuals who failed to observe the rules or refused to participate, of which there was always a fraction, were regarded as outsiders who had failed the collective. They could be, and often were, punished on behalf of the community for failing to value its collective protection. Looters were shot or imprisoned; MPVO officials who abandoned their posts were court-martialled; blackout infringements brought a statutory fine, or worse; pacifists in Britain who refused fire duty were sent to jail. This ideal of civilian community as a collective front line was captured in the award of the George Cross, the highest British civilian award for bravery, to the entire island population of Malta in 1942. Civil defence established a different relationship between home front and fighting front from the one that existed in the First World War, one in which each was tested to the limits of endurance, and in which each played a part in sustaining the war effort.

The community imperatives provoked by bombing did not exclude a wide range of popular individual responses when trying to cope with its violent consequences. Some of those responses were conditioned by the authorities, who could use bombing as a means to sustain commitment to war or to mobilize hatred of the enemy. Propaganda in all the major states subject to attack focused on the barbarous nature of the enemy and, by implication, the civilized and decent nature of their own society. The theme of barbarism seemed to match the destruction of cities and the loss of cultural treasures that resulted, and possessed a deep historical resonance. The term 'barbarian' helped to emphasize the difference between the threatened community and racial alien or outsider: in Italy the American pilots were portrayed in propaganda images as black men; in Germany it was the Jews who were said to pull the strings of Allied bombing; in Britain the term 'Hun' served several purposes at the same time, both reducing all Germans, whether supporters of Hitler or not, to a shared harsh identity and signalling that Germans were by definition barbarians. One of the wartime critics of British bombing, the MP Richard Stokes, complained in a speech that the RAF might 'out-barbarian the Huns', but the Air Ministry publicity department made persistent and persuasive efforts throughout the war to contrast decent British bombing with the enemy's mindless terrorism.[35]

Nevertheless, the evidence in most bombed communities suggests that sustained hatred for what the enemy was doing was not easily prompted by propaganda or widely shared, and was more common among communities where there had been little or no bombing. Those subject to heavy bombing had too many other primary concerns – the search for welfare and accommodation, and anxiety about the private sphere of family life and possessions – to contribute to public clamour for revenge. They sought more immediate means for coping with the psychological and social consequences of bombing: sometimes through superstition or a rediscovered religiosity, sometimes with consoling rumours or, more rarely, through literature or art. In many cases, what popular public criticism existed was directed against the authorities rather than the enemy. A captured German soldier, in a bugged conversation recorded in November 1944, told his companion what he had recently seen when on leave in Berlin: 'I was able to see how the people behaved after a big air attack. You should have heard them shouting "Down with Hitler! He is a criminal against the German nation!" and see them chalking it up in big letters.'[36]

In most cases, however, protest against the authorities was muted or non-existent. In Germany and the Soviet Union there were possibly fatal consequences for sustained dissent. In Britain criticism and discussion was allowed up to a point, though censorship and control of information was widespread, and critics of Britain's war effort during the Blitz were isolated and unpopular. Only in Italy was the capacity of the state to compel compliance and divert protest gradually eroded as the bombing intensified. In circumstances where the urban population was closely monitored for civil defence purposes and subject to a web of small rules and regulations that could not be violated without risk, there was little political space for those who wanted to use bombing to prompt social protest. Most regimes seem to have allowed a certain amount of open grumbling and resentment as a safety valve during and after a raid, a degree of latitude generally understood by the public, but no more than that. There was some opportunity for non-political protest through prolonged absenteeism from work, or refusal to return after evacuation, but the evidence suggests it was not widespread since workers generally needed to work to survive, or could be compelled to return to work. 'Germany has two alternatives,' claimed another bugged soldier in August 1944, 'war and work for all, or peace and unemployment.'[37] Rates of return to work in Britain during the Blitz suggested that work and pay were key considerations even in the face of further danger. What was disliked by the bombed populations was perceived inequality of sacrifice. Ruhr workers wished the bombers would go on to Berlin rather than penalize the wrong people; in Italy in 1943 the northern cities waited to hear news that Rome had at last been bombed; in London the unfortunate inhabitants of the dock areas hoped that bombs would fall on the favoured West End; in bombed and shelled Leningrad, the worst thing for the starving population to bear was the knowledge that the party elite were still eating well. None of these forms of social friction amounted to a serious challenge to war-willingness, which was sustained by fear of defeat and the demonization of the enemy. The post-war USSBS survey of German morale and the wartime Gallup polls in Britain each showed that bombing was low on the list of concerns, whereas fear of blockade, or invasion and occupation, or ultimate defeat, or national extinction played a much greater part.

The third component of bombing strategy was its use for specific political purposes other than trying to encourage the enemy population to revolt. There were many situations in which bombing was used to try to extract a political dividend or to fulfil a political pledge. The bombing of Bulgaria, with which this book opens, is an obvious instance. Bombing Romania in 1943–4 was also designed to try to win Romania away from the Axis alliance through the impact of air attack and its threat. Secret intelligence sources suggested that the bombing of Ploeşti in August 1943 had 'an excellent psychological effect'. The airmen apparently waved to the population below during the raid, and those who were forced to parachute onto Romanian soil from damaged aircraft carried letters in Romanian explaining that they were Americans and not Russians, as well as sums of Balkan currency and packs of Camel cigarettes to hand out.[38] Bombing was at its most significant as a political gambit in the earlier part of the war when the British government used the RAF as a means to win support among the occupied populations and from the United States by showing that Britain was capable of fighting back. Secret intelligence from French sources encouraged the RAF to attack targets in France working for the Germans principally for its political effects: 'These bombardments thus have a fundamental importance for France in the future,' wrote one sympathetic Frenchman in 1941, 'for they will prove to the population at one and the same time that England is there, that she is strong and powerful and that she dominates the air.'[39] In London it was supposed that bombing gave encouragement to the occupied peoples even if the direct economic effect of the attacks was at best very limited. 'The Dutch at least (like the Norwegians),' minuted the British Air Minister in summer 1940, 'like our bombing them.'[40]

The most significant attempt to use bombing to serve political ends came with the many arguments between the Western Allies and the Soviet Union over the establishment of a 'Second Front' in Europe in 1942 and 1943. In the absence of a pledge to launch an offensive in northern France in 1942 and its uncertainty in 1943, Churchill used the bomber offensive instrumentally as a means to mitigate the effect on the Soviet leadership, and Stalin in particular, of the confused nature of Western strategy. At the famous meeting between Churchill and Stalin in Moscow on 12 August 1942, the prime minister first told Stalin that a second front on the northern French coast was not possible that year (the minutes indicate here that Stalin became glum, then glummer, and finally restless), but then indicated that bombing would continue with increasing severity. The course of the subsequent discussion is worth recording:

M. STALIN agreed that bombing was of tremendous importance ... It was not only German industry that should be bombed, but the population too. This was the only way of breaking German morale.

THE PRIME MINISTER ... As regards the civil population, we looked upon it as a military target. We sought no mercy and we would show no mercy.

M. STALIN said that was the only way.

THE PRIME MINISTER said we hoped to shatter twenty German cities as we had shattered Cologne, Lübeck, Düsseldorf, and so on. More and more aeroplanes and bigger and bigger bombs ... If need be, as the war went on, we hoped to shatter almost every dwelling in almost every German city. (These words had a very stimulating effect upon the meeting, and thenceforward the atmosphere became progressively more cordial.)[41]

In this as in most other cases in which bombing was used to make a political point or to buy Allied collaboration, the actual effect is open to question. Bombing as a 'Second Front' did not satisfy Stalin, as is often suggested, since the following day he drafted a short note for Churchill in which he made it clear that the British failure to divert part of the German army to the west 'inflicts a moral blow to the whole of Soviet public opinion, which calculates on the creation of a second front'.[42] The effects of bombing on Bulgaria and Romania were simply overshadowed by the approaching Red Army, while the bombing of occupied Europe provoked growing resentment the longer it went on.

If the political, moral and economic impact of the bomber offensives produced ambiguous, though not negligible results, it is clear that they had significant effects, both direct and indirect, on military strategy and operations. The bomber offensives created battlefields in the European skies in which ground anti-air defences of increasing scientific sophistication combined with day-fighter and night-fighter screens to try to prevent the bombing from taking place. For the bomber force it was essential to create the conditions for air superiority without which the imposition of higher and higher loss rates made it difficult to sustain operations. These battles were carried on at great cost and continued over the whole period of the war. They constituted in their own right, irrespective of the ambition to damage the enemy's economy and morale, a field of battle that absorbed a growing proportion of military resources and involved a major scientific, intelligence and productive effort. The bombing battlefield had not been fully anticipated before the war except by Douhet, who placed air superiority at the centre of his argument for air power, but it soon became a major military arena. The Battle of Britain and the subsequent Blitz were predicated on the need to win air superiority over southern Britain to make invasion possible, and then to suppress the revival of British air power and to compel Britain to maintain substantial air defence forces for the rest of the war. German bombing in the Soviet Union or Axis bombing against Malta also created battlefields between bombers and the guns, fighter aircraft, air warning systems and large numbers of uniformed men and women assigned to combat them. German failure in each of these theatres gave a strategic breathing space to the enemy, and highlighted the extent to which the balance between air defence and air offence was moving in the defenders' favour.

The greatest battle, as Speer called it, was the struggle for air superiority over Germany and German-occupied Europe. Neither the British nor the American air forces had anticipated how difficult this would be. The RAF had no effective counter-force strategy in place when bombing began and developed one piecemeal as losses to anti-aircraft fire and night-fighters threatened to terminate the offensive. The United States air forces built into their planning the idea that the German Air Force constituted an 'intermediate target', but found in the end that German air power, as it grew in size and effectiveness in 1943 and 1944, was the principal objective, whose defeat would not only pave the way for more effective bombing, but would have serious repercussions for German front-line operations, including defence against Operation Overlord.

Achieving air superiority, wrote Spaatz to Doolittle in January 1944, was 'the critical deciding factor in Germany's defeat'.[43] Although some of the bombing effort was devoted to hitting the German aircraft industry, it was not this that won air superiority but the introduction of the long-range fighter and the technical and tactical innovations that made it possible to suppress the German Air Force (and the V-weapons campaign) in ways that had not been achieved by German air forces in the Battle of Britain. Right up to the end of the war, a large proportion of the American air effort over Germany was devoted to maintaining the suppression of German air power by attacks on the whole air force infrastructure. The diversion of a large part of the German fighter force to the home front, the establishment of a dense web of ground anti-aircraft defences, and the recruitment of more than a million men, women and boys to man them distorted German strategy and starved the fronts in the Soviet Union, Italy and France of vital aircraft, both fighters and bombers. It was this form of military distortion that affected Britain's capacity to act more forcefully between 1940 and 1942, as it later inhibited the German war effort between 1943 and 1945. Bombing cities or industries where there existed a cushion of spare capacity had much less effect than the battle for air supremacy and the large call that the bomber war had on the productive and scientific resources of both sides. This suggests that in the end, for all the exaggerated expectations of the new forms of total war, the fight between military forces still dictated the difference between victory and defeat as it had done in the Great War.

This was a paradoxical outcome. A war that was supposed to be waged from the air against the economies and social commitment of both sides, ended up as a major military campaign fought between rival air forces, much more like the tactical bombing campaigns in the field, though larger in scale and more prolonged. At times strategic forces were actually used for tactical purposes, to force a breakthrough for ground forces or to speed up a campaign, though often with very mixed results. The bombings of Warsaw, Minsk, Stalingrad and Cassino were as destructive as anything carried out by independent strategic forces against a distant target but were carried out in order to meet direct operational requirements at or near the fighting front. In these cases bombing proved every bit as blunt an instrument as it was when used to destroy an urban or industrial target, since it often produced exceptional levels of destruction without necessarily achieving the object. The obliteration of Brest and Lorient did not prevent German submarines from continuing to operate; the destruction of Caen held up Allied forces as they tried to navigate its debris-strewn streets; the bombing of Stalingrad created an ideal landscape for urban guerrilla warfare and arguably prevented the German Army from seizing the city in September 1942. The obliteration of Aachen, at General Bradley's request, did not materially speed up the American advance into Germany. Following the deaths of American troops at the opening of Operation Cobra, Eisenhower told Bradley that he did not think that heavy bombers could be used in support of ground troops, which he regarded as 'a job for the artillery'.[44] In August 1944 Doolittle complained to Spaatz that the Eighth Bomber Force was simply an inapposite instrument for regular use in support of ground operations, 'due to the complication of our equipment, the comparatively short combat life of the average crew member, and the fact that some of the concepts of tactical bombing are diametrically opposed to those of strategic bombing'. Doolittle highlighted the regular loss of American troops to friendly fire and suggested that fighters and fighter-bombers were much more useful adjuncts to the battlefield than heavy bombers.[45] This was why the Soviet military leaders wanted a firm bomb line in eastern Europe in early 1945, to prevent American or British bombers hitting their own forces. The Soviet Air Force took the view throughout the war that high-quality battlefield aviation – light bombers, fighters and fighter-bombers – represented the most effective way air power could be exercised given the limitations of the prevailing technology, and it is difficult not to see this as a sensible strategic judgement.

None of the evident drawbacks to bombing during the war prevented the escalation of all the major offensives towards more indiscriminate levels of destruction. The issue of escalation is central to any judgement about the broader ethical implications of the bomber offensives.[46] In each case it is possible to show that the circumstances of war, or the evolving technical capability of the force, or the pressure of political considerations, explains the reduction of whatever restraints existed on inflicting damage on civilians. But there was also a moral dimension to escalation. Each of the major bomber offensives violated established rules of engagement about not inflicting deliberate and disproportional damage on civilians and the civilian milieu. German bombing moved from trying to destroy the infrastructure of RAF Fighter Command to the V-2 rocket campaign four years later; British attacks against city targets where civilians would be killed were declared illegal in autumn 1939, but Bomber Command ended up obliterating Dresden in 1945;

THE BALANCE SHEET OF BOMBING

the American air forces were publicly committed to raids on precise targets but finally authorized unsighted bombing of cities through cloud and smoke. In each case crew were originally told to bring their bombs back if a military or industrial target was not clearly visible, but as standard practice this was soon abandoned in favour of allowing the pilot to find a secondary 'target of opportunity'.

Escalation did not happen without a conscious realization that thresholds were being crossed. Hitler's insistence that only he could order retaliatory 'terror' attacks indicates the German understanding about what constituted legitimate acts of war and what did not (although this scarcely inhibited him in the campaign in Russia against 'Jewish-Bolshevism'). In the United States, the air force made anxious efforts to ensure that the public accepted the higher moral claim of precision bombing, and when the destruction of Dresden became news, Arnold and Spaatz immediately conspired to preserve the image.[47] In Britain, where the RAF was the only major air force to target civilians deliberately, every effort was made to maintain the subterfuge that it was the Germans who inflicted terror, while the RAF hit only military targets, even to the extent of briefing crews before a raid in a language designed to disguise the real intention. This view became so embedded in RAF propaganda that officers later in the war came to accept that it must be true. After the first V-weapons attacks, the plans department in the Air Ministry suggested that since Germany had now deliberately adopted 'terror tactics' against civilians, it was time to retaliate in kind. The Director of Intelligence could see little point in 'declaring our intention to be a savage one after our actions in the past have inevitably been extremely savage'. The response to this claim says much about the duplicity of the British position. 'Whatever the Germans may say about our so-called "terror raids",' wrote Air Marshal Douglas Colyer, 'we have so far held firmly to the fact that our attacks were directed against definite military objectives.'[48] That it was possible to argue this case at all depended on defining military objective in such a way that it became in effect meaningless. By the end of the war the definition used by the United States air forces was simply 'any objective the continued existence of which will materially contribute to the enemy's ability to wage war', which allowed very wide latitude in choosing targets where civilian deaths were unavoidable.[49]

It would be easy to condemn each air force for rapidly violating whatever sense it had that civilian targeting was not a legitimate act of war. The legal position is scarcely open to doubt: bombing deliberately

carried out in conditions in which heavy civilian casualties and destruction of civilian property were bound to occur, violated every accepted
norm in the conduct of modern warfare, whether it was done by German, British or American air forces.[50] The legal issue was well understood
at the time. In summer 1945 the victorious Allies at first intended to add
the bombing of cities to the indictment they were drawing up for the
major German war criminals. On the advice of the British Foreign
Office this particular charge was quietly withdrawn since it was
self-evident that German defence lawyers would have little difficulty in
tarring Allied bombing with the same brush.[51] The only German airman
to be put on trial for bombing was Alexander Löhr, tried and executed
by the Yugoslav authorities for his part in the bombing of Belgrade in
1941. Had bombing of civilians not been regarded as legally problematic, the major powers would not have agreed only four years later, in
the new Geneva Convention of 1949, conditions 'relative to the protection of civilian persons in time of war', which allowed in the event of
conflict for protective areas for children, mothers, the elderly, and any
civilians not directly connected with the war effort; or in 1977 to have
agreed to draw up additional protocols to give protection in international law more generally to civilians, civilian services and the civilian
milieu, which could not be the deliberate objects of military attack or
the victims of careless bombing and shelling of objectives in civilian
areas.[52]

The real issue is to understand how this process of escalating violence came to be justified at the time; in other words, how operations
that were not easily defined as legal could nevertheless be regarded as
ethically acceptable by those ordering the bombardment. This is a much
more complex question and its answer rests on a number of moral
assumptions that were relative to the wartime situation. The simplest
answer is that both sides responded to what they saw as the violations
carried out by the other. In Britain the bombing of Germany could
always be given a wartime moral justification with the argument that
the German Air Force began the campaign against civilian targets, if not
at Guernica or Warsaw, then certainly with the bombing of British cities
in the autumn of 1940. The idea that German forces had 'sowed the
wind' and would as a result 'reap the whirlwind' of heavy retaliatory
bombing ran through much of the public defence of bombing during the
war, and since. The morality of a tooth for a tooth had a raw biblical
sense to it which could be widely endorsed even by those who only a
few years before had campaigned for the international abolition of

bomber aircraft. Indeed, this preference was reflected in the biblical terms chosen for many of the major RAF campaigns – Operation Gomorrah, Operation Millennium, Operation Chastise. German bombing of British cities, on the other hand, was justified as retaliation or revenge for the bombing carried out by British aircraft since May 1940. Much of the justificatory language associated with German bombing in 1940, in 1942 and 1943, and with the V-weapon campaign in 1944, was founded on vengeance. Bombing encouraged a vicious circle in which being bombed could be used as the moral instrument to legitimize bombing the enemy. The United States public had to borrow this morality second-hand, since German aircraft never threatened American cities. One of the fruits of the British propaganda fed to America during the Blitz was the absence of any anguished debate there on the ethics or otherwise of bombing Axis cities.

Behind the justification for bombing as well-merited punishment lay deeper fears about national extinction and political subjection, which were taken to be the terms in which total war had to be waged. The insistent idea that the Second World War was fought for the highest of stakes was not only needed in order to justify national mobilization on a unique scale, but became accepted by a great many Europeans as a historical reality. The official voice on both sides made great play with the idea of 'total war' or 'people's war', but the resonance those terms had among European populations reflected the popular perception of just how dangerous the enemy was and how urgent the need to take any measure, however legally or morally dubious, to defend the spirit of democracy, or the prospect of liberty, or the future of the German race and culture. The sense of an apocalyptic struggle, whether against fascism or communism or the alleged Jewish world conspiracy, was certainly not fully understood or accepted by the populations made to fight against them, but in every combatant power the idea that a war on such a scale must be about issues of life or death blunted many of the doubts about whether the way the war was conducted abided by liberal notions of *jus in bello*, justice in war. The escalating scale and destructiveness of bombing reflected the absolute nature of the way the contest was presented and the moral relativism that this prompted. The difficult thing to do would have been to halt the bombing on the ground that it damaged civilian lives too heavily. When the bombing offensive against Britain ended in summer 1941, there followed years in which those monitoring public opinion in Germany highlighted the frustrations felt by the German public that bombing on a large scale could not be renewed. When there was evidence that British or American bombing was too small-scale to be effective, the public demand for more and heavier bombardment was used to pressure the air forces to respond. From the perspective of the time the moral obligation to defeat the enemy at all costs overrode any moral or legal constraints intended to ensure that in doing so the laws of war were not compromised too far. The support of many in the Church of England for a bombing campaign, for example, rested on an ethical judgement that the higher moral obligation for Christians was to ensure national survival rather than worry about the means through which it was to be achieved. Moral expediency in war is no novelty, nor should it seem surprising that in the terms in which this particular war was fought, the higher morality was always the appeal to national survival.

Expectations about total war as an expression of national struggle in an acute form helped to underpin the decision to carry out bombing offensives, which of all the forms of military activity in the Second World War directly affected the non-combatant population violently and directly. The moral outrage that might be felt today by such deliberate violations was more limited in an age in which total war was, for better or worse, the language of the day. 'Why should a factory in which lethal weapons are made,' wrote the British legal expert J. M. Spaight, 'be immune from attack if it *can* be attacked?'[53] The Dean of St Paul's in London justified his refusal to sign a petition against bombing in autumn 1941 on the grounds that it promoted a more democratic wartime reality: 'I do not think that the sufferings of civilians under night bombing are necessarily the worst thing in this war ... and I don't think that we civilians have any right to cry out or to try to evade our share in the general suffering'.[54] The view that the front line was no longer the front line of conventional warfare was expressed everywhere, from British wartime propaganda on 'taking it' to Soviet mass mobilization of townspeople for digging anti-tank trenches to German recruitment of schoolchildren to man anti-aircraft emplacements. The view that total war meant war between societies had profound implications for how that war was waged. 'A people is only defeated,' announced the commander-in-chief of Bomber Command to an audience of businessmen in 1941, 'when their Will-to-Win has been broken. How can this be done? Only by carrying the offensive into Germany. How else can the offensive be carried into Germany except by the Bombers?'[55] On just such a syllogism was it possible to justify bombing as an instrument of the national effort against enemy civilian targets.

The balance sheet of bombing shows that whatever concerns may inform current judgements about its morality or effectiveness, there were a great many military and moral arguments used at the time to explain why so much commitment was given to it. These arguments need to be understood if sense is to be made of why the combatant powers fighting in Europe indulged in air campaigns over five years in which more than half a million civilians were killed and wide areas of Europe's urban heritage destroyed by fire and explosive, and sense made of how these campaigns were ethically justified at the time. The historical narrative of the bombing war nevertheless confirms that there existed throughout the conflict a wide gap between what was claimed for bombing and what it actually achieved in material and military terms, just as there existed a wide gap between the legal and ethical claims made on its behalf and the deliberate pursuit of campaigns in which civilian deaths were anticipated and endorsed. The resources devoted to strategic bombing might more usefully have been used in other ways: providing large tactical air forces, strengthening air-sea collaboration, producing more and better tanks, or, above all, concentrating research and production on high-quality air technology (long-range fighters, for example, or guided weapons), which might have made bombing a more effective campaign for all three states that tried it. Strategic bombing proved in the end to be inadequate in its own terms for carrying out its principal assignments and was morally compromised by deliberate escalation against civilian populations. The unintended military impact was its most important consequence. Strategic bombing in its wartime form disappeared as a strategic option in Europe after 1945. Profound changes in available weapons, the transformation of geopolitical reality and post-war ethical sensibilities have all combined to make the bombing war between 1939 and 1945 a unique phenomenon in modern European history, not possible earlier and not reproducible since.

Epilogue

Lessons Learned and Not Learned:

Bombing into the Post-War World

After 1945 the terms in which a bombing war came to be understood were dominated by the reality of nuclear weapons, which were only used at the end of the conflict in the Pacific War. Until the missile age, the long-range intercontinental bomber was designed to deliver a first or second-strike nuclear attack of annihilating power against the enemy. This did not rule out the use of conventional bombing (as the wars in Korea and Vietnam made evident), but it forced the Allied air forces to think about the lessons of the Second World War, both in terms of what the campaigns had achieved and in terms of projected future war.

On one thing the two major air forces, the RAF and the USAAF, were agreed: a third world war if it came would be another total war of even greater proportions than the last. When the post-war RAF chief of staff – now Marshal of the Royal Air Force, Lord Tedder – was invited to give the Lees-Knowles lectures on military affairs in Cambridge in the spring of 1947, he assured his audience that in the future 'war will inevitably be total war and world-wide'.[1] In October 1946 Maj. General Lauris Norstad, head of the Plans and Operations Division in the War Department, and a wartime air commander, briefed President Truman on the shape of the post-war American military. He concluded his presentation by repeating what he had already claimed several times: 'We must plan for the next war to be in fact a total war.'[2] A lecture to the National Industrial Conference Board in spring 1947 by General Brehon Somervell, the officer responsible during the war for creating the Pentagon, began from the premise that the next war would be worse than the last: 'Let no man question that World War III will be a total war of a destructiveness and intensity never yet seen.'[3] It was also understood that this war of the future should not be fought as if it were the Second World War. Tedder told his listeners that the fighting services 'must discard old shibboleths and outworn traditions'; for future security 'we must look *forward from* the past and its lessons, not *back* to the past'. Norstad told the National War College in Washington, DC, shortly after his briefing of the president, that it was a mortal danger 'to cling for security in a *next* war to those things which made for security in a *last* war'.[4]

There were nevertheless important lessons to be drawn. In August 1947 Tedder organized a major RAF exercise codenamed 'Thunderbolt' to study the lessons of the Combined Bomber Offensive for the future of war. Senior airmen, government scientists and politicians were invited, though Portal and Harris, architects of the offensive, chose not to attend. There were five senior American Air Force officers, including General Kepner, victor of the 'Battle of Germany'. The conference opened at the School of Air Support at Old Sarum, near Salisbury, on 11 August and lasted five days.[5] Although some defence was made of the bomber offensive, the general tone of the assembly was critical. The failure to destroy the enemy economy or seriously to dent enemy morale was admitted; so too the slowness of the build-up of Bomber Command during the war and the failure to exploit science fully enough.[6] The exercise was an opportunity to think about the advent of entirely new weapons, including atomic bombs, and to decide how the air force should be organized to exploit them. The result was a vision of future air war not very different from the strategic fantasies of General Douhet, first elaborated in the wake of the Great War in his book *Command of the Air*, and finally translated into English in 1942.

Like Douhet, the key priorities identified were the need to be prepared fully for the moment when a war breaks out, to strike ruthlessly and swiftly using any weapon available, and to target the enemy civilian population as the key to destroying the will to resist in days rather than years. Tedder had identified in his Cambridge lectures the key importance of being ready to strike at once when hostilities began, not an 'embryo Goliath' like Bomber Command after 1939, which took years to develop after the outbreak of war, but 'a fully grown David, ready to act swiftly and decisively'.[7] This meant choosing weapons that could deliver a sudden annihilating blow. During Exercise Thunderbolt the possibility was proposed of using atomic weapons, which Britain did not yet possess; Henry Tizard, the government scientist, thought that 500 atomic bombs might bring about a swift end to any war. Norman Bottomley, Harris's successor as commander-in-chief of Bomber Command, presented a paper on biological warfare as an even more effective instrument for total war since it killed only people rather than destroying cities, as incendiary or atomic bombings had done. Carried in cluster bombs or rocket warheads, biological agents used as a strategic weapon against the civilian population would be, ton for ton, more deadly than poison gas and likely to be available sooner than nuclear weapons.[8] In either case, nuclear war or biological war, air power would deliver the rapid and decisive blow it had failed to deliver effectively enough before 1945.

Douhet was even more in evidence in the conclusions drawn by the American military leadership. In his speech to the National Industrial Conference Board, Somervell described the Third World War in terms every bit as lurid as the scaremongering visions of the 1930s:

What kind of war would the third world conflict be? Would it be a Buck Rogers affair with atomic bombs bursting everywhere, bacteria of all kinds falling on us from the sky like angry winter rain, rockets moving with uncanny precision thousands of miles to the most remote inland target hidden in a cave in the Rockies, with one-half or two-thirds of our population or that of the enemy wiped out or crawling about maimed by radioactive emanations or crippled by loathsome or incurable disease . . . Would it be over as quickly as that, with one or both combatants totally destroyed and their civilization wiped out? God only knows.[9]

Somervell reflected the prevailing post-war view that a future world war would be over quickly, despite all the lessons of the recent conflict, and that it would be even more destructive than the damage inflicted from the air in the wartime offensives. In a speech on 'Strategy' to the National War College in January 1947, General Albert Wedemeyer, architect of the American Victory Program in 1941, told his audience that the next war would swiftly assume 'the characteristics of a war of extermination' involving ultra-destructive atomic and bacteriological weapons. Since the United States had failed to rearm in the 1930s in the face of Axis aggression, Wedemeyer warned against the typical American attitudes of 'indifference and apathy' when confronted by the emergence of yet another totalitarian menace to Europe.[10]

The Soviet Union was regarded as the successor to Hitler's Third Reich, but a state potentially capable of stockpiling weapons of mass destruction and inflicting them in a sudden preemptive strike against the American mainland, which Germany had not been able to do. Norstad told Truman that the Soviet Union was the only possible enemy and that war against Communism 'is the basis of our planning'.[11] Like the RAF, American thinking focused on the need to build up overwhelming striking power in peacetime to counter such a threat and to be prepared to use all and any weapons, including bacteriological, chemical and nuclear payloads, to be certain of victory against an apparently ruthless dictatorship. Arnold's final report for the president in 1945 stressed the need in the future for an atomic capability that would allow 'immediate offensive action with overwhelming force', which the American Air Force had demonstrably lacked in 1941.[12] For American planners this meant retaining a strategic air force capable of mounting an immediate air offensive and in 1948 the Strategic Air Command was activated for this purpose under the former Eighth Air Force wing commander, General Curtis LeMay. He welcomed the assignment and had no regrets about wartime bombing. 'Enemy cities were pulverized or fried to a crisp,' LeMay wrote in 1965. 'It was something they asked for and something they deserved.'[13] The RAF bomber force was less fortunate after 1945. Bomber Command was almost entirely demobilized, its Air Striking Force reduced to 10 squadrons by 1946.[14] By the 1950s Britain could no longer afford to be a major player in the air war of the future. No effective heavy bomber was developed for the post-war force and in 1950 the RAF had to borrow 70 B-29s from the United States.

The possession of nuclear weapons now made the city-busting strategy of the Second World War a possibility. Though the object of a nuclear arsenal was to deter an aggressor, both Britain and the United States prepared plans for the point where deterrence failed. By the early 1960s American air forces, using missiles or aircraft, possessed the means to obliterate most Soviet cities and to kill more than 80 million of their inhabitants in a first or second strike.[15] British planners, working with a much more limited nuclear capability, identified 55 Soviet cities for destruction. A committee set up in 1960 to investigate the strategy was instructed to consider only the effects on the population, 'the aim being to select target cities so as to pose the maximum threat to the greatest possible number of Russian people'. The Air Ministry was particularly interested in learning lessons from the bombing of Germany to decide what level of destruction was needed for 'knocking out' a city. It was calculated that Hamburg had received the equivalent of a 5-kiloton bomb during the war, which encouraged confidence that the large megaton bombs now available really would be able to paralyse a city at a stroke.[16] The principal lesson learned from the bombing campaigns of the Second World War was the need for even greater and more indiscriminate destruction of the enemy if ever the Third World War materialized.

The experience of the bombing war helped to shape the Cold War confrontation of mutual destruction or mutual deterrence. It was under this shadow that European nations began the process of reconstructing the bombed cities and towns and counting the cost of the cultural damage they had sustained. The programmes were ambitious and optimistic despite the threat of nuclear obliteration hanging over them.[17] Recovery was in this sense like recovery from a natural disaster – a volcanic eruption or a major earthquake – in the knowledge that another geological shift might undo the urban rebuilding at a stroke. The reconstruction began at first against a background of economic crisis and legal wrangling over ownership of the ruins, and in many cases the bolder plans were shelved in favour of cheaper or more feasible solutions.[18] The most ambitious building took place in Germany where more than half the urban area in the major cities had been destroyed. Some 39 cities had at least 1 million cubic metres of rubble to clear, but in Berlin the figure was 55 million, in Hamburg 35 million and in Cologne 24 million.[19] Coping with life among the ruins were millions of Germans who lived for years in cellars and shacks, short of food, supplies and schooling. A delegation of British peace workers visiting Lübeck in 1947 were shown weekly food rations consisting of just two pounds of bread, a half litre of skimmed milk, half a herring, one ounce of butter and four ounces of sugar. They found 4,000 people in the port still being fed a watery soup daily from a communal kitchen. Accommodation was rationed in Hamburg to 5.6 square metres per person; the water supply was poor, electricity irregular. The women they met expressed strong sentiments 'against all forms of militarism or war'.[20]

Neither in Germany nor elsewhere in Europe were the heavily bombed and depopulated cities abandoned. In France there was a move to keep the ruined peninsula of the Channel port of St Malo as a memorial to the bombing and to relocate the town on the mainland, but tradition prevailed and St Malo was rebuilt on the existing site. The only place to be moved as a result of bombing was the Italian town of Cassino. The ruins on the mountainside were declared a national monument and a new and larger town was built on more level ground a mile away from the original site. City centres, where much of the damage had occurred, were also generally restored with the exception of Bristol and Kiel, where there was sufficient bomb damage to allow the relocation of the centre to a more geographically convenient quarter.[21] In Germany the reconstruction was slower than elsewhere but here too the cities were restored on their original sites despite the exceptional level of destruction. This strong sense of belonging, even to a ruined landscape, was explained by a senior German officer to his fellow prisoners of war early in 1945:

> If there is such a thing as existence in spirit or will alone, without body or matter, that is the life of the German cities. Only their sentimental appeal still holds them together. Cologne has been evacuated time and time again, but the inhabitants still manage to drift back to the heaps of rubble simply because they once bore the name 'home'. Past associations are so much more powerful than the necessities of war that the evacuees resent leaving and rush back again long before the danger is over.[22]

Nevertheless, German cities were remodelled after the bombing, while their demographic geography changed. By 1950, cities with more than 100,000 people made up 27 per cent of the population in West Germany, whereas they had constituted one-third in 1939; the population of communities with fewer than 20,000 inhabitants increased from 53 per cent to 59 per cent over the same period. Hamburg, where the damage and depopulation had been among the most extensive, almost recovered its pre-war population level by 1950, but experienced a substantial relocation of population within the city limits. The inner zones housed 850,000 people in 1939, but by 1950 only 467,000; the outer zones increased from 848,000 to over 1 million.[23]

The geographical relocation was typical of much of the post-war reconstruction, since the destruction of older urban environments presented an opportunity to build modern residential housing with less congestion and more amenities. Wider roads and open spaces were regarded by town planners as desirable improvements to old-fashioned and inconvenient urban structures. 'The Blitz has been a planner's windfall,' wrote the British scientist Julian Huxley. 'It is the psychological moment to get real planning in our towns.'[24] In reality the expense involved and the persistent arguments between local authorities and architects about what was desirable or expedient left many of the plans on the drawing board. A survey of 100 British cities in 1952 by Charles Madge, one of the founders of Mass Observation, discovered that out of the planned 59 nursery schools only one had been built, out of 50 community centres only four had materialized and out of 33 health centres not one.[25] The American social scientist Leo Grebler investigated 28 Western European cities from four countries in 1954 and found that in general there was little radical urban rebuilding and strong pressures for continuity. The actual amount of damage, even in heavily bombed cities, was less than the immediate images of smashed streets and housing suggested. In Plymouth, one of the most heavily bombed British cities, only 9 per cent of the housing stock was destroyed. In London the same percentage of bomb-damaged area was available for new construction, leaving 91 per cent of the capital as it was. The temptation for municipal authorities all over Europe (who needed to restore local tax revenues) was to use what was still standing as fully as possible and to rebuild around it rather than engage in further demolition.[26] In Germany the extent of the problem of homelessness was amplified by the large-scale refugee problem as Germans expelled from Eastern Europe arrived in the western zones of occupation. This forced migration encouraged the rapid rebuilding and repair of existing structures alongside cheap standard housing built on existing foundations. By 1961, 3.1 million houses had been restored or rebuilt.[27] In no case did Grebler find evidence that the threat of nuclear bombing influenced city planning or house design, a discovery that he attributed partly to 'improvidence or defeatism' in the face of the nuclear menace, but principally to the willingness to take high risks for the sake of restoring what had been temporarily sacrificed in wartime.[28]

The physical rebuilding of Europe after 1945 was bound up with the way bombed populations came to terms with the human costs of the bombing war. The psychological impact was difficult to gauge after 1945 and little effort went into analysing the scale or nature of the traumatic impact on those who experienced air raids. The longer-term effects on civilians have been little studied in comparison with the post-war psychological damage done to soldiers as a result of the stresses of combat. The memory of bombing as an expression of collective public awareness of the victims (though not of the survivors) was also much less developed than the public memory of military losses. Much of that public memory was linked to religious monuments as symbols of the injury to Europe's Christian values in the vortex of total war. In Britain part of Coventry Cathedral was kept in its ruined state as both a local and a national monument; in Germany the Frauenkirche in Dresden was a standing indictment of the firestorm until its rebuilding in the early twenty-first century as a symbol of reconciliation and a final settlement of post-war accounts.[29] The Nicholas Church in Hamburg and the Kaiser Wilhelm Church in the centre of Berlin were also left in their ruined state as a visible reminder to the German people of the cost of war against the home front. In Germany the memorializing of the dead from the bombing has been a process shot through with evident ambiguities. For years the memory was suppressed or subdued because of the difficulty of seeing Germans as victims rather than the collective perpetrators of a barbarous European war. The publication in 2002 of Jörg Friedrich's best-seller, *Der Brand* (*The Fire*), opened up a new wave of debate over the extent to which the victimhood of ordinary people in the bombing war can be reconciled with a persistent collective guilt for the crimes of the Hitler regime.[30] Outside Germany, the memorialization of victims of bombing has been unevenly applied. In Britain there is still no collective monument to the victims of the Blitz and there are relatively few local memorials. Established habits of remembering the fighting man have prevailed over public acknowledgement that in total war civilians are as likely to be victims as soldiers.[31]

The ambiguities have also extended to the way in which those who carried out the bombing have been remembered after 1945. The United States Air Force established a major monument at Madingley, outside Cambridge, where thousands of American aircrew were buried. But Bomber Command was for decades after 1945 denied a collective monument to the dead. The erection of a statue to Harris in 1992 outside the RAF church on London's Strand provoked widespread criticism, protest and demonstrations. A memorial to the dead of Bomber Command was finally erected and dedicated only in 2012, in London's Green Park, but once again it provoked renewed debate about whether those who inflicted such damage on civilian communities ought to be remembered in the same spirit in which the 'Few' of the defensive Battle of Britain have been lionized in British public history. This is not the only example of a surviving tension in the way the bombers and the bombed are remembered. In Bulgaria, almost a century after the serendipitous invention of the modern bomb by the Bulgarian army captain, Simeon Petrov, the United States authorities chose in October 2010 to erect a modest stone monument in the grounds of the American Embassy in Sofia to the 150 American airmen who lost their lives flying over Bulgarian territory or bombing Bulgarian targets. The event was marked by protests from Bulgarian political parties at what was regarded as an unjustifiable celebration of a murderous policy that resulted in widespread Bulgarian deaths. A demonstration organized on 18 December 2010 carried placards that read 'No to the monument of shame!' A

Facebook protest group was organized dedicated 'to remove the monument to American pilots who bombed Sofia'.[32] Nevertheless the monument still stands. It performs the conventional function of honouring the military dead who contributed to the well-known history of European liberation – yet it is also a ready reminder that the price of that liberation was not only the death of 1,350 Bulgarians, but of over half a million other European civilians.

Bibliography and Sources

1. Archive sources
2. Published documents and reports
3. Official histories
4. Contemporary publications and memoirs
5. Publications since 1950

1. ARCHIVE SOURCES
United Kingdom

Air Historical Branch, Northolt, Middlesex
AHB narratives
German document translations, vols I–XII

Bodleian Library, Oxford
Gilbert Murray papers
Arthur Ponsonby papers
Richard Stokes papers

Camden Local Studies Centre
Hampstead Metropolitan Borough Civil Defence papers
Holborn Borough records
St Pancras Borough records

Christ Church, Oxford
Portal papers
Denis Richards Archive

Churchill College Archive Centre, Cambridge
Sidney Bufton papers
Chartwell Archive
Malcolm Christie papers
Winston S. Churchill papers

A. V. Hill papers
John Hodsoll papers

Hull History Centre
Civil Defence papers
Edgar Young papers

Imperial War Museum, London
Enemy Document Section papers
Italian Series (Air Force), Boxes 1–25
Erhard Milch documents
Speer Collection, German private firms
Speer Collection, Hamburg and Flensburg series

London Metropolitan Archive, Clerkenwell
Air Raid Precautions: London Region
Civil Defence papers

London School of Economics
Hugh Dalton papers
Fellowship of Reconciliation papers
National Peace Council
Peace Pledge Union papers
Women's International League of Peace and Freedom

The National Archives, Kew, London
Admiralty
Air Ministry
Defence Ministry
Foreign Office (Ministry of Economic Warfare, Political Warfare Executive)
Home Office
Metropolitan Police
Ministry of Aircraft Production
Ministry of Health
Ministry of Home Security
Ministry of Information
Ministry of Supply
Prime Minister's papers
John Slessor papers
War Office

National Library of Wales, Aberystwyth
H. Stanley Jevons papers

Nuffield College, Oxford

Lord Cherwell papers
Parliamentary Archive, Westminster
Harold Balfour papers
Beaverbrook papers

RAF Museum, Hendon, London
Norman Bottomley papers
Sholto Douglas papers
Arthur Travers Harris papers
Trafford Leigh-Mallory papers
Richard Peirse papers
Robert Saundby papers
Arthur Tedder papers

Royal Society, London
Patrick Blackett papers

Tyne and Wear Archive, Discovery Museum, Newcastle
Civil Defence records (Gateshead, Newcastle, Sunderland, Whitley Bay)

University of East Anglia, Special Collections
Solly Zuckerman Archive

University Library, Cambridge
Baldwin papers
Anthony Boyle papers, interviews with Arthur Harris
Needham papers
Templewood papers

York City Archive
Civil Defence records

France

Château de Vincennes, Archives de la Défense
Archives du secrétariat d'état à l'aviation
Archives du secrétariat général à la défense aérienne, 1940–1944

Germany

Bundesarchiv-Berlin
NS-Partei-Kanzlei
Organisation Todt

Reichsarbeitsministerium
Reichskanzlei
Reichsministerium des Innern
Reichsministerium für Bewaffnung und Munition
Reichspropagandaleitung-NSDAP
Reichswirtschaftsministerium
Statistisches Reichsamt
Wirtschaftsgruppe Gas- und Wasserversorgung

Bundesarchiv-Militärarchiv
Dienststellen für technische Erprobungen der Luftwaffe
Generalluftzeugmeister
Göring-Akten
Kriegswissenschaftliche Abteilung
Luftflotte 3
Luftschutztruppe
Reichsluftschutzbund
Reichsminister der Luftfahrt
Wehrwirtschaft- und Rüstungsstab papers

Italy

Archivio Centrale dello Stato, Rome
Ministero dell'Aeronautica
Ministero dell'Interno

Malta

National Archives of Malta
ARP papers, 1934–1945

Russia

*Central Archive of the Ministry of Defence of the Russian Federation (TsAMO),
    Podolsk*
Generalstab der Luftwaffe, Luftwaffe Führungsstab papers
Luftflotte 4 papers
II Fliegerkorps

Russian State Archive of the Economy, Moscow
People's Commissariat for the Aircraft Industry

Russian State Military Archive, Moscow
MPVO Headquarters papers
MPVO Leningrad station reports
MPVO Staff Moscow, 1940–1960
MPVO Stalingrad station reports

United States of America

Air Force Historical Research Agency, Maxwell AFB, Alabama
Eighth Air Force archive
Mediterranean Allied Air Forces archives

Franklin D. Roosevelt Library, Hyde Park, New York
Morgenthau papers
Franklin D. Roosevelt archive

Library of Congress, Washington, DC
Frank Andrews papers
Henry H. Arnold papers
James Doolittle papers
Ira C. Eaker papers
Curtis LeMay papers
Carl Spaatz papers

National Archives II, College Park, Maryland
RG 18 Army Air Forces
RG 94 Office of the Adjutant-General
RG 107 Robert Lovett papers
RG 165 War Department General Staff
RG 208 Office of War Information
RG 218 Joint Chiefs of Staff
RG 243 USSBS documents

United States Air Force Academy, Colorado Springs
Haywood Hansell papers
Larry Kuter papers
George McDonald papers

United States Military Academy, West Point
Omar Bradley papers
Benjamin A. Dickson papers
George A. Lincoln papers

2. PUBLISHED DOCUMENTS AND REPORTS

Akten zur Deutschen auswärtigen Politik: 1918–1945, 62 vols (Baden-Baden: Vandenhoeck and Ruprecht, 1950–95)

Boberach, Heinz (ed), *Meldungen aus dem Reich: Die geheimen Lageberichte des Sicherheitsdienstes der SS 1938–1945*, 17 vols (Herrsching: Pawlak Verlag, 1984)

Boelcke, Willi (ed), *The Secret Conferences of Dr Goebbels, 1939–1943* (London: Weidenfeld & Nicolson, 1967)

Colville, John, *The Fringes of Power: Downing Street Diaries 1939–1945* (London: Weidenfeld & Nicolson, 2004)

Cox, Sebastian (ed), *The Strategic Air War Against Germany, 1939–1945: The Official Report of the British Bombing Survey Unit* (London: Frank Cass, 1998)

Daniels, Gordon (ed), *A Guide to the Reports of the United States Strategic Bombing Survey* (London: Royal Historical Society, 1981)

Di Pompeo, Corrado, *Più della fame e più dei bombardamenti: Diario dell'occupazione di Roma* (Bologna: Il Mulino, 2009)

Domarus, Max (ed), *Hitler: Reden und Proklomationen*, 3 vols (Munich: Süddeutscher Verlag, 1965)

Donnelly, Peter (ed), *Mrs. Milburn's Diaries: An Englishwoman's Day-to-Day Reflections 1939–1945* (London: Harrap, 1979)

Eberle, Henrik and Uhl, Matthias (eds), *The Hitler Book: The Secret Dossier Prepared for Stalin* (London: John Murray, 2005)

Foreign & Commonwealth Office, *Churchill and Stalin: Documents from the British Archives* (London: F&CO, 2002)

Fröhlich, Elke (ed), *Die Tagebücher von Joseph Goebbels: Sämtliche Fragmente*, 4 vols (Munich: K. G. Saur, 1987)

Fuehrer Conferences on Naval Affairs, 1939–1945 (London: Greenhill Books, 1990)

Gallup, George (ed), *The Gallup International Public Opinion Polls: Great Britain 1937–1975*, 2 vols (New York: Random House, 1976)

Gilbert, Martin (ed), *The Churchill War Papers: Volume II: Never Surrender, May 1940–December 1940* (London: Heinemann, 1994)

Hubatsch, Walther (ed), *Hitlers Weisungen für die Kriegführung* (Munich: Deutscher Taschenbuch Verlag, 1965)

Hunter, Ian (ed), *Winston & Archie: The Collected Correspondence of Winston Churchill and Archibald Sinclair 1915–1960* (London: Politico's, 2005)

Huston, John W. (ed), *American Air Power Comes of Age: General Henry H. 'Hap' Arnold's World War II Diaries*, 2 vols (Maxwell, AL: Air University Press, 2002)

International Committee of the Red Cross, *Protocols Additional to the Geneva Convention of 12 August 1949* (Geneva: ICRC, 1977)

Isby, David (ed), *Fighting the Bombers: The Luftwaffe's Struggle Against the Allied Bomber Offensive* (London: Greenhill Books, 2003)

Kimball, Warren (ed), *Churchill & Roosevelt: The Complete Correspondence*, 4 vols (London: Collins, 1984)

Klemperer, Victor, *To the Bitter End: The Diaries of Victor Klemperer 1942–1945* (London: Weidenfeld & Nicolson, 1999)

Maurer, M. (ed), *The US Air Service in World War I*, 4 vols (Washington, DC: Office of Air Force History, 1978)

Millgate, Helen (ed), *Mr. Brown's War: A Diary of the Second World War* (Stroud: Sutton Publishing, 1999)

Moll, Martin (ed), *'Führer-Erlasse' 1939–1945* (Stuttgart: Franz Steiner Verlag, 1997)

Neitzel, Sönke, *Tapping Hitler's Generals: Transcripts of Secret Conversations, 1942–1945* (Barnsley: Frontline Books, 2007)

Nicolson, Nigel (ed), *Harold Nicolson: Diaries and Letters, 1939–1945* (London: Collins, 1967)

Origo, Iris, *War in Val d'Orcia: An Italian War Diary 1943–1944* (London: Allison & Busby, 2003)

Pontaut, Jean-Marie and Pelletier, Éric (eds), *Chronique d'une France occupée: Les rapports confidentiels de la gendarmerie 1940–1945* (Neuilly-sur-Seine: Michel Lafon, 2008)

Roberts, Adam and Guelff, R. (eds), *Documents on the Laws of War*, 3rd edn (Oxford: Oxford University Press, 2000)

Savelli, Alfredo, *Offesa aerea: mezzi di difesa e protezione* (Milan: Gontrano Martucci, 1936)

Schlange-Schoeningen, Hans, *The Morning After* (London: Gollancz, 1948)

Schramm, Percy (ed), *Kriegstagebuch des OKW: Eine Dokumentation*, 7 vols (Augsburg: Weltbild, 2007)

Speer, Albert, *Spandau: The Secret Diaries* (London: Collins, 1976)

Target: Germany. The U.S. Army Air Forces' Official Story of the VIII Bomber Command's First Year over Europe (London: HMSO, 1944)

Trevor-Roper, Hugh (ed), *Hitler's Table Talk 1941–1944* (London: Weidenfeld & Nicolson, 1973)

Völker, Karl-Heinz, *Dokumente und Dokumentarfotos zur Geschichte der Deutschen Luftwaffe* (Stuttgart: DVA, 1968)

3. OFFICIAL HISTORIES

Air Ministry, *The Rise and Fall of the German Air Force, 1933–1945* (London: Arms and Armour Press, 1983)

British Committee on the Preservation and Restitution of Works of Art, *Works of Art in Italy: Losses and Survival in the War: Part I – South of Bologna* (London: HMSO, 1945); *Part II – North of Bologna* (London: HMSO, 1946)

Collier, Basil, *The Defence of the United Kingdom* (London: HMSO, 1957)

Craven, Wesley F. and Cate, James L., *The Army Air Forces in World War II*, 7 vols (Chicago, IL: Chicago University Press, 1948–58)

Della Volpe, Nicola, *Difesa del territorio e protezione antiaerea, 1915–1943: storia, documenti, immagini* (Rome: Ufficio storico SME, 1986)

Greenhous, Brereton, Harris, Stephen, Johnston, William and Rawling, William, *The Crucible of War 1939–1945: The Official History of the Royal Canadian Air Force,* vol III (Toronto: Toronto University Press/Department of National Defence, 1994)

Hammond, R. J., *Food: Volume III: Studies in Administration and Control* (London: HMSO, 1962)

Herington, John, *Air War against Germany and Italy 1939–1945* (Canberra: Australian War Memorial, 1954)

Herington, John, *Air Power over Europe 1944–1945* (Canberra: Australian War Memorial, 1963)

Hinsley, F. H. et al., *British Intelligence in the Second World War,* 4 vols (London: HMSO, 1979–90)

Hornby, W., *Factories and Plant* (London: HMSO, 1958)

Maurer, M., *Aviation in the U.S. Army, 1919–1939,* 4 vols (Washington, DC: Office of Air Force History, 1987)

O'Brien, Terence, *Civil Defence* (London: HMSO, 1955)

Postan, Michael, *British War Production* (London: HMSO, 1957)

Richards, Denis, *Royal Air Force 1939–1945,* 3 vols (London: HMSO, 1974)

Ritchie, Sebastian, *The RAF, Small Wars and Insurgencies in the Middle East, 1919–1939* (Northolt: Air Historical Branch, 2011)

Statistical Digest of the War (London: HMSO, 1951)

Titmuss, Richard, *Problems of Social Policy* (London: HMSO, 1950)

Wagner, Ray (ed), *The Soviet Air Force in World War II: The Official History* (Newton Abbot: David and Charles, 1973)

Webster, Charles and Frankland, Noble, *The Strategic Air Offensive against Germany,* 4 vols (London: HMSO, 1961)

4. CONTEMPORARY PUBLICATIONS AND MEMOIRS

Anon., *A Woman in Berlin* (London: Virago Press, 2005)

Arnold, Henry H., *Global Mission* (New York: Harper & Row, 1949)

A Warden (anon.), *From Dusk to Dawn* (London: Constable, 1941)

Balfour, Harold, *Wings over Westminster* (London: Hutchinson, 1973)

Below, Nicolaus von, *At Hitler's Side: The Memoirs of Hitler's Luftwaffe Adjutant, 1937–1945* (London: Greenhill Books, 2001)

Birse, A. H., *Memoirs of an Interpreter* (London: Michael Joseph, 1967)

Bond, Horatio (ed), *Fire and the Air War* (Boston, MA: National Fire Protection Association, 1946)

Brittain, Vera, *England's Hour* (London: Continuum, 2005)

Churchill, Winston S., *The Second World War,* 6 vols (London: Cassell, 1948–54)

Ciano, Galeazzo, *Diario 1937–1943,* ed. De Felice, Renzo (Milan: RCS, 1990)

Citrine, Walter, *In Moscow Now* (London: Robert Hale, 1942)

Cot, Pierre, *Triumph of Treason* (Chicago, IL: Ziff-Davis, 1944)

Cowles, Virginia, *Looking for Trouble* (London: Hamish Hamilton, 1941)

Davy, M. Bernard, *Air Power and Civilisation* (London: George Allen & Unwin, 1941)

Deane, John, *The Strange Alliance: The Story of American Efforts at Wartime Co-operation with Russia* (London: John Murray, 1947)

Docherty, James, *Post 381: The Memoirs of a Belfast Air-Raid Warden* (Belfast: The Friar's Bush Press, 1989)

Douglas, Sholto, *Years of Command* (London: Collins, 1966)

Douhet, Giulio, *The Command of the Air*, trans. Dino Ferrari (Washington, DC: Office of Air Force History, 1983)

Flannery, Harry, *Assignment to Berlin* (London: Michael Joseph, 1942)

Gafencu, Grigore, *The Last Days of Europe: A Diplomatic Journey in 1939* (London: Frederick Muller, 1947)

Galbraith, John K., *A Life in Our Times: Memoirs* (London: Andre Deutsch, 1981)

Galland, Adolf, *The First and the Last* (London: Methuen, 1955)

Glover, C. W., *Civil Defence* (London: Chapman & Hall, 1938)

Goldsworthy, Lowes Dickinson, *War: Its Nature, Causes and Cure* (London: George Allen & Unwin, 1923)

Graves, Charles, *Women in Green: The Story of the W.V.S.* (London: Heinemann, 1948)

Green, Henry, *Caught* (London: Hogarth Press, 1943)

Hampe, Erich, *... als alles in Scherben fiel* (Osnabrück: Biblio Verlag, 1979)

Hansell, Haywood, *The Air Plan that Defeated Hitler* (Atlanta, GA: Higgins McArthur, 1972)

Harris, Arthur T., *Bomber Offensive* (London: Collins, 1947)

Harrisson, Tom, *Living Through the Blitz* (London: Collins, 1976)

Hayes, Denis, *Challenge of Conscience: The Story of the Conscientious Objectors of 1939–1949* (London: George Allen & Unwin, 1949)

Heinkel, Ernst, *He 1000* (London: Hutchinson, 1956)

Heller, Joseph, *Catch 22* (London: Vintage, 1994)

Hunt, Irmgard, *On Hitler's Mountain: My Nazi Childhood* (London: Atlantic Books, 2005)

Hyde, H. Montgomery and Nuttall, G. R. Falkiner, *Air Defence and the Civil Population* (London: The Cresset Press, 1937)

Idle, E. Doreen, *War over West Ham: A Study of Community Adjustment* (London: Faber & Faber, 1943)

Iklé, Frederick, 'The Effect of War Destruction upon the Ecology of Cities', *Social Forces*, 29 (1950–51), 383–91

Jameson, Storm (ed), *Challenge to Death* (London: Constable, 1934)

Jesse, F. Tennyson and Harwood, H. M., *While London Burns* (London: Constable, 1942)

Jones, R. V., *Most Secret War: British Scientific Intelligence 1939–1945* (London: Hamish Hamilton, 1978)

Kaplan, Chaim, *Scroll of Agony: The Warsaw Diary of Chaim A. Kaplan* (London: Hamish Hamilton, 1966)

Kempe, A. B. C., *Midst Bands and Bombs* (Maidstone: 'Kent Messenger', 1946)

Kesselring, Albert, *The Memoirs of Field-Marshal Kesselring* (London: Greenhill Books, 2007)

Klibansky, Raymond (ed), *Mussolini's Memoirs 1942–1943* (London: Phoenix Press, 2000)

Klotz, Helmut, *Militärische Lehren des Burgerkrieges in Spanien* (self-published, 1937)

Klukowski, Andrew and Klukowski, Helen (eds), *Diary from the Years of Occupation: Zygmunt Klukowski* (Urbana, IL: Illinois University Press, 1993)

Knocke, Heinz, *I Flew for the Führer* (London: Evans Brothers, 1953)

Ley, Willy, *Bombs and Bombing* (New York: Modern Age Books, 1941)

Lloyd, Hugh, *Briefed to Attack: Malta's Part in the African Victory* (London: Hodder & Stoughton, 1949)

Lucas, Laddie, *Malta: The Thorn in Rommel's Side* (London: Penguin, 1993)

Magaieva, Svetlana and Pleysier, Albert, *Surviving the Blockade of Leningrad* (Lanham, MD: University Press of America, 2006)

Maisky, Ivan, *Memoirs of a Soviet Ambassador* (London: Hutchinson, 1967)

Mitchell, William, *Winged Defense* (New York: G. P. Putnam & Sons, 1925)

Moniushko, Evgenii, *From Leningrad to Hungary: Notes of a Red Army Soldier, 1941–1946* (London: Frank Cass, 2005)

Morison, Frank [Ross, Albert Henry], *War on Great Cities: A Study of the Facts* (London: Faber & Faber, 1938)

Morris, Joseph, *The German Air Raids on Great Britain, 1914–1918* (London: Samson, Low, Marston & Co, 1925)

Morrison, Herbert, *An Autobiography of Lord Morrison of Lambeth* (London: Odhams Press, 1960)

Mumford, Lewis, *The Culture of Cities* (New York: Harcourt Brace, 1938)

New Fabian Research Bureau, *The Road to War, Being an Analysis of the National Government's Foreign Policy* (London: Victor Gollancz, 1937)

Nixon, Barbara, *Raiders Overhead: A Diary of the London Blitz* (London: Scolar Press, 1980)

Nossack, Hans, *The End: Hamburg 1943* (Chicago, IL: Chicago University Press, 2004)

Pile, Frederick, *Ack-Ack: Britain's Defence Against Air Attack During the Second World War* (London: George Harrap, 1949)

Piratin, Philip, *Our Flag Stays Red* (London: Thames Publications, 1948)

Portal, Charles, 'Air Force Co-Operation in Policing the Empire', *Journal of the Royal United Services Institution*, 82 (1937), 343–57

Reck-Malleczewen, Friedrich, *Diary of a Man in Despair* (London: Audiogrove, 1995)

Rostow, Walter W., *Pre-Invasion Bombing Strategy: General Eisenhower's Decision of March 25, 1944* (Aldershot, Hants: Gower, 1981)

Rumpf, Hans, *The Bombing of Germany* (London: White Lion Publishers, 1957)

Schneider, Helga, *The Bonfire of Berlin: A Lost Childhood in Wartime Germany* (London: Vintage Books, 2005)

Shirer, William, *Berlin Diary: The Journal of a Foreign Correspondent 1934–1941* (London: Hamish Hamilton, 1941)

Slessor, John, *The Central Blue: Recollections and Reflections* (London: Cassell, 1956)

Smith, Howard, *Last Train from Berlin* (London: The Cresset Press, 1942)

Southern, George, *Poisonous Inferno: World War II Tragedy at Bari Harbour* (Shrewsbury: Airlife, 2002)

Speer, Albert, *Inside the Third Reich* (London: Weidenfeld & Nicolson, 1970)

Spender, Stephen, *Citizens in War – And After* (London: George Harrap, 1945)

Sperling, Hans, 'Deutsche Bevölkerungsbilanz des 2. Weltkrieges', *Wirtschaft und Statistik*, 8 (1956), 493–500

Stebbing, Edward, *Diary of a Decade: 1939–1950* (Lewes: Book Guild, 1998)

Steer, George, *The Tree of Gernika: A Field Study of Modern War* (London: Hodder and Stoughton, 1938)

Stein, Anja vom, *Unser Köln: Erinnerungen 1910–1960* (Erfurt: Sutton Verlag, 1999)

Stengel, E., 'Air-Raid Phobia', *The British Journal of Medical Psychology*, 20 (1944–46), 135–43

Stewart, Oliver, 'The Doctrine of Strategical Bombing', *Journal of the Royal United Services Institution*, 81 (1936), 97–101

Strachey, John, *Post D: Some Experiences of an Air-Raid Warden* (London: Gollancz, 1941)

Süssmilch, Waltraud, *Im Bunker: Eine Überlebende berichtet vom Bombenkrieg in Berlin* (Berlin: Ullstein, 2004)

Sykes, Frederick, *From Many Angles: An Autobiography* (London: Harrap, 1943)

Tedder, Lord Arthur, *With Prejudice: The War Memoirs of Marshal of the Royal Air Force Lord Tedder* (London: Cassell, 1966)

Twyford, H. P., *It Came to Our Door: Plymouth in the World War* (Plymouth: Underhill, 1945)

Vernon, P. E., 'Psychological Effects of Air-Raids', *The Journal of Abnormal and Social Psychology*, 36 (1941), 457–76

Voyetekhov, Boris, *The Last Days of Sevastopol* (London: Cassell, 1943)

Warlimont, Walter, *Inside Hitler's Headquarters 1939–1945* (London: Weidenfeld & Nicolson, 1964)

Wells, H. G., *The War in the Air* (London: George Bell, 1908)

Werth, Alexander, *Leningrad* (London: Hamish Hamilton, 1944)

Werth, Alexander, *Moscow '41* (London: Hamish Hamilton, 1944)

Wilmott, H. G., 'Air Control in Ovamboland', *Journal of the Royal United Services Institution*, 83 (1938), 823–9

Wintringham, Tom, *The Coming World War* (London: Lawrence Wishart, 1935)

Zuckerman, Solly, *From Apes to Warlords: The Autobiography of Solly Zuckerman, 1904–1946* (London: Hamish Hamilton, 1978)

5. PUBLICATIONS SINCE 1950

Addison, Paul and Crang, Jeremy (eds), *Firestorm: The Bombing of Dresden, 1945* (London: Pimlico, 2006)

Alegi, Gregory, 'Qualità del materiale bellico e dottrina d'impiego italiana nella seconda guerra mondiale: il caso della Regia Aeronautica', *Storia contemporanea*, 18 (1987), 197–219

Altes, A. Korthals, *Luchtgevaar: Luchtaanvallen op Nederland 1940–1945* (Amsterdam: Sijthoff, 1984)

Aly, Götz, *Hitlers Volksstaat: Raub, Rassenkrieg und Nationaler Sozialismus* (Frankfurt am Main: S. Fischer Verlag, 2005)

Austin, Douglas, *Malta and British Strategic Policy, 1925–1943* (London: Frank Cass, 2004)

Baker, Nicholson, *Human Smoke: The Beginnings of World War II and the End of Civilization* (New York: Simon & Schuster, 2008)

Baldoli, Claudia, 'Bombing the Eternal City', *History Today* (May 2012), 11–15

Baldoli, Claudia, 'The "Northern Dominator" and the Mare Nostrum: Fascist Italy's "Cultural War" in Malta', *Modern Italy*, 13 (2008), 5–20

Baldoli, Claudia, 'Spring 1943: The Fiat Strikes and the Collapse of the Italian Home Front', *History Workshop Journal*, 72 (2011), 181–9

Baldoli, Claudia and Fincardi, Marco, 'Italian Society under Anglo-American Bombs: Propaganda, Experience and Legend, 1940–1945', *The Historical Journal*, 52 (2009), 1,017–38

Baldoli, Claudia and Knapp, Andrew, *Forgotten Blitzes: France and Italy under Allied Air Attack, 1940–1945* (London: Continuum, 2012)

Baldoli, Claudia, Knapp, Andrew and Overy, Richard (eds), *Bombing, States and Peoples in Western Europe, 1940–1945* (London: Continuum, 2011)

Balfour, Michael, *Propaganda in War, 1939–1945* (London: Routledge, 1979)

Barber, John, 'The Moscow Crisis of October 1941', in Cooper, Julian, Perrie, Maureen and Rees, E. A. (eds), *Soviet History 1917–1953: Essays in Honour of R. W. Davies* (London: Macmillan, 1995), 201–18

Barker, Rachel, *Conscience, Government and War* (London: Routledge, 1982)

Battesti, Michèle and Facon, Patrick (eds), *Les bembardements alliés sur la France durant la Seconde Guerre Mondiale: stratégies, bilans Matériaux et humains* (Vincennes: Centre d'études d'histoire de la défense)

Beck, Earl, *Under the Bombs: The German Home Front, 1942–1945* (Lexington, KS: Kentucky University Press, 1986)

Beer, Wilfried, *Kriegsalltag an der Heimatfront: Alliierten Luftkrieg und deutsche Gegenmassnahmen zur Abwehr und Schadensbegrenzung dargestellt für den Raum Münster* (Bremen: H. M. Hauschild, 1990)

Beevor, Antony, *Stalingrad: The Fateful Siege 1942–1943* (London: Viking, 1998)

Bell, Amy, 'Landscapes of Fear: Wartime London 1939–1945', *Journal of British Studies*, 48 (2009), 153–75

Bell, Amy, *London Was Ours: Diaries and Memoirs of the London Blitz* (London: I. B. Tauris, 2008)

Bellamy, Christopher, *Absolute War: Soviet Russia in the Second World War* (London: Macmillan, 2007)

Bergander, Götz, *Dresden im Luftkrieg: Vorgeschichte – Zerstörung – Folgen* (Munich: Heyne Verlag, 1985)

Bernard, P., 'A propos de la stratégie aérienne pendant la Première Guerre Mondiale: Mythes et realités', *Revue d'Histoire Moderne et Contemporaine*, 16 (1969), 350–75

Berrington, Hugh, 'When Does Personality Make a Difference? Lord Cherwell and the Area Bombing of Germany', *International Political Science Review*, 10 (1989), 9–34

Best, Geoffrey, *Humanity in Warfare: The Modern History of the International Law of Armed Conflicts* (London: Routledge, 1980)

Bialer, Uri, 'Humanization in Air Warfare in British Foreign Policy on the Eve of the Second World War', *Journal of Contemporary History*, 13 (1978), 79–96

Biddle, Tami Davis, 'British and American Approaches to Strategic Bombing: Their Origin and Implementation in the World War II Bomber Offensive', in Gooch, John (ed), *Airpower: Theory and Practice* (London: Frank Cass, 1995), 91–120

Biddle, Tami Davis, *Rhetoric and Reality in Air Warfare: The Evolution of British and American Ideas about Strategic Bombing 1914–1945* (Princeton, NJ: Princeton University Press, 2002)

Biddle, Tami Davis, 'Wartime Reactions', in Addison and Crang (eds), *Firestorm*, 96–122

Bidlack, Richard, 'The Political Mood in Leningrad during the First Year of the Soviet-German War', *The Russian Review*, 59 (2000), 96–113

Blank, Ralf, 'The Battle of the Ruhr, 1943: Aerial Warfare against an Industrial Region', *Labour History Review*, 77 (2012), 35–48

Blank, Ralf, 'Kriegsalltag und Luftkrieg an der "Heimatfront"', in Echternkamp, Jörg (ed), *Das Deutsche Reich und der Zweite Weltkrieg: Band 9, erster Halbband: Die deutsche Kriegsgesellschaft* (Stuttgart: DVA, 2004), 357–464

Boelcke, Willi, *Die Kosten von Hitlers Krieg* (Paderborn: Schöningh, 1985)

Boiry, Philippe, *Paris sous les bombes: Auteuil septembre 1943* (Paris: L'Harmattan, 2000)

Boog, Horst, 'Strategischer Luftkrieg in Europa 1943–1944', in Boog, Horst, Krebs, Gerhard and Vogel, Detlef, *Das Deutsche Reich und der Zweite Weltkrieg: Band 7: Das Deutsche Reich in der Defensive* (Stuttgart: DVA, 2001)

Boog, Horst (ed), *The Conduct of the Air War in the Second World War: An International Comparison* (Oxford: Berg, 1992)

Boog, Horst et al., *Das Deutsche Reich und der Zweite Weltkrieg: Band 4: Der Angriff auf die Sowjetunion* (Stuttgart: DVA, 1983)

Bothe, M., Partsch, K. J. and Solf, W. A. (eds), *New Rules for Victims of Armed Conflicts: Commentary on the Two 1977 Protocols Additional to the Geneva Convention of 1949* (The Hague: Martinus Nijhoff, 1982)

Botti, Ferruccio, 'Amedeo Mecozzi', in *Actes du colloque international 'Précurseurs et prophètes de l'aviation militaire'* (Paris: Service historique de l'armée de l'air, 1992), 134–9

Bourke, Joanna, *Fear: A Cultural History* (London: Virago, 2005)

Boyd, Alexander, *The Soviet Air Force since 1918* (London: Macdonald and Jane's, 1977)

Braithwaite, Rodric, *Moscow 1941: A City and its People at War* (London: Profile Books, 2006)

Brakman, Steven, Garretsen, Harry and Schramm, Marc, 'The Strategic Bombing of German Cities during World War II and its Impact on City Growth', *Journal of Economic Geography*, 4 (2004), 201–18

Brauer, Jurgen and Tuyll, Hubert van, *Castles, Battles & Bombs: How Economics Explains Military History* (Chicago, IL: Chicago University Press, 2008)

Brinkhus, Jörn, 'Ziviler Luftschutz im "Dritten Reich" – Wandel seiner Spitzenorganisation', in Süss, Dietmar (ed), *Deutschland im Luftkrieg: Geschichte und Erinnerung* (Munich: Oldenbourg Verlag, 2007), 27–40

Brookes, Andrew, *Air War over Russia* (Horsham: Ian Allen, 2003)

Brooks, Geoffrey, *Hitler's Nuclear Weapons* (London: Leo Cooper, 1992)

Brown, Donald, *Somerset Against Hitler: Secret Operations in the Mendips 1939–1945* (Newbury: Countryside Books, 1999)

Brown, Michael, *Put That Light Out! Britain's Civil Defence Services at War 1939–1945* (Stroud: Sutton Publishing, 1999)

Brunswig, Hans, *Feuersturm über Hamburg: Die Luftangriffe auf Hamburg im 2. Weltkrieg und ihre Folgen* (Stuttgart: Motorbuch Verlag, 1985)

Buckley, John, *Air Power in the Age of Total War* (London: UCL Press, 1999)

Bucur, Maria, *Heroes and Victims: Remembering War in Twentieth-Century Romania* (Bloomington, IN: Indiana University Press, 2009)

Budden, Michael, 'Defending the Indefensible? The Air Defence of Malta, 1936–40', *War in History*, 6 (1999), 447–67

Budiansky, Stephen, *Air Power* (New York: Viking, 2004)

Budrass, Lutz, *Flugzeugindustrie und Luftrüstung in Deutschland 1918–1945* (Düsseldorf: Droste Verlag, 1998)

Budrass, Lutz, Scherner, Jonas and Streb, Jochen, 'Fixed-Price Contracts, Learning, and Outsourcing: Explaining the Continuous Growth of Output and Labour Productivity in the German Aircraft Industry during the Second World War', *Economic History Review*, 2nd Ser., 63 (2010), 107–36

Burleigh, Michael, *Moral Combat: A History of World War II* (London: Harper Collins, 2010)

Busch, Dieter, *Der Luftkrieg im Raum Mainz während des Zweiten Weltkrieges 1939–1945* (Mainz: Hase & Koehler, 1988)

Büttner, Gretl, 'Zwischen Leben und Tod', in Hage, Volker (ed), *Hamburg 1943: Literarische Zeugnisse zum Feuersturm* (Frankfurt am Main: Fischer Verlag, 2003), 21–35

Büttner, Ursula, '"Gomorrha" und die Folgen', in Hamburg Forschungsstelle für Zeitgeschichte, *Hamburg im 'Dritten Reich'* (Göttingen: Wallstein Verlag, 2005), 613–32

Caddick-Adams, Peter, *Monte Cassino: Ten Armies in Hell* (London: Preface Publishing, 2012)

Calder, Angus, *The Myth of the Blitz* (London: Jonathan Cape, 1991)

Castioni, Luigi, 'I radar industriali italiani. Ricerche, ricordi, considerazioni per una loro storia', *Storia contemporanea*, 18 (1987), 1,221–65

Cate, Johannes ten, Otto, Gerhard and Overy, Richard (eds), *Die 'Neuordnung' Europas: NS-Wirtschaftspolitik in den besetzten Gebieten* (Berlin: Metropol Verlag, 1997)

Ceadel, Martin, 'The First British Referendum: The Peace Ballot 1934–35', *English Historical Review*, 95 (1980), 810–39

Ceva, Lucio, *Spagna 1936–1939: Politica e guerra civile* (Milan: Franco Angeli, 2010)

Ceva, Lucio and Curami, Andrea, 'Luftstreitkräfte und Luftfahrtindustrie in Italien, 1936–1943', in Boog, Horst (ed), *Luftkriegführung im Zweiten Weltkrieg* (Bonn: E. S. Mittler, 1993), 113–36

Chary, Frederick, *The Bulgarian Jews and the Final Solution 1940–1944* (Pittsburgh, NJ: University of Pittsburgh Press, 1972)

Chauvy, Gérard, *Le drame de l'armée française du front populaire à Vichy* (Paris: Pygmalion, 2010)

Chianese, Gloria, *'Quando uscimmo dai rifugi': Il Mezzogiorno tra guerra e dopoguerra (1943–46)* (Rome: Carocci editore, 2004)

Clodfelter, Mark, *Beneficial Bombing: The Progressive Foundations of American Air Power, 1917–1945* (Lincoln, NE: Nebraska University Press, 2010)

Cluet, M., *L'Architecture du IIIe Reich: Origines intellectuelles et visées idéologiques* (Bern: Peter Lang, 1987)

Coccoli, Carlotta, 'I "fortilizi inespugnabili della civiltà italiana": La protezione antiaerea del patrimonio monumentale italiano durante la seconda guerra mondiale', *Scienza e Beni Culturali*, 26 (2010), 409–18

Connelly, Mark, 'The British People, the Press and the Strategic Air Campaign against Germany, 1939–1945', *Contemporary British History*, 16 (2002), 39–58

Connelly, Mark, *Reaching for the Stars: A New History of Bomber Command in World War II* (London: I. B. Tauris, 2001)

Connelly, Mark, *We Can Take It! Britain and the Memory of the Second World War* (Harlow: Longman, 2004)

Connelly, Mark and Goebel, Stefan, 'Zwischen Erinnerungspolitik und Erinnerungskonsum: Der Luftkrieg in Grossbritannien', in Arnold, Jörg, Süss, Dietmar and Thiessen, Malte (eds), *Luftkrieg: Erinnerungen in Deutschland und Europa* (Göttingen: Wallstein Verlag, 2009), 50–65

Conversino, Mark, *Fighting with the Soviets: The Failure of Operation Frantic 1944–1945* (Lawrence, KS: University Press of Kansas, 1997)

Cooke, Ronald and Nesbit, Roy, *Target: Hitler's Oil. Allied Attacks on German Oil Supplies 1939–1945* (London: William Kimber, 1985)

Cooper, Anthony, *Anti-Aircraft Command 1939–1945: The Other Forgotten Army* (Fleet Hargate, Lincs.: Arcturus Press, 2004)

Cooper, Matthew, 'A House Divided: Policy, Rivalry and Administration in Britain's Military Air Command', *Journal of Strategic Studies*, 3 (1980), 178–201

Cortesi, Elena, 'Evacuation in Italy during the Second World War: Evolution and Management', in Baldoli, Knapp and Overy (eds), *Bombing, States and Peoples*, 59–74

Cortesi, Elena, 'Il "primo sfollamento" (maggio 1940–ottobre 1942)', in Labanca, Nicola (ed), *I bombardamenti aerei sull'Italia* (Bologna: Il Mulino, 2012), 177–94

Corum, James, 'Airpower Thought in Continental Europe between the Wars', in Philip Meilinger (ed), *The Paths to Heaven: The Evolution of Airpower Theory* (Maxwell AFB, AL: Air University Press, 1997), 151–81

Corum, James, 'From Biplanes to Blitzkrieg: The Development of German Air Force Doctrine between the Wars', *War in History*, 3 (1996), 85–101

Corum, James, *The Luftwaffe: Creating the Operational Air War, 1918–1940* (Lawrence, KS: University Press of Kansas, 1997)

Corum, James, *Wolfram von Richthofen: Master of the German Air War* (Lawrence, KS: University Press of Kansas, 2008)

Cox, Sebastian, 'A Comparative Analysis of RAF and Luftwaffe Intelligence in the Battle of Britain', *Intelligence and National Security*, 5 (1990), 425–43

Cox, Sebastian, 'The Dresden Raids: Why and How', in Addison and Crang (eds), *Firestorm*, 18–61

Crampton, Richard, *Bulgaria* (Oxford: Oxford University Press, 2007)

Crane, Conrad C., *Bombs, Cities and Civilians: American Airpower Strategy in World War II* (Lawrence, KS: University Press of Kansas, 1993)

Crane, Conrad C., 'Evolution of U.S. Strategic Bombing of Urban Areas', *Historian*, 50 (1987), 14–39

Creveld, Martin van, *The Age of Airpower* (New York: Public Affairs, 2011)

Creveld, Martin van, *Hitler's Strategy 1940–41: The Balkan Clue* (Cambridge: Cambridge University Press, 1973)

Curami, Andrea, Ferrari, Paolo and Rastelli, Achille, *Alle origini della Breda Meccanica Bresciana* (Brescia: Fondazione Negri, 2009)

Darlow, Steve, *Sledgehammers for Tintacks: Bomber Command Combats the V-1 Menace 1943–1944* (London: Grub Street, 2002)

Daso, Dick, *Hap Arnold and the Evolution of American Airpower* (Washington, DC: Smithsonian Institution, 2000)

Davies, Norman, *Rising '44: The Battle for Warsaw* (London: Macmillan, 2003)

Davies, Thomas, 'France and the World Disarmament Conference of 1932–1934', *Diplomacy & Statecraft*, 15 (2004), 765–80

Davis, Richard G., *Bombing the European Axis Powers: A Historical Digest of the Combined Bomber Offensive, 1939–1945* (Maxwell AFB, AL: Air University Press, 2006)

Davis, Richard G., *Carl A. Spaatz and the Air War in Europe* (Washington, DC: Office of Air Force History, 1993)

Dean, Martin, *Robbing the Jews: The Confiscation of Jewish Property in the Holocaust, 1933–1945* (Cambridge: Cambridge University Press, 2008)

De Simone, Cesare, *Venti angeli sopra Roma: I bombardamenti aerei sulla Città Eterna* (Milan: Mursia, 1993)

Del Boca, Angelo, *I gas di Mussolini* (Rome: Editori Riuniti, 1996)

Diamond, Hannah, *Fleeing Hitler: France 1940* (Oxford: Oxford University Press, 2007)

Diefendorf, Jeffry, *In the Wake of War: The Reconstruction of German Cities after World War II* (New York: Oxford University Press, 1993)

Dobinson, Colin, *AA Command: Britain's Anti-Aircraft Defences in World War II* (London: Methuen, 2001)

Dobinson, Colin, *Building Radar: Forging Britain's Early-Warning Chain, 1935–45* (London: Methuen, 2010)

Dodd, Lindsey, '"Relieving Sorrow and Misfortune"? State, Charity, Ideology and Aid in Bombed-out France, 1940–1944', in Baldoli, Knapp and Overy (eds), *Bombing, States and Peoples*, 75–98

Dodd, Lindsey and Knapp, Andrew, '"How Many Frenchmen Did You Kill?": British Bombing Policy Towards France (1940–1945)', *French History*, 22 (2008), 469–92

Donoughue, Bernard and Jones, G. W., *Herbert Morrison: Portrait of a Politician* (London: Phoenix Press, 2001)

Duffy, James, *Target America: Hitler's Plan to Attack the United States* (Guilford, CT: Lyons Press, 2006)

Duggan, John, *Neutral Ireland and the Third Reich* (Dublin: Gill & Macmillan, 1985)

Dumoulin, Olivier, 'A Comparative Approach to Newsreels and Bombing in the Second World War: Britain, France and Germany', in Baldoli, Knapp and Overy (eds), *Bombing, States and Peoples*, 298–314

Dunning, Christopher, *Courage Alone: The Italian Air Force 1940–1943* (Manchester: Hikoki Publications, 2010)

Dunning, Christopher, *Regia Aeronautica: The Italian Air Force 1923–1945* (Hersham: Ian Allan, 2009)

Dyke, Carl van, *The Soviet Invasion of Finland 1939–1940* (London: Frank Cass, 1997)

Edgerton, David, *Britain's War Machine: Weapons, Resources and Experts in the Second World War* (London: Allen Lane, 2011)

Ehlers, Robert S., 'Bombers, "Butchers", and Britain's Bête Noire: Reappraising RAF Bomber Command's Role in World War II', *Air Power Review*, 14 (2011), 5–18

Ehlers, Robert S., *Targeting the Reich: Air Intelligence and the Allied Bombing Campaigns* (Lawrence, KS: University Press of Kansas, 2009)

Eichholtz, Dietrich, *Geschichte der deutschen Kriegswirtschaft*, 4 vols (Munich: K. G. Saur, 1999)

Emme, E. M., 'Technical Change and Western Military Thought', *Military Affairs*, 24 (1960), 6–19

Erdheim, Stuart, 'Could the Allies Have Bombed Auschwitz-Birkenau?', *Holocaust and Genocide Studies*, 11 (1997), 129–70

Esch, Joris van, 'Restrained Policy and Careless Execution: Allied Strategic Bombing on the Netherlands in the Second World War' (Fort Leavenworth, KS: School of Advanced Military Studies)

Essex, Stephen and Brayshay, Mark, 'Boldness Diminished? The Post-War Battle to Replan a Bomb-Damaged Provincial City', *Urban History*, 35 (2008), 437–61

Evans, Richard, *The Third Reich at War* (London: Allen Lane, 2008)

Ewen, Shane, 'Preparing the British Fire Service for War: Local Government, Nationalisation and Evolutionary Reform, 1935–41', *Contemporary British History*, 20 (2006), 209–31

Farr, Martin, 'The Labour Party and Strategic Bombing in the Second World War', *Labour History Review*, 77 (2012), 133–54

Fedorowich, Kent, 'Axis Prisoners of War as Sources for British Military Intelligence, 1939–42', *Intelligence and National Security*, 14 (1999), 156–78

Feigel, Lara, *The Love-Charm of Bombs* (London: Bloomsbury, 2013)

Ferrari, Paolo, 'Un arma versatile. I bombardamenti strategici anglo-americani e l'industria italiana', in idem (ed), *L'aeronautica italiana: una storia del Novecento* (Milan: Franco Angeli, 2004), 391–432

Field, Geoffrey, *Blood, Sweat and Toil: Remaking the British Working Class, 1939–1945* (Oxford: Oxford University Press, 2011)

Field, Geoffrey, 'Nights Underground in Darkest London: The Blitz, 1940–41', *International Labor and Working-Class History*, 62 (2002), 11–49

Fincardi, Marco, 'Gli italiani e l'attesa di un bombardamento della capitale (1940–1943)', in Labanca (ed), *I bombardamenti aerei*, 213–46

Florentin, Eddy, *Quand les Alliés bombardaient la France, 1940–1945* (Paris: Perrin, 2008)

Flower, Stephen, *Barnes Wallis' Bombs: Tallboy, Dambuster and Grand Slam* (Stroud: Tempus, 2002)

Foedrowitz, Michael, *Bunkerwelten: Luftschutzanlagen in Norddeutschland* (Berlin: Links Verlag, 1998)

Foedrowitz, Michael, *Flak-Towers* (Berlin: Berlin Underworlds' Association, 2008)

Formiconi, Paolo, 'La protezione e la difesa contraerea del regime fascista: evoluzione istituzionale', in Labanca (ed), *I bombardamenti aerei*, 117–30

Förster, Gerhard, *Totaler Krieg und Blitzkrieg* (Berlin: Deutscher Militärverlag, 1967)

Förster, Jürgen, 'Hitler Turns East – German War Policy in 1940 and 1941', in Wegner, Bernd (ed), *From Peace to War: Germany, Soviet Russia and the World, 1939–1941* (Oxford: Berg, 1997)

Fredette, Raymond, *The Sky on Fire: The First Battle of Britain, 1917–1918, and the Birth of the Royal Air Force* (Washington, DC: Smithsonian Institution, 1991)

Freedman, Ariela, 'Zeppelin Fictions and the British Home Front', *Journal of Modern Literature*, 27 (2004), 47–62

Freeman, Roger, *The Mighty Eighth War Diary* (London: Jane's, 1981)

Friedrich, Jörg, *The Fire: The Bombing of Germany 1940–1945* (New York: Columbia University Press)

Frieser, Karl-Heinz (ed), *Das Deutsche Reich und der Zweite Weltkrieg: Band 8: Die Ostfront 1943/44* (Stuttgart: DVA, 2007)

Fritzsche, Peter, *A Nation of Flyers: German Aviation and the Popular Imagination* (Cambridge, MA: Harvard University Press, 1992)

Furse, Anthony, *Wilfrid Freeman: The Genius Behind Allied Survival and Air Supremacy 1939 to 1945* (Staplehurst, Kent: Spellmount, 2000)

Futrell, Robert, *Ideas, Concepts, Doctrine: A History of Basic Thinking in the United States Air Force* (Maxwell AFB, AL: Air University Press, 1971)

Gabriele, Mariano, 'L'offensiva su Malta (1941)', in Rainero, R. and Biagini, A. (eds), *Italia in guerra: il secondo anno, 1941* (Rome: Commissione Italiana di Storia Militare, 1992), 435–50

Gabriele, Mariano, 'L'operazione "C.3"', in Rainero, R. and Biagini, A. (eds), *Italia in guerra: il terzo anno, 1942* (Rome: Commissione Italiana di Storia Militare, 1993), 409–34

Galea, Frederick, *Women of Malta: True Wartime Stories of Christina Ratcliffe and Tamara Marks* (Rabat: Wise Owl Publications, 2006)

Gardiner, Juliet, *The Blitz: The British under Attack* (London: HarperCollins, 2010)

Garrett, Stephen A., *Ethics and Airpower in World War II: The British Bombing of German Cities* (New York: St Martin's Press, 1993)

Gentile, Gian, *How Effective is Strategic Bombing? Lessons Learned from World War II to Kosovo* (New York: New York University Press, 2000)

Gilbert, Martin, *Finest Hour: Winston S. Churchill 1939–1941* (London: Heinemann, 1983)

Gioannini, Marco and Massobrio, Giulio, *Bombardate Italia. Storia della guerra di destruzione aerea 1940–1945* (Milan: Rizzoli, 2007)

Glantz, David, *The Siege of Leningrad 1941–1944* (London: Orion Books, 2004)

Glienke, Stephan, 'The Allied Air War and German Society', in Baldoli, Knapp and Overy (eds), *Bombing, States and Peoples*, 184–205

Goldberg, Arthur (ed), *A History of the United States Air Force, 1907–1957* (Princeton, NJ: Princeton University Press, 1957)

Golücke, Friedhelm, *Schweinfurt und der strategische Luftkrieg 1943* (Paderborn: Friedrich Schöningh, 1980)

Gorinov, M. M., 'Muscovites' Moods, 22 June 1941 to May 1942', in Thurston, Robert and Bonwetsch, Bernd (eds), *The People's War: Responses to World War II in the Soviet Union* (Chicago, IL: Illinois University Press, 2000), 108–36

Goyet, P. le, 'Evolution de la doctrine d'emploi de l'aviation française entre 1919 et 1939', *Revue d'histoire de la Deuxième Guerre Mondiale*, 19 (1969), 3–41

Gray, Peter, 'The Gloves Will Have to Come Off: A Reappraisal of the Legitimacy of the RAF Bomber Offensive against Germany', *Air Power Review*, 13 (2010), 9–40

Gray, Todd, *Looting in Wartime Britain* (Exeter: The Mint Press, 2009)

Grayling, Anthony, *Among the Dead Cities: Was the Allied Bombing of Civilians in World War II a Necessity or a Crime?* (London: Bloomsbury, 2005)

Graystone, Philip, *The Blitz on Hull (1940–45)* (Hull: Lampeda Press, 1991)

Grayzel, Susan, *At Home and Under Fire: Air Raids and Culture in Britain from the Great War to the Blitz* (Cambridge: Cambridge University Press, 2012)

Grayzel, Susan, '"A Promise of Terror to Come": Air Power and the Destruction of Cities in British Imagination and Experience, 1908–39', in Goebel, Stefan and Keene, Derek (eds), *Cities into Battlefields: Metropolitan Scenarios, Experiences and Commemorations of Total War* (Farnham: Ashgate, 2011), 47–62

Grebler, Leo, 'Continuity in the Rebuilding of Bombed Cities in Western Europe', *American Journal of Sociology*, 61 (1956), 463–9

Green, William, *Warplanes of the Third Reich* (London: Macdonald, 1970)

Greenwood, J. T. and Hardesty, Von, 'Soviet Air Forces in World War II', in Paul Murphy (ed), *The Soviet Air Forces* (Jefferson, NC: McFarland & Co., 1984), 29–69

Gregg, John, *The Shelter of the Tubes* (London: Capital Transport, 2001)

Gregor, Neil, 'A *Schicksalsgemeinschaft?* Allied Bombing, Civilian Morale, and Social Dissolution in Nuremberg, 1942–1945', *The Historical Journal*, 43 (2000), 1,051–70

Gretzschel, Matthias, *Als Dresden im Feursturm versank* (Hamburg: Eller & Richter, 2004)

Gribaudi, Gabriella, *Guerra Totale: Tra bombe alleate e violenze naziste: Napoli e il fronte meridionale 1940–44* (Turin: Bollati Boringhieri, 2005)

Gribaudi, Gabriella, 'Tra discorsi pubblici e memorie private. Alcune riflessioni sui bombardamenti e sulla loro legittimazione', in Labanca (ed), *I bombardamenti aerei*, 305–24

Griehl, Manfred, *Junkers Ju88: Star of the Luftwaffe* (London: Arms and Armour, 1990)

Grimm, Barbara, 'Lynchmorde an alliierten Fliegern im Zweiten Weltkrieg', in Süss (ed), *Deutschland im Luftkrieg*, 71–84

Groehler, Olaf, *Bombenkrieg gegen Deutschland* (Berlin: Akademie Verlag 1990)

Groehler, Olaf, *Geschichte des Luftkriegs* (Berlin: Militärverlag der DDR, 1981)

Grosscup, Beau, *Strategic Terror: The Politics and Ethics of Aerial Bombardment* (London: Zed Books, 2006)

Guglielmo, Mark, 'The Contribution of Economists to Military Intelligence During World War II', *Journal of Economic History*, 68 (2008), 109–50

Guinn, Gilbert, *The Arnold Scheme: British Pilots, the American South and the Allies' Daring Plan* (Charleston, NC: History Press, 2007)

Gunston, Bill, *Night Fighters: A Development and Combat History* (Cambridge: Patrick Stephens, 1976)

Haining, Peter, *The Chianti Raiders: The Extraordinary Story of the Italian Air Force in the Battle of Britain* (London: Robson Books, 2005)

Hall, R. Cargill (ed), *Case Studies in Strategic Bombardment* (Washington, DC: Office of Air Force History, 1998)

Hamburg und Dresden im Dritten Reich: Bombenkrieg und Kriegsende (Hamburg: Landeszentrale für politische Bildung, 2000)

Hancock, Eleanor, *The National Socialist Leadership and Total War, 1941–5* (New York: St Martin's Press, 1991)

Hanke, Heinz M., *Luftkrieg und Zivilbevölkerung* (Frankfurt am Main: Peter Lang, 1991)

Hansen, Randall, *Fire and Fury: The Allied Bombing of Germany 1942–1945* (New York: NAL Caliber, 2009)

Hardesty, Von and Grinberg, Ilya, *Red Phoenix Rising: The Soviet Air Force in World War II* (Lawrence, KS: University Press of Kansas, 2012)

Harmon, Christopher C., *'Are We Beasts?' Churchill and the Moral Question of World War II Area Bombing* (Newport, RI: 1991)

Harris, Robert and Paxman, Jeremy, *A Higher Form of Killing: The Secret Story of Gas and Germ Warfare* (London: Chatto & Windus, 1982)

Harvey, Stephen, 'The Italian War Effort and the Strategic Bombing of Italy', *History*, 70 (1985), 32–45

Hayward, Joel, 'Air Power, Ethics, and Civilian Immunity during the First World War and its Aftermath', *Global War Studies*, 7 (2010), 102–30

Hayward, Joel, *Stopped at Stalingrad: The Luftwaffe and Hitler's Defeat in the East 1942–1943* (Lawrence, KS: University Press of Kansas, 1998)

Held, Werner and Nauroth, Holger, *Die deutsche Nachtjagd* (Stuttgart: Motorbuch Verlag, 1992)

Herbert, Ulrich (ed), *Europa und der 'Reichseinsatz': Ausländische Zivilarbeiter, Kriegsgefangene und KZ-Häftlinge in Deutschland 1938–1945* (Essen: Klartext, 1991)

Herf, Jeffrey, *The Jewish Enemy: Nazi Propaganda during World War II and the Holocaust* (Cambridge, MA: Harvard University Press, 2006)

Hesse, Hans and Purpus, Elke, 'Vom Luftschutzraum zum Denkmalschutz – Bunker in Köln', in Marszolek, Inge and Buggeln, Marc (eds), *Bunker: Kriegsort, Zuflucht, Erinnerungsraum* (Frankfurt am Main: Campus Verlag, 2008), 61–74

Hewison, Robert, *Under Siege: Literary Life in London 1939–1945* (London: Weidenfeld & Nicolson, 1977)

Hewitt, Kenneth, 'Place Annihilation: Area Bombing and the Fate of Urban Places', *Annals of the Association of American Geographers*, 73 (1983), 257–84

Higham, Robin, *Two Roads to War: The French and British Air Arms from Versailles to Dunkirk* (Annapolis, MD: Naval Institute Press, 2012)

Hiller, Marlene, 'Stuttgarter erzählen vom Luftkrieg', in idem (ed), *Stuttgart im Zweiten Weltkrieg* (Gerlingen: Bleicher Verlag, 1989), 417–40

Hirschleifer, Jack, 'Some Thoughts on the Social Structure after a Bombing Disaster', *World Politics*, 8 (1955–6), 206–27

Hitchcock, William, *The Bitter Road to Freedom: A New History of the Liberation of Europe* (New York: Free Press, 2008)

Hoch, Anton, 'Der Luftangriff auf Freiburg 1940', *Vierteljahreshefte für Zeitgeschichte*, 4 (1956), 115–44

Holland, James, *Fortress Malta: An Island under Siege, 1940–1943* (London: Orion, 2003)

Holman, Brett, 'The Air Panic of 1935: British Press Opinion between Disarmament and Rearmament', *Journal of Contemporary History*, 46 (2011), 288–307

Holman, Brett, '"Bomb Back, and Bomb Hard": Debating Reprisals during the Blitz', *Australian Journal of Politics and History*, 58 (2012), 394–407

Holman, Brett, 'World Police for World Peace: British Internationalism and the Threat of the Knock-Out Blow from the Air', *War in History*, 17 (2010), 313–32

Hopkins, G. E., 'Bombing and the American Conscience During World War II', *Historian*, 28 (1966), 451–73

Hugh-Jones, Martin, 'Wickham Steed and German Biological Warfare Research', *Intelligence and National Security*, 7 (1992), 379–402

Huyssen, Andreas, 'Air War Legacies: From Dresden to Baghdad', in Bill Niven (ed), *Germans as Victims* (Basingstoke: Palgrave, 2006), 181–93

Hylton, Samuel, *Britain's Darkest Hour: The Hidden History of the Blitz* (Stroud: Sutton Publishing, 2001)

Iklé, Fred, *The Social Impact of Bomb Destruction* (Norman, OK: Oklahoma University Press, 1958)

Inglis, Ruth, *The Children's War: Evacuation 1939–1945* (London: Collins, 1989)

Irons, Roy, *The Relentless Offensive: War and Bomber Command 1939–1945* (Barnsley: Pen and Sword, 2009)

Jackson, Ashley, *The British Empire and the Second World War* (London: Hambledon, 2000)

Jacobs, W. A., 'The British Strategic Air Offensive against Germany in World War II', in Hall (ed), *Case Studies in Strategic Bombardment*, 91–182

Jalland, Pat, *Death in War and Peace: Loss and Grief in England 1914–70* (Oxford: Oxford University Press, 2010)

Jarry, Maud, 'Le bombardement des sites V en France', in Battesti and Facon (eds), *Les bombardements alliés*, 39–48

Johnson, David E., *Fast Tanks and Heavy Bombers: Innovation in the U.S. Army 1917–1945* (Ithaca, NY: Cornell University Press, 1998)

Jones, Edgar, '"LMF": The Use of Psychiatric Stigma in the Royal Air Force during the Second World War', *Journal of Military History*, 70 (2006), 439–58

Jones, Edgar, Woolven, Robin and Wessely, Simon, 'Civilian Morale during the Second World War: Responses to Air-Raids Re-Examined', *Social History of Medicine*, 17 (2004), 463–79

Jones, Helen, *British Civilians in the Front Line: Air Raids, Productivity and Wartime Culture, 1939–1945* (Manchester: Manchester University Press, 2006)

Jones, Helen, 'Civil Defence in Britain, 1938–1945: Friendship during Wartime and the Formation of a Work-Based Identity', *Labour History Review*, 77 (2012), 113–32

Jones, Kevin, 'From the Horse's Mouth: *Luftwaffe* POWs as Sources for Air Ministry Intelligence during the Battle of Britain', *Intelligence and National Security*, 15 (2000), 60–80

Jones, Neville, *The Beginnings of Strategic Air Power: A History of the British Bomber Force 1923–1929* (London: Frank Cass, 1987)

Kagan, F., 'The Evacuation of Soviet Industry in the Wake of "Barbarossa": A Key to Soviet Victory', *Journal of Slavic Military Studies*, 8 (1995), 387–414

Kaldor, Nicholas, 'The German War Economy', *Review of Economic Statistics*, 13 (1946)

Karlsch, Rainer, *Hitlers Bombe: Die geheime Geschichte der deutschen Kernwaffenversuche* (Munich: DVA, 2005)

Katz, Barry, *Foreign Intelligence: Research and Analysis in the Office of Strategic Services, 1942–1945* (Cambridge, MA: Harvard University Press, 1989)

Kerber, Leonid, *Stalin's Aviation Gulag: A Memoir of Andrei Tupolev and the Purge Era*, ed. Von Hardesty (Washington, DC: Smithsonian Institution, 1996)

Kettenacker, Lothar (ed), *Ein Volk von Opfern? Die neue Debatte um den Bombenkrieg 1940–1945* (Berlin: Rohwolt, 2003)

Kirwin, G., 'Allied Bombing and Nazi Domestic Propaganda', *European History Quarterly*, 15 (1985), 341–62

Kitching, Carolyn, *Britain and the Geneva Disarmament Conference: A Study in International History* (Basingstoke: Palgrave, 2003)

Kitson, Simon, 'Criminals or Liberators? French Public Opinion and the Allied Bombings of France, 1940–1945', in Baldoli, Knapp and Overy (eds), *Bombing, States and Peoples*, 279–97

Klee, Katja, *Im 'Luftschutzkeller des Reiches': Evakuierte in Bayern, 1939–1945* (Munich: Oldenbourg Verlag, 1999)

Klemann, Hein with Kudryashov, Sergei, *Occupied Economies: An Economic History of Nazi-Occupied Europe, 1939–1945* (London: Berg, 2012)

Klinkhammer, Lutz, *L'occupazione tedesca in Italia, 1943–1945* (Turin: Bollati Boringhieri, 1996)

Knapp, Andrew, 'The Destruction and Liberation of Le Havre in Modern Memory', *War in History*, 14 (2007), 477–98

Knell, Hermann, *To Destroy a City: Strategic Bombing and its Human Consequences in World War II* (Cambridge, MA: Da Capo Press, 2003)

Knox, MacGregor, *Hitler's Italian Allies: Royal Armed Forces, Fascist Regime and the War of 1940–1943* (Cambridge: Cambridge University Press, 2000)

Koch, Gerhard, *'Der Führer sorgt für unsere Kinder . . .': Die Kinderlandverschickung im Zweiten Weltkrieg* (Paderborn: Ferdinand Schöningh, 1997)

Kochanski, Halik, *The Eagle Unbowed: Poland and the Poles in the Second World War* (London: Allen Lane, 2012)

Konvitz, Josef, 'Représentations urbaines et bombardements stratégiques, 1914–1945', *Annales* (1989), 823–47

Kozak, Warren, *LeMay: The Life and Wars of General Curtis LeMay* (Washington, DC: Regnery Publishing, 2009)

Krauskopf, R. W., 'The Army and the Strategic Bomber 1930–1931', Parts I and II, *Military Affairs*, 2 (1958–9), 84–94, 209–15

Kreis, John F. (ed), *Piercing the Fog: Intelligence and Army Air Forces Operations in World War II* (Washington, DC: Air Force History Program, 1996)

Kristensen, Henrik, Kofoed, Claus and Weber, Frank, *Vestallierede luftangre i Danmark under 2. Verdenskrig*, 2 vols (Aarhus: Aarhus Universitetsforlag, 1988)

Kroener, Bernhard, '"Menschenbewirtschaftung", Bevölkerungsverteilung und pesonelle Rüstung in der zweiten Kriegshälfte (1942–1944)', in Kroener, Bernhard, Müller, Rolf-Dieter and Umbreit, Hans, *Das Deutsche Reich und der Zweite Weltkrieg: Band 5/2: Organisation und Mobilisierung des Deutschen Machtbereichs 1942–1944/45* (Stuttgart: DVA, 1999), 777–995

Kube, Alfred, *Pour le Mérite und Hakenzreuz: Hermann Göring im Dritten Reich* (Munich: Oldenbourg, 1986)

Kumanev, G. A., 'The Soviet Economy and the 1941 Evacuation', in Wieczynski, Joseph (ed), *Operation Barbarossa: The German Attack on the Soviet Union, June 22, 1941* (Salt Lake City, UT: Charles Schlacks, 1993), 168–81

Labanca, Nicola (ed), *I bombardamenti aerei sull'Italia* (Bologna: Il Mulino, 2012)

Lackey, Douglas, 'Four Types of Mass Murderer: Stalin, Hitler, Churchill, Truman', in Primoratz (ed), *Terror from the Sky*, 134–54

Lambourne, Nicola, 'The Reconstruction of the City's Historic Monuments', in Addison and Crang, *Firestorm*, 143–60

Lambourne, Nicola, *War Damage in Western Europe: The Destruction of Historic Monuments During the Second World War* (Edinburgh: Edinburgh University Press, 2001)

Lanari, Manuela and Musso, Stefano, 'Un dramma mal calcolato: sfollamento e istituzioni nella provincia di Torino', in Maida, Bruno (ed), *Guerra e società nella provincia di Torino* (Turin: Blu Edizioni, 2007), 1–68

Lee, Gerald, '"I See Dead People": Air-Raid Phobia and Britain's Behaviour in the Munich Crisis', *Security Studies*, 13 (2003–4), 230–72

Lehman, Eric, *Le ali del potere: La propaganda aeronautica nell'Italia fascista* (Turin: Utet, 2010)

Lemke, Bernd, *Luftschutz in Grossbritannien und Deutschland 1923 bis 1939* (Munich: Oldenbourg Verlag, 2005)

Levy, Richard, 'The Bombing of Auschwitz Revisited: A Critical Analysis', *Holocaust and Genocide Studies*, 10 (1996), 267–98

Linhardt, Andreas, *Feuerwehr im Luftschutz 1926–1945: Die Umstrukturierung des öffentlichen Feuerlöschwesens in Deutschland unter Gesichtspunkten des zivilen Luftschutzes* (Brunswick: VFDB, 2002)

Lowe, Keith, *Inferno: The Devastation of Hamburg, 1943* (London: Viking, 2007)

Ludewig, Joachim, *Rückzug: The German Retreat from France, 1944* (Lexington, KT: Kentucky University Press, 2012)

MacBean, John A. and Hogben, Arthur S., *Bombs Gone: The Development and Use of British Air-Dropped Weapons from 1912 to the Present Day* (Wellinborough: Patrick Stephens, 1990)

McCormack, Timothy and Durham, Helen, 'Aerial Bombardment of Civilians: The Current International Legal Framework', in Tanaka and Young (eds), *Bombing Civilians*, 215–39

McFarland, Stephen and Newton, Wesley, 'The American Strategic Air Offensive Against Germany in World War II', in Hall (ed), *Case Studies in Strategic Bombardment*, 183–252

McFarland, Stephen and Newton, Wesley, *To Command the Sky: The Battle for Air Supremacy over Germany, 1942–1944* (Washington, DC: Smithsonian Institution, 1991)

MacPhail, I. M., *The Clydebank Blitz* (West Dunbartonshire Libraries and Museums, 1974)

Maggiorani, Mauro, 'Uscire dalla città: lo sfollamento', in Dalla Casa, Brunella and Preti, Alberto (eds), *Bologna in Guerra 1940–1945* (Milan: Franco Angeli, 1995), 361–93

Maier, Klaus, *Guernica 26.4.1937: Die deutsche Intervention in Spanien und der 'Fall Guernica'* (Freiburg: Verlag Rombach, 1975)

Maier, Klaus, 'Luftschlacht um England', in Maier, Klaus et al. (eds), *Das Deutsche Reich und der Zweite Weltkrieg: Band 2: Die Errichtung der Hegemonie auf dem europäischen Kontinent* (Stuttgart: DVA, 1979)

Maier, Klaus, 'Total War and German Air Doctrine before the Second World War', in Deist, Wilhelm (ed), *The German Military in the Age of Total War* (Oxford: Berg, 1985), 210–19

Maiolo, Joseph, *Cry Havoc: How the Arms Race Drove the World to War, 1931–1941* (New York: Basic Books, 2006)

Mallett, Robert, *The Italian Navy and Fascist Expansionism, 1935–1940* (London: Frank Cass, 1998)

Manaresi, Franco, 'I bombardamenti di Bologna', in Bersani, Cristina and Monaco, Valeria (eds), *Delenda Bononia: immagini dei bombardamenti 1943–1945* (Bologna: Patron Editori, 1995), 47–55

Manaresi, Franco, 'La protezione antiaerea', in Bersani and Monaco (eds), *Delenda Bononia*, 29–45

Markusen, Eric and Kopf, David, 'Was it Genocidal?', in Primoratz (ed), *Terror from the Sky*, 160–71

Martens, Stefan, *Hermann Göring: Erster Paladin des Führers und Zweiter Mann im Reich* (Paderborn: Schöningh, 1985)

Meilinger, Philip, 'Clipping the Bomber's Wings: The Geneva Disarmament Conference and the Royal Air Force 1932–1934', *War in History*, 6 (1999), 306–30

Meisel, Joseph, 'Air Raid Shelter Policy and its Critics before the Second World War', *Twentieth Century British History*, 5 (1994), 300–19

Melinsky, Hugh, *Forming the Pathfinders: The Career of Air Vice-Marshal Sydney Bufton* (Stroud: The History Press, 2010)

Mets, David R., *Master of Airpower: General Carl A. Spaatz* (Novato, CA: Presidio, 1998)

Middlebrook, Martin and Everitt, Chris, *The Bomber Command War Diaries* (Leicester: Midland Publishing, 2000)

Mierzejewski, Alfred, *The Collapse of the German War Economy: Allied Air Power and the German National Railway* (Chapel Hill, NC: North Carolina University Press, 1988)

Miller, Donald, *Eighth Air Force: The American Bomber Crews in Britain* (London: Aurum Press, 2007)

Miller, Marshall, *Bulgaria During the Second World War* (Stanford, CA: Stanford University Press, 1975)

Mommsen, Hans and Grieger, Manfried, *Das Volkswagenwerk und seine Arbieter im Dritten Reich* (Düsseldorf: Econ, 1997)

Moorhouse, Roger, *Berlin at War: Life and Death in Hitler's Capital 1939–45* (London: Bodley Head, 2010)

Morris, Alan, *First of the Many: The Story of Independent Force*, RAF (London: Jarrolds, 1968)

Müller, Rolf-Dieter, 'Albert Speer und die Rüstungspolitik im Totalen Krieg 1942–1945', in Kroener, Müller and Umbreit, *Das Deutsche Reich und der Zweite Weltkrieg*

Müller, Rolf-Dieter, *Der Bombenkrieg 1939–1945* (Berlin: Ch. Links Verlag, 2004)

Müller, Rolf-Dieter, 'Das Scheitern der wirtschaftlichen "Blitzkriegsstrategie"', in Boog, Horst et al., *Das Deutsche Reich und der Zweite Weltkrieg: Band 4: Der Angriff auf die Sowietunion* (Stuttgart: DVA, 1983), 936–1,029

Murray, Williamson, *Luftwaffe: Strategy for Defeat 1933–1945* (London: George Allen & Unwin, 1985)

Natalini, Andrea, *I rapporti tra aeronautica italiana e tedesca durante la seconda guerra mondiale* (Cosenza: Edizioni Lionelle Giordano, 2004)

Nath, Peter, *Luftkriegsoperationen gegen die Stadt Offenburg im Ersten und Zweiten Weltkrieg* (Offenburg: Historisches Verein für Mittelbaden, 1990)

Neitzel, Sönke, *Der Einsatz der deutschen Luftwaffe über dem Atlantik und der Nordsee 1939–1945* (Bonn: Bernard & Graefe, 1995)

Neufeld, Michael, 'The Guided Missile and the Third Reich: Peenemünde and the Forging of a Technological Revolution', in Renneberg, Monika and Walker, Mark (eds), *Science, Technology and National Socialism* (Cambridge: Cambridge University Press, 1994), 51–71

Neufeld, Michael and Berenbaum, Michael (eds), *The Bombing of Auschwitz: Should the Allies Have Attempted It?* (New York: St Martin's Press/United States Holocaust Memorial Museum, 2000)

Nezzo, Marta, 'The Defence of Works of Art in Italy during the Second World War', in Baldoli, Knapp and Overy (eds), *Bombing, States and Peoples*, 101–20

Nezzo, Marta, 'La protezione delle città d'arte', in Labanca (ed), *I bombardamenti aerei*, 195–212

Nicholas, Lynn, *The Rape of Europa: The Fate of Europe's Treasures in the Third Reich and the Second World War* (London: Macmillan, 1994)

Nielsen, Andreas, *The German Air Force General Staff* (New York: Arno Press, 1959)

O'Neill, Gilda, *Our Street: East End Life in the Second World War* (London: Viking, 2003)

Oram, Alison, '"Bombs don't discriminate!" Women's Political Activism in the Second World War', in Gledhill, Christine and Swanson, Gillian (eds), *Nationalising Femininity: Culture, Sexuality and British Cinema in the Second World War* (Manchester: Manchester University Press, 1996), 55–69

Overy, Richard, 'Allied Bombing and the Destruction of German Cities', in Chickering, Roger, Förster, Stig and Greiner, Bernd (eds), *A World at Total War: Global Conflict and the Politics of Destruction* (Cambridge: Cambridge University Press, 2005), 277–95

Overy, Richard, 'Apocalyptic Fears: Bombing and Popular Anxiety in Inter-War Britain', *S-NODI: pubblici e private nella storia contemporanea*, 2 (Spring 2008), 7–30

Overy, Richard, *The Battle of Britain* (London: Penguin, 2010)

Overy, Richard, *Bomber Command 1939–1945* (London: HarperCollins, 1997)

Overy, Richard, 'From "Uralbomber" to "Amerikabomber": The Luftwaffe and Strategic Bombing', *Journal of Strategic Studies*, 1 (1978), 154–78

Overy, Richard, *Goering: Hitler's Iron Knight*, 3rd edn (London: I. B. Tauris, 2012)

Overy, Richard, *Interrogations: The Nazi Elite in Allied Hands* (London: Allen Lane, 2001)

Overy, Richard, 'The Luftwaffe and the European Economy 1939–1945', *Militärgeshichtliche Mitteilungen*, 55 (1979), 55–78

Overy, Richard, 'Mobilisation for Total War in Germany 1939–1941', *English Historical Review*, 103 (1988), 613–39

Overy, Richard, *The Morbid Age: Britain and the Crisis of Civilisation between the Wars* (London: Allen Lane, 2009)

Overy, Richard, *War and Economy in the Third Reich* (Oxford: Oxford University Press, 1994)

Overy, Richard, 'The "Weak Link": Bomber Command and the German Working Class 1940–1945', *Labour History Review*, 77 (2012), 11–34

Paggi, Leonardo, *Il 'popolo dei morti': la repubblica italiana nata della guerra (1940–1946)* (Bologna: Il Mulino, 2009)

Palmer, Scott, *Dictatorship of the Air: Aviation Culture and the Fate of Modern Russia* (Cambridge: Cambridge University Press, 2006)

Panchasi, Roxanne, *Future Tense: The Culture of Anticipation in France between the Wars* (Ithaca, NY: Cornell University Press, 2009)

Pape, Robert A., *Bombing to Win: Air Power and Coercion in War* (Ithaca, NY: Cornell University Press, 1996)

Park, W. Hays, '"Precision" and "Area" Bombing: Who Did Which, and When?', *Journal of Strategic Studies*, 18 (1995), 145–74

Parton, James, *'Air Force Spoken Here': General Ira Eaker and the Command of the Air* (Bethesda, MD: Adler & Adler, 1986)

Patterson, Ian, *Guernica and Total War* (London: Profile Books, 2007)

Pauw, Hans van der, *Rotterdam in de Tweede Wereldoorlog* (Rotterdam: Uitgeverij Boom, 2006)

Peden, George, *Arms, Economics and British Strategy: From Dreadnoughts to Hydrogen Bombs* (Cambridge: Cambridge University Press, 2007)

Permooser, Irmtraud, *Der Luftkrieg über München 1942–1945: Bomben auf die Hauptstadt der Bewegung* (Oberhachung: Aviatic Verlag, 1996)

Perry, Matt, 'Bombing Billancourt: Labour Agency and the Limitations of the Public Opinion Model of Wartime France', *Labour History Review*, 77 (2012), 49–74

Pettenberg, Heinz, *Starke Verbände im Anflug auf Köln*, ed. Reuter-Pettenberg, Hella (Cologne: J. P. Bachem Verlag, 1981)

Pimlott, Ben, *Hugh Dalton* (London: Macmillan, 1985)

Plokhy, S. M., *Yalta: The Price of Peace* (New York: Penguin, 2010)

Pohl, Hans and Treue, Wilhelm, *Die Daimler-Benz AG in den Jahren 1933 bis 1945* (Wiesbaden: Franz Steiner Verlag, 1986)

Poolman, K., *Focke-Wulf Condor: Scourge of the Atlantic* (London: Macdonald & Jane's, 1978)

Preston, Paul, *We Saw Spain Die: Foreign Correspondents in the Spanish Civil War* (London: Constable, 2008)

Price, Alfred, *Instruments of Darkness: The History of Electronic Warfare 1939–1945* (London: Greenhill Books, 2005)

Price, Alfred, *The Luftwaffe Data Book* (London: Greenhill Books, 1997)

Primoratz, Igor (ed), *Terror from the Sky: The Bombing of German Cities in World War II* (Oxford: Berghahn Books, 2010)

Probert, Henry, *Bomber Harris: His Life and Times* (London: Greenhill Books, 2006)

Pugh, Michael, 'An International Police Force: Lord Davies and the British Debate in the 1930s', *International Relations*, 9 (1988), 335–51

Quellien, Jean, 'Les bombardements pendant la campagne de Normandie', in Battesti and Facon (eds), *Les bombardements alliés*, 59–76

Rankin, Nicholas, *Telegram from Guernica: The Extraordinary Life of George Steer, War Correspondent* (London: Faber & Faber, 2003)

Rastelli, Achille, *Bombe sulla città: Gli attacchi aerei alleati: le vittime civili a Milano* (Milan: Mursia, 2000)

Rauh-Kühne, Cornelia, 'Hitlers Hehler? Unternehmerprofite und Zwangsarbeiter-löhne', *Historische Zeitschrift*, 275 (2002), 1–55

Ray, John, *The Night Blitz, 1940–1941* (London: Arms and Armour, 1996)

Reid, Anna, *Leningrad: Tragedy of a City under Siege 1941–1944* (London: Bloomsbury, 2011)

Reinhard, Oliver, Neutzner, Matthias and Hesse, Wolfgang, *Das rote Leuchten: Dresden und der Bombenkrieg* (Dresden: Sächsische Zeitung, 2005)

Reuth, Ralf, *Goebbels: The Life of Joseph Goebbels. The Mephistophelean Genius of Nazi Propaganda* (London: Constable, 1993)

Reynolds, David, *In Command of History: Churchill Fighting and Writing the Second World War* (London: Allen Lane, 2004)

Ribeill, Georges, 'Aux prises avec les voies ferrées: bombarder ou saboter? Un dilemme revisité', in Battesti and Facon (eds), *Les bombardements alliés*, 135–62

Ribeill, Georges and Machefert-Tassin, Yves, *Une Saison en Enfer: Les bombardements des Alliés sur les rails français (1942–1945)* (Migennes: 2004)

Rice, Randall, 'Bombing Auschwitz: US 15th Air Force and the Military Aspects of a Possible Attack', *War in History*, 6 (1999), 205–30

Richards, Denis, *Portal of Hungerford* (London: Heinemann, 1978)

Richardson, C. O., 'French Plans for Allied Attacks on the Caucasus Oil Fields January–April 1940', *French Historical Studies*, 8 (1973), 130–53

Richardson, Dick and Kitching, Carolyn, 'Britain and the World Disarmament Conference', in Catterall, Peter and Morris, C. J. (eds), *Britain and the Threat to Stability in Europe 1918–1945* (Leicester: Leicester University Press, 1993), 35–56

Ritchie, Sebastian, *Industry and Air Power: The Expansion of British Aircraft Production, 1935–1941* (London: Frank Cass, 1997)

Ritchie, Sebastian, 'A Political Intrigue Against the Chief of the Air Staff: The Downfall of Air Chief Marshal Sir Cyril Newall', *War & Society*, 16 (1998), 83–104

Robinson, Douglas, *The Zeppelin in Combat: A History of the German Naval Airship Division* (London: G. T. Foulis, 1962)

Roberts, Geoffrey, *Victory at Stalingrad* (Harlow: Longman, 2002)

Rochat, Giorgio, *Le guerre italiane 1935–1943: Dall'impero d'Etiopia alla disfatta* (Turin: Einaudi, 2005)

Rochat, Giorgio, *Guerre italiane in Libia e in Etiopia: studi militari 1921–1939* (Paese: Pagus Edizioni, 1991)

Rose, Alexander, 'Radar and Air Defence in the 1930s', *Twentieth Century British History*, 9 (1998), 219–45

Rose, Sonya, *Which People's War? National Identity and Citizenship in Wartime Britain, 1939–1945* (Oxford: Oxford University Press, 2003)

Rugg, Julie, 'Managing "Civilian Deaths due to War Operations": Yorkshire Experiences During World War II', *Twentieth Century British History*, 15 (2004), 152–73

Rumenin, Rumen, *Letyashti Kreposti Nad Bulgariya* (Kyustendil: Ivan Sapunjiev, 2009)

Rüther, Martin, *Köln 31. Mai 1942: Der 1000-Bomber-Angriff* (Cologne: Janus, 1992)

Rüther, Martin (ed), *'Zu Hause könnten sie es nicht schöner haben!': Kinderlandverschickung aus Köln und Umgebung 1941–1945* (Cologne: Emons Verlag, 2000)

Saint-Amour, Paul, 'Air War Prophecy and Interwar Modernism', *Comparative Literature Studies*, 42 (2005), 130–61

Salisbury, Harrison, *The 900 Days: The Siege of Leningrad* (London: Macmillan, 1969)

Sallagar, Frederick, *The Road to Total War* (New York: Van Nostrand Reinhold, 1969)

Samuelson, Lennart, *Tankograd: The Formation of a Soviet Company Town: Cheliabinsk 1900–1950s* (Basingstoke: Palgrave, 2011)

Satia, Priya, 'The Defense of Inhumanity: Air Control and the British Idea of Arabia', *American Historical Review*, 111 (2006), 16–51

Saward, Dudley, *'Bomber Harris': The Authorised Biography* (London: Cassell, 1984)

Scattigno, Anna, 'Il clero in Toscana durante il passaggio del fronte. Diari e cronache parrocchiali', in Labanca (ed), *I bombardamenti aerei*, 247–80

Schaffer, Ronald, 'American Military Ethics in World War II: The Bombing of German Civilians', *The Journal of American History*, 67 (1980), 318–34

Schaffer, Ronald, *Wings of Judgment: American Bombing in World War II* (New York: Oxford University Press, 1985)

Schmidt, Ulf, 'Justifying Chemical Warfare: The Origins and Ethics of Britain's Chemical Warfare Programme, 1915–1939', in Fox, Jo and Welch, David (eds), *Justifying War: Propaganda, Politics and the Modern Age* (Basingstoke: Palgrave, 2012), 129–58

Schmiedel, Michael, 'Les Allemands et la défense passive en France: le cas de Nantes', in Battesti and Facon (eds), *Les bombardements alliés*, 49–56

Schmiedel, Michael, 'Orchestrated Solidarity: The Allied Air War in France and the Development of Local and State-Organised Solidarity Movements', in Baldoli, Knapp and Overy (eds), *Bombing, States and Peoples*, 206–18

Segrè, Claudio, 'Giulio Douhet: Strategist, Theorist, Prophet?', *Journal of Strategic Studies*, 15 (1992), 351–66

Serrien, Pieter, *Tranen over Mortsel: De laatste getuigen over het zwaarste bombardement ooit in België* (Antwerp: Standaard Uitgeverij, 2008)

Sevostyanov, Pavel, *Before the Nazi Invasion: Soviet Diplomacy in September 1939–June 1941* (Moscow: Progress Publishers, 1984)

Sherry, Michael, *The Rise of American Air Power: The Creation of Armageddon* (New Haven, CT: Yale University Press, 1987)

Sijes, B. A., *De Razzia van Rotterdam 10–11 November 1944* (Gravenhage: Martinus Nijhoff, 1951)

Silveri, Umberto and Carli, Maddalena, *Bombardare Roma: Gli Alleati e la "città aperta"(1940–1944)* (Bologna: Il Mulion, 2007)

Smith, Bradley, *Sharing Secrets with Stalin: How the Allies Traded Intelligence, 1941–1945* (Lawrence, KS: University Press of Kansas, 1996)

Spooner, Tony, *Supreme Gallantry: Malta's Role in the Allied Victory, 1939–1945* (London: John Murray, 1996)

Stansky, Peter, *The First Day of the Blitz* (New Haven, CT: Yale University Press, 2007)

Stansky, Peter, 'Henry Moore and the Blitz', in Bean, J. M. (ed), *The Political Culture of Modern Britain: Studies in Memory of Stephen Koss* (London: Hamish Hamilton, 1987), 228–42

Stargardt, Nicholas, *Witnesses of War: Children's Lives under the Nazis* (London: Jonathan Cape, 2005)

Stegemann, Bernd, 'The Italo-German Conduct of the War in the Mediterranean and North Africa', in Schreiber, Gerhard, Stegemann, Bernd and Vogel, Detlef, *Germany and the Second World War: Volume III: The Mediterranean, South-East Europe and North Africa 1939–1941* (Oxford: Oxford University Press, 1995), 641–754

Steiner, Zara, *The Lights that Failed: European International History 1919–1933* (Oxford: Oxford University Press, 2005)

Stenton, Michael, *Radio London and Resistance in Occupied Europe: British Political Warfare 1939–1943* (Oxford: Oxford University Press, 2000)

Stephenson, Jill, 'Bombing and Rural Society in Württemberg', *Labour History Review*, 77 (2012), 93–112

Stephenson, Jill, *Hitler's Home Front: Württemberg under the Nazis* (London: Continuum, 2006)

Stonebridge, Lyndsey, 'Anxiety at a Time of Crisis', *History Workshop Journal*, 45 (1998), 171–98

Stradling, Robert, *Your children will be next: Bombing and Propaganda in the Spanish Civil War, 1936–1939* (Cardiff: University of Wales Press, 2008)

Strobl, Gerwin, *The Germanic Isle: Nazi Perceptions of Britain* (Cambridge: Cambridge University Press, 2000)

Suchenwirth, Richard, *Command and Leadership in the German Air Force: USAF Historical Studies, No. 174* (New York: Arno Press/Air University, 1969)

Süss, Dietmar, 'Steuerung durch Information? Joseph Goebbels als "Kommissar der Heimatfront" und die Reichsinspektion für den zivilen Luftschutz', in Hachtmann, Rüdiger and Süss, Winfried (eds), *Hitlers Kommissare: Sondergewalten in der nationalsozialistischen Diktatur* (Göttingen: Wallstein Verlag, 2006), 183–206

Süss, Dietmar, *Tod aus der Luft: Kriegsgesellschaft und Luftkrieg in Deutschland und England* (Munich: Siedler Verlag, 2011)

Süss, Dietmar, 'Wartime Societies and Shelter Politics in National Socialist Germany and Britain', in Baldoli, Knapp and Overy (eds), *Bombing, States and Peoples*, 23–42

Sweetman, John, 'The Smuts Report of 1917: Merely Political Window Dressing?', *Journal of Strategic Studies*, 4 (1981), 152–74

Tanaka, Yuki and Young, Marilyn (eds), *Bombing Civilians: A Twentieth-Century History* (New York: The New Press, 2009)

Taylor, Frederick, *Dresden: Tuesday 13 February 1945* (London: Bloomsbury, 2004)

Tewes, Ludger, *Jugend im Krieg: von Luftwaffenhelfern und Soldaten 1939–1945* (Essen: Reimar Hobbing, 1989)

Thetford, Owen, *Aircraft of the Royal Air Force since 1918* (London: Guild Publishing, 1988)

Thomas, Hugh, *John Strachey* (London: Eyre Methuen, 1973)

Thoms, David, *War, Industry and Society: The Midlands 1939–1945* (London: Routledge, 1989)

Thorpe, Andrew, *Parties at War: Political Organization in Second World War Britain* (Oxford: Oxford University Press, 2009)

Tiratsoo, Nick, 'The Reconstruction of Blitzed British Cities 1945–55: Myths and Reality', *Contemporary British History*, 14 (2000), 27–44

Tooze, Adam, 'No Room for Miracles: German Industrial Output in World War II Reassessed', *Geschichte und Gesellschaft*, 31 (2005), 439–64

Tooze, Adam, *Wages of Destruction: The Making and Breaking of the Nazi Economy* (London: Allen Lane, 2006)

Torrie, Julia, *'For Their Own Good': Civilian Evacuations in Germany and France, 1939–1945* (New York: Berghahn Books, 2010)

Truelle, J., 'La production aéronautique militaire française jusqu'en Juin 1940', *Revue d'histoire de la Deuxième Guerre Mondiale*, 19 (1969), 75–110

Underwood, Jeffery, *The Wings of Democracy: The Influence of Air Power on the Roosevelt Administration 1933–1941* (College Station: Texas A & M University Press, 1991)

Uziel, Daniel, *The Propaganda Warriors: The Wehrmacht and the Consolidation of the German Home Front* (Bern: Peter Lang, 2008)

Vaizey, Hester, *Surviving Hitler's War: Family Life in Germany, 1939–48* (Basingstoke: Palgrave, 2010)

Verhoeyen, Etienne, *La Belgique occupée: De l'an 40 à la libération* (Brussels: De Boeck, 1994)

Villa, Andrea, *Guerra aerea sull'Italia (1943–1945)* (Milan: Angelo Guerini, 2010)

Voldman, Danièle, 'Les populations civiles, enjeux du bombardement des villes (1914–1945)', in Audoin-Rouzeau, Stéphane, Becker, Annette, Ingrao, Christian and Rousso, Henri (eds), *La violence de guerre 1914–1945* (Paris: Éditions complexes, 2002), 151–74

Wakefield, Kenneth, *The First Pathfinders: The Operational History of Kampfgruppe 100* (London: William Kimber, 1981)

Wakelam, Randall, *The Science of Bombing: Operational Research in RAF Bomber Command* (Toronto: Toronto University Press, 2009)

Wark, Wesley, 'British Intelligence on the German Air Force and Aircraft Industry, 1933–1939', *The Historical Journal*, 25 (1982), 627–48

Wasson, Sara, *Urban Gothic of the Second World War: Dark London* (Basingstoke: Palgrave, 2010)

Wells, Mark, *Courage and Air Warfare: The Allied Aircrew Experience in the Second World War* (London: Frank Cass, 1995)

Werner, Wolfgang, *'Bleib übrig': Deutsche Arbeiter in der nationalsozialistischen Kriegswirtschaft* (Düsseldorf: Schwann, 1983)

Westermann, Edward, *Flak: German Anti-Aircraft Defenses, 1914–1945* (Lawrence, KS: University Press of Kansas, 2001)

Westermann, Edward, 'Hitting the Mark but Missing the Target: Luftwaffe Deception Operations, 1939–1945', *War in History*, 10 (2003), 206–21

White, Joseph, 'Target Auschwitz: Historical and Hypothetical German Responses to Allied Attack', *Holocaust and Genocide Studies*, 16 (2002), 54–76

Whiting, K. R., 'Soviet Aviation and Air Power under Stalin', in Higham, Robin and Kipp, Jacob (eds), *Soviet Aviation and Air Power: A Historical View* (London: Brasseys, 1978), 50–63

Wiese, Gernot, 'Die Versorgungslage in Deutschland', in Salewski, Michael and Schulze-Wegener, Guntram (eds), *Kriegsjahr 1944: Im Grossen und im Kleinen* (Stuttgart: Franz Steiner Verlag, 1995), 340–46

Wiggam, Marc, 'The Blackout and the Idea of Community in Britain and Germany', in Baldoli, Knapp and Overy (eds), *Bombing, States and Peoples*, 43–58

Willis, Kirk, 'The Origins of British Nuclear Culture, 1895–1939', *Journal of British Studies*, 34 (1995), 59–89

Wills, Clair, *That Neutral Island: A History of Ireland During the Second World War* (London: Faber & Faber, 2007)

Wolf, Werner, *Luftangriffe auf die deutsche Industrie 1942–1945* (Munich: Universitas, 1985)

Wylie, Neville, 'Muted Applause? British Prisoners of War as Observers and Victims of the Allied Bombing Campaign over Germany', in Baldoli, Knapp and Overy (eds), *Bombing, States and Peoples*, 256–78

Wyman, David, *The Abandonment of the Jews: America and the Holocaust 1941–1945* (New York: Pantheon Books, 1984)

Young, Robert, 'The Strategic Dream: French Air Doctrine in the Inter-War Period, 1919–1939', *Journal of Contemporary History*, 9 (1974), 56–76

Zaidi, Waqar, '"Aviation Will Either Destroy or Save Our Civilization": Proposals for the International Control of Aviation, 1920–45', *Journal of Contemporary History*, 46 (2011), 150–78

Zamagni, Vera, 'Italy: How to Lose the War and Win the Peace', in Harrison, Mark (ed), *The Economics of World War II* (Cambridge: Cambridge University Press, 1998), 177–223

Zelinski, Wilbur and Kolinski, Leszek, *The Emergency Evacuation of Cities* (Savage, MD: Rowman & Littlefield, 1991)

Notes

ABBREVIATIONS USED IN THE NOTES

AA	Anti-Aircraft
AAF	American Air Force
ACS	Archivio Centrale dello Stato (Rome)
ACTS	Air Corps Tactical School
ADAP	*Akten zur Deutschen auswärtigen Politik (Documents on German Foreign Policy)*
AEAF	Allied Expeditionary Air Force
AFB	Air Force Base
AFHRA	Air Force Historical Research Agency (Maxwell AFB, AL)
AHB	Air Historical Branch, Northolt (UK)
AI	Air Intelligence (UK)
ARP	Air Raid Precautions
BA-B	Bundesarchiv-Berlin
BA-MA	Bundesarchiv-Militärarchiv, Freiburg
BBSU	British Bombing Survey Unit
BC	Bomber Command
BIOS	British Intelligence Objectives Sub-Committee
BN	Bibliothèque Nationale (Paris)
BUFT	Bufton papers
CamUL	Cambridge University Library
CAS	Chief of the Air Staff (UK)
CC	Coastal Command
CCAC	Churchill College Archive Centre, Cambridge, UK
CCO	Christ Church, Oxford
CCS	Combined Chiefs of Staff
CD	Civil Defence
C-in-C	Commander-in-Chief

CIOS	Combined Intelligence Objectives Sub-Committee
CLSC	Camden Local Studies Centre, London
Cmd.	Command Paper (Fourth series, 1918–56)
CoS	Chiefs of Staff
DBOps	Director of Bombing Operations (UK)
DCAS	Deputy Chief of the Air Staff (UK)
DDBOps	Deputy Director of Bombing Operations (UK)
DRZW	*Das Deutsche Reich und der Zweite Weltkrieg*
DVA	Deutsche Verlags-Anstalt (Stuttgart)
EDS	Enemy Document Section
FCNA	*Fuehrer Conferences on Naval Affairs*
FDRL	Franklin D. Roosevelt Library, Hyde Park, NY
FHL	Friends House, London
FIAT	Field Intelligence Agencies Technical
GCI	Ground Control Interception (radar, British)
GL	Generalluftzeugmeister (Air Force Quartermaster-General)
HHC	Hull History Centre, Hull, UK
HMSO	His/Her Majesty's Stationery Office
HQ	Headquarters
IAC	Italian Armistice Commission
IWM	Imperial War Museum, London
JCS	Joint Chiefs of Staff
JIC	Joint Intelligence Committee (UK)
JPS	Joint Planning Staff
JSM	Joint Staff Mission (Washington DC)
KTB/OKW	*Kriegstagebuch*/Oberkommando der Wehrmacht (*War Diary*, OKW)
LC	Library of Congress, Washington DC
LCC	London County Council
LMA	London Metropolitan Archives
LSE	London School of Economics
MAAF	Mediterranean Allied Air Forces
MAP	Ministry of Aircraft Production
MD	Milch documents
MdAe	Ministero dell'Aeronautica
MEW	Ministry of Economic Warfare
MH	Ministry of Health (UK)

MHS	Ministry of Home Security (UK)
MO-A	Mass Observation Archive
MoI	Ministry of Information (UK)
MP	Metropolitan Police (UK)
MPVO	mestnaia protivovozdushnaia oborona (Main Directorate of Local Air Defence)
NAAF	Northwest African Air Forces
NAM	National Archive of Malta, Rabat
NARA	National Archives and Records Administration, College Park, MD
NC	Nuffield College, Oxford
NFPA	National Fire Protection Association
NID	Naval Intelligence Division (UK)
NIOD	Netherlands War Document Centre, Amsterdam
NSDAP	Nationalsozialistische Deutsche Arbeiterpartei (National Socialist German Workers' Party)
NSV	Nationalsozialistische Volkswohlfahrt (National Socialist People's Welfare)
OEMU	Oxford Extra-Mural Unit
OKW	Oberkommando der Wehrmacht (High Command of the German Armed Forces)
ORS	Operational Research Section
OSS	Office of Strategic Services (US)
OT	Organisation Todt
OTU	Operational Training Unit
PArch	Parliamentary Archives, London
P/w	Prisoner-of-war
PWB	Psychological Warfare Branch (USA)
PWE	Political Warfare Executive
RAFM	RAF Museum, Hendon
RCAF	Royal Canadian Air Force
REDept	Research & Experiments Department, Ministry of Home Security
RG	Record Group
RGAE	Russian State Archive of the Economy, Moscow
RGVA	Russian State Military Archive, Moscow
RI	Reichsgruppe Industrie

RLB	Reichsluftschutzbund (Reich Air Protection League)
RLM	Reich Air Ministry
RVK	Reichsverteidigungskommissar (Reich Defence Commissar)
SAP	Securité Aérienne Publique
SGDA	Secrétariat Générale de la Défense Aérienne
SHAA	Service Historique de l'Armée de l'Air, Vincennes, Paris
SHAEF	Supreme Headquarters Allied Expeditionary Force
SIPEG	Service Interministériel de Protection Contre les Événements de Guerre (Interministerial Protection Service against the Events of War)
TNA	The National Archives, Kew, London
TsAMO	Central Archive of the Ministry of Defence of the Russian Federation, Podolsk
TWA	Tyne and Wear Archive, Discovery Museum, Newcastle-upon-Tyne
UEA	University of East Anglia
USAAF	United States Army Air Forces
USAFA	United States Air Force Academy, Colorado Springs
USMA	United States Military Academy
USSBS	United States Strategic Bombing Survey
USSTAF	United States Strategic and Tactical Air Forces
VCAS	Vice-Chief of the Air Staff (UK)
WMRC	Warwick Modern Records Centre
WVS	Women's Voluntary Services for Air Raid Precautions (UK)
YCA	York City Archives

PROLOGUE: BOMBING BULGARIA

1. AFHRA, 519.12535, Fifteenth Air Force Operations (Bulgaria), Nov 1943–July 1944; Wesley F. Craven, James L. Cate, *The Army Air Forces in World War II: Vol 2* (Chicago: 1949), 584; Marshall L. Miller, *Bulgaria during the Second World War* (Stanford: 1975), 166; Rumen Rumenin, *Letyashti Kreposti Nad Bulgariya* (Kyustendil: 2009), 94–5, 204.
2. BA-MA, RL2/8, German Air Ministry, aircraft deliveries to neutrals and allies, May 1943–Feb 1944.
3. Martin van Creveld, *Hitler's Strategy 1940–1941: The Balkan Clue* (Cambridge: 1973), 109–13, for a full account of the negotiations.
4. Miller, *Bulgaria*, 48–55, 62–8.
5. Richard J. Crampton, *Bulgaria* (Oxford: 2007), 272, 275–6.
6. TNA, PREM 3/79/1, minutes of CoS meeting, 19 Oct 1943.

7. From a leaflet reproduced in Rumenin, *Letyashti Kreposti*, 335.
8. NARA, RG 165, Box 11, Report by the JCS, 'The Bombing of Sofia', enclosure B.
9. Ibid., Ambassador Kelley, Ankara, to State Dept., 18 Oct 1943.
10. TNA, PREM 3/79/1, CCS to Eisenhower, 24 Oct 1943.
11. Ibid., telegram Eden to Churchill, 23 Oct 1943; Eden to Churchill, 29 Oct 1943.
12. Frederick B. Chary, *The Bulgarian Jews and the Final Solution 1940–1944* (Pittsburgh: 1972), 129–32; Miller, *Bulgaria*, 102–6.
13. TNA, PREM 3/79/1, Churchill to Eden and Deputy Prime Minister Attlee, 25 Dec 1943.
14. *Akten zur Deutschen auswärtigen Politik*, Ser E, Band VII, Ambassador Beckerle to von Ribbentrop, 23 Jan 1944, 349–50.
15. TNA, PREM 3/66/10, War Cabinet JIC Report, 'Effects of Allied Bombing of Balkans and Balkan Situation', 29 Jan 1944, 1–2; FDRL, Roosevelt papers, Map Room Files, Box 136, HQ MAAF to War Department, 10 Jan 1944; Rumenin, *Letyashti Kreposti*, 107–9.
16. Miller, *Bulgaria*, 167–8; Walter Warlimont, *Inside Hitler's Headquarters 1939–1945* (London: 1964), 399. Warlimont was in Bulgaria to discuss Operation Gertrude, a contingency plan for the capture of European Turkey if the Turks joined the Allies.
17. Crampton, *Bulgaria*, 273–4.
18. TNA, PREM 3/79/1, Roosevelt to Churchill, 9 Feb 1944.
19. FDRL, Map Room files, CoS to Eisenhower's HQ, 9 Mar 1944; TNA, PREM 3/79/1, CoS, 'Air Operations against Bulgaria', 27 Jan 1944; Churchill to General Wilson, 27 Jan 1944.
20. RAFM, Bottomley papers, AC 71/2/29, Note by the Air Staff for War Cabinet Inter-Service Committee on Chemical Warfare, 23 Jan 1944, Annex 1.
21. TNA, PREM 3/79/1, Churchill to Roosevelt, 11 Feb 1944 and 12 Feb 1944.
22. Ibid., Roosevelt to Churchill, 12 Feb 1944.
23. Ibid., Lord Killearn (Cairo) to the Foreign Office, 24 Feb 1944; Lord Killearn to the Foreign Office, 24 Feb 1944, encl. report from Mr Howard, 1–3; Crampton, *Bulgaria*, 275–6.
24. TNA, PREM 3/79/1, Eden to Churchill, 3 Mar 1944, 1–3, 8.
25. Ibid., Portal to Churchill, 10 Mar 1944.
26. Rumenin, *Letyashti Kreposti*, 125; AFHRA, 519.12535, Fifteenth Air Force Operations (Bulgaria), Nov 1943–July 1944.
27. Miller, *Bulgaria*, 168–80.
28. FDRL, Map Room files, Box 136, CoS to Wilson and General Carl Spaatz, 25 Mar 1944; TNA, PREM 3/66/10, Portal to Wilson and Spaatz, 28 Mar 1944; Portal to Wilson and Spaatz, 11 Apr 1944.
29. TNA, PREM 3/66/10, Joint Staff Mission, Washington, DC, 21 July 1944, 1–2; CoS memorandum, 25 July 1944.
30. TNA, PREM 3/79/5, War Cabinet minute by Anthony Eden, 'Bulgaria', 17 Mar 1945.

31. Percy Schramm (ed), *Kriegstagebuch des OKW: Eine Dokumentation: 1943, Band 3, Teilband 2* (Augsburg: 2007), 1,089.

32. Michael M. Boll (ed), *The American Military Mission in the Allied Control Commission for Bulgaria 1944–1947* (New York: 1985), 38–42.

33. Peter Donnelly (ed), *Mrs. Milburn's Diaries: An Englishwoman's Day-to-Day Reflections 1939–1945* (London: 1979), 100, entry for 14 June 1941.

34. TNA, PREM 3/79/1, note by Churchill on telegram Tedder (MAAF) to Churchill, 29 Dec 1943; note by Churchill on letter from Lord Killearn to the Foreign Office, 9 Mar 1944.

35. TNA, PREM 3/66/10, JSM Report, 21 July 1944, 1.

36. TsAMO f.500, 0.725168d.319, Luftwaffe Generalstab, 'Luftwehrgeographische Beschreibung von Grossbritannien 1938', edn of 6 Mar 1940.

37. Haywood Hansell, *The Air Plan that Defeated Hitler* (Atlanta: 1972), 81–3.

38. TNA, PREM 3/79/1, telegram from British CoS to JSM, Washington, DC, 20 Oct 1943.

39. CamUL, Baldwin papers, vol 1, Londonderry to Baldwin, 17 July 1934.

40. Vera Brittain, *England's Hour* (London: 2005), xiv (first publ. 1941).

41. TNA, AIR 40/288 Air Intelligence (Liaison), 'The Blitz', 14 Aug 1941, App A, 'Morale', 1.

42. On this see Peter Gray, 'The Gloves Will Have to Come Off: A Reappraisal of the Legitimacy of the RAF Bomber Offensive against Germany', *Air Power Review*, 13 (2010), 9–40.

43. There is now a very large literature on these issues. See, e.g., Anthony Grayling, *Among the Dead Cities: Was the Allied Bombing of Civilians in World War II a Necessity or a Crime?* (London: 2005); Jörg Friedrich, *Der Brand: Deutschland im Bombenkrieg 1940–1945* (Munich: 2002); Nicholson Baker, *Human Smoke: The Beginnings of World War II and the End of Civilization* (New York: 2008); Stephen A. Garrett, *Ethics and Airpower in World War II: The British Bombing of German Cities* (New York: 1993); Beau Grosscup, *Strategic Terror: The Politics and Ethics of Aerial Bombardment* (London: 2006); Igor Primoratz (ed), *Terror from the Sky: The Bombing of German Cities in World War II* (Oxford: 2010).

44. LC, Eaker papers, Box I.30, Intelligence section, MAAF, 'What is Germany Saying?' [n.d. but early 1945].

45. See the excellent essays in Yuki Tanaka, Marilyn Young (eds), *Bombing Civilians: A Twentieth-Century History* (New York: 2009).

1. BOMBING BEFORE 1940: IMAGINED AND REAL

1. Lewis Mumford, *The Culture of Cities* (New York: 1938), 274–5, 292.

2. H. G. Wells, *The War in the Air* (London: 1908), 207, 349. Susan Grayzel, '"A Promise of Terror to Come": Air Power and the Destruction of Cities in British Imagination and Experience, 1908–39', in Stefan Goebel, Derek

Keene (eds), *Cities into Battlefields: Metropolitan Scenarios, Experiences and Commemorations of Total War* (Farnham: 2011), 48–51.

3. Kirk Willis, 'The Origins of British Nuclear Culture, 1895–1939', *Journal of British Studies*, 34 (1995), 70–71.

4. Wells, *War in the Air*, 349.

5. Douglas H. Robinson, *The Zeppelin in Combat: A History of the German Naval Airship Division* (London: 1962), 345–51; Joseph Morris, *The German Air Raids on Great Britain, 1914–1918* (London: 1925), 265–72; Colin Dobinson, *AA Command: Britain's Anti-Aircraft Defences of World War II* (London: 2001), 21–2.

6. Raymond H. Fredette, *The Sky on Fire: The First Battle of Britain, 1917–1918, and the Birth of the Royal Air Force* (Washington, DC: 1991), 14–40, 160–72. Frank Morison (pseud. of Albert Henry Ross), *War on Great Cities: A Study of the Facts* (London: 1938), 180.

7. Dobinson, *AA Command*, 32.

8. Ian Patterson, *Guernica and Total War* (London: 2007), 87–8.

9. Grayzel, '"A Promise of Terror to Come"', 51–2.

10. See John Sweetman, 'The Smuts Report of 1917: Merely Political Window Dressing?', *Journal of Strategic Studies*, 4 (1981), 152–6, 164–6; Matthew Cooper, 'A House Divided: Policy, Rivalry and Administration in Britain's Military Air Command', *Journal of Strategic Studies*, 3 (1980), 178–201.

11. TNA, AIR 1/462, Lord Tiverton to Air Board, 3 Sept 1917; AIR 1/463, memorandum for the Supreme War Council, 'Bombing Operations', Jan 1918.

12. CCAC, Lord Weir papers, WEIR 1/2, Sir Henry Norman to Lord Weir (Air Minister), 25 Mar 1918.

13. Edward Westermann, *Flak: German Anti-Aircraft Defenses, 1914–1945* (Lawrence, KS: 2001), 18–27.

14. Air Ministry, Cmd. 100, 'Synopsis of British Air Effort during the War', Apr 1919, 5–6.

15. TNA, AIR 9/8, chief of the air staff, 'Review of the Air Situation and Strategy for the Information of the Imperial War Cabinet', 27 June 1918; AIR 1/460, War Office D. F.O., 'Strategic Bombing Objectives in Order of Importance' [n.d. but autumn 1917]; Frederick Sykes, *From Many Angles: An Auto-Biography* (London: 1943), 224–30.

16. Peter Nath, *Luftkriegsoperationen gegen die Stadt Offenburg im Ersten und Zweiten Weltkrieg* (Offenburg: 1990), 585–92.

17. Alan Morris, *First of the Many: The Story of Independent Force, RAF* (London: 1968), App A; Air Ministry, Cmd. 100, 6 'Synopsis of British Air Effort' United States Bombing Survey: Narrative Summary, in M. Maurer (ed), *The U.S. Air Service in World War I: Vol 4* (Washington, DC: 1978), 500–502.

18. TNA, AIR 8/179, interview with Lord Trenchard on the Independent Force, 11 Apr 1934; AIR 1/460, Lt. General Groves, 'I.F. R.A.F. Policy', 11 Sept 1918; Sykes, *From Many Angles*, 555–8.

19. TNA, AIR 1/2104, British Bombing Commission Report; AIR 9/6, 'The Operation of the Independent Air Force', 12; United States Bombing Survey in Maurer, *U.S. Air Service: Vol 4*, 495–503.

20. TNA, AIR 9/8, War Office staff exercise, address by the chief of the air staff, 3. See too Tami Davis Biddle, *Rhetoric and Reality in Air Warfare: The Evolution of British and American Ideas about Strategic Bombing, 1914–1945* (Princeton, NJ: 2002), 78–80.

21. Giulio Douhet, *The Command of the Air*, trans. Dino Ferrari (Washington, DC: 1983), 181. Reprinted from 1942.

22. Ibid., 187.

23. Goldsworthy Lowes Dickinson, *War: Its Nature, Cause and Cure* (London: 1923), 12–13.

24. Neville Jones, *The Beginnings of Strategic Air Power: A History of the British Bomber Force 1923–1929* (London: 1987), 37–40.

25. Cited in Roxanne Panchasi, *Future Tense: The Culture of Anticipation in France between the Wars* (Ithaca, NY: 2009), 94–6.

26. 'The War of 19–', reproduced in Douhet, *The Command of the Air*, 392–3.

27. Morison, *War on Great Cities*, 183, 194, 203.

28. Tom Wintringham, *The Coming World War* (London: 1935), 38–9.

29. See e.g. Josef Konvitz, 'Représentations urbaines et bombardements stratégiques, 1914–1945', *Annales* (1989), 825–8; Stefan Goebel, Derek Keene, 'Towards a Metropolitan History of Total War: An Introduction', in Goebel and Keene, *Cities into Battlefields*, 6–11, 22–3.

30. H. Montgomery Hyde, G. R. Falkiner Nuttall, *Air Defence and the Civil Population* (London: 1937), 52–3.

31. CamUL, Needham papers, K31, review of *The Protection of the Public from Aerial Attack*, 20 Feb 1937.

32. Cited in Patterson, *Guernica and Total War*, 110.

33. Eric Lehmann, *Le ali del potere: La propaganda aeronautica nell'Italia fascista* (Turin: 2010); Scott W. Palmer, *Dictatorship of the Air: Aviation Culture and the Fate of Modern Russia* (Cambridge: 2006); Peter Fritzsche, *A Nation of Flyers: German Aviation and the Popular Imagination* (Cambridge, MA: 1992), ch 5.

34. Cited in Jones, *Beginnings of Strategic Air Power*, 41, House of Lords speech, 11 July 1928.

35. CCAC, Noel-Baker papers, 8/19, notes for a lecture, 6 Feb 1934.

36. E. Stengel, 'Air-Raid Phobia', *The British Journal of Medical Psychology*, 20 (1944–6), 135–43; P. E. Vernon, 'Psychological Effects of Air-Raids', *The Journal of Abnormal and Social Psychology*, 36 (1941), 457–61.

37. Brett Holman, 'The Air Panic of 1935: British Press Opinion between Disarmament and Rearmament', *Journal of Contemporary History*, 46 (2011), 288–307; Martin Hugh-Jones, 'Wickham Steed and German Biological Warfare Research', *Intelligence and National Security*, 7 (1992), 387–90.

38. CamUL, Needham papers, G57, rough notes 'Can Sci[ence] Save Civilisation?'

39. New Fabian Research Bureau, *The Road to War, Being an Analysis of the National Government's Foreign Policy* (London: 1937), 177–8.

40. Gerald Lee, '"I See Dead People": Air-Raid Phobia and Britain's Behaviour in the Munich Crisis', *Security Studies*, 13 (2003/4), 230–72.

41. Joel Hayward, 'Air Power, Ethics, and Civilian Immunity during the First World War and its Aftermath', *Global War Studies*, 7 (2010), 107–8.

42. Ibid., 127–8. See too Heinz Hanke, *Luftkrieg und Zivilbevölkerung* (Frankfurt am Main: 1991), 71–7.

43. J. Wheeler-Bennett (ed), *Documents on International Affairs: 1932* (Oxford: 1933), 217–27, 'Memorandum by the French Delegation, 14 November 1932'; Philip Meilinger, 'Clipping the Bomber's Wings: The Geneva Disarmament Conference and the Royal Air Force 1932–1934', *War in History*, 6 (1999), 311–21; Thomas Davies, 'France and the World Disarmament Conference of 1932–1934', *Diplomacy & Statecraft*, 15 (2004), 772–3; Waqar Zaidi, '"Aviation Will Either Destroy or Save Our Civilization": Proposals for the International Control of Aviation, 1920–45', *Journal of Contemporary History*, 46 (2011), 155–9.

44. Hanke, *Luftkrieg und Zivilbevölkerung*, 90.

45. *Documents on International Affairs: 1933* (Oxford: 1934), 173–7, 'British Draft Disarmament Convention, 16 March 1933: Article 34'. Carolyn Kitching, *Britain and the Geneva Disarmament Conference: A Study in International History* (Basingstoke: 2003), 59–60, 124–5; Dick Richardson, Carolyn Kitching, 'Britain and the World Disarmament Conference', in Peter Catterall, C. J. Morris (eds), *Britain and the Threat to Stability in Europe 1918–1945* (Leicester: 1993), 38–41, 47–9.

46. Davies, 'France and World Disarmament', 771–2; Hanke, *Luftkrieg und Zivilbevölkerung*, 93–8.

47. Philip Noel-Baker, 'International Air Police Force', in Storm Jameson (ed), *Challenge to Death* (London: 1934), 206–9, 231; CCAC, Noel-Baker papers, 4/497, 'Proposals for the Abolition of National Air Forces', 1 Nov 1934; Brett Holman, 'World Police for World Peace: British Internationalism and the Threat of the Knock-Out Blow from the Air, 1919–1945', *War in History*, 17 (2010), 319–21; Michael Pugh, 'An International Police Force: Lord Davies and the British Debate in the 1930s', *International Relations*, 9 (1988), 335–51;

48. *Documents on German Foreign Policy: Series C: Vol 5* (London: 1966), 355–63, 'Peace Plan of the German Government of March 31 1936'; *Documents on British Foreign Policy: Second Series: Vol VXI* (London: 1977), 262–4, Eden to Sir Eric Phipps (Paris), 2 Apr 1936; 268–70, Eden to Phipps, 2 Apr 1936.

49. *Documents on German Foreign Policy: Series C: Vol 5* 369–72, memorandum of the German Delegation to London, 2 Apr 1936.

50. Hanke, *Luftkrieg und Zivilbevölkerung*, 100–101.

51. 'How Nearly Twelve Million Voted', *Headway*, 17 (1935), 131. Martin Ceadel, 'The First British Referendum: The Peace Ballot 1934–35', *English*

Historical Review, 95 (1980), 818–21, 828–9; Richard Overy, *The Morbid Age: Britain and the Crisis of Civilization between the Wars* (London: 2009), 229–35.

52. Nicholas Rankin, *Telegram from Guernica: The Extraordinary Life of George Steer, War Correspondent* (London: 2003), 53.

53. Angelo Del Boca, *I gas di Mussolini* (Rome: 1996), 76–7, 139–41, 148.

54. See Klaus Maier, *Guernica 26.4.1937: Die deutsche Intervention in Spanien und der 'Fall Guernica'* (Freiburg: 1975), 55–8.

55. Paul Preston, *We Saw Spain Die: Foreign Correspondents in the Spanish Civil War* (London: 2008), 263–4, 275–6.

56. CamUL, Needham papers, K102, Communist Party of Great Britain, 'The Decisive Hour', 2; Patterson, *Guernica and Total War*, 69.

57. Robert Stradling, *Your Children Will be Next: Bombing and Propaganda in the Spanish Civil War, 1936–1939* (Cardiff: 2008), 219.

58. Rankin, *Telegram from Guernica*, 128–9; CamUL, For Intellectual Freedom papers, A4, FIL statement, 31 Mar 1938.

59. Parliamentary Debates, *Hansard*, Ser 5, vol 270, col 632, 10 Nov 1932.

60. Susan Grayzel, *At Home and Under Fire: Air Raids and Culture in Britain from the Great War to the Blitz* (Cambridge: 2012), 124–5, 130–31.

61. Alfredo Savelli, *Offesa aerea: mezzi di difesa e protezione* (Milan: 1936), 85–104.

62. Richard Overy, 'Apocalyptic Fears: Bombing and Popular Anxiety in Inter-War Britain', *S-NODI: pubblici e private nella storia contemporanea*, 2 (Spring 2008), 20–21.

63. Claudia Baldoli, Andrew Knapp, *Forgotten Blitzes: France and Italy under Allied Air Attack, 1940–1945* (London: 2012), 62–3.

64. Julia Torrie, *'For Their Own Good': Civilian Evacuations in Germany and France, 1939–1945* (New York: 2010), 25–7. On the social body see Panchasi, *Future Tense*, 100–107.

65. Torrie, *'For Their Own Good'*, 27–30; Bernd Lemke, *Luftschutz in Grossbritannien und Deutschland 1923 bis 1939* (Munich: 2005), 327–9.

66. Baldoli and Knapp, *Forgotten Blitzes*, 63–4; Terence O'Brien, *Civil Defence* (London: 1955), 329–30; RGVA, f.37878, o.1, d. 722, 'Anti-Chemical Defence during the War', 3 July 1945.

67. Lara Feigel, *The Love-Charm of Bombs* (London: 2013), 36.

68. Lemke, *Luftschutz*, 329–30.

69. 'Anti Air-Raid-Drill', *The War Resister*, Feb 1934, 6–8; FHL, No More War Movement papers, MSS 579/2, National Committee meeting, 1 June 1935; LSE, National Peace Council papers, 16/9, J. D. Bernal, 'Air Raid Precautions', *Peace*, Jan 1938, 152–3.

70. Joseph Meisel, 'Air Raid Shelter Policy and its Critics before the Second World War', *Twentieth Century British History*, 5 (1994), 307–12.

71. WMRC, Gollancz papers, 157/3/M, Towndrow to Victor Gollancz, October 1938.

72. Montgomery Hyde, *Air Defence and the Civil Population*, 216–24.

73. M. Cluet, *L'Architecture du IIIe Reich: Origines intellectuelles et visées idéologiques* (Bern: 1987), 201–4; C. W. Glover, *Civil Defence* (London: 1938), 692–3.

74. Glover, *Civil Defence*, 690, 694.

75. Helmut Klotz, *Militärische Lehren des Burgerkrieges in Spanien* (1937), 52.

76. NARA, RG 165/888.96, memorandum by Gen. Embick, War Plans Divisions, 6 Dec 1935, 3.

77. J. Truelle, 'La production aéronautique militaire française jusqu'en Juin 1940', *Revue d'histoire de la Deuxième Guerre Mondiale*, 19 (1969), 97; Pierre Cot, *Triumph of Treason* (Chicago, IL: 1944), 282–6, 330–35.

78. TNA, AIR 9/77, Draft Air Staff requirement, Specification B19/38.

79. Ferruccio Botti, 'Amadeo Mecozzi', in *Actes du colloque international, 'Précurseurs et prophètes de l'aviation militaire'* (Paris: 1992), 134–9; James Corum, 'Airpower Thought in Continental Europe between the Wars', in Philip Meilinger (ed), *The Paths to Heaven: The Evolution of Airpower Theory* (Maxwell AFB, AL: 1997), 160–61.

80. 'Rougeron's *Aviation de Bombardement*: Part II', *Royal Air Force Quarterly*, 10 (1939), 39–44; on French First World War experience see P. Bernard, 'A propos de la stratégie aérienne pendant la Première Guerre Mondiale: Mythes et realités', *Revue d'Histoire Moderne et Contemporaine*, 16 (1969), 357–61.

81. Cot, *Triumph of Treason*, 274–5; Robert Young, 'The Strategic Dream: French Air Doctrine in the Inter-War Period, 1919–1939', *Journal of Contemporary History*, 9 (1974), 58–9, 66–7; P. le Goyet, 'Evolution de la doctrine d'emploi de l'aviation française entre 1919 et 1939', *Revue d'Histoire de la Deuxième Guerre Mondiale*, 19 (1969), 22–3. Robin Higham, *Two Roads to War: The French and British Air Arms from Versailles to Dunkirk* (Annapolis, MD: 2012), 136–7.

82. K. R. Whiting, 'Soviet Aviation and Air Power under Stalin, 1928–1941', in Robin Higham, Jacob Kipp (eds), *Soviet Aviation and Air Power: A Historical View* (London: 1978), 50–63; J. T. Greenwood and Von Hardesty, 'Soviet Air Forces in World War II', in Paul Murphy (ed), *The Soviet Air Forces* (Jefferson, NC: 1984), 35–9; Alexander Boyd, *The Soviet Air Force since 1918* (London: 1977), 56–8.

83. James Corum, 'From Biplanes to Blitzkrieg: The Development of German Air Doctrine between the Wars', *War in History*, 3 (1996), 87–9.

84. Ibid., 97; Westermann, *Flak*, 40–46.

85. 'Beitrag zur Wehrmachtstudie, 18 Nov 1935', in Karl-Heinz Völker, *Dokumente und Dokumentarfotos zur Geschichte der Deutschen Luftwaffe* (Stuttgart: 1968), 445–6; E. M. Emme, 'Technical Change and Western Military Thought, 1914–45', *Military Affairs*, 24 (1960), 15.

86. 'Luftwaffendienstschrift "Luftkriegführung"', in Völker, *Dokumente und Dokumentarfotos*, 479–82.

87. Westermann, *Flak*, 54–5, 58–9.

88. Corum, 'From Biplanes to Blitzkrieg', 97–8; a different view in Klaus Maier, 'Total War and German Air Doctrine before the Second World War', in Wilhelm Deist (ed), *The German Military in the Age of Total War* (Oxford: 1985), 214–15.

89. Robert F. Futrell, *Ideas, Concepts, Doctrine: A History of Basic Thinking in the United States Air Force* (Maxwell AFB, AL: 1971), 28.

90. NARA, RG 165/888, Maj. Gen. Hugh Drum, 'Information on Aviation and Department of National Defense', 1 May 1934, 3.

91. M. Maurer, *Aviation in the U.S. Army, 1919–1939* (Washington, DC: 1987), 325–9; Alfred Goldberg (ed), *A History of the United States Air Force, 1907–1957* (Princeton, NJ: 1957), 40–41.

92. NARA, RG 18/223, Box 4, memorandum for the CoS, 4 Apr 1932, 9.

93. NARA, RG 18/229, Patrick papers, Fort Leavenworth lecture, March 27 1924, 1–2, 7–8.

94. Ibid., lecture to the Air War College, 'Air Tactics', Nov 1923, 1, 14–15; LC, Mitchell papers, Box 27, 'Aviation in the Next War' and 'Give America Airplanes'; William Mitchell, *Winged Defense* (New York: 1925), 4–6, 214–16.

95. USAFA, Hansell papers, Ser III, Box 1, Folder 1, 'Fairchild lecture', 1 Dec 1964, 8; USAFA, McDonald papers, Ser V, Box 8, Folder 8, 'Development of the U.S. Air Forces' Philosophy of Air Warfare prior to our Entry into World War II' [n.d.], 15–16.

96. LC, Andrews papers, Box 11, Maj. Harold George, 'An Inquiry into the Subject War', 17.

97. Konvitz, 'Représentations urbaines', 834–5. Gian Gentile, *How Effective is Strategic Bombing? Lessons Learned from World War II to Kosovo* (New York: 2000), 16–18; Biddle, *Rhetoric and Reality*, 161–4.

98. LC, Andrews papers, Box 11, Carl Spaatz, 'Comments on Doctrine of the Army Air Corps', 5 Jan 1935; R. W. Krauskopf, 'The Army and the Strategic Bomber 1930–1939: Part I', *Military Affairs*, 22 (1958/9), 94.

99. NARA, RG 94/452.1, General Oscar Westover to General Marlin Craig, 4 Dec 1936; Henry Arnold to Adjutant-General, 11 Sept 1936; Air Corps Materiel Division to the chief of the air corps, 14 Apr 1937; General Embick for the chief of staff, 'Changes in Fiscal Year 1938 Airplane Program', 16 May 1938.

100. NARA, RG 94/452.1, memorandum for the chief of staff (Gen. George Marshall), 21 Sept 1939; RG 94/580, Gen. George Strong to the chief of staff, 10 May 1940; memorandum, 'Army's Second Aviation Objective', 28 Feb 1941; R. W. Krauskopf, 'The Army and the Strategic Bomber 1930–1939: Part II', *Military Affairs*, 22 (1958/9), 211–14. On Roosevelt see Jeffery Underwood, *The Wings of Democracy: The Influence of Air Power on the Roosevelt Administration 1933–1941* (College Station, TX: 1991), 135–7.

101. TNA, AIR 9/8, Notes on a possible 'Locarno War', 2 May 1929.

102. Ibid., CoS Paper 156, 'Note by the First Sea Lord', 21 May 1928; CAS, 'Note upon the memorandum of the Chief of the Naval Staff' [n.d. but May

1928]; 'Notes for Address by CAS to the Imperial Defence College on the War Aims of an Air Force', 9 Oct 1928, 1.

103. RAFM, Saundby papers, AC72/12, Box 3, lecture, 'The Use of Air Power in 1939/45' [n.d.], 2–3; TNA, AIR 9/39, lecture by Air Vice-Marshal A. S. Barratt, 'Air Policy and Strategy', 23 Mar 1936.

104. TNA, AIR 9/8, Address by the CAS, 9 Oct 1928, 5.

105. Richard Overy, 'Allied Bombing and the Destruction of German Cities', in Roger Chickering, Stig Förster, Bernd Greiner (eds), *A World at Total War: Global Conflict and the Politics of Destruction, 1937–1945* (Cambridge: 2005), 278–84.

106. NARA, RG 18/223, Box 1, RAF *War Manual*, Pt I, May 1935, 57.

107. See e.g. Priya Satia, 'The Defense of Inhumanity: Air Control and the British Idea of Arabia', *American Historical Review*, 111 (2006), 25–38. A more favourable interpretation in Sebastian Ritchie, *The RAF, Small Wars and Insurgencies in the Middle East, 1919–1939* (Northolt: 2011), esp. 78–83.

108. John Slessor, *The Central Blue: Recollections and Reflections* (London: 1956), 65–6.

109. H. G. Wilmott, 'Air Control in Ovamboland', *Journal of the Royal United Services Institution*, 83 (1938), 823–9.

110. CCO, Portal papers, Folder 2/File 2, Portal to Churchill, 25 Sept 1941, encl. 'The Moral Effect of Bombing', 1; see too Charles Portal, 'Air Force Co-operation in Policing the Empire', *Journal of the Royal United Services Institution*, 82 (1937), 343–57.

111. Jones, *Beginnings of Strategic Air Power*, 107–8.

112. Ibid., 123.

113. Ibid., 118–21.

114. TNA, AIR 9/92, First Meeting of the Bombing Policy Sub-Committee, 22 Mar 1938, 1–2, 6–9.

115. Ibid., Note on A.T.S. bombing trial results [n.d.].

116. Ibid., minutes of meeting, Deputy Director of Plans, 23 Mar 1939.

117. TNA, AIR 14/225, Ludlow-Hewitt to Under-Secretary of State, Air Ministry, 30 Aug 1938. See too Charles Webster, Noble Frankland, *The Strategic Air Offensive Against Germany*, 4 vols (London: 1961), vol 1, 100.

118. TNA, AIR 9/8, Air Staff memorandum, 15 Jan 1936, 2–3, 5; AIR 9/77, Operational Requirements Committee, minutes of meeting, 11 Aug 1938, 4.

119. TNA, AIR 9/8, note from Harris to deputy chief of the air staff, 24 Sept 1936.

120. USAFA, McDonald papers, Ser V, Box 8, Folder 8, 'Development of the U.S. Air Forces Philosophy of Air Warfare', 3, 15. Michael Sherry, *The Rise of American Air Power: The Creation of Armageddon* (New Haven, CT: 1987), 53–6.

121. NARA, RG 18/223, Box 4, memorandum for the chief of staff, 4 Apr 1932; Arnold to the chief of the air corps, 'Cumulative Production of Airplanes of Mobilization Planning', 24 Mar 1931. On Britain see Sebastian Ritchie, *Industry and Air Power: The Expansion of British Aircraft Production,*

1935–1941 (London: 1997); George Peden, *Arms, Economics and British Strategy: From Dreadnoughts to Hydrogen Bombs* (Cambridge: 2007), 137–40, 158–61. This is the thrust of David Edgerton, *Britain's War Machine: Weapons, Resources and Experts in the Second World War* (London: 2011), esp. ch 1.

122. Oliver Stewart, 'The Doctrine of Strategical Bombing', *Journal of the Royal United Services Institution*, 81 (1936), 97–8.

123. TNA, AIR 9/39, 'Air Policy and Strategy', 23 Mar 1936, 5–6.

124. USAFA, McDonald papers, Ser V, Box 8, Folder 8, 'Development . . .', 13–15.

125. William Shirer, *Berlin Diary: The Journal of a Foreign Correspondent 1934–1941* (London: 1941), 160.

126. Edward Stebbing, *Diary of a Decade: 1939–1950* (Lewes: 1998), 3–4.

2. THE FIRST STRATEGIC AIR OFFENSIVE

1. Grigore Gafencu, *The Last Days of Europe: A Diplomatic Journey in 1939* (London: 1947), 65–6.

2. William Shirer, *Berlin Diary: The Journal of a Foreign Correspondent 1934–1941* (London: 1941), 388–9, entry for 4/5 Sept 1940; Max Domarus, *Hitler: Reden und Proklamationen. Band II: Erster Halbband* (Munich: 1965), 1,580.

3. Heinz(ed) Boberach, *Meldungen aus dem Reich: Die geheimen Lageberichte des Sicherheitsdienstes der SS 1938–1945*, 17 vols (Herrsching: 1984), vol 5, 1,549, Report 9 Sept 1940.

4. See the discussion in Horst Boog, 'Strategischer Luftkrieg in Europa 1943–1944', in Horst Boog, Gerhard Krebs, Detlef Vogel, *Das Deutsche Reich und der Zweite Weltkrieg, Band 7: Das Deutsche Reich in der Defensive* (Stuttgart: 2001), 323–7.

5. Karl-Heinz Völker, *Dokumente und Dokumentarfotos zur Geschichte der Deutschen Luftwaffe* (Stuttgart: 1968), 469–71, doc 200, 'Luftkriegführung', Mar 1940. For the best account see James Corum, *The Luftwaffe: Creating the Operational Air War, 1918–1940* (Lawrence, KS: 1997).

6. TsAMO, f.500, o.12452, d.11, Luftwaffe Generalstab, 'Merkblatt für den Einsatz der Fliegertruppe zur unmittelbaren Unterstützung des Heeres', 1 July 1939, 1–8.

7. TsAMO, f.500, o.12452, d.13, Luftwaffe Führungsstab, 'Bestimmungen für die Verständigung zwischen Truppenteilen am Boden und fliegenden Verbände', 6 Apr 1940.

8. M. Bernard Davy, *Air Power and Civilization* (London: 1941), 129–30.

9. TsAMO, f.500, o.12452, d.386, Luftflotte 4 Report, 'Angriff auf Warschau', 16 Sept 1939.

10. Ibid., operational orders, Luftflotte 4, 23 Sept 1939; AHB, Translations: Second World War, vol 9, VII/132, 'German Bombing of Warsaw and Rotterdam', 1–2.

11. TsAMO, f.500, o.12452, d.386, Foreign Office to von Richthofen, 24 Sept 1939; Heeresgruppe Nord to von Richthofen, 25 Sept 1939.

12. TsAMO, f.500, o.12452, d.386, Luftflotte 4 operational orders 24 Sept 1939; operational orders 25 Sept 1939; telephone message 27 Sept 1939. See too Boog et al., *DRZW: Band 7*, 323–4.

13. AHB Translations, vol 9, VII/132, 'German Bombing of Warsaw and Rotterdam', 1.

14. Andrew Klukowski, Helen Klukowski (eds), *Diary from the Years of Occupation: Zygmunt Klukowski* (Urbana, IL: 1993), 6, 9–10.

15. Chaim Kaplan, *Scroll of Agony: The Warsaw Diary of Chaim A. Kaplan* (London: 1966), 11, 18.

16. TNA, FO 371/23105, Kennard to Foreign Office, 3 Sept 1939.

17. AHB Translations, vol 2, VII/33, German Air Force General Staff, 'The Luftwaffe in Poland', 11 July 1944, 7.

18. Ibid., 2.

19. Kaplan, *Scroll of Agony*, 17–19.

20. James Corum, *Wolfram von Richthofen: Master of the German Air War* (Lawrence, KS: 2008), 173–4. For a figure of 40,000 dead, Halik Kochanski, *The Eagle Unbowed: Poland and the Poles in the Second World War* (London: 2012), 82.

21. FDRL, President's Personal Files 554, Biddle to Roosevelt, 10 Nov 1939.

22. Nicola Della Volpe, *Difesa del territorio e protezione antiaerea, 1915–1943: storia, documenti, immagini* (Rome: 1986), 215, minutes of the 17th Meeting of the Supreme Commission for the Defence, Feb 1940.

23. AHB Translations, vol 9, VII/132, 'German Bombing of Warsaw and Rotterdam', 2.

24. Leo Polak, 'De hel van Rotterdam', *KIJK*, 6 (2010), 22; Hans van der Pauw, *Rotterdam in de Tweede Wereldoorlog* (Rotterdam: 2006), 848–52; A. Korthals Altes, *Luchtgevaar: Luchtaanvallen op Nederland 1940–1945* (Amsterdam: 1984), 45–54. The estimates vary between 800 and 980, but some of the figures include deaths from earlier bombing raids and from artillery fire. Altes suggests a minimum of 600 (54).

25. Albert Kesselring, *The Memoirs of Field-Marshal Kesselring* (London: 2007), 56–8.

26. RAFM, Saundby papers, Box 3, RAF Staff College lectures, Pt 9, 'Operations 1939–1942', Mar 1944, 13.

27. Gérard Chauvy, *Le drame de l'armée française du Front populaire à Vichy* (Paris: 2010), 544–5.

28. Ibid., 27; Air Ministry, *The Rise and Fall of the German Air Force, 1933–1945* (London: 1983), 70–2.

29. Hanna Diamond, *Fleeing Hitler: France 1940* (Oxford: 2007), 45–9. I am also grateful to Martin Alexander for allowing me to see his unpublished article, 'Retreat, Resistance, Resignation: French Responses to Invasion in 1940'.

30. BA-MA, RL2 III/707b, 'Einsatzbereitschaft Luftwaffe und Verluste: Stand 29 Juni 1940'; AHB Translations, vol 7, VII/107, Luftwaffe Strength and Serviceability Tables, Aug 1938–Apr 1945.

31. Nicolaus von Below, *At Hitler's Side: The Memoirs of Hitler's Luftwaffe Adjutant, 1937–1945* (London: 2001), 63.

32. IWM, EDS collection, OKW, Aktennotiz, 12 June 1940; von Below, *At Hitler's Side*, 63–4. See too Henrik Eberle, Matthias Uhl (eds), *The Hitler Book: The Secret Dossier Prepared for Stalin* (London: 2005), 65. The dossier described a dinner on 24 June with Jodl, Keitel and Martin Bormann at which Hitler was alleged to have said: 'The western European problem has now been solved. All that remains for us now is to deal with the Soviet Union.'

33. *Fuehrer Conferences on Naval Affairs, 1939–1945* (London: 1990) hereafter *FCNA*, 110–11, Conference with the Führer, 20 June 1940; Hans-Adolf Jacobsen (ed), *Generaloberst Halder: Kriegstagebuch* (Stuttgart: 1963), 3 vols, II, 3, entry for 1 July 1940.

34. AHB Translations, vol 2, VII/26, 'The Course of the Air War Against England', 22 Nov 1939; VII/30, Col. Schmid, 'Proposal for the Conduct of Air Warfare against Britain', 22 Nov 1939, 2–4.

35. Walther Hubatsch (ed), *Hitlers Weisungen für die Kriegführung* (Munich: 1965), 46–9, Weisung Nr. 9.

36. Galeazzo Ciano, *Diario 1937–1943*, ed. Renzo De Felice (Milan: 1990), 451, entry for 7 July 1940; *FCNA*, 112–13, 'The War Against England', 7 July 1940.

37. Hubatsch, *Hitlers Weisungen*, 71–2, Directive no. 16.

38. von Below, *At Hitler's Side*, 68; Shirer, *Berlin Diary*, 356–7. The speech in Domarus, *Reden: Band II, erster Halbband*, 1,558: 'once again an appeal to reason even in England'.

39. AHB Translations, vol 1, VII/21, 'First Deliberations Regarding a Landing in England', 12 July 1940; Operations Staff memorandum, 13 Aug 1940: 'the Duce could be made to understand that we are fighting this war *together*, and not on parallel lines'. See too Walter Warlimont, *Inside Hitler's Headquarters, 1939–45* (London: 1964), 109–10; Basil Collier, *The Defence of the United Kingdom* (London: 1957), 499–50, App xxviii. For Hitler's agreement see Percy Schramm (ed), *Kriegstagebuch des OKW* (hereafter *KTB/OKW*): *Band 1, Teilband 1, 1940–1941* (Bonn: 2005), 23–4, entry for 12 Aug 1940.

40. von Below, *At Hitler's Side*, 63–4: 'He wished that Britain would terminate this war in the West because the coming conflict with the Soviet Union was unavoidable and he did not want an enemy front and rear.'

41. *FCNA*, 122–5, 'Conference on July 31 1940'; Jürgen Förster, 'Hitler Turns East – German War Policy in 1940 and 1941', in Bernd Wegner (ed), *From Peace to War: Germany, Soviet Russia and the World, 1939–1941* (Oxford: 1997), 117–24.

42. BA-MA, RL2-IV/27, Otto Bechtle, 'Der Einsatz der Luftwaffe gegen England, 1940–1943', 2 Apr 1944, 1.

43. BA-MA, RL8/1, Generalkommando I Fliegerkorps, 'Gedanken über die Führung des Luftkrieges gegen England', 24 July 1940, 1.

44. TsAMO, f.500, o.12452, d.56, *Orientierungsheft Grossbritannien*, 1 June 1939, Anlage 19, 23.

45. Ibid., f.500, o.725168, d.319, *Luftwehrgeographische Beschreibung von Grossbritannien*, 7 Feb 1940, 99.

46. BA-MA, RL8/1, Kriegstagebuch, I Fliegerkorps, 15 July 1940.

47. TNA, AIR 16/432, Home Security Intelligence Summary, 31 July 1940.

48. TNA, MEPO 2/6335, Metropolitan Police reports, Balham HQ, 2 and 9 Sept 1940.

49. TsAMO, f.500, o.12452, d.14, Luftwaffe Führungsstab, 'Bemerkungen zum Einsatz der Luftwaffe', Nr. 8, 26 July 1940, 1–3.

50. AHB Translations, vol 1, VII/21, 'First Deliberations', 12 July 1940, 2–3.

51. BA-MA, RL8/1, I Fliegerkorps, 'Gedanken über die Führung des Luftkrieges gegen England', 24 July 1940, 1.

52. Ibid., 2; TNA, AIR 40/2444, Bechtle lecture, 2 Feb 1944, 2–4.

53. Boberach, *Meldungen aus dem Reich*, vol 5, 1,424, Report 29 July 1940; 1,441, Report 5 Aug 1940.

54. TNA, AIR 20/8693, Testimony of Hermann Göring taken at Nuremberg, 6 Apr 1946 (interviewed by Hilary St George Saunders), 2, 14.

55. von Below, *At Hitler's Side*, 70; AHB Translations, vol 1, VII/21, OKW to Göring, 30 July 1940.

56. Hubatsch, *Hitlers Weisungen*, 75–6; AHB Translations, vol 1, VII/21, OKW (Keitel), 'Operation Sea Lion', 1 Aug 1940.

57. Boberach, *Meldungen aus dem Reich*, vol 5, 1,449, Report 8 Aug 1940; 1,461–2, Report 12 Aug 1940; Shirer, *Berlin Diary*, 366.

58. TNA, AIR 40/2444, Bechtle lecture, 7; Gerwin Strobl, *The Germanic Isle: Nazi Perceptions of Britain* (Cambridge: 2000), 100–101, 164–5, 182–3.

59. AHB Translations, vol 7, VII/107, Quartermaster Strength and Serviceability Tables.

60. Alfred Price, *The Luftwaffe Data Book* (London: 1997), 32–8.

61. On Göring, Richard Overy, *Goering: Hitler's Iron Knight* (3rd edn, London: 2012); Stefan Martens, *Hermann Göring: Erster Paladin des Führers und Zweiter Mann im Reich* (Paderborn: 1985); Alfred Kube, *Pour le Mérite und Hakenkreuz: Hermann Göring im Dritten Reich* (Munich: 1986).

62. Ernest Evans, 'Göring – beinahe Führer: Teil I', *Interavia*, 1 (Aug 1946), 17.

63. BA-B, RL3/246, letter from Heinrich Koppenberg (chairman of Junkers) to Göring, 11 Aug 1939; RL3/247, 'Besprechungsniederschrift 12/13 Jan 1939, Nachbau Ju88'. See too Lutz Budrass, *Flugzeugindustrie und Luftrüstung in Deutschland 1918–1945* (Düsseldorf: 1998), 622–4.

64. Details from Manfred Griehl, *Junkers Ju88: Star of the Luftwaffe* (London: 1990), ch 3; William Green, *Warplanes of the Third Reich* (London: 1970), 448ff.

65. Willy Ley, *Bombs and Bombing* (New York: 1941), 28–31, 40–43; on bomb loads see TsAMO, f.500, o.12452, d.14, 'Bemerkungen zum Einsatz der Luftwaffe', 26 July 1940, 2.

66. Alfred Price, *Instruments of Darkness: The History of Electronic Warfare, 1939–1945* (London: 2005), 21–47.

67. Details in Kenneth Wakefield, *The First Pathfinders: The Operational History of Kampfgruppe 100, 1939–1941* (London: 1981), 28–34.

68. TNA, AIR 20/335, RAF Wireless Intelligence Service, Periodical Summary 15, 7 June 1941.

69. TNA, PREM 3/29 (3), 'Summarised Order of Battle', 9 Aug 1940. Collier, *The Defence of the United Kingdom*, gives a figure of 57 squadrons for 8 August.

70. Colin Dobinson, *AA Command: Britain's Anti-Aircraft Defences of the Second World War* (London: 2001), 234–5, 512, 528–9; Alexander Rose, 'Radar and Air Defence in the 1930s', *Twentieth Century British History*, 9 (1998), 240–45.

71. AHB, 'Battle of Britain: Despatch by Air Chief Marshal Sir Hugh Dowding, 20 Aug 1941', 8.

72. Colin Dobinson, *Building Radar: Forging Britain's Early-Warning Chain, 1935–1945* (London: 2010), 302–5, 318; AHB, 'Battle of Britain Despatch', 9–10.

73. TsAMO, f.500, o.725168, d.110, Operations Staff, 'Die britische Fliegertruppe: 1.1.1941', 5–6, for a good example of this misconception. Aircraft, it was assumed, were directed by radio from the ground. See Sebastian Cox, 'A Comparative Analysis of RAF and Luftwaffe Intelligence in the Battle of Britain', *Intelligence and National Security*, 5 (1990), 426–7, 435–7.

74. TNA, AIR 8/463, Air Ministry minute, 8 July 1940; Air Staff minute, 'Present and Future Strength of the German Air Force', [n.d.]; German figures in AHB Translations, vol 7, VII/107, Quartermaster Strength and Serviceability Tables; Air Fleet strengths from Collier, *Defence of the United Kingdom*, 452, App xi. On aircraft ranges see AIR 20/313, Air Ministry memorandum, 'Extension of the Air Defence of Great Britain Necessitated by the Defeat of France', 5 July 1940.

75. BA-MA, RL2 IV/33, Luftwaffe Staff, 'Angriffe auf England: Materialsammlung, 1940–41'.

76. HHC, TYP Pt I, Damage to Property 1939–1945, reports for 1940.

77. BA-MA, RL2 IV/30, Maj. Leythehauser lecture, 'Einsatzarten und ihre Durchführung im Englandkrieg', 14 Feb 1944, 1–2; on mining RL2 IV/33, 'Angriffe auf England'.

78. TsAMO, f.500, o.725168, d.527, Luftwaffe Kriegsberichte-Kompanie, 'Bomben auf Flugplätze vor London, 18 Aug 1940', 3.

79. Ibid., account by Hellmut Schwatle, 18 Aug 1940, 2; Anton Dietz, 'Erlebnisbericht: Grossangriff auf London', 5.

80. AHB Translations, vol 2, VII/26, 'Course of the Air War', 2. BA-MA, RL2 IV/27, Bechtle lecture, 2 Apr 1944, 3; Klaus Maier, 'Luftschlacht um England', in Maier et al., *DRZW: Band 2: Die Errichtung der Hegemonie auf dem europäischen Kontinent* (Stuttgart: 1979), 384–5.

81. *KTB/OKW: Band 1, Teilband 1*, 59–60, entry for 3 Sept 1940.

82. Ibid., 50, 55, 62, entries for 29 Aug, 30 Aug, 4 Sept 1940.

83. TNA, AIR 16/432, Home Security intelligence summaries, night raids 18–19, 19–20, 22–23, 24–25, 25–26, 28–29 Aug.

84. AHB Translations, vol 2, VII/26, 'Course of the Air War', 3.

85. Shirer, *Berlin Diary*, 380–81, entry for 26 Aug 1940.

86. Elke Fröhlich (ed), *Die Tagebücher von Joseph Goebbels: Sämtliche Fragmente*, 4 vols (Munich: 1987), vol 4, 296, entry for 27 Aug 1940; *KTB/OKW: Band 1, Teilband 1*, 50, entry for 29 Aug 1940.

87. Shirer, *Berlin Diary*, 391.

88. NC, Cherwell papers, F260, RAF Operational Statistics, 'Night Bomber Sorties, 1 Aug 1940–7 Nov 1940'.

89. BA-MA, RL 41/2, RLB, Luftschutz-Bericht, 22 May 1940, 3.

90. Ibid., Luftschutz-Bericht, 31 July 1940, 2; Luftschutz-Bericht, 11 Sept 1940, 2.

91. Boberach, *Meldungen aus dem Reich*, vol 5, 1,525, 2 Sept 1940.

92. von Below, *At Hitler's Side*, 71.

93. Hugh Trevor-Roper, *Hitler's Table Talk 1941–1944* (London: 1973), 697. 'It was the British who started air attacks,' Hitler claimed. 'The Germans are always restrained by moral scruples, which mean nothing to the British.'

94. AHB Translations, vol 2, VII/30, 'Proposal for the Conduct of Air Warfare against Britain', 22 Nov 1939, 3; vol 1, VII/10, 'The Course of the Air War over Central and Western Europe', 1944, 1.

95. *KTB/OKW: Band 1, Teilband 1*, 27, entry for 13 Aug 1940.

96. AHB Translations, vol 2, VII/30, 'Proposal for the Conduct of Air Warfare against Britain', 22 Nov 1939, 4.

97. BA-MA, RL2 IV/30, Maj. Leythehauser lecture, 14 Feb 1944, 1.

98. TsAMO, f.500, o.725168, d.14, 'Bemerkungen zum Einsatz der Luftwaffe', 3 Sept 1940, 4.

99. von Below, *At Hitler's Side*, 73; Maier, 'Luftschlacht', 390–91. TsAMO, f.500, o.725168, d.14, 'Bemerkungen zum Einsatz der Luftwaffe', 3 Sept 1940, 29 Sept 1940, 14 Oct 1940, 11 Jan 1941. On Hitler's rejection of terror attacks in favour of raids on 'war-essential' targets see *KTB/OKW: Band 1, Teilband 1*, 76, entry for 14 Sept 1940.

100. BA-MA, RL8/1, I Fliegerkorps, 'Befehl zum Angriff auf Hafenanlagen in Loge', 6 Sept 1940.

101. TsAMO, f.500, o.725168, d.527, 'Bemerkungen zum Einsatz der Luftwaffe', 21 Sept 1940. This was the phenomenon of 'Abgeflogensein' – to be averse to flying – observed among crew who had had no previous psychiatric response to combat.

102. Ibid., f.500, o.725168, d.527, KBK-Tagesbericht, Kriegserlebnis, 7 Sept 1940, 'Ein Feuergürtel lodert um London', 1, 'Unternehmen: Vergeltung', 1.

103. Fröhlich, *Die Tagebücher von Joseph Goebbels*, 309, 316.

104. *KTB/OKW: Band 1, Teilband 1*, 76, entry for 14 Aug 1940.

105. von Below, *At Hitler's Side*, 70–71, 73; Adolf Galland, *The First and the Last* (London: 1955), 45.

106. On German estimates see *KTB/OKW: Band 1, Teilband 1*, 60, 67, 86. Not only was Fighter Command assumed to have around 300 aircraft left, it was

wrongly claimed that squadron strength had been reduced from 12–15 down
to 5–7 planes.

107. von Below, *At Hitler's Side*, 71.

108. Maier, 'Luftschlacht', 390–91.

109. Fröhlich, *Die Tagebücher von Joseph Goebbels*, 410, entry for 24 Nov
1940.

110. NARA, RG 332, Box 115, interrogation of Wilhelm Keitel [n.d.], 11–12.

111. TsAMO, f.500, 0.725168, d.527, Jagdgeschwader 3, Erfahrungsbericht,
12 Nov 1940, 'Bombenwerfen der Jäger'.

112. Sönke Neitzel, *Der Einsatz der deutschen Luftwaffe über dem Atlantik und
der Nordsee 1939–1945* (Bonn: 1995), 55–6.

113. Ibid., 85. See too K. Poolman, *Focke-Wulf Condor: Scourge of the Atlantic*
(London: 1978), chs 10–11. On the shipping campaign see BA-MA
RL2 IV/48, Luftwaffe Generalstab Studie, 'Zusammenarbeit Marine-Luftwaffe
im Seekrieg gegen England', 28 Feb 1944, 2–7. 'All possibilities offered by the
bombing war must be placed unreservedly in the service of the campaign
against tonnage.'

114. Calculated from Neitzel, *Einsatz über dem Atlantik*, 68.

115. Ibid., 70, 73.

116. Calculated from BA-MA, RL2 IV/27, Bechtle lecture, Anlage, 'Grossangriffe bei Nacht gegen Lebenszentren Englands, 12.8.1940–26.6.1941'.

117. NARA, RG 332 Box 115, Keitel interrogation, 12. 'A great quantity of
motor vehicles and equipment came from America and so the war was continued through attacks on these harbours.'

118. TsAMO, f.500, 0.725168, d.110, Luftwaffe Operations Staff, 'Die britische
Fliegertruppe', 14 Jan 1941, 10–11.

119. Ibid., f.500, 0.725168, d.527, 'Taktische Feindnachrichten Nr. 11', 9 Nov
1940.

120. BA-MA, RL2 IV/33, 'Luftkrieg gegen England: Weisungen und Befehle',
7 Nov 1940.

121. TsAMO, f.500, 0.725168, d.527, 'Taktische Feindnachrichten Nr 15', II Fliegerkorps, 1 Dec 1940, 1–2. On morale see IWM, Italian Series (Air Force), Box
14, 2547, OKL Ic Report, 'Wirkung deutscher Luftangriffe auf England', 1.

122. Calculated from TNA, HO 191/11, MHS, 'Statement of Civilian Casualties
to 31 May 1945', 31 July 1945.

123. TsAMO, f.500, 0.725168, d.527, 'Taktische Feindnachrichten Nr 11', 3.

124. TNA, HO 186/669, Meteorological Office, 'The Frequency with which
aimed Bombing can be carried out during daytime', Aug 1937; 'Note on
possible use of smoke for camouflage', 1 June 1938.

125. TNA, WO 208/3506, Air Intelligence (k), Report 341, 'Report on Four
He111's of K. Gr. 100', 22 June 1941; TsAMO, f.500, 0.725168, d.15,
London map, target areas for *Fliegerkorps* 3 and 4, July 1940; 725168/17,
London map, target areas for *Fliegerkorps* 1 and 2, July 1940. The full target
intelligence maps can be seen in the IWM Archive at Duxford. See e.g. the
materials for 'Zielstammkarte: Ort: Manchester-Clifton-Junction', prepared

in October 1939, which include two maps and two large photographs, each
clearly marked in red with captions for specific targets.

126. TsAMO, f.500, o.725168, d.14, 'Bemerkungen zum Einsatz der Luftwaffe',
11 Jan 1941, 2–4.

127. TNA, AIR 40/288, A.I.9, 'The Blitz', 14 Aug 1941, 1, 5.

128. On training see TNA, AIR 20/335, RAF Wireless Intelligence Periodical
Summary, 16 Sept 1940, assessing material on German navigation training
courses. On the beams, R. V. Jones, *Most Secret War: British Scientific Intelligence 1939–1945* (London: 1978), 96–110.

129. On this and declining use of beams see TNA, AIR 41/17, AHB Narrative, 'The
Air Defence of Great Britain: vol III, June 1940–December 1941', 113–14.

130. TNA, PREM 3/22/4, Sinclair to Churchill, 22 July 1941; Sinclair to
Churchill, 13 Nov 1941.

131. TNA, AIR 41/46, 'No 80 Wing, RAF: Historical Report 1940–1945', 20–22.

132. TsAMO, f.500, o.725168, d.14, 'Bemerkungen zum Einsatz der Luftwaffe',
14 Nov 1940, 7–8.

133. Ibid., 'Bemerkungen zum Einsatz der Luftwaffe', 11 Jan 1941, 3; 8 May
1941, 3–4.

134. TNA, PREM 3/22/4b, 'Radio Countermeasures', Periodical Report 8,
25 Oct 1940. On the history of Trent Park see AIR 40/1177, ADI (K), 'Intelligence from Interrogation', 31 Dec 1945.

135. TNA, WO 208/3506, 'X-Gerät' interrogations, Special Extract 46.

136. Ibid., Special Extract 54, 11 Oct 1940 on London; Special Extract 52, 8 Oct
1940.

137. AHB Translations, vol 5, VII/92, German Aircraft Losses Jan–Dec 1941;
vol 7, VII/107, Luftwaffe Strength and Serviceability Tables. Kesselring
remark from NC, Cherwell papers, G27, Sholto Douglas to Lindemann,
17 Dec 1940, reporting a POW interrogation.

138. IWM, Milch documents, MD 62/5177, 'Monatliche Ausbringungszahlen
1941'; BAB RL3/162, Lieferplan Nr. 18, 1 July 1940. See too Budrass,
Flugzeugindustrie, 705.

139. BAB, RL3/350, GL Amt to Jeschonnek, 7 Mar 1941.

140. TsAMO, f.500, o.725168, d.527, Fliegerkorpsarzt, Fliegerkorps II, 'Front-
fliegerfahrungsberichte', 29 Nov 1940, 1–5.

141. Ibid., f.500, o.725168, d.527, 'Bericht eines Amerikaners am 23.10', 7 Nov
1940; Luftflottenkommando 2, Operations Staff Report, 28 Nov 1940.

142. Ibid., f.500, o.725168, d.527, 'Tagesbefehl: Reichsmarschall Göring',
23 Nov 1940.

143. TNA, AIR 16/380, notes of a conference at the Air Ministry, 18 Oct 1940.

144. PArch, Beaverbrook papers, BBK/D/328, Note, 'Balloon Barrages – Lethal
Devices', 28 Aug 1940.

145. Anthony Cooper, *Anti-Aircraft Command 1939–1945: The Other Forgotten Army* (Fleet Hargate, Lincs.: 2004), 68; Frederick Pile, *Ack-Ack: Britain's
Defence against Air Attack during the Second World War* (London: 1949),
144–5.

146. TNA, AIR 41/17, 'Air Defence of Great Britain: Volume III', 113; Dobinson, *AA Command*, 279–81.

147. TNA, PREM 3/22/1, Note for Churchill from the Night Air Defence Committee, 25 June 1941; Cooper, *Anti-Aircraft Command*, 74–5.

148. Pile, *Ack-Ack*, 172–3.

149. TNA, PREM 3/22/4B, Portal to Churchill, 5 Nov 1940; HO 186/391, Civil Defence Committee memorandum, 5 Aug 1940.

150. Donald Brown, *Somerset Against Hitler: Secret Operations in the Mendips 1939–1945* (Newbury: 1999), 173–7.

151. TNA, AIR 41/46, No 80 Wing, Historical Report, 25–6.

152. TNA, HO 186/391, Camouflage Committee meeting, 20 June 1940; HO 191/1, Camouflage Advisory Panel, minutes of meeting 21 Oct 1939.

153. HHC, TSCD/41, Air Raids Committee minutes, 9 Sept 1939; Works Committee, 'Camouflage of Concrete Roads', 19 Mar 1941.

154. TNA, AIR 16/113, D. Pye to Dowding, 24 Apr 1939; B. Dickens, 'Note on a visit to RAF Bawdsey, 17 May 1940'; AIR 20/2419, Sir Henry Tizard, 'Technical Aids to Night Fighting', 8 May 1941, 7.

155. TNA, PREM 3/22/1, Lindemann to Churchill, 2 Oct 1940; 'Report of Meeting on Night Air Defence', 7 Oct 1940, 3; AIR 20/2419, Douglas note, 8 Oct 1940; AIR 16/524, 'Progress Report of AO C-in-C Fighter Command 10 May–18/19 June 1941', 4.

156. NC, Cherwell papers, G174/5, D. R. Pye to Lindemann, 18 Nov 1939; G175, memorandum by the First Sea Lord, 'Coal Dust for Camouflaged Coastline', 9 Aug 1941; MHS, REDept, 'Note on the Screening of Water by Coal Dust Filters', 17 Apr 1941.

157. TNA, AIR 16/387, Air Ministry to Dowding, 14 Sept 1940; Air Council recommendations, 17 Sept 1940.

158. TNA, AIR 16/387, Dowding to Harold Balfour, Parliamentary Under-Secretary for Air, 27 Sept 1940; minutes of meeting, 1 Oct 1940; Dowding to Churchill, 8 Oct 1940.

159. TNA, AIR 16/380, Dowding to all Fighter Command Groups, 9 Oct 1940; Director of Home Operations to Dowding, 18 Oct 1940; Dowding to Director of Home Operations, 4 Nov 1940.

160. TNA, PREM 4/3/6, Irene Ward to Bracken, encl. memorandum, 'A weak link in the nation's defences', 3.

161. PArch, Beaverbrook papers, BBK/D/32, Dowding to Sinclair, 14 Oct 1940; Dowding to Sinclair, 9 Oct 1940.

162. Sebastian Ritchie, 'A Political Intrigue Against the Chief of the Air Staff: The Downfall of Air Chief Marshal Sir Cyril Newall', *War & Society*, 16 (1998), 83–104.

163. TNA, PREM 3/22/1, Salmond to Churchill, 5 Oct 1940.

164. TNA, AIR 16/622, Douglas to Portal, 6 Dec 1940; Portal to Douglas, 8 Dec 1940; Douglas to Balfour, 14 Dec 1940; Douglas to group headquarters, Fighter Command, 30 Jan 1941.

165. TNA, PREM 3/22/3, Sinclair to Churchill, 15 Nov 1940; Sinclair to Churchill, 13 July 1941; AIR 41/17, 'Air Defence of Great Britain: Volume III', App 8.

166. Details on GCI radar in Dobinson, *Building Radar*, 367–73.

167. TsAMO, f.500, 0.725168, d.107, 'Bemerkungen zum Einsatz der Luftwaffe', 7 Mar 1941, 2.

168. Ibid., 'Bemerkungen zum Einsatz der Luftwaffe', 4 July 1941, 1–2.

169. TNA, AIR 8/463, 'Present and Future Strength of the German Air Force' [n.d. but Oct 1940]; AHB Translations, vol 7, VII/107, Luftwaffe Strength and Serviceability Tables.

170. NC, Cherwell papers, G25, 'Comparative strengths of the German and British air forces', 7 Dec 1940, 1.

171. Ibid., F125, Lindemann to Churchill, 4 Jan 1941.

172. TNA, AIR 8/463, Portal to Churchill, 18 Feb 1941 and 20 Mar 1941.

173. TNA, PREM 3/88/3, Churchill to Gen. Ismay, 26 Dec 1940.

174. PArch, Beaverbrook papers, BBK/D/32, Sinclair to Beaverbrook, 1 Sept 1940; Beaverbrook to Sinclair, 3 Oct 1940; Sinclair to Beaverbrook, 22 Oct 1940; minute for Churchill, 19 Apr 1941.

175. BA-MA, RL2 IV/33, Angriff auf England: Materialsammlung, 'Durchführung – Erfolg: April 1941'.

176. *FCNA*, 179, Directive No 23, 'Basic Principles of the Prosecution of the War against British War Economy'; Boog et al, *DRZW: Band 7*, 327.

177. TsAMO, f.500, 0.725168, d.112, Operations Staff, 'Unterlagen für Luftangriffe auf britische Häfen und Anlagen der Rüstungsindustrie', 25 Jan 1941.

178. Ibid., f.500, 0.725168, d.110, Operations Staff, Report on British targets, 27 Jan 1941, 2.

179. John Duggan, *Neutral Ireland and the Third Reich* (Dublin: 1985), 138–41; Clair Wills, *That Neutral Island: A History of Ireland during the Second World War* (London: 2007), 208–9, 212.

180. von Below, *At Hitler's Side*, 93–4; BA-MA, RL2 IV/33, 'Durchführung – Erfolg: April 1941'; on Italian opera see Harry Flannery, *Assignment to Berlin* (London: 1942), 163–4.

181. BA-MA, RL2 IV/27, Bechtle lecture, 2 Apr 1944, 5–6; Collier, *Defence of the United Kingdom*, 503–5, App xxx.

182. BA-MA, RL2 IV/33, 'Durchführung – Erfolg: April 1941'; losses calculated from AHB Translations, vol 5, VII/92, German Aircraft Losses (West) Jan–Dec 1941.

183. BA-MA, RL2 IV/28, 'Weisung für die Luftkriegführung gegen England, 16.3.1941'.

184. BA-MA, RL2 IV/27, Bechtle lecture, 6–8; RL2 IV/28, 'Weisung 3.7.1941' and 'Weisung 30.7.1941'; RL2 IV/33, 'Durchführung – Erfolg: Juni 1941'.

185. von Below, *At Hitler's Side*, 79. Overheard in conversation with army leaders Franz Halder and Walter von Brauchitsch.

186. TNA, AIR 20/8693, Testimony of Hermann Göring, 6 Apr 1946, 13.

187. *FCNA*, 177–8, Conference with Führer, 4 Feb 1941.

188. Hubatsch, *Hitlers Weisungen*, 119; on the naval war see Neitzel, *Der Einsatz der deutschen Luftwaffe*, 50–51.

189. von Below, *At Hitler's Side*, 84, 103; quotation in Eberle, Uhl (eds), *The Hitler Book*, 69, from a reported conversation in March 1941. See too Warlimont, *Inside Hitler's Headquarters*, 133–4: 'As soon as the campaign in the East was over, the "siege" was to be resumed in full force.'

190. FDRL, President's Secretary's Files, Box 34, 'Great Britain Military Situation', reports to the president, Sept–Dec 1940.

191. Martin van Creveld, *Hitler's Strategy 1940–1941: The Balkan Clue* (Cambridge: 1973), 27–30; von Below, *At Hitler's Side*, 77; Warlimont, *Inside Hitler's Headquarters*, 127–30.

192. Ivan Maisky, *Memoirs of a Soviet Ambassador* (London: 1967), 104, 109–10: 'Hitler cherished much more serious plans,' wrote Maisky, 'he wanted to *conquer* Britain.' For the Soviet view, Pavel Sevostyanov, *Before the Nazi Invasion: Soviet Diplomacy in September 1939–June 1941* (Moscow: 1984), 137–43.

193. AHB Translations, vol 2, VII/28, 'A Survey of German Air Operations 1939–1944', 21 Sept 1944, 4–5.

194. Fröhlich, *Die Tagebücher von Joseph Goebbels*, vol 4, 720, entry for 28 June 1941.

195. TsAMO, f.500, 0.725168, d.527, 'Bericht eines Amerikaners am 23.10', 7 Nov 1940.

196. Ibid., 7 Nov 1940, 3.

197. Michael Postan, *British War Production* (London: 1957), 484–5; Maier, 'Luftschlacht', 402–4.

198. NC, Cherwell papers, G181, 'Bombing of London in September, October and November'.

199. Royal Society, London, Blackett papers, PB/4/4, 'Operational Research: Recollections of Problems Studied, 1940–1945', 100; 'Effects of Bombing Policy', paper for the JIC, Apr 1942; casualty figures from TNA, HO 191/11, 'Statement of Civilian Casualties in the United Kingdom', 31 July 1945.

200. TNA, AIR 40/288, Air Intelligence, 'The Blitz', 14 Aug 1941, App A, Table 1, 'Effects of Blitz'.

201. NARA, RG 107, Box 138, MHS Report, 'German Bombing of Britain', 31 May 1942, 3–5.

202. TNA, AIR 41/17, 'Air Defence of Great Britain: Volume III', App 1, 'Summary of Damage to Key Points 1940 and 1941', 2–4.

203. Ibid., App A, 'Morale', 1.

204. Cooper, *Anti-Aircraft Command*, 74–5.

205. Calculated from Terence O'Brien, *Civil Defence* (London: 1955), 690, App x.

206. TNA, HO 187/1156, 'Manpower in the National Fire Service: Historical Survey'.

207. Gavin Bailey, 'Aircraft for Survival: Anglo-American Aircraft Diplomacy 1938–42', PhD thesis, Dundee University 2010, 162–8; on British fighter strength, TNA, AIR 20/313, Note, 9 Jan 1941.

208. BA-MA, RL 2 IV/30, Maj. Leythehauser lecture, 14 Feb 1944, 5–6, 19–20.

209. BA-B, RL3/157, 'Plan Elch: 13.8.1941'; RL3/146, 'Göring-Flugzeug-Lieferplan', 15 Sept 1941; IWM, FD 5450/45, 'Expanded Air Armament Programme', 6 July 1941. See too Budrass, *Flugzeugindustrie*, 715–21. The special order for aircraft production was backdated to 22 June 1941, the opening day of Barbarossa.

210. Richard Overy, 'From "Uralbomber" to "Amerikabomber": The Luftwaffe and Strategic Bombing', *The Journal of Strategic Studies*, 1 (1978), 169–70. For the Azores see *FCNA*, 199, Conference with the Führer, 22 May 1941; James Duffy, *Target America: Hitler's Plan to Attack the United States* (Guilford, CT: 2006), 51–5, 126–9.

211. TNA, PREM 3/22/3, Churchill to Sinclair, 20 Aug 1941; AIR 2/5245, Douglas to Balfour, 13 Aug 1941.

212. BA-MA, RL 2 IV/28, Luftflotte 3, 'Gefechtskalender Juli–Dez 1941'.

213. BA-MA, RL 2 IV/149, 'Gedanken zum Einsatz der Luftwaffe im Luftkriege über See', 23 Jan 1944, 23–4.

214. Dobinson, *Building Radar*, 483–5.

215. TNA, PREM 3/22/1, 'Night Air Defence: Progress Report', 12 Nov 1941, 2–4.

216. Ibid., Progress report from C-in-C, Anti-Aircraft Command, 20 Apr 1942; Progress report by C-in-C, Fighter Command, for Night Defence Committee, 16 Mar 1943.

217. BA-MA, RL 36/52, 'Bericht über Reise zu Luftflotte 3 von 11–12.3.1943', 13 Mar 1943.

218. Willi Boelcke(ed), *The Secret Conferences of Dr Goebbels: The Nazi Propaganda War 1939–43* (London: 1967), 233–4.

219. IWM, Milch papers, vol 62, conference at Carinhall, 6 Mar 1942.

220. On Paris see AHB Translations, vol 4, VII/79, 'Conference with Reichsmarschall Goering', 6 Mar 1942, 1. Hitler's order in Collier, *Defence of the United Kingdom*, 512, App xxxvi. See too IWM, Milch papers, vol 62/5208, 'Besprechungsnotiz: 16.5.1942'.

221. AHB Translations, vol 4, VII/79, 'Conference with Reichsmarschall Goering', 16 May 1942, 8; on Weston-super-Mare see vol 2, VII/26, 'A Survey of German Air Operations 1939–1944', 21 Sept 1944, 9. Karl Baedeker, *Great Britain* (Leipzig: 1927), 133.

222. Raid details in Collier, *Defence of the United Kingdom*, 513–16, App xxxvii and xxxviii.

223. Boog, 'Strategischer Luftkrieg', 332ff, for discussion of the background to the renewed offensive.

224. BA-MA, RL 36/52, 'Kommando der Eprobungs-Stellen, Besprechung in Rechlin', 13 Mar 1943; 'Aktenvermerk über Besprechung über verstärkten England-Einsatz', 27 Mar 1943.

225. IWM, Milch documents, MD 53/732, telegram from Göring to Milch, 12 Oct 1943; MD 63/6290-308, 'Besprechung beim Reichsmarschall', 9 Oct 1943.

226. BA-MA, RL2 IV/48, 'Zusammenarbeit Marine-Luftwaffe im Seekrieg gegen England', 28 Feb 1944; 'Unterlagen für Lagebesprechung beim Führer', 19 July 1943.

227. AHB Translations, vol 2, VII/37, 'General Kessler to General Jeschonnek', 5 Sept 1943.

228. Boog, 'Strategischer Luftkrieg', 372–7.

229. IWM, Milch documents, 63/5877, 'Besprechung beim Reichsmarschall', Nov 1943.

230. TNA, HO 191/11, 'Chronological Record of Air Attacks on Great Britain and Northern Ireland', 28 Sept 1945.

231. TNA, PREM 3/18/2, Air Ministry, 'Enemy Night Activity, 22/23 February 1944'; PREM 3/22/1, Progress report from C-in-C, Fighter Command, 1/9/43–22/2/44.

232. Boog, 'Strategischer Luftkrieg', 380–85; G. Kirwin, 'Allied Bombing and Nazi Domestic Propaganda', *European History Quarterly*, 15 (1985), 344–5, 355–6.

233. Boog, 'Strategischer Luftkrieg', 385–418. See too Michael Neufeld, 'The Guided Missile and the Third Reich: Peenemünde and the Forging of a Technological Revolution', in Monika Renneberg, Mark Walker (eds), *Science, Technology and National Socialism* (Cambridge: 1994), 62–6; Duffy, *Target America*, 66–73, 78–83.

234. Figures from Collier, *Defence of the United Kingdom*, 523–26; see too Boog, 'Strategischer Luftkrieg', 397, 402.

235. BA-MA, RL36/52, 'Niederschrift über die Besprechung in Berchtesgaden am 29.5.1944', 1–2.

236. Ibid., 'Jägerstab [Fighter Staff] Besprechung beim Herrn Reichsmarschall', 2 July 1944; 'Besprechung beim Herrn Reichsmarschall', 14 July 1944.

237. TNA, PREM 3/18/2, Churchill to Sinclair and Herbert Morrison, 8 June 1943; Sinclair to Churchill, 10 June 1943, enclosing 'Notes on the Protection of Dams and Reservoirs in the United Kingdom'.

238. FDRL, Map Room files, Box 49, message for US Navy Intelligence from Stockholm, 6 Oct 1944; telegram from US military attaché, Madrid, 6 Sept 1944.

239. Ibid., PREM 3/18/2, Portal to Churchill, 22 Mar 1945; War Cabinet paper, 'Protection of London against Low-Flying Attacks', 29 Mar 1945; Hollis to Churchill, 5 Apr 1945, enclosing CoS memorandum, 'Likelihood and Possible Form of a Last Desperate Throw by the German Naval and Air Forces'.

240. Geoffrey Brooks, *Hitler's Nuclear Weapons* (London: 1992), 112, 122–4, 128–30; see too Rainer Karlsch, *Hitlers Bombe: Die geheime Geschichte der deutschen Kernwaffenversuche* (Munich: 2005), 189–92, for plans to create a long-range missile for use against Allied cities, and 228–237, for the argument that an atomic test took place in Germany in March 1945. On the

failure of the German atomic research programme see Rolf-Dieter Müller, 'Albert Speer und die Rüstungspolitik 1942–1945', in Bernhard Kroener, Rolf-Dieter Müller, Hans Umbreit, *DRZW: Band 5/2: Organisation und Mobilisierung des Deutschen Machtbereichs, 1942–1944/45* (Stuttgart: 1999), 738–43.

241. Louis Lochner, *The Goebbels Diaries* (London: 1948), 139, entry from 27 Apr 1942.

242. NARA, RG 332 Box 115, Keitel interrogation, 22.

243. Evans, 'Göring – beinahe Führer', 5.

244. UEA, Zuckerman Archive, SZ/BBSU/75/1, Interrogation Detachment, US Air Headquarters, Enemy Intelligence Summary, Hermann Göring, 1 June 1945.

3. TAKING IT? BRITISH SOCIETY AND THE BLITZ

1. Bodleian Library, Oxford, Ponsonby papers, C682, J. H. A. to Ruth Fry, 16 Sept 1940.

2. TNA, ED 136/111, 'Planning of Evacuation', Jan 1939, 2.

3. TNA, MH 79/178, Home Office, 'Pamphlet on Shelter from Air Attacks', 1939, 3.

4. TNA, PREM 3/27, draft article, 'The War in East London', 28 Sept 1940, 1.

5. TNA, HO 186/927, Regional Commissioner, South-West region to all town clerks, 20 Dec 1940.

6. On citizen warriors see Sonya Rose, *Which People's War? National Identity and Citizenship in Wartime Britain 1939–1945* (Oxford: 2003), ch 5.

7. TNA, PREM 3/28/5, Note for the prime minister, 'Working after the Siren', 10 Sept 1940.

8. Foreword to Stephen Spender, *Citizens in War – and After* (London: 1945), 5.

9. Terence O'Brien, *Civil Defence* (London: 1955), chs iii, v; Bernd Lemke, *Luftschutz in Grossbritannien und Deutschland 1923 bis 1939* (Munich: 2005), 342–62. See too UEA, Zuckerman Archive, OEMU/56/3, memorandum, 'Regional Machinery, Policy, Personnel'.

10. For one example see E. Doreen Idle, *War over West Ham: A Study of Community Adjustment* (London: 1943), 59–63.

11. TNA, PREM 3/27, note by Edward Bridges for Churchill, 'London Regional Commissioners'; HHC, TSCD/1, Note on Civil Defence Regions, 24 Sept 1941.

12. TNA, HO 45/19762, Order in Council, 4 Sept 1939; Cabinet paper, 'Powers of Regional Commissioners', 21 Mar 1939.

13. HHC, TSCD/1, City of Coventry, 'Air Raid Precautions: Outline Scheme of Organisation', Apr 1937; City of Manchester, memorandum, 'Air Raid Precautions', 21 Oct 1936; City of Leeds, 'Local Scheme of Air Raid Precautions', 23 Sept 1936; City of Newcastle-upon-Tyne, 'Report of Special Committee as to Air Raid Precautions, 1 July 1937'.

14. CLSC, JN20/16/C, minutes of Hampstead Civil Defence Committee, 5 Oct 1939.

15. YCA, Acc 89/1a, ARP Emergency Committee, minutes of meetings, 10 Oct, 17 Oct, 27 Oct, 10 Nov 1939.

16. CLSC, JN20/16/C, minutes of Civil Defence Committee, 26 Sept, 25 Oct 1939.

17. Calculated from TNA, HO 186/602, Statistics on Civil Defence Personnel, Summary of all Services, 30 June 1940, 14 Nov 1940.

18. Shane Ewen, 'Preparing the British Fire Service for War: Local Government, Nationalisation and Evolutionary Reform, 1935–41', *Contemporary British History*, 20 (2006), 216–19.

19. TNA, HO 187/1156, 'Manpower in the National Fire Service', historical survey.

20. Henry Green, *Caught* (London: 1943), 16.

21. LMA, LCC/CL/CD/1/252, memorandum by Deputy Chief Officer, London Fire Brigade, 5 June 1940; LCC to London Ambulance Service, 22 July 1940; Clerk of the LCC, memorandum, 'Civil Defence Services: Employment of Conscientious Objectors', 13 Mar 1941. More generally see Denis Hayes, *Challenge of Conscience: The Story of the Conscientious Objectors of 1939–1949* (London: 1949), 182–4; Rachel Barker, *Conscience, Government and War* (London: 1982), 51, 61–5; Rose, *Which People's War?*, 170–79.

22. Charles Graves, *Women in Green: The Story of the W.V.S.* (London: 1948), 14–20; O'Brien, *Civil Defence*, 128–9.

23. HHC, TYW/1/W5, Synopsis of lecture courses in ARP, WVS June 1940; WVS to chief warden, 4 Nov 1941, 'Emergency Cookery Demonstration'.

24. HHC, TYW/1/W6, League of Good Neighbours circular, 'The Housewives' Service'; 'Help Rendered during Air Raids by Women Wardens and League of Good Neighbours', 8 Jan 1942.

25. YCA, Acc 89/2, Notes of meeting with the chief warden, 24 Apr 1940.

26. HHC, TYW/1/W6, 'Duties of Women Wardens' [n.d.]; *The Manchester Guardian*, 6 Sept 1940, 'Hull's Wardens and Shelters'.

27. TWA, MD-NC/276/3, 'Further Report on the Staffing of Dormitory Shelters', 19 Apr 1941; Newcastle Emergency Committee minutes, 3 Aug 1944; O'Brien, *Civil Defence*, 586–7. Pay in 1940 was £3.10.0 for men and £2.7.0 for women; in 1944 the final rates were £4.0.6 for men and £2.16.6 for women.

28. Calculated from O'Brien, *Civil Defence*, 690, App x.

29. John Strachey, *Post D: Some Experiences of an Air-Raid Warden* (London: 1941), 66–7.

30. O'Brien, *Civil Defence*, 678; Graves, *Women in Green*, 139.

31. HHC, TYW/1/A58-1, Circular to wardens from chief warden, 4 July 1940.

32. YCA, Acc 89/1a, Emergency Committee minutes, 15 Apr 1940; ARP Officer to chief warden, 19 Oct 1939.

33. CLSC, JN20/16/C, minutes of Hampstead Civil Defence Committee, 20 Sept 1939.

34. TNA, HO 207/386, London CD Region, 'Instructors Course for Officers', June 1941, 3.

35. TWA, MD-NC/276/5, Newcastle ARP Committee minutes, 12 Apr 1943; O'Brien, *Civil Defence*, 587–8.

36. HHC, TSCD/1, Borough Engineer, Stoke Newington to City Engineer, Hull, 2 Mar 1938, 'Progress Report No 1', 2.

37. HHC, TYW/1/T5, 'Demonstration of Bombs and Their Effects', 13 July 1939; 'Proceedings at Bomb Demonstrations'.

38. TWA, MD-NC/94/15, ARP Special Committee minutes, 2 July 1936.

39. TNA, ED 136/111, Ministry of Health, 'Report on Evacuation Rehearsal', 28 Aug 1939; 'Report on Visit to London Schools', 26 Aug 1939.

40. HHC, TSCD/1, *Leicester Evening Mail*, 25 and 28 Jan 1938; *News Chronicle*, 1 Apr 1939; Manchester Chief Constable, 'Instructions in Connection with Night Exercises 1 April 1939'.

41. YCA, Acc 89/1a, minutes of Emergency Committee, 17 Nov 1939; TNA, HO 186/2944, London Region Operational Circulars, Nov 1939–Aug 1940.

42. Green, *Caught*, 93–4, 178.

43. TNA, INF 1/264, Home Intelligence, summary of daily reports, 28 Mar 1940; HO 186/2201, Factory Department, Ministry of Labour, circular for all factory premises, Apr 1941.

44. TNA, ED 136/111, 'Planning of Evacuation', Jan 1939; Ruth Inglis, *The Children's War: Evacuation 1939–1945* (London: 1989), 1.

45. Richard Titmuss, *Problems of Social Policy* (London: 1950), 171–6; Inglis, *Children's War*, 25–6.

46. TNA, HO 191/28, ARP Department, MHS, 'Statistics of Shelter Provision', 23 Apr 1940.

47. Dietmar Süss, 'Wartime Societies and Shelter Politics in National Socialist Germany and Britain', in Claudia Baldoli, Andrew Knapp, Richard Overy (eds), *Bombing, States and Peoples in Western Europe 1940–1945* (London: 2011), 31–3.

48. George H. Gallup, *The Gallup International Public Opinion Polls: Great Britain 1937–1975*, 2 vols (New York: 1976), 34–5.

49. UEA, Zuckerman Archive, OEMU/59/13, draft 'Shelter habits', Table B, Table C.

50. HHC, Memorandum from borough engineer, Hull, 'Domestic Surface Shelters', 17 May 1939; TWA, CB-GA/13/1, Gateshead Emergency Committee minutes, 5 Apr 1939; minutes, 18 Sept 1941.

51. Idle, *War over West Ham*, 108–9.

52. HHC, TSA/CD/100, ARP domestic shelters canvass sheet; note for City Engineer, 5 July 1940.

53. YCA, Acc 89/1a, Emergency Committee minutes, 16 Jan, 20 Feb, 27 Feb 1940.

54. HHC, TSCD/1, Rate Estimates 1939–40, 24 Jan 1939; TWA, MD-NC/276/5, 'Report of the City Treasurer', 19 June 1944.

55. TNA, PREM 3/27, Note by Minister without Portfolio (Maurice Hankey) for Churchill, 26 Sept 1940; Anderson to Churchill, 6 Sept 1940.

56. O'Brien, *Civil Defence*, 224–6.

57. TNA, HO 186/2066, letter from Anglo-Iranian Oil to ARP Controller, Glamorgan, 24 July 1940; Chief Constable of Liverpool, Police duty form, 20 Aug 1940.

58. O'Brien, *Civil Defence*, 363–5; NC, Lindemann papers, G99, draft memorandum, 'Air-Raid Alarms'.

59. Marc Wiggam, 'The Blackout and the Idea of Community in Britain and Germany', in Baldoli, Knapp, Overy (eds), *Bombing, States and Peoples in Western Europe 1940–1945*, 43–53.

60. TNA, HO 186/720, MHS memorandum, 'Lighting (Restrictions) Order', 9 Jan 1940; Metropolitan Police Commissioner to Home Office, Mar 1941.

61. Peter Donnelly (ed), *Mrs. Milburn's Diaries: An Englishwoman's Day-to-Day Reflections 1939–1945* (London: 1979), 17, entry for 7 Sept 1939.

62. TNA, MH 76/555, Ministry of Health, 'Proposed Shelter Bye-laws', 31 Oct 1940.

63. TNA, INF 1/254, Home Morale Emergency Committee Report, 4 June 1940.

64. CLSC, JN20/16/C, Hampstead Civil Defence Committee, 'Review of ARP Services', 18 Nov 1939.

65. TWA, DX 875/4, 'A Farewell Message from the Regional Commissioner Sir Arthur Lambert', Apr 1945, 4.

66. HHC, TYW/1/A58-1, Circular to Hull wardens from the chief warden, 4 July 1940.

67. *North Devon at War: The Home Front, Part II* (Barnstaple: 1996), 4, 7, 35.

68. A. B. C. Kempe, *Midst Bands and Bombs* (Maidstone: 1946), 120–29.

69. Philip Graystone, *The Blitz on Hull (1940–45)* (Hull: 1991), 9–11.

70. H. Twyford, *It Came to Our Door: Plymouth in the World War* (Plymouth: 1945), 98–9.

71. TWA, DX 875/4, 'Farewell Message from the Regional Commissioner', 12.

72. UEA, Zuckerman Archive, OEMU/59/13, draft report, 'Evacuation' [n.d.], 1.

73. TNA, MH 76/555, memorandum by Minister of Health, 14 Dec 1940; London figures from O'Brien, *Civil Defence*, 396–7.

74. TNA, INF 1/264, report for 9 Sept 1940. See Titmuss, *Social Policy*, 355ff, and Wilbur Zelinski, Leszek Kolinski, *The Emergency Evacuation of Cities* (Savage, MD: 1991), 86–7, 95–6.

75. TNA, HO 186/606, report from Sir George Gater, 31 Mar 1941.

76. On East End, TNA, INF 1/264, Home Intelligence report, 6 Sept 1940; on Plymouth and Southampton, TNA, HO 186/606, Gater report, 1; Note of an Interdepartmental Committee, 5 May 1941. On Liverpool, 'Bombers Over Merseyside: The Authoritative Record of the Blitz 1940–41', *Liverpool Daily Post and Echo*, 1943, 16. On Clydebank, TNA, AIR 40/288, Air Intelligence, 'The Blitz', 14 Aug 1941, Folder 3; I. M. MacPhail, *The Clydebank Blitz* (West Dunbartonshire Libraries and Museums, 1974), 48–9.

77. TNA, HO 186/1861, Town Clerk Hull to Regional Evacuation Officer, 31 July 1941; Regional Commissioner to Harold Scott (MHS), 11 Aug

1941; 'Report on the Trekking Situation in Hull' [n.d.]; minute for the Regional Commissioner on Hull trekkers, 21 July 1943.

78. MacPhail, *Clydebank Blitz*, 64; UEA, Zuckerman Archive, OEMU/50/2, REDept, 'The Effects of Air Raids on the Port of Liverpool', 22 Mar 1943; 'Effects on Labour in Clydebank of the Clydeside Raids of March 1941'.

79. TNA, MH 76/491, London CD Region, 'Air Raid Shelters: Progress Report', May 1941.

80. On Newcastle, TWA, Newcastle City Council, minutes of meetings, 9 Nov 1940, 8 Jan 1941. On London, TNA, MH 76/491, London CD Region, Shelter Census, 5 May 1941.

81. TWA, DX 52/6, *Tynemouth Evening News*, 13 Oct 1944: 'Official Figures of Tynemouth's Air Attacks'; Pat Jalland, *Death in War and Peace: Loss and Grief in England 1914–1970* (Oxford: 2010), 126.

82. MO-A, TC 23, File 5/B, 'Air Raid Alarm', 15 Aug 1940; 'Air Raids', 8 Sept 1940 (both in London).

83. UEA, Zuckerman Archive, OEMU/56/3, Zuckerman to Stradling, 'Memorandum on Attitudes to Shelters', 11 Nov 1941.

84. F. Tennyson Jesse, H. M. Harwood, *While London Burns* (London: 1942), 72, letter 30 Aug 1940.

85. Strachey, *Post D*, 117–26.

86. Donnelly (ed), *Mrs. Milburn's Diaries*, 54; Virginia Cowles, *Looking for Trouble* (London: 1941), 439, 443.

87. Vera Brittain, *England's Hour: An Autobiography, 1939–1941*, 115, 142, 188.

88. Idle, *War over West Ham*, 110–11; John Gregg, *The Shelter of the Tubes* (London: 2001), 18; Phillip Piratin, *Our Flag Stays Red* (London: 1948), 73–4.

89. NC, Cherwell papers, F396, Harrod to Lindemann, 30 Sept 1940.

90. TWA, MD-NC/276/3, ARP Emergency Committee, 'Provision of Deep Shelters', 9 Oct 1940; HO 207/664, Islington town clerk to London Regional HQ, 6 Nov 1940; Ministry Home Security to town clerk, 25 Nov 1940; Idle, *War over West Ham*, 70–71. See too Geoffrey Field, *Blood, Sweat and Toil: Remaking the British Working Class, 1939–1945* (Oxford: 2011), 39–41.

91. Joseph Meisel, 'Air Raid Shelter Policy and its Critics before the Second World War', *Twentieth Century British History*, 5 (1994), 310–11.

92. TNA, INF 1/319, 'A Call to the People: National Committee of the People's Vigilance Movement' [Sept 1940]; Andrew Thorpe, *Parties at War: Political Organization in Second World War Britain* (Oxford: 2009), 129, 201; Dietmar Süss, *Tod aus der Luft: Kriegsgesellschaft und Luftkrieg in Deutschland und England* (Munich: 2011), 324–5.

93. HHC, Edgar Young papers, DYO 2/31, People's Convention papers, 'Speakers' Notes: No. 1'; 'Memorandum on the tasks of the People's Convention', 26 Sept 1941. By the end of 1941 there were only 1,650 supporters countrywide. See too Thorpe, *Parties at War*, 159–60, 198–9.

94. TNA, MEPO 2/6354, Note for Metropolitan Police Commissioner, 27 Sept 1940; MHS to MP Commissioner, 30 Sept 1940.

95. TNA, PREM 3/27, Churchill to Anderson, 21 Sept 1940; Anderson to
    Churchill, 23 Sept 1940; Gregg, *Shelter of the Tubes*, 20–24.

96. TNA, HO 207/363, 'Note on Condition of Tube at S. Kensington', Oct 1940.

97. TNA, PREM 3/27, MacDonald to Churchill, 7 Oct 1940; Churchill to
    MacDonald, 9 Oct 1940. See too Juliet Gardiner, *The Blitz: The British
    under Attack* (London: 2010), 72–5.

98. TNA, PREM 3/27, Kingsley Martin draft, 'The War in East London', 1–4;
    Clementine Churchill note, 'Shelters visited in Bermondsey'; Churchill to
    MacDonald, 10 Dec 1940.

99. UEA, Zuckerman Archive, OEMU/56/4, Zuckerman to Sir Leonard Par-
    sons (Min of Health), 30 Sept 1940; 'Notes on a discussion, Birmingham',
    9 Nov 1940. Solly Zuckerman, *From Apes to Warlords: The Autobiography
    of Solly Zuckerman 1904–1946* (London: 1978), 133–8.

100. TNA, DSIR 4/366, summary of Building Research Laboratory work for
     Service Departments, 27 Mar 1939; List of Enquiries, Aug 1940–Nov 1941.

101. TNA, PREM 3/27, Edward Evans to Churchill, 24 Oct 1940; Ellen Wilkin-
     son to David Robertson (MP for Streatham), 31 Oct 1940.

102. Idle, *War over West Ham*, 64, 99–100.

103. TNA, HO 186/608, report of the Regional Commissioner South, 14 Dec
     1940, 1–2.

104. TNA, HO 186/608, 'Brief Visit to Southampton, December 3 1940', Minis-
     try of Food to Sir George Gater, 5 Dec 1940.

105. Bernard Donoughue, G. W. Jones, *Herbert Morrison: Portrait of a Politician*
     (London: 2001), 284–7; Herbert Morrison, *An Autobiography of Lord
     Morrison of Lambeth* (London: 1960), 182–3.

106. TNA, HO 205/240, 'Air Raid Shelter Health: Report by Horder Commit-
     tee', 18 Sept 1940; Lord Horder to Morrison, memorandum, 'Air Raid
     Shelters', 23 Oct 1940.

107. TNA, MH 76/555, 'Model Shelter Byelaws', 28 Sept 1940; Harold Scott
     (MHS) to all London Region Officers, 19 Dec 1940.

108. TNA, HO 207/386, London Civil Defence Region: Instructors' Course for
     Officers Responsible for Shelters, June 1941, 3; United Synagogue Welfare
     Department to London Homelessness Commissioner, 'Air Raid Victims –
     Special Jewish Facilities', March 1941.

109. TNA, HO 186/927, 'Departmental Reports on Preparations for Heavy Air
     Attacks Next Winter', Aug 1941, 7–9; Morrison to Churchill, 19 Nov 1940.

110. Donoughue, Jones, *Herbert Morrison*, 290; TNA, HO 186/927, 'Depart-
     mental Reports', 8.

111. TNA, MH 76/491, London Civil Defence Region Report, 'Public Shelters',
     31 Jan 1941; 'Progress Report for May 1941', App v.

112. TNA, PREM 3/27, memorandum from Morrison to Churchill, 'Responsi-
     bility for Shelter Administration', 23 Dec 1940; MacDonald to Churchill,
     31 Dec 1940.

113. TNA, HO 207/363, 'Report on Comfort and Amenities in Shelters', 4 Dec
     1940, 4–5.

114. TNA, HO 207/386, memorandum by M. A. Creswick Atkinson (Welfare Director), 'Plan for Welfare in Shelters', 5 Feb 1941; letter from J. Mooney to Creswick Atkinson, 4 July 1941; memorandum, 'Welfare in Public Shelters' [n.d. but Aug 1941]; Central Film Library, list of 16mm films for shelter controllers.

115. TNA, HO 207/386, LCC Education Officer to Creswick Atkinson, 25 Feb 1941.

116. TNA, MH 76/410, MH minute, 'Face Masks', 20 Feb 1941; Regional Officer, MH, Cambridge, 'Hygiene in Public Air Raid Shelters', 8 Mar 1941; MH circular, 'Medical Aid Posts in Air-Raid Shelters', 23 June 1941; TWA, MD-NC/276/3, Newcastle Council, 'Preliminary Report as to Provision and Organisation of Dormitory Shelters', 7 Feb 1941.

117. TWA, Newcastle City Council: Reports, speeches, notes 1940–41, report of the town clerk, 10 Nov 1941; TNA, HO 186/927, 'Departmental Reports', 33–4.

118. Gardiner, *The Blitz*, 129–30.

119. HHC, 'Coventry Conference', notes for the Hull Emergency Committee, 17 Dec 1940.

120. HHC, TSCD/4, 'Town Clerk's Report on the City's Air Raid Welfare Services during raids of 7/8 and 8/9 May 1941', June 1941, 1–10, 29–39.

121. See e.g. the civil defence preparations at the Team Valley Trading Estate on Tyneside: TWA, 1395/61, ARP file 1941–4.

122. LC, Doolittle papers, Box 18, James Doolittle, 'Report on Visit to England from September 7 to October 15 1941', 32–3.

123. UEA, Zuckerman Archive, OEMU/50/2, REDept, 'The Sheffield Gas Supply and Steel Industry'; TNA, PREM 3/28/4, Beaverbrook to Churchill, 9 Sept 1940, enclosing Ministry of Supply, Iron and Steel Control, 'Loss of Production due to Air Raid Warnings and Air Raids'.

124. TNA, PREM 3/28/5, Beaverbrook to Churchill, 30 Aug 1940; Beaverbrook to Edward Bridges, 1 Sept 1940; Anderson to Churchill, 3 Sept 1940.

125. LC, Doolittle papers, Box 18, 'Report on Visit', 31.

126. TNA, PREM 3/28/4, Bevin to Churchill, 1 Nov 1940, enclosing 'Air Watching at the Rogerstone Works'.

127. Helen Jones, *British Civilians in the Front Line: Air Raids, Productivity and Wartime Culture, 1939–45* (Manchester: 2006), 40–41, 47–50, 104; David Thoms, *War, Industry and Society: The Midlands 1939–1945* (London: 1989), 119–21.

128. TNA, HO 186/927, 'Departmental Reports', 30–32, 38; TWA, MD-NC/94/18, Newcastle Air-Raid Damage Emergency Repairs Committee, minutes 4 May 1944; Thoms, *War, Industry, Society*, 120.

129. TNA, AVIA 15/2330, MAP, 'Evacuation of Factories: Outline of Scheme', 25 June 1940; Ministry of Labour, 'Report on Labour Evacuation', 20 June 1940. In general see W. Hornby, *Factories and Plant* (London: 1958), 203–8.

130. PArch, Beaverbrook papers, BBK/D/328, Note from MAP to the Air Ministry, 24 Oct 1940, memorandum on 'Dispersal'.

131. LC, Doolittle papers, Box 18, 'Report on Visit', 30–32; TNA, AVIA 15/3746, Bristol Aeroplane Co, 'Aero Engine Department Dispersal Scheme', 31 Aug 1940; MAP to Bristol Aeroplane, 30 Sept 1940; Bristol Aeroplane to Director Engine Production, MAP, 15 Aug 1940.

132. TNA, HO 186/927, 'Departmental Reports', 29–30.

133. TNA, PREM 3/18/2, minute for Churchill, 'Report on Damage at Woolwich with Action Proposed', 13 Sept 1940; PArch, Beaverbrook papers, BBK/D/329, Beaverbrook to Portal, 24 Feb 1941.

134. TNA, PREM 3/18/2, Beaverbrook to Churchill, 14 Dec 1940; PArch, Beaverbrook papers, BBK/D/24b, Sir Ernest Simon to Beaverbrook, 'Report on Lancashire Blitz Raids, December 20/24', 25 Dec 1940, 1, 3; UEA, Zuckerman Archive, OEMU/57/3, draft report by Zuckerman and J. D. Bernal, 'Birmingham', 10 Jan 1942, 3–4; Thoms, *War, Industry and Society*, 106–12.

135. PArch, Beaverbrook papers, BBK/D/24b, 'Report on Lancashire Blitz'; NARA, RG107 Box 138, MHS memorandum, 'German Bombing of Britain 1941: Industrial Damage Report'; TNA, AIR 40/288, AI9 report, 'The Blitz', 14 Aug 1941, 2. Figures on steel and aircraft from *Statistical Digest of the War* (London: 1951), 105, 152–3.

136. TNA, MAF 83/194, file on ARP in West Africa and Malaya.

137. UEA, Zuckerman Archive, OEMU/50/2, REDept, 'The Effects of Air Raids on the Port of Liverpool', 1, 6–12; NARA, RG107 Box 138, 'German Bombing of Britain', 1.

138. TNA, PREM 3/18/2, War Cabinet, Air Raid Damage and Shelter Report, 11–18 Dec; 'Statistical Summary of Air Raid Losses of Food and Animal Feeds', 23 Dec 1940.

139. TNA, AIR 41/17, 'RAF Narrative: The Air Defence of Great Britain June 1940–December 1941', App 1, 4–5.

140. HHC, TSCD/4, 'Town Clerk's Report on the City's Welfare Services', June 1941; TWA, MD-NC/PH/1/1, 'Medical Officer of Health Annual Report', 1941, 34.

141. TNA, HO 186/927, 'Departmental Reports', 33. For stock figures see R. J. Hammond, *Food: Volume III: Studies in Administration and Control* (London: 1962), 804. Pre-war flour stocks averaged 314,000 tons, but by the end of 1940 were 695,000 tons and the end of 1941, 857,000 tons.

142. Jesse, Harwood, *While London Burns*, 118; Strachey, *Post D*, 48.

143. UEA, Zuckerman Archive, OEMU/57/3, preliminary draft report, 'Birmingham', 10 Jan 1942; NC, Cherwell papers, G192, 'City of Birmingham: Effects of Air Raids on Dwelling House Property', 12 Feb 1942, 3; TWA, DX 15/1, Gateshead Emergency Services Manual, MH circular, 24 Sept 1940.

144. TNA, PREM 3/18/1, Minister of Health to Churchill, 8 Jan 1941; MH, 'Houses Repaired by Local Authorities in Heavily Raided Towns', 5 June 1941.

145. TWA, Gateshead Emergency Services Manual, 'Mutual Assistance in Clearing Debris'.

146. HHC, TSCD/4, Hull City Engineer, 'The Manchester Blitz', 31 Dec 1940;
     TNA, AIR 40/288, Air Intelligence, 'The Blitz', Folder 3, 'Report on Coven-
     try', 14 Aug 1941.
147. TNA, AIR 40/288, 2–4; Donnelly (ed), *Mrs. Milburn's Diaries*, 69, entry
     for 20 Nov 1940.
148. TWA, Gateshead Emergency Services manual, MHS circulars, 204/1940,
     'Salvage of Property and Clearing of Debris'; 74/1941, 'General Organisa-
     tion of Recovery of Goods and Property'.
149. MO-A, TC 15/1/A, 'Demolition in London, 1941', 15–16, 58–9.
150. Todd Gray, *Looting in Wartime Britain* (Exeter: 2009), 185–9.
151. MO-A, TC 15/1/A, 'War Damage: Emergency Repairs and Supplies of
     Materials'.
152. HHC, TYP Part I, Hull City Corporation, Damage to Property 1939–45;
     TNA, PREM 3/18/1, Churchill to Lord Reith (Minister of Works), 9 Dec
     1940; Reith to Churchill, 3 Jan 1941.
153. TNA, PREM 3/18/1, Minister of Health to Churchill, 'Houses Repaired by
     Local Authorities, November 1941'; Minister of Production (Oliver Lyttle-
     ton) to Churchill, 22 Aug 1942.
154. TNA, AIR 20/4768, Note for Director of Bombing Operations, Air Minis-
     try, 6 Apr 1942.
155. Alymer Firebrace, 'Britain's Wartime Fire Service', in Horatio Bond (ed),
     Fire and the Air War (Boston, MA: 1946), 23–5, 33; Ewen, 'Preparing the
     British Fire Service', 221.
156. Green, *Caught*, 179, 183.
157. Firebrace, 'Britain's Wartime Fire Service', 23.
158. Ewen, 'Preparing the British Fire Service', 221; TNA, AIR 40/288, Air Intel-
     ligence, 'Report on Coventry', 14 Aug 1941.
159. TNA, AIR 40/288, 34–7, 49.
160. Michael Brown, *Put That Light Out! Britain's Civil Defence Services at War
     1939–1945* (Stroud: 1999), 102–3.
161. MO-A, TC23 Box 11, 'Seven Months' Experience of Industrial Firewatch-
     ing', 30 Sept 1941.
162. TNA, HO 186/608, memorandum by Lt. Col. G. Symonds (MHS Fire
     Adviser), 4 Dec 1940.
163. PArch, Beaverbrook papers BBK/D/24b, Sir Ernest Simon to Beaverbrook,
     4 Dec 1940, 'Fire Prevention'; 'Report on Lancashire Blitz Raids, December
     20/24 1940', 25 Dec 1940; report by J. R. Scott, 'Air Attacks on Manches-
     ter', 24 Dec 1940; HHC, TSCD/4, Hull City Engineer, 'Manchester Blitz',
     31 Dec 1940.
164. Donoughue, Jones, *Herbert Morrison*, 292–3.
165. Friends House Archive, London (FHA), COR 5/9, Note 'Firewatching Cases'
     [n.d. but Apr 1941]; Stuart Morris to Herbert Morrison, 1 Apr 1942. Hayes,
     Challenge of Conscience, 191–2.
166. FHA, Temp Mss. 914, 914/BM/1, minutes of Central Board meeting, 26 Feb
     1941; 'Firewatching Cases' [n.d. but Apr 1941]; Stuart Morris to Herbert
     Morrison, 1 Apr 1942.

167. TWA, MD-NC/276/4, Fire Prevention Department, 'The Guard Organisation: Progress Report', 15 Dec 1941; 'Fire Guard Organisation', 27 Apr 1943.

168. Firebrace, 'Britain's Wartime Fire Service', 28–9; idem, 'The Reorganization of the British Fire Service', in Bond, Fire and the Air War, 48–50; Ewen, 'Preparing the British Fire Service', 214, 223–4.

169. CCAC, Hodsoll papers, memorandum by Hodsoll, 'Consolidated Lessons of Raiding in Great Britain' [n.d. but 1945], 2.

170. UEA, Zuckerman Archive, OEMU/56/5, Zuckerman to Ministry of Pensions, 28 Aug 1941; Aubrey Lewis (Mill Hill Hospital) to Stradling, 5 Nov 1941; Russell Fraser (Mill Hill Hospital) to Zuckerman, 23 Nov 1941.

171. UEA, Zuckerman Archive, OEMU/57/5, Hull Survey, Tables Ia–VIIf.

172. Ibid., OEMU/56/5, Aubrey Lewis to Zuckerman, 23 June 1942, 1.

173. Ibid., OEMU/57/3, Draft report, 'Hull' [n.d.], 6; Zuckerman, From Apes to Warlords, 142–3, 405, App 2, 'Quantitative Study of Total Effects of Air Raids', 8 Apr 1942.

174. Thoms, War, Industry and Society, 126–9.

175. Süss, 'Wartime Societies and Shelter Politics', 34–5; Edgar Jones, Robin Woolven, Simon Wessely, 'Civilian Morale during the Second World War: Responses to Air Raids Re-Examined', Social History of Medicine, 17 (2004), 463–79.

176. Field, Blood, Sweat and Toil, 43.

177. UEA, Zuckerman Archive, OEMU/57/5, draft report, 'Disturbances in the mental stability of the working population of Hull', App II, Case Histories.

178. Ibid., App II, Case 1 and Case 37.

179. Gallup, The Gallup International Polls, 43. A second poll on war problems taken in August 1941 had a figure of 9 per cent for bombing, but 17 per cent for the Second Front.

180. TNA, INF 1/254, Home Morale Committee, 'First Interim Report, 22 May 1940', 2; Harold Nicolson to Duff Cooper (Minister of Information), 5 June 1940, 'Report of Home Morale Policy Committee', 2.

181. TNA, INF 1/849, Policy Committee minutes, 8 July 1940, 23 July 1940; INF 1/264, Morale: Summary of Daily Reports, 20 July 1940.

182. TNA, HO 186/886, H. Rhodes (MoI) to S. Leslie (MHS), 29 Nov 1940; managing director, Liverpool Post and Echo, to Morrison, 4 Dec 1940; draft memorandum, 'Publication of Casualties'; Duff Cooper to Morrison, 7 Jan 1941.

183. TNA, HO 186/886, Churchill to Morrison, 7 Mar 1941.

184. Cowles, Looking for Trouble, 445.

185. Brittain, England's Hour, 141–2.

186. TNA, MEPO 2/6335, Croydon MP Station, 'Air Raid – Notes', 21 Aug 1940; Tooting MP Station, Aug 1940; East Ham MP Station, 'Air Raid Warning', 24 June 1940. On the class dimension of reaction to the raids see Süss, Tod aus der Luft, 332–3.

187. TNA, INF/264, Daily Morale Summary, 17 June 1940; INF/292 Pt 1, Weekly Home Intelligence Report, 30 Sept–9 Oct, 1; 4–11 Nov, 2.

188. TNA, HO 186/608, MHS memorandum, 'Lessons of Intensive Air Attack: Working of ARP Services' [n.d. but Jan 1941], 14; Gen. Gordon Finlayson, C-in-C Western Command to all Regional Commissioners, 'Notes for Guidance of all Area Commands', 26 Nov 1940.

189. TNA, INF 6/328, *London Can Take It!*, 14 Oct 1940; MoI, *London Can Take It!*, film commentary.

190. Cinema figures from UEA, Zuckerman Archive, OEMU/59/36, 'Cinema Attendances', 9 Aug 1945. Details on the film from Mark Connelly, *We Can Take It! Britain and the Memory of the Second World War* (Harlow: 2004),132–3.

191. TNA, HO 186/1220, MoI Publications Division to S. C. Leslie (author of the booklet), 12 Jan 1943; Robert Fraser (MoI) to Leslie, 29 Jan 1943.

192. Cowles, *Looking for Trouble*, 446.

193. TNA, INF/174a, Director of Broadcasting Division, MoI, to Controller-General, BBC, 26 Feb 1941; Mary Adams (Home Intelligence) to Kenneth Clark, 28 Feb 1941, encl. 'Script of Broadcast on Swansea Blitz'; 'A Cardiffian Woman' to Churchill, 5 Mar 1941.

194. Edward Stebbing, *Diary of a Decade, 1939–1950* (Lewes: Book Guild, 1998), 68, 80.

195. TNA, INF 1/292, Weekly Home Intelligence Report, 30 Sept–9 Oct, 1; Report, 18–24 Dec, 1; INF 1/849, Policy Committee minutes, 3 Apr 1941, 1; INF 1/249, Home Planning Committee, minutes 26 Dec, 30 Dec 1940.

196. Angus Calder, *The Myth of the Blitz* (London: 1991); Rose, *Which People's War*; and more controversially Samuel Hylton, *Britain's Darkest Hour: The Hidden History of the Blitz* (Stroud: 2001).

197. James Doherty, *Post 381: The Memoirs of a Belfast Air Raid Warden* (Belfast: 1989), 92.

198. Firebrace, 'Britain's Wartime Fire Service', 26.

199. Barbara Nixon, *Raiders Overhead: A Diary of the London Blitz* (London: 1980), 25–7.

200. TNA, INF 1/292 Pt I, Weekly Morale Report, 30 Sept–9 Oct, 1; AIR 40/288, Air Intelligence, 'The Blitz', 14 Aug 1941, App A, 'Morale', 2.

201. Jesse, *While London Burns*, 81–2.

202. UEA, Zuckerman Archive, OEMU/57/5, Hull Survey, Table IIb. Fear as an expression of anticipatory silence followed by terrifying sound is explored in Peter Adey, 'Holding Still: The Private Life of an Air Raid', *M/C Journal*, 12 (2009), 3–5.

203. Royal Society, London, Blackett papers, PB/4/4, 'Notes on effects of bombing on civilian population', 15 Aug 1941; 'confusion, depression and possible loss of morale', in TNA, HO 186/608, 'Notes for the Guidance of Area Commands', 26 Nov 1940; AIR 40/288, Air Intelligence, 'The Blitz', 3, 'damage beyond a certain point produces depression and defeatism'.

204. Nigel Nicolson (ed), *Harold Nicolson: Diaries and Letters 1939–1945* (London: 1967), 126, entry for 8 Nov 1940.

205. A Warden (anon.), *From Dusk to Dawn* (London: 1941), 71–2.

206. TNA, HO 186/608, Midlands Regional Commissioner to MHS, 5 Dec 1940; TWA, MB-WB/27/1, Whitley and Monkseaton Urban District Council, 'After the Raid', 28 Jan 1942, 6.

207. Cited in Robert Hewison, *Under Siege: Literary Life in London 1939–1945* (London: 1977), 40.

208. A Warden (anon.), *From Dusk to Dawn*, 23; Sara Wasson, *Urban Gothic of the Second World War: Dark London* (Basingstoke: 2010), 145.

209. Wasson, *Urban Gothic*, 33; Hewison, *Under Siege*, 44–52.

210. Brett Holman, '"Bomb Back, and Bomb Hard": Debating Reprisals during the Blitz', *Australian Journal of Politics and History*, 58 (2012), 403–5.

211. LSE Archive, Peace Pledge Union papers, Coll. Misc. 825, PPU Information Service, no 22, 6 Nov 1940, 2.

212. FHA, Foley papers, Mss. 448, Box 2, file 4, press review 23 Aug 1941, letter to *Daily Mail* from Lady Hilda Wittenham.

213. Stebbing, *Diary of a Decade*, 51; Donnelly (ed), *Mrs. Milburn's Diaries*, 77. TNA, INF/266, Reginald L. to Duff Cooper, 4 Dec 1940; MoI, internal memorandum, 5 Dec 1940.

214. MO-A, TC 23, File 12/A, 'Report on Reprisals from the RAF', 6 Dec 1940. On the policy of avoiding 'reprisal' see Süss, *Tod aus der Luft*, 105–6.

215. FHA, Foley papers, Mss. 448, Box 3, file 2, Note on British Institute of Public Opinion.

216. Ibid., Mss. 448, Box 2, file 2, 'The Bombing Restrictions Committee: Its Origin, Purpose and Publications', Nov 1944; LSE, Peace Pledge Union Papers, Coll. Misc. 825, PPU Information Service, no 24, 7 Jan 1941, 'The Case against Reprisals'.

217. TNA, AIR 40/288, 'The Blitz', App A, 'Morale', 1.

218. MO-A, TC15/1/A, 'Demolition in London 1941', 23–4, 40–45, 47. Air marshal story in Newcastle University Special Collections, Twentieth-Century Pamphlets, Box 7, Tom Harrisson, 'Mass Observation', *World Review*, Aug 1940, 66.

219. Gallup, *Gallup International Polls*, 37, 43. A good example of a diary is Helen Millgate (ed), *Mr. Brown's War: A Diary of the Second World War* (Stroud: 1999), 63–75. Also Jesse, Harwood, *While London Burns*, where news of bombing in letters to their American friends ebbs away after October.

220. TWA, DX 52/1, minute book, Percy Crescent and Cockburn Terrace Fire-Fighting Scheme, North Shields, meetings of 2 Feb, 4 Feb, 6 Feb, 12 Feb 1941; Fire-Watching Rotas, 1941, 1943, 1944.

221. HHC, TSCD/4, 'Coventry Conference for ARP Controllers', 17 Dec 1940, 2.

222. TNA, HO 186/608, 'Notes for the Guidance of Area Commands', 26 Nov 1940.

223. Ibid., AIR 40/288, 'The Blitz', App A, 'Morale', 1.

224. Ibid., 1; TWA, MD-NC/276/3, Office of Northern Regional Commissioner memorandum, 'Air Raid Damage', 13 Mar 1941.

225. TNA, HO 186/927, Regional Commissioner, South-West region, to all town clerks, 'Intensive Air Attacks – Co-ordination of Services', 20 Dec 1940.

226. Brittain, *England's Hour*, 123.

227. Donnelly, *Mrs. Milburn's Diaries*, 80–81, entry for 14 Jan 1941.

228. UEA, Zuckerman Archive, OEMU/56/3, Report on Interview with Head Shelter Wardens of Lewisham Borough, Oct 1941, 3–4.

229. Cited in Jalland, *Death in War and Peace*, 134–5.

230. Julie Rugg, 'Managing "Civilian Deaths Due to War Operations": Yorkshire Experiences During World War II', *Twentieth Century British History*, 15 (2004), 164–8.

231. Cowles, *Looking for Trouble*, 439.

232. TNA, AIR 40/288, 'The Blitz', 7–8; UEA, Zuckerman Archive, OEMU/57/3, draft report, 'Birmingham', 10 Jan 1942; Report prepared by Zuckerman and J. D. Bernal, 'A Quantitative Study of the Total Effect of Air Raids', 2 Apr 1942, 8.

233. TNA, HO 186/608, minutes of meeting, 3 Dec 1940.

234. MO-A, TC23 Box 11, File 11E, opinion poll, 2 Aug 1941; File 11/K, Warden posts general report, 13 June 1941.

235. TWA, CB.SU/3/1, Sunderland ARP Committee, report on damage, 1 May 1942, 5 June 1942, 11 Oct 1942, 16 Oct 1942, 14 Mar 1943, 22 Mar 1943, 16 May 1943, 24 May 1943.

236. TNA, HO 186/927, MHS, 'Departmental Reports on Preparations for Heavy Attacks', Aug 1941, 22–3.

237. O'Brien, *Civil Defence*, 548–58, 690.

238. TNA, HO 186/2315, LCC, 'Note on Crash Raids' [n.d. but Oct 1942], 3.

239. TNA, PREM 3/27, Morrison and Bevin to Churchill, 9 Oct 1941; MH 76/491, London Civil Defence Region, Progress report on air-raid shelters, Dec 1941.

240. HHC, TSA/CD/87, memorandum, Hull City Engineer, 22 Nov 1941; TSCD/41, meeting of Emergency Works Committee, 8 Apr 1942.

241. HHC, TSA/CD/87, Ministry of Food, instructions to town clerks, 9 Aug 1941; TNA, HO 186/2347, City of Leicester: Emergency Feeding Scheme, July 1943.

242. TNA, HO 199/140, Home Security Office, Bristol, report on bombing in Weston-super-Mare, 29 June 1942; Report re. Weston-super-Mare, 30 June 1942; MHS Report on the South-Western Region for the month of June 1942.

243. TNA, HO 186/2315, Town Clerk Norwich to Eastern Regional Commissioner, 3 June 1942, 'Memorandum in Connection with the Recent Raids on Norwich', 1–4.

244. UEA, Zuckerman Archive, OEMU 50/2/4, REDept, 'Effects on Labour of Air Raids', 19 Oct 1942, 1–5.

245. TNA, HO 186/2315, Notes of meeting at Home Office, 'Crash Raids', 20 Oct 1942; 'Mass Raids: an appreciation of Civil Defence under altered conditions of enemy action', 9 Oct 1942.

246. TNA, HO/2315, County Borough of East Ham, 'Civil Defence Services: Modification in Tactical Dispositions in Case of Crash Raids', 6 July 1943;

Hodsoll (MHS) to Sir Edward Warner, 5 Nov 1943, 'Crash Raiding'; draft report for Regional Commissioners, 'Reporting of Damage Caused by Intensive Raids' [n.d. but Dec 1943].

247. TWA, MD-NC/276/5, Newcastle Fire Prevention Department, 'Fire Guard Organisation', 27 Apr 1943; Emergency Committee meeting minutes, 20 Sept 1943.

248. HHC, TYW/1/A23, Hull ARP controller to chief warden, 25 Feb 1944; TYW/1/T2, Home Security circular, 'Refresher Courses at Home Security Schools'.

249. TWA, DX 1306/1, Tynemouth civil defence Musical and Dramatic Society minute book, 1943–4.

250. Doherty, *Post 381*, 121–3.

251. TNA, MH 79/500, MH minute, 'Shelters – L.P.T.B. Tube Stations', 2 Mar 1944; London Transport Board report, 'Tube Shelters', 29 Feb 1944; O'Brien, *Civil Defence*, 546–7.

252. TNA, MH 79/500, MH minute, 'Provision of Shelters – London Region', 25 Feb 1944; London Transport Board report, 'Tube Shelters', 29 Feb 1944; 'Air Raid Shelter Provision', March 1944; London Tube Shelter Population, Feb to Oct 1944.

253. TNA, HO 186/2944, London Civil Defence Region, 'Reporting the First Flare by Civil Defence', Mar 1944.

254. Stebbing, *Diary of a Decade*, 243–52 (three entries only; on the one raid directly over Stebbing's house he wrote that he was too lazy and too cold to get out of bed); Millgate (ed), *Mr. Brown's War*, 205 (one entry on a raid in Feb).

255. TNA, HO 186/2271, Note of a meeting at the Home Office, 7 July 1943; 'Long Range Rocket: London Region Appreciation', 16 July 1943.

256. TNA, HO 186/2271, War Cabinet minutes, 3 Feb 1944; Churchill to Morrison, 13 Feb 1944.

257. TNA, HO 186/2944, 'London Regional Narrative: History of Operations in London Region', 1945, 28; O'Brien, *Civil Defence*, 652–3.

258. Hewison, *Under Siege: Literary Life in London 1939–1945*, 168; Stebbing, *Diary of a Decade*, 262–3.

259. UEA, Zuckerman Archive, OEMU/59/13/1, Regional Information Office, 'Flying Bomb Attack on London', 12 July 1944, 1.

260. Ibid., OEMU/59/13/3, MoI, 'Effect of the Flying Bomb on Industrial Workers', 1–2.

261. Ibid., OEMU/59/13, British Institute of Public Opinion, survey third week of Aug 1944; 'Effects of Rockets and Flying Bombs' [n.d.]; MO-A, TC 23 File 12/E, observer report, London, 30 June 1944.

262. Titmuss, *Social Policy*, 426–7.

263. CCAC, Hodsoll papers, HDSL 5/4, 'Review of Civil Defence 1944', 2–7.

264. TNA, HO 186/2299, 'Lessons from Recent Raids: Flying Bomb' [n.d.], 1.

265. UEA, Zuckerman Archive, OEMU/59/9, MHS REDept, 'Casualty Rate of Flying Bombs at Night', 4 July 1944; 'Flying Bombs: Casualties in London Region', 20 Dec 1944.

266. TNA, MH 79/500, London Tube Shelter Population, Feb–Oct 1944; HO 191/11, 'Statement of Civilian Casualties', 31 July 1945.

267. MO-A, TC 23 File 12/G, some notes on reaction to V2, March 1945.

268. UEA, Zuckerman Archive, OEMU/59/13, draft 'Shelter Habits', Table A, Table B. Numbers sheltering from rockets varied between 29 per cent of families with a private shelter to 0 per cent using public shelters with or without a family.

269. TNA, MH 79/500, London Tube Shelter Population, Feb–Oct 1945; Titmuss, *Social Policy*, 428–9.

270. HHC, TYP Pt I, War Damage Returns, Hull, 1939–45; TNA, HO 186/2944, London Region Narrative, 1945, 28. Total casualties in TNA, HO 191/11, 'Statement of Civilian Casualties in the United Kingdom', 31 July 1945.

271. MO-A, TC 23 File 12/H, 'The Lifting of the Blackout', 28 Sept 1944; 'A Note on Relaxation of the Blackout', 17 Sept 1944; Wiggam, 'The Blackout and the Idea of Community', 54–5.

272. TWA, MD-NC/276/5, Emergency Committee minutes, 31 July 1944; TSCD/41, 'Report of City Engineer to Emergency Committee', 22 Sept 1944. On reducing civil defence numbers see HHC, TYW/1/A23, Regional Commissioners to ARP Controllers, 14 Apr 1944; Hull ARP Controller to chief warden, 16 Aug 1944; minute ARP Controller, Hull, 28 Sept 1944; Home Office, North-Eastern region to Hull town clerk, 11 July 1947, 'Collection and Disposal of Steel Shelter Material'; Home Office to town clerk, 6 Dec 1947. On London TNA, MEPO 2/6463, Sir Ernest Gowers to MP Commissioner Sir Philip Game, 16 July 1942; MP Commissioner to Westminster town clerk, 'Shelters: Improper Use', 13 Sept 1945.

273. HHC, TYW/1/A-58, Home Office, Leeds to Hull town clerk, 14 June 1945.

274. TNA, HO 207/226, Daily Tube Shelter Returns, 30 Jan, 9 Apr 1945; memorandum, 'How the Tube Shelter Occupancy Figures Read for the Last Few Nights', 8 May 1945.

275. Royal Society, London Blackett papers, PB/4/4, Note on effects of bombing on civilian population, 15 Aug 1941, 3.

4. THE UNTOLD CHAPTER:
THE BOMBING OF SOVIET CITIES

1. PArch, Balfour papers, BAL/1, Moscow Diary 1941, entries for 27–28 Sept, 2 Oct 1941.

2. Alexander Werth, *Moscow '41* (London: 1944), 86, 93–5.

3. Walter Citrine, *In Russia Now* (London: 1942), 55–6.

4. RGVA, f.37878, o.1, d.297, Report on air attacks against Moscow between 21 July and 22 Aug 1941; Horst Boog et al., *DRZW: Band 4: Der Angriff auf die Sowjetunion* (Stuttgart: 1983), 692.

5. RGVA, f.37878, o.1, d.443, report of MPVO HQ, air attacks on the territory of the Soviet Union, Jan–June 1942, 15–36.

6. Richard Suchenwirth, *Command and Leadership in the German Air Force: USAF Historical Studies, no. 174* (New York: 1969), 254, citing an intelligence briefing by Gen. Josef Schmid.

7. Walther Hubatsch (ed), *Hitlers Weisungen für die Kriegführung* (Munich: 1965), 100, Directive no. 21, 'Case Barbarossa', 18 Dec 1940.

8. LC, Spaatz papers, Box 134, Interrogation of Reich Marshal Hermann Goering, 10 May 1945, 10; UEA, Zuckerman Archive, SZ/BBSU/75/1, USAAF HQ, Air P/W Interrogation Detachment, Enemy Intelligence Summaries, Hermann Goering, 1 June 1945, 8.

9. James Corum, *Wolfram von Richthofen: Master of the German Air War* (Lawrence, KS: 2008), 272–3.

10. Andrew Brookes, *Air War Over Russia* (Hersham, Surrey: 2003), 67, citing *Pravda* for 6 Feb 1939.

11. Leonid Kerber, *Stalin's Aviation Gulag: A Memoir of Andrei Tupolev and the Purge Era*, ed Von Hardesty (Washington, DC: 1996), 5–13.

12. *Protivovozdushnaia oborona strany (1914–1995)* (Moscow: 1998), 88–92.

13. Brookes, *Air War Over Russia*, 31, 63.

14. *Protivovozdushnaia oborona strany*, 92–104.

15. Lt. Gen. Beregovoi, 'Voiska VNOS PVO Strany v pervom periode voiny', *Voenno-istoricheskiy zhurnal*, 7 (1975), 13–21; Gen. P. Batitsky, 'Voiska protivovozduzhnoi oborony strany', *Voenno-istoricheskiy zhurnal*, 8 (1967), 20–22.

16. RGVA, f.37878, o.1, d.297, MPVO HQ, Operational Report, June 1941–Feb 1942, 1–9.

17. F. Kagan, 'The Evacuation of Soviet Industry in the Wake of "Barbarossa": A Key to Soviet Victory', *Journal of Slavic Military Studies*, 8 (1995), 396–8, 406; G. A. Kumanev, 'The Soviet Economy and the 1941 Evacuation', in Joseph L. Wieczynski (ed), *Operation Barbarossa: The German Attack on the Soviet Union, June 22, 1941* (Salt Lake City, UT: 1993), 189, 191–3.

18. RGAE, f.29, o.1, d.1792/1961, 2; Brookes, *Air War Over Russia*, 63–4.

19. Olaf Groehler, *Bombenkrieg gegen Deutschland* (Berlin: 1990), 160–61; Rolf-Dieter Müller, *Der Bombenkrieg 1939–1945* (Berlin: 2004), 100.

20. Harry Flannery, *Assignment to Berlin* (London: 1942), 271–2.

21. Groehler, *Bombenkrieg gegen Deutschland*, 164–5.

22. Hubatsch (ed), *Hitlers Weisungen*, 164, Directive no. 33, 19 July 1941.

23. Ibid., 173, Directive no. 34a, 12 Aug 1941. See too Walter Warlimont, *Inside Hitler's Headquarters 1939–45* (London: 1964), 186–8.

24. Henrik Eberle, Matthias Uhl (eds), *The Hitler Book: The Secret Dossier Prepared for Stalin* (London: 2005), 77.

25. RGVA, f.37878, o.1, d.297, MPVO HQ, Operational Report, June 1941–Feb 1942, 10–14.

26. Von Hardesty, Ilya Grinberg, *Red Phoenix Rising: The Soviet Air Force in World War II* (Lawrence, KS: 2012), 57–9, 68; Brookes, *Air War Over Russia*, 70.

27. TsAMO, f.500, 0.957971, d.425, Luftwaffe Operations Staff, Foreign Air Forces East, 'SU-Grossgerät zur Flugabwehr', 8 Mar 1944, 4–6.

28. Boog et al., *DRZW: Band 4*, 692–3.

29. RGVA, f.37878, o.1, d.297, MPUO HQ, Operational Report, June 1941–Feb 1942, 98.

30. Corum, *Wolfram von Richthofen*, 272–4; David Glantz, *The Siege of Leningrad 1941–1944: 900 Days of Terror* (London: 2004), 47. Leningrad survived the ordeal, but was besieged for more than two years.

31. Glantz, *Siege of Leningrad*, 72–3; Harrison Salisbury, *The 900 Days: The Siege of Leningrad* (London: 1969), 297–8. Figures for German and Soviet aircraft from Ray Wagner (ed), *The Soviet Air Force in World War II: The Official History* (Newton Abbot: 1973), 48–52. The figures fluctuated a good deal over time and should be regarded as indicative only.

32. Cited in Anna Reid, *Leningrad: Tragedy of a City under Siege 1941–1944* (London: 2011), 139.

33. RGVA, f.37878, o.1, d.443, MPVO HQ, Operational Report no. 2, Dec 1941 and Jan 1942, 1–3; Report no. 3, Feb 1942, 1; Report no. 5, Mar 1942; Report no. 9, Apr 1942; Report no. 50, June 1942, 1–2.

34. Ibid., f.37878, o.1, d.297, MPVO HQ, Operations of the German Air Force over the territory of the USSR, 22 June 1941–22 July 1941.

35. Ibid., f.37878, o.1, d.189, Reports on the enemy's air raids over the territory of the USSR, 17 July 1941–Feb 1942, MPVO HQ, 1–3, 5–6; F.37878, o.1, d.443, Report no. 9, Apr 1942.

36. Ibid., f.37878, o.1, d.189, 9–11, Report from Lt. Penkov, Ivanovo region, to Major Sosulin, MPVO HQ, 13 Dec 1941; 54–7, Report for Col. Baskov, Operational Dept., MPVO, from Lt. Col. Starchenko, Rostov MPVO-NKVD.

37. Ibid., 39–53, telegrams to MPVO HQ from Yaroslav region.

38. P. Batitsky, 'Voiska protivovozduzhnoi' 20–22.

39. RGVA, f.37878, o.1, d.445, Total number of hits on railroads from July–Dec 1941 to Jan–June 1942, 2; Summary of the enemy's air raids on USSR's railway facilities from 1 Jan to 1 July 1942, Report by Gen. Kovalev, Head of War Communications, 10–12, 15.

40. TsAMO, f.500, 0.801858, d.218, German Air Force operations staff, 'Bemerkungen zum Einsatz der Luftwaffe, Nr. 19', 5 Nov 1941, 10–12; 'Bemerkungen Nr. 20', 22 Jan 1942, 8–9.

41. RGVA, f.37878, o.1, d.445, Report by Gen. Kovalev, 6–7, 8, 12–13, 22, 25.

42. Ibid., f.37878, o.1, d.443, MPVO HQ, Report no. 24, June 1942; Report no. 50, July 1942; f.37878, o.1, d.444, 'Enemy aviation targeting railways and railway stations of the Soviet Union in May–July 1942', 2–4.

43. Ibid., f.37878, o.1, d.444, MPVO HQ, Report no. 68, 19 Aug 1942.

44. Boris Voyetekhov, *The Last Days of Sevastopol* (London: 1943), 68–9, 71, 78–9.

45. Joel Hayward, *Stopped at Stalingrad: The Luftwaffe and Hitler's Defeat in the East 1942–1943* (Lawrence, KS: 1998), 100–101, 110–17; Corum, *Wolfram von Richthofen*, 293–8.

46. Brookes, *Air War Over Russia*, 90.

47. RGVA, f.37878, o.1, d.438, 124, Stalingrad MPVO summative report of activities of enemy aviation in Aug 1942.

48. TsAMO, f.500, o.725109, d.1080, Operational Staff, German Air Force, 'Sowjetunion: Einzelbildunterlagen von Werken der Flugrüstungsindustrie, der Kraftwagen und Kampfwagenherstellung', 1 Feb 1942; o.725168, d.386, 'Übersicht der Archivunterlagen: Band 1: Rüstungsindustrie'.

49. RGVA, f.37878, o.1, d.438, 125, Summative report, Aug 1942. See too Hardesty, Grinberg, *Red Phoenix*, 125, for Gen. Yeremenko's vivid description of the damage done by the burning oil-storage tanks, which, as at Rotterdam, were responsible for much of the damage.

50. Hayward, *Stopped at Stalingrad*, 188–9.

51. A. H. Birse, *Memoirs of an Interpreter* (London: 1967), 148–9.

52. RGVA, f.37878, o.1, d.444, MPVO HQ, Lt. Gen. Osokin, Military dispatches on the consequences of enemy air raids on the territory of the Soviet Union in Aug 1942, 17 Sept 1942; f.37878, o.1, d.438, 125, Summative report, Aug 1942. The figure was incomplete since some of the injured were drowned trying to cross to the east side of the river.

53. Ibid., report for Sept 1942, 15 Oct 1942; report for Nov 1942, 1 Dec 1942.

54. Williamson Murray, *Luftwaffe: Strategy for Defeat 1933–1945* (London: 1985), 141–4.

55. LC, Spaatz papers, Box 134, Interrogation of Reich Marshal Hermann Goering, 10 May 1945, 10.

56. TsAMO, f.500, o.801858, d.218, German Air Force operations staff, 'Bemerkungen zum Einsatz der Luftwaffe, Nr. 19', 5 Nov 1941, 11–12.

57. Scott Palmer, *Dictatorship of the Air: Aviation Culture and the Fate of Modern Russia* (Cambridge: 2006), 115–21.

58. RGVA, f.37878, o.1, d.722, Lt. Col. Nechaev, MPVO HQ, 'The state of the MPVO in People's Commissariats of transport and industry at the time of the MPVO system transfer to the NKVD', 24 Aug 1945.

59. Ibid., 52, 57; Maj. Bychkov, MPVO HQ, 'Organisational Structure of the MPVO during the War', 12 July 1945.

60. RGVA, f.37878, o.1, d.189, Report on state of preparedness of the city of Kursk for Air Defence [n.d.].

61. Ibid., f.37878, o.1, d.722, Col. M. Linin, Chief of Anti-Chemical Defence, MPVO, 'Anti-Chemical Defence during the War', 3 July 1945; Maj. Bychkov, MPVO HQ, 'Organisational Structure of the MPVO', 12 July 1945.

62. Lennart Samuelson, *Tankograd: The Formation of a Soviet Company Town: Cheliabinsk 1900–1950s* (Basingstoke: 2011), 219.

63. Ibid., 65–72; on Stalingrad, RGVA, f.37878, o.1, d.189, Lt. Ageev (MPVO, Stalingrad station), 'Operational review of the activities of MPVO headquarters and agencies in the Stalingrad region until 14 Jan 1942'.

64. RGVA, f.37878, o.1, d.701, MPVO HQ, Lt. Gen. Osokin, 'Report on the Activities of the GU MPVO/NKVD over the Period of the War to December 1 1944', 6 Jan 1945; f.37878, o.1, d.722, 'Organisational Structure of the MPVO', 74–81.

65. RGVA, f.37878, o.1, d.722, 10, 'Financial systems of the MPVO' [n.d.].

66. Ibid., f.37878, o.1, d.701, 'Report on the Activities of GU MPVO/NKVD over the Period of the War', 6 Jan 1945; f.37878, o.1, d.722, 'Anti-Chemical Defence during the War', 3 July 1945; 'The State of the MPVO in People's Commissariats', 24 Aug 1945.

67. Rodric Braithwaite, *Moscow 1941: A City and its People at War* (London: 2006), 189–90.

68. RGVA, f.37878, o.1, d.701, 'Report on the Activities of the GU MPVO/NKVD over the Period of the War', 6 Jan 1945; f.37878, o.1, d.722, 3, 'Growth of the Collective Defence in the Cities'; 17–20, 'Prospects: Protection of the People from Air Raids in the Future', Apr 1945; 'Anti-Chemical Defence during the War', 3 July 1945. For a good description of basement shelters and the construction programme in Leningrad see Evgenii Moniushko, *From Leningrad to Hungary: Notes of a Red Army Soldier, 1941–1946* (London: 2005), 7–9.

69. Henry Cassidy, *Moscow Dateline, 1941–1943* (London: 1943), 68; Braithwaite, *Moscow 1941*, 190–91.

70. Braithwaite, *Moscow 1941*, 187–90.

71. PArch, Balfour papers, BAL/1, Moscow Diary, entry for 27 Sept 1941; Cassidy, *Moscow Dateline*, 66; Moniushko, *From Leningrad to Hungary*, 19–20.

72. Werth, *Moscow '41*, 112–13.

73. Air Ministry, *The Rise and Fall of the German Air Force, 1933–1945* (London: 1983), 168.

74. RGVA, f.37878, o.1, d.443, MPVO HQ, Report no. 2, 'on the consequences of air-raids of the enemy aviation between December 1941 and January 1942', Feb 1942; Report no. 9, 'on the consequences of air raids of enemy aviation in April 1942', May 1942.

75. Ibid., f.37878, o.1, d.443, 1st dept., MPVO HQ, Col. Baksov, 'Report on the activity of divisions and groups of the MPVO from the start of the war until February 1942', [n.d.].

76. Citrine, *In Russia Now*, 59–60; John Barber, 'The Moscow Crisis of October 1941', in Julian Cooper, Maureen Perrie, E. A. Rees (eds), *Soviet History 1917–1953: Essays in Honour of R. W. Davies* (London: 1995), 201–18; M. M. Gorinov, 'Muscovites' Moods, 22 June 1941 to May 1942', in Robert Thurston, Bernd Bonwetsch (eds), *The People's War: Responses to World War II in the Soviet Union* (Chicago, IL: 2000), 123–4.

77. RGVA, f.37878, o.1, d.443, 'Report on the enemy aviation and the work of divisions and groups of the MPVO from the start of the war until February 1942'; Salisbury, *The 900 Days*, 297.

78. Reid, *Leningrad*, 143; Salisbury, *The 900 Days*, 291, 298. On alarms see Moniushko, *From Leningrad to Hungary*, 30.

79. Svetlana Magaieva, Albert Pleysier, *Surviving the Blockade of Leningrad* (Lanham, MD: 2006), 39, 42.

80. RGVA, f.37878, o.1, d.443, Report no. 5, 10 Apr 1942; Report no. 9, May 1942; Moniushko, *From Leningrad to Moscow*, 17.

81. Magaieva, Pleysier, *Surviving the Blockade*, 66.

82. Moniushko, *From Leningrad to Hungary*, 18–19.

83. RGVA, f.37878, o.1, d.443, Report no. 9, May 1942.

84. Ibid., f.37878, o.1, d.438, 21–3, MPVO, Summative report on the enemy's air raids over the city of Stalingrad in Apr 1942; 77–82, Summative report, July 1942.

85. Ibid., 124–5, Summative report, Aug 1942.

86. Ibid., 126–7.

87. Ibid., f.37878, o.1, d.722, 'Prospects: Protection of the People from air Raids', April 1945; 'Anti-Chemical Defence during the War', 3 July 1945; 'The state of the MPVO in People's Commissariats of transport and industry', 24 Aug 1945.

88. Ibid., f.37878, o.1, d.537, Reports on military messages received by the MPVO HQ on the activity of enemy aviation on the territory of the USSR during Jan 1945; Reports between 16 and 20 Feb 1945; Report on operational and organizational questions from 1 Mar 1943 until 1 Mar 1944; Lt. Gen. Soskin, 'Analysis of the Consequences of the Air Raids and the Activity of the MPVO in 1944', 30 Apr 1945.

89. RGVA, f.37878, o.1, d.722, 'The state of the MPVO in People's Commissariats of transport and industry', 24 Aug 1945.

90. Ibid., f.37878, o.1, d.701, 'Report on the Activities of the GU, MPVO/NKVD over the Period of the War' 6 Jan 1945.

91. Alexander Werth, *Leningrad* (London: 1944), 163.

92. RGVA, f.37878, o.1, d.537, Lt. Gen. Osokin, 'Conclusions on the activity of enemy aviation conducting intelligence works and air raids, 1 January until 31 December 1944', 30 Apr 1945; f.37878, o.1, d.723, 'The activity of the MPVO during the Great Patriotic War', 18 Sept 1945.

93. Werth, *Leningrad*, 162.

94. Ibid., 72.

95. Magaieva, Pleysier, *Surviving the Blockade*, 42.

96. Richard Bidlack, 'The Political Mood in Leningrad during the First Year of the Soviet-German War', *The Russian Review*, 59 (2000), 101–2, 106.

97. RGVA, f.37878, o.1, d.722, 'Participation of the MPVO in the reconstruction of the national economy', 21–4.

98. Ernst Heinkel, *He 1000* (London: 1956), 232.

99. IWM, MD, vol LI, 479, Jeschonnek to Milch, 28 Oct 1942.

100. BA-MA, RL 3/16, GL Office, 'Auszug aus der Führerbesprechung', 3/4/5 Jan 1943.

101. Andreas Nielsen, *The German Air Force General Staff* (New York: 1959), 155. Gerhard Förster, *Totaler Krieg und Blitzkrieg* (Berlin: 1967), 150.

102. LC, Spaatz papers, Box 134, Interrogation of Gen. Koller, 25 Sept 1945, 1–2.

103. For details see Richard Overy, 'From "Uralbomber" to "Amerikabomber":
     The Luftwaffe and Strategic Bombing', *Journal of Strategic Studies*, 1 (1978),
     166–7.

104. Heinkel, *He 1000*, 230.

105. NARA, Microfilm T321, Roll 10, frames 6778–9, Luftwaffe-Führungsstab,
     'Kurze Studie: Kampf gegen die russische Rüstungsindustrie', 9 Nov 1943.

106. IWM, MD, vol XV, GL conference, 19 June 1942, in which the head of air
     force development complained about Heinkel's 'egoistic company interests';
     BA-MA, RL3/16, Lucht (Technical Office) to Milch, 9 Sept 1942, 'Festigkeit
     der He177'; Heinkel to Air Ministry, 12 Sept 1942. See too Lutz Budrass,
     Flugzeugindustrie und Luftrüstung in Deutschland 1918–1945 (Düsseldorf:
     1998), 847–58, on the competitive situation in the industry in 1942–3.

107. BA-MA, RL3/16, Kommando der Erprobungsstelle to Göring, 13 Aug
     1942; IWM, MD, vol XV, GL conference, 19 June 1942.

108. Heinkel, *He 1000*, 233.

109. Horst Boog, 'Strategischer Luftkrieg in Europa 1943–1944', in Boog et al.,
     DRZW: Band 7: Das Deutsche Reich in der Defensive (Stuttgart: 2001),
     348–9.

110. Ibid., 350–51, 355; Albert Speer, *Inside the Third Reich* (London: 1970),
     280–83.

111. NARA, Microfilm T321, Roll 10, frames 6780–82, 'Kurze Studie', 9 Nov 1943.

112. TsAMO, f.500, o.801858, d.218, Operational Staff, 'Taktische Bemerkun-
     gen', July 1943, 11.

113. Boog, 'Strategischer Luftkrieg', 354, 357–62.

114. NARA, Microfilm T321, Roll 10, frame 6765, losses, establishment and out-
     put, bomber units, Jan 1943–Mar 1944; Frames 6754–6, Luftwaffe Führungsstab,
     'Studie über die Flugzeuglage der Kampfverbände', 5 May 1944.

115. RGVA, f.37878, o.1, d.537, 136, 'Comparative table of air raids, bombs
     and losses, Jan–May 1943 and Jan–May 1944'; 169, MPVO, 'Analysis of
     the consequences of the air raids and the activity of the MPVO in 1944:
     Table of material losses of the Soviet Union in 1944'.

116. LC, Spaatz papers, Box 134, USSBS Interview no. 8, 5–6.

117. RGAE, f.29, o.1, d.1792/1961, Production of aircraft and engines 1939–
     1945. There were 43,648 fighter aircraft, 28,947 dive-bombers and 11,397
     bombers.

118. Groehler, *Bombenkrieg gegen Deutschland*, 166–70.

119. Carl van Dyke, *The Soviet Invasion of Finland 1939–40* (London: 1997),
     55–6.

120. Alexsandr Medved, Dmitri Hazonov, 'Hyökkäyset Helsinkiin helmikuussa
     1944', *Sotahistoriallinen Aikakauskirja*, 18 (1999), 134–75. On the Soviet
     claims see Groehler, *Bombenkrieg gegen Deutschland*, 170.

121. Birse, *Memoirs of an Interpreter*, 128–9. The Soviet negotiator in Moscow
     compared Allied ambitions to conduct operations in the Caucasus campaign
     with the 'military intervention' of the Western powers in 1918–19 against
     the Bolshevik revolution.

722   NOTES

122. Mark J. Conversino, *Fighting with the Soviets: The Failure of Operation Frantic 1944–1945* (Lawrence, KS: 1997), 26–30.
123. LC, Doolittle papers, Box 19, Col. Old to Doolittle, 6 July 1944, 4.
124. Conversino, *Fighting with the Soviets*, 88–90.
125. RGAE, f.29, o.1, d.1792/1961, Production of aircraft and engines: Bombers. The figures were 1939: 2; 1940: 10; 1941: 23; 1942: 22; 1943: 29; 1944: 5.
126. Kerber, *Stalin's Aviation Gulag*, 255–60.
127. RGVA, f.37878, o.1, d.722, 17–19, 'Prospects: Protection of the People from Air Raids', April 1945.

5. THE SORCERER'S APPRENTICE: BOMBER COMMAND 1939–42

1. Heinz M. Hanke, *Luftkrieg und Zivilbevölkerung* (Frankfurt am Main: 1991), 187–90. Charles Webster, Noble Frankland, *The Strategic Air Offensive Against Germany*, 4 vols (London: 1961), vol 1, 134–5, give the wrong dates for the German pledge and the Anglo-French declaration.
2. FDRL, President's Secretary's Files, Box 47, Ambassador Potocki to Cordell Hull, 1 Sept 1939.
3. TNA, AIR 9/202, first meeting, Committee on the Humanisation of Aerial Warfare, 8 July 1938; Air Staff memorandum, 'The Restriction of Air Warfare', 25 Feb 1938. Uri Bialer, 'Humanization of Air Warfare in British Foreign Policy on the Eve of the Second World War', *Journal of Contemporary History*, 13 (1978), 79–96.
4. TNA, AIR 14/249, 'Air Ministry Instructions and Notes on the Rules to be Observed by the Royal Air Force in War', 17 Aug 1939, 5–7; AIR 41/5, 'International Law of the Air 1939–1945', supplement to 'Air Power and War Rights' by the former Air Ministry legal adviser J. M. Spaight, 7; Joel Hayward, 'Air Power, Ethics, and Civilian Immunity during the First World War and its Aftermath', *Global War Studies*, 7 (2010), 127–9; Peter Gray, 'The Gloves Will Have to Come Off: A Reappraisal of the Legitimacy of the RAF Bomber Offensive against Germany', *Air Power Review*, 13 (2010), 15–16.
5. TNA, AIR 9/105, Anglo-French staff conversations, 'Preparation of Joint Plan', 19 Apr 1939; 'The Employment of British Bombers in the Event of German Invasion of the Low Countries', 21 Apr 1939.
6. TNA, AIR 14/249, Air Ministry to Bomber Command, 22 Aug 1939; AIR 75/8, Newall to Ludlow-Hewitt, 23 Aug 1939. Gray, 'The Gloves Will Have to Come Off', 22–3.
7. TNA, AIR 75/8, Newall to Gen. Gort, 24 Aug 1939; War Cabinet Annex, 'Air Policy', 13 Oct 1939; AIR 14/446, Air Ministry minute, 30 Aug 1939.
8. TNA, FO 371/23093, Sir Hugh Kennard (Warsaw) to Foreign Office, 11 Sept and 12 Sept 1939.

9. Ibid., AIR 75/8, 'Air Policy: Brief for the Secretary of State for Supreme War Council', 15 Nov 1939, 5–8.

10. Martin Middlebrook, Chris Everitt, *The Bomber Command War Diaries: An Operational Reference Book 1939–1945* (Leicester: 2000), 42, 702–3.

11. FDRL, President's Secretary's Files, Box 32, Chamberlain to Roosevelt, 25 Aug 1939; Roosevelt to Chamberlain, 31 Aug 1939.

12. TNA, AIR 9/131, 'The Employment of the Air Striking Force on the Outbreak of War' [n.d. but Aug 1939], 10. W. A. Jacobs, 'The British Strategic Air Offensive against Germany in World War II', in R. Cargill Hall (ed), *Case Studies in Strategic Bombardment* (Washington, DC: 1998), 109–10.

13. Richard Overy, 'Air Power, Armies and the War in the West, 1940', 32nd Harmon Memorial Lecture (Colorado Springs, CO: 1989), 8–12.

14. Webster, Frankland, *Strategic Air Offensive*, vol 4, 99–102, App 6; Tami Davis Biddle, *Rhetoric and Reality in Air Warfare: The Evolution of British and American Ideas about Strategic Bombing, 1914–1945* (Princeton, NJ: 2002), 178–80.

15. TNA, AIR 9/89, Air (Targets) Intelligence: Country: Germany, 21 Jan 1938.

16. Owen Thetford, *Aircraft of the Royal Air Force since 1918* (London: 1988), 138–41, 273–6.

17. Ibid., 30–34, 313–16, 554–61.

18. Armaments Design Establishment, Ministry of Supply, 'The Development of British Incendiary Bombs during the Period of the 1939–1945 World War', Dec 1946; TNA, AIR 9/92, Air Ministry, 'Bomb Stocks as at 26 April 1939'. On the poor quality of bombs see NC, Cherwell papers, G189, Cherwell to Ministry of Supply, 28 Jan 1942, memorandum, 'Bomb Production'; F255, War Cabinet paper, 'The Possibility of Improving Efficiency of Blast Bombs', 6 Oct 1943.

19. TNA, AIR 14/88, Air Ministry to Ludlow-Hewitt, 27 Oct 1939; AIR 41/5, 'International Law of the Air', 1.

20. TNA, AIR 75/5, Slessor to Newall, 29 Mar 1940; Richard Overy, *Bomber Command, 1939–1945* (London: 1997), 32–3.

21. TNA, AIR 9/102, Draft Plan W.A.5(d), 13 Jan 1940; CamUL, Templewood papers, XII, File 2, interviews with officers from Wellington and Whitley squadrons, 29 Apr 1940.

22. TNA, AIR 41/5, 'International Law of the Air', 12–13.

23. TNA, AIR 14/194, Record of a conference with the Air Staff, 28 Apr 1940, 3.

24. Martin Gilbert (ed), *The Churchill War Papers: Vol II: Never Surrender, May 1940–December 1940* (London: 1994), 17–18, 24–6, 38–43, War Cabinet minutes, 12 May, 13 May, 15 May 1940. Randall Hansen, *Fire and Fury: The Allied Bombing of Germany 1942–1945* (New York: 2009), 20, who also dates the Rotterdam attack incorrectly.

25. Christopher Harmon, *'Are We Beasts?': Churchill and the Moral Question of World War II 'Area Bombing'* (Newport, RI: 1991), 8–10.

26. Martin Gilbert, *Finest Hour: Winston S. Churchill 1939–1941* (London: 1983), 329–30, 334, 342–7; Gilbert (ed), *Churchill War Papers: Vol II*, 17–18,

25, 38–41, War Cabinet minutes: Confidential Annex, 13 May 1940; War Cabinet minutes: Confidential Annex, 15 May 1940.

27. TNA, AIR 14/194, CAS minute, 19 May 1940; DCAS to C-in-C Bomber Command, 30 May 1940.

28. TNA, AIR 14/249, Air Ministry to all Commands, 4 June 1940; AIR 41/5, 'International Law of the Air', 13.

29. TNA, AIR 14/249, Bottomley (Bomber Command SASO) to all Group HQ, 14 June 1940.

30. UEA, Zuckerman Archive, SZ/BBSU/56, Portal to Douglas (DCAS), 16 July 1940; TNA, AIR 14/249, Bomber Command War Orders, proposed amendment, 14 July 1940.

31. Biddle, *Rhetoric and Reality*, 188–9.

32. TNA, AIR 14/249, telegram from Air Ministry to Bomber Command HQ, 10 Sept 1940; AIR 41/5, 'International Law of the Air', 13. Gray, 'The Gloves Will Have to Come Off', 25–6.

33. Richard Overy, 'Allied Bombing and the Destruction of German Cities', in Roger Chickering, Stig Förster, Bernd Greiner (eds), *A World at Total War: Global Conflict and the Politics of Destruction* (Cambridge: 2005), 280–84; Hayward, 'Air Power, Ethics', 124–5.

34. TNA, AIR 75/8, War Cabinet Annex, 'Air Policy', 14 Oct 1939.

35. TNA, AIR 9/79, Air Ministry (Plans), 'Note on the Relative Merit of Oil and Power as Objectives for Air Attack', 16 Oct 1939; AIR 75/8, 'Draft Bombing Plans', 14 Nov 1939.

36. RAFM, Douglas papers, MFC 78/23/2, Trenchard to Portal, 2 May 1940; TNA, 75/8, Portal to Newall, 8 May 1940.

37. TNA, 75/8, 'Draft Bombing Plans', 14 Nov 1939, 3.

38. TNA AIR 14/194, Slessor (Director of Plans) to Air Marshal A. Evill, 22 Oct 1939; 'Note on the Question of Relaxing Bombardment Instructions', 7 Sept 1939.

39. TNA, PREM 3/193/6A, FO Report, 30 May 1940; Halifax to Churchill, 2 June 1940, encl. Report, 'Morale in Germany'.

40. TNA, AIR 75/8, Air Ministry (Plans), 'Plans for Attack of Italian War Industry', 2 June 1940; AIR 20/283, Air Ministry (Bomber Operations), 'Notes on Bomb Attacks', 20 Aug 1940.

41. Martin Hugh-Jones, 'Wickham Steed and German Biological Warfare Research', *Intelligence and National Security*, 7 (1992), 387–90, 393–7; Ulf Schmidt, 'Justifying Chemical Warfare: The Origins and Ethics of Britain's Chemical Warfare Programme, 1915–1939', in Jo Fox, David Welch (eds), *Justifying War: Propaganda, Politics and the Modern Age* (Basingstoke: 2012), 148–50.

42. TNA, AIR 14/206, TC 2, 'Notes on German Air Operations in Poland', 19 Oct 1939.

43. TNA, AIR 41/5, 'International Law of the Air', 9–10.

44. TNA, AIR 14/194, Bomber Command, 'Note on the Question of Relaxing the Bombardment Instructions', 7 Sept 1939; AIR 14/381, Plan W.1, memorandum for C-in-C, Bomber Command, Apr 1938, 1.

45. Harold Balfour, *Wings over Westminster* (London: 1973), 120.

46. TNA, FO 898/311, MEW memorandum, 'Bombing of Open Towns', 19 Apr 1940.

47. CCO, Denis Richards Archive, File IV/Folder A, Salmond to Trenchard, 11 May 1940.

48. Gilbert, *Churchill War Papers: Vol II*, 41, War Cabinet minutes: Confidential Annex, 15 May 1940.

49. Gilbert, *Finest Hour*, 81.

50. Robinson Library, University of Newcastle, Trevelyan papers, draft article, 'Nazism and Civilisation', Mar 1943.

51. National Library of Wales, Jevons papers, I/IV/85, Noel-Baker to H. Stanley Jevons, 6 Nov 1940; Noel-Baker, 'Reprisals? No', *Daily Herald*, 2 Oct 1940. Brett Holman, '"Bomb Back, and Bomb Hard": Debating Reprisals during the Blitz', *Australian Journal of Politics and History*, 58 (2012), 395–9.

52. LSE, Women's International League of Peace and Freedom papers, 1/16, Executive minutes, 3 July 1940; WILPF 2009/05/04, 'Report of Deputation of Pacifist Clergy to the Archbishops of Canterbury and York, 11 June 1940', 2.

53. CamUL, Templewood papers, XII, File 2, transcript of broadcast talk, 27 Apr 1940.

54. Gilbert, *Churchill War Papers: Vol II*, 42–3, War Cabinet minutes: Confidential Annex, 15 May 1940.

55. CCO, Portal papers, Folder 1, Portal to Churchill, 27 Oct 1940.

56. TNA, AIR 9/424, Slessor (DCAS) to Director of Plans, 17 Aug and 24 Aug 1942. The final directive (Joint Planning Staff: Anglo-US Bombing Policy) was produced on 31 August naming 'industrial centres' rather than industrial population.

57. RAFM, Harris papers, H47, Harris to the Under-Secretary of State, Air Ministry, 25 Oct 1943; A. W. Street (Air Ministry) to Harris, 15 Dec 1943. There is an extended discussion of this correspondence in Hansen, *Fire and Fury*, 159–66.

58. Webster, Frankland, *Strategic Air Offensive*, vol 4, 111–24. On forests and game see TNA, AIR 40/1814, MEW note, 'German Forests', 7 Aug 1940.

59. TNA, AIR 20/283, Air Ministry War Room, 'Tonnage of Bombs Dropped 24 June to 27 Aug 1940'. The objectives were oil and fuel, electric power, chemicals and explosives, aircraft industry, enemy aerodromes, aluminium, shipbuilding and docks, and communications.

60. TNA, AIR 9/150, Bomber Command war room, details of raids and tonnages on German port targets to May 1941.

61. Ibid., Bomber Command war room, 'Effort Expended by Bomber Command, May to October 1940'; war room to Air Ministry (Plans), details of

all sorties, 11 Oct 1940. The 1944 figures in Webster, Frankland, *Strategic Air Offensive*, vol 4, 445–6.

62. UEA, Zuckerman Archive, SZ/BBSU/56, Douglas to Newall, 9 July 1940; Portal to Douglas, 16 July 1940.

63. CCO, Portal papers, Walter Monkton (MoI) to Portal, 8 Nov 1940.

64. Edward Westermann, *Flak: German Anti-Aircraft Defenses, 1914–1945* (Lawrence, KS: 2001), 90.

65. TNA, PREM 3/11/1, Churchill note for Newall, 28 July 1940; Newall to Churchill, 19 July 1940, 'Note on Attack of German Forests'; AIR 20/5813, 'Forestry Report on Incendiary Tests with Different Types of Bombs', 10 July 1941; 'Report on a Trial of "Razzle" in Standing Crops', 16 Aug 1940.

66. Westermann, *Flak*, 97, 102–3.

67. UEA, Zuckerman Archive, SZ/BBSU/2, précis of a lecture by Wing-Commander G. Carey Foster.

68. CCO, Denis Richards Archive, File VIII, Folder A, interview transcripts with Sir Ian Jacob and Sir Robert Cochrane.

69. Harmon, *'Are We Beasts?'*, 10–14.

70. Winston S. Churchill, *The Second World War: Vol II* (London: Cassell, 1957), 567; Biddle, *Rhetoric and Reality*, 186–7, for Churchill's views on bombing as a 'way of winning the war'.

71. E.g. Jörg Friedrich, *The Fire: The Bombing of Germany 1940–1945* (New York: 2006), 62; Douglas Lackey, 'Four Types of Mass Murderer: Stalin, Hitler, Churchill, Truman', in Igor Primoratz (ed), *Terror from the Sky: The Bombing of German Cities in World War II* (Oxford: 2010), 134–5, 144–54; Eric Markusen, David Kopf, 'Was It Genocidal?', in ibid., 160–71.

72. David Reynolds, *In Command of History: Churchill Fighting and Writing the Second World War* (London: 2004), 320–22.

73. CamUL, Boyle papers, Add 9429/2c, conversation with Harris, 18 July 1979. Harris also showed the letter to Churchill's biographer, Martin Gilbert. See Gilbert, *Churchill War Papers: Vol II*, 492–3.

74. TNA, AIR 2/7211, 'Note on the Lessons to be Learned from German Mistakes', 19 Sept 1940, 3.

75. CCAC, BUFT DBOps, 'Review of the Present Strategical Air Offensive', 5 Apr 1941, 5, and App C, 'The Blitz Attack by Night'.

76. TNA, AIR 9/132, RE8 Report, 'Consideration of the Types of Bombs for Specific Objectives Based on Experience of German Bombing in this Country', 26 Sept 1940, 2–3.

77. UEA, Zuckerman Archive, OEMU/50/7, 'Notes on the Work of R.E.8', 18 Nov 1942; TNA, HO 191/203, A. R. Astbury, 'History of the Research and Experiments Department, Ministry of Home Security, 1939–1945', 21–3.

78. TNA, DSIR 4/366, Building Research Laboratory, List of Enquiries Aug 1940–Nov 1941.

79. For an excellent account see Randall Wakelam, *The Science of Bombing: Operational Research in RAF Bomber Command* (Toronto: 2009), 24–33.

80. Hugh Berrington, 'When Does Personality Make a Difference? Lord Cherwell and the Area Bombing of Germany', *International Political Science Review*, 10 (1989), 18–21.

81. NC, Cherwell papers, F398, Statistical Section, Harrod papers, 'Bombs and Deaths', 30 Sept 1940; G181, 'Air Raid Casualties' [n.d. but Sept 1940]; 'House Damage in Air Raids', 27 Sept 1940; 'Bombing of London in September, October and November 1940'; G183, 'Notes of a Conversation with Professor Zuckerman', 26 March 1941 (attached two charts of Hanover and Frankfurt with zones of population density).

82. TNA, AIR 9/132, minute by Plans Dept, Air Ministry, 6 Jan 1941; AIR 20/2264, AWAS Report, 'The Bomb Censuses of Liverpool, Birmingham and London', 29 Oct 1940; AWAS Report, 'Bomb Census of Liverpool, Birmingham, London, Coventry, Manchester, Leeds and Special Attacks', Apr 1941.

83. CCAC, BUFT 3/26, draft directive [n.d. but June 1941].

84. TNA, AIR 40/1814, memorandum by O. Lawrence (MEW), 9 May 1941.

85. See Richard Overy, 'The "Weak Link": Bomber Command and the German Working Class 1940–1945', *Labour History Review*, 77 (2012), 22–5.

86. CCAC, BUFT 3/48, 'The Role of the Long-Range Bomber Force'; 'Review of the Present Strategical Air Offensive', 5 Apr 1941, App C, 2.

87. Ibid., 3/13, Notes on Plan ZZ, 19 Nov 1941, App VI, 'Attack on an Area of 150 Square Miles'.

88. TNA, AIR 2/7211, bombing policy memorandum, 19 Nov 1940; AIR 20/25, Air Intelligence to Baker, 23 May 1941.

89. TNA, AIR 20/25, memorandum on bombing policy by Baker, 7 May 1941.

90. RAFM, Peirse papers, AC 71/13/61-2, Notes of a speech by Richard Peirse to the Thirty Club in London, 25 Nov 1941, 3.

91. TNA, AIR 20/4768, memorandum, 23 Sept 1941, 'The Value of Incendiary Weapons in Attacks on Area Targets', 2.

92. CCAC, BUFT DBOps to the director, 6 June 1941.

93. TNA, AIR 40/1351, AI 3c (Air Liaison), 'Air Attack by Fire', 17 Oct 1941.

94. CCAC, BUFT 3/26, report from BOPs 1 (Sq. Leader Morley), 18 Oct 1941.

95. Hugh Melinsky, *Forming the Pathfinders: The Career of Air Vice-Marshal Sydney Bufton* (Stroud: 2010), 59.

96. Webster, Frankland, *Strategic Air Offensive*, vol 1, 157–64.

97. TNA, AIR 9/150, Air Ministry War Room, Bomber Command sorties May–Oct 1940, Nov 1940–Apr 1941; DBOps to DCAS, 11 Sept 1941.

98. CCO, Portal papers, Folder 9, Peirse to Balfour, 27 Nov 1940; Portal to Peirse, 30 Nov 1940.

99. TNA, Air 14/291, meeting at Air Ministry, 10 Dec 1940; HQ no 7 Group to C-in-C, Bomber Command, 4 Jan 1941.

100. CCO, Portal papers, Folder 1/File 1, Churchill to Portal, 1 Nov 1940; Churchill to Portal, 30 Dec 1940.

101. Ibid., Folder 9/File 1940, Peirse to Churchill, 24 Dec 1940; Peirse to Portal [n.d. but Dec 1940]; File 1941, Peirse to Churchill, 1 Jan 1941.

102. John Colville, *The Fringes of Power: Downing Street Diaries 1939–1945* (London: 2004), 241, diary entry for 2 Nov 1940.

103. CCO, Portal Papers, Folder 1/File 1, Portal to Churchill, 7 Dec 1940; Folder 9/File 1940, Portal to Peirse, 5 Dec 1940; Peirse to Churchill, 24 Dec 1940. Details of raid in Middlebrook, Everitt, *Bomber Command War Diaries*, 111, and TNA, AIR 14/2670, Night bomb raid sheets, Dec 1940, 'Results of Night Operations, 16/17 December 1940'.

104. Webster, Frankland, *Strategic Air Offensive*, vol 1, 159–60.

105. CCO, Portal papers, Folder 9/File 2, Peirse to Portal, 28 Feb 1941.

106. UEA, Zuckerman Archive, SZ/BBSU/56, 'Bombing Policy'.

107. Ibid., draft directive, 9 July 1941; Webster, Frankland, *Strategic Air Offensive*, vol 4, 135–7.

108. CCO, Portal papers, Folder 9/File 1940, Peirse to Portal [n.d.].

109. RAFM, Peirse papers, AC 71/13/60, speech to the Thirty Club, 25 Nov 1941, 11.

110. TNA, 41/41, RAF Narrative, 'The RAF in the Bombing Offensive against Germany: Vol III', 87.

111. TNA, PREM 3/193/6A, Minister of Information to Churchill, 1 Jan 1941, 'Conditions in Germany, December 1940', 2.

112. CCAC, Bufton papers, BUFT 3/11, 'Report on the Interrogation of American Legation and Consular Officials in Lisbon, 24–31 July 1941', 4.

113. TNA, AIR 20/4768, Air Staff memorandum, 23 Sept 1941.

114. FO Historical Branch, 'Churchill and Stalin: Documents Collated for the Anglo-Russian Seminar, 8 March 2002', doc 9, Broadcast by Mr Churchill, 22 June 1941, 1, 3.

115. Ibid., doc 11, Telegram from Churchill to Stalin, 7 July 1941.

116. Bradley Smith, *Sharing Secrets with Stalin: How the Allies Traded Intelligence 1941–1945* (Lawrence, KS: 1996), 11.

117. Colville, *The Fringes of Power*, 363, entry for 21 July 1941.

118. RAFM, Bottomley papers, AC 71/2/29, Peck to Bottomley, 6 Apr 1944, enclosing 'Address to Thirty Club, 8 Mar 1944', 1–2.

119. Middlebrook, Everitt, *Bomber Command War Diaries*, 166–7.

120. BA-MA, RL2-IV/28, Luftflotte 3, Gefechtskalender, 'Durchführung und Erfolg Juli 1941'.

121. CCO, Portal papers, Folder 2/File 1, Churchill to Portal, 7 July 1941. On the German response see Percy Schramm(ed), *Kriegstagebuch des OKW: Eine Documentation, 1940–1941, Band 1, Teilband 2* (Augsburg: 2007), 417–20.

122. TNA, PREM 3/13/2, Churchill to Lindemann, 7 July 1941; Churchill to Sinclair and Portal, 12 July 1941.

123. RAFM, Bottomley papers, AC 71/2/115, 'Operational Photography in Bomber Command Sept 1939–April 1945', June 1945, 14–29. Robert S. Ehlers, *Targeting the Third Reich: Air Intelligence and the Allied Bombing Campaigns* (Lawrence, KS: 2009), 96–7.

124. CCO, Portal papers, Folder 9/File 2, Portal to Cherwell, 29 July 1941; Cherwell to Portal, 30 July 1941.

125. Webster, Frankland, *Strategic Air Offensive*, vol 4, 205, 'Report by Mr. Butt to Bomber Command on his Examination of Night Photographs, 18 August 1941'; Melinsky, *Forming the Pathfinders*, 43–4.

126. CCO, Portal papers, Folder 2/File 1, Churchill to Portal, 15 Sept 1941.

127. Ibid., Cherwell to Churchill, 3 Sept 1941; Portal to Churchill, 'Notes on Lord Cherwell's Paper', 11 Sept 1941.

128. RAFM, Bottomley papers, AC 71/2/115, 'Operational Photography', 26.

129. Interview with Robert Kee in Overy, *Bomber Command*, 75.

130. TNA, AIR 41/41, RAF Narrative, vol III, 42. Wakelam, *The Science of Bombing*, 42–6.

131. Overy, *Bomber Command* 74, interview with Wilkie Wanless; TNA, AIR 9/150, Peirse to Balfour, 7 Sept 1941; AIR 20/1979, Bomber Command, aircraft strengths and casualties. Between Sept 1939 and Feb 1941, 93,341 non-operational sorties were flown by day, only 3,157 by night.

132. TNA, AIR 9/150, BOps to DBOps, 27 Nov 1941; AIR 20/283, Baker (DBOps) to Portal, 28 July 1941.

133. Webster, Frankland, *Strategic Air Offensive*, vol 4, 455; TNA, AIR 9/150, DBOps to Deputy Chief of Air Staff, 11 Sept 1941.

134. Thetford, *Aircraft of the Royal Air Force*, 317–22, 488–91; Brereton Greenhous, Stephen Harris, William Johnston, William Rawling, *The Crucible of War 1939–1945: The Official History of the Royal Canadian Air Force, Vol III* (Toronto: 1994), 604–6.

135. Ibid., 605.

136. Sebastian Cox (ed), *The Strategic Air War Against Germany, 1939–1945: The Official Report of the British Bombing Survey Unit* (London: 1998), 37.

137. PArch, Beaverbrook papers, BBK/D/329, Air Ministry to MAP, 4 May 1941. On bombs see John A. MacBean, Arthur S. Hogben, *Bombs Gone: The Development and Use of British Air-Dropped Weapons from 1912 to the Present Day* (Wellingborough: 1990), 66–8; Roy Irons, *The Relentless Offensive: War and Bomber Command 1939–1945* (Barnsley: 2009), 190–91, 205–6.

138. TNA, AIR 20/5813, minute, vice chief of staff, 3 Nov 1941; '4lb Incendiary Bomb', BOps 2b, 2 Jan 1942.

139. NC, Cherwell papers, F222, minute for Churchill from Cherwell, May 1941; G182, H. W. Robinson to Cherwell, 27 Oct 1941; Chart, 'Bombs Dropped on Germany July–Dec 1941'; G189, Cherwell to Ministry of Supply, 28 Jan 1942; PArch, Beaverbrook papers, BBK/D/330, Air Marshal Courtney to Beaverbrook, 27 May 1941. Details on bombs from Irons, *The Relentless Offensive*, 203–5.

140. Cox (ed), *The Strategic Air War*, 36.

141. PArch, Balfour papers, BAL/3, 'Dunkirk Days–Battle of Britain' (Balfour was Under-Secretary of State at the Air Ministry). See CamUL, Boyle papers, Add 9429/2C, Boyle to Harris, 22 July 1979, where Beaverbrook was still remembered as 'one of the instinctive opponents of bombing Germany'.

142. PArch, Beaverbrook papers, BBK/D/329, Portal to Moore-Brabazon, 10 May 1941, 3.

143. Gavin Bailey, 'Aircraft for Survival: Anglo-American Aircraft Supply Diplomacy, 1938–1942' (unpublished PhD thesis, University of Dundee: 2010), 183–91.

144. LC, Arnold papers, Reel 199, handwritten notes, Placentia Bay meeting, 11 Aug 1941.

145. Webster, Frankland, *Strategic Air Offensive*, vol 4, 4–6; Melinsky, *Forming the Pathfinders*, 56–7, 59; Alfred Price, *Instruments of Darkness: The History of Electronic Warfare, 1939–1945* (London: 2005), 97–9.

146. BA-MA, RL2 IV/101, Vorstudien zur Luftkriegsgeschichte: Reichsluftverteidigung: Teil B: Flakabwehr [n.d. 1944], 12–13, 15.

147. RAFM, Saundby papers, AC 72/12 Box 7, 'War in the Ether: Europe 1939–1945', Signals Branch, HQ Bomber Command, Oct 1945, 6.

148. BA-MA, RL2 IV/101, 'Flakabwehr', 15–17.

149. Werner Held, Holger Nauroth, *Die deutsche Nachtjagd* (Stuttgart: 1992), 115–17.

150. BA-MA, RL2 IV/101, 'Flakabwehr', 18–19, 23; Bill Gunston, *Night Fighters: A Development and Combat History* (Cambridge: 1976), 86–9; Price, *Instruments of Darkness*, 55–9.

151. Westermann, *Flak*, 123–4.

152. TNA, AIR 20/283, minute by DBOps (Baker), 10 Nov 1941.

153. Melinsky, *Forming the Pathfinders*, 66–7; Middlebrook, Everitt, *Bomber Command War Diaries*, 210.

154. CCO, Portal papers, Folder 2/File 2, Churchill to Portal, 27 Sept 1941; Portal to Churchill, 25 Sept 1941, enclosing 'Development and Employment of the Heavy Bomber Force', 22 Sept 1941.

155. Ibid., Portal to Churchill, 2 Oct 1941; Churchill to Portal, 7 Oct 1941.

156. TNA, AIR 41/41, RAF Narrative, vol III, 111; Middlebrook, Everitt, *Bomber Command War Diaries*, 217–18; Greenhous et al., *Crucible of War*, 559–60.

157. Mark Connelly, *Reaching for the Stars: A New History of Bomber Command in World War II* (London: 2001), 60–2; Webster, Frankland, *Strategic Air Offensive*, vol 1, 254–6; Anthony Furse, *Wilfrid Freeman, The Genius Behind Allied Survival and Air Supremacy 1939–1945* (Staplehurst, Kent: 2000), 199–200.

158. CCAC, BUFT 3/12, 'Report of a Visit to Groups and Stations by Wing-Commander Morley, 10 Dec 1941'.

159. Royal Society, London, Blackett papers, PB/4/4, 'Note on the Use of the Bomber Force', 3.

160. Webster, Frankland, *Strategic Air Offensive*, vol 1, 328–9.

161. CCAC, BUFT 3/12, minute for DBOps from Bufton, 27 Feb 1942.

162. PArch, Beaverbrook papers, BBK/D/330, telegram from Harris to Portal and Sinclair, 18 Sept 1941; RAFM, Harris to Freeman, 15 Sept 1941, 5.

163. Ibid., 2–3.

164. PArch, Beaverbrook papers, BBK/D/330, telegram from Harris to Portal, 8 Dec 1941.

165. Henry Probert, *Bomber Harris: His Life and Times* (London: 2006), 122–3.

166. Warren Kimball (ed), *Churchill & Roosevelt: The Complete Correspondence: Vol I: Alliance Emerging* (London: 1984), 296, memorandum, Churchill to Roosevelt, Pt I, 'The Atlantic Front'.

167. LC, Arnold papers, Reel 199, Proceedings of the American-British Joint Chiefs of Staff Conferences, 24 Dec 1941, 2.

168. Ibid., Annex 1, American-British Strategy, 2, 5.

169. Kimball (ed), *Churchill & Roosevelt Correspondence: Vol I*, 314–23, Churchill to Roosevelt, 7 (?) Jan 1942.

170. USAFA, Colorado Springs (USAFC), Hansell papers, Series III, Box 1, Folder 2, 'Can We Be Bombed?' [n.d. but late 1939], 22–3.

171. NARA, RG94.580, memorandum from the chief of air staff, 10 May 1940; LC, Andrews papers, Box 11, memorandum for the Executive by Carl Spaatz, 5 Jan 1935, 'Comments on Doctrines of the Army Air Corps', 1.

172. Haywood Hansell, *The Air Plan that Defeated Hitler* (Atlanta, GA: 1972), 53–63, 92–3.

173. Douglas Lackey, 'The Bombing Campaign of the USAAF', in Igor Primoratz (ed), *Terror from the Sky: The Bombing of German Cities in World War II* (Oxford: 2010), 41–5; Ronald Schaffer, 'American Military Ethics in World War II: The Bombing of German Civilians', *The Journal of American History*, 67 (1980), 320–22; Conrad Crane, 'Evolution of U.S. Strategic Bombing of Urban Areas', *Historian*, 50 (1987), 16–17, 21–4.

174. On Roosevelt see Jeffery Underwood, *The Wings of Democracy: The Influence of Air Power on the Roosevelt Administration 1933–1941* (College Station: 1991), chs 7–8.

175. TNA, FO 371/23093, Dept of State communiqué from Ambassador Anthony Biddle, 13 Sept 1939; FDRL, President's personal files, 554, Biddle to Roosevelt, 10 Nov 1939.

176. Michael Sherry, *The Rise of American Air Power: The Creation of Armageddon* (New Haven, CT: 1987), 97–8.

177. NARA, RG 107, Lovett papers, Box 138, memorandum for Lovett, 'Blackout Alarms', 24 Dec 1941; Lovett to Donald Douglas (President, Douglas Aircraft Company), 27 Jan 1942; Office of Civilian Defense to all Regional Directors, 22 Dec 1941.

178. Ibid., Engineer Board, US Army, 'Traffic Control during Blackouts', 5 Oct 1942; Joseph McNarney (Deputy Army CoS) to Vice Chief of Naval Operations, 5 June 1942.

179. Ibid., Box 139, Federal Works Agency, 'Air Raid Protection Code for Federal Buildings', Aug 1942, 13–20, 21–5.

180. Ibid., Box 139, *Civilian Front*, vol 11, 15 May 1943, 7; HQ Army Service Forces, Periodic Report to Lovett, 2.

181. Ibid., Box 139, James Landis, 'We're Not Safe from Air Raids', *Civilian Front*, 15 May 1943.

182. James Parton, *'Air Force Spoken Here': General Ira Eaker and the Command of the Air* (Bethesda, MD: 1986), 128–34, 149. Eight Air Force activation in

Maxwell AFB, Eighth Air Force, 520.056, Statistical Summary 8th Air Force Operations, 1.

183. TNA, AIR 14/792, Eaker to Harris, 30 July 1942; Bottomley to Portal, 8 Feb 1942; Baker to Bottomley, 2 Feb 1942.

184. Richard G. Davis, *Carl A. Spaatz and the Air War in Europe* (Washington, DC: 1993), 67–71.

185. Ibid., 48–53.

186. LC, Arnold papers, Reel 89, Harold George (Asst CoS) to Arnold, 25 Feb 1942.

187. John W. Huston (ed), *American Airpower Comes of Age: General Henry H. 'Hap' Arnold's World War II Diaries*, 2 vols (Maxwell, AL: 2002), vol 1, 282–4, 310.

188. Ibid., vol 1, 304, entry for 30 May 1942.

189. Based on Probert, *Bomber Harris*, chs 2, 4–5.

190. 'Rabbits' in CCO, Portal papers, Folder 9/File 3, Harris to Portal, 2 Mar 1942; 'weaker sisters', RAFM, Harris papers, H51, Harris to Peck (Air Ministry), 1 May 1942; 'Fifth Columnists', CCO, Portal papers, Folder 9/File 3, Harris to Portal, 5 Mar 1942; 'impertinent', RAFM, Harris papers, H9, Harris to Bottomley, 13 Jan 1945.

191. UEA, Zuckerman Archive, SZ/BBSU/3, Air Commodore Pelly to Zuckerman, 8 Jan 1947.

192. RAFM, Harris papers, H53, Harris to Baker (DBOps), 11 Apr 1942.

193. CamUL, Boyle papers, Add 9429/2c, Boyle to Harris, 24 Aug 1979.

194. RAFM, Harris papers, H9, Harris to Bottomley, 29 Mar 1945.

195. Webster, Frankland, *Strategic Air Offensive*, vol 4, 143–8.

196. TNA, AIR 20/4768, memorandum from BOps, 25 Feb 1942.

197. NC, Cherwell papers, G192, note for Cherwell, 23 Feb 1942, on German towns; CCAC, BUFT 3/15, memorandum from Morley (BOps 1), 'The Employment of H.E. Bombs in Incendiary Attack', 18 Nov 1942, 1–2.

198. NC, Cherwell papers, F254, War Cabinet, 'Estimates of Bombing Effect', 9 Apr 1942; F226, minute for Churchill from Cherwell, 30 Mar 1942; TNA, AIR 9/183, Comments on Cherwell paper, 17 Apr 1942.

199. CCO, Portal papers, Folder 9/File 3, Harris to Portal, 5 Mar 1942.

200. RAFM, Harris papers, H47, Harris to Bottomley, 9 Apr 1942.

201. Olaf Groehler, *Bombenkrieg gegen Deutschland* (Berlin: 1990), 98.

202. BA-B, R1501/823, directive from Interior Minister, 6 May 1942, 1. Details of raids from Middlebrook, Everitt, *Bomber Command War Diaries*, 246–52, 259–61; Groehler, *Bombenkrieg*, 50–54.

203. RAFM, Harris papers, H53, Baker to Harris, 21 Mar 1942; Baker to Harris, 9 Apr 1942; TNA, AIR 20/4768, note from Bufton for Baker, 6 Apr 1942; Harris to Baker, 11 Apr 1942.

204. CCAC, BUFT 3/12. Bufton to Harris, 8 May 1942; TNA, AIR 14/1779, chart of attacks on Essen, Duisburg and Düsseldorf.

205. TNA, PREM/3/11/4, Cherwell to Churchill, 30 Mar 1942; Sinclair to Churchill, 6 Apr 1942; Hollis (CoS Committee Minutes) to Churchill, 10 Apr 1942; AIR 9/187, CoS, 13 Apr 1942.

206. Webster, Frankland, *Strategic Air Offensive*, vol 4, 231–8, 'Report by Mr Justice Singleton, 20 May 1942'; TNA, PREM 3/11/4, Singleton to Churchill, 20 May 1942.

207. Ibid., PREM 3/11/4, Cherwell to Churchill, 28 May 1942.

208. CCO, Portal papers, Folder 9/File 3, Cherwell to Portal, 27 Feb 1942; Harris to Portal, 2 Mar 1942; Melinsky, *Forming the Pathfinders*, 68–9.

209. CCAC, BUFT 3/12, 'Tactical Direction of the Bomber Force', 16 May 1942, 1.

210. Ibid., 3/12, Bufton to all squadron and station commanders, Mar 1942; H. Graham to Morley (BOps 1), 1 Apr 1942.

211. Melinsky, *Forming the Pathfinders*, 72–8; Furse, *Wilfrid Freeman*, 205–8; Middlebrook, Everitt, *Bomber Command War Diaries*, 297–8, 301.

212. CCAC, BUFT 3/12, minute by the assistant CoS (operations), 2 Aug 1942.

213. TNA, AIR 14/276, Portal to Harris, 19 May 1942; Harris to Coastal Command, Flying Training and Army Co-Operation, 20 May 1942; Harris to Philip Joubert de la Ferté (CC), 23 May 1942; Bomber Command Operational Order, no 147, 23 May 1942.

214. BA-B, NS 18/1058, report, Leiter IV, Party Chancellery, 31 May 1942; Groehler, *Bombenkrieg*, 65–6.

215. Ibid., 66–7.

216. Details from Middlebrook, Everitt, *Bomber Command War Diaries*, 274, 280–81; Groehler, *Bombenkrieg*, 69.

217. Greenhous et al., *Crucible of War*, 621–2.

218. CCO, Portal papers, Folder 3/File 3, Smuts to Churchill, 30 June 1942; draft telegram Churchill to Smuts, 4 July 1942, rejecting the proposal.

219. RAFM, Harris papers, H11, memorandum for the prime minister, 17 June 1942 (revised 20 Aug); TNA, PREM 3/19, Harris to Churchill, 17 June 1942.

220. RAFM, Harris papers, H63, App A, 'Approximate Allocation of Air Resources, June 15 1942'; TNA, PREM 3/19, Churchill minute to Harris, 6 July 1942; Air Ministry to Cabinet Office, 12 Aug 1942; CCO, Portal papers, Folder 9/File 3, Harris to Portal, 20 Aug 1942. Out of 42 squadrons on establishment, Harris reckoned that 6 were on loan, 6 were re-equipping or forming, 4 were operationally limited (Polish squadrons 'almost useless') and 5 others were unavailable.

221. Parton, *'Air Force Spoken Here'*, 166–7.

222. LC, Spaatz papers, Box 76, Eaker to Spaatz, 27 Aug 1942, 'Accuracy of Bombardment', 2, 4.

223. FDRL, Map Room Files, Box 12, telegram from Harriman to Roosevelt, 14 Aug 1942.

224. TNA, AIR 8/435, Churchill to Sinclair and Portal, 17 Aug 1942; Portal to Churchill, 20 Aug 1942; Harris to Portal, 29 Aug 1942.

225. TNA, PREM 3/19, Harris to Churchill, 4 Sept 1942; Churchill to Harris, 13 Sept 1942; 'better than doing nothing' in CCO, Portal papers, Folder 3/File 1, Churchill to Sinclair, 13 Mar 1943.

226. TNA, PREM 3/19, Amery to Churchill, 1 Sept 1942.

227. CCAC, BUFT 3/12, L. A. C. Cunningham to Morley (BOps 1), 14 Oct 1942.

228. Royal Society, London, Blackett papers, PB/4/4, minutes of CoS discussion, 18 Nov 1942.

229. CCO, Portal papers, Folder 9/File 3, Harris to Portal, 24 Sept 1942. On the arguments over the size of the Canadian component see Greenhous et al., *Crucible of War*, 599–600.

230. TNA, AIR 14/792, Harris to Balfour, 12 Nov 1942; Bottomley to Harris, 28 Nov 1942.

231. CCO, Portal papers, Folder 9/File 3, Harris to Portal, 21 Oct 1942.

232. TNA, AIR 14/1779, Air Vice Marshal Saundby to Tizard, 2 Dec 1942.

233. CCAC, BUFT 3/15, minute for Baker from Bufton, 2 Nov 1942.

234. TNA, AIR 22/203, War Room Manual of Bomber Command Operations 1939–1945, Chart 4, Chart 9.

235. UEA, Zuckerman Archive, OEMU/50/2, REDept, 'The 1000-Bomber Raid on Cologne', 3 Nov 1942.

236. BA-B, NS18/1063, Partei-Kanzlei, Abt. PG, 'Angaben über die Verluste durch Fliegerangriffen', 2 Oct 1942; R3102/10031, Statistisches Reichsamt, 'Die Tätigkeit der feindlichen Luftwaffe über dem Reichsgebiet', 10 Jan 1945; United States Strategic Bombing Survey, 'Overall Report, European War, 30 Sept 1945, 74, 81.

237. TNA, AIR 9/424, note from Churchill for the CoS Committee, 18 Nov 1942.

238. Ibid., War Cabinet, JPS, 'Anglo-US Bombing Policy', 18 Aug 1942.

239. LC, Spaatz papers, Box 66, Directive from Roosevelt to Marshall, 24 Aug 1942; Arnold to Harry Hopkins, 3 Sept 1942, memorandum, 'Plans for Operations against the Enemy', 2.

240. Davis, *Carl A. Spaatz*, 113–16.

241. TNA, AIR 40/1814, MEW to Sinclair, 2 May 1942; see too Balfour, *Wings over Westminster*, 103, who wrote that the division he found between service officers and civil servants in the Air Ministry resulted in 'processes of administration and decision [that] were cumbersome and slow'.

242. CCAC, BUFT 3/12, memorandum by Wing Cdr. A. Morley, 'The Tactical Direction of the Bomber Force', 20 May 1942, 2.

243. Ibid., 3/15, memorandum for DBOps from Bufton, 6 Sept 1942.

6. THE COMBINED BOMBER OFFENSIVE:
GERMANY 1943–5

1. TNA, AIR 75/11, Slessor papers, pencil notes, 'Conduct of the War in 1943'.

2. Ibid., AIR 75/11, draft by Slessor, 'The Bomber Offensive from the United Kingdom: Note by the British Chiefs of Staff', 20 Jan 1943; draft, 'Casablanca

Directive', 21 Jan 1943; John Slessor, *The Central Blue: Recollections and Reflections* (London: 1956), 445–6.

3. LC, Arnold papers, Reel 200, Arnold to Gen. Wedemeyer, 30 Dec 1942.
4. RAFM, Harris papers, H28, Arthur Sulzberger, *The New York Times*, to Harris, 21 Sept 1942; Harris to Francis Drake, 1 Jan 1943; Robert Lovett to Harris, 24 Nov 1942; Harris to Lovett, 24 Dec 1942; H51, Richard Peck (Air Ministry) to Harris, 22 Dec 1942; Telegram from air attaché, Washington, DC, to Air Ministry, 11 Jan 1943.
5. UEA, Zuckerman Archive, SZ/BBSU/29, Air Commodore Pelly to Zuckerman, 14 Jan 1946.
6. TNA, PREM 3/14/2, cypher telegram, Churchill to the Air Ministry, 17 Aug 1942; Portal to Churchill, 20 Aug 1942; Stalin to Churchill, 19 Jan 1943. For Harris's views AIR 8/435, Portal and Sinclair to Churchill, 18 Aug 1942; Harris to Portal, 29 Aug 1942.
7. Ibid., AIR 8/435, Stalin to Churchill, 3 Mar 1943; CCO, Portal papers, Folder 3/File 3, Churchill to Portal, 10 Sept 1942; Churchill to Stalin, 11 Sept 1942.
8. Ibid., Portal papers, Folder 3/File 3, Churchill, 'Note on Air Policy', 22 Oct 1942; Folder 3/File 4, Churchill to Portal, 26 Oct 1942; Portal to Churchill, 7 Nov 1942; LC, Eaker papers, Box I.20, Spaatz to Eaker, 9 Dec 1942; Eaker to Spaatz, 29 Jan 1943.
9. LC, Arnold papers, Reel 200, Arnold to Gen. Stratemeyer, 26 Feb 1943.
10. Slessor, *Central Blue*, 438–9; TNA, AIR 75/11, draft, 'Future Strategy', 25 Sept 1942; draft for the CoS, 'Anglo-American Bomber Offensive against Italy and Germany in 1943'.
11. LC, Spaatz papers, Box 66, Arnold to Harry Hopkins, 3 Sept 1942, encl. memorandum, 'Plans for Operations against the Enemy'.
12. Ibid., Box 66, AWPD-42, 'Requirements of Air Ascendancy', 6–7.
13. FDRL, Map Room papers, Box 165, Folder 6, JCS minutes of meetings, 13 Jan and 14 Jan 1943; LC, Arnold papers, Reel 200, JCS, minutes of meetings, 14 Jan 1943, 11–12.
14. CCO, Portal papers, Folder 3/File 4, Churchill to Harry Hopkins, 14 Oct 1942; 'Note on Air Policy', 22 Oct 1942; Churchill to Portal, Sinclair and Harris, 26 Oct 1942.
15. TNA, PREM 3/19, Churchill to Harris, 18 Sept 1942; AIR 9/424, Air Staff minute, 10 Oct 1942.
16. CCO, Portal papers, Folder 3/File 4, Sinclair to Churchill, 23 Oct 1942; Portal to Churchill, 28 Oct 1942; Portal to Churchill, 7 Nov 1942; Tami Davis Biddle, 'British and American Approaches to Strategic Bombing: Their Origins and Implementation in the World War II Bomber Offensive', in John Gooch (ed), *Airpower: Theory and Practice* (London: 1995), 119–20.
17. LC, Spaatz papers, Box 97, 'Casablanca Notes', 15 Jan 1943; John W. Huston (ed), *American Airpower Comes of Age: General Henry H. 'Hap' Arnold's World War II Diaries*, 2 vols (Maxwell, AL: 2002), vol 1, 462; AFHRA, CD A5835, 'Eighth Air Force: Growth, Development and Operations', Air Force

Plans, exhibit 3, 'The Case for Day Bombing'; James Parton, *Air Force Spoken Here': General Ira Eaker and the Command of the Air* (Bethesda, MD: 1986), 217–20; Tami Davis Biddle, *Rhetoric and Reality in Air Warfare: The Evolution of British and American Ideas about Strategic Bombing, 1914–1945* (Princeton, NJ: 2002), 214–15.

18. LC, Spaatz papers, Box 97, 'Casablanca Notes', 17 and 19 Jan 1943; FDRL, Map Room Files, Box 165, Folder 7, ANFA Meeting minutes, 18 Jan 1943.

19. Parton, *'Air Force Spoken Here'*, 221. The sentence ran 'It keeps German defenses alerted around the clock, 24 hours of the day.'

20. LC, Spaatz papers, Box 97, 'Casablanca Notes', 18 and 20 Jan 1943; Henry H. Arnold, *Global Mission* (New York: 1949), 395–7; Parton, *'Air Force Spoken Here'*, 221–2.

21. TNA, AIR 8/1076, Churchill to Attlee, 21 Jan 1943.

22. Charles Webster, Noble Frankland, *The Strategic Air Offensive Against Germany*, 4 vols (London: 1961), vol 4, 153–4, 'Combined Chiefs of Staff Directive for the Bomber Offensive from the United Kingdom'.

23. LC, Spaatz papers, Box 97, 'Casablanca Notes', 25 Jan to 31 Jan 1943; TNA, AIR 8/425, Bottomley to Harris, 4 Feb 1943.

24. Slessor, *Central Blue*, 448.

25. TNA, AIR 9/424, Note by Director of Plans, 24 Aug 1942; Joint Planning Staff, 'Anglo-U.S. Bombing Policy', 18 Aug 1942.

26. LC, Spaatz papers, Box 66, Report on AWPD-42, 19 Sept 1942.

27. CCO, Portal papers, Folder 4/File 1, Arnold to Portal, 10 Dec 1942; Portal to Churchill, 20 Dec 1942.

28. LC, Eaker papers, Box I.20, Eaker to Portal, 30 Aug 1943.

29. Ibid., Spaatz papers, Box 67, 'Status of the Combined Bomber Offensive from U.K.', 7 Aug 1943, 1.

30. TNA, AIR 14/739A, Harris to Eaker, 15 Apr 1943.

31. Ibid., Harris to Portal, 9 Apr 1943, encl. 'The United States Contribution to the Bomber Offensive in 1943', 2.

32. Ibid., War Cabinet, CoS, 'An Estimate of the Effects of an Anglo-American Bomber Offensive against Germany', 3 Nov 1942.

33. TNA, FO 837/1315, 'Bombers' Baedeker: Guide to the Economic Importance of German Towns and Cities', Jan 1943 edition.

34. RAFM, Harris papers, Misc. Box A, Folder 4, 'One Hundred Towns of Leading Economic Importance to the German War Effort'.

35. LC, Eaker papers, Box I.20, Portal to Eaker, 28 Feb 1943.

36. TNA, AIR 14/1779, minutes of meeting in the Air Ministry, 1 Mar 1943, 2.

37. LC, Spaatz papers, Box 67, Eaker to Spaatz, 13 Apr 1943, encl. Air War Plans memorandum, 'The Combined Bomber Offensive from the United Kingdom'.

38. Ibid., Box 67, 'Status of Combined Bomber Offensive', 7 Aug 1943, 1.

39. Ibid., Box 67, memorandum from Arnold to Spaatz, 'Report of the Committee of Operations Analysts with Respect to Economic Targets within the Western Axis', 8 Mar 1943.

40. LC, Eaker papers, Box I.20, Eaker to Portal, 2 Apr 1943; TNA, AIR 8/1103, Arnold to Portal, 24 Mar 1943; Portal to Eaker, 9 Apr 1943; Parton, 'Air Force Spoken Here', 250–53.

41. CCAC, BUFT, 3/42, Bufton to Portal, 8 Apr 1943; 'The Bombing Offensive from the U. K.', and covering note from RAF liaison at Eaker's HQ; Stephen McFarland, Wesley Newton, To Command the Sky: The Battle for Air Supremacy over Germany, 1942–1944 (Washington, DC: 1991), 92–4.

42. TNA, AIR 8/1103, Harris to Eaker, 15 Apr 1943. Air Ministry views on German fighters, AIR 9/423, memorandum, Director of Plans, 22 Mar 1943.

43. LC, Eaker papers, Box I.16, Col. C. Cabell to Eaker, 27 May 1943; Box I.20, Eaker to Portal, 1 June 1943.

44. Ibid., Eaker papers, Box I.16, Kuter to Eaker, 6 July 1943; Eaker to Kuter, 22 July 1943; TNA, AIR 8/1103, CCS meeting, 4 June 1943; minute, Bottomley to Portal, 10 June 1943. Webster, Frankland, Strategic Air Offensive, vol 4, 160, Bottomley to Harris, 3 Sept 1943.

45. LC, Eaker papers, Box I.19, Lovett to Eaker, 28 July 1943.

46. CCO, Portal papers, Folder 3/File 4, Portal to Churchill, 9 Nov 1942.

47. TNA, AIR 20/2025, Air Ministry statistics, RAF personnel, establishment and casualties, 1939–45.

48. RAFM, Harris papers, H67, 'Establishment and Strength of Ancillary Staff, 31 July 1943'.

49. UEA, Zuckerman Archive, SZ/BBSU/3, Exercise Thunderbolt, précis no. 10, 'Administrative Aspects of the Bomber Offensive'; SZ/BBSU/2, minute for Zuckerman from Claude Pelly, 21 June 1946; LC, Eaker papers, Box I.20, Harris to Balfour, 12 Jan 1943, on the transition from grass to concrete runways.

50. Ibid., Eaker to Harris, 4 Jan 1943; Box I.21, Eighth Air Force memorandum, 'Supply and Maintenance' [n.d.]; 'Report of Lt. General Ira Eaker on USAAF Activities in the United Kingdom', 31 Dec 1943, 3. Brereton Greenhouse, Stephen Harris, William Johnston and William Rawling, The Crucible of War 1939–1945: The Official History of the Royal Canadian Air Force, vol III (Toronto: 1994), 616, 631, 636.

51. PArch, Balfour papers, BAL/4, RCAF Station, Trenton, 'The British Commonwealth Air Training Plan 1939–1945', Ottawa 1949, 3–8.

52. Gilbert Guinn, The Arnold Scheme: British Pilots, the American South and the Allies' Daring Plan (Charleston, SC: 2007), 484, 541.

53. John Herington, Air War Against Germany and Italy 1939–1945 (Canberra: 1954), 450–51, 452, 454, 547–51.

54. Greenhous et al., Crucible of War, 616, 627–9, 634–5.

55. LC, Eaker papers, Box I.21, 'Report of Lt. General Ira Eaker', 1; Donald Miller, Eighth Air Force: The American Bomber Crews in Britain (London: 2007), 71–2.

56. AFHRA, Disc A5835, 'Eighth Air Force: Growth, Development and Operations 1 December 1942–31 December 1943', Air Force Supply and Maintenance, chart of Serviceability B-17s, B-24s.

57. LC, Eaker papers, Box I.20, Eighth Air Force, 'Supply and Maintenance' [n.d]; 'Report of Lt. General Ira Eaker', 7.

58. LC, Arnold papers, Reel 89, Spaatz to Arnold, 28 May 1943, encl. 'Organization of the Eighth Air Force' by Follett Bradley; 'The Bradley Plan for the United Kingdom' [n.d.], charts i, iv; Summary of Personnel Requirements for the VIII Air Force Service Command; Gen. Barney Giles to Eaker, 26 Aug 1943; Parton, 'Air Force Spoken Here', 289.

59. LC, Eaker papers, Box I.19, Lovett to Arnold, 19 June 1943.

60. Ibid., Box I.17, Arnold to Eaker, 10 June 1943; Eaker to Arnold, 12 June 1943.

61. Ibid., Box I.17, Arnold to Gen. Devers, 29 June 1943.

62. Ibid., Box I.16, Eaker to Col. Edgar Sorensen, Washington, DC, 11 Jan 1943.

63. LC, Spaatz papers, Box 143, Hansell to Eaker and Longfellow, 26 Feb 1943, 4–5.

64. AFHRA, 520.056-188, Eighth Air Force Statistical Summary, Aircraft Loss Rate. In January the figure was 7.5%, in February, 8.1%, in March 3.2% and in April 7.8%.

65. LC, Eaker papers, Box I.16, Brig. Gen. J. Bevans (Assistant Chief of Staff, Personnel) to Eaker, 1 May 1943; Eaker to Arnold, 22 June 1943.

66. Miller, Eighth Air Force, 221.

67. LC, Spaatz papers, Box 70, Brig. Gen. C. Chauncey to all Eighth Air Force commanders, 18 Dec 1942.

68. Ibid., HQ Eighth Air Force, Provost Marshal's 'Report on Conduct of Troops with Regard to the British', 1, 3–4.

69. Ibid., Eighth Air Force, 'Anglo-American Relations', 20 Sept 1943.

70. NC, Cherwell papers, G195, letter from MAP to War Cabinet, 12 Dec 1942; R. Ewell (Office of Scientific Research and Development) to Cherwell, 12 Dec 1942.

71. LC, Eaker papers, Box I.19, Lovett to Arnold, 19 June 1943: 'The B-17 and B-24 are still useful types but their effectiveness will be reduced sharply by the end of the year.'

72. Ibid., Box I.17, Telegram from Arnold to Eaker, 10 June 1943.

73. Ibid., Telegram from Eaker to Arnold, 12 June 1943.

74. LC, Spaatz papers, Box 316, Gen. Anderson's Diary, 1943–5, entries for 22 Feb, 15 Mar, 1 May, 29 May.

75. LC, Eaker papers, Box I.17, Eaker to Arnold, 29 June 1943. Parton, 'Air Force Spoken Here', 271–8, for a full account of the acrimonious exchange.

76. LC, Eaker papers, Box I.17, Arnold to Eaker, 29 June 1943.

77. TNA, AIR 20/283, Bomber Command Operations, Feb–Nov 1943, 2 Jan 1944.

78. Greenhous et al., Crucible of War, 658–60; Randall Wakelam, The Science of Bombing: Operational Research in RAF Bomber Command (Toronto: 2009), 119–21, 139.

79. RAFM, Saundby papers, AC 72/12, Box 7, Signals Branch, HQ Bomber Command, 'War in the Ether: Europe 1939–1945', Oct 1945, 14–16.

'Boozer' was unable to detect enemy AI radar at more than 1,500 yards, while 'Monica' and 'Boozer' interfered with each other when used together.

80. RAFM, Harris papers, H55, speech to the 21st Army Group HQ, 14 May 1945; TNA, AIR 20/283, Bomber Command Operations; CCO, Portal papers, Folder 5, 'Comparison of Bombing Effort during the Year 1943', 10 Feb 1944.
81. Greenhous et al., *Crucible of War*, 657–67, for a lucid account of the Ruhr operations.
82. Ralf Blank, 'The Battle of the Ruhr, 1943: Aerial Warfare against an Industrial Region', *Labour History Review*, 77 (2012), 35–48.
83. Nikolaus von Below, *At Hitler's Side: The Memoirs of Hitler's Luftwaffe Adjutant 1937–1945* (London: 2001), 169–70.
84. Willi Boelcke (ed), *The Secret Conferences of Dr Goebbels, 1939–1943* (London: 1967), 388–9.
85. Heinz Boberach (ed), *Meldungen aus dem Reich: Die geheimen Lageberichte des Sicherheitsdienstes der SS 1938–1945*, 17 vols (Herrsching: 1984), vol xiii, 4,983, 5,021, reports for 22 Mar, 29 Mar 1943.
86. Edward Westermann, *Flak: German Anti-Aircraft Defenses, 1914–1945* (Lawrence, KS: 2001), 200–202.
87. Ibid., 201–2; Greenhous et al., *Crucible of War*, 662–3.
88. John A. MacBean, Arthur S. Hogben, *Bombs Gone: The Development and Use of British Air-Dropped Weapons from 1912 to the Present Day* (Wellingborough: 1990), 158–61.
89. TNA, AIR 14/840, minute for the C-in-C by Saundby, 14 Feb 1943.
90. Ibid., Harris minute, 15 Apr 1943.
91. MacBean, Hogben, *Bombs Gone*, 164–9; Martin Middlebrook, Chris Everitt *The Bomber Command War Diaries* (Leicester: 2000), 386–8; Olaf Groehler, *Bombenkrieg gegen Deutschland* (Berlin: 1990), 154–6.
92. UEA, Zuckerman Archive, SZ/AEAF/14, Bomber Command, ORS, 'The Operational Use of Oboe Mark 1A, December 1942–June 1943', 3–4.
93. TNA, AIR 20/283, HQ Bomber Command, ORS Report, 27 May 1943; original evasion instructions in AIR 14/206, Tactical Committee paper 31, revised Feb 1943.
94. TNA, AIR 48/29, USSBS Civilian Defense Division: Final Report, 26 Oct 1945, 3; Hitler's comment in von Below, *At Hitler's Side*, 172.
95. TNA, AIR 8/1109, JIC, 'Effects of Bombing Offensive on German War Effort', 22 July 1943.
96. TNA, AIR 20/476, Air Ministry DoI, 'Effects of Air Raids on Labour and Production', 16 Aug 1943, 1–2; O. Lawrence (MEW) to Morley (BOps 1), 6 Sept 1943; note from Lawrence to Bufton, 24 Oct 1943.
97. CCAC, BUFT 3/42, Gen. Frank Andrews (US Supreme Commander in United Kingdom) to Gen. Marshall and Gen. Arnold, 3 Apr 1943.
98. Roger A. Freeman, *The Mighty Eighth War Diary* (London: 1981), 42–73.
99. TNA, AIR 8/1109, JIC, 'Effects of Bombing Offensive', 1; AIR 9/423, Director of Plans minute, 15 Mar 1943.

100. CCAC, BUFT 3/24, BOps 1 to Group Captain Barnett, 1 Nov 1941; Draft App B [n.d. but late Oct 1941].

101. TNA, AIR 20/4768, BOps memorandum, 25 Feb 1942.

102. UEA, Zuckerman Archive, SZ/OEMU/50/7, 'Note for Advisers' Meeting', 12 Aug 1942.

103. Ibid., 9th Meeting of RE8 Advisory Group, 16 Sept 1942; 10th Meeting of RE8 Advisory Group, 24 Sept 1942; 15th Meeting of RE8 Advisory Group, 29 Oct 1942.

104. Ibid., OEMU/50/8, RE8 Report, 'German Domestic Architecture', 7 Apr 1943, 1–2.

105. CCAC, BUFT 3/26, Minutes of meeting at the Ministry of Works, 9 Oct 1941; R. Ewell (Petroleum Warfare Section) to D. A. C. Dewdney, 22 Dec 1942.

106. CCAC, BUFT 3/24, BOps 1, draft report, 'Incendiary Attack', 8 Nov 1941; BOps 1 to Peirse [n.d. but Nov 1941]; Report for DDBOps, 'Types and Weights of German Incendiary Bombs', 11 Oct 1941.

107. Ibid., BUFT 3/26, DBOps, note on an article in *Die Sirene*, 2 Oct 1942 (the article in the German civil defence journal explained how to fight fires even with the threat of anti-personnel bombs).

108. Ibid., BUFT 3/26, DBOps to Director of Research, Air Ministry [n.d. but late Oct 1942]. Some 40 per cent of explosive incendiaries had 3-minute delay, 5 per cent from 6–10 minutes.

109. Ibid, BUFT, 3/27, BOps 1, 'Present and Future Incendiary Technique as Applied to Area Attack', 13 Oct 1942, 1, 2–4.

110. LC, Spaatz papers, Box 80, Bufton memorandum, 'Incendiary Attack of German Cities', Jan 1943, 3.

111. Armaments Design Establishment, Ministry of Supply, 'The Development of British Incendiary Bombs during the Period of the 1939–1945 World War', Dec 1946, 34–7.

112. CCAC, BUFT 3/28, NFPA, 'Conflagrations in America since 1914', Boston, 1942; NFPA, 'National Defense Fires', Mar 1942.

113. CCAC, BUFT 3/26, R. Ewell to Wing Commander A. Morley (BOps 1), 3 Dec 1942, encl. Laiming to R. Russell (Standard Oil Development Co.), 29 Oct 1942, 3.

114. UEA, Zuckerman Archive, SZ/OEMU/50/8, RE8 Report, 'German Domestic Architecture', 1; LC, Arnold papers, Reel 199, Maj. Gen. O. Echols to Arnold, 28 Apr 1943.

115. James McElroy, 'The Work of the Fire Protection Engineers in Planning Fire Attacks', in *Fire and the Air War: A Symposium of Expert Observations* (Boston, MA: 1946), 122–30.

116. LC, Arnold papers, Reel 199, Arnold to Maj. Gen. Echols, 26 Apr 1943.

117. NARA, RG 107, Lovett papers, Box 9, Joint Magnesium Committee Report, 1 June 1942, 2, 12.

118. LC, Spaatz papers, Box 76, HQ Eighth Air Force, A-5 Division memorandum, 'Theory and Tactics of Incendiary Bombing', including Table II, 'Incendiary Bombing Data for German Cities'.

119. AFHRA, 520.805, Eighth Air Force Chemical Section History, 1–4; Report for May 1945, 2.

120. TNA, AIR 40/1271, Target Committee, Report of 87th Meeting, 9 Apr 1943.

121. TNA, AIR 48/33, USSBS, Hamburg Field Report no. 1, 2. There were 78 in 1940, 38 in 1941, 10 in 1942. On 1943 see BA-B, R3102/10046, 'Zerstörung von Wohnraum in deutschen Städten, 1942–43'.

122. TNA, FO 837/1315, 'Bomber's Baedeker', Jan 1943, 131–7.

123. TNA, AIR 14/1779, Report for Dickens and Tizard from RE8, 'Apparent Relative Effectiveness of I.B. and H.E. Attack against German Towns', 7 Jan 1943.

124. RAFM, Saundby papers, AC 72/12, Box 7, 'War in the Ether: Europe 1939–1945', Oct 1945, 33–6.

125. Details in Alfred Price, *Instruments of Darkness: The History of Electronic Warfare, 1939–1945* (London: 2005), 124–33, 153–4.

126. TNA, PREM 3/11/8, Tizard memorandum for Churchill, 22 July 1943; Churchill to Ismay, 23 July 1943; Portal to Sinclair, 24 July 1943; Churchill, note for Ismay, 30 July 1943.

127. For an excellent account of the operations see Keith Lowe, *Inferno: The Devastation of Hamburg 1943* (London: 2007), Pt 2.

128. Westermann, *Flak*, 213–14.

129. Groehler, *Bombenkrieg*, 112.

130. Ibid., 112–13; Westermann, *Flak*, 214–15; Freeman, *The Mighty Eighth*, 78–9.

131. Horatio Bond, 'The Fire Attacks on German Cities', in *Fire and the Air War*, 95–7; Hans Brunswig, *Feuersturm über Hamburg: Die Luftangriffe auf Hamburg im 2. Weltkrieg und ihre Folgen* (Stuttgart: 1985), 269–71.

132. TNA, AIR 20/7287, Home Office, Jan 1946, 'Secret Report by the Police President of Hamburg on the Heavy Raids on Hamburg, 1 Dec 1943', 21–2; Groehler, *Bombenkrieg*, 113–14. Even escape into Hamburg's waterways proved fatal as people plunged into near-boiling water.

133. Civil Defense Liaison Office, *Fire Effects of Bombing Attacks*, prepared for the National Security Resources Board, Nov 1950, 8–9; Horatio Bond, 'Fire Casualties of the German Attacks', in *Fire and the Air War*, 113–18.

134. Groehler, *Bombenkrieg*, 119; TNA, AIR 20/7287, 'Secret Report of the Police President of Hamburg', 17; Brunswig, *Feuersturm über Hamburg*, 278–9; Ursula Büttner, '"Gomorrha" und die Folgen', in Hamburg Forschungsstelle für Zeitgeschichte, *Hamburg im 'Dritten Reich'* (Göttingen: 2005), 618, 764.

135. TNA, AIR 40/425, Immediate Interpretation Report, 27 July 1943.

136. IWM, MD, vol 63, 'Besprechung beim Reichsmarschall, 13 July 1943.

137. BA-MA, RL3/213, Flugzeug-Programme, Studie 1013, 16 Dec 1943.

138. IWM, MD, vol 63, 'Niederschrift der Besprechung des Reichsmarschall mit Industrierat', 14 Oct 1943.

139. Ibid., vol 52, minute on radar, 7 May 1943; Göring decree, 'Verantwort-lichkeit und Durchführung des Funkmess- und Funknavigationsprogramms', 2 May 1943; Price, *Instruments of Darkness*, 136–9, 150.

140. BA-MA, R22 IV/101, Vorstudien zur Luftkriegsgeschichte, Heft 8: Reichs-luftverteidigung: Teil B, Flakabwehr, 28–30; Westermann, *Flak*, 216–19. See Ludger Tewes, *Jugend im Krieg: von Luftwaffenhelfern und Soldaten 1939–1945* (Essen: 1989), 37–50.

141. TNA, AIR 20/4761, DoI to Bufton, 21 Aug 1943.

142. LC, Eaker papers, Box I.19, Lovett to Eaker, 28 July 1943; Eaker to Lovett, 9 Aug 1943.

143. TNA, AIR 8/1109, Harris to Portal, 12 Aug 1943.

144. TNA, AIR 14/1779, Bomber Command, ORS, Survey of Damage to Cities, 29 Nov 1943.

145. TNA, AIR 14/739A, HQ Bomber Command, Intelligence Staff, 'Progress of RAF Bomber Offensive Against Germany', 30 Nov 1943, 1–2.

146. TNA, AIR 20/4761, O. Lawrence (MEW) to Morley, 6 Sept 1943; Law-rence to Bufton, 24 Oct 1943.

147. TNA, FO 837/26, 'Note from Economic Intelligence', 17 Sept 1943; 'Notes on Economic Intelligence', MEW meeting, 1 Oct 1943.

148. LC, Spaatz papers, Box 203, J. K. Galbraith, 'Preliminary Appraisal of Achievement of Strategic Bombing of Germany' [n.d.], 6.

149. FHA, Foley papers, MSS 448 3/2, *Daily Telegraph* article, 6 Aug 1943.

150. Ibid., Thomas Foley to Kingsley Martin (editor *New Statesman*), 3 Nov 1943; 'What Happened in Hamburg', leaflet reprint of article in *Baseler Nachrichten*; 2/2, Corder Catchpool (Bombing Restriction Committee) to Foley, 8 Jan 1943; Bombing Restriction Committee leaflet, 'Bomb, Burn and Ruthlessly Destroy' [n.d. but late 1943], 2.

151. LC, Eaker papers, Box I.19, Lovett to Eaker, 1 July 1943.

152. LC, Spaatz papers, Box 67, 'Status of Combined Bomber Offensive from U.K.', 8 Aug 1943, 4.

153. TNA, AIR 8/1109, Telegram Harris to Portal, 12 Aug 1943.

154. TNA, AIR 8/435, Telegram Portal to VCAS, 19 Aug 1943; VCAS to Por-tal, 21 Aug 1943.

155. LC, Spaatz papers, Box 67, USSTAF DoI, 'An Evaluation of the Effects of the Bomber Offensive on "Overlord" and "Dragoon"', 5 Sept 1944, 1.

156. TNA, AIR 14/783, Portal to Harris, 7 Oct 1943, encl. 'Effort (Planned and Effected) USAF 8th Bomber Command'.

157. TNA, AIR 14/739A, 'Conduct of the Strategic Bomber Offensive before Preparatory Stage of "Overlord"', 17 Jan 1944; LC, Spaatz papers, Box 143, Arnold to Spaatz, 24 Apr 1944.

158. TNA, AIR 8/1167, 'Report by Chief of Air Staff and Commanding General US Eighth Air Force', 7 Nov 1943, 3–4.

159. LC, Eaker papers, Box I.20, HQ Bomber Command, 'Outline of Future Intentions for the Continuation and Intensification of the Bomber Offen-sive', 4 Nov 1943.

160. TNA, AIR 8/425, Harris to Portal and Sinclair, 7 Dec 1943.
161. Details in Groehler, *Bombenkrieg*, 131–3; Freeman, *The Mighty Eighth*, 89–91.
162. Groehler, *Bombenkrieg*, 133–4; Friedhelm Golücke, *Schweinfurt und der strategische Luftkrieg 1943* (Paderborn: 1980), 356–7.
163. Ibid., 134; Richard G. Davis, *Bombing the European Axis Powers: A Historical Digest of the Combined Bomber Offensive, 1939–1945* (Maxwell AFB, AL: 2006), 158–61; Parton, 'Air Force Spoken Here', 300–02.
164. Parton, 'Air Force Spoken Here', 316.
165. Freeman, *The Mighty Eighth*, 119; Davis, *Bombing the European Axis Powers*, 176, 182–4.
166. AFHRA, 520.056-188, Statistical Summary, Eighth Air Force Operations, 'Aircraft Loss Rate on Combat Missions'.
167. TNA, AIR 20/283, Bomber Command operational statistics, Feb–Nov 1943, 1 Jan 1944; AIR 20/2025, Strength of Air Force Personnel, Operational Squadrons, 1940–1945.
168. Details from Middlebrook, Everitt, *Bomber Command War Diaries*, 422–8.
169. TNA, AIR 40/345, Air Intelligence 3c, Raid Assessment Summary, 31 Oct 1943.
170. Groehler, *Bombenkrieg*, 144–7.
171. TNA, AIR 20/4761, RE8 report, 'The Economic Effects of Attacks in Force on German Targets, March–December 1943', Table 2.
172. TNA, AIR 22/203, Bomber Command War Room, Total Wastage 1939–1945.
173. LC, Eaker papers, Box I.19, Lovett to Eaker, 19 Sept 1943.
174. TNA, AIR 8/1103, paper prepared for the Chief of Air Staff, 11 Oct 1943, 4.
175. TNA, AIR 14/783, Portal to Harris, 7 Oct 1943, encl. Air Staff memorandum, 'Extent to which the Eighth U.S.A.A.F. and Bomber Command have been able to implement the G.A.F. Plan', 1.
176. RAFM, Harris papers, H47, Bottomley to Harris, 'Special Brief for Schweinfurt Operation', 25 July 1943; Harris to Bottomley, 20 Dec 1943, 3.
177. TNA, AIR 14/739A, Harris to Bottomley, 28 Dec 1943.
178. TNA, AIR 8/425, Bottomley to Harris, 23 Dec 1943; AIR 20/4761, 'Bomber Command's Comments on R.E.8's Paper', 13 Mar 1944.
179. TNA, AIR 48/65, USSBS, Military Analysis Division, Report no. 2, 'Weather Factors in Combat Bombardment Operations in the European Theater', 3 Nov 1945, 1–3, 15, 23.
180. LC, Spaatz papers, Box 143, Col. D. Zimmerman (Director of Weather) to Hansell, 7 Sept 1942, 2.
181. Ibid., Box 173, Report by AAF Scientific Advisory Group, 'War and Weather', May 1946, 4–6.
182. LC, LeMay papers, Box 8, 305th Bomb Group: Summary of Events, 1 Nov 1942 to 31 Dec 1943.
183. CCAC, BUFT 3/50, 'Area Attack Employing "Gee"' [n.d. but early 1942], 1.

184. Ibid., 3/51, Harris to Portal, 12 Dec 1944.

185. Transcript of interview with Maurice Chick, Nov 1995, 49–50.

186. LC, Spaatz papers, Box 76, Col. William Garland to Anderson, 28 Feb 1943; Anderson to all Wing Commanders, 11 Sept 1943, encl. ORS Report, 'Effect of Spacing between Combat Wings on Bombing Accuracy', 11 Sept 1943, 2.

187. LC, Spaatz papers, Box 76, Anderson to LeMay, 8 Sept 1943.

188. LC, Eaker papers, Box I.20, Eaker to Portal, 15 Mar 1943; Eaker to Gen. Larry Kuter, 20 Sept 1943.

189. Davis, *Bombing the European Axis Powers*, 176–8; Freeman, *The Mighty Eighth*, 118–19; W. Hays Park, '"Precision" and "Area" Bombing: Who Did Which, and When?', *Journal of Strategic Studies*, 18 (1995), 149–57.

190. LC, Spaatz papers, Box 80, Hugh Odishaw (MIT), 'Radar Bombing in the Eighth Air Force', July 1946, 88–9.

191. Ibid., Eighth Air Force ORS to Doolittle, 13 June 1944, encl. 'Bombing Accuracy'; Hays Park, '"Precision" and "Area" Bombing', 154–6.

192. LC, Spaatz papers, Box 80, Odishaw, 'Radar Bombing in the Eighth Air Force', 106.

193. TNA, AIR 20/283, Bomber Command Operations, Feb 1943 to Nov 1943.

194. UEA, Zuckerman Archive, SZ/AEAF/14, Bomber Command ORS, 'The Operational Use of Oboe Mark IA: December 1942–June 1943'; 'The H2S Blind-Bombing Attack on Ludwigshafen, 17/18 November 1943', 18 Dec 1943; ORS, 'Accuracy of H2S as a Blind-Bombing Device', 16 Dec 1943. See too Wakelam, *The Science of Bombing*, 119–21, 158.

195. TNA, AIR 48/67, USSBS Military Analysis Division Report no. 4, 3 Nov 1945, 3–4 and Exhibit B, 'Sample Field Order from Bomber Command'.

196. LC, Eaker papers, Box I.21, 'Target Selection Principles Developed by the Eighth Air Force' [n.d. but late 1943?], 1–5.

197. Mark Guglielmo, 'The Contribution of Economists to Military Intelligence During World War II', *Journal of Economic History*, 68 (2008), 132–4; Barry Katz, *Foreign Intelligence: Research and Analysis in the Office of Strategic Services, 1942–1945* (Cambridge, MA: 1989), 114–18; Walter W. Rostow, *Pre-Invasion Bombing Strategy: General Eisenhower's Decision of March 25, 1944* (Aldershot: 1981), 16–21.

198. LC, Spaatz papers, Box 143, Col. R. Garrison (Adjutant General's office), 'Procedure Followed in Planning an Operation', 9 July 1943, 1–8, and Annex I, 'Procedure in Planning an Operation: Duties and Responsibilities', 1–5.

199. LC, LeMay papers, Box 4, HQ 1st Bombardment Wing, 'Operational Procedure', 12 Oct 1942; HQ 1st Bombardment Wing, 'Tactics and Techniques of Bombardment' [n.d.].

200. Freeman, *The Mighty Eighth*, 93–4, report by Lt. Col. Beirne Lay; other quotations from interviews with Harold Nash, 3 Nov 1995, 20; Peter Hinchcliffe, 24 Oct 1995, 15; Barney D'Ath-Weston, 22.

201. AFHRA, Disc A5385, 'Growth, Development and Operations': Motion Picture Attendance, 1 Dec 1942–30 Nov 1943; Stage Show Attendance.

202. Ibid., Eighth Air Force: Combat Crew Casualties; Mark Wells, *Courage and Air Warfare: The Allied Aircrew Experience in the Second World War* (London: 1995), 31–2.

203. NARA, RG 107, Lovett papers, Box 9, Office of the Air Surgeon, Psychological Branch, 'Report on Survey of Aircrew Personnel in the Eighth, Ninth, and Fifteenth Air Forces', Apr 1944, 35.

204. FDRL, President's Secretary's Files, Box 82, memorandum from Roosevelt to Gen. Watson, encl. report from Lt. Col. John Murray on psychiatry in the Army Air Force, 4 Jan 1944, 3–4. See too Miller, *Eighth Air Force*, 128–34.

205. Wells, *Courage and Air Warfare*, 51.

206. LC, Eaker papers, Box I.16, Col. C. Cabell (HQ AAF) to Eaker, 27 May 1943.

207. NARA, RG 107, Box 9, 'Report on Survey of Aircrew Personnel', 82–5, 88; Wells, *Courage and Air Warfare*, 174.

208. Edgar Jones, '"LMF": The Use of Psychiatric Stigma in the Royal Air Force during the Second World War', *The Journal of Military History*, 70 (2006), 440–41, 443–4.

209. TNA, AIR 49/357, E. C. Jewesbury, 'Work and Problems of an RAF Neuropsychiatric Centre', July 1943, 10–11.

210. Ibid., 16–17.

211. Wells, *Courage and Air Warfare*, 204–5; Jones, '"LMF"', 452.

212. LC, Eaker papers, Box I.19, Eaker to Col. George Brownwell (War Dept., Washington, DC), 28 Nov 1943.

213. NARA, RG 107, Box 9, 'Report on Survey of Aircrew Personnel', 58, 86.

214. CCO, Portal papers, Folder 5, 'Comparison of Bombing Effort During the Year 1943', 10 Feb 1944.

215. TNA, AIR/739, A. F. Inglis (AI) to Harris, 13 Dec 1943; Harris to Bottomley, 28 Dec 1943.

216. TNA, PREM 3/193/6A, JIC Report, 'Probabilities of a German Collapse', 9 Sept 1943, encl. 'Annex: Similarities between Germany's Situation in August 1918 and August 1943', 6.

217. TNA, AIR 8/1167, JIC Report, 'Effects of Bombing Offensive on German War Effort', 12 Nov 1943, Annex by PWE and AI, 'Allied Air Attacks and German Morale', 1, 3, 6–8; PREM 3/193/6A, Desmond Morton to Churchill, 21 Jan 1944.

218. LC, Spaatz papers, Box 67, 'Plan for the Completion of the Combined Bomber Offensive', 5 Mar 1944, Annex, 'Prospect for Ending War by Air Attack against German Morale', 1.

219. LC, Arnold papers, Reel 193, 'Germany's War Potential: An Appraisal by the Committee of Historians for the Commanding General of the Army Air Forces', Dec 1943, 1, 2, 20–23.

220. FDRL, Map Room Files, Box 73, OSS Bulletin, 11 Mar 1944, 1. For a general discussion of American opinion see Richard Overy, '"The Weak Link?": The Perception of the German Working Class by RAF Bomber Command,

1940–1945', *Labour History Review*, 77 (2012), 20–21; Katz, *Foreign Intelligence*, 63–70.

221. RAFM, Bottomley papers, AC 71/2/53, Lecture on Bombing, Spring 1944, 7.

222. USAFA, McDonald papers, Box 8, Folder 8, 'Extracts from News Digest, 30 March 1944', Internal Conditions, 'The Air Offensive', 1.

223. LC, Arnold papers, Reel 193, 'Germany's War Potential', 2.

224. LC, Doolittle papers, Box 19, Doolittle to all Eighth Air Force Commanders, 19 Jan 1944, 1.

225. LC, Eaker papers, Box I.19, Lovett to Arnold, 19 Jun 1943, 2.

226. USAFA, Hansell papers, Ser III, Box 1, Folder 2, 'Salient Features of Various Plans: AWPD-1', 3.

227. Stephen McFarland, Wesley Newton, *To Command the Sky: The Battle for Air Superiority over Germany, 1942–1944* (Washington, DC: 1991), 103–4.

228. Details from John F. Guilmartin, 'The Aircraft that Decided World War II: Aeronautical Engineering and Grand Strategy, 1933–1945', 44th Harmon Memorial Lecture (Colorado Springs, CO: 2001), 16–18, 20–23; Richard G. Davis, *Carl A. Spaatz and the Air War in Europe* (Washington, DC: 1993), 361–4.

229. FDRL, President's Secretary's Files, Box 82, Roosevelt to Arnold, 10 Nov 1942; Arnold to Roosevelt, 12 Nov 1942.

230. McFarland, Newton, *To Command the Sky*, 138–40.

231. Freeman, *The Mighty Eighth*, 148, 183–4, 202–3, 206–7.

232. AFHRA, Disc A5835, Eighth Air Force Tactical Development, 1942–1945, 1; McFarland, Newton, *To Command the Sky*, 106, 112.

233. Ibid., 114–15, 145; Davis, *Carl A. Spaatz*, 302; Parton, '*Air Force Spoken Here*', 273–6, 288.

234. David R. Mets, *Master of Airpower: General Carl A. Spaatz* (Novato, CA: 1998), 179–80.

235. Parton, '*Air Force Spoken Here*', 336–9; Mets, *Master of Airpower*, 180–81.

236. LC, Spaatz papers, Box 84, Spaatz to Doolittle, 26 Jan 1944; Box 143, Spaatz to Doolittle, 28 Jan 1944.

237. LC, Doolittle papers, Box 19, Doolittle to Spaatz, 11 Mar 1944; Davis, *Carl A. Spaatz*, 299–300.

238. AFHRA, Disc A1722, Army Air Forces Evaluation Board, Eighth Air Force, 'Tactical Development August 1942–May 1945', 50.

239. Ibid., 50–55; Davis, *Carl A. Spaatz*, 358–63; McFarland, Newton, *To Command the Sky*, 141, 164–6.

240. IWM, MD, vol 61/5139, minutes of GL meeting, 28 Aug 1943.

241. Von Below, *At Hitler's Side*, 176–7.

242. McFarland, Newton, *To Command the Sky*, 118–20; Air Ministry, *The Rise and Fall of the German Air Force 1933–1945* (London: 1983), 239, 297–8.

243. Lt. Gen. Josef Schmid, 'German Dayfighting in the Defense of the Reich 15 Sept 1943 to the End of the War', in David Isby (ed), *Fighting the Bombers: The Luftwaffe's Struggle against the Allied Bomber Offensive* (London: 2003), 133–40; Josef Schmid, 'German Nightfighting from June 1943 to May 1945', in ibid., 88–9, 95–7; Westermann, *Flak*, 235–6.

244. On German intelligence appreciation of Allied operations see TsAMO, f.500, o.957971, d.450, Führungsstab 1c, 'Einzelnachrichten des 1c Dienstes West der Luftwaffe', 29 Apr 1944; f.500, o.957971, d.448, 'Einzelnachrichten des 1c Dienstes West: Britische Nachteinsatz', 6 May 1944; f.500, o.957971, d.433, 'Einzelnachrichten des 1c Dienstes West', 16 June 1944.

245. Price, *Instruments of Darkness*, 175–8, 184–6, 195–6, 205–6. On 'Carpet' and countermeasures see RAFM, Saundby papers, AC 72/12, Box 7, 'War in the Ether', 45–6.

246. Westermann, *Flak*, 234–5.

247. Ibid., 238–41.

248. BA-MA, RL2 IV/101, Vorstudien zur Luftkriegsgeschichte, Heft 8, 32–3; Air Ministry, *Rise and Fall of the German Air Force*, 283–5.

249. Westermann, *Flak*, 247–9.

250. BA-B, RL3/237, GL C-Amt, Studie 1036; Lutz Budrass, *Flugzeugindustrie und Luftrüstung in Deutschland 1918–1945* (Düsseldorf: 1998), 868–9; Horst Boog, 'Strategischer Luftkrieg in Europa 1943–1944', in Horst Boog et al., *Das Deutsche Reich und der Zweite Weltkrieg: Band 7: Das Deutsche Reich in der Defensive* (Stuttgart: 2001), 309–11.

251. IWM, EDS AL/1746, Karl-Otto Saur interrogation, 10 Aug 1945, 6.

252. IWM, MD, vol 56, 2701-13, memorandum by Milch, 'Der Jägerstab'.

253. Calculated from Budrass, *Flugzeugindustrie und Luftrüstung*, 836. Serviceability rates in Webster, Frankland, *Strategic Air Offensive*, vol 4, 501.

254. McFarland, Newton, *To Command the Sky*, 135; Schmid, 'German Dayfighting', 147.

255. AFHRA, Disc A5835, Tactical Development, 99. Elementary training declined from 100 hours in 1942 to 70 in 1943 and 52 in 1944; Fighter School hours declined from 60 to 40; OTU hours were 50 in 1942, 16–18 in 1943, 20 in 1944.

256. Schmid, 'German Dayfighting', 140–42.

257. Adolf Galland, *The First and the Last* (London: 1955), 189, 200–01.

258. LC, Spaatz papers, Box 143, Anderson to Spaatz, 28 Feb 1944, 2.

259. LC, Spaatz papers, Box 94, statistics on total tonnage dropped by USAAF and RAF, Jan 1944 to May 1944.

260. TNA, AIR 14/739A, 'Conduct of Strategic Bomber Offensive before Preparatory Stage of "Overlord"', 17 Jan 1944, 4–5.

261. Ibid., HQ Bomber Command, Air Intelligence, 'Progress of RAF Bomber Offensive against German Industry', 19 Feb 1944; Harris to Balfour, 2 Mar 1944.

262. CCO, Denis Richards Archive, File IV/Folder B, Portal to Sinclair, 29 Jan 1944.

263. W. A. Jacobs, 'The British Strategic Air Offensive against Germany in World War, II', in R. Cargill Hall (ed), *Case Studies in Strategic* Bombardment (Washington, DC: 1998), 139–40.

264. TNA, FO 935/126, REDept, 'Preliminary Attack Assessment, Berlin', 23 Mar 1944, 1, 3.

265. Webster, Frankland, *Strategic Air Offensive*, vol 2, 193.

266. Williamson Murray, *Luftwaffe: Strategy for Defeat 1933–1945* (London: 1985), 198–9.

267. Stephen McFarland, Wesley Newton, 'The American Strategic Air Offensive against Germany in World War II', in R. Cargill Hall (ed), *Case Studies in Strategic Bombardment* (Washington, DC: 1998), 214–16; Davis, *Carl A. Spaatz*, 322–6.

268. UEA, Zuckerman Archive, SZ/BBSU/101, 'Analysis of M.E.W. Estimates of German War Production' [n.d.], 10.

269. LC Spaatz papers, Box 68, HQ USSTAF, 'The Allied Air Offensive against Germany and Principal Criticisms by the Enemy Leaders', June 1945, Table C, Interrogation of Hermann Göring, 1 June 1945.

270. TNA, AIR 10/3873, BBSU, 'German Experience in the Underground Transfer of War Industries', 12.

271. Budrass, *Flugzeugindustrie und Luftrüstung*, 868; Boog, 'Strategischer Luftkrieg' 101–3.

272. LC, Spaatz papers, Box 67, Committee of Experts, 'Plan for the Completion of the Combined Bomber Offensive', 5 Mar 1944, 2–4; Katz, *Foreign Intelligence*, 19–20; F. H. Hinsley et al., *British Intelligence in the Second World War* (London: 1988), vol 3, pt ii, 497–9.

273. Rostow, *Pre-Invasion Bombing Strategy*, 53–5.

274. Davis, *Carl A. Spaatz*, 398–400; Rostow, *Pre-Invasion Bombing Strategy*, 68.

275. Davis, *Carl A. Spaatz*, 370–79; Murray, *Luftwaffe*, 215.

276. LC, Eaker papers, Box I.35, 'Decline of the GAF: Report from Captured Personnel', forwarded to Military Intelligence Division, 15 Mar 1945, 6.

277. Heinz Knocke, *I Flew for the Führer* (London: 1953), 148–9.

278. Davis, *Carl A. Spaatz*, 379–81.

279. TsAMO, f.500, 0.957971, d.448, 'Einzelnachrichten des 1c Dienstes West der Luftwaffe', 6 May 1944, 12.

280. Ian McLachlan, Russell Zorn, *Eighth Air Force Bomber Stories* (Yeovil: 1991), 110–11.

281. AFHRA, Disc A1722, Eighth Air Force, 'Tactical Development August 1942–May 1945', 99.

282. Boog, 'Strategischer Luftkrieg', 110; Webster, Frankland, *Strategic Air Offensive*, vol 4, 495; 'Nightfighter Direction: Interrogation of Major G. S. Sandmann', in Isby (ed), *Fighting the Bombers*, 211.

283. Von Rohden, 'Reich Air Defense', in Isby (ed), *Fighting the Bombers*, 38.

284. USAFA, McDonald papers, Ser V, Box 12, Folder 1, JIC Report, 'German Strategy and Capacity to Resist', 14 Aug 1944, 1.

285. AHB, Translations, vol 1, VII/7, 8th Abteilung report, 22 Sept 1944, 'A Forecast of Air Developments in 1945', 1.

286. IWM, MD, vol 53, 706–11, Report by Chief of German Air Force Operations Staff (Karl Koller), 'Erforderliche Mindeststärke der fliegenden Verbände der deutschen Luftwaffe zur Behauptung des mitteleuropäischen Raumes', 19 May 1944.

287. Calculated from Webster, Frankland, *Strategic Air Offensive*, vol 4, 497.

288. LC, Eaker papers, Box I.35, 'Decline of the G.A.F.', 6: 'Neither in the East nor South did 50, 80, or 100 of our aircraft ever fly in a body and carry out any major operation. In Russia they flew in "Rotten" of two or "Schwärme" of four . . . our fighter arm had to conduct the fight in a strength to which it was never accustomed.'

289. Sönke Neitzel, *Tapping Hitler's Generals: Transcripts of Secret Conversations, 1942–1945* (Barnsley: 2007), 114–15, recording of Gen. Bernhard Ramcke, 16 Oct 1944.

290. LC, Spaatz papers, Box 134, US Military Intelligence Service, HQ Air P/w, Interrogation of Hermann Göring, 1 Jun 1945, 2.

291. Dik Daso, *Hap Arnold and the Evolution of American Airpower* (Washington, DC: 2000), esp 152–68; on the problems of adjusting to defensive warfare see Boog, 'Strategischer Luftkrieg', 249–58.

292. AHB, Translations, VII/VII, 'A Forecast of Air Developments in 1945', 2–3.

293. LC, Spaatz papers, Box 143, Spaatz to Arnold, 30 Sept 1944.

294. TNA, AIR 14/739A, Harris to Coryton (Air Ministry), 19 July 1944; CCO, Portal papers, Folder 5, Portal to Churchill, 5 Aug 1944.

295. Mark Connelly, 'The British People, the Press and the Strategic Air Campaign against Germany, 1939–1945', *Contemporary British History*, 16 (2002), 54–5.

296. Hugh Thomas, *John Strachey* (London: 1973), 219.

297. TNA, PREM 3/193/6A, JIC Report, 'German Strategy and Capacity to Resist', 16 Oct 1944.

298. AHB, Translations, VII/VII, 'A Forecast of Air Developments'; VII/IX, 'War Appreciation No. 17', 15 Jan 1945, 8.

299. LC, Spaatz papers, Box 143, Spaatz to Arnold, 22 July 1944; Spaatz to Arnold, 3 Sept 1944. See too JIC warnings in Hinsley et al., *British Intelligence in the Second World War*, vol 3, pt ii, 595–9.

300. LC, Doolittle papers, Box 18, Doolittle to Arnold, 2 Aug 1944; Box 19, Doolittle to Spaatz, 18 Oct 1944.

301. NARA, RG 107, Lovett papers, Box 139, Memorandum for Lovett from HQ Army Service Forces, encl. 'Periodic Report of Readiness for Chemical Warfare, 1 January 1945', 2.

302. Robert Harris, Jeremy Paxman, *A Higher Form of Killing: The Secret Story of Gas and Germ Warfare* (London: 1982), 110–16.

303. TNA, PREM 3/193/6A, HQ AF, Algiers to the War Office, 30 Oct 1943 (initialled by Churchill, 1 Nov 1943).

304. NARA, RG 218, Box 3, 'Analysis of Foreign Weapons Division', report for the Commanding General, Army Service Forces, 26 Oct 1943, forwarded to Arnold. On German plans the best account is Rolf-Dieter Müller, 'Albert Speer und die Rüstungspolitik im Totalen Krieg 1942–45', in Bernhard Kroener, Rolf-Dieter Müller, Hans Umbreit, *DRZW: Band 5/2: Organisation und Mobilisierung des Deutschen Machtbereichs 1942–1944/45* (Stuttgart: 1999), 713–16.

305. NARA, RG 218, Box 19, memorandum for the Gas Warfare Subcommittee, HQ USAAF, 21 Jan 1944, 3; Maj. Gen. William Porter (Chief, Chemical Warfare Service) to JCS, 'Present Status of Development of Toxic Gases', 6 Dec 1943.

306. RAFM, Bottomley papers, AC 71/2/29, War Cabinet Inter-Service Committee on Chemical Warfare, Note by the Air Staff, 23 Jan 1944, 2–3, and Annex 1, 'Appreciation on Strategic Gas Effort', 5.

307. Ibid., AC 71/2/75, Memorandum by Norman Bottomley, 'Possibility of the Use of Gas by the Germans to Counter "Overlord"', 1–3.

308. CCAC, Churchill papers, CHAR D.217/4, Churchill to Ismay for the CoS, 6 July 1944; Hinsley et al., *British Intelligence in the Second World War*, vol 3, pt ii, 576–80.

309. Müller, 'Albert Speer und die Rütungspolitik', 714–15.

310. CCAC, BUFT 3/51, 'Plan for Retaliatory Gas Attack on Germany'; NARA, RG 107, Box 139, HQ Army Service Forces memorandum, 'Co-Ordinated Anglo-American Chemical Warfare Procurement and Supply Program', 10 Mar 1945, 2–3.

311. NARA, RG 218, Box 1, Report for the JCS, 6 Jan 1944, 1.

312. Details in RAFM, Bottomley papers, B2320, Inter-Service Sub-Committee on Biological Warfare, 22 Dec 1945, App A, 'Biological Warfare: Report to the Secretary of War', 1–5; NARA, RG 218, Box 1, JCS paper, 20 Dec 1943, 'Implications of Recent Intelligence Regarding Alleged German Secret Weapons'.

313. NARA, RG 218, Box 1, 'Defensive Measures against Bacteriological Warfare', 25 May 1944; Memorandum for Col. Newsome from General Staff, Operations Division, 10 Apr 1944 (shown to Gen. Marshall and forwarded to Field Marshal John Dill).

314. Müller, 'Albert Speer und die Rüstungspolitik', 720–26.

315. See e.g. USAFA, Hansell papers, Ser III, Box 1, Folder 1, 'Fairchild Lecture', 1 Dec 1964, 18–24.

316. Figures from Davis, *Carl A. Spaatz*, App 8; Mets, *Master of Airpower*, 251; Henry Probert, *Bomber Harris: His Life and Times* (London: 2006), 305–6.

317. LC, Spaatz papers, Box 143, Spaatz to Arnold, 30 Sept 1944.

318. Mets, *Master of Airpower*, 258–9; Davis, *Carl A. Spaatz*, 488–90.

319. CCAC, BUFT 3/43, memorandum by Sq. Ldr. John Strachey (BOps), 13 Aug 1944; Draft operation, 'Thunderclap', 15 Aug 1944; Bufton memorandum, 2 Aug 1944, 'Operation Thunderclap'.

320. Directives in Webster, Frankland, *Strategic Air Offensive*, vol 4, 174–6; directive from Bottomley to Harris, 13 Oct 1944. See too Davis, *Carl A. Spaatz*, 494–5.

NOTES   751

321. Solly Zuckerman, *From Apes to Warlords: The Autobiography of Solly Zuckerman, 1904–1946* (London: 1978), 301–4; Hugh Melinsky, *Forming the Pathfinders: The Career of Air Vice-Marshal Sydney Bufton* (Stroud: 2010), 130–33.

322. Webster, Frankland, *Strategic Air Offensive*, vol 4, 177–9, '1st November 1944: Directive No. 2 for the Strategic Air Forces in Europe'.

323. 'Expert' in CCAC, BUFT 3/51, Harris to Portal, 12 Dec 1944; Melinsky, *Forming the Pathfinders*, 135. See too CamUL, Andrew Boyle papers, Add 9429/1B, Harris to Boyle, 13 June 1979: 'He [Bufton] was a prime example in my view of a Junior Officer in the Air Ministry imagining he could run the Command.'

324. CCAC, BUFT 3/51, Harris to Portal, 12 Dec 1944. See the full discussion of the correspondence in Melinsky, *Forming the Pathfinders*, 133–5; Probert, *Bomber Harris*, 309–11.

325. USSBS, 'Oil Division: Final Report', Washington, DC, 25 Aug 1945, fig 7.

326. LC, Spaatz papers, Box 76, 'Conference on Bombing Accuracy', HQ USSTAF, 22–23 Mar 1945; Box 80, Hugh Odishaw, 'Radar Bombing in the Eighth Air Force', 94. See too Davis, *Carl A. Spaatz*, 503–8.

327. Davis, *Carl A. Spaatz*, 508.

328. AHB, Translations, VII/23, GAF Air Historical Branch, 'Some Effects of the Allied Air Offensive on German Economic Life', 7 Dec 1944, 1–2; Davis, *Carl A. Spaatz*, 510–12. The best account is Alfred Mierzejewski, *The Collapse of the German War Economy: Allied Air Power and the German National Railway* (Chapel Hill, NC: 1988), 191, Table A3.

329. Mierzejewski, *Collapse of the German War Economy*, 193, Table A5.

330. AHB, Translations, VII/38, Speer to Field Marshal Keitel, 'Report on the Effects of Allied Air Activity against the Ruhr', 7 Nov 1944.

331. AFHRA, 520.056-188, Statistical Summary Eighth Air Force Operations: Aircraft Loss Rates on Combat Operations.

332. Fighter losses in Murray, *Luftwaffe*, 364; jet production in Boog, 'Strategischer Luftkrieg', 307–8.

333. CCAC, BUFT 3/51, Bufton to Bottomley, 9 June 1945; RAFM, Saundby papers, AC 72/12, Box 7, 'War in the Ether', App B, 'Bomber Command Loss Rate on German Targets'.

334. Schmid, 'German Nightfighting', in Isby (ed), *Fighting the Bombers*, 105–6.

335. Details in RAFM, Saundby papers, AC 72/12, Box 7, 'War in the Ether', Oct 1945, 53–8 and App F; Saundby (HQ Bomber Command) to all group commanders, 13 Oct 1944 on keeping radar silence. See too Bill Gunston, *Night Fighters: A Development and Combat History* (Cambridge: 1976), 125–7; Werner Held, Holger Nauroth, *Die deutsche Nachtjagd* (Stuttgart: 1992), 222–30.

336. Von Below, *At Hitler's Side*, 220–21.

337. LC, Eaker papers, Box I.35, 'Decline of the G.A.F.', 12.

338. Galland, *First and Last*, 246–9, 251–2, 283–5; LC, Spaatz papers, Box 68, Memorandum by George McDonald (G-2, HQ USSTAF), 'The Allied Air

Offensive against Germany and Principal Criticisms by Enemy Leaders', Table F, interrogation of Gen. Galland, 16 May 1945.

339. CCAC, BUFT 3/51, Morley (BOps 2) to SHAEF A-3, 21 Jan 1945.

340. USAFA, McDonald papers, Ser V, Box 12, Folder 1, JIC SHAEF, 'Bombing Policy in Germany', 6 Oct 1944.

341. NARA, RG 107, Box 28, Lovett to Arnold, 9 Jan 1945, 2–3.

342. RAFM, Harris papers, Misc. Box A, Folder 4, 'One Hundred Towns of Leading Economic Importance'.

343. AFHRA, Disc MAAF 233, Air Ministry to HQ 15th Air Force, 14 Oct 1944, additions to target list (as well as Dresden, the additions were Eberswalde, Plauen, Jenbach, Obergrafendorf).

344. CCAC, BUFT 3/51, Combined Strategic Targets Committee, 'Target Priorities for Attack of Industrial Areas', 27 Nov 1944.

345. CCO, Portal papers, Folder 5, Portal to Churchill, 4 Oct 1944.

346. Ibid., Folder 6, Report by A. H. Birse (Churchill's interpreter) 'Notes on Air Chief Marshal Sir A. Tedder's Meeting with Marshal Stalin', 15 Jan 1945.

347. Probert, *Bomber Harris*, 318; UEA, Zuckerman Archive, SZ/BBSU/58, Note by the Air Staff, 'Strategic Bombing in Relation to the Present Russian Offensive', 25 Jan 1945; Hinsley et al., *British Intelligence in the Second World War*, vol 3, pt ii, 611.

348. Ian Hunter (ed), *Winston & Archie: The Collected Correspondence of Winston Churchill and Archibald Sinclair 1915–1960* (London: 2005), 410–11, Sinclair to Churchill, 26 Jan 1945; Churchill to Sinclair, 26 Jan 1945; Sinclair to Churchill, 27 Jan 1945.

349. CCO, Portal papers, Folder 6, Portal to Churchill, 28 Jan 1945.

350. Webster, Frankland, *Strategic Air Offensive*, vol 4, 301, Bottomley to Harris, 27 Jan 1945; Sebastian Cox, 'The Dresden Raids: Why and How', in Paul Addison, Jeremy Crang (eds), *Firestorm: The Bombing of Dresden, 1945* (London: 2006), 22–5; Hinsley et al., *British Intelligence in the Second World War*, vol 3, pt ii, 611.

351. CCAC, BUFT 3/51, 'Strategic Bombing in Reaction to the Present Russian Offensive', note by the Air Staff for CoS Meeting, 31 Jan 1945, 1.

352. Davis, *Carl A. Spaatz*, 546–8.

353. S. M. Plokhy, *Yalta: The Price of Peace* (New York: 2010), 213–14; AFHRA, K239.046-38, Joseph Angell, 'Historical Analysis of the 14–15 February Bombings of Dresden' [n.d. but 1953], 12.

354. RAFM, Harris papers, H136, 'Notes on Bomber Command' [n.d. but 1961 or 1962], 7.

355. Freeman, *The Mighty Eighth*, 432; Davis, *Carl A. Spaatz*, 551–3; Groehler, *Bombenkrieg*, 388–9, 398–400; Richard Overy, 'The Post-War Debate', in Addison, Crang (eds), *Firestorm*, 129–30.

356. Götz Bergander, *Dresden im Luftkrieg: Vorgeschichte – Zerstörung – Folgen* (Munich: 1985), 256–7; Groehler, *Bombenkrieg*, 412; Matthias Gretzschel, 'Dresden im Dritten Reich', in *Hamburg und Dresden im Dritten Reich: Bombenkrieg and Kriegsende. Sieben Beiträge* (Hamburg: 2000), 97.

357. Tami Davis Biddle, 'Wartime Reactions', in Addison, Crang (eds), *Firestorm*, 107–10.

358. Ibid., 113.

359. CamUL, Boyle papers, Add 9429/1B, Harris to Boyle, 13 June 1979.

360. CCAC, BUFT 3/51, HQ Bomber Command, 'Bomber Command's "Battle of the Ruhr"', 24 Mar 1945.

361. Greenhous et al., *Crucible of War*, 862.

362. CCO, Portal papers, Folder 6, Portal to Churchill, 20 Apr 1945; Hunter, *Winston & Archie*, 414, Churchill to Sinclair, 19 Apr 1945.

363. Webster, Frankland, *Strategic Air Offensive*, vol 4, 183–4, Strategic Directive no. 4, 16 Apr 1945.

364. Davis, *Carl A. Spaatz*, 582–4.

365. Mets, *Master of Airpower*, 283–4.

366. TNA, HO 196/30, RE8 Report, 25 May 1945.

367. LC, Spaatz papers, Box 143, Spaatz to commanding generals, 8th, 9th and 15th Air Forces, 24 Aug 1944.

368. Arnold, *Global Mission*, 490–91; USSBS, 'Over-all Report (European War)', Washington, DC, 30 Sept 1945, vol 2, ix; Gordon Daniels (ed), *A Guide to the Reports of the United States Strategic Bombing Survey* (London: 1981), xix–xxii; Gian Gentile, *How Effective is Strategic Bombing? Lessons Learned from World War II to Kosovo* (New York: 2000), 33–54.

369. NC, Cherwell papers, F247, Churchill to Sinclair, 3 Jan 1945; on the problems surrounding the survey see Sebastian Cox (ed), *The Strategic Air War Against Germany, 1939–1945: The Official Report of the British Bombing Survey Unit* (London: 1998), xvii–xix.

370. UEA, Zuckerman Archive, SZ/BBSU/1, BBSU Advisory Committee, minutes of 1st meeting, 6 June 1945; Note for Air Ministry and SHAEF, 13 June 1945; Cox (ed), *The Strategic Air War Against Germany*, xx–xxi.

371. TNA, AIR 14/1779, Minutes of meeting, 27 Feb 1945, on the future of the RE8 Department. The personnel were absorbed into the Air Ministry establishment on 1 March 1945.

372. CCAC, BUFT 3/51, 'Proposals for the Establishment of a British Strategic Bombing Unit', 30 May 1945, 1–3.

373. CCAC, BUFT 3/65, ADI (K) Report, 'Factors in Germany's Defeat', 17 May 1945.

374. LC, Spaatz papers, Box 68, HQ USSTAF, 'The Allied Air Offensive against Germany and Principal Criticisms by Enemy Leaders', 4–5, 6.

375. Ibid., Table D, Ninth Air Force interrogation of Hermann Göring, 1 June 1945; interrogation of Milch, 23 May 1945; Table E, SHAEF interrogation of Speer, 3 June 1945; Gentile, *How Effective is Strategic Bombing?*, 69.

376. Gentile, *How Effective is Strategic Bombing?*, 7; LC, Spaatz papers, Box 134, 'Interrogation of Reich Marshal Hermann Goering', 10 May 1945, 5.

377. LC, Spaatz papers, Box 134, USSBS Interrogation no. 8, Lt. Gen. Karl Koller, 23–24 May 1945, 6–7.

378. USSBS, Over-all Report (European Theatre), 25–6, 37–8, 73–4; Gentile, *How Effective is Strategic Bombing?*, 55–6. For a convincing case on the diminishing returns from bombing, see the recent economic analysis by Jurgen Brauer, Hubert van Tuyll, *Castles, Battles & Bombs: How Economics Explains Military History* (Chicago, IL: 2008), 211–13, 217–19, 235–6.

379. Cox (ed), *The Strategic Air War Against Germany*, 129–34.

380. Ibid., 154.

381. Ibid., 94–7.

382. CCAC, BUFT 3/51, Bufton to Portal, 3 Jan 1945. The report was passed on to Harris by Portal, but with the reference to Hamburg deleted.

383. UEA, Zuckerman Archive, SZ/BBSU/3, Exercise Thunderbolt, précis no. 8, 'The Course of the Combined Bomber Offensive from January 1943 to April 1944', 2; précis no. 18, 'The Course of the Combined Strategic Bomber Offensive from 14 April 1944 to the End of the European War', 3–4.

384. Ibid., Zuckerman Archive, SZ/BBSU/2, précis of lecture by Wing Commander G. A. Carey Foster, 'On the Effects of Strategic Bombing on Germany's Capacity to Make War'.

385. Ibid., Zuckerman Archive, SZ/BBSU/3, Zuckerman, rough notes on Exercise Thunderbolt, 13–16 Aug 1947.

386. Ibid., Zuckerman Archive, SZ/BBSU/103, Nicholas Kaldor typescript, 'The Nature of Strategic Bombing', 4–6; Kaldor typescript, 'Capacity of German Industry', 2–5.

387. Nicholas Kaldor, 'The German War Economy', *Review of Economic Statistics*, 13 (1946), 20ff; see Richard Overy, 'Mobilization for Total War in Germany 1939–1941', *English Historical Review*, 103 (1988), 613–39, and more recently Adam Tooze, 'No Room for Miracles: German Industrial Output in World War II Reassessed', *Geschichte und Gesellschaft*, 31 (2005), 439–64.

388. Webster, Frankland, *Strategic Air Offensive*, vol 4, 469–70, 494, App 49 (iii), 49 (xxii).

389. Richard Overy, 'The Economy of the German "New Order"', in Johannes ten Cate, Gerhard Otto, Richard Overy (eds), *Die 'Neuordnung' Europas: NS-Wirtschaftspolitik in den besetzten Gebieten* (Berlin: 1997), 14–26; on financial contributions, Willi Boelcke, *Die Kosten von Hitlers Krieg* (Paderborn: 1985), 98, 110. On labour Ulrich Herbert (ed), *Europa und der 'Reichseinsatz'. Ausländische Zivilarbeiter, Kriegsgefangene und KZ-Häftlinge in Deutschland 1938–1945* (Essen: 1991), 7–8. The totals were: POWs 1,930,087; forced labourers, 5,976,673. On booty policy and its results, Götz Aly, *Hitlers Volksstaat: Raub, Rassenkrieg und Nationaler Sozialismus* (Frankfurt am Main: 2005), 59ff.

390. UEA, Zuckerman Archive, SZ/BBSU/103, 'Nature of Strategic Bombing', 6–7.

391. LC, Spaatz papers, J. K. Galbraith, 'Preliminary Appraisal of Achievement of Strategic Bombing of Germany', 2.

392. TNA, AIR 48/33, USSBS, Civilian Defense Report no. 4, Hamburg Field Report, vol 1, 83.

393. Details from BA-B, R3102/10031, Reichsministerium für Rüstung- und Kriegswirtschaft, 'Vorläufige Zusammenstellung des Arbeiterstundenausfalls durch Feindeinwirkung', Tables 1 and 4, 4 Jan 1945.

394. Albert Speer, *Spandau: The Secret Diaries* (London: 1976), 360, entry for 12 Apr 1959: 'No-one has yet seen that this was the greatest lost battle on the German side.'

395. CCAC, BUFT 3/51, note by Bufton, 'Part Played by the RAF in the Crossing of the Rhine – 24 March 1945'.

396. UEA, Zuckerman Archive, SZ/BBSU/3, Portal to Tedder, 10 Sept 1947.

397. Air Ministry, *Rise and Fall of the German Air Force*, 274, 302. Boog, 'Strategischer Luftkrieg', 287.

398. Cox (ed), *The Strategic Air War Against Germany*, 97; Air Ministry, *Rise and Fall of the German Air Force*, 274, 298; Golücke, *Schweinfurt und der strategische Luftkrieg*, 153–9; IWM, MD, vol 53, 877, German Flak Office to Milch, 12 Aug 1943.

399. John K. Galbraith, *A Life in Our Times: Memoirs* (London: 1981), 240.

400. UEA, Zuckerman Archive, SZ/BBSU/2, Carey Lecture, 8; TNA, AIR 10/3866, Report of the British Bombing Survey Unit, 38; NARA, RG 107, Box 138, Statistical Control Division, 'An Estimate of Costs of AAF Strategic Air Forces Fighting Germany', 12 Apr 1945. Since this last figure covered the period up to 31 Dec 1944, it is likely that the final figure was between 12 and 13 per cent.

401. TNA, AIR 20/2025, Casualties of RAF, Dominion and Allied Personnel at RAF Posting Disposal, 31 May 1947.

402. Greenhous et al., *Crucible of War*, 864.

403. TNA, AIR 22/203, War Room Manual of Bomber Command Operations 1939–1945, 9.

404. Davis, *Carl A. Spaatz*, App 4, App 9.

7. THE LOGIC OF TOTAL WAR: GERMAN SOCIETY UNDER THE BOMBS

1. LC, Spaatz papers, Box 134, 'Interrogation of Hermann Goering, Augsburg, 10 May 1945'; Hopper to Spaatz, 12 May 1945.

2. Spaatz papers, Box 203, 'Jeeping the Targets in a Country that Was', 17–22 Apr 1945, 1, 19.

3. CCAC, BUFT 3/51, Bufton to Brig. Gen. F. Maxwell, 17 May 1945.

4. UEA, Zuckerman Archive, SZ/BBSU/1, 'Notes on the "pocket"', 28 Apr 1945, 4–5, 7, 10.

5. Bernd Lemke, *Luftschutz in Grossbritannien und Deutschland 1923 bis 1939* (Munich: 2005), 255.

6. BA-B, R 1501/1513, RLM, 'Grundsätze für die Führung des Luftschutzes', Feb 1942, 5.

7. BA-B, NS 18/1333, Göring, Goebbels and Wilhelm Frick (Interior Minister) to all Reichsverteidigungskommissare, 7 May 1942, 'Aufgabenverteilung bei Luftschutzmassnahmen'.

8. Lemke, *Luftschutz*, 258–61.

9. Jörn Brinkhus, 'Ziviler Luftschutz im "Dritten Reich" – Wandel seiner Spitzenorganisation', in Dietmar Süss (ed), *Deutschland im Luftkrieg: Geschichte und Erinnerung* (Munich: 2007), 27–30.

10. Andreas Linhardt, *Feuerwehr im Luftschutz 1926–1945: Die Umstruktierung des öffentlichen Feuerlöschwesens in Deutschland unter Gesichtspunkten des zivilen Luftschutzes* (Brunswick: 2002), 37–8, 85–7, 114–20, 134–9, 204–5.

11. BIOS Report no. 18, 'Fire Fighting Equipment and Methods in Germany during the Period 1939–1945' (London: 1949), 7–9.

12. Lemke, *Luftschutz*, 254–6.

13. BA-B, R1501/823, Luftschutzgesetz, 7 Durchführungsverordnung, 31 Aug 1943, 519–20.

14. TNA, AIR 48/29, USSBS, 'Civilian Defense Division: Final Report, 26 Oct 1945', 117–26.

15. BA-MA, RL 41/3, RLB, Luftschutz-Berichte, 21 May 1941, 1. Leitsätze für Luftschutz-Warte.

16. BA-B, R1501/1513, RLM, 'Grundsätze für die Führung des Luftschutzes', Feb 1942, 6.

17. BA-MA, RL41/7, RLB, Rundschreiben, 2 Oct 1942, 'Führungsaufgaben'; 16 Oct 1942, 'Besonderer Einsatz von Amtsträgerinnen bei Terrorangriffen'.

18. Linhardt, *Feuerwehr im Luftschutz*, 108–9.

19. BA-B, R1501/1516, Deutsche Gemeindetag to Göring, 3 Nov 1938; Interior Ministry to all Reich provinces, 21 Apr 1939.

20. Ibid., Air Ministry to all Regional Air Commands, Nov 1941.

21. BA-MA, RL41/2, RLB, Luftschutz-Berichte, 8 May 1940, 2 and 10 July 1940, 1.

22. Lemke, *Luftschutz*, 328–9.

23. BA-B, R1510/1515, Interior Ministry to Landesregierungen, Oberpräsidenten, 6 Jan 1940, 17 May 1940, 26 Sept 1940.

24. TNA, AIR 20/7287, Home Office, 'Secret Report by the Police President of Hamburg', 1 Dec 1943, 3–4.

25. Wilfried Beer, *Kriegsalltag an der Heimatfront: Alliierten Luftkrieg und deutsche Gegenmassnahmen zur Abwehr und Schadensbegrenzung dargestellt für den Raum Münster* (Bremen: 1990), 108–10.

26. BA-MA, RL 41/2, RLB, Luftschutz-Berichte, vol 6, 10 July 1940; BA-B, R1501/823, Luftschutzgesetz: Zehnte Durchführungsverordnung: Luftschutzmässiges Verhalten.

27. BA-MA, RL 41/6 RLB-Präsidium, material for the press, 10 Aug 1943, 1. On shelter rules see Dietmar Süss, 'Wartime Societies and Shelter Politics in

National Socialist Germany and Britain', in Claudia Baldoli, Andrew Knapp, Richard Overy (eds), *Bombing, States and Peoples in Western Europe 1940–1945* (London: 2011), 29–31.

28. TNA, AIR 48/29, USSBS, 'Civilian Defense Division: Final Report', 141–7; Marc Wiggam, 'The Blackout and the Idea of Community in Britain and Germany', in Baldoli, Knapp, Overy (eds), *Bombing, States and Peoples*, 50–51.

29. BA-MA, RL 41/2, RLB, Luftschutz-Berichte, 6 and 14 Feb 1940, 12 Mar 1940; 9 and 8 Jan 1943.

30. BA-B, R1501/1515, Interior Ministry to all Reichsverteidigungskommissare, 27 Oct 1939.

31. Wilbur Zelinski, Leszek Kosinski, *The Emergency Evacuation of Cities* (Savage, MD: 1991), 160–64; on Hitler see BA-B, R1501/1515, Interior Ministry minute, 8 Oct 1940. On the programme of child evacuation see Gerhard Kock, *'Der Führer sorgt für unsere Kinder ...' Die Kinderlandverschickung im Zweiten Weltkrieg* (Paderborn: 1997), 69, 122, 351; Julia Torrie, *'For Their Own Good': Civilian Evacuations in Germany and France, 1939–1945* (New York: 2010), 52–3. On the experience of Cologne see Martin Rüther, 'Die Erweiterte Kinderlandverschickung in Köln, Bonn und Umgebung', in idem (ed), *'Zu Hause könnten sie es nicht schöner haben!': Kinderlandverschickung aus Köln und Umgebung 1941–1945* (Cologne: 2000), 69–71, 75.

32. Anton Hoch, 'Der Luftangriff auf Freiburg 1940', *Vierteljahreshefte für Zeitgeschichte*, 4 (1956), 115–44.

33. Beer, *Kriegsalltag ... für den Raum Münster*, 107.

34. William Shirer, *Berlin Diary: The Journal of a Foreign Correspondent, 1934–1941* (London: 1941), 273–4, 364; Harry Flannery, *Assignment to Berlin* (London: 1942), 40–41.

35. Heinz Boberach (ed), *Meldungen aus dem Reich: Die geheimen Lageberichte des Sicherheitsdienstes der SS 1938–1945*, 17 vols (Herrsching: 1984), vol 4, 1,140–1, Special Report, 16 May 1940; 1,152, Special Report, 20 May 1940.

36. BA-MA, RL 41/2, RLB, Luftschutz-Berichte, 6 and 22 May 1940, 10 July 1940.

37. Ibid., 11 Sept 1940, 6 Nov 1940.

38. BA-B, R1501/823, Interior Ministry to all Statthalter, Reichsverteidigungs-Kommissare, Oberpräsidenten, 16 May 1940.

39. TNA, AIR 48/29, USSBS, 'Civilian Defense Division: Final Report', 33–6.

40. Wolfgang Werner, *'Bleib übrig': Deutsche Arbeiter in der nationalsozialistischen Kriegswirtschaft* (Düsseldorf: 1983), 34–41.

41. BA-B, R1501/1071, Labour Ministry, 'Änderung über Erstattung von Lohnausfällen', 22 Oct 1940; Ministry of Labour to all Provincial Labour Offices, 8 Feb 1941; Ministry of Labour Decree, 19 Nov 1941.

42. BA-B, NS 18/1060, Propaganda Ministry to Party Chancellery, 9 Oct 1941; 'Bericht wegen Lohnausfall bei Luftalarm und Fliegerschäden', 23 Oct 1941, 1–3.

43. BA-B, R1501/1071, General Plenipotentiary for Labour to all Gau Labour Offices, 15 Nov 1943; Reichsministerialblatt, vol 72, 18 Feb 1944, 'Erlass

über Massnahmen des Arbeitsrechts und Arbeitseinsatzes bei Fliegeralarm und Fliegerschäden'.

44. BA-MA, RL 41/3, RLB, Luftschutz-Berichte, 7 and 26 Mar 1941, 1–2.
45. Ibid., 27 Aug 1941, 3–4.
46. BA-B, R1501/823, Interior Ministry to the Gemeindetag, 2 Oct 1940.
47. BA-B, NS 18/1333, Party Chancellery to Tiessler (Propaganda Ministry), 27 Apr 1942.
48. Martin Dean, *Robbing the Jews: The Confiscation of Jewish Property in the Holocaust, 1933–1945* (Cambridge: 2008), 223–4, 239.
49. BA-MA, RL 41/2, RLB, Luftschutz-Berichte, 6 and 31 July 1940, 2.
50. Jill Stephenson, 'Bombing and Rural Society in Württemberg', *Labour History Review*, 77 (2012), 98–100; Edward Westermann, 'Hitting the Mark, but Missing the Target: Luftwaffe Deception Operations, 1939–1945', *War in History*, 10 (2003), 208–13; BA-MA, RL 41/7, RLB, Rundschreiben, 11 Jan 1943.
51. BA-B, R1501/823, '7th Durchführungsverordnung (Beschaffung von Selbstschutzgerät)', 31 Aug 1943.
52. BA-MA, RL 41/2, RLB, Luftschutz-Berichte, 6 and 25 Sept 1940, 4 Dec 1940.
53. TNA, AIR 20/7287, 'Secret Report by the Police President of Hamburg, 1 Dec 1943', 2; Ursula Büttner, '"Gomorrha" und die Folgen', in Hamburg Forschungsstelle für Zeitgeschichte, *Hamburg im 'Dritten Reich'* (Göttingen: 2005), 616.
54. Beer, *Kriegsalltag . . . für den Raum Münster*, 123–5.
55. TsAMO, f.500, o.12452, d.139, minutes of meeting in the Air Ministry, 17 Oct 1940, 2–3.
56. Michael Foedrowitz, *Bunkerwelten: Luftschutzanlagen in Norddeutschland* (Berlin: 1998), 9–12; Ralf Blank, 'Kriegsalltag und Luftkrieg an der "Heimatfront"', in Jörg Echternkamp, *Das Deutsche Reich und der Zweite Weltkrieg* (Stuttgart: 2004), 395–6.
57. BA-MA, RL 41/3, Luftschutz-Berichte, 7 and 19 Nov 1941, 2.
58. Hans Hesse, Elke Purpus, 'Vom Luftschutzraum zum Denkmalschutz – Bunker in Köln', in Inge Marszolek, Marc Buggeln (eds), *Bunker: Kriegsort, Zuflucht, Errinerungsraum* (Frankfurt am Main: 2008), 66–8.
59. Blank, 'Kriegsalltag und Luftkrieg', 396–7; Olaf Groehler, *Bombenkrieg gegen Deutschland* (Berlin: 1990), 245–7.
60. Groehler, *Bombenkrieg gegen Deutschland*, 245–6; Richard Evans, *The Third Reich at War* (London: 2008), 454–5.
61. Howard Smith, *Last Train from Berlin* (London: 1942), 116; Dietmar Süss, 'Wartime Societies and Shelter Politics in National Socialist Germany and Britain', in Baldoli, Knapp, Overy (eds), *Bombing, States and Peoples*, 25–6; Blank, 'Kriegsalltag und Luftkrieg', 403–5. See too Roger Moorhouse, *Berlin at War: Life and Death in Hitler's Capital 1939–1945* (London: 2010), 310–11.
62. Details in Michael Foedrowitz, *Flak-Towers* (Berlin: 2008), 3–4, 11–13, 17–18.

63. Büttner, "'Gomorrha'", 614–15; Beer, *Kriegsalltag . . . für den Raum Münster*, 19–21.

64. Figures calculated from BA-B, NS18/1063, Partei-Kanzlei, 'Angaben über die Verluste nach Fliegerangriffen', 2 Oct 1942.

65. BA-MA, RL 41/7, RLB, Landesgruppe Hesse-Rheinland, Rundschreiben, 2 Oct 1942; Merkblatt über Aussehen, Wirkung und Bekämpfung Brandabwurfmitteln.

66. BA-MA, RL 41/3, Luftschutz-Berichte, 7 and 23 Apr 1941, 2–3.

67. TsAMO, f.500, 0.393761c, d.34, RLM, Arbeitsstab-Luftschutz, 'Anordnung auf Grund der letzten Erfahrungen aus Luftangriffen', 19 Feb 1941, 1–3, 4–5; 0.12452, d.139, minutes of meeting in the Air Ministry, 10 Oct 1940, 7.

68. Ibid., OKW, 'Weisungen für den Einsatz der Luftschutzkräfte und die Verwendung der Wehrmacht', 7 Mar 1941.

69. BA-B, R1501/823, Interior Ministry to all Reichsverteidigungs-Kommissare, Reichsstatthalter, 2 May 1941. See Torrie, *'For Their Own Good'*, 129–30.

70. Groehler, *Bombenkrieg gegen Deutschland*, 264–6. On the NSV see Armin Nolzen, "'Sozialismus der Tat?' Die Nationalsozialistische Volkswohlfahrt (NSV) und der allierte Luftkrieg gegen das Deutsche Reich', in Süss (ed), *Deutschland im Luftkrieg*, 58–9.

71. BA-MA, RL 41/3, Luftschutz-Berichte, 16 July 1941.

72. BA-B, NS 18/1058, action report to NSDAP Rechsleitung, 'Angriff auf Lübeck', 6 Apr 1942.

73. Ibid., Gauleiter Hildebrandt to Party Reichsleitung, 26 Apr 1942; Gauleitung Mecklenburg to Goebbels, Bormann, 27 Apr 1942 (1).

74. Ibid., Gauleitung Mecklenburg to Goebbels, Bormann, 27 Apr 1942 (2); 28 Apr 1942; 29 Apr 1942.

75. Ibid., Gauleiter Hildebrandt to Führer HQ, 2 May 1942.

76. BA-B, NS 18/1333, Goebbels to all Gauleiter, Reichsstatthalter, Reichsverteidigungskommissare, 28 Apr 1942; see too Dietmar Süss, 'Steuerung durch Information? Joseph Goebbels als "Kommissar der Heimatfront" und die Reichsinspektion für den zivilen Luftschutz', in Rüdiger Hachtmann, Winfried Süss (eds), *Hitlers Kommissare: Sondergewalten in der nationalsozialistischen Diktatur* (Göttingen: 2006), 185–7; Brinkhus, 'Ziviler Luftschutz', in Süss (ed), *Deutschland im Luftkrieg*, 34–5.

77. Nolzen, "'Sozialismus der Tat?'", 60–62.

78. Cited in Eleanor Hancock, *The National Socialist Leadership and Total War, 1941–5* (New York: 1991), 103.

79. BA-B, NS 18/1333, Circular to all Reich Defence Commissars, 'Aufgabenverteilung bei Luftschutzmassnahmen', 7 May 1942; note for Goebbels, 7 May 1942.

80. BA-B, R1501/3791, Arbeitsstab L5 (Air Ministry), 'Abgrenzung von Befehlsbefugnissen', 17 Dec 1942; Göring Directive, 17 Dec 1942, 3.

81. Süss, 'Steuerung durch Information?', 188–91; Brinkhus, 'Ziviler Luftschutz', 34–6.

82. BA-B, R1501/823, RVK Hamburg, 'Richtlinien für die Tätigkeit eines Einsatzstabes bei katastrophen Luftangriffen', 9 Apr 1942; Interior Ministry to all Reich authorities, 6 May 1942.

83. BA-B, R3101/31135, 'Polizeiliche Anordnung über die Luftschutzdienst-pflicht', 27 Aug 1943; BA-MA, RL 41/7, RLB, Rundschreiben, 2 Oct 1942, based on a Göring Decree, 12 Aug 1942.

84. Dieter Busch, Der Luftkrieg im Raum Mainz während des Zweiten Welt-krieges 1939–1945 (Mainz: 1988), 67.

85. BA-B, R13/XVII/21, draft Führer Decree, Aug 1943; Armaments Ministry, 'Durchführungsanordnung zum Führererlass', 23 Aug 1943.

86. BA-B, R1501/938, Verwaltungsbezirk Schöneberg, 'Übersicht über die Sam-melunterkünfte für Obdachlose', Aug 1942.

87. Ibid., Interior Ministry memorandum, 'Besprechung im Rathaus Schöneberg', 9 Apr 1943, 1–3.

88. BA-B, R1501/823, Interior Ministry, 6 May 1942, 'Planmässige Vorberei-tung der Hilfsmassnahmen', 2–4.

89. BA-B, R1501/904, Interior Ministry, 'Richtlinien für die Durchführung von Bauarbeiten zur Beseitigung von Fliegerschäden', 12 Apr 1943.

90. BA-B, R1501/938, memorandum on activity of Baugruppe Pfeil, 9 Mar 1943.

91. BA-B, R1501/949, Stadt der Reichsparteistadt Nürnberg, 'Übersicht über die Fliegerschäden aus dem Luftangriffen vom 28/29.8.1942 bis 8/9.3 1943', 3 May 1943.

92. Ibid., Finance Ministry, Justice Ministry, minutes of meeting, 'Ausgaben für Kriegssachschäden', 17 Feb 1944, 1.

93. Stephan Glienke, 'The Allied Air War and German Society', in Baldoli, Knapp, Overy (eds), Bombing, States and Peoples, 186–8.

94. BA-B, NS 18/1062, Party Chancellery, 'Vorlage: Material und Arbeitskräfte für die Beseitigung von Fliegerschäden' [n.d.].

95. BA-B, R1501/938, ration cards for bomb victims, Berlin, Mar 1943; report from Wirtschaftsamt Schöneberg, 9 Apr 1943, 1–6.

96. RAFM, Harris papers, H51, Summary of the Foreign Press, 29 Aug 1942, Die Weltwoche, 12 June 1942.

97. BA-B, R1501/938, memorandum from Bezirksamt Schöneberg on the work of the Quartieramt (accommodation office), 9 Apr 1943, 1–2, 3–4.

98. BA-B, R1501/949, Stadt der Reichsparteitage Nürnberg, 3 May 1943.

99. Ibid., minutes of meeting, 'Ausgaben für Kriegssachschäden', 17 Feb 1944, 2.

100. TNA, AIR 48/33, USSBS, Civilian Defense Report no. 4: Hamburg Field Report, vol 1, 2, 30.

101. TNA, AIR 20/7287, 'Secret Report of the Police President of Hamburg on the Heavy Raids on Hamburg July/August 1943', 1 Dec 1943, 2–12; AIR 48/33, USSBS, Hamburg Field Report, vol 1, 45.

102. BA-B, NS 18/573, Luftkriegsmeldedienst, Luftangriffe, 14–17 May 1943, 22–23 June 1943; NS 18/1060, Luftangriffe auf deutsche Reichsgebiet, 27–28 May 1943.

103. Hamburg und Dresden im Dritten Reich: Bombenkrieg und Kriegsende:

Sieben Beiträge (Hamburg: 2000), 31–3; BA-B. NS 18/1060, Luftkriegs-meldedienst, Luftangriffe auf deutsche Reichsgebiet, 29–30 July 1943.

104. Büttner, '"Gomorrha" und die Folgen', 47, 69.

105. TNA, AIR 20/7287, 'Secret Report by the Police President of Hamburg', 22; BA-B, R1501/3791, report from Reich Health Leader (Leonardo Conti), 'Ärztliche Erfahrungen im Luftschutz', 27 Mar 1944.

106. BA-B, R1501/949, memorandum by Goebbels, 'Reichsinspektion zur Durchführung ziviler Luftkriegsmassnahmen', 28 Jan 1944, 3.

107. TNA, AIR 20/7287, 'Secret Report by the Police President of Hamburg', 23.

108. TNA, AIR 48/33, Hamburg Field Report, vol 1, 36. The fire service also calculated injury to a further 46,252; AIR 20/7287, 'Secret Report by the Police President of Hamburg', 17, 75.

109. Hans Nossack, *The End: Hamburg 1943* (Chicago, IL: 2004) 17–18, 44 (originally published in Germany in 1948 as *Der Untergang*).

110. Gretl Büttner, 'Zwischen Leben und Tod', in Volker Hage (ed), *Hamburg 1943: Literarische Zeugnisse zum Feuersturm* (Frankfurt am Main: 2003), 30–31.

111. BA-B, R1501/3791, Conti to the ILA, 5 Aug 1943; Dr Illig (Hamburg) to Conti, 5 Aug 1943; City Medical Council (Hanover) to Conti, 13 Aug 1943.

112. BA-B, R1501/37723, Luftschutz-Chemiker, Hamburg to Interior Ministry, 5 Nov 1943, encl. report, 'Trinkwasser-Notversorgung'.

113. BA-B, R1501/3791, RVK, Hamburg to Conti, 17 Aug 1943, 2–3; minute by Dr Cropp, Interior Ministry, 3 Aug 1943.

114. TNA, AIR 48/29, USSBS, Civilian Defense Division: Final Report, 72.

115. Hans Brunswig, *Feuersturm über Hamburg: Die Luftangriffe auf Hamburg im 2. Weltkrieg und ihre Folgen* (Stuttgart: 1985), 300–301.

116. Boberach (ed), *Meldungen aus dem Reich*, vol 14, 5,562–3, report for 2 Aug 1943. Göring visit in Brunswig, *Feuersturm*, 296.

117. Albert Speer, *Inside the Third Reich* (London: 1970), 284.

118. BA-B, R13/XVII/21, Armaments Ministry, 'Durchführungsanordnung zum Führererlass', 23 Aug 1943.

119. BA-B, R1501/949, 'Bericht über die Dienstreise des Reichsrichter Dr Danckelmann nach Hamburg, 20 bis 22 Juni 1944', 3–5.

120. Fred Iklé, *The Social Impact of Bomb Destruction* (Norman, OK: 1958), 67–8.

121. BA-MA, RL 41/7, RLB, Rundschreiben, July 1943.

122. TsAMO, f.500, 0.393761c, d.34, Arbeitsstab-LS, Erfahrungsbericht no. 18, 6 Oct 1943, 4; no. 22, 20 Jan 1944, 1; no. 23, 5 Mar 1944, 4.

123. Ibid., Erfahrungsbericht no. 20, 4 Dec 1943, 1.

124. TNA, AIR 20/7287, 'Secret Report by the Police President', 1 Dec 1943, 87–90.

125. BA-MA, RL41/6, RLB, Presse-Material, 2 Nov 1943; TsAMO, f.500, 0.393761c, d.34, Arbeitsstab-LS, Erfahrungsbericht Nr. 18, 7.

126. Ibid., f.500, 0.393761c, d.34, Erfahrungsbericht Nr. 17, 23 Sept 1943, 9; BA-MA, RL41/6, RLB, Presse-Material, 10 Aug 1943, 1; 2 Nov 1943, 1.

127. Heinz Pettenberg, *Starke Verbände im Anflug auf Köln*, ed. Hella Reuter-Pettenberg (Cologne: 1981), 90–91, entry for 31 May 1942.

128. Details from Linhardt, *Feuerwehr im Luftschutz*, 171–2, 173, 178, 180–82; Hans Rumpf, *The Bombing of Germany* (London: 1957), 186–7.

129. Kock, '*Der Führer sorgt für unsere Kinder*', 139–43; Katja Klee, *Im 'Luftschutzkeller des Reiches': Evakuierte in Bayern, 1939–1945* (Munich: 1999), 165–7.

130. BA-B, R1501/823, Interior Ministry to all local authorities, 27 July 1942.

131. BA-B, R1501/1515, Interior Ministry to provincial governments, 2 Feb 1943; Kock, '*Der Führer sorgt für unsere Kinder*', 141.

132. Groehler, *Bombenkrieg gegen Deutschland*, 266–7.

133. BA-B, R1501/3791, State Secretary Ganzenmüller, Transport Ministry, 'Transport Questions in Evacuation of Air War Regions', June 1943, 1; Groehler, *Bombenkrieg gegen Deutschland*, 282; Klee, *Im 'Luftschutzkeller des Reiches'*, 171.

134. BA-B, R3102/10044, Statistical Office, 'Stand der Umquartierung aus luftgefährdeten Gebieten', 15 Sept 1943.

135. BA-B, NS 18/1062, minute for Tiessler, Party Chancellery, 'Attitude of the Evacuees in the Reception Areas', 11 May 1943.

136. BA-B, NS 18/1333, Propaganda Ministry, Inter-Ministerial Committee to all Gauleiter, 19 Aug 1943, 1, 4.

137. Jill Stephenson, *Hitler's Home Front: Württemberg under the Nazis* (London: 2006), 299–301, 306–11; Glienke, 'Allied Air War and German Society', 196–8; Torrie, '*For Their Own Good*', 100–106. On tensions between evacuees and local populations see Nicholas Stargardt, *Witnesses of War: Children's Lives under the Nazis* (London: 2005), 256–9.

138. BA-B, R1501/3791, Mayor of Berlin to Reichsgesundheitsführer, Conti, 21 Aug 1943; RVK, Hamburg to Conti, 17 Aug 1943, 'Verteilung von Ärzten'.

139. Ibid., NSDAP, Hauptamt für Volkswohlfahrt to Conti, 13 July 1943.

140. BA-B, R1501/3809, Conti papers, 'Gedanken zur artzlichen Planwirtschaft', 12 Oct 1943; R1501/3791, Meeting of the Inter-Ministerial Committee, 21 July 1943; Reich Health Leader to Oberpräsident Münster, 30 July 1943.

141. BA-B, R1501/3791, memorandum to Reich Health Leader, 29 June 1943; Generalreferent für Luftkriegsschäden to Speer, 29 June 1943; RVK, Westfalen-Nord to Conti, 22 July 1943.

142. Ibid., President, German Red Cross, to all provincial offices, 2 July 1943; Conti to all RVK, 'Gesundheitliche Versorgung der Zivilbevölkerung bei Luftgrossangriffen', 5 July 1943.

143. BA-B, NS 18/1062, Karl Brandt, Führer HQ, circular report, 8 Oct 1941. Hitler's decision was taken on 24 August.

144. BA-BV, R1501/3809, Brandt to the Interior Ministry (Conti), Bormann and Hans Lammers, 21 June 1943; Brandt to Lammers, 30 June 1943; Brandt memorandum, 'Aufstellung der im Rahmen des Führerauftrages durch zuführenden Massnahmen'.

145. Süss, 'Wartime Societies and Shelter Politics', 36–8; Dietmar Süss, *Tod aus der Luft: Kriegsgesellschaft und Luftkrieg in Deutschland und England*

(Munich: 2011), 368–72. See too Peter Heinl, 'Invisible Psychological Ruins: Unconscious Long-Term War Trauma', workshop paper, Reading University, 13 Mar 2009. Heinl was able to explain serious psychiatric and psychosomatic conditions among a cohort of elderly Germans by exposing their childhood experiences under bombing.

146. BA-B, NS 18/1063, Notice for Tiessler, 17 Mar 1943.

147. Boberach (ed), *Meldungen aus dem Reich*, vol 13, 4,983, 22 Mar 1943.

148. BA-MA, RL 41/7, RLB, measures to be taken as a result of recent air raids, Sept 1943.

149. BA-B, NS 18/1333, Propaganda Ministry, 'Vorlage für den Herrn Minister', 28 Sept 1942. See too Nicholas Stargardt, *Witnesses of War: Children's Lives Under the Nazis* (London: 2005), 253–4.

150. BA-B, NS 18/1333, 'Vorlage für den Herrn Minister, 3 Juli 1943, Vermeidung von Gerüchten über die Bombardierung von Vulkanen'.

151. Waltraud Süssmilch, *Im Bunker: Eine Überlebende berichtet vom Bombenkrieg in Berlin* (Berlin: 2004), 7.

152. Friedrich Reck-Malleczewen, *Diary of a Man in Despair* (London: 1995), 188–9.

153. BA-B, NS 18/1058, conference with Goebbels, 20 May 1943, report by Mayor Ellgering; Michael Balfour, *Propaganda in War, 1939–1945* (London: 1979), 341.

154. Elke Fröhlich (ed), *Die Tagebücher von Joseph Goebbels: Teil II, Band 7: Januar–März 1943* (Munich: 1993), 540.

155. Ralf Reuth, *Goebbels: The Life of Joseph Goebbels. The Mephistophelean Genius of Nazi Propaganda* (London: 1993), 315–16; Eleanor Hancock, *The National Socialist Leadership and Total War, 1941–5* (New York: 1991), 69–73; Daniel Uziel, *The Propaganda Warriors: The Wehrmacht and the Consolidation of the German Home Front* (Bern: 2008), 303–4.

156. Boberach (ed), *Meldungen aus dem Reich*, vol 13, 5,217, 6 May 1943.

157. Uziel, *Propaganda Warriors*, 318–19; BA-B, NS 18/1333, Propaganda Ministry, 'Vorlage für den Herrn Minister', 28 Sept 1942; Bormann, Party Chancellery, 'Führungshinweis Nr. 7', 4 Nov 1943.

158. BA-B, NS 18/1063, NSDAP Propagandaleitung notice, 17 Mar 1943.

159. Ralf Blank, 'The Battle of the Ruhr, 1943: Aerial Warfare against an Industrial Region', *Labour History Review*, 77 (2012), 45.

160. Uziel, *Propaganda Warriors*, 316–17; Balfour, *Propaganda in War*, 343–4.

161. Boberach (ed), *Meldungen aus dem Reich*, vol 13, 5,187, 29 Apr 1943; vol 14, 5,699, 2 Sept 1943.

162. Uziel, *Propaganda Warriors*, 319–21; Blank, 'The Battle of the Ruhr', 45–6.

163. Cited in Jeffrey Herf, *The Jewish Enemy: Nazi Propaganda during World War II and the Holocaust* (Cambridge, MA: 2006), 215–16, 230; see too Balfour, *Propaganda in War*, 343–4.

164. BA-B, NS 18/1063, Propaganda-Kompanie Rundspruch, 13 Mar 1942, 'Todesanzeigen für Opfer bei Fliegerangriffen'; Reichspropagandamt Weser-Ems to Hans Fritzsche, Propaganda Ministry, 23 Feb 1942.

165. Ibid., OKW to Reichspropagandaleitung, 18 May 1942; Goebbels notice, 7 May 1943. Nicole Kramer, '"Kämpfende Mutter" und "gefallene Heldinnen" – Frauen im Luftschutz', in Süss (ed), *Deutschland im Luftkrieg*, 94–6.

166. Boberach (ed), *Meldungen aus dem Reich*, vol 14, 5,698, 2 Sept 1943. For a full account of the Witten incident see Torrie, 'For Their Own Good', 97–105.

167. Süssmilch, *Im Bunker*, 41–2.

168. Nossack, *The End*, 33; Rumpf, *The Bombing of Germany*, 202.

169. Boberach (ed.), *Meldungen aus dem Reich*, vol 14, 5,620, 16 Aug 1943.

170. Boberach (ed), *Meldungen aus dem Reich*, vol 14, 5,716, 6 Sept 1943; see too Glienke, 'Allied Air War', 191–2.

171. Hester Vaizey, *Surviving Hitler's War: Family Life in Germany, 1939–48* (Basingstoke: 2010), 65.

172. Nossack, *The End*, 31–2.

173. Ibid., 32.

174. Adam Tooze, 'No Room for Miracles: German Industrial Output in World War II Reassessed', *Geschichte und Gesellschaft*, 31 (2005), 439–64; Lutz Budrass, Jonas Scherner, Jochen Streb, 'Fixed-Price Contracts, Learning, and Outsourcing: Explaining the Continuous Growth of Output and Labour Productivity in the German Aircraft Industry during the Second World War', *Economic History Review*, 2nd Ser, 63 (2010), 107–36.

175. IWM, S363, Saur papers, Kartei des Technischen Amtes, 17, speech by the Führer, 23 Sept 1944.

176. BA-B, R7/2249, Bezirksgruppe Nordwest, Wirtschaftsgruppe Eisenschaffende Industrie, 'Zusammenhänge und Lage der nordwestlichen Eisenindustrie', 17 Aug 1945.

177. IWM, MD, vol 13, minutes of GL meeting, 27 Apr 1942.

178. Ibid., MD, vol 56, letter from Technical Office to Milch, 22 Oct 1942, 'Verlegung luftgefährdeter Betriebe'.

179. Edward Westermann, 'Hitting the Mark, but Missing the Target: Luftwaffe Deception Operations, 1939–1945', *War in History*, 10 (2003), 213–14; Werner Wolf, *Luftangriffe auf die deutsche Industrie 1942–1945* (Munich: 1985), 129–30.

180. Smith, *Last Train from Berlin*, 117–18.

181. Westermann, 'Hitting the Mark', 214–16.

182. Richard Overy, 'Guns or Butter? Living Standards, Finance and Labour in Germany, 1939–1942', in idem, *War and Economy in the Third Reich* (Oxford: 1994), 278, 293–5.

183. Rolf-Dieter Müller, 'Das Scheitern der wirtschaftlichen "Blitzkriegsstrategie"', in Horst Boog et al., *DRZW: Band 4: Der Angriff auf die Sowjetunion* (Stuttgart: 1983), 936–49, 1,022–9; Rolf-Dieter Müller, 'Albert Speer und die Rüstungspolitik 1942–1945' in *DRZW: Band 5/2: Organisation und Mobilisierung des deutschen Machtbereichs* (Stuttgart: 1999), 275–317.

184. CIOS Report, Item 21, Metallurgy, 'German Iron and Steel Industry: Ruhr

and Salzgitter Areas', June 1945, 11, 17; USSBS Report 69, *Fr. Krupp AG: Friedrich Alfred Hütte. Heavy Industry Plant Report No. 2* (Washington, DC: 12 Sept 1945), 1.

185. USSBS, Special Paper 3, *The Effects of Strategic Bombing upon the Operations of the Hermann Göring Works during World War II* (Washington, DC: 1946), 60; Control Office for Germany and Austria, 'German Industrial Complexes: The Hermann Göring Complex', June 1946, 42.

186. Müller, 'Albert Speer und die Rüstungspolitik', 620, 630–31, 632, 642. The argument developed by Adam Tooze, *Wages of Destruction: The Making and Breaking of the Nazi Economy* (London: 2006), 598–600, that bombing brought the expansion of arms production to a halt, remains unconvincing given the substantial increases in military output throughout the period from March 1943 to summer 1944.

187. IWM, Box S368, Report 54, Interrogation of Albert Speer, 13 July 1945, 3–4, 7–8. Air supply figures calculated from BA-MA, RL3/38, GL-Office, 'Überblick über den Rüstungsstand der Luftwaffe: 1 Januar 1945'; RL3/36, GL-Technical Office Report, 'Über die Gründe der erhöhten Lieferungen im Rahmen des Luftwaffenprogrammes von März bis Juni 1944'. On the overall effect of losses see Müller, 'Albert Speer und die Rüstungspolitik', 648–58.

188. BA-B, R13/XVII/21, draft Führer Decree, Aug 1943, on the repair of 'Damage Regions'; Ministry of Armaments and Munitions, 'Durchführungsanordnung zum Führererlass', 23 Aug 1943.

189. TsAMO, f.500, 0.393761c, d.34, LS-Arbeitsstab [luftschutz–Air Protection], Erfahrungsbericht, 15 Nov 1943, 12.

190. BA-B, R3101/31135, Economics Ministry to all Reich authorities, 1 Oct 1943.

191. Wolf, *Luftangriffe auf die deutsche Industrie*, 69–74.

192. BA-B, R1501/1071, Four Year Plan, Price Commissar Decree, 4 Sept 1942.

193. Ibid., Plenipotentiary for Labour Supply (Fritz Sauckel) to Reich Trustees of Labour, 9 July 1943.

194. IWM, Box S368, Report 85, Interrogation of Dr Theodor Hupfauer (Ministry of War Production, Chief of Labour Supply), 10 Sept 1945, 3; Hans Pohl, Wilhelm Treue, *Die Daimler-Benz AG in den Jahren 1933 bis 1945* (Wiesbaden: 1986), 173–4, 179.

195. IWM, Box S368, Report 85, Hupfauer interrogation, 8, 14.

196. TsAMO, f.500, 0.393761c, d.34, LS-Arbeitsstab, Erfahrungsberichte, 1 July 1944, 1–2.

197. See the intelligence report from interrogation of the former Italian consul general in Frankfurt, TNA, PREM 3/193/6A, HQ Algiers to War Office, 30 Oct 1943: 'workers particularly were depressed for they now had a reasonable standard of living which they knew would disappear if war lost'. Also LC, Spaatz papers, Box 203, Propaganda Research Section, 'Morale in Hamburg', 29 Jan 1942, based on conversations with Hamburg workers from a Belgian source who identified three principal fears: fear of unemployment and starvation; fear of retribution by the Allies; fear of the dismemberment of Germany.

198. Martin Moll (ed), 'Führer-Erlasse' 1939–1945 (Stuttgart: 1997), 345, decree of 28 June 1943.

199. BA-B, R3101/31170, Führer Decree, 'über Sicherstellung vom Raumen zur Aufnahme von Rüstungsfertigungen aus luftgefährdeten Gebieten'; Armaments Ministry order, 'Betriebsverlagerung und Verlagerung von Lager', 14 July 1943.

200. IWM, MD, vol 56, Air Ministry Technical Office to Milch, 22 Oct 1942; report from Planning Office for Milch, 14 Oct 1942.

201. Ibid., Planning Office to Milch on dispersal policy, 17 Nov 1942; BA-MA, RL36/52, report on conferences of 22, 23, 26, 28, 29 and 30 July 1943, 'über die Massnahmen zur Verstärkung der Luftverteidigung'.

202. Details from Friedhelm Golücke, Schweinfurt und der strategische Luftkrieg 1943 (Paderborn: 1980), 351–3, 357–8, 363–4, 368–70, 372, 378–80.

203. BA-B, RL3/36, GL-Technical Office Report, 'Über die Gründe'.

204. Details in USSBS, Report 7, 'Erla Maschinenwerke GmbH, Leipzig', 1–2, 6; Report 9, 'Gothaer Waggonfabrik AG, Gotha', 1–2, 13; Report 14, 'Wiener-Neustädter Flugzeugwerke', 1–2, 9–12.

205. IWM, MD, vol 51, Main Committee Iron Production (Dr Helmut Rohland) to all industry heads, 27 Mar 1944, 2.

206. IWM, EDS MI 14/133, Army High Command, 'Studie über Rüstung', 25 Jan 1944.

207. IWM, EDS AL/1746, interrogation of Karl-Otto Saur, 10 Aug 1945; Box S368, Report 90, 'Rationalisation in the Components Industry', 34; Dietrich Eichholtz, Geschichte der deutschen Kriegswirtschaft, 4 vols (Munich: 1999), vol 2, 316–17.

208. BA-B, R3101/11921, Economics Ministry, Weekly Reports on Economic Conditions, 7 Feb 1944, 1; 27 May 1944, 1; 28 Sept 1944, 1; 21 Oct 1944, 7. See too Bernhard Kroener, '"Menschenbewirtschaftung", Bevölkerungsverteilung und personelle Rüstung in der zweiten Kriegshälfte (1942–1944)', in Kroener, Müller, Umbreit, DRZW: Band 5/2, 931–4.

209. BA-B, R3101/11921, Economics Ministry Weekly Report, 14 Feb 1944, 1; IWM, Box S366, FIAT Report, 'Statistical Material on the German Manpower Position during the War Period', 31 July 1945. On Daimler-Benz, see Pohl, Treue, Die Daimler-Benz AG, 145.

210. BA-B, R3101/11921, Economics Ministry Weekly Report, 18 Dec 1944, 7. See too Cornelia Rauh-Kühne, 'Hitlers Hehler? Unternehmerprofite und Zwangsarbeiterlöhne', Historische Zeitschrift, 275 (2002), 40–41.

211. BA-B, R3101/11921, Economics Ministry Weekly Report, 18 Dec 1944, 7. The proportion of hours lost for each category was as follows: air raids 2.5%, illness 5.7%, leave 3.0%, truancy 1.3%, workplace problems 3.5%.

212. BA-B, R3102/10031, Statistical Office, 'Vermerk über die Auswirkung der feindlichen Luftangriffe auf die Arbeiterstundenleistung der Industrie', 27 Jan 1945, 2.

213. IWM, Box S126, BBSU, 'MS notes on Ford Cologne'.

214. TNA, AIR 10/3873, BBSU, 'German Experience in the Underground Trans-

fer of War Industries', App 1, 'Survey of Natural Underground Facilities in Greater Germany', 1 July 1943; BA-B, R3101/31170, Mining Office, Bavaria to Mines Department, Economics Ministry, 29 July 1943; Dortmund Mining Office to Mines Department, 7 Aug 1943. For an excellent overview of the underground programme see Paul Clemence, 'German Underground Factories of the Second World War: An Essential Folly', unpublished PhD thesis, University of Exeter, 2008, chs 2–3.

215. TNA, AIR 10/3873, BBSU, 'German Experience', 5.

216. CIOS Report XXX-80, 'Bavarian Motor Works: A Production Survey' (1946), 44–5, 50–51; Hans Mommsen, Manfried Grieger, *Das Volkswagenwerk und seine Arbeiter im Dritten Reich* (Düsseldorf: 1997), 844–5, 879, 1,027; Rauh-Kühne, 'Hitlers Hehler?', 44–5.

217. TNA, AIR 10/3873, BBSU, 'German Experience', 10, 14–15.

218. BA-B, R3101/11921, Economics Ministry weekly reports, 12 Feb 1944, 1; 11 Mar 1944, 1; 28 July 1944, 1; 23 Sept 1944, 1.

219. IWM, Box S368, FIAT Report 67, 'Causes in the Decline of German Industrial Production', 13 Dec 1945, 5, interrogation of Wilhelm Schaaf, 13, Saur interrogation.

220. Ibid., Box S368, Report 52, Interrogation of S. Stieler von Heydekampf, 6 Oct 1945, 10.

221. LC, Spaatz papers, Box 203, J. K. Galbraith, 'Preliminary Appraisal of Achievement of Strategic Bombing of Germany', 2.

222. BA-B, R3102/10031, Statistical Office, 'Statistik der Luftkriegsschädenbetroffene Industriebetriebe: November 1944'; Statistical Office, 'Die Tätigkeit der feindlichen Luftwaffe über den Reichsgebiete im September 1944'.

223. IWM, Box S368, FIAT Report 67, interrogation of Karl-Otto Saur, 12.

224. IWM, EDS MI 14/133, OKH, General-Quartermaster Planning Office, 'Sturm-Programm', 9 Jan 1945, 1–6.

225. IWM, Box S369, SHAEF-G2, interrogation of Albert Speer, 7 June 1945, 3; Box S368, FIAT Report 83, 5 Apr 1946, App 1, 'Speer's Outside Organization'; on the autarkic zones, BA-B, R12 I/9, Reichsgruppe Industrie to all Economic Groups, 5 Mar 1945, 'Verkehrsnot: Bildung eines Verkehrsstabes'; RI to Economic Groups, 8 Mar 1945, 'Einsatz von Rüstungsbevollmächtigten'.

226. Rumpf, *The Bombing of Germany*, 130–31.

227. BA-B, R1501/949, Himmler to all Reich authorities, 21 Feb 1944.

228. Irmtraud Permooser, *Der Luftkrieg über München, 1942–1945: Bomben auf die Hauptstadt der Bewegung* (Oberhachung: 1996), 359; Busch, *Der Luftkrieg im Raum Mainz*, 367.

229. Süssmilch, *Im Bunker*, 55.

230. Linhardt, *Feuerwehr im Luftschutz*, 172–4; Brinkhus, 'Ziviler Luftschutz', 38–9. On the 'Air Protection Regiments' (*Luftschutz-Regimenten*) see e.g. RL13/4, Einsatz LS-Regiment 7, Luftgau VII, 26 Feb–25 Mar 1945.

231. BA-MA, RL 41/7, RLB, Hesse-Rheinland, Rundschreiben, 9 June 1944.

232. BA-B, R1501/1513, Interior Ministry to RVK, Gauleiter, Reichsstatthalter,

6 Jan 1944, encl. 'Erlass des Führers über die Errichtung einer Reichs-inspektion der zivilen Luftkriegsmassnahmen', 21 Dec 1943.

233. BA-B, R1501/949, Himmler to all RVK, 10 Sept 1944, 'Vorbereitungen für die Verteidigung des Reiches'. On Goebbels' new office, Süss, 'Steuerung durch Information', 202–4; Reuth, *Goebbels*, 324–7.

234. BA-B, R1501/1513, Gauleitung Sudetenland to NSDAP-Leitung, 3 Feb 1944; Report from Reich Defence Commissar Hannover-Ost, Aug 1944.

235. BA-B, R3101/31135, Polizeiliche Anordnung über die Luftschutzdienst-pflicht im Selbstschutz, 27 Aug 1943.

236. BA-B, R1501/949, Propaganda Ministry (Berndt) to the Inter-Ministerial Committee, 29 Jan 1944, encl. memorandum from Goebbels, 2.

237. Süssmilch, *Im Bunker*, 54–5.

238. BA-MA, RL 41/7, RLB, Hesse-Rheinland, Rundschreiben, 6 May 1944.

239. BA-B, R1501/906, Speer to all OT-Einsatzgruppenleiter and RVK Bau-beauftragten, 28 Sept 1944, 2.

240. BA-B, R3101/11922, Reichsgruppe Handwerk memorandum, 9 June 1943; Reichsgruppe Handwerk to Transport Ministry, 23 Aug 1943; Reichsgruppe Handwerk to Economics Ministry, 22 May 1944; Finance Ministry to Economics Ministry, 15 July 1944.

241. BA-B, R3102/10031, Otto Ohlendorf (Economics Ministry) to Reich Statistical Office, 9 Mar 1944.

242. Ibid., Economics Ministry note, 'Fliegerschäden in Monat Oktober 1944'; 'Fliegerschäden Januar/Dezember 1943'.

243. Ibid., Air Ministry, LS-Arbeitsstab, 'Übersicht über Luftangriffe und Bombenabwürfe im Heimatkriegsgebiet', Nov 1944.

244. BA-B, R1501/3723, Interior Ministry to all Reich authorities, 24 June 1944.

245. Ibid., Interior Ministry (Murray), 'Für die Trinkwasserversorgung bereit-gestellte Tankfahrzeuge', June 1944; Generalinspektor für Wasser- und Energie, memorandum for Wirtschaftsgruppe Wasser, 'Luftschutz an Wasserversorgungsanlagen', 7 Aug 1944.

246. Ibid., Eastern German Brewing Association to Interior Ministry, 13 Sept 1943; 'Brunnenvorhaben in Gross-Berlin', 30 June 1944; Interior Ministry memorandum, 30 June 1944.

247. BA-B, R13/XVII/21, Wirtschaftsgruppe Gas- und Wasserversorgung, Angriff auf Leipzig, 6 Dec 1943; Luftangriffsmeldung, 4 Sept 1943; on gas capacity see 'Durchschnittliche Tagesleistung der 950 Erzeugerwerke von Stadtgas, Julibis November 1943', which shows spare capacity on each date approximately double the capacity damaged by bombing.

248. Ibid., R13/XVII/49, 'Fliegergeschädigte Werke, Stand 1.6.1944'; General-inspektor für Wasser und Energie to Wirtschaftsgruppe, 22 Nov 1944; Generalinspektor to Niederrheinische Licht- und Kraftwerke AG, 1 Nov 1944, approving the permanent closure of the Mönchengladbach gasholder.

249. Anon., *A Woman in Berlin* (London: 2005), 19.

250. BA-B, R3102/10031, list of damaged cultural and artistic treasures, 15 May

1944; Stadtsynodalverband, Berlin, 'Fliegerschäden an kirchlichen Gebäude 28 April bis 1 Juni 1944'.

251. Permooser, *Der Luftkrieg über München*, 372–5.

252. Busch, *Der Luftkrieg im Raum Mainz*, 361.

253. BA-B, R1501/949, Goebbels memorandum, 28 Jan 1944, 3.

254. Ibid., Himmler to all Reich authorities, 21 Feb 1944.

255. BA-B, R3102/10044, NSDAP, Reichsleitung, Hauptamt für Volkswohlfahrt, Stand der Umquartierung, 11 Jan 1945. See too Groehler, *Bombenkrieg gegen Deutschland*, 281–2; Zelinski, Kosinski, *Emergency Evacuation of Cities*, 167–8, 171–3; Klee, *Im 'Luftschutzkeller des Reiches'*, 150–51, 172–3.

256. Iklé, *Social Impact of Bomb Destruction*, 66–7.

257. Boberach (ed), *Meldungen aus dem Reich*, vol 14, 5,645, 19 Aug 1943.

258. Groehler, *Bombenkrieg gegen Deutschland*, 447.

259. BA-B, R3102/10031, Economics Ministry, 'Fliegerschäden in Monat August 1944'; 'Fliegerschäden in Monat Oktober 1944'; Reich Statistical Office, 'Die Tätigkeit der feindlichen Luftwaffe über dem Reichsgebiet, Oktober 1944', 10 Jan 1945, 9.

260. TNA, AIR 48/29, USSBS, Civilian Defense Division: Final Report, 3 (using LS-Arbeitsstab figures for Greater Germany). These figures can also be found in BA-B, R3102/1003, Arbeitsstab, monthly reports.

261. BA-B, NS18/1063, Partei Kanzlei, Abt. PG, 'Angaben über die Verluste nach Fliegerangriffen', 2 Oct 1942; Groehler, *Bombenkrieg gegen Deutschland*, 316–20.

262. Hans Sperling, 'Deutsche Bevölkerungsbilanz des 2.Weltkrieges', *Wirtschaft und Statistik*, 8 (1956), 498–9.

263. Groehler, *Bombenkrieg gegen Deutschland*, 320; Blank, 'Kriegsalltag und Luftkrieg', 459–60.

264. Calculated from Martin Middlebrook and Chris Everitt, *The Bomber Command War Diaries* (Leicester: 2000), 657–701.

265. Anon., *Woman in Berlin*, 22–3.

266. Boberach (ed), *Meldungen aus dem Reich*, vol 16, 6,466, 6 Apr 1944.

267. Ibid., vol 17, 6,618, 29 June 1944; 6,646, 14 July 1944; 6,697–8, 8 Aug 1944.

268. Ibid., vol 16, 6,298, 3 Feb 1944; 6,414, Mar 1944; vol 17, 6,509–10, 4 May 1944; 6,565, 1 June 1944; Neil Gregor, 'A *Schicksalsgemeinschaft*? Allied Bombing, Civilian Morale, and Social Dissolution in Nuremberg, 1942–1945', *The Historical Journal*, 43 (2000), 1,051–70.

269. USSBS, Report 64b, 'Effects of Bombing on German Morale', 19–20.

270. Ibid., 16. The percentages were: military reverses, 48%; Allied superiority, 24%; air raids, 15%; war shortages, 2%; miscellaneous, 11%.

271. Dietmar Süss, 'Nationalsozialistische Deutungen des Luftkrieges', in idem, *Deutschland im Luftkrieg*, 104–8. On living standards see Gernot Wiese, 'Die Versorgungslage in Deutschland', in Michael Salewski, Guntram Schulze-Wegener (eds), *Kriegsjahr 1944: Im Grossen und im Kleinen* (Stuttgart: 1995), 340–46.

272. Hans Schlange-Schoeningen, *The Morning After* (London: 1948), 229, entry for 1 Jan 1945.

273. Boberach (ed), *Meldungen aus dem Reich*, vol 16, 6,302–4, 7 Feb 1944, 'Gefühlsmässige Einstellung der Bevölkerung gegenüber den Feinden'.

274. Barbara Grimm, 'Lynchmorde an allierten Fliegern im Zweiten Weltkrieg', in Süss (ed), *Deutschland im Luftkrieg*, 75–6; Neville Wylie, 'Muted Applause? British Prisoners of War as Observers and Victims of the Allied Bombing Campaign over Germany', in Baldoli, Knapp, Overy (eds), *Bombing, States and Peoples*, 266–7; Blank, 'Kriegsalltag und Luftkrieg', 449–50.

275. Boberach (ed), *Meldungen aus dem Reich*, vol 17, 6,566, 1 June 1944; Hugh Trevor-Roper (ed), *Hitler's Table Talk, 1941–1944* (London: 1973), 696, entry for 6 Sept 1942; Grimm, 'Lynchmorde', 79–80.

276. Nossack, *The End*, 34; criticism of Goebbels in Boberach (ed), *Meldungen aus dem Reich*, vol 17, 6,566.

277. Marlene Hiller, 'Stuttgarter erzählen vom Luftkrieg', in idem (ed), *Stuttgart im Zweiten Weltkrieg* (Gerlingen: 1989), 425.

278. Süssmilch, *Im Bunker*, 10, 14–15.

279. BA-MA, RL 13/2, Luftschutz-Regiment 3 to Luftgaukommando III, Einsatzbericht, 9 Aug 1944.

280. BA-MA, RL 13/4, LS-Regiment 7, Luftgau VII, Erfahrungsbericht 26 Feb–25 Mar 1945; LS-Regiment, Abteilung 22 to LS-Regimentstab, 25 Feb 1945, 'Einsatzbericht: Nürnberg von 20 bis 23 Februar 1945'.

281. Matthias Gretzschel, *Als Dresden im Feuersturm versank* (Hamburg: 2004), 148–9; Victor Klemperer, *To the Bitter End: The Diaries of Victor Klemperer 1942–1945* (London: 1999), 387. The fullest account of the raid is Frederick Taylor, *Dresden: Tuesday 13 February 1945* (London: 2004).

282. Klemperer, *To the Bitter End*, 393, entry for 22–24 Feb 1945.

283. Erich Hampe, . . . *als alles in Scherben fiel* (Osnabrück: 1979), 119–21.

284. Oliver Reinhard, Matthias Neutzner, Wolfgang Hesse, *Das rote Leuchten: Dresden und der Bombenkrieg* (Dresden: 2005), 101–2.

285. Gretzschel, *Als Dresden im Feuersturm versank*, 149; idem, 'Dresden im Dritten Reich', in *Hamburg und Dresden im Dritten Reich*, 97–8.

286. Klemperer, *To the Bitter End*, 398, entry for 19 Feb 1945; Matthias Neutzner, '"Wozu leben wir nun noch? Um zu warten, bis die Russen kommen?" Die Dresdner Bevölkerung vom 13/14 Februar bis zum 17 April 1945', in *Hamburg und Dresden im Dritten Reich*, 100.

287. Schlange-Schoeningen, *The Morning After*, 232–3.

288. Süssmilch, *Im Bunker*, 21–2.

289. Anon., *Woman in Berlin*, 48.

290. Irmgard Hunt, *On Hitler's Mountain: My Nazi Childhood* (London: 2005), 220, 222–3, 225.

291. Süssmilch, *Im Bunker*, 221–2.

8. ITALY: THE WAR OF BOMBS AND WORDS

1. British Committee on the Preservation and Restitution of Works of Art, *Works of Art in Italy: Losses and Survival in the War: Part I – South of Bologna* (London: 1945); *Part II – North of Bologna* (London: 1946).

2. IWM, London, Italian Series (Air Force), Box 22, E2566, Italian Air Staff study, 'Contributo italiano allo sforzo bellico: Attività della RA dall' 8 settembre 1943 all' 8 maggio 1945', 15–16.

3. Gregory Alegi, 'Qualità del materiale bellico e dottrina d'impiego italiana nella seconda guerra mondiale: il caso della Regia Aeronautica', *Storia contemporanea*, 18 (1987), 1,213.

4. Eric Lehman, *Le ali del potere: La propaganda aeronautica nell'Italia fascista* (Turin: 2010), 78–81, 88–90.

5. IWM, London, Italian Series (Air Force), Box 23/E3003, Ministero dell'Aeronautica, 'Raccolta straci dei voli della Eccel. Il Capo del Governo, Benito Mussolini' (n.d. but late 1942). He undertook 38 flights in 1939, 29 in 1940, 15 in 1941 and 35 in the first nine months of 1942.

6. Valentino Pivetti, 'La potenza dell'arma aerea e la guerra di rapido corso', *Rivista Aeronautica*, 15 (Mar 1939), 491–2.

7. Lucio Ceva, *Spagna 1936–1939: Politica e guerra civile* (Milan: 2010), 333–4.

8. Francesco Pricolo, 'L'aviazione italiana nell'anno XVIII', *Rivista Aeronautica*, 16 (Feb 1940), 186.

9. Vincenzo Lioy, 'Bilancio di guerra aerea', *Rivista Aeronautica*, 16 (Apr 1940), 1–2; Bruno Montanari, 'I inseguamenti della guerra' *Rivista Aeronautica*, 17 (Feb 1941), 251–3. On the idea of moral collapse, Anacheto Bronzuoli, 'Guerre passate e guerra futura', *Rivista Aeronautica*, 15 (Dec 1939), 399–400.

10. Ferruccio Botti, 'Amedeo Mecozzi', in *Actes du colloque international 'Précurseurs et prophètes de l'aviation militaire'* (Paris: 1992), 133–6, 139–40.

11. Piero Incerpi, 'Attacco al suolo nell'azione a "catena"', *Rivista Aeronautica*, 15 (Feb 1939), 263, 269; Pricolo, 'L'aviazione italiana', 187.

12. Ibid., 185.

13. Ceva, *Spagna 1936–1939*, 314–15, 318–19, 330; Joseph Maiolo, *Cry Havoc: How the Arms Race Drove the World to War, 1931–1941* (New York: 2006), 218–19.

14. Giorgio Rochat, *Guerre italiane in Libia e in Etiopia: studi militari 1921–1939* (Paese: 1991), 123, 128, 132–5.

15. Ceva, *Spagna 1936–1939*, 315, 330, 336–40.

16. Ibid., 316, 333–4, 336. The figures on raids are derived from contemporary records of the Spanish Republican Ministry of Defence.

17. Pivetti, 'La potenza dell'arma aerea: Parte 2', *Rivista Aeronautica*, 15 (Apr 1939), 36.

18. IWM, Italian Series, Box 25, Superaereo, Ufficio statistica operative, 'Relazi-one statistica sull'attività operativa dell'aeronautica dall'inizio delle ostilità al 30 settembre 1942', 3, figure for 1 June 1940; the figure of 1,332 is given for 10 June 1940 in G. Bignozzi, B. Catalanotto, *Storia degli Aerei d'Italia* (Rome: 1962), 121. Total air strength on paper was 3,214.

19. Lucio Ceva, Andrea Curami, 'Luftstreitkräfte und Luftfahrtindustrie in Italien, 1936–1943', in Horst Boog (ed), *Luftkriegführung im Zweiten Weltkrieg* (Bonn: 1993), 115–16.

20. See MacGregor Knox, *Hitler's Italian Allies: Royal Armed Forces, Fascist Regime and the War of 1940–1943* (Cambridge: 2000), 62, 64, 141, 164; Ceva, Curami, 'Luftstreitkräfte', 115. On radar see Luigi Castioni, 'I radar industriali italiani. Ricerche, ricordi, considerazioni per una loro storia', *Storia contemporanea*, 18 (1987), 1,223–4, 1,249.

21. Alegi, 'Qualità del materiale bellico', 1,200–201; Ceva, Curami, 'Luftstreit-kräfte', 116–18; Knox, *Hitler's Italian Allies*, 64; Maiolo, *Cry Havoc*, 219.

22. Vera Zamagni, 'Italy: How to Lose the War and Win the Peace', in Mark Harrison (ed), *The Economics of World War II* (Cambridge: 1998), 182–5, 196; Alessandro Massignani, 'L'industria bellica italiana e la Germania nella seconda guerra mondiale', *Italia Contemporanea*, 190 (1993), 192–95.

23. Andrea Natalini, *I rapporti tra aeronautica italiana e tedesca durante la seconda guerra mondiale* (Cosenza: 2004), 21–5.

24. Ibid., 27–31.

25. IWM, Italian Series, Box 25, 'Relazione statistica sull'attività operativa', 12; Box 14, E2547, Corpo Aereo Italiano, report on operations October 1940. Small raids were also made on Colchester and Orford Ness.

26. Peter Haining, *The Chianti Raiders: The Extraordinary Story of the Italian Air Force in the Battle of Britain* (London: 2005), 114.

27. Natalini, *I rapporti tra aeronautica italiana e tedesca*, 42.

28. Claudia Baldoli, Andrew Knapp, *Forgotten Blitzes: France and Italy under Allied Air Attack, 1940–1945* (London: 2012), 123; Amedeo Mecozzi, 'L'ala fascista domina la guerra', *Rivista Aeronautica*, 16 (Dec 1940), 497–507.

29. IWM, Italian Series, Box 14, E2545, Ministero dell'Aeronautica, Servizio Informazioni Aeronautiche, circulars on the experience of war gathered by German aviation, 5 Nov 1940; 'Esperienze di guerra e notizie varie sulla Gran Bretagna', 31 Mar 1941.

30. IWM, Italian Series, Box 14, E2547, Col Luigi Overta (Corpo Aereo Ital-iano), 'Cenni sull'impiego del bombardamento dell'aeronautica del Reich', 29 Mar 1941.

31. Andrea Zotti, 'La teoretica e l'esperienza', *Rivista Aeronautica*, 17 (May 1941), 214–16, 220.

32. IWM, Italian Series, Box 11, E2541, Stato maggiore dell'aeronautica, 'Ore di volo belliche, 10 giugno 1940 al 30 giugno 1941'.

33. *The Jerusalem Post*, 25 Sept 2012, 'How Italy Bombed Tel Aviv in World War II'.

34. Calculated from the statistics in IWM, Box 25, 'Relazione statistica sull'attività operativa', 13, 16.

35. Ibid., 54, 56a, 56b; Knox, *Hitler's Italian Allies*, 163.

36. Alegi, 'Qualità del materiale bellico', 1,201–2, 1,209, 1,213. On training units see IWM, Italian Series, Box 19, E2560, Stato maggiore dell'aeronautica, 'Costituzione dei "Gruppi Complementari" presso i reparti', 12 Aug 1941.

37. IWM, Italian Series, Box 19, E2560, report from Commander 30th Stormo to Commander of Air Forces in Sicily (n.d. but Aug 1941), 1–2.

38. 'Appunti per il potenziamento dell'arma aerea', *Rivista Aeronautica*, 17 (Aug 1941), 301. On the lead role of the group commander see 'La posizione del comandante nella formazione bombardiera', *Rivista Aeronautica*, 16 (June 1940), 411.

39. NAM, Box 24/4, Air Raid Report Book, 1942–4. The last raid occurred on 16 August 1944.

40. Claudia Baldoli, 'The "Northern Dominator" and the Mare Nostrum: Fascist Italy's "Cultural War" in Malta', *Modern Italy*, 13 (2008), 8–14.

41. NAM, Box 1/1, minutes of meeting of ARP Committee, 14 Dec 1934; Note, 'Passive Defence of Malta', 11 Jan 1935; Note by the Lt. Gov., 27 Mar 1935, 'Programme for Development of Passive Defence Measures, Malta'.

42. NAM, Box 1/1, minute, C. H. Sampson, ARP officer, Sept 1939. On decontamination, 'Estimate of Personnel Requiring Instruction in Anti-Gas School'.

43. Michael Budden, 'Defending the Indefensible? The Air Defence of Malta, 1936–1940', *War in History*, 6 (1999), 462–3.

44. IWM, Italian Series, Box 22, E2567, Stato maggiore della R. Aeronautica, 'La situazione della base di Malta da giugno 1940 all'ottobre 1942', 31 Oct 1942, 1–2.

45. Ibid., 2–3; Box 11, E2541, 'Azioni offensive su Malta dall' 11-6-40 al 19-4-41'.

46. Ibid., 'Velivoli perduti in Azioni su Malta dall'11-6-40 al 19-4-41'; NAM, Box 23/1, HQ ARP Malta, 'List of Raids and Raiders 1940–1942'; TNA, AIR 23/5707, Report from HQ RAF Malta to Air Ministry, 23 July 1940.

47. Budden, 'Defending the Indefensible?', 460–64; Douglas Austin, *Malta and British Strategic Policy, 1925–1943* (London: 2004), 82–4, 91–6; Robert Mallett, *The Italian Navy and Fascist Expansionism, 1935–1940* (London: 1998), 193–5. Italian intelligence greatly exaggerated the size of Malta's defences, assuming at least 105 aircraft on the island in June 1940, a figure not reached until almost two years later.

48. TNA, AIR 2/7397, Air Ministry to C-in-C, Bomber Command, 28 Oct and 29 Oct 1940; HQ RAF Malta to Air Ministry, 4 Nov 1940; Air Ministry, Plans to DCAS, 3 Nov 1940.

49. TNA, AIR 23/7375, Air Ministry propaganda department to RAF commander, Malta, 4 Dec 1940.

50. Ibid., Air Ministry to RAF commander, Malta, 18 Jan 1941.

51. TNA, AIR 2/7397, HQ RAF Malta to Air Ministry, 9 Nov 1940; Portal to deputy chief of staff (Harris), 10 Nov 1940.

52. NAM, Box 16/1, Note on Evacuation; Census of Population, Northern Region, 20 Aug 1942; Regional Protection Office, Western Region, Census, 19 Aug 1942; Local Government Office, 'Evacuation Scheme'.

53. Frederick Galea, *Women of Malta: True Wartime Stories of Christina Ratcliffe and Tamara Marks* (Rabat: 2006), 30–35; NAM, Box 16/1, 'Evacuation of Marsaskala: General Instructions', 19 July 1940.

54. TNA, HO 192/59, REDept to the War Office, 19 Oct 1942; R & E Report, 'Effects of Bombs on Tunnel Shelters', 21 Aug 1942.

55. Galea, *Women of Malta*, 45–6, testimony of Christina Ratcliffe.

56. IWM, Italian Series, Box 25, 'Relazione statistica sull'attività operativa', 7. The figures were 30,825 hours of daylight bombing, 9,659 by night. On shelter policy see Austin, *Malta and British Strategic Policy*, 87–8.

57. NAM, Box 14/14, List of Regional Protection Officers, Deputy Regional Protection Officers in Malta and Gozo; Box 21/6, transcript, 'Broadcast by His Excellency the Officer Administering the Government', 27 June 1940, 3–4.

58. NAM, Box 21/6, memorandum from Lt. Gov.'s office, 18 June 1940; Box 21/7, ARP Department, Malta, 'Curfew', 2 July 1940; ARP Officer, Malta to Adjutant of police 'specials', 27 Nov 1940; ARP officer to police superintendent, Msida centre, 12 Nov 1940.

59. NAM, Box 21/6, Information Office, Valletta, to all secretaries of clubs, schoolmasters and schoolmistresses, 14 June 1940; 'Broadcast by His Excellency', 27 June 1940, 3.

60. Galea, *Women of Malta*, 53, 59–60, testimony of Tamara Marks.

61. See reports Sept–Oct 1941 in IWM, Italian Series, Box 10, E2532, operational reports, 29 Gruppo (Bombardamento), 30 Sept, 15 Oct, 17 Oct, 18 Oct, 30 Oct 1941.

62. James Holland, *Fortress Malta: An Island under Siege 1940–1943* (London: 2003), 87–91.

63. Galea, *Women of Malta*, 86, testimony of Tamara Marks.

64. Giorgio Rochat, *Le guerre italiane 1935–1943: Dall'impero d'Etiopia alla disfatta* (Turin: 2005), 333ff.

65. Natalini, *I rapporti tra aeronautica italiana e tedesca*, 61–2.

66. Bernd Stegemann, 'The Italo-German Conduct of the War in the Mediterranean and North Africa', in Gerhard Schreiber, Bernd Stegemann, Detlef Vogel, *Germany and the Second World War: Vol. III: The Mediterranean, South-East Europe, and North Africa 1939–1941* (Oxford: 1995), 654.

67. IWM, Italian Series, Box 14, E2545, X Corps, Ufficio di collegamento per la R. Aeronautica, 'Dislocazione reparti di volo del corpo aereo tedesco', 15 Apr 1941; Air Ministry, *The Rise and Fall of the German Air Force, 1933–1945* (London: 1983), 126–7.

68. Rochat, *Le guerre italiane*, 345; IWM, Italian Series, Box 11, E2541, 'Azioni offensive su Malta dall' 11-6-40 al 19-4-41'.

69. *Fuehrer Conferences on Naval Affairs 1939–1945* (London: 1990), 185, 'Report by the C-in-C Navy to the Fuehrer, March 18 1941'.

70. IWM, Italian Series, Box 22, E2567, 'La situazione della base aero-navale di Malta dall'inizio delle operazioni ad oggi', 31 Oct 1942, 4.

71. For an excellent account of the naval war off Malta see Austin, *Malta and British Strategic Policy*, 127–35. See too Mariano Gabriele, 'L'offensiva su Malta (1941)', in R. Rainero, A. Biagini (eds), *Italia in guerra: il secondo anno, 1941* (Rome: 1992), 444–5.

72. *Fuehrer Conferences on Naval Affairs*, 240, 'Report by the C-in-C Navy to the Fuehrer at Wolfschanze, 13 November 1941'.

73. Natalini, *I rapporti tra aeronautica italiana e tedesca*, 80–83, 86–7; Air Ministry, *Rise and Fall of the German Air Force*, 131–3.

74. IWM, Italian Series, Box 23, E3003, Fliegerführer Sizilien: Einsatzbefehle, 17 and 18 Dec 1941, 1 Jan 1942; HQ II Fliegerkorps, 'Befehl zur Bekämpf-ung von Blockadebrechern für Malta', 13 Jan 1942.

75. Natalini, *I rapporti tra aeronautica italiana e tedesca*, 89.

76. Hugh Lloyd, *Briefed to Attack: Malta's Part in the African Victory* (London: 1949), 131–4.

77. TNA, AIR 23/5721, HQ RAF Malta, 'Attacks on Malta February–October 1942'. The raids on 5 April involved 208 aircraft, those on 7 April involved 228. See too Budden, 'Defending the Indefensible?', 464–5; Ashley Jackson, *The British Empire and the Second World War* (London: 2000), 132.

78. TNA, AIR 23/5721, HQ RAF Malta, 'Casualties in Combat off Malta', Oct 1942. The figures cover the period February to October 1942.

79. Renzo De Felice (ed), *Galeazzo Ciano: Diario 1937–1943* (Milan: 1990), 621, entry for 26 May 1942.

80. Mariano Gabriele, 'L'operazione "C.3" (1942)', in R. Rainero, A. Biagini (eds), *Italia in guerra: Il terzo anno, 1942* (Rome: 1993), 409ff.

81. IWM, Italian Series, Box 22, E2568, Ministero dell'Aeronautica, 'Esigenza "C.3" per l'occupazione dell'isola di Malta', 3–4, 12.

82. Ciano, *Diario*, 614–15, entry for 29–30 Apr; *Fuehrer Conferences on Naval Affairs*, 277–8, telegram from Rome to OKW, 12 Apr 1942, and letter from Lt. Comm. Wolf Junge, 1 May 1942.

83. Ibid., 285, Report on a Conference between the C-in-C Navy and the Fuehrer, 15 June 1942.

84. IWM, Italian Series, Box 22, E2568, 'Esigenza "C.3" per l'occupazione', 25–7; see too Ciano, *Diario*, 619, entry for 12 May 1942 on the tides, and 619–20, entry for 13 May on Italian perception of Maltese defences.

85. TNA, AIR 23/5681, HQ RAF Malta, 'Note on Fighter Strength', 7 Oct 1942.

86. Air Ministry, *Rise and Fall of the German Air Force*, 135–7; Knox, *Hitler's Italian Allies*, 99–100.

87. IWM, Italian Series, Box 22, E2568, 'Esigenza "C.3" per l'occupazione', 7–8; Budden, 'Defending the Indefensible?', 465–6; Austin, *Malta and British Strategic Policy*, 186–8. RAF losses in Tony Spooner, *Supreme Gallantry: Malta's Role in the Allied Victory, 1939–1945* (London: 1996), 7–8.

88. Elke Fröhlich (ed), *Die Tagebücher von Joseph Goebbels Sämltiche Fragmente,* 4 vols (Munich: 1987), vol 2, pt 4, 58.

89. NAM, Air Raid Report Book, 1942–4. On injuries caused see 6 July 1942 (hitting bullets with a hammer), 9 July 1942 (playing with a rocket), 13 July 1942 (playing with an incendiary bomb), 28 July 1942 (child injured playing with an anti-personnel bomb). On the prohibitions, Box 14/2, ARP, HQ minute, 19 June 1943.

90. NAM, Box 14/14, memorandum, Supervisor of Shelter Construction, Nov 1942; Select Committee for Shelters to the President of the Council of Government, 3 Feb 1942, report on shelter provision, 3.

91. NAM, Box 25/6, Regional Protection Officer, Western Region, 'Emergency Feeding Plan', July 1943, 1–2; Lt. Gov.'s office to all RPOs, 13 Apr 1943.

92. NAM, Box 29/2, 'Report from Select Committee on Shelters to the President of Council of Government', 3 Feb 1942; Notes on Shelter Report, 'following approved' (n.d.).

93. NAM, ARP, Box 19/3, 'Report on the Food Situation in Malta', for the Lt. Gov., 22 June 1942, 2–4; on rabbits, ARP, Box 21/6, memorandum for the Lt. Gov., 18 June 1940. See too Austin, *Malta and British Strategic Policy,* 88–9.

94. Galea, *Women of Malta,* 115–16.

95. NAM, ARP, Box 19/3/A, Report on the Food Situation, 22 June 1942, 1, 4.

96. NAM, ARP, Box 19/3/B, minutes of second meeting of the Food and Distribution Board, 13 July 1942; Food Control Committee Report, 6 June 1942; Box 19/3/A, Report on the Food Situation, App 2, 'Stock Table June 1 1942', App 5, 'Civilian Ration Scales'.

97. TNA, AIR 23/5715, minutes of coordinating committee of the Malta Defence Committee, 28 Sept 1942; minutes of Malta Defence Committee, 18 Nov 1942.

98. Galea, *Women of Malta,* 43–4, 87.

99. Austin, *Malta and British Strategic Policy,* 89.

100. Laddie Lucas, *Malta: The Thorn in Rommel's Side* (London: 1993), 32.

101. Spooner, *Supreme Gallantry,* 11.

102. Ibid., 65–6.

103. NAM, ARP, Box 19/3/A, Report on the Food Situation, 22 June 1942, 5.

104. IWM, Italian Series, Box 22, E2567, 'La situazione della base aero-navale di Malta', 31 Oct 1942, 9.

105. TNA, AIR 23/5683, circular to Governor of Malta, 'Scorched Earth', 29 Jan 1942; 'Memorandum of the Application by the Army of the Scorched Earth Policy', Troop Commander, Malta, 15 Apr 1942; Malta Defence Committee, 'Scorched Earth Policy', June 1942, 1–2.

106. NAM, ARP, Box 25/6, Lt. Gov.'s office, 'Civil Organisation in the Event of an Enemy Landing or Attempted Landing', 7 May 1943, 2–4.

107. TNA, AIR 23/5715, Defence Committee, Malta, minutes of meeting, 27 Feb 1943; NAM, ARP, Box 14/2, ARP Department to all Superintendents, 6 Nov 1943.

108. TNA, AIR 2/7197, HQ British Air Force in France to the Air Ministry, 26 Apr 1940. See too Baldoli, Knapp, *Forgotten Blitzes*, 19–20.

109. TNA, AIR 75/8, Slessor papers, 'Operation Haddock: Plan for Attack of Italian War Industry', 2 June 1940.

110. TNA, AIR 35/325, Report for the Air Ministry, 'Haddock Force – Historical Diary', 20 June 1940, 2–9; Denis Richards, *Royal Air Force 1939–1945: Vol 1: The Fight at Odds* (London: 1974), 145–7.

111. Stephen Harvey, 'The Italian War Effort and the Strategic Bombing of Italy', *History*, 70 (1985), 38.

112. TNA, AIR 20/283, Air Ministry, Notes on bomb attacks, 20 Aug 1940.

113. CCO, Portal papers, Folder 9, Walter Monckton (MoI) to Portal, 8 Nov 1940.

114. TNA, AIR 23/7375, Air Intelligence, HQ RAF, Malta, to Malta Information Office, 28 Nov 1940.

115. TNA, AIR 23/7375, Air Ministry to C-in-C, Malta, 18 Jan 1941; HQ RAF Mediterranean to Luqa airbase, 13 Feb 1941; War Office, Deputy Director Military Intelligence to C-in-C, Malta, 21 Apr 1941.

116. TNA, AIR 2/7397, Air Ministry to HQ Middle East, 5 Sept 1941.

117. TNA, AIR 23/5752, Wellington Operations from Malta; Marco Gioannini, Giulio Massobrio, *Bombardate l'Italia. Storia della guerra di distruzione aerea 1940–1945* (Milan: 2007), online appendix.

118. TNA, AIR 2/7397, HQ RAF Med to Bomber Command HQ, 1 Nov 1940; HQ Malta to HQ Middle East, 14 Nov 1940; HQ Malta to HQ Middle East, 23 Nov 1940.

119. TNA, AIR 8/436, Cadogan (FO) to Portal, 21 Oct 1941; Portal to Cadogan, 26 Oct 1941.

120. TNA, AIR 2/7397, Cadogan to Freeman (DCAS), 8 Jan 1942; Freeman to Cadogan, 9 Jan 1942.

121. TNA, AIR 2/7397, reports on raids in October and November 1941 classified 9 of the 16 raids as nuisance raids, using fewer than 7 aircraft. On British policy see Baldoli, Knapp, *Forgotten Blitzes*, 20–21, 25.

122. TNA, AIR 8/435, minute by Churchill for Portal and Sinclair, 3 Dec 1942.

123. TNA, AIR 19/215, Portal to Churchill, 29 Nov 1942; Portal to Churchill 1 Dec 1942.

124. UEA, Zuckerman Archive, SZ/OEMU/50, Ministry of Home Security, RE8, 'Note on Italian Construction and its Vulnerability to I.B. and H.E. Bombs', 30 Dec 1942; RE8, 'Note on Italian Domestic Architecture', 4 Nov 1943, 1. On the Milan raid, CCAC, BUFT 3/26, Memorandum BOps, 15 Nov 1942, 'Milan: Daylight Raid 24 October 1942'.

125. CCAC, BUFT 3/26, BOps to Director of Tactics, 31 May 1943.

126. Knox, *Hitler's Italian Allies*, 101.

127. IWM, Italian Series, Box 25, 'Relazione statistica sull'attività operativa', 8.

128. Paolo Formiconi, 'La protezione e la difesa contraerea del regime fascista: evoluzione istituzionale', in Nicola Labanca (ed), *I bombardamenti aerei sull'Italia* (Bologna: 2012), 123–5.

129. IWM, Italian Series, Box 1, E2476, Ufficio operazioni aeronautica, memorandum for the commanding general, 5 Mar 1943, 1–2.

130. IWM, Italian Series, Box 2, E2485, Relazioni critiche mensili dei reparti intercettori, Dec 1942, Jan and May 1943. On radios see Box 3, E2489, Superaereo to department of air armament, 'Riunione del 28 novembre 1942; tipo di onda per la caccia notturna', 1 Dec 1942.

131. IWM, Italian Series, Box 3, E2489, Liaison officer of XII Fliegerkorps, 'Protocollo della riunione, 9 June 1943'; Box 1, E2476, Comando Supremo to Superaereo, Superesercito, Supermarina, 13 Mar 1943 'Difesa contra-aerea'; Comando supremo, memorandum for Gen. Addetto, 10 Mar 1943.

132. IWM, Italian Series, Box 2, E2485, Relazioni critiche mensili dei reparti intercettori, Maggio 1943, 1–2.

133. IWM, Italian Series, Box 3, E2489, maps of 'Nuovo progetto di schieramento di caccia notturna', 9 June 1943, July 1943, 15 Aug 1943; Castioni, 'I radar industriali italiani', 1,250–51, 1,254.

134. IWM, Italian Series, Box 1/E2470, Anti-aircraft CoS to Gen. Presso, 20 Feb 1943; Gen. von Pohl to Italian Army Staff (Air Defence), 15 Mar 1943.

135. Natalini, *I rapporti tra aeronautica italiana e tedesca*, 157–61. Night-fighters in IWM, Italian Series, Box 3, E2489, Ministero dell'Aeronautica, 'Appunto per il Duce', May 1943, 4.

136. Natalini, *I rapporti tra aeronautica italiana e tedesca*, 162–4; IWM, Italian Series, Box 3, E2489, Ministero dell'Aeronautica, 'Appunto per il Duce', May 1943.

137. IWM, Italian Series, Box 10/E2528, Italian Embassy, Berlin to the Minister for Air, 25 July 1941; Italian Embassy to Minister for Air, 23 July 1941, encl. 'Collaborazione industriale aeronautica fra Italia e Germania'.

138. Nicola della Volpe, *Difesa del territorio e protezione antiaerea (1915–1943)* (Rome: 1986), 194–203, doc 17, 'Istruzione sulla protezione antiaerea'.

139. ACS, MdAe, Busta 82, Ministry of War to all ministries, 18 Feb 1939; Volpe, *Difesa del territorio*, 36. Active air defence was allocated 252 million lire in 1938–9 but civil defence only 20.8 million.

140. ACS, MdAe, Busta 82, Gen. Valle to Mussolini, 23 Apr 1939, encl. Air Staff memorandum, 18 Apr 1939.

141. Volpe, *Difesa del territorio*, 209–10, doc 18, Army Council meeting, 8 May 1939.

142. ACS, MdAe, Busta 82, Ministry of War to all prefects and regional military authorities, 10 June 1940.

143. Baldoli, Knapp, *Forgotten Blitzes*, 54; Volpe, *Difesa del territorio*, 46–8.

144. Baldoli, Knapp, *Forgotten Blitzes*, 71–3.

145. ACS, MdAe, Busta 82, War Ministry to all ministries and prefects, 29 May 1940; Interior Ministry to Air Ministry, 2 Oct 1940; Comando della 3 Zona Aerea to Air Ministry, 11 Nov 1940; note from secretary to the Duce to the Air Ministry, 16 Nov 1940.

146. TNA, AIR 20/5384, Genoa prefect to Interior Ministry, 18 June 1940.

147. ACS, MdAe, Busta 82, Commissariat for War Production to the War Ministry, 24 June 1940.

148. Franco Manaresi, 'La protezione antiaerea', in Cristina Bersani, Valeria Monaco (eds), *Delenda Bononia: immagini dei bombardamenti 1943–1945* (Bologna: 1995), 29–30.

149. Carlotta Coccoli, 'I "fortilizi inespugnabili della civiltà italiana": La protezione antiaerea del patrimonio monumentale italiano durante la seconda guerra mondiale', *Scienza e Beni Culturali*, 26 (2010), 410–12.

150. Marta Nezzo, 'The Defence of Works of Art in Italy during the Second World War', in Baldoli, Knapp, Overy (eds), *Bombing, States and Peoples*, 104–6.

151. ACS, MdAe, Busta 56, Telecommunications inspectorate report for Air Ministry, 'Danni di guerra a stabilimenti ausiliari', 9 Feb 1943; Director General of Construction, Air Ministry, 15 Jan 1943; TNA, AIR 20/5387, Italian Ministry of Public Works, 'Damage Caused by Air Raids on Piemonte – October and November 1942'; report from Prefect in Genoa on air raids of 13–14 and 15–16 and 18 Nov 1942 (both translations from Italian originals).

152. ACS, MdAe, Busta 46, Ministry of War to all ministries, 15 Nov 1942; memorandum for the Comando Supremo, 19 Nov 1942, 1–2.

153. ACS, MdAe, Busta 46, Air Ministry memorandum for Mussolini, 10 Dec 1942, 'Dislocamento dell'industrie aeronautiche'; Air Ministry, 'Appunti per il Duce', 15 Dec 1942; Office of Air Ministry Inspectorate, minutes of meeting with Ministry of Corporations, 14 Dec 1942.

154. ACS, MdAe, Busta 56, memorandum, 'Ripresa produzione officine Alfa Romeo, Pomigliano', 14 June 1943.

155. Cited in Leonardo Paggi, *Il 'popolo dei morti': la repubblica italiana nata della guerra (1940–1946)* (Bologna: 2009), 108–9.

156. Iris Origo, *War in Val d'Orcia: An Italian War Diary 1943–1944* (London: 2003), 28–9, entry for 30 Jan 1943.

157. ACS, MdAe, Busta 55, Air Ministry minute, 18 July 1943; Busta 46, memorandum by Col. Galante, 30 Nov 1942.

158. ACS, Ministero dell'Interno, Busta 21, Police HQ Genoa to Ministry, 14 Nov 1942; Prefect of Turin to Ministry, 19 Dec 1942; sticker samples, 'Merda!'.

159. Elena Cortesi, 'Evacuation in Italy during the Second World War: Evolution and Management', in Baldoli, Knapp, Overy, *Bombing, States and Peoples*, 60–62.

160. Paggi, *Il 'popolo dei morti'*, 107, 110–11; Cortesi, 'Evacuation in Italy', 62–3.

161. Paggi, *Il 'popolo dei morti'*, 110–12; Manuela Lanari, Stefano Musso, 'Un dramma mal calcolato: sfollamento e istituzioni nella provincia di Torino', in Bruno Maida (ed), *Guerra e società nella provincia di Torino* (Turin: 2007), 14, 24–6, 28–9.

162. TNA, AIR 19/215, Sinclair to Churchill, 4 Dec 1942.

163. FDRL, Map Room Files, Box 72, OSS Bulletin, 7 Apr 1943; OSS Report, 19 Apr 1943 (from Bern).

164. TNA, FO 898/175, 'Report on Colonel Thornhill's Mission on Political Warfare in General Eisenhower's Command', 16 Nov 1943, App 10 and App 14.

165. ACS, Ministero dell'Interno, Busta 21, Office of Carabinieri, Genoa, to Ministry of Interior, 16 Nov 1942.

166. TNA, FO 898/175, Allied Force HQ, Algiers, PWB memorandum, 'Combat Propaganda – Leaflet Distribution', 15 June 1943.

167. Cesare de Simone, *Venti angeli sopra Roma: I bombardamenti aerei sulla Città Eterna* (Milan: 1993), 266. On Fascist propaganda see Claudia Baldoli, Marco Fincardi, 'Italian Society under Anglo-American Bombs: Propaganda, Experience and Legend, 1940–1945', *The Historical Journal*, 52 (2009), 1,032–4, 1,037.

168. ACS, Ministero dell'Interno, Busta 21, Appunto per il Duce, 7 July 1943.

169. TNA, AIR 2/7397, Air Ministry to C-in-C Bomber Command, 28 Oct 1940; Air Ministry to C-in-C Bomber Command, 29 Oct 1940; Sinclair to Churchill, 24 Feb 1941; Churchill to Sinclair, 28 Feb 1941.

170. TNA, AIR 8/436, HQ RAF Middle East to Air Ministry, 4 Sept 1941; Sir Miles Lampson (ambassador in Cairo) to the Foreign Office, 17 Sept 1941; AIR 2/7397, Air Ministry to HQ RAF Middle East, 27 Mar 1941; Air Ministry to HQ RAF Middle East, 5 Sept 1941.

171. TNA, AIR 8/436, Portal to Cadogan (Permanent Secretary, Foreign Office), 26 Oct 1941.

172. TNA, AIR 19/215, Note for Sinclair, 'Bombing of Targets in Rome', Dec 1942; Sinclair to Churchill, 4 Dec 1942, 1–2.

173. TNA, AIR 19/215, marginalia on 'Bombing Targets in Rome', Dec 1942; Sinclair to Churchill, 4 Dec 1942; Sinclair to Portal, 11 Dec 1942; Foreign Office to British Embassy, Bern, 17 Dec 1942.

174. CCO, Portal papers, Folder 4/File 2, Eden to Churchill, 14 July 1943; TNA, AIR 19/215, Portal to Sinclair, 3 Dec 1942; Portal to Churchill, 13 July 1943.

175. Warren Kimball (ed), *Churchill & Roosevelt: The Complete Correspondence*, 4 vols (London: 1984), vol 2, 234–5, Churchill to Roosevelt, 10 June 1943; 250–51, Roosevelt to Churchill, 14 June 1943.

176. TNA, AIR 19/215, RAF Delegation, Washington to Air Ministry, 26 June 1943.

177. Ibid., Archbishop Temple to Sinclair, 9 July 1943; Note by the assistant chief of the air staff (ACAS) (Information), 'Air Attacks on Objectives in Rome', 4 July 1943; Minute by ACAS, 15 July 1943; Sinclair to Temple, 17 July 1943.

178. LC, Eaker papers, Box I.36, North-West African Strategic Air Forces (NWASAF), Report and Evaluation, Rome, 19 July 1943: Rome Railroad Yards, Mission Report.

179. Claudia Baldoli, 'Bombing the Eternal City', *History Today* (May 2012), 11; Simone, *Venti angeli sopra Roma*, 262–4.

180. Marco Fincardi, 'Gli italiani e l'attesa di un bombardamento della capitale (1940–1943)', in Labanca (ed), *I bombardamenti aerei sull'Italia*, 239.

181. FDRL, Map Room Files, Box 33, CCS to Eisenhower, 25 June 1943; Eisenhower to War Dept., Washington, DC, 18 July 1943.

182. FDRL, Map Room Files, Box 72, OSS Bulletin, 30 July 1943; Fincardi, 'Gli italiani e l'attesa di un bombardamento della capitale', 233–4, 242–3.

183. Raymond Klibansky (ed), *Mussolini's Memoirs 1942–1943* (London: 2000), 51–55.

184. TNA, FO 898/175, Report of Col. Thornhill's Mission, 16 Nov 1943, App 14.

185. LC, Spaatz papers, Box 94, Total tonnage dropped Aug 1942–May 1944.

186. TNA, AIR 20/5387, Ministry of Public Works, Statistics on Bomb Damage, 10 June 1940–31 Mar 1943. The list did not include buildings lost in Milan, Genoa and Palermo.

187. Paggi, *Il 'popolo dei morti'*, 114–17.

188. Cited in Gloria Chianese, *'Quando uscimmo dai rifugi': Il Mezzogiorno tra guerra e dopoguerra (1943–46)* (Rome: 2004), 35–6. On Naples see Gabriella Gribaudi, *Guerra totale: Tra bombe alleate e violenza naziste: Napoli e il fronte meridionale 1940–44* (Turin: 2005), ch 3.

189. See Gabriella Gribaudi, 'Tra discorsi pubblici e memorie private. Alcune riflessioni sui bombardamenti e sulla loro legittimazione', in Labanca (ed), *I bombardamenti aerei*, 315–18; Marco Gioannini, 'Bombardare l'Italia. Le strategie alleate e le vittime civili' in idem, 92–3.

190. Claudia Baldoli, 'Spring 1943: The Fiat Strikes and the Collapse of the Italian Home Front', *History Workshop Journal*, 72 (2011), 183–6.

191. TNA, AIR 20/5383, Report from the Comune of Rome, May 1943; province of Genoa, 'Situation during the Month of May 1943'; province of Turin, 'Situation during the Month of May 1943'; province of Palermo, 'Report for the Month May 1943'.

192. Origo, *War in Val d'Orcia*, 35, 39–40, entry for 1 Apr 1943.

193. Paggi, *Il 'popolo dei morti'*, 119; the prayer in Origo, *War in Val d'Orcia*, 36. The best account of the role of religion in Italian efforts to cope with bombing is Claudia Baldoli, 'Religion and Bombing in Italy', in Baldoli, Knapp, Overy, *Bombing, States and Peoples*, 136–53.

194. TNA, AIR 19/215, VCAS (Air Marshal Evill) to Sinclair, 31 July 1943; CCO, Portal papers, Folder 3/File 3, Portal to Tedder, 30 July 1943.

195. TNA, FO 898/496, leaflet, 'Fuori i tedeschi – oppure ferro e fuoco', 29 July 1943; leaflet, 'Il governo', 14 Aug 1943.

196. FDRL, Map Room Files, Box 33, CCS to Eisenhower (n.d.); message for the President from Gen. Marshall, 2 Aug 1943; Churchill to Roosevelt, 3 Aug 1943; memorandum for the President from Admiral Leahy, 16 Aug 1943; CCS to Eisenhower, 15 Aug 1943; Simone, *Venti angel sopra Roma*, 301.

197. FDRL, Map Room Files, Box 72, OSS Bulletin, 3 Aug 1943; Report, 17 Aug 1943, 'Italy: Badoglio's Position vis-à-vis the Germans'. Details of raids in Chianese, *'Quando uscimmo dai rifugi'*, 31; Gioannini, Massobrio, *Bombardate l'Italia*, 360–61, 365–6.

198. The best guide to the complex web of command and the thicket of acronyms is Wesley F. Craven, James L. Cate, *The Army Air Forces in World War II: Vol III, Europe: Argument to V-E Day* (Chicago, IL: 1951), 326–35.

199. AFHRA, Disc MAAF 233, American Embassy (Economic Warfare Division) to NAAF, 16 Dec 1943, 2, 4–5.

200. Ibid., HQ NAAF (Norstad) to commanding general NAAF, 14 Nov 1943.

201. Ibid., Cabell to Eaker, Bombing Directive, 1 Mar 1945.

202. LC, Spaatz papers, Box 94, Total tonnage AAF-RAF, Jan–May 1944.

203. Richard G. Davis, *Carl A. Spaatz and the Air War in Europe* (Washington, DC: 1993), App 10 and App 18.

204. TNA, AIR 8/777, Harris to Portal, 13 Nov 1942.

205. Harvey, 'The Italian War Effort', 41.

206. TNA, AIR 20/283, Statistics on Bombing, Feb–Nov 1943.

207. Air Ministry, *Rise and Fall of the German Air Force*, 219, 258–60, 265–6.

208. Davis, *Carl A. Spaatz*, App 24.

209. Joseph Heller, *Catch 22* (London: 1994), 55.

210. Ronald Schaffer, *Wings of Judgment: American Bombing in World War II* (New York: 1985), 47–8; Solly Zuckerman, *From Apes to Warlords: The Autobiography of Solly Zuckerman, 1904–1946* (London: 1978), 211.

211. TNA, AIR 19/215, HQ MAAF (Eaker) to Air Ministry, 7 Apr 1944.

212. Schaffer, *Wings of Judgment*, 49–50.

213. TNA, AIR 19/215, Slessor to Air Ministry, 29 Feb 1944; Ismay to Churchill, 1 Mar 1944; conclusions of CoS meeting, 2 Mar 1944.

214. AFHRA, Disc MAAF 233, Norstad to Allied Tactical Air Forces, Bombing Directive: Florence Marshalling Yards, 2 Mar 1944.

215. TNA, AIR 19/215, Slessor to Sinclair, 7 May 1944.

216. FDRL, Map Room Files, Box 33, Marshall to Eisenhower, 27 Sept 1943; JCS to Eisenhower, 2 Nov 1943; TNA, AIR 8/438, FO to JSM, Washington, DC, 23 Sept 1943; CCS memorandum, 'Rome Open City', 24 Sept 1943; Osborne (Ambassador Holy See) to Foreign Office, 14 Oct 1943.

217. TNA, AIR 19/215, Osborne to Foreign Office (War Cabinet distribution), 6 Nov 1943; Resident Minister Algiers (Harold Macmillan) to Foreign Office, 8 Nov 1943.

218. FDRL, Map Room Files, Box 33, JCS memorandum for the President, 4 Dec 1943; memorandum for the President from Admiral Leahy, 5 Dec 1943; Roosevelt to Cordell Hull, 7 Dec 1943.

219. TNA, WO 204/12508, Maj. F. Jones, 'Report on the Events Leading to the Bombing of the Abbey of Monte Cassino on 15 February 1944', 14 Oct 1949, 7–13.

220. Ibid., 20–23.

221. James Parton, *'Air Force Spoken Here': General Ira Eaker and the Command of the Air* (Bethesda, MD: 1986), 363–4.

222. Peter Caddick-Adams, *Monte Cassino: Ten Armies in Hell* (London: 2012), 145–6.

223. TNA, AIR 8/777, Wilson to the CoS, 9 Mar 1944.

224. John Slessor, *The Central Blue: Recollections and Reflections* (London: 1956), 576–7.

225. TNA, WO 204/12508, 'Report on the Events', 31–3; App 3, Doc 26A, HQ Fifth Army memorandum, 'Monte Cassino Abbey', 28 Feb 1944.

226. Slessor, *Central Blue*, 574, reproducing his memorandum for Portal, 16 Apr 1944.

227. Zuckerman, *Apes to Warlords*, 198, 210–11.

228. Slessor, *Central Blue*, 566–8.

229. AFHRA, Disc MAAF 233, MAAF Bombing Directive, 18 Feb 1944.

230. TNA, AIR 20/2050, Summary of MAAF Effort, Operation 'Strangle', 15 Mar–11 May 1944.

231. Ibid., Summary of MAAF Effort: Operation 'Diadem', 12 May–22 June; Parton, *'Air Force Spoken Here'*, 383–4.

232. AFHRA, Disc MAAF 230, memorandum by Lt. Col. W. Ballard, Analysis Section, MAAF, 28 Sept 1944, 2.

233. UEA, Zuckerman Archive, SZ/BBSU/1/49, Interview with Kesselring, 23 Aug 1945, 3.

234. Paolo Ferrari,'Un arma versatile. I bombardamenti strategici anglo-americani e l'industria italiana', in idem (ed), *L'aeronautica italiana: una storia del Novecento* (Milan: 2004), 401–2; Massignani, 'L'industria bellica italiana', 195; Natalini, *I rapporti tra aeronautica italiana e tedesca*, 165–6.

235. Lutz Klinkhammer, *L'occupazione tedesca in Italia, 1943–1945* (Turin: 1996), 78–84; Natalini, *I rapporti tra aeronautica italiana e tedesca*, 166–7.

236. Andrea Villa, *Guerra aerea sull'Italia (1943–1945)* (Milan: 2010), 217–18.

237. Achille Rastelli, *Bombe sulla città: Gli attacchi aerei alleati: le vittime civili a Milano* (Milan: 2000), 145–7, 184. The figure of 197 dead recorded from the other 17 raids is clearly an incomplete figure, but an indication that most raids at this stage of the war in a city with wide experience of bombing were relatively small.

238. Villa, *Guerra aerea*, 219–20; Natalini, *I rapporti tra aeronautica italiana e tedesca*, 167.

239. AFHRA, Disc MAAF 230, MAAF, Target Committee, minutes of meeting, 23 Feb 1945, 4.

240. Villa, *Guerra aerea*, 226–7. For other estimates see Zamagni, 'Italy: How to Lose the War', 207–12.

241. Ferrari, 'Un arma versatile', 397–9. Housing loss in Zamagni, 'Italy: How to Lose the War', 212, who shows that because of additional housing built between 1938 and 1941, the stock of housing was almost the same in 1945 as in 1938.

242. FDRL, Map Room Files, Box 72, OSS Bulletin, 'The Situation in Italy', Bern station, 27 Sept 1943.

243. TNA, AIR 8/777, D'Arcy Osborne to the Foreign Office, 22 Mar 1944.

244. TNA, AIR 19/215, Eden to Sinclair, 15 May 1944.

245. Ibid., Sinclair to Eden, 17 May 1944; CCO, Portal papers, Folder 5, Evill to Churchill, 6 May 1944.

246. Origo, *War in Val d'Orcia*, 71–2, entry for 1 Aug 1944.

247. Corrado Di Pompeo, *Più della fame e più dei bombardamenti: Diario dell'occupazione di Roma* (Bologna: 2009), 107, 112, entries for 25 Feb and 25 Mar 1944.

248. For a full account see Klinkhammer, *L'occupazione tedesca*, 318–66.

249. Baldoli, 'Religion and Bombing in Italy', 146–7.

250. Simone, *Venti angeli sopra Roma*, 301.

251. Anna Scattigno, 'Il clero in Toscana durante il passaggio del fronte. Diari e cronache parrocchiali', in Labanca (ed), *I bombardamenti aerei*, 253–8.

252. Franco Manaresi, 'I bombardamenti aerei di Bologna', in Bersani, Monaco (eds), *Delenda Bononia*, 47–8; Manaresi, 'La protezione antiaerea', in idem, 40.

253. Ibid., 34–5.

254. ACS, Ministero dell'Interno, Busta 106, memorandum for the Milan Prefect, 4 Mar 1943, 'Ricoveri pubblici'.

255. Baldoli, Knapp, *Forgotten Blitzes*, 188–9.

256. TNA, AIR 20/5387, Province of Palermo, Report for the month, May 1943; Inspector of Air Raid Protection, Rome, 'Report concerning Air Attack on Rome 13 August 1943', 13–14.

257. Cortesi, 'Evacuation in Italy', 65–6.

258. Lanari, Musso, 'Un dramma mal calcolato', 28–9.

259. Calculated from Mauro Maggiorani, 'Uscire dalla città: lo sfollamento', in Brunella Dalla Casa, Alberto Preti (eds), *Bologna in Guerra, 1940–1945* (Milan: 1995), 376.

260. Cortesi, 'Evacuation in Italy', 70–71.

261. Baldoli, Knapp, *Forgotten Blitzes*, 144–9.

262. The only full account is George Southern, *Poisonous Inferno: World War II Tragedy at Bari Harbour* (Shrewsbury: 2002).

263. NARA, RG107, Box 139, HQ Army Service Forces for Lovett, 'United States Chemical Warfare Committee: Periodic Report of Readiness for Chemical Warfare as of January 1 1945', 114–15.

264. AFHRA, Disc MAAF 230, Brig. Gen. Cabell (Operations) to Eaker, 'Employment of Chemical Weapons by the Allied Air Forces', 12 Aug 1944; Operational Memorandum, 'Chemical Warfare – Policy for Offensive Action', 11 Aug 1944.

265. Coccoli, 'I "fortilizi inespugnabili della civiltà italiana"', 414; Marta Nezzo, 'La protezione delle città d'arte', in Labanca (ed), *I bombardamenti aerei*, 202.

266. Nezzo, 'La protezione della città d'arte', 205–6; Nezzo, 'The Defence of Works of Art', 112–13.

267. Coccoli, 'I "fortilizi inespugnabili della civiltà italiana"', 415; Nezzo, 'La protezione della città d'arte', 202–3.

268. Lynn Nicholas, *The Rape of Europa: The Fate of Europe's Treasures in the Third Reich and the Second World War* (London: 1994), 260.
269. Baldoli, Knapp, *Forgotten Blitzes*, 228–9.
270. Ibid., 236–8.
271. TNA, AIR 8/777, Osborne to the Foreign Office, 22 Mar 1944; Baldoli, Knapp, *Forgotten Blitzes*, 238–9.
272. Chianese, *'Quando uscimmo dai rifugi'*, 41, for figure on Sicily.
273. ISTAT, *Morti e disperse per cause belliche negli anni 1940–45* (Rome: 1957), Table 2.8. For a discussion of the problems of assessing wartime casualties see Baldoli, Knapp, *Forgotten Blitzes*, App, 260–62.
274. ACS, Ministero dell'Interno, Busta 22, Railway Commissariat, Palermo to Interior Ministry, 1 Apr 1943; TNA, FO 898/496, PWE, 'Foglio volante', 5 July 1943.

9. BOMBING FRIENDS, BOMBING ENEMIES: GERMANY'S NEW ORDER

1. *Target: Germany. The U.S Army Air Forces' Official Story of the VIII Bomber Command's First Year over Europe* (London: 1944).
2. USSBS, 'Over-All Report (European Theatre)', Washington, DC, 30 Sept 1945, 2. The figures are France 21.8%, Other 7.5%, Austria, Hungary, Balkans 6.7%.
3. TNA, FO 898/313, memorandum by Ritchie Calder, PWE, 'Bombing (military, economic and morale objectives)', 1–5.
4. TNA, AIR 19/217, War Cabinet, 24 July 1940, memorandum by the Air Minister, 'Bombardment Policy in France'.
5. TNA, AIR 20/5831, AI to Air Ministry (Plans), 17 Aug 1940, encl. 'Fringe Targets: Norway, Denmark, Holland, Belgium and France'.
6. TNA, AIR 20/5831, AI to Air Ministry (Plans), 20 Aug 1940 'France: Targets within 30 Miles of Coast Dunkirk – Bordeaux'; 13 Feb 1941, 'France: Fringe Targets within 30 miles of the Coast of Occupied France'; 6 Feb 1941, 'Belgium: Fringe Targets from North to South' (included three rated three-star); 'Norway: Industrial Fringe Targets from North to South' (seven marked three-star).
7. Ibid., Air Marshal Leigh-Mallory to AI (AI9), 1 July 1941.
8. Ibid., 'Information received from Lt. Commander Molenburg', 7 Aug 1940.
9. TNA, FO 371/28541, British Embassy, Bern to French Department (FO), 31 July 1941.
10. TNA, FO 898/312, Mr. Harman (FO) to Air Commodore Groves (PWE), 14 Feb 1942; Mr. Harman to Brigadier Brookes (PWE), 18 Feb 1942; PWE, 'Extrait du journal clandestin belge "Le Peuple" du mois d'avril 1942'.
11. Joris van Esch, 'Restrained Policy and Careless Execution: Allied Strategic Bombing on the Netherlands in the Second World War', School of Advanced Military Studies, Fort Leavenworth, KS (2011), 18–19.

12. TNA, AIR 40/1720, Report from Military Intelligence Division, G2, MAAF, 30 May 1944, on 'Centre de documentation des services speciaux', Annex 1, 'Comparative Table of Bombing in France since 1940' (based on Bulletin de Securité Militaire, Direction Technique des Services Speciaux, 21 May 1944).

13. TNA, FO 371/28541, French department, FO, to W. Mackenzie (Air Ministry), 15 May 1941; FO to Mackenzie, 31 May 1941; W. Law (MoL) to FO, 7 May 1941.

14. TNA, AIR 2/7503, Samuel Hoare (British ambassador to Spain) to the FO, 27 Sept 1941, encl. 'Note verbale' from Le Havre Municipal Council; FO 371/28541, Hoare to FO, 19 Aug 1941, encl. 'Note verbale' from the French Embassy in Madrid. See too Claudia Baldoli, Andrew Knapp, *Forgotten Blitzes: France and Italy under Allied Air Attack, 1940–1945* (London: 2012), 35.

15. TNA, FO 371/28541, Air Vice Marshal Medhurst to Mack (FO), 17 Oct 1941; AIR 2/7503, Minute by DBOps for FO, 25 Oct 1941.

16. For a full account of German exploitation in 1940–41 see Hein Klemann, Sergei Kudryashov, *Occupied Economies: An Economic History of Nazi-Occupied Europe, 1939–1945* (London: 2012), 75–88.

17. TNA, FO 371/28541, War Cabinet paper, 'Air Policy – Attack on Factories in Occupied France', 6 Nov 1941; AIR 19/217, War Cabinet conclusions, 20 Oct 1941. On RAF restrictions on bombing Paris, CCO, Portal papers, Folder 2/File 1, Portal to Churchill, 7 Sept 1941.

18. Michael Stenton, *Radio London and Resistance in Occupied Europe: British Political Warfare 1939–1943* (Oxford: 2000), 13, 88; Ben Pimlott, *Hugh Dalton* (London: 1985), 331–5, 343.

19. Stenton, *Radio London and Resistance*, 100.

20. CCO, Portal papers, Folder 9/File 3, AI, 'Air Activity over Norway', 24 Apr 1942.

21. TNA, FO 898/313, Ritchie Calder, 'Notes for Morale Bombing', 18 Aug 1941; Calder to Reginald Leeper, 'RAF and Morale-Making in Occupied Countries', 25 Aug 1941, 1–2; Calder memorandum, 'Bombing (military, economic and morale objectives)', Mar 1942, 1, 4–5.

22. TNA, FO 898/437, PWE memorandum, 'Why Drop Nickels?', Sept 1943, 1.

23. Ibid., 4.

24. TNA, FO 898/319, PWE Report, 14 Apr 1942.

25. TNA, FO 898/319, Directive for BBC European Service, 'Plan for Propaganda (Occupied Countries) to Accompany RAF Attacks', Mar 1942.

26. TNA, FO 898/234, T. G. Harman to Leeper (PWE), 'Plan for Propaganda to Belgium', 26 Feb 1941; Report on an interview with mademoiselle Depuich [Oct 1941], 2; 'Plan of Propaganda to Holland', 6.

27. TNA, AIR 19/217, paper from the Air Ministry (Plans) for the War Cabinet, 11 Nov 1941; Director of Plans (Air Ministry) to Churchill, 8 Jan 1942; Norman Bottomley to Acting C-in-C, Bomber Command, 5 Feb

1942; FO 371/28541, War Cabinet, 6 Nov 1941; FO 371/31999, Attlee to Churchill, 8 Jan 1942.

28. TNA, AIR 20/4768, Directorate of Bombing, 'Incendiary Attacks in Occupied Countries', 13 Nov 1941.

29. RAFM, Harris papers, H47, Bottomley to Harris, 'Psychological Aspects of Bombing Policy', 14 Apr 1942.

30. TNA, FO 898/313, PWE, 'Progress Report No. 1', Mar 1942.

31. TNA, AIR 19/217, Baker to Bottomley, 4 Mar 1942; casualty figures from Matt Perry, 'Bombing Billancourt: Labour Agency and the Limitations of the Public Opinion Model of Wartime France', *Labour History Review*, 77 (2012), 49, and Service Historique de l'Armeé de l'Air (SHAA), Vincennes, Paris, 3D/48/Dossier 2, Direction de Défense Passive, Bulletin de Renseignements, 30 Mar 1942.

32. SHAA, 3D/112/Dossier 3, propagande anglo-saxonne, 'Aux populations de la France occupée'; TNA, FO 898/319, P. C. Groves (PWE) to the BBC, 6 Feb 1942.

33. Ibid., memorandum by I. Black (PWE), 'The Bombardment of Paris Factories', 5 Mar 1942.

34. Ibid., US Embassy London to Sinclair, encl. message from Admiral Leahy, 13 Mar 1942; Eden to Sinclair, 16 Mar 1942.

35. Perry, 'Bombing Billancourt', 61–2.

36. TNA, FO 898/319, PWE Report, 'The Bombing of French Factories', 10 Apr 1942; PWE Report, 'Evidence of Effect of RAF Bombing on Morale in Enemy-Occupied Territories', 14 Apr 1942, 3.

37. TNA, AIR 19/217, Sir Samuel Hoare (Madrid) to FO, 9 June 1942; US Embassy Berne to Secretary of State, 22 June 1942.

38. Lindsey Dodd, Andew Knapp, '"How Many Frenchmen Did You Kill?": British Bombing Policy Towards France (1940–1945)', *French History*, 22 (2008), 474–80.

39. Simon Kitson, 'Criminals or Liberators? French Public Opinion and the Allied Bombings of France, 1940–1945', in Claudia Baldoli, Andrew Knapp, Richard Overy (eds), *Bombing, States and Peoples in Western Europe, 1940–1945* (London: 2011), 279–84.

40. TNA, AIR 8/428, Harris to Portal, 7 Apr 1942: 'Real Blitzes as Opposed to Dock Bombing'.

41. TNA, AIR 9/187, Slessor to all air commands, 'Bombardment Policy', 29 Oct 1942.

42. TNA, AIR 19/217, Bottomley to Harris, 14 Jan 1943; Baldoli, Knapp, *Forgotten Blitzes*, 25–6; Dodd, Knapp, '"How Many Frenchmen Did You Kill?"', 479–80.

43. Arthur T. Harris, *Bomber Offensive* (London: 1947), 136–7.

44. TNA, ADM 199/2467, Naval Intelligence Division (NID) to Assistant Chief of Naval Staff, 'U/Boat Bases – West Coast of France', 13 Jan 1943; HQ Eighth Bomber Command to NID, 18 Feb 1943.

45. TNA, FO 898/319, PWE minute, 'Campaign to the French Coastal Popula-tions', 1 June 1942; Peck to Baker, enclosing leaflet, 'Aux ouvriers français des ports de l'ouest', June 1942.

46. TNA, ADM 199/2467, NID Report, 'The Bombing of the U-Boat Bases', 11 Mar 1943; NID, 'Factual Statement on the Lorient Base and on Bombing Attacks'.

47. SHAA, 3D/322/Dossier 1, Air Force Report, 'Bombardement de l'Arsenal et de la ville de Lorient, Janvier–Mars 1943', 6–7, 9.

48. TNA, FO 898/319, PWE, draft statement on the bombing of Lorient; Air Ministry (VCAS) to PWE, 23 Feb 1943.

49. TNA, ADM 199/2467, NID note, 'Lorient'; AIR 19/218, Bottomley to Harris, 6 Apr 1943. See too Charles Webster, Noble Frankland, *The Strategic Air Offensive Against Germany*, 4 vols (London: 1961), vol 2, 96–7.

50. Stephen Flower, *Barnes Wallis' Bombs: Tallboy, Dambuster and Grand Slam* (Stroud: 2002), 124–5, 189–90, 192–5, 412.

51. TNA, ADM 199/2467, NID, French division, 'France: Reaction to the Paris and Anvers Raids', 18 Apr 1943.

52. TNA, FO 371/36038, Air Ministry to FO, 30 Dec 1942; Political Intelli-gence Dept, FO, 'Avis no. 7', BBC French Service, 29 Dec 1942.

53. Eddy Florentin, *Quand les Alliés bombardaient la France 1940–1945* (Paris: 2008), 159–61.

54. SHAA, 3D/322/Dossier 1, 'Bombardement du centre industriel de Boulogne-Billancourt, 4 Avril 1943', BN, Défense Passive, Bulletin de Ren-seignements, Mar–May 1943, table V.

55. TNA, FO 371/36038, minute by William Strang (FO), 16 Apr 1943; AIR 19/218, Massigli to Eden, 16 Apr 1943.

56. TNA, AIR 19/218, telegram JSM, Washington, DC, to Air Ministry, 28 Apr 1943; Sinclair to Eden, 9 May 1943; Air Vice Marshal Evill to Eaker, 10 May 1943; Sinclair to Eden, 5 June 1943.

57. Richard Overy, 'The Luftwaffe and the European Economy 1939–1945', *Militärgeschichtliche Mitteilungen*, 55 (1979), 58–60.

58. Florentin, *Quand les Alliés bombardaient la France*, 238–43.

59. Roger Freeman, *The Mighty Eighth War Diary* (London: 1981), 112, 115.

60. BN, Bulletin de Renseignements, Oct 1943, 8–11.

61. TNA, AIR 40/1720, MAAF Military Intelligence Division Report from Centre de Documentation des Services Spéciaux, 7, 18.

62. SHAA, 3D/322/Dossier 1, 'Bombardement de l'usine Dunlop, 16 septembre, 1943', 1.

63. Ibid., Armée de l'Air, 'Bombardements aériens en territoire français: Avant propos: 1944' [May 1944], 1–3.

64. Ibid., 'Bombardement de St. Étienne, 26 Mai 1944', 7–8.

65. BN, Bulletin d'Information de la Défense Passive, May 1944, 7–8; SHAA, 3D/322/Dossier 1, 'Bombardement de la gare d'Avignon, 27 Mai, 25 Juin 1944', 4.

66. Baldoli, Knapp, *Forgotten Blitzes*, 51–3, 55.

67. Ibid., 92–3, 99.
68. BA-MA, RL13/21, Luftschutz-Abteilung 15, Allgemeiner Erfahrungs-bericht, 30 Apr 1942.
69. SHAA, 3D/44/Dossier 2, Admiral Duplat to General Pintor (President of Italian Armistice Commission), 17 Nov 1940; IAC to French delegation, 1 Apr 1941; IAC to French delegation, 23 Sept 1941.
70. Ibid., German Armistice Commission (Air Force) to French delegation, 27 Nov 1941.
71. Ibid., Note for the French delegation at Wiesbaden, 3 Feb 1942; note from Direction des Services de l'Armistice to French delegation, 3 June 1942; Secrétariat à l'Aviation, 'Obscurissement de la zone non occupée', 6 Aug 1942.
72. Ibid., memorandum of the German Armistice Commission to the French delegation, 27 Nov 1941, 1.
73. BA-MA, RL7/141, Intelligence Report, Air Fleet 3, 'Aufbau der franz-ösischen Heimatluftverteidigung', 1 May 1943; Intelligence Report, Air Fleet 3, 1 Aug 1943.
74. SHAA, 3D/44/Dossier 1, SGDA, CoS to the Interior Ministry, 5 June 1943, encl. memorandum from Air Fleet 3, 16 Feb 1943; Direction de la Défense Aérienne to SGDA, Bureau C, 24 June 1943.
75. BA-MA, RL7/141, Intelligence Report, Air Fleet 3, 1 May 1943; SGDA to Secrétariat Générale à la Défense Terrestre, 27 Apr 1943.
76. SHAA, 3D/279/Dossier 2, Commandant de Groupe de SAP, Lyon, 20 Feb 1943; Dossier 1, Defence Secretary to Minister of Industrial Production, 'Service d'alerte', 1 Oct 1943; SGDA, Bureau A, 'Recapitulation des effectifs des formations de SAP', 13 Sept 1943; SGDA to Director of Air Services, Northern Zone, 20 Sept 1943. The main centres in the south were at Lyon, Montpellier, Marseille, Limoges and Toulouse; in the north at Paris, Tours, Dijon, Bordeaux and Reims.
77. SHAA, 3D/43/Dossier 1, Plenipotentiary Air Fleet 3 to SGDA, 20 Aug 1943; 3D/44/Dossier 1, Plenipotentiary Air Fleet 3 to SGDA, 4 July 1943.
78. Baldoli, Knapp, Forgotten Blitzes, 92–3.
79. SHAA, 3D/44/Dossier 1, SGDA to Air Fleet 3, 20 Mar 1944; 'Formations et effectifs réels, Défense Passive', 15 Jan 1944; Ministry of Interior, 'Instruction: Service de protection', 26 Apr 1944.
80. BA-MA, RL7/141, Plenipotentiary of Air Fleet 3, 'Tätigkeitsbericht 1.2–15.3.1944', 19 Mar 1944; SHAA, 3D/44/Dossier 1, SGDA to Plenipotentiary Air Fleet 3, 20 Mar 1944.
81. BA-MA, RL13/24, Kriegstagebuch [War Diary] of LS-Abt. 34, entries for 15, 16 and 29–30 Jan 1943; SHAA, 3D/322/Dossier 1, 'Bombardement de l'Arsenal et de la ville de Lorient', May 1944, 4–5, 8.
82. Michael Schmiedel, 'Les Allemands et la défense passive en France: le cas de Nantes', in Michèle Battesti, Patrick Facon (eds), Les bombardements alliés sur la France durant la Seconde Guerre Mondiale: Stratégies, bilans matériels et humains (Vincennes: 2009), 53–5.

83. BN, Bulletin de Renseignements, Oct 1943, 'L'Oeuvre accomplice par le Service Municipal de la ville de Nantes'.

84. Julia Torrie, 'For Their Own Good': Civilian Evacuations in Germany and France, 1939–1945 (New York: 2010), 115–17.

85. Ibid., 125–7.

86. SHAA, 3D/44/Dossier 1, SIPEG to Directorate of Passive Defence, 26 Jan 1944; Pierre Laval to all ministries, 4 Feb 1944, 1.

87. Michael Schmiedel, 'Orchestrated Solidarity: The Allied Air War in France and the Development of Local and State-Organised Solidarity Movements', in Baldoli, Knapp, Overy (eds), Bombing, States and Peoples, 207–11.

88. Schmiedel, 'Orchestrated Solidarity', 211–13; Torrie, 'For Their Own Good', 153–4; Baldoli, Knapp, Forgotten Blitzes, 150–51.

89. SHAA, 3D/44/ Dossier 1, Laval to all ministers, 4 Feb 1944, 1–2, 5; SIPEG to Directorate of Passive Defence, 26 Jan 1944.

90. Ibid., Laval to all ministers, 2–3; Torrie, 'For Their Own Good', 159; Baldoli, Knapp, Forgotten Blitzes, 153–4.

91. Olivier Dumoulin, 'A Comparative Approach to Newsreels and Bombing in the Second World War: Britain, France and Germany', in Baldoli, Knapp, Overy (eds), Bombing, States and Peoples, 302–3; Baldoli, Knapp, Forgotten Blitzes, 118–19.

92. Lindsey Dodd, '"Relieving Sorrow and Misfortune"? State, Charity, Ideology and Aid in Bombed-out France, 1940–1944', in Baldoli, Knapp, Overy (eds), Bombing, States and Peoples, 83–5.

93. Ibid., 80–81, 86–7.

94. Torrie, 'For Their Own Good', 135–7.

95. Stenton, Radio London and Resistance, 110.

96. TNA, FO 898/457, PWE, 'Annual Dissemination of Leaflets by Aircraft and Balloon 1939–1945'.

97. LC, Spaatz papers, Box 157, memorandum, CoS of Eighth Air Force, 11 Aug 1942; USAAF Adjutant-General to commander of Eighth Air Force, 25 Sept 1943.

98. Ibid., Box 157, Frank Kaufman, Chief (Leaflet Section) PWB to Robert Bruce Lockhart (PWE), 22 Apr 1944, 'Leaflet Production and Dissemination Program between now and D-Day'; Political Warfare Division (SHAEF), 'The Leaflet Propaganda Front', 19 June 1944, 3.

99. Philippe Boiry, Paris sous les bombes: Auteuil septembre 1943 (Paris: 2000), 37–8.

100. TNA, AIR 40/1720, MAAF Intelligence Division Report, 30 May 1944, 1, 8. See too Kitson, 'Criminals or Liberators?', 285–8.

101. TNA, AIR 40/1720, MAAF Intelligence Division Report, 30 May 1944, 13–15.

102. TNA, FO 371/41984, minute for Churchill from Desmond Morton, 9 May 1944; Direction Technique des Services Spéciaux, 'Les bombardements alliés et leurs repercussions sur le moral français', 25 Apr 1944.

103. Ibid., 'France: Cardinals' Message to British and U.S. Episcopates', 14 May 1944; Archbishop of Westminster to French Cardinals, 20 May 1944.

104. Patrick Facon, 'Les bombardements Alliés sur la France durant la Seconde Guerre Mondiale: Enjeux, thématiques et problématiques', in Battesti, Facon (eds), *Les bombardements alliés*, 13–14.

105. Baldoli, Knapp, *Forgotten Blitzes*, 211–13.

106. TNA, AIR 40/1720, MAAF, Military Intelligence Division Report, 30 May 1944, 17–18.

107. Baldoli, Knapp, *Forgotten Blitzes*, 210–11; Torrie, 'For Their Own Good', 113.

108. Jean-Marie Pontaut, Éric Pelletier, *Chronique d'une France occupée: Les rapports confidentiels de la gendarmerie 1940–1945* (Neuilly-sur-Seine: 2008), 444, 'Rapport du commandant de gendarmerie de la Charente', July 1943.

109. BA-MA, RL7/141, Intelligence Report, Air Fleet 3, 1 Aug 1943, 2; minute, 14 July 1943, 'Überwachung der einzustehenden französischen Eisenbahn-flakbatterien'; Intelligence Report, Air Fleet 3, 2 Sept 1943.

110. BA-MA, RL7/141, Intelligence Report, Air Fleet 3, 1 Oct 1943; SHAA, 3D/43/Dossier 1, Sec. Gen. of Air Defence to Col. von Merhart, 18 Sept 1943; Plenipotentiary of the German Air Force, Paris, to Col. Cornillon (Liaison Service), 18 Nov 1943.

111. BA-MA, RL7/141, Intelligence Report, Air Fleet 3, 1 Aug 1943, 2.

112. UEA, Zuckerman Archive, SZ/AEAF/7, War Cabinet Defence Committee, 5 Apr 1944, 1.

113. TNA, AIR 40/1882, Bottomley to Portal, 18 Jan 1944; Bufton to Harris, 14 Jan 1944.

114. TNA, AIR 37/752, Harris memorandum for Leigh-Mallory, 'The Employment of the Night Bomber Force in Connection with the Invasion of the Continent', 13 Jan 1944.

115. LC, Spaatz papers, Box 143, Spaatz to Eisenhower [n.d. but Apr 1944].

116. Ibid., Arnold to Spaatz, 24 Apr 1944; see too Anderson to Spaatz, 28 Feb 1944, 3, 'there be complete accord . . . as to the continuation of POINTBLANK'.

117. Walter W. Rostow, *Pre-Invasion Bombing Strategy: General Eisenhower's Decision of March 25, 1944* (Aldershot: 1981), 13–14, 88–98; Solly Zuckerman, *From Apes to Warlords: The Autobiography of Solly Zuckerman 1904–1946* (London: 1978), 220–24, 231–45.

118. Lord Arthur Tedder, *With Prejudice: The War Memoirs of Marshal of the Royal Air Force Lord Tedder* (London: 1966), 520–25.

119. CCO, Portal papers, Folder 5, Portal to Churchill, 29 Mar 1944; UEA, Zuckerman Archive, SZ/AEAF/7, Defence Committee minutes, 5 Apr 1944; Defence Committee minutes, 13 Apr 1944.

120. CCO, Portal papers, Folder 5, Portal to Churchill, 13 Apr 1944; UEA, Zuckerman Archive, SZ/AEAF/7, Defence Committee, Note by the

Secretary, 'Bombing Policy'; Zuckerman memorandum, 'Estimates of Civilian Casualties', 6 Apr 1944.

121. Ibid., 'Number of Fatal Casualties' [n.d. but Apr 1944]; 'Casualties among French Civilians Resulting from Rail Centre Attacks'.

122. Warren Kimball (ed), *Churchill & Roosevelt: The Complete Correspondence: Vol III, Alliance Declining* (London: 1984), 122–3, Churchill to Roosevelt, 7 May 1944, and 127, Roosevelt to Churchill, 11 May 1944; Tedder, *With Prejudice*, 531–2.

123. BN, Bulletin de Renseignements, Apr 1944, 16; Bulletin d'Information de la Défense Passive, Aug 1944, 18.

124. SHAA, 3D/322/Dossier 1, 'Tableau des projectiles explosifs lancés de janvier 1942 à août 1944'.

125. BN, Bulletin d'Information de la Défense Passive, May 1944, 7–8.

126. Details from BN, Bulletin d'Information de la Défense Passive, June 1944, 1–3, 6–7, 10–11, 13.

127. SHAA, 3D/322/Dossier 1, 'Bombardement de St. Étienne, 26 mai 1944', 4, 7–8; 'Bombardement de Marseille, 27 mai 1944', 1, 4–6; BN, Bulletin d'Information de la Défense Passive, 'Bombardement de Saint-Étienne, 26 mai 1944', 2–4; 'Bombardement de Marseille, 27 mai 1944', 2–5; statistics on human losses from Georges Ribeill, Yves Machefert-Tassin, *Une Saison en Enfer: Les bombardements des Alliés sur les rails français (1942–1945)* (Migennes: 2004), 142–3.

128. TNA, FO 371/41984, memorandum from the French Commissariat for Foreign Affairs, 'Allied Bombardment of Metropolitan France', 5 May 1944; AIR 19/218, telegram for the War Cabinet from the British chargé d'affaires in Algiers, 8 June 1944. See too Baldoli, Knapp, *Forgotten Blitzes*, 233–5, for a fuller discussion of the views of the French Resistance.

129. FDRL, Map Room Files, Box 73, Deputy Director OSS to the White House, 17 May 1944, encl. OSS Bulletin from Madrid.

130. Baldoli, Knapp, *Forgotten Blitzes*, 29.

131. FDRL, Map Room Files, Box 72, OSS Bulletin, 8 Feb 1944.

132. CCAC, BUFT 3/51, SHAEF Report, 'The Effect of the Overlord Plan to Disrupt Enemy Rail Communications', 1–2.

133. Georges Ribeill, 'Aux prises avec les voies ferrées: bombarder ou saboter? Un dilemme revisité', in Battesti, Facon (eds), *Les bombardements alliés*, 162.

134. TNA, AIR 37/719, Solly Zuckerman, 'Times for Re-Establishment of Traffic through Bombed Rail Centres and Junctions and across Bridges', 11 Aug 1944, 2, and App 9, 11; Ribeill, Machefert-Tassin, *Une Saison en Enfer*, 138–9.

135. Ibid., 153–5, 204; TNA, AIR 37/719, Railway Research Service, London, 'German Military Movements in France and Belgium August 1944', 13 Oct 1944, App B.

136. Steve Darlow, *Sledgehammers for Tintacks: Bomber Command Combats the V-1 Menace 1943–1944* (London: 2002), 195–7.

137. Joachim Ludewig, *Rückzug: The German Retreat from France, 1944* (Lexington, KT: 2012), 23–4.

138. Maud Jarry, 'Le bombardement des sites V en France', in Battesti, Facon (eds), *Les bombardements alliés*, 39–43.

139. TNA, AIR 40/1882, Report from Dewdney (RE8) to Bufton, 15 Apr 1944 'Crossbow – Large Sites'.

140. TNA, AIR 19/218, Sinclair to Portal, 9 July 1944.

141. TNA, AIR 40/1882, Air Marshal Colyer to Director of Intelligence, 2 July 1944; AI Report, 'Examination of "Crossbow" Sites in the Cherbourg Peninsula', 6 July 1944.

142. Jean Quellien, 'Les bombardements pendant la campagne de Normandie', in Battesti, Facon (eds), *Les bombardements alliés*, 61–8.

143. BN, Bulletin de Renseignements, June, July and August 1944; Quellien, 'Les bombardements', 70–71.

144. TNA, AIR 37/761, AEAF HQ, 'Observations of RAF Bomber Command's Attack on Caen July 7 1944', 14 July 1944, 3–5.

145. William Hitchcock, *The Bitter Road to Freedom: A New History of the Liberation of Europe* (New York: 2008), 32–3, 34, 44.

146. USMA, Bradley papers, War Diary, vol 3, entry for 24 July 1944; LC, Spaatz papers, Box 84, USSTAF HQ, 'Report of Investigation of Tactical Bombing, 25 July 1944', 14 Aug 1944, 3–4.

147. USMA, Bradley papers, War Diary, vol 3, entry for 25 July 1944. Eisenhower was reported as saying 'I don't believe they [strategic bombers] can be used in support of ground troops.'

148. USMA, Bradley papers, memorandum by Bradley, 'Combined Air and Ground Operations West of St. Lô on Tuesday 25 July 1944'; Bradley memorandum for the record, 19 Nov 1944.

149. Andrew Knapp, 'The Destruction and Liberation of Le Havre in Modern Memory', *War in History*, 14 (2007), 477–82.

150. TNA, AIR 8/842, minute by Portal, 7 Jan 1945; Bottomley to Portal, 9 Jan 1945; Bottomley to Portal, 25 Jan 1945; Florentin, *Quand les Alliés bombardaient la France*, 596–7.

151. Ibid., 597–8.

152. TNA, AIR 40/1720, MAAF Intelligence Division Report, 30 May 1944, 14.

153. Baldoli, Knapp, *Forgotten Blitzes*, gives a figure of 54,631 for overall deaths; Florentin, *Quand les Alliés bombardaient la France*, 600–601, gives both the official figure (53,601) and the post-war estimate of 67,078, which seems to have been derived from the assertion that of the 133,000 civilian dead in France, half came from bombing. Danièle Voldman suggests a figure of at least 70,000, but does not explore how this figure is arrived at. See Voldman, 'Les populations civiles, enjeux du bombardement des villes (1914–1945)', in Stéphane Audoin-Rouzeau, Annette Becker, Christian Ingrao, Henry Rousso (eds), *La violence de guerre 1914–1945* (Paris: 2002), 161–2.

154. LC, Spaatz papers, Box 143, Notes by Spaatz for Eisenhower, Apr 1944.

155. LC, Doolittle papers, Doolittle to Spaatz, 10 Aug 1944; Doolittle to Eisenhower, 5 Aug 1944.

156. TNA, AIR 19/218, Portal to Eaker, 3 June 1943.

157. CCO, Portal papers, Folder 9/File 2, Stefan Zamoyski to Peirse, 4 Jan 1941, encl. letter from Polish Army HQ, 30 Dec 1940; Peirse to Sikorski, 15 Jan 1941; Tami Davis Biddle, *Rhetoric and Reality in Air Warfare: The Evolution of British and American Ideas about Strategic Bombing, 1914–1945* (Princeton, NJ: 2002), 191–2.

158. TNA, AIR 19/218, Eden to Sinclair, 7 July 1944; Sinclair to Eden, 15 July 1944; Sinclair to Vice CoS (RAF), 26 July 1944; Richard Levy, 'The Bombing of Auschwitz Revisited: A Critical Analysis', *Holocaust and Genocide Studies*, 10 (1996), 268–9, 272–3. See too Michael Neufeld, Michael Berenbaum (eds), *The Bombing of Auschwitz: Should the Allies have Attempted it?* (New York: 2000), 263–4, 266–7, for the full correspondence.

159. TNA, AIR 19/218, Bottomley to ACAS (Intelligence), 2 Aug 1944; V. Cavendish-Bentinck (JIC) to Bottomley, 13 Aug 1944. See too Stuart Erdheim, 'Could the Allies Have Bombed Auschwitz-Birkenau?', *Holocaust and Genocide Studies*, 11 (1997), 131–7.

160. David Wyman, *The Abandonment of the Jews: America and the Holocaust 1941–1945* (New York: 1984), 290–91, 295; Levy, 'The Bombing of Auschwitz Revisited', 277–8. The McCloy letters of 14 August and 18 November 1944 are reproduced in Neufeld, Berenbaum (eds), *The Bombing of Auschwitz*, 274, 279–80.

161. TNA, AIR 19/218, Richard Law (FO) to Sinclair, 1 Sept 1944; Air Ministry to Spaatz, 1 Sept 1944.

162. Neufeld, Berenbaum (eds), *The Bombing of Auschwitz*, has 15 papers arguing the case for or against.

163. AFHRA, Disc MAAF 233, Economic Warfare Division to Maj. Ballard, NAAF, 'Strategic Target Priority List', 16 Dec 1943. Oświęcim was number 14 out of 15 priority targets.

164. Joseph White, 'Target Auschwitz: Historical and Hypothetical German Responses to Allied Attack', *Holocaust and Genocide Studies*, 16 (2002), 58–9; Randall Rice, 'Bombing Auschwitz: US 15th Air Force and the Military Aspects of a Possible Attack', *War in History*, 6 (1999), 205–30.

165. Norman Davies, *Rising '44: The Battle for Warsaw* (London: 2003), 310–11.

166. TNA, AIR 8/1169, Portal to Slessor, 5 Aug 1944; Slessor to Portal, 6 Aug 1944; Slessor to Portal, 9 Aug 1944.

167. Ibid., AMSSO to British Mission, Moscow, 8 Aug 1944; Slessor to Portal, 16 Aug 1944. See too Halik Kochanski, *The Eagle Unbowed: Poland and the Poles in the Second World War* (London: 2012), 419.

168. TNA, AIR 8/1169, Despatches from MAAF on Dropping Operations to Warsaw [n.d.]; Davies, *Rising '44*, 311; Kochanski, *Eagle Unbowed*, 408–11. The successful drops included 4.5 million rounds of ammunition, 14,000 hand grenades, 250 anti-tank guns and 1,000 Sten guns.

169. TNA, FO 898/151, PWE, 'Rumanian Policy', 2 Dec 1943; PWE minute, 'Air Attack on Bucharest', 20 Mar 1944.

170. C. O. Richardson, 'French Plans for Allied Attacks on the Caucasus Oil Fields January–April 1940', *French Historical Studies*, 8 (1973), 136–42; Ronald Cooke, Roy Nesbit, *Target: Hitler's Oil. Allied Attacks on German Oil Supplies 1939–45* (London: 1985), 25–8, 37–8.

171. TNA, AIR 9/138, Air Ministry (Plans) for the CAS, 'Appreciation on the Attack of the Russian Oil Industry', 2 Apr 1940, 1–2; memorandum by Air Ministry (Plans), 'Russian Oil Industry in the Caucasus', 30 May 1940.

172. Ibid., 'Memorandum on the Russian Petroleum Industry in the Caucasus', App E, 'Calculation of Effort'; Cooke, Nesbit, *Target: Hitler's Oil*, 49–51.

173. TNA, AIR 9/138, letter from E. A. Berthoud (British Embassy, Cairo) to HQ RAF Middle East, 13 June 1941; Air Ministry (Plans) to HQ RAF Middle East, 13 June 1941; Air Ministry to British C-in-C (India) [n.d. but June 1941].

174. TNA, PREM 3/374/6, HQ RAF Middle East to Air Marshal Evill, 14 June 1942.

175. TNA, FO 898/176, PWB, Allied Forces HQ, 'Psychological Warfare in the Mediterranean Theater', 31 Aug 1945, 4–5, 15.

176. LC, Spaatz papers, Box 157, Col. Earl Thomson to Director of Intelligence, USSTAF Europe, 1 Feb 1944.

177. Ibid., Box 157, Carl Spaatz article for *Air Force Star*, 'Leaflets: An Important Weapon of Total War', 5.

178. Ibid., Box 157, Lt. Col. Lindsey Braxton to Spaatz [n.d. but Feb 1944]; Thomson to Director of Intelligence, USSTAF, 1 Feb 1944. For an example of whole bundles falling see TNA, FO 898/437, H. Knatchbull-Hugesson (British Embassy, Ankara) to Ministry of Information, 18 Jan 1944, on Bulgarian leaflets.

179. TNA, FO 898/176, 'Psychological Warfare in the Mediterranean Theater', 31 Aug 1945, 14; FO 898/318, Dr Vojacek to PWE, 19 Feb 1943; Dr Vojacek to PWE, 11 Jan 1943.

180. TNA, FO 898/318, memorandum by Elizabeth Barker (PWE), 'Probable Effects of Intensified Large-Scale Bombing of Densely Populated Areas in South-Eastern Europe', 26 Jan 1944; PWE memorandum, 'The Bombing of Romania, Austria, Czechoslovakia and Jugoslavia' [n.d.].

181. TNA, FO 898/318, PWE Regional Director (Czechoslovakia) to Calder, 25 Jan 1944.

182. TNA, FO 898/437, Wing Commander Burt-Andrews to Elizabeth Barker, 10 Dec 1943; FO 898/318, Barker memorandum, 26 Jan 1944, 2.

183. Charles Webster, Noble Frankland, *The Strategic Air Offensive Against Germany, 1939–1945*, 4 vols (London: 1961), vol 4, 508–9, 518.

184. TNA, AIR 20/3238, HQ RAF Middle East to Air Ministry, 26 Apr 1942; Air Ministry memorandum, 'Tactical Appreciation on the Interruption of Axis Supplies of Oil from Romania', 21 Dec 1942; Churchill to Portal, 28 Feb 1943; Portal to Churchill, 9 Mar 1943.

185. TNA, PREM 3/374/6, Churchill to Eden, 10 Mar 1943; Ismay to Church-ill, 18 May 1943; Eisenhower to CCS, 25 May 1943.

186. TNA, AIR 20/3238, Air Ministry to Mediterranean Air Command, 31 May 1943; Portal to Tedder, 2 June 1943.

187. TNA, AIR 20/3238, Eisenhower to CCS, 25 May 1943; PREM 3/374/6, minute by Ismay, 19 June 1943; Ismay to Churchill, 23 June 1943.

188. TNA, AIR 20/3238, Lt. Col. W. Forster to E. Berthoud (Cairo Embassy), 3 Aug 1943.

189. Cooke, Nesbit, *Target: Hitler's Oil*, 86–7.

190. TNA, AIR 20/3238, HQ RAF Middle East to Air Ministry, 3 Aug 1943; Report, 'Bombing of Roumanian Oilfields', 9 Aug 1943. For details of both raids see Wesley F. Craven, James L. Cate, *The Army Air Forces in World War II: Europe: Torch to Pointblank* (Chicago, IL: 1949), 481–4; Cooke, Nesbit, *Target: Hitler's Oil*, 89–96.

191. TNA, AIR 20/3238, H. Knatchbull-Hugesson to the Foreign Office, 8 Aug 1943.

192. AFHRA, Disc MAAF/233, HQ MAAF, 'Notes on Strategic Bombardment Conference, Gibraltar, 8–10 November 1943', 11 Nov 1943, 2; Richard G. Davis, *Bombing the European Axis Powers: A Historical Digest of the Combined Bomber Offensive, 1939–1945* (Maxwell AFB, AL: 2006), 322–4.

193. FDRL, Map Room Files, Box 136, Arnold to Spaatz, 17 Mar 1944; CoS to Wilson and Spaatz, 22 Mar 1944; AFHRA, Disc MAAF/233, Air Ministry to Eaker, 11 Apr 1944.

194. *Akten zur Deutschen auswärtigen Politik: Serie E, Band VIII: 1 Mai 1944 bis 8 Mai 1945* (Göttingen: 1979), 99–100, Joachim von Ribbentrop to Bucharest Embassy, 6 June 1944.

195. *ADAP: Serie E, Band VIII*, 114, OKW to Ambassador Ritter, 7 June 1944 (appointment from 4 June 1944).

196. TNA, AIR 23/7776, Fifteenth Air Force, 'The Air Battle of Ploesti', Mar 1945, 2, 6, 61–8, 81.

197. Cooke, Nesbit, *Target: Hitler's Oil*, 105–6; AFRHA, Disc MAAF/233, HQ MAAF, Operation Order for Mining the Danube, 25 Apr 1944.

198. *ADAP: Serie E, Band VIII*, 383–4, Budapest Embassy to the German Foreign Office, 30 Aug 1944; Karl-Heinz Frieser (ed), *DRZW: Band 8: Die Ostfront 1943/44* (Stuttgart: 2007), 782–800.

199. NARA, RG 107, Lovett papers, Box 28, Eaker to Robert Lovett, 18 Sept 1944; FDRL, President's Secretary's Files, Box 82, Arnold to Roosevelt, 22 Sept 1944.

200. TNA, WO 204/1068, Air Ministry to Air Force HQ, Algiers, 4 Apr 1944.

201. AFHRA, MAAF/233, HQ MAAF, Intelligence Section, 'The Balkan Situation – Possibilities of Air Attack', 24 Apr 1944, 13.

202. Ibid., Portal to Spaatz and Wilson, 30 May 1944.

203. NARA, RG 107, Box 28, Eaker to Lovett, 18 Sept 1944, 2–3; Davis, *Bombing the European Axis Powers*, 323.

204. AFHRA, Disc MAAF/233, HQ MAAF, Intelligence Section, 'Priority List of Strategic Targets in MAAF Area', 31 July 1944.
205. Ibid., HQ MAAF, Operational Instruction 111, 21 Mar 1945, 1–2.
206. Ibid., HQ MAAF, cypher message to all air staff, 24 Apr 1944. See too John Deane, *The Strange Alliance: The Story of American Efforts at Wartime Co-operation with Russia* (London: 1947), 128–9.
207. TNA, AIR 20/3229, HQ MAAF to Air Ministry, 9 Nov 1944; JSM Washington to AMSSO (Moscow), 19 Nov 1944; Deane, *The Strange Alliance*, 132–4.
208. TNA, AIR, 20/3229 Spaatz to Arnold, 29 Nov 1944; US Joint Chiefs to John Deane, Military Mission, Moscow; Joint Planning Staff memorandum, 'Co-ordination of Allied Operations', 23 Jan 1945.
209. FDRL, President's Secretary's Files, Box 82, Arnold to Roosevelt, 17 Sept 1944, 2.
210. Gordon Daniels (ed), *A Guide to the Reports of the United States Strategic Bombing Survey* (London: 1981), xxii; Wagenführ story in John K. Galbraith, *A Life in Our Times: Memoirs* (London: 1981), 235–6.
211. See e.g. Maria Bucur, *Heroes and Victims: Remembering War in Twentieth-Century Romania* (Bloomington, IN: 2009), 198–9, 212–13.
212. A. Korthals Altes, *Luchtgevaar: Luchtaanvallen op Nederland 1940–1945* (Amsterdam: 1984), 332.
213. http://www.groningerarchieven.nl 'Groningers gedood door Engelse-bommen'.
214. Altes, *Luchtgevaar*, 332.
215. TNA, FO 898/312, Foreign Office to Brigadier Brooks (PWE), 14 Feb 1942.
216. TNA, AIR 9/187, Slessor (ACAS) to all air commands, 29 Oct 1942, 'Bombardment Policy', 3.
217. Pieter Serrien, *Tranen over Mortsel: De laatste getuigen over het zwaarste bombardement ooit in België* (Antwerp: 2008), 12–19. See too the report in TNA, ADM 199/2467, NID, minute on bombing of Antwerp, 20 Apr 1943.
218. TNA, AIR 40/399, HQ VIII Bomber Command, ORS Report on 5 Apr 1943 operations, 18 May 1943.
219. Serrien, *Tranen over Mortsel*, 41, from an anonymous letter on the bombing.
220. TNA, FO 898/312, Foreign Office to Director of Political Warfare (Operations), 9 Apr 1943.
221. TNA, AIR 19/218, Sinclair to Portal, 30 Apr 1943; Sinclair to Portal, 3 May 1943; Air Marshal Evill to Eaker, 10 May 1943, encl. App A, 'Targets in Occupied Countries Recommended for Attack by the Eighth Air Force'; Air Ministry to Harris, 21 May 1943.
222. TNA, AIR 19/218, Portal to Eaker, 3 June 1943; Sinclair to Eden, 5 June 1943; Eden to Sinclair, 11 June 1943.

223. Ibid., draft leaflet, 'An Urgent Warning to the Belgian People', 16 June 1943; Bottomley to Harris and Eaker, 25 June and 15 July 1943; E. Micheils van Verduyren (Netherlands FO) to Sir Nevile Bland (British ambassador), 23 June 1943.

224. Joris van Esch, 'Restrained Policy and Careless Execution: Allied Strategic Bombing on The Netherlands in the Second World War', US School of Advanced Military Studies, Fort Leavenworth, KS (2011), 35–6.

225. Altes, *Luchtgevaar*, 167–9.

226. LC, Eaker papers, Box I/20, Eaker to Portal, 28 Jul 1943; TNA, AIR 19/218, Portal to Eaker, 25 Jul 1943.

227. Pieter Serrien, 'Bombardementen in België tijdens WOII', in http://pieter serrien.wordpress.com/2010/10/11.

228. Esch, 'Restrained Policy and Careless Execution', 37–8.

229. B. A. Sijes, *De Razzia van Rotterdam 10–11 November 1944* (Gravenhage: 1951), 27–9.

230. On aircraft see Overy, 'The Luftwaffe and the European Economy', 58–60.

231. NARA, T901, Roll 2018, Reichsgruppe Industrie, 'Anlagen zu den Ergebnissen der Industrieberichterstattung: Belgien, Oktober 1943'; ibid., 'Niederlande, November 1943'.

232. Altes, *Luchtgevaar*, 334–6.

233. Netherlands Institute of War Documentation, Amsterdam, File 222, *Haagische Courant*, 30 May 1944; *Het Nieuws van den Dag*, 30 Jan 1942.

234. TNA, FO 898/234, Stockholm Despatch to PWE, 25 Nov 1943 (based on information from a Dutch visitor to Sweden).

235. AFHRA, US Strategic Air Forces in Europe, 519.12535, 'Heavy Bombers: Targets in Low Countries'.

236. Serrien, 'Bombardementen in België', 2–3.

237. Esch, 'Restrained Policy and Careless Execution', 39–44; Altes, *Luchtgevaar*, 189–98, 203–2. The figure of 800 dead includes those classified as missing, those who died of wounds and a number of German personnel.

238. LC, Spaatz papers, Box 157, PWB chief, Leaflet Section, to Bruce Lockhart (PWE), 22 Apr 1944; Esch, 'Restrained Policy and Careless Execution', 43–4.

239. Henrik Kristensen, Claus Kofoed, Frank Weber, *Vestallierede luftangreb i Danmark under 2. Verdenskrig*, 2 vols (Aarhus: 1988), vol 2, 731–2.

240. Ibid., 742–3, 745–7, 748.

241. LC, Spaatz papers, Box 67, 'Status of Combined Bomber Offensive: First Phase, April 1–August 31 [1943]'.

242. TNA, AIR 2/8002, memorandum by the Norwegian Minister of Foreign Affairs, 1 Dec 1943; Laurence Collier (FO) to Eden, 26 Nov 1943.

243. Ibid., Air Ministry, 'Priority Targets in Norway' [n.d. but Apr 1944]; Norwegian High Command, 'Comments on Priority Targets in Norway', 31 May 1944.

244. Ibid., Norwegian Embassy to Air Ministry, 2 Nov 1944; Norwegian Embassy to Collier, 13 Dec 1944; Maurice Dean (Air Ministry) to Foreign

Office, 11 Jan 1945; on the raid, Martin Middlebrook, Chris Everitt, *The Bomber Command War Diaries* (Leicester: 2000), 609.

245. AFHRA, Disc MAAF/233, HQ MAAF, Intelligence Section, 'V-Weapons', 27 Mar 1945; Altes, *Luchtgevaar*, 302–3; TNA, AIR 37/999, SHAEF Air Defense Division, 'An Account of the Continental Crossbow Operation 1944–1945', 1, 13.

246. Serrien, 'Bombardementen in België', 3.

247. CCAC, Hodsoll papers, HDSL 5/4, Sir John Hodsoll, 'Review of Civil Defence 1944', 1, 13; TNA, AIR 37/999, 'Continental Crossbow', 24.

248. TNA, AIR 37/999, SHAEF, 'Continental Crossbow', 7–9, 19–20, 23.

249. Serrien, 'Bombardementen in België', 1, 3–4.

250. Altes, *Luchtgevaar*, 293; Esch, 'Restrained Policy and Careless Execution', 45–7.

251. Altes, *Luchtgevaar*, 324; Esch, 'Restrained Policy and Careless Execution', 5. The figure of 8,000 was calculated by the Netherlands Institute of War Documentation, Amsterdam. Uncertainty over the exact figure derives partly from the difficulty in distinguishing between deaths from aerial bombing and deaths from artillery bombardment or ground strafing.

252. TNA, AIR 2/7894, Arthur Street (Air Ministry) to Orme Sargent (FO), 'Draft Broadcast to the Dutch People', 21 Mar 1945; E. Michiels van Verduynen (Dutch ambassador) to Eden, 15 June 1945.

253. Ibid., Street to Alexander Cadogan (FO), 30 June 1945.

254. Ibid., Mary C. van Pesch-Wittop Koning to King George VI, 20 Dec 1945.

255. Ibid., A. Rumbold (FO) to M. Low (Air Ministry), 4 Mar 1946; Low to Rumbold, 18 Mar 1946.

256. TNA, AIR 19/218, Sinclair to Eden, 5 June 1943; Eden to Sinclair, 11 June 1943.

10. THE BALANCE SHEET OF BOMBING

1. John K. Galbraith, *A Life in Our Times: A Memoir* (London: 1981), 219, 240.

2. LC, Spaatz papers, Box 84, Brig. Gen. John Samford to USAAF Director of Information, 20 Sept 1946.

3. UEA, Zuckerman Archive, SZ/BBSU/29, ACAS (Ops) to Zuckerman, 'Comments by Sir John Slessor', 14 Jan 1947, 1–2.

4. Royal Society, London, Blackett papers, PB/4/4, 'Note on the Use of the Bomber Force' [spring 1942], 1.

5. TNA, AIR 20/8693, Testimony of Hermann Wilhelm Göring at Nürnberg, 6 Apr 1945, interrogation by Hilary St George Saunders (a later official historian of the RAF).

6. LC, Spaatz papers, Box 134, USSBS Interview no. 8, Lt. Gen. Karl Koller, 23–24 May 1945, 3.

7. UEA, Zuckerman Archive, SZ/BBSU/29, 'Comments by Sir John Slessor', 3.

8. TNA, AIR 14/739A, Portal to Harris, 4 Mar 1944; HQ Bomber Command, Air Intelligence Section, 'Progress of RAF Bomber Offensive Against German Industry', 19 Feb 1944, 4.

9. LC, Spaatz papers, Box 134, Excerpt from the Interrogation of General Koller, 25 Sept 1945, 3.

10. UEA, Zuckerman Archive, SZ/BBSU/28, minute for Air Commodore Pelly, 3 Jan 1946.

11. TNA, AIR 14/1779, Air Warfare Analysis Section paper, Feb 1945, 1.

12. CamUL, Andrew Boyle papers, Add 9429/2c, Conversation with Harris, 18 July 1979.

13. Michael Neufeld, 'The Guided Missile and the Third Reich: Peenemünde and the Forging of a Technological Revolution', in Monika Renneberg, Mark Walker (eds), *Science, Technology and National Socialism* (Cambridge: 1994), 64–6.

14. NARA, RG 107/138, Statistical Control Division, 'One Million Tons of Bombs', 30 Sept 1944.

15. UEA, Zuckerman Archive, SZ/BBSU/58, Bottomley (DCAS) to Portal, 3 Apr 1945, 'Area Bombing', 1.

16. Royal Society, London, Blackett papers, PB/4/2, John Jewkes to Blackett, 3 Oct 1939, encl. 'A Note on Economic Intelligence Service in Connection with Air Warfare', 2, 4.

17. LC, Spaatz papers, Box 134, USSBS Interview no. 8, 2.

18. NC, Cherwell papers, G195, Cherwell to Churchill, 6 Nov 1942.

19. UEA, Zuckerman Archive, SZ/BBSU/103, Nicholas Kaldor, 'The Nature of Strategic Bombing' [n.d. but 1945].

20. Ibid., 4.

21. Ibid., SZ/BBSU/1, Interview with Kesselring, 23 Aug 1945, 3.

22. Ibid., SZ/BBSU/90, Transcript of conversation between Lord Zuckerman and Albert Speer, Heidelberg, 28–29 Aug 1974, 4, 6; Notes of a meeting with Albert Speer, 28–29 Aug 1974, 4–6.

23. Royal Society, London, Blackett papers, PB/4/2, Note by P. S. Blackett, 18 July 1936, 2.

24. CCO, Portal papers, Folder 2/File 2, Churchill to Portal, 7 Oct 1941, 2.

25. UEA, Zuckerman Archive, SZ/BBSU/29, 'Comments by Sir John Slessor', 2.

26. NC, Cherwell papers, G193, Cherwell to Tizard, 22 Apr 1942; G192, 'City of Birmingham: Effects of Air Raids on Dwelling House Property', 12 Feb 1942.

27. UEA, Zuckerman Archive, SZ/BBSU/29, 'Comments by Sir John Slessor', 2.

28. Steven Brakman, Harry Garretsen, Marc Schramm, 'The Strategic Bombing of German Cities during World War II and its Impact on City Growth', *Journal of Economic Geography*, 4 (2004), 201–18, who conclude that the evidence for the German Federal Republic shows 'that large, temporary shocks will have at most a temporary impact'.

29. FDRL, Map Room Files, Box 72, OSS Report 49, 'Germany: Air Bombardment and Morale', 11 Aug 1943; Report 60, 17 Sept 1943.

30. Ibid., OSS Report 76, Bern station, 'Germany: Problems of the Bombed-Out Refugees', 15 Nov 1943; Report 89, Bern station, 'Germany', 21 Dec 1943.

31. UEA, Zuckerman Archive, SZ/BBSU/29, Bottomley to Air Marshal William Dickson, 8 Feb 1947, 7 Feb 1947; 'Comments by Sir John Slessor', 2.

32. John Deane, *The Strange Alliance: The Story of American Efforts at Wartime Co-operation with Russia* (London: 1947), 37. Deane visited Stalingrad in late 1943, and was accommodated, he claimed, in the one building left standing.

33. British Red Cross Society Archive, London, J/WO/1/2/2, War Organisation, Second Annual Report, 2.

34. Hans Nossack, *The End: Hamburg 1943* (Chicago, IL: 2004), 41.

35. LSE, Fellowship of Reconciliation papers, Box 16, letter from R. R. Stokes to the *Sunday Dispatch*, 29 Dec 1943.

36. LC, Eaker papers, Box I.30, MAAF Intelligence Section, 'What is the German Saying?', item (c), 11 Nov 1944.

37. Ibid., item (i), lieutenant, German Air Force Artillery, 4 Aug 1944.

38. FDRL, Map Room Files, Box 72, OSS Report 50, Bern station, 12 Aug 1943.

39. TNA, FO 371/28541, British Embassy, Bern, to the Foreign Office (French desk), 31 July 1941, encl. memorandum on bombing French industry.

40. TNA, AIR 19/217, War Cabinet memorandum, 'Bombardment Policy in France', 24 July 1940.

41. Foreign & Commonwealth Office, *Churchill and Stalin: Documents from the British Archives* (London: 2002), doc 29, Conversation between Mr Churchill and Marshal Stalin, 12 Aug 1942, 4.

42. Ibid., doc 30, Aide-Mémoire by Mr Stalin to Mr Churchill and Mr Harriman.

43. LC, Spaatz papers, Box 84, Spaatz to Doolittle, 26 Jan 1944.

44. USMA, Bradley papers, War Diary, vol 3, 25 July 1944.

45. LC, Doolittle papers, Box 18, Doolittle to Spaatz, 10 Aug 1944, 2.

46. See the study by Frederick Sallagar, *The Road to Total War* (New York: 1969), esp. ch 11, 'Pressures for Escalation'.

47. Conrad C. Crane, 'Evolution of U.S. Strategic Bombing of Urban Areas', *Historian*, 50 (1987), 23–5, 31–2.

48. TNA, AIR 40/1882, DoI memorandum, 'Crossbow Retaliations', 3 July 1944; Colyer to DoI, 2 July 1944.

49. AFHRC, Disc MAAF 233, Director of Operations, Mediterranean Allied Air Forces, 'Bombardment Policy', 21 Mar 1945, 1.

50. There is still a great deal of debate about this, occasioned largely by the spurious claim that The Hague Rules for the conduct of air warfare drawn up in 1923 were never ratified, or that defended towns lacked the right to immunity of 'undefended towns'. The existing Hague Convention on the

rules of war, drawn up in 1907, makes clear that the intention of the existing rules governing warfare was to define as illegitimate those acts of war
designed deliberately to damage civilian lives and property. See Timothy
McCormack, Helen Durham, 'Aerial Bombardment of Civilians: The Current International Legal Framework', in Yuki Tanaka, Marilyn Young (eds),
Bombing Civilians: A Twentieth-Century History (New York: 2009), 218–
19, 228–30; Igor Primoratz, 'Can the Bombing be Morally Justified?', in
idem (ed), *Terror from the Sky: The Bombing of German Cities in World
War II* (Oxford: 2010), 113–30; Anthony Grayling, *Among the Dead
Cities: Was the Allied Bombing of Civilians in World War II a Necessity or
a Crime?* (London: 2005), 271–81. It is worth trying to answer the question: could Montgomery's troops on entering Hamburg in 1945 have
legitimately machine-gunned 37,000 of the civilian population? Allied
armies could not deliberately kill any civilians except spies or *francs-tireurs*.

51. Richard Overy, 'The Nuremberg Trials: International Law in the Making',
in Philippe Sands (ed), *From Nuremberg to The Hague: The Future of International Criminal Justice* (Cambridge: 2003), 10–11.

52. *Geneva Conventions of August 12, 1949, for the Protection of War Victims*
(Washington, DC: 1949), 164–9; Adam Roberts, R. Guelff (eds), *Documents on the Laws of War*, 3rd edn (Oxford: 2000), 419–21; M. Bothe, K. J.
Partsch, W. A. Solf (eds), *New Rules for Victims of Armed Conflicts: Commentary on the Two 1977 Protocols Additional to the Geneva Convention
of 1949* (The Hague: 1982), 274–80, 292–318; International Committee of
the Red Cross, *Protocols Additional to the Geneva Convention of 12 August
1949* (Geneva: 1977), 34–9.

53. FHA, Foley papers, Mss 448, Box 1/5, J. M. Spaight, 'Bombing Policy',
12 Sept 1941.

54. Ibid., Box 1/1, Rev. Canon F. Cockin to Thomas Foley, 1 Oct 1941.

55. RAFM, Peirse papers, AC 71/13/61–2, speech to the Thirty Club, 25 Nov
1941, 11.

EPILOGUE: LESSONS LEARNED AND NOT LEARNED: BOMBING INTO THE POST-WAR WORLD

1. Lord Tedder, 'Air Power in War: The Lees Knowles Lectures', Air Ministry
pamphlet 235, Sept 1947, 13.

2. USMA, Lincoln papers, Box 5, File 5/2, Presentation to the President by Maj.
Gen. Lauris Norstad, 29 Oct 1946, 'Postwar Military Establishment', 11. Also
5, 'future war' will be 'truly total', and 6, 'We must prepare for total war.'

3. USMA, Lincoln papers, Box 5, File 5/3, 'Industrial Mobilization', lecture to the
General Session of the National Industrial Conference Board, 28 May 1947.

4. Tedder, 'Air Power and War', 12–13; USMA, Lincoln papers, Box 5, File
5/2, address by Lauris Norstad, National War College, 'U.S. Vital Strategic
Interests', 22 Nov 1946, 2 (emphasis in both originals).

5. RAFM, Bottomley papers, AC 71/2/97, Director of Command and Staff Training to Bottomley, 23 Apr 1947; TNA, AIR 20/6361, Air Ministry Exercise Thunderbolt, vol I, Aug 1947, foreword by Lord Tedder; UEA, Zuckerman Archive, SZ/BBSU/3/75, Exercise Thunderbolt, Joining Instructions, Pt II.

6. UEA, Zuckerman Archive, SZ/BBSU/3/75, Exercise Thunderbolt: Precis Folder, 10–17 Aug 1947; on the economy, TNA, AIR 20/6361, Air Ministry Exercise Thunderbolt, Presentation and Report, vol II, item 20: 'neither the day nor the night offensive succeeded in their strategic task of destroying the enemy's economy'.

7. Tedder, 'Air Power and War', 13, See too TNA, AIR 20/6361, Exercise Thunderbolt, vol II, item 20, 130.

8. RAFM, Bottomley papers, B2318, 'Thunderbolt Exercise: Note on the Potentialities of Biological Warfare', 13 Aug 1947; Note by Bottomley [n.d. but Aug 1947].

9. USMA, Lincoln papers, Box 5, 5/3, Somervell address, 'Industrial Mobilization', 7.

10. Ibid., Box 5, 5/2, Draft address by Gen. Wedemeyer to the National War College on 'Strategy', 15 Jan 1947, 4, 16, 21.

11. Ibid., Box 5, 5/2, Norstad, 'Presentation Given to the President', 27 Oct 1946, 1, 6.

12. Ibid., Box 5, 5/3, Maj. Gen. O. Weyland, Air Force-Civilian Seminar, Maxwell AFB, 20 May 1947.

13. Warren Kozak, LeMay: The Life and Wars of General Curtis LeMay (Washington, DC: 2009), 277–81.

14. TNA, AIR 8/799, Air Ministry (Plans), memorandum for the Defence Committee, 16 Oct 1946, 1.

15. D. A. Rosenberg, 'American Atomic Strategy and the Hydrogen Bomb Decision', Journal of American History, 66 (1979), 68.

16. TNA, DEFE 10/390, Joint Inter-Service Group for Study of All-Out Warfare (JIGSAW) papers, minutes of meeting 23 Feb 1960, 1–2; meeting 2 June 1960, 1; meeting 4 Aug 1960, 2.

17. Kenneth Hewitt, 'Place Annihilation: Area Bombing and the Fate of Urban Places', Annals of the Association of American Geographers, 73 (1983), 278–81.

18. On Britain see Nick Tiratsoo, 'The Reconstruction of Blitzed British Cities 1945–55: Myths and Reality', Contemporary British History, 14 (2000), 27–44; Stephen Essex, Mark Brayshay, 'Boldness Diminished? The Post-War Battle to Replan a Bomb-Damaged Provincial City', Urban History, 35 (2008), 437–61.

19. Jeffry Diefendorf, In the Wake of War: The Reconstruction of German Cities after World War II (New York: 1993), 14–15.

20. LSE archive, Women's International League of Peace and Freedom papers, 2009/52/3, Mary Phillips (Women's International League), 'Germany Today: Report on Visit to British Zone May 9 to 27 1947', 2–3, 5.

21. Leo Grebler, 'Continuity in the Rebuilding of Bombed Cities in Western Europe', *American Journal of Sociology*, 61 (1956), 465–6.

22. LC, Eaker papers, Box I.30, MAAF Intelligence Section, 'What is the German Saying?', recording 'G'.

23. Fred Iklé, *The Social Impact of Bomb Destruction* (Norman, OK: 1958), 213–15, 218–20.

24. Cited in Tiratsoo, 'The Reconstruction of Blitzed British Cities', 28.

25. Ibid., 36.

26. Grebler, 'Continuity in Rebuilding', 467–8.

27. Steven Brackman, Harry Garretsen, Marc Schramm, 'The Strategic Bombing of German Cities during World War II and its Impact on City Growth', *Journal of Economic Geography*, 4 (2004), 205, 212.

28. Grebler, 'Continuity in Rebuilding', 467.

29. Nicola Lambourne, 'The Reconstruction of the City's Historic Monuments', in Paul Addison, Jeremy Crang (eds), *Firestorm: The Bombing of Dresden, 1945* (London: 2006), 151–2, 156–60.

30. Andreas Huyssen, 'Air War Legacies: From Dresden to Baghdad', in Bill Niven (ed), *Germans as Victims* (Basingstoke: 2006), 184–9; Peter Schneider, 'Deutsche als Opfer? Über ein Tabu der Nachkriegsgeneration', in Lothar Kettenacker (ed), *Ein Volk von Opfern? Die neue Debatte um den Bombenkrieg 1940–1945* (Berlin: 2003), 158–65.

31. Mark Connelly, Stefan Goebel, 'Zwischen Erinnerungspolitik und Erinnerungskonsum: Der Luftkrieg in Grossbritannien', in Jörg Arnold, Dietmar Süss, Malte Thiessen (eds), *Luftkrieg: Erinnerungen in Deutschland und Europa* (Göttingen: 2009), 55–60, 65.

32. I am grateful to Professor Dobrinka Parusheva for supplying me with information on the Bulgarian protests.

Index

Page references in *italic* indicate tables.

National Youth movement 565
Resistance movement/workers 559,
    569, 570–71, 572, 575, 576
Secours National (National
    Assistance) 569
transport network damage/bombing
    66, 296, 552, 557, 562, 570, 572,
    573, 574, 575, 576, 577, 578, 583
Vichy regime 182, 549, 551, 557,
    562–5, 568–72
welfare assistance 569
Franco, Francisco 33
Frank, Hans 64
Frankfurt 410, 472, 474
Frankland, Noble xxvi
Freeman, Wilfred, 280, 287, 291, 295
Freemasons 571
Freiburg im Breisgau 419
French *see* France/the French
Freya radar 322, 515
Frick, Wilhelm 430
Friedrich, Jorg: *Der Brand* 641
Friedrichshafen 20
fringe bombing, and the German New
    Order 118, 252, 270, 321, 323,
    547–606, 624
Fritz X gliding bombs 230
Front Line 175
Fry, Ruth 126
fuel
    aviation *see* aviation fuel
    oil industry *see* oil industry
FuG 218 radar scanning equipment 388
Fuller, J. F. C. 27
Futurism 487

Gafencu, Grigore 59
Galbraith, J. K. 408, 466, 609
Galland, Adolf 88–9, 389–90, 400
Gallup Polls (British Institute of Public
    Opinion) 180–81
gas masks 36, 37, 54–5, 135, 136, 215,
    217, 222, 516
gas supply, Germany 471–2
gas warfare 30, 32–3, 44, 106, 283,
    380–81, 543, 620 *see also* bombs,
    aerial: gas; Chemical Warfare
    Service, US

and ARP/civil defence training 135,
    149, 216, 217
decontamination *see* decontamination
Gater, Sir George 185
Gateshead 138, 142
'Gee' navigation 273–4, 289,
    290–91, 294
Geelen 597
Geilenberg, Edmund 465
Geisler, Hans 502
Geneva
    Convention 630
    Disarmament Conference (1932)
        30–31
    League of Nations Assembly 32
    Protocol (1925) 30, 33
Genoa 511, 513, 515, 516, 517–18, 519,
    526, 537, 542, 543
George, David Lloyd, 1st Earl 22
George, Harold 45, 281
germ warfare 30, 381–2, 620, 635–6, 637
German Air Force 59, 60, 68–73, 388
    Air Corps X 502, 503
    and air defence centralization 362–6
    Air Defence Regiment 34 in
        France 565
    Air Fleet 1 61–2, 204, 205
    Air Fleet 2 67, 74, 503; Air Corps II
        503
    Air Fleet 3 67, 74, 109, 116, 117, 118,
        119, 562–3, 564; Air Corps IV 67
    Air Fleet 4 62, 208, 212; Air Corps IV
        209; Air Corps VIII 204, 209
    Air Fleet 5 67, 74, 75, 109
    Air Protection Regiments 468, 481–2
    air strategy and bombing policies: Blitz
        bombing *see* Blitz bombing;
        Blitzkrieg, linked to ground
        campaign 60–61; blockade 68,
        90–91, 92–3, 106, 107, 114,
        119–20, 124, 161, 614; Crash
        Raids 190; and defeat 375; and
        destruction of the enemy bomber
        366; first strategic air offensive
        (Sept. 1940–June 1941) 89–125,
        107, 112, 255–6; food supply
        targeting 60, 68, 107, 111;
        Guidelines for the Conduct of Air

from perspective of total war 632
and propaganda 588
Soviet 221
as a target of strategic bombing 15–16,
20, 23, 85, 257, 258, 263–5, 278,
308, 383–4, 395, 615, 616–24
morality *see* ethics
Morison, Frank: *War on Great Cities* 26
Morrison, Herbert 128, 151–2, 153, 156,
167–8, 173, 194
Morrison shelters 193, 195
Morton, Desmond 240
Mortsel 597–8, 606
Moscow 197–8, 201, 203, 205, 206, 214
blackout 198, 218
bombing 197–8, 202, 203, 204,
218–19; casualties 198, 203, 219
Kremlin 203
metro 197, 217
shelters 217
Mosquito bomber 295, 321, 586,
601, 602
MPVO (Main Directorate of Local Air
Defence) 213–15, 216–20, 221–3,
224–5, 622
Mumford, Lewis: *The Culture of
Cities* 19
München Gladbach (Mönchengladbach)
84, 239, 243
Munich 298, 309, 322, 445, 468, 472–3,
472, 474
crisis 29
Münster, Westphalia 420, 424, 426
Murmansk 224
Murray, Gilbert 181
Mussolini, Benito 33, 64, 486, 487–8,
489, 490, 492–3, 494, 525, 543
and the bombing of Italy 512, 521,
522, 546
and Hitler 493, 503, 505, 525
and Malta 496, 497, 498, 504, 505, 509
Mussolini, Bruno 488
Mustang fighter/fighter-bomber (P-51)
233, 357–8, 359, 361, 369, 377,
383, 390, 535, 592
mustard gas bombs 33, 543
decontamination training 190
Mutual Aid schemes, British 163, 189

Nagasaki 12, 327, 613
Nantes 561, 565–6
Naples 499, 512, 516, 526, 542, 543, 544
narcosis therapy 353
National Fire Service (NFS, British) 168
National Liberation Revolutionary Army,
Bulgaria 7
National Peace Council 38
National Republican Air Force 487, 515
National Service Bill (Britain, 1941) 168
National Socialism 249–50, 356–7, 380,
389, 411, 428–30
National Socialist Party 411, 413, 415,
429–31, 448, 450, 478, 479;
Chancellery 422, 429, 430;
hierarchy 428–9
'People's Community' 37, 414, 485
propaganda 447–8, 568, 622
SA (Sturmabteilung) 428, 429–30,
446, 480
SS *see* SS (Schutzstaffel)
National Socialist People's Welfare (NSV)
427, 429, 430
navigation and target-finding aids
Knickebein 76, 77, 95, 96
with radar 103, 119, 275, 347, 388–9;
Gee 273–4, 289, 290–91, 294; H2S
294–5, 318, 321–2, 342, 346,
347–8, 363, 388, 531; H2X 346,
347, 386–7; *Lichtenstein* 119, 275;
Neptun-R 119; Oboe 294–5, 318,
321, 346, 347; Perfectos 388–9;
Serrate IV 389
sky-marking 322, 325
and the weather 345, 386–7
X-Gerät 76–7, 95–6
Y-Gerät 77, 95–6
Naxos-Z homing device 363
Naxxar 500, 501
Nazism *see* National Socialism
Needham, Joseph 28
Neptun-R radar aid 119
Netherlands/the Dutch *see also* Low
Countries
aircraft industry 599
air-raid violations 553–5
British leaflet numbers dropped in 554
civil defence 600

and the 'Transportation Plan' 370,
396, 573, 593–4
and 'Window' 332–3
Porton Down Experimental Station,
Wiltshire 328
Portsmouth 82, *107*, *112*, 165
Portugal 31
Posen 109
post-war reconstruction 638–40
Potsdam 397
Pound, Sir Dudley 558
Prague 467
Preston *107*
Pricolo, Francesco 488, 489, 503
prisoners of war
American 8–9
German 475, *475*, 476
Pritt, Denis 147
propaganda
and bombing policies/campaigns 64,
480, 522, 540, 552–5, 556, 557,
569–70, 575, 587–9, 622 *see also*
leaflet drops
British: fed to America 631; RAF
propaganda over hitting civilian
targets 629
and German morale 323, 446–7, 478
leaflet *see* leaflet drops
and morale 588
National Socialist 447–8, 568, 622
shells 587, 588
Propaganda Ministry, German 83, 87,
422, 430, 444, 446, 448
prostitution 152
protest, social *see* social protest
Prussia 413
Soviet attacks on German targets in
East Prussia 202
psychiatric health *see* mental health
Psychological Warfare Branch (PWB), US
522, 525, 587, 588
PVO (*protivovozdushnaia
oborona strany*) 200–201,
203–5, 206
PWB *see* Psychological Warfare Branch,
US
PWE *see* Political Warfare Executive
(PWE), British

Quadrant conference, Quebec 339
Queensborough, Almeric Paget,
1st Baron 180

radar aids to navigation *see under*
navigation and target-finding aids
radar detection 40, 78–9, 117, 363, 492,
514, 579
Carpet jammer 363
Flensburg detector 388
Freya 322, 515
FuG 218 scanning equipment 388
inland Ground Control Interception
radars 104, 117
Nürnberg device 363
Piperack jamming device 388–9
radio counter-measures 322
SN 2 scanning equipment 363, 388
SN 3 scanning equipment 388
'Window' radar-blinding strategy 121,
332–3, 335, 363
Wismar modification 363
Würzburg 275, 332, 363, 515
Würzlaus device 363
radar gun-laying equipment 99
Raeder, Erich 68, 70, 88, 502, 503
RAF *see* Royal Air Force
rail and transport network damage/
bombing
Allied Transportation Plan 367, 370,
384–5, 387, 538, 557, 573–6, 592,
593–4, 616
Britain 163
Bulgaria 1, 2, 7, 14
and disproportionality 614, 615
France 66, 296, 552, 557, 562, 570,
572, 573, 574, 575, 576, 577,
578, 583
Germany 23, 239, 244, 247, 263–4, 367,
384, 385, 386, 387, 390, 396, 400,
401, 402, 404, 465–6, 467, 615–16
Italy 519, 523–4, 533, 536–8, 539,
540, 557, 616
Low Countries 597, 600
Poland 62
Romania 593–4
Soviet Union 201, 205–8, 213, 222–3,
225, 230